AMERICAN CONSTITUTIONAL LAW
Volume 1

AMERICAN CONSTITUTIONAL LAW

Volume 1
The Structure of Government

Tenth Edition

RALPH A ROSSUM
Claremont McKenna College

G. ALAN TARR
Rutgers University, Camden

WESTVIEW
PRESS

Westview Press was founded in 1975 in Boulder, Colorado, by notable publisher and intellectual Fred Praeger. Westview Press continues to publish scholarly titles and high-quality undergraduate- and graduate-level textbooks in core social science disciplines. With books developed, written, and edited with the needs of serious nonfiction readers, professors, and students in mind, Westview Press honors its long history of publishing books that matter.

Copyright © 2017 by Westview Press
Published by Westview Press,
An imprint of Perseus Books
A division of Hachette Book Group
2465 Central Avenue
Boulder, CO 80301
www.westviewpress.com

Every effort has been made to secure required permissions for all text, images, maps, and other art reprinted in this volume.

Westview Press books are available at special discounts for bulk purchases in the United States by corporations, institutions, and other organizations. For more information, please contact the Special Markets Department at the Perseus Books Group, 2300 Chestnut Street, Suite 200, Philadelphia, PA 19103, or call (800) 810-4145, ext. 5000, or e-mail special.markets@perseusbooks.com.

A CIP catalog record for the print version of this book is available from the Library of Congress
PB ISBN: 978-0-8133-4996-1
EBOOK ISBN: 978-0-8133-5030-1

10 9 8 7 6 5 4 3 2 1

About the Authors

Ralph A. Rossum is Henry Salvatori Professor of American Constitutionalism at Claremont McKenna College. He earned his PhD from the University of Chicago and is the author of several books, including *Understanding Clarence Thomas: The Jurisprudence of Constitutional Restoration* (2014), *The Supreme Court and Tribal Gaming:* California v. Cabazon Band of Mission Indians (2011); *Antonin Scalia's Jurisprudence: Text and Tradition* (2006); *Federalism, the Supreme Court, and the Seventeenth Amendment: The Irony of Constitutional Democracy* (2001); *Congressional Control of the Judiciary: The Article III Option* (1988); *The American Founding: Politics, Statesmanship, and the Constitution* (1981); *Reverse Discrimination: The Constitutional Debate* (1979); and *The Politics of the Criminal Justice System: An Organizational Analysis* (1978). He has served in the US Department of Justice as deputy director of its Bureau of Justice Statistics and as a board member of its National Institute of Corrections. He currently serves as a member of the California Advisory Committee, US Commission on Civil Rights.

G. Alan Tarr is Director of the Center for State Constitutional Studies and Board of Governors Professor of Political Science at Rutgers University, Camden. He received his doctorate from the University of Chicago. Professor Tarr is the author of several books, including *Judicial Process and Judicial Policymaking* (6th edition, 2013), *Without Fear or Favor: Judicial Independence and Judicial Accountability in the States* (2012), *Understanding State Constitutions* (1998), and *State Supreme Courts in State and Nation* (1988). He is coeditor of the three-volume *State Constitutions for the Twenty-First Century* (2005), *Constitutional Dynamics in Federal Systems: Subnational Perspectives* (2012), *Constitutional Origins, Structure, and Change in Federal Countries* (2005), and several other volumes. Three times the recipient of fellowships from the National Endowment for the Humanities and more recently a Fulbright Fellow, Professor Tarr has served as a consultant to the US Department of State, the American Bar Association, the National Center for State Courts, and several state governments. He has lectured on American constitutionalism and federalism throughout the United States, as well as in Africa, Asia, Europe, North America, and South America.

To the Memory of Herbert J. Storing

Contents

4   THE LEGISLATIVE BRANCH 112

5   THE EXECUTIVE BRANCH 167

6   WAR AND FOREIGN AFFAIRS 203

CASES

7   FEDERALISM 273

CASES

8 THE EXERCISE OF NATIONAL POWER 353

CASES

9 THE EXERCISE OF STATE POWER 416

CASES

Preface

American Constitutional Law, Tenth Edition, is designed as a basic text for courses in national powers and civil liberties. This substantially revised and updated edition features the major constitutional controversies and cases either not included in, or decided since the publication of, the Ninth Edition. This is perhaps our most extensive revision of the casebook from one edition to another; we have added sixteen new cases and deleted and moved twenty-six cases to our new website (www.westviewconlaw.com).

Volume I now includes: *National Labor Relations Board v. Noel Canning* (2014), which restricted the president's power to make recess appointments; *Zivotofsky v. Kerry* (2015), which affirmed the president's exclusive power to recognize foreign states; *Comptroller of the Treasurer of Maryland v. Wynne* (2015), which reflected the Court's continued embrace of the dormant commerce clause; *Adoptive Couple v. Baby Girl* (2013), which revealed the Court's increasing willingness to depart from the standard canons of construction of federal Indian law; *Taylor v. City of Gadsden* (2013), in which a federal district judge rejected a contract clause objection to a city's changes in the public pensions of police and fire personnel; and *Horne v. Department of Agriculture* (2015) and *Koons v. St. Johns River Management District* (2013)—two recent Takings Clause cases.

Volume II now includes: *McDonald v. Chicago* (2010), which incorporated the Second Amendment to apply to the states; *Walker v. Texas Division, Sons of Confederate Veterans Inc.* (2015) and *McCullen v. Coakley* (2014), both of which addressed free speech issues; *Burwell v. Hobby Lobby Stores Inc.* (2014), which concerned the protection of religious liberty; *Los Angeles v. Patel* (2015), *Maryland v. King* (2014), and *Riley v. California* (2014), all of which dealt with Fourth Amendment questions; *Shelby County v. Holder* (2013), which found Section 4 of the Voting Rights Act unconstitutional, and *Obergefell v. Hodges* (2015), the Court's landmark decision regarding same-sex marriage.

As in previous editions, our approach to these subjects is based on three major premises. First, the study of the Constitution and constitutional law is of fundamental importance to a full and coherent understanding of the principles, prospects, and problems of America's democratic republic. Cases should be examined not merely to foster an appreciation of what court majorities have thought of particular issues at certain points in time (although that is obviously important), but also to gain a deeper and fuller understanding of the principles at the very heart of the American constitutional system. To that end, this text emphasizes precedent-setting cases and presents comprehensive expositions of alternative constitutional positions. Substantial excerpts from cases and other constitutionally significant pronouncements have been included so that students can grapple with the arguments and justifications for these alternative positions. To ensure that the best arguments on all sides of a constitutional question are presented, we have included extensive extracts of both concurring and dissenting opinions.

Second, no interpretation of the Constitution can be evaluated properly without an appreciation of what those who initially drafted and ratified the Constitution sought to accomplish. The text incorporates documentary evidence in seeking to identify and explain the original purposes of the Constitution and the means provided for the achievement of those purposes. This inquiry into the Framers' understanding of the Constitution, in turn, furnishes one of the criteria for evaluating judicial decisions and constitutionally significant pronouncements from the executive and legislative branches.

Third, the study of the Constitution involves much more than an examination of its judicial interpretation. The Constitution is not merely what the Supreme Court says it is; its words are not so many empty vessels into which justices can pour meaning. Accordingly, this volume examines the interpretations of a variety of sources. The original intent of the framers, the original understanding of the ratifiers, and the original public meaning of the words and phrases of the Constitution are important sources. Another, equally indispensable source is, of course, the Supreme Court, whose decisions have influenced so profoundly our understanding of the Constitution and its principles. And because other governmental bodies have contributed significantly to the overall interpretation of the Constitution, this text includes decisions of the lower federal courts and state judiciaries and also extrajudicial materials of constitutional significance such as certain congressional acts and resolutions and executive orders.

As we approach constitutional questions throughout this text, we begin by turning to the Framers. We do so, however, not so much for specific answers as for general guidance concerning what the Constitution was designed to accomplish. Obviously, no interpretation can be expected to conform strictly to the expectations of the Framers. Other legitimate approaches may also contribute to an understanding of the Constitution, relying variously on analysis of the text itself, judicial precedent, constitutional doctrine, logical reasoning, adaptation of constitutional provisions to changing circumstances, and a concern for the consequences of any particular decision. All these approaches are described in Chapter 1.

The structure of the volumes might be seen as a reflection of James Madison's observation in *The Federalist,* No. 51, that "in framing a government which is to be administered by men over men, the great difficulty lies in this: you must first enable the government to control the governed; and in the next place; oblige it to control itself." Chapter 1 explores in general how the Constitution was designed to resolve this difficulty, and Chapter 2 introduces the reader to the actual process of constitutional adjudication. The remainder of this two-volume work systematically examines how the Constitution and its amendments not only grant the national and state governments sufficient power to control the governed but also oblige these governments to control themselves. Chapters 3 through 6 of Volume I consider the distribution of power in the national government, specifically exploring how the constitutional scheme of separation of powers and checks and balances both grants and controls power. Because of the importance of the distribution of power among the branches of the national government, we devote separate chapters to the judiciary, Congress, the presidency, and war and foreign affairs. Chapters 7 through 11 of Volume I consider the distribution of power between the national government and the states and between the national government and Native American tribal governments, focusing on how the division of power among various governments in the United States helps to advance the ends of the Constitution. Chapter 12 (also included as Chapter 4 in Volume II) and Chapters 3 through 11 of Volume II shift to an examination of the distribution of power between the government and the individual. The emphasis in these chapters is not so much on institutional contrivances that oblige the government to control itself as on the Bill of Rights and those subsequent amendments that guarantee specific rights and liberties, an emphasis that illuminates the way in which our most precious rights and liberties have increasingly become dependent for their vindication not upon constitutional structure but upon what *The Federalist* called mere "parchment barriers."

With the exception of the first two chapters, each chapter opens with an introductory essay that is then followed by cases and, where appropriate, extrajudicial materials. Each essay ends with extensive notes that provide valuable explanatory details and references to additional materials and a list of suggested readings, including essays in *The Federalist,* additional cases, and scholarly books and articles. Each case also has its own introductory headnote, which provides historical perspective, indicates where the case stands in relation to current law, and gives the final court vote. Some cases have endnotes that elaborate on the short- and long-term consequences of the decision. The text includes three appendixes: the Constitution of the United States, a list of Supreme Court justices, and a table of cases.

We encourage our readers to visit our newly revamped and updated website at westviewconlaw.com for additional cases and other resources in understanding the Supreme Court and constitutional law, including links to primary sources and relevant blogs and websites. The additional cases, numbering more than 150 and formatted identically to those included in the casebooks, are organized by volume and chapter. With the exceptions of Chapters 1 and 2, each of the chapters will have the deleted cases found in past editions, cases that we edited for the website in the past but were never included in subsequent editions, and new cases decided after the publication of the Tenth Edition. Check back every September for new cases and updated resources.

We would like to thank the excellent editorial staff at Westview Press for so smoothly and efficiently bringing the Tenth Edition into print. We express particular gratitude to Senior Editor Ada Fung; Associate Managing Editor Krista Anderson; our project editor, Cisca Schreefel; and our copyeditor, George DeStefano. We would also like to thank the peer reviewers who provided us with helpful and insightful feedback, including: Joseph Knippenberg (Oglethorpe University); Vincent Muñoz (University of Notre Dame); Michael Zarkin (Westminster College); and the many others who wished to remain anonymous.

Any errors of fact or interpretation are, of course, solely our responsibility. Finally, we wish to express our gratitude to our wives, Constance and Susan, for their patience, understanding, and loving support throughout this decades-long project.

Ralph A. Rossum
G. Alan Tarr

Note to the Reader

The authors of *American Constitutional Law* have adopted a convention to inform the reader of how each justice then serving on the Supreme Court voted in each of the cases presented in these two volumes. The convention is perhaps best explained by an example. At the end of the headnote to *Kelo v. City of New London* (2005), a case found in "Economic Due Process and the Takings Clause" (Chapter 12 in Volume I and Chapter 4 in Volume II), the following language is found: "Opinion of the Court: <u>Stevens</u>, Kennedy, Souter, Ginsburg, Breyer. Concurring opinion: <u>Kennedy</u>. Dissenting opinions: <u>O'Connor</u>, Rehnquist, Scalia, Thomas; <u>Thomas</u>." This language indicates that (1) the Court in *Kelo* was divided 5–4 on the question before it; (2) Justice Stevens wrote the opinion of the Court in which Justices Kennedy, Souter, Ginsburg, and Breyer joined (for any opinion, be it the opinion of the Court, the judgment of the Court, a concurrence, or a dissent, the author's name is listed first and underscored, followed by the names of the other justices who join in that opinion—listed in order of seniority); (3) Justice Kennedy wrote a separate concurring opinion (concurring opinions are listed separately from opinions in which justices concur only in the judgment of the Court); (4) Justices O'Connor, Scalia, and Thomas and Chief Justice Rehnquist dissented; (5) Justice O'Connor wrote a dissenting opinion in which Chief Justice Rehnquist and Justices Scalia and Thomas joined; and (6) Justice Thomas wrote a separate dissenting opinion (each concurring or dissenting opinion is separated from the others by a semicolon). Throughout the casebook, the name of any justice who wrote an opinion in a case is underscored whether or not excerpts from that opinion are actually included in the text.

For additional cases and resources, please visit www.westviewconlaw.com

1

Interpretation of the Constitution

We are under a Constitution, but the Constitution is what the Court says it is."[1] In the century since Charles Evans Hughes, then governor of New York and later chief justice of the United States Supreme Court, uttered these now famous words, they have been repeated so often and in so many contexts that they have assumed a prescriptive as well as a descriptive character. But exactly how valid is this prescription for understanding the US Constitution?

Hughes's observation certainly contains some truth. Many provisions of the Constitution are not self-defining and so have been the objects of judicial interpretation and construction. Various criminal procedural protections found in Amendments Four through Eight immediately spring to mind. What, after all, makes a particular search or seizure "unreasonable"? What is sufficient to establish "probable cause"? What constitutes "due process of law"? What is a "speedy" trial? What is an "excessive" fine or bail? What is "cruel and unusual punishment"? Hughes's claim also portrays accurately the perspective of lower-court judges and practicing attorneys. However erroneous they might believe the Supreme Court's understanding of a particular constitutional provision, lower-court judges feel obliged to adhere to the Court's interpretation. And lawyers usually seek to accomplish their objectives within the framework of the prevailing Court view rather than attempting to convince the justices to abandon that view.

Yet, Hughes's assertion is also misleading in several respects. Above all, it fails to recognize that governmental bodies other than the Supreme Court also contribute to an overall interpretation of the Constitution. By passing the War Powers Resolution of 1973, for example, the US Congress undertook to define the constitutional limits of the president's powers to initiate and conduct undeclared war, an issue the Supreme Court has refused to consider. Likewise, in the Speedy Trial Act of 1984, Congress took upon itself constitutional interpretation in the sphere of criminal procedure, declaring that a defendant not brought to trial within one hundred days of arrest can move for a dismissal of the charges. In so doing, it gave meaning to a constitutional provision that the Supreme Court itself has acknowledged to be vaguer than any other procedural right. And in the Voting Rights Act of 1982, Congress held that the Fifteenth Amendment (barring states from denying citizens the right to vote "on account of race, color, or previous condition of servitude") bans not only intentional discrimination against the voting rights of minorities (what the Supreme Court had held) but any electoral scheme that has the effect of preventing minority voters from electing "representatives of their choice." Constitutionally significant pronouncements have also emanated from the executive branch and from the lower federal and state courts. (Statements made by President Abraham Lincoln have had more to do with defining the outer bounds of presidential prerogative than have any statements of the Court, just as actions taken by President Franklin D. Roosevelt altered the balance of power between the national government and the states far more than any judicial opinion.)

Another problem with Hughes's assertion is that it obscures the extent to which the meaning of the Constitution is clear and uncontroversial. Most constitutional provisions are settled; what questions are raised about them pertain not to fundamental meaning but rather to specific application. Relatively few constitutional provisions have sparked protracted debate and controversy: the Commerce Clause of Article I, Section 8, authorizing Congress to regulate commerce among the several states; the First Amendment's establishment of religion and free exercise clauses as well as its guarantees of freedom of speech and of the press; the language of the Fifth and Fourteenth Amendments that no person shall be deprived of life, liberty, or property without due process of law; and the Fourteenth Amendment's pronouncement that no person shall be denied the equal protection of the laws. Although these provisions are extremely important, the intense debate over them tends to obscure how ably the Constitution has governed our political actions for the past two and a quarter centuries. By focusing exclusively on these provisions and arguing, implicitly or explicitly, that they are fundamentally without meaning until construed by the Court, some jurists and legal scholars have reinforced the view that the Constitution is deficient in decisive respects and therefore unworthy of vital public support. As a result, the Constitution is deprived of what James Madison, in *The Federalist,* No. 49, called "that veneration which time bestows on everything, and without which perhaps the wisest and freest governments would not possess the requisite stability." This is of no minor concern, for, as Madison continues, "the most rational government will not find it a superfluous advantage, to have the prejudices of the community on its side."

Still another problem with the view that the Constitution means only what the Court says it means is that it denies that the Constitution is capable of being understood not only by those who made and ratified it but also by those who continue to live under it. As Justice Joseph Story put it in his *Commentaries on the Constitution of the United States:*

> Every word employed in the Constitution is to be expounded in its plain, obvious, and common sense, unless the context provides some ground to control, qualify, or enlarge it. Constitutions are not designed for metaphysical or logical subtleties, for niceties of expression, for critical propriety, for elaborate shades of meaning, or for the exercise of philosophical acuteness or judicial research. They are instruments of a practical nature, founded on the common business of human life, adapted to common wants, designed for common use, and fitted for common understandings. The people make them; the people adopt them; the people must be supposed to read them, with the help of common sense, and cannot be presumed to admit in them any recondite meaning or extraordinary gloss.[2]

In a popular government, the people should take an active interest in the Constitution that gives form to their politics and protection to their liberties; they should not be discouraged from doing so by talk that the Constitution is some obscure document capable of being understood only by Supreme Court justices or by those trained in the law.

A related problem: the view that the Constitution is whatever the Court says it is implies that the Constitution has no meaning in and of itself. If all meaning must be poured into it by the Court, we are unlikely to turn to it for basic instruction on the principles, problems, and prospects of the American regime. The proudest claim of those responsible for framing and ratifying the Constitution was, as stated in *The Federalist,* No. 10, that it provided "a Republican remedy for the diseases most incident to Republican Government." If we strip the Constitution of all independent meaning, we are unlikely to remember the Founders' answers to the basic questions and dilemmas of democratic government—and what is even more regrettable, we are likely to forget the questions themselves.

Yet another effect of presenting the Constitution as devoid of any independent meaning is that it encourages uncritical acceptance of Supreme Court decisions. If the Constitution has only that meaning ascribed to it by the Supreme Court, on what basis, other than subjective preference, can anyone object to the Court's interpretations? On what constitutional basis, for example, can one object to the Supreme Court's decisions in *Dred Scott v. Sandford* (1857), declaring that African Americans could not be citizens, and in *Plessy v. Ferguson* (1896), upholding racial segregation? Students of the Court implicitly acknowledge this problem by routinely paying lip service to Hughes's assertion and then criticizing at length judicial interpretations that they find wanting in fidelity to the language of the Constitution, in scholarship, in craftsmanship, or in deference to the popularly elected branches.

Finally, Hughes's claim ignores the influence that political institutions can have on political behavior. The Court is seen as influencing the Constitution; rarely is the influence that the Constitution might have on the Court, or on politics more generally, even considered.

APPROACHES TO CONSTITUTIONAL INTERPRETATION

To avoid these problems, we will argue, along with Justice Felix Frankfurter, that the "ultimate touchstone of constitutionality is the Constitution itself and not what the [judges] have said about it."[3] But what, in fact, does the Constitution mean? How are we to understand its provisions and give them effect? In searching for satisfactory answers to these questions, students of the Constitution have proposed several approaches to constitutional interpretation, each of which has its own strengths and weaknesses.[4]

Textual Analysis

One approach to constitutional interpretation involves explicating the constitutional text simply on the basis of the words found there. The basic claim of this approach seems unarguable: if the Constitution is to control the outcome of a case, and if its text is plain, then constitutional interpretation should stop right there. As Justice Noah Swayne observed in *United States v. Hartwell* (1868): "If the language be clear, it is conclusive. There cannot be construction where there is nothing to construe."

On today's Supreme Court, the late Justice Antonin Scalia is most closely associated with the textualist approach. He argued that the Court is to interpret the text alone and nothing else. Thus in *Coy v. Iowa* (1988), he upheld the right of a defendant, under the Sixth Amendment, literally to "be confronted with the witnesses against him" and overturned his conviction because Iowa law allowed the two thirteen-year-old girls he was charged with sexually assaulting to testify behind a large screen that shielded them from the defendant. For Scalia, the text was unequivocal and governing: "Simply as a matter of English, it confers at least 'a right to meet face to face all those who appear and give evidence at trial.' Simply as a matter of Latin as well, since the word 'confront' ultimately derives from the prefix 'con-' (from 'contra' meaning 'against' or 'opposed') and the noun 'frons' (forehead). Shakespeare was thus describing the root meaning of confrontation when he had Richard the Second say: 'Then call them to our presence—face to face, and frowning brow to brow, ourselves will hear the accuser and the accused freely speak.'"

Textualism, however, has its limitations. Although many provisions of the Constitution are perfectly clear, others require extensive construction. Consider Article II, section 4, authorizing the impeachment of "the President, Vice President, and all civil officers of the United States" for "high Crimes and Misdemeanors"—a phrase some believe includes not only criminal offenses but also noncriminal behavior amounting to a serious dereliction of duty. Moreover, even if the meanings of all relevant words are perfectly plain, problems of emphasis remain. As Justice Stephen Breyer has noted, "All controversies of importance involve if not a conflict at least an interplay of principles."[5] In many cases, two or more constitutional provisions come into play, and the justices must decide which is to be given priority. To provide just one example of this problem, consider adverse pretrial publicity in a criminal case. Does the First Amendment guarantee of the freedom of speech and the press supersede the Sixth Amendment guarantee of a trial "by an impartial jury"? As this example indicates, the constitutional text in and of itself cannot resolve all the questions that the Constitution raises.

Precedent

When textual analysis alone is inadequate, many students of the Constitution turn to previously decided cases, searching for answers on the basis of precedent, or stare decisis ("to
stand by decided matters"). That is, they seek guidance from how judges have interpreted
a provision in prior cases.

Reliance on precedent, the primary mode of legal reasoning in Anglo-American law,
adds stability, continuity, and predictability to the entire legal enterprise. But judges have
relied on precedent only sporadically in constitutional law. Very good arguments can be
adduced either to adhere to or to depart from precedent. No Supreme Court case presents
these opposing arguments better than *Payne v. Tennessee* (1991), a 5–4 decision that overturned two recent precedents also decided by 5–4 votes—*Booth v. Maryland* (1987) and
South Carolina v. Gathers (1989)—and held that "victim-impact" statements in the penalty
stage of capital punishment cases do not violate the Eighth Amendment's prohibition of
"cruel and unusual punishment." Justice Thurgood Marshall in dissent attacked the *Payne*
majority for departing from precedent, claiming that nothing "has changed since this
Court decided both *Booth* and *Gathers*" other than "this Court's own personnel" and concluding that "this truncation of the Court's duty to stand by its own precedents is astonishing." Justice Scalia in a concurring opinion replied that what would be truly astonishing is
"the notion that an important constitutional decision with plainly inadequate rational
support must be left in place for the sole reason that it once attracted five votes."

Many jurists and scholars believe that interpreters should look to the Constitution itself, rather than to prior interpretations of that document, in deciding cases. Then, too,
constitutional cases deal with momentous social and political issues that only temporarily
take the form of litigation, and there is wide recognition that these issues cannot be resolved satisfactorily on the same basis as other legal problems. To some critics, relying on
precedent for constitutional interpretation is rather like driving a car down a busy street
while looking only through the rearview mirror: we get a good notion of where we have
been but not where we should be going. As Thomas Hobbes observed in *A Dialogue Between a Philosopher and a Student of the Common Laws of England*, "Precedents prove only
what was done, but not what was well done."[6] This difficulty seems especially troublesome
in constitutional law. Most areas of law lack clearly defined ends or purposes and so must
evolve by way of precedent. The common law, for example, is based mainly on long-standing usage or judicial precedent. Constitutional law, on the other hand, has before it certain
"directions, goals, and ideals" that are easily discernible in the Constitution. Once discerned, these guideposts make it possible for the Court to decide matters of political and
social import not in terms of what previous Courts have held, but in light of what is most
conducive to achieving the goals or purposes of the Constitution.[7]

Constitutional Doctrine

When neither the constitutional text nor precedent provides an adequate account of the
meaning of the Constitution, arguments from "constitutional doctrine" might be raised.
Constitutional doctrines are formulas—sometimes nothing more than slogans—extracted
from a combination of the constitutional text and a series of related cases. The Equal Protection Clause of the Fourteenth Amendment provides several examples of the development
and use of constitutional doctrines. When considered as it applies to questions of race, this
clause typically is understood to prohibit discrimination (although the word *discrimination* is
nowhere to be found in the amendment); when considered as it applies to questions of legislative apportionment, it typically is understood to require "one person, one vote" (another
phrase not found in the text). Similarly, the First Amendment's Establishment Clause, which

charges Congress to "make no law respecting an establishment of religion," has been inter-preted by many as erecting a high "wall of separation" between church and state. In these il-lustrations, the enunciated constitutional doctrines serve as mediating principles that stand between specific controversies and the Constitution, giving meaning and content to ideals that may—or may not—be embodied in the text.

Although these examples suggest that constitutional doctrines broaden the scope of the constitutional text they reference, this is not invariably the case. Take the protection against self-incrimination. The Fifth Amendment does not use the term *self-incrimination;* rather, it reads: "No person . . . shall be compelled in any criminal case to be a witness against himself." Unlike certain other reformulations of constitutional provisions, such as "separation of church and state" for the Establishment Clause, "freedom of expres-sion" for "the freedom of speech, or of the press," and "interstate commerce" for "com-merce among the several states," this reformulation is narrower than the constitutional guarantee itself. Individuals can be witnesses against themselves in ways that do not in-criminate them; they can, in criminal cases, injure their civil interests or disgrace them-selves. Thus, unlike the constitutional doctrine limiting the Fifth Amendment to "self-incrimination," the words of the amendment would seem to apply as well to any disclosures that would expose either criminal defendants or witnesses to civil liability or public condemnation.

Over time, many of these doctrines have come to give the constitutional provision in question its only meaning as a guide for decision. This substitution for the original texts may have profound implications. As such doctrines become increasingly important, public debate tends to center on the meaning of the doctrines and not on the meaning of the Constitution itself. In reference to the Equal Protection Clause, for example, the contem-porary debate over affirmative action and diversity has focused almost exclusively on such questions as whether this policy is discriminatory against; the question of what "equal protection of the law" truly means has been all but forgotten. Equally disturbing is the fact that reducing constitutional provisions to doctrines often interferes with thoughtful con-sideration of the constitutional issues.

The "one person, one vote" rule provides a case in point. On only the most elemental level does this rule have meaning; after all, the question of permitting certain voters the opportunity to vote two, five, or ten times has never been raised by any of the legislative reapportionment cases. In *Baker v. Carr* (1962), for example, the central issue was how much the voter's one vote was to be worth—a question that moved Justice Frankfurter to ask:

> What is this question of legislative apportionment? Appellants invoke the right to vote and have their votes counted. But they are permitted to vote and their votes are counted. They go to the polls, they cast their ballots, they send their represen-tatives to the state councils. Their complaint is simply that the representatives are not sufficiently numerous or powerful—in short, that Tennessee has adopted a basis of representation with which they are not satisfied. Talk of "debasement" or "dilution" is circular talk. One cannot speak of "debasement" or "dilution" of the value of a vote until there is first defined a standard of reference as to what a vote should be worth.

Emphasis on "one person, one vote" merely obscured these questions and added to doctrinal confusion. Because of this problem, Justice Abe Fortas broke from the Court majority in the legislative reapportionment cases, declaring that such "admittedly complex and subtle" matters must be governed by "substance, not shibboleth." He complained that formulas such as "one person, one vote," "are not surgical instruments"; rather, "they have a tendency to hack deeply—to amputate."[8] The ease of applying such formulas may make them attractive, but this may come at the price of clarity in constitutional understanding.

Logical Reasoning

Another approach to constitutional interpretation emphasizes the use of logical reasoning as exemplified in the syllogism, a formal argument consisting of a major premise, a minor premise, and a conclusion.[9] The major premise sets forth a proposition, such as "A law repugnant to the Constitution is void." The minor premise contains an assertion related to the major premise: "This particular law is repugnant to the Constitution." From these premises the conclusion logically follows: "This particular law is void." The foregoing example represents the essence of Chief Justice John Marshall's reasoning in *Marbury v. Madison* (1803), which formally established the Court's power of judicial review (that is, the power to void legislative or executive acts that the Court finds unconstitutional).

Marshall himself was well aware, however, that logical analysis is an insufficient method of interpreting the Constitution. If the validity of the major premise is assumed, the soundness of the conclusion depends on whether what is asserted in the minor premise is true.[10] But logic cannot determine whether a particular law is repugnant to the Constitution. Justice Owen Roberts made things too simple in *United States v. Butler* (1936) by arguing that "when an act of Congress is appropriately challenged in the courts as not conforming to the constitutional mandate the judicial branch of the Government has only one duty—to lay the article of the Constitution which is invoked beside the statute which is challenged and to decide whether the latter squares with the former." Whether an act in fact squares with the Constitution is a question that must be left to informed opinion and judgment—informed opinion about the purposes for which the Constitution was established and judgment of as to whether the law in question is consistent with those purposes.

Logical analysis, therefore, must be supplemented with a clear understanding of what *The Federalist,* No. 10, calls the "great objects" of the Constitution. Even Marshall, the justice most commonly identified with the use of logical analysis, ultimately based his constitutional interpretations on his understanding of the ends the Constitution was designed to serve. Marshall believed that the Constitution points beyond itself to the purposes and policies that it serves; in the difficult (and most interesting) cases, constitutional interpretation must turn upon an understanding of the Constitution's proper ends. He confidently observed in *McCulloch v. Maryland* (1819) that the nature of the Constitution demands "that only its great outlines should be marked, its important objects designated." As for the "minor ingredients" that compose these objects, he was convinced that they could be "deduced from the nature of the objects themselves."

The Living Constitution

Based on changing conditions and the lessons of experience, the adaptive, or "living Constitution," approach holds that constitutional interpretation can and must be influenced by present-day values and take account of changing conditions in society. One of its critics writes that its proponents regard the Constitution as a "morphing document"[11] that means, from age to age, whatever the society, and more particularly the Court, thinks it ought to mean. The "living Constitution" approach has been enshrined in the Court's interpretation of the Eighth Amendment's prohibition against cruel and unusual punishments. The Court has held, beginning with *Trop v. Dulles* (1957), that this prohibition is not "static" but changes from generation to generation to comport with what Chief Justice Earl Warren called "the evolving standards of decency that mark the progress of a maturing society."

Proponents of this approach concede that these adaptations must be reconcilable with the language of the Constitution. But, they insist, the meaning of the Commerce Clause, or what is protected by the Fourth Amendment or by the Due Process or Equal Protection Clauses, or the reach of the Eighth Amendment can legitimately change over time. For example, no one voting to adopt or ratify the Fourteenth Amendment in 1868 would have believed that they were, therefore, requiring the states to grant licenses for same-sex marriage. However, Justice Kennedy, relying equally on a "living Constitution" interpretation of both the Due Process and Equal Protection Clauses of the Fourteenth Amendment, would conclude for a five-member majority in *Obergefell v. Hodges* (2015) that a proper contemporary understanding of the principles enshrined by these clauses in the Constitution required exactly that. As Kennedy argued, "the nature of injustice is that we may not always see it in our own times. The generations that wrote and ratified the Bill of Rights and the Fourteenth Amendment did not presume to know the extent of freedom in all of its dimensions, and so they entrusted to future generations a charter protecting the right of all persons to enjoy liberty as we learn its meaning. When new insight reveals discord between the Constitution's central protections and a received legal stricture, a claim to liberty must be addressed." And, he continued, "Indeed, in interpreting the Equal Protection Clause, the Court has recognized that new insights and societal understandings can reveal unjustified inequality within our most fundamental institutions that once passed unnoticed and unchallenged."

The rationale for the living Constitution approach is well stated by Justice Oliver Wendell Holmes in *Missouri v. Holland* (1920):

> When we are dealing with words that also are a constituent act, like the Constitution of the United States, we must realize that they have called into life a being the development of which could not have been foreseen completely by the most gifted of its begetters. It was enough for them to realize or to hope that they had created an organism; it has taken a century and has cost their successors much sweat and blood to prove that they created a nation. The case before us must be considered in the light of our whole experience and not merely in that of what was said a hundred years ago.

Defenders of this approach also like to cite Chief Justice Marshall's observation in *McCulloch* that "we must never forget that it is a constitution we are expounding," one that is "intended to endure for ages to come, and consequently, to be adapted to the various crises of human affairs." However, Marshall was not asserting in *McCulloch* that the Court should adapt the Constitution but was arguing instead that the powers of the Constitution should be understood as broad enough to provide Congress with sufficient latitude to confront various crises in the future.[12]

Like the other approaches to constitutional interpretation considered thus far, the adaptive or "living Constitution" approach has its problems. Most important, too much adaptation can render the Constitution and its various provisions so pliant that the original document is no longer able to provide guidance concerning what is to be done. Some who embrace the adaptive approach seek not merely an adaptation *within* the Constitution but rather an adaptation *of* the Constitution; they want not only to devise new means to the ends of the Constitution but to adopt entirely new ends as well.[13] Justice Byron White's frustration in *New York v. United States* (1992) with the Court's insistence that Congress act in conformity with federalism and the Tenth Amendment is a case in point:

> The Court rejects this . . . argument by resorting to generalities and platitudes about the purpose of federalism being to protect individual rights. Ultimately, I suppose, the entire structure of our federal constitutional government can be traced

to an interest in establishing checks and balances to prevent the exercise of tyranny against individuals. But these fears seem extremely far distant to me in a situation such as this. We face a crisis of national proportions in the disposal of low-level radioactive waste. . . . For me, the Court's civics lecture has a decidedly hollow ring at a time when action, rather than rhetoric, is needed to solve a national problem.

Justice William Brennan's objections to capital punishment also illustrate the problems of the adaptive approach. He consistently argued that the objective of the Cruel and Unusual Punishments Clause of the Eighth Amendment is the promotion of "human dignity" and, by insisting that capital punishment is a denial of human dignity, concluded that capital punishment is unconstitutional,[14] despite the fact that the Constitution permits capital trials when preceded by a "presentment or indictment of a Grand Jury," permits a person to be "put in jeopardy of life" provided it is not done twice "for the same offense," and permits both the national government and the states to deprive persons of their lives provided it is done with "due process of law."

The consequence of such an approach may be an increased politicization of the federal judiciary. As Justice Scalia pointed out in *A Matter of Interpretation:* "If the people come to believe that the Constitution . . . means, not what it says or what it was understood to mean, but what it *should* mean, in light of the 'evolving standards of decency that mark the progress of a maturing society'—well, then, they will look for qualifications other than impartiality, judgment, and lawyerly acumen in those whom they select to interpret it." In fact, "they will look for judges who agree with *them* as to what the evolving standards have evolved to; who agree with *them* as to what the Constitution *ought* to be."[15]

The ultimate objection to the "living Constitution" is its essentially arbitrary quality—if it evolves in a way one likes, it is the "unfolding of the American dream;" if it evolves in a way one does not, it is not only a breach of the nation's pledge to adhere to its original principles but also the unfolding of an American nightmare.

Consequentialism

A consequentialist approach to interpretation will read a constitutional or statutory text with an eye to what will be the "practical consequences" of a Court's decision on the "contemporary conditions, social, industrial, and political of the community to be affected." In his book, *Active Liberty*, Justice Breyer proudly proclaims himself a consequentialist. Thus, for example, in campaign finance reform cases, he declares that "restrictions on speech, even when political speech is at issue," are reasonable and lawful; the campaign reform law's negative consequences on "those primarily wealthier citizens who wish to engage in more electoral communication" are more than offset by its positive consequences on the "public's confidence in, and ability to communicate through, the electoral process." And, concerning federalism issues, he asks, "Why should courts try to answer difficult federalism questions on the basis of logical deduction from text or precedent alone? Why not ask about the consequences of decision-making on the active liberty that federalism seeks to further."[16] Another example: In *District of Columbia v. Heller* (2008), Breyer dissented from the Court's majority opinion that held that the Second Amendment secures an individual right to keep and bear arms for self-defense because of its "unfortunate consequences," including threatening "to leave cities without effective protection against gun violence and accidents."

Most justices who employ consequentialist arguments in constitutional cases lack Breyer's candor in admitting that they are doing so; they simply do it. Some representative examples: in *Linkletter v. Walker* (1965), Justice Tom Clark wrote for a seven-member majority refusing to apply *Mapp v. Ohio* (1961) retroactively, because it would "tax the administration of justice to the utmost," that is, it would allow every person in prison serving a sentence where at trial illegally seized evidence was admitted to seek a new hearing, a new trial, or outright release. In *Planned Parenthood v. Casey* (1992), Justices O'Connor, Kennedy, and Souter in their joint plurality opinion refused to overrule *Roe v. Wade* (1972), despite their "reservations" that it was correctly decided because of the negative consequences that would have on the Court's legitimacy. "A decision to overrule *Roe's* essential holding under the existing circumstances would address error, if error there was, at the cost of both profound and unnecessary damage to the Court's legitimacy, and to the Nation's commitment to the rule of law." In *Blakely v. Washington* (2004), Justice O'Connor wrote for the four justices in dissent, rejecting the majority's decision that the right to trial by jury required that every element of a crime that increases its penalty must be submitted to a jury and proved beyond a reasonable doubt because it would "trim or eliminate altogether" federal and state sentencing guidelines schemes. In *United States v. Windsor* (2013), Justice Kennedy insisted that the Supreme Court had jurisdiction in that case to declare unconstitutional the Defense of Marriage Act (DOMA) for two consequentialist reasons. To begin with, "the costs, uncertainties, and alleged harm and injuries [inflicted by DOMA] likely would continue for a time measured in years before the issue is resolved." In addition, the Obama Administration's refusal to defend DOMA would otherwise "preclude judicial review" and would thereby make "the Court's role in determining the constitutionality of a law . . . secondary to the President's." And, in *Harris v. Quinn* (2014), Justice Kagan, in her dissent, justified the suppression of free speech for a class of public employees on the grounds that "thousands of contracts involving millions of employees" would have to be renegotiated.

Breyer admits that his approach makes it easy for a judge to be "willful, in the sense of enforcing [his] individual views."[17] It is a temptation to which many on the Court have succumbed—and for a very long time. Indeed, Justice Scalia has claimed that consequentialism "is nothing but an invitation to judicial lawmaking."[18]

Originalism

Originalism is an umbrella term, referring to original intent, original understanding, and original public meaning. While these three terms are often used interchangeably and the approaches overlap somewhat, each can be seen as a distinct approach to constitutional interpretation. The first approach, *original intent*, seeks to identify what the delegates to the Constitutional Convention in Philadelphia collectively intended to accomplish when they drafted the Constitution in the summer of 1787. Those who pursue an original intent approach do so because they believe that "interpreting a document means to attempt to discern the intent of the author."[19] Therefore, they focus on the text of the Constitution, on the records of the Constitutional Convention, on what the delegates said about the Constitution as it was being drafted. Madison's notes figure most prominently for them, but other delegates also took notes and many of the delegates wrote letters and essays during and after the Convention that provide for them insight into the Framers' intentions.

The second approach to originalism is *original understanding*. It focuses on identifying what the various provisions of the Constitution meant to those who brought the Constitution into existence, the delegates of the state ratifying conventions of 1787 and 1788. Those who pursue an original understanding approach point out that the Constitutional Convention met in secret under a rule that declared that "nothing spoken in the House be printed, or otherwise published, or communicated without leave," and, as a consequence, the public did not become aware of its records and what was said there until decades after ratification of the Constitution. Therefore, the best way to discern the original understanding of the Constitution is to look at what the delegates said at the ratifying conventions and at what arguments were made by the various Federalist and Anti-Federalist writers attempting to influence the election of those delegates. Those who advocate an original understanding approach cite James Madison, who declared on the floor of the House on April 16, 1796:

> Whatever veneration might be entertained for the body of men who formed our Constitution, the sense of that body could never be regarded as the oracular guide in expounding the Constitution. As the instrument came from them it was nothing more than the draft of a plan, nothing but a dead letter, until life and validity were breathed into it by the voice of the people, speaking through the several State Conventions. If we were to look, therefore, for the meaning of the instrument beyond the face of the instrument, we must look for it, not in the General Convention, which proposed, but in the State Conventions, which accepted and ratified the Constitution.

The third approach to originalism is *original public meaning*, which is closely tied to textualism and is most closely associated with the late Justice Scalia. This approach seeks to ascertain the meaning of the particular constitutional text in question at the time of its adoption by consulting dictionaries of the era and other founding-era documents "to discern the then-customary meaning of the word and phrases in the Constitution." As Scalia put it in *A Matter of Interpretation*:

> I will consult the writings of some men who happened to be delegates to the Constitutional Convention–Hamilton's and Madison's writings in *The Federalist*, for example. I do so, however, not because they were Framers and therefore their intent is authoritative and must be the law; but rather because their writings, like those of other intelligent and informed people of the time, display how the text of the Constitution was originally understood. Thus, I give equal weight to Jay's pieces in *The Federalist*, and to Jefferson's writings, even though neither of them was a Framer. What I look for in the Constitution is precisely what I look for in a statute: the original meaning of the text, not what the original draftsmen intended.[20]

Scalia's majority opinion in *District of Columbia v. Heller* (2008), in which he held that the Second Amendment protects an individual's right to keep and bear arms for purposes of self-defense, demonstrates his original public meaning approach to constitutional interpretation. In it, he turned to dictionaries and legal encyclopedias from the late eighteenth century to determine what such words as "keep," "bear," "arms," and "well-regulated militia" meant to those who adopted and ratified the Second Amendment.

Although original intent, original understanding, and original public meaning typically lead to the same result, they do not always do so. Consider, for example, the question of state sovereign immunity where the text of Article III, § 2 suggests the states could be sued in federal court without their consent; where Alexander Hamilton in *The Federalist*, No. 81 and John Marshall in the Virginia State Ratifying Convention said they could not; where the Supreme Court in 1793 in *Chisholm v. Georgia* said they could; and finally where Congress and the state legislatures through their adoption and ratification of the Eleventh Amendment two years later said they could not. Consider also the tension between original intent and original understanding regarding the legal effect of treaties. James Wilson was one of the most prominent delegates to the Constitutional Convention—he more than any other delegate shaped the executive branch. He chaired the important Committee on Detail that turned the various resolutions approved by the delegates into a draft of the eventual Constitution; he considered treaties to be self-executing, having "the operation of law" without requiring implementing legislation.

Wilson's original intent position differed completely from Hamilton's original understanding view in *The Federalist*, No. 75 that treaties "are not rules prescribed by the sovereign to the subject [i.e., they do not apply directly to the people and therefore do not have the operation of law], but agreements between sovereign and sovereign."

On the current Supreme Court, Justice Clarence Thomas looks simultaneously to original public meaning, original intent, and original understanding to identify what is, in fact, the Constitution's original general meaning.[21] In so doing, he incorporates Scalia's narrower original public meaning approach and also asks what the text meant to the society that adopted it, but he then widens his originalist focus to consider evidence of the original intent of the Framers and the original understanding of the ratifiers and to ask why the text was adopted. Thomas thus views the proper inquiry as being what ends did the Framers seek to achieve, what evils did they seek to avert, and what means did they employ to achieve those ends and avert those evils when they proposed and ratified those texts.

Originalism as an approach to constitutional interpretation is enjoying a revival. In 1987, Scalia's first year on the Court, originalist arguments were made in only 7 percent of constitutional cases, but twenty years later, with Scalia and Thomas together on the Court, they were made in nearly 35 percent of all cases.[22] Originalist arguments are prevailing in a variety of cases—especially in cases involving the rights of criminal defendants. There has been such a dramatic increase in the number of books, law review articles, and legal briefs advancing originalist analyses that Justice Elena Kagan, during her Senate confirmation hearings stated: "We are all originalists."

That, however, has not shielded originalism from criticism. Some object to the very idea of originalism; as Walton H. Hamilton has famously noted, "It is a little presumptuous for one generation, through a Constitution, to impose its will on posterity. Posterity has its own problems, and to deal with them adequately, it needs freedom of action, unhampered by the dead hand of the past."[23] Originalists, however, deny that they are attempting to impose the founding generation's will on posterity. Rather, they seek to understand the intentions of the Framers, the understanding of the ratifiers, and the original meaning of the words and phrases they employed not because their judgments must be embraced unreservedly, but because they wrote and ratified the very Constitution we are called on to interpret; therefore, they are the best possible guides to discovering the ends and means of the constitutional order under which we live. As long as that order remains in force, we need to know as much about the Constitution as possible, including the purposes it was designed to achieve and the evils it was designed to avert. When constitutional questions are raised, therefore, this approach turns to the founding generation not for specific answers but rather for general guidance as to what the Constitution was to accomplish and how constitutional questions can be resolved in a manner consistent with these overall intentions.

Others such as Justice William Brennan criticize originalism as "little more than arrogance cloaked as humility. It is arrogant to pretend that from our vantage we can gauge accurately the intent of the Framers on application of principle to specific, contemporary questions."[24] Or, as Justice Robert Jackson put it in *Youngstown Sheet & Tube Company v. Sawyer* (1952), "Just what our forefathers did envision, or would have envisioned had they foreseen modern conditions, must be divined from materials almost as enigmatic as the dreams Joseph was called to interpret for Pharaoh." If the problem Brennan and Jackson identify is a lack of evidence as to original intent, understanding, and meaning it must be noted that with the tremendous outpouring of historical scholarship surrounding and following the bicentennial celebrations of the Declaration of Independence, the Constitution, and the Bill of Rights, we are awash in originalist sources. Since 1976, the Wisconsin Historical Society has published twenty-six volumes (with four more to come) of *The Documentary History of the Ratification of the Constitution*. In 1987, Philip B. Kurland and

Ralph Lerner published *The Founders' Constitution*, a five-volume work that includes original sources critical to the drafting and ratification of each article, clause, and paragraph of the US Constitution. In 1981, Herbert J. Storing published *The Complete Anti-Federalist*, a seven-volume collection of all the significant pamphlets, newspaper articles and letters, essays, and speeches that were written in opposition to the Constitution during the ratification debate. And, since 1972, the First Federal Congress Project published twenty volumes of *The Documentary History of the First Federal Congress of the United States of America*.

Still others dismiss originalism as simply a means of cloaking the justices' policy predilections. Christopher L. Eisgruber argues that originalism is flexible enough that those who employ it reach conclusions at odds with their political preferences "between very rarely and never."[25] Frank Cross agrees: "The justices are able to manipulate (or ignore) originalist materials to produce results they desire to reach on ideological or other grounds. . . . Originalism does not generally explain decisions, but is used to make them more appealing."[26] To these critics, originalists offer two responses. First, they note that this charge can be leveled against other approaches to constitutional interpretation as well. Second, they argue that a justice's consistent commitment to the originalist approach acts as a check, particularly when compared to the multiple approaches sometimes employed by other justices.

THE APPROACHES IN PERSPECTIVE

Textual analysis, precedent, constitutional doctrine, logical analysis, adaptation, consequentialism, and the identification of original intent, original understanding, and original public meaning have all been used by justices of the Supreme Court as they have engaged in constitutional interpretation, and therefore these approaches all have contributed to our contemporary understanding of the Constitution. In this book, we are especially guided by the originalist approaches to constitutional interpretation, following the prudent counsel given by Justice Joseph Story in his *Commentaries on the Constitution of the United States:*

> In construing the Constitution of the United States, we are, in the first instance, to consider, what are its nature and objects, its scope and design, as apparent from the structure of the instrument, viewed as a whole and also viewed in its component parts. Where its words are plain, clear and determinate, they require no interpretation. . . . Where the words admit of two senses, each of which is conformable to general usage, that sense is to be adopted, which without departing from the literal import of the words, best harmonizes with the nature and objects, the scope and design of the instrument. . . . In examining the Constitution, the antecedent situation of the country and its institutions, the existence and operations of the state governments, the powers and operations of the Confederation, in short all the circumstances, which had a tendency to produce, or to obstruct its formation and ratification, deserve careful attention.[27]

Originalist approaches explore what Story calls the Constitution's "nature and objects, its scope and design." They begin by identifying the ends (i.e., "objects") the Framers intended the Constitution to achieve and the means (i.e., the "scope and design") they used to achieve these ends; based on that understanding, they proceed to evaluate the decisions of the Supreme Court and the lower federal and state judiciaries and the constitutionally significant pronouncements of the executive and legislative branches. But, what are these ends and means? The remainder of this chapter is a brief introduction to this important question.

THE ENDS OF THE CONSTITUTION

In spelling out the ends of the Constitution, we can begin with the Preamble and by quoting Justice Joseph Story: "It is an admitted maxim in the ordinary course of the administration of justice, that the preamble of a statute is a key to open the mind of the makers, as to the mischiefs, which are to be remedied, and the objects, which are to be accomplished by the provisions of the statute. . . . There does not seem any reason why, in a fundamental law or constitution of government, an equal attention should not be given to the intention of the framers, as stated in the preamble."[28] The Preamble states that the Constitution was ordained and established by "We the People of the United States" in order "to form a more perfect Union, establish Justice, insure domestic Tranquility, provide for the common defense, promote the general Welfare, and secure the Blessings of Liberty to ourselves and our Posterity." The Preamble, when read in conjunction with the rest of the Constitution and the documentary history concerning its drafting and ratification, makes clear that the Founders set out to establish an efficient and powerful guarantor of rights and liberties based on the principle of qualitative majority rule, that is, the principle that the majority not only should rule but should rule well. In *The Federalist,* No. 10, James Madison explicitly stated this goal: "To secure the public good and private rights against the danger of [an overbearing majority], and at the same time to preserve the spirit and form of popular government is then the great object to which our inquiries are directed. Let me add that it is the desideratum by which alone this form of government can be rescued from the opprobrium under which it has so long labored and be recommended to the esteem and adoption of mankind."

As Madison and his colleagues were well aware, the "great object" of their inquiries presented daunting difficulties. They were irrevocably committed to popular or republican government, but, historically, popular governments led inevitably to majority tyranny. In such governments, measures were decided "not according to the rules of justice, and the rights of the minor party; but by the superior force of an interested and over-bearing majority." Minority rights were disregarded—as were the "permanent and aggregate interests of the community." Because popular governments too easily allowed for "unjust combinations of the majority as a whole," they typically had proved to be "incompatible with personal security, or the rights of property" and "as short in their lives, as they have been violent in their deaths." Such, according to Madison, was the great "opprobrium" under which "this form of government" had "so long labored."

The most commonly prescribed palliative for the problems of majority tyranny was to render the government powerless. However eager a majority might be to "concert and carry into effect its schemes of oppression," if the government were sufficiently impotent, it would pose no real threat. As William Symmes commented in the Massachusetts State Constitutional Ratifying Convention, "Power was never given . . . but it was exercised, nor ever exercised but it was finally abused."[29] The implication was clear: to prevent abuses, power must be consciously and jealously withheld.

This prescription was not without its shortcomings, however. Carried to an extreme, it rendered government not only powerless but also altogether unworkable. To this view, the leading Framers justifiably and appropriately responded that, although the spirit of jealousy was extremely valuable, when carried too far it impinged on another equally important principle of government—that of "strength and stability in the organization of our government, and vigor in its operations."[30] They understood that a strong and stable government was necessary not only to cope with the problems that society faces, but also to render liberty fully secure. In order that popular government "be recommended to the esteem and adoption of mankind," they realized they would have to solve the twofold problem raised by majority rule: to establish a constitution capable of avoiding democratic tyranny, on the one hand, and democratic ineptitude, on the other. This problem had overwhelmed the government under the Articles of Confederation and led to the calling of the Federal Convention. Under the Articles, the member states were so powerful and their legislative assemblies so dominant and unchecked that the tyrannical impulses of the majority continually placed in jeopardy the life, liberty, and property of the citizenry; the central federal government was so infirm and its responsibilities so few and limited that its situation often "bordered on anarchy." The Framers fully appreciated the challenge they faced. As Madison noted in *The Federalist,* No. 51, "In framing a government which is to be administered by men over men, the great difficulty lies in this: You must first enable the government to control the governed; and in the next place, oblige it to control itself." As we shall see, the Framers rose to this challenge by arranging the various articles and provisions of the Constitution so that they not only granted the federal and state governments sufficient power to control the governed but also obliged them to control themselves through a number of institutional arrangements and contrivances.

CONSTITUTIONAL MEANS TO CONSTITUTIONAL ENDS

The Framers' solution to the problems of republican government was altogether consistent with republican principles. *The Federalist* is replete with references to this matter. Recognizing that "a dependence on the people is no doubt the primary control on the government," the Framers also understood that experience had "taught mankind the necessity of auxiliary precautions." This understanding was fundamentally shaped by their assessment of human nature. They believed humankind to be driven by self-interest and consumed by the desire for distinction. Humans were seen as "ambitious, rapacious, and vindictive" creatures whose passions for "power and advantage" are so powerful and basic that it is folly to expect that they can be controlled adequately by traditional republican reliance on pure patriotism; respect for character, conscience, or religion; or even the not-very-lofty maxim that "honesty is the best policy." Inevitably, human avarice and lust for power divide individuals into parties, inflame them with mutual animosity, and render them much more disposed to oppress one another than to cooperate for the common good. Humans are predictable in such matters. They will form factions, whether there are readily apparent reasons to do so or not. As their passions lead them in directions contrary to the "dictates of reason and justice," their reason is subverted into providing arguments for self-indulgence rather than incentives to virtue.

Given these sentiments, it is hardly surprising that the Framers placed little faith in improving human nature through moral reformation or in the activities of "enlightened statesmen." The only hope for republican government, they concluded, was the establishment of institutions that would depend on "the ordinary depravity of human nature." Appreciating that human passion and pride are elemental forces that can never be stifled or contained by "parchment barriers," they sought to harness and direct these forces through the process of mutual checking. Consequently, they included in the Constitution checks and controls that might "make it the interest, even of bad men, to act for the public good."[31] Self-interest, the Framers contended, was one check that nothing could overcome and the principal hope for security and stability in a republican government. The rather ignoble but always reliable inclination of people to follow their own "sober second thoughts of self-interest" would serve to minimize the likelihood of majority tyranny.[32] As the observant Alexis de Tocqueville would later describe it, the Framers relied on institutional mechanisms to check one personal interest with another and to direct the passions with the very same instruments that excite them.

What kinds of institutional mechanisms—what constitutional means—could incorporate and redirect human self-interest in such a way as to enable the federal and state governments to control the governed and, at the same time, oblige those governments to control themselves? The answer to that question can be found in the three principal concepts underpinning the Constitution: the extended republic; separation of powers and checks and balances; and federalism.

The Extended Republic

The multiplicity of interests in the extended commercial republic established by the Constitution represents one of the principal mechanisms by which the Framers sought to establish an energetic government based on the principle of qualitative majority rule. The advantages of an extended republic can be best seen by examining the defects of a small republic.

As Madison noted in *The Federalist,* No. 10, the smaller the republic, "the fewer probably will be the distinct parties and interests composing it; the fewer the distinct parties and interests, the more frequently will a majority be found of the same party; and the smaller the compass within which they are placed, the more easily will they concert and execute their plans of oppression." Thus arises democratic tyranny, which can be prevented only by rendering the government impotent and thereby fostering democratic ineptitude. In contrast, the larger the republic, the greater the variety of interests, parties, and sects present within it and the more moderate and diffused the conflict. In the words of *The Federalist,* No. 10, "Extend the sphere, and you take in a greater variety of parties and interests; you make it less probable that a majority of the whole will have a common motive to invade the rights of other citizens; or if such a common motive exists, it will be more difficult for all who feel it to discover their own strength, and to act in unison with each other."

Because of the "greater variety" of economic, geographic, religious, political, cultural, and ethnic interests that an extended republic takes in, rule by a majority is effectively replaced by rule by ever-changing coalitions of minorities that come together on one particular issue to act as a majority but break up on the next. The coalition of minorities that acts as a majority on the issue of import duties is not likely to remain intact on such issues as national defense or governmental aid to private schools. The very real possibility that allies in one coalition might be opponents in the next encourages a certain moderation in politics, in terms of both the political objectives sought and the political tactics employed. Political interests become reluctant to raise the political stakes too high: by scoring too decisive a political victory on one issue, an interest might find that it has only weakened itself by devastating a potential ally and thus rendering itself vulnerable to similar treatment in the future. Accordingly, politics is moderated not through idle appeals to conscience and beneficence, but rather through the reliance on the inclination of individuals to look after their own self-interest. As Madison observed in *The Federalist,* No. 51, this diversity of interests ensures that "a coalition of a majority of the whole society" will seldom take place "on any other principles than those of justice and the common good." The extended republic thus helped to make it possible for the Framers to give the national government sufficient power to prevent democratic ineptitude without raising the specter of democratic tyranny.

The Framers' recognition of and reliance on the moderating effects brought about by an extended republic are apparent in such constitutional provisions as the Contract Clause in Article I, Section 10, which prohibits any state from passing laws "impairing the obligation of contracts." Note that only the states are restrained, but the federal government is not— and for good reasons. It was thought that no state, however large, was or would be extensive enough to contain a variety of interests wide enough to prevent majorities from acting oppressively and using their legislative power to nullify contracts for their own advantage. Consequently, the states had to have their power to do so limited by the Constitution. The federal government, by contrast, was large enough and contained the multiplicity of interests necessary to prevent oppression of this sort and so had no need of constitutional constraint. Thus majority tyranny could be avoided simply by relying on the popular principle to operate naturally in an extended republic. The elegant simplicity of this mechanism was pointed out by Madison in *The Federalist,* No. 10: "In the extent and proper structure of the Union, therefore, we behold a Republican remedy for the disease most incident to Republican Government."

Separation of Powers and Checks and Balances

For the Framers, the "great desideratum of politics" was the formation of a "government that will, at the same time, deserve the seemingly opposite epithets—efficient and free."[33] The extended republic was one means by which they sought to realize this objective; a government of separated institutions sharing powers was another. They were aware, as Madison stated in *The Federalist,* No. 47, that "the accumulation of all powers legislative, executive, and judiciary in the same hands, whether of one, a few, or many, and whether hereditary, self-appointed, or elective may justly be pronounced the very definition of tyranny," and therefore that the preservation of liberty requires that the three great departments of power should be separate and distinct. Thus, they sought to construct a government consisting of three coordinate and equal branches, with each performing a blend of functions, thereby balancing governmental powers. Their goal was to structure the government so that, in the words of *The Federalist,* No. 51, the three branches would, "by their mutual relations, be the means of keeping each other in their proper places."

This the Framers succeeded in doing. They began by giving most legislative power to the Congress, most executive power to the president, and most judicial power to the Supreme Court and to such inferior federal courts as Congress might establish. They then set out to divide and arrange the remaining powers in such a manner that each branch could be a check on the others. Thus, they introduced the principle of bicameralism, under which Congress was divided into the House of Representatives and the Senate, and they arranged for the president to exercise certain important legislative powers by requiring yearly addresses on the State of the Union and by providing him with a conditional veto power. (Some Framers assumed that the Congress would also be restrained by the Supreme Court's unstated power of judicial review.) The Framers sought to keep the president in check by requiring senatorial confirmation of executive appointees and judicial nominees, mandating that the Senate advise on and consent to treaties, and allowing for impeachment by the Congress. Finally, they supplied the means for keeping the Supreme Court in its "proper place" by giving the Congress budgetary control over the judiciary, the power of impeachment, and the power to regulate the Court's appellate jurisdiction. On top of these specific arrangements, they provided for staggered terms of office (two years for the House, six years for the Senate, four years for the president, and tenure "for good behavior" for the judiciary) to give each branch a further "constitutional control over the others."

Because they knew that the various branches of the government, even though popularly elected, might from time to time be activated by "an official sentiment opposed to that of the General Government and perhaps to that of the people themselves,"[34] they regarded separation of powers as essential to ensure the fidelity of these popular agents. Separation of powers would provide for a "balance of the parts" that would consist "in the independent exercise of their separate powers and, when their powers are separately exercised, then in their mutual influence and operation on one another. Each part acts and is acted upon, supports and is supported, regulates and is regulated by the rest." This balance would ensure that, even if these separate parts were to become activated by separate interests, they would nonetheless move "in a line of direction somewhat different from that, which each acting by itself, would have taken; but, at the same time, in a line partaking of the natural direction of each, and formed out of the natural direction of the whole—the true line of publick liberty and happiness."[35] Not only would such a separation and balancing of powers prevent any branch of government from tyrannizing the people, but it would also thwart the majority from tyrannizing the minority. In creating an independent executive and judiciary, the Framers provided a means of temporarily blocking the will of tyrannical majorities as expressed through a compliant or demagogic legislature. Although separation of powers cannot permanently frustrate the wishes of the people, on those occasions when "the interests of the people are at variance with their inclinations," it so structures these institutions that they are able to "withstand the temporary delusions" of the people, in order to give them what *The Federalist,* No. 71, described as the "time and opportunity for more cool and sedate reflection." The prospects for democratic tyranny are dimmed accordingly.

And, in addition to keeping society free, separation of powers was seen by the Framers as helping to render the government efficient—as minimizing the prospects for democratic ineptitude. Realizing that the democratic process of mutual deliberation and consent can paralyze the government when swift and decisive action is necessary, the Framers reasoned that government would be more efficient if its various functions were performed by separate and distinct agencies. According to James Wilson, a leading Framer:

> In planning, forming, and arranging laws, deliberation is always becoming, and always useful. But in the active scenes of government, there are emergencies, in which the man . . . who deliberates is lost. Secrecy may be equally necessary as dispatch. But can either secrecy or dispatch be expected, when, to every enterprise, mutual communication, mutual consultation, and mutual agreement among men, perhaps of discordant views, of discordant tempers, and discordant interests, are indispensably necessary? How much time will be consumed! and when it is consumed, how little business will be done! . . . If, on the other hand, the executive power of government is placed in the hands of one person, who is to direct all the subordinate officers of that department; is there not reason to expect, in his plans and conduct, promptitude, activity, firmness, consistency, and energy?[36]

For the Framers, then, separation of powers not only forestalled democratic tyranny but also provided for an independent and energetic executive able to ensure what *The Federalist,* No. 37, called "that prompt and salutary execution of the laws, which enter into the very definition of good Government."

Federalism

The American constitutional system rests on a federal arrangement in which power is shared by the national government and the states. The primary purpose of this arrangement was to provide for a strong central government; however, it has also had the effect of promoting qualitative majority rule. The federalism created by the Framers can best be understood when contrasted with the confederalism that existed under the Articles of Confederation. Confederalism was characterized by three principles:

1. The central government exercised authority only over the individual governments (i.e., states) of which it was composed, never over the individual citizens of whom those governments were composed. Even this authority was limited; the resolutions of the federal authority amounted to little more than recommendations that the states could (and did) disregard.
2. The central government had no authority over the internal affairs of the individual states; its rule was limited mainly to certain external tasks of mutual interest to the member states.
3. Each individual state had an "exact equality of suffrage" derived from the equality of sovereignty shared by all states.[37]

The consequences of these principles on the operation of the federal government were disastrous. They rendered the Articles of Confederation so weak that they were reduced, in Alexander Hamilton's words from *The Federalist*, No. 9, "to the last stage of national humiliation." There was obviously a need for a "more perfect union" and for new arrangements capable of rendering the political structure "adequate to the exigencies of Government and the preservation of the Union."[38]

The new federal structure erected by the Framers corrected each of the difficulties inherent in confederalism. To begin with, the power of the new federal government was enhanced considerably. Not only could it now operate directly on the individual citizen, just as the state governments could, but it could also deal with internal matters: for example, it now could regulate commerce among the several states, establish uniform rules of bankruptcy, coin money, establish a postal system, tax, and borrow money. Moreover, the federal government was made supreme over the states. As Article VI spelled out: "This Constitution, and the laws of the United States which shall be made in pursuance thereof . . . shall be the supreme law of the land."

If the federalism the Framers created strengthened the central government, it also contributed to qualitative majority rule by preserving the presence of powerful states capable of checking and controlling not only the central government but each other as well. Federalism granted the new central government only those powers expressly or implicitly delegated to it in the Constitution and allowed the states to retain all powers not prohibited to them. The states were permitted to regulate intrastate commerce and the health, safety, and welfare of the citizenry (i.e., the police power) and even were authorized to exercise certain powers concurrently with the central government—for example, the power of taxation and the power to regulate interstate commerce—so long as these powers were not exercised in a manner inconsistent with constitutional limitations or federal regulations. Finally, the Framers' federalism also contributed to qualitative majority rule by blending federal elements into the structure and procedures of the central government itself. To take only the most obvious example, it mixed into the Senate the federal principle of equal representation of all states. When joined with bicameralism and separation of powers, this principle directly contributed to qualitative majority rule. For a measure to become law, it would have to pass the Senate—where, because of the federal principle of equal representation of all states, the presence of a nationally distributed majority (with the moderating tendencies that provides) would be virtually guaranteed.

This division of power between the federal and state governments also provided another remedy for the ills of democratic ineptitude. As James Wilson emphasized, with two levels of government at their disposal, the people are in a position to assign their sovereign power to whichever level they believe to be more productive in promoting the common good. Moreover, efficiency is gained in still another way. The federal system permits the states to serve as experimental social laboratories in which new policies and procedures can be implemented. If these experiments prove to be successful, they can be adopted elsewhere; if they fail, the damage is limited to the particular state in question. Because the risks are lessened, experimentation is encouraged, and the chances of positive reform and better governance are increased accordingly. In a wholly national or unitary system, on the other hand, experimentation can take place only on a national scale, and social inertia and a commitment to the status quo are encouraged.

The enhanced efficiency of the federal system, in turn, dims the prospect of democratic tyranny. As Madison observed in *The Federalist,* No. 20, "Tyranny has perhaps oftener grown out of the assumptions of power, called for, on pressing exigencies, by a defective constitution, than by the full exercise of the largest constitutional authorities."

The Framers saw the multiplicity of interests present in an extended republic, separation of powers and checks and balances, and federalism as contributing to a government that is at once "efficient and free." These institutional mechanisms, operating in conjunction with each other, were designed to prevent the twin evils of democratic ineptitude and democratic tyranny. The Framers' intention was to institute an energetic and efficient government based on the principle of qualitative majority rule, and they systematically and consistently employed these means to achieve that end. This understanding is at the core of the approach to constitutional interpretation, used where appropriate, in the discussion of the constitutional provisions that follows.

NOTES

1. Chief Justice Hughes subsequently qualified these remarks. "The remark has been used, regardless of its context, as if permitting the inference that I was picturing constitutional interpretation by the courts as a matter of judicial caprice. This was farthest from my thought. . . . I was speaking of the essential function of the courts under our system of interpreting and applying constitutional safeguards." *The Autobiographical Notes of Charles Evans Hughes,* edited by David J. Danielski and J. S. Tulshin (Cambridge, MA: Harvard University Press, 1973), 143.

2. Joseph Story, *Commentaries on the Constitution of the United States* (Boston: Hilliard and Gray, 1833), 1: 436–437.

3. *Graves v. O'Keefe* (1939), Justice Frankfurter concurring.

4. See book 3, chapter 5, "Rules of Interpretation," in Story, *Commentaries on the Constitution of the United States,* 1:382–442. See also Francis Lieber, *Legal and Political Hermeneutics,* 2nd ed. (Boston: Charles C. Little & James Brown, 1839), reprinted in *Cardozo Law Review* 16, no. 6 (1995): 1879–2105.

5. Stephen Breyer, *Active Liberty: Interpreting Our Democratic Constitution* (New York: Alfred A. Knopf, 2005), 19.

6. Thomas Hobbes, *A Dialogue Between a Philosopher and a Student of the Common Laws of England,* edited by Joseph Cropsey (Chicago: University of Chicago Press, 1971), 129.

7. See J. Skelly Wright, "Professor Bickel, the Scholarly Tradition, and the Supreme Court," *Harvard Law Review* 84, no. 4 (1971): 785.

8. *Avery v. Midland County* (1968), Justice Fortas dissenting.

9. Scalia and Garner state that "the most rigorous form of logic, and hence the most persuasive, is the syllogism." Antonin Scalia and Bryan A. Garner, *Making Your Case: The Art of Persuading Judges* (St. Paul, MN: Thomson, West, 2008), 41.

10. Ibid., 42.

11. The phrase is Justice Scalia's. See Antonin Scalia, *A Matter of Interpretation: Federal Courts and the Law* (Princeton, N.J.: Princeton University Press, 1997), 47.

12. See Christopher Wolfe, "A Theory of U.S. Constitutional History," *Journal of Politics* 43, no. 2 (1981): 301.

13. See Walter F. Berns, *Taking the Constitution Seriously* (New York: Simon and Schuster, 1987), 236: "The Framers . . . provided for a Supreme Court and charged it with the task, not of keeping the Constitution in tune with the times but, to the extent possible, of keeping the times in tune with the Constitution."

14. William J. Brennan, "The Constitution of the United States: Contemporary Ratification," presentation at the Text and Teaching Symposium, Georgetown University, Washington, DC, October 12, 1985.

15. Scalia, *Matter of Interpretation,* 46–47 (emphases in the original).

16. The quotations above come from Breyer, *Active Liberty*, see pp. 6, 18, 48–49, 63, and 97.

17. Ibid, pp. 97, 18.

18. Scalia, *Matter of Interpretation*, 21.

19. Lino Graglia, "Interpreting the Constitution: Posner on Bork," 44 *Stanford Law Review* (1991–1992): 1019, 1024.

20. Scalia, *Matter of Interpretation*, 34.

21. Ralph A. Rossum, *Understanding Clarence Thomas: The Jurisprudence of Constitutional Restoration* (Lawrence: University Press of Kansas, 2014).

22. Jeffrey S. Sutton, "The Role of History in Judging Disputes about the Meaning of the Constitution," *Texas Tech Law Review* 41 (2009): 1173, 1176.

23. Walton H. Hamilton, "The Constitution—Apropos of Crosskey," *University of Chicago Law Review* 21, no. 1 (1953): 82.

24. See Brennan, "Constitution of the United States."

25. Christopher L. Eisgruber, *Constitutional Self-Government* (Cambridge, MA: Harvard University Press, 2007), p. 40.

26. Frank Cross, *The Failed Promise of Originalism* (Palo Alto, CA: Stanford University Press, 2013), p. 190.

27. Story, *Commentaries on the Constitution of the United States,* 1:387–388. See also 322, 404, 412, and 417.

28. Ibid., 443–444.

29. Jonathan Elliot, ed., *The Debates in the Several State Conventions on the Adoption of the Federal Constitution as Recommended by the General Convention in Philadelphia in 1787,* 5 vols., 2nd ed. (Philadelphia: Lippincott, 1866), 2:74.

30. Alexander Hamilton in the New York State Ratifying Convention, in Elliot, *Debates in the Several State Conventions,* 2:301.

31. David Hume, *Political Essays,* edited by Charles W. Handel (Indianapolis: Bobbs-Merrill, 1953), 13.

32. The phrase is Frederick Douglass's. See his "The Destiny of Colored Americans," *North Star,* November 16, 1849.

33. Robert Green McCloskey, ed., *The Works of James Wilson* (Cambridge, MA: Belknap Press of Harvard University Press, 1967), 791.

34. James Wilson, in Farrand, *Records of the Federal Convention of 1787,* 1:359.

35. McCloskey, *Works of James Wilson,* 300.

36. Ibid., 294, 296. See also *The Federalist,* No. 70.

37. See Martin Diamond, "What the Framers Meant by Federalism," in *A Nation of States: Essays on the American Federal System,* edited by Robert A. Goldwin, 2nd ed. (Chicago: Rand McNally College Publications, 1974), 25–42.

38. Resolution of the Congress calling for the Federal Convention of 1787, in Farrand, *Records of the Federal Convention of 1787,* 3:14.

SELECTED READINGS

The Federalist, Nos. 1, 6, 9, 10, 15, 37, 39, 47–51, 63, 70–72, 78.

Amar, Akhil Reed. *America's Constitution: A Biography.* New York: Random House, 2006.

Anastaplo, George. *The Constitution of 1787: A Commentary.* Baltimore, MD: Johns Hopkins University Press, 1989.

Balkin, Jack M. *Living Originalism.* Cambridge, MA: Harvard University Press, 2011.

Barber, Sotirios A., and James E. Fleming. *Constitutional Interpretation: The Basic Questions.* New York: Oxford University Press, 2007.

Baude, William. "Is Originalism Our Law?" *Columbia Law Review* 115 (2015): 1–86.

Breyer, Stephen. *Active Liberty: Interpreting Our Democratic Constitution.* New York: Alfred A. Knopf, 2005.

Calabresi, Steven G., ed. *Originalism: A Quarter-Century of Debate.* Washington, DC: Regnery, 2007.

Cornell, Saul. *The Other Founders: Anti-Federalism and Dissenting Tradition in America, 1788–1828.*

Chapel Hill: University of North Carolina Press, 1999.

Cross, Frank. *The Failed Promise of Originalism.* Palo Alto, CA: Stanford University Press, 2013.

Diamond, Martin. "Democracy and *The Federalist*: A Reconsideration of the Framers' Intent." *American Political Science Review* 53, no. 1 (1959): 52–68.

Douglas, William O. "Stare Decisis." *Columbia Law Review* 49 (1949): 725–758.

Elliot, Jonathan, ed. *The Debates in the Several State Conventions on the Adoption of the Federal Constitution as Recommended by the General Convention in Philadelphia in 1787.* 2nd ed. 5 vols. Philadelphia: Lippincott, 1866.

Farrand, Max, ed. *The Records of the Federal Convention of 1787.* 4 vols. New Haven, CT: Yale University Press, 1937.

Faulkner, Robert K. *The Jurisprudence of John Marshall.* Princeton, NJ: Princeton University Press, 1968.

Hickok, Eugene W., ed. *The Bill of Rights: Original Meaning and Current Understanding.* Charlottesville: University Press of Virginia, 1991.

Kesler, Charles R., ed. *Saving the Revolution: The Federalist Papers and the American Founding.* New York: Free Press, 1987.

Kurland, Philip B., and Ralph Lerner, eds. *The Founders' Constitution.* 5 vols. Chicago: University of Chicago Press, 1987.

Levinson, Sanford. *Framed: America's 51 Constitutions and the Crisis of Governance.* New York: Oxford University Press, 2012.

_____. "On Interpretation: The Adultery Clause of the Ten Commandments." *Southern California Law Review* 58, no. 2 (1985): 719–725.

Levy, Leonard W., and Dennis J. Mahoney, eds. *The Framing and Ratification of the Constitution.* New York: Macmillan, 1987.

Maier, Pauline. *Ratification: The People Debate the Constitution, 1787–1788.* New York: Simon & Schuster, 2010.

McClellan, James. *Liberty, Order, and Justice: An Introduction to the Constitutional Principles of American Government.* 2nd ed. Indianapolis: Liberty Fund, 1999.

McDowell, Gary L. *The Language of Law and the Foundations of American Constitutionalism.* New York: Cambridge University Press, 2010.

McGinnis, John O., and Michael B. Rappaport. *Originalism and the Good Constitution.* Cambridge, MA: Harvard University Press, 2013.

Meese, Edwin. "Toward a Jurisprudence of Original Intention." *Benchmark* 2, no. 1 (1986): 1–10.

O'Connor, Mike. *A Commercial Republic: America's Enduring Debate over Democratic Capitalism.* Lawrence: University Press of Kansas, 2014.

Rehnquist, William H. "The Notion of a Living Constitution." *Texas Law Review* 54 (May 1976): 693–707.

Rossum, Ralph A. *Antonin Scalia's Jurisprudence: Text and Tradition.* Lawrence: University Press of Kansas, 2006.

_____. *Understanding Clarence Thomas: The Jurisprudence of Constitutional Restoration.* Lawrence: University Press of Kansas, 2014.

_____, and Gary L. McDowell, eds. *The American Founding: Politics, Statesmanship, and the Constitution.* Port Washington, NY: Kennikat Press, 1981.

Ryan, James E., "Does It Take A Theory? Originalism, Active Liberty, and Minimalism, *Stanford Law Review* 58 (2006): 1623–1660.

Scalia, Antonin. *A Matter of Interpretation: Federal Courts and the Law.* Princeton, NJ: Princeton University Press, 1997.

Scalia, Antonin, and Bryan A. Garner. *Reading Law: Interpretation of Legal Texts.* St. Paul, MN: West, 2012.

Storing, Herbert J., ed. *The Complete Anti-Federalist.* 7 vols. Chicago: University of Chicago Press, 1981.

Strauss, David A. *The Living Constitution.* New York: Oxford University Press, 2010.

Tillman, Seth Barrett, "*The Federalist Papers* as Reliable Historical Source Materials for Constitutional Interpretation." *West Virginia Law Review* 105 (2003): 601–619.

Watson, Bradley C. S. *Living Constitution, Dying Faith: Progressivism and the New Science of Jurisprudence.* Wilmington, DE: ISI Press, 2009.

Whittington, Keith E. *Constitutional Interpretation: Textual Meaning, Original Intent, and Judicial Review.* Lawrence: University Press of Kansas, 1999.

Wolfe, Christopher. *How to Read the Constitution: Originalism, Constitutional Interpretation, and Judicial Power.* Lanham, MD: Rowman & Littlefield, 1996.

Wood, Gordon S. *The Creation of the American Republic, 1776–1787.* Chapel Hill: University of North Carolina Press, 1969.

2

Constitutional Adjudication

CHAPTER OUTLINE

More than 180 years ago, Alexis de Tocqueville observed that "there is hardly a political question in the United States which does not sooner or later turn into a judicial one."[1] Today, as then, Americans transform policy disputes into constitutional issues and seek resolution of those disputes in courts in general and in the United States Supreme Court in particular. The Supreme Court's political and legal roles are thus intertwined. By deciding cases that raise important issues concerning the extent, distribution, and uses of governmental power, the Court inevitably participates in governing.

The Supreme Court's dual responsibilities as an interpreter of the Constitution and as an agency of government provide the focus for this chapter. Five basic questions are considered: Who is selected to serve on the Supreme Court? What is the Supreme Court's position in the federal judicial system? How are political questions transformed into legal issues and brought before the justices? How do the justices go about deciding cases? And what happens after the Supreme Court decides? The chapter's final sections offer a framework for analyzing judicial decisions and survey source materials in constitutional law.

THE JUSTICES OF THE SUPREME COURT

Appointment and Tenure

Supreme Court justices are appointed by the president with the advice and consent of the Senate and, like other federal judges, hold office during "good behavior." Only one justice has ever been impeached by the House of Representatives (Samuel Chase in 1804), and the Senate failed to convict him. For most justices, appointment to the Court represents the culmination of their careers, and the vast majority remain on the bench until death or retirement. Justice William O. Douglas, for example, served thirty-six years on the Court, and Justice Oliver Wendell Holmes did not retire until he was ninety-one.

Historically, vacancies on the Court have occurred about every two or three years, so presidents serving two full terms often have a considerable impact on the composition of the Court. Thus President Ronald Reagan named four justices to the Court during his two terms, and Presidents Bill Clinton and Barack Obama each named two justices during their first terms. Yet openings do not occur according to a fixed schedule. Thus, Clinton did not appoint any justices during his second term, and President George W. Bush none during his first term. Recent advances in life expectancy have meant that justices tend to serve longer today than in earlier eras: three current justices—Anthony Kennedy, Ruth Bader Ginsburg, and Stephen Breyer—are more than seventy-five years old. This longevity makes the choice of who is appointed to the Court all the more crucial. When Justice Sandra Day O'Connor announced her retirement in 2005, the average tenure for currently sitting justices was more than nineteen years, and no new justice had been appointed for eleven years. Table 2.1 lists the justices serving on the Supreme Court as of 2016.

Choosing Justices

In appointing justices, presidents typically select persons with distinguished careers in public life. Among justices appointed up to 2016, twenty-five had served in Congress, and more than twenty had held cabinet posts. Although prior judicial experience is not a requirement, all but one justice appointed since 1975 had served as an appellate judge. Most important, presidents seek appointees who share their political affiliation (roughly 90 percent of appointees have been members of the president's party) and their constitutional views. Thus, President Reagan sought proponents of "judicial restraint," whereas President Clinton pledged to appoint justices sympathetic to abortion rights. Presidents also consider demographic factors

TABLE 2.1 **Justices of the US Supreme Court, 2016**

	Born	Home State	Position Before Appointment	Prior Judicial Experience	Party Affiliation	Year Appointed	Appointing President
John Roberts	1955	Indiana	US Court of Appeals	Yes	Republican	2005 (Chief)	G. W. Bush
Anthony Kennedy	1936	California	US Court of Appeals	Yes	Republican	1988	Reagan
Clarence Thomas	1948	Georgia	US Court of Appeals	Yes	Republican	1991	G. H. W. Bush
Ruth Bader Ginsburg	1933	New York	US Court of Appeals	Yes	Democrat	1993	Clinton
Stephen Breyer	1938	California	US Court of Appeals	Yes	Democrat	1994	Clinton
Samuel Alito	1950	New Jersey	US Court of Appeals	Yes	Republican	2006	G. W. Bush
Sonia Sotomayor	1954	New York	US Court of Appeals	Yes	Democrat	2009	Obama
Elena Kagan	1960	New York	Solicitor General	No	Democrat	2010	Obama

Note: When Justice Antonin Scalia died in February, 2016, President Barack Obama nominated Merrick Garland, Chief Judge of the United States Court of Appeals for the District of Columbia, to replace him. But as of July 2016, the seat remains vacant.

in their appointments. President Lyndon Johnson chose Thurgood Marshall as the first African American on the Supreme Court; when Marshall retired, President George H. W. Bush replaced him with another African American, Clarence Thomas. President Reagan appointed Sandra Day O'Connor as the first woman on the Court, and in 2009 President Obama selected Sonia Sotomayor as the first Latina appointee. In recent years there has been some criticism that those chosen for the Court are too similar in their backgrounds and experience. Of the current justices, all attended either Harvard or Yale Law School, and all but one had served on federal courts of appeals before their appointment to the Court.

The Impact of Appointments

Through their appointment of Supreme Court justices, presidents can influence the orientation of the Supreme Court. For example, appointments by President George W. Bush from 2001–2009 produced a more conservative Court, while those appointed by President Barack Obama aligned with the liberal wing of the Court. However, presidents do not always see their choices seated on the Court. For example, Harriet Miers asked President Bush to withdraw her nomination in 2005 following widespread criticism from the President's conservative political base. The Senate also can refuse to confirm nominees—between 1968 and 1992, six nominees were rejected by the Senate or withdrew when it became apparent they could not be confirmed. Even when the Senate does confirm nominees, the process has sometimes been contentious—for example, Justice Clarence Thomas was approved by only a 52–48 vote after accusations of sexual harassment were leveled against him during confirmation hearings. Moreover, once on the Court, justices might not behave as the president expected. The president might have misjudged the prospective justice's views, those views might change after the justice is appointed, or new issues might arise that the president did not anticipate when choosing a justice. When a justice fails to meet a president's expectations, there is nothing a president can do about it, and so presidents recognize they must be careful in whom they choose. Thus, in explaining his choice of John Roberts for Chief Justice, President Bush commented: "I believed Roberts would be a natural leader. I didn't worry about him drifting away from his principles over time."[2]

The politics of the appointment process have changed over time, particularly in the Senate. Until the 1920s, Senate deliberations on prospective justices were secret. Nominees did not testify, and they were confirmed or rejected without a roll-call vote, so it was impossible to know how individual senators had voted. Now, however, nominees testify before the Senate Judiciary Committee in public hearings, as do groups and individuals supporting or opposing the nominees. Since 1982, when President Reagan nominated Sandra Day O'Connor to the Court, these hearings have been televised. This opened up the process and made it easier for groups to mobilize opinion for and against nominees and to influence votes on confirmation by threatening to hold senators electorally accountable. Yet whether groups mobilize depends on the character and views of the nominee. When President Reagan nominated conservative jurist Robert Bork for the Supreme Court, liberal groups successfully organized to oppose him. In contrast, President Clinton's appointees to the Supreme Court, Ruth Bader Ginsburg and Stephen Breyer, were uncontroversial and overwhelmingly confirmed by the Senate. Many liberal groups mobilized in unsuccessful attempts to block George W. Bush's appointments of John Roberts and Samuel Alito to the Supreme Court; and when President Obama nominated Sonja Sotomayor and Elena Kagan for the Supreme Court, Democratic senators overwhelmingly supported the nominees, while Republican senators almost unanimously opposed them.

THE SUPREME COURT IN THE FEDERAL JUDICIAL SYSTEM

Article III of the Constitution establishes the United States Supreme Court and authorizes "such inferior Courts as the Congress may from time to time ordain and establish." Acting under this authority, Congress has created a three-tiered system of federal courts, with the Supreme Court at the apex of the system and the federal courts of appeals and federal district courts below it. During the twentieth century, Congress added to this system various specialized courts, such as the Court of Military Appeals, the Foreign Intelligence Surveillance Court, and the Court of International Trade.

The district courts are the primary trial courts of the federal judicial system, with a single judge presiding over trials in civil or criminal cases. Ninety-four federal district courts serve the fifty states, the District of Columbia, and various US territories. Every state has at least one district court, with more populous states divided into multiple districts. California, New York, and Texas each have four district courts.

The thirteen courts of appeals serve as the first-level appellate courts of the federal judicial system, hearing appeals from the district courts, from federal administrative agencies, and from various specialized courts. The courts of appeals typically hear cases as three-judge panels, which are randomly chosen for each case, and decide cases by majority vote. Occasionally, however, a court of appeals might hear a case *en banc*, that is, with the court's entire membership participating in the decision of the case. Most courts of appeals are organized into regional "circuits" made up of three or more states. The Seventh Circuit, for example, includes Wisconsin, Illinois, and Indiana. The Court of Appeals for the District of Columbia hears large numbers of appeals from federal administrative agencies and serves as a sort of state supreme court for the District of Columbia. The Court of Appeals for the Federal Circuit has a subject-matter jurisdiction, hearing cases involving international trade, veterans' benefits, and government contracts, among other matters.

The Supreme Court initially consisted of six justices. Congress changed the size of the Court several times—sometimes for political purposes—before finally establishing the number of justices at nine in 1869. When President Franklin Roosevelt proposed to increase the number of justices after the Court had struck down several New Deal laws, hoping to appoint justices more sympathetic to his views, Congress refused to expand the Court. Since then, there has been no serious effort to expand the Court or to limit the justices' tenure.

HOW CASES GET TO THE SUPREME COURT

Since 2000, the Supreme Court has annually received more than seven thousand petitions for review but decided less than 2 percent of the cases appealed to it with full opinions. In its 2013 term, for example, it received 7,541 petitions for review but decided only seventy-three cases. The cases the Court decides must fall within its jurisdiction; that is, it can decide only those cases it is empowered to hear by the Constitution or by statute. Once this requirement is met, the Court has broad discretion in determining what cases it will decide. The range of discretion available to the Court has increased over time, and this expanded discretion has led to significant shifts in its caseload.

The Jurisdiction of the Supreme Court

The Supreme Court has both an original jurisdiction (over those cases in which the Court functions as a trial court) and an appellate jurisdiction (over those cases in which the Court reviews the decisions of other courts). Article III, Section 2, of the Constitution defines the Court's original jurisdiction but confers its appellate jurisdiction subject to "such Exceptions, and under such Regulations, as Congress shall make."

Original Jurisdiction. The Supreme Court's original jurisdiction extends to cases involving foreign diplomatic personnel and to cases in which a state is a party. The Court seldom decides more than a couple of cases under its original jurisdiction each term. Two developments have minimized the number of cases initiated in the Supreme Court. First, the Eleventh Amendment, adopted in 1798, withdrew part of the Court's original jurisdiction by prohibiting those who were not citizens of a state from suing it in federal court.[3] And second, during the twentieth century, Congress deflected many potential original-jurisdiction cases to the federal district courts by giving those courts concurrent jurisdiction. Currently, the Supreme Court retains exclusive original jurisdiction over only legal disputes between two states, which commonly deal with boundaries or with water or mineral rights. Because hearing testimony in even these few cases would be a major drain on the time and energies of the Court, it typically appoints a "Special Master"—usually a retired judge—to conduct hearings and report back to it. In deciding these cases, the justices often endorse the findings of the Special Master.

Appellate Jurisdiction. The Supreme Court hears most of its cases on appeal from the federal courts of appeals—in its 2014 term, these made up 89 percent of its docket. It may also hear appeals from federal district courts or from one of the fifty state court systems. In all cases, the Court operates as the court of last resort: its decisions are final in that there is no court to which one can appeal to reverse them. The Court's interpretation of statutes can only be reversed by congressional legislation, and given political polarization, this rarely occurs.[4] Its constitutional rulings can only be overturned by constitutional amendment or by subsequent Supreme Court decisions. In the absence of such changes in the law, all courts are obliged to follow the Supreme Court's direction in matters of federal law. The Court's decisions are also final in the sense that the Court generally decides cases only after litigants have exhausted their available appeals to other courts (Figure 2.1). As Justice Robert Jackson put it in *Brown v. Allen* (1953): "We are not final because we are infallible, but we are infallible only because we are final."

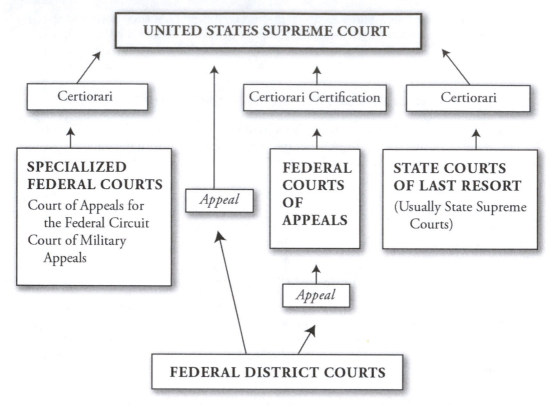

FIGURE 2.1 **How Cases Reach the Supreme Court**

Cases initiated in state courts usually reach the US Supreme Court on appeal from state supreme courts, although the Court may hear a case on appeal from another state court when no further appeal is available in the state system. In *Thompson v. City of Louisville* (1960), for example, the justices accepted a case directly from the police court of Louisville, Kentucky, because under state law the defendant's fine was too low for appeal to any higher state court.[5] Cases initiated in federal district courts normally come to the Court following review by the appropriate court of appeals, but the Court can expedite consideration of cases. In *United States v. Nixon* (1974), which involved President Richard Nixon's refusal during the Watergate Scandal to surrender tapes of his conversations subpoenaed for use in a criminal prosecution, the importance of the dispute prompted the Court to hear the case immediately after the federal district court ruled.

Over the course of time, the Supreme Court has gained virtually total discretion in determining what cases it hears. Early in the twentieth century, cases on appeal (that is, cases in which the party appealing had a right to Supreme Court review) accounted for more than 80 percent of the Court's docket. Because many of these cases raised no significant legal issue, the justices lobbied for a reduction in the burden of obligatory review. Congress responded with the Judiciary Act of 1925, which drastically reduced the categories of cases in which parties had a right of appeal to the Court. In 1988, again at the urging of the justices, Congress eliminated almost all the Court's remaining mandatory jurisdiction, thereby according the Court nearly complete control of its appellate docket.

Even before 1988, the justices had considerable control over what cases they decided. For one thing, more than 90 percent of the petitions for review came to the Court on writs of certiorari.[6] These petitions ranged from professionally drafted legal presentations in so-called paid cases to lay-drafted petitions submitted *in forma pauperis*.[7] In determining which certiorari petitions to accept, the Court has full discretion. As the Supreme Court's Rule 10 states, "A review on writ of certiorari is not a matter of right but of judicial discretion, and will be granted only when there are special and important reasons therefore."[8] In recent years, the Court has used its discretion to reduce dramatically the number of cases it hears each term. During the early 1980s, the justices granted review in more than 180 cases per term. In its 2014 term, however, the Court decided only sixty-seven cases with full opinion. Former Justice David Souter suggested that this change did not reflect a conscious choice; rather, "it just happened." Whatever the explanation, the Court's increasing selectivity underscores the importance of the process by which the justices choose what cases they will hear.

The Decision to Decide

Because the justices receive more than 7,000 petitions for certiorari each year, they have established procedures and criteria for determining which cases warrant review. It might be, as Chief Justice Earl Warren once suggested, that the standards that guide the justices' determinations "cannot be captured in any rule or guidelines that would be meaningful."[9] But if so, how does the Court decide what to decide?

The Case-Selection Process. The mechanics of case selection are clear. Each justice has several law clerks (distinguished law school graduates selected annually by the justice after they have already served a year's clerkship for another federal judge) whose duties include screening the petitions for review and preparing memos summarizing the materials. The influx of cases in recent decades has prompted eight justices to pool their clerks for memo writing, so that the case memos each clerk prepares will be distributed to the justices in the "cert pool." Justice Alito has his clerks independently evaluate all petitions for certiorari. Having evaluated the filings with the aid of the clerks' memos, the chief justice prepares a "discuss list" of the petitions he believes deserve collective consideration. Other justices can then add cases to the list. Unless a justice requests that a petition be discussed in conference, it is automatically denied. More than 70 percent of all petitions are disposed of in this manner.

Collective consideration of the petitions on the discuss list occurs during the three- or four-day conference before the beginning of the Court's term in October and at weekly conferences during the term. In the preterm conference, which is devoted exclusively to case selection, the justices dispose of the hundreds of petitions that have accumulated over the summer months. No case is accepted for review, at either the preterm or the regular weekly conference, unless at least four justices vote to hear it (the so-called rule of four).

Criteria for Case Selection. The justices do not publish or explain their votes to grant or deny review in particular cases, although occasionally a justice may file a dissent from a denial of certiorari. Although the considerations affecting case selection likely vary from justice to justice and case to case, one can identify some factors that affect the Court's decisions on petitions for certiorari.

One factor is the Court's responsibility to promote uniformity and consistency in federal law. This may involve the interpretation of federal statutes as well as of the Constitution—indeed, in its 2013 term, only twenty of the seventy-four cases the Court decided raised constitutional issues. Supreme Court Rule 10, "Considerations Governing Review on Certiorari," recognizes this supervisory responsibility in its list of the factors that might prompt the Court to grant certiorari: (1) important questions of federal law on which the Court has not previously ruled, (2) conflicting interpretations of federal law by lower courts, (3) lower-court decisions that conflict with previous Supreme Court decisions, and

(4) lower-court departures "from the accepted and usual course of judicial proceedings." This list is neither exhaustive nor binding: review may be granted on the basis of other factors or denied when a listed factor is present. At times the Court might deny review even when lower courts have reached conflicting decisions on an issue. For example, for several years the justices refused to review challenges to states' use of roadblocks to detect drunk drivers, even though state courts had disagreed about whether the roadblocks violated the constitutional prohibition on unreasonable searches and seizures. Only in 1990, after rejecting several earlier petitions for certiorari, did the Court address the issue.[10]

In denying certiorari despite disagreement among lower courts, the justices may rely on another case-selection criterion—the intrinsic importance of the issues raised in a case. Although occasionally the Court reaches out to correct a gross miscarriage of justice, the justices tend to be less concerned with correcting the errors of lower courts than with confronting "questions whose resolution will have immediate importance far beyond the particular facts and parties involved."[11] This criterion, of course, cannot be applied automatically. Some cases, because of the momentous political or legal issues they raise, seem to demand Supreme Court review. *National Federation of Independent Business v. Sebelius* (2012), which involved a challenge to President Obama's health-care reforms, fell into that category. Many other cases, including most *in forma pauperis* petitions, raise relatively minor issues that do not warrant the Court's attention. In some cases, the choice as to whether to hear a case might be controversial. For example, commentators disagreed sharply about whether the Court should have heard the case of *Bush v. Gore* (2000), which arose from the dispute over the counting of ballots in Florida in the 2000 presidential election. Whenever the choice is not so clear, additional factors come into play.

A concern in some decisions on whether to grant review is the effect the case might have on the long-term influence of the Court. The Court may seek to safeguard its influence by avoiding unproductive involvement in political disputes, as when it refused to hear cases challenging the constitutionality of the Vietnam War. But this has not always been the case, as shown by the Court's willingness in *Bush v. Gore* (2000) to involve itself in the contested presidential election of 2000. The justices also attempt to select cases in which the issues are clear and sufficiently well-defined so as to facilitate wise and persuasive constitutional decisions.

Finally, the Court sometimes seeks to avoid unnecessarily inflaming public opinion by limiting the number of controversial issues it addresses at one time and by considering public reaction in choosing cases in which to announce important rulings. Thus, for thirteen years after *Brown v. Board of Education* (1954), which outlawed state-mandated school segregation, it refused to consider constitutional challenges to state laws prohibiting interracial marriage.[12] The Court chose *Gideon v. Wainwright* (1963) to announce that indigent defendants had a right to counsel at trial in part because it involved a relatively minor offense rather than a violent crime. Yet the Court does not always avoid controversial issues, as illustrated by its decision in *Obergefell v. Hodges* (2015) to uphold a challenge to state laws prohibiting same-sex marriage.

Even more important than maintaining the Court's influence are the justices' constitutional views—their notions of which constitutional issues are most important and how those issues should be resolved. Specifically, justices might vote to hear a case when they believe that review would further their conception of desirable constitutional policy. In some cases, certain justices might favor review if they believe that a majority of the Court will support their constitutional position, particularly if they disagree with the lower court's decision. Alternatively, if they expect to be in a minority on the Court, they might oppose review rather than risk creation of an unfavorable precedent—a practice referred to as a defensive denial of certiorari.

The Changing Agenda. Our discussion of case selection has focused thus far on the factors underlying the selection of particular cases for review. However, the quotation from De Tocqueville that opens the chapter suggests a broader perspective. If political questions tend to become judicial questions, then the cases from which the justices select presumably reflect the broad political issues confronting the nation. Put differently, if the Court seeks to decide cases of national importance, then the nation's political concerns necessarily furnish the Court's basic agenda.

The historical record confirms this. Prior to the Civil War, the paramount political issue was the distribution of political power between the federal and state governments (with slavery and property rights underlying elements in many of these disputes). So the constitutional cases considered by the Court characteristically required it to define the respective spheres of the federal and state governments. After the Civil War, the nation underwent rapid industrialization and saw the growth of large corporations. Governmental efforts to deal with these developments played a major role in the Court's constitutional decisions from the 1870s until the late 1930s. In the wake of the New Deal, an expansion in the scope of governmental activity, facilitated by Court rulings permitting extensive regulation of economic activity, created new conflicts between government and the individual. Accordingly, the Court's constitutional decisions primarily involved the delineation of individual rights. Although this emphasis on rights has continued, in recent years there has been renewed concern about the reach of government, and this has been reflected in the Supreme Court's renewed attention to issues of federalism and the scope of federal power. In *Shelby County v. Holder* (2013), the Court struck down a provision of the Voting Rights Act of 1965 that required certain jurisdictions, primarily in the South, to obtain permission from the Department of Justice before putting election laws into effect. And in *National Federation of Independent Business v. Sebelius* (2012), while narrowly refusing to hold the Affordable Care Act (otherwise known as Obamacare) unconstitutional, the Court did strike down a provision involving the expansion of Medicaid on the grounds that it unduly coerced states to agree to the expansion or lose all their Medicaid funding.

HOW THE SUPREME COURT DECIDES CASES

In deciding cases, the justices first inform themselves about the facts and legal issues in the case and about the more general consequences that can be expected from a ruling. After oral argument, they discuss the case in closed conference and reach a tentative decision. Finally, through the process of opinion writing and continuing discussion, the justices confirm (or, in rare instances, reconsider) the decision reached in conference, clarify and develop the bases for the ruling, and attempt to reconcile intracourt differences.

The Court's decisions thus have a dual aspect. The litigants in a case may be most concerned with winning or losing: for a convicted felon challenging the constitutionality of a police search that uncovered incriminating evidence, avoiding prison is the primary goal. In announcing decisions, however, the Court justifies its rulings on the basis of legal principles whose ramifications extend far beyond the confines of the individual case. Indeed, the justices use their discretion to review cases that have broad societal importance. This combination of the specific and the general, of immediate results and broader implications, is a crucial aspect of the Court's decision making.

Informing and Persuading the Court

In weighing the merits of a particular case, the Court relies on three sources of information: the briefs of the contending parties, *amicus curiae* (literally, "friend of the court") briefs, and oral argument. In all cases heard by the Court, the lawyers for both parties file legal briefs and argue the case orally before the justices. Other interested parties may submit amicus briefs, which increase the range of information available to the justices.

Legal Briefs. A legal brief is first and foremost a partisan document—an attempt to persuade a court to rule in favor of one's client or position. Persuasion takes the form of marshaling and then interpreting favorably the facts and the legal materials (precedents, statutes, constitutional provisions) involved in the case. For amicus briefs and for those submitted by the litigants, the ultimate goal is to gain a favorable ruling.

Amicus briefs differ from the briefs filed by the litigants. They usually are filed by groups that are interested primarily in the general constitutional issue the case raises, rather than in the fate of the particular litigants. Some organizations file amicus briefs out of concern for the effects the Court's decision might have on them or on their members. For other organizations, the principal concern is ideological: they wish to see the Constitution interpreted in a particular way. *Grutter v. Bollinger* (2003), which involved an affirmative-action program for admission to the University of Michigan Law School, illustrates the range of groups that might be involved on one side or the other of a contentious issue. Among those filing amicus briefs urging the justices to uphold the university's program were several universities that also had affirmative-action programs, the American Psychological Association, the National Urban League, the General Motors Corporation, and several members of Congress. Among those filing briefs opposing the Michigan program were the Asian American Legal Foundation, the Center for Individual Freedom, the National Association of Scholars, and the George W. Bush administration.

Although legal briefs commonly focus on the interpretation of constitutional provisions, statutes, and precedents relevant to the case, they may also include nonlegal materials. For example, attorneys may use social science research to document conditions within society, indicate the effects of governmental policies, or forecast the likely consequences of a Court ruling. The prototype for such briefs was the famous "Brandeis brief" filed in *Muller v. Oregon* (1908). At issue in *Muller* was the constitutionality of an Oregon statute limiting female workers to a ten-hour workday, which the plaintiff challenged as an arbitrary interference with economic liberty. In response, Louis Brandeis, then counsel for the state of Oregon and later a Supreme Court justice, claimed that the law served important public purposes—a claim supported by more than one hundred pages of social and economic data demonstrating that long working hours were dangerous to the health and safety of working women. Brandeis's success in *Muller* prompted counsel in later cases to adopt a similar approach. In *Brown v. Board of Education,* for example, legal arguments for outlawing racial segregation in public education were supplemented by the results of psychological tests showing the adverse effects of segregation on African American children. More recently, contending parties in cases involving the constitutionality of the death penalty have included in their briefs extensive data on the deterrent effect of capital punishment and on the tendency to impose death sentences on those convicted of murdering white victims.

Oral Argument. In oral argument, the attorneys for each party have their last opportunity to influence the Court's decision. In the early nineteenth century, when the Court's docket was less crowded, the greatest lawyers in the country would spend several days arguing a case before the justices. Nowadays, oral presentations are usually limited to a half hour for each party, although in particularly important cases more time can be allotted. In *Bush v. Gore,* the Court allotted forty-five minutes for each side, and in *National Federation of Independent Business v. Sebelius,* it allowed each side three hours of argument over three days to address the variety of issues in the case.

Despite the time constraints, oral argument provides an opportunity for influencing the justices, many of whom view it as vital for clarifying the written arguments presented in the briefs. Through their questions, the justices test the soundness of the opposing legal positions, and weaknesses in an argument or lack of preparation by attorneys soon becomes apparent. The justices' questions can also indicate issues on which they are undecided, and effective response to their inquiries can improve a client's chances. As Justice John Marshall Harlan observed, oral argument "may in many cases make the difference between winning and losing, no matter how good the briefs are."[13]

The Decision-Making Process

On Wednesdays and Fridays during its annual term (early October to late June), the Court meets in conference to consider the cases on which it has most recently heard oral argument. The confidentiality of these deliberations is jealously guarded—only the justices themselves, without law clerks or other Court staff, are present at conference.

Deliberations begin only after the justices shake hands—a ritual meant to symbolize that the inevitable disagreements are legal, not personal. The chief justice initiates discussion by indicating his views of the case at hand and his vote. The associate justices, in descending order of seniority, similarly present their views and votes, and the tallying of votes produces a tentative decision. Although the discussion at conference can on occasion be quite heated, Chief Justice William Rehnquist noted that, for the most part, justices merely announce their conclusions rather than seek to persuade their fellow justices.[14] If the chief justice has voted with the majority, he determines who will write the opinion of the Court (majority opinion), assigning the opinion to another member of the majority or retaining it for himself. If the chief justice is in the minority, the senior justice aligned with the majority assigns the opinion of the Court. The other justices are free to express their views in concurring or dissenting opinions, and in recent decades the number of separate opinions has risen dramatically.

How do the justices decide how they will vote? Some scholars maintain that the justices' votes simply reflect their ideological orientations. According to this view, Justice Clarence Thomas votes as he does because he is a conservative, whereas Justice Ruth Bader Ginsburg votes as she does because she is a liberal. Other scholars insist that justices are not free to decide simply on the basis of their preferences—the law constrains the choices they make and directs their decisions. Still other scholars argue that the justices behave strategically: that in seeking to advance their constitutional or ideological views, they take into account the institutional context in which they operate and the likely reaction of the President, Congress, and other political actors.

Accounts of the justices' deliberations indicate that in conference, they rely on legal arguments to buttress their positions and persuade their colleagues. This emphasis on legal argument suggests that the justices acknowledge their duty to put aside their personal preferences and base their decisions on the Constitution, although whether they succeed in doing so may well be another matter. The requirement that decisions be legally justifiable rarely promotes consensus. Conscientious justices can and often do disagree about the difficult legal issues facing them. In recent terms, dissenting opinions were filed in about half of the cases the Court decided. In the Court's 2014 term, for example, 41 percent of the Court's rulings were unanimous, but in 26 percent of the cases the justices were divided 5–4. Although interaction among the justices might have some effect on their votes and opinions, the decision-making process is more individual than collective in nature. As Justice Lewis Powell put it, "For the most part, perhaps as much as 90 percent of our total time, we function as nine small, independent law firms."[15] This high degree of individuality reflects both the well-developed constitutional views the members of the Court bring to their cases and the limited resources available for changing the views of their colleagues.

The vote in conference is only the initial step. Discussion of cases continues after conference, as the opinion of the Court and any concurring or dissenting opinions are prepared and circulated among the justices for their comments. Reviewing these opinions gives the justices an opportunity to reconsider their initial positions, and a particularly persuasive opinion might lead to a change of vote. On a closely divided Court, defection by a single justice can produce a new majority and, therefore, a different decision.

The likelihood of such a vote shift should not be exaggerated. A study of one ten-year period found that the justices' final votes differed from their votes in conference only about 9 percent of the time.[16] Even if no votes are changed, the period between the conference and the announcement of the Court's decision represents a crucial stage in the decisional process. The justices who compose the majority carefully review the draft opinion of the Court, and they might require changes in its language or argument before they will endorse it. One study found that in the majority of cases the opinion of the Court went through three or more drafts.[17] Even after prolonged discussions, deep-seated differences can prevent a Court majority from coalescing behind a single opinion. In *Furman v. Georgia* (1971), all five members of the Court majority wrote separate opinions presenting quite disparate grounds for invalidating Georgia's death penalty statute. More recently, justices have taken to joining opinions of the Court only "in part," agreeing to some sections but not to others.

The justices' close scrutiny of the opinion of the Court reflects in part a concern for the soundness of the legal arguments it presents, because public and congressional acceptance of a decision might be affected by the persuasiveness of the arguments supporting it. The justices also realize that the justifications for their decision play a large role in future decisions. The importance of this consideration was highlighted in the decision handed down in *United States v. Nixon,* in which the Court unanimously rejected the president's claim of executive privilege and voted to compel him to release the Watergate tapes. Before that decision was announced, several justices refused to join Chief Justice Warren Burger's opinion for the Court because they felt that it provided too much support for future claims of executive power. Only after the chief justice agreed to extensive revisions of the original opinion did all the justices join it.

THE IMPACT OF SUPREME COURT DECISIONS

Most Supreme Court decisions not only resolve disputes between particular litigants but also have consequences for the nation as a whole. In ruling on the constitutionality of a particular program or practice, the Court also indicates the likely validity of similar programs or practices. In interpreting a constitutional provision, the Court announces standards that can guide future decisions involving that provision. In elaborating constitutional principles, the Court can educate the public about what our basic principles of government require.

Yet judicial decisions do not always achieve their intended results. Decisions can be misunderstood, misrepresented, or ignored. Those responsible for carrying out the Court's mandates might seek to evade their responsibilities, or they might find ways to negate the effectiveness of the mandates; opposition to Court rulings might lead to attempts to overturn them or to limit their effects. Rather than resolving conflicts, then, Court decisions sometimes merely aggravate them.

Legal Obligation

A Supreme Court decision invalidating a governmental program imposes legal obligations on three distinct sets of actors. Most immediately, the losing party in the case must either abandon the program or remedy its constitutional defects. In a case such as *Regents of the University of California v. Bakke* (1978), in which the Court ruled that the goal of the affirmative-action plan in question (increased minority-group representation in the medical profession) was legitimate but the means employed to achieve this goal were unconstitutional, the university merely had to revise its program so that the goal could be achieved constitutionally. When the aim of an invalidated program is itself unconstitutional, however, any alternative program designed to accomplish that aim would likewise be unconstitutional.

Because of the Court's hierarchical position in the American judicial system, its decisions on matters of federal law are also binding precedent for all other courts, both federal and state. This means that should a litigant challenge a program similar to one invalidated by the Court, lower-court judges are obliged to invalidate it. Moreover, in deciding other cases in which a federal statute or constitutional provision comes into play, judges must treat the Court's interpretation as authoritative. As Judge Learned Hand of the Second Circuit Court of Appeals put it, "I have always felt that it was the duty of an inferior court to suppress its own opinions and to try to prophesy what the appellate court would do. God knows, I have often been wrong in that too; but I have at least been obedient, which is as I conceive it a judge's prime duty."[18]

Finally, by striking down a program as unconstitutional, the Court can also oblige other governmental units to discontinue programs similar to the invalidated one. This underscores the crucial importance of the opinion of the Court: the broader the basis for the ruling, the broader the range of affected programs. The progress of school-desegregation decisions illustrates this point. In a series of decisions handed down between 1938 and 1954, the Court ruled that certain racially segregated school systems had violated the Equal Protection Clause of the Fourteenth Amendment by failing to provide equal educational facilities for African American students. However, because these rulings were tied to the conditions in specific districts, their effects were not felt outside those districts. Then, in 1954 the Court ruled in *Brown v. Board of Education* that separate public school systems for African Americans and whites were *inherently* unequal, thereby obliging all states operating such systems to dismantle them. By choosing the broader basis for its decision in *Brown,* the Court ensured that its ruling would have nationwide effect.

Yet there is considerable controversy over what obligations a Court ruling imposes on government officials. Although they cannot legitimately defy the Court's decision in a specific case, officials are not obliged in every instance to endorse the Court's interpretation of the Constitution. Such a requirement would imply that the Constitution is what the Court says it is or that the Court can never err in its reading of the Constitution. For example, in the wake of the Court's infamous decision in *Dred Scott v. Sandford* (1857)—declaring that African Americans could not be citizens—Abraham Lincoln, although professing respect for the Court and acknowledging the authority of its ruling in the case, denied that the Court had correctly interpreted the Constitution and indicated his intention to seek a reversal of the Court's position. Similarly, critics of the Supreme Court's ruling in *Roe v. Wade* (1973), which recognized a constitutional right to abortion, adopted various restrictions on abortion that were susceptible to legal challenge, expecting that the resulting litigation would provide an opportunity for the Court to reconsider its position. This strategy succeeded only in part: the Court in *Planned Parenthood of Southeastern Pennsylvania v. Casey* (1992) refused to overrule *Roe,* but it did uphold some regulations of abortion. Those seeking to persuade the Court to reverse direction may also count on changes in the Court's membership to accomplish their goal. Thus, in *Stenberg v. Carhart* (2000), a 5–4 majority struck down restrictions on late-term abortions, but after the appointment of Chief Justice Roberts and Justice Alito, the Court in *Gonzales v. Carhart* (2007) upheld very similar restrictions, also by a 5–4 vote.

Response to Court Mandates

In invalidating a program or practice, the Supreme Court imposes an obligation to cease the unconstitutional activity or to take steps to remedy the constitutional violation. In most cases, those affected by the Court's rulings comply with the legal requirements. The mere existence of legal obligations does not guarantee compliance, however, and the Court's mandates have not always been carried out.

Communication of Court Mandates. If its decisions are to achieve their intended effects, the Court must identify clearly what actions are to be undertaken or what practices eliminated, and it must communicate that mandate to the appropriate officials. Rulings that are unclear or that fail to reach their intended audience are unlikely to have much effect.

Confusion over the exact scope or meaning of Court mandates can stem from disagreement on the Court. Not once during the 1960s, for example, did a majority of the justices agree on standards defining what kinds of sexually explicit materials were protected by the First Amendment. As a result, the Court handed down decisions marked by a multiplicity of opinions, each offering a different standard for determining whether movies or publications were obscene. State and local officials who tried to respect constitutional limitations while enforcing obscenity legislation consequently received little guidance from the Court.

Even when the justices agree among themselves, ambiguities in the opinion of the Court can create uncertainty about the scope of the ruling, as happened in *Escobedo v. Illinois* (1964). In *Escobedo,* the Court for the first time recognized that suspects had a right to counsel during police interrogations. However, because the opinion of the Court did not clearly define that right, lower courts developed widely divergent interpretations of the ruling. Over an eighteen-month period, 150 cases raising *Escobedo*-type issues were appealed to the Supreme Court. Only after the Court clarified its position in *Miranda v. Arizona* (1966) did lower courts consistently enforce the right to counsel prior to trial.[19]

Finally, the meaning of a Court ruling might be obscured as it is transmitted to its intended audience. The transmission to police officers of the Supreme Court's landmark criminal-justice decisions of the 1960s illustrates how such confusion can occur. In determining what the Court required, police officers typically relied on numerous sources for information, such as police training sessions, local officials, and the mass media. Often, the Court's message was simplified and distorted in the course of transmission. A study of the initial response to *Miranda* in four Wisconsin police departments, for example, found that despite the clarity of the Court's guidelines, more than half the officers in three departments incorrectly identified what the decision required.[20] However, this tends to pose a problem only in the short run.

Noncompliance. A more serious concern is noncompliance, the refusal to undertake or refrain from actions as required by Supreme Court rulings. State and federal courts at times have failed to follow or enforce Court decisions, with state supreme courts, in particular, displaying a penchant for ignoring Court precedent. More frequently, however, noncompliance crops up among state or local officials who resist Court directions to implement unpopular decisions or to observe new and potentially burdensome limitations on their powers. Southern school boards, for instance, sought to evade the Court's school desegregation requirements; in the 1970s, some northern school boards did the same. Many school districts initially ignored Court decisions requiring the elimination of prayer and Bible reading from their schools. When police officers believed that Court decisions hampered their efforts to control crime, they sought to evade limitations on their power to conduct searches and interrogate suspects.

That individuals evade, or seek to evade, their legal responsibilities is nothing new: the very existence of courts testifies to the need to enforce legal norms. Yet noncompliance, particularly if it is widespread, poses a threat to the Court's effectiveness because its capacity to enforce its decisions is limited. As Alexander Hamilton noted in *The Federalist,* No. 78, the judiciary lacks control over "either the sword or the purse" and must "ultimately depend upon the aid of the executive arm even for the efficacy of its judgments." Should the executive prove reluctant to enforce the Court's decisions vigorously, as happened initially after *Brown v. Board of Education,* the Court must depend on the willingness of litigants to initiate cases challenging instances of noncompliance. Even then, it cannot always rely on the lower courts to enforce its rulings. In sum, the Court's effectiveness ultimately depends less on its ability to punish noncompliance than on its ability to persuade the targets of its decisions to comply voluntarily.

Political Impact

In addition to imposing legal obligations, Supreme Court decisions influence public opinion, political activity, and the development of public policy. By upholding a challenged governmental enactment, the justices authoritatively dispose of constitutional objections to its validity and can thereby promote public acceptance of the law. The Court's decision in *Heart of Atlanta Motel v. United States* (1964), which upheld a controversial section of the Civil Rights Act of 1964, resolved constitutional questions about the national government's power to ban racial discrimination in public accommodations. Its decisions in *National Labor Relations Board v. Jones & Laughlin Steel Corporation* (1937) and in subsequent cases validated New Deal efforts to regulate the national economy. As these examples indicate, Supreme Court decisions have played a crucial role in legitimating the federal government's expanding exercise of power. In addition, the Court's legitimation of one state's law might dispose other states to adopt similar measures. The full development of so-called Jim Crow laws, for example, did not occur until after the Court, in *Plessy v. Ferguson* (1896), upheld a Louisiana statute establishing racial segregation in public transportation.

Even when the justices do not invalidate governmental policies, their rulings may still have political repercussions. The justices' interpretation of federal statutes has at times prompted campaigns for congressional action to overturn those interpretations. Thus, after a series of rulings during the late 1980s that narrowly construed federal civil rights statutes, civil rights groups prevailed on Congress to pass the Civil Rights Act of 1991, reversing several of those decisions. Even rulings upholding governmental action against constitutional challenge can, by focusing attention on an issue, elicit a political response. For example, after the Court, in *Goldman v. Weinberger* (1986), rejected the claim of an Orthodox Jewish psychologist that he had a constitutional right to wear a yarmulke while on active duty in a military hospital, Congress enacted legislation establishing a statutory right to do so.

Decisions invalidating state or federal policies also have produced varied effects. An adverse Court ruling may activate the political forces supporting a program to seek alternative means of accomplishing their objectives. Five constitutional amendments have been adopted, in whole or in part, to overturn Supreme Court decisions.[21] During the 1970s and 1980s, opponents of Court decisions sought, unsuccessfully, to strip the Court of its power to hear cases involving school prayer, busing, and abortion. And after the Court in *Kelo v. City of New London* (2005) ruled that states could use their power of eminent domain to condemn private residences and then transfer the property to other private landowners to promote economic development, voters in several states adopted amendments to their state constitutions prohibiting state and local officials from using eminent domain to transfer property from one private owner to another.

The response to the Supreme Court's abortion decisions illustrates the political dynamics that may be created by judicial rulings. The Supreme Court's decision in *Roe v. Wade*, striking down state restrictions on abortion, galvanized the pro-life movement, which supported legislation making it more difficult to obtain abortions as well as a constitutional amendment outlawing abortion. During the late 1980s and early 1990s, the Court's validation of state laws limiting abortion activated pro-choice forces, who attempted to blunt the effects of these decisions by supporting candidates sympathetic to their cause and by pushing for the adoption of state and federal laws protecting abortion rights. More recently, the Court's ruling in *Stenberg v. Carhart* (2000), striking down a Nebraska law outlawing certain types of late-term ("partial-birth") abortions, led pro-life advocates to push for a federal law prohibiting the practice. Congress enacted the law, and pro-choice groups immediately challenged it in federal court. Because the Supreme Court would likely rule on the law's constitutionality, both pro-life and pro-choice groups sought to influence who would fill the vacancies on the Court produced by the retirement of Justice O'Connor and the death of Chief Justice Rehnquist. As it turned out, the justices appointed to those vacancies provided crucial votes upholding the congressional statute in *Gonzales v. Carhart* (2007).

Controversial decisions may generate both support and opposition. For example, *Brown v. Board of Education* produced not only intransigent resistance by segregationists but also efforts by civil rights groups to solidify and extend the gains they had made. Such decisions have the added effect of subtly changing the political context in which conflicts between such forces occur, by giving proponents of the Court's view the political advantage of being able to claim that the Constitution supports their position. Finally, the broad public support for the Court has promoted public acceptance of politically charged decisions such as *Bush v. Gore* (2000).

In sum, Supreme Court decisions establish government policy, just as decisions made by the executive or legislative branches do, and thereby shape American society. Indeed, if the Court is to fulfill its constitutional functions, it cannot avoid making policy. The important question to ask is whether its policies can be constitutionally justified.

ANALYZING SUPREME COURT DECISIONS

Because judicial opinions provide justifications for constitutional positions, when reading cases one should bear in mind the modes of constitutional interpretation outlined in Chapter 1. Often it is helpful to "brief," or outline, a case to analyze its major elements (see Box 2.1). In general, one should look for the following elements that are common to all court cases.

Components of Supreme Court Decisions

Title and Citation. Case titles derive from the names of the parties to the controversy. The party listed first is seeking reversal of an unfavorable lower-court decision, whereas the party listed second typically wants that decision affirmed. If the case comes to the Court on appeal, the parties are referred to as the appellant and the appellee. If the case comes on a writ of certiorari, they are referred to as the petitioner and the respondent.

Facts of the Case. Because Supreme Court cases arise as disputes between particular litigants, Court decisions represent attempts to apply constitutional principles to unique situations. Full understanding of a judicial decision therefore requires an appreciation of the facts underlying the case, which have been established by testimony at trial. Supreme

BOX 2.1 A Sample Case Brief

Texas v. Johnson
491 U.S. 397 (1989)

Facts of the Case

Gregory Johnson burned an American flag as a form of political protest. He was arrested and convicted of violating a Texas statute that forbade desecration of the American flag. He appealed his conviction, claiming that his action was protected by the First Amendment. The Texas Court of Criminal Appeals overturned his conviction, and the Supreme Court granted certiorari.

The Law

The Free Speech Clause of the First Amendment, made applicable to states by the Due Process Clause of the Fourteenth Amendment.

Legal Questions

1. Does Johnson's conduct constitute expressive conduct, thus implicating the First Amendment? *Yes.*
2. Did Johnson's burning of the flag disturb the peace? *No.*
3. Is the state's interest in preserving the flag as a national symbol related to the suppression of free expression? *Yes.*
4. Does the Supreme Court's test for expressive conduct enunciated by *United States v. O'Brien* apply here? *No.*
5. Does the state have a valid interest in promoting respect for the flag as a symbol of the nation? *Yes.*
6. Can government prohibit flag desecration as a means of promoting that interest? *No.*
7. Is the Texas law constitutional? *No.*

Opinion of the Court (Brennan)

Johnson's burning of the American flag was an attempt to convey a political message. When Texas banned flag desecration to promote respect for the flag, it prevented the use of the flag to communicate messages, such as Johnson's, that are critical of the government and of the nation. However, the First Amendment forbids government from prohibiting the expression of ideas and communication of messages merely because they are offensive or disagreeable, and therefore the Texas statute is unconstitutional.

Concurring Opinion (Kennedy)

Commitment to the Constitution requires overturning Johnson's conviction, however distasteful it may be to do so.

Dissenting Opinion (Rehnquist)

The American flag's unique position as a symbol of the nation justifies special protections against its desecration. Texas's flag desecration statute does not prevent Johnson from communicating his criticism of the government, because his speech and other actions expressing that criticism were not prohibited or interfered with. The statute only prohibits one means of conveying his message, and it does so in response to the profound regard that Americans have for their flag.

Dissenting Opinion (Stevens)

The rules developed for other forms of symbolic expression do not apply here, because of the flag's status as a special symbol of the nation.

Evaluation

The Court's ruling extended the range of expressive actions entitled to First Amendment protection. Forty-eight states and the national government had statutes banning flag desecration, so the effects of the Court's ruling were felt nationwide. Efforts to amend the Constitution to overturn the Court's ruling failed, and a congressional flag-desecration statute that was passed in the wake of this decision was subsequently invalidated by the Court.

Court justices might differ in interpreting the facts, however; disagreement about the facts, as well as about the proper interpretation of the Constitution, can produce divisions on the Court. The opinion of the Court typically summarizes the relevant facts before elaborating the Court's justification for its decision. Summaries of the facts in those cases precede most of the cases presented in this volume.

The Law. Constitutional rulings by the Supreme Court involve the interpretation of three elements of law: constitutional provisions, statutes or administrative regulations (or both), and Supreme Court precedents. Large bodies of law have sprung from most constitutional provisions, so it is important to note precisely which provision the Court is interpreting. For example, if a constitutional challenge is raised under the Fourteenth Amendment, the first thing to determine is whether the challenge is based on the Due Process Clause or the Equal Protection Clause.

Legal Questions. A Court decision can be viewed as a response to a particular legal question or a series of questions. Identifying these questions is vital to proper analysis of the opinions in a case. One way to do so is to frame the questions in a yes-or-no format (see Box 2.1 for an example). Usually, the Court's answers to the legal questions in a case can be determined from a close reading of the opinion of the Court. However, in cases in which five justices are unable to agree on a single opinion, one must search all opinions in the case for points of majority agreement.

Opinion of the Court. This opinion announces the Court's decision and offers the justification for that ruling. Because the decision can serve as a precedent in future cases, close attention should be paid to the chain of reasoning supporting the decision and to its possible implications. Often the best approach is to trace how the Court arrived at its answers to each of the legal questions previously identified.

Concurring Opinions. Members of the Court majority might write concurring opinions because they agree with the Court's decision but disagree with its justification, in which case the concurring opinion will offer an alternative justification. They might also write concurring opinions even if they agree with both the decision and its justification in order either to clarify their own view of the case or to respond to arguments made in a dissenting opinion. Determining the basis for the concurrence should be the initial step in analyzing a concurring opinion.

Dissenting Opinions. Dissenting opinions attempt to demonstrate why the Court's decision is wrong. They might point to alleged errors in reasoning, misinterpretation of precedents or constitutional provisions, or misunderstanding of the facts in a case. Analysis of dissenting opinions should focus on the bases for disagreement with the opinion of the Court.

Evaluation. No analysis of a case is complete without an evaluation of the decision. Is the opinion of the Court convincing? Is the decision consistent with previous Court decisions? If not, does the Court provide persuasive reasons for departing from precedent? What are the likely effects of the Court's decision?

NOTES

1. Alexis de Tocqueville, *Democracy in America*, edited by J. P. Mayer (Garden City, NY: Doubleday, 1969), 270.

2. George W. Bush, *Decision Point* (New York: Crown, 2010), 98.

3. The Eleventh Amendment was adopted to overturn the Supreme Court's ruling in *Chisholm v. Georgia* (1793), which held that a state could be sued in federal court, by a citizen of another state, without its consent.

4. Richard L. Hasen, "End of the Dialogue? Political Polarization, the Supreme Court, and Congress," *Southern California Law Review* 86 (January 2013): 205–262.

5. "Shufflin' Sam" Thompson had been arrested for loitering while waiting in a bar for his bus and

shuffling his feet in time to music from a jukebox. When he protested his arrest, he was also charged with disorderly conduct. He was convicted on both charges and fined $10 for each. Because Kentucky law provided no opportunity to appeal fines of less than $20, Thompson petitioned for Supreme Court review. The Court accepted the case and ruled unanimously that the convictions were not supported by evidence and therefore amounted to a denial of due process of law.

6. Cases may also come to the Supreme Court by certification. Under this rarely used procedure, a lower federal court requests instruction from the Supreme Court on a point of law.

7. "Paid" cases are those in which the petitioners have paid the $300 filing fee and have supplied the prescribed copies of briefs and other legal materials. An *in forma pauperis* case is one in which an impoverished petitioner requests review of a lower-court decision. These cases generally involve criminal appeals filed by prisoners who cannot afford expert legal assistance. In such cases, the Court waives the filing fee and the other requirements.

8. The Supreme Court establishes the procedural rules governing appeals to the Court and the operations of the Court.

9. "Retired Chief Justice Warren Attacks, . . .Freund Study Group's Composition and Proposal," *American Bar Association Journal* 59 (July 1973): 728.

10. *Michigan Department of State Police v. Sitz*, 496 U.S. 444 (1990).

11. Chief Justice Fred Vinson in "Work of the U.S. Supreme Court," *Texas Bar Journal* 12 (1949): 551.

12. It eventually struck down such laws in the [aptly named] *Loving v. Virginia*, 388 U.S. 1 (1967).

13. Harlan's statement is reported in Lewis, *Gideon's Trumpet*, 162n23.

14. William H. Rehnquist, *The Supreme Court: How It Was, How It Is*, rev. ed. (New York: Knopf, 2001), 254–255.

15. Lewis F. Powell Jr., "What the Justices Are Saying . . . ," *American Bar Association Journal* 62 (1976): 1454.

16. Saul Brenner, "Fluidity on the United States Supreme Court: A Reexamination," *American Journal of Political Science* 24 (1980): 526–535.

17. Forrest Maltzman, James F. Spriggs II, and Paul J. Wahlbeck, *Crafting Law on the Supreme Court: The Collegial Game* (New York: Cambridge University Press, 2000), 116, table 4.2.

18. Hand's comment is contained in an intracourt memorandum quoted in Marvin Schick, *Learned Hand's Court* (Baltimore, MD: Johns Hopkins University Press, 1970), 167.

19. On the initial state-court responses to *Escobedo v. Illinois* and *Miranda v. Arizona*, see Neil T. Romans, "The Role of State Supreme Courts in Judicial Policy Making: *Escobedo, Miranda,* and the Use of Impact Analysis," *Western Political Quarterly* 27 (1974): 526–535.

20. Neil A. Milner, *The Court and Local Enforcement: The Impact of* Miranda (Beverly Hills, CA: Sage, 1971), 225, table 11–2.

21. The Eleventh Amendment overruled *Chisholm v. Georgia* (1793); the Fourteenth Amendment, *Dred Scott v. Sandford* (1857); the Sixteenth Amendment, *Pollock v. Farmers' Loan & Trust Co.* (1895); the Twenty-Fourth Amendment, *Breedlove v. Suttles* (1937); and the Twenty-Sixth Amendment, *Oregon v. Mitchell* (1970).

SELECTED READINGS

Abraham, Henry J. *Justices, Presidents, and Senators: A Political History of U.S. Supreme Court Appointments from Washington to Bush II.* Lanham, MD: Rowman & Littlefield, 2007.

Baum, Lawrence. *The Supreme Court.* 11th ed. Washington, DC: CQ Press, 2012.

Dickson, Dale, ed. *The Supreme Court in Conference (1940–1985): The Private Discussions Behind Nearly 300 Supreme Court Decisions.* New York: Oxford University Press, 2001.

Epstein, Lee, and Jack Knight. *The Choices Justices Make.* Washington, DC: CQ Press, 1998.

Farber, Daniel A., and Suzanna Sherry, *Judgment Calls: Principles and Politics in Constitutional Law.* New York: Oxford University Press, 2009.

Hall, Kermit L., James W. Ely, and Joel B. Grossman, eds. *The Oxford Companion to the Supreme Court of the United States.* 2nd ed. New York: Oxford University Press, 2005.

Hall, Matthew E. K. *The Nature of Supreme Court Power.* New York: Cambridge University Press, 2011.

Keck, Thomas M. *Judicial Politics in Polarized Times.* Chicago: University of Chicago Press, 2014.

Lewis, Anthony. *Gideon's Trumpet.* New York: Random House, 1964.

Maltz, Earl, ed. *Rehnquist Justice: Understanding the Court Dynamic.* Lawrence: University Press of Kansas, 2003.

Murphy, Walter F. *Elements of Judicial Strategy.* Chicago: University of Chicago Press, 1964.

O'Brien, David M. *Storm Center: The Supreme Court in American Politics.* 10th ed. New York: W. W. Norton, 2014.

Perry, H. W., Jr. *Deciding to Decide: Agenda Setting in the United States Supreme Court.* Cambridge, MA: Harvard University Press, 1991.

Powe, Lucas A., Jr. *The Warren Court and American Politics.* Cambridge, MA: Belknap Press of Harvard University Press, 2000.

Rehnquist, William H. *The Supreme Court: How It Was, How It Is.* Rev. ed. New York: Knopf, 2001.

Rosenberg, Gerald N. *The Hollow Hope: Can Courts Bring About Social Change?* 2nd ed. Chicago: University of Chicago Press, 2008.

Rossum, Ralph A. *Antonin Scalia's Jurisprudence: Text and Tradition.* Lawrence: University Press of Kansas, 2006.

Rossum, Ralph A. *Understanding Clarence Thomas: The Jurisprudence of Constitutional Restoration.* Lawrence: University Press of Kansas, 2014.

Segal, Jeffrey A., and Harold J. Spaeth. *The Supreme Court and the Attitudinal Model Revisited.* New York: Cambridge University Press, 2002.

Silverstein, Mark. *Judicious Choices: The New Politics of Supreme Court Confirmations.* 2nd ed. New York: W. W. Norton, 2007.

Sweet, Martin J. *Merely Judgment: Ignoring, Evading, and Trumping the Supreme Court.* Charlottesville: University Press of Virginia, 2010.

Tarr, G. Alan. *Judicial Process and Judicial Policymaking.* 6th ed. Belmont, CA: Cengage, 2014.

Tribe, Laurence, and Joshua Matz. *Uncertain Justice: The Roberts Court and the Constitution.* New York: Henry Holt & Co., 2014.

Whittington, Keith E. *Political Foundations of Judicial Supremacy: The Presidency, the Supreme Court, and Constitutional Leadership in U.S. History.* Princeton, NJ: Princeton University Press, 2007.

Wolfe, Christopher, ed. *That Eminent Tribunal: Judicial Supremacy and the Constitution.* Princeton, NJ: Princeton University Press, 2004.

3

The Judicial Power

CHAPTER OUTLINE

The significance the Framers attached to the courts and the judicial power can be surmised by noting the placement, brevity, and generality of the judicial article. To begin with, Article III, establishing the federal judiciary, follows Article I, establishing the legislative branch, and Article II, establishing the executive branch. By so arranging the articles, the Framers addressed each branch, in the words of James Wilson—a member of the Constitutional Convention and an original justice on the Supreme Court—"as its greatness deserves to be considered."[1] Furthermore, Article III is only about one-sixth as long as the legislative article and only about one-third as long as the executive article. Article I specifies in great detail the qualifications of representatives and senators (including age and citizenship requirements), the size of the two houses of Congress, the procedures they must follow, and the powers they are authorized or prohibited to exercise. Article II is likewise quite detailed in its discussion of the president's qualifications, mode of appointment, powers, and responsibilities. By contrast, Article III merely vests the judicial power of the United States in one Supreme Court (its size is unspecified) and in "such inferior Courts as the Congress may from time to time ordain and establish." Article III imposes no qualifications on the judges—not even the requirement of citizenship—and outlines no procedures the courts are obliged to follow.

The Framers left the judicial article as brief and incomplete as they did because they believed what Alexander Hamilton would later declare in *The Federalist,* No. 78: "The judiciary is beyond comparison the weakest of the three departments of power." Like him, they understood the judiciary to be "the least dangerous to the political rights of the constitution; because it will be least in a capacity to annoy or injure them." They recognized that in any republican government, the greatest threat of tyranny would come from the legislative branch, which, as James Madison declared in the Constitutional Convention, "had evinced a powerful tendency . . . to absorb all power into its vortex." Consequently, they devoted much of their time and energies during the Constitutional Convention to designing institutional arrangements and drafting specific delegations of power that would obviate the threat of legislative tyranny. Most of their discussions and decisions concerning the judiciary—its powers and functions—were influenced by that objective. The establishment of the judicial branch was one more means by which they sought to check legislative oppression. They did not perceive the judiciary itself to be a potential source of oppression; to the extent that it might pose any danger, they believed it could be adequately checked by the same Congress that the judiciary helped to curb.

Although the judiciary is "the weakest of the three departments" of government, the courts are not entirely without power. Article III of the Constitution assigns to them the "judicial power" of the United States—a mandate never delineated clearly in the Constitution but usually understood to confer the power to decide conflicts between litigants and to issue writs and orders to carry them into effect. Also included under the umbrella of "judicial power" are the punishment of criminal contempts (to maintain the dignity of the court itself) and of civil contempts (to secure the rights of one party in a suit by forcing the other party to obey the court's ruling) and the issuance of writs of mandamus (ordering people or officials to do particular things), injunctions (ordering them to refrain from doing particular things), and habeas corpus (protecting citizens from illegal imprisonment).

Over and above these universally accepted powers, the federal courts have come to exercise the far more important power of judicial review, that is, the power to invalidate those actions of the other branches of the federal government that are, in the view of courts, contrary to the Constitution. Although this authority to determine the meaning and application of the Constitution is nowhere defined or even mentioned in the Constitution itself, the federal judiciary in general and the Supreme Court in particular have come to wield it to such an extent as to have raised in the minds of some observers the specter of judicial supremacy or even of an emerging imperial judiciary. In this chapter, we examine the establishment of and general justification for the power of judicial review and discuss the various restraints on its exercise imposed externally by the legislative and executive branches and internally by the courts themselves.

THE POWER OF JUDICIAL REVIEW

Because the power of judicial review is not explicitly spelled out in the Constitution, it cannot be defended by mere reference to a relevant constitutional text, and its defenders have had to engage in other forms of constitutional interpretation. Two of the earliest and most influential of these interpretations were made by Alexander Hamilton in *The Federalist,* No. 78, and Chief Justice John Marshall in *Marbury v. Madison* (1803). In *The Federalist,* Hamilton argued syllogistically that because "the interpretation of the law is the proper and peculiar province of the courts" and because the Constitution is a law (albeit a "fundamental" one), the courts must interpret the Constitution. He continued: "It therefore belongs to them to ascertain its meaning as well as the meaning of any particular act proceeding from the legislative body. If there should happen to be an irreconcilable variance between the two, that which has the superior obligation and validity ought of course to be preferred; or in other words, the Constitution ought to be preferred to the statute, the intention of the people to the intention of their agents."

In addition to justifying judicial review on the basis of logical reasoning, Hamilton also justified it based on the "natural feebleness of the judiciary." This feebleness arises from the judiciary's inherent incapacity, in comparison with the popularly elected branches, to injure the political rights of the Constitution.

> Whoever attentively considers the different departments of power must perceive, that, in a government in which they are separated from each other, the judiciary, from the nature of its functions, will always be the least in a capacity to annoy or injure them. The executive not only dispenses the honors, but holds the sword of the community. The legislature not only commands the purse, but prescribes the rules by which the duties and rights of every citizen are to be regulated. The judiciary, on the contrary, has no influence over either the sword or the purse; no direction either of the strength or of the wealth of the society; and can take no active resolution whatever. It may truly be said to have neither FORCE nor WILL, but merely judgment; and must ultimately depend upon the aid of the executive arm even for the efficacy of its judgments.

Hamilton also defended judicial review as the means by which the Constitution, created by the Framers, will remain "limited" in nature. "By a limited constitution, I understand one which contains certain specific exceptions to the legislative authority; such for instance as that it shall pass no bills of attainder, no *ex post facto* laws, and the like." According to Hamilton, "Limitations of this kind can be preserved in practice no other way than through the medium of the courts of justice; whose duty it must be to declare all acts contrary to the manifest tenor of the constitution void." Without judicial review, all the reservations of particular rights and privileges would amount to nothing.

Hamilton's argument in *The Federalist,* No. 78, however, must be understood in historical context. His arguments were primarily in response to a series of essays written by an Anti-Federalist using the pseudonym of Brutus. Brutus sought to discredit the Constitution by, among other things, focusing on the power of the federal judiciary and presenting it as an instrument for consolidating national powers at the expense of the states.[2] In his response in *The Federalist,* No. 78, Hamilton was not so much advocating judicial review as attempting to turn Brutus's arguments against him when he suggested that the Court's power was intended to hold Congress in check and thereby safeguard the states against national aggrandizement by a Congress seeking consolidation. If Congress were to act "contrary to the manifest tenor of the Constitution" and were to attempt to scuttle the federal structure that the Framers had established, Hamilton argued, the Court could be trusted to invalidate those congressional efforts.

Hamilton's argument in *The Federalist,* No. 78, concerning how Congress's tendencies toward national aggrandizement would be checked, was completely contrary to the argument he made on the same subject in *The Federalist,* No. 33. In No. 78, written after Brutus's essays, he relied exclusively on the Court; in No. 33, written before Brutus, Hamilton never even mentioned the Court. In No. 33, Hamilton discussed the Necessary and Proper Clause, regarded by many Anti-Federalists as a source of unlimited power for Congress, and asked: "Who is to judge the necessity and propriety of the laws to be passed for executing the powers of the Union?" His answer: Congress is to judge "in the first instance the proper exercise of its powers; and its constituents in the last." If Congress were to use the Necessary and Proper Clause "to overpass the just bounds of its authority and make a tyrannical use of its powers," Hamilton argued, "the people whose creature it is must appeal to the standard they have formed, and take such measures to redress the injury done to the constitution, as the exigency may suggest and prudence justify." He made no reference to the Supreme Court exercising judicial review to negate such congressional actions. All this prompted constitutional historian Leonard W. Levy to characterize Hamilton's remarks in No. 78 "as evidence of shrewd political tactics, not of the framers' intention to vest judicial review in the Supreme Court over acts of Congress."[3]

Chief Justice Marshall's defense of judicial review in *Marbury* begins in much the same way as Hamilton's defense in No. 78. In Marshall's own words, "It is emphatically the province and duty of the judicial department to say what the law is. Those who apply the rule to particular cases, must, of necessity, expound and interpret that rule." This argument led him to the conclusion that "a law repugnant to the Constitution is void." Applying that rule in *Marbury,* he found a small portion of Section 13 of the Judiciary Act of 1789 to be unconstitutional because, he argued, it attempted to expand the original jurisdiction of the Supreme Court in violation of Article III, Section 2, of the Constitution.

The Judiciary Act of 1789 put "flesh on the bare bones" of the judicial article; with it, the First Congress created the entire federal judiciary. (The text of the act is found in Chapter 7.) Section 13, *inter alia,* expressly gave the Supreme Court power, in cases of appellate jurisdiction, to issue "writs of mandamus, in cases warranted by the principles and usages of law, to any courts appointed, or persons holding office under the authority of the United States." Marshall, however, construed Section 13 as giving the Supreme Court power to issue writs of mandamus in original jurisdiction, thereby expanding the original jurisdiction of the Supreme Court. Marshall's statutory construction of Section 13 is highly questionable. As Akhil Amar has written, "The statutory sentence that the *Marbury* Court flamboyantly refused to enforce did not say what the Court accused it of saying. Rather than adding to the Court's original jurisdiction, the sentence simply provided that if and when the Court already had jurisdiction (whether original or appellate), the justices would be empowered to issue certain technical writs—in particular writs of prohibition and mandamus."[4] Marshall then engaged in equally questionable constitutional construction by arguing that Article III, Section 2, prohibits Congress from expanding the Court's original jurisdiction. This is questionable, for although Article III, Section 2, bars Congress from reducing the Court's original jurisdiction, it does not prohibit Congress from expanding that jurisdiction by "excepting" into original jurisdiction cases otherwise within the Court's appellate jurisdiction.[5]

George Anastaplo has pointed out the "serious consequences" of Marshall's argument in *Marbury:* "Once the Court insisted that 'excepting' a case from the appellate jurisdiction of the Supreme Court could never mean adding it to the original jurisdiction of the Supreme Court, then it tacitly conceded that it must mean that cases may be altogether removed by Congress from the jurisdiction of the Supreme Court." He continues: "It is revealing that in the very case in which the Supreme Court insisted upon its power of judicial review, it also tacitly recognized a power in Congress to remove cases altogether from the Court's jurisdiction, which means that Congress could routinely remove from review by the Court any cases within its appellate jurisdiction which might result in declarations of the unconstitutionality of acts of Congress. This, alone, should make one wonder about how much sense judicial review makes in our system."[6]

To Anastaplo's criticism of Marshall's argument, Justice John Bannister Gibson of the Pennsylvania Supreme Court added another: Gibson in his dissenting opinion in *Eakin v. Raub* (1825) insisted that "the ordinary and essential powers of the judiciary do not extend to the annulling of an act of the legislature." Rather, "It is the business of the judiciary, to interpret the laws, not scan the authority of the lawgiver; and without the latter, it cannot take cognizance of a collision between a law and the Constitution. . . . But it has been said to be emphatically the business of the judiciary to ascertain and pronounce what the law is, and that this necessarily involves a consideration of the Constitution. It does so: but how far? If the judiciary will inquire into anything beside the form of enactment, where shall it stop?"

Chief Justice Marshall in *Marbury* declared for the first time a federal statute to be unconstitutional by "faulting Congress for doing what Congress, in truth, never did."[7] Why would Marshall have done so? To answer that question, some history must be recounted. After Thomas Jefferson was elected president, but before he took office, the lame-duck Federalist Congress passed the Judiciary Act of 1801, which expanded both the organization and the jurisdiction of the federal courts. Among other things, it abolished the three existing circuit courts created by the Judiciary Act of 1789, replacing them with six new circuits, thereby enabling the outgoing Adams administration to appoint sixteen new circuit judges—the famous "midnight appointees." The outgoing Congress also passed a separate law creating forty-two new justices of the peace for the District of Columbia. (Marbury was one of four of these justices of the peace appointed by Adams whose commissions had not been delivered when Jefferson was inaugurated.)

The Jeffersonians were outraged over these court-packing efforts by the Federalists and proposed to repeal the Judiciary Act of 1801, thereby ousting these judges en masse. This prompted an extensive debate over Congress's constitutional authority to remove judges from the bench by abolishing the courts on which they served.[8] The Federalists insisted that repeal would violate the constitutional provision guaranteeing federal judges tenure during good behavior. The Jeffersonians responded that since the Constitution gave Congress the power to establish lower federal courts, it also gave them the power to abolish them. The Jeffersonians prevailed, and the Repeal Act was passed on March 8, 1802, the immediate effect of which was to restore the judicial system established in the Judiciary Act of 1789.

The Federalists predicted that the Supreme Court would declare the Repeal Act unconstitutional. Fearing that prospect and seeking to delay and perhaps even dissuade the displaced circuit judges from attacking the validity of the Repeal Act before the Supreme Court, the Jeffersonians enacted another law providing for annual rather than semiannual sessions of the Supreme Court; the effect was to postpone the June 1802 term of the Court until February 1803.

The Jeffersonians' delaying tactic failed. On the docket of the February 1803 term of the Court were both *Marbury v. Madison* and a challenge to the Repeal Act, *Stuart v. Laird.*

These cases put Chief Justice Marshall in an unenviable position, facing two equally unacceptable choices. He could rule on behalf of Marbury and the Federalist circuit judges, but these decisions would likely have had two consequences: they would probably have been flouted by the legislative and executive branches, thereby exposing just how weak the federal judiciary really was, and they would probably have sufficiently infuriated the Jeffersonian Congress to impeach Marshall, as it had already successfully done to Federalist judge John Pickering and as it was presently attempting to do to Justice Samuel Chase. Alternatively, he could rule against Marbury and the fellow Federalist judges, but again with the consequence of exposing the Court's weakness. Ultimately, Marshall avoided making either choice. Displaying political genius of the first order, he exercised judicial review to invalidate a few words in Section 13 of the Judiciary Act of 1789 and therefore the Court's ability to provide Marbury the remedy he sought. Since Madison and the Jeffersonians won (as Marbury was denied his commission as a justice of the peace), they could not flout his decision and had no grounds for his impeachment. The only branch whose power was diminished as a result of his exercise of judicial review was the Supreme Court—it could no longer issue writs of mandamus in original jurisdiction, but, of course, it was able to claim for itself the vastly greater power to invalidate acts of Congress and in a way that provided the Jeffersonians with no recourse, that is, no way to object.

Marbury was brilliant politically if suspect constitutionally. *Stuart v. Laird* presented more of a challenge, and here Marshall folded his tent. Marshall, who had participated in the case at the circuit-court level, chose not to participate (interestingly, his personal involvement in *Marbury*—he was Adams's secretary of state who had failed to deliver the commission to Marbury—did not stop him from participating in that case), and Justice William Paterson delivered the opinion for an otherwise unanimous Supreme Court affirming the Jeffersonians' argument that Congress's power to establish inferior courts included the power to abolish them and upholding the Repeal Act. The attorneys challenging the constitutionality of the Repeal Act argued:

> By the constitution the judges both of the supreme and the inferior courts are to hold their offices during good behavior. . . . The words *during good behavior* can not mean *during the will of congress.* The people have a right to the services of those judges who have been constitutionally appointed, and who have been unconstitutionally removed from office. It is the right of the people that their judges should be independent; that they should not stand in dread of any man who, as Mr. Henry said in the Virginia convention, has the congress at his heels. It is admitted that the powers of courts and judges may be altered and modified, but cannot be totally withdrawn. By the repealing law the powers of both are entirely taken away.

On the face of it, the Repeal Act seemed to raise much greater constitutional questions than the "writs of mandamus" language in Section 13 of the Judiciary Act of 1789. Yet, interestingly enough, the Court opinion in *Stuart v. Laird* never so much as acknowledged a possible constitutional problem. Justice Paterson simply refused even to address this issue and blithely declared that "Congress [has] constitutional authority to establish from time to time such inferior tribunals as they may think proper, and to transfer a cause from one such tribunal to another. In this last particular, there are no words in the Constitution to prohibit or restrain the exercise of legislative power." Akhil Amar rightly describes this as "judicial capitulation. . . . The trivial statutory section that the Court struck down in *Marbury* paled in significance to the prominent provisions that the Court felt obliged to uphold in *Stuart*. For all *Marbury*'s bold notes, John Marshall was sounding his judicial trumpet in retreat."[9] Judicial review appeared to be more a means for the Court to participate in the political arena than required by the internal logic of the Constitution; it is not surprising that the Court would not exercise judicial review again until *Dred Scott v. Sandford* (also found in Chapter 7) fifty-four years later, when it interjected itself into the poisonous politics of states' rights and the slavery question.

Hamilton's argument on behalf of judicial review in *The Federalist,* No. 78, and Marshall's argument in *Marbury,* strike many defenders of judicial review as insufficient and in need of reinforcement, which they believe can be found in the principle of separation of powers. They argue that it was the intention of the Framers that the Court should have the power of judicial review to check and balance the other branches, just as Congress and the president have other powers at their disposal to check the Court. This line of reasoning, however, suffers from one principal difficulty: the Constitution simply does not make explicit provision for judicial review, but it does explicitly provide for impeachment; congressional control of the Court's appellate jurisdiction; congressional determination of the size, shape, and composition of the entire federal judiciary; presidential appointment of judges subject to Senate confirmation; congressional appropriations for the courts; and so forth. Separation of powers, from which judicial review is inferred, is itself never explicitly mentioned in the Constitution; rather, it is inferred from the specific powers that the Constitution assigns to the branches. Judicial review is no more than an inference drawn from an inference.[10]

Federalism, much more than separation of powers, has played a legitimate role in the evolution of the judicial role. In *Fletcher v. Peck* (1810), *Martin v. Hunter's Lessee* (1816), and *Cohens v. Virginia* (1821), the Marshall Court expanded its authority beyond that staked out in *Marbury* by asserting its powers to review the constitutionality of actions taken not only by the other branches of the national government but also by the states. In *Fletcher,* it invalidated for the first time an act of a state legislature. Then, in *Martin* and *Cohens,* it defended the legitimacy of Supreme Court review of state-court judgments in (respectively) civil and criminal cases that presented federal constitutional questions. These decisions, unlike *Marbury,* rested squarely on two explicit constitutional provisions: Article III, Section 2, which provides that "the judicial Power shall extend to *all* [emphasis added] Cases in Law and Equity, arising under this Constitution, the Laws of the United States, and Treaties made, or which shall be made, under their Authority"; and Article VI, Section 2, which declares that "this Constitution and the Laws of the United States which shall be made in Pursuance thereof; and all Treaties made, or which shall be made, under the Authority of the United States, shall be the supreme Law of the land; and the Judges in every State shall be bound thereby, any Thing in the Constitution or Laws of any State to the Contrary notwithstanding." Because it is based on clear constitutional texts, "judicial review" by federal courts of the legislative, executive, and judicial conduct of the states is clearly different from judicial review by federal courts of the acts of the federal legislative and executive branches, so it is unfortunate that they are both referred to as simply judicial review.

Also unfortunate is the extraordinary length to which the Supreme Court has gone in interpreting these texts. Its contemporary reliance on and understanding of the Supremacy Clause is apparent in *Cooper v. Aaron* (1958); in this remarkable opinion, the Court held that its interpretations of the Constitution are as much "the supreme Law of the Land" as the Constitution itself. These words mark a profound transformation of the Court from the time of the Founding. An institution that, as Akhil Amar notes, was described in Article III as simply "'supreme' over other judges"[11] has come to understand itself as supreme over all the institutions of government and to describe its interpretations of the Constitution as "the supreme Law of the Land."

Interestingly, judicial review has not only been justified as consistent with the principles of separation of powers and federalism but also, in turn, has become a principal means of defending these principles. For example, in *Plaut v. Spendthrift Farm, Inc.* (1995), the

Supreme Court struck down a congressional measure that retroactively allowed for the reopening of final judgments in federal courts. The Court held that "the doctrine of separation of powers is a *structural safeguard* rather than a remedy to be applied only when specific harm, or risk of specific harm, can be identified. In its major features (of which the conclusiveness of judicial judgments is assuredly one) it is a prophylactic device, establishing high walls and clear distinctions because low walls and vague distinctions will not be judicially defensible in the heat of interbranch conflict." It continued: "Separation of powers, a distinctively American political doctrine, profits from the advice authored by a distinctively American poet: 'Good fences make good neighbors.'"

Of course, the "good fences" of separation of powers are to be respected no less by the judiciary than by Congress. This was Justice Thomas's argument in *Wellness International Network v. Sharif* (2015). In that case, Justice Sotomayor held in a 6–3 decision that non-Article III bankruptcy judges can exercise the power of Article III judges so long as the parties consent to that exercise of power. Thomas sounded a clarion call to his colleagues. "The majority today authorizes non-Article III courts to adjudicate, with consent, claims that we have held to require an exercise of the judicial power based on its assessment that few 'structural interests' are implicated by consent to the adjudication. . . . That reasoning is flawed. It matters not whether we think the particular violation threatens the structure of our Government. Our duty is to enforce the Constitution as written, not as revised by private consent, innocuous or otherwise." Thomas insisted "that each branch of the Government is limited to the exercise of those powers granted to it. Every violation of the separation of powers thus involves an exercise of power in excess of the Constitution. And because the only authorities capable of granting power are the Constitution itself, and the people acting through the amendment process, individual consent cannot authorize the Government to exceed constitutional boundaries." He pointed out that "two potential violations of the separation of powers" occur whenever bankruptcy courts adjudicate claims based on consent. "First, the bankruptcy courts purport to exercise power that the Constitution vests exclusively in the judiciary, even though they are not Article III courts because bankruptcy judges do not enjoy the tenure and salary protections required by Article III. Second, the bankruptcy courts act pursuant to statutory authorization that is itself invalid. For even when acting pursuant to an enumerated power, such as the bankruptcy power, Congress exceeds its authority when it purports to authorize a person or entity to perform a function that requires the exercise of a power vested elsewhere by the Constitution." He concluded by observing that "consent to adjudication by non-Article III judges may waive whatever individual right to impartial adjudication Article III implies, thereby lifting that affirmative barrier on Government action." But, he insisted, "Non-Article III courts must still act within the bounds of their constitutional authority. That is, they must act through a power properly delegated to the Federal Government and not vested by the Constitution in a different governmental actor. Because the judicial power is vested exclusively in Article III courts, non-Article III courts may not exercise it."

That the "good fences" of separation of powers are to be respected by the judiciary was also Justice Scalia's argument when he debated Justice Brennan in *Young v. United States ex rel. Vuitton* (1987) over whether the federal courts have the constitutional power to prosecute contemnors for disobedience to court judgments and to appoint attorneys to conduct contempt prosecutions. Their differing answers show fundamentally differing views of the principle of separation of powers. Justice Brennan insisted that "the ability to punish disobedience to judicial orders is essential to ensuring that the Judiciary has a means to vindicate its own authority without complete dependence on other Branches." Otherwise, he feared, courts will be "at the mercy of another Branch in deciding whether such proceedings should be initiated." Scalia countered by noting that the constitutional scheme of separation of powers "leaves open the theoretical possibility that the actions of one Branch may be brought to naught by the actions or inactions of another," and that just as Congress "is dependent on the Executive and the courts for enforcement of the laws it enacts," and just as the executive "cannot perform its function of enforcing the laws if Congress declines to appropriate the necessary funds for that purpose," or if the courts "decline to entertain its valid prosecutions," so, too, the courts are not "immune from this interdependence."

If *Plaut v. Spendthrift Farm, Inc.* shows how the Supreme Court has used judicial review to protect the principle of separation of powers, *Printz v. United States* (1997) shows how the Court has used judicial review to protect federalism. *Printz* (the opinion is found in Chapter 7) invalidated those provisions of the Brady Handgun Violence Prevention Act that commandeered state and local law enforcement officers to conduct background checks on handgun purchasers. Relying on *New York v. United States* (1992), which held that Congress cannot compel the states to enact or enforce a federal regulatory program, the Court majority declared that "Congress cannot circumvent that prohibition by conscripting the State's officers directly. The Federal Government may neither issue directives requiring the States to address particular problems, nor command the States' officers, or those of their political subdivisions, to administer or enforce a federal regulatory program. It matters not whether policymaking is involved, and no case-by-case weighing of the burdens or benefits is necessary; such commands are fundamentally incompatible with our constitutional system of dual sovereignty."

Justifying its exercise of judicial review on the grounds of separation of powers or federalism, the Court as of July 1, 2014, has struck down in whole or part a total of 177 different federal laws, voided 955 different state statutes and 124 municipal ordinances, and held preempted by federal law 241 state and local laws.[12] These statistics, however, do not reflect what defenders of judicial review consider the most significant effect of the Court's power of judicial review. In giving the Court the power to strike down an unconstitutional legislative action, judicial review ipso facto empowers the Court to validate a legislative action as being within constitutionally granted powers and not violating constitutional limitations.[13] The significance of this legitimating function was pointed out by Chief Justice Charles Evans Hughes: "Far more important to the development of the country than the decisions holding acts of Congress to be invalid, have been those in which the authority of Congress has been sustained and adequate national power to meet the necessities of a growing country has been found to exist within constitutional limitations."[14] Together, the validating function and the checking function of judicial review have contributed mightily to the power of the Court—and to its vulnerability.

EXTERNALLY IMPOSED RESTRAINTS ON JUDICIAL REVIEW

The Court's power of judicial review has often brought it into conflict with those whose measures it has invalidated. Given the necessarily problematic nature of the Court's power to review the acts of the coequal branches of the national government, it should come as no surprise that most such controversies have involved Congress and the executive. Individually or together, these branches have imposed or threatened to impose on the Court such sanctions as impeachment, court packing, congressional review of judicial decisions, remedial constitutional amendments, the requirement of an extraordinary majority of the Court to invalidate legislation, and presidential refusal to enforce a decision.[15] (At the state level, nullification and even resort to force have greeted Court decisions.) Historically more important than any of those measures, however, have been sporadic congressional attempts to reduce the Court's appellate jurisdiction. Article III, Section 2, of the Constitution grants to the Supreme Court "appellate Jurisdiction, both as to Law and Fact, with such Exceptions, and under such Regulations, as the Congress shall make." In the post–Civil War period, for example, Congress invoked this constitutional authority in withdrawing from the Court's appellate jurisdiction a politically embarrassing case on which the justices had already heard argument. In *Ex parte McCardle* (1869), the Court agreed unanimously that such drastic action lay within Congress's power and dismissed the case for want of jurisdiction.

The unanimous *McCardle* decision reflects the prevailing view that Congress's power over the appellate jurisdiction of the Supreme Court is plenary, or absolute. Some scholars have argued, however, that Congress's power to make exceptions is constitutionally limited to such exceptions as will not interfere with the essential role of the Court. According to Leonard Ratner, a leading proponent of this position, "Reasonably interpreted, the clause means 'with such exceptions and under such regulations as Congress may make, not inconsistent with the essential functions of the Supreme Court under this Constitution.'"[16]

Ratner's argument is fraught with difficulties. To begin with, it is contrary to the clear words of the Constitution. Absolutely nothing in the unqualified letter of the Exceptions Clause either expressly or implicitly suggests that congressional authority under Article III, Section 2, is limited to making "inessential exceptions." In addition, along with raising the problem of determining the Court's essential role, any circumscription of Congress's power makes the Court the final arbiter in any controversy over the extent of its own powers. In other words, despite the express grant of power to Congress given in the Constitution, Ratner and others of like mind maintain that no statute can constitutionally deprive the Court of its essential role *and* that that role is to be whatever the Court says it is. As Charles Rice points out in rebuttal, "It is hardly in keeping with the spirit of checks and balances to read such a virtually unlimited power into the Constitution. If the Framers intended so to permit the Supreme Court to define its own jurisdiction even against the will of Congress, it is fair to say that they would have made that intention explicit."[17] In fact, such an intention clearly contradicts the thinking of the Framers. Nothing in the records of the Federal Convention of 1787 or of the various state ratifying conventions contravenes the position set forth in *The Federalist,* No. 80, in which, in reviewing in detail the powers of the federal judiciary, Hamilton observed that "if some partial inconveniences should appear to be connected with the incorporation of any of them into the plan, it ought to be recollected that the national legislature will have ample authority to make such exceptions and to prescribe such regulations as will be calculated to obviate or remove these inconveniences."

Finally, the assertion that Congress's power under the Exceptions Clause is limited contradicts the firm, consistent, and unwavering understanding of the Supreme Court. No justice has ever denied Congress's broad power under Article III. As one scholar has observed, "The government body most ready to assert the power of Congress to deprive the Court of its appellate jurisdiction has been the Court itself."[18] In his dissent in *Glidden Co. v. Zdanok* (1962), Justice William Douglas did declare that "there is a serious question whether the *McCardle* case could command a majority today"; this passage is frequently cited to suggest that the contemporary Supreme Court would not accept congressional restrictions of its appellate jurisdiction equivalent to those upheld in *McCardle.* The context of Justice Douglas's dictum, however, suggests something quite different: namely, if Congress were to attempt to deprive the Supreme Court of jurisdiction over a case that is already before the Court, it is questionable whether *McCardle* would be followed today. Douglas subsequently expressed his understanding of the broader question of Congress's power over the appellate jurisdiction of the Supreme Court in his concurrence in *Flast v. Cohen* (1968): "As respects our appellate jurisdiction, Congress may largely fashion it as Congress desires by reason of the express provisions of Section 2, Article III. See *Ex Parte McCardle.*"

In the face of these formidable objections, those who would deny Congress's plenary power under the Exceptions Clause have failed to gain acceptance for their point of view.[19] Both the Warren and the Burger Courts were the targets of Court-curbing initiatives. In 1957, the Jenner-Butler Bill, prohibiting the Supreme Court from hearing appeal cases that dealt with national security issues, failed by the narrowest of margins in the Senate.[20] Two decades later, Senator Jesse Helms's amendment to S. 210 (the bill creating the Department of Education), which would have forbidden the Supreme Court from hearing cases challenging state-sanctioned voluntary school prayers, passed the Senate but ultimately died in the House when the Ninety-Sixth Congress adjourned. During the early 1980s, scores of bills were introduced in Congress that would have deprived the Supreme Court of appellate jurisdiction either to hear cases involving such issues as abortion rights and voluntary prayer in public schools or to order school busing to achieve racial integration.[21]

COURT-IMPOSED RESTRAINTS ON JUDICIAL REVIEW

To minimize the likelihood of Congress or the executive seeking to impose restraints on its exercise of judicial review, the Court has developed a set of policies (Alexander Bickel calls them "passive virtues"[22]) restricting the general circumstances under which it and the lower courts will engage in constitutional adjudication. The part these restraints (at once both constitutionally based yet self-imposed) play in the exercise of judicial power is no less important than the part played by judicial review itself. As Professor John Roche has observed, "Judicial self-restraint and judicial power seem to be the opposite sides of the same coin: it has been by judicious application of the former that the latter has been maintained. A tradition beginning with Marshall's coup in *Marbury v. Madison* . . . suggests that the Court's power has been maintained by a wise refusal to employ it in unequal combat."[23] The Court's self-declared limitations on its power of judicial review fall into the following categories.

Cases and Controversies

Article III, Section 2, declares that the judicial power of the federal courts shall extend to "cases" and "controversies," that is, to litigation involving a real conflict of interests or rights between contending parties. According to its interpretation of this mandate, the federal judiciary generally will not entertain hypothetical, feigned, or collusive suits or render advisory opinions.[24] In recent years, though, this self-imposed barrier to litigation has been lowered by the Supreme Court itself. Whereas in 1955 Justice Robert Jackson could call this restriction "perhaps the most significant . . . limitation upon judicial power," by 1976 Archibald Cox felt compelled to acknowledge that the Court had moved "away from the view that constitutional adjudication is only collateral to the essential judicial task of deciding lawsuits and towards the notion that the primary function of the Supreme Court of the United States is to ensure that other organs of government observe constitutional limitations."[25]

Standing to Sue

Closely related to the need for the presence of a case or controversy is the requirement that the party bringing suit must have standing to sue. Standing was described by the Supreme Court in *Sierra Club v. Morton* (1972) as "a sufficient stake in an otherwise justiciable controversy to obtain judicial resolution of that controversy." The Court traditionally understood that parties invoking judicial power had to show that they had sustained, or were in immediate danger of sustaining, some direct injury as a result of the enforcement of some statute or regulation. Article III, Section 2, limits the jurisdiction of the federal courts to "cases" and "controversies," and traditionally, the Court understood the doctrine of standing as holding that there is no case or controversy when there are no adverse parties with personal interests in the matter.

That traditional understanding, however, changed in the 1960s. The Warren Court brought about a "sea-change . . . in the judicial attitude towards the doctrine of standing."[26] That "sea-change" began in *Baker v. Carr* (1962), when the Court noted that "a personal stake in the outcome of the controversy" was necessary not because of the constitutional limitation of the federal courts' jurisdiction to cases and controversies but because of the pragmatic argument that it leads to better Supreme Court opinions. "A personal stake," Justice Brennan held for the Court majority, "assures that concrete adverseness which sharpens the presentation of issues upon which the court so largely depends for illumination of difficult constitutional questions." That pragmatic argument, however, is badly flawed. As Justice Scalia has remarked:

> Standing, in other words, is only meant to assure that the courts can do their work well, and not to assure that they keep out of affairs better left to the other branches. . . . [I]f the purpose of standing is "to assure that concrete adverseness which sharpens the presentation of issues," the doctrine is remarkably ill designed to that end. Often the very best adversaries are national organizations such as the NAACP or the American Civil Liberties Union that have a keen interest in the abstract question at issue in the case, but no "concrete injury in fact" whatever. Yet the doctrine of standing clearly excludes them, unless they can attach themselves to some particular individual who happens to have some personal interest (however minor) at stake.[27]

The change in the Warren Court's attitude toward the doctrine of standing that began in *Baker v. Carr* became manifestly apparent in *United States v. Students Challenging Regulatory Agency Procedures* [*SCRAP*] (1973). In that case, the Court held that a group of law students at George Washington University had standing to challenge the failure of the Interstate Commerce Commission to prepare an environmental impact statement before it permitted a railroad freight surcharge to take effect. The students claimed standing to sue based on their assertions that they used parks and forests, that these areas would be less desirable if littered, that litter would increase if the use of recycled goods were reduced, that a reduction in their use would result if the cost of these goods increased, and that the cost of these goods would increase if the freight surcharge went into effect. They further claimed standing by asserting that they breathed the air within the Washington metropolitan area and that this air would suffer from increased pollution caused by the modified rate structure. After the Supreme Court held that the alleged injuries sustained by the plaintiffs in *SCRAP* were adequate to support their suits, any claim that standing still required particularized injury rang hollow, and any restraint that standing had once imposed on the federal courts to keep them from assuming the constitutionally assigned powers of the other branches evanesced.

The loose criteria for standing outlined in *SCRAP* made it much easier for litigants to bring policy disputes before the judiciary. To avoid becoming entangled in these disputes, the more judicially restrained Burger Court soon began tightening them and insisted that plaintiffs show something more than a generalized grievance to gain standing. In *Valley Forge Christian College v. Americans United for Separation of Church and State* (1982), the Court rejected the respondents' assertion that they had standing by virtue of an "'injury in fact' to their shared individuated right to a government that 'shall make no law respecting an establishment of religion.'" As Justice William Rehnquist observed for the Court majority, "Although they claim that the Constitution has been violated, they claim nothing else. They fail to identify any personal injury suffered by the plaintiffs as a consequence of the alleged constitutional error, other than the psychological consequence presumably produced by observation of conduct with which one disagrees. That is not sufficient to confer standing under Article III, even though the disagreement is phrased in constitutional terms." Moreover, he continued, "Their claim that the government has violated the Establishment Clause does not provide a special license to roam the country in search of governmental wrongdoing and to reveal their discoveries in federal court. The federal courts were simply not constituted as ombudsmen of the general welfare."

Likewise, in *Allen v. Wright* (1984), the Burger Court denied standing to African American parents who sought to challenge the Internal Revenue Service for its failure to deny tax-exempt status to private schools that they alleged were practicing racial discrimination. The parents claimed that the tax exemptions harmed them directly and interfered with their children's opportunity to receive an education in desegregated public schools. Justice Sandra Day O'Connor dismissed the parents' claims as "speculative." She spoke for a six-member majority when she declared:

> The links in the chain of causation between the challenged Government conduct and the asserted injury are far too weak for the chain as a whole to sustain respondents' standing. . . . The idea of separation of powers that underlies standing doctrine explains why our cases preclude the conclusion that respondents' alleged injury "fairly can be traced to the challenged action" of the IRS. . . . Carried to its logical end, [respondents'] approach would have the federal courts as virtually continuing monitors of the wisdom and soundness of Executive action; such a role is appropriate for the Congress acting through its committees and the "power of the purse"; it is not the role of the judiciary, absent actual present or immediately threatened injury resulting from unlawful governmental action. The Constitution, after all, assigns to the Executive Branch, and not to the Judicial Branch, the duty to "take Care that the Laws be faithfully executed." We could not recognize respondents' standing in this case without running afoul of that structural principle.

Although these Burger Court–era decisions were important, and although Justice O'Connor's insistence that the "structural principle" of separation of powers and the constitutional language of the Take Care Clause both demanded a revitalized standing doctrine, it was not until in *Lujan v. Defenders of Wildlife* in 1992 that the Rehnquist Court finally spelled out the three elements of standing that Justice Antonin Scalia described as the "irreducible constitutional minimum" that all parties invoking federal jurisdiction must establish: "First, the plaintiff must have suffered an 'injury in fact'—an invasion of a legally protected interest which is (a) concrete and particularized, and (b) 'actual or imminent,' not 'conjectural' or 'hypothetical.' Second, there must be a causal connection between the injury and the conduct complained of. . . . Third, it must be 'likely' . . . that the injury will be 'redressed by a favorable decision.'" Applying these three elements to the facts of the case, the Court denied standing to wildlife conservationists who argued that they were injured by the secretary of the interior because he did not require the director of the Agency for International Development (AID) to consult with him under the provisions of the Endangered Species Act of 1973 before the agency helped to fund the rehabilitation of the Aswan High Dam on the Nile River and the completion of the Mahaweli Project in Sri Lanka, thereby threatening the traditional habitat of the endangered Nile crocodile and the Asian elephant and leopard that the respondent conservationists hoped someday to observe.

In *Lujan,* Scalia also held for a six-member majority that Congress could not confer standing on private citizens by allowing them to claim they had suffered a "procedural injury" because of the secretary's failure to consult. "Whether the courts were to act on their own, or at the invitation of Congress, in ignoring the concrete injury requirement described in our cases, they would be discarding a principle fundamental to the separate and distinct constitutional role of the Third Branch—one of the essential elements that identifies those 'Cases' and 'Controversies' that are the business of the courts rather than of the political branches." (Although see *Massachusetts v. EPA* [2007], in which the Court held that states as they seek to protect their "quasi-sovereign interests" are "entitled to special solicitude in our standing analysis" and therefore have standing not available to private citizens to challenge actions by the executive branch.)

Lujan figured prominently in *Hollingsworth v Perry* (2013), in which the Court refused to reach the merits of whether California's Proposition 8, defining marriage as a union between a man and woman, was constitutional, because the petitioners, the ballot measure's official proponents, lacked standing. When Proposition 8 was declared unconstitutional by a federal district court judge and when state officials refused to appeal that decision, the Court of Appeals for the Ninth Circuit allowed the petitioners to assert its constitutionality. But, when the petitioners lost before the appellate court and petitioned the Supreme Court to reverse that decision, Chief Justice Roberts held for a five-member majority that the "petitioners do not have standing," and, as a consequence, "we have no authority to decide this case on the merits, and neither did the Ninth Circuit." As he explained, "To have standing, a litigant must seek relief for an injury that affects him in a 'personal and individual way.' He must possess a 'direct stake in the outcome' of the case. Here, however, petitioners had no 'direct stake' in the outcome of their appeal. Their only interest in having the District Court order reversed was to vindicate the constitutional validity of a generally applicable California law. We have repeatedly held that such a 'generalized grievance,' no matter how sincere, is insufficient to confer standing. A litigant raising only a generally available grievance about government—claiming only harm to his and every citizen's interest in proper application of the Constitution and laws, and seeking relief that no more directly and tangibly benefits him than it does the public at large—does not state an Article III case or controversy."

Standing also proved decisive in *Clapper v. Amnesty International* (2013). A 2008 amendment to the Foreign Intelligence Surveillance Act (FISA) authorizes the Attorney General and the Director of National Intelligence, after they have obtained approval from a FISA court, to acquire foreign intelligence information by jointly authorizing the surveillance of individuals who are not "United States persons" and are reasonably believed to be located outside the United States. On the day the amendment was enacted, Amnesty International and other human rights organizations who claimed to be "United States persons" filed suit, alleging that their work required them to engage in sensitive international communications with individuals who they believed would be likely targets of surveillance and seeking a declaration that the amendment was unconstitutional, as well as an injunction against the surveillance it authorized. They claimed that they would suffer an injury in fact and that they therefore had standing to seek relief because there was an objectively reasonable likelihood that their communications would be acquired under the amendment at some point in the future. They also argued that they were suffering present injury because the risk of FISA-authorized surveillance already had forced them to take costly and burdensome measures to protect the confidentiality of their international communications. Justice Alito found their claims unavailing. Regarding their future injury, he found it "too speculative to satisfy the well-established requirement that threatened injury must be 'certainly impending.' And even if respondents could demonstrate that the threatened injury is certainly impending, they still would not be able to establish that this injury is fairly traceable" to the FISA amendment. And regarding their claim of present injury, he declared that "respondents cannot manufacture standing by choosing to make expenditures based on hypothetical future harm that is not certainly impending." He concluded for a five-member majority that "respondents lack Article III standing."

Although *Lujan* considerably tightened the requirements for standing, one large qualification to this statement must be noted: even the current Roberts Court continues to uphold the Warren Court's decision in *Flast v. Cohen* providing an important exception to the prohibition of taxpayer suits. In *Frothingham v. Mellon* (1923), the Court considered for the first time the contention that taxpayers qua taxpayers have standing and rejected it unequivocally. It was not enough for a taxpayer to show that "he suffers in some indefinite way in common with people generally." Justice George Sutherland held for a unanimous Court that a taxpayer's interest in the moneys of the Treasury "is shared by millions of others; is comparatively minute and indeterminable; and the effect upon future taxation, of any payment out of the funds, so remote, fluctuating and uncertain, that no basis is afforded for an appeal to the preventive powers of a court of equity." Standing, the Court concluded, requires the demonstration of a personal interest that is sharp and distinct from the interests of taxpayers in general.

In *Flast v. Cohen* (1968), the Warren Court introduced an important exception to *Frothingham:* it gave a federal taxpayer standing to challenge, on Establishment Clause grounds, federal expenditures authorized under the Elementary and Secondary Education Act of 1965 that would assist denominational schools in the purchase of textbooks. Never before had an improper expenditure of federal funds been held to injure a federal taxpayer in such a fashion as to confer standing to sue, but Chief Justice Earl Warren wrote for an eight-member majority of the Court that federal taxpayers would be allowed to challenge congressional spending if the legislation in question emanated from the Taxing and Spending Clause of Article I, Section 8, and if the taxpayers could show a nexus between their status as taxpayers and a specific constitutional limitation upon the exercise of the spending power. He concluded his opinion by declaring that the "taxpayer-appellants in this case have satisfied both nexuses to support their claim of standing under the test we announce today. Their constitutional challenge is made to an exercise by Congress of its power under Art. I, §8, to spend for the general welfare, and the challenged program involves a substantial expenditure of federal tax funds. In addition, appellants have alleged that the challenged expenditures violate the Establishment and Free Exercise Clauses of the First Amendment."

Efforts to enlarge the scope of *Flast* have been unavailing, but so, too, have efforts to restrict or overturn it. For example, in *United States v. Richardson* (1974), the Court held that a taxpayer as such had no standing to challenge the constitutionality of that provision of the Central Intelligence Agency Act that permits the CIA, unlike other federal agencies, to keep its budget secret. Chief Justice Burger, holding for a five-member majority that the taxpayer's challenge was not addressed to the Taxing and Spending Clause but only to a statute regulating the CIA, declared that taxpayers were barred from using the courts as forums to air "general grievances" about governmental policies and procedures. The Burger Court in *Richardson* (as well as in *Schlesinger v. Reservists' Committee to Stop the War,* announced the same day) and the Roberts Court in *DaimlerChrysler Corporation v. Cuno* (2006) flatly refused to expand the scope of *Flast* beyond the nexus of the Taxing and Spending Clause and the First Amendment. But, as *Hein v. Freedom from Religion Foundation* (2007) dramatically illustrates, the Roberts Court also seems equally unwilling to restrict or overturn it.

When the Freedom from Religion Foundation challenged the Bush administration's "Faith-Based and Community Initiatives" program on the grounds that it violated the Establishment Clause of the First Amendment, the plaintiffs argued that *Flast* should be expanded to grant federal taxpayers standing to challenge executive-branch programs on Establishment Clause grounds so long as the activities in question are financed by a congressional appropriation, even when there is no statutory program and the funds are from appropriations for general administrative expenses. In *Hein,* five justices rejected their contention, but those five justices split as to the reasons.

Justice Samuel Alito, joined by Chief Justice Roberts and Justice Kennedy, adhered to the principle of judicial minimalism and simply applied *Flast* to the facts before them and found that "the link between congressional action and constitutional violation that supported taxpayer standing in *Flast* is missing here." The Freedom from Religion Foundation did "not challenge any specific congressional action or appropriation," nor did it ask the Court to invalidate any congressional enactment or legislatively created program as unconstitutional. "That is because the expenditures at issue here were not made pursuant to any Act of Congress. Rather, Congress provided general appropriations to the Executive Branch to fund its day-to-day activities. These appropriations did not expressly authorize, direct, or even mention the expenditures of which respondents complain. Those expenditures resulted from executive discretion, not congressional action." He refused to extend *Flast* to apply to the executive branch, because to do so would "enlist the federal courts to superintend, at the behest of any federal taxpayer, the speeches, statements, and myriad daily activities of the President, his staff, and other Executive Branch officials. This . . . would 'open the Judiciary to an arguable charge of providing government by injunction.' It would deputize federal courts as 'virtually continuing monitors of the wisdom and soundness of Executive action,' and that, most emphatically, 'is not the role of the judiciary.'"

Two other justices—Justice Scalia joined by Justice Thomas—also denied that the plaintiffs had standing; they did so, however, not by applying *Flast* but by arguing that it should be overturned: "*Flast* is wholly irreconcilable with the Article III restrictions on federal-court jurisdiction that this Court has repeatedly confirmed are embodied in the doctrine of standing." Unlike Alito, Scalia refused to be bound by precedent. "*Flast*'s lack of a logical theoretical underpinning has rendered our taxpayer-standing doctrine such a jurisprudential disaster that our appellate judges do not know what to make of it. . . . I can think of few cases less warranting of *stare decisis* respect. It is time—it is past time—to call an end. *Flast* should be overruled."

Four justices, however, thought *Flast* not only was good law but should also be extended to apply to the executive branch. Justice Souter wrote for the dissenters: "The controlling, plurality opinion declares that *Flast* does not apply, but a search of that opinion for a suggestion that these taxpayers have any less stake in the outcome than the taxpayers in *Flast* will come up empty: the plurality makes no such finding, nor could it. Instead, the controlling opinion closes the door on these taxpayers because the Executive Branch, and not the Legislative Branch, caused their injury. I see no basis for this distinction in either logic or precedent, and respectfully dissent."

Mootness

Another barrier to judicial review is mootness, a doctrine closely related to the Court's insistence on standing and its refusal to render advisory opinions. When plaintiffs who clearly have standing to sue at the outset of litigation confront a change either in the facts or in the law that deprives them of a necessary stake in the outcome, the issue involved in the suit is rendered moot. The mootness doctrine requires that the case or controversy exist at all stages of review, not merely at the time the complaint was filed.

Although the Court in the main adheres to the mootness doctrine, fidelity to this technical barrier to adjudication is by no means absolute, as the contrasting holdings in *Roe v. Wade* (1973) and *DeFunis v. Odegaard* (1974) illustrate. In *Roe,* the plaintiff was an (initially) pregnant woman who challenged the constitutionality of abortion laws; her suit was initiated in 1970, but the Court's decision was not handed down until January 1973. Even though the plaintiff was no longer pregnant, the Court refused to dismiss the case as moot. Justice Harry Blackmun spoke for the Court: "Pregnancy provides a classic justification for a conclusion of nonmootness. It truly could be 'capable of repetition, yet evading review.'"

In *DeFunis,* on the other hand, the Court invoked the mootness doctrine to avoid ruling on the emotionally charged issue of affirmative action or reverse discrimination. Under a lower-court order, Marco DeFunis Jr. was admitted to the law school at the University of Washington, and by a Supreme Court stay he was able to remain in law school while he litigated his claim that the law school had practiced reverse discrimination and violated the Equal Protection Clause when it denied him admission while accepting minority applicants with lower grades and test scores. He was in his final term when the Supreme Court handed down its decision, and the Court in its *per curiam* opinion found that fact sufficient to render the case moot: "Since he was now registered for his final term, it is evident that he will be given an opportunity to complete all academic and other requirements for graduation, and, if he does so, will receive his diploma regardless of any decision this Court might reach on the merits of this case."

The Court majority did not find persuasive Justice William Brennan's objection that "any number of unexpected events—illness, economic necessity, even academic failure— might prevent his graduation at the end of the term. Were that misfortune to befall, and were petitioner required to register for yet another term, the prospect that he would again face the hurdle of the admissions policy is real, not fanciful."

Ripeness

Another technical barrier to adjudication of constitutional claims is the requirement that a suit not be brought to the courts prematurely, while the relationships between the parties are still developing or in flux. Unless a dispute is sufficiently real, well developed, and specific—in a word, ripe—any decision reached by the courts necessarily will hinge on a series of predictions about the probable conduct of the parties, and those predictions will in turn depend on contingencies and guesses about the future. Because no principled judgment is possible in such circumstances, the courts have developed the ripeness requirement to avoid having to speculate about contingencies and uncertainties.

Nonjusticiable Political Questions

The presence of a case or controversy, standing to sue, the absence of mootness, and ripeness are characteristics that make a jurisdictional issue a justiciable one, that is, a case that the Supreme Court will decide. A different kind of restraint on judicial review comes into play when the Court considers a case to be nonjusticiable despite clear jurisdictional authority. The most common and controversial nonjusticiable cases are those in which the plaintiffs seek adjudication of questions that, in the view of the courts, can be better solved through the political process.

The first explicit application of the political-questions doctrine occurred in *Luther v. Borden* (1849), in which the Court held that enforcement of Article IV, Section 4, of the Constitution, guaranteeing a republican form of government for all states, was the exclusive responsibility of the popularly elected branches. Until the Court's decision in *Baker v. Carr* in 1962, questions involving legislative and congressional reapportionment were also deemed to be political. Specifically, in the crucial case of *Colegrove v. Green* (1946), Justice Felix Frankfurter held for a plurality of the Court that districting was a political question beyond the reach of the Court, warning that "courts ought not to enter this political thicket." Sixteen years later, however, the justices did exactly that in *Baker*, in which the Court directed a federal court in Tennessee to hear a case challenging legislative malapportionment as unconstitutional under the Equal Protection Clause. Justice Brennan's opinion for the Court in *Baker* is generally considered to be the authoritative statement by the Court on the political-questions doctrine.

In his opinion for the Court, Brennan declared that a political question is present if there is "a textually demonstrable constitutional commitment of the issue to a coordinate political department; or a lack of judicially discoverable and manageable standards for resolving it; or the impossibility of deciding without an initial policy determination of a kind clearly for nonjudicial discretion; or the impossibility of a court's undertaking independent resolution without expressing lack of the respect due coordinate branches of government; or an unusual need for unquestioning adherence to a political decision already made; or the potentiality of embarrassment from multifarious pronouncements by various departments on one question."

Applying these *Baker* factors in *United States Department of Commerce v. Montana* (1992), the Court concluded that Montana's constitutional challenge to a congressional statute that authorized the allocation to that state of one (not two) representatives in Congress after the 1990 census did not raise a political question unamenable to judicial resolution. Justice John Stevens wrote for a unanimous Court when he declared: "The controversy between Montana and the Government turns on the proper interpretation of the relevant constitutional provisions. As our previous rejection of the political question doctrine in this context should make clear, the interpretation of the apportionment provisions of the Constitution is well within the competence of the Judiciary." A year later in *Nixon v. United States* (1993), however, it held a legal controversy over the Senate's conduct in the impeachment and removal of a federal judge to be a political question because of the "textually demonstrable commitment" to the Senate of the power to try impeachments and because of the lack of "manageable judicial standards" to review the Senate's actions.

Avoiding the Constitutional Issue

In his concurrence in *Ashwander v. Tennessee Valley Authority* (1936), Justice Louis Brandeis spelled out yet another policy that the Court generally has followed to avoid antagonizing its coequal branches through too-frequent review of their actions:

> The Court will not pass on a constitutional question, although properly presented by the record, if there is also present some other ground on which the case may be disposed of. This rule has found some varied application. Thus, if a case can be decided on either of two grounds, one involving a constitutional question, the other a question of statutory construction or general law, the Court will decide only the latter. . . . Appeals from the highest court of a state challenging its decision of a question under the federal Constitution are frequently dismissed because the judgment can be sustained on an independent state ground.

Presumption of Constitutionality

In general, the Court presumes that a statute is constitutional unless the opposite is clearly demonstrated. Justice Bushrod Washington provided the rationale for this policy in his opinion for the Court in *Ogden v. Saunders* (1827): "It is but a decent respect due to the wisdom, integrity, and patriotism of the legislative body, by which any law is passed, to presume in favor of its validity." It must be emphasized, however, that today this presumption of constitutionality is confined almost exclusively to economic and social legislation. In the contemporary era, the Court usually has regarded as presumptively unconstitutional any legislation that burdens "insular and discrete minorities" or that infringes upon First Amendment freedoms.[28]

THE EXPANDING ROLE OF THE COURTS

Although the set of policies described here is not exhaustive, it does indicate the range and variety of techniques and devices available to the judiciary when it wishes to avoid adjudicating constitutional claims. These techniques are not always employed. As Henry J. Abraham notes, they are little more than "maxims of judicial self-restraint." Different Courts and different justices have cleaved to them with varying degrees of fidelity.[29] Generally speaking, in recent decades, the Supreme Court has displayed less fidelity to these "passive virtues" than earlier Courts did. Perceiving that its role includes representing those interests in society that have failed to receive representation elsewhere in the government, it no longer embraces Justice Brandeis's observation that "the most important thing that we do is not doing."[30] Rather, it has felt compelled to lower the technical barriers to adjudication and, by reaching the constitutional merits of a case, to vindicate the rights of its clientele groups. Because the Burger, Rehnquist, and Roberts Courts have not raised these barriers appreciably, the federal judiciary as a whole has been faced with an expanded range of issues on which it must render final judgment.

Along with this lowering of barriers to constitutional adjudication, two other factors have contributed to an increased level of judicial activity in recent decades. The enormous expansion in the scope of government itself inevitably has raised the level of legal regulation and has thereby provided new opportunities for litigation. At the same time, special interest groups have displayed an increasing willingness to use the courts to pursue political objectives. With the easing of technical restrictions on constitutional adjudication, myriad organizations and lobbies—including civil rights groups, consumer groups, public interest groups, and environmental groups—have concluded that they might fare better in the courts than in the legislative and executive branches, and thus they have sought to achieve their public policy objectives through litigation.[31]

Not only has the range of issues that the judiciary adjudicates expanded considerably, but the kind of response demanded from the courts by these new issues is also entirely different from past judicial responses. Previously, in the constitutional realm, the courts were called upon simply to protect the public from what the other branches of government might have wished to impose on it. Increasingly, however, they are now expected to participate more actively in the policy-making process and to expand what the popular branches must do, even when they do not wish, or know how, to act. Put another way, the courts are expected to be prescriptive as well as proscriptive and to address themselves not only to the government's "sins of commission" but also to its "sins of omission." This expectation that the judiciary should engage in policy making has set off a lively debate: one side argues that the judiciary lacks the institutional capacity necessary to make effective policy (they stress that the very attributes of the adjudicative process that render courts so well suited for specific, retrospective grievance resolution also render them most ill-suited for society-wide, prospective policy making) and that it should therefore confine itself simply to applying the law;[32] the other side argues that the judiciary is indeed capable of dealing with complex policy issues (they contend that, compared with the popularly elected branches and the bureaucracy, it does so quite well) and that it should consequently go beyond mere application of the law and seek to achieve justice.[33] *DeShaney v. Winnebago County Department of Social Services* (1989) shows the Court debating an invitation to expand the Due Process Clause of the Fourteenth Amendment (and therewith its own power) in an emotionally laden case. Chief Justice Rehnquist for the majority relies on the actual words of the Constitution and on precedent to argue against further judicial control of the popular branches, while Justice Blackmun in his dissent invokes "compassion" as his "only guide and comfort" to press for an expanded judicial role. Interestingly, this same debate was replayed in several exchanges between Senator Joseph Biden and Judge John Roberts during Roberts's 2005 Senate confirmation hearing to succeed Rehnquist, for whom Roberts had once clerked, as chief justice. Biden repeatedly sought to ascertain how Roberts's understanding of himself as a father, a husband, and a man would influence his judgments concerning a constitutional right to privacy, to physician-assisted suicide, or to an abortion. His goal was straightforward: he sought to ascertain what kind of justice Roberts would administer if confirmed. In turn, Roberts was equally resolute, repeatedly refusing to reveal what he, in his heart of hearts, considered to be justice and speaking instead only of what the law as found in the Constitution and as passed by Congress would require of him.

THE COURTS, JUDICIAL REVIEW, AND THE PROBLEM OF LEGITIMACY

Ever since *Marbury v. Madison,* the Supreme Court's first exercise of judicial review, the federal judiciary has had to grapple with the problem of legitimacy. How large a role should a nonmajoritarian institution play in shaping American public policy? How often and to what extent should federal judges substitute their judgment for that of the other branches of government at either the federal or the state level? For many students of the Court, these questions took on an added immediacy and urgency as a result of the Supreme Court's decision on December 12, 2000, in *Bush v. Gore* (the opinion is found in Chapter 10 of Volume II). In *Bush v. Gore,* the Court held that the manual recount of presidential ballots ordered by the Florida Supreme Court was unconstitutional and barred any further recount of disputed ballots, thereby ensuring the election of George W. Bush as president of the United States. Seven justices (Chief Justice Rehnquist and Justices Breyer, Kennedy, O'Connor, Scalia, Souter, and Thomas) concluded that the Florida Supreme Court violated the Equal Protection Clause when it ordered a standardless manual recount of "undervotes" (i.e., ballots on which the vote-counting machines had failed to detect a vote for president of the United States) in Miami-Dade County and all counties where the "undervote" had not been subjected to a manual tabulation.

Only five justices, however, were willing to join the Court's *per curiam* opinion halting the continuation of the recount on the grounds that the state legislature had made clear its intention to conclude all recounts by December 12 to secure "safe harbor" protection for the state's electors (Justices Breyer and Souter dissented, arguing that the state should be allowed to attempt to complete a recount before the meeting of the Electoral College on December 18).

The reaction to the Court's *per curiam* opinion from many, both on and off the Court, was harsh and called into question the Court's legitimacy. Justice Stevens in his dissent complained that although "we may never know with complete certainty the identity of the winner of this year's Presidential election, the identity of the loser is perfectly clear. It is the Nation's confidence in the judge as an impartial guardian of the rule of law." Justice Stephen Breyer agreed, accusing the Court of ruling on a "highly politicized matter" and thereby risking "a self-inflicted wound" that harms "not just the Court but the

Nation." The Court, he charged, was guilty of judicial activism when it should have been guided by a "sense of self-restraint" and by Justice Louis Brandeis's famous dictum that "the most important thing we do is not doing." Political commentators were even more vitriolic. Mary McCrory entitled her essay on *Bush v. Gore* "Supreme Travesty of Justice," Eric Foner labeled his "Partisanship Rules," Randall Kennedy chose "Contempt of Court," and Jeffrey Rosen called his "The Supreme Court Commits Suicide." Anthony Lewis began his opinion piece, "A Failure of Reason," by quoting what he called "the despairing comment of one law professor," who, after reading the Court's *per curiam* opinion, asked: "How can I convince my students now that the integrity of legal reasoning matters?"[34]

Yet the furor quickly subsided: *Bush v. Gore* may have been "self-inflicted," but it proved to be a superficial, not a mortal, wound. Many of the Court's sharpest critics in *Bush v. Gore* were soon again applauding the Court when it subsequently invalidated the Child Pornography Prevention Act of 1996 in *Ashcroft v. Free Speech Coalition* (2002), Texas's antisodomy statute in *Lawrence v. Texas* (2003), and the juvenile death penalty in *Roper v. Simmons* (2005), and, perhaps most dramatically, when it upheld the Affordable Care Act (better known as Obamacare) in *National Federation of Independent Business v. Sebelius* (2012). And, of course, many of the Court's most enthusiastic defenders in *Bush v. Gore* were equally disappointed when they found themselves on the losing side of the Court's activism, proving once again that results-oriented jurisprudence is practiced across the ideological landscape.

It is clear that Judge Gibson's apprehensions in *Eakin v. Raub* (1825) have never been completely allayed, and debate over the appropriate role, function, or purpose of the federal judiciary continues to this day among judges and students of public law. At the heart of this debate has been the question of judicial activism versus judicial self-restraint, with advocates for both positions finding support in *The Federalist,* No. 78.

Those who favor judicial activism stress that the judiciary "was designed to be an intermediate body between the people and the legislature, in order among other things to keep the latter within the limits assigned to their authority." They see the judiciary as a "noble guard,"[35] protecting the people from the tyrannical excesses that might otherwise be visited upon them by their more immediate representatives and justify an activist judiciary on the grounds that it helps to promote qualitative, not simply quantitative, majority rule.

Those who favor judicial self-restraint or passivity also begin with *The Federalist,* No. 78. Reminding the judiciary that it is by far the weakest of the three branches of government, having neither the power of the purse nor the power of the sword but only that of judgment, they caution the Court to avoid placing itself in "continuous jeopardy of being over-powered, awed, or influenced by its coordinate branches." Agreeing with James Bradley Thayer, they argue that the judiciary should

> only disregard [a legislative] act when those who have the right to make laws have not merely made a mistake, but have made a very clear one—so clear that it is not open to rational question. That is the standard of duty to which the Courts bring legislative acts; that is the test which they apply—not merely their own judgment as to constitutionality, but their conclusion as to what judgment is permissible to another department which the Constitution has charged with the duty of making it. This rule recognizes that, having regard to the great, complex, ever-unfolding exigencies of government, much which will seem unconstitutional to one man, or body of men, may reasonably not seem so to another; that the Constitution often admits of different interpretations; that the Constitution does not impose upon the legislature any one specific opinion, but leaves open this range of choice; and that whatever choice is rational is constitutional.[36]

Unless the federal judiciary employs this "reasonable doubt" test in exercising judicial review, the argument goes, the people will lose that "political experience and moral education and stimulus that comes from fighting the question out in the ordinary way and correcting their own errors."[37]

The federal judiciary periodically has swung between activism and self-restraint, alternately attracted to and repelled by the implications of these two basic positions.[38] Whatever its stand of the moment, it historically has sought to reassure the popularly elected branches by emphasizing its inherent weakness and by deliberately avoiding unnecessary conflicts with these branches, principally through the erection of technical barriers to adjudication. In recent years, however, the judiciary has increasingly embraced the arguments of judicial activism, eased restrictions on adjudication, and become an active participant in policy making. As the federal judiciary expands both the reach and the vulnerability of its judicial powers (and, by so doing, reveals the limitations of its capacity to make policy), its legitimacy in the eyes of the public will depend as never before on the qualities of the judges themselves. As Alexis de Tocqueville reminded us more than 170 years ago, "[The judges] are all-powerful so long as people respect the law; but they . . . [are] impotent against popular neglect or contempt of the law." Because of the intractability of public opinion, Tocqueville pointed out, judges must be more than "good citizens and men of the information and integrity which are indispensable to all magistrates"; they must also be "statesmen, wise to discern the signs of the time, not afraid to brave the obstacles that can be subdued, nor slow to turn away from the current when it threatens to sweep them off, and the supremacy of the Union and obedience due to the laws along with them."[39] Whether the judicial power will continue to serve as a means to the ends of the Constitution will in large measure depend on the presence of these qualities in the members of the federal judiciary.

NOTES

1. Robert Green McCloskey, ed., *The Works of James Wilson* (Cambridge, MA: Belknap Press of Harvard University Press, 1967), 290.

2. "The Essays of Brutus," in *The Complete Anti-Federalist,* edited by Herbert J. Storing, 7 vols. (Chicago: University of Chicago Press, 1981), essay 11, 2:421.

3. Leonard W. Levy, "Judicial Review, History, and Democracy," in *Judicial Review and the Supreme Court,* edited by Leonard W. Levy (New York: Harper & Row, 1967), 6.

4. Akhil Reed Amar, *America's Constitution: A Biography* (New York: Random House, 2005), 232.

5. William W. Van Alstyne, "A Critical Guide to *Marbury v. Madison,*" *Duke Law Journal* (January 1969): 33.

6. George Anastaplo, *The Constitution of 1787: A Commentary* (Baltimore, MD: Johns Hopkins University Press, 1989), 141. See also Alex Glashausser, "A Return to Form for the Exceptions Clause," *Boston College Law Review* 51 (November 2010): 1383–1450.

7. Amar, *America's Constitution,* 233.

8. An excellent treatment of this debate is found in William S. Carpenter, *Judicial Tenure in the United States* (New Haven, CT: Yale University Press, 1918), 51–100.

9. Amar, *America's Constitution,* 223.

10. Whatever the understanding of separation of powers, it is significant to note that the Supreme Court did not wield the power of judicial review again until the *Dred Scott* decision in 1857. Although several constitutional law scholars have recently begun to write of a second Marshall Court decision that held a provision of a congressional act unconstitutional—the obscure case of *Hodgson v. Bowerbank* (1809)—this revisionist interpretation has been convincingly rebutted by Dennis J. Mahoney, "A Historical Note on *Hodgson v. Bowerbank,*" *University of Chicago Law Review* 49 (1982): 725–740.

11. Amar, *America's Constitution,* 207.

12. Congressional Research Service, *The Constitution of the United States: Analysis and Interpretation,* Interim Edition (Senate Document No. 112–9) (Washington, DC: Government Printing Office, 2014), 2287–2579.

13. Charles L. Black Jr., *The People and the Court* (New York: Macmillan, 1960).

14. Charles Evans Hughes, *The Supreme Court of the United States* (New York: Columbia University Press, 1928), 96–97.

15. Walter F. Murphy, *Congress and the Court* (Chicago: University of Chicago Press, 1962), 63.

16. Leonard G. Ratner, "Congressional Power over the Appellate Jurisdiction of the Supreme Court," *University of Pennsylvania Law Review* 109 (December 1960): 157. See also Henry M. Hart Jr., "The Power of Congress to Limit the Jurisdiction of Federal Courts: An Exercise in Dialectic," *Harvard Law Review* 66 (June 1953): 1362.

17. Charles Rice, "Limiting Federal Court Jurisdiction: The Constitutional Basis for the Proposals in Congress Today," *Judicature* 65, no. 4 (1981): 195. See also Ralph A. Rossum, "Congress, the Constitution, and the Appellate Jurisdiction of the Supreme Court: The Letter and Spirit of the Exceptions Clause," *William and Mary Law Review* 24 (April 1983): 385–428.

18. Comment, "Removal of Supreme Court Appellate Jurisdiction: A Weapon Against Obscenity?" *Duke Law Journal* (1969): 297.

19. For citations to congressional attempts to limit the Supreme Court's appellate jurisdiction, see Gerald Gunther, "Congressional Power to Curtail Federal Court Jurisdiction: An Opinionated Guide to the Ongoing Debate," *Stanford Law Review* 36 (1984): 895–898.

20. See Murphy, *Congress and the Court.*

21. See Ralph A. Rossum, *Congressional Control of the Judiciary: The Article III Option* (Washington, DC: Center for Judicial Studies, 1988).

22. Alexander M. Bickel, *The Least Dangerous Branch: The Supreme Court at the Bar of Politics* (New York: Bobbs-Merrill, 1962), 111–198.

23. John P. Roche, "Judicial Self-Restraint," *American Political Science Review* 49 (September 1955): 722.

24. See *Muskrat v. United States* (1911). Although the federal courts do not render advisory opinions, they do render declaratory judgments. An advisory opinion is advice on a hypothetical question given by the judiciary to the executive or to the legislature. A declaratory judgment, by way of contrast, grows out of an adjudication of an actual controversy between adverse parties and differs from an ordinary judgment principally in that it involves no compulsory process.

25. Robert H. Jackson, *The Supreme Court in the American System of Government* (Cambridge, MA: Harvard University Press, 1955), 11; Archibald Cox, *The Role of the Supreme Court in American Government* (New York: Oxford University Press, 1976), 101.

26. Antonin Scalia, "The Doctrine of Standing as an Essential Element in the Separation of Powers," *Suffolk University Law Review* 17 (Winter 1983): 882.

27. Ibid., 891–892.

28. See, for example, *United States v. Carolene Products Co.* (1938), n4; and *New York Times v. United States* (1971).

29. Henry J. Abraham, *The Judicial Process*, 7th ed. (New York: Oxford University Press, 1998). See also Wallace Mendelson, "Mr. Justice Douglas and Government by Judiciary," *Journal of Politics* 38, no. 4 (1976): 918–937.

30. Alexander M. Bickel, ed., *The Unpublished Opinions of Mr. Justice Brandeis: The Supreme Court at Work* (Cambridge, MA: Harvard University Press, 1957), 17.

31. The critique is presented in Donald L. Horowitz, *The Courts and Social Policy* (Washington, DC: Brookings Institution Press, 1977), 33–56. For a contrasting point of view, see R. Cavanaugh and A. Sarat, "Thinking About Courts: Towards and Beyond a Jurisprudence of Judicial Competence," *Law and Society Review* 14, no. 2 (1980): 371–420; and Stephen L. Wasby, "Arrogation of Power or Accountability? 'Judicial Imperialism' Revisited," *Judicature* 65, no. 4 (1981): 208–219.

32. As Alexander M. Bickel declared in The Supreme Court and the Idea of Progress (New Haven, CT: Yale University Press, 1970), p. 175: "The judicial process is too principle-prone and principle-bound—it has to be, there is no other justification or explanation for the role it plays. It is also too remote from conditions, and deals, case by case, with too narrow a slice of reality. It is not accessible to all the varied interests that are in play in any decision of great consequence. It is, very properly, independent. It is passive. It has difficulty controlling the stages by which it approaches a problem. It rushes forward too fast, or it lags; its pace hardly ever seems just right. For all these reasons, it is, in a vast, complex, changeable society, a most unsuitable instrument for the formation of policy."

33. See Gerald N. Rosenberg, *The Hollow Hope: Can Courts Bring About Social Change?* (Chicago: University of Chicago Press, 1991), who warns these organizations against this strategy, which he describes as "the 'lawyers' vision of change without pain'" (341). In addition, he argues that, because "U.S. courts can almost never be effective producers of significant social reform" (338), they "act as 'fly-paper' for social reforms who succumb to the 'lure of litigation'" (341). He concludes this influential book by remarking: "American courts are not

all-powerful institutions. They were designed with severe limitations and placed in a political system of divided powers. To ask them to produce significant social reform is to forget their history and ignore their constraints. It is to cloud our vision with a naive and romantic belief in the triumph of rights over politics. And while romance and even naiveté have their charms, they are not best exhibited in courtrooms" (343).

34. All of these articles, and more, can be found in E. J. Dionne Jr. and William Kristol, eds., Bush v. Gore: *The Court Cases and the Commentary* (Washington, DC: Brookings Institution Press, 2001).

35. McCloskey, *Works of James Wilson,* 330.

36. James Bradley Thayer, "The Origin and Scope of the American Doctrine of Constitutional Law," *Harvard Law Review* 7 (October 1893): 144. See also Philip B. Kurland, *Mr. Justice Frankfurter and the Supreme Court* (Chicago: University of Chicago Press, 1971), 5, who identifies six basic assumptions of the doctrine of self-restraint: "One is history and the obligation that constitutionalism imposes to adhere to the essential meaning put in the document by its framers. A second is the intrinsically undemocratic nature of the Supreme Court. A third is a corollary of the second, an abiding respect for the judgments of those branches of the government that are elected representatives of their constituents. A fourth is the recognition that judicial error at this level is more difficult of correction than other forms of judicial action. A fifth is respect for the judgments of earlier courts. But (sixth), the essential feature of judicial restraint that has gained most attention and aroused the greatest doubts—probably because few men are themselves big enough to abide by its command—is the notion of rejection of personal preference."

37. James Bradley Thayer, *John Marshall* (Boston: Houghton Mifflin, 1901), 106–107. See also Sanford Gabin, *Judicial Review and the Reasonable Doubt Test* (New York: Kennikat Press, 1980); and Raoul Berger, *Government by Judiciary,* 2nd ed. (Indianapolis: Liberty Fund, 1997).

38. See Wallace Mendelson, "The Politics of Judicial Activism," *Emory Law Journal* 24 (1975): 43–66, who argues that periods of judicial activism coincide with periods of party decline: "Judicial pretension appears to have thrived only in periods of unusual weakness in our political processes; at other times it has been effectively rebuffed. In short, 'government by judges' seems no more than flaws in the party system permit it to be" (44).

39. Alexis de Tocqueville, *Democracy in America* (New York: Random House, 1945), 1:157.

SELECTED READINGS

The Federalist, Nos. 78, 80.

Berger, Raoul. *Congress Versus the Supreme Court.* Cambridge, MA: Harvard University Press, 1969.

Bickel, Alexander M. *The Least Dangerous Branch: The Supreme Court at the Bar of Politics.* New York: Bobbs-Merrill, 1962.

Chayes, Abram. "The Role of the Judge in Public Law Litigation." *Harvard Law Review* 89 (1976): 1281–1316.

Chemerinsky, Erwin. *The Case Against the Supreme Court.* New York: Viking, 2014.

Choper, Jesse H. *Judicial Review and the National Political Process.* Chicago: University of Chicago Press, 1980.

Clinton, Robert Lowry. *Marbury v. Madison and Judicial Review.* Lawrence: University Press of Kansas, 1989.

Curry, Lynne. *The DeShaney Case: Child Abuse, Family Rights, and the Dilemma of State Intervention.* Lawrence: University Press of Kansas. 2007.

Ely, John Hart. *Democracy and Distrust: A Theory of Judicial Review.* Cambridge, MA: Harvard University Press, 1980.

Glidden, William B. *The Supreme Court versus Congress: Disrupting the Balance of Power.* Santa Barbara, CA: Praeger, 2015.

Hamburger, Philip. *Law and Judicial Duty.* Cambridge, MA: Harvard University Press, 2008.

Hickok, Eugene W., and Gary L. McDowell. *Justice vs. Law: Courts and Politics in American Society.* New York: Free Press, 1993.

Horowitz, Donald L. *The Courts and Social Policy.* Washington, DC: Brookings Institution Press, 1977.

Levy, Leonard W., ed. *Judicial Review and the Supreme Court.* New York: Harper & Row, 1967.

McDowell, Gary L. "Coke, Corwin, and the Constitution: The 'Higher Law Background' Reconsidered." *Review of Politics* 55 (Summer 1993): 393–420.

———. *Curbing the Courts: The Constitution and the Limits of Judicial Power.* Baton Rouge: Louisiana State University Press, 1988.

Nelson, William E. *Marbury v. Madison: The Origins and Legacy of Judicial Review.* Lawrence: University Press of Kansas. 2000.

Pacelle, Richard L. *The Supreme Court in a Separation of Powers System: The Nation's Balance Wheel.* New York: Routledge, 2015.

Perry, Michael J. *The Constitution in the Courts: Law or Politics?* New York: Oxford University Press, 1994.

Rosenberg, Gerald N. *The Hollow Hope: Can Courts Bring About Social Change?* Chicago: University of Chicago Press, 1991.

Rossum, Ralph A. *Federalism, the Supreme Court, and the Seventeenth Amendment: The Irony of Constitutional Democracy.* Lanham, MD: Lexington Books, 2001.

Ruger, Theodore W. "A Question Which Convulses a Nation: The Early Republic's Greatest Debate About the Judicial Review Power." *Harvard Law Review* 117 (January 2004): 826–897.

Sandler, Ross, and David Schoenbrod. *Democracy by Decree: What Happens When Courts Run Government.* New Haven, CT: Yale University Press, 2003.

Scalia, Antonin. "The Doctrine of Standing as an Essential Element of the Separation of Powers." *Suffolk University Law Review* 17 (1983): 881–899.

Strumm, Philippa. *The Supreme Court and "Political Questions": A Study in Judicial Evasion.* Tuscaloosa: University of Alabama Press, 1974.

Tarr, G. Alan. *Judicial Process and Judicial Policymaking.* 6th Edition. Boston, MA. Wadsworth, 2014

_____. *Without Fear or Favor: Judicial Independence and Judicial Accountability in the States.* Stanford, CA: Stanford University Press, 2012.

Thayer, James Bradley. "The Origin and Scope of the American Doctrine of Constitutional Law." *Harvard Law Review* 7 (October 1893): 129–156.

Tribe, Laurence, and Joshua Matz, *Uncertain Justice: The Roberts Court and the Constitution.* New York: Henry Holt, 2014.

Van Alstyne, William W. "A Critical Guide to *Marbury v. Madison.*" *Duke Law Journal* (January 1969): 1–47.

Whittington, Keith E. *Political Foundations of Judicial Supremacy: The Presidency, the Supreme Court, and Constitutional Leadership in U.S. History.* Princeton, NJ: Princeton University Press, 2007.

Wolfe, Christopher. *The Rise of Modern Judicial Review: From Constitutional Interpretation to Judge-Made Law.* Rev. ed. Lanham, MD: Rowman & Littlefield, 1994.

Marbury v. Madison
5 U.S. (1 Cranch) 137 (1803)

Before yielding control of the government to the Jeffersonians in 1801, the Federalist-controlled "lame-duck" Congress created a number of new judicial posts. To fill the forty-two justice-of-the-peace posts mandated for the District of Columbia, President John Adams nominated members of the Federalist Party, including one William Marbury. His commission, which had been confirmed by the Senate and signed by the president, was sealed by John Marshall, who, although appointed by President Adams as chief justice, was also serving as secretary of state. In the rush of the closing hours of the Adams administration, Marshall was unable to deliver Marbury's commission. When James Madison took over as Thomas Jefferson's secretary of state on March 4, he found Marbury's commission (and three others) and refused to deliver them. Marbury then brought suit in the Supreme Court to compel delivery of his commission, relying on Section 13 of the Judiciary Act of 1789, which, he claimed, gave the Supreme Court original jurisdiction in such a case. Despite his involvement in this matter, and with a bare quorum of four of the six justices participating, Chief Justice Marshall used this occasion to establish for the Court the power of judicial review. Opinion of the Court: <u>Marshall</u>,* Paterson, Chase, Washington. Not participating: Cushing, Moore.

THE CHIEF JUSTICE delivered the opinion of the Court.

In the order in which the court has viewed this subject, the following questions have been considered and decided.

1. Has the applicant a right to the commission he demands?
2. If he has a right, and that right has been violated, do the laws of his country afford him a remedy?
3. If they do afford him a remedy, is it a *mandamus* issuing from this court?

. . . It is . . . the opinion of the court,

---

1. That, by signing the commission of Mr. Marbury, the President of the United States appointed him a justice of peace, for the county of Washington in the District of Columbia; and that the seal of the United States, affixed thereto by the Secretary of State, is conclusive testimony of the verity of the signature, and of the completion of the appointment; and that the appointment conferred on him a legal right to the office for the space of five years.
2. That, having this legal title to the office, he has a consequent right to the commission; a refusal to deliver which, is a plain violation of that right, for which the laws of this country afford him a remedy.

It remains to be enquired whether,

3. He is entitled to the remedy for which he applies. This depends on,
1. The nature of the writ applied for and
2. The power of this court.

. . . This, then, is a plain case for mandamus, either to deliver the commission, or a copy of it from the record; and it only remains to be enquired, whether it can issue from this court.

The act to establish the judicial courts of the United States authorizes the Supreme Court "to issue writs of mandamus in cases warranted by the principles and usages of law, to any courts appointed, or persons holding office, under the authority of the United States."

The Secretary of State, being a person holding an office under the authority of the United States, is precisely within the letter of the description, and if this court is not authorized to issue a writ of mandamus to such an officer, it must be because the law is unconstitutional, and therefore absolutely incapable of conferring the authority, and assigning the duties which its words purport to confer and assign.

The Constitution vests the whole judicial power of the United States in one supreme court, and such inferior courts as Congress shall, from time to time, ordain and establish. This power is expressly extended to all cases arising under the laws of the United States; and, consequently, in some form, may be exercised over the present case; because the right claimed is given by a law of the United States.

In the distribution of this power it is declared that "the Supreme Court shall have original jurisdiction in all cases affecting ambassadors, other public ministers and consuls, and those in which a state shall be a party. In all other cases, the Supreme Court shall have appellate jurisdiction." It has been insisted at the bar, that, as the original grant of jurisdiction to the Supreme and inferior courts, is general, and the clause assigning original jurisdiction to the Supreme Court contains no negative or restrictive words, the power remains to the legislature to assign original jurisdiction to that court in other cases than those specified in the article which has been recited; provided those cases belong to the judicial power of the United States.

If it had been intended to leave it in the discretion of the legislature to apportion the judicial power between the Supreme and inferior courts according to the will of that body, it would certainly have been useless to have proceeded further than to have defined the judicial power, and the tribunals in which it should be vested. The subsequent part of the section is mere surplusage, is entirely without meaning. If Congress remains at liberty to give this court appellate jurisdiction, where the Constitution has declared their jurisdiction shall be original; and original jurisdiction where the Constitution has declared it shall be appellate, the distribution of jurisdiction made in the Constitution is form without substance.

Affirmative words are often, in their operation, negative of other objects than those affirmed; and in this case, a negative or exclusive sense must be given to them, or they have no operation at all.

It cannot be presumed that any clause in the Constitution is intended to be without effect; and, therefore, such a construction is inadmissible unless the words require it.

. . . To enable this court, then to issue a mandamus, it must be shown to be an exercise of appellate jurisdiction, or to be necessary to enable them to exercise appellate jurisdiction.

It has been stated at the bar that the appellate jurisdiction may be exercised in a variety of forms, and that, if it be the will of the legislature that a mandamus should be used for that purpose, that will must be obeyed. This is true, yet the jurisdiction must be appellate, not original.

It is the essential criterion of appellate jurisdiction that it revises and corrects the proceedings in a cause already instituted, and does not create that cause. Although, therefore, a mandamus may be directed to courts, yet to issue such a writ to an officer for the delivery of a paper is in effect the same as to sustain an original action for that paper, and, therefore, seems not to belong to appellate, but to original jurisdiction. Neither is it necessary, in such a case as this, to enable the court to exercise its appellate jurisdiction.

The authority, therefore, given to the Supreme Court by the act establishing the judicial courts of the United States, to issue writs of mandamus to public officers, appears not to be warranted by the Constitution; and it becomes necessary to inquire whether a jurisdiction so conferred can be exercised.

The question, whether an act repugnant to the Constitution can become the law of the land, is a question deeply interesting to the United States; but, happily, not of an intricacy proportioned to its interest. It seems only necessary to recognize certain principles, supposed to have been long and well established, to decide it.

That the people have an original right to establish, for their future government, such principles as, in their opinion, shall most conduce to their own happiness is the basis on which the whole American fabric had been erected. The exercise of this original right is a very great exertion; nor can it, nor ought it, to be frequently repeated. The principles, therefore, so established, are deemed fundamental. And as the authority from which they proceed is supreme, and can seldom act, they are designed to be permanent.

This original and supreme will organizes the government, and assigns to different departments their respective powers. It may either stop here, or establish certain limits not to be transcended by those departments.

The government of the United States is of the latter description. The powers of the legislature are defined and limited; and that those limits may not be mistaken, or forgotten, the Constitution is written. To what purpose are powers limited, and to what purpose is that limitation committed to writing, if these limits may, at any time, be passed by those intended to be restrained? The distinction between a government with limited and unlimited powers is abolished if those limits do not confine the persons on whom they are imposed, and if acts prohibited and acts allowed are of equal obligation. It is a proposition too plain to be contested, that the Constitution controls any legislative act repugnant to it; or, that the legislature may alter the Constitution by an ordinary act.

Between these alternatives there is no middle ground. The Constitution is either a superior paramount law, unchangeable by ordinary means, or it is on a level with ordinary legislative acts, and, like other acts, is alterable when the legislature shall please to alter it.

If the former part of the alternative be true, then a legislative act contrary to the Constitution is not law: if the latter part be true, then written constitutions are absurd attempts on the part of the people to limit a power in its own nature illimitable.

Certainly all those who have framed written constitutions contemplate them as forming the fundamental and paramount law of the nation, and consequently, the theory of every such government must be, that an act of the legislature, repugnant to the constitution, is void.

This theory is essentially attached to a written constitution, and is, consequently, to be considered by this court as one of the fundamental principles of our society. It is not therefore to be lost sight of in the further consideration of this subject.

If an act of the legislature, repugnant to the Constitution, is void, does it, notwithstanding its invalidity, bind the courts, and oblige them to give it effect? Or, in other words, though it be not law, does it constitute a rule as operative as if it was a law? This would be to overthrow in fact what was established in theory; and would seem, at first view, an absurdity too gross to be insisted on. It shall, however, receive a more attentive consideration.

It is emphatically the province and duty of the judicial department to say what the law is.

Those who apply the rule to particular cases must, of necessity, expound and interpret that rule. If two laws conflict with each other, the courts must decide on the operation of each.

So if a law be in opposition to the Constitution; if both the law and the Constitution apply to a particular case, so that the court must either decide that case conformably to the law, disregarding the Constitution; or conformably to the Constitution, disregarding the law; the court must determine which of these conflicting rules governs the case. This is of the very essence of judicial duty.

If, then, the courts are to regard the Constitution, and the Constitution is superior to any ordinary act of the legislature, the Constitution, and not such ordinary act, must govern the case to which they both apply.

Those, then, who controvert the principle that the Constitution is to be considered, in court, as a paramount law, are reduced to the necessity of maintaining that courts must close their eyes on the Constitution, and see only the law.

This doctrine would subvert the very foundation of all written constitutions. It would declare that an act which, according to the principles and theory of our government, is entirely void, is yet, in practice, completely obligatory. It would declare that if the legislature shall do what is expressly forbidden, such act, notwithstanding the express prohibition, is in reality effectual. It would be giving to the legislature a practical and real omnipotence, with the same breath which professes to restrict their powers within narrow limits. It is prescribing limits and declaring that those limits may be passed at pleasure.

That it thus reduces to nothing what we have deemed the greatest improvement on political institutions—a written constitution—would of itself be sufficient, in America, where written constitutions have been viewed with so much reverence, for rejecting the construction. But the peculiar expressions of the Constitution of the United States furnish additional arguments in favor of its rejection.

The judicial power of the United States is extended to all cases arising under the Constitution.

Could it be the intention of those who gave this power to say that, in using it, the

Constitution should not be looked into? That a case arising under the Constitution should be decided without examining the instrument under which it rises?

This is too extravagant to be maintained.

In some cases then, the Constitution must be looked into by the judges. And if they can open it at all, what part of it are they forbidden to read or to obey? There are many other parts of the Constitution which serve to illustrate this subject.

It is declared that "no tax or duty shall be laid on articles exported from any state." Suppose a duty on the export of cotton, of tobacco, or of flour; and a suit instituted to recover it. Ought judgment to be rendered in such a case? Ought the judges to close their eyes on the Constitution, and see only the law?

The Constitution declares that "no bill of attainder or *ex post facto* law shall be passed." If, however, such a bill should be passed and a person should be prosecuted under it; must the court condemn to death those victims who the Constitution endeavours to preserve?

"No person," says the Constitution, "shall be convicted of treason unless on the testimony of two witnesses to the same overt act, or on confession in open court." Here the language of the Constitution is addressed especially to the courts. It prescribes, directly for them, a rule of evidence not to be departed from. If the legislature should change that rule, and declare *one* witness, or a confession *out* of court, sufficient for conviction, must the constitutional principle yield to the legislative act?

From these, and many other selections which might be made, it is apparent that the framers of the Constitution contemplated that instrument as a rule for the government of *courts,* as well as of the legislature. Why otherwise does it direct the judges to take an oath to support it?

This oath certainly applies in an especial manner to their conduct in their official character. How immoral to impose it on them, if they were to be used as the instruments, and the knowing instruments, for violating what they swear to support?

The oath of office, too, imposed by the legislature, is completely demonstrative of the legislative opinion on this subject. It is in these words: "I do solemnly swear that I will administer justice without respect to persons, and do equal right to the poor and to the rich; and that I will faithfully and impartially discharge all the duties incumbent on me as _____, according to the best of my abilities and understanding agreeably to the *Constitution* and laws of the United States."

Why does a judge swear to discharge his duties agreeably to the Constitution of the United States, if that Constitution forms no rule for his government? If it is closed upon him, and cannot be inspected by him? If such be the real state of things, this is worse than solemn mockery. To prescribe, or take this oath, becomes equally a crime.

It is also not entirely unworthy of observation that, in declaring what shall be the *supreme* law of the land, the *Constitution* itself is first mentioned; and not the laws of the United States generally, but those only which shall be made in *pursuance* of the Constitution, have that rank. Thus, the particular phraseology of the Constitution of the United States confirms and strengthens the principle, supposed to be essential to all written constitutions, that a law repugnant to the Constitution is void; and that *courts,* as well as other departments, are bound by that instrument.

The rule must be

Discharged.

Eakin v. Raub
12 Sergeant & Rawle (Pennsylvania Supreme Court) 330 (1825)

In this otherwise unimportant case, Justice John Bannister Gibson of the Pennsylvania Supreme Court effectively presents, in a dissenting opinion, the opposite side of the argument made by Chief Justice Marshall in Marbury v. Madison. *Because the facts of the case and the opinion of the Court do not contribute to an understanding of Judge Gibson's argument, they have been omitted.*

JUSTICE GIBSON, dissenting . . .

I am aware, that a right to declare all unconstitutional acts void . . . is generally held as a professional dogma; but I apprehend, rather as a matter of faith than of reason. I admit, that I once embraced the same doctrine, but without examination, and I shall, therefore, state the arguments that impelled me to abandon it, with great respect for those by whom it is still maintained. . . .

. . . The constitution is said to be a law of superior obligation; and consequently, that if it were to come into collision with an act of the legislature, the latter would have to give way; this is conceded. But it is a fallacy, to suppose, that they can come into collision *before the judiciary*. . . . The ordinary and essential powers of the judiciary do not extend to the annulling of an act of the legislature.

The constitution and the *right* of the legislature to pass the act, may be in collision; but is that a legitimate subject for judicial determination? If it be, the judiciary must be a peculiar organ, to revise the proceedings of the legislature, and to correct its mistakes; and in what part of the constitution are we to look for this proud preeminence? Viewing the matter in the opposite direction, what would be thought of an act of assembly in which it should be declared that the supreme court had, in a particular case, put a wrong construction on the constitution of the *United States,* and that the judgment should therefore be reversed? It would, doubtless, be thought a usurpation of judicial power. But it is by no means clear, that to declare a law void, which has been enacted according to the forms prescribed in the constitution, is not a usurpation of legislative power. . . . It is the business of the judiciary, to interpret the laws, not scan the authority of the lawgiver; and without the latter, it cannot take cognizance of a collision between a law and the constitution. So that to affirm that the judiciary has a right to judge of the existence of such collision, is to take for granted the very thing to be proved; and that a very cogent argument may be made in this way, I am not disposed to deny. . . . and pronounce what the law is; and that this necessarily involves a consideration of the constitution. It does so:

but how far? If the judiciary will inquire into anything beside the form of enactment, where shall it stop? There must be some point of limitation to such an inquiry; for no one will pretend, that a judge would be justifiable in calling for the election returns, or scrutinizing the qualifications of those who composed the legislature. . . .

Everyone knows how seldom men think exactly alike on ordinary subjects; and a government constructed on the principle of assent by all its parts, would be inadequate to the most simple operations. The notion of a complication of counterchecks has been carried to an extent in theory, of which the framers of the constitution never dreamt. When the entire sovereignty was separated into its elementary parts, and distributed to the appropriate branches, all things incident to the exercise of its powers were committed to each branch exclusively. The negative which each part of the legislature may exercise, in regard to the acts of the other, was thought sufficient to prevent material infractions of the restraints which were put on the power of the whole; for, had it been intended to interpose the judiciary as an additional barrier, the matter would surely not have been left in doubt. The judges would not have been left to stand on the insecure and ever-shifting ground of public opinion, as to constructive power; they would have been placed on the impregnable ground of an express grant; they would not have been compelled to resort to the debates in the convention, or the opinion that was generally entertained at the time. . . .

But the judges are sworn to support the constitution, and are they not bound by it as the law of the land? In some respects they are. In the very few cases in which the judiciary, and not the legislature, is the immediate organ to execute its provisions, they are bound by it, in preference to any act of assembly to the contrary; in such cases, the constitution is a rule to the courts. But what I have in view in this inquiry is, the supposed right of the judiciary, to interfere, in cases where the constitution is to be carried into effect through the instrumentality of the legislature, and where that organ must necessarily first decide on the constitutionality of its own act. The oath to support the constitution is not peculiar to the judges, but is taken indiscriminately by every officer of the government, and is designed rather as a test of the political principles of the man, than to bind the officer in the discharge of his duty: otherwise, it were difficult to determine, what operation it is to have in the case of a recorder of deeds, for instance, who, in the execution of his office, has nothing to do with the constitution. But granting it to relate to the official conduct of the judge, as well as every other officer, and not to his political principles, still, it must be understood in reference to supporting the constitution, *only as far as that may be involved in his official duty;* and consequently, if his official duty does not comprehend an inquiry into the authority of the legislature, neither does his oath. . . .

But do not the judges do a *positive* act in violation of the constitution, when they give effect to an unconstitutional law? Not if the law has been passed according to the forms established in the constitution. The fallacy of the question is, in supposing that the judiciary adopts the acts of the legislature as its own; whereas, the enactment of a law and the interpretation of it are not concurrent acts, and as the judiciary is not required to concur in the enactment, neither is it in the breach of the constitution which may be the consequence of the enactment; the fault is imputable to the legislature, and on it the responsibility exclusively rests. . . .

But it has been said, that this construction would deprive the citizen of the advantages which are peculiar to a written constitution, by at once declaring the power of the legislature, in practice, to be illimitable. . . . But there is no magic or inherent power in parchment and ink, to command respect, and protect principles from violation. In the business of government, a recurrence to first principles answers the end of an observation at sea, with a view to correct the dead-reckoning; and for this purpose, a written constitution is an instrument of inestimable value. It is of inestimable value also, in rendering its principles familiar to the mass of the people; for, after all, there is no effectual guard against legislative usurpation, but

public opinion, the force of which, in this country, is inconceivably great. . . . Once let public opinion be so corrupt, as to sanction every misconstruction of the constitution, and abuse of power, which the temptation of the moment may dictate, and the party which may happen to be predominant, will laugh at the puny efforts of a dependent power to arrest it in its course.

For these reasons, I am of opinion that it rests with the people, in whom full and absolute sovereign power resides, to correct abuses in legislation, by instructing their representatives to repeal the obnoxious act. What is wanting to plenary power in the government, is reserved by the people, for their own immediate use; and to redress an infringement of their rights in this respect, would seem to be an accessory of the power thus reserved. It might, perhaps, have been better to vest the power in the judiciary; as it might be expected, that its habits of deliberation, and the aid derived from the arguments of counsel, would more frequently lead to accurate conclusions. On the other hand, the judiciary is not infallible; and an error by it would admit of no remedy but a more distinct expression of the public will, through the extraordinary medium of a convention; whereas, an error by the legislature admits of a remedy by an exertion of the same will, in the ordinary exercise of the right of suffrage—a mode better calculated to attain the end, without popular excitement. It may be said, the people would probably not notice an error of their representatives. But they would as probably do so, as notice an error of the judiciary; and besides, it is a *postulate* in the theory of our government, and the very basis of the superstructure, that the people are wise, virtuous, and competent to manage their own affairs: and if they are not so, in fact, still, every question of this sort must be determined according to the principles of the constitution, as it came from the hands of its framers, and the existence of a defect which was not foreseen would not justify those who administer the government, in applying a corrective in practice, which can be provided only by a convention. . . .

Cooper v. Aaron
358 U.S. 1 (1958)

After the Arkansas governor Orval Faubus and state legislature openly resisted the Supreme Court's school desegregation decision of 1954 (Brown v. Board of Education), *the Little Rock School Board petitioned the United States District Court for the Eastern District of Arkansas to suspend for two and one-half years the implementation of the school board's plan for desegregation of a previously all-white high school. It feared continuation of the racial tensions and turmoil that had made it impossible for respondents to attend the high school until federal troops were sent there by President Dwight D. Eisenhower. The district court granted petitioners' request. The Court of Appeals for the Eighth Circuit reversed, however, and the Supreme Court granted certiorari. In reasserting its supremacy to determine constitutional law, every justice signed the opinion as the author, thereby underscoring their unanimity. Justice Frankfurter also prepared a concurring opinion, which he released one week after the Court handed down its decision.* Opinion of the Court: <u>Warren</u>, <u>Black</u>, <u>Frankfurter</u>, <u>Douglas</u>, <u>Burton</u>, <u>Clark</u>, <u>Harlan</u>, <u>Brennan</u>, <u>Whittaker</u>. Concurring opinion: <u>Frankfurter</u>.

THE CHIEF JUSTICE, JUSTICE BLACK, JUSTICE FRANKFURTER, JUSTICE DOUGLAS, JUSTICE BURTON, JUSTICE CLARK, JUSTICE HARLAN, JUSTICE BRENNAN, AND JUSTICE WHITTAKER delivered the opinion of the Court.

As this case reaches us it raises questions of the highest importance to the maintenance of our federal system of government. It necessarily involves a claim by the Governor and Legislature of a State that there is no duty on state officials to obey federal court orders resting on this Court's considered interpretation of the United States Constitution. Specifically it involves actions by the Governor and Legislature of Arkansas upon the premise that they are not bound by our holding in *Brown v. Board of Education* [1954]. That holding was that the Fourteenth Amendment forbids States to use their governmental powers to bar children on racial grounds from attending schools where there is state participation through any arrangement, management, funds or property.

We are urged to uphold a suspension of the Little Rock School Board's plan to do away with segregated public schools in Little Rock until state laws and efforts to upset and nullify our holding in *Brown v. Board of Education* have been further challenged and tested in the courts. We reject these contentions. . . .

In affirming the judgment of the Court of Appeals which reversed the District Court we have accepted without reservation the position of the School Board, the Superintendent of Schools, and their counsel that they displayed entire good faith in the conduct of these proceedings and in dealing with the unfortunate and distressing sequence of events which has been outlined. We likewise have accepted the findings of the District Court as to the conditions at Central High School during the 1957–1958 school year, and also the findings that the educational progress of all the students, white and colored, of that school has suffered and will continue to suffer if the conditions which prevailed last year are permitted to continue.

The significance of these findings, however, is to be considered in light of the fact, indisputably revealed by the record before us, that the conditions they depict are directly traceable to the actions of legislators and executive officials of the State of Arkansas, taken in their official capacities, which reflect their own determination to resist this Court's decision in the *Brown* case and which have brought about violent resistance to that decision in Arkansas. In its petition for certiorari filed in this Court, the School Board itself describes the situation in this language: "The legislative, executive, and judicial departments of the state government opposed the desegregation of Little Rock schools by enacting laws, calling out troops, making statements vilifying federal law and federal courts, and failing to utilize state law enforcement agencies and judicial processes to maintain public peace."

One may well sympathize with the position of the Board in the face of the frustrating conditions which have confronted it, but, regardless of the Board's good faith, the actions of the other state agencies responsible for those conditions compel us to reject the Board's legal position.

Had Central High School been under the direct management of the State itself, it could hardly be suggested that those immediately in charge of the school should be heard to assert their own good faith as a legal excuse for delay in implementing the constitutional rights of these respondents, when vindication of those rights was rendered difficult or impossible by the actions of other state officials. The situation here is in no different posture because the members of the School Board and the Superintendent of Schools are local officials; from the point of view of the Fourteenth Amendment, they stand in this litigation as the agents of the State. . . .

The controlling legal principles are plain. The command of the Fourteenth Amendment is that no "State" shall deny to any person within its jurisdiction the equal protection of the laws. "A State acts by its legislative, its executive, or its judicial authorities. It can act in no other way. The constitutional provision, therefore, must mean that no agency of the State, or of the officers or agents by whom its powers are exerted, shall deny to any person within its jurisdiction the equal protection of the laws. Whoever, by virtue of public position under a State government . . . denies or takes away the equal protection of the laws, violates the constitutional inhibition; and as he acts in the name and for the State, and is clothed with the State's power, his act is that of the State. This must be so, or the constitutional prohibition has no meaning." *Ex parte Virginia*, 100 U.S. 339 [1880]. Thus the prohibitions of the Fourteenth Amendment extend to all action of the State denying equal protection of the laws; whatever the agency of the State taking the action, or whatever the guise in which it is taken. In short, the constitutional rights of children not to be discriminated against in school admission on grounds of race or color declared by this Court in the *Brown* case can neither be nullified openly and directly by state legislators or state executive or judicial officers, nor nullified indirectly by them through evasive schemes for segregation whether attempted "ingeniously or ingenuously." *Smith v. Texas* [1940].

What has been said, in the light of the facts developed, is enough to dispose of the case. However, we should answer the premise of the actions of the Governor and Legislature that they are not bound by our holding in the *Brown* case.

It is necessary only to recall some basic constitutional propositions which are settled doctrine.

Article VI of the Constitution makes the Constitution the "supreme Law of the Land." In 1803, Chief Justice MARSHALL, speaking for a unanimous Court, referring to the Constitution as "the fundamental and paramount law of the nation," declared in the notable case of *Marbury v. Madison* that "It is emphatically the province and duty of the judicial department to say what the law is." This decision declared the basic principle that the federal judiciary is supreme in the exposition of the law of the Constitution, and that principle has ever since been respected by this Court and the Country as a permanent and indispensable feature of our constitutional system. It follows that the interpretation of the Fourteenth Amendment enunciated by this Court in the *Brown* case is the supreme law of the land, and Art. VI of the Constitution makes it of binding effect on the States "any Thing in the Constitution or Laws of any State to the Contrary notwithstanding." Every state legislator and executive and judicial officer is solemnly committed by oath taken pursuant to Art. VI, §3 "to support this Constitution."

No state legislator or executive or judicial officer can war against the Constitution without violating his undertaking to support it. Chief Justice MARSHALL spoke for a unanimous Court in saying that: "If the legislatures of the several states may, at will, annul the judgments of the courts of the United States, and destroy the rights acquired under those judgments, the constitution itself becomes a solemn mockery. . . ." *United States v. Peters* [1809].

It is, of course, quite true that the responsibility for public education is primarily the concern of the States, but it is equally true that such responsibilities, like all other state activity, must be exercised consistently with federal constitutional requirements as they apply to state action. The Constitution created a government dedicated to equal justice under law. The Fourteenth Amendment embodied and emphasized that ideal. State support of segregated schools through any arrangement, management, funds, or property cannot be squared with the Amendment's command that no State shall deny to any person within its jurisdiction the equal protection of the laws. The right of a student not to be segregated on racial grounds in schools so maintained is indeed so fundamental and pervasive that it is embraced in the concept of due process of law. *Bolling v. Sharpe* [1954]. The basic decision in *Brown* was unanimously reached by this Court only after the case had been briefed and twice argued and the issues had been given the most serious consideration. Since the first *Brown* opinion three new Justices have come to the Court. They are at one with the Justices still on the Court who participated in that basic decision as to its correctness, and that decision is now unanimously reaffirmed. The principles announced in that decision and the obedience of the States to them, according to the command of the Constitution, are indispensable for the protection of the freedoms guaranteed by our fundamental charter for all of us. Our constitutional ideal of equal justice under law is thus made a living truth.

JUSTICE FRANKFURTER, concurring.

While unreservedly participating with my brethren in our joint opinion, I deem it appropriate also to deal individually with the great issue here at stake. . . .

We are now asked to hold that the illegal, forcible interference by the State of Arkansas with the continuance of what the Constitution commands, and the consequences in disorder that it entrained, should be recognized as justification for undoing what the School Board had formulated, what the District Court in 1955 had directed to be carried out, and what was in process of obedience. No explanation that may be offered in support of such a request can obscure the inescapable meaning that law should bow to force. To yield to such a claim would be to enthrone official lawlessness, and lawlessness if not checked is the precursor of anarchy. Violent resistance to law cannot be made a legal reason for its suspension without loosening the fabric of our society. What could this mean but to acknowledge that disorder under the aegis of a State has moral superiority over the law of the Constitution? For those in authority thus to defy the law of the land is profoundly subversive not only of our constitutional system but of the presuppositions of a democratic society.

The duty to abstain from resistance to "the supreme Law of the Land," U.S. Const., Art. VI, §2, as declared by the organ of our Government for ascertaining it, does not require immediate approval of it nor does it deny the right of dissent. Criticism need not be stilled. Active obstruction or defiance is barred. Our kind of society cannot endure if the controlling authority of the Law as derived from the Constitution is not to be the tribunal specially charged with the duty of ascertaining and declaring what is "the supreme Law of the Land." Particularly is this so where the declaration of what "the supreme Law" commands on an underlying moral issue is not the dubious pronouncement of a gravely divided Court but is the unanimous conclusion of a long-matured deliberative process. . . .

That the responsibility of those who exercise power in a democratic government is not to reflect inflamed public feeling but to help form its understanding, is especially true when they are confronted with a problem like a racially discriminating public school system. This is the lesson to be drawn from the heartening experience in ending enforced racial segregation in the public schools in cities with Negro populations of large proportions. Compliance with decisions of this Court, as the constitutional organ of the supreme Law of the Land, has often, throughout our history, depended on active support by state and local authorities. It presupposes such support. To withhold it, and indeed to use political power to try to paralyze the supreme Law, precludes the maintenance of our federal system as we have known and cherished it for one hundred and seventy years. . . .

Plaut v. Spendthrift Farm, Inc.
514 U.S. 211 (1995)

In 1987, petitioners alleged in a civil action that respondents committed fraud and deceit in 1983 *and 1984 in the sale of stock in violation of the Securities Exchange Act of 1934. The District*

Court for the Eastern District of Kentucky dismissed petitioners' action with prejudice following the Supreme Court's 1991 decision in Lampf, Pleva, Lipkind, Prupis & Petigrow v. Gilbertson, *501 U.S. 350, which required suits such as the petitioners' be commenced within one year after the discovery of the facts constituting the violation and within three years after such violation. Once the district court's judgment had become final, Congress enacted §27A(b) of the Securities Exchange Act, which provided for reinstatement on motion of any action commenced before* Lampf *but dismissed thereafter as time barred, if the action would have been timely filed under applicable pre-*Lampf *state law. Although finding the statute's terms required that petitioners' ensuing §27A(b) motion be granted, the district court denied the motion on the ground that §27A(b) was unconstitutional. The Court of Appeals for the Sixth Circuit affirmed. The Supreme Court granted certiorari.* Opinion of the Court: <u>Scalia</u>, Rehnquist, O'Connor, Kennedy, Souter, Thomas. Concurring in the judgment: <u>Breyer</u>. Dissenting opinion: <u>Stevens</u>, Ginsburg.

JUSTICE SCALIA delivered the opinion of the Court.

Respondents submit that §27A(b) violates both the separation of powers and the Due Process Clause of the Fifth Amendment. Because the latter submission, if correct, might dictate a similar result in a challenge to state legislation under the Fourteenth Amendment, the former is the narrower ground for adjudication of the constitutional questions in the case, and we therefore consider it first. *Ashwander v. TVA* (1936) (Brandeis, J., concurring). We conclude that in §27A(b) Congress has exceeded its authority by requiring the federal courts to exercise "the judicial Power of the United States," U.S. Const., Art. III, §1, in a manner repugnant to the text, structure and traditions of Article III. . . .

Article III establishes a "judicial department" with the "province and duty . . . to say what the law is" in particular cases and controversies. *Marbury v. Madison* (1803). The record of history shows that the Framers crafted this charter of the judicial department with an expressed understanding that it gives the Federal Judiciary the power, not merely to rule on cases, but to *decide* them, subject to review only by superior courts in the Article III hierarchy—with an understanding, in short, that "a judgment conclusively resolves the case" because "a 'judicial Power' is one to render dispositive judgments." By retroactively commanding the federal courts to reopen final judgments, Congress has violated this fundamental principle.

. . . The Framers of our Constitution lived among the ruins of a system of intermingled legislative and judicial powers, which had been prevalent in the colonies long before the Revolution, and which after the Revolution had produced factional strife and partisan oppression. In the 17th and 18th centuries colonial assemblies and legislatures functioned as courts of equity of last resort, hearing original actions or providing appellate review of judicial judgments. Often, however, they chose to correct the judicial process through special bills or other enacted legislation. It was common for such legislation not to prescribe a resolution of the dispute, but rather simply to set aside the judgment and order a new trial or appeal.

. . . The sense of a sharp necessity to separate the legislative from the judicial power, prompted by the crescendo of legislative interference with private judgments of the courts, triumphed among the Framers of the new Federal Constitution. The Convention made the critical decision to establish a judicial department independent of the Legislative Branch by providing that "the judicial Power of the United States shall be vested in one supreme Court, and in such inferior Courts as the Congress may from time to time ordain and establish." Before and during the debates on ratification, Madison, Jefferson, and Hamilton each wrote of the factional disorders and disarray that the system of legislative equity had produced in the years before the framing; and each thought that the separation of the legislative from the judicial power in the new Constitution would cure them. Madison's *Federalist* No. 48, the famous description of the process by which "[t]he legislative department is every where extending the sphere of its activity, and drawing all power into its impetuous vortex," referred to the report of the Pennsylvania Council of Censors to show that in that State "cases belonging to the judiciary department [had been] frequently drawn within legislative cognizance and determination." Madison relied as well on Jefferson's Notes on the State of Virginia, which mentioned, as one example of the dangerous concentration of governmental powers into the hands of the legislature, that "the Legislature . . . in many instances decided rights which should have been left to judiciary controversy."

If the need for separation of legislative from judicial power was plain, the principal effect to be accomplished by that separation was even plainer. As Hamilton wrote in his exegesis of Article III, §1, in *The Federalist* No. 81:

> It is not true . . . that the parliament of Great Britain, or the legislatures of the particular states, can rectify the exceptionable decisions of their respective courts, in any other sense that might be done by a future legislature of the United States. The theory neither of the British, nor the state constitutions, authorises the revisal of a judicial sentence, by a legislative act. . . . A legislature without exceeding its province cannot reverse a determination once made, in a particular case; though it may prescribe a new rule for future cases.

The essential balance created by this allocation of authority was a simple one. The Legislature would be possessed of power to "prescrib[e] the rules by which the duties and rights of every citizen are to be regulated," but the power of "[t]he interpretation of the laws" would be "the proper and peculiar province of the courts." *The Federalist* No. 78. The Judiciary would be, "from the nature of its functions, . . . the [department] least dangerous to the political rights of the constitution," not because its acts were subject to legislative correction, but because the binding effect of its acts was limited to particular cases and controversies. Thus, "though individual oppression may now and then proceed from the courts of justice, the general liberty of the people can never be endangered from that quarter: . . . so long as the judiciary remains truly distinct

from both the legislative and executive." *The Federalist* No. 78.

Judicial decisions in the period immediately after ratification of the Constitution confirm the understanding that it forbade interference with the final judgments of courts. . . .

Section 27A(b) effects a clear violation of the separation-of-powers principle we have just discussed. It is, of course, retroactive legislation, that is, legislation that prescribes what the law *was* at an earlier time, when the act whose effect is controlled by the legislation occurred—in this case, the filing of the initial Rule 10b-5 action in the District Court. When retroactive legislation requires its own application in a case already finally adjudicated, it does no more and no less than "reverse a determination once made, in a particular case." *The Federalist* No. 81. . . .

It is true, as petitioners contend, that Congress can always revise the judgments of Article III courts in one sense: When a new law makes clear that it is retroactive, an appellate court must apply that law in reviewing judgments still on appeal that were rendered before the law was enacted, and must alter the outcome accordingly.

. . . But a distinction between judgments from which all appeals have been forgone or completed, and judgments that remain on appeal (or subject to being appealed), is implicit in what Article III creates: not a batch of unconnected courts, but a judicial *department* composed of "inferior Courts" and "one supreme Court." Within that hierarchy, the decision of an inferior court is not (unless the time for appeal has expired) the final word of the department as a whole. It is the obligation of the last court in the hierarchy that rules on the case to give effect to Congress's latest enactment, even when that has the effect of overturning the judgment of an inferior court, since each court, at every level, must "decide according to existing laws." Having achieved finality, however, a judicial decision becomes the last word of the judicial department with regard to a particular case or controversy, and Congress may not declare by retroactive legislation that the law applicable *to that very case* was something other than what the courts said it was. Finality of a legal judgment is determined by statute, just as entitlement to a government benefit is a statutory creation; but that no more deprives the former of its constitutional significance for separation-of-powers analysis than it deprives the latter of its significance for due process purposes.

To be sure, §27A(b) reopens (or directs the reopening of) final judgments in a whole class of cases rather than in a particular suit. We do not see how that makes any difference. The separation-of-powers violation here, if there is any, consists of depriving judicial judgments of the conclusive effect that they had when they were announced, not of acting in a manner—viz., with particular rather than general effect—that is unusual (though, we must note, not impossible) for a legislature. To be sure, a general statute such as this one may reduce the perception that legislative interference with judicial judgments were prompted by individual favoritism; but it is legislative interference with judicial judgments nonetheless. Not favoritism, nor even corruption, but *power* is the object of the separation-of-powers prohibition. The prohibition is violated when an individual final judgment is legislatively rescinded for even the *very best* of reasons, such as the legislature's genuine conviction (supported by all the law professors in the land) that the judgment was wrong; and it is violated 40 times over when 40 final judgments are legislatively dissolved.

It is irrelevant as well that the final judgments reopened by §27A(b) rested on the bar of a statute of limitations. The rules of finality, both statutory and judge-made, treat a dismissal on statute-of-limitations grounds the same way they treat a dismissal for failure to state a claim, for failure to prove substantive liability, or for failure to prosecute: as a judgment on the merits.

. . . Apart from the statute we review today, we know of no instance in which Congress has attempted to set aside the final judgment of an Article III court by retroactive legislation. That prolonged reticence would be amazing if such interference were not understood to be constitutionally proscribed.

. . . [T]he doctrine of separation of powers is a *structural safeguard* rather than a remedy to be applied only when specific harm, or risk of specific harm, can be identified. In its major feature (of which the conclusiveness of judicial judgments is assuredly one) it is a prophylactic device, establishing high walls and clear distinctions because low walls and vague distinctions will not be judicially defensible in the heat of interbranch conflict. . . . We think legislated invalidation of judicial judgments deserves the same categorical treatment accorded by *Chadha* to congressional invalidation of executive action. The delphic alternative suggested by the concurrence (the setting aside of judgments) is all right so long as Congress does not "impermissibly tr[y] to *apply*, as well as *make*, the law," simply prolongs doubt and multiplies confrontation. Separation of powers, a distinctively American political doctrine, profits from the advice authored by a distinctively American poet: "Good fences make good neighbors."

We know of no previous instance in which Congress has enacted retroactive legislation requiring an Article III court to set aside a final judgment, and for good reason. The Constitution's separation of legislative and judicial powers denies it the authority to do so. Section 27A(b) is unconstitutional to the extent that it requires federal courts to reopen final judgments entered before its enactment. The judgment of the Court of Appeals is affirmed.

JUSTICE BREYER, concurring in the judgment.

I agree with the majority that §27A(b) of the Securities Exchange Act of 1934 is unconstitutional. In my view, the separation of powers inherent in our Constitution means that at least *sometimes* Congress lacks the power under Article I to reopen an otherwise closed court judgment. And the statutory provision here at issue, §27A(b), violates a basic "separation of powers" principle—one intended to protect individual liberty. Three features of this law—its exclusively retroactive effect, its application to a limited number of individuals, and its reopening of closed judgments—taken together, show that Congress here impermissibly tried to *apply*, as well as *make*, the law. Hence, §27A(b) falls outside the scope of Article I. But, it is far less clear, and unnecessary for the purposes of this case to decide, that separation of powers "is violated" *whenever* an "individual final judgment is legislatively rescinded" or that it is "violated 40 times over when 40 final judgments are legislatively dissolved." I therefore write separately.

[B]ecause the law before us *both* reopens final judgments *and* lacks the liberty-protecting assurances that prospectivity and greater generality would have provided, we need not, and we should not, go further—to make of the reopening itself, an absolute, always determinative distinction, a "prophylactic device," or a foundation for the building of a new "high wal[l]" between the branches. Indeed, the unnecessary building of such walls is, in itself, dangerous, because the Constitution blends, as well as separates, powers in its effort to create a government that will work for, as well as protect the liberties of, its citizens. That doctrine does not "divide the branches into watertight compartments," nor "establish and divide fields of black and white." And, important separation of powers decisions of this Court have sometimes turned, not upon absolute distinctions, but upon degree. As the majority invokes the advice of an American poet, one might consider as well that poet's caution, for he not only notes that "Something there is that doesn't love a wall," but also writes, "Before I built a wall I'd ask to know / What I was walling in or walling out."

JUSTICE STEVENS, with whom JUSTICE GINSBURG joins, dissenting.

The majority's rigid holding unnecessarily hinders the Government from addressing difficult issues that inevitably arise in a complex society. This Court, for example, lacks power to enlarge the time for filing petitions for certiorari in a civil case after 90 days from the entry of final judgment, no matter how strong the equities. If an Act of God, such as a flood or an earthquake, sufficiently disrupted communications in a particular area to preclude filing for several days, the majority's reasoning would appear to bar Congress from addressing the resulting inequity. If Congress passed remedial legislation that retroactively granted movants from the disaster area extra time to file petitions or motions for extensions of time to file, today's holding presumably would compel us to strike down the legislation as an attack on the finality of judgments. Such a ruling, like today's holding, would gravely undermine federal courts' traditional power "to set aside a judgment whose enforcement would work inequity."

. . . The Court has drawn the wrong lesson from the Framers' disapproval of colonial legislatures' appellate review of judicial decisions. The Framers rejected that practice, not out of a mechanistic solicitude for "final judgments," but because they believed the impartial application of rules of law, rather than the will of the majority, must govern the disposition of individual cases and controversies. Any legislative interference in the adjudication of the merits of a particular case carries the risk that political power will supplant even handed justice, whether the interference occurs before or after the entry of final judgment. Section 27A(b) neither commands the reinstatement of any particular case nor directs any result on the merits. Congress recently granted a special benefit to a single litigant in a pending civil rights case, but the Court saw no need even to grant certiorari to review that disturbing legislative favor. In an ironic counterpoint, the Court today places a higher priority on protecting the Republic from the restoration to a large class of litigants of the opportunity to have Article III courts resolve the merits of their claims.

"We must remember that the machinery of government would not work if it were not allowed a little play in its joints." *Bain Peanut Co. of Texas v. Pinson* (1931) (Holmes, J.). The three Branches must cooperate in order to govern. We should regard favorably, rather than with suspicious hostility, legislation that enables the judiciary to overcome impediments to the performance of its mission of administering justice impartially, even when, as here, this Court had created the impediment. Rigid rules often make good law, but judgments in areas such as the review of potential conflicts among the three coequal Branches of the Federal Government partake of art as well as science. That is why we have so often reiterated the insight of Justice Jackson:

The actual art of governing under our Constitution does not and cannot conform to judicial definitions of the power of any of its branches based on isolated clauses or even single Articles torn from context. While the Constitution diffuses power the better to secure liberty, it also contemplates that practice will integrate the dispersed powers into a workable government. It enjoins upon its branches separateness but interdependence, autonomy but reciprocity. *Youngstown Sheet & Tube Co. v. Sawyer* (1952) (concurring opinion).

We have the authority to hold that Congress has usurped a judicial prerogative, but even if this case were doubtful I would heed Justice Iredell's admonition in *Calder v. Bull* (1798) that "the Court will never resort to that authority, but in a clear and urgent case." An appropriate regard for the interdependence of Congress and the judiciary amply supports the conclusion that §27A(b) reflects constructive legislative cooperation rather than a usurpation of judicial prerogatives.

Accordingly, I respectfully dissent.

Ex parte McCardle
74 U.S. (7 Wallace) 506 (1869)

During the post–Civil War period, Radical Republicans in Congress imposed upon the Southern states a Reconstruction program. William McCardle, a Mississippi newspaper editor and opponent of Reconstruction, was held for trial before a military commission on charges that he had allowed to be published articles alleged to be "incendiary and libelous." As a civilian, McCardle asserted that he was being unlawfully restrained and sought a writ of habeas corpus before the Supreme Court under an 1867 statute. The Radical Republican leaders in Congress feared that the Supreme Court—already hostile to Reconstruction—would use the occasion provided by McCardle to declare much of the Reconstruction program unconstitutional. Consequently, Congress, over President Andrew Johnson's veto, repealed the 1867 act on which McCardle's appeal was based. By this time, the Court had already heard full arguments in the case, but it had not yet announced its decision. Opinion of the Court: <u>Chase</u>, Nelson, Grier, Clifford, Swayne, Miller, Davis, Field.

THE CHIEF JUSTICE delivered the opinion of the Court.

The first question necessarily is that of jurisdiction; for, if the act of March, 1868, takes away the jurisdiction defined by the act of February, 1867, it is useless, if not improper, to enter into any discussion of other questions.

It is quite true, as was argued by the counsel for the petitioner, that the appellate jurisdiction of this court is not derived from acts of Congress. It is, strictly speaking, conferred by the Constitution. But it is conferred "with such exceptions and under such regulations as Congress shall make."

It is unnecessary to consider whether, if Congress had made no exceptions and no regulations, this court might not have exercised general appellate jurisdiction under rules prescribed by itself. For among the earliest acts of the first Congress, at its first session, was the act of September 24th, 1789, to establish the judicial courts of the United States. That act provided for the organization of this court, and prescribed regulations for the exercise of its jurisdiction.

The source of that jurisdiction, and the limitations of it by the Constitution and by statute, have been on several occasions subjects of consideration here. In the case of *Durousseau v. The United States* [1810] . . . particularly, the whole matter was carefully examined, and the court held, that while "the appellate powers of this court are not given by the judicial act, but are given by the Constitution," they are, nevertheless, "limited and regulated by that act, and by such other acts as have been passed on the subject." The court said, further, that the judicial act was an exercise of the power given by the Constitution to Congress "of making exceptions to the appellate jurisdiction of the Supreme Court." "They have described affirmatively," said the court, "its jurisdiction, and this affirmative description has been understood to imply a negation of the exercise of such appellate power as is not comprehended within it." The principle that the affirmation of appellate jurisdiction implies that negation of all such jurisdiction not affirmed having been thus established, it was an almost necessary consequence that acts of Congress, providing for the exercise of jurisdiction, should come to be spoken of as acts granting jurisdiction, and not as acts making exceptions to the constitutional grant of it.

The exception to appellate jurisdiction in the case before us, however, is not an inference from the affirmation of other appellate jurisdiction. It is made in terms. The provision of the act of 1867, affirming the appellate jurisdiction of this court in cases of *habeas corpus* is expressly repealed. It is hardly possible to imagine a plainer instance of positive exception.

We are not at liberty to inquire into the motives of the legislature. We can only examine into its power under the Constitution; and the power to make exceptions to the appellate jurisdiction of this court is given by express words.

What, then, is the effect of the repealing act upon the case before us? We cannot doubt as to this. Without jurisdiction the court cannot proceed at all in any cause. Jurisdiction is power to declare the law, and when it ceases to exist, the only function remaining to the court is that of announcing the fact and dismissing the cause. And this is not less clear upon authority than upon principle.

Several cases were cited by the counsel for the petitioner in support of the position that jurisdiction of this case is not affected by the repealing act. But none of them, in our judgment, afford any support to it. They are all cases of the exercise of judicial power by the legislature, or of legislative interference with courts in the exercising of continuing jurisdiction.

On the other hand, the general rule, supported by the best elementary writers, is, that "when an act of the legislature is repealed, it must be considered, except as to transactions past and closed, as if it never existed." . . .

It is quite clear, therefore, that this court cannot proceed to pronounce judgment in this case, for it has no longer jurisdiction of the appeal; and judicial duty is not less fitly performed by declining ungranted jurisdiction than in exercising firmly that which the Constitution and the laws confer.

Lujan v. Defenders of Wildlife
504 U.S. 555 (1992)

The respondent and other wildlife conservation and environmental groups brought an action in US District Court for the District of Minnesota against the secretary of the interior, challenging a regulation promulgated by his department implementing Section 7 of the Endangered Species Act (ESA) of 1973 and arguing that it failed to follow Congress's intentions. In Section 7 of the ESA, Congress sought to protect endangered species by requiring that all federal agencies consult with the secretary of the interior to ensure that any action funded by the agency not jeopardize the continued existence or habitat of any endangered or threatened species. The Interior Department's regulation implementing Section 7 extended the ESA's coverage to federally funded projects only in the United States and on the high seas but did not apply it to actions funded in foreign countries. The district court dismissed the case for lack of standing, and the Court of Appeals for the Eighth *Circuit reversed and remanded. On cross-motions for summary judgment, the district court then rejected the secretary's renewed objection to standing, granted the respondents' motion, and ordered the secretary to publish a new regulation extending coverage to foreign countries. The Supreme Court granted certiorari. Opinion of the Court:* Scalia*, White, Rehnquist, Kennedy, Souter, Thomas. Concurring in part and concurring in the judgment:* Kennedy*, Souter. Concurring in the judgment:* Stevens*. Dissenting opinion:* Blackmun*, O'Connor.*

JUSTICE SCALIA delivered the opinion of the Court.

This case involves a challenge to a rule promulgated by the Secretary of the Interior interpreting §7 of the Endangered Species Act of 1973 (ESA), in such fashion as to render it applicable only to actions within the United

States or on the high seas. The preliminary issue, and the only one we reach, is whether the respondents here, plaintiffs below, have standing to seek judicial review of the rule. . . .

While the Constitution of the United States divides all power conferred upon the Federal Government into "legislative Powers," "[t]he executive Power," and "[t]he judicial Power," it does not attempt to define those terms. To be sure, it limits the jurisdiction of federal courts to "Cases" and "Controversies," but an executive inquiry can bear the name "case" and a legislative dispute can bear the name "controversy." Obviously, then, the Constitution's central mechanism of separation of powers depends largely upon common understanding of what activities are appropriate to legislatures, to executives, and to courts. In *The Federalist*, No. 48, Madison expressed the view that "[i]t is not infrequently a question of real nicety in legislative bodies whether the operation of a particular measure will, or will not, extend beyond the legislative sphere," whereas "the executive power [is] restrained within a narrower compass and . . . more simple in its nature," and "the judiciary [is] described by landmarks still less uncertain." One of those landmarks, setting apart the "Cases" and "Controversies" that are of the justiciable sort referred to in Article III—"serv[ing] to identify those disputes which are appropriately resolved through the judicial process,"—is the doctrine of standing. Though some of its elements express merely prudential considerations that are part of judicial self-government, the core component of standing is an essential and unchanging part of the case-or-controversy requirement of Article III.

Over the years, our cases have established that the irreducible constitutional minimum of standing contains three elements: First, the plaintiff must have suffered an "injury in fact"—an invasion of a legally protected interest which is (a) concrete and particularized, and (b) "actual or imminent, not 'conjectural' or 'hypothetical.'" Second, there must be a causal connection between the injury and the conduct complained of—the injury has to be "fairly . . . trace[able] to the challenged action of the defendant, and not . . . th[e] result [of] the independent action of some third party

not before the court." Third, it must be "likely," as opposed to merely "speculative," that the injury will be "redressed by a favorable decision."

The party invoking federal jurisdiction bears the burden of establishing these elements. . . .

When the suit is one challenging the legality of government action or inaction, the nature and extent of facts that must be averred (at the summary judgment stage) or proved (at the trial stage) in order to establish standing depends considerably upon whether the plaintiff is himself an object of the action (or forgone action) at issue. If he is, there is ordinarily little question that the action or inaction has caused him injury, and that a judgment preventing or requiring the action will redress it. When, however, as in this case, a plaintiff's asserted injury arises from the government's allegedly unlawful regulation (or lack of regulation) of *someone else,* much more is needed. In that circumstance, . . . it becomes the burden of the plaintiff to adduce facts showing that those choices have been or will be made in such manner as to produce causation and permit redressability of injury. Thus, when the plaintiff is not himself the object of the government action or inaction he challenges, standing is not precluded, but it is ordinarily "substantially more difficult" to establish.

We think the Court of Appeals failed to apply the foregoing principles in denying the Secretary's motion for summary judgment. Respondents had not made the requisite demonstration of (at least) injury and redressability.

Respondents' claim to injury is that the lack of consultation with respect to certain funded activities abroad "increas[es] the rate of extinction of endangered and threatened species." Of course, the desire to use or observe an animal species, even for purely aesthetic purposes, is undeniably a cognizable interest for purpose of standing. "But the 'injury in fact' test requires more than an injury to a cognizable interest. It requires that the party seeking review be himself among the injured." . . .

With respect to this aspect of the case, the Court of Appeals focused on the affidavits of two Defenders' members—Joyce Kelly and Amy Skilbred. Ms. Kelly stated that she traveled to Egypt in 1986 and "observed the traditional habitat of the endangered Nile crocodile there and intend[s] to do so again, and hope[s] to observe the crocodile directly," and that she "will suffer harm in fact as a result of [the] American . . . role . . . in overseeing the rehabilitation of the Aswan High Dam on the Nile . . . and [in] develop[ing] . . . Egypt's . . . Master Water Plan." Ms. Skilbred averred that she traveled to Sri Lanka in 1981 and "observed th[e] habitat" of "endangered species such as the Asian elephant and the leopard" at what is now the site of the Mahaweli Project funded by the Agency for International Development (AID), although she "was unable to see any of the endangered species"; "this development project," she continued, "will seriously reduce endangered, threatened, and endemic species habitat including areas that I visited . . . [which] may severely shorten the future of these species;" that threat, she concluded, harmed her because she "intend[s] to return to Sri Lanka in the future and hope[s] to be more fortunate in spotting at least the endangered elephant and leopard." When Ms. Skilbred was asked at a subsequent deposition if and when she had any plans to return to Sri Lanka, she reiterated that "I intend to go back to Sri Lanka," but confessed that she had no current plans: "I don't know [when]. There is a civil war going on right now. I don't know. Not next year, I will say. In the future."

We shall assume for the sake of argument that these affidavits contain facts showing that certain agency-funded projects threaten listed species—though that is questionable. They plainly contain no facts, however, showing how damage to the species will produce "imminent" injury to Mss. Kelly and Skilbred. That the women "had visited" the areas of the projects before the projects commenced proves nothing. And the affiants' profession of an "inten[t]" to return to the places they had visited before— where they will presumably, this time, be deprived of the opportunity to observe animals of the endangered species—is simply not enough. Such "some day" intentions—without any description of concrete plans, or indeed even any specification of *when* the some day will be—do not support a finding of the "actual or imminent" injury that our cases require.

Besides relying upon the Kelly and Skilbred affidavits, respondents propose a series of novel standing theories. The first, inelegantly styled "ecosystem nexus," proposes that any person who uses *any part* of a "contiguous ecosystem" adversely affected by a funded activity has standing even if the activity is located a great distance away. . . .

To say that the Act protects ecosystems is not to say that the Act creates (if it were possible) rights of action in persons who have not been injured in fact, that is, persons who use portions of an ecosystem not perceptibly affected by the unlawful action in question.

Respondents' other theories are called, alas, the "animal nexus" approach, whereby anyone who has an interest in studying or seeing the endangered animals anywhere on the globe has standing; and the "vocational nexus" approach, under which anyone with a professional interest in such animals can sue. Under these theories, anyone who goes to see Asian elephants in the Bronx Zoo, and anyone who is a keeper of Asian elephants in the Bronx Zoo, has standing to sue because the Director of AID did not consult with the Secretary regarding the AID-funded project in Sri Lanka. This is beyond all reason. Standing is not "an ingenious academic exercise in the conceivable," but as we have said requires, at the summary judgment stage, a factual showing of perceptible harm. It is clear that the person who observes or works with a particular animal threatened by a federal decision is facing perceptible harm, since the very subject of his interest will no longer exist. It is even plausible—though it goes to the outermost limit of plausibility—to think that a person who observes or works with animals of a particular species in the very area of the world where the species is threatened by a federal decision is facing such harm, since some animals that might have been the subject of his interest will no longer exist. It goes beyond the limit, however, and into pure speculation and fantasy, to say that anyone who observes or works with an endangered species, anywhere in the world, is appreciably harmed by a single project affecting some portion of that species with which he has no more specific connection.

The Court of Appeals found that respondents had standing for an additional reason: because they had suffered a "procedural injury." . . .

The court held that the citizen-suit provision creates a "procedural righ[t]" to consultation in all "persons"—so that *anyone* can file suit in federal court to challenge the Secretary's (or presumably any other official's) failure to follow the assertedly correct consultative procedure, notwithstanding their inability to allege any discrete injury flowing from that failure. We reject this view.

We have consistently held that a plaintiff raising only a generally available grievance about government—claiming only harm to his and every citizen's interest in proper application of the Constitution and laws, and seeking relief that no more directly and tangibly benefits him than it does the public at large—does not state an Article III case or controversy. For example, in *Frothingham v. Mellon* (1923), we dismissed for lack of Article III standing a taxpayer suit challenging the propriety of certain federal expenditures. We said: "The party who invokes the power [of judicial review] must be able to show not only that the statute is invalid but that he has sustained or is immediately in danger of sustaining some direct injury as the result of its enforcement, and not merely that he suffers in some indefinite way in common with people generally. . . ."

More recent cases are to the same effect.

To be sure, our generalized-grievance cases have typically involved Government violation of procedures assertedly ordained by the Constitution rather than the Congress. But there is absolutely no basis for making the Article III inquiry turn on the source of the asserted right. Whether the courts were to act on their own, or at the invitation of Congress, in ignoring the concrete injury requirement described in our cases, they would be discarding a principle fundamental to the separate and distinct constitutional role of the Third Branch—one of the essential elements that identifies those "Cases" and "Controversies" that are the business of the courts rather than of the political branches. Vindicating the *public* interest (including the public interest in government observance of the Constitution and laws) is the function of Congress and the Chief Executive. The question presented here is whether the public interest in proper administration of the laws (specifically, in agencies' observance of a particular, statutorily prescribed procedure) can be converted into an individual right by a statute that denominates it as such, and that permits all citizens (or, for that matter, a subclass of citizens who suffer no distinctive concrete harm) to sue. If the concrete injury requirement has the separation-of-powers significance we have always said, the answer must be obvious: To permit Congress to convert the undifferentiated public interest in executive officers' compliance with the law into an "individual right" vindicable in the courts is to permit Congress to transfer from the President to the courts the Chief Executive's most important constitutional duty, to "take Care that the Laws be faithfully executed." It would enable the courts, with the permission of Congress, "to assume a position of authority over the governmental acts of another and co-equal department," and to become "'virtually continuing monitors of the wisdom and soundness of Executive action.'" We have always rejected that vision of our role. . . .

We hold that respondents lack standing to bring this action and that the Court of Appeals erred in denying the summary judgment motion filed by the United States. The opinion of the Court of Appeals is hereby reversed, and the cause remanded for proceedings consistent with this opinion.

JUSTICE BLACKMUN, with JUSTICE O'CONNOR, dissenting.

I part company with the Court in this case in two respects. First, I believe that respondents have raised genuine issues of fact—sufficient to survive summary judgment—both as to injury and as to redressability. Second, I question the Court's breadth of language in rejecting standing for "procedural" injuries. I fear the Court seeks to impose fresh limitations on the constitutional authority of Congress to allow citizen-suits in the federal courts for injuries deemed "procedural" in nature. I dissent.

The Court expresses concern that allowing judicial enforcement of "agencies' observance of a particular, statutorily prescribed procedure" would "transfer from the President to the courts the Chief Executive's most important constitutional duty, to 'take Care that the Laws be faithfully executed,' Art. II, sec 3."

In fact, the principal effect of foreclosing judicial enforcement of such procedures is to transfer power into the hands of the Executive at the expense—not of the courts—but of Congress, from which that power originates and emanates.

Under the Court's anachronistically formal view of the separation of powers, Congress legislates pure, substantive mandates and has no business structuring the procedural manner in which the Executive implements these mandates. To be sure, in the ordinary course, Congress does legislate in black-and-white terms of affirmative commands or negative prohibitions on the conduct of officers of the Executive Branch. In complex regulatory areas, however, Congress often legislates, as it were, in procedural shades of gray. That is, it sets forth substantive policy goals and provides for their attainment by requiring Executive Branch officials to follow certain procedures, for example, in the form of reporting, consultation, and certification requirements.

In conclusion, I cannot join the Court on what amounts to a slash-and-burn expedition through the law of environmental standing.

Hein v. Freedom from Religion Foundation
551 U.S. 587 (2007)

President George W. Bush, by executive orders, established a Faith-Based and Community Initiatives program. It provided for a White House office and several centers within federal agencies to ensure that faith-based community groups would be eligible to compete for federal financial support. No congressional legislation specifically authorized these entities (they were created entirely within the executive branch), nor did Congress enact any law specifically appropriating money to their activities (they are funded through general executive-branch appropriations). The Freedom from Religion Foundation, an organization opposed to government endorsement of religion, along with three of its members, brought this suit alleging that Jay F. Hein, director of the White House Office of Faith-Based and Community Initiatives, and others working with him violated the Establishment Clause of the First Amendment by organizing conferences that were designed to promote religious community groups over secular ones. The only asserted basis for standing was that the individual respondents were federal taxpayers opposed to executive-branch use of congressional appropriations for these conferences. The United States District Court for the Western District of Wisconsin dismissed the claims for lack of standing, concluding that under Flast v. Cohen (1968), federal taxpayer standing is limited to Establishment Clause challenges to the constitutionality of exercises of congressional power under the taxing and spending clause of Article I, Section 8. Because petitioners acted on the president's behalf and were not charged with administering a congressional program, the court held that the challenged activities did not authorize taxpayer standing under Flast. The Seventh Circuit reversed; it read Flast as granting federal taxpayers standing to challenge executive-branch programs on Establishment Clause grounds so long as the activities are financed by a congressional appropriation, even where there is no statutory program and the funds are from appropriations for general administrative expenses. According to the court, a taxpayer has standing to challenge anything done by a federal agency so long as the marginal or incremental cost to the public of the alleged Establishment Clause violation is greater than zero. The Supreme Court granted certiorari. Judgment of the Court: <u>Alito</u>, Roberts, Kennedy. Concurring opinion: <u>Kennedy</u>. Concurring in the judgment: <u>Scalia</u>, Thomas. Dissenting opinion: <u>Souter</u>, Stevens, Ginsburg, Breyer.

JUSTICE ALITO announced the judgment of the Court and delivered an opinion in which THE CHIEF JUSTICE and JUSTICE KENNEDY join.

This is a lawsuit in which it was claimed that conferences held as part of the President's Faith-Based and Community Initiatives program violated the Establishment Clause of the First Amendment because, among other things, President Bush and former Secretary of Education Paige gave speeches that used "religious imagery" and praised the efficacy of faith-based programs in delivering social services. The plaintiffs contend that they meet the standing requirements of Article III of the Constitution because they pay federal taxes.

It has long been established, however, that the payment of taxes is generally not enough to establish standing to challenge an action taken by the Federal Government. In light of the size of the federal budget, it is a complete fiction to argue that an unconstitutional federal expenditure causes an individual federal taxpayer any measurable economic harm. And if every federal taxpayer could sue to challenge any Government expenditure, the federal courts would cease to function as courts of law and would be cast in the role of general complaint bureaus.

In *Flast v. Cohen* (1968), we recognized a narrow exception to the general rule against federal taxpayer standing. Under *Flast*, a plaintiff asserting an Establishment Clause claim has standing to challenge a law authorizing the use of federal funds in a way that allegedly violates the Establishment Clause. In the present case, Congress did not specifically authorize the use of federal funds to pay for the conferences or speeches that the plaintiffs challenged. Instead, the conferences and speeches were paid for out of general Executive Branch appropriations. The Court of Appeals, however, held that the plaintiffs have standing as taxpayers because the conferences were paid for with money appropriated by Congress.

The question that is presented here is whether this broad reading of *Flast* is correct. We hold that it is not. We therefore reverse the decision of the Court of Appeals.

I

In 2001, the President issued an executive order creating the White House Office of Faith-Based and Community Initiatives within the Executive Office of the President. The purpose of this new office was to ensure that "private and charitable community groups, including religious ones . . . have the fullest opportunity permitted by law to compete on a level playing field, so long as they achieve valid public purposes" and adhere to "the bedrock principles of pluralism, nondiscrimination, evenhandedness, and neutrality." The office was specifically charged with the task of eliminating unnecessary bureaucratic, legislative, and regulatory barriers that could impede such organizations' effectiveness and ability to compete equally for federal assistance.

By separate executive orders, the President also created Executive Department Centers for Faith-Based and Community Initiatives within several federal agencies and departments. These centers were given the job of ensuring that faith-based community groups would be eligible to compete for federal financial support without impairing their independence or autonomy, as long as they did "not use direct Federal financial assistance to support any inherently religious activities, such as worship, religious instruction, or proselytization." To this end, the President directed that "no organization should be discriminated against on the basis of religion or religious belief in the administration or distribution of Federal financial assistance under social service programs," and that "all organizations that receive Federal financial assistance under social services programs should be prohibited from discriminating against beneficiaries or potential beneficiaries of the social services programs on the basis of religion or religious belief." Petitioners, who have been sued in their official capacities, are the directors of the White House Office and various Executive Department Centers.

No congressional legislation specifically authorized the creation of the White House Office or the Executive Department Centers. Rather, they were "created entirely within the executive branch . . . by Presidential executive order." Nor has Congress enacted any law specifically appropriating money for these entities' activities. Instead, their activities are funded through general Executive Branch appropriations. For example, the Department of Education's Center is funded from money appropriated for the Office of the Secretary of Education, while the Department of Housing and Urban Development's Center is funded through that Department's salaries and expenses account.

The respondents are Freedom from Religion Foundation, Inc., a nonstock corporation "opposed to government endorsement of religion," and three of its members. Respondents brought suit . . . alleging that petitioners violated the

Establishment Clause by organizing conferences at which faith-based organizations allegedly "are singled out as being particularly worthy of federal funding . . . , and the belief in God is extolled as distinguishing the claimed effectiveness of faith-based social services." Respondents further alleged that the content of these conferences sent a message to religious believers "that they are insiders and favored members of the political community" and that the conferences sent the message to nonbelievers "that they are outsiders" and "not full members of the political community." In short, respondents alleged that the conferences were designed to promote, and had the effect of promoting, religious community groups over secular ones.

The only asserted basis for standing was that the individual respondents are federal taxpayers who are "opposed to the use of Congressional taxpayer appropriations to advance and promote religion." In their capacity as federal taxpayers, respondents sought to challenge Executive Branch expenditures for these conferences, which, they contended, violated the Establishment Clause.

The District Court dismissed the claims against petitioners for lack of standing. . . . A divided panel of the United States Court of Appeals for the Seventh Circuit reversed. . . . In dissent, Judge Ripple opined that the majority's decision reflected a "dramatic expansion of current standing doctrine" that "cuts the concept of taxpayer standing loose from its moorings." Noting that "the executive can do nothing without general budget appropriations from Congress," he criticized the majority for overstepping *Flast*'s requirement that a "plaintiff must bring an attack against a disbursement of public funds made in the exercise of *Congress'* taxing and spending power."

II

Article III of the Constitution limits the judicial power of the United States to the resolution of "Cases" and "Controversies," and "'Article III standing . . . enforces the Constitution's case-or-controversy requirement.'" . . .

The constitutionally mandated standing inquiry is especially important in a case like this one, in which taxpayers seek "to challenge laws of general application where their own injury is not distinct from that suffered in general by other taxpayers or citizens." This is because "the judicial power of the United States defined by Article III is not an unconditioned authority to determine the constitutionality of legislative or executive acts." The federal courts are not empowered to seek out and strike down any governmental act that they deem to be repugnant to the Constitution. Rather, federal courts sit "solely, to decide on the rights of individuals," *Marbury v. Madison* (1803), and must "'refrain from passing upon the constitutionality of an act . . . unless obliged to do so in the proper performance of our judicial function, when the question is raised by a party whose interests entitle him to raise it.'" . . .

In *Flast,* the Court carved out a narrow exception to the general constitutional prohibition against taxpayer standing. The taxpayer-plaintiff in that case challenged the distribution of federal funds to religious schools under the Elementary and Secondary Education Act of 1965, alleging that such aid violated the Establishment Clause. The Court set out a two-part test for determining whether a federal taxpayer has standing to challenge an allegedly unconstitutional expenditure:

> First, the taxpayer must establish a logical link between that status and the type of legislative enactment attacked. Thus, a taxpayer will be a proper party to allege the unconstitutionality only of exercises of congressional power under the taxing and spending clause of Art. I, §8, of the Constitution. It will not be sufficient to allege an incidental expenditure of tax funds in the administration of an essentially regulatory statute. . . . Secondly, the taxpayer must establish a nexus between that status and the precise nature of the constitutional infringement alleged. Under this requirement, the taxpayer must show that the challenged enactment exceeds specific constitutional limitations imposed upon the exercise of the congressional taxing and spending power and not simply that the enactment is generally beyond the powers delegated to Congress by Art. I, §8.

The Court held that the taxpayer-plaintiff in *Flast* had satisfied both prongs of this test: The plaintiff's "constitutional challenge [was] made to an exercise by Congress of its power under Art. I, §8, to spend for the general welfare," and she alleged a violation of the Establishment Clause, which "operates as a specific constitutional limitation upon the exercise by Congress of the taxing and spending power conferred by Art. I, §8."

III

Respondents argue that this case falls within the *Flast* exception, which they read to cover any "expenditure of government funds in violation of the Establishment Clause." But this broad reading fails to observe "the rigor with which the *Flast* exception to the *Frothingham* [*v. Mellon* (1923)] principle ought to be applied."

The expenditures at issue in *Flast* were made pursuant to an express congressional mandate and a specific congressional appropriation. The plaintiff in that case challenged disbursements made under the Elementary and Secondary Education Act of 1965. That Act expressly appropriated the sum of $100 million for fiscal year 1966, and authorized the disbursement of those funds to local educational agencies for the education of low-income students. The Act mandated that local educational agencies receiving such funds "make provision for including special educational services and arrangements (such as dual enrollment, educational radio and television, and mobile educational services and equipment)" in which students enrolled in private elementary and secondary schools could participate. In addition, recipient agencies were required to ensure that "library resources, textbooks, and other instructional materials" funded through the grants "be provided on an equitable basis for the use of children and teachers in private elementary and secondary schools."

The expenditures challenged in *Flast*, then, were funded by a specific congressional appropriation and were disbursed to private schools (including religiously affiliated schools) pursuant to a direct and unambiguous congressional mandate. Indeed, the *Flast* taxpayer-plaintiff's constitutional claim was premised on the contention that if the Government's actions were "'within the authority and intent of the Act, the Act is to that extent unconstitutional and void.'" And the judgment reviewed by this Court in *Flast* solely concerned the question whether "if [the challenged] expenditures are authorized by the Act the statute constitutes a 'law respecting an establishment of religion' and law 'prohibiting the free exercise thereof'" under the First Amendment.

Given that the alleged Establishment Clause violation in *Flast* was funded by a specific congressional appropriation and was undertaken pursuant to an express congressional mandate, the Court concluded that the taxpayer-plaintiffs had established the requisite "logical link between [their taxpayer] status and the type of legislative enactment attacked." In the Court's words, "their constitutional challenge [was] made to an exercise by Congress of its power under Art. I, §8, to spend for the general welfare." But as this Court later noted, *Flast* "limited taxpayer standing to challenges directed 'only [at] exercises of congressional power'" under the Taxing and Spending Clause.

The link between congressional action and constitutional violation that supported taxpayer standing in *Flast* is missing here. Respondents do not challenge any specific congressional action or appropriation; nor do they ask the Court to invalidate any congressional enactment or legislatively created program as unconstitutional. That is because the expenditures at issue here were not made pursuant to any Act of Congress. Rather, Congress provided general appropriations to the Executive Branch to fund its day-to-day activities. These appropriations did not expressly authorize, direct, or even mention the expenditures of which respondents complain. Those expenditures resulted from executive discretion, not congressional action. . . .

In short, this case falls outside the "the narrow exception" that *Flast* "created to the general rule against taxpayer standing established in *Frothingham*." Because the expenditures that respondents challenge were not expressly authorized or mandated by any specific congressional enactment, respondents' lawsuit is not directed at an exercise of congressional power and thus lacks the requisite "logical nexus" between taxpayer status "and the type of legislative enactment attacked."

IV

Respondents argue that it is "arbitrary" to distinguish between money spent pursuant to congressional mandate and expenditures made in the course of executive discretion, because "the injury to taxpayers in both situations is the very injury targeted by the Establishment Clause and *Flast*—the expenditure for the support of religion of funds exacted from taxpayers." The panel majority below agreed, based on its observation that "there is so much that executive officials could do to promote religion in ways forbidden by the establishment clause."

But *Flast* focused on congressional action, and we must decline this invitation to extend its holding to encompass discretionary Executive Branch expenditures. . . .

While respondents argue that Executive Branch expenditures in support of religion are no different from legislative extractions, *Flast* itself rejected this equivalence: "It will not be sufficient to allege an incidental expenditure of tax funds in the administration of an essentially regulatory statute."

Because almost all Executive Branch activity is ultimately funded by some congressional appropriation, extending the *Flast* exception to purely executive expenditures would effectively subject every federal action—be it a conference, proclamation or speech—to Establishment Clause challenge by any taxpayer in federal court. To see the wide swathe of activity that respondents' proposed rule would cover, one need look no further than the amended complaint in this action, which focuses largely on speeches and presentations made by Executive Branch officials. Such a broad reading would ignore the first prong of *Flast*'s standing test, which requires "a logical link between [taxpayer] status and the type of legislative enactment attacked."

It would also raise serious separation-of-powers concerns. . . . The constitutional requirements for federal-court jurisdiction—including the standing requirements and Article III—"are an essential ingredient of separation and equilibration of powers." "Relaxation of standing requirements is directly related to the expansion of judicial power," and lowering the taxpayer standing bar to permit challenges of purely executive actions "would significantly alter the allocation of power at the national level, with a shift away from a democratic form of government." The rule respondents propose would enlist the federal courts to superintend, at the behest of any federal taxpayer, the speeches, statements, and myriad daily activities of the President, his staff, and other Executive Branch officials. This . . . would "open the Judiciary to an arguable charge of providing 'government by injunction.'" It would deputize federal courts as "'virtually continuing monitors of the wisdom and soundness of Executive action,'" and that, most emphatically, "is not the role of the judiciary."

Both the Court of Appeals and respondents implicitly recognize that unqualified federal taxpayer standing to assert Establishment Clause claims would go too far, but neither the Court of Appeals nor respondents has identified a workable limitation. The Court of Appeals, as noted, conceded only that a taxpayer would lack standing where "the marginal or incremental cost to the taxpaying public of the alleged violation of the establishment clause" is "zero." . . . [I]f we take the Court of Appeals' test literally—*i.e.*, that any marginal cost greater than zero suffices—taxpayers might well have standing to challenge some (and perhaps many) speeches. As Judge Easterbrook observed: "The total cost of presidential proclamations and speeches by Cabinet officers that touch on religion (Thanksgiving and several other holidays) surely exceeds $500,000 annually; it may cost that much to use Air Force One and send a Secret Service detail to a single speaking engagement." At a minimum, the Court of Appeals' approach (asking whether the marginal cost exceeded zero) would surely create difficult and uncomfortable line-drawing problems. Suppose that it is alleged that a speech writer or other staff member spent extra time doing research for the purpose of including "religious imagery" in a speech. Suppose that a President or a Cabinet officer attends or speaks at a prayer breakfast and that the time spent was time that would have otherwise been spent on secular work.

Respondents take a somewhat different approach, contending that their proposed expansion of *Flast* would be manageable because they would require that a challenged expenditure be "fairly traceable to the conduct alleged to violate the Establishment Clause." Applying this test, they argue, would "screen out . . . challenge[s to] the content of one particular speech, for example the State of the Union address, as an Establishment Clause violation."

We find little comfort in this vague and ill-defined test. As an initial matter, respondents fail to explain why the (often substantial) costs that attend, for example, a Presidential address are any less "traceable" than the expenses related to the Executive Branch statements and conferences at issue here. Indeed, respondents concede that even lawsuits involving *de minimis* amounts of taxpayer money can pass their proposed "traceability" test.

Moreover, the "traceability" inquiry, depending on how it is framed, would appear to prove either too little or too much. If the question is whether an allegedly unconstitutional executive action can somehow be traced to taxpayer funds *in general*, the answer will always be yes: Almost all Executive Branch activities are ultimately funded by *some* congressional appropriation, whether general or specific, which is in turn financed by tax receipts. If, on the other hand, the question is whether the challenged action can be traced to the contributions of a *particular* taxpayer-plaintiff, the answer will almost always be no: As we recognized in *Frothingham*, the interest of any individual taxpayer in a particular federal expenditure "is comparatively minute and indeterminable . . . and constantly changing."

Respondents set out a parade of horribles that they claim could occur if *Flast* is not extended to discretionary Executive Branch expenditures. For example, they say, a federal agency could use its discretionary funds to build a house of worship or to hire clergy of one denomination and send them out to spread their faith. Or an agency could use its funds to make bulk purchases of Stars of David, crucifixes, or depictions of the star and crescent for use in its offices or for distribution to the employees or the general public. Of course, none of these things has happened,

even though *Flast* has not previously been expanded in the way that respondents urge. In the unlikely event that any of these executive actions did take place, Congress could quickly step in. And respondents make no effort to show that these improbable abuses could not be challenged in federal court by plaintiffs who would possess standing based on grounds other than taxpayer standing.

Over the years, *Flast* has been defended by some and criticized by others. But the present case does not require us to reconsider that precedent. The Court of Appeals did not apply *Flast*; it extended *Flast*. It is a necessary concomitant of the doctrine of *stare decisis* that a precedent is not always expanded to the limit of its logic. That . . . is the approach we take here. We do not extend *Flast*, but we also do not overrule it. We leave *Flast* as we found it.

JUSTICE SCALIA says that we must either overrule *Flast* or extend it to the limits of its logic. His position is not "insane," inconsistent with the "rule of law," or "utterly meaningless." But it is wrong. JUSTICE SCALIA does not seriously dispute either (1) that *Flast* itself spoke in terms of "legislative enactments" and "exercises of congressional power," or (2) that in the four decades since *Flast* was decided, we have never extended its narrow exception to a purely discretionary Executive Branch expenditure. We need go no further to decide this case. Relying on the provision of the Constitution that limits our role to resolving the "Cases" and "Controversies" before us, we decide only the case at hand.

For these reasons, the judgment of the Court of Appeals for the Seventh Circuit is reversed.

JUSTICE SCALIA, with whom JUSTICE THOMAS joins, concurring in the judgment.

. . . If this Court is to decide cases by rule of law rather than show of hands, we must surrender to logic and choose sides: Either *Flast v. Cohen* should be applied to (at a minimum) *all* challenges to the governmental expenditure of general tax revenues in a manner alleged to violate a constitutional provision specifically limiting the taxing and spending power, or *Flast* should be repudiated. For me, the choice is easy. *Flast* is wholly irreconcilable with the Article III restrictions on federal-court jurisdiction that this Court has repeatedly confirmed are embodied in the doctrine of standing.

I

There is a simple reason why our taxpayer-standing cases involving Establishment Clause challenges to government expenditures are notoriously inconsistent: We have inconsistently described the first element of the "irreducible constitutional minimum of standing," which minimum consists of (1) a "concrete and particularized" "'injury in fact'" that is (2) fairly traceable to the defendant's alleged unlawful conduct and (3) likely to be redressed by a favorable decision. See *Lujan v. Defenders of Wildlife* (1992). We have alternately relied on two entirely distinct conceptions of injury in fact, which for convenience I will call "Wallet Injury" and "Psychic Injury."

Wallet Injury is the type of concrete and particularized injury one would expect to be asserted in a *taxpayer* suit, namely, a claim that the plaintiff's tax liability is higher than it would be, but for the allegedly unlawful government action. The stumbling block for suits challenging government expenditures based on this conventional type of injury is quite predictable. The plaintiff cannot satisfy the traceability and redressability prongs of standing. It is uncertain what the plaintiff's tax bill would have been had the allegedly forbidden expenditure not been made, and it is even more speculative whether the government will, in response to an adverse court decision, lower taxes rather than spend the funds in some other manner.

Psychic Injury, on the other hand, has nothing to do with the plaintiff's tax liability. Instead, the injury consists of the taxpayer's *mental displeasure* that money extracted from him is being spent in an unlawful manner. This shift in focus eliminates traceability and redressability problems. Psychic Injury is directly traceable to the improper *use* of taxpayer funds, and it is redressed when the improper use is enjoined, regardless of whether that injunction affects the taxpayer's purse. *Flast* and the cases following its teaching have invoked a peculiarly restricted version of Psychic Injury, permitting taxpayer displeasure over unconstitutional spending to support standing *only if* the constitutional provision allegedly violated is a specific limitation on the taxing and spending power. Restricted or not, this conceptualizing of injury in fact in purely mental terms conflicts squarely with the familiar proposition that a plaintiff lacks a concrete and particularized injury when his only complaint is the generalized grievance that the law is being violated. . . .

As the following review of our cases demonstrates, we initially denied taxpayer standing based on Wallet Injury, but then found standing in some later cases based on the limited version of Psychic Injury described above. The basic logical flaw in our cases is thus twofold: We have never explained why Psychic Injury was insufficient in the cases in which standing was denied, and we have never explained why Psychic Injury, however limited, is cognizable under Article III.

Two pre-*Flast* cases are of critical importance. In *Frothingham v. Mellon*, decided with *Massachusetts v. Mellon* (1923), the taxpayer challenged the constitutionality of the Maternity Act of 1921, alleging in part that the federal funding provided by the Act was not authorized by any provision of the Constitution. The Court held that the taxpayer lacked standing. After emphasizing that "the effect upon future taxation . . . of any payment out of [Treasury] funds" was "remote, fluctuating and uncertain," the Court concluded that "the party who invokes the power [of judicial review] must be able to show not only that the statute is invalid but that he has sustained or is immediately in danger of sustaining some direct injury as the result of its enforcement, and not merely that he suffers in some indefinite way in common with people generally." The Court was thus describing the traceability and redressability problems with Wallet Injury, and rejecting Psychic Injury as a generalized grievance rather than concrete and particularized harm.

The second significant pre-*Flast* case is *Doremus v. Board of Education of Hawthorne* (1952). There the taxpayers challenged under the Establishment Clause a state law requiring public-school teachers to read the Bible at the beginning of each school day. Relying extensively on *Frothingham,* the Court denied standing. After first emphasizing that there was no allegation that the Bible reading increased the plaintiffs' taxes or the cost of running the schools, and then reaffirming that taxpayers must allege more than an indefinite injury suffered in common with people generally, the Court concluded that the "grievance which [the plaintiffs] sought to litigate here is not a direct dollars-and-cents injury but is a religious difference." In addition to reiterating *Frothingham*'s description of the unavoidable obstacles to recovery under a taxpayer theory of Wallet Injury, *Doremus* rejected Psychic Injury in unmistakable terms. The opinion's deprecation of a mere "religious difference," in contrast to a real "dollars-and-cents injury," can only be understood as a flat denial of standing supported only by taxpayer disapproval of the unconstitutional use of tax funds. If the Court had thought that Psychic Injury was a permissible basis for standing, it should have sufficed that public employees were being paid in part to violate the Establishment Clause.

Sixteen years after *Doremus,* the Court took a pivotal turn. In *Flast v. Cohen,* taxpayers challenged the Elementary and Secondary Education Act of 1965, alleging that funds expended pursuant to the Act were being used to support parochial schools. . . . The Court held that the taxpayers had standing. Purportedly in order to determine whether taxpayers have the "personal stake and interest" necessary to satisfy Article III, a two-pronged nexus test was invented. The first prong required the taxpayer to "establish a logical link between [taxpayer] status and the type of legislative enactment." . . . The second prong required the taxpayer to "establish a nexus between [taxpayer] status and the precise nature of the constitutional infringement alleged." The Court elaborated that this required "the taxpayer [to] show that the challenged enactment exceeds specific constitutional limitations imposed upon the exercise of the congressional taxing and spending power and not simply that the enactment is generally beyond the powers delegated to Congress by Art. I, §8." The Court held that the Establishment Clause was the type of specific limitation on the taxing and spending power that it had in mind because "one of the specific evils feared by" the Framers of that Clause was that the taxing and spending power would be used to favor one religion over another or to support religion generally.

Because both prongs of its newly minted two-part test were satisfied, *Flast* held that the taxpayers had standing. Wallet Injury could not possibly have been the basis for this conclusion, since the taxpayers in *Flast* were no more able to prove that success on the merits would reduce their tax burden than was the taxpayer in *Frothingham*. Thus, *Flast* relied on Psychic Injury to support standing, describing the "injury" as the taxpayer's allegation that "his tax money is being extracted and spent in violation of specific constitutional protections against such abuses of legislative power."

But that created a problem: If the taxpayers in *Flast* had standing based on Psychic Injury, and without regard to the effect of the litigation on their ultimate tax liability, why did not the taxpayers in *Doremus* and *Frothingham* have standing on a similar basis? Enter the magical two-pronged nexus test. It has often been pointed out, and never refuted, that the criteria in *Flast*'s two-part test are *entirely unrelated* to the purported goal of ensuring that the plaintiff has a sufficient "stake in the outcome of the controversy." In truth, the test was designed for a quite different goal. Each prong was meant to disqualify from standing one of the two prior cases that would otherwise contradict the holding of *Flast*. The first prong distinguished *Doremus* as involving a challenge to an "incidental expenditure of tax funds in the administration of an essentially regulatory statute," rather than a challenge to a taxing and spending statute. Did the Court proffer any reason why a taxpayer's Psychic Injury is less concrete and particularized, traceable, or redressable when the challenged expenditures are incidental to an essentially regulatory statute (whatever that means)? Not at all. *Doremus* had to be evaded, and so it was. In reality, of course, there is simply no material difference between *Flast* and *Doremus* as far as Psychic Injury is concerned: If taxpayers upset with the government's giving money to parochial schools had standing to sue, so should the taxpayers who disapproved of the government's paying public-school teachers to read the Bible.

Flast's dispatching of *Frothingham* via the second prong of the nexus test was only marginally less disingenuous. Not only does the relationship of the allegedly violated provision to the taxing and spending power have no bearing upon the concreteness or particularity of the Psychic Injury, but the existence of that relationship does not even genuinely distinguish *Flast* from *Frothingham*. It is impossible to maintain that the Establishment Clause is a more direct limitation on the taxing and spending power than the constitutional limitation invoked in *Frothingham, which is contained within the very provision creating the power to tax and spend.* Article I, §8, cl. 1, provides: "The Congress shall have Power To lay and collect Taxes . . . , to pay the Debts and provide for the common Defence *and general Welfare* of the United States." (Emphasis added.) Though unmentioned in *Flast,* it was precisely this limitation upon the permissible purposes of taxing and spending upon which Mrs. Frothingham relied. . . .

III

Is a taxpayer's purely psychological displeasure that his funds are being spent in an allegedly unlawful manner ever sufficiently concrete and particularized to support Article III standing? The answer is plainly no. . . .

We twice have noted explicitly that *Flast* failed to recognize the vital separation-of-powers aspect of Article III standing. See *Spencer v. Kemna* (1998); *Lewis v. Casey* (1996). And once a proper understanding of the relationship of standing to the separation of powers is brought to bear, Psychic Injury, even as limited in *Flast,* is revealed for what it is: a contradiction of the basic propositions that the function of the judicial power "is, solely, to decide on the rights of individuals," *Marbury v. Madison* (1803), and that generalized grievances affecting the public at large have their remedy in the political process.

Overruling prior precedents, even precedents as disreputable as *Flast,* is nevertheless a serious undertaking, and I understand the impulse to take a minimalist approach. But laying just claim to be honoring *stare decisis* requires more than beating *Flast* to a pulp and then sending it out to the lower courts weakened, denigrated, more incomprehensible than ever, and yet somehow technically alive. Even before

the addition of the new meaningless distinction devised by today's plurality, taxpayer standing in Establishment Clause cases has been a game of chance. In the proceedings below, well-respected federal judges declined to hear this case en banc, not because they thought the issue unimportant or the panel decision correct, but simply because they found our cases so lawless that there was no point in, quite literally, second-guessing the panel. We had an opportunity today to erase this blot on our jurisprudence, but instead have simply smudged it.

My call for the imposition of logic and order upon this chaotic set of precedents will perhaps be met with the snappy epigram that "the life of the law has not been logic: it has been experience." O. Holmes, *The Common Law* 1 (1881). But what experience has shown is that *Flast*'s lack of a logical theoretical underpinning has rendered our taxpayer-standing doctrine such a jurisprudential disaster that our appellate judges do not know what to make of it. And of course the case has engendered no reliance interests, not only because one does not arrange his affairs with an eye to standing, but also because there is no relying on the random and irrational. I can think of few cases less warranting of *stare decisis* respect. It is time—it is past time—to call an end.

Flast should be overruled.

JUSTICE SOUTER, with whom JUSTICE STEVENS, JUSTICE GINSBURG, and JUSTICE BREYER join, dissenting.

Flast v. Cohen (1968), held that plaintiffs with an Establishment Clause claim could "demonstrate the necessary stake as taxpayers in the outcome of the litigation to satisfy Article III requirements." Here, the controlling, plurality opinion declares that *Flast* does not apply, but a search of that opinion for a suggestion that these taxpayers have any less stake in the outcome than the taxpayers in *Flast* will come up empty: the plurality makes no such finding, nor could it. Instead, the controlling opinion closes the door on these taxpayers because the Executive Branch, and not the Legislative Branch, caused their injury. I see no basis for this distinction in either logic or precedent, and respectfully dissent.

I

We held in *Flast* . . . that the "'injury' alleged in Establishment Clause challenges to federal spending" is "the very 'extraction and spending' of 'tax money' in aid of religion." . . . Here, there is no dispute that taxpayer money in identifiable amounts is funding conferences, and these are alleged to have the purpose of promoting religion. The taxpayers therefore seek not to "extend" *Flast,* but merely to apply it. When executive agencies spend identifiable sums of tax money for religious purposes, no less than when Congress authorizes the same thing, taxpayers suffer injury. And once we recognize the injury as sufficient for Article III, there can be no serious question about the other elements of the standing enquiry: the injury is indisputably "traceable" to the spending, and "likely to be redressed by" an injunction prohibiting it.

The plurality points to the separation of powers to explain its distinction between legislative and executive spending decisions, but there is no difference on that point of view between a Judicial Branch review of an executive decision and a judicial evaluation of a congressional one. We owe respect to each of the other branches, no more to the former than to the latter, and no one has suggested that the Establishment Clause lacks applicability to executive uses of money. It would surely violate the Establishment Clause for the Department of Health and Human Services to draw on a general appropriation to build a chapel for weekly church services (no less than if a statute required it), and for good reason: if the Executive could accomplish through the exercise of discretion exactly what Congress cannot do through legislation, Establishment Clause protection would melt away. . . .

Because the taxpayers in this case have alleged the type of injury this Court has seen as sufficient for standing, I would affirm.

Luther v. Borden
48 U.S. (7 Howard) 1 (1849)

In 1841, Rhode Island was still operating under a system of government established in 1663 under a colonial charter, granted by Charles II, that made no provision for amendment and strictly limited the right to vote. Dissident groups, protesting especially the limits on suffrage, combined that year to form a popular convention and draft a new constitution. In elections held in 1842, Thomas Dorr was elected governor. The old charter government continued to operate, however; when it responded to the insurgent government by declaring martial law, the charter governor appealed to President John Tyler for military support. Although no federal troops were ever sent, the Dorr Rebellion was soon crushed, and the insurgent government collapsed.

On instructions from the charter government to gather up the dispersed and defeated insurgents, Luther Borden and other state militiamen set out to arrest Martin Luther, a Dorr supporter. In the process, they broke into and searched his home, whereupon Luther sued for illegal trespass, alleging that under Article IV, Section 4, which guarantees to each state a republican form of government, the charter government had been supplanted by the more representative insurgent government, and that, as a consequence, was not the lawful government of the state. Because the charter government was not the lawful government, Luther continued, Borden and his men could not defend their actions by claiming to be agents of the state. Borden responded that the charter government was the lawful government and that his search was legitimate. Luther moved to Massachusetts in order to bring the case before the federal courts on the basis of diversity of citizenship. The federal courts were thus invited to determine which of the two governments was the lawful government of Rhode Island. After a federal circuit court ruled in Borden's favor, Luther brought the case to the Supreme Court on a writ of error. Opinion of the Court: <u>Taney</u>, *McLean, Wayne, Nelson, Grier. Dissenting opinion:* <u>Woodbury</u>, *Catron, Daniel. Not participating: McKinley.*

THE CHIEF JUSTICE delivered the opinion of the Court.

The fourth section of the fourth article of the Constitution of the United States provides that the United States shall guarantee to every State in the Union a republican form of government, and shall protect each of them against invasion; and on the application of the legislature or of the executive (when the legislature cannot be convened) against domestic violence.

Under this article of the Constitution it rests with Congress to decide what government is the established one in a State. For as the United States guarantee to each State a republican government, Congress must necessarily decide what government is established in the State before it can determine whether it is republican or not. And when the senators and representatives of a State are admitted into the councils of the Union, the authority of the government under which they are appointed, as well as its republican character, is recognized by the proper constitutional authority. And its decision is binding on every other department of the government, and could not be questioned in a judicial tribunal. It is true that the contest in this case did not last long enough to bring the matter to this issue; and as no senators or representatives were elected under the authority of the government of which Mr. Dorr was the head, Congress was not called upon to decide the controversy. Yet the right to decide is placed there, and not in the courts.

So, too, as relates to the clause in the above-mentioned article of the Constitution, providing for cases of domestic violence. It rested with Congress, too, to determine upon the means proper to be adopted to fulfill this guarantee. They might, if they had deemed it most advisable to do so, have placed it in the power of a court to decide when the contingency had happened which required the federal government to interfere. But Congress thought otherwise, and no doubt wisely; and by the act of February 28, 1795, provided, that "in case of an insurrection in any State against the government thereof, it shall be lawful for the President of the United States, on application of the legislature of such State or of the executive (when the legislature cannot be convened), to call forth such number of the militia of any other State or States, as may be applied for, as he may judge sufficient to suppress such insurrection."

By this act, the power of deciding whether the exigency had arisen upon which the government of the United States is bound to interfere, is given to the President. He is to act upon the application of the legislature or of the executive, and consequently he must determine what body of men constitute the legislature, and who is the governor, before he can act. The fact that both parties claim the right to the government cannot alter the case, for both cannot be entitled to it. If there is an armed conflict, like the one of which we are speaking, it is a case of domestic violence, and one of the parties must be in insurrection against the lawful government. And the President must, of necessity, decide which is the government, and which party is unlawfully arrayed against it, before he can perform the duty imposed upon him by the act of Congress.

After the President has acted and called out the militia, is a Circuit Court of the United States authorized to inquire whether his decision was right? Could the court, while the parties were actually contending in arms for the possession of the government, call witnesses before it and inquire which party represented a majority of the people? If it could, then it would become the duty of the court (provided it came to the conclusion that the President had decided incorrectly) to discharge those who were arrested or detained by the troops in the service of the United States or the government which the President was endeavoring to maintain. If the judicial power extends so far, the guarantee contained in the Constitution of the United States is a guarantee of anarchy, and not of order. Yet if this right does not reside in the courts when the conflict is raging, if the judicial power is at that time bound to follow the decision of the political, it must be equally bound when the contest is over. It cannot, when peace is restored, punish as offenses and crimes the acts which it before recognized, and was bound to recognize, as lawful.

It is true that in this case the militia were not called out by the President. But upon the application of the governor under the charter government, the President recognized him as the executive power of the State, and took measures to call out the militia to support his authority if it should be found necessary for the general government to interfere; and it is admitted in the argument, that it was the knowledge of this decision that put an end to the armed opposition to the charter government, and prevented any further efforts to establish by force the proposed constitution. The interference of the President, therefore, by announcing his determination, was as effectual as if the militia had been assembled under his orders. And it should be equally authoritative. For certainly no court of the United States, with a knowledge of this decision, would have been justified in recognizing the opposing party as the lawful government, or in treating as wrongdoers or insurgents the officers of the government which the President had recognized, and was prepared to support by an armed force. In the case of foreign nations, the government acknowledged by the President is always recognized by the courts of justice. And this principle has been applied by the act of Congress to the sovereign States of the Union.

It is said that this power in the President is dangerous to liberty, and may be abused. All power may be abused if placed in unworthy hands. But it would be difficult, we think, to point out any other hands in which this power would be more safe, and at the same time equally effectual. When citizens of the same State are in arms against each other, and the constituted authorities unable to execute the laws, the interposition of the United States must be prompt, or it is of little value. The ordinary course of proceedings in courts of justice would be utterly unfit for the crisis. And the elevated office of the President, chosen as he is by the people of the United States, and the high responsibility he could not fail to feel when acting in a case of so much moment, appear to furnish as strong safeguards against a wilful abuse of power as human prudence and foresight could well provide. At all events, it is conferred upon him by the Constitution and laws of the United States, and must therefore be respected and enforced in its judicial tribunals. . . .

Undoubtedly, if the President in exercising this power shall fall into error, or invade the rights of the people of the State, it would be in the power of Congress to apply the proper remedy. But the courts must administer the law as they find it. . . .

Much of the argument on the part of the plaintiff turned upon political rights and political questions, upon which the court has been urged to express an opinion. We decline doing so. The high power has been conferred on this court of passing judgment upon the acts of the State sovereignties, and of the legislative and executive branches of the federal government, and of determining whether they are beyond the limits of power marked out for them respectively by the Constitution of the United States. This tribunal, therefore, should be the last to overstep the boundaries which limit its own jurisdiction. And while it should always be ready to meet any question confided to it by the Constitution, it is equally its duty not to pass beyond its appropriate sphere of action, and to take care not to involve itself in discussions which properly belong to other forums. No one we believe, has ever doubted the proposition, that, according to the institutions of this country, the sovereignty in every State resides in the people of the State, and that they may alter and change their form of government at their own pleasure. But whether they have changed it or not by abolishing an old government, and establishing a new one in its place, is a question to be settled by the political power. And when that power has decided, the courts are bound to take notice of its decision, and to follow it.

The judgment of the circuit court must therefore be

Affirmed.

Baker v. Carr
369 U.S. 186 (1962)

The Tennessee Constitution provides that representation in both houses of the state legislature shall be based on population and that legislators shall be apportioned every ten years on the basis of the federal census. Despite the constitutional requirement, the legislature had not reapportioned since 1901 when, in 1959, Charles Baker and other qualified voters in Tennessee brought suit in federal court against Joe Carr, Tennessee secretary of state, and other public officials, alleging deprivation of federal constitutional rights. The plaintiffs argued that the state's system of apportionment was "utterly arbitrary" and thereby deprived them of equal protection of the laws under the Fourteenth Amendment "by virtue of debasement of their votes." A three-member district court, relying on Colegrove v. Green *(1946), dismissed their suit, whereupon the case went to the Supreme Court on appeal.* Opinion of the Court: <u>Brennan</u>, Black, Douglas, Clark, Stewart, Warren. Concurring opinions: <u>Douglas</u>; <u>Clark</u>; <u>Stewart</u>. Dissenting opinions: <u>Frankfurter</u>, Harlan; <u>Harlan</u>, Frankfurter. Not participating: Whittaker.

JUSTICE BRENNAN delivered the opinion of the Court.

We hold today only (a) that the District Court possessed jurisdiction of the subject matter; (b) that a justiciable cause of action is stated upon which appellants would be entitled to appropriate relief; and (c) because appellees raise the issue before this Court, that the appellants have standing to challenge the Tennessee apportionment statutes. Beyond noting that we have no cause at this stage to doubt the District Court will be able to fashion relief if violations of constitutional rights are found, it is improper now to consider what remedy would be most appropriate if appellants prevail at the trial.

JURISDICTION OF THE SUBJECT MATTER

The District Court was uncertain whether our cases withholding federal judicial relief rested upon a lack of federal jurisdiction or upon the inappropriateness of the subject matter for judicial consideration—what we have designated "nonjusticiability." The distinction between the two grounds is significant. In the instance of nonjusticiability, consideration of the cause is not wholly and immediately foreclosed; rather, the Court's inquiry necessarily proceeds to the point of deciding whether the duty asserted can be judicially identified and its breach judicially determined, and whether protection for the right asserted can be judicially molded. In the instance of lack of jurisdiction the cause either does not "arise under"

the Federal Constitution, laws or treaties (or fall within one of the other enumerated categories of Art. III, §2), or is not a "case or controversy" within the meaning of that section; or the cause is not one described by any jurisdictional statute. Our conclusion . . . that this cause presents no nonjusticiable "political question" settles the only possible doubt that it is a case or controversy. Under the present heading of "Jurisdiction of the Subject Matter" we hold only that the matter set forth in the complaint does arise under the Constitution. . . .

STANDING

A federal court cannot "pronounce any statute, either of a state or of the United States, void, because irreconcilable with the constitution, except as it is called upon to adjudge the legal rights of litigants in actual controversies." *Liverpool, N.Y. & P. Steamship Co. v. Commissioners of Emigration* [1885]. . . . Have the appellants alleged such a personal stake in the outcome of the controversy as to assure that concrete adverseness which sharpens the presentation of issues upon which the court so largely depends for illumination of difficult constitutional questions? This is the gist of the question of standing. It is, of course, a question of federal law. . . .

We hold that the appellants do have standing to maintain this suit. Our decisions plainly support this conclusion. Many of the cases have assumed rather than articulated the premise in deciding the merits of similar claims. . . .

These appellants seek relief in order to protect or vindicate an interest of their own, and of those similarly situated. Their constitutional claim is, in substance, that the 1901 statute constitutes arbitrary and capricious state action, offensive to the Fourteenth Amendment in its irrational disregard of the standard of apportionment prescribed by the State's Constitution or of any standard, effecting a gross disproportion of representation to voting population. The injury which appellants assert is that this classification disfavors the voters in the counties in which they reside, placing them in a position of constitutionally unjustifiable inequality *vis-à-vis* voters in irrationally favored counties. . . .

It would not be necessary to decide whether appellants' allegations of impairment of their votes by the 1901 apportionment will, ultimately, entitle them to any relief, in order to hold that they have standing to seek it. If such impairment does produce a legally cognizable injury, they are among those who have sustained it. They are asserting "a plain, direct and adequate interest in maintaining the effectiveness of their votes," . . . not merely a claim of "the right possessed by every citizen 'to require that the government be administered according to law.'" . . .

JUSTICIABILITY

In holding that the subject matter of this suit was not justiciable, the District Court relied on *Colegrove v. Green* (1946) . . . and subsequent *per curiam* cases. . . . We understand the District Court to have read the cited cases as compelling the conclusion that since the appellants sought to have a legislative apportionment held unconstitutional, their suit presented a "political question" and was therefore nonjusticiable. We hold that this challenge to an apportionment presents no nonjusticiable "political questions." The cited cases do not hold the contrary.

Of course the mere fact that the suit seeks protection of a political right does not mean it presents a political question. Such an objection "is little more than a play upon words." . . . Rather, it is argued that apportionment cases, whatever the actual wording of the complaint, can involve no federal constitutional right except one resting on the guaranty of a republican form of government, and that complaints based on that clause have been held to present political questions which are nonjusticiable.

We hold that the claim pleaded here neither rests upon nor implicates the Guaranty Clause and that its justiciability is therefore not foreclosed by our decisions of cases involving that clause. The District Court misinterpreted *Colegrove v. Green* and other decisions of this Court on which it relied. Appellants' claim that they are being denied equal protection is justiciable, and if "discrimination is sufficiently shown, the right to relief under the equal protection clause is not diminished by the fact that the discrimination relates to political rights." *Snowden v. Hughes* (1944). . . . To show why we reject the argument based on the Guaranty Clause, we deem it necessary first to consider the contours of the "political question" doctrine.

Our discussion requires review of a number of political question cases, in order to expose the attributes of the doctrine. . . . That review reveals that in the Guaranty Clause cases and in the other "political question" cases, it is the relationship between the judiciary and the coordinate branches of the Federal Government, and not the federal judiciary's relationship to the States, which gives rise to the "political question." . . .

The nonjusticiability of a political question is primarily a function of the separation of powers. Much confusion results from the capacity of the "political question" label to obscure the need for case-by-case inquiry. Deciding whether a matter has in any measure been committed by the Constitution to another branch of government, or whether the action of that branch exceeds whatever authority has been committed, is itself a delicate exercise in constitutional interpretation, and is a responsibility of this Court as ultimate interpreter of the Constitution. . . .

. . . Prominent on the surface of any case held to involve a political question is found a textually demonstrable constitutional commitment of the issue to a coordinate political department; or a lack of judicially discoverable and manageable standards for resolving it; or the impossibility of deciding without an initial policy determination of a kind clearly for nonjudicial discretion; or the impossibility of a court's undertaking independent resolution without expressing lack of the respect due coordinate branches of government; or an unusual need for unquestioning adherence to a political decision already made; or the potentiality of embarrassment from multifarious pronouncements by various departments on one question.

Unless one of these formulations is inextricable from the case at bar, there should be no dismissal for nonjusticiability on the ground of a political question's presence. The doctrine of which we treat is one of "political questions," not one of "political cases." The courts cannot reject as "no law suit" a bona fide controversy as to whether some action denominated "political" exceeds constitutional authority. . . .

But it is argued that this case shares the characteristics of decisions that constitute a category not yet considered, cases concerning the Constitution's guaranty, in Art. IV, §4, of a republican form of government. . . .

. . . A natural beginning is to note whether any of the common characteristics which we have been able to identify and label descriptively are present. We find none: The question here is the consistency of state action with the Federal Constitution. We have no question decided, or to be decided, by a political branch of government coequal with this Court. Nor do we risk embarrassment of our government abroad, or grave disturbance at home if we take issue with Tennessee as to the constitutionality of her action here challenged. Nor need the appellants, in order to succeed in this action, ask the Court to enter upon policy determinations for which judicially manageable standards are lacking. Judicial standards under the Equal Protection Clause are well developed and familiar, and it has been open to courts since the enactment of the Fourteenth Amendment to determine, if on the particular facts they must, that a discrimination reflects *no* policy, but simply arbitrary and capricious action.

This case does, in one sense, involve the allocation of political power within a State, and the appellants might conceivably have added a claim under the Guaranty Clause. Of course, as we have seen, any reliance on that clause would be futile. But because any reliance on the Guaranty Clause could not have succeeded it does not follow that appellants may not be heard on the equal protection claim which in fact they tender. True, it must be clear that the Fourteenth Amendment claim is not so enmeshed with those political question elements which render Guaranty Clause claims nonjusticiable as actually to present a political question itself. But we have found that not to be the case here. . . .

We conclude then that the nonjusticiability of claims resting on the Guaranty Clause which arises from their embodiment of questions that were thought "political," can have no bearing upon the justiciability of the equal protection claim presented in this case. Finally, we emphasize that it is the involvement in Guaranty Clause claims of the elements thought to define

"political questions," and no other feature, which could render them nonjusticiable. Specifically, we have said that such claims are not held nonjusticiable because they touch matters of state governmental organization. . . .

We conclude that the complaint's allegations of a denial of equal protection present a justiciable constitutional cause of action upon which appellants are entitled to a trial and a decision. The right asserted is within the reach of judicial protection under the Fourteenth Amendment.

The judgment of the District Court is reversed and the cause is remanded for further proceedings consistent with this opinion.

Reversed and remanded.

JUSTICE CLARK, concurring. . . .

Although I find the Tennessee apportionment statute offends the Equal Protection Clause, I would not consider intervention by this Court into so delicate a field if there were any other relief available to the people of Tennessee. But the majority of the people of Tennessee have no "practical opportunities for exerting their political weight at the polls" to correct the existing "invidious discrimination." Tennessee has no initiative and referendum. I have searched diligently for other "practical opportunities" present under the law. I find none other than through the federal courts. The majority of the voters have been caught up in a legislative strait jacket. Tennessee has an "informed, civically militant electorate" and "an aroused popular conscience," but it does not sear "the conscience of the people's representatives." This is because the legislative policy has riveted the present seats in the Assembly to their respective constituencies, and by the votes of their incumbents a reapportionment of any kind is prevented. The people have been rebuffed at the hands of the Assembly; they have tried the constitutional convention route, but since the call must originate in the Assembly it, too, has been fruitless. They have tried Tennessee courts with the same result and Governors have fought the tide only to flounder. It is said that there is recourse in Congress and perhaps that may be, but from a practical standpoint this is without substance. To date Congress has never undertaken such a task in any State. We therefore must conclude that the people of Tennessee are stymied and without judicial intervention will be saddled with the present discrimination in the affairs of their state government. . . .

JUSTICE FRANKFURTER, whom JUSTICE HARLAN joins, dissenting.

We were soothingly told at the bar of this Court that we need not worry about the kind of remedy a court could effectively fashion once the abstract constitutional right to have courts pass on a state-wide system of electoral districting is recognized as a matter of judicial rhetoric, because legislatures would heed the Court's admonition. This is not only an euphoric hope. It implies a sorry confession of judicial impotence in place of a frank acknowledgment that there is not under the Constitution a judicial remedy for every political mischief, for every undesirable exercise of legislative power. The Framers carefully and with deliberate forethought refused so to enthrone the judiciary. In this situation, as in others of like nature, appeal for relief does not belong here. Appeal must be to an informed, civically militant electorate. In a democratic society like ours, relief must come through an aroused popular conscience that sears the conscience of the people's representatives. In any event there is nothing judicially more unseemly nor more self-defeating than for this Court to make in terrorem pronouncements, to indulge in merely empty rhetoric, sounding a word of promise to the ear, sure to be disappointing to the hope. . . .

In sustaining appellants' claim, based on the Fourteenth Amendment, that the District Court may entertain this suit, this Court's uniform course of decision over the years is overruled or disregarded. Explicitly it begins with *Colegrove v. Green* . . . but its roots run deep in the Court's historic adjudicatory process. . . .

The *Colegrove* doctrine, in the form in which repeated decisions have settled it, was not an innovation. It represents long judicial thought and experience. From its earliest opinions this Court has consistently recognized a class of controversies which do not lend themselves to judicial standards and judicial remedies. . . .

The influence of . . . converging considerations—the caution not to undertake decision where standards meet for judicial judgment are lacking, the reluctance to interfere with matters of state government in the absence of an unquestionable and effectively enforceable mandate, the unwillingness to make courts arbiters of the broad issues of political organization historically committed to other institutions and for whose adjustment the judicial process is ill-adapted—has been decisive of the settled line of cases, reaching back more than a century, which holds that Article IV, Section 4, of the Constitution, guaranteeing to the States "a Republican Form of Government," is not enforceable through the courts. . . .

The present case involves all of the elements that have made the Guarantee Clause cases nonjusticiable. It is, in effect, a Guarantee Clause claim masquerading under a different label. But it cannot make the case more fit for judicial action that appellants invoke the Fourteenth Amendment rather than Article IV, Section 4, where, in fact, the gist of their complaint is the same—unless it can be found that the Fourteenth Amendment speaks with greater particularity to their situation. . . .

What, then, is this question of legislative apportionment? Appellants invoke the right to vote and to have their votes counted. But they are permitted to vote and their votes are counted. They go to the polls, they cast their ballots, they send their representatives to the state councils. Their complaint is simply that the representatives are not sufficiently numerous or powerful—in short, that Tennessee has adopted a basis of representation with which they are dissatisfied. Talk of "debasement" or "dilution" is circular talk. One cannot speak of "debasement" or "dilution" of the value of a vote until there is first defined a standard of reference as to what a vote should be worth. What is actually asked of the Court in this case is to choose among competing bases of representation—ultimately, really among competing theories of political philosophy—in order to establish an appropriate frame of government for the State of Tennessee and thereby for all the states of the Union.

What Tennessee illustrates is an old and still widespread method of representation—representation by local geographical division, only in part respective of population—in preference to others, others, forsooth, more appealing. Appellants contest this choice and seek to make this Court the arbiter of the disagreement. They would make the Equal Protection Clause the character of adjudication, asserting that the equality which it guarantees comports, if not the assurance of equal weight to every voter's vote, at least the basic conception that representation ought to be proportionate to the population, a standard by reference to which the reasonableness of apportionment plans may be judged.

To find such a political conception legally enforceable in the broad and unspecific guarantee of equal protection is to rewrite the Constitution. . . . Certainly, "equal protection" is no more secure a foundation for judicial judgment of the permissibility of varying forms of representative governments than is "Republican Form." Indeed since "equal protection of the laws" can only mean an equality of persons standing in the same relation to whatever governmental action is challenged, the determination whether treatment is equal presupposes a determination concerning the nature of the relationship. This, with respect to apportionment, means an inquiry into the theoretic base of representation in an acceptably republican state. For a court could not determine the equal-protection issue without in fact first determining the Republican-Form issue, simply because what is reasonable for equal protection purposes will depend upon what frame of government, basically, is allowed. To divorce "equal protection" from "Republican Form" is to talk about half a question.

The notion that representation proportioned to the geographic spread of population is so universally accepted as a necessary element of equality between man and man that it must be taken to be the standard of a political equality preserved by the Fourteenth Amendment—that it is, in appellants' words "the basic principle of representative government"—is, to put it bluntly, not true. However desirable and however desired by some among the great political thinkers and framers of our government, it has never been generally practiced, today or in the past. It was not the English system, it was not the colonial system, it was not the system chosen for the national government by the Constitution, it was not the system exclusively or even predominantly practiced by the States today. Unless judges, the judges of this Court, are to make their private views of political wisdom the measure of the Constitution—views which in all honesty cannot but give the appearance, if not reflect the reality, of involvement with the business of partisan politics so inescapably a part of apportionment controversies—the Fourteenth Amendment, "itself a historical product," . . . provides no guide for judicial oversight of the representation problem. . . .

Manifestly, the Equal Protection Clause supplies no clearer guide for judicial examination of apportionment methods than would the Guarantee Clause itself. Apportionment, by its character, is a subject of extraordinary complexity, involving—even after the fundamental theoretical issues concerning what is to be represented in a representative legislature have been fought out or compromised—considerations of geography, demography, electoral convenience, economic and social cohesions or divergencies among particular local groups, communications, the practical effects of political institutions like the lobby and the city machine, ancient traditions and ties of settled usage, respect for proven incumbents of long experience and senior status, mathematical mechanics, censuses compiling relevant data, and a host of others. Legislative responses throughout the country to the apportionment demands of the 1960 Census have glaringly confirmed that these are not factors that lend themselves to evaluations of a nature that are the staple of judicial determinations or for which judges are equipped to adjudicate by legal training or experience or native wit. And this is the more so true because in every strand of this complicated, intricate web of values meet the contending forces of partisan politics. The practical significance of apportionment is that the next election results may differ because of it. Apportionment battles are overwhelmingly party or intraparty contests. It will add a virulent source of friction and tension in federal-state relations to embroil the federal judiciary in them.

Nixon v. United States
506 U.S. 224 (1993)

Walter Nixon, a federal district court judge, was convicted of two counts of lying to a grand jury and sentenced to prison. However, he refused to resign from the federal bench and, therefore, continued to receive his judicial salary while in prison. In May 1989, the House of Representatives adopted articles of impeachment, charging him with lying to a grand jury and with bringing disrepute on the federal judiciary. The Senate invoked its own Impeachment Rule XI, under which the presiding officer appoints a committee of senators to receive evidence and take testimony. The committee that was appointed held four days of hearings, during which it heard ten witnesses, including Nixon. Pursuant to Senate rules, it then submitted a report and a transcript of the proceeding to the full Senate. After receiving briefs from the parties and after three hours of oral argument, the Senate voted to convict Nixon of lying to a grand jury, and he was removed from office.

Nixon subsequently sued, claiming that the Senate's use of a committee to hear evidence violated the constitutional requirement that the Senate "try" all impeachments. After the district court and the court of appeals dismissed his suit as nonjusticiable, as a political question, the Supreme Court granted certiorari. Opinion of the Court: <u>Rehnquist</u>, Stevens, O'Connor, Scalia, Kennedy, Thomas. Concurring opinion: <u>Stevens</u>. Concurring in the judgment: <u>White</u>, Blackmun; <u>Souter</u>.

THE CHIEF JUSTICE delivered the opinion of the Court.

A controversy is nonjusticiable—i.e., involves a political question—where there is "a textually demonstrable constitutional commitment of the issue to a coordinate political department; or a lack of judicially discoverable and manageable standards for resolving it." . . . *Baker v. Carr* (1962). But the courts must, in the first instance, interpret the text in question and determine whether and to what extent the issue is textually committed.

As the discussion that follows makes clear, the concept of a textual commitment to a coordinate political department is not completely separate from the concept of a lack of judicially discoverable and manageable standards for resolving it; the lack of judicially manageable standards may strengthen the conclusion that there is a textually demonstrable commitment to a coordinate branch. In this case, we must examine Art I, §3, cl 6, to determine the scope of authority conferred upon the Senate by the Framers regarding impeachment. It provides: "The Senate shall have the sole Power to try all Impeachments. When sitting for that Purpose, they shall be on Oath or Affirmation. When the President of the United States is tried, the Chief Justice shall preside: And no Person shall be convicted without the Concurrence of two thirds of the Members present."

The language and structure of this Clause are revealing. The first sentence is a grant of authority to the Senate, and the word "sole" indicates that this authority is reposed in the Senate and nowhere else. The next two sentences specify requirements to which the Senate proceedings shall conform: the Senate shall be on oath or affirmation, a two-thirds vote is required to convict, and when the President is tried the Chief Justice shall preside.

Petitioner argues that the word "try" in the first sentence imposes by implication an additional requirement on the Senate in that the proceedings must be in the nature of a judicial trial. From there petitioner goes on to argue that this limitation precludes the Senate from delegating to a select committee the task of hearing the testimony of witnesses, as was done pursuant to Senate Rule XI.

There are several difficulties with this position which lead us ultimately to reject it. The word "try," both in 1787 and later, has considerably broader meanings than those to which petitioner would limit it. Based on the variety of definitions, however, we cannot say that the Framers used the word "try" as an implied limitation on the method by which the Senate might proceed in trying impeachments.

The conclusion that the use of the word "try" in the first sentence of the Impeachment Trial Clause lacks sufficient precision to afford any judicially manageable standard of review of the Senate's actions is fortified by the existence of the three very specific requirements that the Constitution does impose on the Senate when trying impeachments: the members must be under oath, a two-thirds vote is required to convict, and the Chief Justice presides when the President is tried. These limitations are quite precise, and their nature suggests that the Framers did not intend to impose additional limitations on the form of the Senate proceedings by the use of the word "try" in the first sentence.

Petitioner devotes only two pages in his brief to negating the significance of the word "sole" in the first sentence of Clause 6. As noted above, that sentence provides that "[t]he Senate shall have the sole Power to try all Impeachments." We think that the word "sole" is of considerable significance. Indeed, the word "sole" appears only one other time in the Constitution—with respect to the House of Representatives' "*sole* Power of Impeachment." Art I, §2, cl 5. The common sense meaning of the word "sole" is that the Senate alone shall have authority to determine whether an individual should be acquitted or convicted. The dictionary definition bears this out. "Sole" is defined as "having no companion," "solitary," "being the only one," and "functioning . . . independently and without assistance or interference." If the courts may review the actions of the Senate in order to determine whether that body "tried" an impeached official, it is difficult to see how the Senate would be "functioning . . . independently and without assistance or interference."

Petitioner also contends that the word "sole" should not bear on the question of justiciability because Art II, §2, cl 1, of the Constitution grants the President pardon authority "except in Cases of Impeachment." He argues that such a limitation on the President's pardon power would not have been necessary if the Framers thought that the Senate alone had authority to deal with such questions. But the granting of a pardon is in no sense an overturning of a judgment of conviction by some other tribunal; it is "[a]n executive action that mitigates or sets aside *punishment* for a crime." Authority in the Senate to determine procedures for trying an impeached official, unreviewable by the courts, is therefore not at all inconsistent with authority in the President to grant a pardon to the convicted official.

Petitioner finally argues that even if significance be attributed to the word "sole" in the first sentence of the clause, the authority granted is to the Senate, and this means that "the Senate—not the courts, not a lay jury, not a Senate Committee—shall try impeachments." It would be possible to read the first sentence of the Clause this way, but it is not a natural reading. Petitioner's interpretation would bring into judicial purview not merely the sort of claim made by petitioner, but other similar claims based on the conclusion that the word "Senate" has imposed by implication limitations on procedures which the Senate might adopt. Such limitations would be inconsistent with the construction of the Clause as a whole, which, as we have noted, sets out three express limitations in separate sentences.

The history and contemporary understanding of the impeachment provisions support our reading of the constitutional language. The parties do not offer evidence of a single word in the history of the Constitutional Convention or in contemporary commentary that even alludes to the possibility of judicial review in the context of the impeachment powers. This silence is quite meaningful in light of the several explicit references to the availability of judicial review as a check on the Legislature's power with respect to bills of attainder, *ex post facto* laws, and statutes.

The Framers labored over the question of where the impeachment power should lie. Significantly, in at least two considered scenarios the power was placed with the Federal Judiciary. Despite these proposals, the Convention ultimately decided that the Senate would have "the sole Power to Try all Impeachments." According to Alexander Hamilton, the Supreme Court was not the proper body because the Framers "doubted whether the members of that tribunal would, at all times, be endowed with so eminent a portion of fortitude as would be called for in the execution of so difficult a task" or whether the Court "would possess the degree of credit and authority" to carry out its judgment if it conflicted with the accusation brought by the Legislature—the people's representative. In addition, the Framers believed the

Court was too small in number. "The awful discretion, which a court of impeachments must necessarily have, to doom to honor or to infamy the most confidential and the most distinguished characters of the community, forbids the commitment of the trust to a small number of persons."

There are two additional reasons why the Judiciary, and the Supreme Court in particular, were not chosen to have any role in impeachments. First, the Framers recognized that most likely there would be two sets of proceedings for individuals who commit impeachable offenses—the impeachment trial and a separate criminal trial. In fact, the Constitution explicitly provides for two separate proceedings. The Framers deliberately separated the two forums to avoid raising the specter of bias and to ensure independent judgments.

Certainly judicial review of the Senate's "trial" would introduce the same risk of bias as would participation in the trial itself.

Second, judicial review would be inconsistent with the Framers' insistence that our system be one of checks and balances. In our constitutional system, impeachment was designed to be the *only* check on the Judicial Branch by the Legislature.

Judicial involvement in impeachment proceedings, even if only for purposes of judicial review, is counterintuitive because it would eviscerate the "important constitutional check" placed on the Judiciary by the Framers. Nixon's argument would place final reviewing authority with respect to impeachments in the hands of the same body that the impeachment process is meant to regulate.

Nevertheless, Nixon argues that judicial review is necessary in order to place a check on the Legislature. The Framers anticipated this objection and created two constitutional safeguards to keep the Senate in check. The first safeguard is that the whole of the impeachment power is divided between the two legislative bodies, with the House given the right to accuse and the Senate given the right to judge. This split of authority "avoids the inconvenience of making the same persons both accusers and judges; and guards against the danger of persecution from the prevalency of a factious spirit in either of those branches." The

second safeguard is the two-thirds supermajority vote requirement. Hamilton explained that "[a]s the concurrence of two-thirds of the senate will be requisite to a condemnation, the security to innocence, from this additional circumstance, will be as complete as itself can desire."

In addition to the textual commitment argument, we are persuaded that the lack of finality and the difficulty of fashioning relief counsel against justiciability. We agree with the Court of Appeals that opening the door of judicial review to the procedures used by the Senate in trying impeachments would "expose the political life of the country to months, or perhaps years, of chaos." This lack of finality would manifest itself most dramatically if the President were impeached. The legitimacy of any successor, and hence his effectiveness, would be impaired severely, not merely while the judicial process was running its course, but during any retrial that a differently constituted Senate might conduct if its first judgment of conviction were invalidated. Equally uncertain is the question of what relief a court may give other than simply setting aside the judgment of conviction. Could it order the reinstatement of a convicted federal judge, or order Congress to create an additional judgeship if the seat had been filled in the interim?

For the foregoing reasons, the judgment of the Court of Appeals is affirmed.

JUSTICE WHITE, with JUSTICE BLACKMUN, concurring in the judgment.

Petitioner contends that the method by which the Senate convicted him on two articles of impeachment violates Art I, §3, cl 6 of the Constitution, which mandates that the Senate "try" impeachments. The Court is of the view that the Constitution forbids us even to consider his contention. I find no such prohibition and would therefore reach the merits of the claim. I concur in the judgment because the Senate fulfilled its constitutional obligation to "try" petitioner.

The majority states that the question raised in this case meets two of the criteria for political questions set out in *Baker v. Carr* (1962). It concludes first that there is "'a textually demonstrable constitutional commitment of the issue to a coordinate political department.'" It also finds that the question cannot be resolved for "a lack of judicially discoverable and manageable standards."

The majority finds a clear textual commitment in the Constitution's use of the word "sole" in the phrase "the Senate shall have the sole Power to try all Impeachments." The significance of the Constitution's use of the term "sole" lies in the fact that it appears exactly twice, in parallel provisions concerning impeachment. That the word "sole" is found only in the House and Senate Impeachment Clauses demonstrates that its purpose is to emphasize the distinct role of each in the impeachment process. As the majority notes the Framers, following English practice, were very much concerned to separate the prosecutorial from the adjudicative aspects of impeachment. While the majority is thus right to interpret the term "sole" to indicate that the Senate ought to "'functio[n] independently and without assistance or interference,'" it wrongly identifies the judiciary, rather than the House, as the source of potential interference with which the Framers were concerned when they employed the term "sole."

The majority also claims support in the history and early interpretations of the Impeachment Clauses, noting the various arguments in support of the current system made at the Constitutional Convention and expressed powerfully by Hamilton in *The Federalist*, Nos. 65 and 66.

The majority's review of the historical record thus explains why the power to try impeachments properly resides with the Senate. It does not explain, however, the sweeping statement that the judiciary was "not chosen to have any role in impeachments." Not a single word in the historical materials cited by the majority addresses judicial review of the Impeachment Trial Clause. And a glance at the arguments surrounding the Impeachment Clauses negates the majority's attempt to infer nonjusticiability from the Framers' arguments in support of the Senate's power to try impeachments.

The historical evidence reveals above all else that the Framers were deeply concerned about placing in any branch the "awful discretion, which a court of impeachments must

necessarily have." *The Federalist*, No. 65. Viewed against this history, the discord between the majority's position and the basic principles of checks and balances underlying the Constitution's separation of powers is clear. In essence, the majority suggests that the Framers conferred upon Congress a potential tool of legislative dominance yet at the same time rendered Congress' exercise of that power one of the very few areas of legislative authority immune from any judicial review. While the majority rejects petitioner's justiciability argument as espousing a view "inconsistent with the Framers' insistence that our system be one of checks and balances," it is the Court's finding of nonjusticiability that truly upsets the Framers' careful design. In a truly balanced system, impeachments tried by the Senate would serve as a means of controlling the largely unaccountable judiciary, even as judicial review would ensure that the Senate adhered to a minimal set of procedural standards in conducting impeachment trials.

The majority also contends that the term "try" does not present a judicially manageable standard. This argument comes in two variants. The first, which asserts that one simply cannot ascertain the sense of "try" which the Framers employed and hence cannot undertake judicial review, is clearly untenable. To begin with, one would intuitively expect that, in defining the power of a political body to conduct an inquiry into official wrongdoing, the Framers used "try" in its legal sense. That intuition is borne out by reflection on the alternatives. The third clause of Art I, §3 cannot seriously be read to mean that the Senate shall "attempt" or "experiment with" impeachments. It is equally implausible to say that the Senate is charged with "investigating" impeachments given that this description would substantially overlap with the House of Representatives' "sole" power to draw up articles of impeachment. Art I, §2, cl 5.

The other variant of the majority position focuses not on which sense of "try" is employed in the Impeachment Trial Clause, but on whether the legal sense of that term creates a judicially manageable standard. The majority concludes that the term provides no "identifiable textual limit." Yet, as the Government itself conceded at oral argument, the term "try" is hardly so elusive as the majority would have it. Were the Senate, for example, to adopt the practice of automatically entering a judgment of conviction whenever articles of impeachment were delivered from the House, it is quite clear that the Senate will have failed to "try" impeachments. Indeed in this respect, "try" presents no greater, and perhaps fewer, interpretive difficulties than some other constitutional standards that have been found amenable to familiar techniques of judicial construction, including, for example, "Commerce . . . among the several States," and "due process of law."

The majority's conclusion that "try" is incapable of meaningful judicial construction is not without irony. One might think that if any class of concepts would fall within the definitional abilities of the judiciary, it would be that class having to do with procedural justice. Examination of the remaining question—whether proceedings in accordance with Senate Rule XI are compatible with the Impeachment Trial Clause—confirms this intuition.

Petitioner bears the rather substantial burden of demonstrating that simply by employing the word "try," the Constitution prohibits the Senate from relying on a fact-finding committee. It is clear that the Framers were familiar with English impeachment practice and with that of the States employing a variant of the English model at the time of the Constitutional Convention. Hence there is little doubt that the term "try" as used in Art I, §3, cl 6 meant that the Senate should conduct its proceedings in a manner somewhat resembling a judicial proceeding. Indeed, it is safe to assume that Senate trials were to follow the practice in England and the States, which contemplated a formal hearing on the charges, at which the accused would be represented by counsel, evidence would be presented, and the accused would have the opportunity to be heard.

Petitioner argues, however, that because committees were not used in state impeachment trials prior to the Convention, the word "try" cannot be interpreted to permit their use. It is, however, a substantial leap to infer from the absence of a particular device of parliamentary procedure that its use has been forever barred by the Constitution.

It is also noteworthy that the delegation of fact-finding by judicial and quasi-judicial bodies was hardly unknown to the Framers. Jefferson, at least, was aware that the House of Lords sometimes delegated fact-finding in impeachment trials to committees and recommended use of the same to the Senate (T. Jefferson, *A Manual of Parliamentary Practice for the Use of the Senate of the United States*). The States also had on occasion employed legislative committees to investigate whether to draw up articles of impeachment. Particularly in light of the Constitution's grant to each House of the power to "determine the Rules of its Proceedings," the existence of legislative and judicial delegation strongly suggests that the Impeachment Trial Clause was not designed to prevent employment of a fact-finding committee.

In short, textual and historical evidence reveals that the impeachment Trial Clause was not meant to bind the hands of the Senate beyond establishing a set of minimal procedures. Without identifying the exact contours of these procedures, it is sufficient to say that the Senate's use of a fact-finding committee under Rule XI is entirely compatible with the Constitution's command that the Senate "try all impeachments." Petitioner's challenge to his conviction must therefore fail.

JUSTICE SOUTER, concurring in the judgment.

I agree with the Court that this case presents a nonjusticiable political question. Because my analysis differs somewhat from the Court's, however, I concur in its judgment by this separate opinion.

Whatever considerations feature most prominently in a particular case, the political question doctrine is "essentially a function of the separation of powers," existing to restrain courts "from inappropriate interference in the business of the other branches of Government," *United States v. Munoz-Flores* (1990), and deriving in large part from prudential concerns about the respect we owe the political departments. Not all interference is inappropriate or disrespectful, however, and application of the doctrine ultimately turns, as Learned Hand put it, on "how importunately the occasion demands an answer."

This occasion does not demand an answer. The impeachment Trial Clause commits to the Senate "the sole Power to try all Impeachments," subject to three procedural requirements: the Senate shall be on oath or affirmation; the Chief Justice shall preside when the President is tried; and conviction shall be upon the concurrence of two-thirds of the Members present. It seems fair to conclude that the Clause contemplates that the Senate may determine, within broad boundaries, such subsidiary issues as the procedures for receipt and consideration of evidence necessary to satisfy its duty to "try" impeachments. Other significant considerations confirm a conclusion that this case presents a nonjusticiable political question: the "unusual need for unquestioning adherence to a political decision already made,"

as well as "the potentiality of embarrassment from multifarious pronouncements by various departments on one question."

One can, nevertheless, envision different and unusual circumstances that might justify a more searching review of impeachment proceedings. If the Senate were to act in a manner seriously threatening the integrity of its results, convicting, say, upon a coin-toss, or upon a summary determination that an officer of the United States was simply "a bad guy" judicial interference might well be appropriate. In such circumstances, the Senate's action might be so far beyond the scope of its constitutional authority, and the consequent impact on the Republic so great, as to merit a judicial response despite the prudential concerns that would ordinarily counsel silence.

DeShaney v. Winnebago County Department of Social Services
489 U.S. 189 (1989)

The petitioner in this case, Joshua DeShaney, was subjected to a series of beatings by his father, Randy DeShaney, with whom he lived. The respondents, a county department of social services and several of its social workers, received complaints that Joshua was being abused by his father and took various steps to protect him; they did not, however, remove him from his father's custody. Joshua's father finally beat him so severely that he suffered massive and permanent brain damage and was rendered profoundly retarded. Although Joshua's father was subsequently tried and convicted of child abuse, Joshua and his mother sued the respondents under 42 U.S.C. Section 1983, alleging that they had deprived Joshua of his "liberty interest in bodily integrity," in violation of his rights under the substantive component of the Fourteenth Amendment's Due Process Clause, by failing to intervene to protect him from his father's violence. The US District Court for the Eastern District of Wisconsin granted summary judgment for the respondents, the Court of Appeals for the Seventh Circuit affirmed, and the Supreme Court granted certiorari. Opinion of the Court: Rehnquist, White, Stevens, O'Connor, Scalia, Kennedy. Dissenting opinions: Brennan, Marshall, Blackmun; Blackmun.

THE CHIEF JUSTICE delivered the opinion of the Court.

Petitioner is a boy who was beaten and permanently injured by his father, with whom he lived. The respondents are social workers and other local officials who received complaints that petitioner was being abused by his father and had reason to believe that this was the case, but nonetheless did not act to remove petitioner from his father's custody. Petitioner sued respondents claiming that their failure to act deprived him of his liberty in violation of the Due Process Clause of the Fourteenth Amendment to the United States Constitution. We hold that it did not. . . .

The Due Process Clause of the Fourteenth Amendment provides that "[n]o State shall . . . deprive any person of life, liberty, or property, without due process of law." Petitioners contend that the State deprived Joshua of his liberty interest in "free[dom] from . . . unjustified intrusions on personal security," . . . by failing to provide him with adequate protection against his father's violence. The claim is one invoking the substantive rather than procedural component of the Due Process Clause; petitioners do not claim that the State denied Joshua protection without according him appropriate procedural safeguards, . . . but that it was categorically obligated to protect him in these circumstances. . . .

But nothing in the language of the Due Process Clause itself requires the State to protect the life, liberty, and property of its citizens against invasion by private actors. The Clause is phrased as a limitation on the State's power to act, not as a guarantee of certain minimal levels of safety and security. It forbids the State itself to deprive individuals of life, liberty, or property without "due process of law," but its language cannot fairly be extended to impose an affirmative obligation on the State to ensure that those interests do not come to harm through other means. Nor does history support such an expansive reading of the constitutional text. Like its counterpart in the Fifth Amendment, the Due Process Clause of the Fourteenth Amendment was intended to prevent government "from abusing [its] power, or employing it as an instrument of oppression." . . . Its purpose was to protect the people from the State, not to ensure that the State protected them from each other. The Framers were content to leave the extent of governmental obligation in the latter area to the democratic political processes.

Consistent with these principles, our cases have recognized that the Due Process Clauses generally confer no affirmative right to governmental aid, even where such aid may be necessary to secure life, liberty, or property interests of which the government itself may not deprive the individual. . . . As we said in *Harris v. McRae* [1980], "[al]though the liberty protected by the Due Process Clause affords protection against unwarranted *government* interference . . . , it does not confer an entitlement to such [governmental aid] as may be necessary to realize all the advantages of that freedom." . . . If the Due Process Clause does not require the State to provide its citizens with particular protective services, it follows that the State cannot be held liable under the Clause for injuries that could have been averted had it chosen to provide them. As a general matter, then, we conclude that a State's failure to protect an individual against private violence simply does not constitute a violation of the Due Process Clause.

Petitioners contend, however, that even if the Due Process Clause imposes no affirmative obligation on the State to provide the general public with adequate protective services, such a duty may arise out of certain "special relationships" created or assumed by the State with respect to particular individuals. . . . Petitioners argue that such a "special relationship" existed here because the State knew that Joshua faced a special danger of abuse at his father's hands, and specifically proclaimed, by word and by deed, its intention to protect him against that danger. . . . Having actually undertaken to protect Joshua from this danger—which petitioners concede the State played no part in creating—the State acquired an affirmative "duty," enforceable through the Due Process Clause, to do so in a reasonably competent fashion. . . .

We reject this argument. It is true that in certain limited circumstances the Constitution imposes upon the State affirmative duties of care and protection with respect to particular individuals. In *Estelle v. Gamble* (1976) we recognized that the Eighth Amendment's prohibition against cruel and unusual punishment . . . requires the State to provide adequate medical care to incarcerated prisoners. . . .

In *Youngberg v. Romeo* (1982) we extended this analysis beyond the Eighth Amendment setting, holding that the substantive component of the Fourteenth Amendment's Due Process Clause requires the State to provide involuntarily committed mental patients with such services as are necessary to ensure their "reasonable safety" from themselves and others. . . .

But these cases afford petitioners no help. Taken together, they stand only for the proposition that when the State takes a person into its custody and holds him there against his will, the Constitution imposes upon it a corresponding duty to assume some responsibility for his safety and general well-being. . . . The rationale for this principle is simple enough: when the State by the affirmative exercise of its power so restrains an individual's liberty that it renders him unable to care for himself, and at the same time fails to provide for his basic human needs—*e.g.*, food, clothing, shelter, medical care, and reasonable safety—it transgresses the substantive limits on state action set by the Eighth Amendment and the Due Process Clause. . . . The affirmative duty to protect arises not from the State's knowledge of the individual's predicament or from its expressions of intent to help him, but from the limitation which it has imposed on his freedom to act on his own behalf. . . . In the substantive due process analysis, it is the State's affirmative act of restraining the individual's freedom to act on his own behalf—through incarceration, institutionalization, or other similar restraint of personal liberty—which is the "deprivation of liberty" triggering the protections of the Due Process Clause, not its failure to act to protect his liberty interests against harms inflicted by other means.

The *Estelle-Youngberg* analysis simply has no applicability in the present case. Petitioners concede that the harms Joshua suffered did not occur while he was in the State's custody, but while he was in the custody of his natural father, who was in no sense a state actor. While the State may have been aware of the dangers that Joshua faced in the free world, it played no part in their creation, nor did it do anything to render him any more vulnerable to them. That the State once took temporary custody of Joshua does not alter the analysis, for when it returned him to his father's custody, it placed him in no worse position than that in which he would have been had it not acted at all; the State does not become the permanent guarantor of an individual's safety by having once offered him shelter. Under these circumstances, the State had no constitutional duty to protect Joshua.

It may well be that, by voluntarily undertaking to protect Joshua against a danger it concededly played no part in creating, the State acquired a duty under state tort law to provide him with adequate protection against that danger. . . . But the claim here is based on the Due Process Clause of the Fourteenth Amendment, which, as we have said many times, does not transform every tort committed by a state actor into a constitutional violation. . . . Because . . . the State had no constitutional duty to protect Joshua against his father's violence, its failure to do so—though calamitous in hindsight—simply does not constitute a violation of the Due Process Clause.

Judges and lawyers, like other humans, are moved by natural sympathy in a case like this to find a way for Joshua and his mother to receive adequate compensation for the grievous harm inflicted upon them. But before yielding to that impulse, it is well to remember once again that the harm was inflicted not by the State of Wisconsin, but by Joshua's father. The most that can be said of the state functionaries in this case is that they stood by and did nothing when suspicious circumstances dictated a more active role for them. In defense of them it must also be said that had they moved too soon to take custody of the son away from the father, they would likely have been met with charges of improperly intruding into the parent-child relationship, charges based on the same Due Process Clause that forms the basis for the present charge of failure to provide adequate protection.

The people of Wisconsin may well prefer a system of liability which would place upon the State and its officials the responsibility for failure to act in situations such as the present one. They may create such a system, if they do not have it already, by changing the tort law of the State in accordance with the regular law-making process. But they should not have it thrust upon them by this Court's expansion of the Due Process Clause of the Fourteenth Amendment.

JUSTICE BRENNAN, with whom JUSTICE MARSHALL and JUSTICE BLACKMUN join, dissenting. . . .

To the Court, the only fact that seems to count as an "affirmative act of restraining the individual's freedom to act on his own behalf" is direct physical control. . . . I would not, however, give *Youngberg* and *Estelle* such a stingy scope. I would recognize, as the Court apparently cannot, that "the State's knowledge of [an] individual's predicament [and] its expressions of intent to help him" can amount to a "limitation of his freedom to act on his own behalf" or to obtain help from others. . . . Thus, I would read *Youngberg* and *Estelle* to stand for the much more generous proposition that, if a State cuts off private sources of aid and then refuses aid itself, it cannot wash its hands of the harm that results from its inaction.

Wisconsin has established a child-welfare system specifically designed to help children like Joshua. Wisconsin law places upon the local departments of social services such as respondent (DSS or Department) a duty to investigate reported instances of child abuse. . . . While other governmental bodies and private persons are largely responsible for reporting of possible cases of child abuse, Wisconsin law channels all such reports to the local departments of social services for evaluation and, if necessary, further action. . . . Even when it is the sheriff's office or police department that receives a report of suspected child abuse, that report is referred to local social services departments for action . . . ; the only exception to this occurs when the reporter fears for the child's *immediate* safety. In this way, Wisconsin law invites—indeed, directs—citizens and other governmental entities to depend on local departments of social services such as respondent to protect children from abuse. . . .

In these circumstances, a private citizen, or even a person working in a government agency other than DSS, would doubtless feel that her job was done as soon as she had reported her suspicions of child abuse to DSS. Through its child-welfare program, in other words, the State of Wisconsin has relieved ordinary citizens and governmental bodies other than the Department of any sense of obligation to do anything more than report their suspicions of child abuse to DSS. If DSS ignores or dismisses these suspicions, no one will step in to fill the gap. Wisconsin's child-protection program thus effectively confined Joshua De-Shaney within the walls of Randy DeShaney's violent home until such time as DSS took action to remove him. Conceivably, then, children like Joshua are made worse off by the existence of this program when the persons and entities charged with carrying it out fail to do their jobs. . . .

As the Court today reminds us, "the Due Process Clause of the Fourteenth Amendment was intended to prevent government 'from abusing [its] power, or employing it as an instrument of oppression.'" . . . My Disagreement with the Court arises from its failure to see that inaction can be every bit as abusive of power as action, that oppression can result when a State undertakes a vital duty and then ignores it. Today's opinion construes the Due Process Clause to permit a State to displace private sources of protection and then, at the critical moment, to shrug its shoulders and turn away from the harm that it has promised to try to prevent. Because I cannot agree that our Constitution is indifferent to such indifference, I respectfully dissent.

JUSTICE BLACKMUN, dissenting.

Today, the Court purports to be the dispassionate oracle of the law, unmoved by "natural sympathy." But, in this pretense, the Court itself retreats into a sterile formalism which prevents it from recognizing either the facts of the case before it or the legal norms that should apply to those facts. As JUSTICE BRENNAN demonstrates, the facts here involve not mere passivity, but active state intervention in the life of Joshua DeShaney—intervention that triggered a fundamental duty to aid the boy once the State learned of the severe danger to which he was exposed. . . . The Court today claims that its decision, however harsh, is compelled by existing legal doctrine. On the contrary, the question presented by this case is an open one, and our Fourteenth Amendment precedents may be read more broadly or narrowly depending upon how one chooses to read them. Faced with the choice, I would adopt a "sympathetic" reading, one which comports with dictates of fundamental justice and recognizes that compassion need not be exiled from the province of judging. Cf. A. Stone, *Law, Psychiatry, and Morality* 262 (1984) ("We will make mistakes if we go forward, but doing nothing can be the worst mistake. What is required of us is moral ambition. Until our composite sketch becomes a true portrait of humanity we must live with our uncertainty; we will grope, we will struggle, and our compassion may be our only guide and comfort").

4

The Legislative Branch

Aware of the inadequacies of the Articles of Confederation, the Framers of the Constitution set out to create a national government powerful enough for a large and diverse nation. Broad powers were conferred on the legislative branch of government, which the Framers expected to be the most powerful of the three branches. But before examining these powers, let us address four preliminary questions:

1. What principles underlie interpretation of the scope of the national legislative power?
2. What powers and privileges does the Constitution grant to Congress to facilitate its legislative activity?
3. What nonlegislative powers does the Constitution confer on Congress?
4. Given the growth of the federal bureaucracy, what constitutional means does Congress have for ensuring that it continues to make basic policy decisions?

THE SCOPE OF CONGRESSIONAL POWER

Article I of the Constitution grants Congress a broad array of legislative powers, including taxing and spending powers, the power to declare war, and the power to regulate commerce. Various constitutional amendments—in particular, the Thirteenth, Fourteenth, Fifteenth, and Sixteenth Amendments—confer important additional powers. Finally, the Necessary and Proper Clause (Article I, Section 8) gives Congress the authority to "make all laws which shall be necessary and proper for carrying into Execution the foregoing Powers, and all other Powers vested by this Constitution in the Government of the United States, or in any Department or Officer thereof."

Although the Constitution vests broad powers in Congress, it also imposes restrictions on congressional power. Some of these restrictions, such as the ban on *ex post facto* laws (criminal laws that have a retroactive effect), were incorporated into the original Constitution. Others were added with the ratification of the Bill of Rights, the first ten amendments to the Constitution. Most important, Congress can exercise only the powers explicitly or implicitly conferred on it by the Constitution.

This distinguishes Congress from the British Parliament, which (at least in theory) can pass any law it wishes. It also means that Congress, unlike the legislature under the Articles of Confederation, is not limited to those powers expressly granted to it. How broad are Congress's implied powers? The answer to this question depends on the interpretation of the Necessary and Proper Clause. By inserting this clause, the Framers sought to give Congress flexibility in dealing with complex and changing conditions. Yet some critics—most notably, Thomas Jefferson—charged that if Congress were allowed too much discretion in determining how it would achieve its objectives, this "sweeping clause" could transform a government of limited powers into one of unlimited powers. A government that was limited in its aims but unlimited in the means it could use to achieve them would be little different from a government of unlimited powers. These critics therefore proposed that the phrase *necessary and proper* be interpreted as limiting, rather than expanding, congressional power. According to this view, Congress could exercise implied powers only insofar as such powers were essential for carrying out its enumerated powers. For example, if Congress's enumerated powers could be implemented without chartering a national bank, then the power to charter a bank was not necessary and hence was not authorized.

This restrictive interpretation of congressional power was rejected in *McCulloch v. Maryland* (1819), in which the Supreme Court recognized Congress's power to charter the Bank of the United States and invalidated a Maryland tax on that bank. Speaking for a unanimous Court, Chief Justice John Marshall argued for a broad construction of congressional powers. Acknowledging that the Constitution did not specifically authorize Congress to charter a bank, Marshall reasoned that this omission was not determinative. In establishing "a constitution intended to endure for ages to come," Marshall argued, the Framers deliberately avoided cluttering it with excessive detail, choosing instead merely to sketch the "great outlines" of congressional power. To determine whether Congress possessed a particular power, therefore, it was necessary to read the Constitution in light of the ends it was created to achieve.

Because the Constitution confers on Congress considerable responsibility for the economic prosperity of the nation, Marshall went on, it must be interpreted as furnishing Congress with sufficient power for securing that end; any other interpretation would be contradictory and self-defeating. In addition, the Constitution must provide Congress with "that discretion, with respect to the means by which the powers it confers are to be carried into execution, which will enable that body to perform the high duties assigned to it, in the manner most beneficial to the people." To confine Congress to only those means essential for carrying out its enumerated powers would be to jeopardize the ends for which the Constitution was established. Therefore, Marshall concluded, "Let the end be legitimate, let it be within the scope of the constitution, and all means which are appropriate, which are plainly adapted to that end, which are not prohibited, but consist with the letter and spirit of the constitution, are constitutional."

Marshall's opinion in *McCulloch* has served as a model for interpreting the constitutional grants of power. By focusing on the ends the Framers sought to achieve, Marshall ensured that Congress neither overstepped its bounds nor was denied powers commensurate with its responsibilities. In allowing Congress to choose how best to achieve those ends, Marshall recognized that flexibility of response was essential for effective government. Although bitterly attacked at the time, his opinion remains the primary rationale for the broad exercise of congressional power.[1]

But as federal power has expanded, some justices have worried that broad congressional discretion over the means for achieving its ends could transform a government of limited powers into a government of unlimited powers. This concern is reflected in two recent cases: *United States v. Comstock* (2010) and *National Federation of Independent Business v. Sebelius* (2012). In *Comstock*, the Court upheld under the Necessary and Proper Clause a federal law that authorized the federal government to require the civil commitment of sexually dangerous offenders after their prison sentences had expired. Speaking for the Court, Justice Stephen Breyer noted that the law constituted a "modest addition" to long-standing federal laws and served the purpose of protecting against prisoners that had come into states as a result of federal incarceration. Justices Samuel Alito and Anthony Kennedy concurred in the judgment but were troubled by the breadth of the Court's language, which they viewed as imposing no clear limits on federal power. Justice Clarence Thomas in dissent, joined by Justice Antonin Scalia, challenged the Court to identify a specific enumerated power that the statute was designed to carry into execution. In *Sebelius* (see Chapter 8), a five-member majority ruled that the Necessary and Proper Clause did not offer a basis for upholding the "individual mandate" of the Affordable Care Act, which required persons who did not have health insurance to purchase it or pay a penalty for failing to do so. (The Court ultimately upheld that provision as an exercise of Congress's taxing power.) Speaking for the Court, Chief Justice John Roberts insisted that the Act would "work a substantial expansion of federal authority" and so "even if the individual mandate was 'necessary' to the Act's insurance reforms, such an expansion of federal power is not a 'proper' means for making those reforms effective." In response, Justice Ruth Bader Ginsburg argued that the Affordable Care Act was an exercise of congressional power under the Commerce Clause (Article I, section 8, paragraph 3) because it regulated health care, a major part of the American economy, and that the individual mandate was constitutionally proper as a means closely related to making such regulation effective.

Interestingly, both the majority and the dissenters on this issue claimed to be following Marshall's lead, even as they disagreed sharply about where his principles led.

POWERS THAT FACILITATE LEGISLATIVE ACTIVITY

McCulloch v. Maryland leads to the conclusion that, having vested Congress with important responsibilities, the Constitution provided lawmakers with the powers and privileges necessary to fulfill those duties. To promote the efficient transaction of legislative business, the Framers gave each house of Congress a limited control over its membership and the power to discipline members who engage in improper conduct. To secure legislative independence, they inserted into Article I both the Speech and Debate Clause, which protects members of Congress from legal inquiry into their legislative activities, and other provisions guaranteeing Congress control over its own proceedings.[2] The Framers also promoted well-informed deliberations through the Necessary and Proper Clause, under whose authority Congress has undertaken investigations, subpoenaed witnesses to testify, and punished refusals to supply pertinent information. Although the existence of these powers and privileges has long been recognized, their scope has periodically been the subject of controversy and litigation.

Membership, Qualifications, and Discipline

The Connecticut Compromise at the Constitutional Convention guaranteed each state equal representation in the Senate but apportioned representation in the House of Representatives on the basis of population. Initially, states had one representative in the House for every 30,000 residents.[3] When population increases threatened to make the House too large, impeding the transaction of legislative business, Congress by statute capped the size of the House at 435. Each state was guaranteed one representative, with the remaining representatives allocated among the states on the basis of population. The problem remained, however, of how to deal with fractional remainders—that is, the remainders left when a state's total population was divided by the population of the ideal district. To solve this problem, Congress in 1941 adopted the "method of equal proportions" proposed by the National Academy of Sciences. In *U.S. Department of Commerce v. Montana* (1992), the Supreme Court upheld Congress's choice, ruling that it had broad leeway in choosing among alternative approaches for dealing with fractional remainders. Then in *Utah v. Evans* (2002), the Court recognized that the Constitution accords the Census Bureau considerable discretion in determining how to achieve an accurate count for apportionment purposes, upholding the bureau's use of "imputation" (a method of inference based on the characteristics of neighboring housing units) in estimating the population of units that did not reply to census inquiries.

Although each state draws up the electoral districts for its House seats, it operates within severe constraints. As the Supreme Court ruled in *Wesberry v. Sanders* (1964), the districts within a state must meet the standard of "one person, one vote." Even minor deviations from equal-population districts can lead to invalidation. For example, in *Karcher v. Daggett* (1983) the Court struck down a New Jersey apportionment scheme even though the variation between the most and least populous districts was less than 1 percent. In *Wisconsin v. City of New York* (1996), however, the Court refused to require a statistical adjustment of census data to remedy possible undercounting of population, even though undercounting could affect the apportionment of members of Congress among the states. (Issues relating to apportionment and representation are discussed in Chapter 10 of Volume II.)

Article I, Section 5, of the Constitution gives each house of Congress control over the admission of members and authorizes it to impose sanctions on them (including expulsion) for improper conduct. The Constitution does not specify the grounds for expelling or otherwise disciplining members of Congress; that lies within the discretion of each house. In fact, neither the Senate nor the House has been eager to sanction its members—as of 2015, only fifteen senators and five representatives had been expelled, all but two for disloyalty during the Civil War. Yet these figures mask the full impact of congressional disciplinary powers, for members of Congress may prefer to resign rather than suffer condemnation by their colleagues. For example, Speaker of the House Jim Wright resigned in 1989 in the face of disclosures about financial dealings likely to lead to expulsion or censure, and Senator Robert Packwood resigned in 1995 when faced with the prospect of expulsion for sexual harassment.

Whereas the Constitution does not specify the grounds for disciplining or expelling members, it does prescribe qualifications of age, citizenship, and residency for serving as a senator or a representative. During the Constitutional Convention, some delegates proposed restrictive property qualifications to serve in the Senate, but these were rejected. The delegates also rejected proposals that the House and Senate be permitted to establish additional qualifications to maintain the integrity and reputation of their chambers. For more than seventy years thereafter, no one with the constitutional qualifications for office was denied a seat in Congress. After the Civil War, however, both houses departed from the original understanding by refusing to seat unregenerate Confederates. In 1900, the House denied admission to a Mormon who had allegedly violated the law outlawing polygamy, and in 1920, it refused to seat a Socialist accused of publishing disloyal articles during World War I. In *Powell v. McCormack* (1969), the Supreme Court decisively rejected such practices and reaffirmed the original understanding of the constitutional qualifications as maximum requirements to which the House and Senate could not add.

Powell did not resolve whether the *states* could add eligibility requirements for their members of Congress. This issue arose in *U.S. Term Limits, Inc. v. Thornton* (1995), in which the Court considered the constitutionality of an Arkansas law limiting the number of terms that its members of Congress could serve.[4] The justices in *Thornton* invalidated the Arkansas law by a 5–4 vote. The majority and dissenters in *Thornton* both consulted the same historical records: the debates at the Constitutional Convention, the debates during ratification, post-ratification practices in the states, and congressional resolution of controversies over seating members. However, they repeatedly clashed over the conclusions to be drawn from these materials.

Their differences reflect a more fundamental disagreement about the character of the Union created by the Constitution. According to the dissenters in *Thornton,* the states retain the power to regulate the national electoral process unless the Constitution has withdrawn that power, because the Tenth Amendment guarantees that all "powers not delegated to the United States by the Constitution, nor prohibited by it to the States, are reserved to the States respectively, or to the people." Congress can override the states' imposition of term limits, because Article I, Section 4, gives it the power to alter state regulations regarding the "Times, Places, and Manner of holding elections." But in the absence of such action by Congress, states remain free to establish qualifications for their members of Congress beyond those enunciated in Article I, Section 5.

The Court majority in *Thornton* argued that, although members of Congress are elected from separate constituencies, they become, once elected, "a uniform national body representing the interests of a single people" rather than "delegates appointed by separate, sovereign states." This explains why the Constitution provides for a uniform salary to be paid by the national Treasury, limits the state role in federal elections, and allows the representatives of all states to judge disputes about the qualifications of representatives of a single state. In addition, the majority rejected the dissenters' reliance on the Tenth Amendment, contending that it reserves to the states only those powers they possessed when the Constitution was adopted. Because no national electoral process existed before the ratification of the Constitution, no power to regulate that process existed in the states. Thus, states can regulate the national electoral process only if authorized to do so by Congress, and Congress had given them no such authority.

By the time the Court's ruling in *Thornton* was announced, twenty-two states had set term limits on their members of Congress, usually in conjunction with similar limits on their state legislators. *Thornton* meant that those congressional term limits could no longer be enforced. Proponents of term limits then sought a constitutional amendment limiting congressional terms, but no such amendment was ever endorsed by Congress.

The Speech and Debate Clause

Article I, Section 6, guarantees members of Congress that "for any Speech or Debate in either House, they shall not be questioned in any other Place." This safeguard against executive harassment or intimidation of legislators originated during the British Parliament's struggle for legislative supremacy. It excited little controversy for most of the nation's history. But in the second half of the twentieth century, the Supreme Court decided several cases involving the Speech and Debate Clause, and the deep divisions on the Court in these cases reveal basic disagreements about the purposes the clause was designed to serve.

The justices have disagreed, first of all, about who is protected by the Speech and Debate Clause. Even though the clause expressly protects only senators and representatives, the Court has concluded that today its protection cannot be so limited. Some congressional employees perform tasks so essential to the legislative process that denying them protection would defeat the basic purpose of the provision. Thus, in *Gravel v. United States* (1972), which involved a grand jury investigation into how Senator Mike Gravel obtained and arranged to publish top-secret government documents, all the justices recognized that Gravel's legislative aide was entitled to the same immunity from legal inquiry as the senator. The justices, however, have not extended similar protection to other congressional employees. In *Dombrowski v. Eastland* (1967), the Court ruled that the counsel for a Senate committee could be sued for conspiring to violate the civil rights of various activists, even though the committee chairman could not. In *Doe v. McMillan* (1973), the Court permitted parents to sue the public printer and superintendent of documents, who had publicly distributed a committee report that allegedly defamed and invaded the privacy of their children.

A more fundamental disagreement involves the range of activities protected by the Speech and Debate Clause. The Court recognized in *Kilbourn v. Thompson* (1881) that the clause covers not only debate within Congress but also all things "generally done in a session of the House by one of its members in relation to the business before it." But what activities constitute "legislative acts" and are immune from inquiry or prosecution? In *Gravel* the Court held that the clause did not foreclose inquiry into how Gravel obtained and arranged for the publication of the Pentagon Papers. Noting that the Constitution specified "Speech or Debate," the *Gravel* majority insisted that it protected only those activities directly related to such "internal" legislative functions as deliberation and voting. This distinction between internal and external functions also underlay the Court's ruling in *Hutchinson v. Proxmire* (1979). The majority in *Hutchinson* concluded that, although the clause protected speeches on the Senate floor in which Senator William Proxmire attacked a government agency's funding of allegedly worthless research, he could be sued for libel for reproducing those speeches in a newsletter to his constituents. The dissenters argued that legislators in a representative government have a responsibility to inform the electorate about governmental operations, and publication of material introduced in congressional hearings and of speeches dealing with the expenditure of public funds is a legitimate and appropriate means of fulfilling this responsibility, and so, they argued, is protected by the Speech and Debate Clause.

Bribery prosecutions of members of Congress have also raised Speech and Debate Clause issues. Because the clause protects both speeches delivered in Congress and the motivations for making them, the Court has held that such speeches and motivations cannot be used in establishing criminal violations. However, a prosecutor could introduce evidence at trial that a member of Congress had taken a bribe, because the clause "does not prohibit inquiry into activities that are casually or incidentally related to legislative affairs but not part of the process itself."[5] This interpretation has blocked members of Congress from using the Speech and Debate Clause as a shield for corruption.

Congressional Investigations

Since 1792, when the House of Representatives appointed a committee to inquire into General St. Clair's defeat in battle by a Native American tribe, congressional committees have conducted investigations to gather information for legislation, to oversee the implementation of laws, to scrutinize the actions of the president and other members of the executive branch, or to pursue various other ends. The House of Representatives and the Senate grant most of their committees the power to hold hearings, to subpoena witnesses and materials, and to cite for contempt witnesses who refuse to cooperate. Committees can also grant immunity to reluctant witnesses, thereby compelling them to testify. Most investigations proceed without fanfare or dispute, furnishing Congress with the information it needs to discharge its constitutional responsibilities. Some, however, have excited great controversy and prompted allegations of constitutional violations.

The most controversial and contentious investigations during the twentieth century were conducted by the House Un-American Activities Committee (HUAC). HUAC's investigations into Communist subversion occurred during the late 1940s and 1950s, during the height of the Cold War between the United States and the Soviet Union. Empowered by the House to investigate subversive and un-American activities and propaganda, HUAC called more than 3,000 witnesses, many for questioning about their own or their acquaintances' political beliefs and affiliations. Some witnesses invoked the protection of the Fifth Amendment's privilege against self-incrimination and refused to testify. Others claimed that the committee's inquiries exceeded its legitimate authority and declined to appear before the committee or answer its questions. HUAC cited more than 140 uncooperative witnesses for contempt of Congress.[6]

In appealing their contempt convictions, witnesses asserted that the committee's inquiries were unconstitutional because they did not serve a valid legislative purpose. In making this claim, witnesses did not challenge Congress's power to investigate—the Supreme Court had recognized in *McGrain v. Daugherty* (1927) that the Necessary and Proper Clause authorized Congress to conduct investigations to secure the information it needed for wise legislation. But they insisted that if the power to investigate derives from the power to legislate, then investigations that do not further the process of legislation have no constitutional warrant. Such was the case, they charged, with HUAC's inquiries. The committee sought not to obtain information for legislation but to punish individuals by exposing their political beliefs, so its investigations were unconstitutional.

This argument enjoyed some success in *Watkins v. United States* (1957), in which the Court overturned the contempt conviction of a labor union official who refused to answer committee questions. Although *Watkins* rested on narrow grounds, Chief Justice Earl Warren pointedly noted that congressional committees had no power "to expose for the sake of exposure." Members of Congress responded not by reining in HUAC but by introducing bills to withdraw the Supreme Court's jurisdiction over congressional investigations. Although none of these bills became law, two years later the Supreme Court in *Barenblatt v. United States* (1959) retreated, rejecting the claim that HUAC's inquiries served no valid legislative purpose. The decisive consideration, the Court suggested, was not the motivation of individual committee members but the scope of Congress's legislative authority. As long as the subject under investigation was one on which Congress could legislate, the Court would assume that the investigation was designed to secure information for possible legislation. This willingness to infer a valid legislative purpose from the subject under investigation virtually eliminated the *McGrain* requirement as a check on investigations.

Some witnesses also protested that the committee's inquiries into political beliefs and affiliations violated their First Amendment rights of freedom of speech and freedom of association. In *Barenblatt,* however, the Court argued that these rights had to be balanced against the congressional committee's interest in obtaining information it needed to carry out its responsibilities. Applying this balancing test, the Court consistently upheld congressional inquiries against First Amendment challenges.

In sum, the Court's rulings on congressional investigations reveal a combination of deference and intervention. On the one hand, the Court has avoided directly confronting Congress by curtailing the scope of its power to investigate. On the other hand, it has reaffirmed that witnesses before Congress retain their constitutional rights; in *McGrain, Watkins,* and other cases, it indicated that it would police the activities of congressional committees.

NONLEGISLATIVE POWERS

Along with lawmaking responsibilities, the Constitution assigns to Congress the power of impeachment and important powers pertaining to the proposal and ratification of constitutional amendments.

Impeachment

Members of the executive and judicial branches can be removed from office upon impeachment by a majority vote in the House of Representatives and conviction by a two-thirds vote in the Senate. For most of the nation's history, the full membership of the Senate participated in impeachment trials. But during the 1980s, the Senate altered this procedure for impeachments of judges, so that a special bipartisan committee of twelve senators heard testimony and gathered evidence, with the full Senate convened only to hear final arguments, review the trial record, and vote on the articles of impeachment. When this new procedure was challenged in *Nixon v. United States* (1993), the Supreme Court ruled that it involved a "political question" not appropriate for judicial resolution. Some concurring justices denied that the case raised a political question but endorsed the Senate's new procedure as constitutional.

In assigning the impeachment power to Congress, the Framers generally followed English parliamentary practice, but they departed from it in two respects. Conviction by the House of Lords typically led to the imposition of criminal penalties, including death. Under the Constitution, however, impeachment and conviction carry only political penalties—removal from office and, if the Senate so votes, ineligibility for future office. By eliminating criminal sanctions, the Framers sought to overcome legislative reluctance to use impeachment to punish official misconduct and to ensure impeached officials a trial by jury in subsequent prosecutions for any criminal offenses. The Constitution also departed from English practice by limiting impeachable offenses to "Treason, Bribery, or other high Crimes and Misdemeanors." Parliament had used impeachment as a political weapon in its struggles with the Crown, but the Framers did not wish Congress to use the impeachment power to intimidate the executive. By specifying the grounds for impeachment and by defining treason in the Constitution (Article III, Section 3), they sought instead to create a check on executive misconduct that would not be subject to abuse.

Impeachment has been employed primarily to remove federal judges from office. Of the sixteen cases in which the Senate has sat as a court of impeachment, twelve targeted federal judges, and the only convictions were of seven judges, who were removed from office. However, attempts to impeach presidents—Andrew Johnson in 1868, Richard Nixon in 1974, and Bill Clinton in 1998–1999—aroused the greatest political and constitutional controversy. Conflict has focused on the constitutional grounds for impeachment, and in particular the definition of "high Crimes and Misdemeanors." Both political considerations and genuine uncertainty about the Framers' intent have fueled these debates.

During the effort to impeach President Nixon, conflict centered on whether the phrase *high Crimes and Misdemeanors* meant that only criminal acts qualified as impeachable offenses. The Constitutional Convention's rejection of "maladministration" as a ground for impeachment underscored the Framers' determination to prevent impeachments motivated solely by political disagreements. Yet the emphasis on "abuse or violation of some public trust" in *The Federalist,* No. 65, suggests that a criminal violation is not necessary for impeachment. This was the position taken by the House committee in recommending the impeachment of President Nixon.

The charges against President Clinton during his impeachment—perjury and obstruction of justice—were offenses under criminal law, so debate shifted to two other issues. The first was whether the offenses with which Clinton was charged were sufficiently serious to warrant impeachment. In 1989 Walter Nixon, a federal district court judge, had been impeached and convicted for perjury before a grand jury; Clinton's supporters, however, insisted that different standards should apply when the removal of the president was contemplated. The second issue was whether acts of private immorality, however reprehensible, could justify impeachment. Clinton's supporters contended that his sexual liaison with intern Monica Lewinsky was private, that it did not involve an "abuse or violation of some public trust," and thus could not be the basis for impeachment. Those favoring impeachment denied that the president's actions were private, insisting that the president has a constitutional responsibility, as the nation's chief law enforcement officer, to set a high standard of adherence to the law. The positions taken on these issues largely tracked partisan divisions within the House and Senate, with Republicans overwhelmingly voting for, and Democrats voting against, impeachment. President Clinton was acquitted of all charges.

It may be that no precise definition of *high Crimes and Misdemeanors* is possible. The Framers' concern about the proper forum for trying impeachments, as voiced in both the Constitutional Convention and *The Federalist,* suggests a recognition that ultimately these terms would be defined in the judgment of specific cases.

Constitutional Amendment

The Framers' experience with the Articles of Confederation, under which constitutional amendments required the approval of all thirteen states, revealed that making constitutional change too difficult could block needed reforms. Yet their experience with the "mutability" of state laws also cautioned against making amendment too easy. Under the Constitution, either Congress or a convention made up of delegates elected in the various

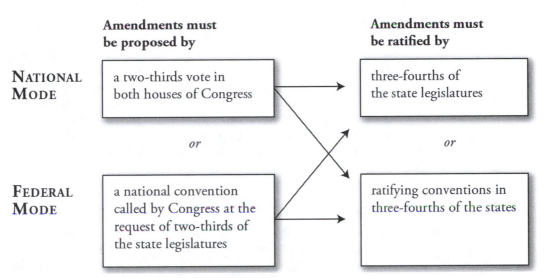

FIGURE 4.1 **Methods of Amending the Constitution**

states can propose amendments (Figure 4.1). Although the Framers expected that Congress would be more aware of defects in the constitutional system and thus more likely to propose remedies, they sought to ensure that it could not block popular demands for constitutional change.[7] The ratification process reflects the federal character of the American political system. It requires that amendments be supported not merely by a numerical majority but also by a geographically dispersed majority. As a final guarantee that constitutional changes would coincide with state public opinion, the Framers required ratification by state legislatures or specially elected conventions in each state. Thus far, only the Twenty-First Amendment, which repealed Prohibition, has been ratified by conventions in the states.

As of 2016, all constitutional amendments have been adopted by the less-cumbersome national mode, under which Congress proposes amendments for adoption and determines the mode of ratification. Because Article V leaves numerous procedural questions unresolved, Congress, acting under the Necessary and Proper Clause, has assumed a supervisory authority over the ratification process: recording state ratifications, determining when amendments have been adopted, and, in the twentieth century, establishing time limits for ratification. In *Dillon v. Gloss* (1921), the Supreme Court upheld Congress's power to establish a "reasonable" period for ratification. In *Coleman v. Miller* (1939), the justices refused to review what was "reasonable," asserting that the political-questions doctrine limits judicial review of Congress's actions.

Congress's exercise of its supervisory power over the amendment process can be controversial. When Congress in 1972 proposed the Equal Rights Amendment (ERA), which would have outlawed gender discrimination, it set a time limit of seven years for ratification. In 1978, as the deadline neared without three-quarters of the state legislatures having ratified the amendment, Congress extended the deadline for another thirty months. Noting that five state legislatures had voted to rescind their earlier ratifications, it also prohibited such action. Both of these steps raised serious constitutional issues, but because the extended deadline passed without the amendment being ratified, they ultimately had no effect on the Constitution.[8] More recently, Congress has recognized some limits on its supervisory power. In 1992, it accepted as valid the ratification of an amendment proposed by the First Congress, despite a two-century gap between the first state's and the last state's ratification.

SAFEGUARDING LEGISLATIVE POWER

Given the broad scope of national governmental concerns, it is not surprising that Congress has increasingly found it necessary to delegate power to the executive branch. In doing so, however, the legislators have often given executive officials broad discretion in defining policy aims and devising measures to achieve those aims—raising the concern that such delegations have produced a basic shift in the locus of national policy making. Whatever the accuracy of this assessment, questions remain about whether the Constitution limits Congress's power to delegate this authority and about the extent to which Congress can retain control over the direction of national policy.

Delegation of Power

Congressional delegations of power have occurred throughout American history. In 1813, the Supreme Court, in *Brig Aurora v. United States,* upheld a statute authorizing the president to lift restrictions on trade with France and Great Britain if those nations ceased interfering with American shipping. Twelve years later, in *Wayman v. Southard* (1825), the justices upheld a provision of the Judiciary Act of 1789 that directed the courts "to make and establish all necessary rules" for the transaction of judicial business.

In upholding these laws, the Court acknowledged that the Constitution limits congressional delegations: whatever powers are surrendered, the determination of basic policy must remain with Congress. The laws challenged in *Brig Aurora* and *Wayman* met this requirement by providing clear standards governing the use of the delegated powers. In *Brig Aurora,* Congress had specified the conditions under which the president was to act and the acts to be performed; in *Wayman,* it had decided the most important matters and merely authorized those operating under the law to "fill up the details." In contrast, a congressional delegation without adequate standards—one that allows executive officials to make basic policy—would constitute a transfer of legislative power to the executive branch and thus be unconstitutional.

The requirement that Congress furnish standards has not impeded broad congressional delegations of power. Not until 1935 did the Court invalidate a congressional delegation. Although in *Panama Refining Company v. Ryan* (1935) and *Schechter Poultry Corporation v. United States* (1935) it struck down provisions of the National Industrial Recovery Act, those cases marked both the zenith and the end of effective judicial supervision. Since 1935, the Supreme Court has not invalidated a single delegation of congressional power.

Mistretta v. United States (1989), a constitutional challenge to the Sentencing Reform Act of 1984, illustrates the Court's current approach in delegation cases. The act authorized the United States Sentencing Commission, made up of three federal judges and four lay members, to establish mandatory sentencing guidelines for all persons convicted in federal courts. The Court upheld this broad grant of power, concluding that this complicated task was precisely the sort appropriate for delegation and that Congress had furnished adequate standards to guide the commission in its work. In solitary dissent, Justice Antonin Scalia insisted that the act represented a dangerous innovation. Previously, the realization that delegations aggrandized the executive branch, "[Congress's] primary competitor for political power," had served as a check on Congress. By permitting Congress to delegate power outside the three branches of government, Scalia asserted, the Court in *Mistretta* removed the primary structural impediment to excessive congressional delegations. (In *United States v. Booker* [2005], the Supreme Court ruled that the statute making the sentencing guidelines mandatory was unconstitutional, not because of an excessive delegation but because the law infringed on the Sixth Amendment's guarantee of trial by jury.)

The Legislative Veto

Rather than limiting administrative policy making through precisely drawn statutes, Congress has sought to safeguard its constitutional position by supervising the exercise of delegated power. One weapon Congress has relied on is the legislative veto, under which it delegates power to the president or an administrative agency with the proviso that it can veto the exercise of that power. These conditional grants of power have taken various forms. The Budget and Impoundment Control Act of 1974 provided for a veto by congressional inaction: the president had to spend appropriated funds unless Congress affirmatively endorsed his failure to do so within forty-five days. The War Powers Resolution, in contrast, permitted Congress to terminate presidential commitments of troops by a concurrent resolution (one passed by both houses of Congress) not subject to presidential veto. Other statutes granted a single house of Congress—or even congressional committees—a veto over administrative regulations or actions of executive-branch officials.

Such a one-house veto figured in *Immigration and Naturalization Service v. Chadha* (1983), the Supreme Court's only ruling on the constitutionality of the legislative veto. Under the Immigration and Nationality Act, the attorney general was authorized to allow deportable aliens to remain in the country, but a single house of Congress could overturn the attorney general's decision by majority vote. This procedure, the Court ruled in *Chadha,* violated the Constitution. Although Chief Justice Warren Burger acknowledged in the opinion of the Court that the legislative veto might promote efficiency, he insisted that it contravened "explicit and unambiguous provisions of the Constitution" defining the respective roles of Congress and the president in legislating. Whereas Article I directs that laws be enacted by majority vote in each house, the legislative veto in *Chadha* allowed action that was legislative in character and effect by majority vote in only one house, thus contravening the constitutional requirement of bicameralism. Whereas the Presentment Clause required that all legislation be submitted to the president before becoming law, the legislative veto enabled Congress to take legislative action without the threat of a presidential veto. Thus, the legislative veto circumvented the procedures prescribed by the Constitution to ensure due deliberation, check ill-advised legislation, and maintain the separation of powers.

Justice Byron White noted in dissent that the Court's interpretation of the Presentment Clause doomed not just the one-house veto in *Chadha* but "nearly 200 other statutory provisions in which Congress has reserved a legislative veto." Yet congressional efforts to exert control over the broad powers it delegates to the executive branch did not end with *Chadha,* as Congress has devised various ingenious mechanisms for maintaining control. For example, if an executive-branch agency uses the broad power delegated to it to adopt a regulation that offends Congress, legislators may attach language to an appropriations bill denying the use of the funds to implement the regulation, confident that the president would not veto the bill because of this provision. Congress has also by statute required executive agencies to notify congressional committees before implementing a program, in the expectation that the agency would not proceed if the committee that oversaw it expressed disapproval. Finally, Congress developed a variation on the legislative veto that is arguably consistent with *Chadha.* Under this procedure, Congress grants broad discretion to executive officials with the proviso that a congressional committee retains the power to veto exercises of that discretion. Given the Court's ruling in *Chadha,* this veto is not legally binding. Nevertheless, executive officials typically agree to abide by the veto, lest Congress reduce their flexibility of action by a less-generous delegation of power. Thus, despite *Chadha,* the legislative veto—and congressional efforts to continue broad delegations of power without losing control over policy making—is far from dead.

CONCLUSIONS

Several conclusions flow from our review of the constitutional provisions defining Congress's powers and regulating their exercise. First, Congress's constitutional powers are very broad. In addition to conferring on Congress important enumerated powers, the Constitution, through the Necessary and Proper Clause, provides extensive additional powers that allow Congress the necessary flexibility to fulfill its constitutional responsibilities. In addition, the Supreme Court, by foreclosing review through the "political-questions doctrine," has acknowledged Congress's broad discretion in the exercise of such nonlegislative powers as supervising the amendment process and hearing impeachments.

Second, the Constitution has provided Congress with important auxiliary powers and privileges that enable it to fulfill its constitutional responsibilities more effectively. Not only does the Constitution expressly confer on members of Congress various immunities that safeguard the independence of the legislative branch, but the Supreme Court has also recognized that the Constitution permits Congress to obtain necessary information for legislation by conducting investigations and punishing witnesses who refuse to supply pertinent information. Yet the Court's interpretation of these auxiliary powers and privileges offers considerable contrast. On the one hand, the justices have attempted to regulate congressional investigations without imposing requirements that would curtail the scope of congressional investigatory authority. On the other hand, in construing the Speech and Debate Clause, they have been much more willing to define the privilege narrowly and to rule against members of Congress.

Finally, the Constitution's generous grants of power have not ensured that Congress will play the decisive role in defining government policy. In recent decades, the executive branch has increasingly dominated policy development. The Supreme Court's permissive interpretation of the nondelegation doctrine has facilitated the transfer of responsibility to the executive branch. Congress has attempted to maintain control less by curtailing the scope of its delegations of power than by regulating the use of delegated power. The Supreme Court's invalidation of the legislative veto in *Chadha* deprived Congress of one weapon for overseeing the executive branch. Congress, however, has shown considerable ingenuity in developing other mechanisms for asserting its control over public policy.

NOTES

1. For the most forceful attacks on *McCulloch* and Marshall's responses, see Gerald Gunther, ed., *John Marshall's Defense of* McCulloch v. Maryland (Stanford, CA: Stanford University Press, 1969).

2. Several constitutional provisions safeguard legislative independence. Each house of Congress can choose its own officers (Article I, Section 2, Paragraph 5, and Section 3, Paragraph 5) and can determine the "Elections, Returns, and Qualifications of its own Members" (Article I, Section 5, Paragraph 1). Each house can also determine the rules of its proceedings and discipline or expel members (Article I, Section 5, Paragraph 2). Finally, members of Congress are generally immune from arrest during their attendance in Congress.

3. As a result of a compromise at the Constitutional Convention, the population base for

determining representation in the House of Representatives originally included all free inhabitants and three-fifths of all slaves but excluded "all Indians not taxed."

4. The Arkansas law imposed term limits indirectly, denying a place on the ballot to representatives who had served three or more terms and senators who had served two or more terms. In theory, legislators could seek reelection as write-in candidates, but the Court in Thornton concluded that, given the unlikelihood of success of write-in candidacies, the Arkansas law operated as a term limit.

5. United States v. Brewster, 408 U.S. 501, 528 (1972).

6. The figures in this paragraph are drawn from Carl Beck's *Contempt of Congress: A Study of the Prosecutions Initiated by the Committee on Un-American*

Activities (New Orleans: Hauser Press, 1959), appx. B, 217–241.

7. Alexander Hamilton emphasized in *The Federalist*, No. 85, that when two-thirds of the states apply to Congress to call a convention for proposing amendments, Congress has no discretion and must do so.

8. A federal district court ruled in *Idaho v. Freeman*, 529 F. Supp. 1107 (1981), that the ERA deadline extension and prohibition on rescission were unconstitutional. The Supreme Court stayed the ruling and granted certiorari, but the deadline for ratification passed before the Court ruled in the case, rendering it moot.

SELECTED READINGS

The Federalist, Nos. 33, 44, 52–66, 85.

Ackerman, Bruce A. *We the People: Foundations.* Cambridge, MA: Belknap Press of Harvard University Press, 1991.

Barber, Sotirios. *Welfare and the Constitution.* Princeton, NJ: Princeton University Press, 2003.

Baude, William. "Sharing the Necessary and Proper Clause," *Harvard Law Review Forum* 128 (2014): 39–48.

Chafetz, Josh. *Democracy's Privileged Few: Legislative Privilege and Democratic Norms in the British and American Constitutions.* New Haven, CT: Yale University Press, 2007.

Craig, Barbara H. *Chadha: The Story of an Epic Constitutional Struggle.* New York: Oxford University Press, 1988.

Devins, Neal, and Keith E. Whittington, eds. *Congress and the Constitution.* Durham, NC: Duke University Press, 2005.

Fisher, Louis. *Constitutional Conflicts between Congress and the President.* 6th ed. Lawrence: University Press of Kansas, 2014.

Gerhardt, Michael J. *The Federal Impeachment Process: A Constitutional and Historical Analysis.* 2nd ed. Chicago: University of Chicago Press, 2000.

Guide to Congress. 10th ed. Washington, DC: CQ Press, 2012.

Hamilton, James. *The Power to Probe: A Study in Congressional Investigations.* New York: Random House, 1976.

Korn, Jessica. *The Power of Separation: American Constitutionalism and the Myth of the Legislative Veto.* Princeton, NJ: Princeton University Press, 1996.

Kyvig, David E. *Explicit and Authentic Acts: Amending the U.S. Constitution, 1776–1995.* Lawrence: University Press of Kansas, 1996.

Lawson, Gary, Geoffrey P. Miller, Robert G. Natelson, and Guy I. Seidman. *The Origins of the Necessary and Proper Clause.* New York: Cambridge University Press, 2010.

Levinson, Sanford, ed. *Responding to Imperfection: The Theory and Practice of Constitutional Amendment.* Princeton, NJ: Princeton University Press, 1995.

Manning, John F. "The Supreme Court, 2013 Term–Foreword: The Means of Constitutional Power," *Harvard Law Review* 128 (2014): 1–84.

Pickerill, J. Mitchell. *Constitutional Deliberation in Congress: The Impact of Judicial Review in a Separated System.* Durham, NC: Duke University Press, 2004.

Schoenbrod, David. *Power Without Responsibility: How Congress Abuses the People Through Delegation.* New Haven, CT: Yale University Press, 1993.

Vile, John R. *Encyclopedia of Constitutional Amendments, Proposed Amendments, and Amending Issues.* 2nd ed. Santa Barbara, CA: ABC-Clio, 2003.

McCulloch v. Maryland
17 U.S. (Wheat.) 316 (1819)

In 1816, Congress chartered the Second Bank of the United States, one branch of which was established in Baltimore the next year. In 1818, the Maryland Legislature passed a statute taxing "all banks or branches thereof" operating in Maryland but not chartered by the state. The act levied a tax of approximately 2 percent of the value of all notes issued or, alternatively, an annual fee of $15,000; it also provided for a $500 penalty for every violation. When James McCulloch, cashier of the Baltimore branch, issued notes and refused to pay the tax, suit was brought on behalf of the State of Maryland to recover the penalties. A judgment was rendered against McCulloch in lower court and affirmed by the Maryland Court of Appeals, the state's highest court. From there, the case was brought to the United States Supreme Court by a writ of error. Opinion of the Court: <u>Marshall</u>, *Washington, Johnson, Livingston, Todd, Duval, Story.*

THE CHIEF JUSTICE delivered the opinion of the Court.

In the case now to be determined, the defendant, a sovereign State, denies the obligation of a law enacted by the legislature of the Union, and the plaintiff, on his part, contests the validity of an act which has been passed by the legislature of that State. The constitution of our country, in its most interesting and vital parts, is to be considered; the conflicting powers of the government of the Union and of its members, as marked in that constitution, are to be discussed; and an opinion given, which may essentially influence the great operations of the government. No tribunal can approach such a question without a deep sense of its importance, and of the awful responsibility involved in the decision. But it must be decided peacefully, or remain a source of hostile legislation, perhaps of hostility of a still more serious nature, and if it is to be so decided, by this tribunal alone can the decision be made. On the Supreme Court of the United States has the constitution of our country devolved this important duty.

The first question made in the cause is, has Congress power to incorporate a bank? The government of the Union is acknowledged by all to be one of enumerated powers. That principle is now universally admitted. But the question respecting the extent of the powers actually granted, is perpetually arising, and will probably continue to arise, as long as our system shall exist. In discussing these questions, the conflicting powers of the general and State governments must be brought into view, and the supremacy of their respective laws, when they are in opposition, must be settled.

It has been truly said, that this can scarcely be considered as an open question, entirely unprejudiced by the former proceedings of the nation respecting it. The principle now contested was introduced at a very early period of our history, has been recognized by many successive legislatures, and has been acted upon by the judicial department, in cases of peculiar delicacy, as a law of undoubted obligation.

It will not be denied, that a bold and daring usurpation might be resisted, after an acquiescence still longer and more complete than this. But it is conceived that a doubtful question, one on which human reason may pause, and the human judgment be suspended, in the decision of which the great principles of liberty are not concerned, but the respective powers of those who are equally representatives of the people, are to be adjusted; if not put at rest by the practice of the government, ought to receive a considerable impression from that practice. An exposition of the constitution, deliberately established by legislative acts, on the faith of which an immense property has been advanced, ought not to be lightly disregarded.

The power now contested was exercised by the first Congress elected under the present constitution. The bill for incorporating the bank of the United States did not steal upon an unsuspecting legislature, and pass unobserved. Its principle was completely understood, and was opposed with equal zeal and ability. After being resisted, first in the fair and open field of debate, and afterwards in the executive cabinet, with as much persevering talent as any measure has ever experienced, and being supported by arguments which convinced minds as pure and as intelligent as this country can boast, it became a law. The original act was permitted to expire; but a short experience of the embarrassments to which the refusal to revive it exposed the government, convinced those who were most prejudiced against the measure of its necessity, and induced the passage of the present law. It would require no ordinary share of intrepidity to assert that a measure adopted under these circumstances was a bold and plain usurpation, to which the constitution gave no countenance.

If any one proposition could command the universal assent of mankind, we might expect it would be this—that the government of the Union, though limited in its powers, is supreme within its sphere of action. This would seem to result necessarily from its nature. It is the government of all; its powers are delegated by all; it represents all, and acts for all. The nation, on those subjects on which it can act, must necessarily bind its component parts. But this question is not left to mere reason: The people have, in express terms, decided it, by saying, "this constitution, and the laws of the United States, which shall be made in pursuance thereof," "shall be the supreme law of the land," and by requiring that the members of the State legislatures, and the officers of the executive and judicial departments of the States, shall take the oath of fidelity to it.

The government of the United States, then, though limited in its powers, is supreme; and its laws, when made in pursuance of the constitution, form the supreme law of the land, "any thing in the constitution or laws of any State to the contrary notwithstanding."

Among the enumerated powers, we do not find that of establishing a bank or creating a corporation. But there is no phrase in the instrument which, like the articles of confederation, excludes incidental or implied powers; and which requires that every thing granted shall be expressly and minutely described. Even the 10th amendment, which was framed for the purpose of quieting the excessive jealousies which had been excited, omits the word "expressly," and declares only that the powers "not delegated to the United States, nor prohibited to the States, are reserved to the States or to the people;" thus leaving the question, whether the particular power which may become the sub-

ject of contest has been delegated to the one government, or prohibited to the other, to depend on a fair construction of the whole instrument. The men who drew and adopted this amendment had experienced the embarrassments resulting from the insertion of this word in the articles of confederation, and probably omitted it to avoid those embarrassments.

A constitution, to contain an accurate detail of all the subdivisions of which its great powers will admit, and of all the means by which they may be carried into execution, would partake of the prolixity of a legal code, and could scarcely be embraced by the human mind. It would probably never be understood by the public. Its nature, therefore, requires, that only its great outlines should be marked, its important objects designated, and the minor ingredients which compose those objects be deduced from the nature of the objects themselves. That this idea was entertained by the framers of the American constitution, is not only to be inferred from the nature of the instrument, but from the language. Why else were some of the limitations, found in the ninth section of the 1st article, introduced? It is also, in some degree, warranted by their having omitted to use any restrictive term which might prevent its receiving a fair and just interpretation. In considering this question, then, we must never forget, that it is *a constitution* we are expounding.

Although, among the enumerated powers of government, we do not find the word "bank" or "incorporation," we find the great powers to lay and collect taxes; to borrow money; to regulate commerce; to declare and conduct a war; and to raise and support armies and navies. The sword and the purse, all the external relations, and no inconsiderable portion of the industry of the nation, are entrusted to its government. It can never be pretended that these vast powers draw after them others of inferior importance, merely because they are inferiors. Such an idea can never be advanced. But it may with great reason be contended, that a government, entrusted with such ample powers, on the due execution of which the happiness and prosperity of the nation so vitally depends, must also be entrusted with ample means for their execution. The power being given, it is the interest of the nation to facilitate its execution. It can never be their interest, and cannot be presumed to have been their intention, to clog and embarrass its execution by withholding the most appropriate means. Throughout this vast republic revenue is to be collected and expended, armies are to be marched and supported. The exigencies of the nation may require that the treasure raised in the north should be transported to the south, that raised in the east conveyed to the west, or that this order should be reversed. Is that construction of the constitution to be preferred which would render these operations difficult, hazardous, and expensive? Can we adopt that construction, (unless the words imperiously require it), which would impute to the framers of that instrument, when granting these powers for the public good, the intention of impeding their exercise by withholding a choice of means? If, indeed, such be the mandate of the constitution, we have only to obey; but that instrument does not profess to enumerate the means by which the powers it confers may be executed; nor does it prohibit the creation of a corporation, if the existence of such a being be essential to the beneficial exercise of those powers. It is, then, the subject of fair inquiry, how far such means may be employed.

It is not denied, that the powers given to the government imply the ordinary means of execution. That, for example, of raising revenue, and applying it to national purposes, is admitted to imply the power of conveying money from place to place, as the exigencies of the nation may require, and of employing the usual means of conveyance. But it is denied that the government has its choice of means; or, that it may employ the most convenient means, if, to employ them, it be necessary to erect a corporation.

But the constitution of the United States has not left the right of Congress to employ the necessary means, for the execution of the powers conferred on the government, to general reasoning. To its enumeration of powers is added that of making "all laws which shall be necessary and proper, for carrying into execution the foregoing powers, and all other powers vested by this constitution, in the government of the United States, or in any department thereof."

The counsel for the State of Maryland have urged various arguments, to prove that this clause, though in terms a grant of power, is not so in effect; but is really restrictive of the general right, which might otherwise be implied, of selecting means for executing the enumerated powers. The argument on which most reliance is placed, is drawn from the peculiar language of this clause. Congress is not empowered by it to make all laws, which may have relation to the powers conferred on the government, but such only as may be "*necessary and proper*" for carrying them into execution. The word "*necessary*," is considered as controlling the whole sentence, and as limiting the right to pass laws for the execution of the granted powers, to such as are indispensable, and without which the power would be nugatory. That it excludes the choice of means, and leaves to Congress, in each case, that only which is most direct and simple.

Is it true, that this is the sense in which the word "necessary" is always used? Does it always import an absolute physical necessity, so strong, that one thing, to which another may be termed necessary, cannot exist without that other? We think it does not. To employ the means necessary to an end, is generally understood as employing any means calculated to produce the end, and not as being confined to those single means, without which the end would be entirely unattainable. Almost all compositions contain words, which, taken in their rigorous sense, would convey a meaning different from that which is obviously intended.

It is essential to just construction, that many words which import something excessive, should be understood in a more mitigated sense—in that sense which common usage justifies. The word "necessary" is of this description. It admits of all degrees of comparison; and is often connected with other words, which increase or diminish the impression the mind receives of the urgency it imports. A thing may be necessary, very necessary, absolutely or indispensably necessary. To no mind would the same idea be conveyed, by these several phrases. This comment on the word is well illustrated by the passage cited at the bar, from the 10th section of the 1st article of the constitution. It is, we think, impossible to compare the sentence which prohibits a State from laying "imposts, or duties on imports or exports, except what may be *absolutely necessary* for executing its inspection laws," with that which authorizes Congress "to make all laws which shall be necessary and proper for carrying into execution" the powers of the general government, without feeling a conviction that the convention understood itself to change materially the meaning of the word "necessary," by prefixing the word "absolutely." This provision is made in a constitution intended to endure for ages to come, and, consequently, to be adapted to the various *crises* of human affairs. To have prescribed the means by which government should, in all future time, execute its powers, would have been to change, entirely, the character of the instrument, and give it the properties of a legal code. To have declared that the best means shall not be used, but those alone without which the power given would be nugatory, would have been to deprive the legislature of the capacity to avail itself of experience, to exercise its reason, and to accommodate its legislation to circumstances. If we apply this principle of construction to any of the powers of the government, we shall find it so pernicious in its operation that we shall be compelled to discard it.

Take, for example, the power "to establish post offices and post roads." This power is executed by the single act of making the establishment. But, from this has been inferred the power and duty of carrying the mail along the post road, from one post office to another. And, from this implied power, has again been inferred the right to punish those who steal letters from the post office, or rob the mail. It may be said, with some plausibility, that the right to carry the mail, and to punish those who rob it, is not indispensably necessary to the establishment of a post office and post road. This right is indeed essential to the beneficial exercise of the power, but not indispensably necessary to its existence. So, of the punishment of the crimes of stealing or falsifying a record or process of a Court of the United States, or of perjury in such Court. To punish these offences is certainly conducive to the due administration of justice. But courts may exist, and may decide the causes brought before them, though such crimes escape punishment.

If this limited construction of the word "necessary" must be abandoned in order to punish, whence is derived the rule which would reinstate it, when the government would carry its powers into execution by means not vindictive in their nature? If the word "necessary" means "needful," "requisite," "essential," "conducive to," in order to let in the power of punishment for the infraction of law; why is it not equally comprehensive when required to authorize the use of means which facilitate the execution of the powers of government without the infliction of punishment?

But the argument which most conclusively demonstrates the error of the construction contended for by the counsel for the State of Maryland, is founded on the intention of the Convention, as manifested in the whole clause. This clause, as construed by the State of Maryland, would abridge, and almost annihilate this useful and necessary right of the legislature to select its means. That this could not be intended, is, we should think, had it not been already controverted, too apparent for controversy. We think so for the following reasons.

1st. The clause is placed among the powers of Congress, not among the limitations on those powers. *2nd.* Its terms purport to enlarge, not to diminish the powers vested in the government. It purports to be an additional power, not a restriction on those already granted. No reason has been, or can be assigned for thus concealing an intention to narrow the discretion of the national legislature under words which purport to enlarge it. The framers of the constitution wished its adoption, and well knew that it would be endangered by its strength, not by its weakness. Had they been capable of using language which would convey to the eye one idea, and, after deep reflection, impress on the mind another, they would rather have disguised the grant of power, than its limitation. If, then, their intention had been, by this clause, to restrain the free use of means which might otherwise have been implied, that intention would have been inserted in another place, and would have been expressed in terms resembling these. "In carrying into execution the foregoing powers, and all others," &c. "no laws shall be passed but such as are necessary and proper." Had the intention been to make this clause restrictive, it would unquestionably have been so in form as well as in effect.

We admit, as all must admit, that the powers of the government are limited, and that its limits are not to be transcended. But we think the sound construction of the constitution must allow to the national legislature that discretion, with respect to the means by which the powers it confers are to be carried into execution, which will enable that body to perform the high duties assigned to it, in the manner most beneficial to the people. Let the end be legitimate, let it be within the scope of the constitution, and all means which are appropriate, which are plainly adapted to that end, which are not prohibited, but consist with the letter and spirit of the constitution, are constitutional.

Should Congress, in the execution of its powers, adopt measures which are prohibited by the constitution; or should Congress, under the pretext of executing its powers, pass laws for the accomplishment of objects not entrusted to the government; it would become the painful duty of this tribunal, should a case requiring such a decision come before it, to say that such an act was not the law of the land. But where the law is not prohibited, and is really calculated to effect any of the objects entrusted to the government, to undertake here to inquire into the degree of its necessity, would be to pass the line which circumscribes the judicial department, and to tread on legislative ground. This court disclaims all pretensions to such a power.

After the most deliberate consideration, it is the unanimous and decided opinion of this Court, that the act to incorporate the Bank of the United States is a law made in pursuance of the constitution and is a part of the supreme law of the land.

We proceed to inquire—Whether the State of Maryland may, without violating the constitution, tax that branch?

The argument on the part of the State of Maryland, is, not that the States may directly resist a law of Congress, but that they may exercise their acknowledged powers upon it, and that the constitution leaves them this right in the confidence that they will not

abuse it. That the power to tax involves the power to destroy; that the power to destroy may defeat and render useless the power to create; that there is a plain repugnance, in conferring on one government a power to control the constitutional measures of another, which other, with respect to those very measures, is declared to be supreme over that which exerts the control, are propositions not to be denied. But all inconsistencies are to be reconciled by the magic of the word CONFIDENCE. Taxation, it is said, does not necessarily and unavoidably destroy. To carry it to the excess of destruction would be an abuse, to presume which, would banish that confidence which is essential to all government.

But is this a case of confidence? Would the people of any one State trust those of another with a power to control the most insignificant operations of their State government? We know they would not. Why, then, should we suppose that the people of any one State should be willing to trust those of another with a power to control the operations of a government to which they have confided their most important and most valuable interests? In the legislature of the Union alone, are all represented. The legislature of the Union alone, therefore, can be trusted by the people with the power of controlling measures which concern all, in the confidence that it will not be abused. This, then, is not a case of confidence, and we must consider it as it really is.

If we apply the principle for which the State of Maryland contends, to the constitution generally, we shall find it capable of changing totally the character of that instrument. We shall find it capable of arresting all the measures of the government, and of prostrating it at the foot of the States. The American people have declared their constitution, and the laws made in pursuance thereof, to be supreme; but this principle would transfer the supremacy, in fact, to the States. It has also been insisted, that, as the power of taxation in the general and State governments is acknowledged to be concurrent, every argument which would sustain the right of the general government to tax banks chartered by the States, will equally sustain the right of the States to tax banks chartered by the general government.

But the two cases are not on the same reason. The people of all the States have created the general government, and have conferred upon it the general power of taxation. The people of all the States, and the States themselves, are represented in Congress, and, by their representatives, exercise this power. When they tax the chartered institutions of the States, they tax their constituents; and these taxes must be uniform. But, when a State taxes the operations of the government of the United States, it acts upon institutions created, not by their own constituents, but by people over whom they claim no control. It acts upon the measures of a government created by others as well as themselves, for the benefit of others in common with themselves. The difference is that which always exists, and always must exist, between the action of the whole on a part, and the action of a part on the whole—between the laws of a government declared to be supreme, and those of a government which, when in opposition to those laws, is not supreme.

The Court has bestowed on this subject its most deliberate consideration. The result is a conviction that the States have no power, by taxation or otherwise, to retard, impede, burden, or in any manner control, the operations of the constitutional laws enacted by Congress to carry into execution the powers vested in the general government. This is, we think, the unavoidable consequence of that supremacy which the constitution has declared. We are unanimously of opinion, that the law passed by the legislature of Maryland, imposing a tax on the Bank of the United States, is unconstitutional and void.

United States v. Comstock
561 U.S. 126 (2010)

Federal law (18 U. S. C. §4248) allows a district court to order the civil commitment of a mentally ill, sexually dangerous federal prisoner beyond the date he would otherwise be released. Under the statute, the government must certify to a federal judge that a prisoner (1) has previously "engaged or attempted to engage in sexually violent conduct or child molestation," (2) currently "suffers from a serious mental illness, abnormality, or disorder," and (3) "as a result of" that mental illness, abnormality, or disorder is "sexually dangerous to others," in that "he would have serious difficulty in refraining from sexually violent conduct or child molestation if released." When such a certification is filed, the statute automatically stays the individual's release from prison. In this case, the government instituted civil-commitment proceedings against Comstock and four other prisoners. Each prisoner filed a motion to dismiss the civil-commitment proceeding on the ground that, in enacting the statute, Congress exceeded its powers under the Necessary and Proper Clause. Agreeing, the District Court granted dismissal, the Fourth Circuit affirmed, and the Supreme Court granted certiorari. Opinion of the Court: Breyer, Roberts, Stevens, Ginsburg, Sotomayor. Concurring in the judgment: Kennedy, Alito. Dissenting opinion: Thomas, Scalia (in part).

JUSTICE BREYER delivered the opinion of the Court.

A federal civil-commitment statute authorizes the Department of Justice to detain a mentally ill, sexually dangerous federal prisoner beyond the date the prisoner would otherwise be released. We have previously examined similar statutes enacted under state law to determine whether they violate the Due Process Clause. But here we ask whether the Federal Government has the authority under Article I of the Constitution to enact this federal civil-commitment program or whether its doing so falls beyond the reach of a government of enumerated powers. We conclude that the Constitution grants Congress the authority to enact §4248 as "necessary and proper for carrying into Execution" the powers "vested by" the "Constitution in the Government of the United States."

II

We base this conclusion on five considerations, taken together.

First, the Necessary and Proper Clause grants Congress broad authority to enact federal legislation. Nearly 200 years ago, this Court stated that the Federal "Government is acknowledged by all to be one of enumerated powers," *McCulloch*, which means that "every law enacted by Congress must be based on one or more of" those powers, *United States* v. *Morrison* (2000). But, at the same time, "a government, entrusted with such" powers "must also be entrusted with ample means for their execution." *McCulloch.* Accordingly, the Necessary and Proper Clause makes clear that the Constitution's grants of specific federal legislative authority are accompanied by broad power to enact laws that are "convenient, or useful" or "conducive" to the authority's "beneficial exercise." Chief Justice Marshall emphasized that the word "necessary" does not mean "absolutely necessary." In language that has come to define the scope of the Necessary and Proper Clause, he wrote: "Let the end be legitimate, let it be within the scope of the constitution, and all means which are appropriate, which are plainly adapted to that end, which are not prohibited, but consist with the letter and spirit of the constitution, are constitutional."

We have since made clear that, in determining whether the Necessary and Proper Clause grants Congress the legislative authority to enact a particular federal statute, we look to see whether the statute constitutes a means that is rationally related to the implementation of a constitutionally enumerated power. *Sabri* v. *United States* (2004). We have also recognized that the Constitution "addresse[s]" the "choice of means" "primarily. . . . . . to the judgment of Congress. If it can be seen that the means adopted are really calculated to attain the end, the degree of their necessity, the extent to which they conduce to the end, the closeness of the relationship between the means adopted and the end to be attained, are matters for congressional determination alone." *Burroughs* v. *United States* (1934). Thus, the Constitution, which nowhere speaks explicitly about the creation of federal crimes beyond those related to "counterfeiting," "treason," or "Piracies and Felonies committed on the high Seas" or "against the Law of Nations," Art. I, §8, cls. 6, 10; Art. III, §3, nonetheless grants Congress

broad authority to create such crimes. And Congress routinely exercises its authority to enact criminal laws in furtherance of, for example, its enumerated powers to regulate interstate and foreign commerce, to enforce civil rights, to spend funds for the general welfare, to establish federal courts, to establish post offices, to regulate bankruptcy, to regulate naturalization, and so forth.

Similarly, Congress, in order to help ensure the enforcement of federal criminal laws enacted in furtherance of its enumerated powers, "can cause a prison to be erected at any place within the jurisdiction of the United States, and direct that all persons sentenced to imprisonment under the laws of the United States shall be confined there." *Ex parte Karstendick* (1876). Moreover, Congress, having established a prison system, can enact laws that seek to ensure that system's safe and responsible administration by, for example, requiring prisoners to receive medical care and educational training, and can also ensure the safety of the prisoners, prison workers and visitors, and those in surrounding communities by, for example, creating further criminal laws governing entry, exit, and smuggling, and by employing prison guards to ensure discipline and security. Neither Congress' power to criminalize conduct, nor its power to imprison individuals who engage in that conduct, nor its power to enact laws governing prisons and prisoners, is explicitly mentioned in the Constitution. But Congress nonetheless possesses broad authority to do each of those things in the course of "carrying into Execution" the enumerated powers "vested by" the "Constitution in the Government of the United States."

Second, the civil-commitment statute before us constitutes a modest addition to a set of federal prison-related mental-health statutes that have existed for many decades. We recognize that even a longstanding history of related federal action does not demonstrate a statute's constitutionality. A history of involvement can nonetheless be "helpful in reviewing the substance of a congressional statutory scheme," *Gonzales* [*v. Raich*]; and, in particular, the reasonableness of the relation between the new statute and pre-existing federal interests.

Here, Congress has long been involved in the delivery of mental health care to federal prisoners, and has long provided for their civil commitment. In 2006, Congress enacted the particular statute before us. It differs from earlier statutes in that it focuses directly upon persons who, due to a mental illness, are sexually dangerous. Notably, many of these individuals were likely already subject to civil commitment under §4246, which, since 1949, has authorized the postsentence detention of federal prisoners who suffer from a mental illness and who are thereby dangerous (whether sexually or otherwise). Aside from its specific focus on sexually dangerous persons, §4248 is similar to the provisions first enacted in 1949. In that respect, it is a modest addition to a longstanding federal statutory framework.

Third, Congress reasonably extended its longstanding civil-commitment system to cover mentally ill and sexually dangerous persons who are already in federal custody, even if doing so detains them beyond the termination of their criminal sentence. For one thing, the Federal Government is the custodian of its prisoners. As federal custodian, it has the constitutional power to act in order to protect nearby (and other) communities from the danger federal prisoners may pose. If a federal prisoner is infected with a communicable disease that threatens others, surely it would be "necessary and proper" for the Federal Government to take action, pursuant to its role as federal custodian, to refuse (at least until the threat diminishes) to release that individual among the general public, where he might infect others. And if confinement of such an individual is a "necessary and proper" thing to do, then how could it not be similarly "necessary and proper" to confine an individual whose mental illness threatens others to the same degree?

Moreover, §4248 is "reasonably adapted" to Congress' power to act as a responsible federal custodian (a power that rests, in turn, upon federal criminal statutes that legitimately seek to implement constitutionally enumerated authority. Congress could have reasonably concluded that federal inmates who suffer from a mental illness that causes them to "have serious difficulty in refraining from sexually violent conduct," would pose an especially high danger to the public if released. And Congress could also have reasonably concluded that a reasonable number of such individuals would likely *not* be detained by the States if released from federal custody, in part because the Federal Government itself severed their claim to "legal residence in any State" by incarcerating them in remote federal prisons. Here Congress' desire to address the specific challenges identified above, taken together with its responsibilities as a federal custodian, supports the conclusion that §4248 satisfies "review for means-end rationality," *i.e.*, that it satisfies the Constitution's insistence that a federal statute represent a rational means for implementing a constitutional grant of legislative authority.

Fourth, the statute properly accounts for state interests. Respondents and the dissent contend that §4248 violates the Tenth Amendment because it "invades the province of state sovereignty" in an area typically left to state control. But the Tenth Amendment's text is clear: "The powers *not delegated to the United States* by the Constitution, nor prohibited by it to the States, are reserved to the States respectively, or to the people." The powers "delegated to the United States by the Constitution" include those specifically enumerated powers listed in Article I along with the implementation authority granted by the Necessary and Proper Clause. Virtually by definition, these powers are not powers that the Constitution "reserved to the States." If a power is delegated to Congress in the Constitution, the Tenth Amendment expressly disclaims any reservation of that power to the States."

Nor does this statute invade state sovereignty or otherwise improperly limit the scope of "powers that remain with the States." To the contrary, it requires *accommodation* of state interests: The Attorney General must inform the State in which the federal prisoner "is domiciled or was tried" that he is detaining someone with respect to whom those States may wish to assert their authority, and he must encourage those States to assume custody of the individual. He must also immediately "release" that person "to the appropriate official of" either State "if such State will assume responsibility." And either State has the right, at any time, to assert its authority over the individual, which will prompt the individual's immediate transfer to State custody.

Fifth, the links between §4248 and an enumerated Article I power are not too attenuated. Respondents argue that, when legislating pursuant to the Necessary and Proper Clause, Congress' authority can be no more than one step removed from a specifically enumerated power. But this argument is irreconcilable with our precedents. Take *Greenwood v. United States* (1956) as an example. In that case we upheld the (likely indefinite) civil commitment of a mentally incompetent federal defendant who was accused of robbing a United States Post Office. The underlying enumerated Article I power was the power to "Establish Post Offices and Post Roads." But, as Chief Justice Marshall recognized in *McCulloch*, "the power 'to establish post offices and post roads' . . . is executed by the single act of *making* the establishment . . . [F]rom this has been inferred the power and duty of *carrying* the mail along the post road, from one post office to another. And, from this *implied* power, has *again* been inferred the right to *punish* those who steal letters from the post office, or rob the mail." And, as we have explained, from the implied power to punish we have *further* inferred both the power to imprison and the federal civil-commitment power.

Our necessary and proper jurisprudence contains multiple examples of similar reasoning. Nor need we fear that our holding today confers on Congress a general "police power, which the Founders denied the National Government and reposed in the States." As the Solicitor General repeatedly confirmed at oral argument, §4248 is narrow in scope. It has been applied to only a small fraction of federal prisoners. Indeed, the Solicitor General argues that "the Federal Government would not have the power to commit a person who has been released from prison and whose period of supervised release is also completed." Far from a "general police power," §4248 is a reasonably adapted and narrowly tailored means of pursuing the Government's legitimate interest in the responsible administration of its prison system.

To be sure, as we have previously acknowledged, "the Federal Government undertakes activities today that would have been unimag-inable to the Framers in two senses; first, because the Framers would not have conceived that *any* government would conduct such activities; and second, because the Framers would not have believed that the *Federal* Government, rather than the States, would assume such responsibilities. Yet the powers conferred upon the Federal Government by the Constitution were phrased in language broad enough to allow for the expansion of the Federal Government's role." As Chief Justice Marshall observed nearly 200 years ago, the Necessary and Proper Clause is part of "a constitution intended to endure for ages to come, and, consequently, to be adapted to the various crises of human affairs."

The judgment of the Court of Appeals for the Fourth Circuit with respect to Congress' power to enact this statute is reversed, and the case is remanded for further proceedings consistent with this opinion.

JUSTICE ALITO, concurring in the judgment.

I am concerned about the breadth of the Court's language, but I am persuaded, on narrow grounds, that it was "necessary and proper" for Congress to enact the statute at issue in this case in order to "carr[y] into Execution" powers specifically conferred on Congress by the Constitution.

Section 4248 was enacted to protect the public from federal prisoners who suffer from "a serious mental illness, abnormality, or disorder" and who, if released, would have "serious difficulty in refraining from sexually violent conduct or child molestation." Under this law, if neither the State of a prisoner's domicile nor the State in which the prisoner was tried will assume the responsibility for the prisoner's "custody, care, and treatment," the Federal Government is authorized to undertake that responsibility. The statute recognizes that, in many cases, no State will assume the heavy financial burden of civilly committing a dangerous federal prisoner who, as a result of lengthy federal incarceration, no longer has any substantial ties to any State.

I entirely agree with the dissent that "[t]he Necessary and Proper Clause empowers Congress to enact only those laws that 'carr[y] into Execution' one or more of the federal powers enumerated in the Constitution," but §4248 satisfies that requirement because it is a necessary and proper means of carrying into execution the enumerated powers that support the federal criminal statutes under which the affected prisoners were convicted. The Necessary and Proper Clause provides the constitutional authority for most federal criminal statutes. In other words, most federal criminal statutes rest upon a congressional judgment that, in order to execute one or more of the powers conferred on Congress, it is necessary and proper to criminalize certain conduct, and in order to do that it is obviously necessary and proper to provide for the operation of a federal criminal justice system and a federal prison system.

The only additional question presented here is whether, in order to carry into execution the enumerated powers on which the federal criminal laws rest, it is also necessary and proper for Congress to protect the public from dangers created by the federal criminal justice and prison systems. In my view, the answer to that question is "yes." Just as it is necessary and proper for Congress to provide for the apprehension of escaped federal prisoners, it is necessary and proper for Congress to provide for the civil commitment of dangerous federal prisoners who would otherwise escape civil commitment as a result of federal imprisonment.

JUSTICE THOMAS, with whom JUSTICE SCALIA joins in all but Part III-A-1-b, dissenting.

The Court holds today that Congress has power under the Necessary and Proper Clause to enact a law authorizing the Federal Government to civilly commit "sexually dangerous persons" beyond the date it lawfully could hold them on a charge or conviction for a federal crime. I disagree. The Necessary and Proper Clause empowers Congress to enact only those laws that "carr[y] into Execution" one or more of the federal powers enumerated in the Constitution. Because §4248 "Execut[es]" no enumerated power, I must respectfully dissent.

Congress has no power to act unless the Constitution authorizes it to do so. The Constitution plainly sets forth the "few and defined" powers that Congress may exercise. Article I "vest[s]" in Congress "all legislative Powers herein granted," and carefully enumerates those powers in §8. The Necessary and Proper Clause, authorizes Congress "[t]o make all Laws which shall be necessary and proper for carrying into Execution the foregoing Powers, and all other Powers vested by this Constitution in the Government of the United States, or in any Department or Officer thereof." Federal legislation is a valid exercise of Congress' authority under the Clause if it satisfies a two-part test: First, the law must be directed toward a "legitimate" end, which McCulloch defines as one "within the scope of the Constitution"— that is, the powers expressly delegated to the Federal Government by some provision in the Constitution. Second, there must be a necessary and proper fit between the "means" (the federal law) and the "end" (the enumerated power or powers) it is designed to serve.

McCulloch accords Congress a certain amount of discretion in assessing means-end fit under this second inquiry. However, unless the end itself is "legitimate," the fit between means and end is irrelevant. This limitation was of utmost importance to the Framers. During the State ratification debates, Anti-Federalists expressed concern that the Necessary and Proper Clause would give Congress virtually unlimited power. Federalist supporters of the Constitution swiftly refuted that charge, explaining that the Clause did not grant Congress any freestanding authority, but instead made explicit what was already implicit in the grant of each enumerated power. McCulloch firmly established this understanding in our constitutional jurisprudence. Since then, our precedents uniformly have maintained that the Necessary and Proper Clause is not an independent fount of congressional authority, but rather "a caveat that Congress possesses all the means necessary to carry out the specifically granted 'foregoing' powers of §8 'and all other Powers vested by this Constitution.'"

Section 4248 establishes a federal civil-commitment regime for certain persons in the custody of the Federal Bureau of Prisons (BOP). No enumerated power in Article I, §8, expressly delegates to Congress the power to enact a civil-commitment regime for sexually dangerous persons, nor does any other provision in the Constitution vest Congress or the other branches of the Federal Government with such a power. Accordingly, §4248 can be a valid exercise of congressional authority only if it is "necessary and proper for carrying into Execution" one or more of those federal powers actually enumerated in the Constitution.

Section 4248 does not fall within any of those powers. The Government identifies no specific enumerated power or powers as a constitutional predicate for §4248, and none are readily discernable. Indeed, it is clear, on the face of the Act and in the Government's arguments urging its constitutionality, that §4248 is aimed at protecting society from acts of sexual violence, not toward "carrying into Execution" any enumerated power or powers of the Federal Government.

To be sure, protecting society from violent sexual offenders is certainly an important end. But the Constitution does not vest in Congress the authority to protect society from every bad act that might befall it. In my view, this should decide the question. Congress may act under that Clause only when its legislation "carr[ies] into Execution" one of the Federal Government's enumerated powers. Section 4248 does not execute *any* enumerated power. Section 4248 is therefore unconstitutional.

III

A, 1, b

Instead of asking the simple question of what enumerated power §4248 "carr[ies] into Execution" at *McCulloch*'s first step, the Court surveys other laws Congress has enacted and concludes that, because §4248 is related to those laws, the "links" between §4248 and an enumerated power are not "too attenuated"; hence, §4248 is a valid exercise of Congress' Necessary and Proper Clause authority. This unnecessarily confuses the analysis and, if followed to its logical extreme, would result in an unwarranted expansion of federal power.

The Court observes that Congress has the undisputed authority to "criminalize conduct" that interferes with enumerated powers; to "imprison individuals who engage in that conduct"; to "enact laws governing [those] prisons"; and to serve as a "custodian of its prisoners." From this, the Court assumes that §4248 must

also be a valid exercise of congressional power because it is "'reasonably adapted'" to *those* exercises of Congress' incidental—and thus unenumerated—authorities. But that is not the question. The Necessary and Proper Clause does not provide Congress with authority to enact any law simply because it furthers *other laws* Congress has enacted in the exercise of its incidental authority; the Clause plainly requires a showing that every federal statute "carr[ies] into Execution" one or more of the Federal Government's *enumerated* powers.

B, 1

I cannot agree with *Justice Alito* that §4248 is a necessary and proper incident of Congress' power "to protect the public from dangers created by the federal criminal justice and prison systems." A federal criminal defendant's "sexually dangerous" propensities are not "created by" the fact of his incarceration or his relationship with the federal prison system. The fact that the Federal Government has the authority to imprison a person for the purpose of punishing him for a federal crime—sex-related or otherwise—does not provide the Government with the additional power to exercise indefinite civil control over that person.

The Court submits that §4248 does not upset the balance of federalism or invade the States' reserved powers because it "requires accommodation of state interests" by instructing the Attorney General to release a committed person to the State in which he was domiciled or tried if that State wishes to "'assume responsibility'" for him. This right of first refusal is mere window dressing. For once it is determined that Congress has the authority to provide for the civil detention of sexually dangerous persons, Congress "is acting within the powers granted it under the Constitution," and "may impose its will on the States." Section 4248's right of first refusal is thus not a matter of constitutional necessity, but an act of legislative grace.

29 States appear as *amici* and argue that §4248 is constitutional. They tell us that they do not object to Congress retaining custody of "sexually dangerous persons" after their criminal sentences expire because the cost of detaining such persons is "expensive"—approximately

$64,000 per year—and these States would rather the Federal Government bear this expense. Congress' power, however, is fixed by the Constitution; it does not expand merely to suit the States' policy preferences, or to allow State officials to avoid difficult choices regarding the allocation of state funds. Absent congressional action that is in accordance with, or necessary and proper to, an enumerated power, the duty to protect citizens from violent crime, including acts of sexual violence, belongs solely to the States.

* * *

In [today's ruling], the Court endorses the precise abuse of power Article I is designed to prevent—the use of a limited grant of authority as a "pretext for the accomplishment of objects not intrusted to the government." *McCulloch*.

I respectfully dissent.

Powell v. McCormack
395 U.S. 486 (1969)

During the Eighty-Ninth Congress, a special subcommittee reported that Adam Clayton Powell, a representative from the Eighteenth Congressional District in New York, had deceived House authorities regarding travel expenses. It also presented evidence that Powell had ordered illegal salary payments to his wife. No action was taken prior to adjournment, but after Powell was reelected to serve in the Ninetieth Congress, the Democratic members voted to remove him from his chairmanship of the Committee on Education and Labor. When other representatives were sworn in, Powell was not given the oath of office. Instead, the House authorized the Speaker of the House to appoint a select committee to determine Powell's eligibility to serve. When the committee reported that Powell had engaged in various improprieties, the House voted by 307–116 to exclude Powell and declared his seat vacant. Powell, together with thirteen voters from his congressional district, then sued the Speaker of the House and various House employees who had participated in his exclusion, seeking a declaratory judgment that his exclusion was unconstitutional and back pay for the period during which he was excluded. While the case was pending, the Ninetieth Congress ended, and Powell was elected to, and seated by, the Ninety-First Congress. After the district court dismissed the case "for want of jurisdiction of the subject matter," and the court of appeals affirmed, the Supreme Court granted certiorari. Opinion of the Court: <u>Warren</u>, Black, Douglas, Harlan, Brennan, White, Fortas, Marshall. Concurring opinion: <u>Douglas</u>. Dissenting opinion: <u>Stewart</u>.

THE CHIEF JUSTICE delivered the opinion of the Court.

SPEECH OR DEBATE CLAUSE

Respondents assert that the Speech or Debate Clause of the Constitution, Art. I, §6, is an absolute bar to petitioners' action. The Court first articulated in *Kilbourn* [*v. Thompson*] and followed in *Dombrowski v. Eastland* the doctrine that, although an action against a Congressman may be barred by the Speech or Debate Clause, legislative employees who participated in the unconstitutional activity are responsible for their acts. That House employees are acting pursuant to express orders of the House does not bar judicial review of the constitutionality of the underlying legislative decision. *Kilbourn* decisively settles this question, since the Sergeant at Arms was held liable for false imprisonment even though he did nothing more than execute the House Resolution that Kilbourn be arrested and imprisoned. Respondents' suggestions thus ask us to distinguish between affirmative acts of House employees and situations in which the House orders its employees not to act or between actions for damages and claims for salary. We can find no basis in either the history of the Speech or Debate Clause or our cases for either distinction.

The purpose of the protection afforded legislators is not to forestall judicial review of legislative action but to insure that legislators are not distracted from or hindered in the performance of their legislative tasks by being called into court to defend their actions. Freedom of legislative activity and the purposes of the

Speech or Debate Clause are fully protected if legislators are relieved of the burden of defending themselves . . . [T]hough this action may be dismissed against the Congressmen petitioners are entitled to maintain their action against House employees and to judicial review of the propriety of the decision to exclude petitioner Powell.

JUSTICIABILITY

Respondents maintain that even if this case is otherwise justiciable, it presents only a political question. It is well established that the federal courts will not adjudicate political questions. Respondents' first contention is that this case presents a political question because under Art. I, §5, there has been a "textually demonstrable constitutional commitment" to the House of the "adjudicatory power" to determine Powell's qualifications. Thus it is argued that the House, and the House alone, has power to determine who is qualified to be a member. In order to determine whether there has been a textual commitment to a co-ordinate department of the Government, we must interpret the Constitution. In other words, we must first determine what power the Constitution confers upon the House through Art. I, §5, before we can determine to what extent, if any, the exercise of that power is subject to judicial review.

Respondents maintain that the House has broad power under §5, and, they argue, the House may determine which are the qualifications necessary for membership. On the other hand, petitioners allege that the Constitution provides that an elected representative may be denied his seat only if the House finds he does not meet one of the standing qualifications expressly prescribed by the Constitution.

In order to determine the scope of any "textual commitment" under Art. I, §5, we necessarily must determine the meaning of the phrase to "be the Judge of the Qualifications of its own Members." Petitioners argue that the records of the debates during the Constitutional Convention; available commentary from the post-Convention, pre-ratification period; and early congressional applications of Art. I, §5, support their construction of the section. Respondents insist, however, that a careful examination of the pre-Convention practices of the English Parliament and American colonial assemblies demonstrates that by 1787, a legislature's power to judge the qualifications of its members was generally understood to encompass exclusion or expulsion on the ground that an individual's character or past conduct rendered him unfit to serve. When the Constitution and the debates over its adoption are thus viewed in historical perspective, argue respondents, it becomes clear that the "qualifications" expressly set forth in the Constitution were not meant to limit the long-recognized legislative power to exclude or expel at will, but merely to establish "standing incapacities," which could be altered only by a constitutional amendment. Our examination of the relevant historical materials leads us to the conclusion that petitioners are correct and that the Constitution leaves the House without authority to *exclude* any person, duly elected by his constituents, who meets all the requirements for membership expressly prescribed in the Constitution.

CONVENTION DEBATES

On August 10, the Convention considered the Committee of Detail's proposal that the "Legislature of the United States shall have authority to establish such uniform qualifications of the members of each House, with regard to property, as to the said Legislature shall seem expedient." The debate on this proposal discloses much about the views of the Framers on the issue of qualifications. For example, James Madison urged its rejection, stating that the proposal would vest

> an improper & dangerous power in the Legislature. The qualifications of electors and elected were fundamental articles in a Republican Govt. and ought to be fixed by the Constitution. If the Legislature could regulate those of either, it can by degrees subvert the Constitution. A Republic may be converted into an aristocracy or oligarchy as well by limiting the number capable of being elected, as the number authorized to elect. It was a power also, which might be made subservient to the views of one faction agst. another. Qualifications founded on artificial distinctions may be devised, by the stron-

ger in order to keep out partisans of [a weaker] faction.

Oliver Ellsworth, of Connecticut, noted that a legislative power to establish property qualifications was exceptional and "dangerous because it would be much more liable to abuse." Gouverneur Morris then moved to strike "with regard to property" from the Committee's proposal. His intention was "to leave the Legislature entirely at large." Hugh Williamson, of North Carolina, expressed concern that if a majority of the legislature should happen to be "composed of any particular description of men, of lawyers for example, the future elections might be secured to their own body." [T] he Convention rejected both Gouverneur Morris' motion and the Committee's proposal. Later the same day, the Convention adopted without debate the provision authorizing each House to be "the judge of the . . . . . . qualifications of its own members."

One other decision made the same day is very important to determining the meaning of Art. I, §5. When the delegates reached the Committee of Detail's proposal to empower each House to expel its members, Madison "observed that the right of expulsion was too important to be exercised by a bare majority of a quorum: and in emergencies [one] faction might be dangerously abused." He therefore moved that "with the concurrence of two-thirds" be inserted. With the exception of one State, whose delegation was divided, the motion was unanimously approved without debate, although Gouverneur Morris noted his opposition. The importance of this decision cannot be overemphasized. None of the parties to this suit disputes that prior to 1787 the legislative powers to judge qualifications and to expel were exercised by a majority vote. Indeed, without exception, the English and colonial antecedents to Art. I, §5, cls. 1 and 2, support this conclusion. Thus, the Convention's decision to increase the vote required to expel, because that power was "too important to be exercised by a bare majority," while at the same time not similarly restricting the power to judge qualifications, is compelling evidence that they considered the latter already limited by the standing qualifications previously adopted.

Petitioners also argue that the post-Convention debates over the Constitution's ratification support their interpretation of §5. For example, they emphasize Hamilton's reply to the antifederalist charge that the new Constitution favored the wealthy and well-born:

The truth is that there is no method of securing to the rich the preference apprehended but by prescribing qualifications of property either for those who may elect or be elected. But this forms no part of the power to be conferred upon the national government. Its authority would be expressly restricted to the regulation of the *times*, the *places*, the manner of elections. The qualifications of the persons who may choose or be chosen, as has been remarked upon other occasions, are defined and fixed in the Constitution, and are unalterable by the legislature. *The Federalist Papers.*

POST-RATIFICATION

As clear as these statements appear, respondents dismiss them as "general statements directed to other issues." They suggest that far more relevant is Congress' own understanding of its power to judge qualifications as manifested in post-ratification exclusion cases. Unquestionably, both the House and the Senate have excluded members-elect for reasons other than their failure to meet the Constitution's standing qualifications. For almost the first 100 years of its existence, however, Congress strictly limited its power to judge the qualifications of its members to those enumerated in the Constitution.

The abandonment of such restraint, however, was among the casualties of the general upheaval produced in [the Civil] war's wake. In 1868, the House voted for the first time in its history to exclude a member-elect. It refused to seat two duly elected representatives for giving aid and comfort to the Confederacy. From that time until the present, congressional practice has been erratic, and on the few occasions when a member-elect was excluded although he met all the qualifications set forth in the Constitution, there were frequently vigorous dissents.

Had these congressional exclusion precedents been more consistent, their precedential value still would be quite limited. That an unconstitutional action has been taken before surely does not render that same action any less unconstitutional at a later date. Particularly in view of the Congress' own doubts in those few cases where it did exclude members-elect, we are not inclined to give its precedents controlling weight. The relevancy of prior exclusion cases is limited largely to the insight they afford in correctly ascertaining the draftsmen's intent. Obviously, therefore, the precedential value of these cases tends to increase in proportion to their proximity to the Convention in 1787. And, what evidence we have of Congress' early understanding confirms our conclusion that the House is without power to exclude any member-elect who meets the Constitution's requirements for membership.

Respondents concede that Powell met these. Thus, there is no need to remand this case to determine whether he was entitled to be seated in the 90th Congress. Therefore, we hold that, since Adam Clayton Powell, Jr., was duly elected by the voters of the 18th Congressional District of New York and was not ineligible to serve under any provision of the Constitution, the House was without power to exclude him from its membership.

U.S. Term Limits, Inc. v. Thornton
514 U.S. 779 (1995)

In November 1992, voters in Arkansas adopted Amendment 73 to their state constitution. Sections 1 and 2 of the amendment directly limited the reeligibility of state legislators and elected officials of Arkansas's executive branch. Section 3 sought through more indirect means to combat what the amendment's preamble referred to as "entrenched incumbency," leading to "an electoral system that is less free, less competitive and less representative than the system established by the Founding Fathers." More specifically, Section 3 provided: (1) Any person having been elected to three or more terms as a member of the United States House of Representatives from Arkansas shall not be certified as a candidate and shall not be eligible to have his or her name placed on the ballot for election to the United States House of Representatives from Arkansas, and (2) any person having been elected to two or more terms as a member of the United States Senate from Arkansas shall not be certified as a candidate and shall not be eligible to have his or her name placed on the ballot for election to the United States Senate from Arkansas. Section 3 was challenged in state court, with petitioners asserting that a state could not limit the number of terms that members of its congressional delegation could serve. After the trial court ruled that Section 3 violated Article I of the United States Constitution and the Arkansas Supreme Court affirmed the trial court's ruling, the US Supreme Court granted certiorari.

Opinion of the Court: <u>Stevens</u>, Kennedy, Souter, Ginsburg, Breyer. Concurring opinion: <u>Kennedy</u>. Dissenting opinion: <u>Thomas</u>, Rehnquist, O'Connor, Scalia.

JUSTICE STEVENS delivered the opinion of the Court.

Today's cases present a challenge to an amendment to the Arkansas State Constitution that prohibits the name of an otherwise-eligible candidate for Congress from appearing on the general election ballot if that candidate has already served three terms in the House of Representatives or two terms in the Senate. The Arkansas Supreme Court held that the amendment violates the Federal Constitution. We agree with that holding. Such a state imposed restriction is contrary to the "fundamental principle of our representative democracy," embodied in the Constitution, that "the people should choose whom they please to govern them." *Powell v. McCormack* (1969).

Allowing individual States to adopt their own qualifications for congressional service would be inconsistent with the Framers' vision of a uniform National Legislature representing the people of the United States. If the qualifications set forth in the text of the Constitution are to be changed, that text must be amended.

As the opinions of the Arkansas Supreme Court suggest, the constitutionality of Amendment 73 depends critically on the resolution of two distinct issues. The first is whether the Constitution forbids States from adding to or altering the qualifications specifically enumerated in the Constitution. The second is, if the Constitution does so forbid, whether the fact that Amendment 73 is formulated as a ballot access restriction rather than as an outright disqualification is of constitutional significance.

Petitioners argue that whatever the constitutionality of additional qualifications for membership imposed by Congress, the historical and textual materials discussed in *Powell* do not support the conclusion that the Constitution prohibits additional qualifications imposed by States. In the absence of such a constitutional prohibition, petitioners argue, the Tenth Amendment and the principle of reserved powers require that States be allowed to add such qualifications. We disagree for two independent reasons.

First, we conclude that the power to add qualifications is not within the "original powers" of the States, and thus is not reserved to the States by the Tenth Amendment. Second, even if States possessed some original power in this area, we conclude that the Framers intended the Constitution to be the exclusive source of qualifications for members of Congress, and that the Framers thereby "divested" States of any power to add qualifications.

Contrary to petitioners' assertions, the power to add qualifications is not part of the original powers of sovereignty that the Tenth Amendment reserved to the States. Petitioners' Tenth Amendment argument misconceives the nature of the right at issue because that Amendment could only "reserve" that which existed before. As Justice Story recognized, "the states can exercise no powers whatsoever, which exclusively spring out of the existence of the national government, which the constitution does not delegate to them. No state can say, that it has reserved, what it never possessed."

Each Member of Congress is "an officer of the union, deriving his powers and qualifications from the constitution, and neither created by, dependent upon, nor controllable by, the states . . . Those officers owe their existence and functions to the united voice of the whole, not of a portion, of the people." Representa-

tives and Senators are as much officers of the entire union as is the President. States thus "have just as much right, and no more, to prescribe new qualifications for a representative, as they have for a president. It is no original prerogative of state power to appoint a representative, a senator, or president for the union."

We believe that the Constitution reflects the Framers' general agreement with the approach later articulated by Justice Story. For example, Art. I, §5, cl. 1 provides: "Each House shall be the Judge of the Elections, Returns and Qualifications of its own Members." The text of the Constitution thus gives the representatives of all the people the final say in judging the qualifications of the representatives of any one State. For this reason, the dissent falters when it states that "the people of Georgia have no say over whom the people of Massachusetts select to represent them in Congress."

Two other sections of the Constitution further support our view of the Framers' vision. First, consistent with Story's view, the Constitution provides that the salaries of representatives should "be ascertained by Law, and paid out of the Treasury of the United States," Art. I, §6, rather than by individual States. The salary provisions reflect the view that representatives owe their allegiance to the people, and not to States. Second, the provisions governing elections reveal the Framers' understanding that powers over the election of federal officers had to be delegated to, rather than reserved by, the States. It is surely no coincidence that the context of federal elections provides one of the few areas in which the Constitution expressly requires action by the States, namely that "[t]he Times, Places and Manner of holding Elections for Senators and Representatives, shall be prescribed in each State by the legislature thereof." This duty parallels the duty under Article II that "Each State shall appoint, in such Manner as the Legislature thereof may direct, a Number of Electors." Art. II, §1, cl. 2. These Clauses are express delegations of power to the States to act with respect to federal elections.

In short, as the Framers recognized, electing representatives to the National Legislature was a new right, arising from the Constitution itself. The Tenth Amendment thus provides no basis for concluding that the States possess reserved power to add qualifications to those that are fixed in the Constitution. Instead, any state power to set the qualifications for membership in Congress must derive not from the reserved powers of state sovereignty, but rather from the delegated powers of national sovereignty. In the absence of any constitutional delegation to the States of power to add qualifications to those enumerated in the Constitution, such a power does not exist.

THE PRECLUSION OF STATE POWER

Even if we believed that States possessed as part of their original powers some control over congressional qualifications, the text and structure of the Constitution, the relevant historical materials, and, most importantly, the "basic principles of our democratic system" all demonstrate that the Qualifications Clauses were intended to preclude the States from exercising any such power and to fix as exclusive the qualifications in the Constitution.

The Convention and Ratification Debates

The available affirmative evidence indicates the Framers' intent that States have no role in the setting of qualifications. In *Federalist Paper* No. 52, dealing with the House of Representatives, Madison addressed the "qualifications of the electors and the elected." Madison first noted the difficulty in achieving uniformity in the qualifications for electors, which resulted in the Framers' decision to require only that the qualifications for federal electors be the same as those for state electors. Madison argued that such a decision "must be satisfactory to every State, because it is comfortable to the standard already established, or which may be established, by the State itself." Madison then explicitly contrasted the state control over the qualifications of electors with the lack of state control over the qualifications of the elected.

The qualifications of the elected, being less carefully and properly defined by the State constitutions, and being at the same time more susceptible of uniformity, have been very properly considered and regulated by the convention. A representative of the United States must be of the age of

twenty-five years; must have been seven years a citizen of the United States; must, at the time of his election be an inhabitant of the State he is to represent; and, during the time of his service must be in no office under the United States. Under these reasonable limitations, the door of this part of the federal government is open to merit of every description, whether native or adoptive, whether young or old, and without regard to poverty or wealth, or to any particular profession of religious faith.

The provisions in the Constitution governing federal elections confirm the Framers' intent that States lack power to add qualifications. The Framers feared that the diverse interests of the States would undermine the National Legislature, and thus they adopted provisions intended to minimize the possibility of state interference with federal elections. For example, to prevent discrimination against federal electors, the Framers required in Art. I, §2, cl. 1, that the qualifications for federal electors be the same as those for state electors. As Madison noted, allowing States to differentiate between the qualifications for state and federal electors "would have rendered too dependent on the State governments that branch of the federal government which ought to be dependent on the people alone." *The Federalist,* No. 52. Similarly, in Art. I, §4, cl. 1, though giving the States the freedom to regulate the "Times, Places and Manner of holding Elections," the Framers created a safeguard against state abuse by giving Congress the power to "by Law make or alter such Regulations." The Convention debates make clear that the Framers' overriding concern was the potential for State abuse of the power to set the "Times, Places and Manner" of elections. Madison noted that "[i]t was impossible to foresee all the abuses that might be made of the discretionary power."

In light of the Framers' evident concern that States would try to undermine the National Government, they could not have intended States to have the power to set qualifications. Indeed, one of the more anomalous consequences of petitioners' argument is that it accepts federal supremacy over the procedural aspects of determining the times, places, and manner of elections while allowing the states *carte blanche* with respect to the substantive qualifications for membership in Congress.

We also find compelling the complete absence in the ratification debates of any assertion that States had the power to add qualifications. In those debates, the question whether to require term limits, or "rotation," was a major source of controversy. The draft of the Constitution that was submitted for ratification contained no provision for rotation. In arguments that echo in the preamble to Arkansas' Amendment 73, opponents of ratification condemned the absence of a rotation requirement, noting that "there is no doubt that senators will hold their office perpetually; and in this situation, they must of necessity lose their dependence, and their attachments to the people." Even proponents of ratification expressed concern about the "abandonment in every instance of the necessity of rotation in office." At several ratification conventions, participants proposed amendments that would have required rotation.

The Federalists' responses to those criticisms and proposals addressed the merits of the issue, arguing that rotation was incompatible with the people's right to choose. Regardless of which side has the better of the debate over rotation, it is most striking that nowhere in the extensive ratification debates have we found any statement by either a proponent or an opponent of rotation that the draft constitution would permit States to require rotation for the representatives of their own citizens. If the participants in the debate had believed that the States retained the authority to impose term limits, it is inconceivable that the Federalists would not have made this obvious response to the arguments of the pro-rotation forces. The absence in an otherwise freewheeling debate of any suggestion that States had the power to impose additional qualifications unquestionably reflects the Framers' common understanding that States lacked that power.

In short, if it had been assumed that States could add additional qualifications, that assumption would have provided the basis for a powerful rebuttal to the arguments being advanced. The failure of intelligent and experienced advocates to utilize this argument must reflect a general agreement that its premise was unsound, and that the power to add qualifications was one that the Constitution denied the States.

Congressional Experience

Congress' subsequent experience with state-imposed qualifications provides further evidence of the general consensus on the lack of state power in this area. Congress first confronted the issue in 1807 when it faced a challenge to the qualifications of William McCreery, a Representative from Maryland who allegedly did not satisfy a residency requirement imposed by that State. In recommending that McCreery be seated, the Report of the House Committee on Elections noted:

> The committee proceeded to examine the Constitution, with relation to the case submitted to them, and find that qualifications of members are therein determined, without reserving any authority to the State Legislatures to change, add to, or diminish those qualifications; and that, by that instrument, Congress is constituted the sole judge of the qualifications prescribed by it, and are obliged to decide agreeably to the Constitutional rules . . .

The Senate experience with state-imposed qualifications further supports our conclusions. In 1887, for example, the Senate seated Charles Faulkner of West Virginia, despite the fact that a provision of the West Virginia Constitution purported to render him ineligible to serve. The Senate Committee on Privileges and Elections unanimously concluded that "no State can prescribe any qualification to the office of United States Senator in addition to those declared in the Constitution of the United States."

Democratic Principles

Our conclusion that States lack the power to impose qualifications vindicates that same "fundamental principle of our representative democracy" that we recognized in *Powell,* namely that "the people should choose whom they please to govern them." Additional qualifications pose the same obstacle to open elections whatever their source. The egalitarian ideal, so valued by the Framers, is thus compromised to the same degree by additional qualifications imposed by States as by those imposed by Congress. Similarly, we believe that state-imposed qualifications, as much as congressionally imposed qualifications, would undermine the second critical idea recognized in *Powell:* that an aspect of sovereignty is the right of the people to vote for whom they wish. Again, the source of the qualification is of little moment in assessing the qualification's restrictive impact. Finally, state-imposed restrictions, unlike the congressionally imposed restrictions at issue in *Powell,* violate a third idea central to this basic principle: that the right to choose representatives belongs not to the States, but to the people.

Consistent with these views, the constitutional structure provides for a uniform salary to be paid from the national treasury, allows the States but a limited role in federal elections, and maintains strict checks on state interference with the federal election process. The Constitution also provides that the qualifications of the representatives of each State will be judged by the representatives of the entire Nation. The Constitution thus creates a uniform national body representing the interests of a single people.

Permitting individual States to formulate diverse qualifications for their representatives would result in a patchwork of state qualifications, undermining the uniformity and the national character that the Framers envisioned and sought to ensure. Such a patchwork would also sever the direct link that the Framers found so critical between the National Government and the people of the United States.

State Practice

Petitioners attempt to overcome this formidable array of evidence against the States' power to impose qualifications by arguing that the practice of the States immediately after the adoption of the Constitution demonstrates their understanding that they possessed such power. One may properly question the extent to which the States' own practice is a reliable indicator of the contours of restrictions that the Constitution imposed on States, especially when no court has ever upheld a state-imposed qualification of any sort. But petitioners' argument is unpersuasive even on its own terms.

At the time of the Convention, States widely supported term limits in at least some circumstances. The Articles of Confederation contained a provision for term limits. As we have noted, some members of the Convention had sought to impose term limits for Members of Congress. In addition, many States imposed term limits on state officers, four placed limits on delegates to the Continental Congress, and several States voiced support for term limits for Members of Congress. Despite this widespread support, no State sought to impose any term limits on its own federal representatives. Thus, a proper assessment of contemporaneous state practice provides further persuasive evidence of a general understanding that the qualifications in the Constitution were unalterable by the States. In sum, the available historical and textual evidence, read in light of the basic principles of democracy underlying the Constitution and recognized by this Court in Powell, reveal the Framers' intent that neither Congress nor the States should possess the power to supplement the exclusive qualifications set forth in the text of the Constitution.

Petitioners argue that, even if States may not add qualifications, Amendment 73 is constitutional because it is not such a qualification, and because Amendment 73 is a permissible exercise of state power to regulate the "Times, Places and Manner of Holding Elections." We reject these contentions. In our view, Amendment 73 is an indirect attempt to accomplish what the Constitution prohibits Arkansas from accomplishing directly. Indeed, it cannot be seriously contended that the intent behind Amendment 73 is other than to prevent the election of incumbents.

Petitioners do, however, contest the Arkansas Supreme Court's conclusion that the Amendment has the same practical effect as an absolute bar. They argue that the possibility of a write-in campaign creates a real possibility for victory, especially for an entrenched incumbent. But even if petitioners are correct that incumbents may occasionally win reelection as write-in candidates, there is no denying that the ballot restrictions will make it significantly more difficult for the barred candidate to win the election. In our view, an amendment with the avowed purpose and obvious effect of evading the requirements of the Qualifications Clauses by handicapping a class of candidates cannot stand.

The merits of term limits, or "rotation," have been the subject of debate since the formation of our Constitution, when the Framers unanimously rejected a proposal to add such limits to the Constitution. It is not our province to resolve this longstanding debate. We are, however, firmly convinced that allowing the several States to adopt term limits for congressional service would effect a fundamental change in the constitutional framework. Any such change must come not by legislation adopted either by Congress or by an individual State, but rather—as have other important changes in the electoral process—through the Amendment procedures set forth in Article V. The Framers decided that the qualifications for service in the Congress of the United States be fixed in the Constitution and be uniform throughout the Nation. That decision reflects the Framers' understanding that Members of Congress are chosen by separate constituencies, but that they become, when elected, servants of the people of the United States. They are not merely delegates appointed by separate, sovereign States; they occupy offices that are integral and essential components of a single National Government. In the absence of a properly passed constitutional amendment, allowing individual States to craft their own qualifications for Congress would thus erode the structure envisioned by the Framers, a structure that was designed, in the words of the Preamble to our Constitution, to form a "more perfect Union."

The judgment is affirmed.

JUSTICE THOMAS, with whom THE CHIEF JUSTICE, JUSTICE O'CONNOR, and JUSTICE SCALIA join, dissenting.

It is ironic that the Court bases today's decision on the right of the people to "choose whom they please to govern them." The Court holds that neither the elected legislature of that State nor the people themselves (acting by ballot initiative) may prescribe any qualifications for those representatives. The majority therefore defends the right of the people of Arkansas to "choose whom they please to govern them" by invalidating a provision that won nearly 60% of the votes cast in a direct election and that carried every congressional district in the State.

I dissent. Nothing in the Constitution deprives the people of each State of the power to prescribe eligibility requirements for the candidates who seek to represent them in Congress. The Constitution is simply silent on this question. And where the Constitution is silent, it raises no bar to action by the States or the people.

Because the majority fundamentally misunderstands the notion of "reserved" powers, I start with some first principles. Contrary to the majority's suggestion, the people of the States need not point to any affirmative grant of power in the Constitution in order to prescribe qualifications for their representatives in Congress, or to authorize their elected state legislators to do so. When they adopted the Federal Constitution, of course, the people of each State surrendered some of their authority to the United States (and hence to entities accountable to the people of other States as well as to themselves). In each State, the remainder of the people's powers—"[t]he powers not delegated to the United States by the Constitution, nor prohibited by it to the States"—are either delegated to the state government or retained by the people. The Federal Government and the States thus face different default rules: where the Constitution is silent about the exercise of a particular power—that is, where the Constitution does not speak either expressly or by necessary implication—the Federal Government lacks that power and the States enjoy it.

These basic principles are enshrined in the Tenth Amendment, which declares that all powers neither delegated to the Federal Government nor prohibited to the States "are reserved to the States respectively, or to the people." Any ambiguity in the Tenth Amendment's use of the phrase "the people" is cleared up by the body of the Constitution itself. Article I begins by providing that the Congress of the United States enjoys "[a]ll legislative

Powers herein granted." §1, and goes on to give a careful enumeration of Congress' powers, §8. It then concludes by enumerating certain powers that are prohibited to the States. The import of this structure is the same as the import of the Tenth Amendment: if we are to invalidate Arkansas' Amendment 73, we must point to something in the Federal Constitution that deprives the people of Arkansas of the power to enact such measures.

The majority begins by announcing an enormous and untenable limitation on the principle expressed by the Tenth Amendment. According to the majority, the States possess only those powers that the Constitution affirmatively grants to them or that they enjoyed before the Constitution was adopted; the Tenth Amendment "could only 'reserve' that which existed before." The majority's essential logic is that the state governments could not "reserve" any powers that they did not control at the time the Constitution was drafted. But it was not the state governments that were doing the reserving. The Constitution derives its authority instead from the consent of the people of the States. Given the fundamental principle that all governmental powers stem from the people of the States, it would simply be incoherent to assert that the people of the States could not reserve any powers that they had not previously controlled.

The majority also sketches out what may be an alternative (and narrower) argument. The majority suggests that it would be inconsistent with the notion of "national sovereignty" for the States or the people of the States to have any reserved powers over the selection of Members of Congress. The majority apparently reaches this conclusion in two steps. First, it asserts that because Congress as a whole is an institution of the National Government, the individual Members of Congress "owe primary allegiance not to the people of a State, but to the people of the Nation." Second, it concludes that because each Member of Congress has a nationwide constituency once he takes office, it would be inconsistent with the Framers' scheme to let a single State prescribe qualifications for him.

While the majority is correct that the Framers expected the selection process to create a "direct link" between members of the House of Representatives and the people, the link was between the Representatives from each State and the people of that State; the people of Georgia have no say over whom the people of Massachusetts select to represent them in Congress. This arrangement must baffle the majority, whose understanding of Congress would surely fit more comfortably within a system of nationwide elections. But the fact remains that when it comes to the selection of Members of Congress, the people of each State have retained their independent political identity. As a result, there is absolutely nothing strange about the notion that the people of the States or their state legislatures possess "reserved" powers in this area.

In a final effort to deny that the people of the States enjoy "reserved" powers over the selection of their representatives in Congress, the majority suggests that the Constitution expressly delegates to the States certain powers over congressional elections. Such delegations of power, the majority argues, would be superfluous if the people of the States enjoyed reserved powers in this area.

Only one constitutional provision—the Times, Places and Manner Clause of Article I, §4—even arguably supports the majority's suggestion. Contrary to the majority's assumption, however, this Clause does not delegate any authority to the States. Instead, it simply imposes a duty upon them. The majority gets it exactly right: by specifying that the state legislatures "shall" prescribe the details necessary to hold congressional elections, the Clause "expressly requires action by the States." This command meshes with one of the principal purposes of Congress' "make or alter" power: to ensure that the States hold congressional elections in the first place, so that Congress continues to exist.

I take it to be established, then, that the people of Arkansas do enjoy "reserved" powers over the selection of their representatives in Congress. Purporting to exercise those reserved powers, they have agreed among themselves that the candidates covered by §3 of Amendment 73—those whom they have already elected to three or more terms in the House of Representatives or to two or more terms in the Senate—should not be eligible to appear on the ballot for reelection, but should nonetheless be returned to Congress if enough voters are sufficiently enthusiastic about their candidacy to write in their names. Whatever one might think of the wisdom of this arrangement, we may not override the decision of the people of Arkansas unless something in the Federal Constitution deprives them of the powers to enact such measures.

The majority settles on "the Qualifications Clauses" as the constitutional provisions that Amendment 73 violates. The Qualifications Clauses do prevent the individual States from abolishing all eligibility requirements for Congress. This restriction on state power reflects that fact that when the people of one State send immature, disloyal, or unknowledgeable representatives to Congress, they jeopardize not only their own interests but also the interests of the people of other States. Because Congress wields power over all the States, the people of each State need some guarantee that the legislators elected by the people of other States will meet minimum standards of competence. The Qualifications Clauses provide that guarantee: they list the requirements that the Framers considered essential to protect the competence of the National Legislature.

If the people of a State decide that they would like their representatives to possess additional qualifications, however, they have done nothing to frustrate the policy behind the Qualifications Clauses. Anyone who possesses all the constitutional qualifications, plus some qualifications required by state law, still has all of the federal qualifications. Accordingly, the fact that the Constitution specifies certain qualifications that the Framers deemed necessary to protect the competence of the National Legislature does not imply that it strips the people of the individual States of the power to protect their own interests by adding other requirements for their own representatives.

The majority responds that "a patchwork of state qualifications" would "undermin[e] the uniformity and the national character that the Framers envisioned and sought to ensure." Yet the Framers thought it perfectly consistent with the "national character" of Congress for the Senators and Representatives from each State to be chosen by the legislature or the people of that State. The majority never explains why Congress' fundamental character permits this state-centered system, but nonetheless prohibits the people of the States and their state legislatures from setting any eligibility requirements for the candidates who seek to represent them.

In discussing the ratification period, the majority stresses two principal data. One of these pieces of evidence is no evidence at all—literally. The majority devotes considerable space to the fact that the recorded ratification debates do not contain any affirmative statement that the States can supplement the constitutional qualifications. For the majority, this void is "compelling" evidence that "unquestionably reflects the Framers' common understanding that States lacked that power." The majority reasons that delegates at several of the ratifying conventions attacked the Constitution for failing to require Members of Congress to rotate out of office. If supporters of ratification had believed that the individual States could supplement the constitutional qualifications, the majority argues, they would have blunted these attacks by pointing out that rotation requirements could still be added State by State.

But the majority's argument cuts both ways. The recorded ratification debates also contain no affirmative statement that the States cannot supplement the constitutional qualifications. While ratification was being debated, the existing rule in America was that the States could prescribe eligibility requirements for their delegates to Congress, even though the Articles of Confederation gave Congress itself no power to impose such qualifications. If the Federal Constitution had been understood to deprive the States of this significant power, one might well have expected its opponents to seize on this point in arguing against ratification. The fact is that arguments based on the absence of recorded debate at the ratification conventions are suspect, because the surviving records of those debates are fragmentary.

If one concedes that the absence of relevant records from the ratification debates is not strong evidence for either side, then the majority's only significant piece of evidence from the ratification period is *Federalist* No. 52. Contrary to the majority's assertion, however, this essay simply does not talk about "the lack of state control over the qualifications of the elected," whether "explicitly" or otherwise.

It is true that *Federalist* No. 52 contrasts the Constitution's treatment of the qualifications of voters in elections for the House of Representatives with its treatment of the qualifications of the Representatives themselves. As Madison noted, the Framers did not specify any uniform qualifications for the franchise in the Constitution; instead, they simply incorporated each State's rules about eligibility to vote in elections for the most numerous branch of the state legislature. By contrast, Madison continued, the Framers chose to impose some particular qualifications that all members of the House had to satisfy. But while Madison did say that the qualifications of the elected were "more susceptible of uniformity" than the qualifications of electors, he did not say that the Constitution prescribes anything but uniform minimum qualifications for congressmen. That, after all, is more than it does for congressional electors.

It is radical enough for the majority to hold that the Constitution implicitly precludes the people of the States from prescribing any eligibility requirements for the congressional candidates who seek their votes. In order to invalidate §3 of Amendment 73, however, the majority must go farther. The bulk of the majority's analysis addresses the issues that would be raised if Arkansas had prescribed "genuine, unadulterated, undiluted term limits."

But as the parties have agreed, Amendment 73 does not actually create this kind of disqualification. It does not say that covered candidates may not serve any more terms in Congress if reelected, and it does not indirectly achieve the same result by barring those candidates from seeking reelection. It says only that if they are to win reelection, they must do so by write-in votes.

One might think that this is a distinction without a difference. As the majority notes, "[t]he uncontested data submitted to the Arkansas Supreme Court" show that write-in candidates have won only six congressional elections in this century. But while the data's accuracy is indeed "uncontested," petitioners filed an equally uncontested affidavit challenging the data's relevance. As political science professor James S. Fay swore to the Arkansas Supreme Court, "[m]ost write-in candidacies in the past have been waged by fringe candidates, with little public support and extremely low name identification." To the best of Professor Fay's knowledge, in modern times only two incumbent Congressmen have ever sought reelection as write-in candidates. One of them was Dale Alford of Arkansas, who had first entered the House of Representatives by winning 51% of the vote as a write-in candidate in 1958; Alford then waged a write-in campaign for reelection in 1960, winning a landslide 83% of the vote against an opponent who enjoyed a place on the ballot.

The other incumbent write-in candidate was Philip J. Philbin of Massachusetts, who—despite losing his party primary and thus his spot on the ballot—won 27% of the vote in his unsuccessful write-in candidacy. According to Professor Fay, these results—coupled with other examples of successful write-in campaigns, such as Ross Perot's victory in North Dakota's 1992 Democratic presidential primary—"demonstrate that when a write-in candidate is well-known and well-funded, it is quite possible for him or her to win an election."

[Today's] decision reads the Qualifications Clauses to impose substantial implicit prohibitions on the States and the people of the States. I would not draw such an expansive negative inference from the fact that the Constitution requires Members of Congress to be a certain age, to be inhabitants of the States that they represent, and to have been United States citizens for a specified period. Rather, I would read the Qualifications Clauses to do no more than what they say. I respectfully dissent.

Gravel v. United States
408 U.S. 606 (1972)

In 1971, Senator Mike Gravel received from Daniel Ellsberg, a Defense Department consultant, a copy of the so-called Pentagon Papers, a *classified Defense Department study on how the United States became involved in the Vietnam War. Gravel then convened a meeting of the Sen-*

ate Subcommittee on Public Buildings and Grounds (of which he was chairman), read excerpts from the papers, and introduced all forty-seven volumes of the study into the record as an exhibit. Press reports indicated that the senator had also arranged with Beacon Press for private publication of the Pentagon Papers. A federal grand jury, impaneled to investigate possible violations of federal law in the release of the papers, subpoenaed Leonard Rodberg, a Gravel aide, to testify about his role in obtaining and arranging for publication of the Pentagon Papers. Senator Gravel intervened, contending that requiring Rodberg to testify about activities he undertook in Gravel's service would violate the Speech or Debate Clause. Opinion of the Court: <u>White</u>, Burger, Blackmun, Powell, Rehnquist. Dissenting opinions: <u>Stewart</u> (in part); <u>Douglas</u>; <u>Brennan</u>, Douglas, Marshall.

JUSTICE WHITE delivered the opinion of the Court.

Because the claim is that a Member's aide shares the Member's constitutional privilege, we consider first whether and to what extent Senator Gravel himself is exempt from process or inquiry by a grand jury investigating the commission of a crime. His insistence is that the Speech or Debate Clause at the very least protects him from criminal or civil liability and from questioning elsewhere than in the Senate, with respect to the events occurring at the subcommittee hearing at which the Pentagon Papers were introduced into the public record. To us this claim is incontrovertible. The Speech or Debate Clause was designed to assure a co-equal branch of the government wide freedom of speech, debate, and deliberation without intimidation or threats from the Executive Branch. It thus protects Members against prosecutions that directly impinge upon or threaten the legislative process.

Even so, the United States strongly urges that because the Speech or Debate Clause confers a privilege only upon "Senators and Representatives," Rodberg himself has no valid claim to constitutional immunity from grand jury inquiry. In our view both courts below correctly rejected this position. It is literally impossible, in view of the complexities of the modern legislative process, with Congress almost constantly in session and matters of legislative concern constantly proliferating, for Members of Congress to perform their legislative tasks without the help of aides and assistants; the day-to-day work of such aides is so critical to the Members' performance that they must be treated as the latter's alter egos; and if they are not so recognized, the central role of the Speech or Debate Clause—to prevent intimidation of legislators by the Executive and accountability before a possibly hostile judiciary—will inevitably be diminished and frustrated.

The United States fears the abuses that history reveals have occurred when legislators are invested with the power to relieve others from the operation of otherwise valid civil and criminal laws. But these abuses, it seems to us, are for the most part obviated if the privilege applicable to the aide is viewed, as it must be, as the privilege of the Senator, and invocable only by the Senator or by the aide on the Senator's behalf* and if in all events the privilege available to the aide is confined to those services that would be immune legislative conduct if performed by the Senator himself. This view places beyond the Speech or Debate Clause a variety of services characteristically performed by aides for Members of Congress, even though within the scope of their employment. Thus our refusal to distinguish between Senator and aide in applying the Speech or Debate Clause does not mean that Rodberg is for all purposes exempt from grand jury questioning.

We are convinced also that the Court of Appeals correctly determined that Senator Gravel's alleged arrangement with Beacon Press to publish the Pentagon Papers was not protected speech or debate within the meaning of Art. I, §6, cl. 1, of the Constitution. Historically, the English legislative privilege was not viewed as protecting republication of an otherwise immune libel on the floor of the House. Prior cases have read the Speech or Debate Clause "broadly to effectuate its purposes," and have included within its reach anything "generally done in a session of the House by one of its members in relation to the business before it."

---

*It follows that an aide's claim of privilege can be repudiated and thus waived by a senator.

But the Clause has not been extended beyond the legislative sphere. That Senators generally perform certain acts in their official capacity as Senators does not necessarily make all such acts legislative in nature. Members of Congress are constantly in touch with the Executive Branch of the Government and with administrative agencies—they may cajole, and exhort with respect to the administration of a federal statute—but such conduct, though generally done, is not protected legislative activity. The heart of the Clause is speech or debate in either House. Insofar as the Clause is construed to reach other matters, they must be an integral part of the deliberative and communicative processes by which Members participate in committee and House proceedings with respect to the consideration and passage or rejection of proposed legislation or with respect to other matters which the Constitution places within the jurisdiction of either House.

Here, private publication by Senator Gravel through the cooperation of Beacon Press was in no way essential to the deliberations of the Senate; nor does questioning as to private publication threaten the integrity or independence of the Senate by impermissibly exposing its deliberation to executive influence. We cannot but conclude that the Senator's arrangements with Beacon Press were not part and parcel of the legislative process.

JUSTICE BRENNAN, with whom JUSTICE DOUGLAS and JUSTICE MARSHALL join, dissenting.

In holding that Senator Gravel's alleged arrangement with Beacon Press to publish the Pentagon Papers is not shielded from extra-senatorial inquiry by the Speech or Debate Clause, the Court adopts what for me is a far too narrow view of the legislative function. The Court excludes from the sphere of protected legislative activity a function that I had supposed lay at the heart of our democratic system. I speak, of course, of the legislator's duty to inform the public about matters affecting the administration of government.

The informing function has been cited by numerous students of American politics, both within and without the Government, as among the most important responsibilities of legislative office. Though I fully share these views on the educational values served by the informing function, there is yet another, and perhaps more fundamental, interest at stake. It requires no citation of authority to state that public concern over current issues—the war, race relations, governmental invasions of privacy—has transformed itself in recent years into what many believe is a crisis of confidence, in our system of government and its capacity to meet the needs and reflect the wants of the American people. Communication between Congress and the electorate tends to alleviate that doubt by exposing and clarifying the workings of the political system, the policies underlying new laws and the role of the Executive in their administration. To the extent that the informing function succeeds in fostering public faith in the responsiveness of Government, it is not only an "ordinary" task of the legislator but one that is essential to the continued vitality of our democratic institutions.

Unlike the Court, therefore, I think that the activities of Congressmen in communicating with the public are legislative acts protected by the Speech or Debate Clause. I agree with the Court that not every task performed by a legislator is privileged; intervention before Executive departments is one that is not. But the informing function carries a far more persuasive claim to the protections of the Clause. It has been recognized by this Court as something "generally done" by Congressmen, the Congress itself has established special concessions designed to lower the cost of such communication, and, most important, the function furthers several well-recognized goals of representative government. To say in the face of these facts that the informing function is not privileged merely because it is not necessary to the internal deliberations of Congress is to give the Speech or Debate Clause an artificial and narrow reading unsupported by reason.

Whether the Speech or Debate Clause extends to the informing function is an issue whose importance goes beyond the fate of a single Senator or Congressman. What is at stake is the right of an elected representative to inform, and the public to be informed, about matters relating directly to the workings of our Government. The dialogue between Congress and people has been recognized, from the days of our founding, as one of the necessary elements of a representative system. We should not retreat from that view merely because, in the course of that dialogue, information may be revealed that is embarrassing to the other branches of government or violates their notions of necessary secrecy. A Member of Congress who exceeds the bounds of propriety in performing this official task may be called to answer by the other Members of his chamber. We do violence to the fundamental concepts of privilege, however, when we subject that same conduct to judicial scrutiny at the instance of the Executive.

Equally troubling in today's decision is the Court's refusal to bar grand jury inquiry into the source of documents received by the Senator and placed by him in the hearing record. The receipt of materials for use in a congressional hearing is an integral part of the preparation for that legislative act. It would accomplish little toward the goal of legislative freedom to exempt an official act from intimidating scrutiny, if other conduct leading up to the act and intimately related to it could be deterred by a similar threat. I would hold that Senator Gravel's receipt of the Pentagon Papers, including the name of the person from whom he received them, may not be the subject of inquiry by the grand jury.

I would go further, however, and also exclude from grand jury inquiry any knowledge that the Senator or his aides might have concerning how the source himself first came to possess the Papers. This immunity, it seems to me, is essential to the performance of the informing function. Corrupt and deceitful officers of the government do not often post for public examination the evidence of their own misdeeds. That evidence must be ferreted out, and often is, by fellow employees and subordinates. Their willingness to reveal that information and spark congressional inquiry may well depend on assurances from their contact in Congress that their identities and means of obtaining the evidence will be held in strictest confidence. To permit the grand jury to frustrate that expectation through an inquiry of the Congressman and his aides can only dampen the flow of information to the Congress and thus to the American people. There is a similar risk, of course, when the Member's own House requires him to break the confidence. But the danger, it seems to me, is far less if the Member's colleagues, and not an "unfriendly executive" or "hostile judiciary," are charged with evaluating the propriety of his conduct. In any event, assuming that a Congressman can be required to reveal the sources of his information and the methods used to obtain that information, that power of inquiry, as required by the Clause, is that of the Congressman's House, and of that House only.

I respectfully dissent.

McGrain v. Daugherty
273 U.S. 135 (1927)

A Senate select committee investigating the Department of Justice's failure to prosecute key figures in the Teapot Dome scandal and other violators of federal statutes subpoenaed Mally Daugherty, a banker and the brother of the former attorney general, but Daugherty failed to appear. Acting on a warrant issued by the Senate, McGrain, the deputy sergeant at arms of the Senate, took Daugherty into custody so that the committee might question him. Daugherty successfully petitioned for a writ of habeas corpus from a federal district court, which ruled that the Senate had exceeded its constitutional powers in detaining him. The case was then appealed to the Supreme

Court. Opinion of the Court: Van Devanter, Taft, Holmes, McReynolds, Brandeis, Sutherland, Butler, Sanford. Not participating: Stone.

JUSTICE VAN DEVANTER delivered the opinion of the Court.

The principal questions involved are (a) whether the Senate—or the House of Representatives, both being on the same plane in this regard—has power, through its own process, to compel a private individual to appear before it or one of its committees and give testimony needed to enable it efficiently to exercise a legislative function belonging to it under the

Constitution, and (b) whether it sufficiently appears that the process was being employed in this instance to obtain testimony for that purpose.

We are not now concerned with the right of the Senate to propound or the duty of the witness to answer specific questions, for as yet no questions have been propounded to him. He is asserting that the Senate is without power to interrogate him, even if the questions propounded be pertinent and otherwise legitimate—which for present purposes must be assumed. There is no provision expressly investing either house with power to make investigations and exact testimony to the end that it may exercise its legislative function advisedly and effectively. So the question arises whether this power is so far incidental to the legislative function as to be implied. We are of the opinion that the power of inquiry—with process to enforce it—is an essential and appropriate auxiliary to the legislative function. It was so regarded and employed in American legislatures before the Constitution was framed and ratified. Both houses of Congress took this view of it early in their history, and both houses have employed the power accordingly up to the present time. So, when their practice in the matter is appraised according to the circumstances in which it was begun and to those in which it has been continued, it falls nothing short of a practical construction, long continued, of the constitutional provisions respecting their powers, and therefore should be taken as fixing the meaning of those provisions, if otherwise doubtful.

We are further of opinion that the provisions are not of doubtful meaning, but are intended to be effectively exercised, and therefore to carry with them such auxiliary powers as are necessary and appropriate to that end. A legislative body cannot legislate wisely or effectively in the absence of information respecting the conditions which the legislation is intended to affect or change; and where the legislative body does not itself possess the requisite information—which not infrequently is true—recourse must be had to others who do possess it. Experience has taught that mere requests for such information often are unavailing, and also that information which is volunteered is not always accurate or complete; so some means of compulsion are essential to obtain what is needed.

We come now to the question whether it sufficiently appears that the purpose for which the witness's testimony was sought was to obtain information in aid of the legislative function. It is quite true that the resolution directing the investigation does not in terms avow that it is intended to be in aid of legislation; but it does show that the subject to be investigated was the administration of the Department of Justice—whether its functions were being properly discharged or were being neglected or misdirected, and particularly whether the Attorney General and his assistants were performing or neglecting their duties in respect of the institution and prosecution of proceedings to punish crimes and enforce appropriate remedies against the wrongdoers—specific instances of alleged neglect being recited. Plainly the subject was one on which legislation could be had and would be materially aided by the information which the investigation was calculated to elicit. The only legitimate object the Senate could have in ordering the investigation was to aid it in legislating; and we think the subject matter was such that the presumption should be indulged that this was the real object.

We conclude that the investigation was ordered for a legitimate object; that the witness wrongfully refused to appear and testify before the committee and was lawfully attached; that the Senate is entitled to have him give testimony pertinent to the inquiry, either at its bar or before the committee; and that the district court erred in discharging him from custody under the attachment.

Watkins v. United States
354 U.S. 178 (1957)

As part of its investigation into Communist influence in the labor movement, the House Un-American Activities Committee summoned John *Watkins, an organizer for the United Auto Workers, to testify before it. Watkins willingly answered questions about his own personal involvement in*

Communist Party activities and about persons whom he believed were still Communist Party members. He refused to respond, however, to questions about persons who had previously been active in the Communist Party but were no longer involved with it, maintaining that an inquiry into their activities was not pertinent to the committee's investigation. He was cited for contempt by the committee and subsequently convicted in federal district court. The court of appeals upheld his conviction, and the Supreme Court granted certiorari. Opinion of the Court: <u>Warren</u>, Black, Douglas, Harlan, Brennan. Concurring opinion: <u>Frankfurter</u>. Dissenting opinion: <u>Clark</u>. Not participating: Burton, Whittaker.

THE CHIEF JUSTICE delivered the opinion of the Court.

We start with several basic premises on which there is general agreement. The power of the Congress to conduct investigations is inherent in the legislative process. That power is broad. It encompasses inquiries concerning the administration of existing laws as well as proposed or possibly needed statutes. It includes surveys of defects in our social, economic or political system for the purpose of enabling the Congress to remedy them. It comprehends probes into departments of the Federal Government to expose corruption, inefficiency or waste. But, broad as is this power of inquiry, it is not unlimited. There is no general authority to expose the private affairs of individuals without justification in terms of the functions of the Congress. Nor is the Congress a law enforcement or trial agency. These are functions of the executive and judicial departments of government. No inquiry is an end in itself; it must be related to, and in furtherance of, a legitimate task of the Congress. Investigations conducted solely for the personal aggrandizement of the investigators or to "punish" those investigated are indefensible.

It is unquestionably the duty of all citizens to cooperate with Congress in its efforts to obtain the facts needed for intelligent legislative action. It is their unremitting obligation to respond to subpoenas, to respect the dignity of the Congress and its committees and to testify fully with respect to matters within the province of proper investigation. This, of course, assumes that the constitutional rights of witnesses will be respected by the Congress as they are in a court of justice. The Bill of Rights is applicable to investigations as to all forms of government action.

Abuses of the investigative process may imperceptibly lead to abridgment of protected freedoms. The mere summoning of a witness and compelling him to testify, against his will, about his beliefs, expressions or associations is a measure of governmental interference. And when those forced revelations concern matters that are unorthodox, unpopular, or even hateful to the general public, the reaction in the life of the witness may be disastrous. This effect is even more harsh when it is past beliefs, expressions or associations that are disclosed and judged by current standards rather than those contemporary with the matters exposed. Nor does the witness alone suffer the consequences. Those who are identified by witnesses and thereby placed in the same glare of publicity are equally subject to public stigma, scorn and obloquy. Beyond that, there is the more subtle and immeasurable effect upon those who tend to adhere to the most orthodox and uncontroversial views and associations in order to avoid a similar fate at some future time. That this impact is partly the result of nongovernmental activity by private persons cannot relieve the investigators of their responsibility for initiating the reaction.

Petitioner has earnestly suggested that the difficult questions of protecting these rights from infringement by legislative inquiries can be surmounted in this case because there was no public purpose served in his interrogation. The sole purpose of the inquiry, he contends, was to bring down upon himself and others the violence of public reaction because of their past beliefs, expressions and associations. In support of this argument, petitioner has marshaled an impressive array of evidence that some Congressmen have believed that such was their duty, or part of it.

We have no doubt that there is no congressional power to expose for the sake of exposure. But a solution to our problem is not to be found in testing the motives of committee members for this purpose. Such is not our function. Their motives alone would not vitiate an investigation which had been instituted by a House of Congress if that assembly's legislative purpose is being served. Petitioner's contentions do point to a situation of particular significance from the standpoint of the constitutional limitations upon congressional investigations. The theory of a committee inquiry is that the committee members are serving as the representatives of the parent assembly in collecting information for a legislative purpose. An essential premise in this situation is that the House or Senate shall have instructed the committee members on what they are to do with the power delegated to them. It is the responsibility of the Congress, in the first instance, to insure that compulsory process is used only in furtherance of a legislative purpose. That requires that the instructions to an investigating committee spell out that group's jurisdiction and purpose with sufficient particularity. Those instructions are embodied in the authorizing resolution. That document is the committee's charter. The more vague the committee's charter is, the greater becomes the possibility that the committee's specific actions are not in conformity with the will of the parent House of Congress.

The authorizing resolution of the Un-American Activities Committee defines the Committee's authority as follows:

> The Committee on Un-American Activities, as a whole or by subcommittee, is authorized to make from time to time investigations of (1) the extent, character, and objects of un-American propaganda activities in the United States, (2) the diffusion within the United States of subversive and un-American propaganda that is instigated from foreign countries or of a domestic origin and attacks the principle of the form of government as guaranteed by our Constitution, and (3) all other questions in relation thereto that would aid Congress in any necessary remedial legislation.

It would be difficult to imagine a less explicit authorization resolution. Combining the language of the resolution with the construction it has been given, it is evident that the preliminary control of the Committee exercised by the House of Representatives is slight or non-existent. No one could reasonably deduce from the charter the kind of investigation that the Committee was directed to make. In fulfillment of their obligation under [the statute for contempt of Congress], the courts must accord to the defendants every right which is guaranteed to defendants in all other criminal cases. Among these is the right to have available, through a sufficiently precise statute, information revealing the standard of criminality before the commission of the alleged offense. Applied to persons prosecuted under §192, this raises a special problem in that the statute defines the crimes as a refusal to answer "any question pertinent to the question under inquiry." Part of the standard of criminality, therefore, is the pertinency of the questions propounded to the witness.

It is obvious that a person is entitled to have knowledge of the subject to which the interrogation is deemed pertinent. That knowledge must be available with the same degree of explicitness and clarity that the Due Process Clause requires in the expression of any element of a criminal offense. The "vice of vagueness" must be avoided here as in all other crimes. There are several sources that can outline the "question under inquiry" in such a way that the rules against vagueness are satisfied. The authorizing resolution, the remarks of the chairman or members of the committee, or even the nature of the proceedings themselves, might sometimes make the topic clear.

The first possibility is that the authorizing resolution itself will so clearly declare the "question under inquiry" that a witness can understand the pertinency of questions asked him. The Government does not contend that the authorizing resolution of the Un-American Activities Committee could serve such a purpose. No aid is given as to the "question under inquiry" in the action of the full Committee that authorized the creation of the Subcommittee before which petitioner appeared. The Committee adopted a formal resolution giving the Chairman the power to appoint subcommittees "for the purpose of performing any and all acts which the Committee as a whole is authorized to do." The Government believes that the topic of inquiry before the Subcommittee concerned Communist infiltration in labor. In his introductory remarks, the Chairman made reference to a bill, then pending before the Committee, which would have penalized labor unions controlled or dominated by persons who were, or had been, members of a "Communist-action" organization, as defined in the Internal Security Act of 1950. The Subcommittee, it is contended, might have been endeavoring to determine the extent of such a problem. This view is corroborated somewhat by the witnesses who preceded and followed petitioner before the Subcommittee. Looking at the entire hearings, however, there is strong reason to doubt that the subject revolved about labor matters. The published transcript is entitled: Investigation of Communist Activities in the Chicago Area, and six of the nine witnesses had no connection with labor at all.

The most serious doubts as to the Subcommittee's "question under inquiry," however, stem from the precise questions that petitioner has been charged with refusing to answer. Under the terms of the statute, after all, it is these which must be proved pertinent. Petitioner is charged with refusing to tell the Subcommittee whether or not he knew that certain named persons had been members of the Communist Party in the past. The Subcommittee's counsel read the list from the testimony of a previous witness who had identified them as Communists. Although this former witness was identified with labor, he had not stated that the persons he named were involved in union affairs. Of the thirty names propounded to petitioner, seven were completely unconnected with organized labor.

The final source of evidence as to "the question under inquiry" is the Chairman's response when petitioner objected to the questions on the grounds of lack of pertinency. The Chairman then announced that the Subcommittee was investigating "subversion and subversive propaganda." This is a subject at least as broad and indefinite as the authorizing resolution of the Committee, if not more so.

Having exhausted the several possible indicia of the "question under inquiry," we remain unenlightened as to the subject to which the questions asked petitioner were pertinent.

Fundamental fairness demands that no witness be compelled to make such a determination with so little guidance. Unless the subject matter has been made to appear with undisputable clarity, it is the duty of the investigative body, upon objection of the witness on grounds of pertinency, to state for the record the subject under inquiry at that time and the manner in which the propounded questions are pertinent thereto.

The statement of the Committee Chairman in this case, in response to petitioner's protest, was woefully inadequate to convey sufficient information as to the pertinency of the questions to the subject under inquiry. Petitioner was thus not accorded a fair opportunity to determine whether he was within his rights in refusing to answer, and his conviction is necessarily invalid under the Due Process Clause of the Fifth Amendment.

We are mindful of the complexities of modern government and the ample scope that must be left to the Congress as the sole constitutional depository of legislative power. Equally mindful are we of the indispensable function, in the exercise of that power, of congressional investigations. The conclusions we have reached in this case will not prevent the Congress, through its committees, from obtaining any information it needs for the proper fulfillment of its role in our scheme of government. The legislature is free to determine the kinds of data that should be collected. It is only those investigations that are conducted by use of compulsory process that give rise to a need to protect the rights of individuals against illegal encroachment. That protection can be readily achieved through procedures which prevent the separation of power from responsibility and which provide the constitutional requisites of fairness for witnesses.

The Watkins decision provoked an immediate reaction in Congress. Senator Albert Jenner of Indiana introduced legislation withdrawing the Supreme Court's jurisdiction over "any function or practice of, or the jurisdiction of, any committee or sub-committee of the United States Congress or any action or proceedings against a witness charged with contempt of Congress." Although favorably reported by a Senate Committee, Jenner's bill was tabled by the Senate. Prior to its reintroduction, several of its supporters were defeated in the congressional elections of 1958, and the Supreme Court allayed congressional fears in Barenblatt v. United States. *As a result, the bill restricting the Court's jurisdiction was handily defeated in 1959.*

Schechter Poultry Corporation v. United States
295 U.S. 495 (1935)

The National Industrial Recovery Act of 1933 was a major element in President Franklin Roosevelt's New Deal program to stimulate the economy and reduce unemployment. Under the act, trade associations were to propose industry-wide codes of fair competition governing wages, hours, and modes of competition; these codes would take legal effect when the president endorsed them by executive order. The act specified that the trade associations should be truly representative, that the codes should not tend to produce monopolies, and that the codes should promote economic recovery. The Schechter brothers were convicted for violating the Live Poultry Code by filing false sales and price reports and selling diseased chickens. They challenged their convictions, contending that the National Industrial Recovery Act constituted an unconstitutional delegation of legislative power and that their business activities were not part of interstate commerce and thus could not be regulated by the federal government. After a court of appeals generally sustained the district court, the Supreme Court granted certiorari. Opinion of the Court: Hughes, Van Devanter, McReynolds, Brandeis, Sutherland, Butler, Roberts. Concurring opinion: Cardozo, Stone.

THE CHIEF JUSTICE delivered the opinion of the Court.

We are told that the provision of the statute authorizing the adoption of codes must be viewed in the light of the grave national crisis with which Congress was confronted. Undoubtedly, the conditions to which power is addressed are always to be considered when the exercise of power is challenged. Extraordinary conditions may call for extraordinary remedies. But the argument necessarily stops short of an attempt to justify action which lies outside the sphere of constitutional authority. Extraordinary conditions do not create or enlarge constitutional power. Such assertions of extraconstitutional authority were anticipated and precluded by the explicit terms of the Tenth Amendment—"The powers not delegated to the United States by the Constitution, nor prohibited by it to the States, are reserved to the States respectively, or to the people."

The question of the delegation of legislative power. The Congress is not permitted to abdicate or to transfer to others the essential legislative functions with which it is thus vested. We have repeatedly recognized the necessity of adapting legislation to complex conditions involving a host of details with which the national legislature cannot deal directly. We pointed out in [*Panama Refining Company v. Ryan* (1935)] that the Constitution has never been regarded as denying to Congress the necessary resources of flexibility and practicality, which will enable it to perform its function in laying down policies and establishing standards, while leaving to selected instrumentalities the making of subordinate rules within prescribed limits and the determination of facts to which the policy as declared by the legislature is to apply. But we said that the constant recognition of the necessity and validity of such provisions, and the wide range of administrative authority which has been developed by means of them, cannot be allowed to obscure the limitations of the authority to delegate, if our constitutional system is to be maintained. Accordingly, we look to the statute to see whether Congress has overstepped these limitations—whether Congress in authorizing "codes of fair competition" has itself established the standards of legal obligation, thus performing its essential legislative function, or, by the failure to enact such standards, has attempted to transfer that function to others.

What is meant by "fair competition" as the term is used in the Act? Does it refer to a category established in the law, and is the authority to make codes limited accordingly? Or is it used as a convenient designation for whatever set of laws the formulators of a code for a particular trade or industry may propose and the President may approve (subject to certain restrictions), or the President may himself prescribe, as being wise and beneficent provisions for the government of the trade or industry in order to accomplish the broad purposes of rehabilitation, correction and expansion which are stated in the first section of Title I? The Government urges that the codes will "consist of rules of competition deemed fair for each industry by representative members of that industry—by the persons most vitally concerned and most familiar with its problems." Instances are cited in which Congress has availed itself of such assistance. But would it be seriously contended that Congress could delegate its legislative authority to trade or industrial associations or groups so as to empower them to enact the laws they deem to be wise and beneficent for the rehabilitation and expansion of their trade or industries? The answer is obvious. Such a delegation of legislative power is unknown to our law and is utterly inconsistent with the constitutional prerogatives and duties of Congress.

The question, then, turns upon the authority which §3 of the Recovery Act vests in the President to approve or prescribe. If the codes have standing as penal statutes, this must be due to the effect of the executive action. But Congress cannot delegate legislative power to the President to exercise an unfettered discretion to make whatever laws he thinks may be needed or advisable for the rehabilitation and expansion of trade or industry.

Section 3 of the Recovery Act is without precedent. It supplies no standards for any trade, industry or activity. It does not undertake to prescribe rules of conduct to be applied to particular states of fact determined by appropriate administrative procedure. Instead of prescribing rules of conduct, it authorizes the making of codes to prescribe them. For that legislative undertaking, section 3 sets up no standards, aside from the statement of the general aims of rehabilitation, correction and expansion described in section 1. In view of the scope of that broad declaration, and of the nature of the few restrictions that are imposed, the discretion of the President in approving or prescribing codes, and thus enacting laws for the government of trade and industry throughout the country, is virtually unfettered. We think that the code-making authority thus conferred is an unconstitutional delegation of legislative power. On both the grounds we have discussed, the attempted delegation of legislative power, and the attempted regulation of intrastate transactions which affect interstate commerce only indirectly, we hold the code provisions here in question to be invalid and that the judgment of conviction must be reversed.

JUSTICE CARDOZO, concurring.

The delegated power of legislation which has found expression in this code is not canalized within banks that keep it from overflowing. It is unconfined and vagrant. This court has held that delegation may be unlawful though the act to be performed is definite and single, if the necessity, time and occasion of performance have been left in the end to the discretion of the delegate. *Panama Refining Co. v. Ryan.* I thought that ruling went too far. Here, in the case before us, is an attempted delegation not confined to any single act nor to any class or group of acts identified or described by reference to a standard. Here in effect is a roving commission to inquire into evils and upon discovery correct them. The code does not confine itself to the suppression of methods of competition that would be classified as unfair according to accepted business standards or accepted norms of ethics. It sets up a comprehensive body of rules to promote the welfare of the industry, if not the welfare of the nation, without reference to standards, ethical or commercial, that could be known or predicted in advance of its adoption. One of the new rules, the source of ten counts in the indictment, is aimed at an established practice, not unethical or oppressive, the practice of selective buying. Many others could be instanced as open to the same objection if the sections of the code were to be examined one by one.

Even if the statute itself has fixed the meaning of fair competition by way of contrast with practices that are oppressive or unfair, the code outruns the bounds of the authority conferred. What is excessive is not sporadic or superficial. It is deep-seated and pervasive.

Mistretta v. United States
488 U.S. 361 (1989)

The Sentencing Act of 1984 was designed to elim-inate the wide disparity in sentences that resulted from the broad sentencing discretion available to federal judges. In place of such discretion, the act proposed a system of determinate sentencing, with mandatory sentencing guidelines to ensure similar sentences for comparable offenders and offenses. To devise this system, the act created the US Sentenc-ing Commission, an independent commission within the judicial branch, with seven voting members (three of them federal judges) appointed by the president. The commission was charged with developing sentencing guidelines, on the basis of criteria outlined in the act, that would prescribe the range of sentences for various catego-ries of offenses and offenders. If a federal judge departs from the guidelines in a particular case because of an aggravating or mitigating factor not considered by the commission, the judge must give reasons for the deviation, and the sentence is sub-ject to appellate review. After the commission an-nounced its guidelines, their constitutionality was widely challenged: prior to the Supreme Court's decision in this case, more than 150 district judges had declared the guidelines unconstitu-tional, whereas more than 100 had upheld them. This case involved a challenge to the guidelines by John Mistretta, who was charged in connection with a sale of cocaine. After the district court re-jected Mistretta's claim that the guidelines in-volved an excessive delegation of congressional power and violated the separation of powers, he pleaded guilty and was sentenced under the guidelines. When Mistretta filed a notice of ap-peal to the court of appeals, both he and the United States petitioned the Supreme Court for certiorari prior to judgment, and the Court granted the request. Opinion of the Court: <u>Blackmun</u>, Rehnquist, Brennan (in part), White, Marshall, Stevens, O'Connor, Ken-nedy. Dissenting opinion: <u>Scalia</u>.

JUSTICE BLACKMUN delivered the opinion of the Court.

DELEGATION OF POWER

Petitioner argues that in delegating the power to promulgate sentencing guidelines for every federal criminal offense to an independent Sen-tencing Commission, Congress has granted the Commission excessive legislative discretion in violation of the constitutionally based nondele-gation doctrine. We do not agree. The separa-tion-of-powers principle, and the nondelegation doctrine in particular, do not prevent Congress from obtaining the assistance of its coordinate Branches. In a passage now enshrined in our jurisprudence, Chief Justice Taft, writing for the Court, explained our approach to such co-operative ventures: "In determining what [Con-gress] may do in seeking assistance from another branch, the extent and character of that assis-tance must be fixed according to common sense and the inherent necessities of the government coordination." *J. W. Hampton, Jr., & Co. v. United States* (1928). So long as Congress "shall lay down by legislative act an intelligible princi-ple to which the person or body authorized to [exercise the delegated authority] is directed to conform, such legislative action is not a forbid-den delegation of legislative power." The Act sets forth more than merely an "intelligible principle" or minimal standards. One court has aptly put it: "The statute outlines the policies which prompted establishment of the Commis-sion, explains what the Commission should do and how it should do it, and sets out specific directives to govern particular situations." *United States v. Chambless* (1988). Developing proportionate penalties for hundreds of differ-ent crimes by a virtually limitless array of of-fenders is precisely the sort of intricate, labor-intensive task for which delegation to an expert body is especially appropriate. Although Congress has delegated significant discretion to the Commission to draw judgments from its analysis of existing sentencing practice and al-ternative sentencing models, "Congress is not confined to that method of executing its policy which involves the least possible delegation of discretion to administrative officers." *Yakus v. United States* (1944).

SEPARATION OF POWERS

Having determined that Congress has set forth sufficient standards for the exercise of the

Commission's delegated authority, we turn to Mistretta's claim that the Act violates the constitutional principle of separation of powers. This Court consistently has given voice to, and has reaffirmed, the central judgment of the Framers of the Constitution that, within our political scheme, the separation of governmental powers into three coordinate Branches is essential to the preservation of liberty. Madison, in writing about the principle of separated powers, said: "No political truth is certainly of greater intrinsic value or is stamped with the authority of more enlightened patrons of liberty." *The Federalist* No. 47. In applying the principle of separated powers in our jurisprudence, we have sought to give life to Madison's view of the appropriate relationship among the three coequal Branches. Accordingly, we have recognized, as Madison admonished at the founding, that while our Constitution mandates that "each of the three general departments of government [must remain] entirely free from the control of coercive influence, direct or indirect, of either of the others," *Humphrey's Executor v. United States* (1935), the Framers did not require—and indeed rejected—the notion that the three Branches must be entirely separate and distinct. In adopting this flexible understanding of separation of powers, we simply have recognized Madison's teaching that the greatest security against tyranny—the accumulation of excessive authority in a single branch—lies not in a hermetic division between the Branches, but in a carefully crafted system of checked and balanced power within each Branch.

LOCATION OF THE COMMISSION

The Sentencing Commission unquestionably is a peculiar institution within the framework of our Government. Although placed by the Act in the Judicial Branch, it is not a court and does not exercise judicial power. Our constitutional principles of separated powers are not violated, however, by mere anomaly or innovation. Congress' decision to create an independent rulemaking body to promulgate sentencing guidelines and to locate that body within the Judicial Branch is not unconstitutional unless Congress has vested in the Commission powers that are more appropriately performed by the other Branches or that undermine the integrity of the Judiciary. Although the judicial power of the United States is limited by express provision of Article III to "Cases" and "Controversies," we have never held, and have clearly disavowed in practice, that the Constitution prohibits Congress from assigning to courts or auxiliary bodies within the Judicial Branch administrative or rulemaking duties that, in the words of Chief Justice Marshall, are "necessary and proper for carrying into execution all the judgments which the judicial department has the power to pronounce." *Wayman v. Southard* (1825).

Given the consistent responsibility of federal judges to pronounce sentence within the statutory range established by Congress, we find that the role of the Commission in promulgating guidelines for the exercise of that judicial function bears considerable similarity to the role of this Court in establishing rules of procedure under the various enabling acts. Such guidelines, like the Federal Rules of Criminal and Civil Procedure, are court rules—rules, to paraphrase Chief Justice Marshall's language in *Wayman,* for carrying into execution judgments that the judiciary has the power to pronounce. Just as the rules of procedure bind judges and courts in the proper management of the cases before them, so the Guidelines bind judges and courts in the exercise of their uncontested responsibility to pass sentence in criminal cases. In other words, the Commission's functions, like this Court's function in promulgating procedural rules, are clearly attendant to a central element of the historically acknowledged mission of the Judicial Branch.

Although the Guidelines are intended to have substantive effects on public behavior (as do the rules of procedure), they do not bind or regulate the primary conduct of the public or vest in the Judicial Branch the legislative responsibility for establishing minimum and maximum penalties for every crime. They do no more than fetter the discretion of sentencing judges to do what they have done for generations—impose sentences within the broad limits established by Congress.

Given their limited reach, the special role of the Judicial Branch in the field of sentencing, and the fact that the Guidelines are promulgated by an independent agency and not a court, it follows that as a matter of "practical consequence" the location of the Sentencing Commission within the Judicial Branch simply leaves with the Judiciary what long has belonged to it.

COMPOSITION OF THE COMMISSION

We now turn to petitioner's claim that Congress' decision to require at least three federal judges to serve on the Commission and to require those judges to share their authority with nonjudges undermines the integrity of the Judicial Branch. The text of the Constitution contains no prohibition against the service of active federal judges on independent commissions such as that established by the Act. The Constitution does include an Incompatibility Clause applicable to national legislators. No comparable restriction applies to judges, and we find it at least inferentially meaningful that at the Constitutional Convention two prohibitions against plural officeholding by members of the judiciary were proposed, but did not reach the floor of the Convention for a vote. Our inferential reading that the Constitution does not prohibit Article III judges from undertaking extrajudicial duties finds support in the historical practice of the Founders after ratification. Subsequent history, moreover, reveals a frequent and continuing, albeit controversial, practice of extrajudicial service. In light of the foregoing history and precedent, we conclude that the principle of separation of powers does not absolutely prohibit Article III judges from serving on commissions such as that created by the Act. The judges serve on the Sentencing Commission not pursuant to their status and authority as Article III judges, but solely because of their appointment by the President as the Act directs. Such power as these judges wield as Commissioners is not judicial power; it is administrative power derived from the enabling legislation. Just as the nonjudicial members of the Commission act as administrators, bringing their experience and wisdom to bear on the problems of sentencing disparity, so too the judges, uniquely qualified on the subject of sentencing, assume a wholly administrative role upon entering into the deliberations of the Commission. In other words, the Constitution, at least as a *per se* matter, does not forbid judges from wearing two hats; it merely forbids them from wearing both hats at the same time.

PRESIDENTIAL CONTROL

The Act empowers the President to appoint all seven members of the Commission with the advice and consent of the Senate. The Act further provides that the President shall make his choice of judicial appointees to the Commission after considering a list of six judges recommended by the Judicial Conference of the United States. The Act also grants the President authority to remove members of the Commission, although "only for neglect of duty or malfeasance in office or for other good cause shown."

Mistretta argues that this power of Presidential appointment and removal prevents the Judicial Branch from performing its constitutionally assigned functions. Since the President has no power to affect the tenure or compensation of Article III judges, even if the Act authorized him to remove judges from the Commission at will, he would have no power to coerce the judges in the exercise of their judicial duties. In any case, Congress did not grant the President unfettered authority to remove Commission members. Instead, precisely to ensure that they would not be subject to coercion even in the exercise of their nonjudicial duties, Congress insulated the members from Presidential removal except for good cause. Under these circumstances, we see no risk that the President's limited removal power will compromise the impartiality of Article III judges serving on the Commission and, consequently, no risk that the Act's removal provision will prevent the Judicial Branch from performing its constitutionally assigned function of fairly adjudicating cases and controversies.

We conclude that in creating the Sentencing Commission—an unusual hybrid in structure and authority—Congress neither delegated excessive legislative power nor upset the constitutionally mandated balance of powers among the coordinate Branches. The judgment of United States District Court for the Western District of Missouri is affirmed.

JUSTICE SCALIA, dissenting.

While the products of the Sentencing Commission's labors have been given the modest name "Guidelines," they have the force and effect of laws, prescribing the sentences criminal defendants are to receive. A judge who disregards them will be reversed. I dissent from today's decision because I can find no place within our constitutional system for an agency created by Congress to exercise no governmental power other than the making of laws.

Petitioner's most fundamental and far-reaching challenge to the Commission is that Congress' commitment of such broad policy responsibility to any institution is an unconstitutional delegation of legislative power. But while the doctrine of unconstitutional delegation is unquestionably a fundamental element of our constitutional system, it is not an element readily enforceable by the courts. Once it is conceded, as it must be, that no statute can be entirely precise, and that some judgments, even some judgments involving policy considerations, must be left to the officers executing the law and to the judges applying it, the debate over unconstitutional delegation becomes a debate not over a point of principle but over a question of degree. In short, I fully agree with the Court's rejection of petitioner's contention that the doctrine of unconstitutional delegation of legislative authority has been violated because of the lack of intelligible, congressionally prescribed standards to guide the Commission.

Precisely because the scope of delegation is largely uncontrollable by the courts, we must be particularly rigorous in preserving the Constitution's structural restrictions that deter excessive delegation. The major one, it seems to me, is that the power to make law cannot be exercised by anyone other than Congress, except in conjunction with the lawful exercise of executive or judicial power. The whole theory of lawful congressional "delegation" is not that Congress is sometimes too busy or too divided and can therefore assign its responsibility of making law to someone else; but rather that a certain degree of discretion, and thus of lawmaking, inheres in most executive or judicial action, and it is up to Congress, by the relative specificity or generality of its statutory commands, to determine—up to a point—how small or how large that degree shall be.

Strictly speaking, there is *no* acceptable delegation of legislative power. As John Locke put it almost three hundred years ago, "[t]he power

of the *legislative* being derived from the people by a positive voluntary grant and institution, can be no other, than what the positive grant conveyed, which being only to make *laws,* and not to make *legislators,* the *legislative* can have no power to transfer their authority of making laws, and place it in other hands." In the present case, however, a pure delegation of legislative power is precisely what we have before us. It is irrelevant whether the standards are adequate, because they are not standards related to the exercise of executive or judicial powers; they are, plainly and simply, standards for further legislation.

The lawmaking function of the Sentencing Commission is completely divorced from any responsibility for execution of the law or adjudication of private rights under the law. The delegation of lawmaking authority to the Commission is, in short, unsupported by any legitimating theory to explain why it is not a delegation of legislative power. To disregard structural legitimacy is wrong in itself—but since structure has purpose, the disregard also has adverse practical consequences. In this case, as suggested earlier, the consequence is to facilitate and encourage judicially uncontrollable delegation.

Until our decision last Term in *Morrison v. Olson* (1988), it could have been said that Congress could delegate lawmaking authority only at the expense of increasing the power of either the President or the courts. Most often, as a practical matter, it would be the President, since the judicial process is unable to conduct the investigations and make the political assessments essential for most policymaking. Thus, the need for delegation would have to be important enough to induce Congress to aggrandize its primary competitor for political power, and the recipient of the policymaking authority, while not Congress itself, would at least be politically accountable.

By reason of today's decision, I anticipate that Congress will find delegation of its lawmaking powers much more attractive in the future. If rulemaking can be entirely unrelated to the exercise of judicial or executive powers, I foresee all manner of "expert" bodies, insulated from the political process, to which Congress will delegate various portions of its lawmaking responsibility. How tempting to create an expert Medical Commission (mostly MDs, with perhaps a few PhDs in moral philosophy) to dispose of such thorny, "no-win" political issues as the witholding of life support systems in federally funded hospitals, or the use of fetal tissue for research. This is an undemocratic precedent that we set—not because of the scope of the delegated power, but because its recipient is not one of the three Branches of Government. The only governmental power the Commission possesses is the power to make law; and it is not the Congress.

Immigration and Naturalization Service v. Chadha
462 U.S. 919 (1983)

Jagdish Rai Chadha, an East Indian born in Kenya, was admitted to the United States in 1966 on a nonimmigrant student visa. When he remained in America after the visa expired in 1972, he became susceptible to deportation under the Immigration and Nationality Act. The act authorized the attorney general to suspend deportation if the alien had resided continuously in the United States for seven years, was of good moral character, and would suffer "extreme hardship" if deported. However, the act reserved to each house of Congress the power to overrule the attorney general's determinations. When Chadha's deportation was suspended and a report of the suspension was transmitted to Congress, the House of Representatives vetoed the action. Chadha challenged the House's authority to order his deportation; when the court of appeals ruled the legislative veto in the act unconstitutional, the case was appealed to the Supreme Court. Opinion of the Court: Burger, Brennan, Marshall, Blackmun, Stevens, O'Connor. Concurring in the judgment: Powell. Dissenting opinions: White; Rehnquist, White.

THE CHIEF JUSTICE delivered the opinion of the Court.

We turn to the question whether action of one House of Congress under §244(c)(2) violates strictures of the Constitution. We begin, of course, with the presumption that the challenged statute is valid. Its wisdom is not the concern of the courts; if a challenged action does not violate the Constitution, it must be sustained. By the same token, the fact that a given law or procedure is efficient, convenient, and useful in facilitating functions of government, standing alone, will not save it if it is contrary to the Constitution. Convenience and efficiency are not the primary objectives—or the hallmarks—of democratic government and our inquiry is sharpened rather than blunted by the fact that Congressional veto provisions are appearing with increasing frequency in statutes which delegate authority to executive and independent agencies.

Explicit and unambiguous provisions of the Constitution prescribe and define the respective functions of the Congress and of the Executive in the legislative process. The very structure of the articles delegating and separating powers under Arts I, II, and III exemplify the concept of separation of powers and we now turn to Art I.

THE PRESENTMENT CLAUSES
The records of the Constitutional Convention reveal that the requirement that all legislation be presented to the President before becoming law was uniformly accepted by the Framers. Presentment to the President and the Presidential veto were considered so imperative that the draftsmen took special pains to assure that these requirements could not be circumvented.

The decision to provide the President with a limited and qualified power to nullify proposed legislation by veto was based on the profound conviction of the Framers that the powers conferred on Congress were the powers to be most carefully circumscribed. The President's role in the lawmaking process also reflects the Framers' careful efforts to check whatever propensity a particular Congress might have to enact oppressive, improvident, or ill-considered measures. The Court also has observed that the Presentment Clauses serve the important purpose of assuring that a "national" perspective is grafted on the legislative process.

BICAMERALISM

The bicameral requirement of Art I, §§1, 7 was of scarcely less concern to the Framers than was the Presidential veto and indeed the two concepts are interdependent. By providing that no law could take effect without the concurrence of the prescribed majority of the Members of both Houses, the Framers reemphasized their belief, already remarked upon in connection with the Presentment Clauses, that legislation should not be enacted unless it has been carefully and fully considered by the Nation's elected officials.

Apart from their fear that special interests could be favored at the expense of public needs, the Framers were also concerned, although not of one mind, over the apprehensions of the smaller states. Those states feared a commonality of interest among the larger states would work to their disadvantage; representatives of the larger states, on the other hand, were skeptical of a legislature that could pass laws favoring a minority of the people. It need hardly be repeated here that the Great Compromise, under which one House was viewed as representing the people and the other the states, allayed the fears of both the large and small states.

We see therefore that the Framers were acutely conscious that the bicameral requirement and the Presentment Clauses would serve essential constitutional functions. The President's participation in the legislative process was to protect the Executive Branch from Congress and to protect the whole people from improvident laws. The division of the Congress into two distinctive bodies assures that the legislative power would be exercised only after opportunity for full study and debate in separate settings. The President's unilateral veto power, in turn, was limited by the power of two thirds of both Houses of Congress to overrule a veto thereby precluding final arbitrary action of one person. It emerges clearly that the prescription for legislative action in Art I, §§1, 7 represents the Framers' decision that the legislative power of the Federal government be exercised in accord with a single, finely wrought and exhaustively considered, procedure.

The Constitution sought to divide the delegated powers of the new federal government into three defined categories, legislative, executive and judicial, to assure, as nearly as possible, that each Branch of government would confine itself to its assigned responsibility. The hydraulic pressure inherent within each of the separate Branches to exceed the outer limits of its power, even to accomplish desirable objectives, must be resisted. Although not "hermetically" sealed from one another, the powers delegated to the three Branches are functionally identifiable. When any Branch acts, it is presumptively exercising the power the Constitution has delegated to it. When the Executive acts, it presumptively acts in an executive or administrative capacity as defined in Art II. And when, as here, one House of Congress purports to act, it is presumptively acting within its assigned sphere.

Beginning with this presumption, we must nevertheless establish that the challenged action under §244(c)(2) is of the kind to which the procedural requirements of Art I, §7 apply. Not every action taken by either House is subject to the bicameralism and presentment requirements of Art I. Whether actions taken by either House are, in law and fact, an exercise of legislative power depends not on their form but upon "whether they contain matter which is properly to be regarded as legislative in its character and effect."

Examination of the action taken here by one House pursuant to §244(c)(2) reveals that it was essentially legislative in purpose and effect. In purporting to exercise power defined in Art I, §8, cl 4 to "establish an uniform Rule of Naturalization," the House took action that had the purpose and effect of altering the legal rights, duties and relations of persons, including the Attorney General, Executive Branch officials and Chadha, all outside the legislative branch. Section 244(c)(2) purports to authorize one House of Congress to require the Attorney General to deport an individual alien whose deportation otherwise would be cancelled under §244. The one-House veto operated in this case to overrule the Attorney General and mandate Chadha's deportation; absent the House action, Chadha would remain in the United States. Congress has acted and its action has altered Chadha's status.

Disagreement with the Attorney General's decision on Chadha's deportation—that is, Congress' decision to deport Chadha—no less than Congress' original choice to delegate to the Attorney General the authority to make that decision, involves determinations of policy that Congress can implement in only one way; bicameral passage followed by presentment to the President. Congress must abide by its delegation of authority until that delegation is legislatively altered or revoked.

Finally, we see that when the Framers intended to authorize either House of Congress to act alone and outside of its prescribed bicameral legislative role, they narrowly and precisely defined the procedure for such action. These exceptions are narrow, explicit, and separately justified; none of them authorize the action challenged here. On the contrary, they provide further support for the conclusion that Congressional authority is not to be implied and for the conclusion that the veto provided for in §244(c)(2) is not authorized by the constitutional design of the powers of the Legislative Branch.

The veto authorized by §244(c)(2) doubtless has been in many respects a convenient shortcut; the "sharing" with the Executive by Congress of its authority over aliens in this manner is, on its face, an appealing compromise. In purely practical terms, it is obviously easier for action to be taken by one House without submission to the President; but it is crystal clear from the records of the Convention, contemporaneous writings, and debates, that the Framers ranked other values higher than efficiency. The records of the Convention and debates in the States preceding ratification underscore the common desire to define and limit the exercise of the newly created federal powers affecting the states and the people. There is unmistakable expression of a determination that legislation by the national Congress be a step-by-step, deliberate and deliberative process. The choices we discern as having been made in the Constitutional Convention impose burdens on governmental processes that often seem clumsy, inefficient, even unworkable, but those hard choices were consciously made by men who had lived under a form of government that permitted arbitrary govern-

mental acts to go unchecked. There is no support in the Constitution or decisions of this Court for the proposition that the cumbersomeness and delays often encountered in complying with explicitly Constitutional standards may be avoided, either by the Congress or by the President.

We hold that the Congressional veto provision in §244(c)(2) is severable from the Act and that it is unconstitutional.

JUSTICE WHITE, dissenting.

Today the Court not only invalidates §244(c)(2) of the Immigration and Nationality Act, but also sounds the death knell for nearly 200 other statutory provisions in which Congress has reserved a "legislative veto."

The prominence of the legislative veto mechanism in our contemporary political system and its importance to Congress can hardly be overstated. It has become a central means by which Congress secures the accountability of executive and independent agencies. Without the legislative veto, Congress is faced with a Hobson's choice: either to refrain from delegating the necessary authority, leaving itself with a hopeless task of writing laws with the requisite specificity to cover endless special circumstances across the entire policy landscape, or in the alternative, to abdicate its lawmaking function to the executive branch and independent agencies. To choose the former leaves major national problems unresolved; to opt for the latter risks unaccountable policymaking by those not elected to fill that role. Accordingly, over the past five decades, the legislative veto has been placed in nearly 200 statutes. [Justice White then reviewed at length the history of the legislative veto.]

Even this brief review suffices to demonstrate that the legislative veto is more than "efficient, convenient, and useful." It is an important if not indispensable political invention that allows the President and Congress to resolve major constitutional and policy differences, assures the accountability of independent regulatory agencies, and preserves Congress' control over lawmaking. Perhaps there are other means of accommodation and accountability, but the increasing reliance of Congress upon the legislative veto suggests that the alternatives to which Congress must now turn are not entirely satisfactory.

The history of the legislative veto also makes clear that it has not been a sword with which Congress has struck out to aggrandize itself at the expense of the other branches—the concerns of Madison and Hamilton. Rather, the veto has been a means of defense, a reservation of ultimate authority necessary if Congress is to fulfill its designated role under Article I as the Nation's lawmaker. While the President has often objected to particular legislative vetoes, generally those left in the hands of congressional committees, the Executive has more often agreed to legislative review as the price for a broad delegation of authority. To be sure, the President may have preferred unrestricted power, but that could be precisely why Congress thought it essential to retain a check on the exercise of delegated authority.

The constitutional question posed today is one of immense difficulty over which the executive and legislative branches—as well as scholars and judges—have understandably disagreed. That disagreement stems from the silence of the Constitution on the precise question: The Constitution does not directly authorize or prohibit the legislative veto. Thus, our task should be to determine whether the legislative veto is consistent with the purposes of Art I and the principles of Separation of Powers which are reflected in that Article and throughout the Constitution. We should not find the lack of a specific constitutional authorization for the legislative veto surprising, and I would not infer disapproval of the mechanism from its absence. From the summer of 1787 to the present the government of the United States has become an endeavor far beyond the contemplation of the Framers. Only within the last half century has the complexity and size of the Federal Government's responsibilities grown so greatly that the Congress must rely on the legislative veto as the most effective if not the only means to insure its role as the Nation's lawmaker. But the wisdom of the Framers was to anticipate that the Nation would grow and new problems of governance would require different solutions. Accordingly, our Federal Government was intentionally chartered with the flexibility to respond to contemporary needs without losing sight of fundamental democratic principles.

This is the perspective from which we should approach the novel constitutional questions presented by the legislative veto. In my view, neither Article I of the Constitution nor the doctrine of separation of powers is violated by this mechanism by which our elected representatives preserve their voice in the governance of the nation.

The terms of the Presentment Clauses suggest only that bills and their equivalent are subject to the requirements of bicameral passage and presentment to the President. This reading is consistent with the historical background of the Presentment Clause itself which reveals only that the Framers were concerned with limiting the methods for enacting new legislation. The Framers were aware of the experience in Pennsylvania where the legislature had evaded the requirements attached to the passing of legislation by the use of "resolves," and the criticisms directed at this practice by the Council of Censors. There is no record that the Convention contemplated, let alone intended, that these Art. I requirements would someday be invoked to restrain the scope of congressional authority pursuant to duly enacted law.

When the Convention did turn its attention to the scope of Congress' lawmaking power, the Framers were expansive. The Necessary and Proper Clause, Art I, §8, cl 18, vests Congress with the power "[t]o make all laws which shall be necessary and proper for carrying into Execution the foregoing Powers [the enumerated powers of §8], and all other Powers vested by this Constitution in the government of the United States, or in any Department or Officer thereof." It is long settled that Congress may "exercise its best judgment in the selection of measures, to carry into execution the constitutional powers of the government," and "avail itself of experience, to exercise its reason, and to accommodate its legislation to circumstances." *McCulloch v. Maryland* [1819].

The Court heeded this counsel in approving the modern administrative state. The Court's holding today that all legislative-type action must be enacted through the lawmaking process ignores that legislative authority is routinely delegated to the Executive Branch, to the independent regulatory agencies, and to private individuals and groups. This Court's decisions sanctioning such delegations make clear that Art. I does not require all action with the effect of legislation to be passed as a law. If Congress may delegate lawmaking power to independent and Executive agencies, it is most difficult to understand Art. I as prohibiting Congress from also reserving a check on legislative power for itself. Absent the veto, the agencies receiving delegations of legislative or quasi-legislative power may issue regulations having the force of law without bicameral approval and without the President's signature. It is thus not apparent why the reservation of a veto over the exercise of that legislative power must be subject to a more exacting test. In both cases, it is enough that the initial statutory authorizations comply with the Art. I requirements.

The Court concedes that certain administrative agency action, such as rulemaking, "may resemble lawmaking" and recognizes that "[t]his Court has referred to agency activity as being 'quasi-legislative' in character." Under the Court's analysis, the Executive Branch and the independent agencies may make rules with the effect of law while Congress, in whom the Framers confided the legislative power, Art I, §1, may not exercise a veto which precludes such rules from having operative force. If the effective functioning of a complex modern government requires the delegation of vast authority which, by virtue of its breadth, is legislative or "quasi-legislative" in character, I cannot accept that Article I—which is, after all, the source of the nondelegation doctrine—should forbid Congress to qualify that grant with a legislative veto.

The central concern of the presentment and bicameralism requirements of Article I is that when a departure from the legal status quo is undertaken, it is done with the approval of the President and both Houses of Congress—or, in the event of a Presidential veto, a two-thirds majority in both Houses. This interest is fully satisfied by the operation of §244(c)(2). The President's approval is found in the Attorney General's action in recommending to Congress that the deportation order for a given alien be suspended. The House and the Senate indicate their approval of the Executive's action by not passing a resolution of disapproval within the statutory period. Thus, a change in the legal status quo—the deportability of the alien—is consummated only with the approval of each of the three relevant actors. The disagreement of any one of the three maintains the alien's pre-existing status: the Executive may choose not to recommend suspension; the House and Senate may each veto the recommendation. The effect on the rights and obligations of the affected individuals and upon the legislative system is precisely the same as if a private bill were introduced but failed to receive the necessary approval.

I do not suggest that all legislative vetoes are necessarily consistent with separation-of-powers principles. A legislative check on an inherently executive function, for example, that of initiating prosecutions, poses an entirely different question. But the legislative veto device here—and in many other settings—is far from an instance of legislative tyranny over the Executive. It is a necessary check on the unavoidably expanding power of the agencies, both Executive and independent, as they engage in exercising authority delegated by Congress.

5

The Executive Branch

CHAPTER OUTLINE

In *The Federalist*, No. 51, James Madison suggested that "in republican government, the legislative authority necessarily predominates." Many contemporary observers of American government would disagree, noting that the development of American political institutions has promoted executive rather than legislative power. The discrepancy between Madison's statement and current realities raises troubling questions. How has the executive branch become so powerful? If American political development has not coincided with Madison's expectations, has the presidency exceeded its constitutional bounds? Put bluntly, can the modern presidency be squared with the Constitution?

Constitutional scholars have long debated these questions. Some maintain that the constitutional system of checks and balances continues to operate. Others assert that those checks no longer effectively constrain the president and that the contemporary American government is largely presidential government. Whereas some scholars contend that the expansion of presidential power has occurred within the constitutional framework, others insist that "the history of the presidency is a history of aggrandizement."[1] This debate cannot be resolved conclusively in these pages. However, analysis of the Framers' conception of the office, the powers constitutionally assigned to the president, and the means by which presidential power has expanded can provide the basis for an informed judgment on the legitimate scope of presidential power.

THE AIMS OF THE FRAMERS

The events leading to the American Revolution created a distrust of executive power that was reflected in the constitutions adopted following independence. The Articles of Confederation, which created a national government of very limited powers, did not even establish a separate executive branch. Every state had a separate executive, but most state governors were rendered politically impotent by short terms of office, restrictions on reeligibility, election by the legislature, the division of executive responsibilities among various officials, or some combination thereof. The results, predictably, were disastrous. At the national level, the absence of a separate executive frustrated effective administration. At the state level, the lack of any effective check on state legislatures led to the adoption of ill-considered and unjust laws. By the time of the Constitutional Convention, most of the Framers were convinced of the need for a vigorous and independent executive. Alexander Hamilton reflected this view when he observed in *The Federalist*, No. 70 that "energy in the executive is a leading character in the definition of good government."

The Framers took several steps to ensure an energetic executive. First, they lodged the executive power in a single person. Only a unified executive, they reasoned, could act with the necessary decisiveness and dispatch. Such a concentration of power would also promote accountability, because a single person could be held responsible for the results of executive action. Second, the Framers established a lengthy term of office and made the president eligible for reelection. An extended tenure, in their view, would not only promote continuity in administration but also give the president both the opportunity and the incentive to undertake long-range projects. The prospect of reelection, meanwhile, would encourage faithful performance of presidential duties and provide a basis for accountability. (The Twenty-Second Amendment, which limits the president to two terms, has altered this part of the Framers' design.) Third, the Framers secured presidential independence by granting to the president powers (e.g., the veto) designed to safeguard his constitutional position and by creating a system of election (the Electoral College) that render him or her independent of Congress. The Electoral College had the additional advantage, according to *The Federalist*, No. 68, of ensuring that only figures of national stature would be elected, thereby affording "a moral certainty that the office of President will seldom fall to the lot of any man who is not in an eminent degree endowed with the requisite qualifications."

Most significantly, the Framers granted to the president extensive powers. Primary among these powers are those enumerated in Article II of the Constitution.

In the legislative sphere, the president:

- Must inform Congress as to the State of the Union (Section 3)
- Can recommend legislation to Congress (Section 3)
- Can call Congress into special session and, if the two houses disagree on the time of adjournment, adjourn it (Section 3)—no longer important with the advent of year-round congressional sessions
- Can veto legislation (Article I, Section 7, Paragraphs 2 and 3)

As chief executive, the president:

- Can appoint executive officers and fill vacancies in such offices (Section 2, Paragraphs 2 and 3)
- Can require the heads of executive departments to furnish advice, in writing, on subjects relating to the duties of their offices (Section 2, Paragraph 1)
- Must take care that the laws are faithfully executed (Section 3)

As chief law enforcer, the president:

- Can grant pardons and reprieves (Section 2, Paragraph 1)
- Must take care that the laws are faithfully executed (Section 3)

More generally, presidents have claimed broad powers to:

- Exercise "the executive Power" vested in the President (Section 1, Paragraph 1)
- "Preserve, protect, and defend the Constitution," as required in the presidential oath of office (Section 1, Paragraph 8)

Presidential powers, however, are not limited to those expressly listed in the Constitution. Much of the debate about the presidency has centered on how far beyond those enumerated powers presidential power extends. What emerges from the Framers' discussions is a commitment to giving the president powers adequate to the responsibilities of the office.

GRANTS OF POWER AND THEIR USE

Presidential power has grown in large measure through the exercise of powers expressly granted in the Constitution. The executive branch has benefited greatly from historical developments that have increased the importance of particular governmental functions, and thereby the power of the branch assigned responsibility for those functions. For example, extensive American involvement in foreign affairs has augmented presidential power, because the Constitution assigns the president a primary role in the conduct of foreign policy (see Chapter 6). In the domestic sphere, the vast expansion in the size of the federal government and in the scope of its activities has enhanced the significance of the president's power to make appointments and to supervise administration.

Presidential power has also been expanded through the more vigorous use of powers granted by the Constitution. Presidential activity in the legislative sphere illustrates this.

From the Founding through the nineteenth century, presidents generally did not exploit the potentialities of the legislative functions assigned to the executive by the Constitution. Because chief executives of that era neither recommended detailed legislative programs to Congress nor consistently used the veto to enforce their legislative priorities, Congress tended to dominate the legislative process. During the twentieth century, however, presidents assumed a more active role in legislation. Woodrow Wilson and the two Roosevelts established the idea that presidents should submit extensive legislative programs and work for their enactment, and they transformed the State of the Union address and other messages to Congress into vehicles for the announcement of presidential programs. Subsequent presidents, Republicans and Democrats, have continued this practice, to the point where in one year President Lyndon Johnson sought congressional action on 469 separate proposals. In recent decades, Congress has usually allowed presidential initiatives to define its legislative agenda, but this is not always the case when Congress and the presidency are controlled by different parties. When the Democratic Party captured control of Congress in 2007, it pursued an agenda significantly different from President George W. Bush's, and when Republicans gained a majority in the House of Representatives in 2011 and in both houses in 2014, they refused to back President Obama's agenda.

Presidential use of the veto presents a parallel case. During the first seventy-five years of the Republic, presidents were reluctant to veto legislation—no president before Andrew Johnson vetoed more than twelve bills—and even then, the veto most frequently was used to prevent enactment of laws the president believed were unconstitutional. As presidents became active participants in the legislative process, however, the veto emerged as a formidable weapon. It is extremely effective in preventing the enactment of legislation—only about 4 percent of all presidential vetoes have been overridden. Given its proven effectiveness, presidential willingness to use the veto increases the executive's influence on Congress. Just as the power to suggest legislation gives presidents considerable control over the issues Congress addresses, the veto power ensures that their views will be taken into account in congressional deliberations, as members of Congress seek to avoid the threat of a veto.

Congressional legislation has also contributed to the growth of presidential power. By enacting broad legislation without clear standards for its exercise, Congress has allowed the executive branch to make important policy decisions, and congressional requirements that the president submit programs or reports have created additional opportunities for presidential leadership. The Budget and Accounting Act of 1921 illustrates how assignment of responsibilities to the president can enhance presidential power. The Act requires that the president submit a budget to Congress each year and thereby provide a basis for congressional action. Inevitably, however, the budget submitted reflects not merely the aggregate requests of the various executive departments but also the policy priorities of the president. Thus, simply by fulfilling their statutory responsibility, presidents may set the agenda for public debate and congressional action. President George W. Bush's tax cut proposals in 2001–2002 shifted the focus of federal activity and expenditures, demonstrating the legislative leverage this process can give the executive. However, President Obama has found it impossible to rally Republicans as well as Democrats behind his budgetary initiatives.

The Line Item Veto Act represented another congressional delegation of important power to the president. For years, presidents had complained that Congress regularly confronted them with two disagreeable alternatives. They were obliged either to sign legislation that included spending programs that they deemed wasteful or unwise or to veto worthwhile legislation because of objections to one or a few provisions. During the twentieth century, most state constitutions relieved governors of this dilemma by authorizing them to veto individual provisions of appropriations bills, and presidents argued that they too needed an item veto. In 1995 Congress—concerned about federal budget deficits—responded to these presidential complaints by enacting the Line Item Veto Act, which granted the president limited item-veto authority. When President Clinton used his item-veto authority to strike tax and spending provisions from congressional enactments, various groups sued, claiming that an item veto could be granted only by constitutional amendment. In *Clinton v. City of New York* (1998), a six-member Court majority agreed, invalidating the Act because it violated the constitutionally prescribed procedure for the enactment of legislation.

IMPLIED POWERS

Presidential power has also increased through the recognition of the implied powers of the office. Chief Justice (and former president) William Howard Taft summarized the basis for claims of implied powers: "The true view of the Executive function is . . . that the President can exercise no power which cannot be fairly and reasonably traced to some specific grant of power or justly implied and included within such express grant as necessary and proper for its exercise." In taking this position, Taft was rejecting an even more expansive view of presidential power enunciated by President Theodore Roosevelt.[2] Yet Taft's view likewise supports a broad exercise of executive power in suggesting that the president is not restricted to the powers enumerated in Article II. Because those grants relate to particular governmental functions and because the Framers intended that the executive fulfill those functions, it follows that they must have provided the executive with the means necessary to carry them out. Thus, the character of the powers assigned to the president points to the existence of implied powers.

Yet acceptance of the principle of implied powers does not prevent disagreements about the scope of those powers. Examination of the president's powers as chief executive and the disputes over executive privilege and presidential immunity illustrate both the bases for claims of implied powers and possible limits on those powers.

The President as Chief Executive

Article II of the Constitution recognizes the president as head of the executive branch, assigning him "the Executive Power" and making him responsible for ensuring "that the laws be faithfully executed." To enable him to meet his responsibilities, it grants him the power to appoint major executive officers. This promotes presidential control over those who execute the laws—a necessary precondition for the effective supervision of administration. It also leads to accountability in the executive. A president who selects executive officials and has authority over them can be held responsible for their actions. But the Constitution limits presidential control over the selection of executive-branch officials in several ways. First, presidential nominees for most major offices must be confirmed by the Senate. Although usually they are—since 1789, only eight nominees for cabinet posts have been rejected—on occasion presidents have been forced to withdraw nominations, and the necessity of securing senatorial confirmation also constrains presidential choices. Congress also by statute defines the offices to be filled as well as the responsibilities of those offices, and it can require Senate approval for appointment to them. Under legislation enacted in 1974, for example, the director of the Office of Management and the Budget must be confirmed by the Senate. Furthermore, Congress can establish qualifications for offices that restrict the president's range of choice in filling them.

Finally, the presidential appointment power extends only to principal officers. Article II authorizes Congress to vest the appointment of "inferior" officers in the president, the courts, or the heads of executive departments. Exactly what distinguishes "principal" from "inferior" officers is far from clear. In *Morrison v. Olson* (1988), for example, the Court ruled that an independent counsel with the power to investigate and prosecute violations of federal law largely free from executive-branch control was an inferior officer and upheld congressional legislation vesting her appointment in a federal court. Yet this congressional power is subject to an important separation-of-powers limitation. Although Congress can designate who will appoint inferior officers, it cannot lodge that power in its own hands. When Congress attempted to vest in the president pro tem of the Senate and the Speaker of the House the power to appoint a majority of the voting members of the Federal Election Commission, the Supreme Court in *Buckley v. Valeo* (1976) unanimously struck down the plan.

The scope of the presidential appointment power arose recently in *National Labor Relations Board v. Noel Canning* (2014). Although Article II conditions the presidential appointment power on "the Advice and Consent of the Senate," it also authorizes the President "to fill up all Vacancies that may happen during the Recess of the Senate, by granting Commissions which shall expire at the End of their next Session." When a number of vacancies opened on the National Labor Relations Board (NLRB), such that a quorum could not be obtained to conduct business, and the Senate delayed votes on President Obama's nominees for the vacant positions, the president took advantage of a period when the Senate was conducting only pro forma sessions to appoint three members to the NLRB, claiming that they were recess appointments. This claim was disputed by the Senate, which claimed it was not in recess. In resolving a challenge to actions taken by the reconstituted NLRB, the Supreme Court unanimously agreed with the Senate, holding that "for purposes of the Recess Appointments Clause, the Senate is in session when it says it is, provided that under its own rules, it retains the capacity to transact Senate business." The Court maintained that such deference to the Senate's position was consistent with the Constitution's delegation of authority to the Senate to determine how it would conduct its own business. Four justices, in a concurring opinion by Justice Antonin Scalia, would have gone considerably further. Scalia argued that the phrase "all Vacancies that may happen during the Recess of the Senate" meant that the vacancies themselves must have occurred during a Senate recess, which was not in the case in *Noel Canning* and in fact rarely occurs. More generally, he insisted that "the recess appointment power is an anachronism," given the modern practice of Congress remaining in session almost continually throughout the year.

If the Constitution gives the president the power to appoint executive-branch officials to promote effective administration, does it also give him the power to remove them? This is vital because the power to remove from office is in effect the power to control behavior in office. Aside from noting that "civil officers" are impeachable, the Constitution is silent on this point. Thus, if the president has a constitutional power to remove officials, it is an implied power.

The First Congress confronted this question in establishing a Department of Foreign Affairs. After prolonged debate, it concluded that the president, acting alone, could remove the secretary of state. Many members of Congress accepted the view, best presented by James Madison, that the removal power was implied in the grant of executive power to the president. Others insisted that Congress could determine who would exercise the removal power. The issue arose intermittently thereafter—most notably during the impeachment trial of President Andrew Johnson—but did not reach the Supreme Court until *Myers v. United States* (1926). In *Myers* the Court upheld the president's removal of a postmaster in violation of legislation establishing a four-year term for postmasters and requiring senatorial consent for their removal. In support of this decision, Chief Justice Taft cited the actions of the First Congress, which he viewed as an authoritative recognition of an implied presidential power of removal of all executive-branch employees. In addition, he insisted that the president's responsibilities required that this implied power be recognized: "Made responsible under the Constitution for the effective enforcement of the law, the President needs as an indispensable aid to meet it the disciplinary influence upon those who act under him of a reserve power of removal."

The Court's ruling in *Myers* has not prevented disputes about the scope of the president's removal power. *Myers* seems to imply that the president has the power to remove all those involved in the execution of the laws. If so, this raises questions about the constitutionality of independent regulatory commissions, such as the Federal Communications Commission, whose members can be removed by the president before the expiration of their terms only for dereliction of duty. However, the Court appears to have retreated from its position in *Myers*. It continues to insist, as in *Bowsher v. Synar* (1986), that those exercising executive functions not be under the control of Congress. But in *Humphrey's Executor v. United States* (1935) and *Wiener v. United States* (1958), it rejected presidential efforts to remove members of independent regulatory commissions before the expiration of their terms of office, contending that the powers they exercised were only partly executive in character. More recently, in *Morrison v. Olson*, it upheld restrictions on the removal of an independent counsel who was investigating and prosecuting official wrongdoing. The Court argued that the restrictions did not substantially impede the president's ability to perform his constitutional duty or unduly interfere with the functioning of the executive branch. In dissent, Justice Scalia insisted that if prosecution of crimes is an executive function, then the president must have control over those exercising the function, lest the unity of the executive be compromised.

Signing Statements

"Signing statements" are written comments issued by presidents at the time they sign into law bills passed by Congress. For most of the nation's history, they excited no controversy, as presidents used them primarily to indicate their understanding of the meaning or significance of laws. This changed during the presidency of Ronald Reagan (1981–1989): he used signing statements to give his own interpretation of statutes and thereby guide and direct executive-branch officials in interpreting or administering laws. Still, such statements arguably fell within the president's authority to supervise and control the activity of subordinate officials within the executive branch, to "take care that the laws be faithfully executed" (Article II, Section 3). Every president since Reagan has used signing statements to influence the implementation of law.

Far more controversial are signing statements in which presidents claim that some provisions of a law are unconstitutional, usually alleging that they intrude on presidential authority, and indicate that they therefore intend to ignore those provisions or to implement them only in ways they believe are constitutional. The legitimacy of such statements emerged as a major issue during the presidency of George W. Bush, because he frequently employed signing statements for this purpose. During his presidency he issued 160 signing statements, of which 126 (79 percent) contained a constitutional objection to provisions of the laws he was signing. Take, for example, his signing statement for the 2008 National Defense Authorization Act, which authorized funding for the defense of the United States and its interests abroad, for military construction, and for national security–related energy programs. President Bush singled out several provisions of the act that "purport to impose requirements that could inhibit the President's ability to carry out his constitutional obligations to take care that the laws be faithfully executed, to protect national security, to supervise the executive branch, and to execute his authority as Commander in Chief." He asserted that "the executive branch shall construe such provisions in a manner consistent with the constitutional authority of the President."[3]

Some critics insist that the executive power vested in the president does not authorize him to ignore duly enacted laws or suspend their operation. Signing statements that announce an intention to disregard provisions of statutes in effect involve the president in rewriting those statutes, in violation of the separation of powers. These critics argue that the Presentment Clause (Article I, Section 7, Paragraph 2) establishes what the Court in *Immigration and Naturalization Service v. Chadha* (1983) termed a "single, finely wrought, and exhaustively considered" procedure for lawmaking. This clause offers the president only three options: he can sign a bill into law, he can let it become law without his signature, or he can veto it. The clause does not authorize a president to approve only part of a piece of legislation—as the Court ruled in *Clinton v. New York* (1998), there is no line-item veto—and this remains true even when the president believes some provisions are unconstitutional. If a president believes that a bill is an unconstitutional intrusion on his powers, the Constitution affords him a remedy: he can veto the legislation.

Defenders of these controversial signing statements respond that the presidential oath of office requires him to "preserve, protect, and defend the Constitution" (Article II, Section 1, Paragraph 8) and that the Constitution is among the laws that the president is charged with faithfully executing (Article VI, Paragraph 2). Therefore, a president may legitimately decline to enforce a law that unconstitutionally encroaches on his powers or otherwise violates the Constitution—indeed, he is obliged not to enforce it. But if a president can refuse to enforce unconstitutional laws, then he certainly can announce to Congress and to the public via signing statements that he will not do so. Presidential veto of laws with unconstitutional provisions is not a realistic alternative. Congress regularly passes omnibus bills lumping together many diverse provisions, and so it becomes impractical for the president to veto every bill that has a constitutional flaw. The only realistic alternative, then, is for presidents to sign bills but refuse to enforce unconstitutional provisions.

Even if one accepts this response, a basic question remains: has the president properly understood the scope of his constitutional authority and of congressional power? The issue is not the legitimacy of signing statements but rather presidents' understanding of the scope of their powers—and Congress's powers—under the Constitution.

Executive Privilege

Executive privilege is the power of the president to refuse to provide information requested by other branches of government. Typically, presidents invoke this power to avoid surrendering documents to congressional committees investigating executive-branch matters or to prevent executive-branch officials from being forced to testify before those committees. The Constitution does not expressly grant the president executive privilege, nor (as noted in Chapter 4) does it expressly grant Congress the power to investigate or demand information. However, presidents have offered three arguments for executive privilege. First, they have maintained that, in order to fulfill their military, diplomatic, and national security responsibilities, they must at times withhold sensitive information from congressional and public scrutiny. Otherwise, they could not successfully carry out the tasks assigned to the executive by the Constitution. Another defense of executive privilege notes that presidents regularly depend on advice from associates and subordinates in policy making. Only by ensuring the confidentiality of these communications, it is argued, can they secure that candid interchange of views needed for wise decisions. Like the "national security" argument, this "candid interchange" argument suggests that the president's constitutional responsibilities by implication support claims of executive privilege. Some presidents have gone even further, asserting that the principle of separation of powers vests the president with control over the executive branch and, thereby, with the authority to control all communications emanating from that branch. This argument has been used to support the most extensive claims of executive privilege, because it implies that the provision of information to the other two branches is entirely a matter of presidential discretion.

Presidential invocation of executive privilege became more frequent after World War II, in part because of increased American involvement in world affairs. For many years, conflicts between the president and Congress over the withholding of information were regularly resolved by interbranch compromises, not by testing the legitimacy of executive privilege in the courts. This changed, however, when during the Watergate investigation President Richard Nixon relied on executive privilege to deny White House tapes and other records to congressional investigating committees, the Watergate special prosecutor, and the courts. When the president refused to turn over sixty-four tapes for use in the Watergate cover-up trial, the issue of executive privilege came to the Supreme Court. In *United States v. Nixon* (1974) a unanimous Supreme Court rejected the broad separation-of-powers argument for executive privilege and ordered the president to turn over the tapes. But it did not reject the notion of implied powers. The justices acknowledged that presidential claims of executive privilege had a basis in the Constitution and that such claims had particular force when information pertaining to war and foreign affairs was concerned. To determine the scope of this implied power, therefore, it was necessary to balance the interest in confidentiality against the need for disclosure of the specific information. For although presidents can claim the powers necessary to fulfill their constitutional responsibilities, so too can Congress and the courts. When these claims conflict, the executive will not always prevail. In *United States v. Nixon,* for example, the Court ruled that the interest in securing evidence necessary for a fair trial outweighed the president's "generalized assertion of privilege."

President Nixon's use of executive privilege to cover up presidential wrongdoing seemed to taint the doctrine of executive privilege, and his immediate successors were reluctant to invoke it in clashes with Congress. However, executive privilege figured prominently in the investigation that led to the impeachment of President Clinton in 1998. During the investigation, the Clinton administration invoked executive privilege to protect the secrecy of discussions between the president and his White House counsel, to safeguard discussions between the first lady and an aide, and to block grand jury questioning of Secret Service agents about what they had observed while guarding the president. When Kenneth Starr, the independent counsel investigating presidential wrongdoing, challenged the president's claims of executive privilege, the federal courts consistently ruled that those claims were not justified. Nevertheless, by invoking executive privilege, the president was able to delay the investigation and buy time to rally public support. Thus, as in President Nixon's case, the personal interests of the president and the interests of the office diverged, with executive privilege being viewed as a device to hide personal wrongdoing rather than as a valid constitutional power of the presidency.

In 2007, President George W. Bush invoked executive privilege, forbidding executive-branch officials and former officials from producing documents that Congress had subpoenaed relating to the dismissal and replacement of nine US attorneys in 2006. In support of this claim of executive privilege, he argued that the Constitution having vested in the president the responsibility for faithful execution of the laws, the president's need to maintain the confidentiality of discussions about the selection of executive-branch personnel is compelling. Only if such discussions are confidential can the president expect to receive candid advice from those involved in the selection process.

Presidential Immunity

When presidential claims of implied powers or privileges do not collide with the claims of a coequal branch of government, the Supreme Court has been more receptive to them. Presidential immunity from civil suit is a case in point. In *Nixon v. Fitzgerald* (1982), the Court ruled that the Constitution implicitly grants the president an absolute immunity from private suit for all actions that fall "within the outer perimeter of his authority." Such an immunity, the Court argued, was necessary so that presidents could fulfill their constitutional responsibilities unimpeded by the threat of private suit. Even those justices who dissented from granting an absolute immunity for official conduct recognized that the Constitution implicitly provided the president with the protection necessary to carry out the responsibilities of the office.

The issue of presidential immunity arose again in litigation stemming from a sexual harassment suit filed against President Clinton for actions allegedly undertaken while he was governor of Arkansas. In *Clinton v. Jones* (1997), the Supreme Court ruled against the president. The Court reiterated that the president enjoys an absolute immunity from civil suits for damages arising out of his official acts. It refused to extend this immunity to suits arising out of the president's private conduct, insisting such suits would not deter the president from vigorous exercise of his constitutional powers.

PREROGATIVE POWERS

A third basis for the expansion of executive power has been presidential exercise of prerogative powers. The concept of prerogative powers derives from the writings of the English political philosopher John Locke, who defined prerogative as the power of the executive "to act according to discretion for the public good, without the prescription of law and sometimes even against it."[4] In the American context, prerogative justifies the use of powers beyond those granted or implied in Article II, including in extraordinary conditions going beyond or against the law. This absence of set limits on presidential power raises the question whether prerogative is compatible with constitutional government.

There is some textual support for prerogative powers. Whereas Article I restricts Congress to "all legislative powers herein granted," Article II vests the "executive power" in the president. The open-ended character of this provision suggests that the president can legitimately claim all powers, perhaps including prerogative powers, characteristically exercised by the executive in other governments. Hamilton's emphasis in *The Federalist,* No. 70, on "energy in the executive"—the ability of the president to respond swiftly and decisively to emergency situations—seems to presuppose the availability of prerogative powers. Yet as Hamilton also made clear in *The Federalist,* No. 67, the powers of the executive in a republican government differ dramatically from those in a monarchy.

So the status of prerogative under the Constitution remains uncertain. Some assertions of prerogative powers have been accepted as justified responses to extraordinary conditions. At the outset of the Civil War, President Abraham Lincoln, acting on his own initiative while Congress was adjourned, ordered several measures of questionable legality (see Chapter 6). He later justified his actions as necessary to preserve the Union: "I did understand, however, that my oath to preserve the constitution to the best of my ability, imposed upon me the duty of preserving, by every indispensable means, that government—that nation—of which that constitution was the organic law. Was it possible to lose the nation, and yet preserve the constitution? I felt that measures, otherwise unconstitutional, might become lawful, by becoming indispensable to the preservation of the constitution, through the preservation of the nation."[5] Once convened, Congress ratified Lincoln's actions, and the verdict of history has supported his forceful assertion of prerogative powers.

The Supreme Court has at times supported the idea of prerogative powers. In *In re Neagle* (1890), it ruled that the president did not need legislative authorization to assign a federal marshal to protect a Supreme Court justice. Although there was no statutory basis for such action, the justices held that the president's responsibility to "ensure that the laws be faithfully executed" extends beyond acts of Congress and includes "the rights, duties, and obligations growing out of the Constitution itself, our international relations, and all the protection implied by the nature of the government under the Constitution." Put differently, because the responsibility for preserving the peace of the nation—a requirement common to all societies—is lodged in the president, so is the power necessary to fulfill that responsibility.

Other assertions of prerogative powers have been viewed less sympathetically. In *Youngstown Sheet & Tube Company v. Sawyer* (1952), the Supreme Court invalidated President Harry Truman's order, given during the (undeclared) Korean War, that the nation's steel mills be seized to prevent a strike. The Court held that, because Congress had designated steps to be followed in such emergencies, its determination bound the president and foreclosed consideration of alternative responses. When President Nixon attempted to justify actions taken during the Watergate scandal by invoking prerogative powers, the public reaction was overwhelmingly negative.

The condemnation of presidential actions in these instances may not indicate a wholesale rejection of prerogative powers. Rather, it may reflect a judgment that the situations in question did not warrant the exercise of such powers. The deeper issue remains: Are prerogative powers necessary in "a constitution intended to endure for ages to come, and consequently to be adapted to the various crises of human affairs"?[6] And if they are, can they be entrusted to the executive without jeopardizing the system of republican government? The problem raised by prerogative powers puts into clear focus the continuing problem of the presidency. When the proposed constitution was submitted for adoption, leading Anti-Federalists charged that, in the words of Patrick Henry, it "squints toward monarchy." The Framers sought to allay this concern by combining energy in the executive with, as *The Federalist,* No. 70, put it, "other ingredients which constitute safety in the republican sense." The continuing debate over the modern presidency, with its greatly expanded powers, is largely a dispute over the success of their efforts.

NOTES

1. The quotation is from Edward S. Corwin, *The President: Office and Powers,* 4th ed. (New York: New York University Press, 1957), 29–30.

2. William Howard Taft, *Our Chief Magistrate and His Powers* (New York: Columbia University Press, 1916), 139. Theodore Roosevelt spelled out his view in his autobiography: "My view was that every officer, and above all every executive officer in high position, was a steward of the people. . . . I declined to adopt the view that what was imperatively necessary for the Nation could not be done by the President unless he could find some specific authorization to do it. My belief was that it was not only his right but his duty to do anything that the needs of the Nation demanded unless such action was forbidden by the

Constitution or the laws." Roosevelt, *An Autobiography* (New York: Charles Scribner's Sons, 1931), 388.

3. This statement is available at www.coherent babble.com/Statements/SShr4986.pdf. This site also contains a list of signing statements issued by President George W. Bush and President Obama.

4. John Locke, *Second Treatise of Government,* edited by C. B. Macpherson (Indianapolis: Hackett, 1980), 84.

5. Abraham Lincoln, letter to A. G. Hodges, April 4, 1864, in *The Complete Works of Abraham Lincoln,* edited by John Nicolay and John Hay (New York: Francis D. Tandy, 1894), 10:65–68.

6. *McCulloch v. Maryland,* 17 U.S. (Wheat.) 316, 415 (1819).

SELECTED READINGS

The Federalist, Nos. 67–77.

Bessette, Joseph M., and Jeffrey Tulis, eds. *The Constitutional Presidency.* Baltimore, MD: Johns Hopkins University Press, 2009.

Farber, Daniel. *Lincoln's Constitution.* Chicago: University of Chicago Press, 2003.

Fisher, Louis. *Constitutional Conflicts between Congress and the President.* 6th rev. ed. Lawrence: University Press of Kansas, 2014.

————. *The Politics of Executive Privilege*. Durham, NC: Carolina Academic Press, 2003.

Kelley, Christopher S., ed. *Executing the Constitution: Putting the President Back into the Constitution*. Albany: State University of New York Press, 2006.

Milkis, Sidney M. *The American Presidency: Origins and Development, 1776–2012*. 6th ed. Washington, DC: CQ Press, 2012.

Pallitto, Robert M., and William G. Weaver. *Presidential Secrecy and the Law*. Baltimore, MD: Johns Hopkins University Press, 2007.

Posner, Eric A., and Adrian Vermeule. *The Executive Unbound: After the Madisonian Republic*. New York: Oxford University Press, 2011.

Prakash, Saikrishna Bagalore. *Imperial from the Beginning: The Constitution of the Original Executive*. New Haven, CT: Yale University Press, 2015.

Rohr, John. *To Run a Constitution: The Legitimacy of the Administrative State*. Lawrence: University Press of Kansas, 1986.

Rozell, Mark J. *Executive Privilege: Presidential Power, Secrecy, and Accountability*. 3rd ed. Lawrence: University Press of Kansas, 2010.

Skowronek, Stephen. *The Politics Presidents Make: Leadership from John Adams to George Bush*. Cambridge, MA: Belknap Press of Harvard University Press, 1993.

————. *Presidential Leadership in Political Time: Reprise and Reappraisal*. Lawrence: University Press of Kansas, 2008.

"Symposium: The Last Word? The Constitutional Implications of Presidential Signing Statements," *William & Mary Bill of Rights Law Journal* 16 (October 2007): 1–314.

Thach, Charles C., Jr. *The Creation of the Presidency, 1775–1789*. Baltimore, MD: Johns Hopkins University Press, 1922.

Thurber, James A., ed. *Rivals for Power: Presidential-Congressional Relations*. Lanham, MD: Rowman & Littlefield, 2013.

National Labor Relations Board v. Noel Canning (2014)
573 U.S. ___ (2014)

The National Labor Relations Board (NLRB) found that a Pepsi-Cola distributor, Noel Canning, had unlawfully refused to reduce to writing and execute a collective-bargaining agreement with a labor union. The Board ordered the distributor to execute the agreement and to make employees whole for any losses. Noel Canning sued in the Court of Appeals for the District of Columbia Circuit, asking that the NLRB order be put aside. He claimed that three of the five NLRB members had been invalidly appointed, leaving the Board without the three lawfully appointed members necessary for it to act. The three members in question had been nominated by President Obama in 2011 but had not been confirmed by the Senate, when the President on January 4, 2012, invoking the Recess Appointments Clause, appointed all three to the Board. Noel Canning argued that the clause did not authorize those appointments, pointing out that on December 17, 2011, the Senate, by unanimous consent, had adopted a resolution (2011 S.J.) under which it would take a series of brief recesses beginning the following day. Pursuant to that resolution, the Senate held pro forma sessions every Tuesday and Friday until it returned for ordinary business on January 23, 2012. The President's January 4 appointments were made between the January 3 and January 6 pro forma sessions. Insisting that each pro forma session terminated the immediately preceding recess, Noel Canning argued that the appointments were made during a three-day adjournment, which is not long enough to trigger the Recess Appointments Clause. The Court of Appeals agreed that the NLRB appointments fell outside the scope of the clause, and the Supreme Court granted certiorari. Opinion of the Court: <u>Breyer</u>, *Kennedy, Ginsburg, Sotomayor, Kagan. Concurring in the judgment:* <u>Scalia</u>, *Roberts, Thomas, Alito.*

JUSTICE BREYER delivered the opinion of the Court.

Ordinarily the President must obtain "the Advice and Consent of the Senate" before appointing an "Office[r] of the United States." U. S. Const., Art. II, §2, cl. 2. But the Recess Appointments Clause gives the President alone the power "to fill up all Vacancies that may happen during the Recess of the Senate, by granting Commissions which shall expire at the End of their next Session." Art. II, §2, cl. 3. We here consider three questions about the application of this Clause.

The first concerns the scope of the words "recess of the Senate." Does that phrase refer only to an inter-session recess (*i.e.,* a break between formal sessions of Congress), or does it also include an intra-session recess, such as a summer recess in the midst of a session? We conclude that the Clause applies to both kinds of recess.

The second question concerns the scope of the words "vacancies that may happen." Does that phrase refer only to vacancies that first come into existence during a recess, or does it also include vacancies that arise prior to a recess but continue to exist during the recess? We conclude that the Clause applies to both kinds of vacancy.

The third question concerns calculation of the length of a "recess." The President made the appointments here at issue on January 4, 2012. At that time the Senate was in recess pursuant to a December 17, 2011, resolution providing for a series of brief recesses punctuated by "*pro forma* sessions," with "no business transacted," every Tuesday and Friday through January 20. We conclude that we cannot ignore these *pro forma* sessions. When the appointments before us took place, the Senate was in the midst of a 3-day recess. Three days is too short a time to bring a recess within the scope of the Clause. Thus we conclude that the President lacked the power to make the recess appointments here at issue.

II

Before turning to the specific questions, we mention two background considerations relevant to all three. First, the Recess Appointments Clause sets forth a subsidiary, not a primary, method for appointing officers of the United States. The Federalist Papers make clear that the Founders intended the method of appointment requiring Senate approval to be the norm (at least for principal officers). The

Recess Appointments Clause reflects the tension between, on the one hand, the President's continuous need for "the assistance of subordinates," *Myers* v. *United States* (1926), and, on the other, the Senate's practice, particularly during the Republic's early years, of meeting for a single brief session each year. We seek to interpret the Clause as granting the President the power to make appointments during a recess but not offering the President the authority routinely to avoid the need for Senate confirmation.

Second, in interpreting the Clause, we put significant weight upon historical practice. For one thing, the interpretive questions before us concern the allocation of power between two elected branches of Government. Long ago Chief Justice Marshall wrote that "a doubtful question, one on which human reason may pause, and the human judgment be suspended, in the decision of which the great principles of liberty are not concerned, but the respective powers of those who are equally the representatives of the people, are to be adjusted; if not put at rest by the practice of the government, ought to receive a considerable impression from that practice." *McCulloch* v. *Maryland* (1819). And we later confirmed that "long settled and established practice is a consideration of great weight in a proper interpretation of constitutional provisions" regulating the relationship between Congress and the President. *The Pocket Veto Case* (1929). There is a great deal of history to consider here. Presidents have made recess appointments since the beginning of the Republic. We have not previously interpreted the Clause, and, when doing so for the first time in more than 200 years, we must hesitate to upset the compromises and working arrangements that the elected branches of Government themselves have reached.

III

The first question concerns the scope of the phrase "the recess of the Senate." The Constitution provides for congressional elections every two years. And the 2-year life of each elected Congress typically consists of two formal 1-year sessions, each separated from the next by an "inter-session recess." All agree that the phrase "the recess of the Senate" covers inter-session recesses. The question is whether it includes intra-session recesses as well. In our view, the phrase "the recess" includes an intra-session recess of substantial length. Its words taken literally can refer to both types of recess. Founding-era dictionaries define the word "recess," much as we do today, simply as "a period of cessation from usual work." We recognize that the word "the" in "*the* recess" might suggest that the phrase refers to the single break separating formal sessions of Congress. That is because the word "the" frequently (but not always) indicates "a particular thing." But the word can also refer "to a term used generically or universally." The Constitution, for example, directs the Senate to choose a President *pro tempore* "in *the* Absence of the Vice-President." Art. I, §3, cl. 5. And the Federalist Papers refer to the chief magistrate of an ancient Achaean league who "administered the government in *the* recess of the Senate." The Federalist No. 18. Reading "the" generically in this way, there is no linguistic problem applying the Clause's phrase to both kinds of recess.

The constitutional text is thus ambiguous. And we believe the Clause's purpose demands the broader interpretation. The Clause gives the President authority to make appointments during "the recess of the Senate" so that the President can ensure the continued functioning of the Federal Government when the Senate is away. The Senate is equally away during both an intersession and an intra-session recess, and its capacity to participate in the appointments process has nothing to do with the words it uses to signal its departure. History also offers strong support for the broad interpretation. We concede that pre-Civil War history is not helpful. But it shows only that Congress generally took long breaks between sessions, while taking no significant intra-session breaks at all. Obviously, if there are no significant intra-session recesses, there will be no intra-session recess appointments. In 1867 and 1868, Congress for the first time took substantial, nonholiday intra-session breaks, and President Andrew Johnson made dozens of recess appointments. The Federal Court of Claims upheld one of those specific appointments, writing "we have no doubt that a vacancy occurring while the Senate was thus temporarily adjourned" during the "first session of the Fortieth Congress" was "legally filled by appointment of the President alone." *Gould* v. *United States* (1884). Attorney General Evarts also issued three opinions concerning the constitutionality of President Johnson's appointments, and it apparently did not occur to him that the distinction between intra-session and inter-session recesses was significant. In all, between the founding and the Great Depression, Congress took substantial intra-session breaks (other than holiday breaks) in four years: 1867, 1868, 1921, and 1929. And in each of those years the President made intra-session recess appointments. Since 1929, and particularly since the end of World War II, Congress has shortened its inter-session breaks as it has taken longer and more frequent intra-session breaks; Presidents have correspondingly made more intra-session recess appointments.

What about the Senate? Since Presidents began making intra-session recess appointments, neither the Senate considered as a body nor its committees, despite opportunities to express opposition to the practice of intra-session recess appointments, has done so. Rather, to the extent that the Senate or a Senate committee has expressed a view, that view has favored a functional definition of "recess," and a functional definition encompasses intra-session recesses. The upshot is that restricting the Clause to inter-session recesses would frustrate its purpose. It would make the President's recess-appointment power dependent on a formalistic distinction of Senate procedure. Moreover, the President has consistently and frequently interpreted the word "recess" to apply to intra-session recesses, and has acted on that interpretation. The Senate as a body has done nothing to deny the validity of this practice for at least three-quarters of a century. And three-quarters of a century of settled practice is long enough to entitle a practice to "great weight in a proper interpretation" of the constitutional provision.

We are aware of, but we are not persuaded by, three important arguments to the contrary. First, some argue that the Founders would likely have intended the Clause to apply only to intersession recesses, for they hardly knew any other. The problem with this argument, however, is that it does not fully describe the relevant founding intent. The question is not: Did the Founders at the time think about intra-session recesses? Perhaps they did not. The question is: Did the Founders intend to restrict the scope of the Clause to the form of congressional recess then prevalent, or did they intend a broader scope permitting the Clause to apply, where appropriate, to somewhat changed circumstances? The Founders knew they were writing a document designed to apply to ever-changing circumstances over centuries. After all, a Constitution is "intended to endure for ages to come," and must adapt itself to a future that can only be "seen dimly," if at all. *McCulloch.* We therefore think the Framers likely did intend the Clause to apply to a new circumstance that so clearly falls within its essential purposes, where doing so is consistent with the Clause's language.

Second, some argue that the intra-session interpretation permits the President to make "illogically" long recess appointments. A recess appointment made between Congress' annual sessions would permit the appointee to serve for about a year, *i.e.,* until the "end" of the "next" Senate "session." But an intra-session appointment made at the beginning or in the middle of a formal session could permit the appointee to serve for 1½ or almost 2 years (until the end of the following formal session). We agree that the intra-session interpretation permits somewhat longer recess appointments, but we do not agree that this consequence is "illogical."

Third, the greater interpretive problem is determining how long a recess must be in order to fall within the Clause. Is a break of a week, or a day, or an hour too short to count as a "recess"? The Clause itself does not say. And Justice Scalia claims that this silence itself shows that the Framers intended the Clause to apply only to an inter-session recess. We disagree. For one thing, the most likely reason the Framers did not place a textual floor underneath the word "recess" is that they did not foresee the *need* for one. They might have expected that the Senate would meet for a single session lasting at most half a year. And they might not have anticipated that intrasession recesses would become lengthier and more significant than inter-session ones. The Framers' lack of clairvoyance on that point is not dispositive. Unlike Justice Scalia, we think it most consistent with our constitutional structure to presume that the Framers would have allowed intra-session recess appointments where there was a long history of such practice. There are a few historical examples of recess appointments made during inter-session recesses shorter than 10 days. But when considered against 200 years of settled practice, we regard these few scattered examples as anomalies. We therefore conclude, in light of historical practice, that a recess of more than 3 days but less than 10 days is presumptively too short to fall within the Clause.

IV

The second question concerns the scope of the phrase "vacancies *that may happen* during the recess of the Senate." Art. II, §2, cl. 3. All agree that the phrase applies to vacancies that initially occur during a recess. But does it also apply to vacancies that initially occur before a recess and continue to exist during the recess? In our view the phrase applies to both kinds of vacancy. We believe that the Clause's language, read literally, permits, though it does not naturally favor, our broader interpretation. We concede that the most natural meaning of "happens" as applied to a "vacancy" (at least to a modern ear) is that the vacancy "happens" when it initially occurs. But that is not the only possible way to use the word. When Attorney General William Wirt advised President Monroe to follow the broader interpretation, he wrote that the "expression seems not perfectly clear. It may mean 'happen to take place:' that is, '*to originate*,' "or it "may mean, also, without violence to the sense, 'happen to exist.' "The broader interpretation, he added, is "most accordant with" the Constitution's "reason and spirit."

In any event, the linguistic question here is not whether the phrase can be, but whether it must be, read more narrowly. The question is whether the Clause is ambiguous. *The Pocket Veto Case*, 279 U. S., at 690. And the broader reading, we believe, is at least a permissible reading of a "'doubtful'" phrase. We consequently go on to consider the Clause's purpose

and historical practice. The Clause's purpose strongly supports the broader interpretation. That purpose is to permit the President to obtain the assistance of subordinate officers when the Senate, due to its recess, cannot confirm them. Historical practice over the past 200 years strongly favors the broader interpretation. The tradition of applying the Clause to pre-recess vacancies dates at least to President James Madison. In light of some linguistic ambiguity, the basic purpose of the Clause, and the historical practice we have described, we conclude that the phrase "all vacancies" includes vacancies that come into existence while the Senate is in session.

V

The third question concerns the calculation of the length of the Senate's "recess." On December 17, 2011, the Senate by unanimous consent adopted a resolution to convene "*pro forma* session[s]" only, with "no business transacted," on every Tuesday and Friday from December 20, 2011, through January 20, 2012. At the end of each *pro forma* session, the Senate would "adjourn until" the following *pro forma* session. During that period, the Senate convened and adjourned as agreed. It held *pro forma* sessions on December 20, 23, 27, and 30, and on January 3, 6, 10, 13, 17, and 20; and at the end of each *pro forma* session, it adjourned until the time and date of the next. We must determine the significance of these sessions—that is, whether, for purposes of the Clause, we should treat them as periods when the Senate was in session or as periods when it was in recess. If the former, the period between January 3 and January 6 was a 3-day recess, which is too short to trigger the President's recess-appointment power. If the latter, however, then the 3-day period was part of a much longer recess during which the President did have the power to make recess appointments.

In our view, the *pro forma* sessions count as sessions, not as periods of recess. We hold that, for purposes of the Recess Appointments Clause, the Senate is in session when it says it is, provided that, under its own rules, it retains the capacity to transact Senate business. The Senate met that standard here. The standard we apply is consistent with the Constitution's broad delegation of authority to the Senate to determine how and when to conduct its business. In addition, the Constitution provides the Senate with extensive control over its schedule. The Constitution thus gives the Senate wide latitude to determine whether and when to have a session, as well as how to conduct the session. This suggests that the Senate's determination about what constitutes a session should merit great respect.

VI

Justice Scalia would render illegitimate thousands of recess appointments reaching all the way back to the founding era. More than that: Calling the Clause an "anachronism," he would basically read it out of the Constitution. He performs this act of judicial excision in the name of liberty. We fail to see how excising the Recess Appointments Clause preserves freedom. In fact, Alexander Hamilton observed in the very first Federalist Paper that "the vigour of government is essential to the security of liberty." And the Framers included the Recess Appointments Clause to preserve the "vigour of government" at times when an important organ of Government, the United States Senate, is in recess. Justice Scalia's interpretation of the Clause would defeat the power of the Clause to achieve that objective.

* * *

We conclude that the Recess Appointments Clause does not give the President the constitutional authority to make the appointments here at issue. Because the Court of Appeals reached the same ultimate conclusion, its judgment is affirmed.

It is so ordered.

JUSTICE SCALIA, with whom THE CHIEF JUSTICE, JUSTICE THOMAS, and JUSTICE ALITO join, concurring in the judgment.

Except where the Constitution or a valid federal law provides otherwise, all "Officers of the United States" must be appointed by the President "by and with the Advice and Consent of the Senate." That general rule is subject to an exception: "The President shall have Power to fill up all Vacancies that may happen during the Recess of the Senate, by granting Commissions which shall expire at the End of their next Session." To prevent the President's recess-appointment power from nullifying the Senate's role in the appointment process, the Constitution cabins that power in two significant ways. First, it may be exercised only in "the Recess of the Senate," that is, the intermission between two formal legislative sessions. Second, it may be used to fill only those vacancies that "happen during the Recess," that is, offices that become vacant during that intermission. Both conditions are clear from the Constitution's text and structure, and both were well understood at the founding. Today's Court . . . sweeps away the key textual limitations on the recess-appointment power. The majority justifies those atextual results on an adverse-possession theory of executive authority: Presidents have long claimed the powers in question, and the Senate has not disputed those claims with sufficient vigor, so the Court should not "upset the compromises and working arrangements that the elected branches of Government themselves have reached."

Myers v. United States
272 U.S. 52 (1926)

According to an act adopted by Congress in 1876, "Postmasters of the first, second, and third classes shall be appointed and may be removed by the President by and with the advice and consent of the Senate, and shall hold their offices for four years unless sooner removed or suspended according to law." Myers was appointed to a first-class postmaster position under this statute in 1917. The postmaster *general, at the direction of President Woodrow Wilson, removed Myers from his post in 1920, prior to the expiration of Myers's term and without Senate approval. Myers protested his removal and sued to recover his lost salary in the US Court of Claims. When the court of claims sustained the removal, the case was appealed to the Supreme Court. Opinion of the Court:* <u>Taft</u>, *Sutherland, Butler,*

Sanford, Stone. Dissenting opinions: <u>Holmes</u>; <u>Brandeis</u>; <u>McReynolds</u>.

THE CHIEF JUSTICE delivered the opinion of the Court.

This case presents the question whether under the Constitution the President has the exclusive power of removing executive officers of the United States whom he has appointed by and with the advice and consent of the Senate.

The question where the power of removal of executive officers appointed by the President by and with the advice and consent of the Senate was vested, was presented early in the first session of the First Congress. There is no express provision respecting removals in the Constitution, except as Section 4 of Article II, above quoted, provides for removal from office by impeachment. Mr. Madison and his associates in the discussion in the House dwelt at length upon the necessity there was for construing Article II to give the President the sole power of removal in his responsibility for the conduct of the executive branch, and enforced this by emphasizing his duty expressly declared in the third section of the Article to "take care that the laws be faithfully executed."

The vesting of the executive power in the President was essentially a grant of the power to execute the laws. But the President alone and unaided could not execute the laws. He must execute them by the assistance of subordinates. This view has since been repeatedly affirmed by this Court. As he is charged specifically to take care that they be faithfully executed, the reasonable implication, even in the absence of express words, was that as part of his executive power he should select those who were to act for him under his direction in the execution of the laws. The further implication must be, in the absence of any express limitation respecting removals, that as his selection of administrative officers is essential to the execution of the laws by him, so must be his power of removing those for whom he cannot continue to be responsible.

The power to prevent the removal of an officer who has served under the President is different from the authority to consent to or reject his appointment. When a nomination is made, it may be presumed that the Senate is, or may become, as well advised as to the fitness of the nominee as the President, but in the nature of things like defects in ability or intelligence or loyalty in the administration of the law of one who has served as an officer under the President, are facts as to which the President, or his trusted subordinates, must be better informed than the Senate, and the power to remove him may, therefore, be regarded as confined, for very sound and practical reasons, to the governmental authority which has administrative control. The power of removal is incident to the power of appointment, not to the power of advising and consenting to appointment, and when the grant of the executive power is enforced by the express mandate to take care that the laws be faithfully executed, it emphasizes the necessity for including within the executive power as conferred the exclusive power of removal.

Made responsible under the Constitution for the effective enforcement of the law, the President needs as an indispensable aid to meet it the disciplinary influence upon those who act under him of a reserve power of removal. In all such cases, the discretion to be exercised is that of the President in determining the national public interest and in directing the action to be taken by his executive subordinates to protect it. In this field his cabinet officers must do his will. He must place in each member of his official family, and his chief executive subordinates, implicit faith. The moment that he loses confidence in the intelligence, ability, judgment or loyalty of any one of them, he must have the power to remove him without delay. To require him to file charges and submit them to the consideration of the Senate might make impossible that unity and co-ordination in executive administration essential to effective action.

The duties of the heads of departments and bureaus in which the discretion of the President is exercised and which we have described, are the most important in the whole field of executive action of the Government. There is nothing in the Constitution which permits a distinction between the removal of the head of a department or a bureau, when he discharges a political duty of the President or exercises his direction, and the removal of executive officers engaged in the discharge of their other normal duties. The imperative reasons requiring an unrestricted power to remove the most important of his subordinates in their most important duties must, therefore, control the interpretation of the Constitution as to all appointed by him.

But this is not to say that there are not strong reasons why the President should have a like power to remove his appointees charged with other duties than those above described. The ordinary duties of officers prescribed by statute come under the general administrative control of the President by virtue of the general grant to him of the executive power, and he may properly supervise and guide their construction of the statutes under which they act in order to secure that unitary and uniform execution of the laws which Article II of the Constitution evidently contemplated in vesting general executive power in the President alone. Laws are often passed with specific provision for the adoption of regulations by a department or bureau head to make the law workable and effective. The ability and judgment manifested by the official thus empowered, as well as his energy and stimulation of his subordinates, are subjects which the president must consider and supervise in his administrative control. Finding such officers to be negligent and inefficient, the president should have the power to remove them. Of course there may be duties so peculiarly and specifically committed to the discretion of a particular officer as to raise a question whether the president may overrule or revise the officer's interpretation of his statutory duty in a particular instance. Then there may be duties of a quasi-judicial character imposed on executive officers and members of executive tribunals whose decisions after hearing affect interests of individuals, the discharge of which the President cannot in a particular case properly influence or control. But even in such a case he may consider the decision after its rendition as a reason for removing the officer, on the ground that the discretion regularly entrusted to that officer by statute has not been on the whole intelligently or wisely exercised. Otherwise he does not discharge his own constitutional duty of seeing that the laws be faithfully executed.

We have devoted much space to this discussion and decision of the question of the presidential power of removal in the First Congress, not because a Congressional conclusion on a constitutional issue is conclusive, but, first, because of our agreement with the reasons upon which it was avowedly based; second, because this was the decision of the First Congress, on a question of primary importance in the organization of the Government, made within two years after the Constitutional Convention and within a much shorter time after its ratification: and, third, because that Congress numbered among its leaders those who had been members of the Convention. It must necessarily constitute a precedent upon which many future laws supplying the machinery of the new Government would be based, and, if erroneous, it would be likely to evoke dissent and departure in future Congresses. It would come at once before the executive branch of the Government for compliance, and might well be brought before the judicial branch for a test of its validity. As we shall see, it was soon accepted as a final decision of the question by all branches of the Government.

An argument *ab inconvenienti* has been made against our conclusion in favor of the executive power of removal by the President, without the consent of the Senate—that it will open the door to a reintroduction of the spoils system. Reform in the federal civil service was begun by the Civil Service Act of 1883. It has been developed from that time, so that the classified service now includes a vast majority of all the civil officers. It may still be enlarged by further legislation. The independent power of removal by the President alone, under present conditions, works no practical interference with the merit system. Political appointments of inferior officers are still maintained in one important class, that of the first, second and third class postmasters, collectors of internal revenue, marshals, collectors of customs and other officers of that kind, distributed through the country. They are appointed by the President with the consent of the Senate. It is the intervention of the Senate in their appointment, and not in their removal, which prevents their classification into the merit system. If such appointments were vested in the heads of departments to which they belong, they could be entirely removed from politics, and that is what a number of Presidents have recommended.

For the reasons given, we must therefore hold that the provision of the law of 1876, by which the unrestricted power of removal of first class postmasters is denied to the President, is in violation of the Constitution, and invalid.

Judgment affirmed.

JUSTICE HOLMES, dissenting.

The arguments drawn from the executive power of the President, and from his duty to appoint officers of the United States (when Congress does not vest the appointment elsewhere), to take care that the laws be faithfully executed, and to commission all officers of the United States, seem to me spider's webs inadequate to control the dominant facts.

We have to deal with an office that owes its existence to Congress and that Congress may abolish tomorrow. Its duration and the pay attached to it while it lasts depend on Congress alone. Congress alone confers on the President the power to appoint to it and at any time may transfer the power to other hands. With such power over its own creation, I have no more trouble in believing that Congress has power to prescribe a term of life for it free from any interference than I have in accepting the undoubted power of Congress to decree its end. I have equally little trouble in accepting its power to prolong the tenure of an incumbent until Congress or the Senate shall have assented to his removal. The duty of the President to see that the laws be executed is a duty that does not go beyond the laws or require him to achieve more than Congress sees fit to leave within his power.

JUSTICE BRANDEIS, dissenting.

The ability to remove a subordinate executive officer, being an essential of effective government, will, in the absence of express constitutional provision to the contrary, be deemed to have been vested in some person or body. But it is not a power inherent in a chief executive. The President's power of removal from statutory civil inferior offices, like the power of appointment to them, comes immediately from Congress. It is true that the exercise of the power of removal is said to be an executive act; and that when the Senate grants or withholds consent to a removal by the President, it participates in an executive act. But the Constitution has confessedly granted to Congress the legislative power to create offices, and to prescribe the tenure thereof; and it has not in terms denied to Congress the power to control removals. To prescribe the tenure involves prescribing the conditions under which incumbency shall cease. For the possibility of removal is a condition or qualification of the tenure. When Congress provides that the incumbent shall hold the office for four years unless sooner removed with the consent of the Senate, it prescribes the term of the tenure.

To imply a grant to the President of the uncontrollable power of removal from statutory inferior executive offices involves an unnecessary and indefensible limitation upon the constitutional power of Congress to fix the tenure of inferior statutory offices. That such a limitation cannot be justified on the ground of necessity is demonstrated by the practice of our governments, state and national. The historical data submitted present a legislative practice, established by concurrent affirmative action of Congress and the President, to make consent of the Senate a condition of removal from statutory inferior, civil, executive offices to which the appointment is made for a fixed term by the President with such consent. They show that the practice has existed, without interruption, continuously for the last fifty-eight years; that, throughout this period, it has governed a great majority of all such offices; that the legislation applying the removal clause specifically to the office of postmaster was enacted more than half a century ago; and that recently the practice has, with the President's approval, been extended to several newly created offices. The data show further, that the insertion of the removal clause in acts creating inferior civil offices with fixed tenures is part of the broader legislative practice, which has prevailed since the formation of our Government, to restrict or regulate in many ways both removal from and nomination to such offices. A persistent legislative practice which involves a delimitation of the respective powers of Congress and the

President, and which has been so established and maintained, should be deemed tantamount to judicial construction, in the absence of any decision by any court to the contrary.

The persuasive effect of this legislative practice is strengthened by the fact that no instance has been found, even in the earlier period of our history, of concurrent affirmative action of Congress and the President which is inconsistent with the legislative practice of the last fifty-eight years to impose the removal clause.

The separation of the powers of government did not make each branch completely autonomous. It left each, in some measure, dependent upon the others, as it left to each power to exercise, in some respects, functions in their nature executive, legislative and judicial. Obviously the President cannot secure full execution of the laws if Congress denies to him adequate means of doing so. The President performs his full constitutional duty, if, with the means and instruments provided by Congress and within the limitations prescribed by it, he uses his best endeavors to secure the faithful execution of the laws enacted. The doctrine of the separation of powers was adopted by the Convention of 1787, not to promote efficiency but to preclude the exercise of arbitrary power. The purpose was, not to avoid friction, but, by means of the inevitable friction incident to the distribution of the governmental powers among three departments, to save the people from autocracy. Nothing in support of the claim of uncontrollable power can be inferred from the silence of the Convention of 1787 on the subject of removal. For the outstanding fact remains that every specific proposal to confer such uncontrollable power upon the President was rejected. In America, as in England, the conviction prevailed then that the people must look to representative assemblies for the protection of their liberties. And protection of the individual, even if he be an official, from the arbitrary or capricious exercise of power was then believed to be an essential of free government.

Morrison v. Olson
487 U.S. 654 (1988)

The Ethics in Government Act of 1978 provides for the appointment of an independent counsel to investigate and prosecute violations of federal criminal laws by high-ranking officials of the executive branch. The executive branch's control over the independent counsel is quite limited: the counsel is appointed by a Special Division of the Court of Appeals (District of Columbia Circuit) and can be removed by the attorney general only for "good cause." The constitutional challenge to the act arose out of a congressional investigation of the Environmental Protection Agency (EPA). In 1982 two subcommittees of the House of Representatives issued subpoenas directing the EPA to produce documents relating to its implementation of the "Superfund Law." At that time Theodore Olson was assistant attorney general for the Office of Legal Counsel, Edward Schmults was deputy attorney general, and Carol Dinkins was assistant attorney general for the Land and Resources Division. President Ronald Reagan ordered the administrator of the EPA to invoke executive privilege to withhold certain documents; after the House voted to hold the administrator in contempt, however, a compromise was reached whereby the House obtained limited access to the documents. In 1984, the House Judiciary Committee began an investigation into the controversy over the withheld documents, at which Olson testified. Following the investigation, the committee issued a report that suggested that Olson had given false and misleading testimony and that Schmults and Dinkins had wrongfully withheld documents, thereby obstructing the investigation. The chairman of the Judiciary Committee sent the report to Attorney General Edwin Meese, requesting that he seek the appointment of an independent counsel to investigate the allegations. Under the act, the attorney general is obliged to request appointment of an independent counsel if there are "reasonable grounds" to believe further investigation or prosecution is warranted. When Meese did so, the special division designated Alexia Morrison as independent counsel. Morrison caused a grand jury to issue subpoenas to Olson, Schmults, and Dinkins, who moved to quash the subpoenas, claiming that the independent-counsel provisions of the act were unconstitutional and that Morrison therefore had no authority to proceed. The district court rejected their motion, but the court of appeals reversed, ruling the act unconstitutional, and Morrison appealed that decision to the Supreme Court. Opinion of the Court: <u>Rehnquist</u>, Brennan, White, Marshall, Blackmun, Stevens, O'Connor. Dissenting opinion: <u>Scalia</u>.

THE CHIEF JUSTICE delivered the opinion of the Court.

This case presents us with a challenge to the independent counsel provisions of the Ethics in Government Act of 1978. We hold today that these provisions of the Act do not violate the Appointments Clause of the Constitution, Art II, §2, cl 2, or the limitations of Article III, nor do they impermissibly interfere with the President's authority under Article II in violation of the constitutional principle of separation of powers.

The Appointments Clause of Article II reads as follows:

> [The President] shall nominate, and by and with the Advice and Consent of the Senate, shall appoint Ambassadors, other public Ministers and Consuls, Judges of the supreme Court, and all other Officers of the United States, whose Appointments are not herein otherwise provided for, and which shall be established by Law: but the Congress may by Law vest the Appointment of such inferior Officers, as they think proper, in the President alone, in the Courts of Law, or in the Heads of Departments.

The initial question is, accordingly, whether appellant is an "inferior" or a "principal" officer. The line between "inferior" and "principal" officers is one that is far from clear, and the Framers provided little guidance into where it should be drawn. We need not attempt here to decide exactly where the line falls between the two types of officers, because in our view appellant clearly falls on the "inferior officer" side of that line. Several factors lead to this conclusion.

First, appellant is subject to removal by a higher Executive Branch official. Although appellant may not be "subordinate" to the Attorney General (and the President) insofar as she possesses a degree of independent discretion to exercise the powers delegated to her under the Act, the fact that she can be removed by the Attorney General indicates that she is to some degree "inferior" in rank and authority. Second, appellant is empowered by the Act to perform only certain, limited duties. An independent counsel's role is restricted primarily to investigation and, if appropriate, prosecution for certain federal crimes. Admittedly, the Act delegates to appellant "full power and independent authority to exercise all investigative and prosecutorial functions and powers of the Department of Justice," but this grant of authority does not include any authority to formulate policy for the Government or the Executive Branch, nor does it give appellant any administrative duties outside of those necessary to operate her office. The Act specifically provides that in policy matters appellant is to comply to the extent possible with the policies of the Department.

Third, appellant's office is limited in jurisdiction. Not only is the Act itself restricted in applicability to certain federal officials suspected of certain serious federal crimes, but an independent counsel can only act within the scope of the jurisdiction that has been granted by the Special Division pursuant to a request by the Attorney General. Finally, appellant's office is limited in tenure. There is concededly no time limit on the appointment of a particular counsel. Nonetheless, the office of independent counsel is "temporary" in the sense that an independent counsel is appointed essentially to accomplish a single task, and when that task is over the office is terminated, either by the counsel herself or by action of the Special Division. Unlike other prosecutors, appellant has no ongoing responsibilities that extend beyond the accomplishment of the mission that she was appointed for and authorized by the Special Division to undertake. In our view, these factors relating to the "ideas of tenure, duration, and duties" of the independent counsel are sufficient to establish that appellant is an "inferior" officer in the constitutional sense. Appellees argue that even if appellant is an "inferior" officer, the Clause does not empower Congress to place the power to appoint such an office outside the Executive Branch. They contend that the Clause does not contemplate congressional authorization of "interbranch appointments," in which an officer of one branch is appointed by officers of another branch. The relevant language of the Appointments Clause is worth repeating. It reads: "but the Congress may by Law vest the Appointment of such inferior Officers, as they think proper, in the President alone, in the courts of Law, or in the Heads of Departments." On its face, the language of this "excepting clause" admits of no limitation on interbranch appointments. Indeed, the inclusion of "as they think proper" seems clearly to give Congress significant discretion to determine whether it is "proper" to vest the appointment of, for example, executive officials in the "courts of Law."

We do not mean to say that Congress' power to provide for interbranch appointments of "inferior officers" is unlimited. In addition to separation of powers concerns, which would arise if such provisions for appointment had the potential to impair the constitutional functions assigned to one of the branches, [*Ex parte*] *Siebold* [1880] itself suggested that Congress' decision to vest the appointment power in the courts would be improper if there was some "incongruity" between the functions normally performed by the courts and the performance of their duty to appoint. In this case, however, we do not think it impermissible for Congress to vest the power to appoint independent counsels in a specially created federal court. Congress of course was concerned when it created the office of independent counsel with the conflicts of interest that could arise in situations when the Executive Branch is called upon to investigate its own high-ranking officers. If it were to remove the appointing authority from the Executive Branch, the most logical place to put it was in the Judicial Branch. In the light of the Act's provision making the judges of the Special Division ineligible to participate in any matters relating to an independent counsel they have appointed, we do not think that appointment of the independent counsels by the court runs afoul of the constitutional limitation on "incongruous" interbranch appointments.

We now turn to consider whether the Act is invalid under the constitutional principle of separation of powers. Two Terms ago we had occasion to consider whether it was consistent with the separation of powers for Congress to pass a statute that authorized a government official who is removable only by Congress to participate in what we found to be "executive powers." *Bowsher v. Synar* (1986). We held in *Bowsher* that "Congress cannot reserve for itself the power of removal of an officer charged with the execution of the laws except by impeachment." A primary antecedent for this ruling was our 1926 decision in *Myers v. United States.*

Unlike both *Bowsher* and *Myers,* this case does not involve an attempt by Congress itself to gain a role in the removal of executive officials other than its established powers of impeachment and conviction. The Act instead puts the removal power squarely in the hands of the Executive Branch; an independent counsel may be removed from office, "only by the personal action of the Attorney General, and only for good cause." There is no requirement of congressional approval of the Attorney General's removal decision, though the decision is subject to judicial review. In our view, the removal provisions of the Act make this case more analogous to *Humphrey's Executor v. United States* (1935), and *Wiener v. United States* (1958) [rulings denying presidential power to remove members of independent commissions before their terms expired], than to *Myers* or *Bowsher.*

We undoubtedly did rely on the terms "quasi-legislative" and "quasi-judicial" to distinguish the officials involved in *Humphrey's Executor* and *Wiener* from those in *Myers,* but our present considered view is that the determination of whether the Constitution allows Congress to impose a "good cause"–type restriction on the President's power to remove an official cannot be made to turn on whether or not that official is classified as "purely executive." But the real question is whether the removal restrictions are of such a nature that they impede the President's ability to perform his constitutional duty, and the functions of the officials in question must be analyzed in that light. It is undeniable that the Act reduces the amount of control or supervision that the

Attorney General and, through him, the President exercises over the investigation and prosecution of a certain class of alleged criminal activity. The Attorney General is not allowed to appoint the individual of his choice; he does not determine the counsel's jurisdiction; and his power to remove a counsel is limited. Nonetheless, the Act does give the Attorney General several means of supervising or controlling the prosecutorial powers that may be wielded by an independent counsel. Most importantly, the Attorney General retains the power to remove the counsel for "good cause," a power that we have already concluded provides the Executive with substantial ability to ensure that the laws are "faithfully executed" by an independent counsel.

JUSTICE SCALIA, dissenting.

That is what this suit is about. Power. The allocation of power among Congress, the President and the courts in such fashion as to preserve the equilibrium the Constitution sought to establish—so that "a gradual concentration of the several powers in the same department," *Federalist* No. 51, can effectively be resisted. Frequently an issue of this sort will come before the Court clad, so to speak, in sheep's clothing: the potential of the asserted principle to effect important change in the equilibrium of power is not immediately evident, and must be discerned by a careful and perceptive analysis. But this wolf comes as a wolf.

By the application of this statute in the present case, Congress has effectively compelled a criminal investigation of a high-level appointee of the President in connection with his actions arising out of a bitter power dispute between the President and the Legislative Branch. Mr. Olson may or may not be guilty of a crime; we do not know. But we do know that the investigation of him has been commenced, not necessarily because the President or his authorized subordinates believe it is the interest of the United States, in the sense that it warrants the diversion of resources from other efforts, and is worth the cost in money and in possible damage to other governmental interests; and not even, leaving aside those normally considered factors, because the President or his authorized subordinates necessarily believe that an

investigation is likely to unearth a violation worth prosecuting; but only because the Attorney General cannot affirm, as Congress demands, that there are no *reasonable grounds to believe* that further investigation is warranted. The decisions regarding the scope of that further investigation, its duration, and, finally, whether or not prosecution should ensue, are likewise beyond the control of the President and his subordinates. If to describe this case is not to decide it, the concept of a government of separate and coordinate powers no longer has meaning.

Art II., §1, cl 1 of the Constitution provides: The executive Power shall be vested in a President of the United States. This does not mean *some of* the executive power, but *all of* the executive power. It seems to me, therefore, that the decision of the Court of Appeals invalidating the present statute must be upheld on fundamental separation-of-powers principles if the following two questions are answered affirmatively: (1) Is the conduct of a criminal prosecution (and of an investigation to decide whether to prosecute) the exercise of purely executive power? (2) Does the statute deprive the President of the United States of exclusive control over the exercise of that power? Surprising to say, the Court appears to concede an affirmative answer to both questions, but seeks to avoid the inevitable conclusion that since the statute vests some purely executive power in a person who is not the President of the United States it is void.

The utter incompatibility of the Court's approach with our constitutional traditions can be made more clear, perhaps, by applying it to the powers of the other two Branches. Is it conceivable that if Congress passed a statute depriving itself of less than full and entire control over some insignificant area of legislation, we would inquire whether the matter was "*so central* to the functioning of the Legislative Branch" as really to require complete control, or whether the statute gives Congress "*sufficient* control over the surrogate legislator to ensure that Congress is able to perform its constitutionally assigned duties"? Of course we would have none of that. Once we determined that a purely legislative power was at issue we would require it to be exercised, wholly and entirely, by Congress. Or to bring the point closer to home, consider a statute giving to non–Article III judges just a tiny bit of purely judicial power in a relatively insignificant field, with substantial control, though not total control, in the courts—perhaps "clear error" review, which would be a fair judicial equivalent of the Attorney General's "for cause" removal power here. Is there any doubt that we would not pause to inquire whether the matter was "*so central* to the functioning of the Judicial Branch" as really to require complete control, or whether we retained "*sufficient* control over the matters to be decided that we are able to perform our constitutionally assigned duties"? We would say that our "constitutionally assigned duties" include *complete* control over all exercises of the judicial power—or, as the plurality opinion said in *Northern Pipeline Construction Co. v. Marathon Pipe Line Co.* (1982), that "[t]he inexorable command of [Article III] is clear and definite: The judicial power of the United States must be exercised by courts having the attributes prescribed in Art III." We should say here that the President's constitutionally assigned duties include *complete* control over investigation and prosecution of violations of the law, and that the inexorable command of Article II is clear and definite: the

executive power must be vested in the President of the United States.

The Court has, nonetheless, replaced the clear constitutional prescription that the executive power belongs to the President with a "balancing test." What are the standards to determine how the balance is to be struck, that is, how much removal of presidential power is too much? Many countries of the world get along with an Executive that is much weaker than ours—in fact, entirely dependent upon the continued support of the legislature. Once we depart from the text of the Constitution, just where short of that do we stop? The most amazing feature of the Court's opinion is that it does not even purport to give an answer. It simply *announces,* with no analysis, that the ability to control the decision whether to investigate and prosecute the President's closest advisors, and indeed the President himself, is not "so central to the functioning of the Executive Branch" as to be constitutionally required to be within the President's control. Evidently, the governing standard is to be what might be called the unfettered wisdom of a majority of this Court, revealed to an obedient people on a case-by-case basis. This is not only not the government of laws that the Constitution established; it is not a government of laws at all.

United States v. Nixon
418 U.S. 683 (1974)

On March 1, 1974, a federal grand jury returned indictments against Attorney General John Mitchell, presidential assistants H. R. Haldeman and John Ehrlichman, and four other officials, charging them with conspiracy to defraud the government and obstruction of justice. The grand jury also named President Richard Nixon as an unindicted coconspirator. Special Prosecutor Leon Jaworski obtained from the trial court a subpoena directing the president to produce as evidence certain tape recordings and memorandums of conversations held in the White House. Although he surrendered some of the subpoenaed materials, President Nixon refused to produce others, basing his right to refuse primarily on a claim of executive privilege. When the trial judge denied this claim, the president appealed the decision to the court of appeals. The special prosecu-

tor petitioned the Supreme Court to expedite the matter by granting certiorari before the court of appeals reached a decision. The Supreme Court agreed to the prosecutor's request, heard oral argument in special session on July 8, and announced its decision on July 24. Six days later, the House Judiciary Committee voted articles of impeachment against the president. Opinion of the Court: <u>Burger</u>, Douglas, Brennan, Stewart, White, Marshall, Blackmun, Powell. Not participating: Rehnquist.

THE CHIEF JUSTICE delivered the opinion of the Court.

JUSTICIABILITY

In the District Court, the President's counsel argued that the court lacked jurisdiction to issue the subpoena because the matter was an intra-branch dispute between a subordinate and superior officer of the Executive Branch and hence not subject to judicial resolution. Since the Executive Branch has exclusive authority and absolute discretion to decide whether to prosecute a case, it is contended that a President's decision is final in determining what evidence is to be used in a given criminal case. The Special Prosecutor's demand for the items therefore presents, in the view of the President's counsel, a political question since it involves a "textually demonstrable" grant of power under Art. II. The mere assertion of a claim of an "intra-branch dispute," without more, has never operated to defeat federal jurisdiction.

Our starting point is the nature of the proceeding for which the evidence is sought—here a pending criminal prosecution. Under the authority of Art. II §2, Congress has vested in the Attorney General the power to conduct the criminal litigation of the United States Government. It has also vested in him the power to appoint subordinate officers to assist him in the discharge of his duties. Acting pursuant to those statutes, the Attorney General has delegated the authority to represent the United States in these particular matters to a Special Prosecutor with unique authority and tenure. The regulation gives the Special Prosecutor explicit power to contest the invocation of executive privilege in the process of seeking evidence deemed relevant to the performance of these specially delegated duties. So long as this regulation is extant it has the force of law. Here at issue is the production or non-production of specified evidence deemed by the Special Prosecutor to be relevant and admissible in a pending criminal case. It is sought by one official of the Executive Branch within the scope of his express authority; it is resisted by the Chief Executive on the ground of his duty to preserve the confidentiality of the communications of the President. Whatever the correct answer on the merits, these issues are "of a type which are traditionally justiciable."

THE CLAIM OF PRIVILEGE

We turn to the claim that the subpoena should be quashed because it demands "confidential conversations between a President and his close advisors that it would be inconsistent with the public interest to produce." The first contention is a broad claim that the separation of powers doctrine precludes judicial review of a President's claim of privilege. The second contention is that if he does not prevail on the claim of absolute privilege, the court should hold as a matter of constitutional law that the privilege prevails over the subpoena *duces tecum.*

In the performance of assigned constitutional duties each branch of the Government must initially interpret the Constitution, and the interpretation of its powers by any branch is due great respect from the others. The President's counsel, as we have noted, reads the Constitution as providing an absolute privilege of confidentiality for all Presidential communications. Many decisions of this Court, however, have unequivocally reaffirmed the holding of *Marbury v. Madison* [1803] that "it is emphatically the province and duty of the judicial department to say what the law is."

In support of his claim of absolute privilege, the President's counsel urges two grounds, one of which is common to all governments and one of which is peculiar to our system of separation of powers. The first ground is the valid need for protection of communications between high Government officials and those who advise and assist them in the performance of their manifold duties; the importance of this confidentiality is too plain to require further discussion. Human experience teaches that those who expect public dissemination of their remarks may well temper candor with a concern for appearances and for their own interests to the detriment of the decision-making process. Whatever the nature of the privilege of confidentiality of Presidential communications in the exercise of Art. II powers, the privilege can be said to derive from the supremacy of each branch within its own assigned area of constitutional duties. Certain powers and privileges flow from the nature of enumerated powers; the protection of the confidentiality of Presidential communications has similar constitutional underpinnings and rests on the doctrine of separation of powers. Here it is argued that the independence of the Executive Branch within its own sphere insulates a President from a judicial subpoena in an ongoing criminal prosecution, and thereby protects confidential Presidential communications.

However, neither the doctrine of separation of powers, nor the need for confidentiality of high-level communications, without more, can sustain an absolute, unqualified Presidential privilege of immunity from judicial process under all circumstances. The President's need for complete candor and objectivity from advisers calls for great deference from the courts. However, when the privilege depends solely on the broad, undifferentiated claim of public interest in the confidentiality of such conversations, a confrontation with other values arises. Absent a claim of need to protect military, diplomatic, or sensitive national security secrets, we find it difficult to accept the argument that even the very important interest in confidentiality of Presidential communications is significantly diminished by production of such material for *in camera* inspection with all the protection that a district court will be obliged to provide.

The impediment that an absolute, unqualified privilege would place in the way of the primary constitutional duty of the Judicial Branch to do justice in criminal prosecutions would plainly conflict with the function of the courts under Art. III. Since we conclude that the legitimate needs of the judicial process may outweigh Presidential privilege, it is necessary to resolve those competing interests in a manner that preserves the essential functions of each branch.

The expectation of a President to the confidentiality of his conversations and correspondence, like the claim of confidentiality of judicial deliberations, for example, has all the values to which we accord deference for the privacy of all citizens and, added to those values, is the necessity for protection of the public interest in candid, objective, and even blunt or harsh opinions in Presidential decision making. But this presumptive privilege must be considered in light of our historic commitment to the rule of law. The ends of criminal justice would be defeated if judgments were to be founded on a partial or speculative presentation of the facts. The very integrity of the judicial system and public confidence in the system depend on full disclosure of all the facts, within the framework of the rules of evidence. To ensure that justice is done, it is imperative to the function of courts that compulsory process be available for the production of evidence needed either by the prosecution or by the defense. In this case the President challenges a subpoena served on him as a third party requiring the production of materials for use in a criminal prosecution; he does so on the claim that he has a privilege against disclosure of confidential communications. He does not place his claim of privilege on the ground they are military or diplomatic secrets. As to these areas of Art. II duties the courts have traditionally shown the utmost deference to Presidential responsibilities. No case of the Court, however, has extended this high degree of deference to a President's generalized interest in confidentiality.

On the other hand, the allowance of the privilege to withhold evidence that is demonstrably relevant in a criminal trial would cut deeply into the guarantee of due process of law and gravely impair the basic function of the courts. Without access to specific facts a criminal prosecution may be totally frustrated. We conclude that when the ground for asserting privilege as to subpoenaed materials sought for use in a criminal trial is based only on the generalized interest in confidentiality, it cannot prevail over the fundamental demands of due process of law in the fair administration of criminal justice. The generalized assertion of privilege must yield to the demonstrated, specific need for evidence in a pending criminal trial.

Clinton v. Jones
520 U.S. 681 (1997)

Paula Corbin Jones sued under 42 U.S.C. sections 1983 and 1985 and under Arkansas law to recover damages from President Bill Clinton, alleging that while Clinton was governor of Arkansas, he made "abhorrent" sexual advances to her and that her rejection of those advances led to punishment by her supervisors in the state job she held at the time. President Clinton filed a motion to dismiss the suit on presidential immunity grounds and requested that all other pleadings and motions be deferred until the immunity issue was resolved. The federal district court granted that request but ultimately refused to dismiss the suit on immunity grounds and ruled that discovery—the pretrial exchange of information between the parties—could go forward, but ordered any trial stayed until the conclusion of the Clinton presidency. The Eighth Circuit affirmed the dismissal denial, but reversed the trial postponement as the "functional equivalent" of a grant of temporary immunity to which petitioner was not constitutionally entitled. The Supreme Court then granted certiorari. Opinion of the Court: Stevens, Rehnquist, O'Connor, Scalia, Kennedy, Souter, Thomas, Ginsburg. Concurring in the judgment: Breyer.

JUSTICE STEVENS delivered the opinion of the Court.

The President submits that in all but the most exceptional cases the Constitution requires federal courts to defer civil suits against the president until his term ends and that, in any event, respect for the office warrants such a stay. Despite the force of the arguments supporting the President's submissions, we conclude that they must be rejected.

It is true that we have often stressed the importance of avoiding the premature adjudication of constitutional questions. That doctrine of avoidance make[s] it appropriate to identify two important constitutional issues not encompassed within the questions presented by the petition for certiorari that we need not address today. First, because the claim of immunity is asserted in a federal court and relies heavily on the doctrine of separation of powers that restrains each of the three branches of the Federal Government from encroaching on the domain of the other two, it is not necessary to consider or decide whether a comparable claim might succeed in a state tribunal. Second, our decision rejecting the immunity claim and allowing the case to proceed does not require us to confront the question whether a court may compel the attendance of the President at any specific time or place. Petitioner's principal submission—that "in all but the most exceptional cases," the Constitution affords the President temporary immunity from civil damages litigation arising out of events that occurred

before he took office—cannot be sustained on the basis of precedent. Only three sitting Presidents have been defendants in civil litigation involving their actions prior to taking office. None of those cases sheds any light on the constitutional issue before us.

The principal rationale for affording certain public servants immunity from suits for money damages arising out of their official acts is inapplicable to unofficial conduct. In cases involving prosecutors, legislators, and judges we have repeatedly explained that the immunity serves the public interest in enabling such officials to perform their designated functions effectively without fear that a particular decision may give rise to personal liability. That rationale provided the principal basis for our holding that a former President of the United States was "entitled to absolute immunity from damages liability predicated on his official acts," [*Nixon v.*] *Fitzgerald* (1982). Our central concern was to avoid rendering the President "unduly cautious in the discharge of his official duties." This reasoning provides no support for an immunity for unofficial conduct. We have never suggested that the President, or any other official, has an immunity that extends beyond the scope of any action taken in an official capacity.

Petitioner's strongest argument supporting his immunity claim is based on the text and structure of the Constitution. He does not contend that the occupant of the Office of the President is "above the law," in the sense that his conduct is entirely immune from judicial scrutiny. The President argues merely for a postponement of the judicial proceedings that will determine whether he violated any law. His argument is grounded in the character of the office that was created by Article II of the Constitution, and relies on separation of powers principles that have structured our constitutional arrangement since the Founding.

As a starting premise, petitioner contends that he occupies a unique office with powers and responsibilities so vast and important that the public interest demands that he devote his undivided time and attention to his public duties. He submits that—given the nature of the office—the doctrine of separation of powers places limits on the authority of the Federal Judiciary to interfere with the Executive Branch that would be transgressed by allowing this action to proceed.

We have no dispute with the initial premise of the argument. It does not follow, however, that separation of powers principles would be violated by allowing this action to proceed. Of course the lines between the powers of the three branches are not always neatly defined. But in this case there is no suggestion that the Federal Judiciary is being asked to perform any function that might in some way be described as "executive." Respondent is merely asking the courts to exercise their core Article III jurisdiction to decide cases and controversies. Whatever the outcome of this case, there is no possibility that the decision will curtail the scope of the official powers of the Executive Branch. The litigation of questions that relate entirely to the unofficial conduct of the individual who happens to be the President poses no perceptible risk of misallocation of either judicial power or executive power.

Rather than arguing that the decision of the case will produce either an aggrandizement of judicial power or a narrowing of executive power, petitioner contends that—as a byproduct of an otherwise traditional exercise of judicial power—burdens will be placed on the President that will hamper the performance of his official duties. We have recognized that "even when a branch does not arrogate power to itself, the separation-of-powers doctrine requires that a branch not impair another in the performance of its constitutional duties." *Loving v. United States* (1996). As a factual matter, petitioner contends that this particular case—as well as the potential additional litigation that an affirmance of the Court of Appeals judgment might spawn—may impose an unacceptable burden on the President's time and energy, and thereby impair the effective performance of his office.

Petitioner's predictive judgment finds little support in either history or the relatively narrow compass of the issues raised in this particular case. In the more than 200-year history of the Republic, only three sitting Presidents have been subjected to suits for their private actions. If the past is any indicator, it seems unlikely that a deluge of such litigation will ever engulf the Presidency. As for the case at hand, if

properly managed by the District Court, it appears to us highly unlikely to occupy any substantial amount of petitioner's time.

Of greater significance, petitioner errs by presuming that interactions between the Judicial Branch and the Executive, even quite burdensome interactions, necessarily rise to the level of constitutionally forbidden impairment of the Executive's ability to perform its constitutionally mandated functions. The fact that a federal court's exercise of its traditional Article III jurisdiction may significantly burden the time and attention of the Chief Executive is not sufficient to establish a violation of the Constitution. Sitting Presidents have responded to court orders to provide testimony and other information with sufficient frequency that such interactions between the Judicial and Executive Branches can scarcely be thought a novelty. President Monroe responded to written interrogatories, President Nixon produced tapes in response to a *subpoena duces tecum,* President Ford complied with an order to give a deposition in a criminal trial, and President Clinton has twice given videotaped testimony in criminal proceedings. Moreover, sitting Presidents have also voluntarily complied with judicial requests for testimony.

In sum, "[i]t is settled law that the separation-of-powers doctrine does not bar every exercise of jurisdiction over the President of the United States." *Fitzgerald.* If the Judiciary may severely burden the Executive Branch by reviewing the legality of the President's official conduct, and if it may direct appropriate process to the President himself, it must follow that the federal courts have power to determine the legality of his unofficial conduct. The burden on the President's time and energy that is a mere by product of such review surely cannot be considered as onerous as the direct burden imposed by judicial review and the occasional invalidation of his official actions. We therefore hold that the doctrine of separation of powers does not require federal courts to stay all private actions against the President until he leaves office. If Congress deems it appropriate to afford the President stronger protection, it may respond with appropriate legislation. Our holding today raises no barrier to a statutory response to these concerns.

The Federal District Court has jurisdiction to decide this case. Like every other citizen who properly invokes that jurisdiction, respondent has a right to an orderly disposition of her claims. Accordingly, the judgment of the Court of Appeals is affirmed.

JUSTICE BREYER, concurring in the judgment.

I agree with the majority that the Constitution does not automatically grant the President an immunity from civil lawsuits based upon his private conduct. However, once the President sets forth and explains a conflict between judicial proceeding and public duties, the matter changes. At that point, the Constitution permits a judge to schedule a trial in an ordinary civil damages action (where postponement normally is possible without overwhelming damage to a plaintiff) only within the constraints of a constitutional principle—a principle that forbids a federal judge in such a case to interfere with the President's discharge of his public duties. I have no doubt that the Constitution contains such a principle applicable to civil suits, based upon Article II's vesting of the entire "executive Power" in a single individual, implemented through the Constitution's structural separation of powers, and revealed both by history and case precedent.

I recognize that this case does not require us now to apply the principle specifically, thereby delineating its contours; nor need we now decide whether lower courts are to apply it directly or categorically through the use of presumptions or rules of administration. Yet I fear that to disregard it now may appear to deny it. I also fear that the majority's description of the relevant precedents deemphasizes the extent to which they support a principle of the President's independent authority to control his own time and energy. Further, if the majority is wrong in predicting the future infrequency of private civil litigation against sitting Presidents, acknowledgement and future delineation of the constitutional principle will prove a practically necessary institutional safeguard.

In re Neagle
135 U.S. 1 (1890)

US marshal David Neagle was appointed by the attorney general to protect Supreme Court justice Stephen Field while he rode circuit in California. When David Terry, a disappointed litigant with a grudge against Field, appeared about to attack the justice, Neagle shot and killed him. After California authorities arrested Neagle and charged him with murder, the US government sought to secure Neagle's release on habeas corpus. In the absence of any law specifically authorizing the president or the attorney general to assign marshals as bodyguards to the justices, the United States relied on a federal statute that made the writ available to those "in custody for an act done or omitted in pursuance of a law of the United States." Opinion of the Court: Miller, Bradley, Harlan, Gray, Blatchford, Brewer. Dissenting opinion: Lamar, Fuller. Not participating: Field.

JUSTICE MILLER delivered the opinion of the Court.

Without a more minute discussion of this testimony, it produces upon us the conviction of a settled purpose on the part of Terry and his wife, amounting to a conspiracy, to murder Justice Field. And we are quite sure that if Neagle had been merely a brother or a friend of Judge Field, travelling with him, and aware of all the previous relations of Terry to the Judge—as he was—of his bitter animosity, his declared purpose to have revenge even to the point of killing him, he would have been justified in what he did in defence of Mr. Justice Field's life, and possibly of his own.

But such a justification would be a proper subject for consideration on a trial of the case for murder in the courts of the State of California, and there exists no authority in the courts of the United States to discharge the prisoner while held in custody by the State authorities for this offence, unless there be found in aid of the defence of the prisoner some element of power and authority asserted under the government of the United States.

This element is said to be found in the facts that Mr. Justice Field, when attacked, was in the immediate discharge of his duty as judge of the Circuit Courts of the United States within California; that the assault upon him grew out of the animosity of Terry and wife, arising out of the previous discharge of his duty as circuit justice in the case for which they were committed for contempt of court; and that the deputy marshal of the United States, who killed Terry in defence of Field's life, was charged with a duty under the law of the United States to protect Field from the violence which Terry was inflicting, and which was intended to lead to Field's death.

It is urged, however, that there exists no statute authorizing any such protection as that which Neagle was instructed to give Judge Field in the present case, and indeed no protection whatever against a vindictive or malicious assault growing out of the faithful discharge of his official duties; and that the language of section 753 of the Revised Statutes, that the party seeking the benefit of the writ of *habeas corpus* must in this connection show that he is "in custody for an act done or omitted in pursuance of a law of the United States," makes it necessary that upon this occasion it should be shown that the act for which Neagle is imprisoned was done by virtue of an act of Congress. It is not supposed that any special act of Congress exists which authorizes the marshals or deputy marshals of the United States in express terms to accompany the judges of the Supreme Court through their circuits, and act as a bodyguard to them, to defend them against malicious assaults against their persons.

But we are of opinion that this view of the statute is an unwarranted restriction of the meaning of a law designed to extend in a liberal manner the benefit of the writ of *habeas corpus* to persons imprisoned for the performance of their duty. And we are satisfied that if it was the duty of Neagle, under the circumstances, a duty which could only arise under the laws of the United States, to defend Mr. Justice Field from a murderous attack upon him, he brings himself within the meaning of the section we have recited.

In the view we take of the Constitution of the United States, any obligation fairly and properly inferrible from that instrument, or any duty of the marshal to be derived from the general scope of his duties under the laws of the United States, is "a law" within the meaning of this phrase. It would be a great reproach to the system of government of the United States, declared to be within its sphere sovereign and supreme, if there is to be found within the domain of its powers no means of protecting the judges, in the conscientious and faithful discharge of their duties, from the malice and hatred of those upon whom their judgments may operate unfavorably.

Where, then, are we to look for the protection which we have shown Judge Field was entitled to when engaged in the discharge of his official duties? The Constitution, section 3, Article 2, declares that the President "shall take care that the laws be faithfully executed," and he is provided with the means of fulfilling this obligation by his authority to commission all the officers of the United States, and, by and with the advice and consent of the Senate, to appoint the most important of them and to fill vacancies. He is declared to be commander-in-chief of the army and navy of the United States. The duties which are thus imposed upon him he is further enabled to perform by the recognition in the Constitution, and the creation by acts of Congress, of executive departments, which have varied in number from four or five to seven or eight, the heads of which are familiarly called cabinet ministers. These aid him in the performance of the great duties of his office, and represent him in a thousand acts to which it can hardly be supposed his personal attention is called, and thus he is enabled to fulfil the duty of his great department, expressed in the phrase that "he shall take care that the laws be faithfully executed." Is this duty limited to the enforcement of acts of Congress or of treaties of the United States according to their express terms, or does it include the rights, duties and obligations growing out of the Constitution itself, our international relations, and all the protection implied by the nature of the government under the Constitution?

We cannot doubt the power of the President to take measures for the protection of a judge of one of the courts of the United States, who, while in the discharge of the duties of his office, is threatened with a personal attack which may probably result in his death. But there is positive law investing the marshals and their deputies with powers which not only justify what Marshal Neagle did in this matter, but which imposed it upon him as a duty. In chapter fourteen of the Revised Statutes of the United States, which is devoted to the appointment and duties of the district attorneys, marshals, and clerks of the courts of the United States, section 788 declares: "The marshals and their deputies shall have, in each State, the same powers, in executing the laws of the United States, as the sheriffs and their deputies in such State may have, by law, in executing the laws thereof." If, therefore, a sheriff of the State of California was authorized to do in regard to the laws of California what Neagle did, that is, if he was authorized to keep the peace, to protect a judge from assault and murder, then Neagle was authorized to do the same thing in reference to the laws of the United States.

That there is a peace of the United States; that a man assaulting a judge of the United States while in the discharge of his duties violates that peace; that in such case the marshal of the United States stands in the same relation to the peace of the United States which the sheriff of the county does to the peace of the State of California; are questions too clear to need argument to prove them.

The result at which we have arrived upon this examination is, that in taking the life of Terry, under the circumstances, he was acting under the authority of the law of the United States, and was justified in so doing; and that he is not liable to answer in the courts of California on account of his part in that transaction.

We therefore affirm the judgment of the Circuit Court authorizing his discharge from the custody of the sheriff of San Joaquin County.

Youngstown Sheet & Tube Company v. Sawyer
343 U.S. 579 (1952)

In order to avert an apparently imminent nation-wide steel strike during the Korean War, President Harry Truman issued an executive order directing the secretary of commerce to seize and operate the nation's steel mills. By taking such a step, he implicitly rejected the remedy offered by the Taft-Hartley Act: the seeking of an injunction against the strike. Reporting his action to Congress, the president justified the seizure by citing his aggregate powers as chief executive and commander in chief. He also noted that Congress could reverse or endorse the seizure. Congress took no action prior to the Supreme Court's consideration of the case, however. Shortly after the seizure, the steel companies obtained from a federal district court an injunction restraining the secretary of commerce from "continuing the seizure and possession of the plants," but on the same day the court of appeals stayed the injunction. The Supreme Court granted certiorari and expedited consideration of the case, announcing its decision less than two months after the seizure. Opinion of the Court: Black, *Frankfurter, Burton, Jackson. Concurring opinions:* Frankfurter; Burton; Jackson; Clark; Douglas. *Dissenting opinion:* Vinson, *Reed, Minton.*

JUSTICE BLACK delivered the opinion of the Court.

We are asked to decide whether the President was acting within his constitutional power when he issued an order directing the Secretary of Commerce to take possession of and operate most of the Nation's steel mills.

The President's power, if any, to issue the order must stem either from an act of Congress or from the Constitution itself. There is no statute that expressly authorizes the President to take possession of property as he did here. Nor is there any act of Congress to which our attention has been directed from which such a power can fairly be implied. Indeed, we do not understand the Government to rely on statutory authorization for this seizure. It is clear that if the President had authority to issue the order he did, it must be found in some provision of the Constitution. And it is not claimed that express constitutional language grants this power to the President. The contention is that presidential power should be implied from the aggregate of his powers under the Constitution. Particular reliance is placed on provisions in Article II which say that "The executive Power shall be vested in a President . . . "; that "he shall take Care that the Laws be faithfully executed"; and that he "shall be Commander in Chief of the Army and Navy of the United States."

The order cannot properly be sustained as an exercise of the President's military power as Commander in Chief of the Armed Forces. The Government attempts to do so by citing a number of cases upholding broad powers in military commanders engaged in day-to-day fighting in a theater of war. Such cases need not concern us here. Even though "theater of war" may be an expanding concept, we cannot with faithfulness to our constitutional system hold that the Commander in Chief of the Armed Forces has the ultimate power as such to take possession of private property in order to keep labor disputes from stopping production. This is a job for the Nation's lawmakers, not for its military authorities.

Nor can the seizure order be sustained because of the several constitutional provisions that grant executive power to the President. In the framework of our Constitution, the President's power to see that the laws are faithfully executed refutes the idea that he is to be a lawmaker. The Constitution limits his functions in the lawmaking process to the recommending of laws he thinks wise and the vetoing of laws he thinks bad. And the Constitution is neither silent nor equivocal about who shall make laws which the President is to execute. The first section of the first article says that "All legislative Powers herein granted shall be vested in a Congress of the United States." After granting many powers to the Congress, Article I goes on to provide that Congress may "make all Laws which shall be necessary and proper for carrying into Execution the foregoing Powers, and all other Powers vested by this Constitution in the Government of the United States, or in any Department or Officer thereof."

The Founders of this Nation entrusted the lawmaking power to the Congress alone in both good and bad times. It would do no good to recall the historical events, the fears of power and the hopes for freedom that lay behind their choice. Such a review would but confirm our holding that this seizure order cannot stand. The judgment of the District Court is

Affirmed.

JUSTICE FRANKFURTER, concurring in the judgment and opinion of the Court.

Congress has frequently—at least 16 times since 1916—specifically provided for executive seizure of production, transportation, communications, or storage facilities. In every case it has qualified this grant of power with limitations and safeguards. Congress in 1947 was again called upon to consider whether governmental seizure should be used to avoid serious industrial shutdowns. A proposal that the President be given powers to seize plants to avert a shutdown where the "health or safety" of the Nation was endangered, was thoroughly canvassed by Congress and rejected. No room for doubt remains that the proponents as well as the opponents of the bill which became the Labor Management Relations Act of 1947 clearly understood that as a result of that legislation the only recourse for preventing a shutdown in any basic industry, after failure of mediation, was Congress. Perhaps as much so as is true of any piece of modern legislation, Congress acted with full consciousness of what it was doing and in the light of much recent history.

It cannot be contended that the President would have had power to issue this order had Congress explicitly negated such authority in formal legislation. Congress has expressed its will to withhold this power from the President as though it had said so in so many words. The authoritatively expressed purpose of Congress to disallow such power to the President and to require him, when in his mind the occasion arose for such a seizure, to put the matter to Congress and ask for specific authority from it, could not be more decisive if it had been written into §§206–210 of the Labor Management Relations Act of 1947.

JUSTICE JACKSON, concurring in the judgment and opinion of the Court.

A judge, like an executive adviser, may be surprised at the poverty of really useful and unambiguous authority applicable to concrete problems of executive power as they actually present themselves. Just what our forefathers did envision, or would have envisioned had they foreseen modern conditions, must be divined from materials almost as enigmatic as the dreams Joseph was called upon to interpret for Pharaoh. A century and a half of partisan debate and scholarly speculation yields no net result but only supplies more or less apt quotations from respected sources on each side of any question. They largely cancel each other. And court decisions are indecisive because of the judicial practice of dealing with the largest questions in the most narrow way.

The actual art of governing under our Constitution does not and cannot conform to judicial definitions of the power of any of its branches based on isolated clauses or even single Articles torn from context. While the Constitution diffuses power the better to secure liberty, it also contemplates that practice will integrate the dispersed powers into a workable government. It enjoins upon its branches separateness but interdependence, autonomy but reciprocity. Presidential powers are not fixed but fluctuate, depending upon their disjunction or conjunction with those of Congress. We may well begin by a somewhat over-simplified grouping of practical situations in which a President may doubt, or others may challenge, his powers, and by distinguishing roughly the legal consequences of this factor of relativity.

1. When the President acts pursuant to an express or implied authorization of Congress, his authority is at its maximum, for it includes all that he possesses in his own right plus all that Congress can delegate. In these circumstances, and in these only, may he be said (for what it may be worth) to personify the federal sovereignty. If his act is held unconstitutional under these circumstances, it usually means that the Federal Government as an undivided whole lacks power. A seizure executed by the President pursuant to an Act of Congress would be supported by the strongest of presumptions and the widest latitude of judicial interpretation, and the burden of persuasion would rest heavily upon any who might attack it.

2. When the President acts in absence of either a congressional grant or denial of authority, he can only rely upon his own independent powers, but there is a zone of twilight in which he and Congress may have concurrent authority, or in which its distribution is uncertain. Therefore, congressional inertia, indifference or quiescence may sometimes, at least as a practical matter, enable, if not invite, measures on independent presidential responsibility. In this area, any actual test of power is likely to depend on the imperatives of events and contemporary imponderables rather than on abstract theories of law.

3. When the President takes measures incompatible with the expressed or implied will of Congress, his power is at its lowest ebb, for then he can rely only upon his own constitutional powers minus any constitutional powers of Congress over the matter. Courts can sustain exclusive presidential control in such a case only by disabling the Congress from acting upon the subject. Presidential claim to a power at once so conclusive and preclusive must be scrutinized with caution, for what is at stake is the equilibrium established by our constitutional system.

Into which of these classifications does this executive seizure of the steel industry fit? It is eliminated from the first by admission, for it is conceded that no congressional authorization exists for this seizure. Can it then be defended under flexible tests available to the second category? It seems clearly eliminated from that class because Congress has not left seizure of private property an open field but has covered it by three statutory policies inconsistent with this seizure. In choosing a different and inconsistent way of his own, the President cannot claim that it is necessitated or invited by failure of Congress to legislate upon the occasions, grounds and methods for seizure of industrial properties.

This leaves the current seizure to be justified only by the severe tests under the third grouping, where it can be supported only by any remainder of executive power after subtraction of such powers as Congress may have over the subject. In short, we can sustain the President only by holding that seizure of such strike-bound industries is within his domain and beyond control by Congress. Thus, this Court's first review of such seizures occurs under circumstances which leave presidential power most vulnerable to attack and in the least favorable of possible constitutional postures.

That seems to be the logic of an argument tendered at our bar—that the President having, on his own responsibility, sent American troops abroad derives from that act "affirmative power" to seize the means of producing a supply of steel for them. I cannot foresee all that it might entail if the Court should indorse this argument. Nothing in our Constitution is plainer than that declaration of a war is entrusted only to Congress. Of course, a state of war may in fact exist without a formal declaration. But no doctrine that the Court could promulgate would seem to me more sinister and alarming than that a President whose conduct of foreign affairs is so largely uncontrolled, and often even is unknown, can vastly enlarge his mastery over the internal affairs of the country by his own commitment of the Nation's armed forces to some foreign venture.

That military powers of the Commander in Chief were not to supersede representative government of internal affairs seems obvious from the Constitution and from elementary American history. We should not use this occasion to circumscribe, much less to contract, the lawful role of the President as Commander in Chief. I should indulge the widest latitude of interpretation to sustain his exclusive function to command the instruments of national force, at least when turned against the outside world for the security of our society. But, when it is turned inward, not because of rebellion but because of a lawful economic struggle between industry and labor, it should have no such indulgence.

In view of the ease, expedition and safety with which Congress can grant and has granted large emergency powers, certainly ample to embrace this crisis, I am quite unimpressed with the argument that we should affirm possession of them without statute. Such power either has no beginning or it has no end. If it exists, it need submit to no legal restraint. I am

not alarmed that it would plunge us straightway into dictatorship, but it is at least a step in that wrong direction. But I have no illusion that any decision by this Court can keep power in the hands of Congress if it is not wise and timely in meeting its problems. A crisis that challenges the President equally, or perhaps primarily, challenges Congress. If not good law, there was worldly wisdom in the maxim attributed to Napoleon that "The tools belong to the man who can use them." We may say that power to legislate for emergencies belongs in the hands of Congress, but only Congress itself can prevent power from slipping through its fingers.

The essence of our free Government is "leave to live by no man's leave, underneath the law"—to be governed by those impersonal forces which we call law. Our Government is fashioned to fulfill this concept so far as humanly possible. The Executive, except for recommendation and veto, has no legislative power. The executive action we have here originates in the individual will of the President and represents an exercise of authority without law. No one, perhaps not even the President, knows the limits of the power he may seek to exert in this instance and the parties affected cannot learn the limit of their rights. We do not know today what powers over labor or property would be claimed to flow from Government possession if we should legalize it, what rights to compensation would be claimed or recognized, or on what contingency it would end. With all its defects, delays and inconveniences, men have discovered no technique for long preserving free government except that the Executive be under the law, and that the law be made by parliamentary deliberations. Such institutions may be destined to pass away. But it is the duty of the Court to be last, not first, to give them up.

CHIEF JUSTICE VINSON, with whom JUSTICE REED and JUSTICE MINTON join, dissenting.

In passing upon the question of Presidential powers in this case, we must first consider the context in which those powers were exercised. One is not here called upon even to consider the possibility of executive seizure of a farm, a corner grocery store or even a single industrial plant. Such considerations arise only when one ignores the central fact of this case—that the Nation's entire basic steel production would have shut down completely if there had been no Government seizure. Even ignoring for the moment whatever confidential information the President may possess as "the Nation's organ for foreign affairs," the uncontroverted affidavits in this record amply support the finding that "a work stoppage would immediately jeopardize and imperil our national defense." Plaintiffs do not remotely suggest any basis for rejecting the President's finding that any stoppage of steel production would immediately place the Nation in peril.

Focusing now on the situation confronting the President on the night of April 8, 1952, we cannot but conclude that the President was performing his duty under the Constitution to "take Care that the Laws be faithfully executed"—a duty described by President Benjamin Harrison as "the central idea of the office." The President reported to Congress the morning after the seizure that he acted because a work stoppage in steel production would immediately imperil the safety of the Nation by preventing execution of the legislative programs for procurement of military equipment. And, while a shutdown could be averted by granting the price concessions requested by plaintiffs, granting such concessions would disrupt the price stabilization program also enacted by Congress. Rather than fail to execute either legislative program, the President acted to execute both.

Much of the argument in this case has been directed at straw men. We do not now have before us the case of a President acting solely on the basis of his own notions of the public welfare. Nor is there any question of unlimited executive power in this case. The President himself closed the door to any such claim when he sent his Message to Congress stating his purpose to abide by any action of Congress, whether approving or disapproving his seizure action. Here, the President immediately made sure that Congress was fully informed of the temporary action he had taken only to preserve the legislative programs from destruction until Congress could act.

The absence of a specific statute authorizing seizure of the steel mills as a mode of executing the laws—both the military procurement program and the anti-inflation program—has not until today been thought to prevent the President from executing the laws. Unlike an administrative commission confined to the enforcement of the statute under which it was created, or the head of a department when administering a particular statute, the President is a constitutional officer charged with taking care that a "mass of legislation" be executed. Flexibility as to mode of execution to meet critical situations is a matter of practical necessity. Faced with the duty of executing the defense programs which Congress had enacted and the disastrous effects that any stoppage in steel production would have on those programs, the President acted to preserve those programs by seizing the steel mills. The President immediately informed Congress of his action and clearly stated his intention to abide by the legislative will. No basis for claims of arbitrary action, unlimited powers or dictatorial usurpation of congressional power appears from the facts of this case. On the contrary, judicial, legislative and executive precedents throughout our history demonstrate that in this case the President acted in full conformity with his duties under the Constitution.

6

War and Foreign Affairs

Throughout the Vietnam War, congressional opponents of the conflict charged that the president had usurped Congress's war-making powers. Following the invasion of Iraq in 2003, congressional critics complained that the Bush administration had misled them with faulty intelligence on weapons of mass destruction. And more recently, some congressional critics insisted that President Barack Obama needed congressional approval to conduct operations in Libya and against ISIS.

There is nothing novel in these conflicts. Within five years of the ratification of the Constitution, James Madison and Alexander Hamilton—the principal authors of *The Federalist*—clashed over whether President George Washington had the authority to issue a proclamation of American neutrality in the war between France and Great Britain.[1] Since then, disputes over the constitutional distribution of power for the direction of foreign affairs and for the commitment of American troops have been a recurring feature of American politics. The constitutional separation of powers virtually guarantees such interbranch conflict, because the division of powers "is an invitation to struggle for the privilege of directing American foreign policy," and policy and constitutional arguments are frequently intermixed in this struggle.[2]

The scope of the national power over war and foreign affairs has also raised constitutional questions. The Framers clearly intended to lodge power over these subjects in the federal government. As Madison observed in *The Federalist,* No. 42, "If we are to be one nation in any respect, it clearly ought to be in respect to other nations." But this grant of power, in the view of some observers, can pose a threat to the division of power between the federal and state governments and to constitutional protections of individual rights. The difficulty of delineating the limits of the foreign-affairs power, for instance, has fueled suspicions that the federal government might use that power as a pretext to invade state prerogatives. Similar problems attend the protection of individual rights. Indisputably, the Framers sought to create a constitution that was, as Chief Justice John Marshall proclaimed in *McCulloch v. Maryland*, "intended to endure for ages to come, and, consequently, to be adapted to the various crises of human affairs." Less clear is whether this aim is compatible with the protection of individual rights, or whether a successful response to extreme crises might require a temporary sacrifice of those rights. In sum, constitutional conflicts have focused on the distribution of power among the branches of the federal government, between the levels of the federal system, and between the government and the people.

THE INTERBRANCH DISTRIBUTION OF POWER

Table 6.1 summarizes the war and foreign-affairs powers expressly granted in the Constitution to each branch of government. What is most striking is the complete absence of the judiciary. Although the power of judicial review extends to the exercise of governmental power in war and foreign affairs, several interrelated factors have restricted the frequency and importance of judicial intervention in those areas.

One factor is the nonjusticiability of many questions involving war and foreign affairs under the political-questions doctrine (see Chapter 3). For example, although many opponents of the Vietnam War believed it was unconstitutional, efforts to secure a judicial ruling to that effect consistently failed under the political-questions doctrine or because the plaintiffs lacked standing to sue. The Supreme Court also invoked the political-questions doctrine in *Goldwater v. Carter* (1979) to avoid a ruling on whether President Jimmy Carter could unilaterally terminate the nation's mutual-defense treaty with Taiwan.

An additional barrier has been the Court's traditional reluctance even to consider such delicate questions. For instance, the Court used its discretionary jurisdiction to refuse to hear several challenges to the constitutionality of the Vietnam War. This unwillingness to

TABLE 6.1   The Constitutional Distribution of Powers of War and Foreign Affairs

	Presidential Powers	Congressional Powers	Senatorial Powers
Foreign Relations Powers	1. To make treaties (Senate consent required) 2. To appoint envoys (Senate consent required) 3. To receive envoys	1. To regulate foreign commerce 2. To lay duties 3. To define and punish piracies and felonies committed on the high seas and offenses against the law of nations	1. To advise on and consent to treaties 2. To advise on and consent to appointment of envoys
Defense Powers	1. Commander-in-chief power 2. To repel sudden attacks on the United States or its armed forces (not mentioned in the constitutional text but indisputably granted)	1. To raise and support armies 2. To provide and maintain a navy 3. To make rules for the government and regulation of the land and naval forces 4. To provide for calling forth the militia to repel invasions 5. To suspend the writ of *habeas corpus* in cases of rebellion or invasion or when the public safety might require such action 6. To declare war	1. To advise on and consent to appointments
General Powers	1. To inform the Congress about the state of the union and make recommendations 2. To convene both houses of Congress, or either one of them, on extraordinary occasions 3. To veto legislation 4. To execute the laws (which includes unmentioned, delegated rulemaking powers) 5. To appoint (Senate consent generally required)	1. To lay taxes, etc., and provide for the common defense and general welfare 2. To make all laws necessary and proper for carrying into execution congressional powers, and all other powers vested in the government, or in any department or officer thereof 3. To make appropriations 4. To impeach	

rule on foreign-policy issues may discourage potential litigants from pursuing their goals through the courts. Moreover, when the Court has intervened, it has often deferred—because of its limited expertise and the lack of clear constitutional standards—to the judgment of other branches. The Court's decisions upholding the all-male draft registration system (*Rostker v. Goldberg* [1981]) and President Reagan's restrictions on travel to Cuba (*Regan v. Wald* [1984]) reflect this deferential posture. But in *Boumediene v. Bush* (2008), the Court by a 5–4 vote struck down a congressional statute that denied federal courts the authority to hear petitions for a writ of habeas corpus from detained aliens deemed to be enemy combatants, and in *Zivotofsky v. Kerry* (2015) it invalidated a congressional statute authorizing American citizens born in Jerusalem to list Israel as their place of birth on their US passports. Nevertheless, the most important sources of constitutional law relating to war and foreign affairs have been the executive and legislative branches.

Checks and Balances

Interpretations of the war and foreign affairs powers typically have emerged through political interaction between the president and Congress. For example, because both branches have long agreed that the president should serve as the "sole organ of the nation in its external relations," this monopoly on communications with foreign governments has been recognized as constitutionally based.[3] On the other hand, dissatisfaction with the results of presidential control over commitment of troops led Congress to attempt to limit this control through the War Powers Resolution, which was enacted over a presidential veto in 1973. Although these instances of interbranch cooperation and conflict mix policy and constitutional considerations, their outcomes do not represent merely "political" adjustments. For one thing, the participants in interbranch disputes generally have recognized the seriousness of constitutional questions and, rather than simply basing constitutional interpretations on their own policy positions, have sought correct solutions to them. More important, the Constitution itself regulates and in large measure determines the outcomes of such conflicts.

Under the Constitution's system of checks and balances, powers are distributed to the various branches so that each can adequately defend its prerogatives and prevent domination of the government by another branch. These powers, in turn, represent political resources that can be brought to bear in interbranch conflicts. Should the dispute concern the regulation of foreign imports, both Congress and the president have constitutionally defined roles in the legislative process that prevent a single branch from acting alone. Should the president and the Senate conclude a treaty that the House of Representatives opposes, the House can refuse to enact legislation necessary to implement the treaty or can refuse to appropriate money for its implementation. Thus, the constitutional division of power provides each branch with the means to frustrate the pursuit of foreign-policy goals favored by only one branch, thereby placing a premium on interbranch cooperation. (This, of course, assumes that no branch would cooperate if it believed its powers were being usurped in the process. Some critics charge that Congress has been all too willing to cede power to the executive.)

The Constitution also influences the nature and outcomes of interbranch conflicts by imparting a particular character to each branch. The unity of the executive, Hamilton noted in *The Federalist,* No. 70, is conducive to "decision, activity, secrecy, and dispatch." These qualities enable the president to seize the initiative in foreign affairs—as President George W. Bush did in the immediate aftermath of the terrorist attacks on September 11, 2001—and to provide effective leadership during the nation's war efforts. In addition, the unity of the executive frequently allows the president to portray himself as the nation's representative in its dealings with other countries. In contrast, the two houses of Congress are deliberative bodies that more adequately reflect the varying viewpoints and interests in the nation.

These differences in composition have had two important consequences. First, as relations with other countries have increasingly demanded swift and decisive reactions to events, the power of the executive has increased. Second, the success over time of presidential initiatives—that is, whether they will lead to interbranch conflict—depends on the president's ability to convince the people and their representatives of the initiatives' wisdom. President Woodrow Wilson's attempt to secure the participation of the United States in the League of Nations, for example, foundered when the Senate refused to ratify the treaty leading to membership. President Harry Truman, on the other hand, gained congressional backing for the Marshall Plan (which provided aid to rebuild European countries after World War II) by involving influential members in the negotiations establishing the plan. Therefore, although the character of the branches affects the roles they assume in foreign affairs, the constitutional structure again encourages interbranch cooperation.

War and Other Hostilities

The commitment of American troops to combat poses the most severe test of the constitutional division of powers. As the Supreme Court ruled in *The Prize Cases* (1863), when the nation is attacked, the president can recognize that a state of war exists and, as commander in chief, respond accordingly. Even in such circumstances, the president might find it advantageous to seek congressional support for his actions, as President George W. Bush did in the wake of the 9/11 terrorist attacks, in order to demonstrate the nation's unity to foreign foes.

Although the Constitution confers on Congress the choice between war and peace by granting to it the power to declare war, political practice has not always reflected this constitutional division of power. Since World War II, American troops have been involved in hostilities ranging from short-term engagements for limited purposes (for example, safeguarding Americans in Grenada during the Reagan administration) to protracted conflicts in Korea, Vietnam, Iraq, and Afghanistan. Other armed conflicts, like the invasion of Panama and the Gulf War against Iraq in 1991, have fallen somewhere in between these two extremes. In some instances, presidents have asked for and received authorization from Congress before engaging in hostilities, as President George W. Bush did before committing troops to Afghanistan and Iraq. Yet in many instances, presidents have committed troops without formal congressional authorization. Such unilateral presidential commitment of forces is not just a recent phenomenon: during the debates on the War Powers Resolution, one source listed 161 such instances of unilateral presidential action.[4] What is new is the willingness of some presidents to claim this power as a presidential preserve that is beyond congressional control. In support of this claim, presidents have asserted that the commander-in-chief power permits them to deploy troops wherever they wish and to use the armed forces for various purposes short of war, such as protecting the lives and property of American citizens abroad, defending American troops from attack, and protecting American foreign-policy interests.

The president's power to direct the movements of American troops can lead, either inadvertently or by design, to the preemption of congressional decision-making. Once US forces are attacked, public opinion usually supports retaliatory measures, and Congress is left with little choice but to endorse presidential requests for the continuation and expansion of hostilities. In the most blatant instance of presidential war-making, President James Polk in 1846 ordered troops to occupy disputed territory along the Rio Grande, thereby provoking a Mexican attack and in effect forcing Congress to declare war against Mexico. (The House of Representatives subsequently amended a resolution of thanks to General Zachary Taylor to include a condemnation of President Polk for unconstitutionally involving the nation in war.) Similarly, in 1964 President Lyndon Johnson used an alleged attack on American ships operating off North Vietnam to secure passage of the Gulf of Tonkin Resolution, which authorized military action in Vietnam.

In an effort to clarify the limits of unilateral presidential action and to reclaim lost powers, Congress in 1973 adopted the War Powers Resolution, which obliges the president to consult with Congress "in every possible instance" before committing troops "into hostilities or into situations where imminent involvement in hostilities is clearly indicated by the circumstances." If circumstances prevent prior consultation, the law requires the president to report his actions to Congress within forty-eight hours. Furthermore, the president is required to terminate any use of military forces within sixty days after submitting such a report (with a possible extension of thirty days), unless Congress specifically authorizes their continued use. Finally, the law reserves to Congress a legislative veto over troop commitments, that is, the power to compel the withdrawal of troops by an unvetoable concurrent resolution.

The War Powers Resolution has not restored the constitutional division of powers, neither preventing presidential commitment of troops nor promoting consultation beforehand. For example, President Bill Clinton initiated air strikes against the Serbs in Bosnia without congressional authorization, and President Obama did so in Libya. At times, presidents have refused to acknowledge the applicability of the resolution to their commitment of troops—President Reagan's deployment of marines in Lebanon is a prime example—thereby preventing the start of the sixty-day time limit for congressional authorization.

Even when the presidents have notified Congress or its leadership, as President George H. W. Bush did before dispatching troops to Panama in 1989, they have done so to announce a decision rather than to seek advice. In addition, congressional control after the commitment of troops has been limited. When President Reagan's Grenada incursion succeeded, Congress was hard-pressed to object to the unilateral presidential action; when President Carter's effort to rescue American hostages in Iran failed in 1980, Congress was more concerned with the details of the failure than with the lack of consultation. On the other hand, when a president seeks sustained American involvement in a conflict, the resolution's requirement that Congress specifically authorize prolonged troop commitments provides it with a weapon to ensure consultation.

Some critics have charged that the War Powers Resolution infringes on presidential authority and undermines the conduct of foreign policy. In 1995, congressional Republicans sought to repeal the resolution on that basis, although their effort failed. Certainly, presidents have been reluctant to comply with its provisions, and some have raised doubts about its constitutionality. Yet disputes over presidential initiation of hostilities tend to be resolved through interbranch interaction rather than by judicial decision.

THE FOUNDATION AND EXTENT OF THE FOREIGN-AFFAIRS POWER

The conduct of foreign affairs is preeminently a federal, rather than a state, concern. The Constitution recognizes this not only by granting pertinent powers to the president and to Congress but also by expressly denying them to the states. Thus, Article I, Section 10, of the Constitution prohibits states from entering into alliances or other agreements with foreign nations and forbids them from engaging in war unless actually invaded or in imminent danger of invasion. The Supreme Court has recognized that the exercise of national powers in foreign affairs supersedes state prerogatives. Thus, in *American Insurance Association v. Garamendi* (2003), the Court struck down a California law designed to force European companies to pay unpaid insurance policies of victims of the Holocaust. However, *Garamendi* focused on the conflict between federal and state policies, leaving unanswered whether the Constitution precludes all state involvement in foreign affairs. In *Arizona v. United States* (2012), the Court noted the strong connection between immigration policy and relations with other countries, as "foreign countries [might have] concerns about the status, safety, and security of their nationals in the United States." Nonetheless, it did not conclude that only the federal government could address immigration issues. Rather, it held that Arizona could act to combat illegal immigration into the state as long as its policies did not conflict with or interfere with federal immigration law (see Chapter 9).

Although the federal government has authority over foreign relations, the constitutional foundation for that authority is somewhat sketchy. For one thing, the Constitution's assignment of particular powers to each branch does not exhaust the range of powers necessary for the conduct of foreign affairs. The power to terminate treaties, the legal status of executive agreements, the circumstances under which the president may commit American troops to hostilities—none of these matters is expressly dealt with in the Constitution. Moreover, although the Constitution in no way limits federal authority over foreign affairs, it does not explicitly grant a comprehensive foreign-affairs power.

This problem of "missing powers" has generated two radically different justifications for federal control. The so-called extrapolation approach suggests that the particular powers assigned to the various branches or denied to the states necessarily imply the missing powers required for the conduct of foreign affairs. Thus, the power to make treaties implies the power to break them, the power to make war implies the power to make peace, the power to receive ambassadors (thereby granting diplomatic recognition) implies the power to refuse recognition by not receiving ambassadors, and so on. According to this view, a complete picture of the extent and distribution of the powers over foreign affairs can be derived from the express grants of power in the Constitution.

A contrasting approach, outlined by Justice George Sutherland in *United States v. Curtiss-Wright Export Corporation* (1936), bases federal control over foreign affairs on an extra-constitutional foundation. The Constitution, Sutherland maintained, distributed only the "internal powers" of government, that is, those powers pertaining to domestic affairs. In Sutherland's view, the powers pertaining to foreign affairs—external powers—had already been lodged in the federal government as an inheritance from the British Crown at the time that the United States became a sovereign nation, and thus they did not rest on a delegation from the people or the states. What is assumed to be an incomplete grant of powers under the extrapolation approach, therefore, becomes for Sutherland merely the assignment of those powers that do not belong naturally to either the legislative or the executive branch. And for Sutherland most powers not expressly listed in the Constitution reside in the executive branch.

Both approaches have difficulties. The extrapolation approach requires an extraordinarily broad reading of specific constitutional provisions that is at variance with how grants of authority in domestic affairs are interpreted. Proponents of extrapolation argue, for example, that the power to appoint ambassadors includes the power to direct their activities and thus to define the ends, or policy objectives, to which those activities shall be directed. But the appointment power might just as readily be read as a narrow and specific grant of power that has nothing to do with setting foreign-policy goals. In addition, this approach does not resolve conflicts about the distribution of powers. Although the president might infer the power to set foreign-policy objectives from the power to appoint ambassadors, Congress might conclude that its power to declare war carries with it a power to decide on policies that might propel the nation into war.

The Sutherland approach, on the other hand, relies on a questionable interpretation of history. The fact that several states during the post-Independence period acted autonomously in foreign affairs appears to belie Sutherland's claim that sovereignty—and hence control over foreign affairs—passed directly from the Crown to a federal government. In addition, there is no discussion of a preexisting foreign-affairs power in the Constitution, in the records of the Constitutional Convention, or in other contemporary sources. It hardly seems credible that such a departure from the system of delegated powers would not have occasioned discussion. Moreover, Sutherland's claim that, unless the Constitution specifies otherwise, the powers over foreign affairs reside in the presidency is itself controversial.

The limitations of both approaches are evident in *Zivotofsky v. Kerry* (2015), which struck down a congressional statute allowing those born in Jerusalem to list Israel as their birthplace on their US passports and on consular reports of births abroad. Such a listing was controversial because no president had ever recognized Israeli sovereignty over Jerusalem and because the listing might be perceived as indicating a change in US policy on the issue. Speaking for the Court, Justice Anthony Kennedy acknowledged that *Curtiss-Wright* gave too broad a scope to presidential power over foreign affairs. But he argued that the constitutional grant to the president of the powers to send ambassadors, receive ambassadors, and enter into treaties carried with them an exclusive power to recognize or not recognize foreign governments. This power in turn included a power to determine the territory over which the US would recognize those governments' authority. Thus the congressional statute, by undermining the president's determination of American policy regarding Jerusalem, invaded powers assigned by the Constitution to the president and was unconstitutional. In one dissent, Chief Justice John Roberts noted that "never before has this Court accepted a President's direct defiance of an Act of Congress in the field of foreign affairs," reiterating Justice Jackson's admonition in *Youngstown Sheet & Tube v. Sawyer* (see Chapter 5) that when the president acts contrary to an act of Congress, his authority is at its lowest ebb. In another dissent, Justice Antonin Scalia acknowledged the president's power to recognize foreign governments but denied that it was exclusive. Congress in the exercise of its constitutional powers could also express its own views on questions of statehood and territory.

Whatever their differences, both the extrapolation approach and Sutherland's extraconstitutional approach assign the foreign-affairs power to the federal government. Yet the scope of this power remains a matter of controversy. In *Curtiss-Wright,* Sutherland contended that federal control over external affairs could be complete only if the line between external and internal affairs—and between external and internal powers—reflected changing world conditions. Sixteen years earlier, Justice Oliver Wendell Holmes had advanced a similar argument in *Missouri v. Holland* (1920), which upheld congressional legislation in pursuance of a treaty regulating the killing of migratory birds. To Holmes, neither the Framers' failure to anticipate treaties about migratory birds nor a lower court's invalidation of similar legislation before the treaty's ratification was decisive. As long as the treaty addressed a matter of national concern that could be regulated through an international agreement, it constituted a valid exercise of the foreign-affairs power. Even if congressional legislation exceeded the express constitutional grants of power to Congress, it might still be valid if necessary and proper to implement a treaty or other exercise of the foreign-affairs power.

Not surprisingly, the notion that the federal government might expand its sphere of domestic control through the foreign-affairs power has been disputed. Defenders of state prerogatives have asserted that this interpretation threatens the division of power between nation and state, particularly because contemporary multilateral treaties (e.g., the United Nations covenant on the elimination of racial discrimination) might involve matters of exclusively domestic concern. During the early 1950s, this concern led Senator John Bricker of Ohio to propose a constitutional amendment that would have required congressional legislation before any treaty became effective as internal law in the United States. Bricker's effort dramatized the concern that the states might lack constitutional protection against national foreign-policy decisions. However, opponents of the Bricker Amendment insisted that ratification of treaties by the Senate, in which the states are equally represented, afforded the states adequate protection.

Controversy over the domestic effects of international treaties arose more recently in *Medellin v. Texas* (2008). Medellin, a Mexican citizen convicted of rape and murder in Texas courts, claimed that the state had violated his rights by not allowing him to contact his consulate, as guaranteed by the Vienna Convention, a treaty to which the United States was a party. He further noted that the International Court of Justice (ICJ) had ruled that the United States had violated the treaty by not allowing him and other foreign nationals to consult their consulates. The Texas Court of Criminal Appeals, however, held that the ICJ ruling was not binding on Texas courts and reaffirmed Medellin's conviction. Further complicating the issue was a memorandum written by President George W. Bush in the wake of the ICJ ruling, ordering the Texas courts to comply with the ICJ's rulings by rehearing the cases. Medellin insisted that the Constitution gives the president broad power to ensure that treaties are enforced and that this power extends to the treatment of treaties in state-court proceedings.

By a 6–3 vote, however, the justices rejected Medellin's claim. Although acknowledging that the Supremacy Clause of the Constitution (Article VI, Section 2) recognizes treaties as part of the supreme law of the land and thus superior to state enactments, the Court noted that some treaties are non-self-executing, that is, they are not enforceable in US courts unless implemented by Congress, and nothing in the text of the Vienna Convention gave evidence that it was self-executing. Although acknowledging that a president may take action to enforce a non-self-executing treaty under his responsibility to "faithfully execute the laws," the justices maintained that this did not extend to "unilaterally making the treaty binding on domestic courts." Thus, the responsibility to pass implementing legislation rested with Congress, and its failure to enact such law meant that the states were not obliged to give the treaty effect within their borders.

WAR AND INDIVIDUAL RIGHTS

The Framers of the Constitution sought to design a system of government that could respond successfully to crises of war and foreign affairs. In *The Federalist,* No. 23, Hamilton acknowledged that the achievement of this aim required a broad grant of power to the national government: "The circumstances that endanger the safety of nations are infinite, and for this reason no constitutional shackles can wisely be imposed on the power to which the care of it is committed. This power ought to be coextensive with all the possible combinations of such circumstances; and ought to be under the direction of the same councils which are appointed to preside over the common defense."

Because war places a premium on swift and decisive action, Congress in wartime has characteristically concentrated broad governmental power in the executive. During World War I, Congress delegated to President Wilson virtually standardless regulatory power over major sectors of the economy, private communications with foreign countries, and numerous other concerns. Even before the United States' entry into World War II, the Lend-Lease Act empowered the president to transfer "defense articles" to the "government of any country whose defense he deems vital to the defense of the United States" under any terms that he deemed satisfactory. During the war, President Franklin Roosevelt was authorized to direct war production, to control the prices of goods, to introduce rationing, and generally to regulate the economic life of the country.

At times, presidents have relied on their own authority rather than on congressional delegations of power. President Abraham Lincoln's actions during the ten weeks between the fall of Fort Sumter, South Carolina, and the convening of Congress exemplify this. During that period, Lincoln enlarged the army and navy, called up the state militias, spent unappropriated funds, and instituted a blockade of Southern ports. In defending his actions, he asserted that the "war power," derived from the Commander-in-Chief Clause and his responsibility to ensure that "the laws be faithfully executed," provided a sufficient constitutional justification. He also submitted his extraordinary exercise of power to Congress, which promptly ratified his actions.

Several times during the twentieth century, presidents claimed the power to act in crisis situations even when there was no declared war. During the "police action" in Korea,

President Truman seized the steel mills to prevent a strike that would have stopped steel production, and during the Vietnam conflict, President Richard Nixon attempted to halt publication of the Pentagon Papers, a classified study of how the United States became involved in the war. Although the Supreme Court in both instances rejected the claims of executive power, the justices were careful not to say that the national government as a whole lacked sufficient power to deal with such crises.

Both governmental practice and judicial decisions, then, confirm that the national government has broad powers to deal with crises in external affairs and that the exercise of these powers can justify temporarily overriding the constitutional separation of powers. Do war and other emergencies also permit the temporary suspension or dilution of constitutionally protected rights? The US Constitution, unlike the constitutions in many other countries, does not directly answer that question. The most important constitutional recognition of how hostilities might affect rights is found in Article I, Section 9, which authorizes suspension of the writ of habeas corpus "when in Cases of Rebellion or Invasion the public Safety may require it." The Third Amendment ensures that soldiers can be quartered in private houses only in wartime and only "in a manner to be prescribed by law"—that is, only by vote of the people's representatives. This latter provision has, perhaps unsurprisingly, produced no litigation.

Nevertheless, the status of rights during wartime and other emergencies has been debated throughout American history. During the Civil War, President Lincoln suspended the writ of habeas corpus to all persons "guilty of any disloyal practice" and authorized trial and punishment of such persons by courts-martial and military tribunals. Early in World War II, President Roosevelt issued an executive order, later supported by congressional action, that led to the forced evacuation from the West Coast of 112,000 residents of Japanese ancestry, many of whom were American citizens. During both World War I and World War II, the government imposed restrictions on speech deemed detrimental to the war effort, and during the Cold War with the Soviet Union, it imposed various restrictions on freedom of speech and association.

Finally, in the wake of the 9/11 attacks on the United States, the federal government took decisive—and in some instances controversial—action to deal with the threat of terrorism. President George W. Bush issued an executive order authorizing trial by military tribunals for noncitizens allegedly implicated in terrorist activities. He also ordered the indefinite detention without charges, access to counsel, or hearings of alien "enemy combatants" at a facility in Guantánamo Bay, Cuba, and of "enemy combatants" with American citizenship within the United States. Congress enacted the USA PATRIOT Act, which substantially augmented federal powers to investigate and gather information in order to head off future terrorist attacks. This act promoted cooperation and sharing of information between law enforcement and intelligence agencies, permitted government tracing and tracking of e-mails and other electronic communications when there were "reasonable grounds" for such inquiries, permitted "roving" wiretaps of cell phones and other devices, expanded governmental authority to conduct "sneak-and-peek" searches in which the suspect was not notified of the search, and expanded governmental powers to deny admission to foreign nationals and to detain or deport them, if (among other things) they espoused terrorism or were suspected of intending to engage in activities "that could endanger the welfare, safety, or security of the United States."

Shortly after 9/11, President Bush also unilaterally authorized the National Security Agency (NSA) to conduct wiretaps on overseas communications to and from US residents, in order to obtain information on potential terrorist activity. This electronic eavesdropping, conducted without seeking search warrants from the Foreign Intelligence Surveillance Court, remained secret until it was revealed by the *New York Times* in late 2005. In the wake of this revelation, Congress enacted legislation authorizing such eavesdropping.

But further revelations of NSA wiretapping, involving domestic phone calls by Americans, emerged in 2013 from the material published by Edward Snowden, a former CIA officer and government contractor. In May, 2015, the Federal Court of Appeals for the Second Circuit ruled that the PATRIOT Act did not authorize bulk collection of domestic phone data, but Congress responded a month later by passing the USA Freedom Act, which re-enacted the expiring provision of the PATRIOT Act while prohibiting the bulk collection of call data after six months. The Federal Intelligence Surveillance Court then authorized the resumption of the bulk collection of domestic phone data for the six-month period. The scope of the federal government's search authority, consistent with the Fourth Amendment, therefore remains in flux.

Throughout American history as well, there have been challenges to government actions during wartime by those who believed that their constitutional rights had been violated. In *Ex parte Milligan* (1866) and *Korematsu v. United States* (1944), the Supreme Court ruled directly on Lincoln's and Roosevelt's actions. Four alternative interpretations of the extent of governmental power during wartime emerged from these cases. According to the broadest interpretation of governmental power, which was espoused by the four concurring justices in *Milligan* and by the Court majority in *Korematsu,* the fundamental consideration is that the government's power to wage war is the power to wage war successfully. From this, it follows that the federal government possesses all powers necessary and proper to the successful prosecution of the war. Thus, when an area of the country is an actual or potential theater of military operations, the government can engage in actions that would violate the Constitution during peacetime. As long as the actions are "reasonably expedient military precautions" relating to national security, they are constitutionally permissible under the Necessary and Proper Clause.

The Supreme Court in *Milligan* took a more restrictive view of governmental power, asserting that all constitutional limitations on governmental action apply with equal force during wartime. According to the *Milligan* majority, the decisive factor is the Framers' decision not to insert exceptions for wartime in the Bill of Rights. Their judgment that the government did not need the power to suspend constitutionally protected rights, based as it was on a personal familiarity with war during the American Revolution, is binding on future generations. Therefore, any action that infringes on rights during peacetime remains unconstitutional during wartime, because "the Constitution of the United States is a law for rulers and ruled, equally in war and in peace."

Justice Frank Murphy, dissenting in *Korematsu,* proposed a third approach. According to Murphy, military necessity can justify the deprivation of individual rights, but judges should not accept uncritically government assertions of necessity. When the government undertakes the radical step of suspending rights, judges must scrutinize closely the bases for this action. Only when such deprivations can be "reasonably related to a public danger that is so immediate, imminent, and impending as not to admit of delay and not to permit the intervention of ordinary constitutional processes," Murphy concluded, should they be upheld. Even in wartime, then, the judiciary has a major role in enforcing constitutional limitations.

In his dissent in *Korematsu,* Justice Robert Jackson offered a distinctive interpretation of governmental power in wartime. Jackson maintained that what is expedient on military grounds might not be constitutionally permissible—a situation that obviously creates a dilemma for the Supreme Court. On the one hand, the judiciary cannot expect the federal government to refrain from actions it deems essential to the public safety merely because of judicial disapproval. On the other hand, should the Court endorse unconstitutional actions on the basis of alleged military necessity, it would provide a precedent for abuses of power whenever "any authority can bring forward a plausible claim of an urgent need." Because the Constitution does not provide sufficient power to deal with all the exigencies of war, necessity—self-preservation—and not constitutionality will inevitably (and properly) be the standard for governmental action during wartime. The Supreme Court, Jackson argued, should play no role in such situations.

The government's response to the 2001 terrorist attacks on the United States once again raised the issue of the status of rights in time of war or national emergency. Civil-liberties groups criticized various aspects of the PATRIOT Act, particularly its authorization of "sneak-and-peek" searches, its expansion of wiretapping authority, and its expansion of executive power to detain and deport aliens. In contrast, proponents of the act claimed that it gave the federal government the tools it needed to combat a serious threat to the nation's security and the rights of its citizens.[5] As of 2015, the Supreme Court had not considered the constitutionality of any provisions of the PATRIOT Act. However, Congress's insertion of sunset provisions in the PATRIOT Act, mandating that certain provisions expire at the end of 2005 unless reenacted, created the opportunity for an assessment of the act's effectiveness and its effect on civil liberties. In 2005 and 2011, Congress extended the most controversial provisions in the act.

President Bush's executive order authorizing trial of suspected terrorists by military tribunal was likewise controversial. Although *Milligan* suggested limits on the use of such tribunals, the Bush administration relied on the Supreme Court's decision in *Ex parte Quirin* (1942) for constitutional authorization for the use of such tribunals. In *Quirin* the Court reviewed a petition for a writ of habeas corpus from German saboteurs apprehended on American soil during World War II. Convicted by a military tribunal specially convened by President Roosevelt to hear their cases, the saboteurs claimed that their convictions were unconstitutional and that they should have been tried in civilian courts, which were operating in the states in which they were apprehended. However, the Supreme Court unanimously upheld the convictions and the constitutionality of the military tribunal. The justices distinguished *Milligan*, because that case involved a citizen noncombatant rather than enemy combatants who had violated the laws of war by secretly infiltrating military lines without wearing identifying military uniforms for the purpose of hostile actions. When military tribunals were established in the wake of September 11 to try noncitizen members of terrorist networks, President Bush insisted that *Quirin* supported the constitutionality of those tribunals.

The Bush administration's decision to hold as "enemy combatants" both nonAmericans and American citizens apprehended during military operations in Afghanistan or in other circumstances also prompted legal challenges. In *Rumsfeld v. Padilla* (2004), a five-member majority ruled that Jose Padilla's habeas corpus petition had been filed in the wrong court and thus refused to address whether American citizens apprehended in the United States could be designated as enemy combatants and held indefinitely without charges being filed. But in *Hamdi v. Rumsfeld* (2004), the Court concluded that the Due Process Clause required that American citizens be informed of the basis for their designation as enemy combatants and given the opportunity to rebut the government's assertions before a neutral decision maker. The Court divided, however, on what procedures were constitutionally required. A plurality of justices, in an opinion by Justice Sandra Day O'Connor, sought to balance the individual's strong liberty interest and the government's concern that those who fought with the enemy not be released to resume their activities. Justice O'Connor suggested the possibility that the demands of due process "could be met by an appropriately authorized and properly constituted military tribunal." Justice David Souter, joined by Justice Ruth Bader Ginsburg, concluded that Congress had not authorized the president to detain American citizens as "enemy combatants." Justice Antonin Scalia, joined by Justice John Paul Stevens in dissent, noted the narrow scope of what was decided: the Court's ruling applied "only to citizens accused of being enemy combatants, who are detained within the territorial jurisdiction of a federal court." Yet for these individuals, he argued, the Constitution offered the government only two options—suspend the writ of habeas corpus or commence criminal proceedings. Only Justice Clarence Thomas concluded that the president in time of war could hold Americans indefinitely as "enemy combatants" without a hearing.

In *Rasul v. Bush* (2004), the Court considered the rights of aliens held as "enemy combatants." By a 6–3 vote, the justices concluded that the federal courts had jurisdiction under the federal habeas corpus statute to hear petitions from aliens captured during hostilities in Afghanistan who were being held in indefinite detention at the US Naval Base at Guantánamo Bay, Cuba. Speaking for the Court, Justice Stevens distinguished *Johnson v. Eisentrager* (1950), an earlier ruling that enemy aliens detained outside the United States were not entitled to habeas corpus relief. Although Guantánamo Bay was outside the country, he argued that it was effectively under the jurisdiction of the United States. Moreover, as Justice Anthony Kennedy noted in his concurring opinion, whereas the petitioners in *Eisentrager* had received a full trial by military commission, the detainees in Guantánamo were being held indefinitely without access to counsel and without any legal proceeding to determine their status. The Court's ruling brought an angry rejoinder from Justice Scalia, who distinguished sharply between the rights guaranteed to citizens and those provided to aliens, between those available within the United States and those available beyond its borders. In the wake of the Court's ruling, the Defense Department established a Combatant Status Review Tribunal at Guantánamo, with authority to explain to detainees the grounds for their detention and to provide them an opportunity to contest their designation as enemy combatants.[6]

Rasul involved the interpretation of a federal statute rather than of the Constitution, and it thus could be overturned by congressional amendment of the statute. It nonetheless represented a significant extension of judicial authority. For the first time, the Supreme Court undertook to review actions against foreign enemies taken by the executive branch beyond the borders of the United States. To its proponents, *Rasul* showed the judiciary meeting its responsibility to ensure due process for all those accused of wrongdoing. But to its critics, *Rasul* represented an inappropriate attempt by the judiciary to supervise the exercise of the commander-in-chief power, a power the Constitution expressly conferred on the president.

In *Hamdan v. Rumsfeld* (2006), the Supreme Court by a 5–3 vote invalidated President Bush's executive order authorizing trial of detainees by military tribunal. Speaking for the Court, Justice John Paul Stevens insisted that even if the president possessed the power to convene military commissions, those tribunals would have to be either sanctioned by the "laws of war," as codified by Congress in Article 21 of the Uniform Code of Military Justice, or authorized by statute. Congress responded by enacting the Military Commissions Act of 2006, which authorized trying enemy combatants by military commission. But this act also was challenged, and in *Boumediene v. Bush* (2008), a five-member majority in an opinion by Justice Anthony Kennedy held that the detainees at Guantánamo Bay had the constitutional privilege of habeas corpus. It also ruled that the procedures established by the Detainee Treatment Act (DTA), under which the determinations of Combat Status Review Tribunals (military tribunals) were subject to limited review by a federal court of appeals, did not provide an adequate substitute. The Court in *Johnson v. Eisentrager* had ruled that aliens held outside American territory had no right to habeas corpus. But Justice Kennedy argued that the US government's "effective control" over the base at Guantánamo Bay, rather than political sovereignty, was determinative. "The Constitution," he wrote, "grants Congress and the President the power to acquire, dispose of, and govern territory, not the power to decide when and where its terms apply." Even when the United States acts outside its borders, its powers are not "absolute and unlimited" but are subject "to such restrictions as are expressed in the Constitution." These restrictions include the right to habeas corpus, unless Congress has suspended the writ, as it had not in this instance.

Having determined that noncitizens on foreign soil have constitutional rights that federal courts could enforce, the Court next examined whether the Detainee Treatment Act

(DTA) adequately protected those rights, concluding that it did not. Particularly troubling to the Court majority was the limited review allowed to the court of appeals in reviewing the rulings of Combatant Status Review Tribunals and the statute's failure to provide opportunities for detainees to present new evidence before the court of appeals. In dissent, Chief Justice John Roberts maintained that the DTA fully protected the constitutional rights of aliens held as enemy combatants, in fact, the "statutory scheme provides the combatants held at Guantanamo greater procedural protections than have ever been afforded alleged enemy detainees—whether citizens or aliens—in our national history." In cases involving complicated national security concerns, he insisted, courts should defer to the joint judgment of Congress and the president. Otherwise, as Justice Scalia noted in his dissent, questions of "how to handle enemy prisoners in war will ultimately lie with the branch that knows the least about national security concerns."

Another area of constitutional controversy was warrantless wiretapping within the United States. When President Bush's wiretapping program was disclosed in late 2005, he defended the program as necessary to forestall future terrorist attacks. As legal authority for the program, he cited both his constitutional powers as commander in chief and the 2001 Authorization for Use of Military Force (AUMF), enacted by Congress a week after the 9/11 attacks. The AUMF empowered the president to "use all necessary and appropriate force" against "nations, organizations, or persons that he determined planned, authorized, committed or aided the terrorist attacks" of 9/11 "in order to prevent any future acts of international terrorism against the United States." The wiretaps, President Bush argued, were vital to detecting plans for future attacks by al-Qaeda and related organizations and thus were authorized by the AUMF.

Critics of the warrantless wiretapping insisted that the Foreign Intelligence Surveillance Act required that the president obtain authorization from the Foreign Intelligence Surveillance Court before conducting such domestic wiretapping. Beyond that, they objected to the broad claim of unilateral presidential power underlying the program. The commander-in-chief power, they insisted, authorizes the president to direct the use of military forces but does not extend to all activities related to the war effort occurring far from the field of battle. As these competing views illustrate, the scope of national power—and executive power in particular—during time of war remains a perplexing and contentious issue.

NOTES

1. Hamilton defended the president's power to issue the Neutrality Proclamation in the "Pacificus" letters. See Alexander Hamilton, *The Works of Alexander Hamilton*, edited by Henry Cabot Lodge, 12 vols. (New York: Federal Edition, 1904), 4:76. Madison challenged this view, at times quoting Hamilton's statements in *The Federalist* in the "Helvidius" letters. Alexander Hamilton and James Madison, *The Pacificus-Helvidius Debates—1793–1794* (Indianapolis, IN: Liberty Fund, 2007).

2. Edward S. Corwin, *The President: Office and Powers*, 4th rev. ed. (New York: New York University Press, 1957), 171.

3. John Marshall applied this label to the president during a debate in the House of Representatives in 1800.

4. American Enterprise Institute, *The War Powers Bill*, Legislative Analysis, no. 19 (April 17, 1972): 47–55.

5. For a survey of competing views, see Howard Ball, *The USA Patriot Act of 2001: Balancing Civil Liberties and National Security* (Santa Barbara, CA: ABC-Clio, 2004), chaps. 3–4.

6. On the federal government's response to *Rasul v. Bush,* see Louis Fisher, *Military Tribunals and Presidential Power: American Revolution to the War on Terrorism* (Lawrence: University Press of Kansas, 2005), 249–252.

SELECTED READINGS

The Federalist, Nos. 23–26, 64, 70, 75.

Ely, John Hart. *War and Responsibility: Constitutional Lessons of Vietnam and Its Aftermath.* Princeton, NJ: Princeton University Press, 1993.

Farber, Daniel. *Lincoln's Constitution.* Chicago, IL: University of Chicago Press, 2004.

Fisher, Louis. *Military Tribunals and Presidential Power: American Revolution to the War on Terrorism.* Lawrence: University Press of Kansas, 2005.

Genovese, Michael A. *Presidential Prerogative: Imperial Power in an Age of Terrorism.* Stanford, CA: Stanford University Press, 2011.

Griffin, Steven M. *Long Wars and the Constitution.* Cambridge, MA: Harvard University Press, 2013.

Hamilton, Alexander, and James Madison. *The Pacificus-Helvidius Debates of 1793–94*, ed. Morton J. Frisch. Indianapolis, IN: Liberty Fund, 2007.

Irons, Peter H. *Justice at War.* New York: Oxford University Press, 1983.

Posner, Eric A., and Adrian Vermeule. *Terror in the Balance: Security, Liberty, and the Courts.* New York: Oxford University Press, 2007.

Posner, Richard A. *Not a Suicide Pact: The Constitution in a Time of National Emergency.* New York: Oxford University Press, 2006.

Ramsey, Michael D. *The Constitution's Text in Foreign Affairs.* Cambridge, MA: Harvard University Press, 2007.

Rehnquist, William H. *All the Laws but One: Civil Liberties in Wartime.* New York: Knopf, 1998.

Silverstein, Gordon. *Imbalance of Power: Constitutional Interpretation and the Making of American Foreign Policy.* New York: Oxford University Press, 1997.

Stone, Geoffrey R. *Perilous Times: Free Speech in Wartime from the Sedition Act of 1798 to the War on Terrorism.* New York: W. W. Norton, 2004.

Treanor, William M. "Fame, the Founding, and the Power to Declare War." *Cornell Law Review* 82 (1997): 695–772.

Tushnet, Mark, ed. *The Constitution in Wartime: Beyond Alarmism and Complacency.* Durham, NC: Duke University Press. 2005.

Zeisberg, Mariah. *War Powers: The Politics of Constitutional Authority.* Princeton, NJ: Princeton University Press, 2013.

The Prize Cases
67 U.S. (2 Bl.) 635 (1863)

In April 1861, after the initial outbreak of Civil War hostilities but before the convening of a special session of Congress, President Abraham Lincoln proclaimed a blockade of Confederate ports. During the period between the issuance of the president's proclamation and the passage of congressional legislation endorsing the blockade, several ships were seized as blockade runners and their cargoes confiscated. The owners of the ships challenged the legality of the blockade, and questions arising from the litigation were certified to the Supreme Court. Opinion of the Court: <u>Grier,</u> Wayne, Swayne, Miller, Davis. Dissenting opinion: <u>Nelson</u>, Taney, Catron, Clifford.

JUSTICE GRIER delivered the opinion of the Court.

Let us inquire whether, at the time this blockade was instituted, a state of war existed which would justify a resort to these means of subduing the hostile force. If a war be made by invasion of a foreign nation, the President is not only authorized but bound to resist force by force. He does not initiate the war, but is bound to accept the challenge without waiting for any special legislative authority. And whether the hostile "party be a foreign invader, or States organized in rebellion, it is nonetheless a war, although the declaration of it be *unilateral.*"

Whether the President in fulfilling his duties, as Commander-in-chief, in suppressing an insurrection, has met with such armed hostile resistance, and a civil war of such alarming proportions as will compel him to accord to them the character of belligerents, is a question to be decided *by him,* and this Court must be governed by the decisions and acts of the political department of the Government to which this power was entrusted. "He must determine what degree of force the crisis demands." The proclamation of blockade is itself official and conclusive evidence to the Court that a state of war existed which demanded and authorized a recourse to such a measure, under the circumstances peculiar to the case.

If it were necessary to the technical existence of a war, that it should have a legislative sanction, we find it in almost every act passed at the extraordinary session of the Legislature of 1861, which was wholly employed in enacting laws to enable the Government to prosecute the war with vigor and efficiency. And finally, in 1861, we find Congress passing an act "approving, legalizing, and making valid all the acts, proclamations, and orders of the President, &c., as if they had been *issued and done under the previous express authority* and direction of the Congress of the United States." Without admitting that such an act was necessary under the circumstances, it is plain that if the President had in any manner assumed powers which it was necessary should have the authority or sanction of Congress, this ratification has operated to perfectly cure the defect. We are of the opinion that the President had a right, *jure belli,* to institute a blockade of ports in possession of the States in rebellion, which neutrals are bound to regard.

JUSTICE NELSON, dissenting.

The right of making war belongs exclusively to the supreme or sovereign power of the State. This power in all civilized nations is regulated by the fundamental laws or municipal constitution of the country. By our Constitution this power is lodged in Congress.

An idea seemed to be entertained that all that was necessary to constitute a war was organized hostility in the district of country in a state of rebellion. Now, in one sense, no doubt this is war, and may be a war of the most extensive and threatening dimensions and effects, but it is a statement simply of its existence in a material sense, and has no relevancy or weight when the question is what constitutes war in a legal sense, in the sense of the law of nations, and of the Constitution of the United States?

Ample provision has been made under the Constitution and laws against any sudden and unexpected disturbance of the public peace from insurrection at home or invasion from abroad. The whole military and naval power of the country is put under the control of the President to meet the emergency. But it is the exercise of a power under the municipal laws of the country and not under the law of nations.

I am compelled to the conclusion that no civil war existed between this Government and the States in insurrection till recognized by the Act of Congress 13th of July, 1861; that the President does not possess the power under the Constitution to declare war or recognize its existence within the meaning of the law of nations, which carries with it belligerent rights, and thus change the country and all its citizens from a state of peace to a state of war; that this power belongs exclusively to the Congress of the United States, and, consequently, that the President had no power to set on foot a blockade under the law of nations, and that the capture of the vessel and cargo in this case, and in all cases before us in which the capture occurred before the 13th of July, 1861 are illegal and void, and that the decrees of condemnation should be reversed and the vessel and cargo restored.

The War Powers Resolution
87 Stat. 555 (1973)

As criticism of the Vietnam War mounted during the early 1970s, members of Congress sought to reassert congressional control over the use of American troops. In 1972, the Senate passed a war-powers bill that listed the circumstances under which the president could commit American troops to hostilities, but this bill was rejected by the House of Representatives. The following resolution, passed over President Richard Nixon's veto in 1973, does not specify when troops may be used, but it does require presidential consultation with Congress, when possible, and it allows Congress to terminate American involvement in hostilities.

§1541 (a) It is the purpose of this joint resolution to fulfill the intent of the framers of the Constitution of the United States and insure that the collective judgment of both the Congress and the President will apply to the introduction of United States Armed Forces into hostilities, or into situations where imminent involvement in hostilities is clearly indicated by the circumstances, and to the continued use of such forces in hostilities or in such situations.

(b) Under article I, section 8, of the Constitution, it is specifically provided that the Congress shall have the power to make all laws necessary and proper for carrying into execution, not only its own powers but also all other powers vested by the Constitution in the Government of the United States, or in any department or officer hereof.

(c) The constitutional powers of the President as Commander-in-Chief to introduce United States Armed Forces into hostilities, or into situations where imminent involvement in hostilities is clearly indicated by the circumstances, are exercised only pursuant to (1) a declaration of war, (2) specific statutory authorization, or (3) a national emergency created by attack upon the United States, its territories or possessions, or its armed forces.

§1542 The President in every possible instance shall consult with Congress before introducing United States Armed Forces into hostilities or into situations where imminent involvement in hostilities is clearly indicated by the circumstances, and after every such introduction shall consult regularly with the Congress until United States Armed Forces are no longer engaged in hostilities or have been removed from such situations.

§1543 (a) In the absence of a declaration of war, in any case in which United States Armed Forces are introduced—(1) into hostilities or into situations where imminent involvement in hostilities is clearly indicated by the circumstances; (2) into the territory, airspace or waters of a foreign nation, while equipped for combat, except for deployments which relate solely to supply, replacement, repair, or training of such forces; or (3) in numbers which substantially enlarge United States Armed Forces equipped for combat already located in a foreign nation; the President shall submit within 48 hours to the Speaker of the House of Representatives and to the President pro tempore of the Senate a report, in writing, setting forth— (A) the circumstances necessitating the introduction of the United States Armed Forces; (B) the constitutional and legislative authority under which such introduction took place; and (C) the estimated scope and duration of the hostilities or involvement.

(b) The President shall provide such other information as the Congress may request in the fulfillment of its constitutional responsibilities with respect to committing the Nation to war and to the use of United States Armed Forces abroad

§1544 (b) Within sixty calendar days after a report is submitted or is required to be submitted pursuant to section 1543(a)(1) of this title, whichever is earlier, the President shall terminate any use of United States Armed Forces with respect to which such report was submitted (or required to be submitted), unless the Congress (1) has declared war or has enacted a specific authorization for such use of United States Armed Forces, (2) has extended by law such sixty-day period, or (3) is physically unable to meet as a result of an armed attack upon the United States. Such sixty-day period shall be extended for not more than an additional thirty days if the President determines and certifies to the Congress in writing that unavoidable military necessity respecting the safety of United States Armed Forces requires the continued use of such armed forces in the course of bringing about a prompt removal of such forces.

(c) Notwithstanding subsection (b) of this section, at any time that United States Armed Forces are engaged in hostilities outside the territory of the United States, its possessions and territories without a declaration of war or specific statutory authorization, such forces shall be removed by the President if the Congress so directs by concurrent resolution.

§1547 Authority to introduce United States Armed Forces into hostilities or into situations wherein involvement in hostilities is clearly indicated by the circumstances shall not be inferred—(1) from any provision of law (whether or not in effect before November 7, 1973), including any provision contained in any appropriation Act, unless such provision specifically authorizes the introduction of United States Armed Forces into hostilities or into such situations and states that it is intended to constitute specific statutory authorization within the meaning of this joint resolution; or (2) from any treaty heretofore or hereafter ratified unless such treaty is implemented by legislation specifically authorizing the introduction of United States Armed Forces into hostilities or into such situations and stating that it is intended to constitute specific statutory authorization within the meaning of this joint resolution.

(d) Nothing in this joint resolution(1) is intended to alter the constitutional authority of the Congress or of the President, or the provisions of existing treaties; or (2) shall be construed as granting any authority to the President with respect to the introduction of United States Armed Forces into hostilities or into situations wherein involvement in hostilities is clearly indicated by the circumstances which authority he would not have had in the absence of this joint resolution.

Authorization for Use of Military Force
115 Stat. 224 (2001)

The authorization known as the AUMF became law on September 18, 2001. It passed the Senate by a vote of 98–0 and the House by a vote of 420–1. The circumstances of its adoption are outlined in the authorization.

To authorize the use of United States Armed Forces against those responsible for the recent attacks launched against the United States.

Whereas, on September 11, 2001, acts of treacherous violence were committed against the United States and its citizens; and

Whereas, such acts render it both necessary and appropriate that the United States exercise its rights to self-defense and to protect United States citizens both at home and abroad; and

Whereas, in light of the threat to the national security and foreign policy of the United States posed by these grave acts of violence; and

Whereas, such acts continue to pose an unusual and extraordinary threat to the national security and foreign policy of the United States; and

Whereas, the President has authority under the Constitution to take action to deter and prevent acts of international terrorism against the United States: Now, therefore, be it

Resolved by the Senate and House of Representatives of the United States of America in Congress assembled,

SECTION 1—SHORT TITLE

This joint resolution may be cited as the 'Authorization for Use of Military Force'.

SECTION 2—AUTHORIZATION FOR USE OF UNITED STATES ARMED FORCES

(a) IN GENERAL—That the President is authorized to use all necessary and appropriate force against those nations, organizations, or persons he determines planned, authorized, committed, or aided the *terrorist* attacks that occurred on September 11, 2001, or harbored such organizations or persons, in order to prevent any future acts of international terrorism against the United States by such nations, organizations or persons.

(b) War Powers Resolution Requirements

(1) SPECIFIC STATUTORY AUTHORIZATION—Consistent with section 8(a)(1) of the War Powers Resolution, the Congress declares that this section is intended to constitute specific statutory authorization within the meaning of section 5(b) of the War Powers Resolution.

(2) APPLICABILITY OF OTHER REQUIREMENTS—Nothing in this resolution supercedes any requirement of the War Powers Resolution.

United States v. Curtiss-Wright Export Corporation
299 U.S. 304 (1936)

On May 28, 1934, Congress passed a joint resolution authorizing the president to prohibit the sale of arms and munitions to the warring countries of Bolivia and Paraguay, should he determine that such a prohibition would "contribute to the reestablishment of peace between those countries." In pursuance of this authority, President Franklin Roosevelt immediately embargoed the sale of war matériel to those countries. The defendants in this case, charged with conspiring to sell arms to Bolivia in violation of the embargo, contended that the presidential proclamation was invalid because Congress could not constitutionally delegate such broad power to the president. When a federal district court upheld this contention, the United States appealed directly to the Supreme Court. Opinion of the Court: <u>Sutherland,</u> Hughes, Van Devanter, Brandeis, Butler, Roberts, Cardozo. Dissenting opinion: <u>McReynolds</u>. Not participating: Stone.

JUSTICE SUTHERLAND delivered the opinion of the Court.

Whether, if the Joint Resolution had related solely to internal affairs it would be open to the challenge that it constituted an unlawful delegation of legislative power to the Executive, we find it unnecessary to determine. The whole aim of the resolution is to affect a situation entirely external to the United States, and falling within the category of foreign affairs. The determination which we are called to make, therefore, is whether the Joint Resolution, as applied to that situation, is vulnerable to attack under the rule that forbids a delegation of the law-making power. In other words, assuming (but not deciding) that the challenged delegation, if it were confined to internal affairs, would be invalid, may it nevertheless be sustained on the ground that its exclusive aim is to afford a remedy for a hurtful condition within foreign territory?

It will contribute to the elucidation of the question if we first consider the differences between the powers of the federal government in respect of foreign or external affairs and those in respect of domestic or internal affairs. That there are differences between them, and that these differences are fundamental, may not be doubted.

The two classes of powers are different, both in respect of their origin and their nature. The broad statement that the federal government can exercise no powers except those specifically enumerated in the Constitution, and such implied powers as are necessary and proper to carry into effect the enumerated powers, is categorically true only in respect of our internal affairs. In that field, the primary purpose of the Constitution was to carve from the general mass of legislative powers *then possessed by the states* such portions as it was thought desirable to vest in the federal government, leaving those not included in the enumeration still in the states. Since the states severally never possessed international powers, such powers could not have been carved from the mass of state powers but obviously were transmitted to the United States from some other source. During the colonial period, those powers were possessed exclusively by and were entirely under the control of the Crown. By the Declaration of Independence, "the Representatives of the United States of America" declared the United (not the several) Colonies to be free and independent states, and as such to have "full Power to levy War, conclude Peace, contract Alliances, establish Commerce and to do all other Acts and Things which Independent States may of right do."

As a result of the separation from Great Britain by the colonies acting as a unit, the powers of external sovereignty passed from the Crown not to the colonies severally, but to the colonies in their collective and corporate capacity as the United States of America. Even before the Declaration, the colonies were a unit in foreign affairs, acting through a common agency—namely the Continental Congress, composed of delegates from the thirteen colonies. That agency exercised the powers of war and peace, raised an army, created a navy, and finally adopted the Declaration of Independence. Rulers come and go; governments end and forms of government change; but sovereignty survives. A political society cannot endure without a supreme will somewhere. Sovereignty is never held in suspense. When, therefore, the external sovereignty of Great Britain in respect of the colonies ceased, it immediately passed to the Union.

The Union existed before the Constitution, which was ordained and established among other things to form "a more perfect Union." Prior to that event, it is clear that the Union, declared by the Articles of Confederation to be "perpetual," was the sole possessor of external sovereignty and in the Union it remained without change save in so far as the Constitution in express terms qualified its exercise. The Framers' Convention was called and exerted its powers upon the irrefutable postulate that though the states were several, their people in respect of foreign affairs were one.

It results that the investment of the federal government with the powers of external sovereignty did not depend upon the affirmative grants of the Constitution. The powers to declare and wage war, to conclude peace, to make treaties, to maintain diplomatic relations with other sovereignties, if they had never been mentioned in the Constitution, would have vested in the federal government as necessary concomitants of nationality. As a member of the family of nations, the right and power of the United States in that field are equal to the right and power of the other members of the international family. Otherwise, the United States is not completely sovereign.

Not only, as we have shown, is the federal power over external affairs in origin and essential character different from that over internal affairs, but participation in the exercise of the power is significantly limited. In this vast external realm, with its important, complicated, delicate and manifold problems, the President alone has the power to speak or listen as a representative of the nation. As [John] Marshall said in his great argument of March 7, 1800, in the House of Representatives, "The President is the sole organ of the nation in its external relations, and its sole representative with foreign nations." It is important to bear in mind that we are here dealing not alone with an authority vested in the President by an exertion of legislative power, but with such an authority plus the very delicate, plenary and exclusive power of the President as the sole organ of the federal government in the field of international relations—a power which does not require as a basis for its exercise an act of Congress, but which, of course, like every other governmental power, must be exercised in subordination to the applicable provisions of the Constitution. It is quite apparent that if, in the maintenance of our international relations, embarrassment—perhaps serious embarrassment—is to be avoided and success for our aims achieved, congressional legislation which is to be made effective through negotiation and inquiry within the international field must often accord to the President a degree of discretion and freedom from statutory restriction which would not be admissible were domestic affairs alone involved. Moreover, he, not Congress, has the better opportunity of knowing the conditions which prevail in foreign countries, and especially is this true in time of war. He has his confidential sources of information. He has his agents in the form of diplomatic, consular and other officials. Secrecy in respect of information gathered by them may be highly necessary, and the premature disclosure of it productive of harmful results. Indeed, so clearly is this true that the first President refused to accede to a request to lay before the House of Representatives the instructions, correspondence and documents relating to the negotiation of the Jay Treaty—a refusal the wisdom of which was recognized by the House itself and has never since been doubted.

The marked difference between foreign affairs and domestic affairs in this respect is recognized by both houses of Congress in the very form of their requisitions for information from the executive departments. In the case of every department except the Department of State, the resolution directs the official to furnish the information. In the case of the State Department, dealing with foreign affairs, the President is requested to furnish the information "if not incompatible with the public interest." A statement that to furnish the information is not compatible with the public interest rarely, if ever, is questioned.

When the President is to be authorized by legislation to act in respect of a matter intended to affect a situation in foreign territory, the legislator properly bears in mind the important consideration that the form of the President's action—or, indeed, whether he shall act at all—may well depend, among other things, upon the nature of the confidential information which he has or may thereafter receive, or upon the effect which his action may have upon our foreign relations. This consideration, in connection with what we have already

said on the subject, discloses the unwisdom of requiring Congress in this field of governmental power to lay down narrowly definite standards by which the President is to be governed. As this court said in *Mackenzie v. Hare* (1915), "As a government, the United States is invested with all the attributes of sovereignty. As it has the character of nationality it has the powers of nationality, especially those which concern its relations and intercourse with other countries. We should hesitate long before limiting or embarrassing such powers."

In the light of the foregoing observations, it is evident that this court should not be in haste to apply a general rule which will have the effect of condemning legislation like that under review as constituting an unlawful delegation of legislative power. The principles which justify such legislation find overwhelming support in the unbroken legislative practice which has prevailed almost from the inception of the national government to the present day.

The result of holding that the joint resolution here under attack is void and unenforceable as constituting an unlawful delegation of legislative power would be to stamp this multitude of comparable acts and resolutions as likewise invalid. And while this court may not, and should not, hesitate to declare acts of Congress, however many times repeated, to be unconstitutional if beyond all rational doubt it finds them to be so, an impressive array of legislation such as we have just set forth, enacted by nearly every Congress from the beginning of our national existence to the present day, must be given unusual weight in the process of reaching a correct determination of the problem. A legislative practice such as we have here, evidenced not by only occasional instances, but marked by the movement of a steady stream for a century and a half of time, goes a long way in the direction of proving the presence of unassailable ground for the constitutionality of the practice, to be found in the origin and history of the power involved, or in its nature, or in both combined.

The judgment of the court below must be reversed and the cause remanded for further proceedings in accordance with the foregoing opinion.

Missouri v. Holland
252 U.S. 346 (1920)

In 1913, Congress passed legislation regulating the hunting of migratory birds. When two federal district courts ruled that the legislation was unconstitutional in that it lay beyond Congress's enumerated powers under the Constitution, the government accepted the decisions without appeal. In 1916, however, the United States entered into a treaty with Great Britain regulating the hunting of birds that migrated between the United States and Canada; two years later, Congress passed the Migratory Bird Treaty Act in pursuance of that treaty. A lower federal court denied the State of Missouri's challenge to the legislation, and Missouri appealed. Opinion of the Court: <u>Holmes</u>, White, McKenna, Day, McReynolds, Brandeis, Clarke. Dissenting (without opinion): Van Devanter, Pitney.

JUSTICE HOLMES delivered the opinion of the Court.

The question raised is the general one whether the treaty and statute are void as an interference with the rights reserved to the States. To answer this question it is not enough to refer to the Tenth Amendment, reserving the powers not delegated to the United States, because by Article II, §2, the power to make treaties is delegated expressly, and by Article VI treaties made under the authority of the United States, along with the Constitution and laws of the United States made in pursuance thereof, are declared the supreme law of the land. If the treaty is valid there can be no dispute about the validity of the statute under Article I, §8, as a necessary and proper means to execute the powers of the Government. The language of the Constitution as to the supremacy of treaties being general, the question before us is narrowed to an inquiry into the ground upon which the present supposed exception is placed.

It is said that a treaty cannot be valid if it infringes the Constitution, that there are limits, therefore, to the treaty-making power, and that one such limit is that what an act of Congress could not do unaided, in derogation of the powers reserved to the States, a treaty cannot do. An earlier act of Congress that attempted by itself and not in pursuance of a treaty to regulate the killing of migratory birds within the States had been held bad in the District Court.

Whether the two cases were decided rightly or not, they cannot be accepted as a test of the treaty power. Acts of Congress are the supreme law of the land only when made in pursuance of the Constitution, while treaties are declared to be so when made under the authority of the United States. It is open to question whether the authority of the United States means more than the formal acts prescribed to make the convention. We do not mean to imply that there are no qualifications to the treaty-making power; but they must be ascertained in a different way. It is obvious that there may be matters of the sharpest exigency for the national well being that an act of Congress could not deal with but that a treaty followed by such an act could, and it is not lightly to be assumed that, in matters requiring national action, "a power which must belong to and somewhere reside in every civilized government" is not to be found. We are not yet discussing the particular case before us but only are considering the validity of the test proposed. With regard to that we may add that when we are dealing with words that also are a constituent act, like the Constitution of the United States, we must realize that they have called into life a being the development of which could not have been foreseen completely by the most gifted of its begetters. It was enough for them to realize or to hope that they had created an organism; it has taken a century and has cost their successors much sweat and blood to prove that they created a nation. The case before us must be considered in the light of our whole experience and not merely in that of what was said a hundred years ago. The treaty in question does not contravene any prohibitory words to be found in the Constitution. The only question is whether it is forbidden by some invisible radiation from the general terms of the Tenth Amendment. We must consider what this country has become in deciding what that Amendment has reserved.

The State as we have intimated founds its claim of exclusive authority upon an assertion of title to migratory birds, an assertion that is embodied in statute. The whole foundation of the State's rights is the presence within their jurisdiction of birds that yesterday had not arrived, tomorrow may be in another State and in a week a thousand miles away. If we are to be accurate we cannot put the case of the State upon higher ground than that the treaty deals with creatures that for the moment are within the state borders, that it must be carried out by officers of the United States within the same territory, and that but for the treaty the State would be free to regulate this subject itself.

Here a national interest of very nearly the first magnitude is involved. It can be protected only by national action in concert with that of another power. The subject-matter is only transitorily within the State and has no permanent habitat therein. But for the treaty and the statute there soon might be no birds for any powers to deal with. We see nothing in the Constitution that compels the Government to sit by while a food supply is cut off and the protectors of our forests and our crops are destroyed. It is not sufficient to rely upon the States. The reliance is vain, and were it otherwise, the question is whether the United States is forbidden to act. We are of opinion that the treaty and statute must be upheld.

Decree affirmed.

Medellin v. Texas
552 U.S.491 (2008)

In 1969, the United States ratified the Vienna Convention on Consular Relations (Vienna Convention) and the Optional Protocol Concerning the Compulsory Settlement of Disputes to the Vienna Convention. Article 36 of the Vienna Convention provides that if a person detained by a foreign country "so requests, the competent authorities of the receiving State shall, without delay, inform the consular post of the sending State" of such detention, and "inform the [detainee] of his right" to request assistance from the consul of his own state. Claiming that the United States had violated the convention in its treatment of fifty-one Mexican nationals in the United States, Mexico brought suit against the United States before the International Court of Justice (ICJ). In the Case Concerning Avena and Other Mexican Nationals (Avena), *the ICJ held that, based on violations of the Vienna Convention, the fifty-one named Mexican nationals were entitled to review and reconsideration of their state-court convictions and sentences in the United States, regardless of any forfeiture of the right to raise Vienna Convention claims because of a failure to comply with state rules governing challenges to criminal convictions. In 2005, after* Avena, *President George W. Bush sent a memorandum to the attorney general affirming that the United States would "discharge its international obligations" under* Avena *"by having State courts give effect to the decision." In 2006, likewise after*

Avena *but in a case not involving the individuals named in that case, the Supreme Court held in* Sanchez-Llamas v. Oregon, *548 U.S. 331 (2006), that, contrary to the ICJ's determination, the Vienna Convention did not preclude the application of state default rules. José Ernesto Medellín, convicted and sentenced in Texas state court for murder, was one of the fifty-one Mexican nationals named in the* Avena *decision. Relying on the ICJ's decision and the president's memorandum, Medellín filed an application for a writ of habeas corpus in state court. The Texas Court of Criminal Appeals dismissed Medellín's application, given Medellín's failure to raise his Vienna Convention claim in a timely manner under state law, and the US Supreme Court granted certiorari.* Opinion of the Court: <u>Roberts</u>, Scalia, Kennedy, Thomas, Alito. Concurring in the judgment: <u>Stevens</u>. Dissenting opinion: <u>Breyer</u>, Souter, Ginsburg.

THE CHIEF JUSTICE delivered the opinion of the Court.

We granted certiorari to decide two questions. *First,* is the ICJ's judgment in *Avena* directly enforceable as domestic law in a state court in the United States? *Second,* does the President's Memorandum independently require the States to provide review and reconsideration of the claims of the 51 Mexican nationals named in *Avena* without regard to state procedural default rules? We conclude that neither *Avena* nor the President's Memorandum constitutes directly enforceable federal law that pre-empts state limitations on the filing of successive habeas petitions. We therefore affirm the decision below.

II

Medellin first contends that the ICJ's judgment in *Avena* constitutes a "binding" obligation on courts of the United States. He argues that "by virtue of the Supremacy Clause, the treaties requiring compliance with the *Avena* judgment are *already* the 'Law of the Land' by which all state and federal courts in this country are 'bound.'" No one disputes that the *Avena* decision constitutes an *international* law obligation on the part of the United States. But not all international law obligations automatically constitute binding federal law enforceable in United States courts. The question we confront here is whether the *Avena* judgment has automatic *domestic* legal effect such that the judgment of its own force applies in state and federal courts.

This Court has long recognized the distinction between treaties that automatically have effect as domestic law, and those that—while they constitute international law commitments—do not by themselves function as binding federal law. The distinction was well explained by Chief Justice Marshall's opinion in *Foster v. Neilson* (1829), which held that a treaty is "equivalent to an act of the legislature," and hence self-executing, when it "operates of itself without the aid of any legislative provision." When, in contrast, "[treaty] stipulations are not self-executing they can only be enforced pursuant to legislation to carry them into effect." *Whitney v. Robertson* (1888). In sum, while treaties "may comprise international commitments, they are not domestic law unless Congress has either enacted implementing statutes or the treaty itself conveys an intention that it be 'self-executing' and is ratified on these terms."

A

The interpretation of a treaty, like the interpretation of a statute, begins with its text. Because a treaty ratified by the United States is "an agreement among sovereign powers," we have also considered as "aids to its interpretation" the negotiation and drafting history of the treaty as well as "the post-ratification understanding" of signatory nations.

As a signatory to the Optional Protocol, the United States agreed to submit disputes arising out of the Vienna Convention to the ICJ. The Protocol says nothing about the effect of an ICJ decision and does not itself commit signatories to comply with an ICJ judgment. The Protocol is similarly silent as to any enforcement mechanism. The obligation on the part of signatory nations to comply with ICJ judgments derives not from the Optional Protocol, but rather from Article 94 of the United Nations Charter—the provision that specifically addresses the effect of ICJ decisions. Article 94(1) provides that "each Member of the United Nations *undertakes to comply* with the decision of the [ICJ] in any case to which it is a party." The Executive Branch contends that the phrase "undertakes to comply" is not "an acknowledgement that an ICJ decision will have immediate legal effect in the courts of U.N. members," but rather "a *commitment* on the part of U.N. Members to take *future* action through their political branches to comply with an ICJ decision." We agree with this construction of Article 94. The U.N. Charter's provision of an express diplomatic—that is, nonjudicial—remedy is itself evidence that ICJ judgments were not meant to be enforceable in domestic courts. Medellin's view that ICJ decisions are automatically enforceable as domestic law is fatally undermined by the enforcement structure established by Article 94.

It is, moreover, well settled that the United States' interpretation of a treaty "is entitled to great weight." *Sumitomo Shoji America, Inc. v. Avagliano* (1982). The Executive Branch has unfailingly adhered to its view that the relevant treaties do not create domestically enforceable federal law. The pertinent international agreements, therefore, do not provide for implementation of ICJ judgments through direct enforcement in domestic courts, and "where a treaty does not provide a particular remedy, either expressly or implicitly, it is not for the federal courts to impose one on the States through lawmaking of their own."

B

The dissent faults our analysis because it "looks for the wrong thing (explicit textual expression about self-execution) using the wrong standard (clarity) in the wrong place (the treaty language)." Given our obligation to interpret treaty provisions to determine whether they are self-executing, we have to confess that we do think it rather important to look to the treaty language to see what it has to say about the issue. That is after all what the Senate looks to in deciding whether to approve the treaty.

As against this time-honored textual approach, the dissent proposes a multifactor, judgment-by-judgment analysis that would "jettison relative predictability for the open-ended rough-and-tumble of factors." *Jerome B. Grubart, Inc. v. Great Lakes Dredge & Dock Co.* (1995). The dissent's novel approach to deciding which (or, more accurately, when) treaties give rise to directly enforceable federal law is arrestingly indeterminate. Treaty language is barely probative. Determining whether treaties themselves create federal law is sometimes committed to the political branches and sometimes to the judiciary. Of those committed to the judiciary, the courts pick and choose which shall be binding United States law—trumping not only state but other federal law as well—and which shall not. They do this on the basis of a multifactor, "context-specific" inquiry. Even then, the same treaty sometimes gives rise to United States law and sometimes does not, again depending on an ad hoc judicial assessment.

The dissent's approach risks the United States' involvement in international agreements. It is hard to believe that the United States would enter into treaties that are sometimes enforceable and sometimes not. Such a treaty would be the equivalent of writing a blank check to the judiciary. Senators could never be quite sure what the treaties on which they were voting meant. Only a judge could say for sure and only at some future date. This uncertainty could hobble the United States' efforts to negotiate and sign international agreements.

The dissent's contrary approach would assign to the courts—not the political branches—the primary role in deciding when and how international agreements will be enforced. To read a treaty so that it sometimes has the effect of domestic law and sometimes does not is tantamount to vesting with the judiciary the power not only to interpret but also to create the law.

C

Our conclusion that *Avena* does not by itself constitute binding federal law is confirmed by the "postratification understanding" of signatory nations. There are currently 47 nations that are parties to the Optional Protocol and 171 nations that are parties to the Vienna Convention. Yet neither Medellin nor his *amici* have identified a single nation that treats ICJ judgments as binding in domestic courts. Moreover, the consequences of Medellin's argument give pause. An ICJ judgment, the argument goes, is not only binding domestic law but is also unassailable. As a result, neither Texas nor this Court may look behind a judgment and quarrel with its reasoning or result. Even the dissent flinches at reading the relevant treaties to give rise to self-executing ICJ judgments in all cases. It admits that "Congress is unlikely to authorize automatic judicial enforceability of *all* ICJ judgments, for that could include some politically sensitive judgments and others better suited for enforcement by other branches." Our point precisely. But the lesson to draw from that insight is hardly that the judiciary should decide which judgments are politically sensitive and which are not. In short, and as we observed in *Sanchez-Llamas,* "nothing in the structure or purpose of the ICJ suggests that its interpretations were intended to be conclusive on our courts."

D

The dissent worries that our decision casts doubt on some 70-odd treaties under which the United States has agreed to submit disputes to the ICJ according to "roughly similar" provisions. Again, under our established precedent, some treaties are self-executing and some are not, depending on the treaty. That the judgment of an international tribunal might not automatically become domestic law hardly means the underlying treaty is "useless." Such judgments would still constitute international obligations, the proper subject of political and diplomatic negotiations. And Congress could elect to give them wholesale effect (rather than the judgment-by-judgment approach hypothesized by the dissent) through implementing legislation, as it regularly has. In sum, while the ICJ's judgment in *Avena* creates an international law obligation on the part of the United States, it does not of its own force constitute binding federal law that pre-empts state restrictions on the filing of successive habeas petitions.

III

Medellin next argues that the ICJ's judgment in *Avena* is binding on state courts by virtue of the President's February 28, 2005 Memorandum. The United States contends that while the *Avena* judgment does not of its own force require domestic courts to set aside ordinary rules of procedural default, that judgment became the law of the land with precisely that effect pursuant to the President's Memorandum and his power "to establish binding rules of decision that preempt contrary state law." Accordingly, we must decide whether the President's declaration alters our conclusion that the *Avena* judgment is not a rule of domestic law binding in state and federal courts. The United States maintains that the President's constitutional role "uniquely qualifies" him to resolve the sensitive foreign policy decisions that bear on compliance with an ICJ decision and "to do so expeditiously." We do not question these propositions. Such considerations, however, do not allow us to set aside first principles. The President's authority to act, as with the exercise of any governmental power, "must stem either from an act of Congress or from the Constitution itself."

The United States marshals two principal arguments in favor of the President's authority "to establish binding rules of decision that preempt contrary state law." The Solicitor General first argues that the relevant treaties give the President the authority to implement the *Avena* judgment and that Congress has acquiesced in the exercise of such authority. The United States also relies upon an "independent" international dispute-resolution power wholly apart from the asserted authority based on the pertinent treaties. Medellin adds the additional argument that the President's Memorandum is a valid exercise of his power to take care that the laws be faithfully executed.

The United States maintains that the President's Memorandum is authorized by the Optional Protocol and the U.N. Charter. That is, because the relevant treaties "create an obligation to comply with *Avena*," they "*implicitly* give the President authority to implement that treaty-based obligation." As a result, the President's Memorandum is well grounded in the first category of the *Youngstown* framework. We disagree. The President has an array of political and diplomatic means available to enforce international obligations, but unilaterally converting a non-self-executing treaty into a self-executing one is not among them. The responsibility for transforming an international obligation arising from a non-self-executing treaty into domestic law falls to Congress. The requirement that Congress, rather than the President, implement a non-self-executing treaty derives from the text of the Constitution, which divides the treaty-making power between the President and the Senate. The Constitution vests the President with the authority to "make" a treaty. If the Executive determines that a treaty should have domestic effect of its own force, that determination may be implemented "in making" the treaty, by ensuring that it contains language plainly providing for domestic enforceability. If the treaty is to be self-executing in this respect, the Senate must consent to the treaty by the requisite two-thirds vote, consistent with all other constitutional restraints. Once a treaty is ratified without provisions clearly according it domestic effect, however, whether the treaty will ever have such effect is governed by the fundamental constitutional principle that "the power to make the necessary laws is in Congress; the power to execute in the President." *Hamdan v. Rumsfeld* (2006).

Each of the two means described above for giving domestic effect to an international treaty obligation under the Constitution—for making law—requires joint action by the Executive and Legislative Branches: The Senate can ratify a self-executing treaty "made" by the Executive, or, if the ratified treaty is not self-executing, Congress can enact implementing legislation approved by the President. It should not be surprising that our Constitution does not contemplate vesting such power in the Executive alone. As Madison explained in *The Federalist* No. 47, under our constitutional system of checks and balances, "the magistrate in whom the whole executive power resides cannot of himself make a law." That would, however, seem an apt description of the asserted executive authority unilaterally to give the effect of domestic law to obligations under a non-self-executing treaty.

The United States nonetheless maintains that the President's Memorandum should be given effect as domestic law because "this case involves a valid Presidential action in the context of Congressional 'acquiescence.'" Even if we were persuaded that congressional acquiescence could support the President's asserted authority to create domestic law pursuant to a non-self-executing treaty, such acquiescence does not exist here. The United States first locates congressional acquiescence in Congress's failure to act following the President's resolution of prior ICJ controversies. A review of the Executive's actions in those prior cases, however, cannot support the claim that Congress acquiesced in this particular exercise of Presidential authority, for none of them remotely involved transforming an international obligation into domestic law and thereby displacing state law.

The United States also directs us to the President's "related" statutory responsibilities and to his "established role" in litigating foreign policy concerns as support for the President's asserted authority to give the ICJ's decision in *Avena* the force of domestic law. Congress has indeed authorized the President to represent the United States before the United Nations, the ICJ, and the Security Council, but the authority of the President to represent the United States before such bodies speaks to the President's *international* responsibilities, not any unilateral authority to create domestic law.

None of this is to say, however, that the combination of a non-self-executing treaty and the lack of implementing legislation precludes the President from acting to comply with an international treaty obligation. It is only to say that the Executive cannot unilaterally execute a non-self-executing treaty by giving it domestic effect.

2

We thus turn to the United States' claim that independent of the United States' treaty obligations, the Memorandum is a valid exercise of the President's foreign affairs authority to resolve claims disputes with foreign nations. The United States relies on a series of cases in which this Court has upheld the authority of the President to settle foreign claims pursuant to an executive agreement. In these cases this Court has explained that, if pervasive enough, a history of congressional acquiescence can be treated as a "gloss on 'Executive Power' vested in the President by §1 of Art. II."

We find that our claims-settlement cases do not support the authority that the President asserts in this case. The claims-settlement cases involve a narrow set of circumstances: the making of executive agreements to settle civil claims between American citizens and foreign governments or foreign nationals. They are based on the view that "a systematic, unbroken, executive practice, long pursued to the knowledge of the Congress and never before questioned," can "raise a presumption that the [action] had been [taken] in pursuance of its consent." The President's Memorandum is not supported by a "particularly longstanding practice" of congressional acquiescence, but rather is what the United States itself has described as "unprecedented action." Indeed, the Government has not identified a single instance in which the President has attempted (or Congress has acquiesced in) a Presidential directive issued to state courts.

The judgment of the Texas Court of Criminal Appeals is affirmed.

JUSTICE BREYER, with whom JUSTICE SOUTER and JUSTICE GINSBURG join, dissenting.

The Constitution's Supremacy Clause provides that "all Treaties which shall be made under the Authority of the United States, shall be the supreme Law of the Land; and the Judges in every State shall be bound thereby." The Clause means that the "courts" must regard "a treaty as equivalent to an act of the legislature, whenever it operates of itself without the aid of any legislative provision." *Foster v. Neilson* (1829). The United States has signed and ratified a series of treaties obliging it to comply with ICJ judgments in cases in which it has given its consent to the exercise of the ICJ's adjudicatory authority. President Bush has determined that domestic courts should enforce this particular ICJ judgment. And Congress has done nothing to suggest the contrary. Under these circumstances, I believe the treaty obligations, and hence the judgment, resting as it does upon the consent of the United States to the ICJ's jurisdiction, bind the courts no less than would "an act of the federal legislature."

To understand the issue before us, the reader must keep in mind three separate ratified United States treaties and one ICJ judgment against the United States. The first treaty, the Vienna Convention, contains two relevant provisions. The first requires the United States and other signatory nations to inform arrested foreign nationals of their separate Convention-given right to contact their nation's consul. The second says that these rights (of an arrested person) "shall be exercised in conformity with the laws and regulations" of the arresting nation, *provided that the "laws and regulations enable full effect to be given to the purposes for which" those "rights are intended."* The second treaty, the Optional Protocol, concerns the "compulsory settlement" of Vienna Convention disputes. It provides that for parties that elect to subscribe to the Protocol, "disputes arising out of the interpretation or application of the [Vienna] Convention" shall be submitted to the "compulsory jurisdiction of the International Court of Justice." It authorizes any party that has consented to the ICJ's jurisdiction (by signing the Optional Protocol) to bring another such party before that Court. The third treaty, the United Nations Charter, says that every signatory Nation "undertakes to comply with the decision of the International Court of Justice in any case to which it is a party." In an annex to the Charter, the Statute of the International Court of Justice states that an ICJ judgment has "binding force between the parties and in respect of that particular case."

The ICJ judgment in *Avena* requires that the United States reexamine "by means of its own choosing" certain aspects of the relevant state criminal proceedings of 51 of these individual Mexican nationals. The President has determined that this should be done. The critical question here is whether the Supremacy Clause requires Texas to follow, *i.e.,* to enforce, this ICJ judgment. The Court says "no." And it reaches its negative answer by interpreting the labyrinth of treaty provisions as creating a legal obligation that binds the United States internationally, but which, for Supremacy Clause purposes, is not "automatically enforceable as domestic law." Rather, here (and presumably in any other ICJ judgment rendered pursuant to any of the approximately 70 U.S. treaties in force that contain similar provisions for submitting treaty-based disputes to the ICJ for decisions that bind the parties) Congress must enact specific legislation before ICJ judgments entered pursuant to our consent to compulsory ICJ jurisdiction can become domestic law.

In my view, the President has correctly determined that Congress need not enact additional legislation. The majority places too much weight upon treaty language that says little about the matter. The words "undertake to comply," for example, do not tell us whether an ICJ judgment rendered pursuant to the parties' consent to compulsory ICJ jurisdiction does, or does not, automatically become part of our domestic law. To answer that question we must look instead to our own domestic law, in particular, to the many treaty-related cases interpreting the Supremacy Clause. Those cases, including some written by Justices well aware of the Founders' original intent, lead to the conclusion that the ICJ judgment before us is enforceable as a matter of domestic law without further legislation.

The case law provides no simple magic answer to the question whether a particular treaty provision is self-executing. But the case law does make clear that, insofar as today's majority looks for language about "self-execution" in the treaty itself and insofar as it erects "clear statement" presumptions designed to help find an answer, it is misguided. The many treaty provisions that this Court has found self-executing contain no textual language on the point. In a word, for present purposes, the absence or presence of language in a treaty about a provision's self-execution proves nothing at all. At best the Court is hunting the snark. At worst it erects legalistic hurdles that can threaten the application of provisions in many existing commercial and other treaties and make it more difficult to negotiate new ones.

The case law also suggests practical, context-specific criteria that this Court has previously used to help determine whether, for Supremacy Clause purposes, a treaty provision is self-executing. In making this determination, this Court has found the provision's subject matter of particular importance. Does the treaty provision declare peace? Does it promise not to engage in hostilities? If so, it addresses itself to the political branches. Alternatively, does it concern the adjudication of traditional private legal rights such as rights to own property, to conduct a business, or to obtain civil tort recovery? If so, it may well address itself to the Judiciary. Enforcing such rights and setting their boundaries is the bread-and-butter work of the courts.

One might also ask whether the treaty provision confers specific, detailed individual legal rights. Does it set forth definite standards that judges can readily enforce? Other things being equal, where rights are specific and readily enforceable, the treaty provision more likely "addresses" the judiciary. Alternatively, would direct enforcement require the courts to create a new cause of action? Would such enforcement engender constitutional controversy? Would it create constitutionally undesirable conflict with the other branches? In such circumstances, it is not likely that the provision contemplates direct judicial enforcement.

Such questions, drawn from case law stretching back 200 years, do not create a simple test, let alone a magic formula. But they do help to constitute a practical, context-specific judicial approach, seeking to separate run-of-the-mill judicial matters from other matters, sometimes more politically charged, sometimes more clearly the responsibility of other branches, sometimes lacking those attributes that would permit courts to act on their own without more ado. And such an approach is all that we need to find an answer to the legal question now before us.

Applying the approach just described, I would find the relevant treaty provisions self-executing as applied to the ICJ judgment before us (giving that judgment domestic legal effect) for the following reasons, taken together. *First,* the language of the relevant treaties strongly supports direct judicial enforceability, at least of judgments of the kind at issue here. The Optional Protocol bears the title "Compulsory Settlement of Disputes," thereby emphasizing the mandatory and binding nature of the procedures it sets forth. And the Protocol contrasts proceedings of the compulsory kind with an alternative "conciliation procedure," the recommendations of which a party may decide "not" to "accept."

Second, the Optional Protocol here applies to a dispute about the meaning of a Vienna Convention provision that is itself self-executing and judicially enforceable. *Third,* logic suggests that a treaty provision providing for "final" and "binding" judgments that "settl[e]" treaty-based disputes is self-executing insofar as the judgment in question concerns the meaning of an underlying treaty provision that is itself self-executing. What sense would it make (1) to make a self-executing promise and (2) to promise to accept as final an ICJ judgment interpreting that self-executing promise, yet (3) to insist that the judgment itself is not self-executing (*i.e.,* that Congress must enact specific legislation to enforce it)? I am not aware of any satisfactory answer to these questions.

Fourth, the majority's very different approach has seriously negative practical implications. The United States has entered into at least 70 treaties that contain provisions for ICJ dispute settlement similar to the Protocol before us. Many of these treaties contain provisions similar to those this Court has previously found self-executing—provisions that involve, for example, property rights, contract and commercial rights, trademarks, civil liability for personal injury, rights of foreign diplomats, taxation, domestic-court jurisdiction, and so forth. If the Optional Protocol here, taken together with the U.N. Charter and its annexed ICJ Statute, is insufficient to warrant enforcement of the ICJ judgment before us, it is difficult to see how one could reach a different conclusion in any of these other instances. And the consequence is to undermine longstanding efforts in those treaties to create an effective international system for interpreting and applying many, often commercial, self-executing treaty provisions.

Fifth, other factors, related to the particular judgment here at issue, make that judgment well suited to direct judicial enforcement. The specific issue before the ICJ concerned "review and reconsideration" of the "possible prejudice" caused in each of the 51 affected cases by an arresting State's failure to provide the defendant with rights guaranteed by the Vienna Convention. This review will call for an understanding of how criminal procedure works, including whether, and how, a notification failure may work prejudice. As the ICJ itself recognized, "it is the judicial process that is suited to this task."

Sixth, to find the United States' treaty obligations self-executing as applied to the ICJ judgment (and consequently to find that judgment enforceable) does not threaten constitutional conflict with other branches; it does not require us to engage in nonjudicial activity; and it does not require us to create a new cause of action.

Seventh, neither the President nor Congress has expressed concern about direct judicial enforcement of the ICJ decision. To the contrary, the President *favors* enforcement of this judgment. Thus, insofar as foreign policy impact, the interrelation of treaty provisions, or any other matter within the President's special treaty, military, and foreign affairs responsibilities might prove relevant, such factors favor, rather than militate against, enforcement of the judgment before us.

For these seven reasons, I would find that the United States' treaty obligation to comply with the ICJ judgment in *Avena* is enforceable in court in this case without further congressional action.

Zivotofsky v. Kerry
576 U.S. ___ (2015)

In 1948, President Harry Truman formally recognized Israel, but neither he nor any later president officially acknowledged any country's sovereignty over the contested city of Jerusalem. This position is reflected in State Department policy regarding passports and consular reports of birth abroad, which lists "Jerusalem" rather than a country name as the place of birth for those born there. In 2002, Congress passed the Foreign Relations Authorization Act, Section 214 of which is entitled "United States Policy with Respect to Jerusalem as the Capital of Israel." Subsection 214(d) states that "for purposes of the registration of birth, certification of nationality, or issuance of a passport of a United States citizen born in the city of Jerusalem, the Secretary shall, upon the request of the citizen or the citizen's legal guardian, record the place of birth as Israel." When signing the Act into law, President George W. Bush issued a signing statement declaring that §214 would, "if construed as mandatory rather than advisory, impermissibly interfere with the president's constitutional authority to formulate the position of the United States, speak for the Nation in international affairs, and determine the terms on which recognition is given to foreign states." Petitioner Menachem Binyamin Zivotofsky was born to United States citizens living in Jerusalem, and his parents sought both a passport and a consular report of birth listing his place of birth as "Jerusalem, Israel." When the Embassy refused to do so, they sued. The US District Court dismissed Zivotofsky's suit, reasoning that it presented a nonjusticiable political question and that Zivotofsky lacked standing. The Court of Appeals for the District of Columbia Circuit reversed on the standing issue, but affirmed the District Court's political question determination. The Supreme Court granted certiorari and vacated the judgment that the case raised a political question. On remand the Court of Appeals held the statute unconstitutional, and the Supreme Court again granted certiorari. Opinion of the Court: <u>Kennedy</u>, Ginsburg, Breyer, Sotomayor, Kagan. Concurring opinion: <u>Breyer</u>. Concurring in the judgment in part and dissenting in part: <u>Thomas</u>. Dissenting opinions: <u>Roberts</u>, Alito; <u>Scalia</u>, Roberts, Alito.

JUSTICE KENNEDY delivered the opinion of the Court.

II

In considering claims of Presidential power this Court refers to Justice Jackson's familiar tripartite framework from *Youngstown Sheet & Tube Co. v. Sawyer*, 343 U.S. 579 (1952) (concurring opinion). In this case the Secretary contends that §214(d) infringes on the President's exclusive recognition power by "requiring the President to contradict his recognition position regarding Jerusalem in official communications with foreign sovereigns." In so doing the Secretary acknowledges the President's power is "at its lowest ebb." Because the President's refusal to implement §214(d) falls into Justice Jackson's third category, his claim must be "scrutinized with caution," and he may rely solely on powers the Constitution grants to him alone. To determine whether the President possesses the exclusive power of recognition the Court examines the Constitution's text and structure, as well as precedent and history bearing on the question.

A

Recognition is a "formal acknowledgement" that a particular "entity possesses the qualifications for statehood" or "that a particular regime is the effective government of a state." It may also involve the determination of a state's territorial bounds. Recognition at international law is a precondition of regular diplomatic relations.

Despite the importance of the recognition power in foreign relations, the Constitution does not use the term "recognition," either in Article II or elsewhere. The Secretary asserts that the President exercises the recognition power based on the Reception Clause, which directs that the President "shall receive Ambassadors and other public Ministers." Art. II, §3. The Reception Clause received little attention at the Constitutional Convention. In fact, during the ratification debates, Alexander Hamilton claimed that the power to receive ambassadors was "more a matter of dignity than of authority," a ministerial duty largely "without consequence." *The Federalist*, No. 69. At the time of the founding, however, promi-

nent international scholars suggested that receiving an ambassador was tantamount to recognizing the sovereignty of the sending state. This in fact occurred early in the Nation's history when President Washington recognized the French Revolutionary Government by receiving its ambassador. After this incident the import of the Reception Clause became clear—causing Hamilton to change his earlier view. He wrote that the Reception Clause "includes th[e power] of judging, in the case of a revolution of government in a foreign country, whether the new rulers are competent organs of the national will, and ought to be recognised, or not." As a result, the Reception Clause provides support, although not the sole authority, for the President's power to recognize other nations.

The inference that the President exercises the recognition power is further supported by his additional Article II powers. It is for the President, "by and with the Advice and Consent of the Senate," to "make Treaties, provided two thirds of the Senators present concur." Art. II, §2, cl. 2. In addition, "he shall nominate, and by and with the Advice and Consent of the Senate, shall appoint Ambassadors" as well as "other public Ministers and Consuls." As a matter of constitutional structure, these additional powers give the President control over recognition decisions. Because these specific Clauses confer the recognition power on the President, the Court need not consider whether or to what extent the Vesting Clause, which provides that the "executive Power" shall be vested in the President, provides further support for the President's action here. Art. II, §1, cl. 1.

The text and structure of the Constitution grant the President the power to recognize foreign nations and governments. The question then becomes whether that power is exclusive. The various ways in which the President may unilaterally effect recognition—and the lack of any similar power vested in Congress—suggest that it is. So, too, do functional considerations. Put simply, the Nation must have a single policy regarding which governments are legitimate in the eyes of the United States and which are not. Foreign countries need to know, before entering into diplomatic relations or commerce with the United States, whether their ambassadors will be received; whether their officials will be immune from suit in federal court; and whether they may initiate lawsuits here to vindicate their rights. These assurances cannot be equivocal.

Recognition is a topic on which the Nation must "speak with one voice." *American Ins. Assn.* v. *Garamendi*, 539 U.S. 396 (2003). That voice must be the President's. Between the two political branches, only the Executive has the characteristic of unity at all times. And with unity comes the ability to exercise, to a greater degree, "decision, activity, secrecy, and dispatch." *The Federalist*, No. 70. The President is capable, in ways Congress is not, of engaging in the delicate and often secret diplomatic contacts that may lead to a decision on recognition. He is also better positioned to take the decisive, unequivocal action necessary to recognize other states at international law. These qualities explain why the Framers listed the traditional avenues of recognition—receiving ambassadors, making treaties, and sending ambassadors—as among the President's Article II powers. The President since the founding has exercised this unilateral power to recognize new states—and the Court has endorsed the practice.

It remains true that many decisions affecting foreign relations—including decisions that may determine the course of our relations with recognized countries—require congressional action. Although the President alone effects the formal act of recognition, Congress' powers, and its central role in making laws, give it substantial authority regarding many of the policy determinations that precede and follow the act of recognition itself. If Congress disagrees with the President's recognition policy, there may be consequences. Formal recognition may seem a hollow act if it is not accompanied by the dispatch of an ambassador, the easing of trade restrictions, and the conclusion of treaties. And those decisions require action by the Senate or the whole Congress. [But] the formal act of recognition is an executive power that Congress may not qualify. If the President is to be effective in negotiations over a formal recognition determination, it must be evident to his counterparts abroad that he speaks for the Nation on that precise question.

B

No single precedent resolves the question whether the President has exclusive recognition authority and, if so, how far that power extends. In part that is because, until today, the political branches have resolved their disputes over questions of recognition. The relevant cases, though providing important instruction, address the division of recognition power between the Federal Government and the States or between the courts and the political branches, not between the President and Congress. However, a fair reading of the cases shows that the President's role in the recognition process is both central and exclusive.

The Secretary [of State] now urges the Court to define the executive power over foreign relations in even broader terms. He contends that under the Court's precedent the President has "exclusive authority to conduct diplomatic relations," along with "the bulk of foreign-affairs powers." In support of his submission that the President has broad, undefined powers over foreign affairs, the Secretary quotes *United States* v. *Curtiss-Wright Export Corp.*, which described the President as "the sole organ of the federal government in the field of international relations." This Court declines to acknowledge that unbounded power. A formulation broader than the rule that the President alone determines what nations to formally recognize as legitimate—and that he consequently controls his statements on matters of recognition—presents different issues and is unnecessary to the resolution of this case.

In a world that is ever more compressed and interdependent, it is essential the congressional role in foreign affairs be understood and respected. For it is Congress that makes laws, and in countless ways its laws will and should shape the Nation's course. The Executive is not free from the ordinary controls and checks of Congress merely because foreign affairs are at issue. It is not for the President alone to determine the whole content of the Nation's foreign policy. That said, judicial precedent and historical practice teach that it is for the President alone to make the specific decision of what foreign power he will recognize as legitimate.

C

Having examined the Constitution's text and this Court's precedent, it is appropriate to turn to accepted understandings and practice. In separation-of-powers cases this Court has often "put significant weight upon historical practice." *NLRB* v. *Noel Canning*, (2014) From the first Administration forward, the President has claimed unilateral authority to recognize foreign sovereigns. For the most part, Congress has acquiesced in the Executive's exercise of the recognition power. On occasion, the President has chosen, as may often be prudent, to consult and coordinate with Congress. However, the most striking thing about the history of recognition is what is absent from it: a situation like this one, where Congress has enacted a statute contrary to the President's formal and considered statement concerning recognition. The weight of historical evidence indicates Congress has accepted that the power to recognize foreign states and governments and their territorial bounds is exclusive to the Presidency.

III

As the power to recognize foreign states resides in the President alone, the question becomes whether §214(d) infringes on the Executive's consistent decision to withhold recognition with respect to Jerusalem. If the power over recognition is to mean anything, it must mean that the President not only makes the initial, formal recognition determination but also that he may maintain that determination in his and his agent's statements. This conclusion is a matter of both common sense and necessity. If Congress could command the President to state a recognition position inconsistent with his own, Congress could override the President's recognition determination. Congress in effect would exercise the recognition power. As Justice Jackson wrote in *Youngstown*, when a Presidential power is "exclusive," it "disables the Congress from acting upon the subject."

Although the statement required by §214(d) would not itself constitute a formal act of recognition, it is a mandate that the Executive contradict his prior recognition determination

in an official document issued by the Secretary of State. The flaw in §214(d) is further underscored by the undoubted fact that that the purpose of the statute was to infringe on the recognition power—a power the Court now holds is the sole prerogative of the President. To allow Congress to control the President's communication in the context of a formal recognition determination is to allow Congress to exercise that exclusive power itself. As a result, the statute is unconstitutional.

* * *

In holding §214(d) invalid the Court does not question the substantial powers of Congress over foreign affairs in general or passports in particular. This case is confined solely to the exclusive power of the President to control recognition determinations, including formal statements by the Executive Branch acknowledging the legitimacy of a state or government and its territorial bounds. The judgment of the Court of Appeals for the District of Columbia Circuit is

Affirmed.

JUSTICE THOMAS, concurring in the judgment in part and dissenting in part.

Our Constitution allocates the powers of the Federal Government over foreign affairs in two ways. First, it expressly identifies certain foreign affairs powers and vests them in particular branches, either individually or jointly. Second, it vests the residual foreign affairs powers of the Federal Government—*i.e.,* those not specifically enumerated in the Constitution—in the President by way of Article II's Vesting Clause.

Section 214(d) ignores that constitutional allocation of power insofar as it directs the President, contrary to his wishes, to list "Israel" as the place of birth of Jerusalem-born citizens on their passports. The President has long regulated passports under his residual foreign affairs power, and this portion of §214(d) does not fall within any of Congress' enumerated powers. By contrast, §214(d) poses no such problem insofar as it regulates consular reports of birth abroad. Unlike passports, these reports were developed to effectuate the naturalization laws, and they continue to serve the role of identifying persons who need not be naturalized to obtain U.S. citizenship. The regulation of these reports does not fall within the President's foreign affairs powers, but within Congress' enumerated powers under the Naturalization and Necessary and Proper Clauses. I concur only in the portion of the Court's judgment holding §214(d) unconstitutional as applied to passports. I respectfully dissent from the remainder of the Court's judgment.

CHIEF JUSTICE ROBERTS, with whom JUSTICE ALITO joins, dissenting.

Today's decision is a first: Never before has this Court accepted a President's direct defiance of an Act of Congress in the field of foreign affairs. We have instead stressed that the President's power reaches "its lowest ebb" when he contravenes the express will of Congress, "for what is at stake is the equilibrium established by our constitutional system." *Youngstown Sheet & Tube Co.* v. *Sawyer*, 343 U.S. 579 (1952) (Jackson, J., concurring).

The Constitution allocates some foreign policy powers to the Executive, grants some to the Legislature, and enjoins the President to "take Care that the Laws be faithfully executed." Art. II, §3. The Executive may disregard "the expressed or implied will of Congress" only if the Constitution grants him a power "at once so conclusive and preclusive" as to "disable the Congress from acting upon the subject." For our first 225 years, no President prevailed when contradicting a statute in the field of foreign affairs.

In this case, the President claims the exclusive and preclusive power to recognize foreign sovereigns. I have serious doubts about that position. The majority places great weight on the Reception Clause, which directs that the Executive "shall receive Ambassadors and other public Ministers." But that provision, framed as an obligation rather than an authorization, appears alongside the *duties* imposed on the President by Article II, Section 3, not the *powers* granted to him by Article II, Section 2. Indeed, the People ratified the Constitution with Alexander Hamilton's assurance that executive reception of ambassadors "is more a matter of dignity than of authority" and "will be without consequence in the ad-

ministration of the government." *The Federalist*, No. 69. In short, at the time of the founding, "there was no reason to view the reception clause as a source of discretionary authority for the president." The majority's other asserted textual bases are even more tenuous. The President does have power to make treaties and appoint ambassadors. But those authorities are *shared* with Congress, so they hardly support an inference that the recognition power is *exclusive*. Precedent and history lend no more weight to the Court's position.

But even if the President does have exclusive recognition power, he still cannot prevail in this case, because the statute at issue *does not implicate recognition*. The relevant provision, §214(d), simply gives an American citizen born in Jerusalem the option to designate his place of birth as Israel "for purposes of" passports and other documents. The State Department itself has explained that "identification"—not recognition—"is the principal reason that U.S. passports require 'place of birth.'" Congress has not disputed the Executive's assurances that §214(d) does not alter the longstanding United States position on Jerusalem. At most, the majority worries that there may be a *perceived* contradiction based on a *mistaken* understanding of the effect of §214(d), insisting that some "observers interpreted §214 as altering United States policy regarding Jerusalem." To afford controlling weight to such impressions, however, is essentially to subject a duly enacted statute to an international heckler's veto. I respectfully dissent.

JUSTICE SCALIA, with whom THE CHIEF JUSTICE and JUSTICE ALITO join, dissenting.

The People adopted a Constitution that divides responsibility for the Nation's foreign concerns between the legislative and executive departments. This case arises out of a dispute between the Executive and Legislative Branches about whether the United States should treat Jerusalem as a part of Israel. The Constitution contemplates that the political branches will make policy about the territorial claims of foreign nations the same way they make policy about other international matters: The President will exercise his powers on the basis of his views, Congress its powers on the basis of its views. That is just what has happened here.

I

Before turning to Presidential power under Article II, I think it well to establish the statute's basis in congressional power under Article I. Congress's power to "establish an uniform Rule of Naturalization," Art. I, §8, cl. 4, enables it to grant American citizenship to someone born abroad. The naturalization power also enables Congress to furnish the people it makes citizens with papers verifying their citizenship— say a consular report of birth abroad (which certifies citizenship of an American born outside the United States) or a passport (which certifies citizenship for purposes of international travel). As the Necessary and Proper Clause confirms, every congressional power "carries with it all those incidental powers which are necessary to its complete and effectual execution." *Cohens v. Virginia*, 6 Wheat. 264 (1821). Even on a miserly understanding of Congress's incidental authority, Congress may make grants of citizenship "effectual" by providing for the issuance of certificates authenticating them.

One would think that if Congress may grant Zivotofsky a passport and a birth report, it may also require these papers to record his birthplace as "Israel." The birthplace specification promotes the document's citizenship-authenticating function by identifying the bearer, distinguishing people with similar names but different birthplaces from each other, helping authorities uncover identity fraud, and facilitating retrieval of the Government's citizenship records. To be sure, recording Zivotovsky's birthplace as "Jerusalem" rather than "Israel" would fulfill these objectives, but when faced with alternative ways to carry its powers into execution, Congress has the "discretion" to choose the one it deems "most beneficial to the people." *McCulloch* v. *Maryland*, 4 Wheat. 316 (1819). It thus has the right to decide that recording birthplaces as "Israel" makes for better foreign policy. Or that regardless of international politics, a passport or birth report should respect its bearer's conscientious belief that Jerusalem belongs to Israel.

No doubt congressional discretion in executing legislative powers has its limits; Congress's chosen approach must be not only "necessary" to carrying its powers into execution, but also "proper." Congress thus may not transcend boundaries upon legislative authority stated or implied elsewhere in the Constitution. But as we shall see, §214(d) does not transgress any such restriction.

II

The Court holds that the Constitution makes the President alone responsible for recognition and that §214(d) invades this exclusive power. I agree that the Constitution *empowers* the President to extend recognition on behalf of the United States, but I find it a much harder question whether it makes that power exclusive. Fortunately, I have no need to confront these matters today—nor does the Court—because §214(d) plainly does not concern recognition. Section 214(d) does not require the Secretary to make a formal declaration about Israel's sovereignty over Jerusalem. And nobody suggests that international custom infers acceptance of sovereignty from the birthplace designation on a passport or birth report, as it does from bilateral treaties or exchanges of ambassadors. Section 214(d) performs a more prosaic function than extending recognition. Just as foreign countries care about what our Government has to say about their borders, so too American citizens often care about what our Government has to say about their identities. The State Department does not grant or deny recognition in order to accommodate these individuals, but it does make exceptions to its rules about how it records birthplaces. Section 214(d) requires the State Department to make a further accommodation. Granting a request to specify "Israel" rather than "Jerusalem" does not recognize Israel's sovereignty over Jerusalem, just as granting a request to specify "Belfast" rather than "United Kingdom" does not derecognize the United Kingdom's sovereignty over Northern Ireland.

III

The Court complains that §214(d) requires the Secretary of State to issue official documents implying that Jerusalem is a part of Israel; that it appears in a section of the statute bearing the title "United States Policy with Respect to Jerusalem as the Capital of Israel"; and that foreign "observers interpreted [it] as altering United States policy regarding Jerusalem." But these features do not show that §214(d) recognizes Israel's sovereignty over Jerusalem. They show only that the law displays symbolic support for Israel's territorial claim. That symbolism may have tremendous significance as a matter of international diplomacy, but it makes no difference as a matter of constitutional law.

Even if the Constitution gives the President sole power to extend recognition, it does not give him sole power to make all decisions relating to foreign disputes over sovereignty. To the contrary, a fair reading of Article I allows Congress to decide for itself how its laws should handle these controversies. Read naturally, power to "regulate Commerce with foreign Nations," §8, cl. 3, includes power to regulate imports from Gibraltar as British goods or as Spanish goods. Read naturally, power to "regulate the Value . . . of foreign Coin," §8, cl. 5, includes power to honor (or not) currency issued by Taiwan. And so on for the other enumerated powers.

The Constitution likewise does not give the President exclusive power to determine which claims to statehood and territory "are legitimate in the eyes of the United States." Congress may express its own views about these matters by declaring war, restricting trade, denying foreign aid, and much else besides. To take just one example, in 1991, Congress responded to Iraq's invasion of Kuwait by enacting a resolution authorizing use of military force. No doubt the resolution reflected Congress's views about the legitimacy of Iraq's territorial claim.

* * *

International disputes about statehood and territory are neither rare nor obscure. A President empowered to decide all questions relating to these matters, immune from laws embodying congressional disagreement with his position, would have uncontrolled mastery of a vast share of the Nation's foreign affairs.

That is not the chief magistrate under which the American People agreed to live when they adopted the national charter. They believed that "the accumulation of all powers, legislative, executive, and judiciary, in the same hands may justly be pronounced the very definition of tyranny." *The Federalist*, No. 47. For this reason, they did not entrust either the President or Congress with sole power to adopt uncontradictable policies about *any* subject—foreign-sovereignty disputes included. They instead gave each political department its own powers, and with that the freedom to contradict the other's policies. Under the Constitution they approved, Congress may require Zivotofsky's passport and birth report to record his birthplace as Israel, even if that requirement clashes with the President's preference for neutrality about the status of Jerusalem.

Ex parte Milligan
71 U.S. (4 Wall.) 2 (1866)

In 1862, President Abraham Lincoln ordered that all persons "guilty of any disloyal practice affording aid and comfort to rebels" should be subject to trial and punishment by "courts-martial or military commissions." Two years later, a military commission acting under this authority tried and convicted Lambdin P. Milligan, a notorious Confederate sympathizer in Indiana, on charges of disloyalty. Because the civil courts were functioning and Indiana was not a battle zone, Milligan charged that the commission lacked jurisdiction over him and sought a writ of habeas corpus in circuit court. He also contended that trial before the military commission violated his constitutional right to trial by jury. After failing to reach agreement on the issues Milligan raised, the circuit court certified the questions to the Supreme Court. Opinion of the Court: <u>Davis</u>, Nelson, Grier, Clifford, Field. Concurring opinion: <u>Chase</u>, Wayne, Swayne, Miller.*

JUSTICE DAVIS delivered the opinion of the Court.

Milligan, not a resident of one of the rebellious states, or a prisoner of war, but a citizen of Indiana for twenty years past, and never in the military or naval service, is, while at his home, arrested by the military power of the United States, imprisoned and, on certain criminal charges preferred against him, tried, convicted, and sentenced to be hanged by a military commission, organized under the direction of the military commander of the military district of Indiana. Had this tribunal the legal power and authority to try and punish this man?

No graver question was ever considered by this court, nor one which more nearly concerns the rights of the whole people; for it is the birthright of every American citizen when charged with crime, to be tried and punished according to law. The provisions of that instrument on the administration of criminal justice are too plain and direct to leave room for misconstruction or doubt of their true meaning. Those applicable to this case are found in that clause of the original Constitution which says "that the trial of all crimes, except in case of impeachment, shall be by jury;" and in the fourth, fifth, and sixth articles of the amendments.

Even these provisions, expressed in such plain English words, that it would seem the ingenuity of man could not evade them, are now, after the lapse of more than seventy years, sought to be avoided. The Constitution of the United States is a law for rulers and people, equally in war and in peace, and covers with the shield of its protection all classes of men, at all times and under all circumstances. No doctrine, involving more pernicious consequences, was ever invented by the wit of man than that any of its provisions can be suspended during any of the great exigencies of government. Such a doctrine leads directly to anarchy or despotism, but the theory of necessity on which it is based is false; for the government, within the Constitution, has all the powers granted to it which are necessary to preserve its existence, as has been happily proved by the result of the great effort to throw off its just authority.

Have any of the rights guaranteed by the Constitution been violated in the case of Milligan? and if so, what are they?

Every trial involves the exercise of judicial power; and from what source did the Military Commission that tried him derive their authority? Certainly no part of the judicial power of the country was conferred on them: because the Constitution expressly vests it "in one Supreme Court and such inferior courts as the Congress may from time to time ordain and establish," and it is not pretended that the commission was a court ordained and established by Congress. They cannot justify on the mandate of the President: because he is controlled by law, and has his appropriate sphere of duty, which is to execute, not to make, the laws.

But it is said that the jurisdiction is complete under the "laws and usages of war." It can serve no useful purpose to inquire what those laws and usages are, whence they originated, where found, and on whom they operate; they can never be applied to citizens in states which have upheld the authority of the government, and where the courts are open and their process unobstructed. This court has judicial knowledge that in Indiana the Federal authority was always unopposed, and its courts always open to hear criminal accusations and redress grievances; and no usage of war could sanction a military trial there for any offense whatever of a citizen in civil life, in nowise connected with the military service. Congress could grant no such power; and to the honor of our national legislature be it said, it has never been provoked by the state of the country even to attempt its exercise. One of the plainest constitutional provisions was, therefore, infringed when Milligan was tried by a court not ordained and established by Congress, and not composed of judges appointed during good behavior.

Another guarantee of freedom was broken when Milligan was denied a trial by jury. This privilege is a vital principle, underlying the whole administration of criminal justice; it is not held by sufferance, and cannot be frittered away on any plea of state or political necessity. When peace prevails, and the authority of the government is undisputed, there is no difficulty in preserving the safeguards of liberty; for the ordinary modes of trial are never neglected, and no one wishes it otherwise; but if society is disturbed by civil commotion—if the passions of men are aroused and the restraints of law weakened, if not disregarded—these safeguards need, and should receive, the watchful care of those intrusted with the guardianship of the Constitution and laws.

It is claimed that martial law covers with its broad mantle the proceedings of this Military Commission. The proposition is this: That in a time of war the commander of an armed force (if in his opinion the exigencies of the country demand it, and of which he is to judge), has the power, within the lines of his military district, to suspend all civil rights and their remedies, and subject citizens as well as soldiers to the rule of his will; and in the exercise of his lawful authority cannot be restrained, except by his superior officer or the President of the United States.

This nation, as experience has proved, cannot always remain at peace, and has no right to expect that it will always have wise and humane rulers, sincerely attached to the principles of the Constitution. Wicked men, ambitious of power, with hatred of liberty and contempt of law, may fill the place once occupied by Washington and Lincoln; and if this right is conceded, and the calamities of war again befall us, the dangers to human liberty are frightful to contemplate.

It is insisted that the safety of the country in time of war demands that this broad claim for martial law shall be sustained. If this were true, it could be well said that a country, preserved at the sacrifice of all the cardinal principles of liberty, is not worth the cost of preservation. Happily, it is not so. Martial rule can never exist where the courts are open, and in the proper and unobstructed exercise of their jurisdiction. It is also confined to the locality of actual war. Because, during the late Rebellion it could have been enforced in Virginia, where the national authority was overturned and the courts driven out, it does not follow that it should obtain in Indiana, where that authority was never disputed, and justice was always administered.

THE CHIEF JUSTICE delivered the following opinion.

The opinion which has just been read asserts not only that the Military Commission held in Indiana was not authorized by Congress, but that it was not in the power of Congress to authorize it. We cannot agree to this. We think that Congress had power, though not exercised, to authorize the Military Commission which was held in Indiana.

Congress has power to raise and support armies; to provide and maintain a navy; to make rules for the government and regulation of the land and naval forces; and to provide for governing such part of the militia as may be in the service of the United States. It is not denied that the power to make rules for the government of the army and navy is a power to provide for trial and punishment by military courts without a jury. It has been so understood and exercised from the adoption of the Constitution to the present time.

Nor, in our judgment, does the fifth or any other amendment, abridge that power. It is not necessary to attempt any precise definition of the boundaries of this power. But may it not be said that government includes protection and defense as well as the regulation of internal administration? And is it impossible to imagine cases in which citizens conspiring or attempting the destruction of great injury of the national forces may be subjected by Congress to military trial and punishment in the just exercise of this undoubted constitutional power?

But we do not put our opinion, that Congress might authorize such a military commission as was held in Indiana, upon the power to provide for the government of the national forces. Congress has the power not only to raise and support and govern armies, but to declare war. It has, therefore, the power to provide by law for carrying on war. This power necessarily extends to all legislation essential to the prosecution of war with vigor and success, except such as interferes with the command of the force and conduct of campaigns. That power and duty belong to the President as Commander-in-Chief. Both these powers are derived from the Constitution, but neither is defined by that instrument. Their extent must be determined: by their nature, and by the principles of our institutions.

Where peace exists the laws of peace must prevail. What we do maintain is that when the nation is involved in war, and some portions of the country are invaded, and all are exposed to invasion, it is within the power of Congress to determine to what states or districts such great and imminent public danger exists as justifies the authorization of military tribunals for the trial of crimes and offenses against the discipline or security of the army or against the public safety.

In Indiana, for example, at the time of the arrest of Milligan and his co-conspirators, it is established by the papers in the record, that the state was a military district, was the theater of military operations, had been actually invaded, and was constantly threatened with invasion. It appears, also, that a powerful secret association, composed of citizens and others, existed within the state, under military organization, conspiring against the draft, and plotting insurrection, the liberation of the prisoners of war at various depots, the seizure of the state and national arsenals, armed co-operation with the enemy, and war against the national government.

We cannot doubt that, in such a time of public danger, Congress had power, under the Constitution, to provide for the organization of a military commission, and for trial by that commission of persons engaged in this conspiracy. The fact that the Federal courts were open was regarded by Congress as a sufficient reason for not exercising the power; but that fact could not deprive Congress of the right to exercise it. Those courts might be open and undisturbed in the execution of their functions, and yet wholly incompetent to avert threatened danger, or to punish, with adequate promptitude and certainty, the guilty conspirators.

In Indiana, the judges and officers of the courts were loyal to the government. But it might have been otherwise. In times of rebellion and civil war it may often happen, indeed, that judges and marshals will be in active sympathy with the rebels, and courts their most efficient allies. We think that the power of Congress, in such times and in such localities, to authorize trials for crimes against the security and safety of the national forces, may be derived from its constitutional authority to raise and support armies and to declare war, if not from its constitutional authority to provide for governing the national forces.

We have no apprehension that this power, under our American system of government, in which all official authority is derived from the people and exercised under direct responsibility to the people, is more likely to be abused than the power to regulate commerce or the power to borrow money. And we are unwilling to give our assent by silence to expressions of opinion which seem to us calculated, though not intended, to cripple the constitutional powers of the government, and to augment the public dangers in times of invasion and rebellion.

[*Although* Milligan *dealt with presidential actions, the opinion of the Court also stated that Congress could not have authorized the trial of civilians by military tribunals. After the Civil War, many members of Congress believed that the* Milligan *decision cast doubt on the constitutionality of the Reconstruction program in the Southern states. Its suspicions of the Court thus fueled, Congress responded in part by withdrawing the Court's jurisdiction to decide* ex parte McCardle *(see Chapter 3), which questioned the validity of the Reconstruction Acts.*]

Korematsu v. United States
323 U.S. 214 (1944)

In February 1942, President Franklin Roosevelt issued Executive Order 9066, which authorized the creation of military areas from which individuals might be excluded to prevent espionage or sabotage. The order also permitted military commanders to regulate who might enter or remain in such areas. A month later, Congress passed legislation establishing criminal penalties for violations of these regulations. Acting pursuant to the authority delegated to him under the executive order, the commander of the Western Defense Command initially imposed a curfew on residents of Japanese ancestry and ultimately ordered that they be evacuated to inland detention centers. In Hirabayashi v. United States *(1943), the Court upheld the curfew program in a narrow ruling that involved no consideration of the evacuation program. When Toyosaburo Korematsu, an*

American citizen of Japanese ancestry, refused to leave his home in California, he was convicted in federal district court of violating the exclusion order. After the conviction was upheld by the circuit court of appeals, the Supreme Court granted certiorari. Opinion of the Court: <u>Black</u>, Stone, Reed, Frankfurter, Douglas, Rutledge. Concurring opinion: <u>Frankfurter</u>. Dissenting opinions: <u>Roberts</u>; <u>Murphy</u>; <u>Jackson</u>.

JUSTICE BLACK delivered the opinion of the Court.

All legal restrictions which curtail the civil rights of a single racial group are immediately suspect. That is not to say that all such restrictions are unconstitutional. It is to say that courts must subject them to the most rigid scrutiny. Pressing public necessity may sometimes justify the existence of such restrictions; racial antagonism never can.

In the light of the principles we announced in the Hirabayashi case [*Hirabayashi v. United States* (1943)], we are unable to conclude that it was beyond the war power of Congress and the Executive to exclude those of Japanese ancestry from the West Coast war area at the time they did. Nothing short of apprehension by the proper military authorities of the gravest imminent danger to the public safety can constitutionally justify either. But exclusion from a threatened area has a definite and close relationship to the prevention of espionage and sabotage.

It was because we could not reject the finding of the military authorities that it was impossible to bring about an immediate segregation of the disloyal from the loyal that we sustained the validity of the curfew order as applying to the whole group. In the instant case, temporary exclusion of the entire group was rested by the military on the same ground. The judgment that exclusion of the whole group was for the same reason a military imperative answers the contention that the exclusion was in the nature of group punishment based on antagonism to those of Japanese origin.

We uphold the exclusion order as of the time it was made and when the petitioner violated it. In doing so, we are not unmindful of the hardships imposed by it upon a large group of American citizens. But hardships are part of war, and war is an aggregation of hardships. All citizens alike, both in and out of uniform, feel the impact of war in greater or lesser measure. Citizenship has its responsibilities as well as its privileges, and in time of war the burden is always heavier. Compulsory exclusion of large groups of citizens from their homes, except under circumstances of direst emergency and peril, is inconsistent with our basic governmental institutions. But when under conditions of modern warfare our shores are threatened by hostile forces, the power to protect must be commensurate with the threatened danger.

It is said that we are dealing here with the case of imprisonment of a citizen in a concentration camp solely because of his ancestry, without evidence or inquiry concerning his loyalty and good disposition towards the United States. To cast this case into outlines of racial prejudice, without reference to the real military dangers which were presented, merely confuses the issue. Korematsu was not excluded from the Military Area because of hostility to him or his race. He was excluded because we are at war with the Japanese Empire, because the properly constituted military authorities feared an invasion of our West Coast and felt constrained to take proper security measures, because they decided that the military urgency of the situation demanded that all citizens of Japanese ancestry be segregated from the West Coast temporarily, and finally, because Congress, reposing its confidence in this time of war in our military leaders—as inevitably it must—determined that they should have the power to do just this. There was evidence of disloyalty on the part of some, the military authorities considered that the need for action was great, and time was short. We cannot—by availing ourselves of the calm perspective of hindsight—now say that at that time these actions were unjustified.

Affirmed.

JUSTICE FRANKFURTER, concurring.

The provisions of the Constitution which confer on the Congress and the President powers to enable this country to wage war are as much part of the Constitution as provisions looking to a nation at peace. And we have had recent occasion to quote approvingly the statement of former Chief Justice Hughes that the war power of the Government is "the power to wage war successfully." Therefore, the validity of action under the war power must be judged wholly in the context of war. That action is not to be stigmatized as lawless because like action in times of peace would be lawless. To talk about a military order that expresses an allowable judgment of war needs by those entrusted with the duty of conducting war as "an unconstitutional order" is to suffuse a part of the Constitution with an atmosphere of unconstitutionality. To recognize that military orders are "reasonably expedient military precautions" in time of war and yet to deny them constitutional legitimacy makes of the Constitution an instrument for dialectic subtleties not reasonably to be attributed to the hard-headed Framers, of whom a majority had had actual participation in war. If a military order such as that under review does not transcend the means appropriate for conducting war, such action by the military is as constitutional as would be any authorized action by the Interstate Commerce Commission within the limits of the constitutional power to regulate commerce. To find that the Constitution does not forbid the military measures now complained of does not carry with it approval of that which Congress and the Executive did. That is their business, not ours.

JUSTICE MURPHY, dissenting.

This exclusion of "all persons of Japanese ancestry, both alien and non-alien," from the Pacific Coast area on a plea of military necessity in the absence of martial law ought not to be approved. Such exclusion goes over "the very brink of constitutional power" and falls into the ugly abyss of racism.

In dealing with matters relating to the prosecution and progress of a war, we must accord great respect and consideration to the judgments of the military authorities who are on the scene and who have full knowledge of the military facts. The scope of their direction must, as a matter of necessity and common sense, be wide. And their judgments ought not to be overruled lightly by those whose training and duties ill-equip them to deal intelligently with matters so vital to the physical security of the nation. At the same time, however, it is essential that there be definite limits to military discretion, especially where martial law has not been declared. Individuals must not be left impoverished of their constitutional rights on a plea of military necessity that has neither substance nor support. The judicial test of whether the Government, on a plea of military necessity, can validly deprive an individual of any of his constitutional rights is whether the deprivation is reasonably related to a public danger that is so "immediate, imminent, and impending" as not to admit of delay and not to permit the intervention of ordinary constitutional processes to alleviate the danger.

In adjudging the military action taken in light of the then apparent dangers, we must not erect too high or too meticulous standards; it is necessary only that the action have some reasonable relation to the removal of the dangers of invasion, sabotage and espionage. But the exclusion, either temporarily or permanently, of all persons with Japanese blood in their veins has no such reasonable relation. And that relation is lacking because the exclusion order necessarily must rely for its reasonableness upon the assumption that all persons of Japanese ancestry may have a dangerous tendency to commit sabotage and espionage and to aid our Japanese enemy in other ways. That this forced exclusion was the result in good measure of this erroneous assumption of racial guilt rather than bona fide military necessity is evidenced by the Commanding General's Final Report on the evacuation from the Pacific Coast area. In it he refers to all individuals of Japanese descent as "subversive," as belonging to "an enemy race" whose "racial strains are undiluted," and as constituting over 112,000 potential enemies at large today along the Pacific Coast.* In support

---

*Further evidence of the Commanding General's attitude toward individuals of Japanese ancestry is revealed in his voluntary testimony: "I don't want any of them [persons of Japanese ancestry] here. They are a dangerous element. There is no way to determine their loyalty. The west coast contains too many vital installations essential to the defense of the country to allow any Japanese on this coast. The danger of the Japanese was, and is now—if they are permitted to come back—espionage and sabotage. It makes no difference whether he is an American citizen, he is still a Japanese. American citizenship does not necessarily determine loyalty. But we must worry about the Japanese all the time until he is wiped off the map. Sabotage and espionage will make problems as long as he is allowed in this area."

of this blanket condemnation of all persons of Japanese descent, however, no reliable evidence is cited to show that such individuals were generally disloyal, or had generally so conducted themselves in this area as to constitute a special menace to defense installations or war industries, or had otherwise by their behavior furnished reasonable ground for their exclusion as a group.

Justification for the exclusion is sought, instead, mainly upon questionable racial and sociological grounds not ordinarily within the realm of expert military judgment, supplemented by certain semimilitary conclusions drawn from an unwarranted use of circumstantial evidence. No adequate reason is given for the failure to treat these Japanese Americans on an individual basis by holding investigations and hearings to separate the loyal from the disloyal, as was done in the case of persons of German and Italian ancestry. It is asserted merely that the loyalties of this group "were unknown and time was of the essence." Yet nearly four months elapsed after Pearl Harbor before the first exclusion order was issued; nearly eight months went by until the last order was issued; and the last of these "subversive" persons was not actually removed until almost eleven months had elapsed. Leisure and deliberation seem to have been more of the essence than speed. And the fact that conditions were not such as to warrant a declaration of martial law adds strength to the belief that the factors of time and military necessity were not as urgent as they have been represented to be.

I dissent, therefore, from this legalization of racism. All residents of this nation are kin in some way by blood or culture to a foreign land. Yet they are primarily and necessarily a part of the new and distinct civilization of the United States. They must accordingly be treated at all times as the heirs of the American experiment and as entitled to all the rights and freedoms guaranteed by the Constitution.

JUSTICE JACKSON, dissenting.

It is said that if the military commander had reasonable military grounds for promulgating the orders, they are constitutional and become law, and the Court is required to enforce them. There are several reasons why I cannot subscribe to this doctrine.

It would be impracticable and dangerous idealism to expect or insist that each specific military command in an area of probable operations will conform to conventional tests of constitutionality. When an area is so beset that it must be put under military control at all, the paramount consideration is that its measures be successful, rather than legal. The armed services must protect a society, not merely its Constitution. The very essence of the military job is to marshal physical force, to remove every obstacle to its effectiveness, to give it every strategic advantage. Defense measures will not, and often should not, be held within the limits that bind civil authority in peace. No court can require such a commander in such circumstances to act as a reasonable man; he may be unreasonably cautious and exacting. Perhaps he should be. But a commander in temporarily focusing the life of a community on defense is carrying out a military program; he is not making law in the sense the courts know the term. He issues orders, and they may have a certain authority as military commands, although they may be very bad as constitutional law.

But if we cannot confine military expedients by the Constitution, neither would I distort the Constitution to approve all that the military may deem expedient. That is what the Court appears to be doing, whether consciously or not. I cannot say, from any evidence before me, that the orders of General DeWitt were not reasonably expedient military precautions, nor could I say that they were. But even if they were permissible military procedures, I deny that it follows that they are constitutional. If, as the Court holds, it does follow, then we may as well say that any military order will be constitutional and have done with it.

In the very nature of things, military decisions are not susceptible of intelligent judicial appraisal. They do not pretend to rest on evidence, but are made on information that often would not be admissible and on assumptions that could not be proved. Information in support of an order could not be disclosed to courts without danger that it would reach the enemy. Neither can courts act on communications made in confidence. Hence courts can never have any real alternative to accepting the mere declaration of the authority that issued the order that it was reasonably necessary from a military viewpoint.

Much is said of the danger to liberty from the Army program for deporting and detaining these citizens of Japanese extraction. But a judicial construction of the due process clause that will sustain this order is a far more subtle blow to liberty than the promulgation of the order itself. A military order, however unconstitutional, is not apt to last longer than the military emergency. Even during that period a succeeding commander may revoke it all. But once a judicial opinion rationalizes such an order to show that it conforms to the Constitution, or rather rationalizes the Constitution to show that the Constitution sanctions such an order, the Court for all time has validated the principle of racial discrimination in criminal procedure and of transplanting American citizens. The principle then lies about like a loaded weapon ready for the hand of any authority that can bring forward a plausible claim of an urgent need. Every repetition imbeds that principle more deeply in our law and thinking and expands it to new purposes.

I should hold that a civil court cannot be made to enforce an order which violates constitutional limitations even if it is a reasonable exercise of military authority. The courts can exercise only the judicial power, can apply only law, and must abide by the Constitution, or they cease to be civil courts and become instruments of military policy.

Of course the existence of a military power resting on force, so vagrant, so centralized, so necessarily heedless of the individual, is an inherent threat to liberty. But I would not lead people to rely on this Court for a review that seems to me wholly delusive. The military reasonableness of these orders can only be determined by military superiors. If the people ever let command of the war power fall into irresponsible and unscrupulous hands, the courts wield no power equal to its restraint. The chief restraint upon those who command the physical forces of the country, in the future as in the past, must be their responsibility to the political judgments of their contemporaries and to the moral judgments of history.

My duties as a justice as I see them do not require me to make a military judgment as to whether General DeWitt's evacuation and detention program was a reasonable military necessity. I do not suggest that the courts should have attempted to interfere with the Army in carrying out its task. But I do not think they may be asked to execute a military expedient that has no place in law under the Constitution. I would reverse the judgment and discharge the prisoner.

[*In 1948, following condemnation by a presidential commission of the forced evacuation of Japanese Americans, Congress passed the Evacuation Claims Act, under which claimants received more than $37 million. In 1984, another governmental commission concluded that the internment resulted from "race prejudice, wartime hysteria, and a failure of political leadership" and recommended a national apology and further monetary compensation. That same year a federal district court vacated Korematsu's conviction based on newly discovered evidence that the government had deliberately withheld and falsified relevant evidence in the materials it presented in court. In 1988, Congress formally apologized for the internment and established a fund to pay reparations.*]

Ex parte Quirin
317 U.S. 1 (1942)

Quirin and the seven other petitioners in this case were born in Germany, lived in the United States, but returned to Germany between 1933 and 1941. All except petitioner Haupt were citizens of Germany, with which the United States was at war. Haupt claimed to be a US citizen, a claim disputed by the US government. After the declaration of war between the United States and Germany, the petitioners received training in sabotage in Germany. Four were transported by German submarine to Amagansett Beach on Long Island, New York, where they landed under cover of darkness on June 13, 1942, carrying with them a supply of explosives, fuses, and incendiary and timing devices. While landing, they wore German military uniforms or parts of uniforms, but immediately after landing they buried their uniforms and proceeded in civilian dress to New York City. The remaining four petitioners came by German submarine to Ponte Vedra Beach, Florida. On June 17, 1942, they came ashore during the hours of darkness wearing caps of the German Marine Infantry and carrying with them a supply of explosives, fuses, and incendiary and timing devices. They immediately buried their caps and proceeded in civilian dress to various points in the United States. All eight petitioners, who had received instructions in Germany from an officer of the German High Command to destroy war industries and war facilities in the United States, were arrested by agents of the Federal Bureau of Investigation.

On July 2, 1942, the president, as president and commander in chief of the army and navy, appointed a military commission and directed it to try petitioners for offenses against the law of war and the Articles of War, and prescribed regulations for the procedure in the trial and for review of the record of the trial and of any judgment or sentence of the commission. On the same day, by proclamation, the president declared that "all persons who are subjects, citizens or residents of any nation at war with the United States or who give obedience to or act under the direction of any such nation, and who during time of war enter or attempt to enter the United States through coastal or boundary defenses, and are charged with committing or attempting or preparing to commit sabotage, espionage, hostile or warlike acts, or violations of the law of war, shall be subject to the law of war and to the jurisdiction of military tribunals." The proclamation also stated that all such persons were denied access to the courts.

While the petitioners' trial for spying was proceeding before the military tribunal, they sought a writ of habeas corpus, claiming that the military tribunal was unconstitutional and that they should have been tried in civilian courts. The Supreme Court agreed to hear their case in expedited fashion and heard arguments on July 29, 1942. The Court announced its decision upholding the tribunals on July 31, and the German spies were convicted and sentenced. Six of the eight were executed on August 8, and two were imprisoned and ultimately deported after the conclusion of

World War II. Opinion of the Court: <u>Stone,</u> Roberts, Black, Reed, Frankfurter, Douglas, Byrnes, Jackson. Not participating: Murphy.

THE CHIEF JUSTICE delivered the opinion of the Court.

The question for decision is whether the detention of petitioners by respondent for trial by Military Commission, appointed by Order of the President of July 2, 1942, on charges preferred against them purporting to set out their violations of the law of war and of the Articles of War, is in conformity to the laws and Constitution of the United States.

Petitioners' main contention is that the President is without any statutory or constitutional authority to order the petitioners to be tried by military tribunal for offenses with which they are charged; that in consequence they are entitled to be tried in the civil courts with the safeguards, including trial by jury, which the Fifth and Sixth Amendments guarantee to all persons charged in such courts with criminal offenses. In any case it is urged that the President's Order, in prescribing the procedure of the Commission and the method for review of its findings and sentence, and the proceedings of the Commission under the Order, conflict with Articles of War adopted by Congress—particularly Articles 38, 43, 46, 50½ and 70—are illegal and void. The Government challenges each of these propositions.

We are not here concerned with any question of the guilt or innocence of petitioners. Constitutional safeguards for the protection of all who are charged with offenses are not to be disregarded in order to inflict merited punishment on some who are guilty. But the detention and trial of petitioners—ordered by the President in the declared exercise of his powers as Commander in Chief of the Army in time of war and of grave public danger—are not to be set aside by the courts without the clear conviction that they are in conflict with the Constitution or laws of Congress constitutionally enacted.

Congress and the President, like the courts, possess no power not derived from the Constitution. But one of the objects of the Constitution, as declared by its preamble, is to "provide for the common defence." As a means to that end the Constitution gives to Congress the power to 'provide for the common Defence'; 'To raise and support Armies', 'To provide and maintain a Navy'; and 'To make Rules for the Government and Regulation of the land and naval Forces'. Congress is given authority 'To declare War, grant Letters of Marque and Reprisal, and make Rules concerning Captures on Land and Water'; and 'To define and punish Piracies and Felonies committed on the high Seas, and Offenses against the Law of Nations'. And finally the Constitution authorizes Congress 'To make all Laws which shall be necessary and proper for carrying into Execution the foregoing Powers, and all other Powers vested by this Constitution in the Government of the United States, or in any Department or Officer thereof.' The Constitution confers on the President the 'executive Power', and imposes on him the duty to 'take Care that the Laws be faithfully executed'. It makes him the Commander in Chief of the Army and Navy, and empowers him to appoint and commission officers of the United States. The Constitution thus invests the President as Commander in Chief with the power to wage war which Congress has declared, and to carry into effect all laws passed by Congress for the conduct of war and for the government and regulation of the Armed Forces, and all laws defining and punishing offences against the law of nations, including those which pertain to the conduct of war.

By the Articles of War, Congress has provided rules for the government of the Army. It has provided for the trial and punishment, by courts martial, of violations of the Articles by members of the armed forces and by specified classes of persons associated or serving with the Army. But the Articles also recognize the "military commission" appointed by military command as an appropriate tribunal for the trial and punishment of offenses against the law of war not ordinarily tried by court martial. Articles 38 and 46 authorize the President, with certain limitations, to prescribe the procedure for military commissions. Articles 81 and 82 authorize trial, either by court martial or military commission, of those charged with relieving, harboring or corresponding with the enemy and those charged with spying. And

Article 15 declares that "the provisions of these articles conferring jurisdiction upon courts martial shall not be construed as depriving military commissions or other military tribunals of concurrent jurisdiction in respect of offenders or offenses that by statute or by the law of war may be triable by such military commissions or other military tribunals." Article 2 includes among those persons subject to military law the personnel of our own military establishment. But this, as Article 12 provides, does not exclude from that class "any other person who by the law of war is subject to trial by military tribunals" and who under Article 12 may be tried by court martial or under Article 15 by military commission. Similarly the Espionage Act of 1917, which authorizes trial in the district courts of certain offenses that tend to interfere with the prosecution of war, provides that nothing contained in the act "shall be deemed to limit the jurisdiction of the general courts-martial, military commissions, or naval courts-martial."

From the very beginning of its history this Court has recognized and applied the law of war as including that part of the law of nations which prescribes, for the conduct of war, the status, rights and duties of enemy nations as well as of enemy individuals. By the Articles of War, and especially Article 15, Congress has explicitly provided, so far as it may constitutionally do so, that military tribunals shall have jurisdiction to try offenders or offenses against the law of war in appropriate cases. Congress, in addition to making rules for the government of our Armed Forces, has thus exercised its authority to define and punish offenses against the law of nations by sanctioning, within constitutional limitations, the jurisdiction of military commissions to try persons for offenses which, according to the rules and precepts of the law of nations, and more particularly the law of war, are cognizable by such tribunals. And the President, as Commander in Chief, by his Proclamation in time of war has invoked that law. By his Order creating the present Commission he has undertaken to exercise the authority conferred upon him by Congress, and also such authority as the Constitution itself gives the Commander in Chief, to direct the performance of those functions which may constitutionally be performed by the military arm of the nation in time of war.

An important incident to the conduct of war is the adoption of measures by the military command not only to repel and defeat the enemy, but to seize and subject to disciplinary measures those enemies who in their attempt to thwart or impede our military effort have violated the law of war. It is unnecessary for present purposes to determine to what extent the President as Commander in Chief has constitutional power to create military commissions without the support of Congressional legislation. For here Congress has authorized trial of offenses against the law of war before such commissions. We are concerned only with the question whether it is within the constitutional power of the national government to place petitioners upon trial before a military commission for the offenses with which they are charged.

We must therefore first inquire whether any of the acts charged is an offense against the law of war cognizable before a military tribunal, and if so whether the Constitution prohibits the trial. We may assume that there are acts regarded in other countries, or by some writers on international law, as offenses against the law of war which would not be triable by military tribunal here, either because they are not recognized by our courts as violations of the law of war or because they are of that class of offenses constitutionally triable only by a jury. It was upon such grounds that the Court denied the right to proceed by military tribunal in *Ex parte Milligan*. But as we shall show, these petitioners were charged with an offense against the law of war which the Constitution does not require to be tried by jury.

By universal agreement and practice the law of war draws a distinction between the armed forces and the peaceful populations of belligerent nations and also between those who are lawful and unlawful combatants. Lawful combatants are subject to capture and detention as prisoners of war by opposing military forces. Unlawful combatants are likewise subject to capture and detention, but in addition they are subject to trial and punishment by military tribunals for acts which render their belligerency unlawful. The spy who secretly and without uniform passes the military lines of a belliger-

ent in time of war, seeking to gather military information and communicate it to the enemy, or an enemy combatant who without uniform comes secretly through the lines for the purpose of waging war by destruction of life or property, are familiar examples of belligerents who are generally deemed not to be entitled to the status of prisoners of war, but to be offenders against the law of war subject to trial and punishment by military tribunals.

Our Government, by thus defining lawful belligerents entitled to be treated as prisoners of war, has recognized that there is a class of unlawful belligerents not entitled to that privilege, including those who though combatants do not wear "fixed and distinctive emblems." And by Article 15 of the Articles of War Congress has made provision for their trial and punishment by military commission, according to "the law of war."

By a long course of practical administrative construction by its military authorities, our Government has likewise recognized that those who during time of war pass surreptitiously from enemy territory into our own, discarding their uniforms upon entry, for the commission of hostile acts involving destruction of life or property, have the status of unlawful combatants punishable as such by military commission. This precept of the law of war has been so recognized in practice both here and abroad, and has so generally been accepted as valid by authorities on international law that we think it must be regarded as a rule or principle of the law of war recognized by this Government by its enactment of the Fifteenth Article of War.

Citizenship in the United States of an enemy belligerent does not relieve him from the consequences of a belligerency which is unlawful because in violation of the law of war. Citizens who associate themselves with the military arm of the enemy government, and with its aid, guidance and direction enter this country bent on hostile acts are enemy belligerents within the meaning of the Hague Convention and the law of war. It is as an enemy belligerent that petitioner Haupt is charged with entering the United States, and unlawful belligerency is the gravamen of the offense of which he is accused.

Nor are petitioners any the less belligerents if, as they argue, they have not actually committed or attempted to commit any act of depredation or entered the theatre or zone of active military operations. The argument leaves out of account the nature of the offense which the Government charges and which the Act of Congress, by incorporating the law of war, punishes. It is that each petitioner, in circumstances which gave him the status of an enemy belligerent, passed our military and naval lines and defenses or went behind those lines, in civilian dress and with hostile purpose. The offense was complete when with that purpose they entered—or, having so entered, they remained upon—our territory in time of war without uniform or other appropriate means of identification.

Petitioners note the requirement of the Fifth Amendment that no person shall be held to answer for a capital or otherwise infamous crime unless on a presentment or indictment of a grand jury, and that such trials by Article III, 2, and the Sixth Amendment must be by jury in a civil court. Before the Amendments, 2 of Article III, the Judiciary Article, had provided: "The Trial of all Crimes, except in Cases of Impeachment, shall be by Jury," and had directed that "such Trial shall be held in the State where the said Crimes shall have been committed."

Presentment by a grand jury and trial by a jury of the vicinage where the crime was committed were at the time of the adoption of the Constitution familiar parts of the machinery for criminal trials in the civil courts. But they were procedures unknown to military tribunals, which are not courts in the sense of the Judiciary Article, and which in the natural course of events are usually called upon to function under conditions precluding resort to such procedures. As this Court has often recognized, it was not the purpose or effect of §2 of Article III, read in the light of the common law, to enlarge the then existing right to a jury trial. The object was to preserve unimpaired trial by jury in all those cases in which it had been recognized by the common law and in all cases of a like nature as they might arise in the future, but not to bring within the sweep of the guaranty those cases in which it was then well understood that a jury trial could not be demanded as of right.

In the light of this long-continued and consistent interpretation we must conclude that §2

of Article III and the Fifth and Sixth Amendments cannot be taken to have extended the right to demand a jury to trials by military commission, or to have required that offenses against the law of war not triable by jury at common law be tried only in the civil courts.

The fact that "cases arising in the land or naval forces" are excepted from the operation of the Amendments does not militate against this conclusion. Such cases are expressly excepted from the Fifth Amendment, and are deemed excepted by implication from the Sixth. It is argued that the exception, which excludes from the Amendment cases arising in the armed forces, has also by implication extended its guaranty to all other cases; that since petitioners, not being members of the Armed Forces of the United States, are not within the exception, the Amendment operates to give to them the right to a jury trial. But we think this argument misconceives both the scope of the Amendment and the purpose of the exception.

No exception is necessary to exclude from the operation of these provisions cases never deemed to be within their terms. An express exception from Article III, §2, and from the Fifth and Sixth Amendments, of trials of petty offenses and of criminal contempts has not been found necessary in order to preserve the traditional practice of trying those offenses without a jury. It is no more so in order to continue the practice of trying, before military tribunals without a jury, offenses committed by enemy belligerents against the law of war.

Section 2 of the Act of Congress of April 10, 1806, derived from the Resolution of the Continental Congress of August 21, 1776, imposed the death penalty on alien spies "according to the law and usage of nations, by sentence of a general court martial." This enactment must be regarded as a contemporary construction of both Article III, §2, and the Amendments as not foreclosing trial by military tribunals, without a jury, of offenses against the law of war committed by enemies not in or associated with our Armed Forces. It is a construction of the Constitution which has been followed since the founding of our government, and is now continued in the 82nd Article of War. Such a construction is entitled to the greatest respect.

We cannot say that Congress in preparing the Fifth and Sixth Amendments intended to extend trial by jury to the cases of alien or citizen offenders against the law of war otherwise triable by military commission, while withholding it from members of our own armed forces charged with infractions of the Articles of War punishable by death. It is equally inadmissible to construe the Amendments—whose primary purpose was to continue unimpaired presentment by grand jury and trial by petit jury in all those cases in which they had been customary—as either abolishing all trials by military tribunals, save those of the personnel of our own armed forces, or what in effect comes to the same thing, as imposing on all such tribunals the necessity of proceeding against unlawful enemy belligerents only on presentment and trial by jury. We conclude that the Fifth and Sixth Amendments did not restrict whatever authority was conferred by the Constitution to try offenses against the law of war by military commission, and that petitioners, charged with such an offense not required to be tried by jury at common law, were lawfully placed on trial by the Commission without a jury.

Petitioners, and especially petitioner Haupt, stress the pronouncement of this Court in the Milligan case, that the law of war "can never be applied to citizens in states which have upheld the authority of the government, and where the courts are open and their process unobstructed." Elsewhere in its opinion, the Court was at pains to point out that Milligan, a citizen twenty years resident in Indiana, who had never been a resident of any of the states in rebellion, was not an enemy belligerent either entitled to the status of a prisoner of war or subject to the penalties imposed upon unlawful belligerents. We construe the Court's statement as to the inapplicability of the law of war to Milligan's case as having particular reference to the facts before it. From them the Court concluded that Milligan, not being a part of or associated with the armed forces of the enemy, was a non-belligerent, not subject to the law of war save as—in circumstances found not there to be present and not involved here—martial law might be constitutionally established. The Court's opinion is inapplicable to the case presented by the present record.

Accordingly, we conclude that Charge I, on which petitioners were detained for trial by the Military Commission, alleged an offense which the President is authorized to order tried by military commission; that his Order convening the Commission was a lawful order and that the Commission was lawfully constituted; that the petitioners were held in lawful custody and did not show cause for their discharge.

Detention, Treatment, and Trial of Certain Non-Citizens in the War Against Terrorism (2001)

This executive order was issued by President George W. Bush on November 13, 2001, in the wake of the September 11 attacks on the United States.

By the authority vested in me as President and as Commander in Chief of the Armed Forces of the United States by the Constitution and the laws of the United States of America, including the Authorization for Use of Military Force Joint Resolution and sections 821 and 836 of title 10, United States Code, it is hereby ordered as follows:

SECTION 1. FINDINGS.

(a) International terrorists, including members of al Qaida, have carried out attacks on United States diplomatic and military personnel and facilities abroad and on citizens and property within the United States on a scale that has created a state of armed conflict that requires the use of the United States Armed Forces.

(b) In light of grave acts of terrorism and threats of terrorism, including the terrorist attacks on September 11, 2001, on the headquarters of the United States Department of Defense in the national capital region, on the World Trade Center in New York, and on civilian aircraft such as in Pennsylvania, I proclaimed a national emergency on September 14, 2001.

(c) Individuals acting alone and in concert involved in international terrorism possess both the capability and the intention to undertake further terrorist attacks against the United States that, if not detected and prevented, will cause mass deaths, mass injuries, and massive destruction of property, and may place at risk the continuity of the operations of the United States Government.

(d) The ability of the United States to protect the United States and its citizens, and to help its allies and other cooperating nations protect their nations and their citizens, from such further terrorist attacks depends in significant part upon using the United States Armed Forces to identify terrorists and those who support them, to disrupt their activities, and to eliminate their ability to conduct or support such attacks.

(e) To protect the United States and its citizens, and for the effective conduct of military operations and prevention of terrorist attacks, it is necessary for individuals subject to this order pursuant to section 2 hereof to be detained, and, when tried, to be tried for violations of the laws of war and other applicable laws by military tribunals.

(f) Given the danger to the safety of the United States and the nature of international terrorism, and to the extent provided by and under this order, I find consistent with section 836 of title 10, United States Code, that it is not practicable to apply in military commissions under this order the principles of law and the rules of evidence generally recognized in the trial of criminal cases in the United States district courts.

(g) Having fully considered the magnitude of the potential deaths, injuries, and property destruction that would result from potential acts of terrorism against the United States, and the probability that such acts will occur, I have determined that an extraordinary emergency exists for national defense purposes, that this emergency constitutes an urgent and compelling government interest, and that issuance of this order is necessary to meet the emergency.

SEC. 2. DEFINITION AND POLICY.

(a) The term "individual subject to this order" shall mean any individual who is not a United States citizen with respect to whom I determine from time to time in writing that:

(1) there is reason to believe that such individual, at the relevant times, (i) is or was a member of the organization known as al Qaida; (ii) has engaged in, aided or abetted, or conspired to commit, acts of international terrorism, or acts in preparation therefore, that have caused, threaten to cause, or have as their aim to cause injury to or adverse effects on the United States, its citizens, national security, foreign policy, or economy; or (iii) has knowingly harbored one or more individuals described in subparagraphs (i) or (ii) of subsection 2(a)(1) of this order; and

(2) it is in the interest of the United States that such individual be subject to this order.

(b) It is the policy of the United States that the Secretary of Defense shall take all necessary measures to ensure that any individual subject to this order is detained in accordance with section 3, and, if the individual is to be tried, that such individual is tried only in accordance with section 4.

SEC. 3. DETENTION AUTHORITY OF THE SECRETARY OF DEFENSE. ANY INDIVIDUAL SUBJECT TO THIS ORDER SHALL BE—

(a) detained at an appropriate location designated by the Secretary of Defense outside or within the United States;

(b) treated humanely, without any adverse distinction based on race, color, religion, gender, birth, wealth, or any similar criteria;

(c) afforded adequate food, drinking water, shelter, clothing, and medical treatment;

(d) allowed the free exercise of religion consistent with the requirements of such detention; and

(e) detained in accordance with such other conditions as the Secretary of Defense may prescribe.

SEC. 4. AUTHORITY OF THE SECRETARY OF DEFENSE REGARDING TRIALS OF INDIVIDUALS SUBJECT TO THIS ORDER.

(a) Any individual subject to this order shall, when tried, be tried by military commission for any and all offenses triable by military commission that such individual is alleged to have committed, and may be punished in accordance with the penalties provided under applicable law, including life imprisonment or death.

(b) As a military function and in light of the findings in section 1, including subsection (f) thereof, the Secretary of Defense shall issue such orders and regulations, including orders for the appointment of one or more military commissions, as may be necessary to carry out subsection (a) of this section.

(c) Orders and regulations issued under subsection (b) of this section shall include, but not be limited to, rules for the conduct of the proceedings of military commissions, including pretrial, trial, and post-trial procedures, modes of proof, issuance of process, and qualifications of attorneys, which shall at a minimum provide for—

(1) military commissions to sit at any time and any place, consistent with such guidance regarding time and place as the Secretary of Defense may provide;

(2) a full and fair trial, with the military commission sitting as the triers of both fact and law;

(3) admission of such evidence as would, in the opinion of the presiding officer of the military commission (or instead, if any other member of the commission so requests at the time the presiding officer renders that opinion, the opinion of the commission rendered at that time by a majority of the commission), have probative value to a reasonable person;

(4) in a manner consistent with the protection of information classified or classifiable under Executive Order 12958 of April 17, 1995, as amended, or any successor Executive Order, protected by statute or rule from unauthorized disclosure, or otherwise protected by law, (A) the handling of, admission into evidence of, and access to materials and information, and (B) the conduct, closure of, and access to proceedings;

(5) conduct of the prosecution by one or more attorneys designated by the Secretary of Defense and conduct of the defense by attorneys for the individual subject to this order;

(6) conviction only upon the concurrence of two-thirds of the members of the commission present at the time of the vote, a majority being present;

(7) sentencing only upon the concurrence of two-thirds of the members of the commission present at the time of the vote, a majority being present; and

(8) submission of the record of the trial, including any conviction or sentence, for review and final decision by me or by the Secretary of Defense if so designated by me for that purpose.

SEC. 7. RELATIONSHIP TO OTHER LAW AND FORUMS.

(b) With respect to any individual subject to this order—

(1) military tribunals shall have exclusive jurisdiction with respect to offenses by the individual; and

(2) the individual shall not be privileged to seek any remedy or maintain any proceeding, directly or indirectly, or to have any such remedy or proceeding sought on the individual's behalf, in (i) any court of the United States, or any State thereof, (ii) any court of any foreign nation, or (iii) any international tribunal.

Hamdi v. Rumsfeld
542 U.S. 507 (2004)

After the 2001 terrorist attacks by al-Qaeda, Congress authorized the president to "use all necessary and appropriate force against those nations, organizations, or persons he determines planned, authorized, committed, or aided the terrorist attacks" or "harbored such organizations or persons, in order to prevent any future acts of international terrorism against the United States by such nations, organizations or persons." Soon thereafter, the president ordered US armed forces to Afghanistan to subdue al-Qaeda and the Taliban regime that supported it. In the course of this conflict, Yaser Esam Hamdi was captured. Hamdi was imprisoned at the US Naval Base in Guantánamo Bay, Cuba, but upon learning that Hamdi was an American citizen, authorities transferred him to a naval brig in Norfolk, Virginia, and then to one in Charleston, South

Carolina. The government contended that Hamdi was an "enemy combatant" and that this status justified holding him in the United States indefinitely without formal charges or proceedings. Hamdi's father filed a petition for a writ of habeas corpus in the Eastern District of Virginia, alleging that his son's detention was not legally authorized and that detention of a US citizen without charges, access to an impartial tribunal, or assistance of counsel violated his constitutional rights.

The district court initially ordered that counsel be given access to Hamdi, but the United States Court of Appeals reversed. On remand, the government submitted a declaration from Michael Mobbs, a special adviser to the undersecretary of defense for policy, that asserted that Hamdi was a member of a Taliban military unit and had surrendered with his unit to the Northern Alliance. It claimed that because al-Qaeda and the Taliban "were and are hostile forces engaged in armed conflict with the armed forces of the United States," "individuals associated with" those groups "were and continue to be enemy combatants." Finally, it stated that Hamdi was labeled an enemy combatant "based upon his interviews and in light of his association with the Taliban."

The district court concluded that the Mobbs Declaration fell "far short" of supporting Hamdi's detention and ordered the government to turn over numerous materials for in camera review, including copies of all of Hamdi's statements and the notes taken from interviews with him that related to his reasons for going to Afghanistan and his activities therein, a list of all interrogators who had questioned Hamdi and their names and addresses, statements by members of the Northern Alliance regarding Hamdi's surrender and capture, a list of the dates and locations of his capture and subsequent detentions, and the names and titles of the US government officials who made the determinations that Hamdi was an enemy combatant and that he should be moved to a naval brig. The government appealed the production order, and the court of appeals reversed. Hamdi then appealed that ruling, and the Supreme Court granted certiorari. Judgment of the Court: O'Connor, Rehnquist, Kennedy, Breyer. Concurring in part and dissenting in part: Souter, Ginsburg. Dissenting opinions: Scalia, Stevens; Thomas.

JUSTICE O'CONNOR announced the judgment of the Court and delivered an opinion, in which THE CHIEF JUSTICE, JUSTICE KENNEDY, and JUSTICE BREYER join.

II

The threshold question before us is whether the Executive has the authority to detain citizens who qualify as "enemy combatants." The Government maintains that no explicit congressional authorization is required, because the Executive possesses plenary authority to detain pursuant to Article II of the Constitution. We do not reach the question whether Article II provides such authority, however, because we agree with the Government's alternative position, that Congress has in fact authorized Hamdi's detention, through the AUMF [Authorization for Use of Military Force].

The AUMF authorizes the President to use "all necessary and appropriate force" against "nations, organizations, or persons" associated with the September 11, 2001, terrorist attacks. We conclude that detention of individuals falling into the limited category we are considering, for the duration of the particular conflict in which they were captured, is so fundamental and accepted an incident to war as to be an exercise of the "necessary and appropriate force" Congress has authorized the President to use.

There is no bar to this Nation's holding one of its own citizens as an enemy combatant. In Quirin, one of the detainees, Haupt, alleged that he was a naturalized United States citizen. We held that "[c]itizens who associate themselves with the military arm of the enemy government, and with its aid, guidance and direction enter this country bent on hostile acts, are enemy belligerents within the meaning of the law of war." A citizen, no less than an alien, can be "part of or supporting forces hostile to the United States or coalition partners" and "engaged in an armed conflict against the United States." Such a citizen, if released, would pose the same threat of returning to the front during the ongoing conflict.

In light of these principles, it is of no moment that the AUMF does not use specific language of detention. Because detention to prevent a combatant's return to the battlefield is a fundamental incident of waging war, in permitting the use of "necessary and appropriate force," Congress has clearly and unmistakably authorized detention in the narrow circumstances considered here.

Hamdi objects, nevertheless, that Congress has not authorized the indefinite detention to which he is now subject. We understand Congress' grant of authority for the use of "necessary and appropriate force" to include the authority to detain for the duration of the relevant conflict, and our understanding is based on longstanding law-of-war principles. If the practical circumstances of a given conflict are entirely unlike those of the conflicts that informed the development of the law of war, that understanding may unravel. But that is not the situation we face as of this date. Active combat operations against Taliban fighters apparently are ongoing in Afghanistan. The United States may detain, for the duration of these hostilities, individuals legitimately determined to be Taliban combatants who "engaged in an armed conflict against the United States." If the record establishes that United States troops are still involved in active combat in Afghanistan, those detentions are part of the exercise of "necessary and appropriate force," and therefore are authorized by the AUMF.

Ex parte Milligan (1866) does not undermine our holding about the Government's authority to seize enemy combatants. In that case, the Court made repeated reference to the fact that its inquiry into whether the military tribunal had jurisdiction to try and punish Milligan turned in large part on the fact that Milligan was not a prisoner of war, but a resident of Indiana arrested while at home there. Had Milligan been captured while he was assisting Confederate soldiers by carrying a rifle against Union troops on a Confederate battlefield, the holding of the Court might well have been different. Moreover, as Justice Scalia acknowledges, the Court in *Ex parte Quirin* (1942) dismissed the language of *Milligan* that the petitioners had suggested prevented them from being subject to military process. Haupt was accused of being a spy. The Court in *Quirin* found him "subject to trial and punishment by [a] military tribunal" for those acts, and

held that his citizenship did not change this result.

III

Even in cases in which the detention of enemy combatants is legally authorized, there remains the question of what process is constitutionally due to a citizen who disputes his enemy-combatant status. Hamdi argues that he is owed a meaningful and timely hearing and that "extra-judicial detention [that] begins and ends with the submission of an affidavit based on third-hand hearsay" does not comport with the Fifth and Fourteenth Amendments. The Government counters that any more process than was provided below would be both unworkable and "constitutionally intolerable."

First, the Government urges the adoption of the Fourth Circuit's holding below—that because it is "undisputed" that Hamdi's seizure took place in a combat zone, the habeas determination can be made purely as a matter of law, with no further hearing or factfinding necessary. This argument is easily rejected. As the dissenters from the denial of rehearing en banc noted, the circumstances surrounding Hamdi's seizure cannot in any way be characterized as "undisputed," as "those circumstances are neither conceded in fact, nor susceptible to concession in law, because Hamdi has not been permitted to speak for himself or even through counsel as to those circumstances."

The Government's second argument is that further factual exploration is unwarranted and inappropriate in light of the extraordinary constitutional interests at stake. Under the Government's most extreme rendition of this argument, "respect for separation of powers and the limited institutional capabilities of courts in matters of military decision-making in connection with an ongoing conflict" ought to eliminate entirely any individual process, restricting the courts to investigating only whether legal authorization exists for the broader detention scheme. At most, the Government argues, courts should review its determination that a citizen is an enemy combatant under a very deferential "some evidence" standard. Under this review, a court would assume the accuracy of the Government's articulated basis for Hamdi's detention, as set forth in the

Mobbs Declaration, and assess only whether that articulated basis was a legitimate one. In response, Hamdi emphasizes that this Court consistently has recognized that an individual challenging his detention may not be held at the will of the Executive without recourse to some proceeding before a neutral tribunal to determine whether the Executive's asserted justifications for that detention have basis in fact and warrant in law.

Both of these positions highlight legitimate concerns. And both emphasize the tension that often exists between the autonomy that the Government asserts is necessary in order to pursue effectively a particular goal and the process that a citizen contends he is due before he is deprived of a constitutional right. The ordinary mechanism that we use for balancing such serious competing interests, and for determining the procedures that are necessary to ensure that a citizen is not "deprived of life, liberty, or property, without due process of law," is the test that we articulated in *Mathews v. Eldridge* (1976). *Mathews* dictates that the process due in any given instance is determined by weighing "the private interest that will be affected by the official action" against the Government's asserted interest, "including the function involved" and the burdens the Government would face in providing greater process. The *Mathews* calculus then contemplates a judicious balancing of these concerns, through an analysis of "the risk of an erroneous deprivation" of the private interest if the process were reduced and the "probable value, if any, of additional or substitute safeguards." We take each of these steps in turn.

It is beyond question that substantial interests lie on both sides of the scale in this case. Hamdi's "private interest affected by the official action," is the most elemental of liberty interests—the interest in being free from physical detention by one's own government. Nor is the weight on this side of the *Mathews* scale offset by the circumstances of war or the accusation of treasonous behavior. The risk of erroneous deprivation of a citizen's liberty in the absence of sufficient process here is very real. Moreover, as critical as the Government's interest may be in detaining those who actually pose an immediate threat to the national security of the United States during ongoing international conflict, history and common sense teach us that an unchecked system of detention carries the potential to become a means for oppression and abuse of others who do not present that sort of threat.

On the other side of the scale are the weighty and sensitive governmental interests in ensuring that those who have in fact fought with the enemy during a war do not return to battle against the United States. Without doubt, our Constitution recognizes that core strategic matters of warmaking belong in the hands of those who are best positioned and most politically accountable for making them.

The Government also argues at some length that its interests in reducing the process available to alleged enemy combatants are heightened by the practical difficulties that would accompany a system of trial-like process. In its view, military officers who are engaged in the serious work of waging battle would be unnecessarily and dangerously distracted by litigation half a world away, and discovery into military operations would both intrude on the sensitive secrets of national defense and result in a futile search for evidence buried under the rubble of war. To the extent that these burdens are triggered by heightened procedures, they are properly taken into account in our due process analysis.

Striking the proper constitutional balance here is of great importance to the Nation during this period of ongoing combat. But it is equally vital that our calculus not give short shrift to the values that this country holds dear or to the privilege that is American citizenship. It is during our most challenging and uncertain moments that our Nation's commitment to due process is most severely tested; and it is in those times that we must preserve our commitment at home to the principles for which we fight abroad.

With due recognition of these competing concerns, we believe that neither the process proposed by the Government nor the process apparently envisioned by the District Court below strikes the proper constitutional balance when a United States citizen is detained in the United States as an enemy combatant. We therefore hold that a citizen-detainee seeking to challenge his classification as an enemy combatant must receive notice of the factual basis for his classification, and a fair opportunity to rebut the Government's factual assertions before a neutral decisionmaker. At the same time, the exigencies of the circumstances may demand that, aside from these core elements, enemy combatant proceedings may be tailored to alleviate their uncommon potential to burden the Executive at a time of ongoing military conflict. Hearsay, for example, may need to be accepted as the most reliable available evidence from the Government in such a proceeding. Likewise, the Constitution would not be offended by a presumption in favor of the Government's evidence, so long as that presumption remained a rebuttable one and fair opportunity for rebuttal were provided. Thus, once the Government puts forth credible evidence that the habeas petitioner meets the enemy-combatant criteria, the onus could shift to the petitioner to rebut that evidence with more persuasive evidence that he falls outside the criteria.

We think it unlikely that this basic process will have the dire impact on the central functions of warmaking that the Government forecasts. The parties agree that initial captures on the battlefield need not receive the process we have discussed here; that process is due only when the determination is made to continue to hold those who have been seized. The Government has made clear in its briefing that documentation regarding battlefield detainees already is kept in the ordinary course of military affairs. Any factfinding imposition created by requiring a knowledgeable affiant to summarize these records to an independent tribunal is a minimal one. Likewise, arguments that military officers ought not have to wage war under the threat of litigation lose much of their steam when factual disputes at enemy-combatant hearings are limited to the alleged combatant's acts. This focus meddles little, if at all, in the strategy or conduct of war, inquiring only into the appropriateness of continuing to detain an individual claimed to have taken up arms against the United States.

There remains the possibility that the standards we have articulated could be met by an appropriately authorized and properly constituted military tribunal. Indeed, it is notable that military regulations already provide for such process in related instances, dictating that tribunals be made available to determine the status of enemy detainees who assert prisoner-of-war status under the Geneva Convention. In the absence of such process, however, a court that receives a petition for a writ of *habeas corpus* from an alleged enemy combatant must itself ensure that the minimum requirements of due process are achieved. Both courts below recognized as much, focusing their energies on the question of whether Hamdi was due an opportunity to rebut the Government's case against him. The Government, too, proceeded on this assumption, presenting its affidavit and then seeking that it be evaluated under a deferential standard of review based on burdens that it alleged would accompany any greater process. As we have discussed, a habeas court in a case such as this may accept affidavit evidence like that contained in the Mobbs Declaration, so long as it also permits the alleged combatant to present his own factual case to rebut the Government's return. We anticipate that a District Court would proceed with the caution that we have indicated is necessary in this setting, engaging in a factfinding process that is both prudent and incremental. We have no reason to doubt that courts faced with these sensitive matters will pay proper heed both to the matters of national security that might arise in an individual case and to the constitutional limitations safeguarding essential liberties that remain vibrant even in times of security concerns.

The judgment of the United States Court of Appeals for the Fourth Circuit is vacated, and the case is remanded for further proceedings.

JUSTICE SOUTER, with whom JUSTICE GINSBURG joins, concurring in part, dissenting in part, and concurring in the judgment.

Hamdi seeks to challenge the facts claimed by the Government as the basis for holding him as an enemy combatant. And in this Court he presses the distinct argument that the Government's claim, even if true, would not implicate any authority for holding him that would satisfy 18 U.S.C. §4001(a) (Non-Detention Act), which bars imprisonment or detention of a citizen "except pursuant to an Act of Congress." The plurality accepts the Government's position that if Hamdi's designation as an enemy combatant is correct, his detention (at least as to some period) is authorized by an Act of Congress as required by §4001(a), that is, by the Authorization for Use of Military Force (hereinafter Force Resolution). Here, I disagree and respectfully dissent.

Because I find Hamdi's detention forbidden by §4001(a) and unauthorized by the Force Resolution, I would not reach any questions of what process he may be due in litigating disputed issues in a proceeding under the habeas statute or prior to the habeas enquiry itself. For me, it suffices that the Government has failed to justify holding him in the absence of a further Act of Congress, criminal charges, a showing that the detention conforms to the laws of war, or a demonstration that §4001(a) is unconstitutional. I would therefore vacate the judgment of the Court of Appeals and remand for proceedings consistent with this view.

JUSTICE SCALIA, with whom JUSTICE STEVENS joins, dissenting.

Petitioner, a presumed American citizen, has been imprisoned without charge or hearing in the Norfolk and Charleston Naval Brigs for more than two years, on the allegation that he is an enemy combatant who bore arms against his country for the Taliban. His father claims to the contrary, that he is an inexperienced aid worker caught in the wrong place at the wrong time. This case brings into conflict the competing demands of national security and our citizens' constitutional right to personal liberty. Although I share the Court's evident unease as it seeks to reconcile the two, I do not agree with its resolution.

Where the Government accuses a citizen of waging war against it, our constitutional tradition has been to prosecute him in federal court for treason or some other crime. Where the exigencies of war prevent that, the Constitution's Suspension Clause, Art. I, §9, cl. 2, allows Congress to relax the usual protections temporarily. Absent suspension, however, the Executive's assertion of military exigency has not been thought sufficient to permit detention without charge. No one contends that the congressional Authorization for Use of Military Force, on which the Government relies to justify its actions here, is an implementation of the Suspension Clause. Accordingly, I would reverse the decision below.

I

The very core of liberty secured by our Anglo-Saxon system of separated powers has been freedom from indefinite imprisonment at the will of the Executive. The gist of the Due Process Clause, as understood at the founding and since, was to force the Government to follow those common-law procedures traditionally deemed necessary before depriving a person of life, liberty, or property. When a citizen was deprived of liberty because of alleged criminal conduct, those procedures typically required committal by a magistrate followed by indictment and trial.

These due process rights have historically been vindicated by the writ of *habeas corpus*. The writ of *habeas corpus* was preserved in the Constitution—the only common-law writ to be explicitly mentioned. Hamilton lauded "the establishment of the writ of *habeas corpus*" in his Federalist defense as a means to protect against "the practice of arbitrary imprisonments, [one of] the favourite and most formidable instruments of tyranny." *The Federalist* No. 84. Indeed, availability of the writ under the new Constitution (along with the requirement of trial by jury in criminal cases) was his basis for arguing that additional, explicit procedural protections were unnecessary. See *The Federalist* No. 83.

II

The allegations here, of course, are no ordinary accusations of criminal activity. Yaser Esam Hamdi has been imprisoned because the Government believes he participated in the waging of war against the United States. The relevant question, then, is whether there is a different, special procedure for imprisonment of a citizen accused of wrongdoing by aiding the enemy in wartime.

Justice O'Connor, writing for a plurality of this Court, asserts that captured enemy combatants (other than those suspected of war crimes) have traditionally been detained until the cessation of hostilities and then released.

That is probably an accurate description of wartime practice with respect to enemy aliens. The tradition with respect to American citizens, however, has been quite different. Citizens aiding the enemy have been treated as traitors subject to the criminal process.

There are times when military exigency renders resort to the traditional criminal process impracticable. English law accommodated such exigencies by allowing legislative suspension of the writ of *habeas corpus* for brief periods. Our Federal Constitution contains a provision explicitly permitting suspension, but limiting the situations in which it may be invoked: "The privilege of the Writ of *Habeas Corpus* shall not be suspended, unless when in Cases of Rebellion or Invasion the public Safety may require it." Although this provision does not state that suspension must be effected by, or authorized by, a legislative act, it has been so understood, consistent with English practice and the Clause's placement in Article I.

The Suspension Clause was by design a safety valve, the Constitution's only "express provision for exercise of extraordinary authority because of a crisis," *Youngstown Sheet & Tube Co. v. Sawyer* (1952) (Jackson, J., concurring). Very early in the Nation's history, President Jefferson unsuccessfully sought a suspension of *habeas corpus* to deal with Aaron Burr's conspiracy to overthrow the Government. During the Civil War, Congress passed its first Act authorizing Executive suspension of the writ of *habeas corpus*, to the relief of those many who thought President Lincoln's unauthorized proclamations of suspension unconstitutional. Later Presidential proclamations of suspension relied upon the congressional authorization, e.g., Proclamation No. 7 (1863). During Reconstruction, Congress passed the Ku Klux Klan Act, which included a provision authorizing suspension of the writ, invoked by President Grant in quelling a rebellion in nine South Carolina counties.

III

Of course the extensive historical evidence of criminal convictions and habeas suspensions does not necessarily refute the Government's position in this case. When the writ is suspended, the Government is entirely free from judicial oversight. It does not claim such total liberation here, but argues that it need only produce what it calls "some evidence" to satisfy a habeas court that a detained individual is an enemy combatant. Even if suspension of the writ on the one hand, and committal for criminal charges on the other hand, have been the only traditional means of dealing with citizens who levied war against their own country, it is theoretically possible that the Constitution does not require a choice between these alternatives.

I believe, however, that substantial evidence does refute that possibility. Writings from the founding generation suggest that, without exception, the only constitutional alternatives are to charge the crime or suspend the writ. Further evidence comes from this Court's decision in *Ex parte Milligan*. There, the Court issued the writ to an American citizen who had been tried by military commission for offenses that included conspiring to overthrow the Government, seize munitions, and liberate prisoners of war. The Court rejected in no uncertain terms the Government's assertion that military jurisdiction was proper "under the 'laws and usages of war'": "It can serve no useful purpose to inquire what those laws and usages are, whence they originated, where found, and on whom they operate; they can never be applied to citizens in states which have upheld the authority of the government, and where the courts are open and their process unobstructed."

Milligan is not exactly this case, of course, since the petitioner was threatened with death, not merely imprisonment. But the reasoning and conclusion of *Milligan* logically cover the present case. The Government justifies imprisonment of Hamdi on principles of the law of war and admits that, absent the war, it would have no such authority. But if the law of war cannot be applied to citizens where courts are open, then Hamdi's imprisonment without criminal trial is no less unlawful than Milligan's trial by military tribunal.

Milligan responded to the argument, repeated by the Government in this case, that it is dangerous to leave suspected traitors at large in time of war: "If it was dangerous, in the distracted condition of affairs, to leave Milligan unrestrained of his liberty, because he 'conspired against the government, afforded aid and comfort to rebels, and incited the people to insurrection,' the law said arrest him, confine him closely, render him powerless to do further mischief; and then present his case to the grand jury of the district, with proofs of his guilt, and, if indicted, try him according to the course of the common law. If this had been done, the Constitution would have been vindicated, the law of 1863 enforced, and the securities for personal liberty preserved and defended."

The proposition that the Executive lacks indefinite wartime detention authority over citizens is consistent with the Founders' general mistrust of military power permanently at the Executive's disposal. In the Founders' view, the "blessings of liberty" were threatened by "those military establishments which must gradually poison its very fountain." *The Federalist* No. 45. No fewer than 10 issues of the *Federalist* were devoted in whole or part to allaying fears of oppression from the proposed Constitution's authorization of standing armies in peacetime. Many safeguards in the Constitution reflect these concerns. Congress's authority "[t]o raise and support Armies" was hedged with the proviso that "no Appropriation of Money to that Use shall be for a longer Term than two Years." U.S. Const., Art. 1, §8, cl. 12. Except for the actual command of military forces, all authorization for their maintenance and all explicit authorization for their use is placed in the control of Congress under Article I, rather than the President under Article II. As Hamilton explained, the President's military authority would be "much inferior" to that of the British King: "It would amount to nothing more than the supreme command and direction of the military and naval forces, as first general and admiral of the confederacy: while that of the British king extends to the declaring of war, and to the raising and regulating of fleets and armies; all which, by the constitution under consideration, would appertain to the legislature." *The Federalist* No. 69. A view of the Constitution that gives the Executive authority to use military force rather than the force of law against citizens on American soil flies in the face of the mistrust that engendered these provisions.

IV

The Government argues that our more recent jurisprudence ratifies its indefinite imprisonment of a citizen within the territorial jurisdiction of federal courts. It places primary reliance upon *Ex parte Quirin* (1942), a World War II case upholding the trial by military commission of eight German saboteurs, one of whom, Hans Haupt, was a U.S. citizen. The case was not this Court's finest hour.

Quirin would still not justify denial of the writ here. In *Quirin* it was uncontested that the petitioners were members of enemy forces. They were "admitted enemy invaders," and it was "undisputed" that they had landed in the United States in service of German forces. The specific holding of the Court was only that, "upon the conceded facts," the petitioners were "plainly within [the] boundaries" of military jurisdiction. But where those jurisdictional facts are not conceded—where the petitioner insists that he is not a belligerent—*Quirin* left the pre-existing law in place: Absent suspension of the writ, a citizen held where the courts are open is entitled either to criminal trial or to a judicial decree requiring his release.

V

It follows from what I have said that Hamdi is entitled to a habeas decree requiring his release unless (1) criminal proceedings are promptly brought, or (2) Congress has suspended the writ of *habeas corpus*. A suspension of the writ could, of course, lay down conditions for continued detention, similar to those that today's opinion prescribes under the Due Process Clause. But there is a world of difference between the people's representatives' determining the need for that suspension (and prescribing the conditions for it), and this Court's doing so.

VI

Several limitations give my views in this matter a relatively narrow compass. They apply only to citizens, accused of being enemy combatants, who are detained within the territorial jurisdiction of a federal court. This is not likely to be a numerous group; currently we know of only two, Hamdi and Jose Padilla. Where the citizen is captured outside and held outside the United States, the constitutional requirements may be different. Moreover, even within the United States, the accused citizen-enemy combatant may lawfully be detained once prosecution is in progress or in contemplation. The Government has been notably successful in securing conviction, and hence long-term custody or execution, of those who have waged war against the state.

I frankly do not know whether these tools are sufficient to meet the Government's security needs, including the need to obtain intelligence through interrogation. It is far beyond my competence, or the Court's competence, to determine that. But it is not beyond Congress's. If the situation demands it, the Executive can ask Congress to authorize suspension of the writ—which can be made subject to whatever conditions Congress deems appropriate, including even the procedural novelties invented by the plurality today. To be sure, suspension is limited by the Constitution to cases of rebellion or invasion. But whether the attacks of September 11, 2001, constitute an "invasion," and whether those attacks still justify suspension several years later, are questions for Congress rather than this Court. If civil rights are to be curtailed during wartime, it must be done openly and democratically, as the Constitution requires, rather than by silent erosion through an opinion of this Court.

The Founders well understood the difficult tradeoff between safety and freedom. "Safety from external danger," Hamilton declared, "is the most powerful director of national conduct. Even the ardent love of liberty will, after a time, give way to its dictates. The violent destruction of life and property incident to war; the continual effort and alarm attendant on a state of continual danger, will compel nations the most attached to liberty, to resort for repose and security to institutions which have a tendency to destroy their civil and political rights. To be more safe, they, at length, become willing to run the risk of being less free." *The Federalist* No. 8. The Founders warned us about the risk, and equipped us with a Constitution designed to deal with it.

Many think it not only inevitable but entirely proper that liberty give way to security in times of national crisis—that, at the extremes of military exigency, *inter arma silent leges.* Whatever the general merits of the view that war silences law or modulates its voice, that view has no place in the interpretation and application of a Constitution designed precisely to confront war and, in a manner that accords with democratic principles, to accommodate it. Because the Court has proceeded to meet the current emergency in a manner the Constitution does not envision, I respectfully dissent.

JUSTICE THOMAS, dissenting.

The Executive Branch, acting pursuant to the powers vested in the President by the Constitution and with explicit congressional approval, has determined that Yaser Hamdi is an enemy combatant and should be detained. This detention falls squarely within the Federal Government's war powers, and we lack the expertise and capacity to second-guess that decision. As such, petitioner's habeas challenge should fail, and there is no reason to remand the case. The plurality reaches a contrary conclusion by failing adequately to consider basic principles of the constitutional structure as it relates to national security and foreign affairs and by using the balancing scheme of *Mathews v. Eldridge* (1976). I do not think that the Federal Government's war powers can be balanced away by this Court. Arguably, Congress could provide for additional procedural protections, but until it does, we have no right to insist upon them.

But even if I were to agree with the general approach the plurality takes, I could not accept the particulars. The plurality utterly fails to account for the Government's compelling interests and for our own institutional inability to weigh competing concerns correctly. I respectfully dissent.

I

"It is obvious and unarguable that no governmental interest is more compelling than the security of the Nation." *Haig v. Agee* (1981). The national security, after all, is the primary responsibility and purpose of the Federal Government. The Founders intended that the President have primary responsibility—along with the necessary power—to protect the national security and to conduct the Nation's foreign relations. They did so principally because the structural advantages of a unitary Executive are essential in these domains. "Energy in the executive is a leading character in the definition of good government. It is essential to the protection of the community against foreign attacks." *The Federalist* No. 70. The principle "ingredient" for "energy in the executive" is "unity." This is because "decision, activity, secrecy, and dispatch will generally characterise the proceedings of one man, in a much more eminent degree, than the proceedings of any greater number."

Judicial interference in these domains destroys the purpose of vesting primary responsibility in a unitary Executive. I cannot improve on Justice Jackson's words, speaking for the Court: "The President, both as Commander-in-Chief and as the Nation's organ for foreign affairs, has available intelligence services whose reports are not and ought not to be published to the world. It would be intolerable that courts, without the relevant information, should review and perhaps nullify actions of the Executive taken on information properly held secret. Nor can courts sit *in camera* in order to be taken into executive confidences. But even if courts could require full disclosure, the very nature of executive decisions as to foreign policy is political, not judicial. Such decisions are wholly confided by our Constitution to the political departments of the government, Executive and Legislative. They are delicate, complex, and involve large elements of prophecy. They are and should be undertaken only by those directly responsible to the people whose welfare they advance or imperil. They are decisions of a kind for which the Judiciary has neither aptitude, facilities nor responsibility and which has long been held to belong in the domain of political power not subject to judicial intrusion or inquiry."

Several points, made forcefully by Justice Jackson, are worth emphasizing. First, with respect to certain decisions relating to national security and foreign affairs, the courts simply lack the relevant information and expertise to second-guess determinations made by the President based on information properly withheld. Second, even if the courts could compel the Executive to produce the necessary information, such decisions are simply not amenable to judicial determination because "they are delicate, complex, and involve large elements of prophecy." Third, the Court in *Chicago & Southern Air Lines* and elsewhere has correctly recognized the primacy of the political branches in the foreign-affairs and national-security contexts.

Finally, and again for the same reasons, where "the President acts pursuant to an express or implied authorization from Congress, he exercises not only his powers but also those delegated by Congress [, and i]n such a case the executive action 'would be supported by the strongest of presumptions and the widest latitude of judicial interpretation, and the burden of persuasion would rest heavily upon any who might attack it.'" *Dames & Moore.* That is why the Court has explained, in a case analogous to this one, that "the detention ordered by the President in the declared exercise of his powers as Commander in Chief of the Army in time of war and of grave public danger [is] not to be set aside by the courts without the clear conviction that [it is] in conflict with the Constitution or laws of Congress constitutionally enacted." *Ex parte Quirin,* (1942).

I acknowledge that the question whether Hamdi's executive detention is lawful is a question properly resolved by the Judicial Branch, though the question comes to the Court with the strongest presumptions in favor of the Government. The plurality agrees that Hamdi's detention is lawful if he is an enemy combatant. But the question whether Hamdi is actually an enemy combatant is "of a kind for which the Judiciary has neither aptitude, facilities nor responsibility and which has long been held to belong in the domain of political power not subject to judicial intrusion or inquiry." *Chicago & Southern Air Lines.* That is, although it is appropriate for the Court to determine the judicial question whether the President has the asserted authority, we lack the information and expertise to question whether Hamdi is actually an enemy combatant, a question the resolution of which is committed to other branches.

IV

Although I do not agree with the plurality that the balancing approach of *Mathews v. Eldridge* (1976) is the appropriate analytical tool with which to analyze this case, I cannot help but explain that the plurality misapplies its chosen framework, one that if applied correctly would probably lead to the result I have reached. The plurality devotes two paragraphs to its discussion of the Government's interest, though much of those two paragraphs explain why the Government's concerns are misplaced. But: "It is 'obvious and unarguable' that no governmental interest is more compelling than the security of the Nation." The Government seeks to further that interest by detaining an enemy soldier not only to prevent him from rejoining the ongoing fight. Rather, as the Government explains, detention can serve to gather critical intelligence regarding the intentions and capabilities of our adversaries, a function that the Government avers has become all the more important in the war on terrorism.

Additional process, the Government explains, will destroy the intelligence gathering function. It also does seem quite likely that, under the process envisioned by the plurality, various military officials will have to take time to litigate this matter. And though the plurality does not say so, a meaningful ability to challenge the Government's factual allegations will probably require the Government to divulge highly classified information to the purported enemy combatant, who might then upon release return to the fight armed with our most closely held secrets.

The plurality manages to avoid these problems by discounting or entirely ignoring them. Ultimately, the plurality's dismissive treatment of the Government's asserted interests arises from its apparent belief that enemy-combatant determinations are not part of "the actual prosecution of a war," or one of the "central functions of warmaking." This seems wrong: Taking and holding enemy combatants is a quintessential aspect of the prosecution of war.

Undeniably, Hamdi has been deprived of a serious interest, one actually protected by the Due Process Clause. Against this, however, is the Government's overriding interest in protecting the Nation. I acknowledge that under the plurality's approach, it might, at times, be appropriate to give detainees access to counsel and notice of the factual basis for the Government's determination. But properly accounting for the Government's interests also requires concluding that access to counsel and to the factual basis would not always be warranted. Though common sense suffices, the Government thoroughly explains that counsel would often destroy the intelligence gathering function. Equally obvious is the Government's interest in not fighting the war in its own courts and protecting classified information.

For these reasons, I would affirm the judgment of the Court of Appeals.

Boumediene v. Bush
553 U.S. 723 (2008)

After the terrorist attacks on 9/11 and the commencement of hostilities with Afghanistan, the United States began incarcerating aliens whom it designated as "enemy combatants" at the naval base at Guantánamo Bay, Cuba. These detainees included persons captured on the battlefield in Afghanistan and others apprehended in places far removed from the battlefield, such as Bosnia and Gambia. In Hamdi v. Rumsfeld (2004), the Supreme Court held that the detainees were entitled to procedures that allowed them to contest their designation as enemy combatants. In response, the deputy secretary of defense established military commissions, known as Combatant Status Review Tribunals (CSRTs), to review the status of detainees. The petitioners in this case all denied that they

were members of the al-Qaeda terrorist network that carried out the 9/11 attacks or of the Taliban regime that provided sanctuary for al-Qaeda. Each appeared before a separate CSRT, was determined to be an enemy combatant, and sought a writ of habeas corpus in the United States District Court for the District of Columbia. These petitions were consolidated in two separate cases before the district court. In one a judge ruled for the government, and in the other a judge ruled for the petitioners. While these cases were on appeal, Congress passed the Detainee Treatment Act (DTA), stripping federal district courts of jurisdiction over writs of habeas corpus filed by Guantánamo detainees and giving the D.C. Court of Appeals exclusive authority to conduct a limited review of the determinations of the CSRTs. After the Supreme Court in Hamdan v. Rumsfeld *(2006) ruled that these provisions did not apply to cases filed before the DTA was enacted, Congress passed the Military Commissions Act (MCA), which confirmed that the habeas-stripping provision of the DTA applied to pending petitions as well. The court of appeals concluded that this law removed its jurisdiction to consider petitioners' habeas corpus applications, the petitioners appealed that ruling, and the Supreme Court granted certiorari.* Opinion of the Court: <u>Kennedy</u>, Stevens, Souter, Ginsburg, Breyer. Concurring opinion: <u>Souter</u>, Ginsburg, Breyer. Dissenting opinions: <u>Roberts</u>, Scalia, Thomas, Alito; <u>Scalia</u>, Roberts, Thomas, Alito.

JUSTICE KENNEDY delivered the opinion of the Court.

Petitioners present a question not resolved by our earlier cases relating to the detention of aliens at Guantanamo: whether they have the constitutional privilege of *habeas corpus*, a privilege not to be withdrawn except in conformance with the Suspension Clause, Art. I, §9, cl. 2. We hold these petitioners do have the *habeas corpus* privilege. Congress has enacted a statute, the Detainee Treatment Act of 2005 (DTA), that provides certain procedures for review of the detainees' status. We hold that those procedures are not an adequate and effective substitute for *habeas corpus*. Therefore §7 of the Military Commissions Act of 2006 (MCA) operates as an unconstitutional suspension of the writ.

II

As a threshold matter, we must decide whether MCA §7 denies the federal courts jurisdiction to hear *habeas corpus* actions pending at the time of its enactment. We hold the statute does deny that jurisdiction, so that, if the statute is valid, petitioners' cases must be dismissed. The MCA was a direct response to *Hamdan*'s holding that the DTA's jurisdiction-stripping provision had no application to pending cases.

III

In deciding the constitutional questions now presented we must determine whether petitioners are barred from seeking the writ or invoking the protections of the Suspension Clause either because of their status, *i.e.,* petitioners' designation by the Executive Branch as enemy combatants, or their physical location, *i.e.,* their presence at Guantanamo Bay. The Government contends that noncitizens designated as enemy combatants and detained in territory located outside our Nation's borders have no constitutional rights and no privilege of *habeas corpus*. Petitioners contend they do have cognizable constitutional rights and that Congress, in seeking to eliminate recourse to *habeas corpus* as a means to assert those rights, acted in violation of the Suspension Clause.

[*Justice Kennedy then surveyed the history of* habeas corpus, *focusing particularly on whether it operated in territory over which the British government lacked sovereignty. He concluded:*] Recent scholarship points to the inherent shortcomings in the historical record. And given the unique status of Guantanamo Bay and the particular dangers of terrorism in the modern age, the common-law courts simply may not have confronted cases with close parallels to this one. We decline, therefore, to infer too much, one way or the other, from the lack of historical evidence on point.

IV

Drawing from its position that at common law the writ ran only to territories over which the Crown was sovereign, the Government says the Suspension Clause affords petitioners no rights because the United States does not claim sovereignty over the place of detention. We do not question the Government's position that Cuba, not the United States, maintains sovereignty, in the legal and technical sense of the term, over Guantanamo Bay. But we take notice of the obvious and uncontested fact that the United States, by virtue of its complete jurisdiction and control over the base, maintains *de facto* sovereignty over this territory.

A

The Court has discussed the issue of the Constitution's extraterritorial application on many occasions. These decisions undermine the Government's argument that, at least as applied to noncitizens, the Constitution necessarily stops where *de jure* sovereignty ends.

[After reviewing the Court's rulings in *The Insular Cases, Reid v. Covert* (1956), and *Johnson v. Eisentrager* (1950), Justice Kennedy concluded that there was] a common thread uniting the *Insular Cases, Eisentrager,* and *Reid*: the idea that questions of extraterritoriality turn on objective factors and practical concerns, not formalism.

B

The Government's formal sovereignty-based test raises troubling separation-of-powers concerns as well. The political history of Guantanamo illustrates the deficiencies of this approach. The United States has maintained complete and uninterrupted control of the bay for over 100 years. Yet the Government's view is that the Constitution had no effect there, at least as to noncitizens, because the United States disclaimed sovereignty in the formal sense of the term. The necessary implication of the argument is that by surrendering formal sovereignty over any unincorporated territory to a third party, while at the same time entering into a lease that grants total control over the territory back to the United States, it would be possible for the political branches to govern without legal constraint.

Our basic charter cannot be contracted away like this. The Constitution grants Congress and the President the power to acquire, dispose of, and govern territory, not the power to decide when and where its terms apply. Abstaining from questions involving formal sovereignty and territorial governance is one thing. To hold the political branches have the power to switch the Constitution on or off at will is quite another. The former position reflects this Court's recognition that certain matters requiring political judgments are best left to the political branches. The latter would permit a striking anomaly in our tripartite system of government, leading to a regime in which Congress and the President, not this Court, say "what the law is."

These concerns have particular bearing upon the Suspension Clause question in the cases now before us, for the writ of *habeas corpus* is itself an indispensable mechanism for monitoring the separation of powers. The test for determining the scope of this provision must not be subject to manipulation by those whose power it is designed to restrain.

C

As we recognized in *Rasul,* the outlines of a framework for determining the reach of the Suspension Clause are suggested by the factors the Court relied upon in *Eisentrager.* In addition to the practical concerns discussed above, the *Eisentrager* Court found relevant that each petitioner: "(a) is an enemy alien; (b) has never been or resided in the United States; (c) was captured outside of our territory and there held in military custody as a prisoner of war; (d) was tried and convicted by a Military Commission sitting outside the United States; (e) for offenses against laws of war committed outside the United States; (f) and is at all times imprisoned outside the United States." Based on this language from *Eisentrager,* and the reasoning in our other extraterritoriality opinions, we conclude that at least three factors are relevant in determining the reach of the Suspension Clause: (1) the citizenship and status of the detainee and the adequacy of the process through which that status determination was made; (2) the nature of the sites where apprehension and then detention took place; and (3) the practical obstacles inherent in resolving the prisoner's entitlement to the writ.

Applying this framework, we note at the onset that the status of these detainees is a matter of dispute. The petitioners, like those in *Eisentrager,* are not American citizens. But the petitioners in *Eisentrager* did not contest, it seems, the Court's assertion that they were "enemy aliens." In the instant cases, by contrast, the detainees deny they are enemy combatants. They have been afforded some process in CSRT proceedings to determine their status; but, unlike in *Eisentrager,* there has been no trial by military commission for violations of the laws of war. The difference is not trivial. The records from the *Eisentrager* trials suggest that, well before the petitioners brought their case to this Court, there had been a rigorous adversarial process to test the legality of their detention. The *Eisentrager* petitioners were charged by a bill of particulars that made detailed factual allegations against them. To rebut the accusations, they were entitled to representation by counsel, allowed to introduce evidence on their own behalf, and permitted to cross-examine the prosecution's witnesses. In comparison the procedural protections afforded to the detainees in the CSRT hearings are far more limited, and, we conclude, fall well short of the procedures and adversarial mechanisms that would eliminate the need for *habeas corpus* review. Although the detainee is assigned a "Personal Representative" to assist him during CSRT proceedings, the Secretary of the Navy's memorandum makes clear that person is not the detainee's lawyer or even his "advocate." The Government's evidence is accorded a presumption of validity. The detainee is allowed to present "reasonably available" evidence, but his ability to rebut the Government's evidence against him is limited by the circumstances of his confinement and his lack of counsel at this stage. And although the detainee can seek review of his status determination in the Court of Appeals, that review process cannot cure all defects in the earlier proceedings.

As to the second factor relevant to this analysis, the detainees here are similarly situated to the *Eisentrager* petitioners in that the sites of their apprehension and detention are technically outside the sovereign territory of the United States. But there are critical differences between Landsberg Prison, circa 1950, and the United States Naval Station at Guantanamo Bay in 2008. Unlike its present control over the naval station, the United States' control over the prison in Germany was neither absolute nor indefinite. Guantanamo Bay, on the other hand, is no transient possession. In every practical sense Guantanamo is not abroad; it is within the constant jurisdiction of the United States.

As to the third factor, we recognize, as the Court did in *Eisentrager,* that there are costs to holding the Suspension Clause applicable in a case of military detention abroad. *Habeas corpus* proceedings may require expenditure of funds by the Government and may divert the attention of military personnel from other pressing tasks. While we are sensitive to these concerns, we do not find them dispositive. Compliance with any judicial process requires some incremental expenditure of resources. Yet

civilian courts and the Armed Forces have functioned along side each other at various points in our history. The Government presents no credible arguments that the military mission at Guantanamo would be compromised if *habeas corpus* courts had jurisdiction to hear the detainees' claims.

It is true that before today the Court has never held that noncitizens detained by our Government in territory over which another country maintains *de jure* sovereignty have any rights under our Constitution. But the cases before us lack any precise historical parallel. We hold that Art. I, §9, cl. 2, of the Constitution has full effect at Guantanamo Bay. If the privilege of *habeas corpus* is to be denied to the detainees now before us, Congress must act in accordance with the requirements of the Suspension Clause. The MCA does not purport to be a formal suspension of the writ; and the Government, in its submissions to us, has not argued that it is. Petitioners, therefore, are entitled to the privilege of *habeas corpus* to challenge the legality of their detention.

V

In light of this holding the question becomes whether the statute stripping jurisdiction to issue the writ avoids the Suspension Clause mandate because Congress has provided adequate substitute procedures for *habeas corpus*. The Government submits there has been compliance with the Suspension Clause because the DTA review process in the Court of Appeals provides an adequate substitute.

A

The DTA's jurisdictional grant is quite limited. The Court of Appeals has jurisdiction not to inquire into the legality of the detention generally but only to assess whether the CSRT complied with the "standards and procedures specified by the Secretary of Defense" and whether those standards and procedures are lawful. The differences between the DTA and the habeas statute that would govern in MCA §7's absence, are likewise telling. In §2241 Congress confirmed the authority of "any justice" or "circuit judge" to issue the writ. That statute accommodates the necessity for fact-finding that will arise in some cases by allowing the appellate judge or Justice to transfer the case to a district court of competent jurisdiction, whose institutional capacity for factfinding is superior to his or her own. By granting the Court of Appeals "exclusive" jurisdiction over petitioners' cases, Congress has foreclosed that option. This choice indicates Congress intended the Court of Appeals to have a more limited role in enemy combatant status determinations than a district court has in *habeas corpus* proceedings. In passing the DTA Congress did not intend to create a process that differs from traditional *habeas corpus* process in name only. It intended to create a more limited procedure. It is against this background that we must interpret the DTA and assess its adequacy as a substitute for *habeas corpus*.

B

We do not endeavor to offer a comprehensive summary of the requisites for an adequate substitute for *habeas corpus*. We do consider it uncontroversial, however, that the privilege of *habeas corpus* entitles the prisoner to a meaningful opportunity to demonstrate that he is being held pursuant to "the erroneous application or interpretation" of relevant law. And the habeas court must have the power to order the conditional release of an individual unlawfully detained—though release need not be the exclusive remedy and is not the appropriate one in every case in which the writ is granted. These are the easily identified attributes of any constitutionally adequate *habeas corpus* proceeding. But, depending on the circumstances, more may be required. *Habeas corpus* proceedings need not resemble a criminal trial, even when the detention is by executive order. But the writ must be effective. The habeas court must have sufficient authority to conduct a meaningful review of both the cause for detention and the Executive's power to detain.

Petitioners identify what they see as myriad deficiencies in the CSRTs. The most relevant for our purposes are the constraints upon the detainee's ability to rebut the factual basis for the Government's assertion that he is an enemy combatant. As already noted, at the CSRT stage the detainee has limited means to find or present evidence to challenge the Government's case against him. He does not have the

assistance of counsel and may not be aware of the most critical allegations that the Government relied upon to order his detention. The detainee can confront witnesses that testify during the CSRT proceedings. But given that there are in effect no limits on the admission of hearsay evidence—the only requirement is that the tribunal deem the evidence "relevant and helpful"—the detainee's opportunity to question witnesses is likely to be more theoretical than real.

The Government defends the CSRT process, arguing that it was designed to conform to the procedures suggested by the plurality in *Hamdi*. Setting aside the fact that the relevant language in *Hamdi* did not garner a majority of the Court, it does not control the matter at hand. For the writ of *habeas corpus*, or its substitute, to function as an effective and proper remedy in this context, the court that conducts the habeas proceeding must have the means to correct errors that occurred during the CSRT proceedings. This includes some authority to assess the sufficiency of the Government's evidence against the detainee. It also must have the authority to admit and consider relevant exculpatory evidence that was not introduced during the earlier proceeding.

C

We now consider whether the DTA allows the Court of Appeals to conduct a proceeding meeting these standards. The DTA does not explicitly empower the Court of Appeals to order the applicant in a DTA review proceeding released should the court find that the standards and procedures used at his CSRT hearing were insufficient to justify detention. This is troubling. Yet, for present purposes, we can assume congressional silence permits a constitutionally required remedy. The more difficult question is whether the DTA permits the Court of Appeals to make requisite findings of fact. The DTA enables petitioners to request "review" of their CSRT determination in the Court of Appeals; but the "Scope of Review" provision confines the Court of Appeals' role to reviewing whether the CSRT followed the "standards and procedures" issued by the Department of Defense and assessing whether those "standards and procedures" are lawful.

Among these standards is "the requirement that the conclusion of the Tribunal be supported by a preponderance of the evidence allowing a rebuttable presumption in favor of the Government's evidence." Assuming the DTA can be construed to allow the Court of Appeals to review or correct the CSRT's factual determinations, as opposed to merely certifying that the tribunal applied the correct standard of proof, we see no way to construe the statute to allow what is also constitutionally required in this context: an opportunity for the detainee to present relevant exculpatory evidence that was not made part of the record in the earlier proceedings.

VI

B

Although we hold that the DTA is not an adequate and effective substitute for *habeas corpus*, it does not follow that a *habeas corpus* court may disregard the dangers the detention in these cases was intended to prevent. Certain accommodations can be made to reduce the burden *habeas corpus* proceedings will place on the military without impermissibly diluting the protections of the writ.

In the DTA Congress sought to consolidate review of petitioners' claims in the Court of Appeals. Channeling future cases to one district court would no doubt reduce administrative burdens on the Government. This is a legitimate objective that might be advanced even without an amendment to §2241. If, in a future case, a detainee files a habeas petition in another judicial district in which a proper respondent can be served, the Government can move for change of venue to the court that will hear these petitioners' cases, the United States District Court for the District of Columbia. Another of Congress' reasons for vesting exclusive jurisdiction in the Court of Appeals, perhaps, was to avoid the widespread dissemination of classified information. The Government has raised similar concerns here and elsewhere. We make no attempt to anticipate all of the evidentiary and access-to-counsel issues that will arise during the course of the detainees' *habeas corpus* proceedings. We recognize, however, that the Government has a

legitimate interest in protecting sources and methods of intelligence gathering; and we expect that the District Court will use its discretion to accommodate this interest to the greatest extent possible. These and the other remaining questions are within the expertise and competence of the District Court to address in the first instance.

* * *

Our opinion does not undermine the Executive's powers as Commander in Chief. On the contrary, the exercise of those powers is vindicated, not eroded, when confirmed by the Judicial Branch. Within the Constitution's separation-of-powers structure, few exercises of judicial power are as legitimate or as necessary as the responsibility to hear challenges to the authority of the Executive to imprison a person. Some of these petitioners have been in custody for six years with no definitive judicial determination as to the legality of their detention. Their access to the writ is a necessity to determine the lawfulness of their status, even if, in the end, they do not obtain the relief they seek.

The determination by the Court of Appeals that the Suspension Clause and its protections are inapplicable to petitioners was in error. The judgment of the Court of Appeals is reversed. The cases are remanded to the Court of Appeals with instructions that it remand the cases to the District Court for proceedings consistent with this opinion.

JUSTICE SOUTER, with whom JUSTICE GINSBURG and JUSTICE BREYER join, concurring.

A fact insufficiently appreciated by the dissents is the length of the disputed imprisonments. It is in fact the very lapse of four years from the time *Rasul* put everyone on notice that habeas process was available to Guantanamo prisoners, and the lapse of six years since some of these prisoners were captured and incarcerated, that stand at odds with the repeated suggestions of the dissenters that these cases should be seen as a judicial victory in a contest for power between the Court and the political branches. The several answers to the charge of triumphalism might start with a basic fact of

Anglo-American constitutional history: that the power, first of the Crown and now of the Executive Branch of the United States, is necessarily limited by *habeas corpus* jurisdiction to enquire into the legality of executive detention. And one could explain that in this Court's exercise of responsibility to preserve *habeas corpus* something much more significant is involved than pulling and hauling between the judicial and political branches. Instead, though, it is enough to repeat that some of these petitioners have spent six years behind bars. After six years of sustained executive detentions in Guantanamo, subject to habeas jurisdiction but without any actual habeas scrutiny, today's decision is no judicial victory, but an act of perseverance in trying to make habeas review, and the obligation of the courts to provide it, mean something of value both to prisoners and to the Nation.

CHIEF JUSTICE ROBERTS, with whom JUSTICE SCALIA, JUSTICE THOMAS, and JUSTICE ALITO join, dissenting.

Today the Court strikes down as inadequate the most generous set of procedural protections ever afforded aliens detained by this country as enemy combatants. The political branches crafted these procedures amidst an ongoing military conflict, after much careful investigation and thorough debate. The Court rejects them today out of hand, without bothering to say what due process rights the detainees possess, without explaining how the statute fails to vindicate those rights, and before a single petitioner has even attempted to avail himself of the law's operation. And to what effect? The majority merely replaces a review system designed by the people's representatives with a set of shapeless procedures to be defined by federal courts at some future date. One cannot help but think, after surveying the modest practical results of the majority's ambitious opinion, that this decision is not really about the detainees at all, but about control of federal policy regarding enemy combatants.

The Court should have resolved these cases on other grounds. Habeas is most fundamentally a procedural right, a mechanism for contesting the legality of executive detention. The critical threshold question in these cases, prior

to any inquiry about the writ's scope, is whether the system the political branches designed protects whatever rights the detainees may possess. If so, there is no need for any additional process, whether called "habeas" or something else.

Congress entrusted that threshold question in the first instance to the Court of Appeals for the District of Columbia Circuit, as the Constitution surely allows Congress to do. But before the D. C. Circuit has addressed the issue, the Court cashiers the statute, and without answering this critical threshold question itself. The Court does eventually get around to asking whether review under the DTA is, as the Court frames it, an "adequate substitute" for habeas, but even then its opinion fails to determine what rights the detainees possess and whether the DTA system satisfies them. The majority instead compares the undefined DTA process to an equally undefined habeas right— one that is to be given shape only in the future by district courts on a case-by-case basis. This whole approach is misguided.

It is also fruitless. How the detainees' claims will be decided now that the DTA is gone is anybody's guess. But the habeas process the Court mandates will most likely end up looking a lot like the DTA system it replaces, as the district court judges shaping it will have to reconcile review of the prisoners' detention with the undoubted need to protect the American people from the terrorist threat—precisely the challenge Congress undertook in drafting the DTA. All that today's opinion has done is shift responsibility for those sensitive foreign policy and national security decisions from the elected branches to the Federal Judiciary.

I believe the system the political branches constructed adequately protects any constitutional rights aliens captured abroad and detained as enemy combatants may enjoy. I therefore would dismiss these cases on that ground. With all respect for the contrary views of the majority, I must dissent.

II

The majority's overreaching is particularly egregious given the weakness of its objections to the DTA. Simply put, the Court's opinion fails on its own terms. The majority strikes down the statute because it is not an "adequate substitute" for habeas review, but fails to show what rights the detainees have that cannot be vindicated by the DTA system.

Because the central purpose of *habeas corpus* is to test the legality of executive detention, the writ requires most fundamentally an Article III court able to hear the prisoner's claims and, when necessary, order release. Beyond that, the process a given prisoner is entitled to receive depends on the circumstances and the rights of the prisoner. After much hemming and hawing, the majority appears to concede that the DTA provides an Article III court competent to order release. The only issue in dispute is the process the Guantanamo prisoners are entitled to use to test the legality of their detention. *Hamdi* concluded that American citizens detained as enemy combatants are entitled to only limited process, and that much of that process could be supplied by a military tribunal, with review to follow in an Article III court. That is precisely the system we have here. It is adequate to vindicate whatever due process rights petitioners may have. The *Hamdi* plurality concluded that this type of review would be enough to satisfy due process, even for citizens. Congress followed the Court's lead, only to find itself the victim of a constitutional bait and switch.

Hamdi merits scant attention from the Court—a remarkable omission, as *Hamdi* bears directly on the issues before us. *Hamdi* was all about the scope of habeas review in the context of enemy combatant detentions. The petitioner, an American citizen held within the United States as an enemy combatant, invoked the writ to challenge his detention. After "a careful examination both of the writ and of the Due Process Clause," this Court enunciated the "basic process" the Constitution entitled Hamdi to expect from a habeas court under §2241. That process consisted of the right to "receive notice of the factual basis for his classification, and a fair opportunity to rebut the Government's factual assertions before a neutral decisionmaker." In light of the Government's national security responsibilities, the plurality found the process could be "tailored to alleviate [the] uncommon potential to burden the Executive at a time of ongoing military conflict." For example, the Government could rely on hearsay and could claim a presumption in favor of its own evidence.

Hamdi further suggested that this "basic process" on collateral review could be provided by a military tribunal. It pointed to prisoner-of-war tribunals as a model that would satisfy the Constitution's requirements. Only "in the *absence* of such process" before a military tribunal, the Court held, would Article III courts need to conduct full-dress habeas proceedings to "ensure that the minimum requirements of due process are achieved." And even then, the petitioner would be entitled to no more process than he would have received from a properly constituted military review panel, given his limited due process rights and the Government's weighty interests.

Contrary to the majority, *Hamdi* is of pressing relevance because it establishes the procedures American *citizens* detained as enemy combatants can expect from a habeas court proceeding under §2241. The DTA system of military tribunal hearings followed by Article III review looks a lot like the procedure *Hamdi* blessed. If nothing else, it is plain from the design of the DTA that Congress, the President, and this Nation's military leaders have made a good-faith effort to follow our precedent.

D

Despite these guarantees, the Court finds the DTA system an inadequate habeas substitute, for one central reason: Detainees are unable to introduce at the appeal stage exculpatory evidence discovered after the conclusion of their CSRT proceedings. The Court hints darkly that the DTA may suffer from other infirmities, but it does not bother to name them, making a response a bit difficult. As it stands, I can only assume the Court regards the supposed defect it did identify as the gravest of the lot.

If this is the most the Court can muster, the ice beneath its feet is thin indeed. As noted, the CSRT procedures provide ample opportunity for detainees to introduce exculpatory evidence—whether documentary in nature or from live witnesses—before the military tribunals. And if their ability to introduce such evidence is denied contrary to the Constitution or laws of the United States, the D. C. Circuit has the authority to say so on review. If that sort of procedure sounds familiar, it should. Federal appellate courts reviewing factual determinations follow just such a procedure in a variety of circumstances.

III

The majority rests its decision on abstract and hypothetical concerns. Step back and consider what, in the real world, Congress and the Executive have actually granted aliens captured by our Armed Forces overseas and found to be enemy combatants:

The right to hear the bases of the charges against them, including a summary of any classified evidence.

The ability to challenge the bases of their detention before military tribunals modeled after Geneva Convention procedures. Some 38 detainees have been released as a result of this process.

The right, before the CSRT, to testify, introduce evidence, call witnesses, question those the Government calls, and secure release, if and when appropriate.

The right to the aid of a personal representative in arranging and presenting their cases before a CSRT.

Before the D. C. Circuit, the right to employ counsel, challenge the factual record, contest the lower tribunal's legal determinations, ensure compliance with the Constitution and laws, and secure release, if any errors below establish their entitlement to such relief.

In sum, the DTA satisfies the majority's own criteria for assessing adequacy. This statutory scheme provides the combatants held at Guantanamo greater procedural protections than have ever been afforded alleged enemy detainees—whether citizens or aliens—in our national history.

I respectfully dissent.

JUSTICE SCALIA, with whom THE CHIEF JUSTICE, JUSTICE THOMAS, and JUSTICE ALITO join, dissenting.

Today, for the first time in our Nation's history, the Court confers a constitutional right to *habeas corpus* on alien enemies detained abroad by our military forces in the course of an ongoing war. The Chief Justice's dissent, which I join, shows that the procedures prescribed by Congress in the Detainee Treatment Act provide the essential protections that *habeas corpus* guarantees; there has thus been no suspension of the writ, and no basis exists for judicial intervention beyond what the Act allows. My problem with today's opinion is more fundamental still: The writ of *habeas corpus* does not, and never has, run in favor of aliens abroad; the Suspension Clause thus has no application, and the Court's intervention in this military matter is entirely *ultra vires.*

I think it appropriate to begin with a description of the disastrous consequences of what the Court has done today. America is at war with radical Islamists. The enemy began by killing Americans and American allies abroad: 241 at the Marine barracks in Lebanon, 19 at the Khobar Towers in Dhahran, 224 at our embassies in Dar es Salaam and Nairobi, and 17 on the USS *Cole* in Yemen. On September 11, 2001, the enemy brought the battle to American soil, killing 2,749 at the Twin Towers in New York City, 184 at the Pentagon in Washington, D. C., and 40 in Pennsylvania. It has threatened further attacks against our homeland; one need only walk about buttressed and barricaded Washington, or board a plane anywhere in the country, to know that the threat is a serious one. Our Armed Forces are now in the field against the enemy, in Afghanistan and Iraq. Last week, 13 of our countrymen in arms were killed.

The game of bait-and-switch that today's opinion plays upon the Nation's Commander in Chief will make the war harder on us. It will almost certainly cause more Americans to be killed. That consequence would be tolerable if necessary to preserve a time-honored legal principle vital to our constitutional Republic. But it is this Court's blatant *abandonment* of such a principle that produces the decision today. The President relied on our settled precedent in *Johnson v. Eisentrager* (1950), when he established the prison at Guantanamo Bay for enemy aliens. Had the law been otherwise, the military surely would not have transported prisoners there, but would have kept them in Afghanistan, transferred them to another of our foreign military bases, or turned them over to allies for detention. Those other facilities might well have been worse for the detainees themselves.

In the long term, then, the Court's decision today accomplishes little, except perhaps to reduce the well-being of enemy combatants that the Court ostensibly seeks to protect. In the short term, however, the decision is devastating. At least 30 of those prisoners hitherto released from Guantanamo Bay have returned to the battlefield. Some have been captured or killed. But others have succeeded in carrying on their atrocities against innocent civilians. In one case, a detainee released from Guantanamo Bay masterminded the kidnapping of two Chinese dam workers, one of whom was later shot to death when used as a human shield against Pakistani commandoes. Another former detainee promptly resumed his post as a senior Taliban commander and murdered a United Nations engineer and three Afghan soldiers. Still another murdered an Afghan judge. It was reported only last month that a released detainee carried out a suicide bombing against Iraqi soldiers in Mosul, Iraq.

These, mind you, were detainees whom the military had concluded were not enemy combatants. Their return to the kill illustrates the incredible difficulty of assessing who is and who is not an enemy combatant in a foreign theater of operations where the environment does not lend itself to rigorous evidence collection. Astoundingly, the Court today raises the bar, requiring military officials to appear before civilian courts and defend their decisions under procedural and evidentiary rules that go beyond what Congress has specified. As The Chief Justice's dissent makes clear, we have no idea what those procedural and evidentiary rules are, but they will be determined by civil courts and (in the Court's contemplation at least) will be more detainee-friendly than those now applied, since otherwise there would no reason to hold the congressionally prescribed procedures unconstitutional. If they impose a higher standard of proof (from foreign battlefields) than the current procedures require, the number of the enemy returned to combat will obviously increase.

But even when the military has evidence that it can bring forward, it is often foolhardy to release that evidence to the attorneys representing our enemies. And one escalation of procedures that the Court is clear about is affording the detainees increased access to witnesses (perhaps troops serving in Afghanistan?) and to classified information. During the 1995 prosecution of Omar Abdel Rahman, federal prosecutors gave the names of 200 unindicted co-conspirators to the "Blind Sheik's" defense lawyers; that information was in the hands of Osama Bin Laden within two weeks. In another case, trial testimony revealed to the enemy that the United States had been monitoring their cellular network, whereupon they promptly stopped using it, enabling more of them to evade capture and continue their atrocities.

And today it is not just the military that the Court elbows aside. A mere two Terms ago in *Hamdan v. Rumsfeld* (2006), when the Court held (quite amazingly) that the Detainee Treatment Act of 2005 had not stripped habeas jurisdiction over Guantanamo petitioners' claims, four Members of today's five-Justice majority joined an opinion saying the following: "Nothing prevents the President from returning to Congress to seek the authority [for trial by military commission] he believes necessary. Where, as here, no emergency prevents consultation with Congress, judicial insistence upon that consultation does not weaken our Nation's ability to deal with danger. To the contrary, that insistence strengthens the Nation's ability to determine—through democratic means—how best to do so. The Constitution places its faith in those democratic means."

Turns out they were just kidding. For in response, Congress, at the President's request, quickly enacted the Military Commissions Act, emphatically reasserting that it did not want these prisoners filing habeas petitions. It is therefore clear that Congress and the Executive—both political branches—have determined that limiting the role of civilian courts in adjudicating whether prisoners captured abroad are properly detained is important to success in the war that some 190,000 of our men and women are now fighting. But it does not matter. The Court today decrees that no good reason to accept the judgment of the other two branches is "apparent." "The Government," it declares, "presents no credible arguments that the military mission at Guantanamo would be compromised if *habeas corpus* courts had jurisdiction to hear the detainees' claims." What competence does the Court have to second-guess the judgment of Congress and the President on such a point? None whatever. But the Court blunders in nonetheless. Henceforth, as today's opinion makes unnervingly clear, how to handle enemy prisoners in this war will ultimately lie with the branch that knows least about the national security concerns that the subject entails.

The Nation will live to regret what the Court has done today. I dissent.

7

Federalism

CHAPTER OUTLINE

As a central feature of the American constitutional system, federalism is one of the most important contributions the Founders made to the art of government; it represents the paradigm of what is called federal government. Most contemporary definitions of federalism amount to little more than generalized descriptions of the way governing power is divided in the United States between the states and the national government.[1] The Framers, however, did not consider the system they had designed to be federal. As *The Federalist,* No. 39, makes clear, they thought that the Constitution was "in strictness, neither a national nor a federal Constitution, but a composition of both." Furthermore, James Madison argued, the "compound government" created by the Constitution must "be explained by itself, [and] not by similitudes or analogies."[2] In order to appreciate the difficulties facing the Supreme Court when it deals with questions of federalism and to evaluate its decisions in this area, we must attempt to comprehend the Framers' understanding of this "neither wholly federal, nor wholly national" political arrangement and how they thought that it contributed to the overall ends of the Constitution.

FEDERALISM AND THE FOUNDING

It is essential to understand that the Framers recognized only two fundamental modes, or elements, of political organization—the federal and the national[3]—which they thought they had combined into a compound system. Today, in contrast, it is commonplace to speak of three elemental forms: confederal, federal, and national (or unitary). This modern typology treats the confederal and national forms as the extremes, with a confederation preserving the primacy and autonomy of the states and a nation giving unimpeded primacy to the government of the whole society. Federalism, in this view, is a third fundamental mode that stands between these two poles and combines the best characteristics of each. Specifically, federalism is thought to combine states, which confederally retain sovereignty within a certain sphere, with a central body that nationally possesses sovereignty within another sphere. Modern usage has co-opted the simple word *federal* to signify what the Framers considered to be a composition of both federal and national elements.

The Framers, however, saw no more difference between the confederal and the federal than we see, for example, between the words *inflammable* and *flammable:* nothing more was involved than the accidental presence or absence of a nonsignifying prefix. For them, the confederal or federal was opposed to the unitary or national, and they viewed the Constitution as a composition of both elemental modes.

The Founding generation's idea of confederal or federal arrangements, as represented in the Articles of Confederation, was characterized by three operative principles, each of which drastically limited the power of the central authority and preserved the primacy of the member states.[4] First, the central authority did not govern individual citizens: it dealt only with the individual states that composed the federal system and operated primarily by the voluntary consent of those states. Second, the central government had no authority to deal with the internal affairs of the member states; rather, its rule was narrowly confined to certain external tasks of mutual interest to all—for example, war and common defense. Third, each member state had an exact equality of suffrage—an equal vote derived from the equal sovereignty possessed by each state, regardless of size, strength, or wealth.

In the Founders' conception of a national government, in contrast, all power resided in the central authority; local units of government, if retained at all, were mere subdivisions that existed for administrative purposes only. Such powers as these localities possessed were delegated by the central government and could be overridden or withdrawn altogether at its will. The central authority, then, extended to all matters of internal administration and acted directly, through its own officials, not merely on the local governments but upon every citizen as well. Finally, since the central government was independent of the local units, it could continue to exist even if they were to disappear.

Given these two modes from which to choose, confederal or federal association traditionally had been preferred by those who favored republican government; they regarded it as the only way in which the advantages of size could be combined with the blessings of republicanism—which was understood to mean a government in which power resides in the citizens, who elect their representatives and are governed according to law. Proponents of this view argued that, first of all, only small countries with homogeneous populations could possess republican government, for only small countries could secure the public's voluntary attachment to the government and voluntary obedience to the laws; and second, when such small republics seek the advantages and safety of greater size, as inevitably they must, they can preserve their republican character only by uniting in a federal manner. Federalism would be, for them, the protective husk that preserved the kernels of free government.[5]

The leading Framers realized, however, that the traditional republican embrace of federalism, as incorporated in the Articles of Confederation, had reduced the people to "the last stage of national humiliation." As Alexander Hamilton complained in *The Federalist,* "there is scarcely anything that can wound the pride, or degrade the character of an independent nation, which we do not experience." The principles of federalism had rendered the Articles so weak that the situation "sometimes bordered on anarchy." Nor was the government's ineptitude limited to the realm of foreign affairs. Domestically, "the security of private rights" had been rendered precarious, and the "steady dispensation of justice" was interrupted by the practices of many states. Convinced of the need for a more powerful government, many delegates to the Constitutional Convention supported the Virginia Plan. As amended, the plan declared that "a Union of the States merely federal will not accomplish the objects proposed by the Articles of Confederation, namely common defense, security of liberty, and general welfare" and proposed, therefore, that "a *national* Government ought to be established consisting of a *supreme* Legislative, Executive and Judiciary."[6]

At this juncture, a serious question arose: could a national government be formed without jeopardizing republican liberty? Those who favored the establishment of such a government had to persuade their contemporaries that the proposed plan was also compatible with republican government—that federalism as it had been understood to that time was not indispensable to republicanism. To do so, they chose to undermine the prevailing notion that, without federalism, only small countries could possess republican governments. Madison's arguments in this regard were decisive. Turning the small-republic view on its head, he contended that smallness, not largeness, was fatal to republican liberty. History demonstrated that small republics were continuously racked with faction and oppression; indeed, the Constitutional Convention itself had been instigated by the fear for liberty in the small American states. "Was it to be supposed that republican liberty could long exist under the abuses of it practiced in some of the States? . . . Were we not thence admonished to enlarge the sphere as far as the nature of the government would admit?" Because smallness had proven fatal to republicanism, "the only remedy is to enlarge the sphere, and thereby divide the community into so great a number of interests and parties, that in the first place a majority will not be likely at the same moment to have a common interest separate from that of the whole or of the minority; and in the second place, that in case they should have such an interest, they may not be apt to unite in the pursuit of it."[7] The multiplicity of interests present in a large republic was thus the true guardian of republican liberty—*The Federalist,* No. 10, describes it as the republican remedy for the diseases most incident to republican government.

Madison's arguments on behalf of a large extended republic effectively demolished the small-republic argument but failed to convince the delegates to the convention to adopt a wholly national government. Most of the delegates, reluctant to abolish the states altogether, sought some means for preserving their existence and agency. Increasingly, they came to recognize that because, as William Johnson of Connecticut pointed out, the states were both distinct "political societies" and "districts of people composing one political society,"[8] neither a wholly federal nor a wholly national constitution was appropriate. Spurred on by, among others, George Mason of Virginia and James Wilson of Pennsylvania, they realized that it was possible for the people to create and assign power to more than "one set of immediate representatives."[9] The people could have their cake and eat it, too: not only could they preserve the states while establishing a new national government, but they could also have a political structure in which both levels of government operated over the same geographic area. Power would be divided between these two levels according to a simple yet elegant formula: any object of government that was confined in operation and effect wholly within the bounds of a particular state would belong to the government of that state, and any object of government that was extended in its operation and effect beyond the bounds of the particular state would belong to the government of the United States.

Beyond this straightforward division of power between the central government and the states, federalism to the convention delegates also meant the presence of federal elements in the central government itself. They anticipated that the new constitution would "in some respects operate on the States, in others on the people."[10] Because the new central government would act upon both the states and the people, the delegates concluded that both ought to be represented in the new government. Accordingly, they mixed together varying proportions of federal and national elements to create a composition that was neither wholly federal nor wholly national. This blend of elements is apparent in such constitutional provisions as the mode by which the Constitution was to be ratified, the amending process, equal representation of the states in the Senate, election of the Senate by state legislatures, and the Electoral College.

When Alexis de Tocqueville examined the American Constitution, he described it as "neither exactly national nor exactly federal; but the new word which ought to express this novel thing does not yet exist."[11] Although he was correct in declaring that a new word had not been devised, a familiar term from the beginning had been pressed into service to express this novel thing: the term *federal*. Well aware that federalism was generally thought to be essential for a republican government, the Framers seized the word for themselves and called their new compound arrangement *federalism*. This stratagem proved to be of considerable value during the ratification campaign, as it enabled them to present themselves as defenders of federalism and to refer to the adherents of true federalism as Anti-Federalists. But the Framers' identification of their compound government as federal, although an effective ploy at the time, has been the source of much subsequent confusion over exactly what federalism means and what mode of government the American Constitution establishes. Such confusion can be avoided by reference to the Constitution's Preamble. The Constitution was intended neither to provide for a perfect union (i.e., a wholly national government) nor to preserve the radically imperfect union of the Articles of Confederation; rather, it was ordained and established "in order to form a more perfect Union." The phrase *a more perfect Union* is no grammatical solecism; to the contrary, it is an accurate description of the compound government, made up of both federal and national elements, that the convention had devised.

It was, in part, through the means of this "more perfect Union" that the overall ends of the Constitution were to be served. As Madison had observed in *The Federalist*, No. 51, in framing the Constitution the convention's great object was "first [to] enable the government to control the governed; and in the next place, [to] oblige it to control itself." Madison and the other leading Framers recognized that the federal arrangements they had devised could contribute to the realization of both goals. The division of power between the states and the national government allowed them to entrust to the entire federal structure more power than they would have been willing to grant to either the states or the national government alone, and thereby to ensure that the government would have sufficient power to control the governed and to avoid the near anarchy that had existed under the Articles of Confederation. They also appreciated that the federalism they had devised helped to oblige the government to control itself. By creating two levels of government and dividing power between them, the Framers made each level less threatening to liberty. And by interjecting federal elements into the national government itself, they checked the threat of tyranny from regionally concentrated factious majorities. In short, the Framers' federalism helped to provide energetic government organized around the principle of qualitative majority rule.

FEDERALISM AND THE FIRST CONGRESS

The Framers understood that the new Constitution they were establishing was neither wholly national nor wholly federal but a composition of both. The members of the First Congress acted in conformity with this statement as they drafted the Judiciary Act of 1789.

The First Congress has been described as "a sort of continuing constitutional convention."[12] Not only had many of its members—for example, James Madison, Oliver Ellsworth, Elbridge Gerry, Rufus King, Robert Morris, Pierce Butler, William Johnson, and William Paterson—helped to draft and ratify the Constitution, but it was responsible for taking the generalities of the Constitution—what Chief Justice John Marshall in *McCulloch v. Maryland* (1819) called its "great outlines"—and translating them into concrete and functioning institutions. As David P. Currie points out, the First Congress determined its own procedures; established the great executive departments of War, State, Justice, and Treasury; enacted a system of taxation; provided for payment of Revolutionary War debts; created a national bank; provided for national defense; regulated relations with Indian tribes; advised the president on foreign affairs (the Senate); passed statutes regarding naturalization, patents, copyrights, and federal crimes; regulated relations with existing states and admitted new ones; provided for the administration of the territories; established a permanent seat of government; adopted a bill of rights; and set up the federal judiciary.[13] By the time the First Congress adjourned on March 3, 1791, "the country had a much clearer idea of what the Constitution meant than it had had when that body had first met in 1789."[14] It is not surprising that, two months into the Second Congress, Fisher Ames, a Massachusetts congressman, lamented in a November 24, 1791, letter that "Congress is not engaged in very interesting work. The first acts were the pillars of the federal edifice. Now we have only to keep the sparks from catching the shavings; we must watch the broom, that it is not set behind the door with fire on it, etc. etc. Nobody cares much for us now, except the enemies of the excise law, who remonstrate and make a noise."[15]

With the Judiciary Act of 1789, Congress established the Supreme Court, consisting of a chief justice and five associate justices. Significantly, the Congress also exercised its constitutional option to establish a system of inferior federal courts. It did so for two principal reasons. First, it believed that an effective maritime commerce (essential to the new nation) needed a dependable body of admiralty and maritime law and that the most reliable method to ensure the development of these laws would be to entrust them to a new set of federal courts. As historian John Frank has remarked: "The experience of the Confederation convinced virtually every conscientious patriot of the 1780s that the admiralty jurisdiction ought to be totally, effectively, and completely in the hands of the national government, and an extended search has not revealed a criticism from any contemporary source of the constitution granting federal admiralty jurisdiction."[16] The need for district courts with admiralty jurisdiction, in turn, "opened the door for somewhat broader jurisdiction, since it effectively surrendered the argument over the expense of federal district courts."[17]

Second, the Congress exercised its option to create lower federal courts because at least one state, Virginia, had adopted legislation, sponsored by Patrick Henry, prohibiting its judges from "executing federal functions." As Senator Caleb Strong noted, "The State of Virginia by a Law passed since their Adoption of the Constitution, have prohibited their Officers from holding Offices under the United States, and their Courts from having Jurisdiction of Causes arising under the Laws of the Union; by such Laws every State would be able to defeat the Provisions of Congress if the Judiciary powers of the Genl. Government were directed to be exercised by the State Courts."[18]

Thus, Congress established thirteen federal district courts of one judge each—one district for each of the eleven states that had, by that time, ratified the Constitution and two additional districts, in Virginia and Massachusetts, for Kentucky and Maine. It also provided for three circuit courts, each composed of two justices of the Supreme Court sitting in conjunction with one district court judge.

Parts of the Judiciary Act of 1789 were unquestionably national in character. Thus, in addition to establishing inferior federal tribunals rather than simply relying on state courts, the Congress also included Section 25, which brought the state courts directly under federal appellate jurisdiction by providing for appeals from state courts to the federal judiciary. Under Section 25, appeals could be taken to the US Supreme Court whenever the highest state court having jurisdiction of the case ruled against the constitutionality of a federal law or treaty, ruled in favor of the validity of a state act that had been challenged as contrary to the Constitution or federal law, or ruled against a right or privilege claimed under the Constitution or federal law. (Interestingly, however, Congress withheld from the Supreme Court the power to review cases in which state courts invalidated state conduct on federal grounds, even in those cases in which state conduct was invalidated under an overly broad reading of federal laws that in turn defeated other federal rights.)

Although the creation of inferior federal courts and Section 25 were national in character, other provisions of the Judiciary Act were federal. It granted state courts concurrent original jurisdiction in all civil suits at common law and equity, conferring upon the federal courts exclusive jurisdiction only in admiralty and maritime cases and in cases involving the few crimes and offenses cognizable under the authority of the United States. It withheld from the federal trial courts jurisdiction over cases "arising under" the Constitution and laws of the United States, leaving these to be adjudicated in the state courts. (Congress did not provide the federal courts with federal-question jurisdiction until the Judiciary Act of 1875.)

The Judiciary Act of 1789 also set a monetary minimum for Supreme Court review of civil cases, a requirement that Congress did not eliminate for all cases involving constitutional issues until 1891 and did not abolish with respect to Supreme Court review of all federal questions until 1925. It also withheld Supreme Court review of federal criminal cases, something Congress did not provide until 1891. Still another provision that was definitely federal in character was Section 34, called the Rules of Decision Act. It provided that "the laws of the several States, except where the Constitution, treaties, or statutes of the United States shall otherwise require or provide, shall be regarded as rules of decision in trials at common law in the courts of the United States in cases where they apply."

FEDERALISM AND THE MARSHALL COURT

As is true of many compounds, the government created by the Framers is potentially unstable. Under the pressure of events and with the proper catalytic agents present, it might break down into its elemental modes and become either wholly federal or wholly national. A principal responsibility of the Supreme Court, consistent with its claim in *Marbury v. Madison* (1803) that "it is emphatically the province and duty of the judicial department to say what the law is," has been to prevent such an occurrence and to preserve the "mixed nature" of the Constitution. In discharging this responsibility, the Court has often had to counteract whichever element is in danger of gaining ascendancy. For the most part, the justices have accomplished this task by the way in which they have drawn the line between the powers of the national government and those of the states. The line of demarcation cannot be fixed permanently or precisely. As Chief Justice John Marshall remarked in *McCulloch v. Maryland* (1819), "The question respecting the extent of the powers actually granted, is perpetually arising, and will probably continue to arise, as long as our system shall exist." The answers given by the Court to this "perpetually arising" question have helped to maintain a balance of power between the states and the national government, and thereby to preserve the compound nature of our constitutional system.

Initially, under Marshall's leadership, the Court defined state and national powers in such a way as to benefit the national government. At that time, the people felt a "habitual attachment" to their state governments. As Hamilton pointed out, in the Constitutional Convention, the state's "sovereignty is immediately before the eyes of the people: its protection is immediately enjoyed by them. From its hand distributive justice, and all those acts which familiarize and endear government to a people, are dispensed to them." Given that "the passions . . . of avarice, ambition, interest, which govern most individuals and all public bodies, fall into the current of the States and do not flow in the stream of the General Government," the states were likely to be "an overmatch for the General Government."[19] In the face of this imbalance in power, the compound government created by the Framers could easily be broken down into its elemental modes to such an extent that a simple confederation—with all its attendant evils—once again would emerge. To prevent such a calamity, the Marshall Court systematically interpreted the Constitution so as to render secure the power and authority of the general government, as its opinions in *McCulloch* (found in Chapter 4), *Martin v. Hunter's Lessee* (1816), and *Cohens v. Virginia* (1821) make clear.

In *McCulloch,* Chief Justice Marshall set forth three basic rules of constitutional interpretation that in general favored the national government and in particular supported his argument for upholding the constitutionality of the Bank of the United States and invalidating Maryland's tax on that bank. First, he argued that the enumerated powers of the national government ought to be seen as the means to the accomplishment of certain ends. Because these powers helped designate the Constitution's "great outlines" and "important objects," Marshall contended, they should not be considered to be limitations on the national government. A broad and expansive construction of the powers of the national government was essential: "A constitution, to contain an accurate detail of all the subdivisions of which its great powers will admit, and of all the means by which they may be carried into execution, would partake of the prolixity of a legal code, and could scarcely be embraced by the human mind." The United States Constitution was not a statute, and it ought not to be read as one. Emphasizing that "we must never forget that it is *a constitution* we are expounding, . . . intended to endure for ages to come," Marshall advanced the following principle, which he felt would ensure a "sound construction" of the Constitution: "Let the end be legitimate, let it be within the scope of the constitution, and all means which are appropriate, which are plainly adapted to that end, which are not prohibited, but consist with the letter and spirit of the constitution, are constitutional." To Marshall, this principle of constitutional construction was dictated not only by logic, but also by the presence of the Necessary and Proper Clause.

The second basic rule of constitutional interpretation advanced in *McCulloch* was related to the first: the Tenth Amendment, Marshall declared, constitutes no bar to a broad construction of even the incidental or implied powers of the national government. The chief justice drew attention to the fact that, unlike the Articles of Confederation, which required "that everything granted shall be expressly and minutely described," the Tenth Amendment declares only that the powers "not delegated to the United States, nor prohibited to the States, are reserved to the States or to the people." Thus, the answer to the question of whether "the particular power which may become the subject of contest has been delegated to the one government or prohibited to the other, [is] to depend on a fair construction of the whole instrument."

Marshall's third and final rule arose out of his reading of the Supremacy Clause in Article VI. He contended that within its sphere, the national government is supreme, and its policies must prevail, regardless of whatever state powers or functions it may touch: "It is of the very essence of supremacy to remove all obstacles to its action within its own sphere, and so to modify every power vested in subordinate governments, as to exempt its own operations from their own influence."

In *Martin v. Hunter's Lessee* and *Cohens v. Virginia,* the Marshall Court further sought to protect the compound nature of the American constitutional system from the excessive centrifugal forces generated by state loyalties; it therefore established the authority of the Supreme Court to review state court decisions in the civil and criminal realms. In *Martin,* Justice Joseph Story spoke for his judicial brethren when he declared that Section 25 of the Judiciary Act of 1789, which extended federal jurisdiction over civil cases pending in state courts, was "supported by the letter and spirit of the Constitution." He stressed

the importance, and even necessity of uniformity of decisions throughout the whole United States, upon all subjects within the purview of the constitution. Judges of equal learning and integrity, in different states, might differently interpret the statute, or a treaty of the United States, or even the Constitution itself: if there were no revising authority to control these jarring and discordant judgments, and harmonize them into uniformity, the laws, the treaties and the constitution of the United States would be different, in different states, and might, perhaps, never have precisely the same construction, obligation or efficiency, in any two states. The public mischiefs that would attend such a state of things would be truly deplorable; and it cannot be believed, that they could have escaped the enlightened convention which formed the constitution. What, indeed, might then have been only prophecy, has now become fact; and the appellate jurisdiction must continue to be the only adequate remedy for such evils.

In *Cohens,* Chief Justice Marshall rejected the arguments of the State of Virginia that state judiciaries were totally separate from and independent of the federal judiciary. He pointed out, first of all, that the states have "chosen to be, in many respects, and to many purposes, a nation; and for all these purposes, her government is complete; to all these objects, it is competent. The people have declared, that in the exercise of all powers given for these objects, it is supreme." From these facts, Marshall went on, it followed inevitably that in a government that is acknowledged to be supreme with respect to objects of vital interest to the nation, "the exercise of the appellate power over those judgments of the State tribunals which may contravene the Constitution or laws of the United States, is, we believe, essential to the attainment of those objects."

FEDERALISM AND ITS PROTECTION BY SUBSEQUENT COURTS

Marshall's efforts to protect the national elements of the Constitution proved so successful that most subsequent concern by the Supreme Court for the preservation of the government's compound nature has been directed toward retaining its federal elements and ensuring the independent existence and agency of the states. The Court has done so by upholding state actions as consistent with the overall structure and relationships created by the Constitution and by invalidating congressional measures that threaten the federal balance on the grounds that they violate the principles of dual federalism, go beyond the Court's narrow construction of the Commerce Clause, "commandeer" state officials to carry out certain federal mandates, or encroach on the states' sovereign immunity.

Federalism Based on Structure and Relationship

It must be noted that even Chief Justice Marshall, who often favored the claims of the national government over those of the states, emphasized in *Cohens* that although the states are subordinate for some purposes, for other purposes they are sovereign. Marshall argued that the question of whether a state is to be considered sovereign or subordinate must be answered through a "fair construction" of the entire Constitution. As Charles L. Black Jr. has described it, Marshall's method was one of "inference from the structure and relationships created by the Constitution in all its parts," not one of elaborate interpretation or exegesis of a particular constitutional provision.[20]

After Marshall, Courts that attempted to preserve the federal elements in the Constitution have frequently followed his example and reasoned from the total structure that the Constitution created. In *Coyle v. Smith* (1911), for example, the Court denied Congress the power to specify in Oklahoma's Enabling Act the location of the state's capital, arguing that congressional power was limited to admitting states into "a union of States, equal in power, dignity and authority, each competent to exert that residuum of sovereignty not delegated to the United States by the Constitution itself." To allow Congress selectively to impose conditions on some states would destroy the equality of status that the states enjoy as an inherent attribute of the federal Union; in addition, it would mean that the powers of Congress, rather than being defined by the Constitution alone, in this instance could be enlarged or restricted by the conditions imposed on new states by congressional legislation admitting them into the Union. If such legislation were to be sanctioned, finally, new states might bargain away some of the powers reserved to them by the Constitution in an effort to gain admission into the Union.

The same emphasis on reasoning from the total structure of the Constitution is also apparent in *Younger v. Harris* (1971) and *Baldwin v. Montana Fish and Game Commission* (1978). In *Younger,* the Court refused to enjoin, on First Amendment grounds, a pending state criminal prosecution because of its commitment to what Justice Hugo Black called "Our Federalism." Stressing that the Court must be sensitive to the legitimate interests of both the states and the national government, Black declared that this sensitivity requires "a proper respect for state functions, a recognition of the fact that the entire country is made up of a Union of separate state governments, and a continuance of the belief that the National Government will fare best if the States and their institutions are left free to perform their separate functions in their separate ways"; therefore, federal courts should not intervene to protect plaintiffs' rights, allegedly jeopardized by state laws, before the state courts themselves have had the opportunity to hear these challenges to their laws and to demonstrate their own fidelity to the US Constitution.

However, over the years, the federal courts increasingly appeared to honor the *Younger* principle more often in the breach than in the observance. For example, in 1994, when the voters of California passed Proposition 187 (banning state-sponsored health and education benefits for illegal aliens), a federal court immediately enjoined its enforcement and refused to allow California courts to offer authoritative constructions of the law that might have eliminated (or at least reduced) the number of constitutional objections to its implementation. Likewise, in 1996, when the voters of California passed Proposition 209 (barring the state from discriminating against or granting preference to any individual or group on the basis of race, sex, color, ethnicity, or national origin), a federal judge quickly enjoined its implementation before California's own courts could construe its own law and address questions concerning its constitutionality.

"Our Federalism," as defined by Justice Black, appeared to be dead. In *Arizonans for Official English v. Arizona* (1997), however, the Supreme Court made it clear that *Younger* remains good law. When the Arizona electorate approved by ballot initiative Article XXVIII of the Arizona Constitution, declaring English "the official language of the State" and requiring the State to "act in English and in no other language," a state employee who worked as an insurance-claims manager sued the state, its governor, and its attorney general in federal court, alleging that this constitutional provision violated the Free Speech Clause of the First Amendment. After rejecting the attorney general's narrow interpretation of the article and declining to allow the Arizona courts the initial opportunity to construe the article, the federal district court declared the article fatally overbroad after reading it to impose a sweeping ban on the use of any language other than English by all Arizona governmental employees. When the Ninth Circuit affirmed the decision of the district court, an angry Supreme Court vacated the judgment of the court of appeals on the ground of mootness (the state employee had subsequently resigned to take a job in the private sector) and directed the district court to dismiss the action. It read a stern lecture to the courts involved in this case for their failure to help build a "cooperative judicial federalism":

> In litigation generally, and in constitutional litigation most prominently, courts in the United States characteristically pause to ask: Is this conflict really necessary? When anticipatory relief is sought in federal court against a state statute, respect for the place of the States in our federal system calls for close consideration of that core question.
>
> Arizona's Attorney General, in addition to releasing his own opinion on the meaning of Article XXVIII, asked both the District Court and the Court of Appeals to pause before proceeding to judgment; specifically, he asked both federal courts to seek, through the State's certification process, an authoritative construction of the new measure from the Arizona Supreme Court.

Both lower federal courts in this case refused to invite the aid of the Arizona Supreme Court because they found the language of Article XXVIII "plain," and the Attorney General's limiting construction unpersuasive. . . . A more cautious approach was in order. Through certification of novel or unsettled questions of state law for authoritative answers by a State's highest court, a federal court may save "time, energy, and resources and hel[p] build a cooperative judicial federalism."

In *Baldwin v. Montana Fish and Game Commission,* the Court relied on the same logic it employed in *Younger* and reasoned from the total structure of the Constitution to uphold a Montana law that mandated substantially higher hunting fees for nonresidents than for residents. Speaking for a six-member majority, Justice Harry Blackmun contended that this distinction between residents and nonresidents did not violate the Privileges and Immunities Clause of Article IV, Section 2: "Some distinctions between residents and nonresidents merely reflect the fact that this is a Nation composed of individual States, and are permitted; other distinctions are prohibited because they hinder the formation, purpose, or development of a single Union of those States. Only with respect to those 'privileges' and 'immunities' bearing upon the vitality of the Nation as a single entity must the State treat all citizens, resident and nonresident, equally."

Blackmun rejected the contention of Justice William Brennan and other dissenters that the state must justify all distinctions, even those that neither encroach upon the "basic rights" and "essential activities" of the citizenry nor "frustrate the purposes of the formation of the Union."

Dual Federalism

From the appointment of Chief Justice Roger Brooke Taney as Marshall's successor in 1835 until President Franklin D. Roosevelt's clash with the Supreme Court during the New Deal era, the concern over retaining the Constitution's federal elements and ensuring the independent existence of the states most often was manifested in what usually is called *dual federalism*. This doctrine was clearly defined by Justice Peter V. Daniel in the *License Cases* (1847): "Every power delegated to the federal government must be expounded in coincidence with a perfect right in the states to all that they have not delegated; in coincidence, too, with the possession of every power and right necessary for their existence and preservation." Dual federalism assumes that the two levels of government are coequal sovereignties and that each is supreme within its own sphere. Accordingly, the national government cannot undertake any action, even in the exercise of its enumerated powers, that touches upon those functions that the Constitution has reserved to the states. The notorious decision handed down in *Dred Scott v. Sandford* (1857), in which the Court held unconstitutional the Missouri Compromise of 1820 and declared that Congress had no power to limit the spread of slavery in the territories, is based on these assumptions.

The proponents of dual federalism insist that the Constitution is a compact among the states, which have, on certain enumerated issues, ceded a portion of their sovereignty to the national government. All sovereignty not ceded, they argue, is retained. To prevent that retained sovereignty from slipping away, they interpret very narrowly the enumerated powers of the national government in general, and the Necessary and Proper Clause in particular. Also, they strongly emphasize the Tenth Amendment, which they consider to be an affirmative base of power from which the states can challenge the wide-ranging effects of national legislation.

All of these considerations are present in *Hammer v. Dagenhart* (1918), perhaps the Supreme Court's clearest statement of the theory of dual federalism (see Chapter 8). In *Hammer,* the Court, by a 5–4 vote, invalidated a congressional statute that restricted the transportation in interstate commerce of goods produced by child labor. The majority held that despite the express delegation to the national government of the power "to regulate commerce among the several states," the national government was excluded from regulating any matter that was subject to state power.[21] In the words of Justice William R. Day, author of the majority opinion, "The grant of authority over a purely federal [i.e., national] matter was not intended to destroy the local power always existing and carefully reserved to the States in the Tenth Amendment." He admonished all those who would interpret the Constitution to recall that "the powers not expressly delegated to the national government" are reserved to the states and to the people by the Tenth Amendment.

C. Herman Pritchett has pointed out that in the *Hammer* ruling, Justice Day misquoted the Tenth Amendment (the term *expressly* does not appear in the text), ignored judicial precedent (in *McCulloch v. Maryland,* Chief Justice Marshall had held that because the word *expressly* had been intentionally omitted from the amendment, the question of whether a particular power had been delegated to the national government could be answered only by a "fair construction of the whole instrument"), and denied the historical record (in considering the Tenth Amendment, the First Congress rejected a proposal to insert the word *expressly*).[22] These problems did not go unnoticed at the time. Speaking for the four dissenters, Justice Oliver Wendell Holmes declared, "I should have thought that the most conspicuous decisions of this Court had made it clear that the power to regulate commerce and other constitutional powers could not be cut down or qualified by the fact that it might interfere with the carrying out of the domestic policy of any State." Justice Day's argument in effect accorded such primacy to the purely federal elements in the constitutional system that it jeopardized the Constitution's mixed nature and gravely restricted the national government's ability to respond to nationwide problems.

In contending that Congress could not use its admitted powers if they interfered in any way with the states' exercise of their admitted powers, the advocates of dual federalism not only denied the compound nature of the Constitution but also ignored practical necessity. In the end, they did themselves a decided disservice: by the mid-1930s, not surprisingly, the doctrine had fallen into disgrace.[23] Dual federalism was soon replaced by what is often referred to as cooperative federalism—a pragmatic sharing of governmental functions by federal, state, and local authorities that takes little account of whether federal or national elements are present and governing.[24]

The Court's Narrow Construction of the Commerce Clause

The many deficiencies of dual federalism became so painfully apparent that the Court no longer employed it to invalidate a congressional enactment after *Trusler v. Crooks* in 1926.[25] Rather, the Court shifted its ground and found offensive federal legislation unconstitutional based on its narrow reading of the Commerce Clause and its use of the "direct effects/indirect effects" test. To do so, it had to abandon Marshall's expansive understanding of the Commerce Clause as he had articulated it in *Gibbons v. Ogden* (1824) (see Chapter 8). "The word 'commerce,'" the Court came to insist, "is the equivalent of the phrase 'intercourse for the purposes of trade.'" On that basis, it denied that the Congress had plenary power under the Commerce Clause to regulate agriculture in *United States v. Butler* (1936) and mining in *Carter v. Carter Coal Company* (1936).[26]

These were not the first cases in which the Court had narrowed Marshall's expansive definition of commerce as stated in *Gibbons*. In *United States v. E. C. Knight Company,* in 1895, the Court asserted that "commerce succeeds to manufacture, and is not a part of it" and, on that basis, held that the Sherman Anti-Trust Act of 1890 could not be used against the American Sugar Refining Company and its monopoly control of the nation's sugar-refining business. In *E. C. Knight,* the Court conceded that sugar manufacturing, although not commerce, could nevertheless affect interstate commerce. The Court denied, however, that the American Sugar Refining Company was covered by the Sherman Anti-Trust Act, because its monopoly control of sugar refining affected commerce "only incidentally and indirectly." The Court thereby introduced a crucial distinction between intrastate activities having a "direct effect" on commerce (and therefore subject to congressional regulation) and intrastate activities having only an "indirect effect" on commerce (and therefore beyond Congress's reach). This distinction was not used to invalidate, as opposed to merely limit the reach of, a federal statute until the New Deal era, when, in *Schechter Poultry Corporation v. United States* (1935) (found in Chapter 4), it used the "direct effects/indirect effects" test to declare unconstitutional the National Industrial Recovery Act of 1933 because, *inter alia*, Congress was attempting to regulate intrastate acts that only indirectly affected interstate commerce. The next year, in *Carter v. Carter Coal Company,* it again employed this test to find Congress's efforts to regulate coal production unconstitutional.

In *Schechter*, Chief Justice Charles Evans Hughes confidently asserted that the distinction between a direct and an indirect effect was "clear in principle"; however, just one year later in *Carter Coal*, Justice George Sutherland confessed that "[w]hether the effect of a given activity or condition is direct or indirect is not always easy to determine." Struggling to articulate a distinction, he declared that "the word 'direct' implies that the activity or condition invoked or blamed shall operate proximately—not mediately, remotely, or collaterally—to produce the effect. It connotes the absence of an efficient intervening agency or condition." And, he continued, "the extent of the effect bears no logical relation to its character. The distinction between a direct and an indirect effect turns not upon the magnitude of either the cause or the effect, but entirely upon the manner in which the effect has been brought about." He acknowledged that "it is quite true that rules of law are sometimes qualified by considerations of degree," but he insisted that "the matter of degree has no bearing upon the question here, since that question is not what is the extent of the local activity or condition, or the extent of the effect produced upon interstate commerce, but what is the relation between the activity or condition and the effect?" Sutherland's clarification was, of course, completely unhelpful; it came as no surprise that, in *National Labor Relations Board v. Jones & Laughlin Steel Corporation* (1937), decided during its next term, the Court totally abandoned the "direct effect/indirect effect" test and held that, if intrastate activities "have such a close and substantial relation to interstate commerce that their control is essential or appropriate to protect that commerce from burdens and obstructions, Congress cannot be denied the power to exercise that control" (the opinion is found in Chapter 8).

So the matter remained until 1995 when, for the first time in almost six decades,[27] the Supreme Court in *United States v. Lopez* (see Chapter 8) invalidated a federal law—in this case, the Gun-Free School Zones Act of 1990—for exceeding the scope of the Commerce Clause. Chief Justice William Rehnquist wrote for a five-member majority that the act (which made it a federal offense "for any individual knowingly to possess a firearm at a place that the individual knows, or has reasonable cause to believe, is a school zone") "neither regulates a commercial activity nor contains a requirement that the possession be connected in any way to interstate commerce" and consequently "exceeds the authority of Congress 'to regulate Commerce . . . among the several States.'" In his concurring opinion, Thomas pointed out the flaws of what has come to be known as the substantial-effects test:

> After all, if Congress may regulate all matters that substantially affect commerce, there is no need for the Constitution to specify that Congress may enact bankruptcy laws, cl. 4, or coin money and fix the standard of weights and measures, cl. 5, or punish counterfeiters of United States coin and securities, cl. 6. Likewise, Congress would not need the separate authority to establish post-offices and post-roads, cl. 7, or to grant patents and copyrights, cl. 8, or to "punish Piracies and Felonies committed on the high Seas," cl. 10. It might not even need the power to raise and support an Army and Navy, cls. 12 and 13, for fewer people would engage in commercial shipping if they thought that a foreign power could expropriate their property with ease. Indeed, if Congress could regulate matters that substantially affect interstate commerce, there would have been no need to specify that Congress can regulate international trade and commerce with the Indians. As the Framers surely understood, these other branches of trade substantially affect interstate commerce.

Thomas insisted that an interpretation of the Interstate Commerce Clause, based on the "substantial effects" test, "that makes the rest of §8 superfluous simply cannot be correct."

How important as a precedent was *Lopez* remained an open question until *United States v. Morrison* (2000), when the Court held, *inter alia*, that the Congress lacked authority under the Commerce Clause to enact a key provision of the Violence Against Women Act of 1994 (VAWA), which provided a federal civil remedy for victims of gender-motivated violence. In his majority opinion, Chief Justice Rehnquist relied on *Lopez* and expressed the concern of the five-member majority that if the Court were to uphold Congress's authority under the Commerce Clause to enact VAWA, the result would be "to completely obliterate the Constitution's distinction between national and local authority."

> The reasoning that petitioners advance seeks to follow the but-for causal chain from the initial occurrence of violent crime (the suppression of which has always been the prime object of the States' police power) to every attenuated effect upon interstate commerce. If accepted, petitioners' reasoning would allow Congress to regulate any crime as long as the nationwide, aggregated impact of that crime has substantial effects on employment, production, transit, or consumption. Indeed, if Congress may regulate gender-motivated violence, it would be able to regulate murder or any other type of violence since gender-motivated violence, as a subset of all violent crime, is certain to have lesser economic impacts than the larger class of which it is a part.

More significantly still, *Lopez* and *Morrison* figured prominently in *National Federation of Independent Business v. Sebelius* (2012), in which Chief Justice Roberts cited both of these cases in holding for a five-member majority that the individual mandate in the Affordable Care Act (commonly known as Obamacare) requiring all individuals to purchase health insurance and imposing penalties on those who fail to do so was unconstitutional under the Commerce Clause. (However, and of critical importance, Chief Justice Roberts joined a different five-member majority upholding the constitutionality of the individual mandate under Congress's taxing power. See Chapter 8.)

With respect to the Commerce Clause, Roberts wrote that while the Constitution grants Congress the power to "regulate Commerce," that power "presupposes the existence of commercial activity to be regulated. If the power to 'regulate' something included the power to create it, many of the provisions in the Constitution would be superfluous." He offered several examples:

> [T]he Constitution gives Congress the power to "coin Money," in addition to the power to "regulate the Value thereof." And it gives Congress the power to "raise and support Armies" and to "provide and maintain a Navy," in addition to the power to "make Rules for the Government and Regulation of the land and naval Forces." If the power to regulate the armed forces or the value of money included the power to bring the subject of the regulation into existence, the specific grant of such powers would have been unnecessary. The language of the Constitution reflects the natural understanding that the power to regulate assumes there is already something to be regulated.

Roberts argued that the individual mandate did not regulate "existing commercial activity." Rather, it compelled individuals "to become active in commerce by purchasing a product, on the ground that their failure to do so affects interstate commerce." For the Court to construe the Commerce Clause to allow Congress to regulate individuals "precisely because they are doing nothing would open a new and potentially vast domain to congressional authority" and "would bring countless decisions an individual could potentially make within the scope of federal regulation, and . . . empower Congress to make those decisions for him."

The Court's Commandeering Jurisprudence

Although the Court has attempted, for the most part, to protect the original federal design primarily through its use of dual-federalism principles or its narrow construction of the

Commerce Clause, as of late it has also begun to protect it by declaring that Congress lacks the power to "commandeer" state officials into carrying out federal programs. In *New York v. United States* (1992), the Court held unconstitutional a key provision of the Low-Level Radioactive Waste Policy Amendments Act of 1985; this required a state that had failed to provide for the disposal of all of its internally generated low-level radioactive waste by a particular date to take title to and possession of that waste and to become liable for all damages suffered by the generator or owner of that waste as a result of the state's failure to take prompt possession. Justice Sandra Day O'Connor, a former state legislator and state-court judge, asserted for a six-member majority that "no matter how powerful the federal interest involved, the Constitution simply does not give Congress the authority to require the States to regulate. The Constitution instead gives Congress the authority to regulate matters directly and to preempt contrary state regulation. Where a federal interest is sufficiently strong to cause Congress to legislate, it must do so directly; it may not conscript state governments as its agents."

Justice Scalia built on Justice O'Connor's opinion in *Printz v. United States* (1997), when he held for the Court that those provisions of the Brady Handgun Violence Prevention Act that commanded state and local law-enforcement officers to conduct background checks on prospective handgun purchasers were unconstitutional. "We held in *New York* that Congress cannot compel the State to enact or enforce a federal regulatory program. Today we hold that Congress cannot circumvent that prohibition by conscripting the State's officers directly." Scalia observed that conscripting state officers to carry out a federal program violated the states' "residuary and inviolable sovereignty." Scalia went further, however; not only did it violate federalism, but it violated the principle of separation of powers as well:

The Constitution does not leave to speculation who is to administer the laws enacted by Congress; the President, it says, "shall take Care that the Laws be faithfully executed," personally and through officers whom he appoints (save for such inferior officers as Congress may authorize to be appointed by the "Courts of Law" or by "the Heads of Departments" who are themselves presidential appointees). The Brady Act effectively transfers this responsibility to thousands of CLEOs [chief law-enforcement officers, e.g., local sheriffs] in the 50 States, who are left to implement the program without meaningful Presidential control (if indeed meaningful Presidential control is possible without the power to appoint and remove). The insistence of the Framers upon unity in the Federal Executive—to insure both vigor and accountability—is well known. That unity would be shattered, and the power of the President would be subject to reduction, if Congress could act as effectively without the President as with him, by simply requiring state officers to execute its laws.

Interestingly, when Scalia made precisely the same separation-of-powers argument in *Morrison v. Olson* (see Chapter 5), he spoke in dissent and for himself alone. By contrast, in *Printz,* by first sugarcoating this argument with a concern for federalism, Scalia was able to speak for a majority.

The Court's State-Sovereign Immunity Jurisprudence

In *Seminole Tribe of Florida v. Florida* (1996), Chief Justice Rehnquist wrote for a five-member majority that Congress lacked power under the Commerce Clause to abrogate state-sovereign immunity protected by the Eleventh Amendment. Just as he declared in *National League of Cities* that the Tenth Amendment limits what Congress can regulate under the Interstate Commerce Clause, so also he declared in *Seminole Tribe* that the Eleventh Amendment limits what Congress can regulate under the Indian Commerce Clause.

In 1988, pursuant to its powers under the Indian Commerce Clause, Congress passed the Indian Gaming Regulatory Act, which allowed Indian tribes to conduct certain gaming activities provided they are in conformity with the terms of a valid compact between the tribe and the state in which the gaming activities are located. Under the act, Congress imposed on states a duty to negotiate in good faith with a tribe toward the formation of a compact and authorized the tribes to sue a state in federal court in order to compel performance of that duty. When the Seminole Tribe sued the State of Florida for its refusal to enter into good-faith negotiations, Florida moved to dismiss the complaint on the ground that congressional authorization of the suit violated its sovereign immunity from suit in federal court. When the district court denied Florida's motion, the United States Court of Appeals for the Eleventh Circuit reversed, concluding that, under the Eleventh Amendment, the federal courts had no jurisdiction. The Supreme Court agreed.

Rehnquist's majority opinion had to overcome a major textual problem: by its terms, the Eleventh Amendment simply does not bar the kind of suit brought by the Seminole Tribe. It reads as follows: "The Judicial power of the United States shall not be construed to extend to any suit in law or equity, commenced or prosecuted against one of the United States by Citizens of another State, or by Citizens or Subjects of any Foreign State." The members of the Seminole Tribe were not "Citizens of another State, or . . . Citizens or Subjects of any Foreign State" bringing suit under the federal court's state-citizen diversity jurisdiction (granted by Article III in the original Constitution but then subsequently repealed by the Eleventh Amendment); rather, they were bringing suit under the federal court's federal-question (also known as "subject matter" or "arising under") jurisdiction (granted by Article III and left untouched by the Eleventh Amendment).

Although the words of the Eleventh Amendment did not bar the suit filed by the Seminole Tribe, Rehnquist nevertheless proclaimed that a "blind reliance upon the text of the Eleventh Amendment" would be "overly exacting" and would result in a "construction never imagined or dreamed of." The Eleventh Amendment, he insisted, stands "not so much for what it says, as for the presupposition . . . which it confirms." That presupposition, he continued, has two parts: "first, that each State is a sovereign entity in our federal system; and second, that 'it is inherent in the nature of sovereignty not to be amenable to suit without its consent.'"

The Eleventh Amendment was, Rehnquist pointed out, a reaction to "the now-discredited decision in *Chisholm v. Georgia*" (1793) in which the Supreme Court had held that a state could be sued by a citizen of another state or by an alien. The Eleventh Amendment reversed that decision, and, as Rehnquist emphasized, it "dealt in terms only with the problem presented" by *Chisholm*. Because the federal courts in 1793 did not have federal-question jurisdiction and, in fact, would not have it until 1875, Rehnquist concluded that the authors of the Eleventh Amendment did not see a threat to the principle of state-sovereign immunity coming from that quarter but rather only from suits brought under the federal court's diversity jurisdiction and, therefore, barred only those suits. The goal of these drafters, Rehnquist implied, was to protect the principle of state-sovereign immunity from any threat; their means—in retrospective less comprehensive than they should have been—was to bar suits under the federal court's diversity jurisdiction.

In the lead dissent, Justice David Souter argued that *Chisholm* settled the question of whether the states could be sued not only under the federal court's citizen-state diversity jurisdiction but also, "by implication," under their federal-question jurisdiction. "The constitutional text on federal-question jurisdiction, after all, was just as devoid of immunity language as it was on citizen-state diversity." Yet, he pointed out, the Congress drafted the Eleventh Amendment to protect the states only from suits brought against them under the federal courts' diversity jurisdiction. As he went on to say: "If the Framers had meant the Amendment to bar federal-question suits as well, they could not only have made their intention clearer very easily, but could simply have adopted the first post-*Chisholm* proposal adopted by Theodore Sedgwick of Massachusetts on instructions from the Legislature of that Commonwealth." That proposal would have covered expressly what Rehnquist contended the Eleventh Amendment was intended to convey: "No state shall be liable to be made a party defendant, in any of the judicial courts, established, or which shall be established under the authority of the United States, at the suit of any person or persons, whether a citizen or citizens, or a foreigner or foreigners, or any body politic or corporate, whether within or without the United States."

On a single day at the end of its 1998–1999 term, the Court built on *Seminole Tribe* and handed down three separate state-sovereign immunity decisions; it struck down the 1992 amendments to the Patent Remedy Act expressly abrogating state-sovereign immunity in patent cases in *Florida Prepaid Postsecondary Education Expense Board v. College Savings Bank* (1999), the Trademark Remedy Clarification Act of 1992 (TRCA) subjecting states to suit under the Trademark Act of 1946 in *College Savings Bank v. Florida Prepaid Postsecondary Education Expense Board* (1999), and the 1974 amendments to the Fair Labor Standards Act authorizing private actions against the states in their own courts without their consent in *Alden v. Maine* (1999). Each of these cases was decided by the same 5–4 vote, with Chief Justice Rehnquist and Justices Kennedy, O'Connor, Scalia, and Thomas in the majority and Justices Breyer, Ginsburg, Souter, and Stevens in dissent.

In *Florida Prepaid Postsecondary Education Expense Board v. College Savings Bank,* the Court invalidated the Patent Remedy Act of 1992 that expressly abrogated state-sovereign immunity from claims of patent infringement. In the opinion for the Court, Chief Justice Rehnquist rehearsed the three basic conclusions of his *Seminole Tribe* opinion: the Eleventh Amendment stands "not so much for what it says, but for the presupposition . . . which it confirms"; that presupposition precludes suits against a state in federal court under not only diversity but also federal-question jurisdiction unless the state expressly consents to suit or unless Congress expressly abrogates state-sovereign immunity; and Congress has no power to abrogate sovereign immunity under Article I of the Constitution (which was trumped by the Eleventh Amendment) but has power to do so only under Section 5 of the Fourteenth Amendment (which, in turn, trumps the Eleventh Amendment). To the conclusions of *Seminole Tribe,* Rehnquist then added the Court's conclusion of *City of Boerne v. Flores* (1997): Congress's enforcement power under Section 5 is merely "'remedial' in nature."

Rehnquist then asked whether the Patent Remedy Act could be "viewed as remedial or preventive legislation aimed at securing the protections of the Fourteenth Amendment for patent owners." He answered in the negative. The legislative record leading to the passage of the Patent Remedy Act established "no pattern of patent infringement by the States, let alone a pattern of constitutional violations." In fact, he continued, "the evidence before Congress suggested that most state infringement was innocent or at worst negligent" and did not rise to the level of a violation of the Due Process Clause. Consequently, the act was "so out of proportion to the supposed remedial or preventive object" that it could not be understood as "designed to prevent unconstitutional behavior." Accordingly, it could not be sustained under Section 5.

In *College Savings Bank v. Florida Prepaid Postsecondary Education Expense Board,* the Court invalidated the Trademark Remedy Clarification Act of 1992, which subjected states to suits brought under the Trademark Act of 1946 for false and misleading advertising. In his opinion for the Court, Justice Scalia held that Congress lacked the power under Section 5 to pass the TRCA to remedy and prevent state deprivations of property without due process. There simply is no property right, he insisted, to be free from a "competitor's false advertising about its own product"; there was, therefore, no constitutional violation for

Congress to remedy and, hence, no power under Section 5 for Congress to abrogate state-sovereign immunity.

Of these three cases, perhaps the most significant was *Alden v. Maine.* In *Alden,* a group of probation officers filed suit in 1992 in the United States District Court for the District of Maine against their employer, the State of Maine, for its failure to abide by the overtime provisions of the Fair Labor Standards Act of 1938, made applicable by Congress to the states in 1974 and upheld as constitutional by the Supreme Court in *Garcia v. San Antonio Metropolitan Transit Authority* in 1985. Their suit was still pending when the Supreme Court held in *Seminole Tribe* that Congress lacked power under Article I of the Constitution to abrogate state-sovereign immunity from suits in the federal courts. In light of *Seminole Tribe,* the district court dismissed their action, and the Court of Appeals for the First Circuit affirmed. The probation officers then filed the same action in state court, where the state trial court dismissed the suit on the basis of sovereign immunity, and the Maine Supreme Judicial Court affirmed. The United States Supreme Court granted certiorari in order to address the question of the constitutionality of the provisions of the Fair Labor Standards Act authorizing private actions against states in their own courts without their consent.

In the majority opinion, Justice Anthony Kennedy admitted that there is no such thing as "Eleventh Amendment immunity." That phrase, he conceded, "is a convenient shorthand but something of a misnomer, for the sovereign immunity of the States neither derives from nor is limited by the terms of the Eleventh Amendment." Rather, "the States' immunity from suit is a fundamental aspect of the sovereignty which the States enjoyed before the ratification of the Constitution" and which was "confirm[ed]" by the Tenth Amendment. The States, he continued, retain this immunity "today (either literally or by virtue of their admission into the Union upon an equal footing with the other States) except as altered by the plan of the Convention or certain constitutional amendments."

Justice Kennedy observed that the question of whether Congress has authority under Article I to abrogate a state's immunity from suit in its own courts was "a question of first impression" for which "the historical record gives no instruction as to the founding generation's intent." He asserted, however, that "the founders' silence is best explained by the simple fact that no one, not even the Constitution's most ardent opponents, suggested the document might strip the States of the immunity." He went so far as to declare that "it is difficult to conceive that the Constitution would have been adopted if it had been understood to strip the States of immunity from suit in their own courts." Kennedy offered another reason Congress could not abrogate a state's immunity from suit in its own courts: as a consequence of the Court's decisions in *Seminole Tribe* and the two *Florida Prepaid* cases, "Congress cannot abrogate the States' sovereign immunity in federal court; were the rule to be different here, the National Government would wield greater power in the state courts than in its own judicial instrumentalities."

Justice Souter wrote the dissent, insisting that the Supremacy Clause, "which requires state courts to enforce federal law and state-court judges to be bound by it, requires the Maine courts to entertain this federal cause of action." The Court in *Garcia* had declared the Fair Labor Standards Act and its subsequent amendments to be constitutional, that is, to be "made in pursuance" of the Constitution. The act was therefore "the supreme law of the land," and, according to the Supremacy Clause, it thereby bound the judges in every state, "any thing in the Constitution or laws of any state to the contrary notwithstanding." For Souter, state-court judges were therefore bound by *Garcia* and by the clear textual language of the Supremacy Clause, not by the nontextual claims of state-sovereign immunity.

In *Kimel v. Florida Board of Regents* (2000), the Supreme Court continued along the path it had laid out in *City of Boerne* and the two *Florida Prepaid* cases by holding that

Congress exceeded its authority under Section 5 of the Fourteenth Amendment when it amended the Age Discrimination in Employment Act of 1967 (ADEA) to abrogate state-sovereign immunity for suits charging states with discrimination because of an individual's age. Arguing that an ADEA suit against a state could be maintained only if the act were "appropriate legislation" under Section 5 of the Fourteenth Amendment, and relying on *City of Boerne*'s insistence that Section 5 gave Congress only the power to prevent or remedy violations of the Fourteenth Amendment but not to define its substance, and on the language of *City of Boerne* that "there must be a congruence and proportionality between the injury to be prevented or remedied and the means adopted to that end," Justice O'Connor concluded for the majority that the ADEA was not "appropriate legislation." To begin with, she noted that age classifications that are rationally related to a legitimate state interest do not violate the Equal Protection Clause of the Fourteenth Amendment. Furthermore, Congress never identified any pattern of age discrimination by the states that would justify Congress in using its Section 5 enforcement powers to prevent or remedy such conduct. "In light of the indiscriminate scope of the Act's substantive requirements, and the lack of evidence of widespread and unconstitutional age discrimination by the States, we hold that the ADEA is not a valid exercise of Congress's power under Section 5 of the Fourteenth Amendment. The ADEA's proposed abrogation of the States' sovereign immunity is accordingly invalid."

Finally, in 2001, in *Board of Trustees of Univ. of Alabama v. Garrett,* the Supreme Court held, again by a vote of 5–4, that Congress, when it passed the Americans with Disabilities Act of 1990, lacked the authority under Section 5 of the Fourteenth Amendment to abrogate state-sovereign immunity and to allow state employees to recover monetary damages by reason of the state's failure to comply with the act's provisions. Justice Stephen Breyer dissented from Chief Justice Rehnquist's majority opinion, insisting that there was "no reason to require Congress, seeking to determine facts relevant to the exercise of its Section 5 authority, to adopt rules or presumptions that reflect a court's institutional limitations." He drew several clear distinctions between courts and the Congress:

> Unlike courts, Congress can gather facts from across the Nation, assess the magnitude of a problem, and more easily find an appropriate remedy. Unlike courts, Congress directly reflects public attitudes and beliefs, enabling Congress better to understand where, and to what extent, refusals to accommodate a disability amount to behavior that is callous and unreasonable to the point of lacking constitutional justification. Unlike judges, Members of Congress can directly obtain information from constituents who have first-hand experience with discrimination and related issues. Moreover, unlike judges, Members of Congress are elected. . . . To apply a rule designed to restrict courts as if it restricted Congress' legislative power is to stand the underlying principle—a principle of judicial restraint—on its head.

Federal Maritime Commission v. South Carolina State Ports Authority (2002) is perhaps the Court's most extraordinary attempt to protect nonconsenting states from legal actions against them, going far beyond *Seminole Tribe* or *Alden*. In *Seminole Tribe,* the Court departed from the text of the Eleventh Amendment when it held that its "presupposition" barred suits against the states without their consent—not only under the federal courts' state-citizen diversity jurisdiction, but also under their subject-matter jurisdiction. In *Alden,* it departed further still from the text by holding that this "presupposition" barred Congress from authorizing suits against nonconsenting states not only in federal courts but in state courts as well. In *Federal Maritime Commission,* it abandoned the text altogether, holding that this same "presupposition" barred actions against nonconsenting states not only in courts generally but even in federal regulatory agencies.

A cruise ship operator filed a complaint with the Federal Maritime Commission (FMC), alleging that South Carolina's ports authority had violated the Shipping Act of 1984 by denying the operator permission to berth ships at a particular port. When an administrative-law judge dismissed the complaint on the basis that the ports authority, as an arm of the state, was entitled to sovereign immunity from suits by private parties, litigation was set in motion that ultimately reached the Supreme Court. Justice Thomas held for the same five-member majority present in all the state-sovereign immunity cases that "the Eleventh Amendment does not define the scope of the States' sovereign immunity"; rather, "it is but one particular exemplification of that immunity." Declaring that "the preeminent purpose of state-sovereign immunity is to accord States the dignity that is consistent with their status as sovereign entities," and noting the "remarkably strong resemblance" of an FMC administrative proceeding to civil litigation in federal courts (it "walks, talks, and squawks very much like a lawsuit"), he held that

> state sovereign immunity bars the FMC from adjudicating complaints filed by a private party against a nonconsenting State. Simply put, if the Framers thought it an impermissible affront to a State's dignity to be required to answer the complaints of private parties in federal courts, we cannot imagine that they would have found it acceptable to compel a State to do exactly the same thing before the administrative tribunal of an agency, such as the FMC. The affront to a State's dignity does not lessen when an adjudication takes place in an administrative tribunal as opposed to an Article III court. In both instances, a State is required to defend itself in an adversarial proceeding against a private party before an impartial federal officer.

Justice Breyer wrote the lead dissent. He began by observing that "the Court holds that a private person cannot bring a complaint against a State to a federal administrative agency where the agency (1) will use an internal adjudicative process to decide if the complaint is well founded, and (2) if so, proceed to court to enforce the law." He then inquired: "Where does the Constitution contain the principle of law that the Court enunciates? I cannot find the answer to this question in any text, in any tradition, or in any relevant purpose." He found the lack of a textual basis especially troubling. "The Court's principle lacks any firm anchor in the Constitution's text. The Eleventh Amendment cannot help. It says: 'The *Judicial* power of the United States shall not . . . extend to any suit . . . commenced or prosecuted against one of the . . . States by Citizens of another State.' (Emphasis added.)" Federal administrative agencies, however, "do not exercise the 'judicial power of the United States.' Of course, this Court has read the words 'Citizens of another State' as if they also said 'citizen of the same State.' But it has never said that the words 'judicial power of the United States' mean 'the executive power of the United States.' Nor should it."

Interestingly, however, since its decision in *South Carolina State Ports Authority,* the Court suddenly became much more deferential to congressional abrogation of state-sovereign immunity, as *Nevada Department of Human Resources v. Hibbs* (2003) and *Tennessee v. Lane* (2004) make clear. In *Hibbs,* the Court held that state employees could sue their employers in federal court for violation of the family-care leave provisions of the Family and Medical Leave Act (FMLA) because Congress had validly exercised its Section 5 enforcement powers under the Fourteenth Amendment to abrogate the states' Eleventh Amendment immunity to such suits.

Chief Justice Rehnquist held for a six-member majority that Congress had established a history of significant gender discrimination by the states that FMLA was targeted to prevent. "Stereotypes about women's domestic roles are reinforced by parallel stereotypes presuming a lack of domestic responsibilities for men. Because employers continued to regard the family as the woman's domain, they often denied men similar accommodations or discouraged them from taking leave. These mutually reinforcing stereotypes created a self-fulfilling cycle of discrimination that forced women to continue to assume the role of primary family caregiver, and fostered employers' stereotypical views about women's commitment to work and their value as employees." Those perceptions, Rehnquist continued, "lead to subtle discrimination that may be difficult to detect on a case-by-case basis." Congress's chosen remedy, the family-care leave provision of the FMLA, was therefore "congruent and proportional to the targeted violation." By creating an across-the-board, routine employment benefit for all eligible employees, Congress ensured that "family-care leave would no longer be stigmatized as an inordinate drain on the workplace caused by female employees, and that employers could not evade leave obligations simply by hiring men." Rehnquist concluded: "By setting a minimum standard of family leave for *all* eligible employees, irrespective of gender, the FMLA attacks the formerly state-sanctioned stereotype that only women are responsible for family caregiving, thereby reducing employers' incentives to engage in discrimination by basing hiring and promotion decisions on stereotypes."

Then, in *Tennessee v. Lane,* Justice Stevens held for a five-member majority that Title II of the Americans with Disabilities Act—guaranteeing, among other things, the right of disabled persons to physical access to state courts and authorizing them to file suits in federal court for money damages when the right is violated—was a valid exercise of Congress's enforcement authority under Section 5 of the Fourteenth Amendment. He applied the *City of Boerne* "congruence and proportionality" test and concluded that "judged against this backdrop, Title II's affirmative obligation to accommodate persons with disabilities in the administration of justice cannot be said to be 'so out of proportion to a supposed remedial or preventive object that it cannot be understood as responsive to, or designed to prevent, unconstitutional behavior.' It is, rather, a reasonable prophylactic measure, reasonably targeted to a legitimate end." Justice Scalia dissented and in so doing, rejected the congruence and proportionality test he had initially accepted:

> I joined the Court's opinion in *Boerne* with some misgiving. I have generally rejected tests based on such malleable standards as "proportionality," because they have a way of turning into vehicles for the implementation of individual judges' policy preferences. Even so, I signed on to the "congruence and proportionality" test in *Boerne,* and adhered to it in [a number of] later cases. . . . I yield to the lessons of experience. The "congruence and proportionality" standard, like all such flabby tests, is a standing invitation to judicial arbitrariness and policy-driven decisionmaking. Worse still, it casts this Court in the role of Congress's taskmaster. Under it, the courts (and ultimately this Court) must regularly check Congress's homework to make sure that it has identified sufficient constitutional violations to make its remedy congruent and proportional. As a general matter, we are ill advised to adopt or adhere to constitutional rules that bring us into constant conflict with a coequal branch of Government. And when conflict is unavoidable, we should not come to do battle with the United States Congress armed only with a test ("congruence and proportionality") that has no demonstrable basis in the text of the Constitution and cannot objectively be shown to have been met or failed. . . .
>
> I would replace "congruence and proportionality" with another test—one that provides a clear, enforceable limitation supported by the text of §5. Section 5 grants Congress the power "to *enforce,* by appropriate legislation," the other provisions of the Fourteenth Amendment. . . . [O]ne does not "enforce" the right of access to the

courts at issue in this case by requiring that disabled persons be provided access to *all* of the "services, programs, or activities" furnished or conducted by the State. That is simply not what the power to enforce means. . . . Nothing in §5 allows Congress to go *beyond* the provisions of the Fourteenth Amendment to proscribe, prevent, or "remedy" conduct that does not *itself* violate any provision of the Fourteenth Amendment. . . . When congressional regulation . . . goes beyond enforcement to prophylaxis, I shall consider it ultra vires. The present legislation is plainly of the latter sort.

THE POST–CIVIL WAR AMENDMENTS AND THE SHIFTING OF THE FEDERAL BALANCE

With the exception of state-sovereign immunity, the discussion thus far has been confined to the relationship between the national and state governments that was originally established by the Constitution, into which the Framers incorporated a balance of national and federal elements. Now we must consider the extent to which the mixed nature of the constitutional system has been altered by the Civil War amendments and the statutes flowing from them.

At a minimum, the Thirteenth, Fourteenth, and Fifteenth Amendments were intended to safeguard the civil rights of the recently emancipated slaves. Although the protection of such civil rights previously had been among the broad mass of police powers reserved to the states, the last section of each of these amendments gave Congress the "power to enforce" them "by appropriate legislation." Pursuant to these grants of power, Congress passed the Civil Rights Acts of 1866 (which protected the rights of blacks to move about freely, own property, have access to the courts, and make and enforce contracts, and which prohibited any person acting under color of state law from depriving any citizen of rights secured by the Constitution or federal law), of 1870 (which protected voting rights), of 1871 (which created a cause of civil action for deprivations, under color of state law, of secured rights), and of 1875 (which secured for blacks the "full and equal enjoyment" of public accommodations). The pressures generated by the racial problems that these and subsequent civil rights acts were intended to address, together with the catalytic presence of the Civil War amendments themselves, have helped to break down the compound nature of the government and to give primacy to its national elements. The rate at which this process has taken place, however, has been largely determined by Supreme Court decisions interpreting the Thirteenth, Fourteenth, and Fifteenth Amendments and the acts passed pursuant thereto.

Initially, the Court construed these constitutional and statutory provisions narrowly, in order to preserve the federal balance. In 1873, for example, it held in the *Slaughter-House Cases*—found in Chapter 12—that the "privileges and immunities of citizens of the United States" protected from state abridgement by Section 1 of the Fourteenth Amendment were few in number and limited to such rights as access to the nation's seaports and the privilege of habeas corpus writs. That left the vast majority of legal rights and relations under the protection of the state governments. In reaching this decision, the Court majority pronounced itself reluctant to "fetter and degrade the State governments by subjecting them to the control of Congress, in the exercise of powers heretofore universally conceded to them of the most ordinary and fundamental character" and to change "the whole theory of the relations of the State and Federal governments to each other and of both these governments to the people . . . in the absence of language which expresses such a purpose too clearly to admit of doubt." This led Justice Stephen B. Field to file a furious dissent; he insisted that the purpose of the Fourteenth Amendment was exactly that—to shift decisively the federal-state balance by giving vast new powers to the national government at the expense of the states. The Fourteenth Amendment, he insisted,

> recognizes in express terms . . . citizens of the United States, and it makes their citizenship dependent upon the place of their birth, or the fact of their adoption, and not upon the constitution or laws of any State or the condition of their ancestry. A citizen of a State is now only a citizen of the United States residing in that State. The fundamental rights, privileges, and immunities which belong to him as a free man and a free citizen, now belong to him as a citizen of the United States, and are not dependent upon his citizenship of any State. . . . The amendment does not attempt to confer any new privileges or immunities upon citizens, or to enumerate or define those already existing. It assumes that there are such privileges and immunities which belong of right to citizens as such, and ordains that they shall not be abridged by State legislation. If this [amendment] has no reference to privileges and immunities of this character, but only refers, as held by the majority of the court in their opinion, to such privileges and immunities as were before its adoption specially designated in the Constitution or necessarily implied as belonging to citizens of the United States, it was a vain and idle enactment, which accomplished nothing, and most unnecessarily excited Congress and the people on its passage. . . . But if the amendment refers to the natural and inalienable rights which belong to all citizens, the inhibition has a profound significance and consequence.

The Court repeated the narrow view expressed by the majority in the *Slaughter-House Cases* in the *Civil Rights Cases* (1883), where it held that the public accommodations provisions of the Civil Rights Act of 1875 were unconstitutional. Noting that the Fourteenth Amendment reads "no *state* shall . . . ," it declared that the amendment prohibited only state actions of certain types, not "individual invasion of individual rights." Legislation that attempted to prohibit such purely private discrimination, therefore, was beyond the constitutional powers of Congress to enact. Justice John Marshall Harlan strenuously dissented; he argued that Congress has power under Sections 1 and 5 of the Fourteenth Amendment to protect the civil rights of citizens of the United States. Section 1 begins by declaring that "all persons born or naturalized in the United States, and subject to the jurisdiction thereof, are citizens of the United States, and of the State wherein they reside." These words, Harlan observed, made "the colored race . . . , instantly, citizens of the United States, and of their respective States." And that citizenship "may be protected" by Section 5. "Congress is not restricted to the enforcement of prohibitions upon State laws or State action." Rather, it is free to enforce "all of the provisions—affirmative and prohibitive—of the amendment." Harlan insisted it was "a grave misconception to suppose" that Section 5 "has reference exclusively to express prohibitions upon State laws or State action." Quite the contrary, he argued, Section 5 "authorizes Congress, by means of legislation, operating throughout the entire Union, to guard, secure, and protect" any right created by the Fourteenth Amendment. He denied that his construction "in any degree intrench[es] upon the just rights of the States in the control of their domestic affairs. It simply recognizes the enlarged powers conferred by the recent amendments upon the general government."

Although the state-action doctrine promulgated in the *Civil Rights Cases* (see Chapter 8 of Volume II for a detailed discussion) has sharply limited the ability of Congress to enter the domain of the states' police power and to use its Section 5 enforcement powers to protect the civil rights of American citizens, it has not, however, precluded the national government from intervening when the states themselves have violated constitutionally protected rights. To take perhaps the most famous example, the doctrine did not prevent the Supreme Court from declaring in *Brown v. Board of Education* (1954) that the defendant states were guilty of violating the Equal Protection Clause of the Fourteenth Amendment by requiring that schools be racially segregated. Nor has the theory of state action prevented federal prosecution of state officials and others who, while acting under color of state law, have deprived citizens of their constitutionally protected rights. Nonetheless, the state-action doctrine historically has sharply limited the ability of the national government to enter the domain of the states' police power and, to that extent, has helped to preserve the compound quality of the Constitution.

In recent decades, the state-action doctrine has increasingly been sidestepped altogether by those who seek to expand the power of the national government to protect the civil rights of the citizenry. Of decisive importance in this respect is *Jones v. Alfred H. Mayer Company* (1968), in which the Court held that the national government has the power to regulate purely private-property transactions where racial discrimination is present. In his majority opinion, Justice Potter Stewart exhumed the Civil Rights Act of 1866 and held that it "bars all racial discrimination, private as well as public, in the sale or rental of property, and that the statute, thus construed, is a valid exercise of the power of Congress to enforce the Thirteenth Amendment." Making many of the same arguments found in Justice Harlan's dissent in the *Civil Rights Cases,* Stewart insisted that the Thirteenth Amendment authorized Congress not only to dissolve the legal bonds by which slaves had been held to their masters, but also to determine rationally what the badges and the incidents of slavery are and to translate that determination into effective legislation.

Jones was followed by *Griffin v. Breckenridge* (1971) and *Runyon v. McCrary* (1976), in both of which the Court avoided the state-action doctrine and relied on the Thirteenth Amendment to justify congressional bars to wholly private discrimination. In *Griffin,* a unanimous Court, reversing its decision in *Collins v. Handyman* (1951), held that those sections of the Civil Rights Acts of 1866 and 1871 that granted civil remedies against racially motivated conspiracies to deprive individuals of their civil rights were applicable even to wholly private conspiracies. Speaking for the Court, Justice Stewart concluded that "Congress was wholly within its power under Section 2 of the Thirteenth Amendment in creating a statutory cause of action for Negro citizens who have been the victims of conspiratorial, racially discriminatory private action aimed at depriving them of the basic rights that the law secures to all free men." Employing the same arguments, Stewart held in *Runyon* that the section of the Civil Rights Act of 1866 forbidding discrimination in the making and enforcing of contracts prohibits private schools from excluding qualified students solely on the basis of race. In this particular case, blacks had been denied the opportunity to enter into a contract for the provision of educational services in return for the payment of tuition. This, in Justice Stewart's estimation, constituted a "class violation" of the law in question.

Jones and the Court's subsequent decisions make clear how profoundly the Framers' original understanding of federalism was altered by the post–Civil War amendments—so, too, do other Supreme Court decisions, including those incorporating the Bill of Rights into the Fourteenth Amendment so that they apply to the states and those holding that national law preempts state law if considerations of national policy so warrant and if these considerations are consistent with either enumerated powers or broader national security interests. What Madison declared in *The Federalist,* No. 39—that the Constitution is "neither wholly federal, nor wholly national" but "a composition of both"—cannot be asserted in the same way after the ratification of the post–Civil War amendments, for they simply made the Constitution much more national in character.

Subsequent amendments have done likewise; two deserve special mention. The ratification of the Sixteenth Amendment, authorizing a federal income tax, gave Congress access to revenues it has used to influence states to behave in a manner consistent with its wishes (see, for example, *South Dakota v. Dole* in Chapter 8). And the ratification of the Seventeenth Amendment, replacing the election of the Senate by state legislatures with direct election by the people, removed one of the principal structural devices the Framers employed to protect the interests of states as states[28] and made the "residuary and inviolable sovereignty" of the states dependent on congressional discretion or whether an occasional Court majority can be mustered on its behalf (as in *Printz*) or both. By constitutional amendment and judicial construction of those amendments, federalism, one of the principal means employed by the Framers to achieve the ends of the Constitution, has been enfeebled; the result is that we have become more reliant on the two remaining means of separation of powers and the multiplicity of interests present in the extended republic.

NOTES

1. See Martin Diamond, "*The Federalist* on Federalism: 'Neither a National nor a Federal Constitution, but a Composition of Both,'" *Yale Law Journal* 86, no. 6 (1977): 1273–1285.

2. James Madison, "Outline," in *The Writings of James Madison,* edited by Gaillard Hunt, 9 vols. (New York: G. P. Putnam's Sons, 1910), 9:351.

3. The discussion that follows relies heavily on Martin Diamond, "What the Framers Meant by Federalism," in *A Nation of States,* edited by Robert A. Goldwin, 2nd ed. (Chicago: Rand McNally, 1974), 25–42.

4. See Martin Diamond, "The Ends of Federalism," *Publius* 3, no. 2 (1973): 131–132.

5. Herbert J. Storing, foreword to *The Philosophy of the American Constitution,* by Paul Eidelberg (New York: Free Press, 1968).

6. Max Farrand, ed., *The Records of the Federal Convention of 1787,* 4 vols. (New Haven, CT: Yale University Press, 1937), 1:33 (emphasis in the original).

7. Ibid., 134–136.

8. Ibid., 461.

9. Ibid., 339, 405–406.

10. Ibid., 488.

11. Alexis de Tocqueville, *Democracy in America,* edited by Phillips Bradley, 2 vols. (New York: Random House, 1945), 1:165.

12. David P. Currie, *The Constitution in Congress: The Federalist Period, 1789–1801* (Chicago: University of Chicago Press, 1997), 3.

13. Ibid., 4.

14. Ibid., 5.

15. Fisher Ames, *Works of Fisher Ames,* edited by W. B. Allen, 2 vols. (Indianapolis: Liberty Fund, 1983), 2:877.

16. John Frank, "Historical Bases of the Federal Judicial System," *Law and Contemporary Problems* 13 (1948): 3, 9. Congress recognized that admiralty jurisdiction had international ramifications and that uncontrolled state admiralty courts hearing prize disputes had already generated interstate and international resentment.

17. Henry J. Bourguignon, "The Federal Key to the Judiciary Act of 1789," *South Carolina Law Review* 46 (1995): 688.

18. Maeva Marcus et al., eds., *Documentary History of the Supreme Court of the United States, 1789–1800: Organizing the Federal Judiciary; Legislation and Commentaries,* 8 vols. (New York: Columbia University Press, 1992), 4:395–396. This prompted one writer to remark, "Clearly the Virginians had been hoist by their own petard." Julius Goebel Jr., *The Oliver Wendell Holmes Devise History of the Supreme Court of the United States,* vol. 1, *Antecedents and Beginnings to 1801* (New York: Macmillan, 1971), 462.

19. Farrand, *Records,* 1:284–285.

20. Charles L. Black Jr., *Structure and Relationship in Constitutional Law* (Baton Rouge: Louisiana State University Press, 1969), 7.

21. In *Bailey v. Drexel Furniture Company* (1922), the Court relied on *Hammer* to invalidate the Child Labor Tax Law of 1919, which imposed a 10 percent tax on the annual net profits of manufacturers that employed children under the age of sixteen. Chief Justice Taft wrote: "In the act before us, the presumption of validity cannot prevail, because the proof of the contrary is found on the very fact of its provisions. Grant the validity of this law, and all that Congress would need do thereafter, in seeking to take over to its control any one of the great number of subjects . . . the states have never parted with, and which are reserved to them by the Tenth Amendment, would be to enact a detailed measure

of complete regulation of the subject and enforce it by a so-called tax upon departures from it."

22. C. Herman Pritchett, *The American Constitution,* 3rd ed. (New York: McGraw-Hill, 1977), 50–51.

23. See *United States v. Darby Lumber Company* (1941). The defenders of economic due process suffered a similar fate. See Robert G. McCloskey, "Economic Due Process: An Exhumation and Reburial," in *1962 Supreme Court Review,* edited by Philip B. Kurland (Chicago: University of Chicago Press, 1963), 42–43.

24. See Stephen Gardbaum, "New Deal Constitutionalism and the Unshackling of the States," *University of Chicago Law Review* 64 (Spring 1997): 483–567.

25. The Court did not officially repudiate the use of the principle of dual federalism in interpreting the Commerce Clause until *United States v. Darby Lumber Co.* (1941), when it explicitly overturned *Hammer v. Dagenhart.*

26. In the *Carter Coal* case, Justice Sutherland wrote: "The word 'commerce' is the equivalent of the phrase 'intercourse for the purposes of trade.' Plainly, the incidents leading up to and culminating in the mining of coal do not constitute such intercourse. The employment of men, the fixing of their wages, hours of labor and working conditions, the bargaining in respect of these things—whether carried on separately or collectively—each and all constitute intercourse for the purposes of production, not of trade. The latter is a thing apart from the relation of employer and employee, which, in all producing occupations, is purely local in character. Extraction of coal from the mine is the aim and the completed result of local activities. Commerce in the coal mined is not brought into being by force of these activities, but by negotiations, agreements, and circumstances entirely apart from production. Mining brings the subject matter of commerce into existence. Commerce disposes of it."

27. Although the Court in *National League of Cities v. Usery* (1976) invalidated Congress's 1974 amendments to the Fair Labor Standards Act, which applied the act's minimum-wage and maximum-hours provisions to state governments and their political subdivisions, its argument was not that Congress had exceeded its powers under the Commerce Clause to pass these amendments, but rather that its otherwise valid use of the Commerce Clause had run afoul of the Tenth Amendment, which prohibits Congress from exercising its Commerce Clause power "in a fashion that impairs the States' integrity or their ability to function effectively in a federal system." In any case, *National League of Cities* was expressly overruled just nine years later in *Garcia v. San Antonio Metropolitan Transit Authority* (1985).

28. See Ralph A. Rossum, *Federalism, the Supreme Court, and the Seventeenth Amendment: The Irony of Constitutional Democracy* (Lanham, MD: Lexington Books, 2001).

SELECTED READINGS

The Federalist, Nos. 15, 16, 17, 18, 21, 22, 39.

Amar, Akhil. *The Law of the Land: A Grand Tour of our Constitutional Republic.* New York: Basic Books, 2015.

Banks, Christopher P. and John C. Blakeman. *The U.S. Supreme Court and New Federalism: From the Rehnquist to the Roberts Courts.* Lanham, MD: Rowman and Littlefield, 2012.

Berger, Raoul. *Federalism: The Founders' Design.* Norman: University of Oklahoma Press, 1987.

Bourguignon, Henry J. "The Federal Key to the Judiciary Act of 1789." *South Carolina Law Review* 46 (1995): 647–702.

Choper, Jesse H. *Judicial Review and the National Political Process: A Functional Reconsideration of the Role of the Supreme Court.* Chicago: University of Chicago Press, 1980.

Corwin, Edward S. "The Passing of Dual Federalism." *Virginia Law Review* 36 (February 1950): 1–24.

Diamond, Martin. "*The Federalist* on Federalism." *Yale Law Journal* 86 (May 1977): 1273–1285.

Greve, Michael S. *Federalism and the Constitution: Competition v. Cartels.* Fairfax, VA: Mercatus Center, 2015

_____. *The Upside-Down Constitution.* Cambridge, MA: Harvard University Press, 2012.

Hobson, Charles F. "A Nation of States: Federalism in the Framing of the Constitution." In *Our Peculiar Security: The Written Constitution and Limited Government,* edited by Eugene W. Hickok Jr., Gary L. McDowell, and Philip J. Costopoulos. Lanham, MD: Rowman & Littlefield, 1993.

Hoebeke, C. H. *The Road to Mass Democracy: Original Intent and the Seventeenth Amendment.* New Brunswick, NJ: Transaction, 1995.

La Croix, Alison L. *The Ideological Origins of American Federalism.* New York, NY: Cambridge University Press, 2010.

Maltz, Earl M. Dred Scott *and the Politics of Slavery.* Lawrence: University Press of Kansas, 2007.

McConnell, Michael W. "Federalism: Evaluating the Founders' Design." *University of Chicago Law Review* 54 (1987): 1484–1512.

Meltzer, Daniel J. "The *Seminole* Decision and State Sovereign Immunity." In *1996 Supreme Court Review,* edited by Dennis J. Hutchinson, David A. Strauss, and Geoffrey R. Stone. Chicago: University of Chicago Press, 1997.

Nagel, Robert F. *The Implosion of American Federalism.* New York: Oxford University Press, 2001.

Rossum, Ralph A. *Federalism, the Supreme Court, and the Seventeenth Amendment: The Irony of Constitutional Democracy.* Lanham, MD: Lexington Books, 2001.

Vile, M. J. C. *The Structure of American Federalism.* Oxford: Oxford University Press, 1961.

Wechsler, Herbert. "The Political Safeguards of Federalism: The Role of the States in the Composition and Selection of the National Government." In *Federalism: Mature and Emergent,* edited by Arthur W. MacMahon. Garden City, NY: Doubleday, 1955.

Zuckert, Michael P. "Federalism and the Founding: Toward a Reinterpretation of the Constitutional Convention." *Review of Politics* 41 (Spring 1986): 166–210.

The Judiciary Act of 1789
1 Stat. 73 (1789)

On September 24, 1789, Congress passed the Judiciary Act of 1789. Its thirty-five sections took the sketchy provisions of the Constitution's judicial article (Article III) and transformed them into the federal judicial system.

Chap. XX.—*An act to establish the Judicial Courts of the United States.*

Section 1. Be it enacted by the Senate and House of Representatives of the United States of America in Congress assembled, That the supreme court of the United States shall consist of a chief justice and five associate justices, any four of whom shall be a quorum, and shall hold annually at the seat of government two sessions, the one commencing the first Monday of February, and the other the first Monday of August. That the associate justices shall have precedence according to the date of their commissions, or when the commission of two or more of them bear date on the same day, according to their respective ages.

Sec. 2. And be it further enacted, That the United States shall be, and they hereby are divided into thirteen districts, to be limited and called as follows, to wit: one to consist of that part of the State of Massachusetts which lies easterly of the State of New Hampshire, and to be called Maine District; one to consist of the State of New Hampshire, and to be called New Hampshire District; one to consist of the remaining part of the State of Massachusetts, and to be called Massachusetts District; one to consist of the State of Connecticut, and to be called Connecticut District; one to consist of the State of New York, and to be called New York District; one to consist of the State of New Jersey, and to be called New Jersey District; one to consist of the State of Pennsylvania, and to be called Pennsylvania District; one to consist of the State of Delaware, and to be called Delaware District; one to consist of the State of Maryland, and to be called Maryland District; one to consist of the State of Virginia, except that part called the District of Kentucky, and to be called Virginia District; one to consist of the remaining part of the State of Virginia, and to be called Kentucky District; one to consist of the State of South Carolina, and to be called South Carolina District; and one to consist of the State of Georgia, and to be called Georgia District.

Sec. 3. And be it further enacted, That there be a court called a District Court, in each of the aforementioned districts, to consist of one judge, who shall reside in the district for which he is appointed, and shall be called a District Judge, and shall hold annually four sessions. . . .

Sec. 4. And be it further enacted, That the before mentioned districts, except those of Maine and Kentucky, shall be divided into three circuits, and be called the eastern, the middle, and the southern circuit. That the eastern circuit shall consist of the districts of New Hampshire, Massachusetts, Connecticut and New York; that the middle circuit shall consist of the districts of New Jersey, Pennsylvania, Delaware, Maryland and Virginia; and that the southern circuit shall consist of the districts of South Carolina and Georgia, and that there shall be held annually in each district of said circuits, two courts, which shall be called Circuit Courts, and shall consist of any two justices of the Supreme Court, and the district judge of such districts, any two of whom shall constitute a quorum: *Provided,* That no district judge shall give a vote in any case of appeal or error from his own decision; but may assign the reasons of such his decision. . . .

Sec. 7. And be it [further] enacted, That the Supreme Court, and the district courts shall have power to appoint clerks for their respective courts, and that the clerk for each district court shall be clerk also of the circuit court in such district. . . .

Sec. 8. And be it further enacted, That the justices of the Supreme Court, and the district judges, before they proceed to execute the duties of their respective offices, shall take the following oath or affirmation, to wit: "I, A. B., do solemnly swear or affirm, that I will administer justice without respect to persons, and do equal right to the poor and to the rich, and that I will faithfully and impartially discharge and perform all the duties incumbent on me as according to the best of my abilities and understanding, agreeably to the constitution and laws of the United States. So help me God."

Sec. 9. And be it further enacted, That the district courts shall have, exclusively of the courts of the several States, cognizance of all crimes and offences that shall be cognizable under the authority of the United States, committed within their respective districts, or upon the high seas; where no other punishment than whipping, not exceeding thirty stripes, a fine not exceeding one hundred dollars, or a term of imprisonment not exceeding six months, is to be inflicted; and shall also have exclusive original cognizance of all civil causes of admiralty and maritime jurisdiction, including all seizures under laws of impost, navigation or trade of the United States, where the seizures are made, on waters which are navigable from the sea by vessels of ten or more tons burthen, within their respective districts as well as upon the high seas; saving to suitors, in all cases, the right of a common law remedy, where the common law is competent to give it; and shall also have exclusive original cognizance of all seizures on land, or other waters than as aforesaid, made, and of all suits for penalties and forfeitures incurred, under the laws of the United States. And shall also have cognizance, concurrent with the courts of the several States, or the circuit courts, as the case may be, of all causes where an alien sues for a tort only in violation of the law of nations or a treaty of the United States. And shall also have cognizance, concurrent as last mentioned, of all suits at common law where the United States sue, and the matter in dispute amounts, exclusive of costs, to the sum or value of one hundred dollars. And shall also have jurisdiction exclusively of the courts of the several States, of all suits against consuls or vice-consuls, except for offences above the description aforesaid. And the trial of issues in fact, in the district courts, in all causes except civil causes of admiralty and maritime jurisdiction, shall be by jury. . . .

Sec. 11. And be it further enacted, That the circuit courts shall have original cognizance, concurrent with the courts of the several States, of all suits of a civil nature at common law or in equity, where the matter in dispute exceeds, exclusive of costs, the sum or value of five hundred dollars, and the United States are plaintiffs, or petitioner; or an alien is a party, or the suit is between a citizen of the State where the suit is brought, and a citizen of another State. And shall have exclusive cognizance of all crimes and offences cognizable under the authority of the United States, except where this act otherwise provides, or the laws of the United States shall otherwise direct, and concurrent jurisdiction with the district courts of the crimes and offences cognizable therein. . . . And the circuit courts shall also have appellate jurisdiction from the district courts under the regulations and restrictions herein after provided.

Sec. 12. And be it further enacted, That if a suit be commenced in any state court against an alien, or by a citizen of the state in which the suit is brought against a citizen of another state, and the matter in dispute exceeds the aforesaid sum or value of five hundred dollars, exclusive of costs, to be made to appear to the satisfaction of the court; and the defendant shall, at the time of entering his appearance in such state court, file a petition for the removal of the cause for trial into the next circuit court, . . . the cause shall there proceed in the same manner as if it had been brought there by original process. . . .

Sec. 13. And be it further enacted, That the Supreme Court shall have exclusive jurisdiction of all controversies of a civil nature, where a state is a party, except between a state and its citizens; and except also between a state and citizens of other states, or aliens, in which latter case it shall have original but not exclusive jurisdiction. And shall have exclusively all such jurisdiction of suits or proceedings against ambassadors, or other public ministers, or their domestics, or domestic servants, as a court of law can have or exercise consistently with the law of nations; and original, but not exclusive jurisdiction of all suits brought by ambassadors or other public ministers, or in which a consul, or vice-consul, shall be a party. And the trial of issues in fact in the Supreme Court, in all actions at law against citizens of the United States, shall be by jury. The Supreme Court shall also have appellate jurisdiction from the circuit courts and courts of the several states, in the cases herein after specially provided for;

and shall have power to issue writs of prohibition to the district courts, when proceeding as courts of admiralty and maritime jurisdiction, and writs of *mandamus,* in cases warranted by the principles and usages of law, to any courts appointed, or persons holding office, under the authority of the United States.

Sec. 14. And be it further enacted, That all the before-mentioned courts of the United States, shall have power to writs of *scire facias, habeas corpus,* and all other writs not specially provided for by statute, which may be necessary for the exercise of their respective jurisdictions, and agreeable to the principles and usages of law. . . .

Sec. 16. And be it further enacted, That suits in equity shall not be sustained in either of the courts of the United States, in any case where plain, adequate and complete remedy may be had at law. . . .

Sec. 22. And be it further enacted, That final decrees and judgments in civil actions in a district court, where the matter in dispute exceeds the sum or value of fifty dollars, exclusive of costs, may be reexamined, and reversed or affirmed in a circuit court. . . . And upon a like process, may final judgments and decrees in civil actions, and suits in equity in a circuit court, brought there by original process, or removed there from courts of the several States, or removed there by appeal from a district court where the matter in dispute exceeds the sum or value of two thousand dollars, exclusive of costs, be re-examined and reversed or affirmed in the Supreme Court, the citation being in such case signed by a judge of such circuit court, or justice of the Supreme Court, and the adverse party having at least thirty days' notice. . . .

Sec. 25. And be it further enacted, That a final judgment or decree in any suit, in the highest court of law or equity of a State in which a decision in the suit could be had, where is drawn in question the validity of a treaty or statute of, or an authority exercised under the United States, and the decision is against their validity; or where is drawn in question the validity of a statute of, or an authority exercised under any State, on the ground of their being repugnant to the constitution, treaties or laws of the United States, and the decision is in favour of

such their validity, or where is drawn in question the construction of any clause of the constitution or of a treaty, or statute of, or commission held under the United States, and the decision is against the title, right, privilege or exemption specially set up or claimed by either party, under such clause of the said Constitution, treaty, statute or commission, may be reexamined and reversed or affirmed in the Supreme Court of the United States upon a writ of error, the citation being signed by the chief justice, or judge or chancellor of the court rendering or passing the judgment or decree complained of, or by a justice of the Supreme Court of the United States, in the same manner and under the same regulations, and the writ shall have the same effect, as if the judgment or decree complained of had been rendered or passed in a circuit court, and the proceeding upon the reversal shall also be the same, except that the Supreme Court, instead of remanding the cause for a final decision as before provided, may at their discretion, if the cause shall have been once remanded before, proceed to a final decision of the same, and award execution. But no other error shall be assigned or regarded as a ground of reversal in any such case as aforesaid, than such as appears on the face of the record, and immediately respects the before mentioned questions of validity or construction of the said constitution, treaties, statutes, commissions, or authorities in dispute. . . .

Sec. 27. And be it further enacted, That a marshal shall be appointed in and for each district for the term of four years, but shall be removable from office at pleasure, whose duty it shall be to attend the district and circuit courts when sitting therein, and also the Supreme Court in the district in which that court shall sit. . . .

Sec. 29. And be it further enacted, That in cases punishable with death, the trial shall be had in the county where the offence was committed, or where that cannot be done without great inconvenience, twelve petit jurors at least shall be summoned from thence. And jurors in all cases to serve in the courts of the United States shall be designated by lot or otherwise in each State respectively according to the mode of forming juries therein now practised, so far as the laws of the same shall render such designation practicable by the courts or marshals of the United States; and the jurors shall have the same qualifications as are requisite for jurors by the laws of the State of which they are citizens, to serve in the highest courts of law of such State, and shall be returned as there shall be occasion for them, from such parts of the district from time to time as the court shall direct, so as shall be most favourable to an impartial trial, and so as not to incur an unnecessary expense, or unduly to burthen the citizens of any part of the district with such services. . . .

Sec. 34. And be it further enacted, That the laws of the several states, except where the constitution, treaties or statutes of the United States shall otherwise require or provide, shall be regarded as rules of decision in trials at common law in the courts of the United States in cases where they apply.

Cohens v. Virginia
19 U.S. (6 Wheaton) 264 (1821)

In 1802, Congress passed an act authorizing the District of Columbia to conduct lotteries to finance "any important improvements in the City, which the ordinary funds or revenue thereof will not accomplish." Pursuant to this act, the City of Washington passed an ordinance creating a lottery. The State of Virginia had a law that prohibited the sale of lottery tickets except for lotteries authorized by that state. P. J. and M. J. Cohen were arrested for selling the Washington lottery tickets at their office in Norfolk, Virginia. After the Cohens were found guilty in borough court and fined $100, the case went to the US Supreme Court on a writ of error, and the justices unanimously upheld the Cohens' conviction on the grounds that Congress did not authorize the District of Columbia to "force the sale of these lottery tickets in States where such sales may be prohibited by law." Opinion of the Court: <u>Marshall</u>, *Johnson, Livingston, Todd, Duvall, Story. Not participating: Washington.*

THE CHIEF JUSTICE delivered the opinion of the Court.

The questions presented to the Court . . . are of great magnitude, and may be truly said vitally to affect the Union. They exclude the inquiry whether the constitution and laws of the United States have been violated by the judgment which the plaintiffs in error seek to review; and maintain that, admitting such violation, it is not in the power of the government to apply a corrective. They maintain that the nation does not possess a department capable of restraining peaceably, and by authority of law, any attempts which may be made, by a part, against the legitimate powers of the whole; and that the government is reduced to the alternative of submitting to such attempts, or of resisting them by force. They maintain that the constitution of the United States has provided no tribunal for the final construction of itself, or of the laws or treaties of the nation; but that this power may be exercised in the last resort by the Courts of every State in the Union. . . .

If such be the constitution, it is the duty of the Court to bow with respectful submission to its provisions. If such be not the constitution, it is equally the duty of this Court to say so; and to perform that task which the American people have assigned to the judicial department.

1st. The first question to be considered is, whether the jurisdiction of this Court is excluded by the character of the parties, one of them being a State, and the other a citizen of that State?

The second section of the third article of the constitution defines the extent of the judicial power of the United States. Jurisdiction is given to the Courts of the Union in two classes of cases. In the first, their jurisdiction depends on the character of the cause, whoever may be the parties. This class comprehends "all cases in law and equity arising under this constitution, the laws of the United States, and treaties made, or which shall be made, under their authority." This clause extends the jurisdiction of the Court to all the cases described, without making in its terms any exception whatever, and without any regard to the condition of the party. If there be any exception, it is to be implied against the express words of the article.

In the second class, the jurisdiction depends entirely on the character of the parties. In this are comprehended "controversies between two or more States, between a State and citizens of another State," "and between a State and foreign States, citizens or subjects." If these be the parties, it is entirely unimportant what may be the subject of controversy. Be it what it may, these parties have a constitutional right to come into the Court of the Union. . . .

The jurisdiction of the Court, then, being extended by the letter of the constitution to all cases arising under it, or under the laws of the United States, it follows that those who would withdraw any case of this description from that jurisdiction, must sustain the exemption they claim on the spirit and true meaning of the constitution, which spirit and true meaning must be so apparent as to overrule the words which its framers have employed.

The counsel for the defendant in error have undertaken to do this; and have laid down the general proposition, that a sovereign independent State is not suable, except by its own consent.

This general proposition will not be controverted. But its consent is not requisite in each particular case. It may be given in a general law. And if a State has surrendered any portion of its sovereignty, the question whether a liability to suit be a part of this portion, depends on the instrument by which the surrender is made. If, upon a just construction of that instrument, it shall appear that the State has submitted to be sued, then it has parted with this sovereign right of judging in every case on the justice of its own pretensions, and has entrusted that power to a tribunal in whose impartiality it confides.

The American States, as well as the American people, have believed a close and firm Union to be essential to their liberty and to their happiness. They have been taught by experience, that this Union cannot exist without a government for the whole; and they have been taught by the same experience that this government would be a mere shadow, that must disappoint all their hopes, unless invested with large portions of that sovereignty which belongs to independent States. Under the influence of this opinion, and

thus instructed by experience, the American people, in the conventions of their respective States, adopted the present constitution.

If it could be doubted, whether from its nature, it were not supreme in all cases where it is empowered to act, that doubt would be removed by the declaration, that "this constitution, and the laws of the United States, which shall be made in pursuance thereof, and all treaties made, or which shall be made, under the authority of the United States, shall be the supreme law of the land; and the judges in every State shall be bound thereby; any thing in the constitution or laws of any State to the contrary notwithstanding."

This is the authoritative language of the American people; and, if gentlemen please, of the American States. It marks, with lines too strong to be mistaken, the characteristic distinction between the government of the Union, and those of the States. The general government, though limited as to its objects, is supreme with respect to those objects. This principle is a part of the constitution; and if there be any who deny its necessity, none can deny its authority.

To this supreme government ample powers are confided; and if it were possible to doubt the great purposes for which they were so confided, the people of the United States have declared, that they are given "in order to form a more perfect union, establish justice, ensure domestic tranquility, provide for the common defence, promote the general welfare, and secure the blessings of liberty to themselves and their posterity."

With the ample powers confided to this supreme government, for these interesting purposes, are connected many express and important limitations on the sovereignty of the States, which are made for the same purposes. The powers of the Union, on the great subjects of war, peace, and commerce, and on many others, are in themselves limitations of the sovereignty of the States; but in addition to these, the sovereignty of the States is surrendered in many instances where the surrender can only operate to the benefit of the people and where, perhaps, no other power is conferred on Congress than a conservative power to maintain the principles established in the constitution. The maintenance of these principles in their purity, is certainly among the great duties of the government. One of the instruments by which this duty may be peaceably performed, is the judicial department. It is authorized to decide all cases of every description, arising under the constitution or laws of the United States. From this general grant of jurisdiction, no exception is made of those cases in which a State may be a party. When we consider the situation of the government of the Union and of a State, in relation to each other; the nature of our constitution; the subordination of the State governments to that constitution; the great purpose for which jurisdiction over all cases arising under the constitution and laws of the United States, is confided to the judicial department; are we at liberty to insert in this general grant, an exception of those cases in which a State may be a party? Will the spirit of the constitution justify this attempt to control its words? We think it will not. We think a case arising under the constitution or laws of the United States, is cognizable in the Courts of the Union, whoever may be the parties to that case. . . .

The mischievous consequences of the construction contended for on the part of Virginia, are also entitled to great consideration. It would prostrate, it has been said, the government and its laws at the feet of every State in the Union. And would not this be its effect? What power of the government could be executed by its own means, in any State disposed to resist its execution by a course of legislation? The laws must be executed by individuals acting within the several States. If these individuals may be exposed to penalties, and if the Courts of the Union cannot correct the judgments by which these penalties may be enforced, the course of the government may be, at any time, arrested by the will of one of its members. Each member will possess a *veto* on the will of the whole.

The answer which has been given to this argument, does not deny its truth, but insists that confidence is reposed, and may be safely reposed, in the State institutions; and that, if they shall ever become so insane or so wicked as to seek the destruction of the government, they may accomplish their object by refusing to perform the functions assigned to them. . . .

. . . A constitution is framed for ages to come, and is designed to approach immortality as nearly as human institutions can approach it. Its course cannot always be tranquil. It is exposed to storms and tempests, and its framers must be unwise statesmen indeed, if they have not provided it, as far as its nature will permit, with the means of self-preservation from the perils it may be destined to encounter. No government ought to be so defective in its organization, as not to contain within itself the means of securing the execution of its own laws against other dangers than those which occur every day. Courts of justice are the means most usually employed; and it is reasonable to expect that a government should repose on its own Courts, rather than on others. There is certainly nothing in the circumstances under which our constitution was formed; nothing in the history of the times, which would justify the opinion that the confidence reposed in the States was so implicit as to leave in them and their tribunals the power of resisting or defeating in the form of law, the legitimate measures of the Union. . . .

It has been also urged, as an additional objection to the jurisdiction of the Court, that cases between a State and one of its own citizens, do not come within the general scope of the constitution; and were obviously never intended to be made cognizable in the federal Courts. . . .

If jurisdiction depended entirely on the character of the parties, and was not given where the parties have not an original right to come into Court, that part of the 2d section of the 3d article, which extends the judicial power to all cases arising under the constitution and laws of the United States, would be mere surplusage. It is to give jurisdiction where the character of the parties would not give it, that this very important part of the clause was inserted. It may be true, that the partiality of the State tribunals, in ordinary controversies between a State and its citizens, was not apprehended, and therefore the judicial power of the Union was not extended to such cases; but this was not the sole nor the greatest object for which this department was created. A more important, a much more interesting object, was the preservation of the constitution and laws of the United States, so far as they can be preserved by judicial authority; and therefore the jurisdiction of the Courts of the Union was expressly extended to all cases arising under that constitution and those laws. If the constitution or laws may be violated by proceedings instituted by a State against its own citizens, and if that violation may be such as essentially to affect the constitution and the laws, such as to arrest the progress of government in its constitutional course, why should these cases be excepted from that provision which expressly extends the judicial power of the Union to *all* cases arising under the constitution and laws? . . .

It is most true that this Court will not take jurisdiction if it should not: but it is equally true, that it must take jurisdiction if it should. The judiciary cannot, as the legislature may, avoid a measure because it approaches the confines of the constitution. We cannot pass it by because it is doubtful. With whatever doubts, with whatever difficulties, a case may be attended, we must decide it, if it be brought before us. We have no more right to decline the exercise of jurisdiction which is given, than to usurp that which is not given. The one or the other would be treason to the constitution. Questions may occur which we would gladly avoid; but we cannot avoid them. All we can do is, to exercise our best judgment, and conscientiously to perform our duty. In doing this, on the present occasion, we find this tribunal invested with appellate jurisdiction in *all* cases arising under the constitution and laws of the United States. We find no exception to this grant, and we cannot insert one. . . .

2d. The second objection to the jurisdiction of the Court is, that its appellate power cannot be exercised, in any case, over the judgment of a State Court.

This objection is sustained chiefly by arguments drawn from the supposed total separation of the judiciary of a state from that of the Union, and their entire independence of each other. The argument considers the federal judiciary as completely foreign to that of a State; and as being no more connected with it in any respect whatever, than the Court of a foreign State. If this hypothesis be just, the argument

founded on it is equally so; but if the hypothesis be not supported by the constitution, the argument fails with it.

This hypothesis is not founded on any words in the constitution, which might seem to countenance it, but on the unreasonableness of giving a contrary construction to words which seem to require it; and on the incompatibility of the application of the appellate jurisdiction to the judgments of State Courts, with that constitutional relation which subsists between the government of the Union and the governments of those States which compose it.

Let this unreasonableness, this total incompatibility, be examined.

That the United States form, for many, and for most important purposes, a single nation, has not yet been denied. In war, we are one people. In making peace, we are one people. In all commercial regulations, we are one and the same people. In many other respects, the American people are one; and the government which is alone capable of controlling and managing their interests in all these respects, is the government of the Union. It is their government, and in that character they have no other. America has chosen to be, in many respects, and to many purposes, a nation, and for all these purposes, her government is complete; to all these objects, it is competent. The people have declared, that in the exercise of all powers given for these objects, it is supreme. It can, then, in effecting these objects, legitimately control all individuals or governments within the American territory. The constitution and laws of a State, so far as they are repugnant to the constitution and laws of the United States, are absolutely void. These States are constituent parts of the United States. They are members of one great empire—for some purposes sovereign, for some purposes subordinate.

In a government so constituted, is it unreasonable that the judicial power should be competent to give efficacy to the constitutional laws of the legislature? That department can decide on the validity of the constitution or law of a State, if it be repugnant to the constitution or to a law of the United States. Is it unreasonable that it should also be empowered to decide on the judgment of a State tribunal enforcing such unconstitutional law? Is it so very unreasonable as to furnish a justification for controlling the words of the constitution?

We think it is not. We think in a government acknowledgedly supreme, with respect to objects of vital interest to the nation, there is nothing inconsistent with sound reason, nothing incompatible with the nature of government, in making all its departments supreme, so far as respects those objects, and so far as is necessary to their attainment. The exercise of the appellate power over those judgments of the State tribunals which may contravene the constitution or laws of the United States, is, we believe, essential to the attainment of those objects.

The propriety of entrusting the construction of the constitution, and laws made in pursuance thereof, to the judiciary of the Union, has not, we believe, as yet, been drawn into question. It seems to be a corollary from this political axiom, that the federal Courts should either possess exclusive jurisdiction in such cases, or a power to revise the judgment rendered in them, by the State tribunals. If the federal and State Courts have concurrent jurisdiction in all cases arising under the constitution, laws, and treaties of the United States; and if a case of this description brought in a State Court cannot be removed before judgment, nor revised after judgment, then the construction of the constitution, laws, and treaties of the United States, is not confided particularly to their

judicial department, but is confided equally to that department and to the State Courts, however they may be constituted. "Thirteen independent Courts," says a very celebrated statesman (and we have now more than twenty such Courts,) "of final jurisdiction over the same causes, arising upon the same laws, is a hydra in government, from which nothing but contradiction and confusion can proceed."

Dismissing the unpleasant suggestion, that any motives which may not be fairly avowed, or which ought not to exist, can ever influence a State or its Courts, the necessity of uniformity, as well as correctness in expounding the constitution and laws of the United States, would itself suggest the propriety of vesting in some single tribunal the power of deciding, in the last resort, all cases in which they are involved.

We are not restrained, then, by the political relations between the general and State governments, from construing the words of the constitution, defining the judicial power, in their true sense. We are not bound to construe them more restrictively than they naturally import.

They give to the Supreme Court appellate jurisdiction in all cases arising under the constitution, laws, and treaties of the United States. The words are broad enough to comprehend all cases of this description, in whatever Court they may be decided. In expounding them, we may be permitted to take into view those considerations to which Courts have always allowed great weight in the exposition of laws.

Coyle v. Smith
221 U.S. 559 (1911)

Under the 1906 enabling act admitting Oklahoma as a state, Congress specified that the capital should be located in Guthrie until at least 1913. This arrangement was agreed to by the voters of the state at the time of the adoption of the state's constitution. In 1910, however, the Oklahoma Legislature passed an act that provided for the removal of the capital to Oklahoma City. W. H. Coyle, a property owner in Guthrie, brought suit against Thomas P. Smith, secretary of state of Oklahoma, to test the legality of the removal. The Oklahoma Supreme Court upheld the legislative act, and the

case went to the US Supreme Court on a writ of error. Opinion of the Court: Lurton, Hughes, Harlan, Day, Lamar, White, Van Devanter. Dissenting (without opinion): McKenna, Holmes.

JUSTICE LURTON delivered the opinion of the Court.

. . . The only question for review by us is whether the provision of the enabling act was a valid limitation upon the power of the State after its admission, which overrides any subsequent state legislation repugnant thereto.

The power to locate its own seat of government and to determine when and how it shall be changed from one place to another, and to appropriate its own public funds for that purpose, are essentially and peculiarly state powers. That one of the original thirteen States could now be shorn of such powers by an act of Congress would not be for a moment entertained. The question then comes to this: Can a State be placed upon a plane of inequality with its sister States in the Union if the Congress chooses to impose conditions which so operate, at the time of its admission? The argument is, that while Congress may not deprive a State of any power which it possesses, it may, as a condition to the admission of a new State, constitutionally restrict its authority, to the extent at least, of suspending its powers for a definite time in respect to the location of its seat of government. . . .

The power of Congress in respect to the admission of new States is found in the third section of the fourth Article of the Constitution. That provision is that, "new States may be admitted by the Congress into this Union." . . .

. . . "This Union" was and is a union of States, equal in power, dignity and authority, each competent to exert that residuum of sovereignty not delegated to the United States by the Constitution itself. To maintain otherwise would be to say that the Union, through the power of Congress to admit new States, might come to be a union of States unequal in power, as including States whose powers were restricted only by the Constitution, with others whose powers had been further restricted by an act of Congress accepted as a condition of admission. Thus it would result, first, that the powers of Congress would not be defined by the Constitution alone, but in respect to new States, enlarged or restricted by the conditions imposed upon new States by its own legislation admitting them into the Union; and, second, that such new States might not exercise all of the powers which had not been delegated by the Constitution, but only such as had not been further bargained away as conditions of admission. . . .

When a new State is admitted into the Union, it is so admitted with all of the powers of sovereignty and jurisdiction which pertain to the original States, and . . . such powers may not be constitutionally diminished, impaired or shorn away by any conditions, compacts or stipulations embraced in the act under which the new State came into the Union, which would not be valid and effectual if the subject of congressional legislation after admission. . . .

It may well happen that Congress should embrace in an enactment introducing a new State into the Union legislation intended as a regulation of commerce among the States, or with Indian tribes situated within the limits of such new State, or regulations touching the sole care and disposition of the public lands or reservations therein which might be upheld as legislation within the sphere of the plain power of Congress. But in every such case such legislation would derive its force not from any agreement or compact with the proposed new State, nor by reason of its acceptance of such enactment as a term of admission, but solely because the power of Congress extended to the subject, and therefore, would not operate to restrict the State's legislative power in respect of any matter which was not plainly within the regulating power of Congress. . . .

No such question is presented here. The legislation in the Oklahoma enabling act relating to the location of the capital of the State, if construed as forbidding a removal by the State after its admission as a State, is referable to no power granted to Congress over the subject, and if it is to be upheld at all, it must be implied from the power to admit new States. If power to impose such a restriction upon the general and undelegated power of a State be conceded as implied from the power to admit a new State, where is the line to be drawn against restrictions imposed upon new States? . . .

In *Texas v. White* [1869], Chief Justice Chase said in strong and memorable language that, "the Constitution, in all of its provisions looks to an indestructible Union, composed of indestructible States."

In *Lane County v. Oregon* [1869], . . . he said: "The people of the United States constitute one nation, under one government, and this government, within the scope of the powers with which it is invested, is supreme. On the other hand, the people of each State compose a State, having its own government, and endowed with all the functions essential to separate and independent existence. The States disunited might continue to exist. Without the States in union there could be no such political body as the United States."

To this we may add that the constitutional equality of the States is essential to the harmonious operation of the scheme upon which the Republic was organized. When that equality disappears we may remain a free people, but the Union will not be the Union of the Constitution.

Judgment affirmed.

Baldwin v. Montana Fish and Game Commission
436 U.S. 371, 98 S. Ct. 1852, 56 L. Ed. 2d 354 (1978)

Under Montana's elk-hunting license system, non-residents were charged substantially higher fees than residents and were required to purchase a combination hunting-and-fishing license in order to be able to hunt elk. In 1976, for example, a Montana resident could purchase a license solely for elk for $9, whereas a nonresident had to pay $225 for a combination license. Lester Baldwin, a Montana hunting guide, and four nonresident elk hunters brought suit in federal court seeking declaratory and injunctive relief and reimbursement of fees already paid. They contended that Montana's elk-hunting licensing scheme violated the Privileges and Immunities Clause of Article IV, Section 2. A divided three-judge district court denied all relief to the appellants, who appealed to the Supreme Court. Opinion of the Court: <u>Blackmun</u>, Burger, Stewart, Stevens, Powell, Rehnquist. Concurring opinion: <u>Burger</u>. Dissenting opinion: <u>Brennan</u>, White, Marshall.

JUSTICE BLACKMUN delivered the opinion of the Court.

. . . Appellants strongly urge here that the Montana licensing scheme for the hunting of elk violates the Privileges and Immunities Clause of Art. IV, §2, of our Constitution. That Clause is not one the contours of which have been precisely shaped by the process and wear of constant litigation and judicial interpretation over the years since 1789. . . . We are, nevertheless, not without some pronouncements by this Court as to the Clause's significance and reach. . . .

When the Privileges and Immunities Clause has been applied to specific cases, it has been interpreted to prevent a State from imposing unreasonable burdens on citizens of other States in their pursuit of common callings within the State, . . . in the ownership and disposition of privately held property within the State, . . . and in access to the courts of the State. . . .

It has not been suggested, however, that state citizenship or residency may never be used by a State to distinguish among persons. Suffrage, for example, always has been understood to be tied to an individual's identification with a particular State. . . . No one would suggest that the Privileges and Immunities Clause requires a State to open its polls to a person who declines to assert that the State is the only one where he claims a right to vote. The same is true as to qualification for an elective office of the State. . . . Nor must a State always apply all its laws or all its services equally to anyone, resident or nonresident, who may request it so to do. . . . Some distinctions between residents and nonresidents merely reflect the fact that this is a Nation composed of individual States, and are permitted; other distinctions are prohibited because they hinder the formation, the purpose, or the development of a single Union of those States. Only with respect to those "privileges" and "immunities" bearing upon the vitality of the Nation as a single entity must the State treat all citizens, resident and nonresident, equally. Here we must decide into which category falls a distinction with respect to access to recreational big-game hunting.

Many of the early cases embrace the concept that the States had complete ownership over wildlife within their boundaries, and, as well, the power to preserve this bounty for their citizens alone. It was enough to say "that in regulating the use of the common property of the citizens of [a] state, the legislature is [not] bound to extend to the citizens of all the other states the same advantages as are secured to their own citizens." *Corfield v. Coryell* (1825). It appears to have been generally accepted that although the States were obligated to treat all those within their territory equally in most respects, they were not obliged to share those things they held in trust for their own people. In *Corfield,* . . . Mr. Justice Washington, sitting as Circuit Justice, although recognizing that the States may not interfere with the "right of a citizen of one state to pass through, or to reside in any other state, for purposes of trade, agriculture, professional pursuits, or otherwise; to claim the benefit of the writ of *habeas corpus*; to institute and maintain actions of any kind in the courts of the state; to take, hold and dispose of property, either real or personal," . . . nonetheless concluded that access to oyster beds determined to be owned by New Jersey could be limited to New Jersey residents. This holding, and the conception of state sovereignty upon which it relied, formed the basis for similar decisions during later years of the 19th century. . . .

In more recent years, however, the Court has recognized that the States' interest in regulating and controlling those things they claim to "own," including wildlife, is by no means absolute. States may not compel the confinement of the benefits of their resources, even their wildlife, to their own people whenever such hoarding and confinement impedes interstate commerce. . . . And a State's interest in its wildlife and other resources must yield when, without reason, it interferes with a nonresident's right to pursue a livelihood in a State other than his own, a right that is protected by the Privileges and Immunities Clause. . . .

Appellants contend that the doctrine on which *Corfield* . . . relied has no remaining vitality. We do not agree. . . . The fact that the State's control over wildlife is not exclusive and absolute in the face of federal regulation and certain federally protected interests does not compel the conclusion that it is meaningless in their absence. . . .

Appellants have demonstrated nothing to convince us that we should completely reject the Court's earlier decisions. In his opinion in *Coryell,* Mr. Justice Washington, although he seemingly relied on notions of "natural rights" when he considered the reach of the Privileges and Immunities Clause, included in his list of situations, in which he believed the States would be obligated to treat each other's residents equally, only those where a nonresident sought to engage in an essential activity or exercise a basic right. He himself used the term "fundamental," . . . in the modern as well as the "natural right" sense. . . . With respect to such basic and essential activities, interference with which would frustrate the purposes of the formation of the Union, the States must treat residents and nonresidents without unnecessary distinctions.

Does the distinction made by Montana between residents and nonresidents in establishing access to elk hunting threaten a basic right in a way that offends the Privileges and Immunities Clause? Merely to ask the question seems to provide the answer. . . . Elk hunting by nonresidents in Montana is a recreation and a sport. In itself—wholly apart from license fees—it is costly and obviously available only to the wealthy nonresident or to the one so taken with the sport that he sacrifices other values in order to indulge in it and to enjoy what it offers. It is not a means to the nonresident's livelihood. The mastery of the animal and the trophy are the ends that are sought; appellants are not totally excluded from these. The elk supply, which has been entrusted to the care of the State by the people of Montana, is finite and must be carefully tended in order to be preserved.

Appellants' interest in sharing this limited resource on more equal terms with Montana residents simply does not fall within the purview of the Privileges and Immunities Clause. Equality in access to Montana elk is not basic to the maintenance or well-being of the Union. . . . We do not decide the full range of activities that are sufficiently basic to the livelihood of the Nation that the States may not interfere with a nonresident's participation therein without similarly interfering with a resident's participation. Whatever rights or activities may be "fundamental" under the Privileges and Immunities Clause, we are persuaded, and hold, that elk hunting by nonresidents in Montana is not one of them. . . .

JUSTICE BRENNAN, with whom JUSTICE WHITE and JUSTICE MARSHALL join, dissenting.

Far more troublesome than the Court's narrow holding—elk hunting in Montana is not a privilege or immunity entitled to protection under Art. IV, §2, cl. 1, of the Constitution—is the rationale of the holding that Montana's elk-hunting licensing scheme passes constitutional muster. The Court concludes that because elk hunting is not a "basic and essential activit[y]," interference with which would frustrate [the] purposes of the formation of the Union," . . . the Privileges and Immunities Clause of Art. IV, §2 . . . does not prevent Montana from irrationally, wantonly, and even invidiously discriminating against nonresidents seeking to enjoy natural treasures it alone among the 50 States possesses. I cannot agree that the Privileges and Immunities Clause is so impotent a guarantee that such discrimination remains wholly beyond the purview of that provision.

I think the time has come to confirm explicitly that which has been implicit in our modern privileges and immunities decisions, namely that an inquiry into whether a given right is "fundamental" has no place in our analysis of whether a State's discrimination against nonresidents—who "are not represented in the [discriminating] State's legislative halls," . . . —violates the Clause. Rather, our primary concern is the State's justification for its discrimination. . . . A State's discrimination against nonresidents is permissible where (1) the presence or activity of nonresidents is the source or cause of the problem or effect with which the State seeks to deal, and (2) the discrimination practiced against nonresidents bears a substantial relation to the problem they present. . . .

It is clear that under a proper privileges and immunities analysis Montana's discriminatory treatment of nonresident big-game hunters in this case must fall. . . . There are three possible justifications for charging nonresident elk hunters an amount at least 7.5 times the fee imposed on resident big-game hunters.* The first is conservation. . . . There is nothing in the record to indicate that the influx of nonresident hunters created a special danger to Montana's elk or to any of its other wildlife species. . . . Moreover, . . . if Montana's discriminatorily high big-game license fee is an outgrowth of general conservation policy to discourage elk hunting, this too fails as a basis for the licensing scheme. Montana makes no effort similarly to inhibit its own residents. . . .

The second possible justification for the fee differential . . . is a cost justification. . . . The licensing scheme, appellants contend, is simply an attempt by Montana to shift the costs of its conservation efforts, however commendable they may be, onto the shoulders of nonresidents who are powerless to help themselves at the ballot box. . . . The District Court agreed, finding that "[o]n a consideration of [the] evidence . . . and with due regard to the presumption of constitutionality . . . the ratio of 7.5 to 1 cannot be justified on any basis of cost allocation." . . . Montana's attempt to cost-justify its discriminatory licensing practices thus fails under the second prong of a correct privileges and immunities analysis— that which requires the discrimination a State visits upon nonresidents to bear a substantial relation to the problem or burden they pose.

The third possible justification for Montana's licensing scheme . . . is actually no justification at all, but simply an assertion that a State "owns" the wildlife within its borders in trust for its citizens and may therefore do with it what it pleases.

In unjustifiably discriminating against nonresident elk hunters, Montana has not "exercised its police power in conformity with the . . . Constitution." The State's police power interest in its wildlife cannot override the appellants' constitutionally protected privileges and immunities right.

I respectfully dissent and would reverse.

---

*This is the cost ratio of the 1976 nonresident combination license fee ($225) to the 1976 resident combination license fee ($30). Since a Montana resident wishing to hunt only elk could purchase an elk-hunting license for only $9, a nonresident who wanted to hunt only elk had to pay a fee twenty-five times as great as that charged a similarly situated resident of Montana.

Dred Scott v. Sandford
60 U.S. (19 Howard) 393 (1857)

Dred Scott was a Negro slave belonging to Dr. Emerson, a US Army surgeon stationed in Missouri. In 1834, Dr. Emerson was transferred to a military post in Rock Island, Illinois, a state in which slavery was forbidden, and he took Dred Scott with him. Two years later, Dr. Emerson again took Scott with him when he moved to Fort Snelling, in the territory of Louisiana (now Minnesota), an area in which slavery was prohibited by the terms of the Missouri Compromise of 1820. In 1838 Dr. Emerson returned with his slave to Missouri. In 1846 Dred Scott brought suit in a Missouri state court to obtain his freedom on the claim that his residence in a free territory conferred freedom upon him. Scott won, but the judgment was reversed by the Missouri Supreme Court. Seeking further judicial review of his case, abolitionists and other friends of Dred Scott arranged for a fictitious sale of Scott to John Sandford, a citizen of New York and a brother of the widow of the late Dr. Emerson, so that jurisdiction could be taken by the federal circuit court in Missouri. The federal court held against Scott, and he appealed his case to the Supreme Court on a writ of error. Opinion of the Court: <u>Taney</u>, Wayne, Catron, Nelson, Grier, Campbell. Concurring opinions: <u>Wayne</u>; Catron; <u>Nelson</u>; <u>Grier</u>; Campbell. Concurring in the result: <u>Daniel</u>. Dissenting opinions: <u>McLean</u>; <u>Curtis</u>.

THE CHIEF JUSTICE delivered the opinion of the Court.

. . . The question is simply this: can a negro whose ancestors were imported into this country and sold as slaves, become a member of the political community formed and brought into existence by the Constitution of the United States, and as such become entitled to all the rights, and privileges, and immunities, guaranteed by that instrument to the citizen. One of these rights is the privilege of suing in a court of the United States in the cases specified in the Constitution.

It will be observed, that the plea applies to that class of persons only whose ancestors were negroes of the African race, and imported into this country, and sold and held as slaves. The only matter in issue before the Court, therefore, is whether the descendants of such slaves, when they shall be emancipated, or who are born of parents who had become free before their birth, are citizens of a state, in the sense in which the word "citizen" is used in the Constitution of the United States. And this being the only matter in dispute on the pleadings, the Court must be understood as speaking in this opinion of that class only; that is, of those persons who are the descendants of Africans who were . . . imported into this country and sold as slaves.

In discussing this question, we must not confound the rights of citizenship which a State may confer within its own limits, and the rights of citizenship as a member of the Union. It does not by any means follow, because he has all the rights and privileges of a citizen of a State, that he must be a citizen of the United States. He may have all of the rights and privileges of the citizen of a State, and yet not be entitled to the rights and privileges of a citizen in any other State. For previous to the adoption of the Constitution of the United States, every State had the undoubted right to confer on whomsoever it pleased the character of citizen, and to endow him with all its rights. . . .

The question then arises, whether the provisions of the Constitution, in relation to the personal rights and privileges to which the citizen of a State should be entitled, embraced the negro African race, at that time in this country, or who might afterwards be imported, who had then or should afterwards be made free in any State; and to put it in the power of a single State to make him a citizen of the United States, and endue him with the full rights of citizenship in every other State without their consent? Does the Constitution of the United States act upon him whenever he shall be made free under the laws of a State, and raised there to the rank of a citizen, and immediately clothe him with all the privileges of a citizen in every other State, and in its own courts?

The court thinks the affirmative of these propositions cannot be maintained. And if it cannot, the plaintiff in error could not be a citizen of the State of Missouri, within the meaning of the Constitution of the United States, and, consequently, was not entitled to sue in its courts.

It becomes necessary, therefore, to determine who were citizens of the several States when the Constitution was adopted. And in order to do this, we must recur to the Governments and institutions of the thirteen colonies, when they separated from Great Britain and formed new sovereignties, and took their places in the family of independent nations. We must inquire who, at that time, were recognised as the people or citizens of a State, whose rights and liberties had been outraged by the English Government; and who declared their independence, and assumed the powers of Government to defend their rights by force of arms.

In the opinion of the court, the legislation and histories of the times, and the language used in the Declaration of Independence, show, that neither the class of persons who had been imported as slaves, nor their descendants, whether they had become free or not, were then acknowledged as a part of the people, nor intended to be included in the general words used in that memorable instrument.

It is difficult at this day to realize the state of public opinion in relation to that unfortunate race, which prevailed in the civilized and enlightened portions of the world at the time of the Declaration of Independence, and when the Constitution of the United States was framed and adopted. But the public history of every European nation displays it in a manner too plain to be mistaken.

They had for more than a century before been regarded as beings of an inferior order, and altogether unfit to associate with the white race, either in social or political relations; and so far inferior, that they had no rights which the white man was bound to respect; and that the negro might justly and lawfully be reduced to slavery for his benefit. He was bought and sold, and treated as an ordinary article of merchandise and traffic, whenever a profit could be made by it. This opinion was at that time fixed and universal in the civilized portion of the white race. It was regarded as an axiom in morals as well as in politics, which no one thought of disputing, or supposed to be open to dispute; and men in every grade and position in society daily and habitually acted upon it in their private pursuits, as well as in matters of public concern, without doubting for a moment the correctness of this opinion.

And in no nation was this opinion more firmly fixed or more uniformly acted upon than by the English Government and English people. They not only seized them on the coast of Africa, and sold them or held them in slavery for their own use; but they took them as ordinary articles of merchandise to every country where they could make a profit on them, and were far more extensively engaged in this commerce than any other nation in the world.

The legislation of the different Colonies furnishes positive and indisputable proof of this fact. . . .

[They] show that a perpetual and impassable barrier was intended to be erected between the white race and the one which they had reduced to slavery, and governed as subjects with absolute and despotic power, and which they then looked upon as so far below them in the scale of created beings, that intermarriages between white persons and negroes or mulattoes were regarded as unnatural and immoral, and punished as crimes, not only in the parties, but in the person who joined them in marriage. And no distinction in this respect was made between the free negro or mulatto and the slave, but this stigma, of the deepest degradation, was fixed upon the whole race.

The language of the Declaration of Independence is equally conclusive. It [says] "We hold these truths to be self-evident: that all men are created equal; that they are endowed by their Creator with certain unalienable rights; that among them is life, liberty, and the pursuit of happiness; that to secure these rights, Governments are instituted, deriving their just powers from the consent of the governed."

The general words above quoted would seem to embrace the whole human family, and if they were used in a similar instrument at this day would be so understood. But it is too clear for dispute that the enslaved African race were not intended to be included, and formed no part of the people who framed and adopted this declaration; for if the language, as understood in that day, would embrace them, the conduct of the distinguished men who framed the Declaration of Independence would have been utterly and flagrantly inconsistent with the principles they asserted; and instead of the sympathy of mankind, to which they so confidently appealed, they would have deserved and received universal rebuke and reprobation.

Yet the men who framed this declaration were great men—high in literary acquirements—high in their sense of honor, and incapable of asserting principles inconsistent with those on which they were acting. They perfectly understood the meaning of the language they used, and how it would be understood by others; and they knew that it would not in any part of the civilized world be supposed to embrace the negro race, which, by common consent, had been excluded from civilized Governments and the family of nations and doomed to slavery. They spoke and acted according to the then established doctrines and principles, and in the ordinary language of the day, and no one misunderstood them. The unhappy black race were separated from the white by indelible marks, and laws long before established, and were never thought of or spoken of except as property, and when the claims of the owner or the profit of the trader were supposed to need protection.

The legislation of the States . . . shows, in a manner not to be mistaken, the inferior and subject condition of . . . [the Negro] race at the time the Constitution was adopted, and long afterward, throughout the thirteen States by which that instrument was framed; and it is hardly consistent with the respect due to these States, to suppose that they regarded at that time as fellow-citizens and members of the sovereignty, a class of beings whom they had thus stigmatized; whom, as we are bound, out of respect to the State sovereignties, to assume they had deemed it just and necessary thus to stigmatize, and upon whom they had impressed such deep and enduring marks of inferiority and degradation; or, that when they met in convention to form the Constitution, they looked upon them as a portion of their constituents, or deigned to include them in the provisions so carefully inserted for the security and protection of the liberties and rights of their citizens. It cannot be supposed that they intended to secure to them rights, and privileges,

and rank, in the new political body throughout the Union, which every one of them denied within the limits of its own dominion. More especially, it cannot be believed that the large slaveholding States regarded them as included in the word citizens, or would have consented to a Constitution which might compel them to receive them in that character from another State. For if they were so received, and entitled to the privileges and immunities of citizens, it would exempt them from the operation of the special laws and from the police regulations which they considered to be necessary for their own safety. It would give to persons of the Negro race, who were recognized as citizens in any one State of the Union, the right to enter every other State whenever they pleased, singly or in companies, without pass or passport, and without obstruction to sojourn there as long as they pleased, to go where they pleased at every hour of the day or night without molestation, unless they committed some violation of law for which a white man would be punished; and it would give them the full liberty of speech in public and in private upon all subjects upon which its own citizens might speak; to hold public meetings upon political affairs, and to keep and carry arms wherever they went. And all of this would be done in the face of the subject race of the same color, both free and slaves, and inevitably producing discontent and insubordination among them, and endangering the peace and safety of the State. . . .

Undoubtedly, a person may be a citizen, that is, a member of the community who form the sovereignty, although he exercises no share of the political power, and is incapacitated from holding particular offices. Women and minors, who form a part of the political family, cannot vote; and when a property qualification is required to vote or hold a particular office, those who have not the necessary qualification cannot vote or hold the office, yet they are citizens.

So, too, a person may be entitled to vote by the law of the State, who is not a citizen even of the State itself. And in some of the States of the Union foreigners not naturalized are allowed to vote. And the State may give the right to free negroes and mulattoes, but that does not make them citizens of the State, and still less of the United States. And the provisions in the Constitution giving privileges and immunities in other States does not apply to them.

Neither does it apply to a person who, being the citizen of a State, migrates to another State. For then he becomes subject to the laws of the State in which he lives, and he is no longer a citizen of the State from which he removed. And the State in which he resides may then, unquestionably, determine his status or condition, and place him among the class of persons who are not recognised as citizens, but belong to an inferior and subject race; and may deny him the privileges and immunities enjoyed by its citizens. . . .

No one, we presume, supposes that any change in public opinion or feeling, in relation to this unfortunate race, in the civilized nations of Europe or in this country, should induce the court to give to the words of the Constitution a more liberal construction in their favor than they were intended to bear when the instrument was framed and adopted. Such an argument would be altogether inadmissible in any tribunal called on to interpret it. If any of its provisions are deemed unjust, there is a mode prescribed in the instrument itself by which it may be amended; but while it remains unaltered, it must be construed now as it was understood at the time of its adoption. It is not only the same in words, but the same in meaning, and delegates the same powers to the Government, and reserves and secures the same rights and privileges to the citizen; and as long as it continues to exist in its present form, it speaks not only in the same words, but with the same meaning and intent with which it spoke when it came from the hands of its framers, and was voted on and adopted by the people of the United States. Any other rule of construction would abrogate the judicial character of this court, and make it the mere reflex of the popular opinion or passion of the day. This court was not created by the Constitution for such purposes. Higher and graver trusts have been confided to it, and it must not falter in the path of duty. . . .

. . . [T]he court is of opinion, that . . . Dred Scott was not a citizen of Missouri within the meaning of the Constitution of the United States, and not entitled as such to sue in its

courts: and, consequently, that the Circuit Court had no jurisdiction of the case. . . .

We proceed, therefore, to inquire whether the facts relied on by the plaintiff entitled him to his freedom. . . .

In considering this part of the controversy, two questions arise: (1.) Was he, together with his family, free in Missouri by reason of the stay in the territory of the United States? . . . and (2.) If they were not, is Scott himself free by reason of his removal to Rock Island, in the State of Illinois. . . .

We proceed to examine the first question.

The act of Congress [Missouri Compromise] upon which the plaintiff relies, declares that slavery and involuntary servitude, except as a punishment for crime, shall be forever prohibited in all that part of the territory ceded by France, under the name of Louisiana, which lies north of 36°30′ north latitude, and not included within the limits of Missouri. And the difficulty which meets us at the threshold of this part of the inquiry is, whether Congress was authorized to pass this law under any of the powers granted to it by the Constitution; for if the authority is not given by that instrument, it is the duty of this court to declare it void and inoperative, and incapable of conferring freedom upon any one who is held as a slave under the laws of any one of the States.

The counsel for the plaintiff has laid much stress upon that article in the Constitution which confers on Congress the power "to dispose of and make all needful rules and regulations respecting the territory or other property belonging to the United States"; but, in the judgment of the court, that provision has no bearing on the present controversy, and the power there given, whatever it may be, is confined, and was intended to be confined, to the territory which at that time belonged to, or was claimed by, the United States, and was within their boundaries as settled by the treaty with Great Britain, and can have no influence upon a territory afterwards acquired from a foreign Government. It was a special provision for a known and particular territory, and to meet a present emergency, and nothing more. . . .

The language used in the clause, the arrangement and combination of the powers, and the somewhat unusual phraseology it uses, when it speaks of the political power to be exercised in the government of the territory, all indicate the design and meaning of the clause to be such as we have mentioned. It does not speak of *any* territory, nor of *Territories,* but uses language which, according to its legitimate meaning, points to a particular thing. The power is given in relation only to *the* territory of the United States—that is, to a territory then in existence, and then known or claimed as the territory of the United States. . . .

This brings us to examine by what provision of the Constitution the present Federal Government, under its delegated and restricted powers, is authorized to acquire territory outside of the original limits of the United States, and what powers it may exercise therein over the person or property of a citizen of the United States, while it remains a Territory, and until it shall be admitted as one of the States of the Union.

There is certainly no power given by the Constitution to the Federal Government to establish or maintain colonies bordering on the United States or at a distance, to be ruled and governed at its own pleasure; nor to enlarge its territorial limits in any way, except by the admission of new States. That power is plainly given; and if a new State is admitted, it needs no further legislation by Congress, because the Constitution itself defines the relative rights and powers, and duties of the State, and the citizens of the State, and the Federal Government. But no power is given to acquire a Territory to be held and governed permanently in that character. . . .

. : . It may be safely assumed that citizens of the United States who migrate to a Territory belonging to the people of the United States, cannot be ruled as mere colonists, dependent upon the will of the General Government, and to be governed by any laws it may think proper to impose. The principle upon which our Governments rest, and upon which alone they continue to exist, is the union of States, sovereign and independent within their own limits in their internal and domestic concerns, and bound together as one people by a General Government possessing certain enumerated and restricted powers, delegated to it by the people of the several States, and exercising supreme authority within the scope of the powers granted to it, throughout the dominion of the United States. A power, therefore, in the General Government to obtain and hold colonies and dependent territories, over which they might legislate without restriction, would be inconsistent with its own existence in its present form. Whatever it acquires it acquires for the benefit of the people of the several States who created it. It is their trustee acting for them, and charged with the duty of promoting the interests of the whole people of the Union in the exercise of the powers specifically granted. . . .

At the time when the Territory in question was obtained by cession from France, it contained no population fit to be associated together and admitted as a State; and it therefore was absolutely necessary to hold possession of it, as a Territory belonging to the United States, until it was settled and inhabited by a civilized community capable of self-government, and in a condition to be admitted to equal terms with the other States as a member of the Union. But, as we have before said, it was acquired by the General Government, as the representative and trustee of the people of the United States, and it must therefore be held in that character for their common and equal benefit; for it was the people of the several States, acting through their agent and representative, the Federal Government, who in fact acquired the Territory in question, and the Government holds it for their common use until it shall be associated with the other States as a member of the Union.

But until that time arrives, it is undoubtedly necessary that some Government should be established, in order to organize society, and to protect the inhabitants in their persons and property; and as the people of the United States could act in this matter only through the Government which represented them, and through which they spoke and acted when the Territory was obtained, it was not only within the scope of its powers, but it was its duty to pass such laws and establish such a Government as would enable those by whose authority they acted to reap the advantages anticipated from its acquisition, and to gather there a population which would enable it to assume the position to which it was destined among the States of the Union. The power to acquire necessarily carries with it the power to preserve and apply to the purposes for which it was acquired. The form of government to be established necessarily rested in the discretion of Congress. It was their duty to establish the one that would be best suited for the protection and security of the citizens of the United States, and other inhabitants who might be authorized to take up their abode there, and that must always depend upon the existing condition of the Territory, as to the number and character of its inhabitants, and their situation in the Territory. In some cases a Government, consisting of persons appointed by the Federal Government, would best subserve the interests of the Territory, when the inhabitants were few and scattered, and new to one another. In other instances, it would be more advisable to commit the powers of self-government to the people who had settled in the Territory, as being the most competent to determine what was best for their own interests. But some form of civil authority would be absolutely necessary to organize and preserve civilized society, and prepare it to become a State; and what is the best form must always depend on the condition of the Territory at the time, and the choice of the mode must depend upon the exercise of a discretionary power by Congress, acting within the scope of its constitutional authority, and not infringing upon the rights of person or rights of property of the citizen who might go there to reside, or for any other lawful purpose. It was acquired by the exercise of this discretion, and it must be held and governed in like manner, until it is fitted to be a State.

But the power of Congress over the person or property of a citizen can never be a mere discretionary power under our Constitution and form of Government. The powers of the Government and the rights and privileges of the citizen are regulated and plainly defined by the Constitution itself. And when the Territory becomes a part of the United States, the Federal Government enters into possession in the character impressed upon it by those who created it. It enters upon it with its powers over the citizen strictly defined, and limited by the Constitution, from which it derives its own existence, and by virtue of which alone it continues to exist and act as a Government and sovereignty. It has no power of any kind beyond it; and it cannot, when it enters a Territory of the United States, put off its character, and assume discretionary or despotic powers which the Constitution has denied to it. It cannot create for itself a new character separated from the citizens of the United States, and the duties it owes them under of the United States, the Government and the citizen both enter it under the authority of the Constitution, with their respective rights defined and marked out; and the Federal Government can exercise no power over his person or property, beyond what that instrument confers, nor lawfully deny any right which it has reserved.

A reference to a few of the provisions of the Constitution will illustrate this proposition.

For example, no one, we presume, will contend that Congress can make any law in a Territory respecting that establishment of religion, or the free exercise thereof, or abridging the freedom of speech or of the press, or the right of the people of the Territory peaceably to assemble, and to petition the Government for the redress of grievances.

Nor can Congress deny to the people the right to keep and bear arms, nor the right to trial by jury, nor compel any one to be a witness against himself in a criminal proceeding.

These powers, and others, in relation to rights of person, which it is not necessary here to enumerate, are, in express and positive terms, denied to the General Government; and the rights of private property have been guarded with equal care. Thus the rights of property are united with the rights of person, and placed on the same ground by the fifth amendment to the Constitution, which provides that no person shall be deprived of life, liberty, and property, without due process of law. And an act of Congress which deprives a citizen of the United States of his liberty or property, merely because he came himself or brought his property into a particular Territory of the United States, and who had committed no offence against the laws, could hardly be dignified with the name of due process of law. . . .

The powers over person and property of which we speak are not only not granted to Congress, but are in express terms denied, and they are forbidden to exercise them. And this prohibition is not confined to the States, but the words are general, and extend to the whole territory over which the Constitution gives it power to legislate, including those portions of it remaining under Territorial Government, as well as that covered by States. It is a total absence of power everywhere within the dominion of the United States, and places the citizens of a Territory, so far as these rights are concerned, on the same footing with citizens of the States, and guards them as firmly and plainly against any inroads which the General Government might attempt, under the plea of implied or incidental powers. And if Congress itself cannot do this—if it is beyond the powers conferred on the Federal Government—it will be admitted, we presume, that it could not authorize a Territorial Government to exercise them. It could confer no power on any local Government, established by its authority, to violate the provisions of the Constitution.

It seems, however, to be supposed, that there is a difference between property in a slave and other property, and that different rules may be applied to it in expounding the Constitution of the United States. And the laws and usages of nations, and the writing of eminent jurists upon the relation of master and slave and their mutual rights and duties, and the powers which Governments may exercise over it, have been dwelt upon in the argument. . . .

Now, as we have already said in an earlier part of this opinion, upon a different point, the right of property in a slave is distinctly and expressly affirmed in the Constitution. The right to traffic in it, like an ordinary article of merchandise and property, was guaranteed to the citizens of the United States, in every State that might desire it, for twenty years. And the Government in express terms is pledged to protect it in all future time, if the slave escapes from his owner. This is done in plain words— too plain to be misunderstood. And no word can be found in the Constitution which gives Congress a greater power over slave property, or which entitles property of that kind to less protection than property of any other description.

The only power conferred is the power coupled with the duty of guarding and protecting the owner in his rights.

Upon these considerations, it is the opinion of the court that the act of Congress which prohibited a citizen from holding and owning property of this kind in the territory of the United States north of the line therein mentioned, is not warranted by the Constitution, and is therefore void; and that neither Dred Scott himself, nor any of his family, were made free by being carried into this territory; even if they had been carried there by the owner, with the intention of becoming a permanent resident.

But there is another point in the case which depends on State power and State law. And it is contended, on the part of the plaintiff, that he is made free by being taken to Rock Island, in the State of Illinois, independently of his residence in the territory of the United States; and being so made free, he was not again reduced to a state of slavery by being brought back to Missouri.

Our notice of this part of the case will be very brief; for the principle on which it depends was decided in this court, upon much consideration, in the case of *Strader v. Graham* (1851). In that case, the slaves had been taken from Kentucky to Ohio, with the consent of the owner, and afterwards brought back to Kentucky. And this court held that their status or condition, as free or slave, depended upon the laws of Kentucky, when they were brought back into the State, and not of Ohio; and that this court had no jurisdiction to revise the judgment of a State court upon its own laws. . . .

So in this case. As Scott was a slave when taken into the State of Illinois by his owner, and was there held as such, and brought back in that character, his status, as free or slave, depended on the laws of Missouri, and not of Illinois. . . . Upon the whole, therefore, it is the judgment of this court, that it appears by the record before us that the plaintiff in error is not a citizen of Missouri, in the sense in which that word is used in the Constitution; and that the Circuit Court of the United States, for that reason, had no jurisdiction in the case, and could give no judgment in it. Its judgment for the defendant must, consequently, be reversed, and a mandate issued, directing the suit to be dismissed for want of jurisdiction. . . .

JUSTICE MCLEAN, dissenting.

In the argument, it was said that a colored citizen would not be an agreeable member of society. This is more a matter of taste than of law. Several of the States have admitted persons of color to the right of suffrage, and in this view have recognised them as citizens; and this has been done in the slave as well as the free States. On the question of citizenship, it must be admitted that we have not been very fastidious. Under the late treaty with Mexico, we have made citizens of all grades, combinations, and colors. The same was done in the admission of Louisiana and Florida. No one ever doubted, and no court ever held, that the people of these Territories did not become citizens under the treaty. They have exercised all the rights of citizens, without being naturalized under the acts of Congress.

In the formation of the Federal Constitution, care was taken to confer no power on the Federal Government to interfere with this institution [of slavery] in the States. In the provision respecting the slave trade, in fixing the ratio of representation, and providing for the reclamation of fugitives from labor, slaves were referred to as persons, and in no other respect are they considered in the Constitution.

We need not refer to the mercenary spirit which introduced the infamous traffic in slaves, to show the degradation of negro slavery in our country. This system was imposed upon our colonial settlements by the mother country, and it is due to truth to say that the commercial colonies and States were chiefly engaged in the traffic. But we know as a historical fact, that James Madison, that great and good man, a leading member in the Federal Convention, was solicitous to guard the language of that instrument so as not to convey the idea that there could be property in man.

I prefer the lights of Madison, Hamilton, and Jay, as a means of construing the Constitution in all its bearings, rather than to look behind that period into a traffic which is now declared to be piracy, and punished with death by Christian nations. I do not like to draw the sources of our domestic relations from so dark a ground. Our independence was a great epoch in the history of freedom; and while I admit the Government was not made especially for the colored race, yet many of them were citizens of the New England States, and exercised the rights of suffrage when the Constitution was adopted, and it was not doubted by any intelligent person that its tendencies would greatly ameliorate their condition.

Many of the States, on the adoption of the Constitution, or shortly afterward, took measures to abolish slavery within their respective jurisdictions; and it is a well-known fact that a belief was cherished by the leading men, South as well as North, that the institution of slavery would gradually decline, until it would become extinct. The increased value of slave labor, in the culture of cotton and sugar, prevented the realization of this expectation. Like all other communities and States, the South were influenced by what they considered to be their own interests.

But if we are to turn our attention to the dark ages of the world, why confine our view to colored slavery? On the same principles, white men were made slaves. All slavery has its origin in power, and is against right.

The power of Congress to establish Territorial Governments, and to prohibit the introduction of slavery therein, is the next point to be considered.

The prohibition of slavery north of 36°30', and of the State of Missouri, contained in the act admitting that State into the Union, was passed by a vote of 134, in the House of Representatives, to 42. Before Mr. Monroe signed the act, it was submitted by him to his Cabinet, and they held the restriction of slavery in a Territory to be within the constitutional powers of Congress. It would be singular, if in 1804 Congress had power to prohibit the introduction of slaves in Orleans Territory from any other part of the Union, under the penalty of freedom to the slave, if the same power, embodied in the Missouri Compromise, could not be exercised in 1820.

But this law of Congress, which prohibits slavery north of Missouri and of 36°30' is declared to have been null and void by my brethren. And this opinion is founded mainly, as I understand, on the distinction drawn between the [Northwest] ordinance of 1787 and the Missouri Compromise line. In what does the distinction consist? The ordinance, it is said, was a compact entered into by the confederated States before the adoption of the Constitution; and that in the cession of territory authority was given to establish a Territorial Government.

It is clear that the ordinance did not go into operation by virtue of the authority of the Confederation, but by reason of its modification and adoption by Congress under the Constitution. It seems to be supposed, in the opinion of the court, that the articles of cession placed it on a different footing from territories subsequently acquired. I am unable to perceive the force of this distinction. That the ordinance was intended for the government of the Northwestern Territory, and was limited to such Territory, is admitted. It was extended to Southern Territories, with modifications, by acts of Congress, and to some Northern Territories. But the ordinance was made valid by the act of Congress, and without such act could have been of no force. It rested for its validity on the act of Congress, the same, in my opinion, as the Missouri Compromise line.

If Congress may establish a Territorial Government in the exercise of its discretion, it is a clear principle that a court cannot control that discretion. This being the case, I do not see on what ground the act is held to be void. It did not purport to forfeit property, or take it for public purposes. It only prohibited slavery; in doing which, it followed the ordinance of 1787.

JUSTICE CURTIS, dissenting.

I dissent from the opinion pronounced by the Chief Justice, and from the judgment which the majority of the court think it proper to render in this case. . . .

To determine whether any free persons, descended from Africans held in slavery, were citizens of the United States under the Confederation, and consequently at the time of the adoption of the Constitution of the United States, it is only necessary to know whether any such persons were citizens of either of the States under the Confederation, at the time of the adoption of the Constitution.

Of this there can be no doubt. At the time of the ratification of the Articles of Confederation, all free native-born inhabitants of the States of New Hampshire, Massachusetts, New York, New Jersey, and North Carolina, though descended from African slaves, were not only citizens of those States, but such of them as had the other necessary qualifications possessed the franchise of electors, on equal terms with other citizens. . . .

I shall not enter into an examination of the existing opinions of that period respecting the African race, nor into any discussion concerning the meaning of those who asserted, in the Declaration of Independence, that all men are created equal; that they are endowed by their Creator with certain inalienable rights; that among these are life, liberty, and the pursuit of happiness. My own opinion is, that a calm comparison of these assertions of universal abstract truths, and of their own individual opinions and acts, would not leave these men under any reproach of inconsistency; that the great truths they asserted on that solemn occasion, they were ready and anxious to make effectual, wherever a necessary regard to circumstances, which no statesman can disregard without producing more evil than good, would allow; and that it would not be just to them, nor true in itself, to allege that they intended to say that the Creator of all men had endowed the white race, exclusively, with the great natural rights which the Declaration of Independence asserts. But this is not the place to vindicate their memory. As I conceive, we should deal here, not with such disputes, if there can be a dispute concerning this subject, but with those substantial facts evinced by the written constitutions of States, and by the notorious practice under them. And they show, in a manner which no argument can obscure, that in some of the original thirteen States, free colored persons, before and at the time of the formation of the Constitution, were citizens of those States.

Did the Constitution of the United States deprive them or their descendants of citizenship?

That Constitution was ordained and established by the people of the United States through the action, in each State, of those persons who were qualified by its laws to act thereon, in behalf of themselves and all other citizens of that State. In some of the States, as we have seen, colored persons were among those qualified by law to act on this subject. These colored persons were not only included in the body of "the people of the United States by whom the Constitution was ordained and established," but in at least five of the States they had the power to act, and doubtless did act, by their suffrages, upon the question of its adoption. It would be strange, if we were to find in that instrument anything which deprived of their citizenship any part of the people of the United States who were among those by whom it was established.

I can find nothing in the Constitution which deprives of their citizenship any class of persons who were citizens of the United States at the time of its adoption, or who should be native-born citizens of any State after its adoption; nor any power enabling Congress to disfranchise persons born on the soil of any State, and entitled to citizenship of such State by its constitution and laws. And my opinion is, that, under the Constitution of the United States, every free person born on the soil of a State, who is a citizen of that State by force of its Constitution or laws, is also a citizen of the United States. . . .

Confining our view to free persons born within the several States, we find that the Constitution has recognized the general principle of public law, that allegiance and citizenship depend on the place of birth; that it has not attempted practically to apply this principle by designating the particular classes of persons who should or should not come under it; that when we turn to the Constitution for an answer to the question, what free persons, born within the several States, are citizens of the United States, the only answer we can receive from any of its express provisions is, the citizens of the several States are to enjoy the privileges and immunities of citizens in every State, and their franchise as electors under the Constitution depends on their citizenship in the several States. Add to this, that the Constitution was ordained by the citizens of the several States; that they were "the people of the United States," for whom and whose posterity the government was declared in the preamble of the Constitution to be made; that each of them was "a citizen of the United States at the time of the adoption of the Constitution," within the meaning of those words in that instrument; that by them the government was to be and was in fact organized; and that no power is conferred on the Government of the Union to discriminate between them, or to disfranchise any of them—the necessary conclusion is, that those persons born within the several States, who, by force of their respective constitutions and laws, are citizens of the State, are thereby citizens of the United States.

It has been often asserted that the Constitution was made exclusively by and for the white race. It has already been shown that in five of the thirteen original States, colored persons then possessed the elective franchise, and were among those by whom the Constitution was ordained and established. If so, it is not true, in point of fact, that the Constitution was made exclusively by the white race? And that it was made exclusively for the white race is, in my opinion, not only an assumption not warranted by anything in the Constitution, but contradicted by its opening declaration, that it was ordained and established by the people of the United States, for themselves and their posterity. And as free colored persons were then citizens of at least five States, and so in every sense part of the people of the United States, they were among those for whom and whose posterity the Constitution was ordained and established.

I dissent, therefore, from that part of the opinion of the majority of the court, in which it is held that a person of African descent cannot be a citizen of the United States; and I regret I must go further, and dissent both from what I deem their assumption of authority to examine the constitutionality of the act of Congress commonly called the Missouri Compromise act, and the grounds and conclusions announced in their opinion.

Having first decided that they were bound to consider the sufficiency of the plea to the jurisdiction of the Circuit Court, and having decided that this plea showed that the Circuit Court had not jurisdiction, and consequently that this is a case to which the judicial power of the United States does not extend, they have gone on to examine the merits of the case as they appeared on the trial before the court and jury, on the issues joined on the pleas in bar, and so have reached the question of the power of Congress to pass the act of 1820. On so grave a subject as this, I feel obliged to say that, in my opinion, such an exertion of judicial power transcends the limits of the authority of the court, as described by its repeated decisions and, as I understand, acknowledged in this opinion of the majority of the court. . . .

The question here is whether . . . the court [is authorized] to insert into [Article 4, Section 2—concerning Territories] an exception of the exclusion or allowance of slavery, not found therein, nor in any other part of that instrument. To engraft on any instrument a substantive exception not found in it, must be admitted to be a matter attended with great difficulty. And the difficulty increases with the importance of the instrument, and the magnitude and complexity of the interests involved in its construction. To allow this to be done with the Constitution, upon reasons purely political, renders its judicial interpretation impossible—because judicial tribunals, as such, cannot decide upon political considerations. Political reasons have not the requisite certainty to afford rules of juridical interpretation. They are different in different men. They are different in the same men at different times. And when a strict interpretation of the Constitution, according to the fixed rules which govern the interpretation of laws, is abandoned, and the theoretical opinions of individuals are allowed to control its meaning, we have no longer a Constitution; we are under the government of individual men, who for the time being have power to declare what the Constitution is, according to their own views of what it ought to mean. When such a method of interpretation of the Constitution obtains, in place of a republican government, with limited and defined powers, we have a government which is merely an exponent of the will of Congress; or what, in my opinion, would not be preferable, an exponent of the individual political opinions of the members of this court.

If it can be shown by anything in the Constitution itself that when it confers on Congress the power to make all needful rules and regulations respecting the Territory belonging to the United States, the exclusion or the allowance of slavery was excepted; or if anything in the history of this provision tends to show that such an exception was intended by those who framed and adopted the Constitution to be introduced into it, I hold it to be my duty carefully to consider, and to allow just weight to such considerations in interpreting the positive text of the Constitution. But where the Constitution has said all needful rules and regulations, I must find something more than theoretical reasoning to induce me to say it did not mean all.

Looking at the power of Congress over the Territories as of the extent just described, what positive prohibition exists in the Constitution, which restrained Congress from enacting a law in 1820 to prohibit slavery north of 36°30' north latitude?

The only one suggested is that clause in the 5th article of the Amendments of the Constitution which declares that no person shall be deprived of his life, liberty, or property, without due process of law. I will now proceed to examine the question, whether this clause is entitled to the effect thus contributed to it. It is necessary, first, to have a clear view of the nature and incidents of that particular species of property which is now in question.

Slavery being contrary to natural right, is created only by municipal law. This is not only plain in itself, and agreed by all writers on the subject, but is inferable from the Constitution, and has been explicitly declared by this court. The Constitution refers to slaves as "persons held to service in one State, under the laws thereof." Nothing can more clearly describe a status created by municipal law. In *Prigg v. Pennsylvania* (1842), this court said: "The state of slavery is deemed to be a mere municipal regulation, founded on and limited to the range of territorial laws." In *Rankin v. Lydia* (1820), the Supreme Court of Appeals of Kentucky said: "Slavery is sanctioned by the laws of this State, and the right to hold them under our municipal regulations is unquestionable. But we view this as a right existing by positive law of a municipal character, without foundation in the law of nature or the unwritten common law." I am not acquainted with any case or writer questioning the correctness of this doctrine.

The status of slavery is not necessarily always attended with the same powers on the part of the master. The master is subject to the supreme power of the State, whose will controls his action towards his slave, and this control must be defined and regulated by the municipal law. In one State, as at one period of the Roman law, it may put the life of the slave into the hand of the master; others, as those of the United States, which tolerate slavery, may treat the slave as a person when the master takes his life; while in others, the law may recognize a right of the slave to be protected from cruel treatment. In other words, the status of slavery embraces every condition, from that in which the slave is known to the law simply as a chattel, with no civil rights, to that in which he is recognized as a person for all purposes, save the compulsory power of directing and receiving the fruits of his labor. Which of these conditions shall attend the status of slavery, must depend on the municipal law which creates and upholds it.

And not only must the status of slavery be created and measured by municipal law, but the rights, powers and obligations which grow out of that status, must be defined, protected and enforced by such laws. The liability of the master for the torts and crimes of his slave, and of third persons for assaulting or injuring or harboring or kidnapping him, the forms and modes of emancipation and sale, their subjection to the debts of the master, succession by the death of the master, suits for freedom, the capacity of the slave to be party to a suit, or to be a witness, with such police regulations as have existed in all civilized States where slavery has been tolerated, are among the subjects upon which municipal legislation becomes necessary when slavery is introduced.

Is it conceivable that the Constitution has conferred the right on every citizen to become a resident on the Territory of the United States with his slaves, and there to hold them as such, but has neither made nor provided for any municipal regulations which are essential to the existence of slavery?

Is it not more rational to conclude that they who framed and adopted the Constitution were aware that persons held to service under the laws of a State are property only to the extent and under the conditions fixed by those laws; that they must cease to be available as property, when their owners voluntarily place them permanently within another jurisdiction, where no municipal laws on the subject of slavery exist; and that, being aware of these principles, and having said nothing to interfere with or displace them, or compel Congress to legislate in any particular manner on the subject, and having empowered Congress to make all needful rules and regulations respecting the Territory of the United States, it was their intention to leave to the discretion of Congress what regulations, if any, should be made concerning slavery therein? . . .

. . . I am of opinion that so much of the several acts of Congress as prohibited slavery and involuntary servitude within that part of the Territory of Wisconsin lying north of 36°30' north latitude, and west of the river Mississippi, were constitutional and valid laws.

New York v. United States
505 U.S. 144 (1992)

Confronting a dire shortage of disposal sites in thirty-one states for low-level radioactive waste generated by the federal government, hospitals, research institutions, and various industries, Congress enacted the Low-Level Radioactive Waste Policy Amendments Act of 1985. This act, based largely on a proposal submitted by the National Governors' Association, embodied a compromise between sited and unsited states, in which the sited states agreed to extend for seven years the period in which they would accept low-level radioactive waste from other states, and, in exchange, the unsited states agreed to end their reliance on the sited states by 1992. To ensure that these agreements were honored, the act imposed on the states, either alone or in "regional compacts" with other states, the obligation to provide for the disposal of waste generated within their borders and contained three provisions setting forth "incentives" to states to comply with that obligation. The first set of incentives was monetary: states with disposal sites were authorized to impose a surcharge on radioactive waste received from other states. The second set of incentives was access incentives: states and regional compacts with disposal sites were authorized to increase gradually the cost of access to their sites and eventually to deny access altogether. The third incentive was a "take title" provision, which specified that a state or regional compact that failed to provide for the disposal of all internally generated waste by a particular date must, upon the request of the waste's generator or owner, take title to and possession of the waste and become liable for all damages suffered by the generator or owner as a result of the state's failure to take prompt possession. New York State filed suit against the United States in United States District Court for the Northern District of New York, seeking a declaratory judgment that the three incentives' provisions were inconsistent with the Tenth Amendment. The district court dismissed the complaint, and the Second Circuit Court of Appeals affirmed. The US Supreme Court granted certiorari. Opinion of the Court: <u>O'Connor</u>, Rehnquist, Scalia, Kennedy, Souter, Thomas. Concurring in part and dissenting in part: <u>White</u>, Blackmun, Stevens; <u>Stevens</u>.

JUSTICE O'CONNOR delivered the opinion of the Court.

This case implicates one of our Nation's newest problems of public policy and perhaps our oldest question of constitutional law. The public policy issue involves the disposal of radioactive waste: In this case, we address the constitutionality of three provisions of the Low-Level Radioactive Waste Policy Amendments Act of 1985. The constitutional question is as old as the Constitution: It consists of discerning the proper division of authority between the Federal Government and the States. We conclude that while Congress has substantial power under the Constitution to encourage the States to provide for the disposal of the radioactive waste generated within their borders, the Constitution does not confer upon Congress the ability simply to compel the States to do so. We therefore find that only two of the Act's three provisions at issue are consistent with the Constitution's allocation of power to the Federal Government.

In 1788, in the course of explaining to the citizens of New York why the recently drafted Constitution provided for federal courts, Alexander Hamilton observed: "The erection of a new government, whatever care or wisdom may distinguish the work, cannot fail to originate questions of intricacy and nicety; and these may, in a particular manner, be expected to flow from the establishment of a constitution founded upon the total or partial incorporation of a number of distinct sovereignties." *The Federalist,* No. 82. Hamilton's prediction has proved quite accurate. While no one disputes the proposition that "[t]he Constitution created a Federal Government of limited powers," and while the Tenth Amendment makes explicit that "[t]he powers not delegated to the United States by the Constitution, nor prohibited by it to the States, are reserved to the States respectively, or to the people"; the task of ascertaining the constitutional line between federal and state power has given rise to many of the Court's most difficult and celebrated cases. At least as far back as *Martin v. Hunter's Lessee* (1816), the Court has resolved questions "of great importance and delicacy" in determining whether particular sovereign powers have been granted by the Constitution to the Federal Government or have been retained by the States.

These questions can be viewed in either of two ways. In some cases the Court has inquired whether an Act of Congress is authorized by one of the powers delegated to Congress in Article I of the Constitution. In other cases the Court has sought to determine whether an Act of Congress invades the province of state sovereignty reserved by the Tenth Amendment. In a case like this one, involving the division of authority between federal and state governments, the two inquiries are mirror images of each other. If a power is delegated to Congress in the Constitution, the Tenth Amendment expressly disclaims any reservation of that power to the States; if a power is an attribute of state sovereignty reserved by the Tenth Amendment, it is necessarily a power the Constitution has not conferred on Congress.

It is in this sense that the Tenth Amendment "states but a truism that all is retained which has not been surrendered." *United States v. Darby* (1941). As Justice Story put it, "[t]he amendment is a mere affirmation of what, upon any just reasoning, is a necessary rule of interpreting the constitution. Being an instrument of limited and enumerated powers, it follows irresistibly, that what is not conferred, is withheld, and belongs to the state authorities." 3 J. Story, *Commentaries on the Constitution of the United States* 752 (1833). This has been the Court's consistent understanding: "The States unquestionably do retai[n] a significant measure of sovereign authority . . . to the extent that the Constitution has not divested them of their original powers and transferred those powers to the Federal Government." *Garcia v. San Antonio Metropolitan Transit Authority* (1985).

Congress exercises its conferred powers subject to the limitations contained in the Constitution. Thus, for example, under the Commerce Clause Congress may regulate publishers engaged in interstate commerce, but Congress is constrained in the exercise of that power by the First Amendment. The Tenth Amendment likewise restrains the power of Congress, but this limit is not derived from the text of the Tenth Amendment itself, which, as we have discussed, is essentially a tautology. Instead, the Tenth Amendment confirms that the power of the Federal Government is subject to limits that may, in a given instance, reserve power to the States. The Tenth Amendment thus directs us to determine, as in this case, whether an incident of state sovereignty is protected by a limitation on an Article I power.

The actual scope of the Federal Government's authority with respect to the States has changed over the years, but the constitutional structure underlying and limiting that authority has not. In the end, just as a cup may be half empty or half full, it makes no difference whether one views the question at issue in this case as one of ascertaining the limits of the power delegated to the Federal Government under the affirmative provisions of the Constitution or one of discerning the core of sovereignty retained by the States under the Tenth Amendment. Either way, we must determine whether any of the three challenged provisions of the Low-Level Radioactive Waste Policy Amendments of 1985 oversteps the boundary between federal and state authority.

Petitioners do not contend that Congress lacks the power to regulate the disposal of low-level radioactive waste. Space in radioactive waste disposal sites is frequently sold by residents of one State to residents of another. Regulation of the resulting interstate market in waste disposal is therefore well within Congress's authority under the Commerce Clause. Petitioners likewise do not dispute that under the Supremacy Clause Congress could, if it wished, pre-empt state radioactive waste regulation. Petitioners contend only that the Tenth Amendment limits the power of Congress to regulate in the way it has chosen. Rather than addressing the problem of waste disposal by directly regulating the generators and disposers of waste, petitioners argue, Congress has impermissibly directed the States to regulate in this field.

Most of our recent cases interpreting the Tenth Amendment have concerned the authority of Congress to subject state governments to generally applicable laws.

This case presents no occasion to apply or revisit the holdings of any of these cases, as this is not a case in which Congress has subjected a State to the same legislation applicable to private parties.

This case instead concerns the circumstances under which Congress may use the States as implements of regulation; that is, whether Congress may direct or otherwise motivate the States to regulate in a particular field or a particular way. Our cases have established a few principles that guide our resolution of the issue.

As an initial matter, Congress may not simply "commandee[r] the legislative processes of the States by directly compelling them to enact and enforce a federal regulatory program." While Congress has substantial powers to govern the Nation directly, including in areas of intimate concern to the States, the Constitution has never been understood to confer upon Congress the ability to require the States to govern according to Congress' instructions.

The question whether the Constitution should permit Congress to employ state governments as regulatory agencies was a topic of lively debate among the Framers.

The Convention generated a great number of proposals for the structure of the new

Government, but two quickly took center stage. Under the Virginia Plan, as first introduced by Edmund Randolph, Congress would exercise legislative authority directly upon individuals, without employing the States as intermediaries. Under the New Jersey Plan, as first introduced by William Paterson, Congress would continue to require the approval of the States before legislating, as it had under the Articles of Confederation. These two plans underwent various revisions as the Convention progressed, but they remained the two primary options discussed by the delegates. One frequently expressed objection to the New Jersey Plan was that it might require the Federal Government to coerce the States into implementing legislation.

In the end, the Convention opted for a Constitution in which Congress would exercise its legislative authority directly over individuals rather than over States; for a variety of reasons, it rejected the New Jersey Plan in favor of the Virginia Plan. This choice was made clear to the subsequent state ratifying conventions. Oliver Ellsworth, a member of the Connecticut delegation in Philadelphia, explained the distinction to his State's convention: "This Constitution does not attempt to coerce sovereign bodies, states, in their political capacity. . . . But this legal coercion singles out the . . . individual."

Rufus King, one of Massachusetts' delegates, returned home to support ratification by recalling the Commonwealth's unhappy experience under the Articles of Confederation and arguing: "Laws, to be effective, therefore, must not be laid on states, but upon individuals." At New York's convention, Hamilton (another delegate in Philadelphia) exclaimed: "But can we believe that one state will ever suffer itself to be used as an instrument of coercion? The thing is a dream; it is impossible. Then we are brought to this dilemma—either a federal standing army is to enforce the requisitions, or the federal treasury is left without supplies and the government without support. What, sir, is the cure for this great evil? Nothing, but to enable the national laws to operate on individuals, in the same manner as those of the states do."

In providing for a stronger central government, therefore, the Framers explicitly chose a Constitution that confers upon Congress the power to regulate individuals, not States. As we have seen, the Court has consistently respected this choice. We have always understood that even where Congress has the authority under the Constitution to pass laws requiring or prohibiting certain acts, it lacks the power directly to compel the States to require or prohibit those acts.

This is not to say that Congress lacks the ability to encourage a State to regulate in a particular way, or that Congress may not hold out incentives to the States as a method of influencing a State's policy choices. Our cases have identified a variety of methods, short of outright coercion, by which Congress may urge a State to adopt a legislative program consistent with federal interests. Two of these methods are of particular relevance here.

First, under Congress' spending power, "Congress may attach conditions on the receipt of federal funds." *South Dakota v. Dole* (1987) was one such case: The Court found no constitutional flaw in a federal statute directing the Secretary of Transportation to withhold federal highway funds from States failing to adopt Congress' choice of a minimum drinking age.

Second, where Congress has the authority to regulate private activity under the Commerce Clause, we have recognized Congress' power to offer States the choice of regulating that activity according to federal standards or having state law preempted by federal regulation. This arrangement, which has been termed "a program of cooperative federalism," is replicated in numerous federal statutory schemes. These include the Clean Water Act, the Occupational Safety and Health Act of 1970, the Resource Conservation and Recovery Act of 1976, and the Alaska National Interest Lands Conservation Act.

By either of these two methods, as by any other permissible method of encouraging a State to conform to federal policy choices, the residents of the State retain the ultimate decision as to whether or not the State will comply. If a State's citizens view federal policy as sufficiently contrary to local interests, they may elect to decline a federal grant. If state residents would prefer their government to devote its attention and resources to problems other than those deemed important by Congress, they may choose to have the Federal Government rather than the State bear the expense of a federally mandated regulatory program, and they may continue to supplement that program to the extent state law is not pre-empted. Where Congress encourages state regulation rather than compelling it, state governments remain responsive to the local electorate's preferences; state officials remain accountable to the people.

By contrast, where the Federal Government compels States to regulate, the accountability of both state and federal officials is diminished. If the citizens of New York, for example, do not consider that making provision for the disposal of radioactive waste is in their best interest, they may elect state officials who share their view. That view can always be pre-empted under the Supremacy Clause if it is contrary to the national view, but in such a case it is the Federal Government that makes the decision in full view of the public, and it will be federal officials that suffer the consequences if the decision turns out to be detrimental or unpopular. But where the Federal Government directs the States to regulate, it may be state officials who will bear the brunt of public disapproval, while the federal officials who devised the regulatory program may remain insulated from the electoral ramifications of their decision. Accountability is thus diminished when, due to federal coercion, elected state officials cannot regulate in accordance with the views of the local electorate in matters not preempted by federal regulation.

With these principles in mind, we turn to the three challenged provisions of the Low-Level Radioactive Waste Policy Amendments Act of 1985.

The Act's first set of incentives, in which Congress has conditioned grants to the States upon the States' attainment of a series of milestones, is thus well within the authority of Congress under the Commerce and Spending Clauses. Because the first set of incentives is supported by affirmative constitutional grants of power to Congress, it is not inconsistent with the Tenth Amendment.

In the second set of incentives, Congress has authorized States and regional compacts with disposal sites gradually to increase the cost of access to the sites, and then to deny access altogether, to radioactive waste generated in States that do not meet federal deadlines. As a simple regulation, this provision would be within the power of Congress to authorize the States to discriminate against interstate commerce. Where federal regulation of private activity is within the scope of the Commerce Clause, we have recognized the ability of Congress to offer states the choice of regulating that activity according to federal standards or having state law preempted by federal regulation.

This is the choice presented to nonsited States by the Act's second set of incentives: States may either regulate the disposal of radioactive waste according to federal standards by attaining local or regional self-sufficiency, or their residents who produce radioactive waste will be subject to federal regulation authorizing sited States and regions to deny access to their disposal sites. The affected States are not compelled by Congress to regulate, because any burden caused by a State's refusal to regulate will fall on those who generate waste and find no outlet for its disposal, rather than on the State as a sovereign. A State whose citizens do not wish it to attain the Act's milestones may devote its attention and its resources to issues its citizens deem more worthy; the choice remains at all times with the residents of the State, not with Congress. The State need not expend any funds, or participate in any federal program, if local residents do not view such expenditures or participation as worthwhile. Nor must the State abandon the field if it does not accede to federal direction; the State may continue to regulate the generation and disposal of radioactive waste in any manner its citizens see fit.

The Act's second set of incentives thus represents a conditional exercise of Congress' commerce power, along the lines of those we have held to be within Congress' authority. As a result, the second set of incentives does not intrude on the sovereignty reserved to the States by the Tenth Amendment.

The take title provision is of a different character. This third so-called "incentive" offers States, as an alternative to regulating pursuant to Congress' direction, the option of taking title to and possession of the low-level radioactive waste generated within their borders and becoming liable for all damages waste generators suffer as a result of the States' failure to do so promptly. In this provision, Congress has crossed the line distinguishing encouragement from coercion.

Because an instruction to state governments to take title to waste, standing alone, would be beyond the authority of Congress, and because a direct order to regulate, standing alone, would also be beyond the authority of Congress, it follows that Congress lacks the power to offer the States a choice between the two. Unlike the first two sets of incentives, the take title incentive does not represent the conditional exercise of any congressional power enumerated in the Constitution. In this provision, Congress has not held out the threat of exercising its spending power or its commerce power; it has instead held out the threat, should the States not regulate according to one federal instruction, of simply forcing the States to submit to another federal instruction. A choice between two unconstitutionally coercive regulatory techniques is no choice at all. Either way, "the Act commandeers the legislative processes of the States by directly compelling them to enact and enforce a federal regulatory program," an outcome that has never been understood to lie within the authority conferred upon Congress by the Constitution.

The take title provision appears to be unique. No other federal statute has been cited which offers a state government no option other than that of implementing legislation enacted by Congress. Whether one views the take title provision as lying outside Congress' enumerated powers, or as infringing upon the core of state sovereignty reserved by the Tenth Amendment, the provision is inconsistent with the federal structure of our Government established by the Constitution.

Respondents raise a number of objections to this understanding of the limits of Congress' power. [They] . . . focus their attention on the process by which the Act was formulated. They correctly observe that public officials representing the State of New York lent their support to the Act's enactment. A Deputy Commissioner of the State's Energy Office testified in favor of the Act. Senator Moynihan of New York spoke in support of the Act on the floor of the Senate. Respondents note that the Act embodies a bargain among the sited and unsited States, a compromise to which New York was a willing participant and from which New York has reaped much benefit. Respondents then pose what appears at first to be a troubling question: How can a federal statute be found an unconstitutional infringement of State sovereignty when state officials consented to the statute's enactment?

The answer follows from an understanding of the fundamental purpose served by our Government's federal structure. The Constitution does not protect the sovereignty of States for the benefit of the States or state governments as abstract political entities, or even for the benefit of the public officials governing the States. To the contrary, the Constitution divides authority between federal and state governments for the protection of individuals. State sovereignty is not just an end in itself: "Rather, federalism secures to citizens the liberties that derive from the diffusion of sovereign power."

Where Congress exceeds its authority relative to the States, therefore, the departure from the constitutional plan cannot be ratified by the "consent" of state officials. An analogy to the separation of powers among the Branches of the Federal Government clarifies this point. The Constitution's division of power among the three Branches is violated where one Branch invades the territory of another, whether or not the encroached-upon Branch approves the encroachment. In *INS v. Chadha* (1983), we held that the legislative veto violated the constitutional requirement that legislation be presented to the President, despite Presidents' approval of hundreds of statutes containing a legislative veto provision. The constitutional authority of Congress cannot be expanded by the "consent" of the governmental unit whose domain is thereby narrowed, whether that unit is the Executive Branch or the States.

States are not mere political subdivisions of the United States. State governments are neither regional offices nor administrative agencies of the Federal Government. The positions occupied by state officials appear nowhere on the Federal Government's most detailed organizational chart. The Constitution instead "leaves to the several States a residuary and inviolable sovereignty," *The Federalist*, No. 39, reserved explicitly to the States by the Tenth Amendment.

Whatever the outer limits of that sovereignty may be, one thing is clear: The Federal Government may not compel the States to enact or administer a federal regulatory program. The Constitution permits both the Federal Government and the States to enact legislation regarding the disposal of low level radioactive waste. The Constitution enables the Federal Government to preempt state regulation contrary to federal interests, and it permits the Federal Government to hold out incentives to the States as a means of encouraging them to adopt suggested regulatory schemes. It does not, however, authorize Congress simply to direct the States to provide for the disposal of the radioactive waste generated within their borders. While there may be many constitutional methods of achieving regional self-sufficiency in radioactive waste disposal, the method Congress has chosen is not one of them. The judgment of the Court of Appeals is accordingly

Affirmed in part and reversed in part.

JUSTICE WHITE, with JUSTICE BLACK-MUN and JUSTICE STEVENS, concurring in part and dissenting in part.

In *Garcia,* we stated the proper inquiry: "[W]e are convinced that the fundamental limitation that the constitutional scheme imposes on the Commerce Clause to protect the 'States as States' is one of process rather than one of result. Any substantive restraint on the exercise of Commerce Clause powers must find its justification in the procedural nature of this basic limitation, and it must be tailored to compensate for possible failings in the national political process rather than to dictate a 'sacred province of state autonomy.'" Where it addresses this aspect of respondents' argument, the Court tacitly concedes that a failing of the political process cannot be shown in this case because it refuses to rebut the unassailable arguments that the States were well able to look after themselves in the legislative process that

culminated in the 1985 Act's passage. Indeed, New York acknowledges that its "congressional delegation participated in the drafting and enactment of both the 1980 and the 1985 Acts." The Court rejects this process-based argument by resorting to generalities and platitudes about the purpose of federalism being to protect individual rights.

Ultimately, I suppose, the entire structure of our federal constitutional government can be traced to an interest in establishing checks and balances to prevent the exercise of tyranny against individuals. But these fears seem extremely far distant to me in a situation such as this. We face a crisis of national proportions in the disposal of low-level radioactive waste, and Congress has acceded to the wishes of the States by permitting local decisionmaking rather than imposing a solution from Washington. New York itself participated and supported passage of this legislation at both the gubernatorial and federal representative levels, and then enacted state laws specifically to comply with the deadlines and timetables agreed upon by the States in the 1985 Act. For me, the Court's civics lecture has a decidedly hollow ring at a time when action, rather than rhetoric, is needed to solve a national problem.*

---

*With selective quotations from the era in which the Constitution was adopted, the majority attempts to bolster its holding that the take title provision is tantamount to federal "commandeering" of the States. In view of the many Tenth Amendment cases decided over the past two decades in which resort to the kind of historical analysis generated in the majority opinion was not deemed necessary, I do not read the majority's many invocations of history to be anything other than elaborate window-dressing. Certainly nowhere does the majority announce that its rule is compelled by an understanding of what the Framers may have thought about statutes of the type at issue here. Moreover, I would observe that, while its quotations add a certain flavor to the opinion, the majority's historical analysis has a distinctly wooden quality. One would not know from reading the majority's account, for instance, that the nature of federal-state relations changed fundamentally after the Civil War. That conflict produced in its wake a tremendous expansion in the scope of the Federal Government's law-making authority, so much so that the persons who helped to found the Republic would scarcely have recognized the many added roles the National Government assumed for itself. Moreover, the majority fails to mention the New Deal era, in which the Court recognized the enormous growth in Congress' power under the Commerce Clause.

While I believe we should not be blind to history, neither should we read it so selectively as to restrict the proper scope of Congress' powers under Article I, especially when the history not mentioned by the majority fully supports a more expansive understanding of the legislature's authority than may have existed in the late 18th-century.

Given the scanty textual support for the majority's position, it would be far more sensible to defer to a coordinate branch of government in its decision to devise a solution to a national problem of this kind.

Printz v. United States
521 U.S. 898 (1997)

In 1993, Congress enacted the Brady Handgun Violence Prevention Act, which, inter alia, required the attorney general to establish a national system for instantly checking prospective handgun purchasers' backgrounds and commanded the "chief law enforcement officer" (CLEO) of each local jurisdiction to conduct such checks and perform related tasks on an interim basis until the national system became operative. Jay Printz, the sheriff of Ravalli County, Montana, and Richard Mack, the sheriff of Graham County, Arizona, filed actions in separate US district courts challenging the interim provisions' constitutionality. In each case, the district court held that the background-check provision was unconstitutional; they concluded, however, that it was severable from the remainder of the act and effectively left a voluntary background-check system in place. The Ninth Circuit Court reversed, finding none of the interim provisions unconstitutional. The US Supreme Court granted certiorari. Opinion of the Court: <u>Scalia</u>, Rehnquist, O'Connor, Kennedy, Thomas. Concurring opinions: <u>O'Connor</u>; <u>Thomas</u>. Dissenting opinions: <u>Stevens</u>, Souter, Ginsburg, Breyer; <u>Souter</u>; <u>Breyer</u>, Stevens.

JUSTICE SCALIA delivered the opinion of the Court.

The question presented in these cases is whether certain interim provisions of the Brady Handgun Violence Prevention Act, commanding state and local law enforcement officers to conduct background checks on prospective handgun purchasers and to perform certain related tasks, violate the Constitution. . . .

The petitioners here object to being pressed into federal service, and contend that congressional action compelling state officers to execute federal laws is unconstitutional. Because there is no constitutional text speaking to this precise question, the answer to the CLEOs' challenge must be sought in historical understanding and practice, in the structure of the Constitution, and in the jurisprudence of this Court. We treat those three sources, in that order. . . .

Petitioners contend that compelled enlistment of state executive officers for the administration of federal programs is, until very recent years at least, unprecedented. The Government contends, to the contrary, that "the earliest Congresses enacted statutes that required the participation of state officials in the implementation of federal laws." The Government's contention demands our careful consideration, since early congressional enactments "provid[e] 'contemporaneous and weighty evidence' of the Constitution's meaning." . . .

These early laws establish, at most, that the Constitution was originally understood to permit imposition of an obligation on state *judges* to enforce federal prescriptions, insofar as those prescriptions related to matters appropriate for the judicial power. That assumption was perhaps implicit in one of the provisions of the Constitution, and was explicit in another. In accord with the so-called Madisonian Compromise, Article III, §1, established only a Supreme Court, and made the creation of lower federal courts optional with the Congress—even though it was obvious that the Supreme Court alone could not hear all federal cases throughout the United States. And the Supremacy Clause announced that "the Laws of the United States . . . shall be the supreme Law of the Land; and the Judges in every State shall be bound thereby." It is understandable why courts should have been viewed distinctively in this regard; unlike legislatures and executives, they applied the law of other sovereigns all the time. . . .

For these reasons, we do not think the early statutes imposing obligations on state courts imply a power of Congress to impress the state executive into its service. Indeed, it can be argued that the numerousness of these statutes, contrasted with the utter lack of statutes imposing obligations on the States' executive (notwithstanding the attractiveness of that course to Congress), suggests an assumed *absence* of such power. The only early federal law the Government has brought to our attention that imposed duties on state executive officers is the Extradition Act of 1793, which required the "executive authority" of a State to cause the arrest and delivery of a fugitive from justice upon the request of the executive authority of the State from which the fugitive had fled. That was in direct implementation, however, of the Extradition Clause of the Constitution itself, see Art. IV, §2.

Not only do the enactments of the early Congresses, as far as we are aware, contain no evidence of an assumption that the Federal Government may command the States' executive power in the absence of a particularized constitutional authorization, they contain some indication of precisely the opposite assumption. On September 23, 1789—the day before its proposal of the Bill of Rights—the First Congress enacted a law aimed at obtaining state assistance of the most rudimentary and necessary sort for the enforcement of the new Government's laws: the holding of federal prisoners in state jails at federal expense. Significantly, the law issued not a command to the States' executive, but a recommendation to their legislatures. Congress "recommended to the legislatures of the several States to pass laws, making it expressly the duty of the keepers of their gaols, to receive and safe keep therein all prisoners committed under the authority of the United States," and offered to pay 50 cents per month for each prisoner. Act of Sept. 23, 1789. Moreover, when Georgia refused to comply with the request, Congress's only reaction was a law authorizing the marshal in any State that failed to comply with the Recommendation of September 23, 1789, to

rent a temporary jail until provision for a permanent one could be made. . . .

The constitutional practice we have examined above tends to negate the existence of the congressional power asserted here, but is not conclusive. We turn next to consideration of the structure of the Constitution, to see if we can discern among its "essential postulate[s]" a principle that controls the present cases.

It is incontestible that the Constitution established a system of "dual sovereignty." Although the States surrendered many of their powers to the new Federal Government, they retained "a residuary and inviolable sovereignty," *The Federalist,* No. 39. This is reflected throughout the Constitution's text, including (to mention only a few examples) the prohibition on any involuntary reduction or combination of a State's territory, Art. IV, §3; the Judicial Power Clause, Art. III, §2, and the Privileges and Immunities Clause, Act. IV, §2, which speak of the "Citizens" of the States; the amendment provision, Article V, which requires the votes of three fourths of the States to amend the Constitution; and the Guarantee Clause, Art. IV, §4, which "presupposes the continued existence of the states and . . . those means and instrumentalities which are the creation of their sovereign and reserved rights." Residual state sovereignty was also implicit, of course, in the Constitution's conferral upon Congress of not all governmental powers, but only discrete, enumerated ones, Art. I, §8, which implication was rendered express by the Tenth Amendment's assertion that "[t]he powers not delegated to the United States by the Constitution, nor prohibited by it to the States, are reserved to the States respectively, or to the people." . . .

This separation of the two spheres is one of the Constitution's structural protections of liberty. "Just as the separation and independence of the coordinate branches of the Federal Government serve to prevent the accumulation of excessive power in any one branch, a healthy balance of power between the States and the Federal Government will reduce the risk of tyranny and abuse from either front." To quote Madison:

> In the compound republic of America, the power surrendered by the people is

first divided between two distinct governments, and then the portion allotted to each subdivided among distinct and separate departments. Hence a double security arises to the rights of the people. The different governments will control each other, at the same time that each will be controlled by itself. *The Federalist,* No. 51.

The power of the Federal Government would be augmented immeasurably if it were able to impress into its service—and at no cost to itself—the police officers of the 50 States.

We have thus far discussed the effect that federal control of state officers would have upon the first element of the "double security" alluded to by Madison: the division of power between State and Federal Governments. It would also have an effect upon the second element: the separation and equilibration of powers between the three branches of the Federal Government itself. The Constitution does not leave to speculation who is to administer the laws enacted by Congress; the President, it says, "shall take Care that the Laws be faithfully executed," personally and through officers whom he appoints (save for such inferior officers as Congress may authorize to be appointed by the "Courts of Law" or by "the Heads of Departments" who are themselves presidential appointees). The Brady Act effectively transfers this responsibility to thousands of CLEOs in the 50 States, who are left to implement the program without meaningful Presidential control (if indeed meaningful Presidential control is possible without the power to appoint and remove). The insistence of the Framers upon unity in the Federal Executive—to insure both vigor and accountability—is well known. That unity would be shattered, and the power of the President would be subject to reduction, if Congress could act as effectively without the President as with him, by simply requiring state officers to execute its laws.

The dissent of course resorts to the last, best hope of those who defend *ultra vires* congressional action, the Necessary and Proper Clause. It reasons that the power to regulate the sale of handguns under the Commerce Clause, coupled with the power to "make all Laws which shall be necessary and proper for carrying into Execution the foregoing Powers," conclusively establishes the Brady Act's constitutional validity, because the Tenth Amendment imposes no limitations on the exercise of *delegated* powers but merely prohibits the exercise of powers "*not* delegated to the United States." What destroys the dissent's Necessary and Proper Clause argument, however, is not the Tenth Amendment but the Necessary and Proper Clause itself. When a "La[w] . . . for carrying into Execution" the Commerce Clause violates the principle of state sovereignty reflected in the various constitutional provisions we mentioned earlier, it is not a "La[w] . . . *proper* for carrying into Execution the Commerce Clause," and is thus, in the words of *The Federalist,* "merely [an] ac[t] of usurpation" which "deserve[s] to be treated as such." *The Federalist,* No. 33. . . .

Finally, and most conclusively in the present litigation, we turn to the prior jurisprudence of this Court. Federal commandeering of state governments is such a novel phenomenon that this Court's first experience with it did not occur until the 1970's. . . . When we were at last confronted squarely with a federal statute that unambiguously required the States to enact or administer a federal regulatory program, our decision should have come as no surprise. At issue in *New York v. United States* (1992), were the so-called "take title" provisions of the Low-Level Radioactive Waste Policy Amendments Act of 1985, which required States either to enact legislation providing for the disposal of radioactive waste generated within their borders, or to take title to, and possession of the waste—effectively requiring the States either to legislate pursuant to Congress's directions, or to implement an administrative solution. We concluded that Congress could constitutionally require the States to do neither. "The Federal Government," we held, "may not compel the States to enact or administer a federal regulatory program."

The Government contends that *New York* is distinguishable on the following ground: unlike the "take title" provisions invalidated there, the background-check provision of the Brady Act does not require state legislature or executive officials to make policy, but instead issues a final directive to state CLEOs. It is permissible, the Government asserts, for Congress to command state or local officials to assist in the implementation of federal law so long as "Congress itself devises a clear legislative solution that regulates private conduct" and requires state or local officers to provide only "limited, nonpolicymaking help in enforcing that law." . . . Even assuming . . . that the Brady Act leaves no "policymaking" discretion with the States, we fail to see how that improves rather than worsens the intrusion upon state sovereignty. . . . It is an essential attribute of the States' retained sovereignty that they remain independent and autonomous within their proper sphere of authority. It is no more compatible with this independence and autonomy that their officers be "dragooned" (as Judge Fernandez put it in his dissent [from the Ninth Circuit decision]) into administering federal law, than it would be compatible with the independence and autonomy of the United States that its officers be impressed into service for the execution of state laws. . . .

The dissent makes no attempt to defend the Government's basis for distinguishing *New York,* but instead advances what seems to us an even more implausible theory. The Brady Act, the dissent asserts, is different from the "take title" provisions invalidated in *New York* because the former is addressed to individuals— namely CLEOs—while the latter were directed to the State itself. That is certainly a difference, but it cannot be a constitutionally significant one. While the Brady Act is directed to "individuals," it is directed to them in their official capacities as state officers; it controls their actions, not as private citizens, but as the agents of the State. The distinction between judicial writs and other government action directed against individuals in their personal capacity, on the one hand, and in their official capacity, on the other hand, is an ancient one, principally because it is dictated by common sense. We have observed that "a suit against a state official in his or her official capacity is not a suit against the official but rather is a suit against the official's office. . . . As such, it is no different from a suit against the State itself." *Will v. Michigan Dept. of State Police* (1989). And the same must be said of a directive to an

official in his or her official capacity. To say that the Federal Government cannot control the State, but can control all of its officers, is to say nothing of significance. Indeed, it merits the description "empty formalistic reasoning of the highest order." By resorting to this, the dissent not so much distinguishes *New York* as disembowels it. . . .

We held in *New York* that Congress cannot compel the States to enact or enforce a federal regulatory program. Today we hold that Congress cannot circumvent that prohibition by conscripting the State officers directly. The Federal Government may neither issue directives requiring the State to address particular problems, nor command the States' officers, or those of their political subdivisions, to administer or enforce a federal regulatory program. It matters not whether policymaking is involved, and no case-by-case weighing of the burdens or benefits is necessary; such commands are fundamentally incompatible with our constitutional system of dual sovereignty.

Accordingly, the judgment of the Court of Appeals for the Ninth Circuit is

Reversed.

JUSTICE THOMAS, concurring.

Although I join the Court's opinion in full, I write separately to emphasize that the Tenth Amendment affirms the undeniable notion that under our Constitution, the Federal Government is one of enumerated, hence limited, powers. . . . In my "revisionist" view, the Federal Government's authority under the Commerce Clause, which merely allocates to Congress the power "to regulate Commerce . . . among the several states," does not extend to the regulation of wholly *intra*state, point-of-sale transactions. See *United States v. Lopez* (1995) (concurring opinion). Absent the underlying authority to regulate the intrastate transfer of firearms, Congress surely lacks the corollary powers to impress state law enforcement officers into administering and enforcing such regulations.

Although this Court has long interpreted the Constitution as ceding Congress extensive authority to regulate commerce (interstate or otherwise), I continue to believe that we must "temper our Commerce Clause jurisprudence" and return to an interpretation better rooted in the Clause's original understanding. Even if we construe Congress's authority to regulate interstate commerce to encompass those intrastate transactions that "substantially affect" interstate commerce, I question whether Congress can regulate the particular transactions at issue here. The Constitution, in addition to delegating certain enumerated powers to Congress, places whole areas outside the reach of Congress' regulatory authority. The First Amendment, for example, is fittingly celebrated for preventing Congress from "prohibiting the free exercise" of religion or "abridging the freedom of speech." The Second Amendment similarly appears to contain an express limitation on the government's authority. That Amendment provides: "[a] well regulated Militia, being necessary to the security of a free State, the right of the people to keep and bear arms, shall not be infringed." This Court has not had recent occasion to consider the nature of the substantive right safeguarded by the Second Amendment. If, however, the Second Amendment is read to confer a *personal* right to "keep and bear arms," a colorable argument exists that the Federal Government's regulatory scheme, at least as it pertains to the purely intrastate sale or possession of firearms, runs afoul of that Amendment's protections. As the parties did not raise this argument, however, we need not consider it here. Perhaps, at some future date, this Court will have the opportunity to determine whether Justice Story was correct when he wrote that the right to bear arms "has justly been considered, as the palladium of the liberties of a republic." 3 J. Story, *Commentaries* §1890, p. 746 (1833). In the meantime, I join the Court's opinion striking down the challenged provisions of the Brady Act as inconsistent with the Tenth Amendment.

JUSTICE STEVENS, with whom JUSTICE SOUTER, JUSTICE GINSBURG, and JUSTICE BREYER join, dissenting.

When Congress exercises the powers delegated to it by the Constitution, it may impose affirmative obligations on executive and judicial officers of state and local governments as well as ordinary citizens. This conclusion is firmly supported by the text of the Constitution, the early history of the Nation, decisions of this Court, and a correct understanding of the basic structure of the Federal Government. . . .

[S]ince the ultimate issue is one of power, we must consider its implications in times of national emergency. Matters such as the enlistment of air raid wardens, the administration of a military draft, the mass inoculation of children to forestall an epidemic, or perhaps the threat of an international terrorist, may require a national response before federal personnel can be made available to respond. If the Constitution empowers Congress and the President to make an appropriate response, is there anything in the Tenth Amendment, "in historical understanding and practice, in the structure of the Constitution, [or] in the jurisprudence of this Court," that forbids the enlistment of state officers to make that response effective? More narrowly, what basis is there in any of those sources for concluding that it is the Members of this Court, rather than the elected representatives of the people, who should determine whether the Constitution contains the unwritten rule that the Court announces today? Perhaps today's majority would suggest that no such emergency is presented by the facts of these cases. But such a suggestion is itself an expression of a policy judgment. And Congress' view of the matter is quite different from that implied by the Court today. . . .

The text of the Constitution provides a sufficient basis for a correct disposition of this case. Article I, §8, grants the Congress the power to regulate commerce among the States. Putting to one side the revisionist views expressed by Justice Thomas in his concurring opinion in *United States v. Lopez* (1995), there can be no question that that provision adequately supports the regulation of commerce in handguns effected by the Brady Act. Moreover, the additional grant of authority in that section of the Constitution "[t]o make all Laws which shall be necessary and proper for carrying into Execution the foregoing Powers" is surely adequate to support the temporary enlistment of local police officers in the process of identifying persons who should not be entrusted with the possession of handguns. In short, the affirmative delegation of power in Article I provides ample authority for the congressional enactment. . . .

There is not a clause, sentence, or paragraph in the entire text of the Constitution of the United States that supports the proposition that a local police officer can ignore a command contained in a statute enacted by Congress pursuant to an express delegation of power enumerated in Article I. . . .

[T]he historical materials strongly suggest that the Founders intended to enhance the capacity of the federal government by empowering it—as a part of the new authority to make demands directly on individual citizens—to act through local officials. . . . During the debates concerning the ratification of the Constitution, it was assumed that state agents would act as tax collectors for the federal government. Opponents of the Constitution had repeatedly expressed fears that the new federal government's ability to impose taxes directly on the citizenry would result in an overbearing presence of federal tax collectors in the States. Federalists rejoined that this problem would not arise because, as Hamilton explained, "the United States . . . will make use of the State officers and State regulations for collecting" certain taxes. Similarly, Madison made clear that the new central government's power to raise taxes directly from the citizenry would "not be resorted to, except for supplemental purposes of revenue . . . and that the eventual collection, under the immediate authority of the Union, will generally be made by the officers . . . appointed by the several States." The Court's response to this powerful historical evidence is weak. The majority suggests that "none of these statements necessarily implies . . . Congress could impose these responsibilities without the consent of the States." No fair reading of these materials can justify such an interpretation. . . . Bereft of support in the history of the founding, the Court rests its conclusion on the claim that there is little evidence the National Government actually exercised such a power in the early years of the Republic. This reasoning is misguided in principle and in fact. . . . [T]he fact that Congress did elect to rely on state judges and the clerks of state courts to perform a variety of executive functions is surely evidence of a contemporary understanding that their status as state officials did not immunize them from federal service. The majority's description of these early statutes is both incomplete and at times misleading. . . .

[Concerning t]he Court's "structural" arguments . . . , [t]he fact that the Framers intended to preserve the sovereignty of the several States simply does not speak to the question whether individual state employees may be required to perform federal obligations. . . .

As we explained in *Garcia v. San Antonio Metropolitan Transit Authority*, (1985): "[T]he principal means chosen by the Framers to ensure the role of the States in the federal system lies in the structure of the Federal Government itself. It is no novelty to observe that the composition of the Federal Government was designed in large part to protect the States from overreaching by Congress." Given the fact that the Members of Congress are elected by the people of the several States, with each State receiving an equivalent number of Senators in order to ensure that even the smallest States have a powerful voice in the legislature, it is quite unrealistic to assume that they will ignore the sovereignty concerns of their constituents. It is far more reasonable to presume that their decisions to impose modest burdens on state officials from time to time reflect a considered judgment that the people in each of the States will benefit therefrom.

Indeed, the presumption of validity that supports all congressional enactments has added force with respect to policy judgments concerning the impact of a federal statute upon the respective States. The majority points to nothing suggesting that the political safeguards of federalism identified in *Garcia* need be supplemented by a rule, grounded in neither constitutional history nor text, flatly prohibiting the National Government from enlisting state and local officials in the implementation of federal law.

Recent developments demonstrate that the political safeguards protecting Our Federalism are effective. The majority expresses special concern that were its rule not adopted the Federal Government would be able to avail itself of the services of state government officials "at no cost to itself." But this specific problem of federal actions that have the effect of imposing so-called "unfunded mandates" on the States has been identified and meaningfully addressed by

Congress in recent legislation. See Unfunded Mandates Reform Act of 1995, Pub. L. 104–4, 109 Stat. 48.

The statute was designed "to end the imposition, in the absence of full consideration by Congress, of Federal mandates on State . . . governments without adequate Federal funding, in a manner that may displace other essential State . . . governmental priorities." . . . Whatever the ultimate impact of the new legislation, its passage demonstrates that unelected judges are better off leaving the protection of federalism to the political process in all but the most extraordinary circumstances.

Perversely, the majority's rule seems more likely to damage than to preserve the safeguards against tyranny provided by the existence of vital state governments. By limiting the ability of the Federal Government to enlist state officials in the implementation of its programs, the Court creates incentives for the National Government to aggrandize itself. In the name of States' rights, the majority would have the Federal Government create vast national bureaucracies to implement its policies. This is exactly the sort of thing that the early Federalists promised would not occur, in part as a result of the National Government's ability to rely on the magistracy of the states. . . .

In response to this dissent, the majority asserts that the difference between a federal command addressed to individuals and one addressed to the State itself "cannot be a constitutionally significant one." But as I have already noted, there is abundant authority in our Eleventh Amendment jurisprudence recognizing a constitutional distinction between local government officials, such as the CLEOs who brought this action, and State entities that are entitled to sovereign immunity. To my knowledge, no one has previously thought that the distinction "disembowels" the Eleventh Amendment. . . .

The provision of the Brady Act that crosses the Court's newly defined constitutional threshold is more comparable to a statute requiring local police officers to report the identity of missing children to the Crime Control Center of the Department of Justice than to an offensive federal command to a sovereign state. If Congress believes that such a statute will benefit the people of the Nation, and serve the interests of cooperative federalism better than an enlarged federal bureaucracy, we should respect both its policy judgment and its appraisal of its constitutional power. Accordingly, I respectfully dissent.

JUSTICE SOUTER, dissenting.

I join Justice Stevens['s] dissenting opinion, but subject to the following qualifications. While I do not find anything dispositive in the paucity of early examples of federal employment of state officers for executive purposes, for the reason given by Justice Stevens, neither would I find myself in dissent with no more to go on than those few early instances in the administration of naturalization laws, for example, or such later instances as state support for federal emergency action. These illustrations of state action implementing congressional statutes are consistent with the Government's positions, but they do not speak to me with much force.

Alden v. Maine
527 U.S. 706 (1999)

In 1992, the petitioners in this case, a group of probation officers, filed suit against their employer, the State of Maine, in the federal district court. The officers alleged that the state had violated the overtime provisions of the Fair Labor Standards Act of 1938 (FLSA) and sought compensation. While the suit was pending, the Supreme Court decided in Seminole Tribe of Florida v. Florida *(1996) that Congress lacks power under Article I to abrogate the states'* *sovereign immunity—the states' freedom from suit without their own consent—in federal court. Relying on that ruling, the district court then dismissed the officers' suit.*

The officers next filed the same suit in state court. Although the FLSA authorizes private actions against states in their own courts, the trial court dismissed the suit on the basis of the state's sovereign immunity, and the Maine Supreme Judicial Court affirmed. In a similar case, however, the Supreme Court of Arkansas in 1998 reached the opposite result: it rejected the state's claim of sovereign immunity and upheld the right of private parties to sue states under FLSA in state courts. In view of the importance of the issue and the conflict between the two courts, the Supreme Court granted certiorari. Opinion of the Court: <u>Kennedy</u>, Rehnquist, O'Connor, Scalia, Thomas. Dissenting opinion: <u>Souter</u>, Stevens, Ginsburg, Breyer.

JUSTICE KENNEDY delivered the opinion of the Court.

We hold that the powers delegated to Congress under Article I of the United States Constitution do not include the power to subject nonconsenting States to private suits for damages in state courts. We decide as well that the State of Maine has not consented to suits for overtime pay and liquidated damages under the FLSA. On these premises we affirm the judgment sustaining dismissal of the suit.

The Eleventh Amendment makes explicit reference to the States' immunity from suits "commenced or prosecuted against one of the United States by Citizens of another State, or by Citizens or Subjects of any Foreign State." We have, as a result, sometimes referred to the States' immunity from suit as "Eleventh Amendment immunity." The phrase is convenient shorthand but something of a misnomer, for the sovereign immunity of the States neither derives from nor is limited by the terms of the Eleventh Amendment. Rather, as the Constitution's structure, and its history, and the authoritative interpretations by this Court make clear, the States' immunity from suit is a fundamental aspect of the sovereignty which the States enjoyed before the ratification of the Constitution, and which they retain today (either literally or by virtue of their admission into the Union upon an equal footing with the other States) except as altered by the plan of the Convention or certain constitutional Amendments.

Although the Constitution establishes a National Government with broad, often plenary authority over matters within its recognized competence, the founding document "specifically recognizes the States as sovereign entities." *Seminole Tribe of Fla. v. Florida* (1996). Various textual provisions of the Constitution assume the States' continued existence and active participation in the fundamental processes of governance. See *Printz v. United States* (1997). The limited and enumerated powers granted to the Legislative, Executive, and Judicial Branches of the National Government, moreover, underscore the vital role reserved to the States by the constitutional design. Any doubt regarding the constitutional role of the States as sovereign entities is removed by the Tenth Amendment, which, like the other provisions of the Bill of Rights, was enacted to allay lingering concerns about the extent of the national power. . . .

The federal system established by our Constitution preserves the sovereign status of the States in two ways. First, it reserves to them a substantial portion of the Nation's primary sovereignty, together with the dignity and essential attributes inhering in that status. The States "form distinct and independent portions of the supremacy, no more subject, within their respective spheres, to the general authority than the general authority is subject to them, within its own sphere." *The Federalist*, No. 39.

Second, even as to matters within the competence of the National Government, the constitutional design secures the founding generation's rejection of "the concept of a central government that would act upon and through the States" in favor of "a system in which the State and Federal Governments would exercise concurrent authority over the people" who were, in Hamilton's words, "the only proper objects of government." The Framers explicitly chose a Constitution that confers upon Congress the power to regulate individuals, not States. In this the founders achieved a deliberate departure from the Articles of Confederation: Experience under the Articles had "exploded on all hands the practicality of making laws, with coercive sanctions, for the States as political bodies." 2 *Records of the Federal Convention of 1787* (J. Madison).

The States thus retain "residuary and inviolable sovereignty." *The Federalist*, No. 39. They are not relegated to the role of mere provinces or political corporations, but retain the dignity, though not the full authority, of sovereignty.

The generation that designed and adopted our federal system considered immunity from private suits central to sovereign dignity. When the Constitution was ratified, it was well established in English law that the Crown could not be sued without consent in its own courts. . . . Although the American people had rejected other aspects of English political theory, the doctrine that a sovereign could not be sued without its consent was universal in the States when the Constitution was drafted and ratified. The ratification debates, furthermore, underscored the importance of the States' sovereign immunity to the American people. Grave concerns were raised by the provisions of Article III which extended the federal judicial power to controversies between States and citizens of other States or foreign nations. The leading advocates of the Constitution assured the people in no uncertain terms that the Constitution would not strip the States of sovereign immunity. One assurance was contained in *The Federalist* No. 81, written by Alexander Hamilton:

> It is inherent in the nature of sovereignty not to be amenable to the suit of an individual *without its consent*. This is the general sense, and the general practice of mankind; and the exemption, as one of the attributes of sovereignty, is now enjoyed by the government of every State in the Union. Unless therefore, there is a surrender of this immunity in the plan of the convention, it will remain with the States, and the danger intimated must be merely ideal. [T]here is no color to pretend that the State governments would, by the adoption of that plan, be divested of the privilege of paying their own debts in their own way, free from every constraint but that which flows from the obligations of good faith. The contracts between a nation and individuals are only binding on the conscience of the sovereign, and have no pretensions to a compulsive force. They confer no right of action independent of the sovereign Will. To what purpose would it be to authorize suits against States for the debts they owe? How could recoveries be enforced? It is evident that it could

not be done without waging war against the contracting State; and to ascribe to the federal courts, by mere implication, and in destruction of the preexisting right of the State governments, a power which would involve such a consequence, would be altogether forced and unwarrantable.

At the Virginia ratifying convention, James Madison echoed this theme. . . . When Madison's explanation was questioned, John Marshall provided immediate support. Although the state conventions which addressed the issue of sovereign immunity in their formal ratification documents sought to clarify the point by constitutional amendment, they made clear that they, like Hamilton, Madison, and Marshall, understood the Constitution as drafted to preserve the States' immunity from private suits.

Despite the persuasive assurances of the Constitution's leading advocates and the expressed understanding of the only state conventions to address the issue in explicit terms, this Court held, just five years after the Constitution was adopted, that Article III authorized a private citizen of another State to sue the State of Georgia without its consent. *Chisholm v. Georgia* (1793).

The Court's decision "fell upon the country with a profound shock." . . . An initial proposal to amend the Constitution was introduced in the House of Representatives the day after *Chisholm* was announced; the proposal adopted as the Eleventh Amendment was introduced in the Senate promptly following an intervening recess. Congress turned to the latter proposal with great dispatch; little more than two months after its introduction it had been endorsed by both Houses and forwarded to the States. Each House spent but a single day discussing the Amendment, and the vote in each House was close to unanimous.

It might be argued that the *Chisholm* decision was a correct interpretation of the constitutional design and that the Eleventh Amendment represented a deviation from the original understanding. This, however, seems unsupportable. First, despite the opinion of Justice Iredell, the majority failed to address either the practice or the understanding that prevailed in the States at the time the Constitution was adopted. Second, even a casual reading of the opinions suggests the majority suspected the decision would be unpopular and surprising. These concessions undercut the crucial premise that either the Constitution's literal text or the principle of popular sovereignty necessarily overrode widespread practice and opinion.

The text and history of the Eleventh Amendment also suggest that Congress acted not to change but to restore the original constitutional design. Although earlier drafts of the Amendment had been phrased as express limits on the judicial power granted in Article III, the adopted text addressed the proper interpretation of that provision of the original Constitution. By its terms, then, the Eleventh Amendment did not redefine the federal judicial power but instead overruled the Court. . . . Given the outraged reaction to *Chisholm*, as well as Congress' repeated refusal to otherwise qualify the text of the Amendment, it is doubtful that if Congress meant to write a new immunity into the Constitution it would have limited that immunity to the narrow text of the Eleventh Amendment.

Can we suppose that, when the Eleventh Amendment was adopted, it was understood to be left open for citizens of a State to sue their own state in federal courts, whilst the idea of suits by citizens of other states, or of foreign states, was indignantly repelled? Suppose that Congress, when proposing the Eleventh Amendment, had appended to it a proviso that nothing therein contained should prevent a State from being sued by its own citizens in cases arising under the Constitution or laws of the United States, can we imagine that it would have been adopted by the States? The supposition that it would is almost an absurdity on its face. The more natural inference is that the Constitution was understood, in light of its history and structure, to preserve the States' traditional immunity from private suits. As the Amendment clarified the only provisions of the Constitution that anyone had suggested might support a contrary understanding, there was no reason to draft with a broader brush.

Finally, the swiftness and near unanimity with which the Eleventh Amendment was adopted suggest "either that the Court had not captured the original understanding, or that the country had changed its collective mind most rapidly." The more reasonable interpretation, of course, is that regardless of the views of four Justices in *Chisholm*, the country as a whole (which had adopted the Constitution just five years earlier) had not understood the document to strip the States' of their immunity from private suits. Although the dissent attempts to rewrite history to reflect a different original understanding, its evidence is unpersuasive. . . . [T]he scanty and equivocal evidence offered by the dissent establishes no more than what is evident from the decision in *Chisholm*, that some members of the founding generation disagreed with Hamilton, Madison, Marshall, Iredell, and the only state conventions formally to address the matter. The events leading to the adoption of the Eleventh Amendment, however, make clear that the individuals who believed the Constitution stripped the States of their immunity from suit were at most a small minority. . . .

The Court has been consistent in interpreting the adoption of the Eleventh Amendment as conclusive evidence that the decision in *Chisholm* was contrary to the well-understood meaning of the Constitution, and that the views expressed by Hamilton, Madison, and Marshall during the ratification debates, and by Justice Iredell in his dissenting opinion in *Chisholm* reflect the original understanding of the Constitution. . . . Following this approach, the Court has upheld States' assertions of sovereign immunity in various contexts falling outside the literal text of the Eleventh Amendment. In *Hans v. Louisiana* (1890), the Court held that sovereign immunity barred a citizen from suing his own State under the federal-question head of jurisdiction. . . . Later decisions rejected similar requests to conform the principle of sovereign immunity to the strict language of the Eleventh Amendment in holding that non-consenting States are immune from suits brought by federal corporations, foreign nations, or Indian tribes, and in concluding that sovereign immunity is a defense to suits in admiralty, though the text of the Eleventh Amendment addresses only suits "in law or equity." These holdings reflect a settled doctrinal understanding, consistent with the views of the leading advocates of the Constitution's ratification, that sovereign immunity derives not from the Eleventh Amendment but from the structure of the original Constitution itself. The Eleventh Amendment confirmed rather than established sovereign immunity as a constitutional principle; it follows that the scope of the States' immunity from suit is demarcated not by the text of the Amendment alone but by fundamental postulates implicit in the constitutional design.

In this case we must determine whether Congress has the power, under Article I, to subject non-consenting States to private suits in their own courts. As the foregoing discussion makes clear, the fact that the Eleventh Amendment by its terms limits only "[t]he Judicial power of the United States" does not resolve the question. While the constitutional principle of sovereign immunity does pose a bar to federal jurisdiction over suits against nonconsenting States, this is not the only structural basis of sovereign immunity implicit in the constitutional design. Rather, "[t]here is also the postulate that States of the Union, still possessing attributes of sovereignty, shall be immune from suits, without their consent, save where there has been 'a surrender of this immunity in the plan of the convention.'" This separate and distinct structural principle is not directly related to the scope of the judicial power established by Article III, but inheres in the system of federalism established by the Constitution. In exercising its Article I powers Congress may subject the States to private suits in their own courts only if there is "compelling evidence" that the States were required to surrender this power to Congress pursuant to the constitutional design.

Petitioners contend the text of the Constitution and our recent sovereign immunity decisions establish that the States were required to relinquish this portion of their sovereignty. We turn first to these sources.

Article I grants Congress broad power to enact legislation in several enumerated areas of national concern. The Supremacy Clause, furthermore, provides: "This Constitution, and the Laws of the United States which shall be made in Pursuance thereof . . . shall be the supreme Law of the Land; and the Judges in every State shall be bound thereby, any Thing in the Constitution or Laws of any state to the Contrary notwithstanding." U.S. Const., Art. VI. It is contended that, by virtue of these provisions, where Congress enacts legislation subjecting the States to suit, the legislation by necessity overrides the sovereign immunity of the States. As is evident from its text, however, the Supremacy Clause enshrines as "the supreme Law of the Land" only those federal Acts that accord with the constitutional design. Appeal to the Supremacy Clause alone merely raises the question whether a law is a valid exercise of the national power. The Constitution, by delegating to Congress the power to establish the supreme law of the land when acting within its enumerated powers, does not foreclose a State from asserting immunity to claims arising under federal law merely because that law derives not from the State itself but from the national power. We reject any contention that substantive federal law by its own force necessarily overrides the sovereign immunity of the States. When a State asserts its immunity to suit, the question is not the primacy of federal law but the implementation of the law in a manner consistent with the constitutional sovereignty of the States. Nor can we conclude that the specific Article I powers delegated to Congress necessarily include, by virtue of the Necessary and Proper Clause or otherwise, the incidental authority to subject the States to private suits as a means of achieving objectives otherwise within the scope of the enumerated powers. Although some of our decisions had endorsed this contention, they have since been overruled. As we have recognized in an analogous context: "When a La[w] for carrying into Execution the Commerce Clause violates the principle of state sovereignty reflected in the various constitutional provisions, it is not a La[w] *proper* for carrying into Execution the Commerce Clause, and is thus, in the words of *The Federalist*, 'merely [an] ac[t] of usurpation'" which "deserve[s] to be treated as such." *Printz v. United States.*

The dissenting opinion seeks to reopen these precedents, contending that state sovereign immunity must derive either from the common law (in which case the dissent contends it is defeasible by statute) or from natural law (in which case the dissent believes it cannot bar a federal claim). As should be obvious to all, this is a false dichotomy. The text and the structure of the Constitution protect various rights and principles. Many of these, such as the right to trial by jury and the prohibition on unreasonable searches and seizures, derive from the common law. The common-law lineage of these rights does not mean they are defeasible by statute or remain mere common-law rights, however. They are, rather, constitutional rights, and form the fundamental law of the land. Although the sovereign immunity of the States derives at least in part from the common-law tradition, the structure and history of the Constitution make clear that the immunity exists today by constitutional design. . . .

Underlying constitutional form are considerations of great substance. Private suits against nonconsenting States—especially suits for money damages—may threaten the financial integrity of the States. It is indisputable that, at the time of the founding, many of the States could have been forced into insolvency but for their immunity from private suits for money damages. Even today, an unlimited congressional power to authorize suits in state court to levy upon the treasuries of the States for compensatory damages, attorney's fees, and even punitive damages could create staggering burdens, giving Congress a power and a leverage over the States that is not contemplated by our constitutional design. The potential national power would pose a severe and notorious danger to the States and their resources.

A congressional power to strip the States of their immunity from private suits in their own courts would pose more subtle risks as well. The principle of immunity from litigation assures the states and the nation from unanticipated intervention in the processes of government. When the States' immunity from private suits is disregarded, "the course of their public policy and the administration of their public affairs" may become "subject to and controlled by the mandates of judicial tribunals without their consent, and in favor of individual interests." While the States have relinquished their immunity from suit in some special contexts—at least as a practical mat-

ter—this surrender carries with it substantial costs to the autonomy, the decision-making ability, and the sovereign capacity of the States. A general federal power to authorize private suits for money damages would place unwarranted strain on the States' ability to govern in accordance with the will of their citizens. Today, as at the time of the founding, the allocation of scarce resources among competing needs and interests lies at the heart of the political process. While the judgment creditor of the State may have a legitimate claim for compensation, other important needs and worthwhile ends compete for access to the public fisc. Since all cannot be satisfied in full, it is inevitable that difficult decisions involving the most sensitive and political of judgments must be made. If the principle of representative government is to be preserved to the States, the balance between competing interests must be reached after deliberation by the political process established by the citizens of the State, not by judicial decree mandated by the Federal Government and invoked by the private citizen. . . .

The sole remaining question is whether Maine has waived its immunity. The State of Maine regards the immunity from suit as "one of the highest attributes inherent in the nature of sovereignty," and adheres to the general rule that "specific authority conferred by an enactment of the legislature is requisite if the sovereign is to be taken as having shed the protective mantle of immunity." Petitioners have not attempted to establish a waiver of immunity under this standard. Although petitioners contend the State has discriminated against federal rights by claiming sovereign immunity from this FLSA suit, there is no evidence that the State has manipulated its immunity in a systematic fashion to discriminate against federal causes of action. To the extent Maine has chosen to consent to certain classes of suits while maintaining its immunity from others, it has done no more than exercise a privilege of sovereignty concomitant to its constitutional immunity from suit. The State, we conclude, has not consented to suit. . . .

The judgment of the Supreme Judicial Court of Maine is

Affirmed.

JUSTICE SOUTER, with whom JUSTICE STEVENS, JUSTICE GINSBURG, and JUSTICE BREYER join, dissenting.

In *Seminole Tribe of Fla. v. Florida* (1996), a majority of this Court invoked the Eleventh Amendment to declare that the federal judicial power under Article III of the Constitution does not reach a private action against a State, even on a federal question. In the Court's conception, however, the Eleventh Amendment was understood as having been enhanced by a "background principle" of state sovereign immunity (understood as immunity to suit) that operated beyond its limited codification in the Amendment, dealing solely with federal citizen-state diversity jurisdiction. To the *Seminole Tribe* dissenters, of whom I was one, the Court's enhancement of the Amendment was at odds with constitutional history and at war with the conception of divided sovereignty that is the essence of American federalism. Today's issue arises naturally in the aftermath of the decision in *Seminole Tribe*. The Court holds that the Constitution bars an individual suit against a State to enforce a federal statutory right under the Fair Labor Standards Act of 1938 (FLSA), when brought in the State's courts over its objection. In thus complementing its earlier decision, the Court of course confronts the fact that the state forum renders the Eleventh Amendment beside the point, and it has responded by discerning a simpler and more straightforward theory of state sovereign immunity than it found in *Seminole Tribe*: a State's sovereign immunity from all individual suits is a "fundamental aspect" of state sovereignty "confirm[ed]" by the Tenth Amendment. . . .

There is no evidence that the Tenth Amendment constitutionalized a concept of sovereign immunity as inherent in the notion of statehood, and no evidence that any concept of inherent sovereign immunity was understood historically to apply when the sovereign sued was not the font of the law. Nor does the Court fare any better with its subsidiary lines of reasoning, that the state-court action is barred by the scheme of American federalism, a result supposedly confirmed by a history largely devoid of precursors to the action considered here. The Court's federalism ignores the accepted authority of Congress to bind States under the FLSA and to provide for enforcement of federal rights in state court. The Court's history simply disparages the capacity of the Constitution to order relationships in a Republic that has changed since the founding. On each point the Court has raised it is mistaken, and I respectfully dissent from its judgment.

The Court rests its decision principally on the claim that immunity from suit was "a fundamental aspect of the sovereignty which the States enjoyed before the ratification of the Constitution," an aspect which the Court understands to have survived the ratification of the Constitution in 1788 and to have been "confirm[ed]" and given constitutional status by the adoption of the Tenth Amendment in 1791. If the Court truly means by "sovereign immunity" what that term meant at common law, its argument would be insupportable. While sovereign immunity entered many new state legal systems as a part of the common law selectively received from England, it was not understood to be indefeasible or to have been given any such status by the new National Constitution, which did not mention it. Had the question been posed, state sovereign immunity could not have been thought to shield a State from suit under federal law on a subject committed to national jurisdiction by Article I of the Constitution. Congress exercising its conceded Article I power may unquestionably abrogate such immunity.

The Court does not, however, offer today's holding as a mere corollary to its reasoning in *Seminole Tribe,* substituting the Tenth Amendment for the Eleventh as the occasion demands, and it is fair to read its references to a "fundamental aspect" of state sovereignty as referring not to a prerogative inherited from the Crown, but to a conception necessarily implied by statehood itself. The conception is thus not one of common law so much as of natural law, a universally applicable proposition discoverable by reason. This, I take it, is the sense in which the Court so emphatically relies on Alexander Hamilton's reference in *The Federalist,* No. 81 to the States' sovereign immunity from suit as an "inherent" right. . . .

I understand the Court to rely on the Hamiltonian formulation with the object of suggesting that its conception of sovereign immunity as a "fundamental aspect" of sovereignty was a substantially popular, if not the dominant, view in the periods of Revolution and Confederation. There is, after all, nothing else in the Court's opinion that would suggest a basis for saying that the ratification of the Tenth Amendment gave this "fundamental aspect" its constitutional status and protection against any legislative tampering by Congress. The Court's principal rationale for today's result, then, turns on history: was the natural law conception of sovereign immunity as inherent in any notion of an independent State widely held in the United States in the period preceding the ratification of 1788 (or the adoption of the Tenth Amendment in 1791)?

The answer is certainly no. There is almost no evidence that the generation of the Framers thought sovereign immunity was fundamental in the sense of being unalterable. Whether one looks at the period before the framing, to the ratification controversies, or to the early republican era, the evidence is the same. Some Framers thought sovereign immunity was an obsolete royal prerogative inapplicable in a republic; some thought sovereign immunity was a common-law power defeasible, like other common-law rights, by statute; and perhaps a few thought, in keeping with a natural law view distinct from the common-law conception, that immunity was inherent in a sovereign because the body that made a law could not logically be bound by it. Natural law thinking on the part of a doubtful few will not, however, support the Court's position. . . .

The Court's rationale for today's holding based on a conception of sovereign immunity as somehow fundamental to sovereignty or inherent in statehood fails for the lack of any substantial support for such a conception in the thinking of the founding era. The Court cannot be counted out yet, however, for it has a second line of argument looking not to a clause-based reception of the natural law conception or even to its recognition as a "background principle," but to a structural basis in the Constitution's creation of a federal system. Immunity, the Court says, "inheres in the system of federalism established by the Constitution," its "contours [being] determined by the founders' understanding, not by the principles or limitations derived from natural law." That is, the Court believes that the federal constitutional structure itself necessitates recognition of some degree of state autonomy broad enough to include sovereign immunity from suit in a State's own courts, regardless of the federal source of the claim asserted against the State. If one were to read the Court's federal structure rationale in isolation from the preceding portions of the opinion, it would appear that the Court's position on state sovereign immunity might have been rested entirely on federalism alone. If it had been, however, I would still be in dissent, for the Court's argument that state court sovereign immunity on federal questions is inherent in the very concept of federal structure is demonstrably mistaken. The National Constitution formally and finally repudiated the received political wisdom that a system of multiple sovereignties constituted the "great solecism of an *imperium in imperio*." Once "the atom of sovereignty" had been split, the general scheme of delegated sovereignty as between the two component governments of the federal system was clear, and was succinctly stated by Chief Justice Marshall: "In America, the powers of sovereignty are divided between the government of the Union, and those of the States. They are each sovereign, with respect to the objects committed to it, and neither sovereign with respect to the objects committed to the other." *McCulloch v. Maryland* (1819). Hence the flaw in the Court's appeal to federalism. The State of Maine is not sovereign with respect to the national objective of the FLSA. It is not the authority that promulgated the FLSA, on which the right of action in this case depends. That authority is the United States acting through the Congress, whose legislative power under Article I of the Constitution to extend FLSA coverage to state employees has already been decided, see *Garcia v. San Antonio Metropolitan Transit Authority* (1985), and is not contested here. Nor can it be argued that because the State of Maine creates its own court system, it has authority to decide what sorts of claims may be entertained there, and thus in effect to control the right of action in this case. Maine has created state courts of general jurisdiction; once it has done so, the Supremacy Clause of the Constitution, which requires state courts to enforce federal law and state-court judges to be bound by it, requires the Maine courts to entertain this federal cause of action. Maine has advanced no valid excuse for its courts' refusal to hear federal-law claims in which Maine is a defendant, and sovereign immunity cannot be that excuse, simply because the State is not sovereign with respect to the subject of the claim against it. The Court's insistence that the federal structure bars Congress from making States susceptible to suit in their own courts is, then, plain mistaken. . . .

If today's decision occasions regret at its anomalous versions of history and federal theory, it is the more regrettable in being the second time the Court has suddenly changed the course of prior decision in order to limit the exercise of authority over a subject now concededly within the Article I jurisdiction of the Congress. . . . [T]here is much irony in the Court's profession that it grounds its opinion on a deeply rooted historical tradition of sovereign immunity, when the Court abandons a principle nearly as inveterate, and much closer to the hearts of the Framers: that where there is a right, there must be a remedy. The generation of the Framers thought the principle so crucial that several States put it into their constitutions. Yet today the Court has no qualms about saying frankly that the federal right to damages afforded by Congress under the FLSA cannot create a concomitant private remedy. It will not

do for the Court to respond that a remedy was never available where the right in question was against the sovereign. A State is not the sovereign when a federal claim is pressed against it, and even the English sovereign opened itself to recovery and, unlike Maine, provided the remedy to complement the right. To the Americans of the founding generation it would have been clear that if the King would do right, the democratically chosen Government of the United States could do no less.

The Court has swung back and forth with regrettable disruption on the enforceability of the FLSA against the States, but if the present majority had a defensible position one could at least accept its decision with an expectation of stability ahead. As it is, any such expectation would be naive. The resemblance of today's state sovereign immunity to the *Lochner* era's industrial due process is striking. The Court began this century by imputing immutable constitutional status to a conception of economic self-reliance that was never true to industrial life and grew insistently fictional with the years, and the Court has chosen to close the century by conferring like status on a conception of state sovereign immunity that is true neither to history nor to the structure of the Constitution. I expect the Court's late essay into immunity doctrine will prove the equal of its earlier experiment in laissez-faire, the one being as unrealistic as the other, as indefensible, and probably as fleeting.

The Civil Rights Cases
109 U.S. 3 (1883)

The Civil Rights Act of 1875 prohibited any person from denying a citizen "the full and equal enjoyment of the accommodations, advantages, facilities, and privileges of inns, public conveyances on land or water, theatres, and other places of public amusement." In the five cases that were heard together as The Civil Rights Cases, *persons were indicted for violating the act by denying accommodations to blacks in a hotel, a theater, an opera house, and a ladies' car on a train. Two of the five cases went to the Supreme Court on writs of error brought by the plaintiffs in federal circuit courts. The other three were certified to the Supreme Court because the*

lower-court judges disagreed on the constitutionality of the act. Opinion of the Court: <u>Bradley</u>, Waite, Miller, Field, Woods, Matthews, Gray, Blatchford. Dissenting opinion: <u>Harlan</u>.

JUSTICE BRADLEY delivered the opinion of the Court.

It is obvious that the primary and important question in all the cases is the constitutionality of the law: for if the law is unconstitutional none of the prosecutions can stand. . . .

The essence of the law is, not to declare broadly that all persons shall be entitled to the full and equal enjoyment of the accommodations, advantages, facilities, and privileges of inns, public conveyances, and theatres; but that such enjoyment shall not be subject to any conditions applicable only to citizens of a particular race or color, or who had been in a previous condition of servitude. In other words, it is the purpose of the law to declare that, in the enjoyment of the accommodations and privileges of inns, public conveyances, theatres, and other places of public amusement, no distinction shall be made between citizens of different race or color, or between those who have, and those who have not, been slaves. . . .

Has Congress constitutional power to make such a law? Of course, no one will contend that the power to pass it was contained in the Constitution before the adoption of the last three amendments. The power is sought, first, in the Fourteenth Amendment, and the views and arguments of distinguished Senators, advanced whilst the law was under consideration, claiming authority to pass it by virtue of that amendment, are the principal arguments adduced in favor of the power. . . .

The first section of the Fourteenth Amendment (which is the one relied on), after declaring who shall be citizens of the United States, and of the several States, is prohibitory in its character, and prohibitory upon the States. It declares that: "No State shall make or enforce any law which shall abridge the privileges or immunities of citizens of the United States; nor shall any State deprive any person of life, liberty, or property without due process of law; nor deny to any person within its jurisdiction the equal protection of the laws."

It is State action of a particular character that is prohibited. Individual invasion of individual rights is not the subject matter of the amendment. It has a deeper and broader scope. It nullifies and makes void all State legislation, and State action of every kind, which impairs the privileges and immunities of citizens of the United States, or which injures them in life, liberty or property without due process of law, or which denies to any of them the equal protection of the laws. It not only does this, but, in order that the national will, thus declared, may not be a mere *brutum fulmen,* the last section of the amendment invests Congress with power to enforce it by appropriate legislation. To enforce what? To enforce the prohibition. To adopt appropriate legislation for correcting the effects of such prohibited State laws and State acts, and thus to render them effectually null, void, and innocuous. This is the legislative power conferred upon Congress, and this is the whole of it. It does not invest Congress with power to legislate upon subjects which are within the domain of State legislation; but to provide modes of relief against State legislation, or State action, of the kind referred to. It does not authorize Congress to create a code of municipal law for the regulation of private rights; but to provide modes of redress against the operation of State laws, and the action of State officers executive or judicial, when these are subversive of the fundamental rights specified in the amendment. Positive rights and privileges are undoubtedly secured by the Fourteenth Amendment; but they are secured by way of prohibition against State laws and State proceedings affecting those rights and privileges, and by power given to Congress to legislate for the purpose of carrying such prohibition into effect. . . .

An inspection of the law shows that it makes no reference whatever to any supposed or apprehended violation of the Fourteenth Amendment on the part of the States. It is not predicated on any such view. It proceeds *ex directo* to declare that certain acts committed by individuals shall be deemed offences, and shall be prosecuted and punished by proceedings in the courts of the United States. It does not profess to be corrective of any constitutional wrong committed by the States; it does not make its operation to depend upon any such wrong committed. It applies equally to cases arising in States which have the justest laws respecting the personal rights of citizens, and whose authorities are ever ready to enforce such laws, as to those which arise in States that may have violated the prohibition of the amendment. In other words, it steps into the domain of local jurisprudence, and lays down rules for the conduct of individuals in society towards each other, and imposes sanctions for the enforcement of those rules, without referring in any manner to any supposed action of the State or its authorities.

If this legislation is appropriate for enforcing the prohibitions of the amendment, it is difficult to see where it is to stop. Why may not Congress with equal show of authority enact a code of laws for the enforcement and vindication of all rights of life, liberty, and property? If it is supposable that the States may deprive persons of life, liberty, and property without due process of law (and the amendment itself does suppose this), why should not Congress proceed at once to prescribe due process of law for the protection of every one of these fundamental rights, in every possible case, as well as to prescribe equal privileges in inns, public conveyances, and theatres? The truth is, that the implication of a power to legislate in this manner is based upon the assumption that if the States are forbidden to legislate or act in a particular way on a particular subject, and power is conferred upon Congress to enforce the prohibition, this gives Congress power to legislate generally upon that subject, and not merely power to provide modes of redress against such State legislation or action. The assumption is certainly unsound. It is repugnant to the Tenth Amendment of the Constitution, which declares that powers not delegated to the United States by the Constitution, nor prohibited by it to the States, are reserved to the States respectively or to the people. . . .

In this connection it is proper to state that civil rights, such as are guaranteed by the Constitution against State aggression, cannot be impaired by the wrongful acts of individuals, unsupported by State authority in the shape of laws, customs, or judicial or executive proceedings. The wrongful act of an individual, unsupported by any such authority, is simply a private wrong, or a crime of that individual; an invasion of the rights of the injured party, it is true, whether they affect his person, his property, or his reputation; but if not sanctioned in some way by the State, or not done under State authority, his rights remain in full force, and may presumably be vindicated by resort to the laws of the State for redress. An individual cannot deprive a man of his right to vote, to hold property, to buy and sell, to sue in the courts, or to be a witness or a juror; he may, by force or fraud, interfere with the enjoyment of the right in a particular case; he may commit an assault against the person, or commit murder, or use ruffian violence at the polls, or slander the good name of a fellow citizen; but, unless protected in these wrongful acts by some shield of State law or State authority, he cannot destroy or injure the right; he will only render himself amenable to satisfaction or punishment; and amenable therefore to the laws of the State where the wrongful acts are committed. Hence, in all those cases where the Constitution seeks to protect the rights of the citizen against discriminative and unjust laws of the State by prohibiting such laws, it is not individual offences, but abrogation and denial of rights, which it denounces, and for which it clothes the Congress with power to provide a remedy. This abrogation and denial of rights, for which the States alone were or could be responsible, was the great seminal and fundamental wrong which was intended to be remedied. And the remedy to be provided must necessarily be predicated upon that wrong. It must assume that in the cases provided for, the evil or wrong actually committed rests upon some State law or State authority for its excuse and perpetration.

Of course, these remarks do not apply to those cases in which Congress is clothed with direct and plenary powers of legislation over the whole subject, accompanied with an express or implied denial of such power to the States, as in the regulation of commerce with foreign nations, among the several States, and with the Indian tribes, the coining of money, the establishment of post offices and post roads, the declaring of war, etc. In these cases Congress has power to pass laws for regulating the subjects specified in every detail, and the conduct and transactions of individuals in respect thereof. But where a subject is not submitted to the general legislative power of Congress, but is only submitted thereto for the purpose of rendering effective some prohibition against particular State legislation or State action in reference to that subject, the power given is limited by its object, and any legislation by Congress in the matter must necessarily be corrective in its character, adapted to counteract and redress the operation of such prohibited State laws or proceedings of State officers. . . .

The power of Congress to adopt direct and primary, as distinguished from corrective legislation, on the subject in hand, is sought . . . from the Thirteenth Amendment, which abolishes slavery. . . .

It is assumed, that the power vested in Congress to enforce the article by appropriate legislation, clothes Congress with power to pass all laws necessary and proper for abolishing all badges and incidents of slavery in the United States: and upon this assumption it is claimed, that this is sufficient authority for declaring by law that all persons shall have equal accommodations and privileges in all inns, public conveyances, and places of amusement; the argument being, that the denial of such equal accommodations and privileges is, in itself, a subjection to a species of servitude within the meaning of the amendment. Conceding the major proposition to be true, that Congress has a right to enact all necessary and proper laws for the obliteration and prevention of slavery with all its badges and incidents, is the minor proposition also true, that the denial to any person of admission to the accommodations and privileges of an inn, a public conveyance, or a theatre, does subject that person to any form of servitude, or tend to fasten upon him any badge of slavery? If it does not, then power to pass the law is not found in the Thirteenth Amendment. . . .

It would be running the slavery argument into the ground to make it apply to every act of discrimination which a person may see fit to make as to the guests he will entertain, or as to the people he will take into his coach or cab or car, or admit to his concert or theatre, or deal with in other matters of intercourse or business. . . .

When a man has emerged from slavery, and by the aid of beneficent legislation has shaken off the inseparable concomitants of that state, there must be some stage in the progress of his elevation when he takes the rank of a mere citizen, and ceases to be the special favorite of the laws, and when his rights as a citizen, or a man, are to be protected in the ordinary modes by which other men's rights are protected. . . .

On the whole we are of opinion, that no countenance of authority for the passage of the law in question can be found in either the Thirteenth or Fourteenth Amendment of the Constitution; and no other ground of authority for its passage being suggested, it must necessarily be declared void at least so far as its operation in the several States is concerned. . . .

JUSTICE HARLAN, dissenting.

The opinion in these cases proceeds, it seems to me, upon grounds entirely too narrow and artificial. I cannot resist the conclusion that the substance and spirit of the recent amendments of the Constitution have been sacrificed by a subtle and ingenious verbal criticism. . . .

There seems to be no substantial difference between my brethren and myself as to the purpose of Congress; for, they say that the essence of the law is, not to declare broadly that all persons shall be entitled to the full and equal enjoyment of the accommodations, advantages, facilities, and privileges of inns, public conveyances, and theatres; but that such enjoyment shall not be subject to conditions applicable only to citizens of a particular race or color, or who had been in a previous condition of servitude.

The court adjudges, I think erroneously, that Congress is without power, under either the Thirteenth or Fourteenth Amendment, to establish such regulations, and that the first and second sections of the statute are, in all their parts, unconstitutional and void. . . .

The Thirteenth Amendment, it is conceded, did something more than to prohibit slavery as an *institution,* resting upon distinctions of race, and upheld by positive law. My brethren admit that it established and decreed universal *civil freedom* throughout the United States. . . .

That there are burdens and disabilities which constitute badges of slavery and servitude, and that the power to enforce by appropriate legislation the Thirteenth Amendment may be exerted by legislation of a direct and primary character, for the eradication, not simply of the institution, but of its badges and incidents, are propositions which ought to be deemed indisputable. They lie at the foundation of the Civil Rights Act of 1866. Whether that act was authorized by the Thirteenth Amendment alone, without the support which it subsequently received from the Fourteenth Amendment, after the adoption of which it was re-enacted with some additions, my brethren do not consider it necessary to inquire. But I submit, with all respect to them, that its constitutionality is conclusively shown by their opinion. They admit, as I have said, that the Thirteenth Amendment established freedom; that there are burdens and disabilities, the necessary incidents of slavery, which constitute its substance and visible form; that Congress, by the act of 1866, passed in view of the Thirteenth Amendment, before the Fourteenth was adopted, undertook to remove certain burdens and disabilities, the necessary incidents of slavery, and to secure to all citizens of every race and color, and without regard to previous servitude, those fundamental rights which are the essence of civil freedom, namely, the same right to make and enforce contracts, to sue, be parties, give evidence, and to inherit, purchase, lease, sell, and convey, property as is enjoyed by white citizens; that under the Thirteenth Amendment, Congress has to do with slavery and its incidents; and that legislation, so far as necessary or proper to eradicate all forms and incidents of slavery and involuntary servitude, may be direct and primary, operating upon the acts of individuals, whether sanctioned by State legislation or not. These propositions being conceded, it is impossible, as it seems to me, to question the constitutional validity of the Civil Rights Act of 1866. I do not contend that the Thirteenth Amendment invests Congress with authority, by legislation, to define and regulate the entire body of the civil rights which citizens enjoy, or may enjoy, in the several States. But I hold that since slavery . . . was the moving or principal cause of the adoption of that amendment, and since that institution rested wholly upon the inferiority, as a race, of those held in bondage, their freedom necessarily involved immunity from, and protection against, all discrimination against them, because of their race, in respect of such civil rights as belong to freemen of other races. Congress, therefore, under its express power to enforce that amendment, by appropriate legislation, may enact laws to protect that people against the deprivation, *because of their race,* of any civil rights granted to other freemen in the same State; and such legislation may be of a direct and primary character, operating upon States, their officers and

agents, and, also, upon, at least, such individuals and corporations as exercise public functions and wield power and authority under the State. . . .

Congress has not, in these matters, entered the domain of State control and supervision. It does not . . . assume to prescribe the general conditions and limitations under which inns, public conveyances, and places of public amusement, shall be conducted or managed. It simply declares, in effect, that since the nation has established universal freedom in this country, for all time, there shall be no discrimination, based merely upon race or color, in respect of the accommodations and advantages of public conveyances, inns, and places of public amusement.

I am of the opinion that such discrimination practised by corporations and individuals in the exercise of their public or quasi-public functions is a badge of servitude the imposition of which Congress may prevent under its power, by appropriate legislation, to enforce the Thirteenth Amendment; and, consequently, without reference to its enlarged power under the Fourteenth Amendment, the act of March 1, 1875, is not, in my judgment, repugnant to the Constitution.

It remains now to consider these cases with reference to the power Congress has possessed since the adoption of the Fourteenth Amendment. Much that has been said as to the power of Congress under the Thirteenth Amendment is applicable to this branch of the discussion, and will not be repeated. . . .

The assumption that the Fourteenth Amendment consists wholly of prohibitions upon State laws and State proceedings in hostility to its provisions, is unauthorized by its language. The first clause of the first section—"All persons born or naturalized in the United States, and subject to the jurisdiction thereof, are citizens of the United States, and of the State wherein they reside"—is of a distinctly affirmative character. In its application to the colored race, previously liberated, it created and granted, as well citizenship of the United States, as citizenship of the State in which they respectively resided. It introduced all of that race, whose ancestors had been imported and sold as slaves, at once, into the political community known as the "People of the United States." They became, instantly, citizens of the United States, *and* of their respective States. . . .

The citizenship thus acquired, by that race, in virtue of an affirmative grant from the nation, may be protected, not alone by the judicial branch of the government, but by congressional legislation of a primary direct character; this, because the power of Congress is not restricted to the enforcement of prohibitions upon State laws or State action. It is, in terms distinct and positive, to enforce "the *provisions of this article*" of amendment; not simply those of a prohibitive character, but the provisions—*all* of the provisions—affirmative and prohibitive, of the amendment. It is, therefore, a grave misconception to suppose that the fifth section of the amendment has reference exclusively to express prohibitions upon State laws or State action. If any right was created by that amendment, the grant of power, through appropriate legislation, to enforce its provisions, authorizes Congress, by means of legislation, operating throughout the entire Union, to guard, secure, and protect that right. . . .

This construction does not in any degree intrench upon the just rights of the States in the control of their domestic affairs. It simply recognizes the enlarged powers conferred by the recent amendments upon the general government. In the view which I take of those amendments, the States possess the same authority which they have always had to define and regulate the civil rights which their own people, in virtue of State citizenship, may enjoy within their respective limits; except that its exercise is now subject to the expressly granted power of Congress, by legislation, to enforce the provisions of such amendments—a power which necessarily carries with it authority, by national legislation, to protect and secure the privileges and immunities which are created by or are derived from those amendments. That exemption of citizens from discrimination based on race or color, in respect to civil rights, is one of those privileges or immunities, can no longer be deemed an open question in this court. . . .

Government has nothing to do with social, as distinguished from technically legal, rights of individuals. No government ever has brought, or ever can bring, its people into social intercourse against their wishes. Whether one person will permit or maintain social relations with another is a matter with which government has no concern. . . . The rights which Congress, by the act of 1875, endeavored to secure and protect are legal, not social rights. The right, for instance, of a colored citizen to use the accommodations of a public highway, upon the same terms as are permitted to white citizens, is no more a social right than his right, under the law, to use the public streets of a city or a town, or a turnpike road, or a public market, or a post office, or his right to sit. My brethren say, that when a man has emerged from slavery, and by the aid of beneficent legislation has shaken off the inseparable concomitants of that state, there must be some state in the progress of his elevation when he takes the rank of a mere citizen, and ceases to be the special favorite of the laws, and when his rights as a citizen, or a man, are to be protected in the ordinary modes by which other men's rights are protected. It is, I submit, scarcely just to say that the colored race has been the special favorite of the laws. The statute of 1875, now adjudged to be unconstitutional, is for the benefit of citizens of every race and color. What the nation, through Congress, has sought to accomplish in reference to that race, is—what had already been done in every State of the Union for the white race—to secure and protect rights belonging to them as freemen and citizens; nothing more. . . . The supreme law of the land has decreed that no authority shall be exercised in this country upon the basis of discrimination, in respect of civil rights, against freemen and citizens because of their race, color, or previous condition of servitude. To that decree— for the due enforcement of which, by appropriate legislation, Congress has been invested with express power—every one must bow, whatever may have been, or whatever now are, his individual views as to the wisdom or policy, either of the recent changes in the fundamental law, or of the legislation which has been enacted to give them effect.

For the reasons stated I feel constrained to withhold my assent to the opinion of the court.

Jones v. Alfred H. Mayer Company
392 U.S. 409 (1968)

Petitioners Joseph Lee Jones and his wife, alleging that the respondents had refused to sell them a home for the sole reason that the Joneses were black, filed a complaint in federal district court, seeking injunctive and other relief. They relied in part upon 42 U.S.C. Section 1982, which provides that "all citizens of the United States shall have the same right, in every State and Territory, as is enjoyed by white citizens thereof to inherit, purchase, lease, sell, hold, and convey real and personal property." The district court dismissed the complaint, and the Court of Appeals for the Eighth Circuit affirmed, concluding that Section 1982 applies only to state action and does not reach private refusals to sell. The Supreme Court granted certiorari. Opinion of the Court: <u>Stewart</u>, Warren, Black, Brennan, Fortas, Marshall. Concurring opinion: <u>Douglas</u>. Dissenting opinion: <u>Harlan</u>, White.

JUSTICE STEWART delivered the opinion of the Court.

In this case we are called upon to determine the scope and the constitutionality of an Act of Congress, 42 U. S. C. §1982. . . .

For the reasons that follow, we reverse the judgment of the Court of Appeals. We hold that §1982 bars *all* racial discrimination, private as well as public, in the sale or rental of property, and that the statute, thus construed, is a valid exercise of the power of Congress to enforce the Thirteenth Amendment. . . .

We begin with the language of the statute itself. In plain and unambiguous terms, §1982 grants to *all* citizens, without regard to race or color, "the same right" to purchase and lease property "as is enjoyed by white citizens." As the Court of Appeals in this case evidently recognized, that right can be impaired as effectively by "those who place property on the market" as by the State itself. For, even if the State and its agents lend no support to those who wish to exclude persons from their communities on racial grounds, the fact remains that, whenever property "is placed on the market for whites only, whites have a right denied to Negroes." . . .

On its face, therefore, §1982 appears to prohibit *all* discrimination against Negroes in the sale or rental of property—discrimination by private owners as well as discrimination by public authorities. Indeed, even the respondents seem to concede that, if §1982 "means what it says"—to use the words of the respondents' brief—then it must encompass every racially motivated refusal to sell or rent and cannot be confined to officially sanctioned segregation in housing. Stressing what they consider to be the revolutionary implications of so literal a reading of §1982, the respondents argue that Congress cannot possibly have intended any such result. Our examination of the relevant history, however, persuades us that Congress meant exactly what it said. . . .

In its original form, 42 U. S. C. §1982 was part of §1 of the Civil Rights Act of 1866. . . . The crucial language (of that section) was that which guaranteed all citizens "the same right, in every State and Territory in the United States, . . . to inherit, purchase, lease, sell, hold, and convey real and personal property . . . as is enjoyed by white citizens. . . ." To the Congress that passed the Civil Rights Act of 1866, it was clear that the right to do these things might be infringed not only by "State or local law" but also by "custom, or prejudice." Thus, when Congress provided in §1 of the Civil Rights Act that the right to purchase and lease property was to be enjoyed equally throughout the United States by Negro and white citizens alike, it plainly meant to secure that right against interference from any source whatever, whether governmental or private. . . .

In attempting to demonstrate the contrary, the respondents rely heavily upon the fact that the Congress which approved the 1866 statute wished to eradicate the recently enacted Black Codes—laws which had saddled Negroes with "onerous disabilities and burdens, and curtailed their rights . . . to such an extent that their freedom was of little value. . . ." . . . The respondents suggest that the only evil Congress sought to eliminate was that of racially discriminatory laws in the former Confederate States. But the Civil Rights Act was drafted to apply throughout the country, and its language was far broader than would have been necessary to strike down discriminatory statutes.

That broad language, we are asked to believe, was a mere slip of the legislative pen. We disagree. For the same Congress that wanted to do away with the Black Codes *also* had before it an imposing body of evidence pointing to the mistreatment of Negroes by private individuals and unofficial groups, mistreatment unrelated to any hostile state legislation. . . .

Indeed, one of the most comprehensive studies then before Congress stressed the prevalence of private hostility toward Negroes and the need to protect them from the resulting persecution and discrimination. . . .

In this setting, it would have been strange indeed if Congress had viewed its task as encompassing merely the nullification of racist laws in the former rebel States. . . .

The remaining question is whether Congress has power under the Constitution to do what §1982 purports to do: to prohibit all racial discrimination, private and public, in the sale and rental of property. Our starting point is the Thirteenth Amendment, for it was pursuant to that constitutional provision that Congress originally enacted what is now §1982. . . .

It has never been doubted . . . "that the power vested in Congress to enforce the article by appropriate legislation," . . . includes the power to enact laws "direct and primary, operating upon the acts of individuals, whether sanctioned by State legislation or not." . . .

The constitutional question in this case, therefore, comes to this: Does the authority of Congress to enforce the Thirteenth Amendment "by appropriate legislation" include the power to eliminate all racial barriers to the acquisition of real and personal property? We think the answer to that question is plainly yes. . . .

. . . Surely Congress has the power under the Thirteenth Amendment rationally to determine what are the badges and the incidents of slavery, and the authority to translate that determination into effective legislation. Nor can we say that the determination Congress has made is an irrational one. For this Court recognized long ago that, whatever else they may have encompassed, the badges and incidents of slavery—its "burdens and disabilities"—included restraints upon "those fundamental rights which are that essence of civil freedom, namely, the same right . . . to inherit, purchase, lease, sell and convey property, as is enjoyed by white citizens." Just as the Black Codes, enacted after the Civil War to restrict the free exercise of those rights, were substitutes for the slave system, so the exclusion of Negroes from white communities became a substitute for the Black Codes. And when racial discrimination herds men into ghettos and makes their ability to buy property turn on the color of their skin, then it too is a relic of slavery. . . . At the very least, the freedom that Congress is empowered to secure under the Thirteenth Amendment includes the freedom to buy whatever a white man can buy, the right to live wherever a white man can live. If Congress cannot say that being a free man means at least this much, then the Thirteenth Amendment made a promise the Nation cannot keep. . . .

JUSTICE HARLAN, whom JUSTICE WHITE joins, dissenting.

The decision in this case appears to me to be most ill-considered and ill-advised. . . .

The petitioners argue that the respondents' racially motivated refusal to sell them a house entitles them to judicial relief on two separate grounds. First, they claim that the respondents acted in violation of 42 U.S.C. §1982; second, they assert that the respondents' conduct amounted in the circumstances to "state action" and was therefore forbidden by the Fourteenth Amendment even in the absence of any statute.

For reasons which follow, I believe that the Court's construction of §1982 as applying to purely private action is almost surely wrong, and at the least is open to serious doubt. The issues of the constitutionality of §1982, as construed by the Court, and of liability under the Fourteenth Amendment alone, also present formidable difficulties. Moreover, the political processes of our own era have, since the date of oral argument in this case, given birth to [the Civil Rights Act of 1968] embodying "fair housing" provisions which would at the end of this year make available . . . the type of relief which the petitioners now seek. It seems to me that this latter factor so diminishes the public importance of this case that by far the wisest course would be for this Court to refrain from decision and to dismiss the writ as improvidently granted. . . .

Like the Court, I begin analysis of §1982 by examining its language. . . .

The Court finds it "plain and unambiguous," . . . that this language forbids purely private as well as state-authorized discrimination. With all respect, I do not find it so. For me, there is an inherent ambiguity in the term "right," as used in §1982. The "right" referred to may either be a right to equal status under the law, in which case the statute operates only against state-sanctioned discrimination, or it may be an "absolute" right enforceable against private individuals. To me, the words of the statute, taken alone, suggest the former interpretation, not the latter. . . .

The Court rests its opinion chiefly upon the legislative history of the Civil Rights Act of 1866. . . . Those debates do not, as the Court would have it, overwhelmingly support the result reached by the Court, . . . in fact, a contrary conclusion may equally well be drawn.

[*Justice Harlan then engages in a lengthy review of the act's legislative history.*]

The foregoing, I think, amply demonstrates that the Court has chosen to resolve this case by according to a loosely worded statute a meaning which is open to the strongest challenge in light of the statute's legislative history. In holding that the Thirteenth Amendment is sufficient constitutional authority for §1982 as interpreted, the Court also decides a question of great importance. Even contemporary supporters of the aims of the 1866 Civil Rights Act doubted that those goals could constitutionally be achieved under the Thirteenth Amendment, and this Court has twice expressed similar doubts. . . . Thus, it is plain that the course of decision followed by the Court today entails the resolution of important and difficult issues. . . .

8

The Exercise of National Power

CHAPTER OUTLINE

The defects of the Articles of Confederation convinced the Framers of the Constitution that the United States needed a substantially stronger national government. Under the Articles, the national government could not regulate domestic commerce or levy taxes, and its powers were limited to those expressly enumerated. In the absence of a national commerce power, states taxed goods that were in transit for sale in other states and devised regulations to protect local producers from out-of-state competition, thereby impeding the flow of commerce and producing a stagnant national economy. The national government, meanwhile, was forced to rely on state contributions for its revenues. Because the states were notoriously unresponsive to requests for funds, forceful national action was impossible. Without implied powers, moreover, the national government lacked the flexibility necessary for effective responses to changing situations. To correct these problems, the Framers augmented the powers of the national government. Article I, Section 8, of the new Constitution gives Congress the power "to regulate Commerce with foreign Nations, and among the several States, and with the Indian Tribes," the power to tax and to spend "to provide for the common Defense and the general Welfare of the United States," and to exercise all powers necessary and proper for carrying out its enumerated powers.

Since the 1930s, Congress has used these provisions to justify legislation affecting virtually every aspect of American life. On the basis of the commerce power, Congress has regulated interstate and intrastate economic activities of all sorts, to the extent that in 1970 it authorized the president to freeze all wages and prices throughout the United States.[1] It has also relied on the commerce power to deal with noneconomic concerns as diverse as civil rights, kidnapping, and pollution control. Congress has used its taxing power not only to raise revenue but also to encourage or discourage conduct, such as smoking. Relying on the spending power, it dispensed tax revenues through grant programs that at times have accounted for more than 20 percent of the budgets of state and local governments. In 2010, Congress enacted major health care legislation proposed by President Barack Obama that became the basis for a landmark Supreme Court ruling in *National Federation of Independent Business v. Sebelius* (2012).

In recent years, the Supreme Court has often been called upon to reconsider whether this expansion of national power is consistent with the constitutional design of the Founders or whether it undermines the federal system established by the Constitution. The current Court has divided sharply on the question. To arrive at our own assessment, we must trace the emergence of this broad interpretation of national power and analyze the constitutional arguments for and against this development.

THE COMMERCE POWER

Although Congress's power to regulate foreign trade has seldom been challenged, its attempts to regulate commerce "among the several States" have aroused fierce resistance. The range of congressional control over commerce is crucial to American federalism, because in large measure it determines the distribution of power between the national and state governments. Debate over the interpretation of the Commerce Clause has focused on three questions: (1) What activities constitute "commerce"? (2) If the power to regulate commercial activities is divided between the national and state governments, what portion of these activities can Congress regulate? (3) For what purposes can Congress regulate these activities? Various eras have proposed different answers to these questions.

Chief Justice Marshall's Interpretation

Chief Justice John Marshall's opinion in *Gibbons v. Ogden* (1824) provides the starting point for all subsequent interpretation of the Commerce Clause. Although the case was decided on the basis of a conflict between federal and state law, Marshall used *Gibbons* to elaborate a broad interpretation of national power. He observed that constitutional grants of power must be construed in terms of the ends for which they were conferred, because the Framers must have intended that those powers be sufficient to achieve their objectives. Because the federal government was to promote economic prosperity by eliminating state barriers to economic activity and creating a national market for goods and services, Congress must have been provided with the powers necessary to accomplish this purpose. This premise supports an expansive definition of commerce. Because commerce "describes the commercial intercourse between nations, and parts of nations, in all its branches," the commerce power extends beyond buying and selling to encompass all aspects of economic activity. Elastic as well as broad, this power could be used to regulate new forms of commercial intercourse fostered by inventions and changes in business organization, including those unknown to the Framers. Thus in *Pensacola Telegraph Company v. Western Union Telegraph Company* (1878), the Supreme Court recognized the authority of Congress to regulate telegraph companies. With advances in transportation and communications, congressional authority has expanded accordingly.

In Marshall's view, the aims of the Commerce Clause also dictated a wide scope for congressional regulation. Since the commerce power was designed to promote the free flow of goods among the states, he contended, Congress can deal with all obstacles to that flow, no matter how local they might be. Thus, congressional power necessarily extends to "that commerce which concerns more states than one"—a formulation that encompasses but is not limited to interstate commerce. Insofar as intrastate activities affect commerce "among the several States," they too are subject to congressional regulation. As the expansion of business enterprises has produced a more interdependent national economy, the range of economic activities subject to congressional regulation has increased: the principle has remained the same, but its application has changed.

Because the Marshall Court never addressed the use of the commerce power for noncommercial purposes, it never directly considered whether such a use was constitutionally permissible. On the one hand, Marshall in *Gibbons* seems to suggest that Congress can regulate commerce for whatever purposes it wishes. The power to regulate, he noted, is "the power to prescribe the rules by which commerce is to be governed. This power, like all others vested in Congress, is complete in itself, may be exercised to its utmost extent, and acknowledges no limitations, other than are prescribed in the Constitution." On the other hand, he also in *Gibbons* specifically refers to the "immense mass of legislation" left to the states, embracing "inspection laws, quarantine laws, health laws of every description"—in short, laws that regulate commercial activity for noncommercial ends. Moreover, in *McCulloch v. Maryland* and other cases, Marshall emphasized that the Constitution conveyed powers to the national government to achieve certain broad ends. From this, one might conclude that the use of these powers for other ends is improper. In sum, it is likely that Marshall did not believe that Congress could use its commerce power to pursue exclusively noncommercial ends.

Whatever the conclusion on this point, the *Gibbons* opinion affirmed that the Framers vested Congress with broad authority to regulate commerce. Within its sphere Congress was supreme, and that sphere included all economic transactions that affected more than one state. Although Congress did not immediately accept Marshall's implicit invitation to expand its use of the commerce power, his analysis would eventually be relied upon in upholding vigorous congressional action.

Contraction of the Commerce Power: 1888–1936

For almost a century after the Founding, the national commerce power was not a major issue, because Congress enacted little commercial legislation. The passage of the Interstate

Commerce Act (1887), however, heralded a more active national role, and conflict over the scope of congressional power soon reached the Supreme Court. Starting from different premises than Marshall had, the Court in the late nineteenth and early twentieth centuries developed a more restrictive conception of the commerce power and invalidated important congressional statutes.

Underlying the Court's new interpretation of the Commerce Clause was the doctrine of dual federalism (see Chapter 7), which suggests that, in dividing governmental functions between the federal and state governments, the Framers reserved important powers—including the police power—to the states. In exercising their powers, therefore, neither the federal nor the state governments can invade the other's sphere; in particular, the federal government cannot use the pretext of its delegated powers to usurp those powers reserved to the states. The Court, accordingly, must interpret the Commerce Clause—along with other constitutional grants of power—so that the Framers' dual aims of adequate national power and a federal balance are both achieved. Thus, the restrictive interpretation of the national commerce power in *United States v. E. C. Knight Company* (1895) was justified by noting the dire effects that would presumably flow from a broad interpretation of that provision: "If the national power extends to all contracts and combinations in manufacture, agriculture, mining, and other productive industries, whose ultimate result may affect external commerce, comparatively little of business operations and affairs would be left for state control."

Under the influence of dual federalism, the Court attempted to safeguard state power by defining commerce narrowly, restricting the range of commercial activities under congressional control, and limiting the purposes for which the commerce power could be exercised. In *Knight,* which provided the authoritative interpretation of the Sherman Anti-Trust Act, the Court first announced its new definition of commerce. At issue were the activities of the American Sugar Refining Company, which controlled more than 98 percent of the nation's sugar-refining business. In holding that the antitrust act did not apply to the company's activities, the Court contended that congressional power extends only to commerce and that "commerce succeeds to manufacture, and is not a part of it." The implications of this distinction between commerce and production were dramatic: at a stroke, the justices had immunized from congressional regulation major elements of the national economy, including manufacturing, oil production, agriculture, and mining.

This distinction between production and commerce might not have precluded congressional regulation if the Supreme Court had embraced Marshall's interpretation of the scope of congressional power: "That commerce which concerns more states than one." For production, even if not a part of commerce, unquestionably affects it and thus would fall within Congress's orbit. But the dual-federalist Court adopted a more exacting standard. Congress was permitted to regulate the flow of goods in interstate commerce, as well as those local transactions incidental to the transportation of goods in interstate commerce. In *Swift & Company v. United States* (1905), for example, the justices ruled that the national government could prosecute stockyard firms that had conspired to monopolize the sale and distribution of fresh beef, because the purchase of cattle was merely an element in the "current of commerce" among the states. But congressional regulation of intrastate activities was limited to those activities that had a "direct effect," not merely an "indirect effect," on interstate commerce.

This distinction between "direct" and "indirect" effects, which insulated some intrastate activities from congressional regulation, eventually proved unworkable. A vague criterion, it offered little guidance in the analysis of specific cases and contributed to the inconsistency that marked the Court's decisions during the early twentieth century. Judicial efforts to clarify the distinction between direct and indirect effects met with little success. When Justice George Sutherland undertook to do so in *Carter v. Carter Coal Company* (1936), which invalidated congressional regulation of labor relations throughout the mining industry, his explanation revealed the problems with the dual-federalist approach:

> The extent of the effect bears no logical relation to its character. The distinction between a direct and indirect effect turns, not upon the magnitude of either the cause or the effect, but entirely upon the manner in which the effect has been brought about. If the production by one man of a single ton of coal intended for interstate sale and shipment, and actually so sold and shipped, affects interstate commerce indirectly, the effect does not become direct by multiplying the tonnage, or increasing the number of men employed, or adding to the expense or complexities of the business, or by all combined.

Following this logic, the Court in *Carter Coal* held that the distinction between direct and indirect effects turned on the *proximity* of the effect to interstate commerce, rather than on the *extent* of the effect. No matter how severe the effect of intrastate activity on interstate commerce, if the effect was indirect, the remedy lay solely with the states. So Congress could not prevent such major interferences with the flow of commerce as nationwide strikes, because they affected commerce only "indirectly."

Even within Congress's recognized sphere of interstate commerce, the dual-federalist Court discovered a further limitation, holding that Congress could not use this power for noncommercial purposes. Initially, no such restriction was apparent to the Court. In *Champion v. Ames* (1903), the justices sustained a federal statute that prohibited the interstate transportation of lottery tickets, even though it served police-power ends. Following *Champion,* Congress enacted additional regulatory legislation—the Pure Food Act, the Narcotics Acts, and the White Slave Act, to name but a few—and these laws were also upheld. In *Hammer v. Dagenhart* (1918), however, the Court struck down a ban on interstate shipment of goods produced by child labor. Insisting that the regulations in previous cases involved inherently harmful items, the majority in *Hammer* pointed out that items produced by child labor were indistinguishable from other goods except in terms of the workers involved. Thus, the only congressional interest in banning their shipment was to prevent the employment of child labor. Because control over employment practices was vested in the states, the justices concluded, Congress could not interfere in this matter. In reaching this decision, the Court followed the dictates of dual federalism, according to which grants of power to the federal government were conditioned by the reserved powers of the states.

So long as Congress exercised the commerce power sparingly, collisions between Court and Congress were intermittent.[2] With the advent of the Great Depression, however, more active governmental intervention in the economy made confrontation almost inevitable. In 1935–1936, the Court struck down such important New Deal measures as the National Industrial Recovery Act, the Agricultural Adjustment Act, and the Bituminous Coal Conservation Act.[3] The reasons given by the Court for its rulings presaged the invalidation of further New Deal measures. In 1937, following his landslide reelection, President Franklin Roosevelt proposed a plan to expand the membership of the Supreme Court.[4] Although the measure was defended as necessary to help the Court with its workload, in fact the expansion of the Court was intended to give the president a chance to appoint justices more sympathetic to New Deal legislation. While the court-packing bill was before Congress (where it ultimately died), the Court upheld the National Labor Relations Act, signaling a new approach to its interpretation of the Commerce Clause. The retirement of Justices Willis Van Devanter in 1937 and George Sutherland in 1938 and their replacement by Roosevelt appointees solidified support for a broad view of the national commerce power.

The Expansion of the Commerce Power

In *National Labor Relations Board v. Jones & Laughlin Steel Corporation* (1937), the Supreme Court adopted a much broader view of the congressional commerce power. At least one commentator, Bruce Ackerman, has argued that the decision reflected a recognition by the justices that the electorate's overwhelming endorsement of Roosevelt's economic program in the presidential election of 1936 had produced a basic change in the Constitution, accomplished outside the normal channels for constitutional amendment.[5] Other commentators, however, believe that the Court merely applied Marshall's interpretation of the commerce power to twentieth-century economic conditions. Whichever interpretation is correct, the Court's shift was dramatic. Gone were the production-commerce dichotomy and the distinction between direct and indirect effects. Asserting that judgments concerning interstate commerce must take into account "actual experience," the Court in *Jones & Laughlin Steel* recognized that labor-management strife in nationwide industries threatens interstate commerce and so can be regulated by Congress. Other decisions indicated that the scope of congressional power turned on the existence of an effect on interstate commerce, not on the extent of the effect.[6] If Congress indicated that a class of activities had an effect on interstate commerce, then the Court would defer to that legislative judgment. The scope of this power was strikingly confirmed in *Wickard v. Filburn* (1942), in which the Court unanimously upheld congressional legislation governing the growing of wheat by a farmer for home consumption.

Another series of decisions removed restrictions on the purposes for which Congress can employ the commerce power. In *United States v. Darby* (1941), the Court overruled *Hammer v. Dagenhart*, holding that Congress could prohibit the interstate shipment of goods produced by workers receiving substandard wages. Justice Harlan Stone's opinion acknowledged that the *Darby* decision gave Congress wide leeway: "The motive and purpose of a regulation of interstate commerce are matters for the legislative judgment upon the exercise of which the Constitution places no restriction and over which the courts are given no control."

This interpretation encouraged Congress to rely on the commerce power to pursue such noncommercial ends as the protection of civil rights and the suppression of crime. In 1964, for example, Congress banned racial discrimination in public accommodations (restaurants, theaters, hotels, and so on) throughout the nation, and the Court in *Heart of Atlanta Motel v. United States* (1964) upheld this ban as a valid exercise of the commerce power. In later cases, citing *Wickard v. Filburn,* the justices sustained its application to small enterprises whose individual effect on interstate commerce was minimal. In *Perez v. United States* (1971), for example, the Court held that the Commerce Clause gave Congress broad authority to deal with crime.

Previous Court decisions had endorsed congressional efforts to prevent misuse of the channels of interstate commerce, such as the transportation of stolen goods or kidnapped persons, and to protect the instrumentalities of interstate commerce against theft or destruction. In *Perez,* however, the Court for the first time upheld congressional regulation of local criminal activity (loan sharking) that could supply funds for organized crime and thereby affect interstate commerce, even though the activities of the defendant were purely intrastate, were unconnected to organized crime, and had no measurable effect on interstate commerce. Justice William Douglas, writing for the Court, noted that "where the class of activities is regulated and that class is within the reach of federal power, the courts have no power to excise as trivial, individual instances of the class." In recent years, Congress has enacted legislation making crimes that had previously been state concerns, such as carjacking and various firearms offenses, violations of federal law as well.

A New Direction?

From 1937 to 1995, the Supreme Court endorsed an expansive interpretation of the commerce power. Only once during this period, in *National League of Cities v. Usery* (1976), did the justices rule that an enactment exceeded Congress's power under the commerce power, striking down the minimum-wage and overtime-pay provisions of the Fair Labor Standards Act insofar as they were applied to prescribe wages for state employees. Such regulations, a five-member majority held, invaded the "traditional governmental functions" of the states. But nine years later the Court overruled *Usery* by a 5–4 vote in *Garcia v. San Antonio Metropolitan Transit Authority* (1985). Speaking for the Court in *Garcia*, Justice Harry Blackmun contended that the constitutional protection for the division of power between nation and state was primarily political, not judicial. Representation of the states in Congress sufficed to guarantee the vital interests of the states and to safeguard against federal intrusion on state powers. The four dissenters offered a very different assessment: "The Court today surveys the battle scene of federalism and sounds a retreat."

Since 1995, however, the Court has subjected the exercise of the national commerce power to more exacting scrutiny. In *United States v. Lopez* (1995), it struck down a federal law creating gun-free zones near schools. Five years later, in *United States v. Morrison* (2000), the Court struck down a provision of the Violence Against Women Act (VAWA) that established a right to sue perpetrators of gender-based violence in federal court. In both cases, a five-member majority held that Congress had exceeded its power under the Commerce Clause. (Other provisions of VAWA were not challenged, and Congress reauthorized VAWA in 2000, 2005, and 2013.)

The dissenters in *Lopez* and *Morrison* relied on precedent, insisting that the challenged enactments were consistent with the Court's interpretation of the Commerce Clause since the late 1930s. They argued that the Court had regularly upheld congressional regulations so long as Congress had a rational basis for concluding that the regulated activity affected interstate commerce. The dissenters analogized the challenged statutes in *Lopez* and *Morrison* to those upheld in *Wickard v. Filburn* and *Perez v. United States,* noting that in those earlier cases the Court had recognized that Congress could regulate even purely local activities if they might, in aggregate, have a significant impact on the national economy.

According to the Court majorities in *Lopez* and *Morrison,* however, Congress had exceeded its authority. Speaking for the Court in each case, Chief Justice William Rehnquist emphasized that the noncommercial character of the regulated activity distinguished the current cases from earlier cases. Congressional statutes that regulate noncommercial activity in areas of traditional state concern, he implied, were subject to more searching judicial scrutiny in order to maintain the balance of power between nation and state. Insisting that Congress could regulate only activity that had a substantial influence on commerce among the several states, Rehnquist noted in *Lopez* that the connection between gun ownership in school zones and interstate commerce was tenuous at best. To accept Congress's rationale for upholding the statute would in effect remove all limits on congressional regulatory authority. Because this would transform the constitutional system from a federal to a unitary system, such an interpretation could not be proper.

Morrison presented a somewhat different situation, in that Congress had compiled voluminous data purporting to show that crimes of violence motivated by gender did have a substantial effect on interstate commerce. Yet as Chief Justice Rehnquist observed, "simply because Congress may conclude that a particular activity substantially affects interstate commerce does not make it so." Rather than attempting to show why Congress's factual claims were mistaken, the Court in *Morrison,* as it had in *Lopez,* stressed the consequences of endorsing Congress's position. If, under the Commerce Clause, Congress can regulate gender-motivated violence, it can also regulate all ordinary criminal activity and all areas of family law. Thus, once again, the Court majority sought to protect traditional state functions from federal invasion.

Justice Clarence Thomas, concurring in both cases, challenged the Court's Commerce Clause jurisprudence more directly. Fidelity to the original understanding of the Commerce Clause, he argued, would require the Court to reexamine its conclusion that the national commerce power extends to purely intrastate activities as long as they bear a "substantial relationship" to interstate commerce. For Thomas, Congress's power under the Commerce Clause extended only to buying and selling and to transportation related to those activities. Thus, he proposed reviving the distinction between commerce and production that underlay the dual-federalist interpretation of the commerce power.

Lopez and *Morrison* signaled a judicial willingness to police congressional overreaching rather than a fundamental shift in the Court's jurisprudence. In neither case did Congress regulate economic activity, and in both the commerce power was employed to reach activities that concerned Congress for reasons other than their effects on interstate commerce. Congress's broad power to regulate commercial activity for commercial purposes, established in *National Labor Relations Board v. Jones & Laughlin Steel* and subsequent cases, remained unaffected by the Court's recent rulings. This was underlined in *Gonzales v. Raich* (2005), in which the justices rejected a challenge to the federal Controlled Substances Act (regulating drugs), insofar as it interfered with state programs that authorized physicians to prescribe marijuana for medical purposes and permitted patients to grow or purchase marijuana for those purposes. According to the majority, the key difference from *Lopez* and *Morrison* was that Congress was directly regulating economic activity, since there is a thriving (albeit illegal) market for marijuana. To the dissenters, the statute interfered with the states' ability to experiment in an area of traditional state concern and made it difficult to discern any activities not subject to federal regulation under the Commerce Clause. In recent years, several states have authorized the use of marijuana for medicinal purposes, and Colorado and Washington have done so for recreational purposes as well; the Obama administration has indicated that it will not interfere with these state experiments.

THE TAXING POWER

The Framers gave Congress the power to tax so that the national government could raise the revenue necessary to finance its operations. The Constitution imposes only three express limits on this power. Congress may not tax exports, must apportion direct taxes among the states in relation to their populations, and must impose taxes uniformly throughout the nation (Article I, Section 8, Paragraph 1, and Article I, Section 9, Paragraphs 4 and 5). Only the limitation on "direct taxes"—a vague phrase neither discussed in the Constitutional Convention nor defined in the Constitution—has provoked much litigation. In *Hylton v. United States* (1796), the Supreme Court rejected a claim that a tax on carriages was a direct tax, noting that the term applied to head taxes and land taxes. And in *Springer v. United States* (1881), it concluded that the Civil War income tax was not a direct tax. In *Pollock v. Farmer's Loan & Trust Company* (1895), however, it abandoned this position, holding that because taxes on real estate were direct taxes, so were taxes on the income from real estate. This decision, which prevented the imposition of any type of federal income tax, was overturned by the Sixteenth Amendment (1913).

A more serious constitutional issue stems from the uses Congress may make of its taxing power. All taxes, in addition to raising revenues, make goods more expensive and thereby discourage their purchase. But if the Constitution places few restrictions on the goods and activities Congress can tax, does this mean that the taxing power can be used for regulatory—as well as revenue-raising—purposes? During the nineteenth century, debate over this question centered on protective tariffs, which both raised revenue and shielded American industries from foreign competition. In pursuing the latter objective, Congress was using its taxing power for a regulatory purpose. Because the Constitution grants Congress regulatory authority over commerce with foreign nations, however, protective tariffs involve activities that Congress could regulate by other means, if it so chose. Thus, the constitutionality of this use of the taxing power was recognized long before the Supreme Court expressly upheld it in *J. W. Hampton Jr. & Company v. United States* (1928).

During the twentieth century, debate focused on congressional use of the taxing power to reach activities it could not otherwise regulate. In *McCrary v. United States* (1904), the Court endorsed one such use of the taxing power, upholding a heavy excise tax on margarine that had been colored yellow to resemble butter. Although the tax was designed to discourage purchase of the colored margarine, the Court insisted that it could not question the motives underlying the exercise of constitutionally granted powers. Yet it did precisely that in *Bailey v. Drexel Furniture Company* (1922), striking down a law that imposed a 10 percent tax on the profits of businesses employing children. Writing for the Court, Chief Justice William Howard Taft acknowledged that all taxes have regulatory effects but noted that "there comes a time in the extension of the penalizing features of the so-called tax when it loses its character as such and becomes a mere penalty, with the characteristics of regulation and punishment." If Congress cannot regulate an activity—and the Court in *Hammer v. Dagenhart* had ruled that it could not regulate child labor—then it cannot regulate indirectly through the subterfuge of a "so-called tax."

In *United States v. Butler* (1936), the Court employed the *Bailey* rationale to strike down a major piece of New Deal legislation, the Agricultural Adjustment Act of 1933. Since 1937, however, the Court has refused to monitor the motives underlying congressional tax laws. In *Mulford v. Smith* (1939), it upheld an act virtually identical to the one it had invalidated in *Butler* only three years earlier; in *United States v. Kahriger* (1953), it ruled that an occupational tax on gamblers was constitutional, even though the tax's primary aim was to suppress gambling. Although the justices eventually struck down the tax on gamblers on self-incrimination grounds in *Marchetti v. United States* (1968), in doing so they reasserted that only explicit constitutional prohibitions—not the reserved powers of the states—justified invalidation of congressional tax statutes. Thus, the power to tax, like the power to regulate commerce among the several states, is plenary.

THE SPENDING POWER

Article I, Section 8, authorizes Congress "to pay the debts and provide for the common defense and general welfare of the United States." During the ratification debates, critics of the Constitution asserted that this broad grant of power would transform the federal government into a government of indefinite, rather than enumerated, powers. James Madison rejected this interpretation, maintaining in *The Federalist,* No. 41, that the enumeration of congressional powers that followed the general authorization served to "explain and qualify" it. To Madison, then, the spending power was subordinate to, rather than independent of, the Constitution's grants of legislative power. In his famous *Report on Manufactures,* however, Alexander Hamilton challenged Madison's view that the enumeration of powers served to limit the spending power and proposed a more expansive interpretation:

> The phrase is as comprehensive as any that could have been used, because it was not fit that the constitutional authority of the Union to appropriate its revenues should have been restricted within narrower limits than the "general welfare" and because

this necessarily embraces a vast variety of particulars which are susceptible neither of specification nor of definition. It is therefore of necessity left to the discretion of the National Legislature to pronounce upon the objects which concern the general welfare, and for which, under the description, an appropriation of money is requisite and proper.[7]

Throughout most of the nation's history, congressional practice has been guided by the Hamiltonian position, which the Supreme Court expressly endorsed in *United States v. Butler*. Justice Owen Roberts nonetheless insisted in *Butler* that the spending power was limited by the reserved powers of the states, but the Court has since repudiated that position in *Steward Machine Company v. Davis* (1937) and *Helvering v. Davis* (1937).

Under the Hamiltonian interpretation of the spending power, Congress can use its spending power to regulate indirectly matters that it could not regulate directly, by attaching conditions on the funds that it makes available to states and localities. *South Dakota v. Dole* (1987) illustrates how this works. Congress in 1984 appropriated funds to be distributed to the states for highway construction, but it directed the secretary of transportation to withhold 5 percent of those funds from states that allowed persons under twenty-one years of age to purchase alcoholic beverages. This legislation thus placed financial pressure on states that allowed persons under age twenty-one to drink. The states could choose either to continue to maintain their policy and forfeit some federal funds or to raise their drinking age in order to avoid a loss of funds. In *Dole* the Supreme Court, following a long line of precedent, upheld the condition that Congress had imposed on the distribution of highway funds. This condition, the Court noted, was directly related to a major aim of the highway program—namely, safe interstate travel. In addition, because states could choose whether to forgo the federal funds, the Supreme Court held that states were not coerced by Congress's imposition of conditions on the distribution of grant funds to them. Yet, as Justice Sandra Day O'Connor noted in dissent, in practice the potential loss of even some federal funds may serve as a strong inducement to states to change policy. The issue of when persuasion becomes coercion would resurface in *National Federation of Independent Business v. Sebelius*.

Congress's power to spend is not completely unrestricted. All congressional expenditures must provide for the "common defense" or the "general welfare." But in *Helvering v. Davis* (1937), the Court recognized that Congress has primary responsibility for determining whether expenditures promote the general welfare, and courts can challenge only those determinations that are "clearly wrong, a display of arbitrary power, not an exercise of judgment." Expenditures, like all other congressional actions, are also subject to express constitutional limitations, such as the Bill of Rights. The requirement of standing to sue (see Chapter 3), however, has limited judicial enforcement of these restrictions by making it difficult for taxpayers to contest federal expenditures.

HEALTH CARE AND THE CONSTITUTION

In the landmark case of *National Federation of Independent Business v. Sebelius* (2012), the Supreme Court heard a constitutional challenge to the Patient Protection and Affordable Care Act (PPACA), also known as Obamacare. In addition to its practical importance, the Court's ruling provides crucial insight into current judicial understandings of congressional power under the Commerce Clause, the Necessary and Proper Clause, the Taxing Clause, and the Spending Clause.

The Court's decision focused on two elements of the PPACA: the individual mandate and the act's expansion of Medicaid (a program that provides health care for low-income persons). The individual mandate requires most Americans to maintain "minimal essential" health insurance coverage and provides for a "penalty," beginning in 2014, to be paid for noncompliance with the mandate. Those too poor to pay taxes and a few other groups are exempt from the mandate and the penalty. The Medicaid expansion requires states to expand their coverage to all adults under age sixty-five whose income is no higher than 133 percent of the federal poverty line. This would bring 17 million more low-income persons into the Medicaid program by 2021. States that failed to expand their coverage would no longer receive *any* federal Medicaid funds. Plaintiffs argued that both these provisions exceeded congressional power.

The Court splintered badly in its treatment of the individual mandate. Four justices (Alito, Kennedy, Scalia, and Thomas) concluded that the individual mandate exceeded congressional power under the Commerce Clause, the Necessary and Proper Clause, and the Taxing Clause, and would have struck it down as unconstitutional. Four justices (Breyer, Ginsburg, Kagan, and Sotomayor) voted to uphold the individual mandate under all of these clauses. Chief Justice Roberts agreed with the first group of justices as to the Commerce and Necessary and Proper Clauses but agreed with the second group as to the Taxing Clause, thereby providing the decisive vote for upholding the individual mandate. The justices likewise divided on the constitutionality of withholding all federal Medicaid funds from states that declined to expand coverage. Seven justices (Roberts, Alito, Breyer, Kagan, Kennedy, Scalia, and Thomas) held that the threat to withhold those funds exceeded congressional power under the Spending Clause, but five justices (Roberts, Breyer, Ginsburg, Kagan, and Sotomayor) concluded that this constitutional defect did not require striking down the entire law, so the PPACA emerged largely intact. (PPACA survived a further challenge in *King v. Burwell* (2015), in which a six-member majority rejected an interpretation of the language of the statute that would have limited the availability of tax credits and health insurance in states that did not set up their own "health-care exchanges.")

The Commerce and Necessary and Proper Clauses

The federal government maintained that the individual mandate was a valid exercise of congressional power under both the Commerce and the Necessary and Proper Clauses. Because health care is a major component of the national economy, it contended that attempts to comprehensively reform it therefore fell within Congress's commerce power. The PPACA, it noted, was designed to combat a national problem, namely, that many persons were unable or unwilling to obtain health insurance. The federal government argued that the individual mandate (requiring individuals to buy health insurance) was necessary to further its goal: the law prohibited private health insurers from denying coverage based on preexisting conditions, and the cost of this requirement would be underwritten by increasing the pool of the insured and eliminating "free riders." Although the individual mandate in effect required persons to engage in commerce, the federal government insisted that failure to buy insurance itself affected interstate commerce and that the requirement did not represent a major innovation, because everyone eventually participates in the health care market.

Five justices (Roberts, Alito, Kennedy, Scalia, and Thomas) rejected the government's argument. Whereas previous rulings had recognized that Congress could regulate activities that affected commerce among the states, these justices noted that the individual mandate regulated persons not engaged in commerce, requiring them to buy a commercial product against their will. As Chief Justice Roberts wrote, "The Government's logic would justify a mandatory purchase to solve almost any problem. People, for reasons of their own, often fail to do things that would be good for them or good for society. Those failures—joined with the similar failures of others—can readily have a substantial effect on interstate commerce. Under the Government's logic, that authorizes Congress to use its commerce power to compel citizens to act as the Government would have them act." This went far beyond past precedent, they argued, and exceeded congressional authority under the Commerce Clause. Nor did the Necessary and Proper Clause authorize the individual mandate. Although the five justices acknowledged that Congress has broad discretion in choosing the means to accomplish its constitutional ends, that discretion is not unlimited. Congress cannot employ means that are not "consistent with the letter and spirit of the Constitution" or jeopardize the constitutional division of power between nation and state. As the joint opinion of Justices Alito, Kennedy, Scalia, and Thomas put it, "Whereas the precise scope of the Commerce Clause and the Necessary and Proper Clause is uncertain, the proposition that the Federal Government cannot do everything is a fundamental precept." Thus, grants of power to Congress should be interpreted so as to avoid undermining the structure of government established by the Constitution. In taking this position, the Court confirmed that it would continue to scrutinize the exercise of congressional powers.

The Taxing Power

The federal government argued that the monetary assessment imposed on those who failed to purchase health insurance by 2014 should be understood as a tax on those persons and that the individual mandate should thus be upheld under Congress's power to "lay and collect Taxes." By a 5–4 vote, the Court agreed. In characterizing the "shared responsibility payment" (as the PPACA entitled it) as a tax, Roberts noted that the requirement was found in the Internal Revenue Code, enforced by the Internal Revenue Service, and did not apply to those who did not pay federal income tax because their income was too low. The individual mandate also raised revenue, a key element in determining whether an assessment is a tax. The fact that it also influenced behavior was not decisive, as the Court had in the past upheld the use of taxation for regulatory purposes. Roberts noted that "if one chooses to pay [the tax] rather than obtain health insurance, they have fully complied with the law," so it was best understood as a tax that one could choose to pay in lieu of buying health insurance. Having reached that conclusion, he noted that while the Commerce Clause may not authorize Congress to regulate inactivity, "the Constitution does not guarantee that individuals may avoid taxation through inactivity."

The justices who had joined Chief Justice Roberts's interpretation of the Commerce and Necessary and Proper Clauses disagreed. Even if Congress had the power to frame the individual-mandate provision as a tax, it had not done so, choosing instead to frame it as a penalty imposed for violation of the law. Whereas Chief Justice Roberts emphasized the importance of giving a presumption of constitutionality to congressional enactments, the dissenters charged the Court with judicial activism: "To say that the individual mandate merely imposes a tax is not to interpret the statute but to rewrite it." Ultimately, then, the disagreement rested not on the scope of Congress's taxing power but on whether it had exercised that power in enacting the individual mandate.

The Spending Power

The plaintiffs in the case also claimed that by cutting off all federal Medicaid funding to those states that failed to expand Medicaid eligibility as required by the PPACA, Congress was coercing the states to accept the expanded coverage and thereby exceeding its power under the Spending Clause. Seven justices agreed. States could choose to expand Medicaid coverage as required by the PPACA, thereby gaining access to the funds available for this purpose under the statute. But they could not be threatened with the loss of all their Medicaid funding if they failed to do so.

Chief Justice Roberts acknowledged that the Constitution authorizes Congress to spend for the common good and that Congress can use the incentive of federal funds to induce states to participate in governmental programs. However, he insisted that the Constitution imposes limits on congressional inducements. At some point, such inducements cross the line from persuasion to coercion—"pressure turns into compulsion"—and this undue influence violates the Constitution. The withdrawal of all federal Medicaid funds from states that do not expand their coverage, he insisted, crosses this line, because "the 'financial inducement' Congress has chosen is much more than 'relatively mild encouragement'—it is a gun to the head. The threatened loss of over 10 percent of a State's overall budget left the States with no real option but to acquiesce in the Medicaid expansion." The key, he emphasized, is the voluntariness of state participation in a grant program. The states, as sovereigns, cannot be simply commandeered into the service of the federal government nor required by it to regulate. This would undermine the system of federalism created by the Constitution and the system of accountability it fosters. Only when states have a real choice can voters hold state officials accountable for the exercise of that choice.

This marked the first time the Supreme Court had invalidated a federal grant program as coercive. Yet exactly when persuasion becomes coercion remains unclear. As Roberts noted, "It is enough for today that wherever that line may be, this statute is surely beyond it. Congress may not simply conscript state agencies into the national bureaucratic army, and that is what it is attempting to do with the Medicaid expansion." But in failing to fix the line distinguishing persuasion from coercion, the Court virtually guaranteed that future cases would arise challenging federal grant programs.

LIMITATIONS ON NATIONAL POWER

Responding to the deficiencies of the Articles of Confederation, the Framers vested Congress with broad powers to tax, to spend, and to regulate commerce. Yet although these grants of power were broad, they were not unlimited, and controversy has arisen periodically about the scope of these powers. In the aftermath of the New Deal conflict between Franklin Roosevelt and the Supreme Court, the justices interpreted these powers so expansively that commentators questioned whether any constitutional limitations remained on the exercise of national power. Since 1995, however, the Supreme Court has attempted to reimpose some limits, invalidating the provisions of various federal statutes as beyond the scope of the federal commerce power or, as in *National Federation of Independent Business v. Sebelius,* ruling that Congress had exceeded its power under the Commerce Clause, even as it upheld the law on other grounds. Equally important as a check on federal power are the limitations found in the Bill of Rights. It is no coincidence that as the scope of the federal government has expanded, the Court has found increasing occasion to invalidate congressional legislation violating these protections.

Nevertheless, the primary limitation on the exercise of federal power is political, not constitutional, in character. As Chief Justice Marshall observed in *Gibbons v. Ogden,* "The wisdom and the discretion of Congress, their identity with the people, and the influence which their constituents possess at election, are the restraints on which the people must often rely solely, in all representative governments."

NOTES

1. The Economic Stabilization Act of 1970 was upheld against constitutional challenge in *Amalgamated Meat Cutters & Butcher Workmen v. Connally,* 337 F. Supp. 737 (D.D.C. 1971).

2. Between 1888 and 1933, the Supreme Court struck down forty federal laws; from 1934 to 1936, it struck down thirteen. See "The Constitution of the United States of America: Analysis and Interpretation," www.gpoaccess.gov/constitution/index.html.

3. *Schechter Poultry Corp. v. United States* (1935), *United States v. Butler* (1936), and *Carter v. Carter Coal Co.* (1936).

4. This plan is discussed in Robert H. Jackson, *The Struggle for Judicial Supremacy: A Study of a Crisis in American Power Politics* (New York: Alfred A. Knopf, 1941); and Jeff Shesol, *Supreme Power: Franklin Roosevelt vs. the Supreme Court* (New York: W. W. Norton, 2010).

5. Bruce Ackerman, *We the People: Foundations* (Cambridge, MA: Belknap Press of Harvard University Press, 1991).

6. This is illustrated in *NLRB v. Friedman–Harry Marks Clothing Co.* (1937), *NLRB v. Fainblatt* (1939), and *Santa Cruz v. NLRB* (1938).

7. Alexander Hamilton, *The Works of Alexander Hamilton*, edited by Henry Cabot Lodge, 7 vols. (New York: Federal Edition, 1904), 4:151.

SELECTED READINGS

The Federalist, Nos. 30–36, 41–42, 56.

Ackerman, Bruce A. *We the People: Foundations.* Cambridge, MA: Belknap Press, 1991.

Allhof, Fritz, and Mark Hill, eds. *The Affordable Care Act Decision: Philosophical and Legal Implications.* New York: Taylor & Francis, 2014.

Barber, Sotirios A. *Welfare and the Constitution.* Princeton, NJ: Princeton University Press, 2003.

Barnett, Randy E. *Restoring the Lost Constitution: The Presumption of Liberty.* Princeton, NJ: Princeton University Press, 2004.

Corwin, Edward S. "The Passing of Dual Federalism." In *Essays in Constitutional Law,* edited by Robert G. McCloskey. New York: Alfred A. Knopf, 1957.

Cushman, Barry. *Rethinking the New Deal Court: The Structure of a Constitutional Revolution.* New York: Oxford University Press, 1998.

Edling, Max M. *A Revolution in Favor of Government: Origins of the U.S. Constitution and the Making of the American State.* New York: Oxford University Press, 2003.

Epstein, Richard A. *The Classical Liberal Constitution: The Uncertain Quest for Limited Government.* Cambridge, MA: Harvard University Press, 2014.

Frankfurter, Felix. *The Commerce Clause under Marshall, Taney, and Waite.* Chapel Hill: University of North Carolina Press, 1937.

Nelson, Grant S., and Robert J. Pashaw Jr. "Rethinking the Commerce Clause: Applying First Principles to Uphold Federal Commercial Regulation but Preserve State Control over Social Issues." *Iowa Law Review* 85 (1999): 1–173.

Noonan, John T. *Narrowing the Nation's Power: The Supreme Court Sides with the States.* Berkeley: University of California Press, 2002.

Shesol, Jeff. *Supreme Power: Franklin Roosevelt vs. the Supreme Court.* New York: W. W. Norton, 2010.

Sunstein, Cass. *The Partial Constitution.* Cambridge, MA: Harvard University Press, 1993.

"Symposium: Health Care and the Constitution: A Forum on the Supreme Court's Affordable Care Act," *Fordham Law Review* 81 (March 2013): 1697–1879.

White, G. Edward. *The Constitution and the New Deal.* Cambridge, MA: Harvard University Press, 2000.

Gibbons v. Ogden
22 U.S. (9 Wheat.) 1 (1824)

Robert Fulton and Robert Livingston, having obtained from the state of New York an exclusive right to operate steamboats in its waters, licensed Aaron Ogden to operate steamboats between New Jersey and New York. But Thomas Gibbons, armed with a federal license under the Coasting Act of 1793 (in which Congress provided for the licensing of "vessels employed in the coasting trade"), challenged the state-granted monopoly by running two steamboats between Elizabethtown, New Jersey, and New York City. When the New York Court of Chancery enjoined Gibbons from continuing to operate his boats, he appealed the decision to the United States Supreme Court. Opinion of the Court: <u>Marshall</u>, Todd, Duval, Story, Thompson. Concurring opinion: <u>Johnson</u>.

THE CHIEF JUSTICE delivered the opinion of the Court.

As preliminary to the very able discussions of the constitution, which we have heard from the bar, and as having some influence on its construction, reference has been made to the political situation of these states, anterior to its formation. It has been said, that they were sovereign, were completely independent, and were connected with each other only by a league. This is true. But when these allied sovereigns converted their league into a government, when they converted their congress of ambassadors, deputed to deliberate on their common concerns, and to recommend measures of general utility into a legislature, empowered to enact laws on the most interesting subjects, the whole character in which the states appear, underwent a change, the extent of which must be determined by a fair consideration of the instrument by which that change was effected.

This instrument contains an enumeration of powers expressly granted by the people to their government. It has been said, that these powers ought to be construed strictly. But why ought they to be so construed? Is there one sentence in the constitution which gives countenance to this rule? In the last of the enumerated powers, that which grants, expressly, the means for carrying all others into execution, congress is authorized "to make all laws which shall be

necessary and proper" for the purposes. But this limitation on the means which may be used, is not extended to the powers which are conferred; nor is there one sentence in the constitution which has been pointed out by the gentlemen of the bar, or which we have been able to discern, that prescribes this rule. We do not, therefore, think ourselves justified in adopting it. What do gentlemen mean, by a strict construction? If they contend only against that enlarged construction, which would extend words beyond their natural and obvious import, we might question the application of the term, but should not controvert the principle. If they contend for that narrow construction which, in support of some theory not to be found in the constitution, would deny to the government those powers which the words of the grant, as usually understood, import, and which are consistent with the general views and objects of the instrument—for that narrow construction, which would cripple the government, and render it unequal to the objects for which it is declared to be instituted, and to which the powers given, as fairly understood, render it competent—then we cannot perceive the propriety of this strict construction, nor adopt it as the rule by which the constitution is to be expounded.

The words are, "congress shall have power to regulate commerce with foreign nations, and among the several states, and with the Indian tribes." The subject to be regulated is commerce; and our constitution being, as was aptly said at the bar, one of enumeration, and not of definition, to ascertain the extent of the power, it becomes necessary to settle the meaning of the word. The counsel for the appellee would limit it to traffic, to buying and selling, or the interchange of commodities, and do not admit that it comprehends navigation. This would restrict a general term, applicable to many objects, to one of its significations. Commerce, undoubtedly, is traffic, but it is something more—it is intercourse. It describes the commercial intercourse between nations, and parts of nations, in all its branches, and is regulated by prescribing rules for carrying on that intercourse. The mind can scarcely conceive a system for regulating commerce between nations, which shall exclude all laws concerning navigation, which shall be silent on the admission of the vessels of the one nation into the parts of the other, and be confined to prescribing rules for the conduct of individuals, in the actual employment of buying and selling, or of barter. If commerce does not include navigation, the government of the Union has no direct power over that subject, and can make no law prescribing what shall constitute American vessels or requiring that they shall be navigated by American seamen. Yet this power has been exercised from the commencement of the government, has been exercised with the consent of all, and has been understood by all to be a commercial regulation. All America understands, and has uniformly understood, the word "commerce," to comprehend navigation. It was so understood, and must have been so understood, when the constitution was framed. The power over commerce, including navigation, was one of the primary objects for which the people of America adopted their government, and must have been contemplated in forming it. The convention must have used the word in that sense, because all have understood it in that sense; and the attempt to restrict it comes too late.

The word used in the constitution, then, comprehends, and has been always understood to comprehend, navigation within its meaning; and a power to regulate navigation, is as expressly granted, as if that term had been added to the word "commerce." To what commerce does this power extend? The constitution informs us, to commerce "with foreign nations, and among the several states, and with the Indian tribes." It has, we believe, been universally admitted, that these words comprehend every species of commercial intercourse between the United States and foreign nations.

If this be the admitted meaning of the word, in its application to foreign nations, it must carry the same meaning throughout the sentence, and remain a unit, unless there be some plain intelligible cause which alters it. The subject to which the power is next applied, is to commerce, "among the several states." The word "among" means intermingled with. A thing which is among others, is intermingled with them. Commerce among the states, cannot stop at the external boundary line of each state, but may be introduced into the interior. It is not intended to say, that these words comprehend that commerce, which is completely internal, which is carried on between man and man in a state, or between different parts of the same state, and which does extend to or affect other states. Such a power would be inconvenient, and is certainly unnecessary. Comprehensive as the word "among" is, it may very properly be restricted to that commerce which concerns more states than one. The genius and character of the whole government seem to be, that its action is to be applied to all the external concerns of the nation, and to those internal concerns which affect the states generally; but not to those which are completely within a particular state, which do not affect other states, and with which it is not necessary to interfere, for the purpose of executing some of the general powers of the government. The completely internal commerce of a state, then, may be considered as reserved for the state itself.

But in regulating commerce with foreign nations, the power of congress does not stop at the jurisdictional lines of the several states. If congress has the power to regulate it, that power must be exercised whenever the subject exists. If it exists within the states, if a foreign voyage may commence or terminate at a port within a state, then the power of congress may be exercised within a state.

This principle is, if possible, still more clear, when applied to commerce "among the several states." They either join each other, in which case they are separated by a mathematical line, or they are remote from each other, in which case other states lie between them. What is commerce "among" them; and how is it to be conducted? Can a trading expedition between two adjoining states, commence and terminate outside of each? And if the trading intercourse be between two states remote from each other, must it not commence in one, terminate in the other, and probably pass through a third? The power of congress, then, whatever it may be, must be exercised within the territorial jurisdiction of the several states.

We are now arrived at the inquiry—what is the power? It is the power to regulate; that is, to prescribe the rule by which commerce is to be governed. This power, like all others vested in congress, is complete in itself, may be exercised to its utmost extent, and acknowledges no limitations, other than are prescribed in the constitution. If, as has always been understood, the sovereignty of congress, though limited to specified objects, is plenary as to those objects, the power over commerce with foreign nations, and among the several states, is vested in congress as absolutely as it would be in a single government, having in its constitution the same restrictions on the exercise of the power as are found in the constitution of the United States. The wisdom and the discretion of congress, their identity with the people, and the influence which their constituents possess at elections, are, in this, as in many other instances, as that, for example, of declaring war, the sole restraints on which they have relied, to secure them from its abuse. They are the restraints on which the people must often rely solely, in all representative governments.

But it has been urged, with great earnestness, that although the power of congress to regulate commerce with foreign nations, and among the several states, be co-extensive with the subject itself, and have no other limits than are prescribed in the constitution, yet the states may severally exercise the same power, within their respective jurisdictions.

The grant of the power to lay and collect taxes is, like the power to regulate commerce, made in general terms, and has never been understood to interfere with the exercise of the same power by the states; and hence has been drawn an argument which has been applied to the question under consideration. But the two grants are not, it is conceived, similar in their terms or their nature. Although many of the powers formerly exercised by the states, are transferred to the government of the Union, yet the state governments remain, and constitute a most important part of our system. The power of taxation is indispensable to their existence, and is a power which, in its own nature, is capable of residing in, and being exercised by, different authorities, at the same time. We are accustomed to see it placed, for different purposes, in different hands. Taxation is the simple operation of taking small portions from a perpetually accumulating mass, susceptible of almost infinite division; and a power in one to take what is necessary for certain purposes, is not, in its nature, incompatible with a power in another to take what is necessary for other purposes. Congress is authorized to lay and collect taxes, &c., to pay the debts, and provide for the common defense and general welfare of the United States. This does not interfere with the power of the states to tax for the support of their own governments; nor is the exercise of that power by the states, an exercise of any portion of the power that is granted to the United States. In imposing taxes for state purposes, they are not doing what congress is empowered to do. Congress is not empowered to tax for those purposes which are within the exclusive province of the states. When, then, each government exercises the power of taxation, neither is exercising the power of the other. But when a state proceeds to regulate commerce with foreign nations, or among the several states, it is exercising the very power that is granted to congress, and is doing the very thing which congress is authorized to do. There is no analogy, then, between the power of taxation and the power of regulating commerce.

In discussing the question, whether this power is still in the states, in the case under consideration, we may dismiss from it the inquiry, whether it is surrendered by the mere grant to congress, or is retained until congress shall exercise the power. We may dismiss that inquiry, because it has been exercised, and the regulations which congress deemed it proper to make, are now in full operation. The sole question is, can a state regulate commerce with foreign nations and among the states, while congress is regulating it?

The inspection laws are said to be regulations of commerce and are certainly recognised in the constitution, as being passed in the exercise of a power remaining with the states. That inspection laws may have a remote and considerable influence on commerce, will not be denied: but that a power to regulate commerce is the source from which the right to pass them is derived cannot be admitted. The object of inspection laws is to improve the quality of articles produced by the labor of a country: to do them for exportation; or, it may be, for domestic use. They act upon the subject, before it becomes an article of foreign commerce, or of commerce among the states, and prepare it for that purpose. They form a portion of that immense mass of legislation, which embraces everything within the territory of a state, not surrendered to the general government; all which can be most advantageously exercised by the states themselves. Inspection laws, quarantine laws, health laws of every description, as well as laws for regulating the internal commerce of a state, and those which respect turnpike-roads, ferries, &c., are component parts of this mass.

No direct general power over these objects is granted to congress; and, consequently, they remain subject to state legislation. If the legislative power of the Union can reach them, it must be for national purposes; it must be, where the power is expressly given for a special purpose, or is clearly incidental to some power which is expressly given. It is obvious, that the government of the Union, in the exercise of its express powers, that, for example, of regulating commerce with foreign nations and among the states, may use means that may also be employed by a state, in the exercise of its acknowledged powers; that, for example, of regulating commerce within the state.

In our complex system, presenting the rare and difficult scheme of one general government, whose action extends over the whole, but which possesses only certain enumerated powers; and of numerous state governments, which retain and exercise all powers not delegated to the Union, contests respecting power must arise. Were it even otherwise, the measures taken by the respective governments to execute their acknowledged powers, would often be of the same description, and might, sometimes, interfere. This, however, does not prove that the one is exercising, or has a right to exercise, the powers of the other.

Since, however, in exercising the power of regulating their own purely internal affairs, whether of trading or police, the states may sometimes enact laws, the validity of which depends on their interfering with, and being contrary to, an act of congress passed in pursuance

of the constitution, the court will enter upon the inquiry, whether the laws of New York, as expounded by the highest tribunal of that state, have in their application to this case, come into collision with an act of congress and deprived a citizen of a right to which that act entitles him. Should this collision exist, it will be immaterial, whether those laws were passed in virtue of a concurrent power "to regulate commerce with foreign nations and among the several states" or in virtue of a power to regulate their domestic trade and police. In one case and the other, the acts of New York must yield to the law of congress; and the decision sustaining the privilege they confer, against a right given by a law of the Union, must be erroneous. This opinion has been frequently expressed in this court, and is founded, as well on the nature of the government, as on the words of the constitution. In argument, however, it has been contended, that if a law passed by a state, in the exercise of its acknowledged sovereignty, comes into conflict with a law passed by congress in pursuance of the constitution, they affect the subject, and each other, like equal opposing powers. But the framers of our constitution foresaw this state of things, and provided for it, by developing the supremacy not only of itself, but of the laws made in pursuance of it. The nullity of any act, inconsistent with the constitution is produced by the declaration, that the constitution is the supreme law. The appropriate application of that part of the clause which confers the same supremacy on laws and treaties, is to such acts of the state legislatures as do not transcend their powers, but though enacted in the execution of acknowledged state powers, interfere with, or are contrary to the laws of congress, made in pursuance of the constitution, or some treaty made under the authority of the United States. In every such case the acts of congress, or the treaty, is supreme; and the law of the state, though enacted in the exercise of powers not controverted, must yield to it.

But all inquiry into this subject seems to the court to be put completely at rest, by the act already mentioned, entitled, "an act for the enrolling and licensing of steamboats." This act authorizes a steam boat employed, or intended to be employed, only in a river or bay of the

United States, owned wholly or in part by an alien, resident within the United States, to be enrolled and licensed as if the same belonged to a citizen of the United States. This act demonstrates the opinion of congress, that steamboats may be enrolled and licensed, in common with vessels using sails. They are, of course, entitled to the same privileges, and can no more be restrained from navigating waters, and entering ports which are free to such vessels, than if they were wafted on their voyage by the winds, instead of being propelled by the agency of fire. The one element may be as legitimately used as the other, for every commercial purpose authorized by the laws of the Union; and the act of a state inhibiting the use of either, to any vessel having a license under the act of congress, comes, we think, in direct collision with that act.

JUSTICE JOHNSON, concurring.

In attempts to construe the constitution, I have never found much benefit resulting from the inquiry, whether the whole; or any part of it, is to be construed strictly or liberally. The simple, classical, precise, yet comprehensive language in which it is couched, leaves, at most, but very little latitude for construction; and when its intent and meaning are discovered, nothing remains but to execute the will of those who made it, in the best manner to effect the purposes intended. The great and paramount purpose was, to unite this mass of wealth and power, for the protection of the humblest individual; his rights, civil and political, his interests and prosperity, are the sole end; the rest are nothing but the means. The history of the times will sustain the opinion, that the grant of power over commerce, if intended to be commensurate with the evils existing, and the purpose of remedying those evils, could be only commensurate with the power of the states over the subject.

But what was that power? The states were, unquestionably, supreme; and each possessed that power over commerce, which is acknowledged to reside in every sovereign state. The power of a sovereign state over commerce, therefore, amounts to nothing more than a power to limit and restrain it at pleasure. And since the power to prescribe the limits to its freedom, necessarily implies the power to determine what shall remain unrestrained, it follows, that the power must be exclusive: it can reside but in one potentate; and hence, the grant of this power carries with it the whole subject, leaving nothing for the state to act upon.

United States v. E. C. Knight Company
156 U.S. 1 (1895)

By purchasing the stock of four Philadelphia sugar refineries with shares of its own stock, the American Sugar Refining Company acquired control of more than 98 percent of the nation's sugar-refining business. The federal government charged that this action constituted a violation of the Sherman Anti-Trust Act, passed by Congress in 1890, which made it illegal to monopolize or restrain— or seek to monopolize or restrain—interstate or foreign commerce through any contact, combination, or conspiracy. The basic issue in this case was thus the interpretation of the statute: does the acquisition of control over the sugar-refining business constitute a monopoly in interstate commerce? In interpreting the statute, however, the Court sought to construe it so as to render it constitutional. Thus, the Court's construction of the statute depended upon its understanding of the scope of national regulatory authority under the Commerce Clause. Opinion of the Court: <u>Fuller,</u> Field, Gray, Brewer, Brown, Shiras, White, Peckham. Dissenting opinion: <u>Harlan.</u>

THE CHIEF JUSTICE delivered the opinion of the Court.

The fundamental question is, whether conceding that the existence of a monopoly in manufacture is established by the evidence, that monopoly can be directly suppressed under the act of Congress in the mode attempted by this bill.

It cannot be denied that the power of a State to protect the lives, health, and property of its citizens, and to preserve good order and the public morals, "the power to govern men and things within the limits of its dominion," is a power originally and always belonging to the States, not surrendered by them to the general government, nor directly restrained by the Constitution of the United States, and essentially exclusive. On the other hand, the power of Congress to regulate commerce among the several States is also exclusive. That which belongs to commerce is within the jurisdiction of the United States, but that which does not belong to commerce is within the jurisdiction of the police power of the State.

The argument is that the power to control the manufacture of refined sugar is a monopoly over a necessary of life, to the enjoyment of which by a large part of the population of the United States interstate commerce is indispensable, and that, therefore, the general government in the exercise of the power to regulate commerce may repress such monopoly directly and set aside the instruments which have created it. But this argument cannot be confined to necessaries of life merely, and must include all articles of general consumption. Doubtless the power to control the manufacture of a given thing involves in a certain sense the control of its disposition, but this is a secondary and not the primary sense; and although the exercise of that power may result in bringing the operation of commerce into play, it does not control it, and affects it only incidentally and indirectly. Commerce succeeds to manufacture, and is not a part of it. The power to regulate commerce is the power to prescribe the rule by which commerce shall be governed, and is a power independent of the power to suppress monopoly. But it may operate in repression of monopoly whenever that comes within the rules by which commerce is governed or whenever the transaction is itself a monopoly of commerce.

It is vital that the independence of the commercial power and of the police power, and the delimitation between them, however sometimes perplexing, should always be recognized and observed, for while the one furnishes the strongest bond of union, the other is essential to the preservation of the autonomy of the States as required by our dual form of government; and acknowledged evils, however grave and urgent they may appear to be, had better be borne, than the risk be run, in the effort to suppress them, of more serious consequences by resort to expedients of even doubtful constitutionality.

It will be perceived how far-reaching the proposition is that the power of dealing with a monopoly directly may be exercised by the general government whenever interstate or international commerce may be ultimately affected. The regulation of commerce applies to the subjects of commerce and not to matters of internal police. Contracts to buy, sell, or exchange goods to be transported among the several States, the transportation and its instrumentalities, and articles bought, sold, or exchanged for the purposes of such transit among the States, or put in the way of transit, may be regulated, but this is because they form part of interstate trade or commerce. The fact that an article is manufactured for export to another State does not of itself make it an article of interstate commerce, and the intent of the manufacturer does not determine the time when the article or product passes from the control of the State and belongs to commerce.

Contracts, combinations, or conspiracies to control domestic enterprise in manufacture, agriculture, mining, production in all its forms, or to raise or lower prices or wages, might unquestionably tend to restrain external as well as domestic trade, but the restraint would be an indirect result, however inevitable and whatever its extent, and such result would not necessarily determine the object of the contract, combination, or conspiracy. Slight reflection will show that if the national power extends to all contracts and combinations in manufacture, agriculture, mining, and other productive industries, whose ultimate result may affect external commerce, comparatively little of business operations and affairs would be left for state control.

It was in the light of well-settled principles that the act of July 2, 1890, was framed. Congress did not attempt thereby to assert the power to deal with monopoly directly as such. What the law struck at was combinations, contracts, and conspiracies to monopolize trade and commerce among the several States or with foreign nations; but the contracts and acts of the defendants related exclusively to the acquisition of the Philadelphia refineries and the business of sugar refining in Pennsylvania, and bore no direct relation to commerce between the States or with foreign nations. The object was manifestly private gain in the manufacture of the commodity, but not through the control of interstate or foreign commerce. It is true that the bill alleged that the products of these refineries were sold and distributed among the several States, and that all the companies were engaged in trade or commerce with the several States and with foreign nations; but this was no more than to say that trade and commerce served manufacture to fulfill its function. It does not follow that an attempt to monopolize, or the actual monopoly of, the manufacture was an attempt, whether executory or consummated, to monopolize commerce, even though, in order to dispose of the product, the instrumentality of commerce was necessarily invoked. There was nothing in the proofs to indicate any intention to put a restraint upon trade or commerce, and the fact, was we have seen, that trade or commerce might be indirectly affected was not enough to entitle complainants to a decree.

Decree affirmed.

Hammer v. Dagenhart
247 U.S. 251 (1918)

The Federal Child Labor Act of 1916, which was designed to discourage the employment of child labor, prohibited the shipment in interstate commerce of goods produced in factories that employed children under the age of fourteen or permitted children under age sixteen to work either at night or for more than eight hours a day. Dagenhart, whose sons worked in his cotton mill, challenged the act in federal district court. When the district court invalidated the act, the case was appealed to the Supreme Court. Opinion of the Court: Day, *White, Van Devanter, Pitney, McReynolds. Dissenting opinion:* Holmes, *McKenna, Brandeis, Clarke.*

JUSTICE DAY delivered the opinion of the Court.

The controlling question for decision is: Is it within the authority of Congress in regulating commerce among the States to prohibit the transportation in interstate commerce of manufactured goods, the product of a factory in which, within thirty days prior to their removal therefrom, children under the age of fourteen have been employed or permitted to work, or children between the ages of fourteen and sixteen years have been employed or permitted to work more than eight hours in any day, or more than six days in any week, or after the hour of seven o'clock p.m. or before the hour of 6 o'clock a.m.?

[*Justice Day then reviewed the Court's previous decisions regarding the use of the Commerce Clause for noncommercial purposes.*] In each of these instances the use of interstate transportation was necessary to the accomplishment of harmful results. In other words, although the power over interstate transportation was to regulate, that could only be accomplished by prohibiting the use of facilities of interstate commerce to effect the evil intended.

This element is wanting in the present case. The thing intended to be accomplished by this statute is the denial of the facilities of interstate commerce to those manufacturers in the States who employ children within the prohibited ages. The act in its effect does not regulate transportation among the States, but aims to standardize the ages at which children may be employed in mining and manufacturing within the States. The goods shipped are of themselves harmless. The act permits them to be freely shipped after thirty days from the time of their removal from the factory. When offered for shipment, and before transportation begins, the labor of their production is over, and the mere fact that they were intended for interstate commerce transportation does not make their production subject to federal control under the commerce power.

It is further contended that the authority of Congress may be exerted to control interstate commerce in the shipment of child-made goods because of the effects of the circulation of such goods in other States where the evil of this class of labor has been recognized by local legislation, and the right to thus employ child labor has been more rigorously restrained than in the State of production. In other words, that the unfair competition, thus engendered, may be controlled by closing the channels of interstate commerce to manufacturers in those States where the local laws do not meet what Congress deems to be the more just standard of other States.

There is no power vested in Congress to require the States to exercise their police power so as to prevent possible unfair competition. Many causes may cooperate to give one State, by reason of local laws or conditions, an economic advantage over others. The Commerce Clause was not intended to give to Congress a general authority to equalize such conditions.

A statute must be judged by its natural and reasonable effect. The control by Congress over interstate commerce cannot authorize the exercise of authority not entrusted to it by the Constitution. The maintenance of the authority of the States over matters purely local is as essential to the preservation of our institutions as is the conservation of the supremacy of the federal power in all matters entrusted to the Nation by the Federal Constitution. . . .

To sustain this statute would not be in our judgment a recognition of the lawful exertion of congressional authority over interstate commerce, but would sanction an invasion by the federal power of the control of a matter purely local in its character, and over which no authority has been delegated to Congress in conferring the power to regulate commerce among the States. In our view the necessary effect of this act is, by means of a prohibition against the movement in interstate commerce of ordinary commercial commodities, to regulate the hours of labor of children in factories and mines within the States, a purely state authority. Thus the act in a twofold sense is repugnant to the Constitution. It not only transcends the authority delegated to Congress over commerce but also exerts a power as to a purely local matter to which the federal authority does not extend. The far reaching result of upholding the act cannot be more plainly indicated than by pointing out that if Congress can thus regulate matters entrusted to local authority by prohibition of the movement of commodities in interstate commerce, all freedom of commerce will be at an end, and the power of the States over local matters may be eliminated, and thus our system of government be practically destroyed.

JUSTICE HOLMES, dissenting.

The first step in my argument is to make plain what no one is likely to dispute—that the statute in question is within the power expressly given to Congress if considered only as to its immediate effects and that if invalid it is so only upon some collateral ground. The statute confines itself to prohibiting the carriage of certain goods in interstate or foreign commerce. Congress is given power to regulate such commerce in unqualified terms.

The question then is narrowed to whether the exercise of its otherwise constitutional power by Congress can be pronounced unconstitutional because of its possible reaction upon the conduct of the States in a matter upon which I have admitted that they are free from direct control. I should have thought that that matter had been disposed of so fully as to leave no room for doubt. I should have thought that the most conspicuous decisions of this Court had made it clear that the power to regulate commerce and other constitutional powers could not be cut down or qualified by the fact that it might interfere with the carrying out of the domestic policy of any State.

The notion that prohibition is any less prohibition when applied to things now thought evil I do not understand. But if there is any matter upon which civilized countries have agreed—far more unanimously than they have with regard to intoxicants and some other matters over which this country is now emotionally aroused—it is the evil of premature and excessive child labor. I should have thought that if we were to introduce our own moral conceptions where in my opinion they do not belong, this was preeminently a case for upholding the exercise of all its powers by the United States. But I had thought that the propriety of the exercise of a power admitted to exist in some cases was for the consideration of Congress alone and that this Court always had disavowed the right to intrude its judgment upon questions of policy or morals.

The act does not meddle with anything belonging to the States. They may regulate their internal affairs and their domestic commerce as they like. But when they seek to send their products across the state line they are no longer within their rights. If there were no Constitution and no Congress their power to cross the line would depend upon their neighbors. Under the Constitution such commerce belongs not to the States but to Congress to regulate. It may carry out its views of public policy whatever indirect effect they may have upon the activities of the States. The national welfare as understood by Congress may require a different attitude within its sphere from that of some self-seeking State. It seems to me entirely constitutional for Congress to enforce its understanding by all the means at its command.

National Labor Relations Board v. Jones & Laughlin Steel Corporation
301 U.S. 1 (1937)

The National Labor Relations Act (also called the Wagner Act) was designed to protect the rights of workers to form unions and to bargain collectively. The act prohibited a variety of unfair labor practices and authorized the National Labor Relations Board (NLRB) to issue cease-and-desist orders to employers who engaged in such practices. Jones & Laughlin, one of the nation's largest steel producers, violated the act by firing ten workers for engaging in union activities. The company then refused to comply with an NLRB order to reinstate the workers. After a court of appeals declined to enforce the board's order, the Supreme Court granted certiorari.

This decision—the so-called switch in time that saved nine—was announced amid intense controversy over the Supreme Court's rulings. Following his landslide reelection in 1936, President Franklin Roosevelt, frustrated by adverse Supreme Court rulings and sure that the nation supported his program of economic reform, sent to Congress a proposal to expand the number of Supreme Court justices. By upholding the Wagner Act, the Court largely defused the controversy and ensured the defeat of the so-called court-packing scheme. Shortly thereafter, President Roosevelt had the opportunity to name his first justice to the Court, and his appointment of eight justices by 1941 produced unanimous support for the conception of national power over the economy enunciated in this case. Opinion of the Court: <u>Hughes</u>, Brandeis, Stone, Roberts, Cardozo. Dissenting opinion: <u>McReynolds</u>, Van Devanter, Sutherland, Butler.

THE CHIEF JUSTICE delivered the opinion of the Court.

First. The scope of the Act—The Act is challenged in its entirety as an attempt to regulate all industry, thus invading the reserved powers of the States over their local concerns. It is asserted that the references in the Act to interstate and foreign commerce are colorable at best; that the Act is not a true regulation of such commerce or of matters which directly affect it but on the contrary has the fundamental object of placing under the compulsory supervision of the federal government all industrial labor relations within the nation.

The grant of authority to the Board does not purport to extend to the relationship between all industrial employees and employers. Its terms do not impose collective bargaining upon all industry regardless of effects upon interstate or foreign commerce. It purports to reach only what may be deemed to burden or obstruct that commerce and, thus qualified, it must be construed as contemplating the exercise of control within constitutional bounds. It is a familiar principle that acts which directly burden or obstruct interstate or foreign commerce, or its free flow, are within the reach of the congressional power. Acts having that effect are not rendered immune because they grow out of labor disputes. It is the effect upon commerce, not the source of the injury, which is the criterion. Whether or not particular action does affect commerce in such a close and intimate fashion as to be subject to federal control, and hence to lie within the authority conferred upon the Board, is left by the statute to be determined as individual cases arise.

Second. The unfair practices in question—In its present application, the statute goes no further than to safeguard the right of employees to self-organization and to select representatives of their own choosing for collective bargaining or other mutual protection without restraint or coercion by their employer. That is a fundamental right. Employees have as clear a right to organize and select their representatives for lawful purposes as the respondent has to organize its business and select its own officers and agents. Discrimination and coercion to prevent the free exercise of the right of employees to self-organization and representation is a proper subject for condemnation by competent legislative authority. Hence the prohibition by Congress of interference with the selection of representatives for the purpose of negotiation and conference between employers and employees, "instead of being an invasion of the constitutional right of either was based on the recognition of the rights of both." *Texas & N.O.R.C. v. Railway Clerks* (1930).

Third. The application of the Act to employees engaged in production—The principle involved—Respondent says that whatever may be said of employees engaged in interstate commerce, the industrial relations and activities in the manufacturing department of respondent's enterprise are not subject to federal regulation. The argument rests upon the proposition that manufacturing in itself is not commerce.

The congressional authority to protect interstate commerce from burdens and obstructions is not limited to transactions which can be deemed to be an essential part of a "flow" of interstate or foreign commerce. Although activities may be intrastate in character when separately considered if they have such a close and substantial relation to interstate commerce that their control is essential or appropriate to protect that commerce from burdens and obstructions, Congress cannot be denied the power to exercise that control. Undoubtedly the scope of this power must be considered in the light of our dual system of government and may not be extended so as to embrace effects upon interstate commerce so indirect and remote that to embrace them, in view of our complex society, would effectually obliterate the distinction between what is national and what is local and create a completely centralized government. The question is necessarily one of degree.

It is thus apparent that the fact that the employees here concerned were engaged in production is not determinative. The question remains as to the effect upon interstate commerce of the labor practice involved.

Fourth. Effects of the unfair labor practice in respondent's enterprise—Giving full weight to respondent's contention with respect to a break in the complete continuity of the "stream of commerce" by reason of respondent's manufacturing operations, the fact remains that the stoppage of those operations by industrial strife would have a most serious effect upon interstate commerce. In view of respondent's far-flung activities, it is idle to say that the effect would be indirect or remote. It is obvious that it would be immediate and might be catastrophic. We are asked to shut our eyes to the plainest facts of our national life and to deal with the question of direct and indirect effects in an intellectual vacuum. Because there may be but indirect and remote effects upon interstate commerce in connection with a host of local enterprises throughout the country, it does not follow that other industrial activities do not have such a close and intimate relation to interstate commerce as to make the presence of industrial strife a matter of the most urgent national concern. When industries organize themselves on a national scale, making their relation to interstate commerce the dominant factor in their activities, how can it be maintained that their industrial labor relations constitute a forbidden field into which Congress may not enter when it is necessary to protect interstate commerce from the paralyzing consequences of industrial war? We have often said that interstate commerce itself is a practical conception. It is equally true that interferences with that commerce must be appraised by a judgment that does not ignore actual experience.

Experience has abundantly demonstrated that the recognition of the right of employees to self-organization and to have representatives of their own choosing for the purpose of collective bargaining is often an essential condition of industrial peace. Refusal to confer and negotiate has been one of the most prolific causes of strife. This is such an outstanding fact in the history of labor disturbances that it is a proper subject of judicial notice and requires no citation of instances.

Our conclusion is that the order of the Board was within its competency and that the Act is valid as here applied. The judgment of the Circuit Court of Appeals is reversed and the cause is remanded for further proceedings in conformity with this opinion.

JUSTICE MCREYNOLDS, dissenting.

The Court, as we think, departs from well established principles followed in *Schechter Corp. v. United States* [1935] and *Carter v. Carter Coal Co.* [1936]. Six district courts, on the authority of *Schechter*'s and *Carter*'s cases, have held that the Board has no authority to regulate relations between employers and employees engaged in local production. No decision or judicial opinion to the contrary has been cited, and we find none. Every consideration brought forward to uphold the Act before us was applicable to support the acts held unconstitutional in causes decided within two years.

An effect on interstate commerce by the discharge of employees shown here, would be indirect and remote in the highest degree as consideration of the facts will show. [In *Jones & Laughlin*] ten men out of ten thousand were discharged: in the other cases only a few. The immediate effect in the factory may be to create discontent among all those employed and a strike may follow, which, in turn, may result in reducing production, which ultimately may reduce the volume of goods moving in interstate commerce. By this chain of indirect and progressively remote events we finally reach the evil with which it is said the legislation under consideration undertakes to deal. A more remote and indirect interference with interstate commerce or a more definite invasion of the powers reserved to the states is difficult, if not impossible, to imagine.

Wickard v. Filburn
317 U.S. 111 (1942)

The Agricultural Adjustment Act of 1938 imposed limitations on the acreage individual farmers could devote to wheat production. In setting such limits, Congress sought to control the volume of wheat moving in interstate and foreign commerce, in order to avoid surpluses and shortages and thereby prevent abnormally low or high wheat prices. Filburn, who owned a small farm in Ohio, exceeded his allotment of 11.1 acres for the 1941 wheat crop. He produced twenty-three acres of wheat, intending to keep the excess for use on his own farm. Penalized $117.11 for growing the excess wheat, he refused to pay and brought action to prevent collection. When the district court granted an injunction on nonconstitutional grounds, the government appealed. Opinion of the Court: Jackson, Stone, Roberts, Black, Reed, Frankfurter, Douglas, Murphy, Byrnes.

JUSTICE JACKSON delivered the opinion of the Court.

It is urged that under the Commerce Clause of the Constitution, Article I, §8, clause 3, Congress does not possess the power it has in this instance sought to exercise. The question would merit little consideration since our decision in *United States v. Darby* [1941] sustaining the federal power to regulate production of goods for commerce, except for the fact that this Act extends federal regulation to production not intended in any part for commerce but wholly for consumption on the farm.

Appellee says that this is a regulation of production and consumption of wheat. Such activities are, he urges, beyond the reach of Congressional power under the Commerce Clause, since they are local in character, and their effects upon interstate commerce are at most "indirect." In answer the Government argues that the statute regulates neither production nor consumption, but only marketing; and, in the alternative, that if the Act does go beyond the regulation of marketing it is sustainable as a "necessary and proper" implementation of the power of Congress over interstate commerce.

Whether the subject of the regulation in question was "production," "consumption," or "marketing" is not material for purposes for deciding the question of federal power before us. That an activity is of local character may help in a doubtful case to determine whether Congress intended to reach it. But even if appellee's activity be local and though it may not be regarded as commerce, it may still, whatever its nature, be reached by Congress if it exerts a substantial economic effect on interstate commerce, and this irrespective of whether such effect is what might at some earlier time have been defined as "direct" or "indirect." The effect of consumption of home-grown wheat on interstate commerce is due to the fact that it constitutes the most variable factor in the disappearance of the wheat crop. Consumption on the farm where grown appears to vary in an amount greater than 20 percent of average production. The total amount of wheat consumed as food varies but relatively little, and use as seed is relatively constant.

The maintenance by government regulation of a price for wheat undoubtedly can be accomplished as effectively by sustaining or increasing the demand as by limiting the supply. The effect of the statute before us is to restrict the amount which may be produced for market and the extent as well to which one may forestall resort to the market by producing to meet his own needs. That appellee's own contribution to the demand for wheat may be trivial by itself is not enough to remove him from the scope of federal regulation where, as here, his contribution, taken together with that of many others similarly situated, is far from trivial.

It is well established by decisions of this Court that the power to regulate commerce includes the power to regulate the prices at which commodities in that commerce are dealt in and practices affecting such prices. One of the primary purposes of the Act in question was to increase the market price of wheat, and to that end to limit the volume thereof that could affect the market. It can hardly be denied that a factor of such volume and variability as home-consumed wheat would have a substantial influence on price and market conditions. This record leaves us in no doubt that Congress may properly have considered that wheat consumed on the farm where grown, if wholly outside the scheme of regulation, would have a substantial effect in defeating and obstructing its purpose to stimulate trade therein at increased prices.

It is said, however, that this Act, forcing some farmers into the market to buy what they could provide for themselves, is an unfair promotion of the markets and prices of specializing wheat growers. It is of the essence of regulation that it lays a restraining hand on the self-interest of the regulated and that advantages from the regulation commonly fall to others. The conflicts of economic interest between the regulated and those who advantage by it are wisely left under our system to resolution by the Congress under its more flexible and responsible legislative process. Such conflicts rarely lend themselves to judicial determination. And with the wisdom, workability, or fairness, of the plan of regulation we have nothing to do.

Reversed.

Heart of Atlanta Motel v. United States
379 U.S. 241 (1964)

The Heart of Atlanta Motel, located near major highways and interstates, sought patronage from outside Georgia through national advertising campaigns; approximately 75 percent of its patrons were from out of state. Prior to passage of the Civil Rights Act of 1964, which outlawed discrimination in public accommodations, the motel refused to rent rooms to African Americans. It indicated that it intended to continue this policy and sought a declaratory judgment attacking the validity of Title II (the public- *accommodations section). A three-judge district court sustained the challenged legislation, and the case was appealed to the Supreme Court. In a companion case argued at the same time—* Katzenbach v. McClung *(379 U.S. 294)—the Court upheld application of the act to a family-owned restaurant serving a primarily local clientele.* Opinion of the Court: <u>Clark</u>, Warren, Black, Douglas, Harlan, Brennan, Stewart, White, Goldberg. Concurring opinions: <u>Black</u>; <u>Douglas</u>.

JUSTICE CLARK delivered the opinion of the Court.

It is admitted that the operation of the motel brings it within the provisions of §201 (a) of the Act and that appellant refused to provide lodging for transient Negroes because of their race or color and that it intends to continue that policy unless restrained. The sole question posed is, therefore, the constitutionality of the Civil Rights Act of 1964 as applied to these facts. The legislative history of the Act indicates that Congress based the Act on §5 and the Equal Protection Clause of the Fourteenth Amendment as well as its power to regulate interstate commerce under Art. I. §8, cl. 3, of the Constitution.

While the act as adopted carried no congressional findings the records of its passage through each house is replete with evidence of the burdens that discrimination by race or color places upon interstate commerce. This testimony included the fact that our people have become increasingly mobile with millions of people of all races traveling from State to State; that Negroes in particular have been the subject of discrimination in transient accommodations, having to travel great distances to secure the same; that often they have been unable to obtain accommodations and have had to call upon friends to put them up overnight; and that these conditions had become so acute as to require the listing of available lodging for Negroes in a special guidebook. This testimony indicated a qualitative as well as quantitative effect on interstate travel by Negroes. The former was the obvious impairment of the Negro traveler's pleasure and convenience that resulted when he continually was uncertain of finding lodging. As for the latter, there was evidence that this uncertainty stemming from racial discrimination had the effect of discouraging travel on the part of a substantial portion of the Negro community. The voluminous testimony presents overwhelming evidence that discrimination by hotels and motels impedes interstate travel.

[*Justice Clark then reviewed the Court's earlier decisions regarding the use of the Commerce Clause for noncommercial purposes.*] That Congress was legislating against moral wrongs in many of these areas rendered its enactments no less valid. In framing Title II of this Act Congress was also dealing with what it considered a moral problem. But that fact does not detract from the overwhelming evidence of the disruptive effect that racial discrimination has had on commercial intercourse. It was this burden which empowered Congress to enact appropriate legislation and, given this basis for the exercise of its power, Congress was not restricted by the fact that the particular obstruction to interstate commerce with which it was dealing was also deemed a moral and social wrong.

It is said that the operation of the motel here is of a purely local character. But, assuming this to be true, "if it is interstate commerce that feels the pinch, it does not matter how local the operation which applies the squeeze." *United States v. Women's Sportswear Mfrs.* [1949]. Thus the power of Congress to promote interstate commerce also includes the power to regulate the local incidents thereof, including local activities in both the States of origin and destination, which might have a substantial and harmful effect upon that commerce. One need only examine the evidence which we have discussed above to see that Congress may—as it has—prohibit racial discrimination by motels serving travelers, however "local" their operations may appear.

JUSTICE DOUGLAS, concurring.

Though I join the Court's opinion, I am somewhat reluctant here to rest solely on the Commerce Clause. My reluctance is not due to any conviction that Congress lacks power to regulate commerce in the interests of human rights. It is rather my belief that the right of people to be free of state action that discriminates against them because of race, like the "right of persons to move freely from State to State" (*Edwards v. California* [1941]) "occupies a more protected position in our constitutional system than does the movement of cattle, fruit, steel and coal across state lines." . . . Hence I would prefer to rest on the assertion of legislative power contained in §5 of the Fourteenth Amendment which states: "The Congress shall have power to enforce, by appropriate legislation, the provisions of this article"—a power which the Court concedes was exercised at least in part in this Act.

A decision based on the Fourteenth Amendment would have a more settling effect, making unnecessary litigation over whether a particular restaurant or inn is within the commerce definitions of the Act or whether a particular customer is an interstate traveler. Under my construction, the Act would apply to all customers in all the enumerated places of public accommodation. And that construction would put an end to all obstructionist strategies and finally close one door on a bitter chapter in American history.

Garcia v. San Antonio Metropolitan Transit Authority
469 U.S. 528 (1985)

The San Antonio Metropolitan Transit Authority (SAMTA), a public mass-transit authority, is the major provider of public transportation in San Antonio, Texas. In 1979 the Wage and Hour Administration of the US Department of Labor issued an opinion that SAMTA's operations were not immune from the minimum-wage and overtime provisions of the Fair Labor Standards Act (FLSA) under National League of Cities v. Usery, *426 U.S. 833 (1976), in which it was held that the Commerce Clause does not empower Congress to enforce such requirements against the states in "areas of traditional governmental functions." SAMTA then brought action in the US District Court for the Western District of Texas seeking declaratory judgment that municipal ownership and operation of a mass-transit system are traditional governmental functions and, under* National League of Cities, *are exempt from the obligations imposed by the FLSA. In response, the Department of Labor sought enforcement of the overtime and record-keeping requirements of the FLSA; Joe G. Garcia and several other SAMTA employees intervened, seeking overtime pay under the FLSA. The district court granted SAMTA's motion for summary judgment, and the Department of Labor and the SAMTA employees appealed directly to the US Supreme Court.* Opinion of the Court: <u>Blackmun</u>, Brennan, White, Marshall, Stevens. Dissenting opinions: <u>Powell</u>, Burger, Rehnquist, O'Connor; <u>Rehnquist</u>; <u>O'Connor</u>, Powell, Rehnquist.

JUSTICE BLACKMUN delivered the opinion of the Court.

We revisit in these cases an issue raised in *National League of Cities v. Usery* (1976). In that litigation, this Court, by a sharply divided vote, ruled that the Commerce Clause does not empower Congress to enforce the minimum wage and overtime provisions of the Fair Labor Standards Act (FLSA) against the States "in areas of traditional governmental functions." Although *National League of Cities* supplied some examples of "traditional governmental functions," it did not offer a general explanation of how a "traditional" function is to be distinguished from a "nontraditional" one. Since then, federal and state courts have struggled with the task, thus imposed, of identifying a traditional function for purposes of state immunity under the Commerce Clause.

In the present cases, a Federal District Court concluded that municipal ownership and operation of a mass-transit system is a traditional governmental function and thus, under *National League of Cities*, is exempt from the obligations imposed by the FLSA. Faced with the identical question, three Federal Courts of Appeals and one state appellate court have reached the opposite conclusion.

Our examination of this "function" standard applied in these and other cases over the last eight years now persuades us that the attempt to draw the boundaries of state regulatory immunity in terms of "traditional governmental function" is not only unworkable but is inconsistent with established principles of federalism and, indeed, with those very federalism principles on which *National League of Cities* purported to rest. That case, accordingly, is overruled.

The controversy in the present case has focused on the third requirement—that the challenged federal statute trench on "traditional governmental functions." The District Court voiced a common concern: "Despite the abundance of adjectives, identifying which particular state functions are immune remains difficult." Just how troublesome the task has been is revealed by the results reached in other federal cases. Thus courts have held that regulating ambulance services, licensing automobile drivers, operating a municipal airport, performing solid waste disposal, and operating a highway authority are functions protected under *National League of Cities*. At the same time, courts have held that issuance of industrial development bonds, regulation of intrastate natural gas sales, regulation of traffic on public roads, regulation of air transportation, operation of a telephone system, leasing and sale of natural gas, operation of a mental health facility, and provision of in-house domestic services for the aged and handicapped are *not* entitled to immunity. We find it difficult, if not impossible, to identify an organizing principle that places each of the cases in the first group on one side of a line and each of the cases in the second group on the other side. The constitutional distinction between licensing drivers and regulating traffic, for example, or between operating a highway authority and operating a mental health facility, is elusive at best.

We believe, however, that there is a more fundamental problem at work here. The problem is that no distinction that purports to separate out important governmental functions can be faithful to the role of federalism in a democratic society. The essence of our federal system is that within the realm of authority left open to them under the Constitution, the States must be equally free to engage in any activity that their citizens choose for the common weal, no matter how unorthodox or unnecessary anyone else—including the judiciary—deems state involvement to be. Any rule of state immunity that looks to the "traditional," "integral," or "necessary" nature of governmental functions inevitably invites an unelected federal judiciary to make decisions about which state policies it favors and which ones it dislikes.

The central theme of *National League of Cities* was that the States occupy a special position in our constitutional system and that the scope of Congress' authority under the Commerce Clause must reflect that position. What has proved problematic is not the perception that the Constitution's federal structure imposes limitations on the Commerce Clause, but rather the nature and content of those limitations. We doubt that courts ultimately can identify principled constitutional limitations on the scope of Congress' Commerce Clause powers over the States merely by relying on *a priori* definitions of state sovereignty. In part, this is because of the elusiveness of objective criteria for "fundamental" elements of state sovereignty, a problem we have witnessed in the search for "traditional governmental functions." There is, however, a more fundamental reason: the sovereignty of the States is limited by the Constitution itself. A variety of sovereign powers, for example, are withdrawn from the States by Article I, §10. Section 8 of the same Article works an equally sharp contraction of state sovereignty by authorizing Congress to exercise a wide range of legislative powers and (in conjunction with the Supremacy Clause of Article VI) to displace contrary state legislation. By providing for final review of questions of federal law in this Court, Article III curtails the sovereign power of the States' judiciaries to make authoritative determinations of law. Finally, the developed application, through the Fourteenth Amendment, of the greater part of the Bill of Rights to the States limits the sovereign authority that States otherwise would possess to legislate with respect to their citizens and to conduct their own affairs.

The States unquestionably do "retain a significant measure of sovereign authority." They do so, however, only to the extent that the Constitution has not divested them of their original powers and transferred those powers to the Federal Government. In the words of James Madison to the Members of the First Congress: "Interference with the power of the States was no constitutional criterion of the power of Congress. If the power was not given, Congress could not exercise it; if given, they might exercise it, although it should interfere with the laws, or even the Constitution of the States."

As a result, to say that the Constitution assumes the continued role of the States is to say little about the nature of that role. The fact that the States remain sovereign as to all powers not vested in Congress or denied them by the Constitution offers no guidance about where the frontier between state and federal power lies. In short, we have no license to employ free-standing conceptions of state sovereignty when measuring congressional authority under the Commerce Clause.

When we look for the States' "residuary and inviolable sovereignty," *The Federalist* No. 39, in the shape of the constitutional scheme rather than in predetermined notions of sovereign power, a different measure of state sovereignty emerges. Apart from the limitation on federal authority inherent in the delegated nature of Congress' Article I powers, the principal means chosen by the Framers to ensure the role of the States in the federal system lies in the structure of the Federal Government itself. It is no novelty to observe that the composition of the Federal Government was designed in large part to protect the States from overreaching by Congress. The Framers thus gave the States a role in the selection both of the Executive and the Legislative Branches of the Federal Government. The States were vested with indirect influence over the House of Representatives and the Presidency by their control of electoral qualifications and their role in presidential elections. U.S. Const., Art. I, §2, and Art. II, §1. They were given more direct influence in the Senate, where each State received equal representation and each Senator was to be selected by the legislature of his State. Art. I, §3. The significance attached to the States' equal representation in the Senate is underscored by the prohibition of any constitutional amendment divesting a State of equal representation without the State's consent. Art. V.

The extent to which the structure of the Federal Government itself was relied on to insulate the interests of the States is evident in the views of the Framers. James Madison explained that the Federal Government "will partake sufficiently of the spirit [of the States], to be disinclined to invade the rights of the individual States, or the prerogatives of their governments." *The Federalist* No. 46. The Framers chose to rely on a federal system in which special restraints on federal power over the States inhered principally in the workings of the National Government itself, rather than in discrete limitations on the objects of federal authority. State sovereign interests, then, are more properly protected by procedural safeguards inherent in the structure of the federal system than by judicially created limitations on federal power.

We realize that changes in the structure of the Federal Government have taken place since 1789, not the least of which has been the substitution of popular election of Senators by the adoption of the Seventeenth Amendment in 1913, and that these changes may work to alter the influence of the States in the federal political process. Nonetheless, against this background, we are convinced that the fundamental limitation that the constitutional scheme imposes on the Commerce Clause to protect the "States as States" is one of process rather than one of result. Any substantive restraint on the exercise of Commerce Clause powers must find its justification in the procedural nature of this basic limitation, and it must be tailored to compensate for possible failings in the national political process rather than to dictate a "sacred province of state autonomy."

Insofar as the present cases are concerned, then, we need go no further than to state that we perceive nothing in the overtime and minimum wage requirements of the FLSA, as applied to SAMTA, that is destructive of state sovereignty or violative of any constitutional provision. SAMTA faces nothing more than the same minimum-wage and overtime obligations that hundreds of thousands of other employers, public as well as private, have to meet.

In these cases, the status of public mass transit simply underscores the extent to which the structural protections of the Constitution insulate the States from federally imposed burdens. When Congress first subjected state mass transit systems to FLSA obligations in 1966, and when it expanded those obligations in 1974, it simultaneously provided extensive funding for state and local mass transit. In the two decades since it has provided over $22 billion in mass transit aid to States and localities. SAMTA and its immediate predecessor have received a substantial amount of funding, including over $12 million during SAMTA's first two fiscal years alone. In short, Congress has not simply placed a financial burden on the shoulders of States and localities that operate mass-transit systems, but has provided substantial countervailing financial assistance as well, assistance that may leave individual mass-transit systems better off than they would have been had Congress never intervened at all in the area. Congress' treatment of public mass transit reinforces our conviction that the national political process systematically protects States from the risk of having their functions in that area handicapped by Commerce Clause regulation.

This analysis makes clear that Congress' action in affording SAMTA employees the protections of the wage and hour provisions of the FLSA contravened no affirmative limit on Congress' power under the Commerce Clause. The judgment of the District Court therefore must be reversed.

JUSTICE POWELL, with whom THE CHIEF JUSTICE, JUSTICE REHNQUIST, and JUSTICE O'CONNOR join, dissenting.

The Court today, in its 5–4 decision, overrules *National League of Cities v. Usery* (1976), a case in which we held that Congress lacked authority to impose the requirements of the Fair Labor Standards Act on state and local governments. Because I believe this decision substantially alters the federal system embodied in the Constitution, I dissent.

Whatever effect the Court's decision may have in weakening the application of *stare decisis,* it is likely to be less important than what the Court has done to the Constitution itself. A unique feature of the United States is the *federal* system of government guaranteed by the Constitution and implicit in the very name of our country. Despite some genuflecting in the Court's opinion to the concept of federalism, today's decision effectively reduces the Tenth Amendment to meaningless rhetoric when Congress acts pursuant to the Commerce Clause.

To leave no doubt about its intention, the Court renounces its decision in *National League of Cities* because it "inevitably invites an unelected federal judiciary to make decisions about which state policies it favors and which ones it dislikes." In other words, the extent to which the States may exercise their authority, when Congress purports to act under the Commerce Clause, henceforth is to be determined from time to time by political decisions made by members of the federal government, decisions the Court says will not be subject to judicial review. I note that it does not seem to

have occurred to the Court that *it*—an unelected majority of five Justices—today rejects almost 200 years of the understanding of the constitutional status of federalism. In doing so, there is only a single passing reference to the Tenth Amendment. Nor is so much as a dictum of any court cited in support of the view that the role of the States in the federal system may depend upon the grace of elected federal officials, rather than on the Constitution as interpreted by this Court.

Today's opinion does not explain how the States' role in the electoral process guarantees that particular exercises of the Commerce Clause power will not infringe on residual State sovereignty. Members of Congress are elected from the various States, but once in office they are members of the federal government. Although the States participate in the Electoral College, this is hardly a reason to view the President as a representative of the States' interest against federal encroachment. We noted recently "the hydraulic pressure inherent within each of the separate Branches to exceed the outer limits of its power." *Immigration and Naturalization Service v. Chadha* (1983). The Court offers no reason to think that this pressure will not operate when Congress seeks to invoke its powers under the Commerce Clause, notwithstanding the electoral role of the States.

The Court apparently thinks that the State's success at obtaining federal funds for various projects and exemptions from the obligations of some federal statutes is indicative of the "effectiveness of the federal political process in preserving the States' interests." But such political success is not relevant to the question whether the political *processes* are the proper means of enforcing constitutional limitations. The fact that Congress generally does not transgress constitutional limits on its power to reach State activities does not make judicial review any less necessary to rectify the cases in which it does do so. The States' role in our system of government is a matter of constitutional law, not of legislative grace. "The powers not delegated to the United States by the Constitution, nor prohibited by it to the States, are reserved to the States, respectively, or to the people." U.S. Const., Amend. 10.

More troubling than the logical infirmities in the Court's reasoning is the result of its holding, i.e., that federal political officials, invoking the Commerce Clause, are the sole judges of the limits of their own power. This result is inconsistent with the fundamental principles of our constitutional system. At least since *Marbury v. Madison* it has been the settled province of the federal judiciary "to say what the law is" with respect to the constitutionality of acts of Congress. In rejecting the role of the judiciary in protecting the States from federal overreaching, the Court's opinion offers no explanation for ignoring the teaching of the most famous case in our history.

In our federal system, the States have a major role that cannot be preempted by the national government. As contemporaneous writings and the debates at the ratifying conventions make clear, the States' ratification of the Constitution was predicated on this understanding of federalism. Indeed, the Tenth Amendment was adopted specifically to ensure that the important role promised the States by the proponents of the Constitution was realized.

The Framers had definite ideas about the nature of the Constitution's division of authority between the federal and state governments. The Framers believed that the separate sphere of sovereignty reserved to the States would ensure that the States would serve as an effective "counterpoise" to the power of the federal government. The States would serve this essential role because they would attract and retain the loyalty of their citizens. The roots of such loyalty, the Founders thought, were found in the objects peculiar to state government. For example, Hamilton argued that the States "regulat[e] all those personal interests and familiar concerns to which the sensibility of individuals is more immediately awake." *The Federalist* No. 17.

Thus, he maintained that the people would perceive the States as "the immediate and most visible guardian of life and property," a fact which "contributes more than any other circumstance to impressing upon the minds of the people affection, esteem and reverence towards the government." Madison took the same position, explaining that "the people will be more familiarly and minutely conversant" with the business of state governments, and "with the members of these, will a greater proportion of the people have the ties of personal acquaintance and friendship, and of family and party attachments." *The Federalist* No. 46. Like Hamilton, Madison saw the States' involvement in the everyday concerns of the people as the source of their citizens' loyalty.

Thus, the harm to the States that results from federal overreaching under the Commerce Clause is not simply a matter of dollars and cents. Nor is it a matter of the wisdom or folly of certain policy choices. Rather, by usurping functions traditionally performed by the States, federal overreaching under the Commerce Clause undermines the constitutionally mandated balance of power between the States and the federal government, a balance designed to protect our fundamental liberties.

In *National League of Cities,* we spoke of fire prevention, police protection, sanitation, and public health as "typical of [the services] performed by state and local governments in discharging their dual functions of administering the public law and furnishing public services." Not only are these activities remote from any normal concept of interstate commerce, they are also activities that epitomize the concerns of local, democratic self-government. In emphasizing the need to protect traditional governmental functions, we identified the kinds of activities engaged in by state and local governments that affect the everyday lives of citizens. These are services that people are in a position to understand and evaluate, and in a democracy, have the right to oversee. We recognized that "it is functions such as these which governments are created to provide" and that the states and local governments are better able than the national government to perform them. . . .

The Court maintains that the standard approved in *National League of Cities* "disserves principles of democratic self government." In reaching this conclusion, the Court looks myopically only to persons elected to positions in the federal government. It disregards entirely the far more effective role of democratic self government at the state and local levels. One must compare realistically the operation of the state and local governments with that of the federal government. Federal legislation is drafted primarily by the staffs of the congressional committees. In view of the hundreds of bills introduced at each session of Congress and the complexity of many of them, it is virtually impossible for even the most conscientious legislators to be truly familiar with many of the statutes enacted. Federal departments and agencies customarily are authorized to write regulations. Often these are more important than the text of the statutes. As is true of the original legislation, these are drafted largely by staff personnel. The administration and enforcement of federal laws and regulations necessarily are largely in the hands of staff and civil service employees. These employees may have little or no knowledge of the States and localities that will be affected by the statutes and regulations for which they are responsible. In any case, they hardly are as accessible and responsive as those who occupy analogous positions in State and local governments.

In drawing this contrast, I imply no criticism of these federal employees or the officials who are ultimately in charge. The great majority are conscientious and faithful to their duties. My point is simply that members of the immense federal bureaucracy are not elected, know less about the services traditionally rendered by States and localities, and are inevitably less responsive to recipients of such services, than are state legislatures, city councils, boards of supervisors, and state and local commissions, boards, and agencies. It is at these state and local levels—not in Washington as the Court so mistakenly thinks—that "democratic self government" is best exemplified.

The Court emphasizes that municipal operation of an intracity mass-transit system is relatively new in the life of our country. It nevertheless is a classic example of the type of service traditionally provided by local government. It is local by definition. State and local officials of course must be intimately familiar with these services and sensitive to their quality as well as cost. Such officials also know that their constituents and the press respond to the adequacy, fair distribution, and cost of these services. It is this kind of state and local control and accountability that the Framers understood would insure the vitality and preservation of the federal system that the Constitution explicitly requires.

JUSTICE O'CONNOR, with whom JUSTICE POWELL and JUSTICE REHNQUIST join, dissenting.

The Court today surveys the battle scene of federalism and sounds a retreat. Like Justice Powell, I would prefer to hold the field and, at the very least, render a little aid to the wounded. I join Justice Powell's opinion. I also write separately to note my fundamental disagreement with the majority's views of federalism and the duty of this Court. The true "essence" of federalism is that the States *as States* have legitimate interest which the National Government is bound to respect even though its laws are supreme. If federalism so conceived and so carefully cultivated by the Framers of our Constitution is to remain meaningful, this Court cannot abdicate its constitutional responsibility to oversee the Federal Government's compliance with its duty to respect the legitimate interests of the States.

Due to the emergence of an integrated and industrialized national economy, this Court has been required to examine and review a breathtaking expansion of the powers of Congress. In doing so the Court correctly perceived that the Framers of our Constitution intended Congress to have sufficient power to address national problems. But the Framers were not single-minded. The Constitution is animated by an array of intentions. Just as surely as the Framers envisioned a National Government capable of solving national problems, they also envisioned a republic whose vitality was assured by the diffusion of power not only among the branches of the Federal Government, but also between the Federal Government and the States. In the 18th century these intentions did not conflict because technology had not yet converted every local problem into a national one. A conflict has now emerged, and the Court today retreats rather than reconciles the Constitution's dual concerns for federalism and an effective commerce power.

The Framers perceived the interstate commerce power to be important but limited, and expected that it would be used primarily if not exclusively to remove interstate tariffs and to regulate maritime affairs and large-scale mercantile enterprise. This perception of a narrow commerce power is important not because it suggests that the commerce power should be as narrowly construed today. Rather, it explains why the Framers could believe the Constitution assured significant state authority even as it bestowed a range of powers, including the commerce power, on the Congress. In an era when interstate commerce represented a tiny fraction of economic activity and most goods and services were produced and consumed close to home, the interstate commerce power left a broad range of activities beyond the reach of Congress.

In the decades since ratification of the Constitution, interstate economic activity has steadily expanded. Industrialization, coupled with advances in transportation and communications, has created a national economy in which virtually every activity occurring within the borders of a State plays a part. Incidental to this expansion of the commerce power, Congress has been given an ability it lacked prior to the emergence of an integrated national economy. Because virtually every *state* activity, like virtually every activity of a private individual, arguably "affects" interstate commerce, Congress can now supplant the States from the significant sphere of activities envisioned for them by the Framers. It is in this context that recent changes in the workings of Congress, such as the direct election of Senators and the expanded influence of national interest groups become relevant. These changes may well have lessened the weight Congress gives to the legitimate interests of States as States. As a result, there is now a real risk that Congress will gradually erase the diffusion of power between state and nation on which the Framers based their faith in the efficiency and vitality of our Republic.

It is worth recalling the passage in *McCulloch v. Maryland* that lies at the source of the recent expansion of the commerce power. "Let the end be legitimate, let it be within the scope of the constitution," Chief Justice Marshall said, "and all means which are appropriate, which are plainly adapted to that end, which are not prohibited, but consist with the letter *and spirit* of the constitution, are constitutional." The

spirit of the Tenth Amendment, of course, is that the States will retain their integrity in a system in which the laws of the United States are nevertheless supreme.

It is not enough that the "end be legitimate"; the means to that end chosen by Congress must not contravene the spirit of the Constitution. Thus many of this Court's decisions acknowledge that the means by which national power is exercised must take into account concerns for state autonomy. For example, Congress might rationally conclude that the location a State chooses for its capital may affect interstate commerce, but the Court has suggested that Congress would nevertheless be barred from dictating that location because such an exercise of a delegated power would undermine the state sovereignty inherent in the Tenth Amendment. *Coyle v. Oklahoma* (1911).

The problems of federalism in an integrated national economy are capable of more responsible resolution than holding that the States as States retain no status apart from that which Congress chooses to let them retain. The proper resolution, I suggest, lies in weighing state autonomy as a factor in the balance when interpreting the means by which Congress can exercise its authority on the States as States. It is insufficient, in assessing the validity of congressional regulation of a State pursuant to the commerce power, to ask only whether the same regulation would be valid if enforced against a private party. That reasoning, embodied in the majority opinion, is inconsistent with the spirit of our Constitution.

It remains relevant that a *State* is being regulated. As far as the Constitution is concerned, a State should not be equated with any private litigant. Instead, the autonomy of a State is an essential component of federalism. If state autonomy is ignored in assessing the means by which Congress regulates matters affecting commerce, then federalism becomes irrelevant simply because the set of activities remaining beyond the reach of such a commerce power "may well be negligible."

It has been difficult for this Court to craft bright lines defining the scope of the state autonomy protected by National League of Cities. Such difficulty is to be expected whenever constitutional concerns as important as federalism and the effectiveness of the commerce power come into conflict. Regardless of the difficulty, it is and will remain the duty of this Court to reconcile these concerns in the final instance. That the Court shuns the task today by appealing to the "essence of federalism" can provide scant comfort to those who believe our federal system requires something more than a unitary, centralized government. I would not shirk the duty acknowledged by *National League of Cities* and its progeny.

[*With the decision in* Garcia, *state and local governments across the United States were* confronted with the prospect of having to pay up to $3 billion annually in overtime. Senator Pete Wilson of California predicted that his state, with more than eighty-nine thousand state employees, would "be out some $300 million, with the city of Los Angeles accounting for perhaps $50 million." Worried about huge overtime bills and the likelihood of tax hikes to cover these costs, state and local government officials lobbied Congress for relief, and in November 1985 President Reagan signed into law a bill that allowed state and local governments to continue offering compensatory time off in lieu of overtime pay.*]

United States v. Lopez
514 U.S. 549 (1995)

In 1990, Congress enacted the Gun-Free School Zones Act. This act, referred to in the justices' opinions as Section 922(q), made it a federal offense "for any individual knowingly to possess a firearm at a place that the individual knows, or has reasonable cause to believe, is a school zone." Alfonso Lopez, then a senior at Edison High School in San Antonio, Texas, was arrested and charged under the act when he brought to school a concealed .38-caliber handgun and five bullets. He was convicted in federal district court, after the court denied his claim that the statute under which he was charged exceeded Congress's authority under the Commerce Clause. On appeal, the court of appeals reversed, holding that Section 922(q) was invalid in the absence of congressional findings and legislative history demonstrating the connection between commerce and the evil addressed by the statute. The Supreme Court granted certiorari. Opinion of the Court: <u>Rehnquist</u>, O'Connor, Scalia, Kennedy, Thomas. Concurring opinions: <u>Kennedy</u>, O'Connor; <u>Thomas</u>. Dissenting opinions: <u>Stevens</u>; <u>Souter</u>; <u>Breyer</u>, Stevens, Souter, Ginsburg.

THE CHIEF JUSTICE delivered the opinion of the Court.

We start with first principles. The Constitution creates a Federal Government of enumerated powers. As James Madison wrote, "[t]he powers delegated by the proposed Constitution to the federal government are few and defined. Those which are to remain in the State governments are numerous and indefinite." *The Federalist* No. 45.

The Constitution delegates to Congress the power "[t]o regulate Commerce with foreign Nations, and among the several States, and with the Indian Tribes." The Court, through Chief Justice Marshall, first defined the nature of Congress's commerce power in *Gibbons v. Ogden* (1824). The *Gibbons* Court acknowledged that limitations on the commerce power are inherent in the very language of the Commerce Clause: "It is not intended to say that these words comprehend that commerce, which is completely internal, which is carried on between man and man in a State, or between different parts of the same State, and which does not extend to or affect other States. Such a power would be inconvenient, and is certainly unnecessary. Comprehensive as the word 'among' is it may very properly be restricted to that commerce which concerns more States than one." The enumeration presupposes something not enumerated; and that something, if we regard the language or the subject of the sentence, must be the exclusively internal commerce of a State.

[*Chief Justice Rehnquist then reviewed the development of the Supreme Court's interpretation of the Commerce Clause, particularly the Court's shift in interpretation in National Labor Relations Board v. Jones & Laughlin Steel (1937), United States v. Darby (1941), and Wickard v. Filburn (1942).*] Jones & Laughlin Steel, Darby, and *Wickard* ushered in an era of Commerce Clause jurisprudence that greatly expanded the previously defined authority of Congress under that Clause. In part, this was a recognition of the great changes that had occurred in the way business was carried on in this country. Enterprises that had once been local or at most regional in nature had become national in scope. But the doctrinal change also reflected a view that earlier Commerce Clause cases artificially had constrained the authority of Congress to regulate interstate commerce.

But even these modern-era precedents which have expanded congressional power under the Commerce Clause confirm that this power is subject to outer limits. In *Jones & Laughlin Steel,* the Court warned that the scope of the interstate commerce power "must be considered in the light of our dual system of government and may not be extended so as to embrace effects upon interstate commerce so indirect and remote that to embrace them, in view of our complex society, would effectually obliterate the distinction between what is national and what is local and create a completely centralized government." See also *Darby* (Congress may regulate intrastate activity that has a "substantial effect" on interstate commerce); *Wickard* (Congress may regulate activity that "exerts a substantial economic effect on interstate commerce"). Since that time, the Court has heeded that warning and undertaken to decide whether a rational basis existed for concluding that a regulated activity sufficiently affected interstate commerce.

Consistent with this structure, we have identified three broad categories of activity that Congress may regulate under its commerce power. First, Congress may regulate the use of the channels of interstate commerce. Second, Congress is empowered to regulate and protect the instrumentalities of interstate commerce, or persons or things in interstate commerce, even though the threat may come only from intrastate activities. Finally, Congress's commerce authority includes the power to regulate those activities having a substantial relation to interstate commerce, those activities that substantially affect interstate commerce.

We now turn to consider the power of Congress, in the light of this framework, to enact §922(q). The first two categories of authority may be quickly disposed of: §922(q) is not a regulation of the use of the channels of interstate commerce, nor is it an attempt to prohibit the interstate transportation of a commodity through the channels of commerce; nor can §922(q) be justified as a regulation by which Congress has sought to protect an instrumentality of interstate commerce or a thing in interstate commerce. Thus, if §922(q) is to be sustained, it must be under the third category as a regulation of an activity that substantially affects interstate commerce.

First, we have upheld a wide variety of Congressional Acts regulating intrastate economic activity where we have concluded that the activity substantially affected interstate commerce. Examples include the regulation of intrastate coal mining, intrastate extortionate credit transactions, restaurants utilizing substantial interstate supplies, inns and hotels catering to interstate guests, and production and consumption of home-grown wheat. These examples are by no means exhaustive, but the pattern is clear. Where economic activity substantially affects interstate commerce, legislation regulating that activity will be sustained.

Section 922(q) is a criminal statute that by its terms has nothing to do with "commerce" or any sort of economic enterprise, however broadly one might define those terms. Section 922(q) is not an essential part of a larger regulation of economic activity, in which the regulatory scheme could be undercut unless the intrastate activity were regulated. It cannot, therefore, be sustained under our cases upholding regulations of activities that arise out of or are connected with a commercial transaction, which viewed in the aggregate, substantially affects interstate commerce.

The Government's essential contention, *in fine,* is that we may determine here that §922(q) is valid because possession of a firearm in a local school zone does indeed substantially affect interstate commerce. The Government argues that possession of a firearm in a school zone may result in violent crime and that violent crime can be expected to affect the functioning of the national economy in two ways. First, the costs of violent crime are substantial, and, through the mechanism of insurance, those costs are spread throughout the population. Second, violent crime reduces the willingness of individuals to travel to areas within the country that are perceived to be unsafe. The Government also argues that the presence of guns in schools poses a substantial threat to the educational process by threatening the learning environment. A handicapped educational process, in turn, will result in a less productive citizenry. That, in turn, would have an adverse effect on the Nation's economic well-being. As a result, the Government argues that Congress could rationally have concluded that §922(q) substantially affects interstate commerce.

We pause to consider the implications of the Government's arguments. The Government admits, under its "costs of crime" reasoning, that Congress could regulate not only all violent crime, but all activities that might lead to violent crime, regardless of how tenuously they relate to interstate commerce. Similarly, under the Government's "national productivity" reasoning, Congress could regulate any activity that it found was related to the economic productivity of individual citizens: family law (including marriage, divorce, and child custody), for example. Under the theories that the Government presents in support of §922(q), it is difficult to perceive any limitation on federal power, even in areas such as criminal law enforcement or education where States historically have been sovereign. Thus, if we were to accept the Government's arguments, we are hard-pressed to posit any activity by an individual that Congress is without power to regulate.

Justice Breyer rejects our reading of precedent and argues that "Congress could rationally conclude that schools fall on the commercial side of the line." Again Justice Breyer's rationale lacks any real limits because, depending on the level of generality, any activity can be looked upon as commercial. Under the dissent's rationale, Congress could just as easily look at child rearing as "falling on the commercial side of the line" because it provides a "valuable service—namely, to equip [children] with the skills they need to survive in life and, more specifically, in the workplace." We do not doubt that Congress has authority under the Commerce Clause to regulate numerous commercial activities that substantially

affect interstate commerce and also affect the educational process. That authority, though broad, does not include the authority to regulate each and every aspect of local schools. . . .

To uphold the Government's contentions here, we would have to pile inference upon inference in a manner what would bid fair to convert congressional authority under the Commerce Clause to a general police power of the sort retained by the States. Admittedly, some of our prior cases have taken long steps down that road, giving great deference to congressional action. The broad language in these opinions has suggested the possibility of additional expansion, but we decline here to proceed any further. To do so would require us to conclude that the Constitution's enumeration of powers does not presuppose something not enumerated, and that there never will be a distinction between what is truly national and what is truly local. This we are unwilling to do. For the foregoing reasons the judgment of the Court of Appeals is

Affirmed.

JUSTICE THOMAS, concurring.

Although I join the majority, I write separately to observe that our case law has drifted far from the original understanding of the Commerce Clause. In a future case, we ought to temper our Commerce Clause jurisprudence in a manner that both makes sense of our more recent case law and is more faithful to the original understanding of that Clause.

We have said that Congress may regulate not only "Commerce . . . among the several states," but also anything that has a "substantial effect" on such commerce. This test, if taken to its logical extreme, would give Congress a "police power" over all aspects of American life. Unfortunately, we have never come to grips with this implication of our substantial effects formula. Although we have supposedly applied the substantial effects test for the past 60 years, we *always* have rejected readings of the Commerce Clause and the scope of federal power that would permit Congress to exercise a police power; our cases are quite clear that there are real limits to federal power.

While the principal dissent concedes that there are limits to federal power, the sweeping nature of our current test enables the dissent to argue that Congress can regulate gun possession. But it seems to me that the power to regulate "commerce" can by no means encompass authority over mere gun possession, any more than it empowers the Federal Government to regulate marriage, littering, or cruelty to animals, throughout the 50 States. Our Constitution quite properly leaves such matters to the individual States, notwithstanding these activities' effects on interstate commerce. Any interpretation of the Commerce Clause that even suggests that Congress could regulate such matters is in need of reexamination. In an appropriate case, I believe that we must further reconsider our "substantial effects" test with an eye toward constructing a standard that reflects the text and history of the Commerce Clause without totally rejecting our more recent Commerce Clause jurisprudence.

JUSTICE BREYER, with whom JUSTICE STEVENS, JUSTICE SOUTER, and JUSTICE GINSBURG join, dissenting.

The issue in this case is whether the Commerce Clause authorizes Congress to enact a statute that makes it a crime to possess a gun in, or near, a school. In my view, the statute falls well within the scope of the commerce power as this Court has understood that power over the last half-century.

In reaching this conclusion, I apply three basic principles of Commerce Clause interpretation. First, the power to "regulate Commerce . . . among the several States," encompasses the power to regulate local activities insofar as they significantly affect interstate commerce. See, e.g., *Gibbons v. Ogden* (1824), *Wickard v. Filburn* (1942). Second, in determining whether a local activity will likely have a significant effect upon interstate commerce, a court must consider, not the effect of an individual act (a single instance of gun possession), but rather the cumulative effect of all similar instances (i.e., the effect of all guns possessed in or near schools). Third, the Constitution requires us to judge the connection between a regulated activity and interstate commerce, not directly, but at one remove. Courts must give Congress a degree of leeway in determining the existence of a significant factual connection between the

regulated activity and interstate commerce—both because the Constitution delegates the commerce power directly to Congress and because the determination requires an empirical judgment of a kind that a legislature is more likely than a court to make with accuracy. The traditional words "rational basis" capture this leeway. Thus, the specific question before us, as the Court recognizes, is not whether the "regulated activity sufficiently affected interstate commerce," but, rather, whether Congress could have had "*a rational basis*" for so concluding.

Applying these principles to the case at hand, we must ask whether Congress could have had a *rational basis* for finding a significant (or substantial) connection between gun-related school violence and interstate commerce. The answer to this question must be yes. Numerous reports and studies—generated both inside and outside government—make clear that Congress could reasonably have found the empirical connection that its law, implicitly, or explicitly, asserts. And, they report that this widespread violence in schools throughout the Nation significantly interferes with the quality of education in those schools. Based on reports such as these, Congress obviously could have thought that guns and learning are mutually exclusive. And, Congress could therefore have found a substantial educational problem—teachers unable to teach, students unable to learn—and concluded that guns near schools contribute substantially to the size and scope of that problem.

Having found that guns in schools significantly undermine the quality of education in our Nation's classrooms, Congress could also have found, given the effect of education upon interstate and foreign commerce, that gun-related violence in and around schools is a commercial, as well as a human, problem. The economic links I have just sketched seem fairly obvious. Why then is it not equally obvious, in light of those links, that a widespread, serious, and substantial physical threat to teaching and learning also substantially threatens the commerce to which that teaching and learning is inextricably tied? That is to say, guns in the hands of six percent of inner-city high school students and gun-related violence throughout a city's schools must threaten the trade and commerce that those schools support. The only question, then, is whether the latter threat is (to use the majority's terminology) "substantial." And, the evidence of (1) the *extent* of the gun-related violence problem, (2) the *extent* of the resulting negative effect on classroom learning, and (3) the *extent* of the consequent negative commercial effects, when taken together, indicate a threat to trade and commerce that is "substantial." At the very least, Congress could rationally have concluded that the links are "substantial."

In sum, a holding that the particular statute before us falls within the commerce power would not expand the scope of the Clause.

Rather, it simply would apply pre-existing law to changing economic circumstances. It would recognize that, in today's economic world, gun-related violence near the classroom makes a significant difference to our economic, as well as our social, well-being. In accordance with well-accepted precedent, such a holding would permit Congress "to act in terms of economic realities," would interpret the commerce power as "an affirmative power commensurate with the national needs," and would acknowledge that the "commerce clause does not operate so as to render the nation powerless to defend itself against economic forces that Congress decrees inimical or destructive of the national economy." *North American Co. v. SEC* (1946).

Gonzales v. Raich
545 U.S. 1 (2005)

In 1996, California voters passed Proposition 215, the Compassionate Use Act of 1996, which was designed to ensure that "seriously ill" residents of the state had access to marijuana for medical purposes and to encourage federal and state governments to take steps toward ensuring the safe and affordable distribution of the drug to patients in need. The act created an exemption from criminal prosecution for physicians, as well as for patients and primary caregivers who possessed or cultivated marijuana for medicinal purposes with the recommendation or approval of a physician. Angel Raich and Diane Monson were California residents who sought to avail themselves of medical marijuana pursuant to the terms of the Compassionate Use Act. In 2002 county deputy sheriffs and agents from the federal Drug Enforcement Administration came to Monson's home. After a thorough investigation, the county officials concluded that her use of marijuana was entirely lawful as a matter of California law, but the federal agents seized and destroyed all her cannabis plants. She and Raich then sued, seeking an injunction prohibiting the enforcement of the federal Controlled Substances Act (CSA), to the extent it prevented them from possessing, obtaining, or manufacturing cannabis for their personal medical use. The district court denied their motion for a preliminary injunction, but the court of appeals reversed, and the Supreme Court granted certiorari.

Opinion of the Court: Stevens, Kennedy, Souter, Ginsburg, Breyer. Concurring in the judgment: Scalia. Dissenting opinions: O'Connor, Rehnquist (in part), Thomas (in part); Thomas.

JUSTICE STEVENS delivered the opinion of the Court.

California is one of at least nine States that authorize the use of marijuana for medicinal purposes. The question presented in this case is whether the power vested in Congress by Article I, §8, of the Constitution "to make all Laws which shall be necessary and proper for carrying into Execution" its authority to "regulate Commerce with foreign Nations, and among the several States" includes the power to prohibit the local cultivation and use of marijuana in compliance with California law.

I

The case is made difficult by respondents' strong arguments that they will suffer irreparable harm because, despite a congressional finding to the contrary, marijuana does have valid therapeutic purposes. The question before us, however, is not whether it is wise to enforce the statute in these circumstances; rather, it is whether Congress' power to regulate interstate markets for medicinal substances encompasses the portions of those markets that are supplied with drugs produced and consumed locally. Well-settled law controls our answer. The CSA is a valid exercise of federal power, even as applied to the troubling facts of this case. We accordingly vacate the judgment of the Court of Appeals.

II

The main objectives of the CSA were to conquer drug abuse and to control the legitimate and illegitimate traffic in controlled substances. Congress was particularly concerned with the need to prevent the diversion of drugs from legitimate to illicit channels. To effectuate these goals, Congress devised a closed regulatory system making it unlawful to manufacture, distribute, dispense, or possess any controlled substance except in a manner authorized by the CSA.

III

Respondents in this case do not dispute that passage of the CSA, as part of the Comprehensive Drug Abuse Prevention and Control Act, was well within Congress' commerce power. Nor do they contend that any provision or section of the CSA amounts to an unconstitutional exercise of congressional authority. Rather, respondents' challenge is actually quite limited; they argue that the CSA's categorical prohibition of the manufacture and possession of marijuana as applied to the intrastate manufacture and possession of marijuana for medical purposes pursuant to California law exceeds Congress' authority under the Commerce Clause.

In assessing the validity of congressional regulation, none of our Commerce Clause cases can be viewed in isolation. As charted in considerable detail in *United States v. Lopez,* our understanding of the reach of the Commerce Clause, as well as Congress' assertion of authority thereunder, has evolved over time. The Commerce Clause emerged as the Framers' response to the central problem giving rise to the Constitution itself: the absence of any federal commerce power under the Articles of Confederation. For the first century of our history, the primary use of the Clause was to preclude the kind of discriminatory state legislation that had once been permissible. Then, in response to rapid industrial development and an increasingly interdependent national economy, Congress "ushered in a new era of federal regulation under the commerce power," beginning with the enactment of the Interstate Commerce Act in 1887 and the Sherman Antitrust Act in 1890. Cases decided during that "new era," which now spans more than a century, have identified three general categories of regulation in which Congress is authorized to engage under its commerce power. First, Congress can regulate the channels of interstate commerce. Second, Congress has authority to regulate and protect the instrumentalities of interstate commerce, and persons or things in interstate commerce. Third, Congress has the power to regulate activities that substantially affect interstate commerce. Only the third category is implicated in the case at hand.

Our case law firmly establishes Congress' power to regulate purely local activities that are part of an economic "class of activities" that have a substantial effect on interstate commerce. *Wickard v. Filburn* (1942). As we stated in *Wickard,* "even if appellee's activity be local and though it may not be regarded as commerce, it may still, whatever its nature, be reached by Congress if it exerts a substantial economic effect on interstate commerce." We have never required Congress to legislate with scientific exactitude. When Congress decides that the "'total incidence'" of a practice poses a threat to a national market, it may regulate the entire class. In this vein, we have reiterated that when "a general regulatory statute bears a substantial relation to commerce, the *de minimis* character of individual instances arising under that statute is of no consequence."

The similarities between this case and *Wickard* are striking. Like the farmer in *Wickard,* respondents are cultivating, for home consumption, a fungible commodity for which there is an established, albeit illegal, interstate market. Just as the Agricultural Adjustment Act was designed "to control the volume [of wheat] moving in interstate and foreign commerce in order to avoid surpluses" and consequently control the market price, a primary purpose of the CSA is to control the supply and demand of controlled substances in both lawful and unlawful drug markets. In *Wickard,* we had no difficulty concluding that Congress had a rational basis for believing that, when viewed in the aggregate, leaving home-consumed wheat outside the regulatory scheme would have a substantial influence on price and market conditions. Here too, Congress had a rational basis for concluding that leaving home-consumed marijuana outside federal control would similarly affect price and market conditions.

Nonetheless, respondents suggest that *Wickard* differs from this case in three respects: (1) the Agricultural Adjustment Act, unlike the CSA, exempted small farming operations; (2) *Wickard* involved a "quintessential economic activity"—a commercial farm—whereas respondents do not sell marijuana; and (3) the *Wickard* record made it clear that the aggregate production of wheat for use on farms had a significant impact on market prices. Those differences, though factually accurate, do not diminish the precedential force of this Court's reasoning.

The fact that Wickard's own impact on the market was "trivial by itself" was not a sufficient reason for removing him from the scope of federal regulation. That the Secretary of Agriculture elected to exempt even smaller farms from regulation does not speak to his power to regulate all those whose aggregated production was significant, nor did that fact play any role in the Court's analysis. Moreover, even though Wickard was indeed a commercial farmer, the activity he was engaged in—the cultivation of wheat for home consumption—was not treated by the Court as part of his commercial farming operation. And while it is true that the record in the *Wickard* case itself established the causal connection between the production for local use and the national market, we have before us findings by Congress to the same effect.

In assessing the scope of Congress' authority under the Commerce Clause, we stress that the task before us is a modest one. We need not determine whether respondents' activities, taken in the aggregate, substantially affect interstate commerce in fact, but only whether a "rational basis" exists for so concluding. Given the enforcement difficulties that attend distinguishing between marijuana cultivated locally and marijuana grown elsewhere, and concerns about diversion into illicit channels, we have

no difficulty concluding that Congress had a rational basis for believing that failure to regulate the intrastate manufacture and possession of marijuana would leave a gaping hole in the CSA. Thus, as in *Wickard,* when it enacted comprehensive legislation to regulate the interstate market in a fungible commodity, Congress was acting well within its authority to "make all Laws which shall be necessary and proper" to "regulate Commerce . . . among the several States." That the regulation ensnares some purely intrastate activity is of no moment. As we have done many times before, we refuse to excise individual components of that larger scheme.

IV

To support their contrary submission, respondents rely heavily on two of our more recent Commerce Clause cases, *Lopez* and *Morrison.* As an initial matter, the statutory challenges at issue in those cases were markedly different from the challenge respondents pursue in the case at hand. Here, respondents ask us to excise individual applications of a concededly valid statutory scheme. In contrast, in both *Lopez* and *Morrison,* the parties asserted that a particular statute or provision fell outside Congress' commerce power in its entirety. This distinction is pivotal for we have often reiterated that "where the class of activities is regulated and that class is within the reach of federal power, the courts have no power 'to excise, as trivial, individual instances' of the class." *Perez.*

Unlike those at issue in *Lopez* and *Morrison,* the activities regulated by the CSA are quintessentially economic. Respondents acknowledge this proposition, but nonetheless contend that their activities were not "an essential part of a larger regulatory scheme" because they had been "isolated by the State of California, and [are] policed by the State of California," and thus remain "entirely separated from the market." The notion that California law has surgically excised a discrete activity that is hermetically sealed off from the larger interstate marijuana market is a dubious proposition, and, more importantly, one that Congress could have rationally rejected. Indeed, the California exemptions will have a significant impact on both the supply and demand sides of the market for marijuana. The exemption for physicians provides them with an economic incentive to grant their patients permission to use the drug. The exemption for cultivation by patients and caregivers can only increase the supply of marijuana in the California market. The likelihood that all such production will promptly terminate when patients recover or will precisely match the patients' medical needs during their convalescence seems remote; whereas the danger that excesses will satisfy some of the admittedly enormous demand for recreational use seems obvious. Moreover, that the national and international narcotics trade has thrived in the face of vigorous criminal enforcement efforts suggests that no small number of unscrupulous people will make use of the California exemptions to serve their commercial ends whenever it is feasible to do so. Congress could have rationally concluded that the aggregate impact on the national market of all the transactions exempted from federal supervision is unquestionably substantial.

Thus the case for the exemption comes down to the claim that a locally cultivated product that is used domestically rather than sold on the open market is not subject to federal regulation. Given the findings in the CSA and the undisputed magnitude of the commercial market for marijuana, our decisions in *Wickard v. Filburn* and the later cases endorsing its reasoning foreclose that claim.

JUSTICE O'CONNOR, with whom THE CHIEF JUSTICE and JUSTICE THOMAS join as to all but Part III, dissenting.

We enforce the "outer limits" of Congress' Commerce Clause authority not for their own sake, but to protect historic spheres of state sovereignty from excessive federal encroachment and thereby to maintain the distribution of power fundamental to our federalist system of government. One of federalism's chief virtues, of course, is that it promotes innovation by allowing for the possibility that "a single courageous State may, if its citizens choose, serve as a laboratory; and try novel social and economic experiments without risk to the rest of the country." *New State Ice Co. v. Liebmann* (1932) (Brandeis, J., dissenting).

This case exemplifies the role of States as laboratories. The States' core police powers have always included authority to define criminal law and to protect the health, safety, and welfare of their citizens. Exercising those powers, California has come to its own conclusion about the difficult and sensitive question of whether marijuana should be available to relieve severe pain and suffering. Today the Court sanctions an application of the federal Controlled Substances Act that extinguishes that experiment, without any proof that the personal cultivation, possession, and use of marijuana for medicinal purposes, if economic activity in the first place, has a substantial effect on interstate commerce and is therefore an appropriate subject of federal regulation. In so doing, the Court announces a rule that gives Congress a perverse incentive to legislate broadly pursuant to the Commerce Clause—nestling questionable assertions of its authority into comprehensive regulatory schemes—rather than with precision. That rule and the result it produces in this case are irreconcilable with our decisions in *Lopez* and *United States v. Morrison* (2000). Accordingly I dissent.

II

What is the relevant conduct subject to Commerce Clause analysis in this case? Today's decision allows Congress to regulate intrastate activity without check, so long as there is some implication by legislative design that regulating intrastate activity is essential (and the Court appears to equate "essential" with "necessary") to the interstate regulatory scheme. Seizing upon our language in *Lopez* that the statute prohibiting gun possession in school zones was "not an essential part of a larger regulation of economic activity, in which the regulatory scheme could be undercut unless the intrastate activity were regulated," the Court appears to reason that the placement of local activity in a comprehensive scheme confirms that it is essential to that scheme. If the Court is right, then *Lopez* stands for nothing more than a drafting guide: Congress should have described the relevant crime as "transfer or possession of a firearm anywhere in the nation"—thus including commercial and noncommercial activity, and clearly encompassing some activity with assuredly substantial effect on interstate commerce.

I cannot agree that our decision in *Lopez* contemplated such evasive or overbroad legislative strategies with approval. *Lopez* and *Morrison* did not indicate that the constitutionality of federal regulation depends on superficial and formalistic distinctions. Likewise I did not understand our discussion of the role of courts in enforcing outer limits of the Commerce Clause for the sake of maintaining the federalist balance our Constitution requires, as a signal to Congress to enact legislation that is more extensive and more intrusive into the domain of state power. If the Court always defers to Congress as it does today, little may be left to the notion of enumerated powers.

The hard work for courts, then, is to identify objective markers for confining the analysis in Commerce Clause cases. Here, respondents challenge the constitutionality of the CSA as applied to them and those similarly situated. I agree with the Court that we must look beyond respondents' own activities. Otherwise, individual litigants could always exempt themselves from Commerce Clause regulation merely by pointing to the obvious—that their personal activities do not have a substantial effect on interstate commerce. The task is to identify a mode of analysis that allows Congress to regulate more than nothing (by declining to reduce each case to its litigants) and less than everything (by declining to let Congress set the terms of analysis). The analysis may not be the same in every case, for it depends on the regulatory scheme at issue and the federalism concerns implicated.

A number of objective markers are available to confine the scope of constitutional review here. Both federal and state legislation—including the CSA itself, the California Compassionate Use Act, and other state medical marijuana legislation—recognize that medical and non-medical (*i.e.,* recreational) uses of drugs are realistically distinct and can be segregated, and regulate them differently. Respondents challenge only the application of the CSA to medicinal use of marijuana. Moreover, because fundamental structural concerns about dual sovereignty animate our Commerce Clause cases, it is relevant that this case

involves the interplay of federal and state regulation in areas of criminal law and social policy, where "States lay claim by right of history and expertise." California, like other States, has drawn on its reserved powers to distinguish the regulation of medicinal marijuana. To ascertain whether Congress' encroachment is constitutionally justified in this case, then, I would focus here on the personal cultivation, possession, and use of marijuana for medicinal purposes.

Having thus defined the relevant conduct, we must determine whether, under our precedents, the conduct is economic and, in the aggregate, substantially affects interstate commerce. Even if intrastate cultivation and possession of marijuana for one's own medicinal use can properly be characterized as economic, and I question whether it can, it has not been shown that such activity substantially affects interstate commerce. Similarly, it is neither self-evident nor demonstrated that regulating such activity is necessary to the interstate drug control scheme.

The Court suggests that *Wickard,* which we have identified as "perhaps the most far reaching example of Commerce Clause authority over intrastate activity," established federal regulatory power over any home consumption of a commodity for which a national market exists. I disagree. *Wickard* involved a challenge to the Agricultural Adjustment Act of 1938 (AAA), which directed the Secretary of Agriculture to set national quotas on wheat production, and penalties for excess production. The AAA itself confirmed that Congress made an explicit choice not to reach—and thus the Court could not possibly have approved of federal control over—small-scale, noncommercial wheat farming. In contrast to the CSA's limitless assertion of power, Congress provided an exemption within the AAA for small producers. When Filburn planted the wheat at issue in *Wickard,* the statute exempted plantings less than 200 bushels (about six tons), and when he harvested his wheat it exempted plantings less than six acres. *Wickard,* then, did not extend Commerce Clause authority to something as modest as the home cook's herb garden. This is not to say that Congress may never regulate small quantities of commodities possessed or produced for personal use, or to deny that it sometimes needs to enact a zero tolerance regime for such commodities. It is merely to say that *Wickard* did not hold or imply that small-scale production of commodities is always economic, and automatically within Congress' reach.

There is simply no evidence that homegrown medicinal marijuana users constitute, in the aggregate, a sizable enough class to have a discernable, let alone substantial, impact on the national illicit drug market—or otherwise to threaten the CSA regime. Explicit evidence is helpful when substantial effect is not "visible to the naked eye." And here, in part because common sense suggests that medical marijuana users may be limited in number and that California's Compassionate Use Act and similar state legislation may well isolate activities relating to medicinal marijuana from the illicit market, the effect of those activities on interstate drug traffic is not self-evidently substantial.

In this regard, again, this case is readily distinguishable from *Wickard*. To decide whether the Secretary could regulate local wheat farming, the Court looked to "the actual effects of the activity in question upon interstate commerce." Critically, the Court was able to consider "actual effects" because the parties had "stipulated a summary of the economics of the wheat industry." After reviewing in detail the picture of the industry provided in that summary, the Court explained that consumption of homegrown wheat was the most variable factor in the size of the national wheat crop, and that on-site consumption could have the effect of varying the amount of wheat sent to market by as much as 20 percent. With real numbers at hand, the *Wickard* Court could easily conclude that "a factor of such volume and variability as home-consumed wheat would have a substantial influence on price and market conditions" nationwide.

The Government has not overcome empirical doubt that the number of Californians engaged in personal cultivation, possession, and use of medical marijuana, or the amount of marijuana they produce, is enough to threaten the federal regime. Nor has it shown that Compassionate Use Act marijuana users have been or are realistically likely to be responsible for the drug's seeping into the market in a significant way.

III

We would do well to recall how James Madison, the father of the Constitution, described our system of joint sovereignty to the people of New York: "The powers delegated by the proposed constitution to the federal government are few and defined. Those which are to remain in the State governments are numerous and indefinite. The powers reserved to the several States will extend to all the objects which, in the ordinary course of affairs, concern the lives, liberties, and properties of the people, and the internal order, improvement, and prosperity of the State." *The Federalist* No. 45.

Relying on Congress' abstract assertions, the Court has endorsed making it a federal crime to grow small amounts of marijuana in one's own home for one's own medicinal use. This overreaching stifles an express choice by some States, concerned for the lives and liberties of their people, to regulate medical marijuana differently. If I were a California citizen, I would not have voted for the medical marijuana ballot initiative; if I were a California legislator I would not have supported the Compassionate Use Act. But whatever the wisdom of California's experiment with medical marijuana, the federalism principles that have driven our Commerce Clause cases require that room for experiment be protected in this case. For these reasons I dissent.

United States v. Butler
297 U.S. 1 (1936)

The Agricultural Adjustment Act of 1933, in seeking to curtail excess farm production, provided that farmers who reduced their production would be compensated financially. The funds for *this compensation came from a tax, levied by the act, on the processing of agricultural commodities. Butler, the receiver for a cotton-processing firm, refused to pay the tax. The district court ordered*

Butler to pay the tax, the court of appeals reversed, and the government appealed.

Opinion of the Court: <u>Roberts</u>, Hughes, Van Devanter, McReynolds, Sutherland, Butler. Dissenting opinion: <u>Stone</u>, Brandeis, Cardozo.

JUSTICE ROBERTS delivered the opinion of the Court.

The Government asserts that even if the respondents may question the propriety of the appropriation embodied in the statute their attack must fail because Article I, §8 of the Constitution authorizes the contemplated expenditure of the funds raised by the tax. This contention presents the great and the controlling question in the case. We approach its decision with a sense of our grave responsibility to render judgment in accordance with the principles established for the governance of all three branches of the Government. There should be no misunderstanding as to the function of this court in such a case. It is sometimes said that the court assumes a power to overrule or control the action of the people's representatives. This is a misconception. The Constitution is the supreme law of the land ordained and established by the people. All legislation must conform to the principles it lays down. When an act of Congress is appropriately challenged in the courts as not conforming to the constitutional mandate the judicial branch of the Government has only one duty—to lay the article of the Constitution which is invoked beside the statute which is challenged and to decide whether the latter squares with the former. All the court does, or can do, is to announce its considered judgment upon the question. The only power it has, if such it may be called, is the power of judgment. This court neither approves nor condemns any legislative policy. Its delicate and difficult office is to ascertain and declare whether the legislation is in accordance with, or in contravention of, the provisions of the Constitution; and, having done that, its duty ends.

The question is not what power the Federal Government ought to have but what powers in fact have been given by the people. It hardly seems necessary to reiterate that ours is a dual form of government; that in every state there are two governments—the state and the United States. Each State has all governmental powers save such as the people, by their Constitution, have conferred upon the United States, denied to the States, or reserved to themselves. The federal union is a government of delegated powers. It has only such as are expressly conferred upon it and such as are reasonably to be implied from those granted. In this respect we differ radically from nations where all legislative power, without restriction or limitation, is vested in a parliament or other legislative body subject to no restrictions except the discretion of its members.

Article I, §8, of the Constitution vests sundry powers in the Congress. But two of its clauses have any bearing upon the validity of the statute under review. The clause thought to authorize the legislation—the first—confers upon the Congress power "to lay and collect Taxes, Duties, Imports and Excises, to pay the Debts and provide for the common Defence and general Welfare of the United States." It is not contended that this provision grants power to regulate agricultural production upon the theory that such legislation would promote the general welfare. The Government concedes that the phrase "to provide for the general welfare" qualifies the power "to lay and collect taxes." The view that the clause grants power to provide for the general welfare, independently of the taxing power, has never been authoritatively accepted. Mr. Justice Story points out that if it were adopted "it is obvious that under color of the generality of the words, to 'provide for the common defence and general welfare,' the government of the United States is, in reality, a government of general and unlimited powers, notwithstanding the subsequent enumeration of specific powers." The true construction undoubtedly is that the only thing granted is the power to tax for the purpose of providing funds for payment of the nation's debt and making provision for the general welfare.

Nevertheless the Government asserts that warrant is found in this clause for the adoption of the Agricultural Adjustment Act. The argument is that Congress may appropriate and authorize the spending of moneys for the "general welfare"; that the phrase should be liberally construed to cover anything conducive to national welfare; that decision as to what will promote such welfare rests with Congress alone, and the courts may not review its determination; and finally that the appropriation under attack was in fact for the general welfare of the United States.

The Congress is expressly empowered to lay taxes to provide for the general welfare. Funds in the Treasury as a result of taxation may be expended only through appropriation. (Art. I, §9, cl. 7.) They can never accomplish the objects for which they were collected unless the power to appropriate is as broad as the power to tax. The necessary implication from the terms of the grant is that the public funds may be appropriated "to provide for the general welfare of the United States." These words cannot be meaningless, else they would not have been used. The conclusion must be that they were intended to limit and define the granted power to raise and to expend money. How shall they be construed to effectuate the intent of the instrument?

Since the foundation of the Nation sharp differences of opinion have persisted as to the true interpretation of the phrase. Madison asserted it amounted to no more than a reference to the other powers enumerated in the subsequent clauses of the same section; that, as the United States is a government of limited and enumerated powers, the grant of power to tax and spend for the general national welfare must be confined to the enumerated legislative fields committed to the Congress. In this view the phrase is mere tautology, for taxation and appropriation are or may be necessary incidents of the exercise of any of the enumerated legislative powers. Hamilton, on the other hand, maintained the clause confers a power separate and distinct from those later enumerated, is not restricted in meaning by the grant of them, and Congress consequently has a substantive power to tax and to appropriate, limited only by the requirement that it shall be exercised to provide for the general welfare of the United States. Each contention has had the support of those whose views are entitled to weight. This court has noticed the question, but has never found it necessary to decide which is the true construction. Mr. Justice Story, in his Commentaries, espouses the Hamiltonian position. We shall not review the writings of public men and commentators or discuss the legislative practice. Study of all these leads us to conclude that the reading advocated by Mr. Justice Story is the correct one. While, therefore, the power to tax is not unlimited, its confines are set in the clause which confers it, and not in those of §8 which bestow and define the legislative powers of the Congress. It results that the power of Congress to authorize expenditure of public moneys for public purposes is not limited by the direct grants of legislative power found in the Constitution.

But the adoption of the broader construction leaves the power to spend subject to limitations. Story says that if the tax be not proposed for the common defence or general welfare, but for other objects wholly extraneous, it would be wholly indefensible upon constitutional principles. And he makes it clear that the powers of taxation and appropriation extend only to matters of national, as distinguished from local welfare.

We are not now required to ascertain the scope of the phrase "general welfare of the United States" or to determine whether an appropriation in aid of agriculture falls within it. Wholly apart from that question, another principle embedded in our Constitution prohibits the enforcement of the Agricultural Adjustment Act. The act invades the reserved rights of states. It is a statutory plan to regulate and control agricultural production, a matter beyond the powers delegated to the federal government. The tax, the appropriation of the funds raised, and the direction for their disbursement, are but parts of the plan. They are but means to an unconstitutional end.

From the accepted doctrine that the United States is a government of delegated powers, it follows that those not expressly granted, or reasonably to be implied from such as are conferred are reserved to the states or to the people. To forestall any suggestion to the contrary, the Tenth Amendment was adopted. The same proposition, otherwise stated, is that powers not granted are prohibited. None to regulate agricultural production is given, and therefore legislation by Congress for that purpose is forbidden.

It is an established principle that the attainment of a prohibited end may not be accomplished under the pretext of the exertion of powers which are granted. If the taxing power may not be used as the instrument to enforce a regulation of matters of state concern with respect to which the Congress has no authority to interfere, may it, as in the present case, be employed to raise the money necessary to purchase a compliance which the Congress is powerless to command? The Government asserts that whatever might be said against the validity of the plan if compulsory, it is constitutionally sound because the end is accomplished by voluntary cooperation. The regulation is not in fact voluntary. The farmer, of course, may refuse to comply, but the price of such refusal is the loss of benefits. The amount offered is intended to be sufficient to exert pressure on him to agree to the proposed regulation. The power to confer or withhold unlimited benefits is the power to coerce or destroy.

But if the plan were one for purely voluntary cooperation it would stand no better so far as federal power is concerned. At best it is a scheme for purchasing with federal funds submission to federal regulation of a subject reserved to the states. Congress has no power to enforce its commands on the farmer to the ends sought by the Agricultural Adjustment Act. It must follow that it may not indirectly accomplish those ends by taxing and spending to purchase compliance. The Constitution and the entire plan of our government negative any such use of the power to tax and to spend as the act undertakes to authorize. It does not help declare that local conditions throughout the nation have created a situation of national concern; for this is but to say that whenever there is a widespread similarity of local conditions, Congress may ignore constitutional limitations upon its own powers and usurp those reserved to the states. If, in lieu of compulsory regulation of subjects within the states' reserved jurisdiction, which is prohibited, the Congress could invoke the taxing and spending power as a means to accomplish the same end, clause 1 of §8 of Article I would become the instrument for total subversion of the governmental powers reserved to the individual states.

If the act before us is a proper exercise of the federal taxing power, evidently the regulation of all industry throughout the United States may be accomplished by similar exercises of the same power. It would be possible to exact money from one branch of an industry and pay it to another branch in every field of activity which lies within the province of the states. The mere threat of such a procedure might well induce the surrender of rights and the compliance with federal regulation as the price of continuance in business. The judgment is

Affirmed.

JUSTICE STONE, dissenting.

1. The power of courts to declare a statute unconstitutional is subject to two guiding principles of decision which ought never to be absent from judicial consciousness. One is that courts are concerned only with the power to enact statutes, not with their wisdom. The other is that while unconstitutional exercise of power by the executive and legislative branches of the government is subject to judicial restraint, the only check upon our own exercise of power is our own sense of self-restraint. For the removal of unwise laws from the statute books appeal lies not to the courts but to the ballot and to the processes of democratic government.

2. The constitutional power of Congress to levy an excise tax upon the processing of agricultural products is not questioned. The present levy is held invalid, not for any want of power in Congress to lay such a tax to defray public expenditures, including those for the general welfare, but because the use to which its proceeds are put is disapproved.

3. As the present depressed state of agriculture is nationwide in its extent and effects, there is no basis for saying that the expenditure of public money in aid of farmers is not within the specifically granted power of Congress to levy taxes to "provide for the . . . general welfare." The opinion of the Court does not declare otherwise.

It is with these preliminary and hardly controverted matters in mind that we should direct our attention to the pivot on which the decision of the Court is made to turn. It is that a levy unquestionably within the taxing power of Congress may be treated as invalid because it is a step in a plan to regulate agricultural production and is thus a forbidden infringement of state power. The levy is not any the less an exercise of taxing power because it is intended to defray an expenditure for the general welfare rather than for some other support of government. Nor is the levy and collection of the tax pointed to as effecting the regulation. While all federal taxes inevitably have some influence on the internal economy of the states, it is not contended that the levy of a processing tax upon manufacturers using agricultural products as raw material has any perceptible regulatory effect upon either their production or manufacture. Here regulation, if any there be, is accomplished not by the tax but by the method by which its proceeds are expended, and would equally be accomplished by any like use of public funds, regardless of their source.

It is upon the contention that state power is infringed by purchased regulation of agricultural production that chief reliance is placed. It is insisted that, while the Constitution gives to Congress, in specific and unambiguous terms, the power to tax and spend, the power is subject to limitations which do not find their origin in any express provision of the Constitution and to which other expressly delegated powers are not subject.

Such a limitation is contradictory and destructive of the power to appropriate for the public welfare, and is incapable of practical application. The spending power of Congress is in addition to the legislative power and not subordinate to it. This independent grant of the power of the purse, and its very nature, involving in its exercise the duty to insure expenditure within the granted power, presuppose freedom of selection among divers ends and aims, and the capacity to impose such conditions as will render the choice effective. It is a contradiction in terms to say that there is power to spend for the national welfare while rejecting any power to impose conditions reasonably adapted to the attainment of the end which alone would justify the expenditure.

A tortured construction of the Constitution is not to be justified by recourse to extreme examples of reckless congressional spending which might occur if courts could not prevent—expenditures which even if they could be thought to effect any national purpose, would be possible only by action of a legislature lost to all sense of public responsibility. Such suppositions are addressed to the mind accustomed to belief that it is the business of courts to sit in judgment on the wisdom of legislative action. Courts are not the only agency of government that must be assumed to have capacity to govern. Congress and the courts both unhappily may falter or be mistaken in the performance of their constitutional duty. But interpretation of our great charter of government which proceeds on any assumption that the responsibility for the preservation of our institutions is the exclusive concern of any one of the three branches of government, or that it alone can save them from destruction is far more likely, in the long run, "to obliterate the constituent members" of "an indestructible union of indestructible states" than the frank recognition that language, even of a constitution, may mean what it says: that the power to tax and spend includes the power to relieve a nationwide economic maladjustment by conditional gifts of money.

United States v. Kahriger
345 U.S. 22 (1953)

Congress enacted a law levying an annual tax of $50 on persons in the business of taking bets. Persons paying the tax were required to register with the Federal Collector of Internal Revenue, giving their names, addresses, and places of business. Kahriger was indicted for running a gambling business without paying the tax, but the district court dismissed the charge, ruling the law unconstitutional. The government then appealed the case to the Supreme Court. Opinion of the Court: <u>Reed</u>, Warren, Jackson, Burton, Clark, Minton. Concurring opinion: <u>Jackson</u>. Dissenting opinions: <u>Black</u>, Douglas; <u>Frankfurter</u>, Douglas (in part).

JUSTICE REED delivered the opinion of the Court.

The issue raised by this appeal is the constitutionality of the occupational tax provisions of the Revenue Act of 1951, which levy a tax on persons engaged in the business of accepting wagers, and require such persons to register with the Collector of Internal Revenue. The unconstitutionality of the tax is asserted on two grounds. First, it is said that Congress, under the pretense of exercising its power to tax has attempted to penalize illegal intrastate gambling through the regulatory features of the Act and has thus infringed the police power which is reserved to the states. Secondly, it is urged that the registration provisions of the tax violate the privilege against self-incrimination and are arbitrary and vague, contrary to the guarantees of the Fifth Amendment.

It is conceded that a federal excise tax does not cease to be valid merely because it discourages or deters the activities taxed. Nor is the tax invalid because the revenue obtained is negligible. Appellee, however, argues that the sole purpose of the statute is to penalize only illegal gambling in the states through the guise of a tax measure. The instant tax has a regulatory effect. But regardless of its regulatory effect, the wagering tax produces revenue. As such it surpasses both the narcotics and firearms taxes which we have found valid. It is hard to understand why the power to tax should raise more doubts because of indirect effects than other federal powers.

Appellee's second assertion is that the wagering tax is unconstitutional because it is a denial of the privilege against self-incrimination as guaranteed by the Fifth Amendment. Since appellee failed to register for the wagering tax, it is difficult to see how he can now claim the privilege even assuming that the disclosure of violations of law is called for. Assuming that respondent can raise the self-incrimination issue, that privilege has relation only to past acts, not to future acts that may or may not be committed. If respondent wishes to take wagers subject to excise taxes under §3285, he must pay an occupational tax and register. Under the registration provisions of the wagering tax, appellee is not compelled to confess to acts already committed, he is merely informed by the statute that in order to engage in the business of wagering in the future he must fulfill certain conditions.

JUSTICE BLACK, with whom JUSTICE DOUGLAS concurs, dissenting.

The Act creates a squeezing device contrived to put a man in federal prison if he refuses to confess himself into a state prison as a violator of state gambling laws. The coercion of confessions is a common but justly criticized practice of many countries that do not have or live up to a Bill of Rights. But we have a Bill of Rights that condemns coerced confessions, however refined or legalistic may be the technique of extortion. I would hold that this Act violates the Fifth Amendment.

JUSTICE FRANKFURTER, dissenting.

Constitutional issues are likely to arise whenever Congress draws on the taxing power not to raise revenue but to regulate conduct. This is so, of course, because of the distribution of legislative power as between the Congress and the State Legislatures in the regulation of conduct. . . . When oblique use is made of the taxing power as to matters which substantively are not within the powers delegated to Congress, the Court cannot shut its eyes to what is obviously, because designedly, an attempt to control conduct which the Constitution left to the responsibility of the States, merely because Congress wrapped the legislation in the verbal cellophane of a revenue measure. . . .

Congress, which cannot constitutionally grapple directly with gambling in the States, may not compel self-incriminating disclosures for the enforcement of State gambling laws, merely because it does so under the guise of a revenue measure obviously passed not for revenue purposes. The motive of congressional legislation is not for our scrutiny, provided only that the ulterior purpose is not expressed in ways which negative what the revenue words on their face express and which do not seek enforcement of the formal revenue purpose through means that offend those standards of decency in our civilization against which due process is a barrier.

South Dakota v. Dole
483 U.S. 203 (1987)

In 1984, Congress enacted legislation directing the secretary of transportation to withhold 5 percent of federal highway funds from states that permitted purchase or public possession of alcoholic beverages by persons less than twenty-one years of age. South Dakota, which permitted persons nineteen years of age or older to purchase 3.2 percent beer, sought a declaratory judgment that the law exceeded the constitutional limitations on the congressional spending power and violated the Twenty-First Amendment, which it viewed as granting the states exclusive authority to regulate the sale of alcohol within their borders. In support of this latter contention, South Dakota pointed to Section 2 of the amendment, which provides: "The transportation or importation into any State, Territory, or possession of the United States for delivery or use therein of intoxicating liquors, in violation of the laws thereof, is hereby prohibited." After its claims were rejected in federal district court and in the court of appeals, South Dakota appealed the case to the Supreme Court. Opinion of the Court: <u>Rehnquist</u>, White, Marshall, Blackmun, Powell, Stevens, Scalia. Dissenting opinions: <u>Brennan</u>; <u>O'Connor</u>.

THE CHIEF JUSTICE delivered the opinion of the Court.

We need not decide in this case whether [the Twenty-First] Amendment would prohibit an attempt by Congress to legislate directly a national minimum drinking age. Here, Congress has acted indirectly under its spending power to encourage uniformity in the States' drinking ages. As we explain below, we find this legislative effort within constitutional bounds even if Congress may not regulate drinking ages directly.

The Constitution empowers Congress to "lay and collect Taxes, Duties, Imports, and Excises, to pay the Debts and provide for the common Defence and general Welfare of the United States." Art. I, §8, cl. 1. Incident to this power, Congress may attach conditions on the receipt of federal funds, and has repeatedly employed the power "to further broad policy objectives by conditioning receipt of federal moneys upon compliance by the recipient with federal statutory and administrative directives." *Fullilove v.*

Klutznick (1980). The breadth of this power was made clear in *United States v. Butler* (1936), where the Court, resolving a longstanding debate over the scope of the Spending Clause, determined that "the power of Congress to authorize expenditure of public moneys for public purposes is not limited by the direct grants of legislative power found in the Constitution." Thus, objectives not thought to be within Article I's "enumerated legislative fields" may nevertheless be attained through the use of the spending power and the conditional grant of federal funds. We can readily conclude that the provision is designed to serve the general welfare, especially in light of the fact that "the concept of welfare or the opposite is shaped by Congress." *Helvering v. Davis* [1937]. Congress found that the differing drinking ages in the States created particular incentives for young persons to combine their desire to drink with their ability to drive, and that this interstate problem required a national solution. The means it chose to address this dangerous situation were reasonably calculated to advance the general welfare. The conditions upon which States receive the funds, moreover, could not be more clearly stated by Congress. And the State itself, rather than challenging the germaneness of the condition to federal purposes, admits that it "has never contended that the congressional action was unrelated to a national concern in the absence of the Twenty First Amendment." Indeed, the condition imposed by Congress is directly related to one of the main purposes for which highway funds are expended—safe interstate travel.

The basic point of disagreement between the parties—is whether the Twenty-first Amendment constitutes an "independent constitutional bar" to the conditional grant of federal funds. . . . Petitioner, relying on its view that the Twenty-first Amendment prohibits *direct* regulation of drinking ages by Congress, asserts that "Congress may not use the spending power to regulate that which it is prohibited from regulating directly under the Twenty-first Amendment." But our cases show that this "independent constitutional bar" limitation on the spending power is not of the kind petitioner suggests.

Our decisions have recognized that in some circumstances the financial inducement offered by Congress might be so coercive as to pass the point at which "pressure turns into compulsion." *Steward Machine Co. v. Davis* [1937]. . . . Here Congress has offered relatively mild encouragement to the States to enact higher minimum drinking ages than they would otherwise choose. But the enactment of such laws remains the prerogative of the States not merely in theory but in fact. Even if Congress might lack the power to impose a national minimum drinking age directly, we conclude that encouragement to state action found in §158 is a valid use of the spending power. Accordingly, the judgment of the Court of Appeals is

Affirmed.

JUSTICE O'CONNOR, dissenting.

My disagreement with the Court is relatively narrow on the Spending Power issue: it is a disagreement about the application of a principle rather than a disagreement on the principle itself. I agree with the Court that Congress may attach conditions on the receipt of federal funds to further "the federal interest in particular national projects or programs." *Massachusetts v. United States* (1978). In my view, establishment of a minimum drinking age of 21 is not sufficiently related to interstate highway construction to justify so conditioning funds appropriated for that purpose. The Court reasons that Congress wishes that the roads it builds may be used safely, that drunk drivers threaten highway safety, and that young people are more likely to drive while under the influence of alcohol under existing law than would be the case if there were a uniform national drinking age of 21. It hardly needs saying, however, that if the purpose of [this law] is to deter drunken driving, it is far too over- and under-inclusive. It is over-inclusive because it stops teenagers from drinking even when they are not about to drive on interstate highways. It is under-inclusive because teenagers pose only a small part of the drunken driving problem in this Nation.

When Congress appropriates money to build a highway, it is entitled to insist that the highway be a safe one. But it is not entitled to insist as a condition of the use of highway funds that the State impose or change regulations in other areas of the State's social and economic life because of an attenuated or tangential relationship to highway use or safety. Indeed, if the rule were otherwise, the Congress could effectively regulate almost any area of a State's social, political, or economic life on the theory that use of the interstate transportation system is somehow enhanced.

There is a clear place at which the Court can draw the line between permissible and impermissible conditions on federal grants. It is the line identified in the Brief for the National Conference of State Legislatures as *Amici Curiae*:

Congress has the power to spend for the general welfare, it has the power to *legislate* only for delegated purposes. The appropriate inquiry, then, is whether the spending requirement or prohibition is a condition on a grant or whether it is regulation. The difference turns on whether the requirement specifies in some way how the money should be spent, so that Congress' intent in making the grant will be effectuated. Congress has no power under the Spending Clause to impose requirements on a grant that go beyond specifying how the money should be spent. A requirement that is not such a specification is not a condition, but a regulation, which is valid only if it falls within one of Congress' delegated regulatory powers.

This approach harks back to *United States v. Butler* (1936), the last case in which this Court struck down an Act of Congress as beyond the authority granted by the Spending Clause. While *Butler*'s authority is questionable insofar as it assumes that Congress has no regulatory power over farm production, its discussion of the Spending Power and its description of both the power's breadth and its limitations remains sound. The Court's decision in *Butler* also properly recognizes the gravity of the task of appropriately limiting the Spending Power. If the Spending Power is to be limited only by Congress' notion of the general welfare, the reality, given the vast financial resources of the Federal Government, is that the Spending Clause gives "power to the Congress to tear down the barriers, to invade the states' jurisdiction, and to become a parliament of the whole people, subject to no restrictions save such as are self-imposed." *United States v. Butler.* This, of course, as *Butler* held, was not the Framers' plan and it is not the meaning of the Spending Clause.

National Federation of Independent Business v. Sebelius
567 U.S. ___ (2012)

In 2010, Congress enacted the Patient Protection and Affordable Care Act, which aimed to increase the number of Americans covered by health insurance and decrease the cost of health care, with almost all Democrats supporting the measure and all Republicans opposing it. Two key provisions aroused controversy. The "individual mandate" required most Americans to maintain "minimum essential" health insurance coverage and, beginning in 2014, imposed on those who do not comply with the mandate a "shared responsibility payment." The law also expanded Medicaid, a program jointly funded by the federal government and the states that provides health care to the needy, and required states to expand funding to meet the new coverage requirements. If a state failed to comply with this requirement, it could lose not only the federal funding for those requirements but all of its federal Medicaid funds. On the day the president signed the act into law, Florida and twelve other states filed suit in federal district court challenging the constitutionality of the law. Those plaintiffs were later joined by thirteen more states, several individuals, and the National Federation of Independent Business. The plaintiffs alleged that the "individual mandate" provision and the law's expansion of Medicaid exceeded congressional power. Several other suits were also filed, with federal courts of appeals divided as to the constitutionality of the law, and the Supreme Court granted certiorari. Judgment of the Court and, in part, the opinion of the Court: <u>Roberts</u>. Concurring in part and dissenting in part: <u>Ginsburg</u>, Sotomayor, Breyer (in part), Kagan (in part). Dissenting in part and concurring in part: <u>Scalia</u>, Kennedy, Thomas, Alito.

THE CHIEF JUSTICE announced the judgment of the Court and delivered the opinion of the Court with respect to Parts I, II, and III-C, an opinion with respect to Part IV, in which JUSTICE BREYER and JUSTICE KAGAN join, and an opinion with respect to Parts III-A, III-B, and III-D.

Today we resolve constitutional challenges to two provisions of the Patient Protection and Affordable Care Act of 2010: the individual mandate, which requires individuals to purchase a health insurance policy providing a minimum level of coverage; and the Medicaid expansion, which gives funds to the States on the condition that they provide specified health care to all citizens whose income falls below a certain threshold. We do not consider whether the Act embodies sound policies. That judgment is entrusted to the Nation's elected leaders. We ask only whether Congress has the power under the Constitution to enact the challenged provisions.

In our federal system, the National Government possesses only limited powers; the States and the people retain the remainder. Nearly two centuries ago, Chief Justice Marshall observed that "the question respecting the extent of the powers actually granted" to the Federal Government "is perpetually arising, and will probably continue to arise, as long as our system shall exist." *McCulloch v. Maryland* (1819). In this case we must again determine whether the Constitution grants Congress powers it now asserts, but which many States and individuals believe it does not possess. Resolving this controversy requires us to examine both the limits of the Government's power, and our own limited role in policing those boundaries.

The Federal Government "is acknowledged by all to be one of enumerated powers." The enumeration of powers is also a limitation of powers, because "the enumeration presupposes something not enumerated." *Gibbons v. Ogden* (1824). The Constitution's express conferral of some powers makes clear that it does not grant others. And the Federal Government "can exercise only the powers granted to it." The Federal Government has expanded dramatically over the past two centuries, but it still must show that a constitutional grant of power authorizes each of its actions.

The same does not apply to the States, because the Constitution is not the source of their power. The Constitution may restrict state governments—as it does, for example, by forbidding them to deny any person the equal protection of the laws. But where such prohibitions do not apply, state governments do not need constitutional authorization to act. The States thus can and do perform many of the vital functions of modern government—punishing street crime, running public schools, and zoning property for development, to name but a few—even though the Constitution's text does not authorize any government to do so. Our cases refer to this general power of governing, possessed by the States but not by the Federal Government, as the "police power."

Because the police power is controlled by 50 different States instead of one national sovereign, the facets of governing that touch on citizens' daily lives are normally administered by smaller governments closer to the governed. The Framers thus ensured that powers which "in the ordinary course of affairs, concern the lives, liberties, and properties of the people" were held by governments more local and more accountable than a distant federal bureaucracy. *The Federalist* No. 45. The independent power of the States also serves as a check on the power of the Federal Government: "By denying any one government complete jurisdiction over all the concerns of public life, federalism protects the liberty of the individual from arbitrary power." *Bond v. United States* (2011).

This case concerns two powers that the Constitution does grant the Federal Government, but which must be read carefully to avoid creating a general federal authority akin to the police power. The Constitution authorizes Congress to "regulate Commerce with foreign Nations, and among the several States, and with the Indian Tribes." Art. I, §8, cl. 3. Our precedents read that to mean that Congress may regulate "the channels of interstate commerce," "persons or things in interstate commerce," and "those activities that substantially affect interstate commerce." The power over activities that substantially affect interstate commerce can be expansive. That power has been held to authorize federal regulation of such seemingly local matters as a farmer's decision to grow wheat for himself and his livestock, and a loan shark's extortionate collections from a neighborhood butcher shop. See *Wickard v. Filburn* (1942); *Perez v. United States* (1971).

Congress may also "lay and collect Taxes, Duties, Imposts and Excises, to pay the Debts and provide for the common Defence and general Welfare of the United States." U. S. Const., Art. I, §8, cl. 1. Put simply, Congress may tax and spend. This grant gives the Federal Government considerable influence even in areas where it cannot directly regulate. The Federal Government may enact a tax on an activity that it cannot authorize, forbid, or otherwise control. And in exercising its spending power, Congress may offer funds to the States, and may condition those offers on compliance with specified conditions. These offers may well induce the States to adopt policies that the Federal Government itself could not impose. See, e.g., *South Dakota v. Dole* (1987).

The reach of the Federal Government's enumerated powers is broader still because the Constitution authorizes Congress to "make all Laws which shall be necessary and proper for carrying into Execution the foregoing Powers." Art. I, §8, cl. 18. We have long read this provision to give Congress great latitude in exercising its powers: "Let the end be legitimate, let it be within the scope of the constitution, and all means which are appropriate, which are plainly adapted to that end, which are not prohibited, but consist with the letter and spirit of the constitution, are constitutional." *McCulloch.*

Our permissive reading of these powers is explained in part by a general reticence to invalidate the acts of the Nation's elected leaders. "Proper respect for a co-ordinate branch of the government" requires that we strike down an Act of Congress only if "the lack of constitutional authority to pass [the] act in question is clearly demonstrated." *United States v. Harris* (1883). Members of this Court are vested with the authority to interpret the law; we possess neither the expertise nor the prerogative to make policy judgments. Those decisions are entrusted to our Nation's elected leaders, who can be thrown out of office if the people disagree with them. It is not our job to protect the people from the consequences of their political choices.

Our deference in matters of policy cannot, however, become abdication in matters of law. Our respect for Congress's policy judgments can never extend so far as to disavow restraints on federal power that the Constitution carefully constructed. And there can be no question that it is the responsibility of this Court to enforce the limits on federal power by striking down acts of Congress that transgress those limits. The questions before us must be considered against the background of these basic principles.

III

The Government advances two theories for the proposition that Congress had constitutional authority to enact the individual mandate. First, the Government argues that Congress had the power to enact the mandate under the Commerce Clause. Under that theory, Congress may order individuals to buy health insurance because the failure to do so affects interstate commerce, and could undercut the Affordable Care Act's other reforms. Second, the Government argues that if the commerce power does not support the mandate, we should nonetheless uphold it as an exercise of Congress's power to tax. According to the Government, even if Congress lacks the power to direct individuals to buy insurance, the only effect of the individual mandate is to raise taxes on those who do not do so, and thus the law may be upheld as a tax.

A

The Government's first argument is that the individual mandate is a valid exercise of Congress's power under the Commerce Clause and the Necessary and Proper Clause. The Government contends that the individual mandate is within Congress's power because the failure to purchase insurance "has a substantial and deleterious effect on interstate commerce" by creating the cost-shifting problem.

The Constitution grants Congress the power to "regulate Commerce." The power to regulate commerce presupposes the existence of commercial activity to be regulated. The individual mandate, however, does not regulate existing commercial activity. It instead compels individuals to become active in commerce by purchasing a product, on the ground that their failure to do so affects interstate commerce. Construing the Commerce Clause to permit Congress to regulate individuals precisely because they are doing nothing would open a new and potentially vast domain to congressional authority.

Applying the Government's logic to the familiar case of *Wickard v. Filburn* shows how far that logic would carry us from the notion of a government of limited powers. *Wickard* has long been regarded as "perhaps the most far reaching example of Commerce Clause authority over intrastate activity," but the Government's theory in this case would go much further. Under *Wickard* it is within Congress's power to regulate the market for wheat by supporting its price. But price can be supported by increasing demand as well as by decreasing supply. The aggregated decisions of some consumers not to purchase wheat have a substantial effect on the price of wheat, just as decisions not to purchase health insurance have on the price of insurance. Congress can therefore command that those not buying wheat do so, just as it argues here that it may command that those not buying health insurance do so. The farmer in *Wickard* was at least actively engaged in the production of wheat, and the Government could regulate that activity because of its effect on commerce. The Government's theory here would effectively override that limitation, by establishing that individuals may be regulated under the Commerce Clause whenever enough of them are not doing something the Government would have them do.

Indeed, the Government's logic would justify a mandatory purchase to solve almost any problem. People, for reasons of their own, often fail to do things that would be good for them or good for society. Those failures—joined with the similar failures of others—can readily have a substantial effect on interstate commerce. Under the Government's logic, that authorizes Congress to use its commerce power to compel citizens to act as the Government would have them act.

That is not the country the Framers of our Constitution envisioned. James Madison explained that the Commerce Clause was "an addition which few oppose and from which no apprehensions are entertained." *The Federalist* No. 45. While Congress's authority under the Commerce Clause has of course expanded with the growth of the national economy, our cases have "always recognized that the power to regulate commerce, though broad indeed, has limits." The Government's theory would erode those limits, permitting Congress to reach beyond the natural extent of its authority, "everywhere extending the sphere of its activity and drawing all power into its impetuous vortex." *The Federalist* No. 48. Accepting the Government's theory would give Congress the same license to regulate what we do not do, fundamentally changing the relation between the citizen and the Federal Government.

The Government argues that because sickness and injury are unpredictable but unavoidable, "the uninsured as a class are active in the market for health care, which they regularly seek and obtain." But an individual who bought a car two years ago and may buy another in the future is not "active in the car market" in any pertinent sense. The phrase "active in the market" cannot obscure the fact that most of those regulated by the individual mandate are not currently engaged in any commercial activity involving health care, and that fact is fatal to the Government's effort to "regulate the uninsured as a class." Our precedents recognize Congress's power to regulate "class[es] of activities," *Gonzales v. Raich* (2005), not classes of individuals, apart from any activity in which they are engaged. The proposition that Congress may dictate the conduct of an individual today because of prophesied future activity finds no support in our precedent.

The Government next contends that Congress has the power under the Necessary and Proper Clause to enact the individual mandate because the mandate is an "integral part of a comprehensive scheme of economic regulation." The power to "make all Laws which shall be necessary and proper for carrying into Execution" the powers enumerated in

the Constitution, Art. I, §8, cl. 18, vests Congress with authority to enact provisions "incidental to the [enumerated] power, and conducive to its beneficial exercise," *McCulloch*. We have been very deferential to Congress's determination that a regulation is "necessary." But we have also carried out our responsibility to declare unconstitutional those laws that undermine the structure of government established by the Constitution. Such laws, which are not "consist[ent] with the letter and spirit of the constitution," *McCulloch*, are not "proper [means] for carrying into Execution" Congress's enumerated powers. Rather, they are, "in the words of *The Federalist*, 'merely acts of usurpation' which 'deserve to be treated as such.'"

Applying these principles, the individual mandate cannot be sustained under the Necessary and Proper Clause as an essential component of the insurance reforms. Each of our prior cases upholding laws under that Clause involved exercises of authority derivative of, and in service to, a granted power. The individual mandate, by contrast, vests Congress with the extraordinary ability to create the necessary predicate to the exercise of an enumerated power. Such a conception of the Necessary and Proper Clause would work a substantial expansion of federal authority. No longer would Congress be limited to regulating under the Commerce Clause those who by some preexisting activity bring themselves within the sphere of federal regulation. Instead, Congress could reach beyond the natural limit of its authority and draw within its regulatory scope those who otherwise would be outside of it. Even if the individual mandate is "necessary" to the Act's insurance reforms, such an expansion of federal power is not a "proper" means for making those reforms effective.

B

That is not the end of the matter. The Government's second argument [is] that the mandate may be upheld as within Congress's enumerated power to "lay and collect Taxes." The Government asks us to read the mandate not as ordering individuals to buy insurance, but rather as imposing a tax on those who do not buy that product.

The text of a statute can sometimes have more than one possible meaning. To take a familiar example, a law that reads "no vehicles in the park" might, or might not, ban bicycles in the park. And it is well established that if a statute has two possible meanings, one of which violates the Constitution, courts should adopt the meaning that does not do so. Under our precedent, it is therefore necessary to ask whether the Government's alternative reading of the statute—that it only imposes a tax on those without insurance—is a reasonable one.

Under the mandate, if an individual does not maintain health insurance, the only consequence is that he must make an additional payment to the IRS when he pays his taxes. That, according to the Government, means the mandate can be regarded as establishing a condition—not owning health insurance—that triggers a tax—the required payment to the IRS. Under that theory, the mandate is not a legal command to buy insurance. Rather, it makes going without insurance just another thing the Government taxes, like buying gasoline or earning income. And if the mandate is in effect just a tax hike on certain taxpayers who do not have health insurance, it may be within Congress's constitutional power to tax.

The exaction the Affordable Care Act imposes on those without health insurance looks like a tax in many respects. The "[s]hared responsibility payment," as the statute entitles it, is paid into the Treasury by "taxpayer[s]" when they file their tax returns. It does not apply to individuals who do not pay federal income taxes because their household income is less than the filing threshold in the Internal Revenue Code. For taxpayers who do owe the payment, its amount is determined by such familiar factors as taxable income, number of dependents, and joint filing status. The requirement to pay is found in the Internal Revenue Code and enforced by the IRS. This process yields the essential feature of any tax: it produces at least some revenue for the Government.

It is of course true that the Act describes the payment as a "penalty," not a "tax." But that does not control whether an exaction is within Congress's constitutional power to tax. Our precedent reflects this: In 1922, we decided two challenges to the "Child Labor Tax" on the same day. In the first, we held that a suit to enjoin collection of the so-called tax was barred by the Anti-Injunction Act. In the second case, however, we held that the same exaction, although labeled a tax, was not in fact authorized by Congress's taxing power. That constitutional question was not controlled by Congress's choice of label. We have similarly held that exactions not labeled taxes nonetheless were authorized by Congress's power to tax.

The same analysis here suggests that the shared responsibility payment may for constitutional purposes be considered a tax, not a penalty. In distinguishing penalties from taxes, this Court has explained that "if the concept of penalty means anything, it means punishment for an unlawful act or omission." *United States v. Reorganized CF&I Fabricators of Utah, Inc.* (1996). While the individual mandate clearly aims to induce the purchase of health insurance, it need not be read to declare that failing to do so is unlawful. Neither the Act nor any other law attaches negative legal consequences to not buying health insurance, beyond requiring a payment to the IRS. The Government agrees with that reading, confirming that if someone chooses to pay rather than obtain health insurance, they have fully complied with the law.

The joint dissenters argue that we cannot uphold §5000A as a tax because Congress did not "frame" it as such. Our precedent demonstrates that Congress had the power to impose the exaction in §5000A under the taxing power, and that §5000A need not be read to do more than impose a tax. That is sufficient to sustain it. The "question of the constitutionality of action taken by Congress does not depend on recitals of the power which it undertakes to exercise." *Woods v. Cloyd W. Miller Co.* (1948). The Affordable Care Act's requirement that certain individuals pay a financial penalty for not obtaining health insurance may reasonably be characterized as a tax. Because the Constitution permits such a tax, it is not our role to forbid it, or to pass upon its wisdom or fairness.

IV

A

The States also contend that the Medicaid expansion exceeds Congress's authority under the Spending Clause. They claim that Congress is coercing the States to adopt the changes it wants by threatening to withhold all of a State's Medicaid grants, unless the State accepts the new expanded funding and complies with the conditions that come with it. This, they argue, violates the basic principle that the "Federal Government may not compel the States to enact or administer a federal regulatory program."

There is no doubt that the Act dramatically increases state obligations under Medicaid. The current Medicaid program requires States to cover only certain discrete categories of needy individuals—pregnant women, children, needy families, the blind, the elderly, and the disabled. The Medicaid provisions of the Affordable Care Act, in contrast, require States to expand their Medicaid programs by 2014 to cover all individuals under the age of 65 with incomes below 133 percent of the federal poverty line. The Act also establishes a new "[e]ssential health benefits" package, which States must provide to all new Medicaid recipients—a level sufficient to satisfy a recipient's obligations under the individual mandate. The Affordable Care Act provides that the Federal Government will pay 100 percent of the costs of covering these newly eligible individuals through 2016. In the following years, the federal payment level gradually decreases, to a minimum of 90 percent.

The Spending Clause grants Congress the power "to pay the Debts and provide for the general Welfare of the United States." We have long recognized that Congress may use this power to grant federal funds to the States, and may condition such a grant upon the States' "taking certain actions that Congress could not require them to take." At the same time, our cases have recognized limits on Congress's power under the Spending Clause to secure state compliance with federal objectives. Congress may use its spending power to create incentives for States to act in accordance with federal policies. But when "pressure turns into compulsion," the legislation runs contrary to our system of federalism. The Constitution simply does not give Congress the authority to require the States to regulate. That is true whether Congress directly commands a State

to regulate or indirectly coerces a State to adopt a federal regulatory system as its own.

The States argue that the Medicaid expansion is far from the typical case. They object that Congress has crossed the line distinguishing encouragement from coercion in the way it has structured the funding: Instead of simply refusing to grant the new funds to States that will not accept the new conditions, Congress has also threatened to withhold those States' existing Medicaid funds. The States claim that this threat serves no purpose other than to force unwilling States to sign up for the dramatic expansion in health care coverage effected by the Act.

Given the nature of the threat and the programs at issue here, we must agree. We have upheld Congress's authority to condition the receipt of funds on the States' complying with restrictions on the use of those funds, because that is the means by which Congress ensures that the funds are spent according to its view of the "general Welfare." Conditions that do not here govern the use of the funds, however, cannot be justified on that basis. When, for example, such conditions take the form of threats to terminate other significant independent grants, the conditions are properly viewed as a means of pressuring the States to accept policy changes.

In this case, the financial "inducement" Congress has chosen is much more than "relatively mild encouragement"—it is a gun to the head. The threatened loss of over 10 percent of a State's overall budget is economic dragooning that leaves the States with no real option but to acquiesce in the Medicaid expansion.

Nothing in our opinion precludes Congress from offering funds under the Affordable Care Act to expand the availability of health care, and requiring that States accepting such funds comply with the conditions on their use. What Congress is not free to do is to penalize States that choose not to participate in that new program by taking away their existing Medicaid funding. Section 1396c gives the Secretary of Health and Human Services the authority to do just that. It allows her to withhold all "further [Medicaid] payments to the State" if she determines that the State is out of compliance with any Medicaid requirement, including those contained in the expansion. In light of the Court's holding, the Secretary cannot apply §1396c to withdraw existing Medicaid funds for failure to comply with the requirements set out in the expansion. That fully remedies the constitutional violation we have identified.

* * *

The Affordable Care Act is constitutional in part and unconstitutional in part. The individual mandate cannot be upheld as an exercise of Congress's power under the Commerce Clause. That Clause authorizes Congress to regulate interstate commerce, not to order individuals to engage in it. In this case, however, it is reasonable to construe what Congress has done as increasing taxes on those who have a certain amount of income, but choose to go without health insurance. Such legislation is within Congress's power to tax.

As for the Medicaid expansion, that portion of the Affordable Care Act violates the Constitution by threatening existing Medicaid funding. Congress has no authority to order the States to regulate according to its instructions. Congress may offer the States grants and require the States to comply with accompanying conditions, but the States must have a genuine choice whether to accept the offer. The States are given no such choice in this case: They must either accept a basic change in the nature of Medicaid, or risk losing all Medicaid funding. The remedy for that constitutional violation is to preclude the Federal Government from imposing such a sanction. That remedy does not require striking down other portions of the Affordable Care Act.

The Framers created a Federal Government of limited powers, and assigned to this Court the duty of enforcing those limits. The Court does so today. But the Court does not express any opinion on the wisdom of the Affordable Care Act. Under the Constitution, that judgment is reserved to the people.

The judgment of the Court of Appeals for the Eleventh Circuit is affirmed in part and reversed in part.

JUSTICE GINSBURG, with whom JUSTICE SOTOMAYOR joins, and with whom JUSTICE BREYER and JUSTICE KAGAN join as to Parts I, II, III, and IV, concurring in part, concurring in the judgment in part, and dissenting in part.

I would hold that the Commerce Clause authorizes Congress to enact the minimum coverage provision. I would also hold that the Spending Clause permits the Medicaid expansion exactly as Congress enacted it.

I

The provision of health care is today a concern of national dimension, just as the provision of old-age and survivors' benefits was in the 1930's. In enacting the Patient Protection and Affordable Care Act (ACA), Congress comprehensively reformed the national market for health-care products and services. By any measure, that market is immense. Collectively, Americans spent $2.5 trillion on health care in 2009, accounting for 17.6% of our Nation's economy. Unlike the market for almost any other product or service, the market for medical care is one in which all individuals inevitably participate. Virtually every person residing in the United States, sooner or later, will visit a doctor or other health-care professional. Most people will do so repeatedly.

When individuals make those visits, they face another reality of the current market for medical care: its high cost. To manage the risks associated with medical care—its high cost, its unpredictability, and its inevitability—most people in the United States obtain health insurance. Not all U. S. residents, however, have health insurance. The large number of individuals without health insurance, Congress found, heavily burdens the national health-care market.

Medical-care providers deliver significant amounts of care to the uninsured for which the providers receive no payment. [They] do not absorb these bad debts. Instead, they raise their prices, passing along the cost of uncompensated care to those who do pay reliably: the government and private insurance companies. In response, private insurers increase their premiums, shifting the cost of the elevated bills from providers onto those who carry insurance. The net result: Those with health insurance subsidize the medical care of those without it. As economists would describe what happens, the uninsured "free ride" on those who pay for health insurance. Congress found that the cost-shifting just described "increases family [insurance] premiums by on average over $1,000 a year."

Aware that a national solution was required, Congress could have taken over the health-insurance market by establishing a tax-and-spend federal program like Social Security. Such a program, commonly referred to as a single-payer system (where the sole payer is the Federal Government), would have left little, if any, room for private enterprise or the States. Instead of going this route, Congress enacted the ACA, a solution that retains a robust role for private insurers and state governments. To make its chosen approach work, however, Congress had to use some new tools, including a requirement that most individuals obtain private health insurance coverage. In sum, Congress passed the minimum coverage provision as a key component of the ACA to address an economic and social problem that has plagued the Nation for decades: the large number of U. S. residents who are unable or unwilling to obtain health insurance. Whatever one thinks of the policy decision Congress made, it was Congress' prerogative to make it. Reviewed with appropriate deference, the minimum coverage provision, allied to the guaranteed-issue and community-rating prescriptions, should survive measurement under the Commerce and Necessary and Proper Clauses.

II

The Commerce Clause "was the Framers' response to the central problem that gave rise to the Constitution itself." *EEOC v. Wyoming* (1983). What was needed was a "national Government armed with a positive & compleat authority in all cases where uniform measures are necessary." See Letter from James Madison to Edmund Randolph (Apr. 8, 1787). The Framers understood that the "general Interests of the Union" would change over time, in ways they could not anticipate. Accordingly, they recognized that the Constitution was of necessity a "great outlin[e]," not a detailed blueprint, see *McCulloch v. Maryland* (1819), and that its provisions included broad concepts, to be "explained by the context or by the facts of the case." Letter from James Madison to N. P. Trist (Dec. 1831). Consistent with the Framers' intent, we have repeatedly emphasized that Congress' authority under the Commerce Clause is dependent upon "practical" considerations, including "actual experience." *Jones & Laughlin Steel Corp.* (1937).

Until today, this Court's pragmatic approach to judging whether Congress validly exercised its commerce power was guided by two familiar principles. First, Congress has the power to regulate economic activities "that substantially affect interstate commerce." *Gonzales v. Raich* (2005). Second, we owe a large measure of respect to Congress when it frames and enacts economic and social legislation. Straightforward application of these principles would require the Court to hold that the minimum coverage provision is proper Commerce Clause legislation. Beyond dispute, Congress had a rational basis for concluding that the uninsured, as a class, substantially affect interstate commerce. The minimum coverage provision, furthermore, bears a "reasonable connection" to Congress' goal of protecting the health-care market from the disruption caused by individuals who fail to obtain insurance. By requiring those who do not carry insurance to pay a toll, the minimum coverage provision gives individuals a strong incentive to insure. This incentive, Congress had good reason to believe, would reduce the number of uninsured and, correspondingly, mitigate the adverse impact the uninsured have on the national health-care market.

Rather than evaluating the constitutionality of the minimum coverage provision in the manner established by our precedents, The Chief Justice relies on a newly minted constitutional doctrine. The commerce power does not, The Chief Justice announces, permit Congress to "compel individuals to become active in commerce by purchasing a product." The Chief Justice's novel constraint on Congress' commerce power gains no force from our precedent and for that reason alone warrants disapprobation. But even assuming, for the moment, that Congress lacks authority under the Commerce Clause to "compel individuals not engaged in commerce to purchase an unwanted product," such a limitation would be inapplicable here. Everyone will, at some point, consume health-care products and services. Thus, if The Chief Justice is correct that an insurance-purchase requirement can be applied only to those who "actively" consume health care, the minimum coverage provision fits the bill.

The Chief Justice does not dispute that all U. S. residents participate in the market for health services over the course of their lives. But, The Chief Justice insists, the uninsured cannot be considered active in the market for health care, because "the proximity and degree of connection between the [uninsured today] and [their] subsequent commercial activity is too lacking." This argument has multiple flaws. First, more than 60% of those without insurance visit a hospital or doctor's office each year. Second, it is Congress' role, not the Court's, to delineate the boundaries of the market the Legislature seeks to regulate. Third, contrary to The Chief Justice's contention, our precedent does indeed support "the proposition that Congress may dictate the conduct of an individual today because of prophesied future activity." Our decisions acknowledge Congress' authority, under the Commerce Clause, to direct the conduct of an individual today (the farmer in *Wickard,* stopped from growing excess wheat; the plaintiff in *Raich,* ordered to cease cultivating marijuana) because of a prophesied future transaction (the eventual sale of that wheat or marijuana in the interstate market). Congress' actions are even more rational in this case, where the future activity (the consumption of medical care) is certain to occur, the sole uncertainty being the time the activity will take place.

Underlying The Chief Justice's view that the Commerce Clause must be confined to the regulation of active participants in a commercial market is a fear that the commerce power would otherwise know no limits. The joint dissenters express a similar apprehension. This concern is unfounded. First, The Chief Justice could certainly uphold the individual mandate without giving Congress carte blanche to enact any and all purchase mandates. The unique attributes of the health-care market render everyone active in that market and give rise to a significant free-riding problem that does not occur in other markets. Nor would the commerce power be unbridled, absent The Chief Justice's "activity" limitation. Congress would

remain unable to regulate noneconomic conduct that has only an attenuated effect on interstate commerce and is traditionally left to state law.

Other provisions of the Constitution also check congressional overreaching. A mandate to purchase a particular product would be unconstitutional if, for example, the edict impermissibly abridged the freedom of speech, interfered with the free exercise of religion, or infringed on a liberty interest protected by the Due Process Clause. Supplementing these legal restraints is a formidable check on congressional power: the democratic process. As the controversy surrounding the passage of the Affordable Care Act attests, purchase mandates are likely to engender political resistance.

III

Asserting that the Necessary and Proper Clause does not authorize the minimum coverage provision, The Chief Justice focuses on the word "proper." A mandate to purchase health insurance is not "proper" legislation, The Chief Justice urges, because the command "undermines the structure of government established by the Constitution." If long on rhetoric, The Chief Justice's argument is short on substance. The Chief Justice cites only two cases in which this Court concluded that a federal statute impermissibly transgressed the Constitution's boundary between state and federal authority: *Printz v. United States* (1997) and *New York v. United States* (1992). The statutes at issue in both cases, however, compelled state officials to act on the Federal Government's behalf. The minimum coverage provision, in contrast, acts "directly upon individuals, without employing the States as intermediaries." *New York.* The provision is thus entirely consistent with the Constitution's design.

V

Through Medicaid, Congress has offered the States an opportunity to furnish health care to the poor with the aid of federal financing. To receive federal Medicaid funds, States must provide health benefits to specified categories of needy persons, including pregnant women, children, parents, and adults with disabilities. The spending power conferred by the Constitution, the Court has never doubted, permits Congress to define the contours of programs financed with federal funds.

The Chief Justice acknowledges that Congress may "condition the receipt of federal funds on the States' complying with restrictions on the use of those funds," but nevertheless concludes that the 2010 expansion is unduly coercive. His conclusion rests on three premises, each of them essential to his theory. First, the Medicaid expansion is, in The Chief Justice's view, a new grant program, not an addition to the Medicaid program existing before the ACA's enactment. Congress, The Chief Justice maintains, has threatened States with the loss of funds from an old program in an effort to get them to adopt a new one. Second, the expansion was unforeseeable by the States when they first signed on to Medicaid. Third, the threatened loss of funding is so large that the States have no real choice but to participate in the Medicaid expansion. The Chief Justice therefore—for the first time ever—finds an exercise of Congress' spending power unconstitutionally coercive.

Medicaid, as amended by the ACA, however, is not two spending programs; it is a single program with a constant aim—to enable poor persons to receive basic health care when they need it. Given past expansions, plus express statutory warning that Congress may change the requirements participating States must meet, there can be no tenable claim that the ACA fails for lack of notice. Moreover, States have no entitlement to receive any Medicaid funds; they enjoy only the opportunity to accept funds on Congress' terms. Future Congresses are not bound by their predecessors' dispositions; they have authority to spend federal revenue as they see fit. The Federal Government, therefore, is not, as The Chief Justice charges, threatening States with the loss of "existing" funds from one spending program in order to induce them to opt into another program. Congress is simply requiring States to do what States have long been required to do to receive Medicaid funding: comply with the conditions Congress prescribes for participation.

The alternative to conditional federal spending, it bears emphasis, is not state autonomy but state marginalization. In 1965, Congress elected to nationalize health coverage for seniors through Medicare. It could similarly have established Medicaid as an exclusively federal program. Instead, Congress gave the States the opportunity to partner in the program's administration and development. Absent from the nationalized model, of course, is the state-level policy discretion and experimentation that is Medicaid's hallmark; undoubtedly the interests of federalism are better served when States retain a meaningful role in the implementation of a program of such importance.

The Chief Justice ultimately asks whether "the financial inducement offered by Congress passed the point at which pressure turns into compulsion." The financial inducement Congress employed here, he concludes, crosses that threshold: The threatened withholding of "existing Medicaid funds" is "a gun to the head" that forces States to acquiesce.

The Chief Justice sees no need to "fix the outermost line where persuasion gives way to coercion." When future Spending Clause challenges arrive, as they likely will in the wake of today's decision, how will litigants and judges assess whether "a State has a legitimate choice whether to accept the federal conditions in exchange for federal funds"? Are courts to measure the number of dollars the Federal Government might withhold for noncompliance? The portion of the State's budget at stake? And which State's—or States'—budget is determinative? Does it matter that Florida, unlike most States, imposes no state income tax, and therefore might be able to replace foregone federal funds with new state revenue? Or that the coercion state officials in fact fear is punishment at the ballot box for turning down a politically popular federal grant? The coercion inquiry, therefore, appears to involve political judgments that defy judicial calculation.

At bottom, my colleagues' position is that the States' reliance on federal funds limits Congress' authority to alter its spending programs. This gets things backwards: Congress, not the States, is tasked with spending federal money in service of the general welfare. And each successive Congress is empowered to appropriate funds as it sees fit. When the 110th Congress reached a conclusion about Medicaid funds that differed from its predecessors' view, it abridged no State's right to "existing," or "pre-existing," funds. For, in fact, there are no such funds. There is only money States anticipate receiving from future Congresses.

JUSTICE SCALIA, JUSTICE KENNEDY, JUSTICE THOMAS, and JUSTICE ALITO, dissenting.

Congress has set out to remedy the problem that the best health care is beyond the reach of many Americans who cannot afford it. It can assuredly do that, by exercising the powers accorded to it under the Constitution. The question in this case, however, is whether the complex structures and provisions of the Patient Protection and Affordable Care Act (Affordable Care Act or ACA) go beyond those powers. We conclude that they do.

This case is in one respect difficult: it presents two questions of first impression. The first of those is whether failure to engage in economic activity (the purchase of health insurance) is subject to regulation under the Commerce Clause. Failure to act does result in an effect on commerce, and hence might be said to come under this Court's "affecting commerce" criterion of Commerce Clause jurisprudence. But in none of its decisions has this Court extended the Clause that far. The second question is whether the congressional power to tax and spend, U. S. Const., Art. I, §8, cl. 1, permits the conditioning of a State's continued receipt of all funds under a massive state-administered federal welfare program upon its acceptance of an expansion to that program. Several of our opinions have suggested that the power to tax and spend cannot be used to coerce state administration of a federal program, but we have never found a law enacted under the spending power to be coercive. Those questions are difficult.

The case is easy and straightforward, however, in another respect. What is absolutely clear, affirmed by the text of the 1789 Constitution, by the Tenth Amendment ratified in 1791, and by innumerable cases of ours in the 220 years since, is that there are structural limits upon federal power—upon what it can prescribe with respect to private conduct, and upon what it can impose upon the sovereign States. Whatever may be the conceptual limits

upon the Commerce Clause and upon the power to tax and spend, they cannot be such as will enable the Federal Government to regulate all private conduct and to compel the States to function as administrators of federal programs.

That clear principle carries the day here. *Wickard v. Filburn* (1942) held that the economic activity of growing wheat, even for one's own consumption, affected commerce sufficiently that it could be regulated, always has been regarded as the *ne plus ultra* of expansive Commerce Clause jurisprudence. To go beyond that, and to say the failure to grow wheat (which is not an economic activity, or any activity at all) nonetheless affects commerce and therefore can be federally regulated, is to make mere breathing in and out the basis for federal prescription and to extend federal power to virtually all human activity.

As for the constitutional power to tax and spend for the general welfare: The Court has long since expanded that beyond (what Madison thought it meant) taxing and spending for those aspects of the general welfare that were within the Federal Government's enumerated powers. Thus, we now have sizable federal Departments devoted to subjects not mentioned among Congress' enumerated powers, and only marginally related to commerce: the Department of Education, the Department of Health and Human Services, the Department of Housing and Urban Development. The principal practical obstacle that prevents Congress from using the tax-and-spend power to assume all the general-welfare responsibilities traditionally exercised by the States is the sheer impossibility of managing a Federal Government large enough to administer such a system. That obstacle can be overcome by granting funds to the States, allowing them to administer the program. That is fair and constitutional enough when the States freely agree to have their powers employed and their employees enlisted in the federal scheme. But it is a blatant violation of the constitutional structure when the States have no choice.

The Act before us here exceeds federal power both in mandating the purchase of health insurance and in denying nonconsenting States all Medicaid funding. These parts of the Act are central to its design and operation, and all the Act's other provisions would not have been enacted without them. In our view it must follow that the entire statute is inoperative.

I

[*The opinion first argues that the individual mandate exceeds congressional power under the Commerce and Necessary and Proper Clauses. It then turns to the government's claim that the individual mandate is "independently authorized" by the federal taxing power.*]

The phrase "independently authorized" suggests the existence of a creature never hitherto seen in the United States Reports: A penalty for constitutional purposes that is also a tax for constitutional purposes. The two are mutually exclusive. It is important to bear this in mind in evaluating the tax argument of the Government and of those who support it: The issue is not whether Congress had the power to frame the minimum-coverage provision as a tax, but whether it did so.

Our cases establish a clear line between a tax and a penalty: "A tax is an enforced contribution to provide for the support of government; a penalty is an exaction imposed by statute as punishment for an unlawful act." *United States v. Reorganized CF&I Fabricators of Utah, Inc.* (1996). In a few cases, this Court has held that a "tax" imposed upon private conduct was so onerous as to be in effect a penalty. But we have never held—never—that a penalty imposed for violation of the law was so trivial as to be in effect a tax. We have never held that any exaction imposed for violation of the law is an exercise of Congress' taxing power—even when the statute calls it a tax, much less when (as here) the statute repeatedly calls it a penalty. When an act "adopts the criteria of wrongdoing" and then imposes a monetary penalty as the "principal consequence on those who transgress its standard," it creates a regulatory penalty, not a tax. *Child Labor Tax Case* (1922).

So the question is, quite simply, whether the exaction here is imposed for violation of the law. It unquestionably is. The minimum-coverage provision is found in 26 U. S. C. §5000A, entitled "Requirement to maintain minimum essential coverage." It commands that every "applicable individual shall ensure that the individual is covered under minimum essential coverage." And the immediately following provision states that, "if an applicable individual fails to meet the requirement of subsection (a), there is hereby imposed a penalty." And several of Congress' legislative "findings" with regard to §5000A confirm that it sets forth a legal requirement and constitutes the assertion of regulatory power, not mere taxing power.

In the face of all these indications of a regulatory requirement accompanied by a penalty, the Solicitor General assures us that "neither the Treasury Department nor the Department of Health and Human Services interprets Section 5000A as imposing a legal obligation," and that "if [those subject to the act] pay the tax penalty, they're in compliance with the law." These self-serving litigating positions are entitled to no weight. What counts is what the statute says, and that is entirely clear. The nail in the coffin is that the mandate and penalty are located in Title I of the Act, its operative core, rather than where a tax would be found—in Title IX, containing the Act's "Revenue Provisions." In sum, "the terms of the act render it unavoidable," *Parsons v. Bedford* (1830), that Congress imposed a regulatory penalty, not a tax.

For all these reasons, to say that the Individual Mandate merely imposes a tax is not to interpret the statute but to rewrite it. Judicial tax-writing is particularly troubling. We have no doubt that Congress knew precisely what it was doing when it rejected an earlier version of this legislation that imposed a tax instead of a requirement-with-penalty. Imposing a tax through judicial legislation inverts the constitutional scheme, and places the power to tax in the branch of government least accountable to the citizenry.

9

The Exercise of State Power

CHAPTER OUTLINE

A paramount development in American constitutional history has been the expansion of the power of the federal government. This process has been aided by the Supreme Court's broad interpretation of the powers granted to Congress and by constitutional amendments—especially the Fourteenth, Fifteenth, and Sixteenth Amendments—that have conferred additional powers on Congress. Although the Tenth Amendment provides that the states retain those powers not delegated to the federal government, the areas of exclusive state control have progressively narrowed. And as the federal government has come to regulate areas traditionally dominated by the states, collisions between state and federal claims of authority have increased.

CONSTITUTIONAL PRINCIPLES

Alexander Hamilton observed in *The Federalist,* No. 32, that "the State governments would clearly retain all the rights of sovereignty which they before had, and which were not, by the ratification of the Constitution *exclusively* delegated to the United States." This statement suggests that the powers delegated to the federal government can be divided into three categories: exclusive powers, which cannot be exercised by the states; concurrent powers, whose delegation to the federal government does not restrict state power; and powers that are neither altogether exclusive nor altogether concurrent, whose delegation to the federal government limits but does not completely preclude their exercise by the states.

The Constitution grants exclusive authority to the federal government in various ways. Some powers, such as jurisdiction over the seat of government (Washington, DC), are expressly identified as exclusive (Article I, Section 8). Others are both granted to the federal government and denied to the states: for example, the Constitution both authorizes the president to make treaties, with the advice and consent of the Senate (Article II, Section 2), and forbids the states to make them (Article I, Section 10). Finally, some powers granted to the federal government, such as the power to declare war (Article I, Section 8), are by their very nature exclusive and thus cannot be exercised by the states.

In granting yet other powers to the federal government, the Constitution neither expressly nor implicitly precludes state legislation. An example of these concurrent powers is the power to tax. Under the Supremacy Clause (Article VI, Section 2), enactments of the states under their concurrent powers might still be unconstitutional, if they conflict with federal legislation. In this way, the vigorous exercise of federal power can diminish state power. In the absence of conflicting federal legislation, however, the states remain free to exercise their concurrent powers.

Finally, some constitutional grants of power are neither wholly exclusive nor wholly concurrent. If the states exercised these powers to the fullest possible extent, the federal government would be prevented from achieving the ends for which the powers were granted to it. Elimination of all state authority, on the other hand, would imperil legitimate state objectives. By far the most important of the powers that fall into this category is the commerce power. In the words of constitutional scholar Thomas Reed Powell, "Congress may regulate interstate commerce. The states may also regulate interstate commerce, but not too much."[1] The responsibility for deciding what constitutes "too much" has fallen largely to the Supreme Court, which has heard hundreds of cases involving the validity of state regulations affecting interstate commerce.

PREEMPTION

Since the early 1930s, the federal government has entered a variety of policy areas—for example, environmental protection, race relations, and consumer protection—that had previously been predominantly state concerns. This expansion of federal power does not always produce conflict, because federal and state policies are often complementary. When federal and state policies collide, however, the Supremacy Clause (Article VI, Section 2) mandates that federal policy prevail. The process by which valid federal statutes, treaties, and administrative regulations supersede inconsistent state laws is known as *preemption*.

Federal preemption of state law has reached unprecedented levels in recent decades. According to one study, of the 522 congressional enactments from 1789 to 2004 that indicated an intention to preempt state laws, 356 were enacted since 1965.[2] Yet congressional statutes can affect state power even without an express reference to preemption. In such circumstances, the Court might review congressional hearings and floor debates to determine Congress's intention. But if Congress did not consider the effect of its action on state laws, such a search is fruitless, and the Court then must consider, as noted in *Hines v. Davidowitz* (1940), "whether the state action stands as an obstacle to the accomplishment and execution of the full purposes and objectives of Congress." In doing so, the Court examines (1) whether the state regulations conflict with federal requirements, (2) whether the pervasiveness of federal regulation signals an intention to "occupy the field" and exclude state regulation, and (3) whether the state regulations, although not directly in conflict with federal law, nevertheless might frustrate the purposes of that law.

Although these criteria guide its decisions, the Court must analyze preemption claims on a case-by-case basis. As the Supreme Court noted in *Rice v. Santa Fe Elevator Company* (1947), "The historic police powers of the States [are] not to be superseded by the Federal Act unless that [is] the clear and manifest purpose of Congress." In practice, however, the Court has not always honored this presumption against preemption. From 1940, when it ruled in *Hines v. Davidowitz* that congressional legislation precluded state registration of aliens, through the late 1960s, the Court tended to assume the incompatibility of state law with federal initiatives. The Burger Court (1969–1986) was more reluctant to infer preemption in the absence of clear direction from Congress. In *Pacific Gas & Electric Company v. State Energy Resources & Development Commission* (1983), for example, it ruled that although the national government under the Federal Atomic Energy Act had occupied the field of nuclear safety, California's moratorium on the construction of new nuclear power plants could be upheld as an economic regulation. And in *Silkwood v. Kerr-McGee Corporation* (1984), it also upheld a state-authorized award of punitive damages for conduct that created nuclear hazards, because Congress had not intended to preclude states from providing remedies for those suffering injuries from radiation in a nuclear plant. This approach to preemption protected the legitimate concerns of both the state and the federal governments. Whereas the Court's refusal to infer preemption of state laws maximized the exercise of state power, federal concerns were protected, because Congress could override Court rulings by clarifying its preemptive intent. Thus, Congress, rather than the Court, had the final responsibility for maintaining the federal balance.

The Rehnquist Court (1986–2005) reversed the presumption against preemption of state laws. This is reflected in rulings invalidating state laws that touched on foreign affairs (e.g., *Crosby v. National Foreign Trade Council* [2000] and *American Insurance Association v. Garamendi* [2003]). It is also evident in rulings blocking on preemption grounds claims against tobacco companies under state law (*Cipollone v. Liggett Group* [1992]), state laws regulating the display of cigarette advertisements (*Lorillard Tobacco Co. v. Reilly* [2001]), and remedies under state law for design defects in automobiles (*Geier v. American Honda*

Motor Company [2000]). Like the Rehnquist Court, the Roberts Court (2005–) has been quite willing to strike down state laws on preemption grounds. For example, it has limited the power of states to tax the out-of-state activities of a multistate company (*MeadWestvaco Corporation v. Illinois Department of Revenue* [2008]) and ruled that federal law superseded a state law regulating the treatment of animals at slaughterhouses (*National Meat Association v. Harris* [2012]). However, in *Wyeth v. Levine* (2009), the Court held that the Federal Drug Administration's approval of a drug did not preempt litigants from pursuing claims against drug companies under state law for failure to warn of the drug's potential dangers; and in *Oneok, Inc. v. Lear Jet, Inc.* (2015), it held that the federal Natural Gas Act did not preclude lawsuits under state antitrust laws.

As these examples suggest, preemption issues typically involve state laws regulating economic activity. But not always. Distressed by what they perceived as a failure to enforce federal immigration laws, several states and localities in recent years have acted to combat illegal immigration. In *Arizona v. United States* (2012), the Supreme Court considered a challenge to four provisions of an Arizona law targeting illegal immigrants. Section 3 of the Arizona law made it a misdemeanor to fail to comply with federal alien-registration requirements. Section 5 made it a misdemeanor for an illegal immigrant to seek or engage in work in the state. Section 6 authorized state officers to arrest without a warrant a person "the officer has probable cause to believe has committed any public offense that makes the person removable from the United States." And Section 2(B) provided that officers who conduct a stop, detention, or arrest must in some circumstances seek to verify the person's immigration status with the federal government. Of these only the last survived constitutional scrutiny.

Writing for a five-member majority, Justice Anthony Kennedy emphasized that "the Government of the United States has broad, undoubted power over the subject of immigration and the regulation of aliens" and that "the federal power to determine immigration policy is well settled." The Court struck down Section 3 on the ground that Congress had occupied the field of immigrant registration, barring states from legislating on the topic. It invalidated Section 5 because it conflicted with Congress's decision to penalize employers who hired illegal workers but not the workers themselves. In striking down Section 6, the Court highlighted the federal government's enforcement discretion, noting that it may decide not to prosecute immigration violations based on "immediate human concerns" such as the existence of US citizen children or immigrants' longtime residence in the United States. Underlying the Court's argument for federal primacy over immigration were the federal responsibility for the conduct of foreign relations and concerns that "mistreatment of aliens in the United States" under state law might lead to reciprocal mistreatment of Americans abroad.

In his dissent, Justice Antonin Scalia challenged the majority's claim of federal primacy, arguing that the Framers of the Constitution recognized that the states exercised sovereign power over immigration. He denied that "the sovereign states [are] at the mercy of the Federal Executive's refusal to enforce the Nation's immigration laws" and insisted that Arizona has the power to adopt laws designed to protect its citizens and lawful residents from the threat to life and property caused by the influx of illegal immigration and cross-border drug trafficking.

The Court unanimously upheld the Arizona provision authorizing state police to check the immigration status of persons stopped, detained, or arrested if there was reasonable suspicion that they were in the country illegally. It concluded that there were adequate safeguards in place, including the law's ban on racial profiling, which saved it from being invalidated on its face. However, the Court majority left the door open to future claims challenging how the law was applied, noting that "this opinion does not foreclose other preemption and constitutional challenges to the law as interpreted and applied after it goes into effect."

NEGATIVE IMPLICATIONS OF THE COMMERCE CLAUSE

When preemption is not an issue, state laws can violate the Constitution by invading the powers granted to the federal government. In this respect, the Commerce Clause is particularly important. The Framers gave Congress the power to regulate commerce in order to promote economic prosperity throughout the nation, and, as Justice Robert Jackson observed in *H. P. Hood & Sons v. DuMond* (1949), accomplishment of this aim demands some exclusivity of regulation: "Our system, fostered by the Commerce Clause, is that every farmer and every craftsman shall be encouraged by the certainty that he will have free access to every market in the Nation, that no home embargoes will withhold his exports, and no foreign state will by customs duties or regulations exclude them. Likewise, every consumer may look to the free competition from every producing area in the Nation to protect him from exploitation by any."

On the other hand, the states have traditionally exercised considerable power over commerce, not only by regulating commerce for commercial purposes but also by taxing interstate commerce to raise revenue and by enacting "police power" regulations to protect the health, safety, welfare, and morals of the state population. If the Commerce Clause foreclosed all such regulation, the states would be deprived of much of their governing authority.

During the nineteenth century, the Supreme Court was called upon to render several important decisions concerning how the federal commerce power affected state authority to regulate commerce, tax commercial activities, and enforce police-power regulations. Two questions were of particular concern: Was the grant of power to Congress an exclusive mandate that precluded all state regulation? And if not, what standards should govern the exercise of state power over commerce?

The Exclusivity Issue

The case for exclusivity is presented in the dormant-power theory, which suggests that by granting Congress the power to regulate commerce among the several states, the Constitution implicitly prohibited state regulation of that commerce. The scope of state power over commerce, accordingly, could be defined by subtraction: the states can regulate only those commercial transactions that Congress cannot regulate. With the expansion of federal regulatory power during the twentieth century, this theory would virtually eliminate state power over commerce.

The most persuasive argument for this theory was offered by Justice William Johnson in his concurring opinion in *Gibbons v. Ogden* (1824) (see Chapter 8). According to Johnson, economic warfare among the states during the Confederation period was a major concern of the Framers, who attempted to eliminate state barriers to the flow of commerce by vesting exclusive regulatory authority in Congress. If a state enactment conflicts with a congressional regulation, the congressional policy necessarily prevails. But even in failing to regulate, Congress makes a policy choice, for it indicates thereby that commerce should not be regulated. To allow state regulation when Congress fails to act, therefore, would frustrate congressional policy as surely as would permitting state regulations that are inconsistent with congressional action.

Chief Justice John Marshall acknowledged in *Gibbons* that "there is great force in the argument, and the Court is not satisfied that it has been refuted." But adoption of the dormant-power theory, when joined with Marshall's expansive definition of the commerce power, would have stripped the states of much of their traditional regulatory authority. Perhaps for this reason, Marshall twice sidestepped the issue: in *Gibbons*, by concluding that the New York law involved was preempted by congressional legislation; and in *Willson v. Black Bird Creek Marsh Company* (1829), by asserting that the Delaware law authorizing a dam across a navigable stream was an exercise of the police power rather than a regulation of commerce. Some members of the Court majority in *The License Cases* (1847) endorsed the dormant-power theory, but in *Cooley v. Board of Wardens* (1852), the Court decisively rejected it.

Doing so, however, left important questions unanswered. If the federal commerce power does not foreclose all state regulation, does it foreclose any? And if it does, how does one determine the validity of state enactments? To understand how the Court answered these questions, one must return to *Gibbons*. In arguing for the validity of New York's regulation of ferry service in *Gibbons,* the counsel for Ogden maintained that federal and state powers over commerce were altogether concurrent: that is, in conferring the commerce power on Congress, the Constitution did not thereby withdraw any field of endeavor from state regulation. In this respect, the commerce power was analogous to the taxing power: just as the grant to Congress of the power to tax did not interfere with the states' taxing power, the power granted in the Commerce Clause did not limit the states' regulatory authority. Thus, state laws would be invalid only if they conflicted with congressional legislation.

Chief Justice Marshall persuasively disposed of the concurrent-power theory in his opinion in *Gibbons*. The commerce power is not analogous to the taxing power, he noted, since it is not "in its own nature capable of residing in, and being exercised by, different authorities at the same time." In regulating commerce, a state "is exercising the very power that is granted to Congress, and is doing the very thing which Congress is authorized to do." Accordingly, the constitutional grant of power to Congress, by its own force and in the absence of congressional legislation, precludes some state regulations.

Another interpretation of state regulatory authority was provided by the mutual-exclusiveness theory, championed by Thomas Jefferson and other proponents of state power. According to this theory, the Constitution, although conferring the commerce power on Congress, left the states free to exercise the police power—the power to protect the health, safety, welfare, and morals of their citizens. It thereby established separate spheres for state and federal activity, and neither government could trespass on the other's domain. These spheres were distinguished not by what was regulated—state and federal laws might touch the same activities—but by the ends served by regulation. Because the police power resided in the states, then, the validity of a state regulation affecting commerce depended upon whether the regulatory act served legitimate police-power ends.

The Search for a Standard

In his opinions in *Gibbons* and *Black Bird,* Marshall neither endorsed nor rejected the mutual-exclusiveness theory. On the one hand, he recognized that the states had not surrendered all power to enact legislation that affected commerce. He acknowledged in *Gibbons* that the states could enact "inspection laws, quarantine laws, health laws of every description, as well as laws for regulating the internal commerce of the state, and those which respect turnpike-roads, ferries, etc." And in *Black Bird,* he ruled that a state law authorizing the damming of a navigable stream constituted a valid exercise of the police power rather than a regulation of commerce. On the other hand, Marshall also recognized in *Black Bird* that even state legislation that served valid state ends might be "repugnant to the power to regulate commerce in its dormant state, or in conflict with a law passed on the subject." So although states in the exercise of their police power could enact laws that affected commerce, state laws could be struck down if they infringed on the field of regulation that the Commerce Clause reserved to the federal government.

The search for an appropriate standard governing state regulation of commerce ended in *Cooley,* in which the Court adopted the selective-exclusiveness theory. Speaking for the Court, Justice Benjamin Curtis noted that, because the Constitution does not expressly bar state regulation of commerce, such regulations are valid unless "the nature of the power, thus granted to Congress, requires a similar authority should not exist in the states." Whether such a requirement exists can be determined only by examining the nature of the subjects to be regulated. According to Curtis, previous theories upholding or denying state regulatory power were inadequate because no simple standard could take into account the diversity of the subjects to be regulated. Having thus disposed of the dormant-power and concurrent-power theories, he proposed a different approach: "Now the power to regulate commerce, embraces a vast field, containing not only many, but exceedingly various subjects, quite unlike in their nature; some imperatively demanding a single uniform rule, operating equally on the commerce of the United States in every port; and some like the subject now in question, as imperatively demanding that diversity which alone can meet the local necessities of navigation."

By directing attention to the particular factual situation in each case rather than to the nature of national and state power, the *Cooley* standard marked a major advance in Commerce Clause analysis. Exactly how the standard should be applied, however, is not always clear. For one thing, most subjects, rather than demanding federal or state regulation, could "admit of" either. In addition, states might regulate a subject for either legitimate or illegitimate purposes. In *Dean Milk Company v. City of Madison* (1951), for example, the Court observed that a state could regulate milk sold in the state to protect the health of residents but it could not do so to protect its dairy industry from competition. In cases involving state regulations, therefore, the Court has undertaken to balance the national interest in uniformity against the interests served by state regulation.

STATE REGULATION AND THE MODERN COURT

In determining the validity of state regulations that affect interstate commerce, the contemporary Supreme Court's approach in many ways resembles the selective-exclusiveness standard announced in *Cooley*. State regulations that serve no valid purpose or that unduly impede interstate commerce are struck down. But those that serve important state interests and minimally burden commerce are upheld. In determining whether the benefits of state regulation outweigh the burdens on interstate commerce, the Court employs a balancing test.

Discrimination against Interstate Commerce

The Supreme Court has consistently struck down state laws designed to shield local businesses from interstate competition. Such economic protectionism defeats the very purpose of the Commerce Clause—the creation of "a federal free trade unit"—and encourages retaliatory state laws reminiscent of the Confederation period. In *South-Central Timber Development, Inc. v. Wunnicke* (1984), for example, the Court invalidated an Alaska law requiring that timber taken from state lands be processed before being shipped out of state—a measure designed to aid the state's fledgling timber-processing industry. In *Edwards v. California* (1941), it struck down a California law prohibiting any person from knowingly bringing nonresident indigents into the state, ruling that the measure had been designed in part to limit competition for jobs.[3] And despite the Twenty-First Amendment's grant of power to states to regulate the transportation or importation of alcoholic beverages, the Court in *Granholm v. Heald* (2005) invalidated Michigan and New York statutes that prohibited out-of-state wineries from shipping directly to consumers.

A difficult problem is posed by state statutes that discriminate against interstate commerce but that also (at least arguably) serve legitimate state interests. Examples have been plentiful. In *City of Philadelphia v. New Jersey* (1978), a New Jersey statute prohibited the importation of out-of-state wastes, largely for environmental and health reasons. In *Dean Milk Company v. City of Madison,* the municipal ordinance purportedly safeguarded local health by limiting the sale of milk unless it was processed and bottled in an approved plant within five miles of the city's central square. And in *Camps Newfound/Owatonna v. Town of Harrison* (1997), Maine limited its tax exemption to charitable institutions serving state residents, in order to compensate or subsidize those organizations dispensing public benefits the state might otherwise provide. In each case, the Court struck down the challenged legislation, ruling that a legitimate state objective is not enough. When a state law impedes the flow of interstate commerce, the Court indicated, it will be upheld only when it serves a particularly important state end that cannot be achieved by nondiscriminatory legislation. Few state enactments can survive such scrutiny.

The difficulty of the Court's task is illustrated by the recent case of *Comptroller of the Treasury of Maryland v. Wynne* (2015). Maryland imposes both a state income tax and a county income tax. Nonresidents who earn income from sources within Maryland must pay the state income tax. Maryland residents who pay income tax to another state for income earned in that state are allowed a credit against their state income tax bill, but they are still obliged to pay the county income tax on that income. In essence, then, they are taxed twice on that income, whereas they only pay income tax once on income earned within the state. The issue in *Wynne* was whether this double taxation discouraged Maryland residents from engaging in interstate commerce, in violation of the dormant commerce clause. Justice Samuel Alito, speaking for a five-member Court majority, concluded that it did, and he therefore struck down the system of double taxation as discrimination against interstate commerce. In dissent, Justice Ruth Bader Ginsburg argued that states retain the power to tax income regardless of the source from which it is obtained and that that power is not affected by the fact that other states may likewise tax that income or may give tax credits to their residents for income earned out-of-state. Two dissenters—Justices Antonin Scalia and Clarence Thomas—went considerably further, rejecting the very idea of a dormant commerce clause that limited state regulation. Indeed, Justice Scalia denounced it as "a judicial fraud."

Burdens on Commerce

Nondiscriminatory state regulations may also impose diverse requirements that tend to make interstate commerce less convenient and more expensive. The Supreme Court nonetheless has upheld such regulations unless they unduly interfere with interstate commerce. Each case has required the Court to examine the operation of the state law and to balance the benefits it produces against the burden it imposes on interstate commerce.

The Court's case-by-case approach to this issue is reflected in several decisions concerning interstate transportation. Whereas in *Missouri Pacific Company v. Norwood* (1931) the Court upheld state legislation requiring "full-crews" on trains, in *Southern Pacific Company v. Arizona* (1945) it struck down a law restricting the length of trains traveling through Arizona. These divergent rulings reflected the differing operation of the statutes. The train-length law produced negligible safety gains but posed a major obstacle to the flow of interstate train traffic. The "full-crew" laws, on the other hand, had demonstrable safety benefits and did not significantly interfere with interstate transportation.

Similar considerations have governed the Court's treatment of state laws dealing with highway safety. Although such laws burden interstate commerce, particularly when adjoining states impose different requirements, the Court has upheld state regulations that effectively promote highway safety and do not place interstate commerce at a competitive disadvantage. In *South Carolina Highway Department v. Barnwell Brothers, Inc.* (1938), for example, it upheld a South Carolina law that imposed weight and width limitations on trucks operating on state roads. When the safety benefits are negligible, however, the Court has struck down the state legislation. In *Raymond Motor Transportation, Inc. v. Rice* (1978), for example, it invalidated a Wisconsin law that imposed a fifty-five-foot-length limitation on trucks and prohibited double-trailer trucks. The aim of the law was valid, the Court acknowledged, but it imposed a substantial burden on interstate commerce, and Wisconsin had offered no evidence supporting the safety benefits of the limitations. Similarly, in *Kassel v. Consolidated Freightways Corporation* (1981), the justices struck down an Iowa truck-length law, endorsing the trial court's conclusion that the state's safety evidence was unpersuasive.

THE ROLE OF THE COURT

The Supreme Court's balancing of federal and state interests in Commerce Clause cases has been questioned by several justices, most recently, Justices Antonin Scalia and Clarence Thomas, as shown in *Comptroller of the Treasury of Maryland v. Wynne*. They complain that such balancing involves the Court in making policy judgments that Congress and state legislatures are more qualified to make. Moreover, this sort of judicial intervention responsibility is not mandated by the Constitution, as the text of the Commerce Clause addresses federal, not state, regulation. They thus favor a much narrower role for the Court. As long as a state does not discriminate against interstate commerce in order to advantage in-state economic interests, it should be allowed to determine how heavily commerce should be regulated and whether particular regulations effectively promote health and safety. If the regulations impose too heavy a burden on interstate commerce, Congress can always intervene to remedy the situation.[4]

Other justices—most eloquently, Justice Robert Jackson—have defended the Court's traditional approach. The question, they insist, is not one of competence but one of responsibility. More specifically, the Court's responsibility to enforce the Constitution includes enforcement of the negative implications of the Commerce Clause. Furthermore, they point out, Congress lacks the time to oversee the multitude of state regulations that, although of limited importance individually, collectively can pose a serious barrier to interstate commerce and threaten the national common market the Framers sought to create. As Justice Oliver Wendell Holmes argued: "I do not think the United States would come to an end if we lost our power to declare an Act of Congress void. I do think the Union would be imperiled if we could not make that declaration as to the laws of the several States. For one in my place sees how often a local policy prevails with those who are not trained to national views and how often action is taken that embodies what the Commerce Clause was meant to end."[5]

Although the Court has accepted this viewpoint, the more basic concern raised by Justices Scalia and Thomas remains valid. By dividing governing authority between nation and state, the Constitution created a potential for conflict between the levels of government. When state enactments are challenged as inconsistent with the Constitution or federal law, the Court must consider both the aims of the Union and the legitimate regulatory concerns of the states. The sensitivity of the Court's treatment of these valid but competing claims can affect substantially the role that the states play in governing.

NOTES

1. Thomas Reed Powell, *Vagaries and Varieties in Constitutional Interpretation* (New York: Columbia University Press, 1956), ix.

2. Joseph F. Zimmerman, "The Nature and Political Significance of Preemption," *PS: Political Science and Politics* 38 (July 2005): 361.

3. Four justices would have struck down the law as a violation of the Privileges and Immunities Clause of the Fourteenth Amendment. In *Hicklin v. Orbeck* (1978), the Court struck down an "Alaska Hire" law on that basis.

4. Even if the Court declares a state law unconstitutional, Congress can override the Court's ruling and legitimize the regulation. This paradoxical situation is a natural consequence of the congressional power over commerce. Because Congress can prescribe the rules by which commerce is to be governed, it has the power to subject commerce to relevant state regulations. For an example, see *Prudential Insurance Co. v. Benjamin* (1946).

5. Oliver Wendell Holmes, *Collected Legal Papers* (New York: Harcourt, Brace, 1921), 295–296.

SELECTED READINGS

The Federalist, Nos. 31–34, 44–46.

Barber, Sotirios A. *The Fallacies of States' Rights.* Cambridge, MA: Harvard University Press, 2013.

Buzbee, William W., ed. *Preemption Choice: The Theory, Law, and Reality of Federalism's Core Question.* Cambridge: Cambridge University Press, 2009.

Elazar, Daniel J. *American Federalism: A View from the States.* 3rd ed. New York: Harper & Row, 1984.

Epstein, Richard, and Michael Greve, eds. *Federal Preemption: States' Powers, National Interests.* Washington, DC: AEI Press, 2007.

Greve, Michael. *Upside-Down Federalism.* Cambridge, MA: Harvard University Press, 2012.

Kincaid, John. "The Rise of Social Welfare and Onward March of Coercive Federalism." In *Networked Governance: The Future of Intergovernmental Management,* edited by Jack W. Meek and Kurt Thurmaier. Los Angeles: Sage/CQ Press, 2011.

Novak, William J. *The People's Welfare: Law and Regulation in Nineteenth-Century America.* Chapel Hill: University of North Carolina Press, 1996.

Powell, Thomas Reed. *Vagaries and Varieties in Constitutional Interpretation.* New York: Columbia University Press, 1956.

"Symposium on Preemption." *PS: Political Science and Politics* (2005): 359–378.

Young, Ernest A. "The Rehnquist Court's Two Federalisms." *Texas Law Review* 82 (2004): 1–165.

Arizona v. United States
567 U.S. ___ (2012)

In 2010, Arizona enacted the Support Our Law Enforcement and Safe Neighborhoods Act (S.B. 1070), the stated purpose of which was to "discourage and deter the unlawful entry and presence of aliens and economic activity by persons unlawfully present in the United States." The law's provisions established an official state policy of "attrition through enforcement." The United States filed this suit against Arizona, seeking to enjoin S.B. 1070 as preempted, focusing on four provisions of the law. Section 3 made failure to comply with federal alien-registration requirements a state misdemeanor. Section 5 made it a misdemeanor for an unauthorized alien to seek or engage in work in the state. Section 6 authorized state officers to arrest without a warrant a person "the officer has probable cause to believe has committed any public offense that makes the person removable from the United States." And Section 2(B) provided that officers who conduct a stop, detention, or arrest must in some circumstances make efforts to verify the person's immigration status with the federal government. The United States District Court for the District of Arizona issued a preliminary injunction preventing the four provisions at issue from taking effect, the Court of Appeals for the Ninth Circuit affirmed, and the Supreme Court granted certiorari. Opinion of the Court: <u>Kennedy</u>, Roberts, Ginsburg, Breyer, Sotomayor. Opinions dissenting in part and concurring in part: <u>Scalia</u>, Thomas; <u>Thomas</u>; <u>Alito</u>. Not participating: Kagan.

JUSTICE KENNEDY delivered the opinion of the Court.

II

A

The Government of the United States has broad, undoubted power over the subject of immigration and the status of aliens. This authority rests, in part, on the National Government's constitutional power to "establish an uniform Rule of Naturalization," U. S. Const., Art. I, §8, cl. 4, and its inherent power as sovereign to control and conduct relations with foreign nations. The federal power to determine immigration policy is well settled. Immigration policy can affect trade, investment, tourism, and diplomatic relations for the entire Nation, as well as the perceptions and expectations of aliens in this country who seek the full protection of its laws. Perceived mistreatment of aliens in the United States may lead to harmful reciprocal treatment of American citizens abroad.

It is fundamental that foreign countries concerned about the status, safety, and security of their nationals in the United States must be able to confer and communicate on this subject with one national sovereign, not the 50 separate States. See *Chy Lung v. Freeman* (1876); see also *The Federalist* No. 3 (observing that federal power would be necessary in part because "bordering States under the impulse of sudden irritation, and a quick sense of apparent interest or injury" might take action that would undermine foreign relations). This Court has reaffirmed that "one of the most important and delicate of all international relationships has to do with the protection of the just rights of a country's own nationals when those nationals are in another country." *Hines v. Davidowitz* (1941).

Federal governance of immigration and alien status is extensive and complex. Congress has specified categories of aliens who may not be admitted to the United States. Unlawful entry and unlawful reentry into the country are federal offenses. Once here, aliens are required to register with the Federal Government and to carry proof of status on their person. Congress has specified which aliens may be removed from the United States and the procedures for doing so. Aliens may be removed if they were inadmissible at the time of entry, have been convicted of certain crimes, or meet other criteria set by federal law. Removal is a civil, not criminal, matter. A principal feature of the removal system is the broad discretion exercised by immigration officials. Federal officials, as an initial matter, must decide whether it makes sense to pursue removal at all. If removal proceedings commence, aliens may seek asylum and other discretionary relief allowing them to remain in the country or at least to leave without formal removal.

Discretion in the enforcement of immigration law embraces immediate human concerns. Unauthorized workers trying to support their families, for example, likely pose less danger than alien smugglers or aliens who commit a serious crime. The equities of an individual case may turn on many factors, including whether the alien has children born in the United States, long ties to the community, or a record of distinguished military service. Some discretionary decisions involve policy choices that bear on this Nation's international relations. Returning an alien to his own country may be deemed inappropriate even where he has committed a removable offense or fails to meet the criteria for admission. The foreign state may be mired in civil war, complicit in political persecution, or enduring conditions that create a real risk that the alien or his family will be harmed upon return. The dynamic nature of relations with other countries requires the Executive Branch to ensure that enforcement policies are consistent with this Nation's foreign policy with respect to these and other realities.

B

The pervasiveness of federal regulation does not diminish the importance of immigration policy to the States. Arizona bears many of the consequences of unlawful immigration. Hundreds of thousands of deportable aliens are apprehended in Arizona each year. Unauthorized aliens who remain in the State comprise, by one estimate, almost six percent of the population. And in the State's most populous county, these aliens are reported to be responsible for a disproportionate share of serious crime. Statistics alone do not capture the full extent of Arizona's concerns. Accounts in the record suggest there is an "epidemic of crime, safety risks, serious property damage, and environmental problems" associated with the influx of illegal migration across private land near the Mexican border. The problems posed to the State by illegal immigration must not be underestimated. These concerns are the background for the formal legal analysis that follows.

III

Federalism, central to the constitutional design, adopts the principle that both the Na-

tional and State Governments have elements of sovereignty the other is bound to respect. From the existence of two sovereigns follows the possibility that laws can be in conflict or at cross-purposes. The Supremacy Clause provides a clear rule that federal law "shall be the supreme Law of the Land; and the Judges in every State shall be bound thereby, any Thing in the Constitution or Laws of any State to the Contrary notwithstanding." Art. VI, cl. 2. Under this principle, Congress has the power to preempt state law. There is no doubt that Congress may withdraw specified powers from the States by enacting a statute containing an express preemption provision.

State law must also give way to federal law in at least two other circumstances. First, the States are precluded from regulating conduct in a field that Congress, acting within its proper authority, has determined must be regulated by its exclusive governance. The intent to displace state law altogether can be inferred from a framework of regulation "so pervasive that Congress left no room for the States to supplement it" or where there is a "federal interest so dominant that the federal system will be assumed to preclude enforcement of state laws on the same subject." *Rice v. Santa Fe Elevator Corp.* (1947). Second, state laws are preempted when they conflict with federal law. This includes cases where "compliance with both federal and state regulations is a physical impossibility," and those instances where the challenged state law "stands as an obstacle to the accomplishment and execution of the full purposes and objectives of Congress." In preemption analysis, courts should assume that "the historic police powers of the States" are not superseded "unless that was the clear and manifest purpose of Congress." The four challenged provisions of the state law each must be examined under these preemption principles.

IV
A

Section 3 of S. B. 1070 forbids the "willful failure to complete or carry an alien registration document in violation of 8 United States Code section 1304(e) or 1306(a)." In effect, §3 adds a state-law penalty for conduct proscribed by federal law. The United States contends that this state enforcement mechanism intrudes on the field of alien registration, a field in which Congress has left no room for States to regulate. The Court discussed federal alien-registration requirements in *Hines v. Davidowitz.* In 1940, as international conflict spread, Congress added to federal immigration law a "complete system for alien registration." The new federal law struck a careful balance. It punished an alien's willful failure to register but did not require aliens to carry identification cards. There were also limits on the sharing of registration records and fingerprints. The Court found that Congress intended the federal plan for registration to be a "single integrated and all-embracing system." Because this "complete scheme for the registration of aliens" touched on foreign relations, it did not allow the States to "curtail or complement" federal law or to "enforce additional or auxiliary regulations." As a consequence, the Court ruled that Pennsylvania could not enforce its own alien-registration program.

The present regime of federal regulation is not identical to the statutory framework considered in *Hines*, but it remains comprehensive. The framework enacted by Congress leads to the conclusion here, as it did in *Hines*, that the Federal Government has occupied the field of alien registration. Where Congress occupies an entire field, as it has in the field of alien registration, even complementary state regulation is impermissible.

B

Section 5(C) enacts a state criminal prohibition where no federal counterpart exists. The provision makes it a state misdemeanor for "an unauthorized alien to knowingly apply for work, solicit work in a public place or perform work as an employee or independent contractor" in Arizona. Violations can be punished by a $2,500 fine and incarceration for up to six months. The United States contends that the provision upsets the balance struck by the Immigration Reform and Control Act of 1986 (IRCA) and must be preempted as an obstacle to the federal plan of regulation and control.

Congress enacted IRCA as a comprehensive framework for "combating the employment of illegal aliens." *Hoffman Plastic Compounds, Inc. v. NLRB* (2002). The law makes it illegal for employers to knowingly hire, recruit, refer, or continue to employ unauthorized workers. It also requires every employer to verify the employment authorization status of prospective employees. These requirements are enforced through criminal penalties and an escalating series of civil penalties tied to the number of times an employer has violated the provisions. This comprehensive framework does not impose federal criminal sanctions on the employee side (i.e., penalties on aliens who seek or engage in unauthorized work). The legislative background of IRCA underscores the fact that Congress made a deliberate choice not to impose criminal penalties on aliens who seek, or engage in, unauthorized employment. IRCA's framework reflects a considered judgment that making criminals out of aliens engaged in unauthorized work—aliens who already face the possibility of employer exploitation because of their removable status—would be inconsistent with federal policy and objectives.

The ordinary principles of preemption include the well-settled proposition that a state law is preempted where it "stands as an obstacle to the accomplishment and execution of the full purposes and objectives of Congress." Arizona law would interfere with the careful balance struck by Congress with respect to unauthorized employment of aliens. Although §5(C) attempts to achieve one of the same goals as federal law—the deterrence of unlawful employment—it involves a conflict in the method of enforcement. The Court has recognized that a "conflict in technique can be fully as disruptive to the system Congress enacted as conflict in overt policy." *Motor Coach Employees v. Lockridge* (1971). The correct instruction to draw from the text, structure, and history of IRCA is that Congress decided it would be inappropriate to impose criminal penalties on aliens who seek or engage in unauthorized employment. It follows that a state law to the contrary is an obstacle to the regulatory system Congress chose.

C

Section 6 of S. B. 1070 provides that a state officer, "without a warrant, may arrest a person if the officer has probable cause to believe [the person] has committed any public offense that makes [him] removable from the United States." The United States argues that arrests authorized by this statute would be an obstacle to the removal system Congress created.

As a general rule, it is not a crime for a removable alien to remain present in the United States. If the police stop someone based on nothing more than possible removability, the usual predicate for an arrest is absent. When an alien is suspected of being removable, a federal official issues an administrative document called a Notice to Appear. The form does not authorize an arrest. Instead, it gives the alien information about the proceedings, including the time and date of the removal hearing. If an alien fails to appear, an in absentia order may direct removal. The federal statutory structure instructs when it is appropriate to arrest an alien during the removal process. Section 6 attempts to provide state officers even greater authority to arrest aliens on the basis of possible removability than Congress has given to trained federal immigration officers. This state authority could be exercised without any input from the Federal Government about whether an arrest is warranted in a particular case. The result could be unnecessary harassment of some aliens (for instance, a veteran, college student, or someone assisting with a criminal investigation) whom federal officials determine should not be removed. This is not the system Congress created. By nonetheless authorizing state and local officers to engage in these enforcement activities as a general matter, §6 creates an obstacle to the full purposes and objectives of Congress. Section 6 is preempted by federal law.

D

Section 2(B) of S. B. 1070 requires state officers to make a "reasonable attempt to determine the immigration status" of any person they stop, detain, or arrest on some other legitimate basis if "reasonable suspicion exists that the person is an alien and is unlawfully present in the United States." The law also provides that "any person who is arrested shall have the person's immigration status determined before the person is released." The accepted way to perform these status checks is to contact ICE [Immigration Control and Enforcement, a federal agency], which maintains a database of immigration records. Three limits are built into the state provision. First, a detainee is presumed not to be an alien unlawfully present in the United States if he or she provides a valid Arizona driver's license or similar identification. Second, officers "may not consider race, color or national origin except to the extent permitted by the United States [and] Arizona Constitution[s]." Third, the provisions must be "implemented in a manner consistent with federal law regulating immigration, protecting the civil rights of all persons and respecting the privileges and immunities of United States citizens."

1

Consultation between federal and state officials is an important feature of the immigration system. Congress has made clear that no formal agreement or special training needs to be in place for state officers to "communicate with the [federal government] regarding the immigration status of any individual, including reporting knowledge that a particular alien is not lawfully present in the United States." And Congress has obligated ICE to respond to any request made by state officials for verification of a person's citizenship or immigration status. It is true that §2(B) does not allow state officers to consider federal enforcement priorities in deciding whether to contact ICE about someone they have detained. Congress has done nothing to suggest it is inappropriate to communicate with ICE in these situations, however. Indeed, it has encouraged the sharing of information about possible immigration violations. The federal scheme thus leaves room for a policy requiring state officials to contact ICE as a routine matter.

2

Some who support the challenge to §2(B) argue that, in practice, state officers will be required to delay the release of some detainees for no reason other than to verify their immigration status. But §2(B) could be read to avoid these concerns. To take one example, a person might be stopped for jaywalking in Tucson and be unable to produce identification. A person might be held pending release on a charge of driving under the influence of alcohol. As this goes beyond a mere stop, the arrestee would appear to be subject to the categorical requirement in the second sentence of §2(B) that "any person who is arrested shall have the person's immigration status determined before [he] is released." State courts may read this as an instruction to initiate a status check every time someone is arrested, or in some subset of those cases, rather than as a command to hold the person until the check is complete no matter the circumstances. Even if the law is read as an instruction to complete a check while the person is in custody, it is not clear at this stage and on this record that the verification process would result in prolonged detention.

The nature and timing of this case counsel caution in evaluating the validity of §2(B). The Federal Government has brought suit against a sovereign State to challenge the provision even before the law has gone into effect. There is a basic uncertainty about what the law means and how it will be enforced. At this stage, without the benefit of a definitive interpretation from the state courts, it would be inappropriate to assume §2(B) will be construed in a way that creates a conflict with federal law. As a result, the United States cannot prevail in its current challenge. This opinion does not foreclose other preemption and constitutional challenges to the law as interpreted and applied after it goes into effect.

V

The United States has established that §§3, 5(C), and 6 of S. B. 1070 are preempted. It was improper, however, to enjoin §2(B) before the state courts had an opportunity to construe it and without some showing that enforcement of the provision in fact conflicts with federal immigration law and its objectives. The judgment of the Court of Appeals for the Ninth Circuit is affirmed in part and reversed in part. The case is remanded for further proceedings consistent with this opinion.

JUSTICE SCALIA, concurring in part and dissenting in part.

I

As a sovereign, Arizona has the inherent power to exclude persons from its territory, subject only to those limitations expressed in the Constitution or constitutionally imposed by Congress. That power to exclude has long been recognized as inherent in sovereignty. There is no doubt that "before the adoption of the constitution of the United States" each State had the authority to "prevent [itself] from being burdened by an influx of persons." *Mayor of New York v. Miln* (1837). And the Constitution did not strip the States of that authority. To the contrary, two of the Constitution's provisions were designed to enable the States to prevent "the intrusion of obnoxious aliens through other States." Letter from James Madison to Edmund Randolph (Aug. 27, 1782). The Constitution's Privileges and Immunities Clause provided that "[t]he Citizens of each State shall be entitled to all Privileges and Immunities of Citizens in the several States." Art. IV, §2, cl. 1. But if one State had particularly lax citizenship standards, it might still serve as a gateway for the entry of "obnoxious aliens" into other States. This problem was solved "by authorizing the general government to establish a uniform rule of naturalization throughout the United States." *The Federalist* No. 42. In other words, the naturalization power was given to Congress not to abrogate States' power to exclude those they did not want, but to vindicate it.

In *Mayor of New York v. Miln,* this Court considered a New York statute that required the commander of any ship arriving in New York from abroad to disclose "the name, place of birth, and last legal settlement, age and occupation of all passengers with the intention of proceeding to the said city." After discussing the sovereign authority to regulate the entrance of foreigners, the Court said: "The power of New York to pass this law having undeniably existed at the formation of the constitution, the simply inquiry is, whether by that instrument it was taken from the states, and granted to congress; for if it were not, it yet remains with them." And the Court held that it remains.

II

One would conclude from the foregoing that after the adoption of the Constitution there was some doubt about the power of the Federal Government to control immigration, but no doubt about the power of the States to do so. Since the founding era (though not immediately), doubt about the Federal Government's power has disappeared. Indeed, primary responsibility for immigration policy has shifted from the States to the Federal Government. I accept that as a valid exercise of federal power—not because of the Naturalization Clause (it has no necessary connection to citizenship) but because it is an inherent attribute of sovereignty no less for the United States than for the States. As this Court has said, it is an "accepted maxim of international law, that every sovereign nation has the power, as inherent in sovereignty, and essential to self-preservation, to forbid the entrance of foreigners within its dominions." *Fong Yue Ting v. United States* (1893). That is why there was no need to set forth control of immigration as one of the enumerated powers of Congress, although an acknowledgment of that power (as well as of the States' similar power, subject to federal abridgment) was contained in Art. I, §9, which provided that "[t]he Migration or Importation of such Persons as any of the States now existing shall think proper to admit, shall not be prohibited by the Congress prior to the Year one thousand eight hundred and eight."

In light of the predominance of federal immigration restrictions in modern times, it is easy to lose sight of the States' traditional role in regulating immigration—and to overlook their sovereign prerogative to do so. I accept as a given that State regulation is excluded by the Constitution when (1) it has been prohibited by a valid federal law, or (2) it conflicts with federal regulation—when, for example, it admits those whom federal regulation would exclude, or excludes those whom federal regulation would admit. Possibility (1) need not be considered here: there is no federal law prohibiting the States' sovereign power to exclude (assuming federal authority to enact such a law). The mere existence of federal action in

the immigration area—and the so-called field preemption arising from that action, upon which the Court's opinion so heavily relies—cannot be regarded as such a prohibition [as] we are talking about a federal law going to the core of state sovereignty: the power to exclude. Implicit "field preemption" will not do.

Nor can federal power over illegal immigration be deemed exclusive because of what the Court's opinion solicitously calls "foreign countries' concerns about the status, safety, and security of their nationals in the United States." Even in its international relations, the Federal Government must live with the inconvenient fact that it is a Union of independent States, who have their own sovereign powers. Though it may upset foreign powers—and even when the Federal Government desperately wants to avoid upsetting foreign powers—the States have the right to protect their borders against foreign nationals, just as they have the right to execute foreign nationals for murder.

§6

"A peace officer, without a warrant, may arrest a person if the officer has probable cause to believe the person to be arrested has committed any public offense that makes the person removable from the United States." The Government's primary contention is that §6 is pre-empted by federal immigration law because it allows state officials to make arrests "without regard to federal priorities." The Court's opinion focuses on limits that Congress has placed on federal officials' authority to arrest removable aliens and the possibility that state officials will make arrests "to achieve [Arizona's] own immigration policy" and "without any input from the Federal Government." Of course, on this pre-enforcement record there is no reason to assume that Arizona officials will ignore federal immigration policy (unless it be the questionable policy of not wanting to identify illegal aliens who have committed offenses that make them removable). But that is not the most important point. The most important point is that Arizona is entitled to have "its own immigration policy"—including a more rigorous enforcement policy—so long as that does not conflict with federal law. The Court says, as though the point is utterly dispositive, that "it is not a crime for a removable alien to remain present in the United States." It is not a federal crime, to be sure. But there is no reason Arizona cannot make it a state crime for a removable alien (or any illegal alien, for that matter) to remain present in Arizona. Statutory limitations upon the actions of federal officers in enforcing the United States' power to protect its borders do not on their face apply to the actions of state officers in enforcing the State's power to protect its borders. The State has the sovereign power to protect its borders more rigorously if it wishes, absent any valid federal prohibition. The Executive's policy choice of lax federal enforcement does not constitute such a prohibition.

§3

"In addition to any violation of federal law, a person is guilty of willful failure to complete or carry an alien registration document if the person is in violation of 8 [U. S. C.] §1304(e) or §1306(a)." It is beyond question that a State may make violation of federal law a violation of state law as well. We have said that explicitly with regard to illegal immigration: "Despite the exclusive federal control of this Nation's borders, we cannot conclude that the States are without any power to deter the influx of persons entering the United States against federal law, and whose numbers might have a discernible impact on traditional state concerns." *Plyler v. Doe* (1982).

The Court's opinion relies upon *Hines v. Davidowitz*. But that case did not, as the Court believes, establish a "field preemption" that implicitly eliminates the States' sovereign power to exclude those whom federal law excludes. It held that the States are not permitted to establish "additional or auxiliary" registration requirements for aliens. But §3 does not establish additional or auxiliary registration requirements. It merely makes a violation of state law the very same failure to register and failure to carry evidence of registration that are violations of federal law. The Court points out that in some respects the state law exceeds the punishments prescribed by federal law. The answer is that it makes no

difference. It is one thing to say that the Supremacy Clause prevents Arizona law from excluding those whom federal law admits. It is quite something else to say that a violation of Arizona law cannot be punished more severely than a violation of federal law.

§5(C)

"It is unlawful for a person who is unlawfully present in the United States and who is an unauthorized alien to knowingly apply for work, solicit work in a public place or perform work as an employee or independent contractor in this state." Congress has enacted its own restrictions on employers who hire illegal aliens in legislation that also includes some civil (but no criminal) penalties on illegal aliens who accept unlawful employment. The Court concludes from this (reasonably enough) "that Congress made a deliberate choice not to impose criminal penalties on aliens who seek, or engage in, unauthorized employment." But that is not the same as a deliberate choice to prohibit the States from imposing criminal penalties. Congress's intent with regard to exclusion of state law need not be guessed at, but is found in the law's express pre-emption provision, which excludes "any State or local law imposing civil or criminal sanctions (other than through licensing and similar laws) upon those who employ, or recruit or refer for a fee for employment, unauthorized aliens." Common sense suggests that the specification of pre-emption for laws punishing "those who employ" implies the lack of pre-emption for other laws, including laws punishing "those who seek or accept employment."

The Court concludes that §5(C) "would interfere with the careful balance struck by Congress," but that is easy to say and impossible to demonstrate. The Court relies primarily on the fact that "proposals to make unauthorized work a criminal offense were debated and discussed during the long process of drafting [the Immigration Reform and Control Act of 1986]," "but Congress rejected them." There is no more reason to believe that this rejection was expressive of a desire that there be no sanctions on employees, than expressive of a desire that such sanctions be left to the States. To tell the truth, it was most likely expressive of what inaction ordinarily expresses: nothing at all. It is a "naïve assumption that the failure of a bill to make it out of committee, or to be adopted when reported to the floor, is the same as a congressional rejection of what the bill contained."

* * *

The brief for the Government in this case asserted that "the Executive Branch's ability to exercise discretion and set priorities is particularly important because of the need to allocate scarce enforcement resources wisely." But priorities based on the need to allocate "scarce enforcement resources" is not the problem here. After this case was argued and while it was under consideration, the Secretary of Homeland Security announced a program exempting from immigration enforcement some 1.4 million illegal immigrants under the age of 30. The President said at a news conference that the new program is "the right thing to do." Perhaps it is, though Arizona may not think so. But to say, as the Court does, that Arizona contradicts federal law by enforcing applications of the Immigration Act that the President declines to enforce boggles the mind. So the issue is a stark one. Are the sovereign States at the mercy of the Federal Executive's refusal to enforce the Nation's immigration laws?

JUSTICE ALITO, concurring in part and dissenting in part.

I agree with the Court that §2(B) is not preempted. That provision does not authorize or require Arizona law enforcement officers to do anything they are not already allowed to do under existing federal law. I also agree with the Court that §3 is pre-empted by virtue of our decision in *Hines v. Davidowitz*, 312 U.S. 52 (1941). Our conclusion in that case that Congress had enacted an "all-embracing system" of alien registration and that States cannot "enforce additional or auxiliary regulations" forecloses Arizona's attempt here to impose additional, state-law penalties for violations of the federal registration scheme. While I agree with the Court on §2(B) and §3, I part ways on §5(C) and §6.

Cooley v. Board of Wardens
53 U.S. (12 How.) 299 (1852)

In 1803, Pennsylvania passed a law requiring all ships entering or leaving the port of Philadelphia to engage a local pilot or to pay a fine amounting to half the pilotage fee for the "use of the society for the relief of distressed and decayed pilots" and their families. A 1789 act of Congress had provided that "all pilots in the bays, inlets, rivers, harbors, and ports of the United States shall continue to be regulated in conformity with the existing laws of the states, respectively, wherein such pilots may be, or with such laws as the states may respectively hereafter enact for the purpose, until further legislative provision shall be made by Congress." After being fined for failure to engage a pilot, Aaron Cooley challenged the Pennsylvania law as an impermissible regulation of interstate commerce. Opinion of the Court: <u>Curtis</u>, Taney, Catron, McKinley, Nelson, Grier. Concurring opinion: <u>Daniel</u>. Dissenting opinion: <u>McLean</u>, Wayne.

JUSTICE CURTIS delivered the opinion of the Court.

That the power to regulate commerce includes the regulation of navigation, we consider settled. And when we look to the nature of the service performed by pilots, to the relations which that service and its compensations bear to navigation between the several states, and between the ports of the United States and foreign countries, we are brought to the conclusion, that the regulation of the qualifications of pilots, of the modes and times of offering and rendering their services, of the responsibilities which shall rest upon them, of the powers they shall possess, of the compensation they may demand, and of the penalties by which their rights and duties may be enforced, do constitute regulations of navigation, and consequently of commerce, within the just meaning of this clause of the Constitution.

It becomes necessary, therefore, to consider whether this law of Pennsylvania, being a regulation of commerce, is valid. We are brought directly and unavoidably to the consideration of the question, whether the grant of the commercial power to Congress, did *per se* deprive the states of all power to regulate pilots. This question has never been decided by this court, nor, in our judgment, has any case depending upon all the considerations which must govern this one, come before this court. The grant of commercial power to Congress does not contain any terms which expressly exclude the states from exercising an authority over its subject-matter. If they are excluded it must be because the nature of the power, thus granted to Congress, requires that a similar authority should not exist in the states. If it were conceded on the one side, that the nature of this power, like that to legislate for the District of Columbia, is absolutely and totally repugnant to the existence of similar power in the states, probably no one would deny that the grant of the power to Congress, as effectually and perfectly excludes the states from all future legislation on the subject, as if express words had been used to exclude them. And on the other hand, if it were admitted that the existence of this power in Congress, like the power of taxation, is compatible with the existence of a similar power in the states, then it would be in conformity with the contemporary exposition of the Constitution (*Federalist,* No. 32), and with the judicial construction, given from time to time by this court, after the most deliberate consideration, to hold that the mere grant of such a power to Congress, did not imply a prohibition on the states to exercise the same power; that it is not the mere existence of such a power, but its exercise by Congress, which may be incompatible with the exercise of the same power by the states, and that the states may legislate in the absence of congressional regulations.

The diversities of opinion, therefore, which have existed on this subject, have arisen from the different views taken of the nature of this power. But when the nature of a power like this is spoken of, when it is said that the nature of the power requires that it should be exercised exclusively by Congress, it must be intended to refer to the subjects of that power, and to say they are of such a nature as to require exclusive legislation by Congress. Now the power to regulate commerce, embraces a vast field, containing not only many, but exceedingly various subjects, quite unlike in their nature; some imperatively demanding a single uniform rule, operating equally on the commerce of the United States in every port; and some, like the subject now in question, as imperatively demanding that diversity, which alone can meet the local necessities of navigation.

Either absolutely to affirm, or deny that the nature of this power requires exclusive legislation by Congress, is to lose sight of the nature of the subjects of this power, and to assert concerning all of them, what is really applicable but to a part. Whatever subjects of this power are in their nature national, or admit only of one uniform system, or plan of regulation, may justly be said to be of such a nature as to require exclusive legislation by Congress. That this cannot be affirmed of laws for the regulation of pilots and pilotage is plain. The act of 1789 contains a clear and authoritative declaration by the first Congress, that the nature of this subject is such, that until Congress should find it necessary to exert its power, it should be left to the legislation of the states; that it is local and not national; that it is likely to be the best provided for, not by one system, or plan of regulations, but by as many as the legislative discretion of the several states should deem applicable to the local peculiarities of the ports within their limits. Viewed in this light, so much of this act of 1789 as declares that pilots shall continue to be regulated "by such laws as the states may respectively hereafter enact for that purpose," instead of being held to be inoperative, as an attempt to confer on the states a power to legislate, of which the Constitution had deprived them, is allowed an appropriate and important signification. It manifests the understanding of Congress, at the outset of the government, that the nature of this subject is not such as to require its exclusive legislation.

The practice of the states, and of the national government, has been in conformity with this declaration, from the origin of the national government to this time; and the nature of the subject when examined, is such as to leave no doubt of the superior fitness and propriety, not to say the absolute necessity, of different systems of regulation, drawn from local knowledge and experience, and conformed to local wants. How then can we say that by the mere grant of power to regulate commerce, the states are deprived of all the power to legislate on this subject, because from the nature of the power the legislation of Congress must be exclusive. This would be to affirm that the nature of the power is in any case, something different from the nature of the subject to which, in such case, the power extends, and that the nature of the power necessarily demands, in all cases, exclusive legislation by Congress, while the nature of one of the subjects of that power, not only does not require such exclusive legislation, but may be best provided for by many different systems enacted by the states, in conformity with the circumstances of the ports within their limits. In construing an instrument designed for the formation of a government, and in determining the extent of one of its important grants of power to legislate, we can make no such distinction between the nature of the power and the nature of the subject on which that power was intended practically to operate, nor consider the grant more extensive by affirming of the power, what is not true of its subject now in question.

It is the opinion of a majority of the court that the mere grant to Congress of the power to regulate commerce, did not deprive the states of power to regulate pilots, and that although Congress has legislated on this subject, its legislation manifests an intention, with a single exception, not to regulate this subject, but to leave its regulation to the several states. . . .

We are of opinion that this state law was enacted by virtue of a power, residing in the state to legislate; that it is not in conflict with any law of Congress; that it does not interfere with any system which Congress has established by making regulations, or by intentionally leaving individuals to their own unrestricted action; that this law is therefore valid, and the judgment of the Supreme Court of Pennsylvania in each case must be affirmed.

Southern Pacific Company v. Arizona
325 U.S. 761 (1945)

The Arizona Train Limit Law prohibited passenger trains of more than fourteen cars and freight trains of more than seventy cars from operating in the state. When the Southern Pacific Railroad violated these safety restrictions by operating longer trains on interstate routes through the state, Arizona brought action in state court. The trial court ruled in favor of the company, the Arizona Supreme Court reversed, and Southern Pacific appealed to the Supreme Court. Opinion of the Court: <u>Stone</u>, Reed, Frankfurter, Murphy, Jackson, Burton. Concurring in result: <u>Rutledge</u>. Dissenting opinion: <u>Black</u>, Douglas.

THE CHIEF JUSTICE delivered the opinion of the Court.

Although the commerce clause conferred on the national government power to regulate commerce, its possession of the power does not exclude all state power of regulation. In the absence of conflicting legislation by Congress, there is a residuum of power in the state to make laws governing matters of local concern which nevertheless in some measure affect interstate commerce or even, to some extent, regulate it. Thus the states may regulate matters which, because of their number and diversity, may never be adequately dealt with by Congress. When the regulation of matters of local concern is local in character and effect, and its impact on the national commerce does not seriously interfere with its operation, and the consequent incentive to deal with them nationally is slight, such regulation has been generally held to be within state authority. But ever since *Gibbons v. Ogden*, the states have not been deemed to have authority to impede substantially the free flow of commerce from state to state, or to regulate those phases of the national commerce which, because of the need of national uniformity, demand that their regulation, if any, be prescribed by a single authority.

In the application of these principles some enactments may be found to be plainly within and others plainly without state power. But between these extremes lies the infinite variety of cases, in which regulation of local matters may also operate as a regulation of commerce, in which reconciliation of the conflicting claims of state and national power is to be attained only by some appraisal and accommodation of the competing demands of the state and national interests involved.

Hence the matters for ultimate determination here are the nature and extent of the burden which the state regulation of interstate trains, adopted as a safety measure, imposes on interstate commerce, and whether the relative weights of the state and national interests involved are such as to make inapplicable the rule, generally observed, that the free flow of interstate commerce and its freedom from local restraints in matters requiring uniformity of regulation are interests safeguarded by the commerce clause from state interference.

The findings show that the operation of long trains, that is trains of more than fourteen passenger and more than seventy freight cars, is standard practice over the main lines of the railroads of the United States, and that, if the length of trains is to be regulated at all, national uniformity in the regulation adopted, such as only Congress can prescribe, is practically indispensable to the operation of an efficient and economical national railway system. On many railroads passenger trains of more than fourteen cars and freight trains of more than seventy cars are operated, and on some systems freight trains are run ranging from one hundred and twenty-five to one hundred and sixty cars in length. Outside of Arizona, where the length of trains is not restricted, appellant runs a substantial proportion of long trains. In 1939 on its comparable route for through traffic through Utah and Nevada from 66 to 85% of its freight trains were seventy cars in length and over 43% of its passenger trains included more than fourteen passenger cars.

In Arizona, approximately 93% of the freight traffic and 95% of the passenger traffic is interstate. Because of the Train Limit Law appellant is required to haul over 30% more trains in Arizona than would otherwise have been necessary. The record shows a definite relationship between operating costs and the length of trains, the increase in length resulting in a reduction of operating costs per car. The additional cost of operation of trains complying with the Train Limit Law in Arizona amounts for the two railroads traversing that state to about $1,000,000 a year. The reduction in train lengths also impedes efficient operation. More locomotives and more manpower are required; the necessary conversion and reconversion of train lengths at terminals and the delay caused by breaking up and remaking long trains upon entering and leaving the state in order to comply with the law, delays the traffic and diminishes its volume moved in a given time, especially when traffic is heavy.

The unchallenged findings leave no doubt that the Arizona Train Limit Law imposes a serious burden on the interstate commerce conducted by appellant. Compliance with a state statute limiting train lengths requires interstate trains of a length lawful in other states to be broken up and reconstituted as they enter each state according as it may impose varying limitations upon train lengths. The alternative is for the carrier to conform to the lowest train limit restriction of any of the states through which its trains pass, whose laws thus control the carriers' operations both within and without the regulating state.

The trial court found that the Arizona law had no reasonable relation to safety, and made train operation more dangerous. The principal source of danger of accident from increased length of trains is the resulting increase of "slack action" of the train. The length of the train increases the slack since the slack action of a train is the total of the free movement between its several cars. The amount of slack action has some effect on the severity of the shock of train movements, and on freight trains sometimes results in injuries to operatives, which most frequently occur to occupants of the caboose. The amount and severity of slack action, however, are not wholly dependent upon the length of train, as they may be affected by the mode and conditions of operation as to grades, speed, and load.

On comparison of the number of slack action accidents in Arizona with those in Nevada, where the length of trains is now unregulated, the trial court found that with substantially the same amount of traffic in each state the number of accidents was relatively the same in long as in short train operations.

Reduction of the length of trains tends to increase the number of accidents because of the increase in the number of trains. The accident rate in Arizona is much higher than on comparable lines elsewhere, where there is no regulation of length of trains. The record lends support to the trial court's conclusion that the train length limitation increased rather than diminished the number of accidents.

[Arizona's] regulation of train lengths, admittedly obstructive to interstate train operation, and having a seriously adverse effect on transportation efficiency and economy, passes beyond what is plainly essential for safety since it does not appear that it will lessen rather than increase the danger of accident. Examination of all the relevant factors makes it plain that the state interest is outweighed by the interest of the nation in an adequate, economical and efficient railway transportation service, which must prevail.

Reversed.

JUSTICE BLACK, with JUSTICE DOUGLAS, dissenting.

I think that the "findings" of the state court do not authorize today's decision. That court did not find that there is no unusual danger from slack movements in long trains. It did decide on disputed evidence that the long train "slack movement" dangers were more than offset by prospective dangers as a result of running a larger number of short trains, since many people might be hurt at grade crossing. There was undoubtedly some evidence before the state court from which it could have reached such a conclusion. There was undoubtedly as much evidence before it which would have justified a different conclusion. Under those circumstances, the determination of whether it is in the interest of society for the length of trains to be governmentally regulated is a matter of public policy. Someone must fix that policy—either the Congress, or the state, or the courts. A century and a half of constitutional history and government admonishes this Court to leave that choice to the elected legislative representatives of the people themselves, where it properly belongs both on democratic principles and the requirements of efficient government.

When we finally get down to the gist of what the Court today actually decides, it is this: Even though more railroad employees will be injured by "slack action" movements on long trains than on short trains, there must be no regulation of this danger in the absence of "uniform regulations." We are not left in doubt as to why, as against the potential peril of injuries to employees, the Court tips the scales on the side of "uniformity." For the evil it finds in a lack of uniformity is that it (1) delays interstate commerce, (2) increases its cost and (3) impairs its efficiency. All three of these boil down to the same thing, and that is that running shorter trains would increase the cost of railroad operations.

Thus the conclusion that a requirement for long trains will "burden interstate commerce" is a mere euphemism for the statement that a requirement for long trains will increase the cost of railroad operations.

Granholm v. Heald
544 U.S. 460 (2005)

Like many other states, Michigan and New York regulate the sale and importation of alcoholic beverages, including wine. Under Michigan law, most wine producers must distribute their wine through wholesalers in the state, but there is an exception for in-state wineries, which are eligible for "winemaker" licenses that allow direct shipment to in-state consumers. Some Michigan residents brought suit in the United States District Court for the Eastern District of Michigan, challenging the state's direct-shipment laws as discriminating against interstate commerce, and Domaine Alfred, a San Luis Obispo winery, joined in the suit. The plaintiffs contended that Michigan's direct-shipment laws discriminated against interstate commerce in violation of the Commerce Clause. The district court sustained the Michigan scheme, but the Court of Appeals for the Sixth Circuit reversed.

New York's licensing scheme likewise makes exceptions for in-state wineries, so that local wineries can make direct sales to consumers on terms not available to out-of-state wineries. An out-of-state winery may ship directly to New York consumers only if it becomes a licensed New York winery, which requires the establishment of "a branch factory, office or storeroom within the state of New York." Juanita Swedenburg and David Lucas, joined by three of their New York customers, brought suit in the Southern District of New York against the officials responsible for administering New York's Alcoholic Beverage Control Law. The district court granted summary judgment to the plaintiffs, but the Court of Appeals for the Second Circuit reversed. The Supreme Court consolidated these cases and granted certiorari on the following question: Does a state's regulatory scheme that permits in-state wineries directly to ship alcohol to consumers but restricts the ability of out-of-state wineries to do so violate the dormant Commerce Clause in light of Section 2 of the Twenty-First Amendment? Opinion of the Court: <u>Kennedy</u>, Scalia, Souter, Ginsburg, Breyer. Dissenting opinions: <u>Stevens</u>, O'Connor; <u>Thomas</u>, Rehnquist, Stevens, O'Connor.

JUSTICE KENNEDY delivered the opinion of the Court.

These consolidated cases present challenges to state laws regulating the sale of wine from out-of-state wineries to consumers in Michigan and New York. The details and mechanics of the two regulatory schemes differ, but the object and effect of the laws are the same: to allow in-state wineries to sell wine directly to consumers in that State but to prohibit out-of-state wineries from doing so, or, at the least, to make direct sales impractical from an economic standpoint. It is evident that the object and design of the Michigan and New York statutes is to grant in-state wineries a competitive advantage over wineries located beyond the States' borders. We hold that the laws in both States discriminate against interstate commerce in violation of the Commerce Clause, and that the discrimination is neither authorized nor permitted by the Twenty-first Amendment.

II

This Court has held that, in all but the narrowest circumstances, state laws violate the Commerce Clause if they mandate "differential treatment of in-state and out-of-state economic interests that benefits the former and burdens the latter." *Oregon Waste Systems, Inc. v. Department of Environmental Quality of Ore.* (1994). This rule is essential to the foundations of the Union. The mere fact of nonresidence should not foreclose a producer in one State from access to markets in other States. States may not enact laws that burden out-of-state producers or shippers simply to give a competitive advantage to in-state businesses. This mandate "reflect[s] a central concern of the Framers that was an immediate reason for calling the Constitutional Convention: the conviction that in order to succeed, the new Union would have to avoid the tendencies toward economic Balkanization that had plagued relations among the Colonies and later among the States under the Articles of Confederation." *Hughes v. Oklahoma* (1979).

Laws of the type at issue in the instant cases contradict these principles. They deprive citizens of their right to have access to the markets of other States on equal terms. The perceived necessity for reciprocal sale privileges risks generating the trade rivalries and animosities, the alliances and exclusivity, that the Constitution and, in particular, the Commerce Clause were designed to avoid. State laws that protect local wineries have led to the enactment of statutes under which some States condition the right of out-of-state wineries to make direct wine sales to in-state consumers on a reciprocal right in the shipping State. California, for example, passed a reciprocity law in 1986, retreating from the State's previous regime that allowed unfettered direct shipments from out-of-state wineries. The current patchwork of laws—with some States banning direct shipments altogether, others doing so only for out-of-state wines, and still others requiring reciprocity—is essentially the product of an ongoing, low-level trade war. Allowing States to discriminate against out-of-state wine "invites a multiplication of preferential trade areas destructive of the very purpose of the Commerce Clause." *Dean Milk Co. v. Madison* (1951).

B

The discriminatory character of the Michigan system is obvious. Michigan allows in-state wineries to ship directly to consumers, subject only to a licensing requirement. Out-of-state wineries, whether licensed or not, face a complete ban on direct shipment. The differential treatment requires all out-of-state wine, but not all in-state wine, to pass through an in-state wholesaler and retailer before reaching consumers. These two extra layers of overhead increase the cost of out-of-state wines to Michigan consumers. The cost differential, and in some cases the inability to secure a wholesaler for small shipments, can effectively bar small wineries from the Michigan market.

The New York regulatory scheme differs from Michigan's in that it does not ban direct shipments altogether. Out-of-state wineries are instead required to establish a distribution operation in New York in order to gain the privilege of direct shipment. This, though, is just an indirect way of subjecting out-of-state wineries, but not local ones, to the three-tier system. New York and those allied with its interests defend the scheme by arguing that an out-of-state winery has the same access to the State's consumers as in-state wineries: All wine must be sold through a licensee fully accountable to New York; it just so happens that in order to become a licensee, a winery must have a physical presence in the State. There is some confusion over the precise steps out-of-state wineries must take to gain access to the New York market, in part because no winery has run the State's regulatory gauntlet. New York's argument, in any event, is unconvincing.

III

State laws that discriminate against interstate commerce face "a virtually *per se* rule of invalidity." *Philadelphia v. New Jersey* (1978). The Michigan and New York laws by their own terms violate this proscription. The two States, however, contend their statutes are saved by §2 of the Twenty-first Amendment, which provides: "The transportation or importation into any State, Territory, or possession of the United States for delivery or use therein of intoxicating liquors, in violation of the laws thereof, is hereby prohibited."

The States' position is inconsistent with our precedents and with the Twenty-first Amendment's history. Section 2 does not allow States to regulate the direct shipment of wine on terms that discriminate in favor of in-state producers.

A

Before 1919, the temperance movement fought to curb the sale of alcoholic beverages one State at a time. The movement made progress, and many States passed laws restricting or prohibiting the sale of alcohol. This Court upheld state laws banning the production and sale of alcoholic beverages, *Mugler v. Kansas* (1887), but was less solicitous of laws aimed at imports. In a series of cases before ratification of the Eighteenth Amendment the Court, relying on the Commerce Clause, invalidated a number of state liquor regulations. These cases advanced two distinct principles. First, the Court held that the Commerce Clause prevented States from discriminating against imported liquor. Second, the Court held that the Commerce Clause prevented States from passing facially neutral laws that placed an impermissible burden on interstate commerce. For example, in *Bowman v. Chicago & Northwestern R. Co.* (1888), the Court struck down an Iowa statute that required all liquor importers to have a permit. *Bowman* and its progeny rested in part on the since-rejected original-package doctrine. Under this doctrine goods shipped in interstate commerce were immune from state regulation while in their original package. *Bowman* reserved the question whether a State could ban the sale of imported liquor altogether. Iowa responded to *Bowman* by doing just that but was thwarted once again. In *Leisy v. Hardin* (1890), the Court held that Iowa could not ban the sale of imported liquor in its original package.

Leisy left the States in a bind. They could ban the production of domestic liquor, but these laws were ineffective because out-of-state liquor was immune from any state regulation as long as it remained in its original package. To resolve the matter, Congress passed the Wilson Act, which empowered the States to regulate imported liquor on the same terms as domestic liquor. By its own terms, the Wilson Act did not allow States to discriminate against out-of-state liquor; rather, it allowed States to regulate imported liquor only "to the same extent and in the same manner" as domestic liquor.

Although the Wilson Act increased the States' authority to police liquor imports, it did not solve all their problems. In *Vance* and *Rhodes*—two cases decided soon after *Scott*—the Court made clear that the Wilson Act did not authorize States to prohibit direct shipments for personal use and that consumers had the right to receive alcoholic beverages shipped in interstate commerce for personal use. Congress responded to the direct-shipment loophole in 1913 by enacting the Webb-Kenyon Act. The Court construed the Act to close the direct-shipment gap left open by the Wilson Act. States were now empowered to forbid shipments of alcohol to consumers for personal use, provided that the States treated in-state and out-of-state liquor on the same terms.

Michigan and New York now argue the Webb-Kenyon Act went even further and removed any barrier to discriminatory state liquor regulations. We do not agree. First, this reading of the Webb-Kenyon Act conflicts with that given the statute in *Clark Distilling*. *Clark Distilling* recognized that the Webb-Kenyon Act extended the Wilson Act to allow the States to intercept liquor shipments before those shipments reached the consignee. The statute's text does not compel a different result. The Webb-Kenyon Act readily can be construed as forbidding "shipment or transportation" only where it runs afoul of the State's generally applicable laws governing receipt, possession, sale, or use. Last, and most importantly, the Webb-Kenyon Act did not purport to repeal the Wilson Act, which expressly precludes States from discriminating.

B

The ratification of the Eighteenth Amendment in 1919 provided a brief respite from the legal battles over the validity of state liquor regulations. With the ratification of the Twenty-first Amendment 14 years later, however, nationwide Prohibition came to an end. Section 1 of the Twenty-first Amendment repealed the Eighteenth Amendment. Section 2 of the Twenty-first Amendment is at issue here.

Michigan and New York say the provision grants to the States the authority to discriminate against out-of-state goods. The history we have recited does not support this position. To the contrary, it provides strong support for the view that §2 restored to the States the powers they had under the Wilson and Webb-Kenyon Acts. The aim of the Twenty-first Amendment was to allow States to maintain an effective and uniform system for controlling liquor by regulating its transportation, importation, and use. The Amendment did not give States the authority to pass nonuniform laws in order to discriminate against out-of-state goods, a privilege they had not enjoyed at any earlier time.

Some of the cases decided soon after ratification of the Twenty-first Amendment did not take account of this history and were inconsistent with this view. [But] our more recent cases confirm that the Twenty-first Amendment does not supersede other provisions of the Constitution and, in particular, does not displace the rule that States may not give a discriminatory preference to their own producers.

V

States have broad power to regulate liquor under §2 of the Twenty-first Amendment. This power, however, does not allow States to ban, or severely limit, the direct shipment of out-of-state wine while simultaneously authorizing direct shipment by in-state producers. If a State chooses to allow direct shipment of wine, it must do so on evenhanded terms. Without demonstrating the need for discrimination, New York and Michigan have enacted regulations that disadvantage out-of-state wine producers. Under our Commerce Clause jurisprudence, these regulations cannot stand. We affirm the judgment of the Court of Appeals for the Sixth Circuit; and we reverse the judgment of the Court of Appeals for the Second Circuit and remand the case for further proceedings consistent with our opinion.

JUSTICE STEVENS, with whom JUSTICE O'CONNOR joins, dissenting.

The New York and Michigan laws challenged in these cases would be patently invalid under well settled dormant Commerce Clause principles if they regulated sales of an ordinary article of commerce rather than wine. But ever since the adoption of the Eighteenth Amendment and the Twenty-first Amendment, our Constitution has placed commerce in alcoholic beverages in a special category. Section 2 of the Twenty-first Amendment expressly provides that "the transportation or importation into any State, Territory, or possession of the United States for delivery or use therein of intoxicating liquors, in violation of the laws thereof, is hereby prohibited."

Today many Americans, particularly those members of the younger generations who make policy decisions, regard alcohol as an ordinary article of commerce, subject to substantially the same market and legal controls as other consumer products. That was definitely not the view of the generations that made policy in 1919 when the Eighteenth Amendment was ratified or in 1933 when it was repealed by the Twenty-first Amendment. On the contrary, the moral condemnation of the use of alcohol as a beverage represented not merely the convictions of our religious leaders, but the views of a sufficiently large majority of the population to warrant the rare exercise of the power to amend the Constitution on two occasions. The Eighteenth Amendment entirely prohibited commerce in "intoxicating liquors" for beverage purposes throughout the United States and the territories subject to its jurisdiction. While §1 of the Twenty-first Amendment repealed the nationwide prohibition, §2 gave the States the option to maintain equally comprehensive prohibitions in their respective jurisdictions.

My understanding (and recollection) of the historical context reinforces my conviction that the text of §2 should be "broadly and colloquially interpreted." *Carter v. Virginia* (1944) (Frankfurter, J., concurring). Indeed, the fact that the Twenty-first Amendment was the only Amendment in our history to have been ratified by the people in state conventions, rather than by state legislatures, provides further reason to give its terms their ordinary meaning. Because the New York and Michigan laws regulate the "transportation or importation" of "intoxicating liquors" for "delivery or use therein," they are exempt from dormant Commerce Clause scrutiny. As Justice Thomas has demonstrated, the text of the Twenty-first Amendment is a far more reliable guide to its meaning than the unwritten rules that the majority enforces today. I therefore

join his persuasive and comprehensive dissenting opinion.

JUSTICE THOMAS, with whom THE CHIEF JUSTICE, JUSTICE STEVENS, and JUSTICE O'CONNOR join, dissenting.

The Court devotes much attention to the Twenty-first Amendment, yet little to the terms of the Webb-Kenyon Act. This is a mistake, because that Act's language displaces any negative Commerce Clause barrier to state regulation of liquor sales to in-state consumers.

The Webb-Kenyon Act immunizes from negative Commerce Clause review the state liquor laws that the Court holds are unconstitutional. The Act "prohibits" any "shipment or transportation" of alcoholic beverages "into any State" when those beverages are "intended, by any person interested therein, to be received, possessed, sold, or in any manner used in violation of any law of such State." State laws that regulate liquor imports in the manner described by the Act are exempt from judicial scrutiny under the negative Commerce Clause, as this Court has long held. See *McCormick & Co. v. Brown* (1932); *Clark Distilling Co. v. Western Maryland R. Co.* (1917). The Webb-Kenyon Act's language, in other words, "prevents the immunity characteristic of interstate commerce from being used to permit the receipt of liquor through such commerce in States contrary to their laws." *Clark Distilling*.

The Michigan and New York direct-shipment laws are within the Webb-Kenyon Act's terms and therefore do not run afoul of the negative Commerce Clause. Those laws restrict out-of-state wineries from shipping and selling wine directly to Michigan and New York consumers. Any winery that ships wine directly to a Michigan or New York consumer in violation of those state-law restrictions is a "person interested therein" "intending" to "sell" wine "in violation of" Michigan and New York law, and thus comes within the terms of the Webb-Kenyon Act.

This construction of the Webb-Kenyon Act is no innovation. The Court adopted this reading of the Act in *McCormick & Co. v. Brown*, and Congress approved it shortly thereafter in 1935 when it reenacted the Act without alteration. *McCormick* considered a state law that prohibited out-of-state manufacturers (as well as in-state manufacturers) from shipping liquor to a licensed in-state dealer without first obtaining a wholesaler permit. The Court held that by shipping liquor into the State without a license, the out-of-state manufacturer fell "directly within the terms of" the Webb-Kenyon Act, thus violating it. While the law at issue in *McCormick* did not discriminate against out-of-state products, the construction of the Webb-Kenyon Act it adopted applies equally to state laws that so discriminate. If an out-of-state manufacturer shipping liquor to an in-state distributor without a license "sells" liquor "in violation of any law of such State" within the meaning of Webb-Kenyon, as *McCormick* held, an out-of-state winery directly shipping wine to consumers in violation of even a discriminatory state law does so as well. The Michigan and New York laws are indistinguishable in relevant part from the state law upheld in *McCormick*.

The Court answers that the Webb-Kenyon Act's text "readily can be construed as forbidding 'shipment or transportation' only where it runs afoul of the States' generally applicable laws governing receipt, possession, sale, or use." The Court leaves unexplained how this ad hoc exception follows from the Act's text. The Act does not condition a State's ability to regulate the receipt, possession, and use of liquor free from negative Commerce Clause immunity on the character of the state law. It does not mention "discrimination," much less discrimination against out-of-state liquor products. Instead, it

prohibits the interstate shipment of liquor into a State "in violation of any law of such State."

The contrast between the language of the Webb-Kenyon Act and its predecessor, the Wilson Act, casts still more doubt on the Court's reading. The Wilson Act provided that liquor shipped into a State was "subject to the operation and effect of the laws of such State to the same extent and in the same manner as though such liquids or liquors had been produced in such State or Territory." Even if this language does not authorize States to discriminate against out-of-state liquor products, the Webb-Kenyon Act has no comparable language addressing discrimination. The contrast is telling. It shows that the Webb-Kenyon Act encompasses laws that discriminate against both out-of-state wholesalers and out-of-state manufacturers.

The Court begins its opinion by detailing the evils of state laws that restrict the direct shipment of wine. It stresses, for example, the Federal Trade Commission's opinion that allowing the direct shipment of wine would enhance consumer welfare. But the Twenty-first Amendment and the Webb-Kenyon Act took those policy choices away from judges and returned them to the States. Whatever the wisdom of that choice, the Court does this Nation no service by ignoring the textual commands of the Constitution and Acts of Congress. The Twenty-first Amendment and the Webb-Kenyon Act displaced the negative Commerce Clause as applied to regulation of liquor imports into a State. They require sustaining the constitutionality of Michigan's and New York's direct-shipment laws. I respectfully dissent.

Comptroller of the Treasury of Maryland v. Wynne
575 U.S. ___ (2015)

Like many other States, Maryland taxes the income its residents earn both within and outside the state, as well as the income that nonresidents earn from sources within Maryland. But unlike most other states, Maryland does not offer its residents a full credit against the income taxes that they pay to other states, so some of the income earned by Maryland residents outside the state is taxed twice. In 2006, Brian and Karen Wynne claimed an income tax credit for all income taxes

paid to other states, and when the Maryland State Comptroller of the Treasury denied their claim, they sued. The Maryland Tax Court upheld the Comptroller's decision, but the Circuit Court for Howard County reversed on the ground that Maryland's tax system violated the Commerce Clause. The Court of Appeals of Maryland affirmed that ruling, and the Supreme Court granted certiorari. Opinion of the Court: <u>Alito</u>, Roberts, Kennedy, Breyer, Sotomayor.

Dissenting opinions: <u>Scalia</u>, Thomas (as to Parts 1 and 2); <u>Thomas</u>, Scalia (except as to the first paragraph); <u>Ginsburg</u>, Scalia, Kagan.

JUSTICE ALITO delivered the opinion of the Court.

This case involves the constitutionality of an unusual feature of Maryland's personal income tax scheme [under which] some of the income earned by Maryland residents outside the State is taxed twice. Maryland's scheme creates an incentive for taxpayers to opt for intrastate rather than interstate economic activity. We have long held that States cannot subject corporate income to tax schemes similar to Maryland's, and we see no reason why income earned by individuals should be treated less favorably. Maryland admits that its law has the same economic effect as a state tariff, the quintessential evil targeted by the dormant Commerce Clause. We therefore affirm the decision of Maryland's highest court and hold that this feature of the State's tax scheme violates the Federal Constitution.

II

A

The Commerce Clause grants Congress power to "regulate Commerce . . . among the several States." Art. I, § 8, cl. 3. These "few simple words reflected a central concern of the Framers that was an immediate reason for calling the Constitutional Convention: the conviction that in order to succeed, the new Union would have to avoid the tendencies toward economic Balkanization that had plagued relations among the Colonies and later among the States under the Articles of Confederation." *Hughes* v. *Oklahoma*, 441 U.S. 322 (1979). Although the Clause is framed as a positive grant of power to Congress, "we have consistently held this language to contain a further, negative command, known as the dormant Commerce Clause, prohibiting certain state taxation even when Congress has failed to legislate on the subject." *Oklahoma Tax Comm'n* v. *Jefferson Lines, Inc.*, 514 U.S. 175 (1995).

This interpretation of the Commerce Clause has been disputed. But it has deep roots. By prohibiting States from discriminating against or imposing excessive burdens on interstate commerce without congressional approval, it strikes at one of the chief evils that led to the adoption of the Constitution, namely, state tariffs and other laws that burdened interstate commerce. *The Federalist*, Nos. 7, 11, and 42.

Under our precedents, the dormant Commerce Clause precludes States from "discriminating between transactions on the basis of some interstate element." *Boston Stock Exchange v. State Tax Comm'n*, 429 U.S. 318 (1977). This means, among other things, that a State "may not tax a transaction or incident more heavily when it crosses state lines than when it occurs entirely within the State." *Armco Inc.* v. *Hardesty*, 467 U.S. 638 (1984). "Nor may a State impose a tax which discriminates against interstate commerce either by providing a direct commercial advantage to local business, or by subjecting interstate commerce to the burden of multiple taxation." *Northwestern States Portland Cement Co.* v. *Minnesota*, 358 U.S. 450 (1959).

B

Our existing dormant Commerce Clause cases all but dictate the result reached in this case. In *J. D. Adams Mfg. Co.* v. *Storen*, 304 U.S. 307 (1938), Indiana taxed the income of every Indiana resident (including individuals) and the income that every nonresident derived from sources within Indiana. The State levied the tax on income earned by the plaintiff Indiana corporation on sales made out of the State. Holding that this scheme violated the dormant Commerce Clause, we explained that the "vice of the statute" was that it taxed, "without apportionment, receipts derived from activities in interstate commerce." If these receipts were also taxed by the States in which the sales occurred, we warned, interstate commerce would be subjected "to the risk of a double tax burden to which intrastate commerce is not exposed, and which the commerce clause forbids." The next year, in *Gwin, White & Prince, Inc.* v. *Henneford*, 305 U.S. 34 (1939), we reached a similar result. [Finally,] in *Central Greyhound Lines, Inc.* v. *Mealey*, 334 U.S. 653 (1948), New York sought to tax the portion of a domiciliary bus company's gross receipts that were derived from services provided in neighboring States.

Noting that these other States might also attempt to tax this portion of the company's gross receipts, the Court held that the New York scheme violated the dormant Commerce Clause because it imposed an "unfair burden" on interstate commerce.

In all three cases, the Court struck down a state tax scheme that might have resulted in the double taxation of income earned out of the State and that discriminated in favor of intrastate over interstate economic activity. Maryland's tax scheme is unconstitutional for similar reasons.

C

The principal dissent distinguishes these cases on the sole ground that they involved a tax on gross receipts rather than net income. We see no reason why the distinction should matter. The distinction between taxes on gross receipts and net income was based on the notion, endorsed in some early cases, that a tax on gross receipts is an impermissible "direct and immediate burden" on interstate commerce, whereas a tax on net income is merely an "indirect and incidental" burden. This arid distinction between direct and indirect burdens allowed "very little coherent, trustworthy guidance as to tax validity." And so, beginning with Justice Stone's seminal opinion in *Western Live Stock* v. *Bureau of Revenue*, 303 U.S. 250 (1938), the direct-indirect burdens test was replaced with a more practical approach that looked to the economic impact of the tax.

For its part, petitioner distinguishes *J. D. Adams*, *Gwin, White*, and *Central Greyhound* on the ground that they concerned the taxation of corporations, not individuals. Attempting to explain why the dormant Commerce Clause should provide less protection for natural persons than for corporations, petitioner and the Solicitor General argue that States should have a free hand to tax their residents' out-of-state income because States provide their residents with many services. This argument fails because corporations also benefit from state and local services.

The sole remaining attribute that, in the view of petitioner, distinguishes a corporation from an individual for present purposes is the right of the individual to vote to change Maryland's discriminatory tax law. But if a State's tax unconstitutionally discriminates against interstate commerce, it is invalid regardless of whether the plaintiff is a resident voter or nonresident of the State. In addition, the notion that the victims of such discrimination have a complete remedy at the polls is fanciful. It is likely that only a distinct minority of a State's residents earns income out of State. Schemes that discriminate against income earned in other States may be attractive to legislators and a majority of their constituents for precisely this reason. It is even more farfetched to suggest that natural persons with out-of-state income are better able to influence state lawmakers than large corporations headquartered in the State. In short, petitioner's argument would leave no security where the majority of voters prefer protectionism at the expense of the few who earn income interstate.

D

In attempting to justify Maryland's unusual tax scheme, the principal dissent argues that Maryland has the sovereign power to tax all of the income of its residents, wherever earned, and it therefore reasons that the dormant Commerce Clause cannot constrain Maryland's ability to expose its residents (and nonresidents) to the threat of double taxation. The principal dissent, if accepted, would work a sea change in our Commerce Clause jurisprudence. Legion are the cases in which we have considered and even upheld dormant Commerce Clause challenges brought by residents to taxes that the State had the jurisdictional power to impose. If the principal dissent were to prevail, all of these cases would be thrown into doubt. After all, in those cases, as here, the State's decision to tax in a way that allegedly discriminates against interstate commerce could be justified by the argument that a State may tax its residents without any Commerce Clause constraints.

F

1

As previously noted, the tax schemes held to be unconstitutional in *J. D. Adams*, *Gwin, White*, and *Central Greyhound*, had the potential to result in the discriminatory double taxation of income earned out of state and created a powerful incentive to engage in intrastate rather than interstate economic activity. The Maryland scheme's discriminatory treatment of interstate commerce is not simply the result of its interaction with the taxing schemes of other States. Instead, Maryland's tax scheme is inherently discriminatory and operates as a tariff. This identity between Maryland's tax and a tariff is fatal because tariffs are "[t]he paradigmatic example of a law discriminating against interstate commerce."

The principal dissent is left with two arguments. First, the principal dissent claims that the analysis outlined above requires a State taxing based on residence to "recede" to a State taxing based on source. We establish no such rule of priority. To be sure, Maryland could remedy the infirmity in its tax scheme by offering, as most States do, a credit against income taxes paid to other States. But we do not foreclose the possibility that it could comply with the Commerce Clause in some other way. Of course, we do not decide the constitutionality of a hypothetical tax scheme that Maryland might adopt because such a scheme is not before us. That Maryland's existing tax unconstitutionally discriminates against interstate commerce is enough to decide this case.

Second, the principal dissent finds a "deep flaw" with the possibility that "Maryland could eliminate the inconsistency [with its tax scheme] by terminating the special nonresident tax—a measure that would not help the Wynnes at all." This second objection refutes the first. By positing that Maryland could remedy the unconstitutionality of its tax scheme by eliminating the special nonresident tax, the principal dissent accepts that Maryland's desire to tax based on residence need not "recede" to another State's desire to tax based on source.

G

Justice Scalia would uphold the constitutionality of the Maryland tax scheme because the dormant Commerce Clause, in his words, is "a judicial fraud." That was not the view of the Court in *Gibbons* v. *Ogden*, where Chief Justice Marshall wrote that there was "great force" in the argument that the Commerce Clause by itself limits the power of the States to enact laws regulating interstate commerce. Since that time, this supposedly fraudulent doctrine has been applied in dozens of our opinions, joined by dozens of Justices. Perhaps for this reason, petitioner in this case, while challenging the interpretation and application of that doctrine by the court below, did not ask us to reconsider the doctrine's validity.

Justice Scalia does not dispute the fact that State tariffs were among the principal problems that led to the adoption of the Constitution. Nor does he dispute the fact that the Maryland tax scheme is tantamount to a tariff on work done out of State. He argues, however, that the Constitution addresses the problem of state tariffs by prohibiting States from imposing "Imposts or Duties on Imports or Exports." Art. I, §10, cl. 2. But he does not explain why, under his interpretation of the Constitution, the Import-Export Clause would not lead to the same result that we reach under the dormant Commerce Clause.

Justice Thomas also refuses to accept the dormant Commerce Clause doctrine, and he suggests that the Constitution was ratified on the understanding that it would not prevent a State from doing what Maryland has done here. This argument is plainly unsound. First, because of the difficulty of interstate travel, the number of individuals who earned income out of State in 1787 was surely very small. Second, Justice Thomas has not shown that the small number of individuals who earned income out of State were taxed twice on that income. A number of Founding-era income tax schemes appear to have taxed only the income of residents, not nonresidents. Third, even if some persons were taxed twice, it is unlikely that this was a matter of such common knowledge that it must have been known by the delegates to the State ratifying conventions who voted to adopt the Constitution.

The judgment of the Court of Appeals of Maryland is affirmed.

JUSTICE SCALIA, with whom JUSTICE THOMAS joins as to Parts I and II, dissenting.

The Court holds unconstitutional Maryland's refusal to give its residents full credits against income taxes paid to other States. It does this by invoking the negative Commerce Clause, a judge-invented rule under which judges may set aside state laws that they think impose too much of a burden upon interstate commerce. The fundamental problem with our negative Commerce Clause cases is that the Constitution does not contain a negative Commerce Clause. It contains only a Commerce Clause. Unlike the negative Commerce Clause adopted by the judges, the real Commerce Clause says nothing about prohibiting state laws that burden commerce. Much less does it say anything about authorizing judges to set aside state laws *they believe* burden commerce. The clearest sign that the negative Commerce Clause is a judicial fraud is the utterly illogical holding that congressional consent enables States to enact laws that would otherwise constitute impermissible burdens upon interstate commerce. See *Prudential Ins. Co. v. Benjamin*, 328 U.S. 408 (1946). How could congressional consent lift a constitutional prohibition?

The Court's efforts to justify this judicial economic veto come to naught. The Court claims that the doctrine "has deep roots." So it does, like many weeds. But age alone does not make up for brazen invention. And the doctrine in any event is not quite as old as the Court makes it seem. The idea that the Commerce Clause of its own force limits state power "finds no expression" in discussions surrounding the Constitution's ratification. For years after the adoption of the Constitution, States continually made regulations that burdened interstate commerce (like pilotage laws and quarantine laws) without provoking any doubts about their constitutionality. Our first clear *holding* setting aside a state law under the negative Commerce Clause came after the Civil War, more than 80 years after the Constitution's adoption. *Case of the State Freight Tax*, 15 Wall. 232 (1873).

The Court adds that "tariffs and other laws that burdened interstate commerce" were among "the chief evils that led to the adoption of the Constitution." This line of reasoning forgets that interpretation requires heeding more than the Constitution's purposes; it requires heeding the means the Constitution uses to achieve those purposes. The Constitution addresses the evils of local impediments to commerce by prohibiting States from impos-

ing certain especially burdensome taxes—"Imposts or Duties on Imports or Exports" and "Dut[ies] of Tonnage"—without congressional consent. Art. I, §10, cls. 2–3. It also addresses these evils by giving Congress a commerce power under which *it* may prohibit other burdensome taxes and laws. As the Constitution's text shows, however, it does not address these evils by empowering the *judiciary* to set aside state taxes and laws that *it* deems too burdensome. By arrogating this power anyway, our negative Commerce Clause cases have disrupted the balance the Constitution strikes between the goal of protecting commerce and competing goals like preserving local autonomy and promoting democratic responsibility.

Maryland's refusal to give residents full tax credits against income taxes paid to other States has its disadvantages. It threatens double taxation and encourages residents to work in Maryland. But Maryland's law also has its advantages. It allows the State to collect equal revenue from taxpayers with equal incomes, avoids the administrative burdens of verifying tax payments to other States, and ensures that every resident pays the State at least some income tax. Nothing in the Constitution precludes Maryland from deciding that the benefits of its tax scheme are worth the costs.

JUSTICE GINSBURG, with whom JUSTICE SCALIA and JUSTICE KAGAN join, dissenting.

Today's decision veers from a principle of interstate and international taxation repeatedly acknowledged by this Court: A nation or State "may tax *all* the income of its residents, even income earned outside the taxing jurisdiction." *Oklahoma Tax Comm'n v. Chickasaw Nation*, 515 U.S. 450 (1995). As I see it, nothing in the Constitution or in prior decisions of this Court dictates that one of two States, the domiciliary State or the source State, must recede simply because both have lawful tax regimes reaching the same income. True, Maryland elected to deny a credit for income taxes paid to other States in computing a resident's county tax liability. It is equally true, however, that the other States that taxed the Wynnes' income elected not to offer them a credit for their Maryland county income taxes. In this situation, the Constitution does not prefer one lawful basis for state taxation of a person's income over the other. Nor does it require one State to limit its residence-based taxation, should the State also choose to exercise, to the full extent, its source-based authority. States often offer their residents credits for income taxes paid to other States, as Maryland does for state income tax purposes. States do so, however, as a matter of tax policy, not because the Constitution compels that course.

For at least a century, "domicile" has been recognized as a secure ground for taxation of residents' worldwide income. More is given to the residents of a State than to those who reside elsewhere, therefore more may be demanded of them. With this Court's approbation, States have long favored their residents over nonresidents in the provision of local services. A taxpayer's home State, then, can hardly be faulted for making support of local government activities an obligation of every resident, regardless of any obligations residents may have to *other* States. Residents, moreover, possess political means, not shared by outsiders, to ensure that the power to tax their income is not abused.

States deciding whether to tax residents' entire worldwide income must choose between legitimate but competing tax policy objectives. A State might prioritize obtaining equal contributions from those who benefit from the State's protection in roughly similar ways. Or a State might prioritize ensuring that its taxpayers are not subject to double taxation. For at least a century, responsibility for striking the right balance between these two policy objectives has belonged to the States (and Congress), not this Court. Some States have chosen the same balance the Court embraces today. But since almost the dawn of the modern era of state

income taxation, other States have taken the same approach as Maryland does now, taxing residents' entire income, wherever earned, while at the same time taxing nonresidents' entire in-state income. And recognizing that "protection, benefit, and power over [a taxpayer's income] are not confined to either" the State of residence or the State in which income is earned, this Court has long afforded States that flexibility. *Curry* v. *McCanless*, 307 U.S. 357 (1939). This history of States imposing and this Court upholding income tax schemes materially identical to the one the Court confronts here should be the beginning and end of this case.

The majority asserts that Maryland's tax scheme "operates as a tariff," making it "patently unconstitutional." This is a curious claim. The defining characteristic of a tariff is that it taxes interstate activity at a higher rate than it taxes the same activity conducted within the State. Maryland's resident income tax does the exact opposite: It taxes the income of its residents at precisely the same rate, whether the income is earned in-state or out-of-state.

This case is, at bottom, about policy choices: Should States prioritize ensuring that all who live or work within the State shoulder their fair share of the costs of government? Or must States prioritize avoidance of double taxation? As I have demonstrated, achieving even the latter goal is beyond this Court's competence. Resolving the competing tax policy considerations this case implicates is something the Court is even less well equipped to do. For a century, we have recognized that state legislatures and the Congress are constitutionally assigned and institutionally better equipped to balance such issues. I would reverse, so that we may leave that task where it belongs.

10

The Constitution and Native American Tribes

This volume thus far has examined the division of power within the federal government among the legislative, executive, and judicial branches (separation of powers) and the division of power between the federal government and the state governments (federalism). This chapter explores another division of power that is less familiar to many Americans but no less constitutionally interesting—the division of power between the federal government and Native American (Indian) tribal governments.

Within the United States, 566 Native American tribes/nations[1] are officially recognized by the federal government. These tribes are bound together by ethnicity, language, and history, and they govern territorial holdings ("Indian country") that encompass altogether more than 56.2 million acres. These tribes devise their own constitutions, elect their own leaders, and exercise significant governing authority, albeit as "domestic dependent nations" within the borders of the United States.[2] Indeed, "American Indians are unique in the world in that they represent the only aboriginal peoples still practicing a form of self-government in the midst of a wholly new and modern civilization that has been transported to their lands."[3]

NATIVE AMERICAN TRIBES AND THE NEW REPUBLIC

At the time when European colonization of North America began, the Indian population numbered an estimated 12 million or more, organized into various tribes or nations, each sharing a common language and ethnicity. The mode of food production differed from tribe to tribe: many emphasized hunting and gathering, and others engaged in agriculture, but generally tribes held property in common rather than in individual allotments. The systems of government likewise differed, ranging from the sophisticated confederal arrangement of the Iroquois Federation to less formalized structures in many tribes; however, few Indian nations had written constitutions. When European explorers and settlers came to North America, they adopted contradictory positions regarding the status of Indian nations. On the one hand, they recognized the tribes as sovereign entities by entering into treaties with them, and they acknowledged tribal property rights by purchasing land from them. On the other hand, the Europeans also denied tribes the status of nations by purporting to have "discovered" an unoccupied continent, and they rejected Indian property rights by laying down claims to possess and rule the land that they had "discovered." This ambivalence regarding the status of Indian nations has persisted to the present day, at times resulting in efforts to eliminate tribes as distinct entities and at times leading to efforts to reinvigorate tribal self-government.

When the American colonies declared their independence, the United States inherited the problem of how to relate to Indian tribes. The Articles of Confederation assigned Congress the responsibility for "regulating the trade and managing all affairs with the Indians, not members of any of the States, provided that the legislative right of any State within its own limits be not infringed or violated" (Article IX, Section 1). In fact, this grant of authority was less expansive than it appears, because many states maintained extravagant western land claims, which in effect placed most tribes within their borders.

The federal Constitution, by contrast, granted the power to deal with Indian tribes to the federal government exclusively. Indeed, eleven western state constitutions contain "disclaimer provisions," inserted as a condition for their admission to the Union, that expressly recognize their lack of authority over Indian tribes.[4] The most direct grant of authority is found in the Commerce Clause (Article I, Section 8, Paragraph 3), which gives Congress the power "to regulate Commerce with foreign Nations, and among the several States, and with the Indian Tribes." The clause reveals the distinctive position of tribes within the governing scheme—they are not simply foreign nations (otherwise, inclusion of "with the

Indian Tribes" would be redundant), but commerce with them is not simply domestic commerce either (otherwise, it would fall under "among the several States"). The only other mention of Indians occurs in the formula for apportionment of representation and direct taxes (Article I, Section 2, Paragraph 3), which excludes "Indians not taxed" from the population base. This rather obscure phrase, which reappears in the Fourteenth Amendment's discussion of representation (in Section 2), acknowledges Indian nationhood, at least obliquely. It implies that Indians who were taxed, who had assimilated and become part of the American body politic, should be represented in government, whereas those who were not taxed would not be represented because they were not part of the United States but rather were members of another nation.

Other constitutional grants and prohibitions, although not focusing directly on relations with Indian tribes, confirm that such relations are exclusively the domain of the federal government. For example, agreements between the United States and tribes were for the first one hundred years of our constitutional experience likely to take the form of treaties, and the Constitution both awards the treaty power to the president with the advice and consent of the Senate (Article II, Section 2, Paragraph 2) and prohibits states from entering into treaties (Article I, Section 10, Paragraph 1). The Constitution's reaffirmation of previously negotiated treaties (Article VI, Section 1) is particularly important, because most of these treaties were with Indian tribes, thereby confirming that tribal sovereignty predated the Constitution and continued after its adoption. Similarly, the Constitution gives Congress the sole authority to govern territory belonging to the United States (Article IV, Section 3, Paragraph 2), thereby enabling it to set rules for areas within the borders of the United States claimed by and occupied by Indian tribes, a power enhanced by the cession of state territorial holdings to the federal government. And, of course, it gives to the federal government the power to conduct military operations against external foes (Article I, Section 8, Paragraph 11) as well as the power to protect states against violence arising within their borders (Article IV, Section 4).

Although the Constitution makes clear the exclusive authority of the federal government to deal with Indian tribes, it does not clarify the scope of federal power over those tribes or the powers that they retained, that is, their right of self-government. Such an omission is hardly surprising. Insofar as tribes were analogous to foreign nations, there was no reason for the Constitution to define their powers, any more than there was for the Constitution to have defined the powers of France or Great Britain. During the Founding era, the analogy between tribes and foreign nations made intuitive sense, because tribes were often close to military equals of the United States. In addition, the Constitution needed to address the respective spheres of the federal and state governments, because its major aim was to reallocate powers between nation and state. Because that constitutional reallocation did not affect tribal powers—those powers were "both preconstitutional and extraconstitutional"—the adoption of the Constitution afforded no occasion to define their scope.[5] Only when the status of the tribes shifted from rough equals to what Chief Justice John Marshall called "domestic dependent nations" did the respective spheres of the federal government and tribes—or, put differently, tribal sovereignty and the right of tribes to self-government free from federal direction or intrusion—emerge as a major issue.

TRIBAL SOVEREIGNTY AND THE MARSHALL TRILOGY

Over a ten-year period culminating in the early 1830s, Chief Justice John Marshall handed down for the Supreme Court three decisions that have come to be known as the Marshall Trilogy–three decisions that continue to define the nature and extent of tribal sovereignty and the relation of the tribes to the federal government and the states. They were *Johnson v. McIntosh* (1823), *Cherokee Nation v. Georgia* (1831), and *Worcester v. Georgia* (1832).

In *Johnson v. McIntosh*, he held that, because of the principles of discovery and conquest, Indian tribes had no power to grant lands to anyone other than the federal government. The tribes' "rights to complete sovereignty, as independent nations, were necessarily diminished, and their power to dispose of the soil at their own will, to whomever they pleased, was denied by the original fundamental principle, that discovery gave exclusive title to those who made it." Marshall refused to debate the justice of this principle. "Whether agriculturists, merchants, and manufacturers, have a right, on abstract principles, to expel hunters from the territory they possess, or to contract their limits" were questions he would not address. "Conquest gives a title which the Courts of the conqueror cannot deny, whatever the private and speculative opinions of individuals may be, respecting the original justice of the claim which has been successfully asserted."

Although *Johnson v. McIntosh* limited tribal sovereignty, Marshall's opinions in the two *Cherokee Nation* cases confirmed the sovereign status of the tribes. In *Cherokee Nation v. Georgia*, he held that the Cherokees could not be regarded as a "foreign nation" within the meaning of Article III of the Constitution and therefore could not bring a suit in the US Supreme Court, under the Court's original jurisdiction, against the State of Georgia. He invoked the Commerce Clause and declared that it divided "the objects" to which the power of regulating commerce might be directed into "three distinct classes—foreign nations, the several states, and Indian tribes. When forming this article, the convention considered them [the tribes] as entirely distinct." He denominated them "domestic dependent nations. They occupy a territory to which we assert a title independent of their will, which must take effect in point of possession when their right of possession ceases. Meanwhile they are in a state of pupilage. Their relation to the United States resembles that of a ward to his guardian."

And, the next year in *Worcester v. Georgia* (1832), Marshall made it clear that although the right of self-determination of tribal nations is inevitably limited by their "domestic dependent" status, it is not effaced. "A weak state, in order to provide for its safety, may place itself under the protection of one more powerful, without stripping itself of the right of government, and ceasing to be a state." He continued: "The Indian nations had always been considered as distinct, independent, political communities, retaining their original natural rights, as the undisputed possessors of the soil, from time immemorial, with the single exception of that imposed by irresistible power, which excluded them from intercourse with any other European potentate than the first discoverer of the coast of the particular region claimed." Thus, Marshall held that the laws of Georgia could "have no force" in the Cherokee Nation, which "is a distinct community occupying its own territory" and which "the citizens of Georgia have no right to enter, but with the assent of the Cherokees themselves, or in conformity with treaties, and with the acts of congress. The whole intercourse between the United States and this nation, is, by our constitution and laws, vested in the government of the United States."

In brief, the Marshall Trilogy established the position that tribes are nations whose independence is limited in only three essentials: the ability to convey land, deal with foreign powers, and engage in commerce apart from that authorized by Congress. For all internal purposes, however, the tribes are sovereign and free from state intrusion on that sovereignty—unless Congress explicitly acts to grant the states this power.

Two major consequences of the Marshall Trilogy must be noted. The first, based on the tribes' status as "domestic dependent nations" and therefore on what the Supreme Court in *County of Oneida v. Oneida Indian Nation* (1985) called "the unique trust relationship between the United States and the Indians," is the development of the canons of construction of federal Indian law. All treaties, agreements, statutes, and executive orders are to be construed liberally in favor of the tribes, and all ambiguities are to be resolved to their benefit. Additionally, treaties and agreements are to be construed as the tribes would have understood them, and tribal property rights and sovereignty are to be preserved unless Congress's intent to the contrary is clear and unambiguous.

The second consequence has been well over a century of vacillating federal policy towards the tribes. As a trustee, the federal government is obliged to act in the best interests of the tribes—a notion that took root only after the Jackson Administration's policy of Indian Removal and the extreme hardships experienced by the Five Civilized Tribes as they were forced to travel the Trail of Tears from the Southeast to what is now Oklahoma. But, what does it mean to act in the best interests of the tribe? From the early 1850s to the present, people of good will (and, truth to tell, such people have often been in short supply) have been of two minds on this, vibrating between two polar opposites. During some periods of American history, they have believed it is in the best interests of the tribes that their members should be assimilated into American society, and during other periods, they have believed it is in the tribes' best interests that they be preserved and that the federal government promote tribal self-determination.

Thus, the United States has moved from a policy of moving tribes to specified reservations from the mid-nineteenth century to the early 1880s, to:

- a policy of allotting reservation land to individual Indians and the attempted assimilation of tribal members from the early 1880s to the late 1920s. Major legislation during this period included: the Major Crimes Act of 1885, which declared that murder and other serious crimes committed by an Indian in Indian country were federal offenses to be tried in federal court rather than tribal courts; the General Allotment Act of 1887, which authorized the president to allot portions of reservation land to individual Indians; and the Indian Citizenship Act of 1924, a statute that conferred citizenship upon all Indians born within the United States; to
- efforts to provide for tribal autonomy and the preservation of tribes from the late 1920s to the early 1950s. During this period, Congress passed the Indian Reorganization Act of 1934 (also known as the Wheeler-Howard Act), which ended the practice of allotments, fostered the acquisition of new Indian lands and the creation of new reservations, and authorized the tribes to set up legal structures for self-government; to
- a policy of termination and assimilation from the early 1950s to the late 1960s. In 1953, Congress passed Public Law 280, mandating six states to assume criminal and limited civil jurisdiction in Indian county, and it adopted House Concurrent Resolution 108 declaring it the policy of the Congress "as rapidly as possible to make the Indian subject to the same laws and entitled to the same privileges and responsibilities as are applicable to other citizens and to end their status as wards"; to
- a policy of self-determination and self-governance from the late 1960s to the present.
- Key legislation includes the Indian Civil Rights Act of 1968, the Indian Child Welfare Act of 1978, the Indian Gaming Regulatory Act of 1988, and the Tribal Self-Governance Act of 1994.

TRIBAL SELF-DETERMINATION

Perhaps the most fundamental constitutional question involving Native American tribes is their right of self-determination—the power to determine the fundamental character, membership, and future course of the political society of which they are a part. The right of self-determination of tribal nations is inevitably limited by their "domestic dependent" status, but it is not effaced. As Chief Justice John Marshall noted in *Worcester v. Georgia*, "a weak state, in order to provide for its safety, may place itself under the protection of one more powerful, *without stripping itself of the right of government, and ceasing to be a state*" (emphasis added). Thus, the Court held that the laws of Georgia could "have no force" in the Cherokee Nation, which "is a distinct community occupying its own territory" and which "the citizens of Georgia have no right to enter, but with the assent of the Cherokees themselves, or in conformity with treaties, and with the acts of congress."

Moreover, Marshall in *Worcester* insisted that this dependent status, together with the surrender of territory by Indian nations, imposed a fiduciary obligation upon the federal government. This "trust relationship" appeared to promise the tribes federal support and protection. During the late nineteenth century, however, this promise of protection was transformed into a power to direct and control, based on claims of Indian incompetence and an insistence that it was in the Indians' interest to abandon their traditional practices and become "civilized." Thus, Congress sponsored efforts to assimilate Indians by supporting Christian missionaries who might convert and "civilize" the Indians, by banning tribal rituals, and by educating Indian youth at boarding schools off the reservations so as to root out tribal customs and practices.[6] Congress also attempted to eliminate tribal patterns of communal landownership, and it largely replaced tribal self-government with administration by the Bureau of Indian Affairs (on this, more below). In *United States v. Kagama* (1886), the Supreme Court upheld this vast extension of congressional power. Speaking for the Court in *Kagama,* Justice Samuel Miller described the tribes as "the wards of the nation. They are communities dependent on the United States. Dependent largely for their daily food. Dependent for their political rights." From "their very weakness and helplessness," he insisted that "there arises the duty of protection, and with it the power."

With the enactment of the Indian Reorganization Act in 1934, federal policy shifted from assimilation to Indian self-determination through the revival of tribal governments. During the 1950s (and especially with the passage of Public Law 280 in 1953), policy shifted again, this time toward "termination," that is, the unilateral ending of the special relationship between tribes and the federal government. During the presidency of Richard Nixon, policy shifted back once more to self-determination; subsequent presidents have followed Nixon's lead, at least rhetorically, in championing self-determination, reemphasizing the trust relationship, and repudiating termination.[7] Nevertheless, the prevailing Supreme Court case law appears to recognize no constitutional limits to Congress's power to act as trustee for Indian nations, and thus the tribes' right to self-determination seems a matter of congressional grace rather than a matter of right, subject to the vagaries of policy shifts.

TRIBAL AUTHORITY OVER DISPOSITION OF LANDS

During the late eighteenth and early nineteenth centuries, the American desire to expand beyond the coastal regions of the new nation into land claimed by the United States collided with Indian territorial claims. The purchase of land from Indian nations helped finesse the question of ownership, at least initially. But the American appetite for expansion soon outran the tribes' willingness to relinquish their holdings, and thus the question of Indian land rights could not be avoided indefinitely. In a series of rulings over three decades, the Supreme Court under Marshall outlined a doctrine of limited tribal land rights. In *Fletcher v. Peck* (1810) (see Chapter 11), the Court concluded that tribes possessed a "right of occupancy" rather than full title to the land, although tribal consent was nonetheless required before the right of occupancy was extinguished.[8] Elaborating in *Johnson v. McIntosh* (1823), Marshall concluded that the tribes' "power to dispose of the soil at their own will, to whomever they pleased, was denied by the original fundamental principle, that discovery gave exclusive title to those who made it." And in *Cherokee Nation v. Georgia*

(1831), the Court further limited the authority of tribes to dispose of their own lands: "They occupy a territory to which we assert a title independent of their will, which must take effect in point of possession when their right of possession ceases."

Subsequent congressional legislation further diminished even this limited tribal authority over the disposition of tribal lands. In 1887 Congress enacted the General Allotment Act of 1887, which provided for allotment of tribal lands in fee simple to individual Indians and the sale of surplus lands to white homesteaders. Whatever the motivations underlying the Dawes Act—and these ranged from the conviction that Indian progress required individual ownership of land to the desire to open Indian land to non-Indians—its effects were dramatic and disastrous. Before this policy was abandoned in 1934, federal sale of "surplus" lands plus the sale of holdings by individual Indians reduced tribal land from 138 million acres to 52 million acres. The loss of communal control over land and its use also undermined the authority of tribal governments. (Indeed, this was precisely the aim of some supporters of the act; as Theodore Roosevelt explained, "The General Allotment Act is a mighty pulverizing engine to break up the tribal mass.")[9] In addition, by opening the reservations for settlement by non-Indians, the act destroyed close-knit tribal communities, jeopardized the separate development sought by Indian nations, and undermined their efforts to maintain traditional lifestyles. From a practical standpoint, the fact that reservations included large numbers of non-Indian residents—in some instances, even a majority of the reservation population—complicated the exercise of political and judicial jurisdiction. Charles Wilkinson's summary of these political effects of the Dawes Act thus seems altogether accurate: "With the land base slashed back once again and with strange new faces within most reservations, tribal councils and courts went dormant. The BIA [federal Bureau of Indian Affairs] moved in as the real government."[10]

TRIBAL AUTHORITY TO INSTITUTE A GOVERNMENT

Indian nations had instituted their own governments prior to the European colonization of North America, and they never surrendered their authority to create and re-create their political institutions. The federal Constitution does not restrict the form that those governments take: whereas it mandates that state governments be "republican," it imposes no such requirement on tribal governments.

In practice, however, by the late nineteenth century the BIA had largely displaced traditional Indian governments as the effective governing authority in Indian country. To reverse this transformation of Indian nations from self-governing peoples to administered subjects, Congress in 1934 adopted the Indian Reorganization Act (IRA), which sought to reinvigorate Indian self-government by encouraging tribes to draft constitutions. Yet the scope of tribal authority under the IRA was circumscribed. If a tribe voluntarily subjected itself to the IRA (and most tribes did), it was obliged to submit its constitution for approval by the BIA, and any subsequent amendment or revision of the constitution was also subject to BIA approval. Even some tribes, such as the Cherokees, that devised non-IRA constitutions voluntarily subjected themselves to BIA review. When the Cherokees subsequently sought to eliminate that review when revising their constitution in 1999, they found the bureau reluctant to approve the constitution and relinquish control.

TRIBAL AUTHORITY TO ENTER INTO TREATIES

One attribute of nationhood is the power to enter into agreements with other sovereign nations through government-to-government negotiations. Since US independence, Indian tribes have entered into one treaty with the United States under the Continental Congress, nine treaties with the United States under the Articles of Confederation, and 376 treaties with the United States under the US Constitution; after 1871, when the United States formally renounced treaty making with tribes, tribes have continued to negotiate bilateral agreements with the United States ("treaty substitutes") that were approved by both houses of Congress.[11] In the early 1970s, some Indian groups advocated a resumption of treaty making with the federal government.

As Chief Justice Marshall indicated in *Johnson v. McIntosh,* however, the doctrine of discovery, under which the European colonizers purportedly gained title to territory occupied by Indian tribes, had the effect of diminishing the treaty-making authority of Indian nations. One element of the doctrine of discovery was that the European power that had discovered and occupied a territory gained exclusive title to the land. The country that held title could transfer the land to another country, as occurred when Britain ceded territory to the United States at the conclusion of the Revolutionary War. However, the Indian tribes, as mere occupants of land under the authority of one sovereign, could not transfer land to the authority of another sovereign. Thus, although Indian nations could enter into agreements to dispose of land they occupied, the doctrine of discovery decreed that they could dispose of their holdings only to the country that held title to the land. Indeed, as Marshall explained in *Cherokee Nation v. Georgia,* the limit on Indian treaty making went beyond the conveying of land: "They and their country are considered by foreign nations, as well as by ourselves, as being so completely under the sovereignty and dominion of the United States, that any attempt to acquire their lands, or to form a political connexion with them, would be considered by all as an invasion of our territory, and an act of hostility."

At the beginning of the twentieth century, the Supreme Court in *Lone Wolf v. Hitchcock* (1903) undermined the authority of even those treaties that tribes were permitted to negotiate.[12] Rejecting a challenge to congressional action in violation of a treaty, the Court concluded that Congress could unilaterally abrogate treaties with Indian tribes by subsequent legislation, because it had "plenary power" in Indian affairs. This ruling in effect made US-tribal treaties binding only on the contracting tribe, which lacked the power to violate a treaty without suffering repercussions.

Lone Wolf created the danger that, even when Congress enacts general regulatory laws that do not specifically mention tribes, these laws might be interpreted to override treaty commitments by implication, thereby jeopardizing tribal prerogatives. However, the Supreme Court, for the most part, has sought to avoid this result by reading statutes in the light of the special trust relationship between tribes and the federal government, as well as the federal commitment to tribal self-government, and by generally refusing to abrogate treaty rights in the absence of explicit statutory language indicating a congressional intent to do so. Thus, in *Bryan v. Itasca County* (1976), the Court severely limited the reach of Public Law 280 (discussed later) by insisting that the law must be construed in favor of tribal prerogatives of self-government. The Court ruled that Congress intended only to add private causes of action in Indian country to state court jurisdictions, but not state tax or regulatory jurisdictions; if Congress had intended to add them, Congress would have stated so explicitly.

In *Morton v. Mancari* (1974), the Court also ruled in favor of Indian tribal prerogatives, holding that Indian preferential hiring for the Bureau of Indian Affairs represented an exception to the 1972 Equal Employment Act requiring equal treatment in federal employment. The Court so held because Congress had not specifically addressed the question of its applicability to Indian tribes in the act, whereas Congress had specifically addressed it in a 1934 law creating the preference. And in *Santa Clara Pueblo v. Martinez* (1978), the Court disallowed a suit of sexual discrimination against a tribe in federal court because the Indian Civil Rights Act of 1968 did not explicitly subject tribes to civil suits in federal court. By means of these and other cases, the Court has demonstrated that, when there exists a disputed question as to whether Congress intended to restrict Indian self-government, the Court, keeping in mind the trust responsibility imposed upon the former, applies the strictest test of construction in presumption of the Indians' self-government. Thus, in spite of its "plenary power" over tribal relations, the Court has often held Congress to the highest standard of specificity in restricting Indian self-government.

TRIBES AND THEIR RELATION TO THE STATES

Although the Marshall Court made it very clear in *Worcester v. Georgia* that state laws "can have no force" in Indian country, later Courts have not consistently adhered to *Worcester.* Indeed, for a period of approximately seventy-five years, the Court did not recognize Indian sovereignty against the states at all. In *McBratney v. United States* (1882), for example, the Court held that states had jurisdiction on Indian land in cases involving the commission of a crime by a non-Indian against a non-Indian, despite the absence of a specific congressional grant to the states of that power. In *United States v. Kagama,* the Court stated that there are only two sovereign entities, federal and state. In *Cherokee Nation v. Southern Kansas Ry. Co.* (1890), the Court wrote that "the proposition that the Cherokee nation is a sovereign in the sense that the United States is a sovereign, or in the sense that the states are sovereign, . . . finds no support."

It was only in 1959 in *Williams v. Lee* that the Court once again began to reassert the idea that the states could not interfere with tribal self-government. In *Williams,* the Court ruled that Arizona did not have jurisdiction over civil disputes on Navajo land—only tribal courts did. In *Warren Trading Post v. Arizona State Tax Commission* (1965), the Court ruled that tribes are "largely free to run the reservation . . . without state control." And in *McClanahan v. Arizona State Tax Commission* (1973), the Court found that states lack jurisdiction to tax the income of an Indian that was earned on a reservation.

McClanahan was not, however, a complete victory for tribal independence from state control, for the Court did not decide in favor of the Indian tribes on the basis of sovereignty. Rather, it announced that its fundamental guiding principle was "federal pre-emption." As Justice Thurgood Marshall declared: "The trend has been away from the idea of inherent Indian sovereignty as a bar to state jurisdiction and toward reliance on federal pre-emption. . . . The modern cases thus tend to avoid reliance on platonic notions of Indian sovereignty and to look instead to the applicable treaties and statutes which define the limits of state power."

The basis of the Court's decision in *McClanahan* was the Indian Commerce Clause. Essentially, the states cannot interfere with internal Indian affairs, because that is the sole province of Congress. Congress's power to regulate commerce "with the Indian tribes" preempts the ability of the states to interfere with internal Indian affairs. Thus, *McClanahan* represented a vindication not of tribal sovereignty but of Congress's sovereignty. In fact, two years later, in *United States v. Mazurie* (1975), the Court upheld the right of tribes to issue licenses, but only because Congress had delegated that power to the tribes.

TRIBAL AUTHORITY TO ADMINISTER JUSTICE

The right of self-government includes the authority to administer criminal and civil justice within the boundaries of the political society. Indeed, according to one scholar, this jurisdiction represents "the cornerstone of tribal sovereignty."[13] For Indian tribes, however, this power is circumscribed. For cases exclusively involving tribal members, tribes for most of the nineteenth century retained criminal and civil jurisdiction. Thus, in *Ex parte Crow Dog* (1883), the Supreme Court recognized the exclusive power of tribes to make criminal laws and punish Indians who committed crimes against other Indians in Indian country. For cases involving non-Indians or members of other tribes, the United States and Indian nations by treaty apportioned jurisdiction between their sets of courts. The Choctaw and Chickasaw Treaty of 1866, for example, gave those tribes both civil and criminal jurisdiction over non-Indians as well as Indians within their territory.

Since the late nineteenth century, however, tribal authority to administer justice has come under attack. In 1885 Congress responded to *Crow Dog* by enacting the Major Crimes Act, which withdrew tribal jurisdiction over major crimes (such as murder, rape, and robbery) regardless of whether the victim or the alleged perpetrator or both was an Indian, and it placed this jurisdiction in the federal courts. That same year, the secretary of the interior initiated the creation of the Courts of Indian Offenses under the Bureau of Indian Affairs, which were designed to replace traditional Indian courts. In 1953, Congress adopted Public Law 280; it mandated six states—California, Minnesota, Nebraska, Oregon, Wisconsin, and Alaska (although still a federal territory until 1959) to enforce their criminal laws on reservations and granted them adjudicatory jurisdiction over civil suits between Indians or to which Indians were parties that arose on reservations. Public Law 280 also authorized other "non-mandatory" states to assume criminal and civil jurisdiction if they so chose.[14] Acting on that invitation, nine additional states had claimed some or all of the jurisdiction that Public Law 280 allowed before Congress amended the act in 1968 to require tribal consent for state assumption of jurisdiction.[15] In the Indian Civil Rights Act of 1968, Congress restricted the authority of tribes to develop their own standards of due process by extending various guarantees of the Bill of Rights—including most of the Fourth, Fifth, and Sixth Amendments—to Indian country. It also limited the jurisdiction of tribal courts to sentences not exceeding one year's imprisonment and a $5,000 fine or both.[16] Then, in *Oliphant v. Suquamish Indian Tribe* (1978), the Supreme Court ruled that Indian nations have no general criminal jurisdiction over non-Indians even in Indian country.

In *Duro v. Reina* (1990), the United States Supreme Court went further and held that an Indian tribe also lacked sovereign authority to prosecute Indians who were not members of that tribe. Disagreeing with that decision, the next year Congress amended the Indian Civil Rights Act of 1968 to "recognize and affirm" the "inherent power" of Indian tribes to exercise criminal jurisdiction over "all Indians." In *United States v. Lara* (2004), the Court held that this congressional recognition was a relaxation of previous restrictions that Congress had placed on the exercise of the tribes' inherent sovereign authority and not a delegation of federal prosecutorial power to them, and that, therefore, a federal prosecution of an Indian for assaulting a federal police officer did not violate the Double Jeopardy Clause of the Federal Constitution's Fifth Amendment, where the Indian had previously been prosecuted for "violence to a policeman" under the law of an Indian tribe to which the Indian was not a member.

Duro and *Lara* dealt with the criminal jurisdiction of tribal courts. In *Plains Commerce Bank v. Long Family Land and Cattle Company* (2008), the Supreme Court addressed the civil jurisdiction of tribal courts. Plains Commerce Bank, a non-Indian bank, sold land it owned in fee simple on the Cheyenne River Sioux Indian Reservation to non-Indians. The Longs, an Indian couple who had been leasing the land with an option to purchase, claimed the bank discriminated against them by selling the parcel to non-Indians on terms more favorable than the bank offered to sell it to them. The couple sued in the tribal court, claiming discrimination, breach of contract, and bad faith. Over the objection of the Plains Commerce Bank, the tribal court concluded that it had jurisdiction and an Indian jury ruled against the bank. The court awarded the Longs damages plus interest and also gave the Longs an option to purchase that portion of the fee land they still occupied, nullifying the bank's sale of the land to non-Indians. In a 5–4 decision, Chief Justice Roberts noted that "our cases have made clear that once tribal land is converted into fee simple, the tribe loses plenary jurisdiction over it." On that basis, he held that the "Tribal Court lacks jurisdiction to hear the Longs' discrimination claim because the Tribe lacks the civil authority to regulate the Bank's sale of its fee land."

TRIBAL AUTHORITY TO ENGAGE IN "INDIAN GAMING"

Gaming in some form has always been a part of Native American culture. Historically, many Native American tribes played games of chance, traditionally in connection with tribal powwows and ceremonies or celebrations, with little controversy. Certainly, such entertainments were not considered a matter that required governmental intervention and regulation. In 1979, however, the Seminole Tribe of Florida caught the attention of Florida legislators by opening the first "high-stakes" tribal bingo casino on its Hollywood, Florida, reservation lands. Citing criminal authority transferred to it by Congress by means of Public Law 280 and fearing the infiltration of gaming sources by "criminal elements," the State of Florida sought to shut down the Seminole bingo hall in the 1981 case of *Seminole v. Butterworth.* The United States Court of Appeals for the Fifth Circuit, however, engaged in a "civil/regulatory versus criminal/prohibitory analysis" and concluded that, because Florida did not prohibit bingo as contrary to the public policy of the state but rather merely regulated it, it had no power to act against Indian gaming on reservation lands, and the Seminole Tribe was permitted to keep its bingo hall. Several subsequent decisions in other federal courts affirmed this interpretation, and tribal bingo halls began to multiply rapidly in the early 1980s.

For the first several years following *Seminole v. Butterworth,* the position of the federal government—which exercises civil and regulatory power over Indian tribes—was one of general inattention to the explosion of bingo halls. And when Washington, recognizing the tremendous impact that Indian gaming was starting to have, began to assert itself, it did so in a fractured way. On the one hand, the Bureau of Indian Affairs (within the US Department of the Interior) recognized the potential economic boon that bingo had become to tribes, and accordingly adopted a supportive policy. On the other hand, however, the Criminal Division of the Justice Department feared that Indian gaming, like many other gambling enterprises before it, would be taken over by organized crime. That concern was heightened by the introduction of "Las Vegas-style" slot-machine operations to reservation lands as Indian gaming expanded—type and number—in the 1980s.

The corresponding congressional debate on Indian gaming mirrored this difference of opinion. Many members of Congress recognized that tribal gaming revenues had allowed tribes to provide basic governmental services to tribal members, without relying solely on federal aid. That was seen as a benefit, both to the tribes themselves and to members of Congress anxious to use these federal funds for other purposes. Nonetheless, many in Congress were reluctant to grant Indians carte blanche to promote gaming operations that most of the states did not permit the rest of their citizens to operate and that many people viewed with suspicion. Over the next several years, various federal policies on Indian gaming were proposed, but none made it through Congress. The debate was intensified in 1987, though, when the Supreme Court upheld in *California v. Cabazon Band of Mission Indians* the sovereign right of Indians to engage in gaming on tribal lands.

Congress consequently renewed efforts to address the matter of Indian gaming. Most members, however, were uninterested in the details of the debate, believing that the bill did not affect their states, or, alternatively, they were reluctant to involve themselves in an issue with so many powerful competing interests in an election year. The result of this lack of interest was the passage of a law—the Indian Gaming Regulatory Act of 1988 (IGRA)—that few in Congress had seen, and even fewer had read.

IGRA was widely touted by its proponents as a vindication of tribal sovereignty and as a means for Native Americans to promote self-reliance. In some respects, it was; it freed the federally recognized tribes from federal laws prohibiting the use of gaming devices that employ a wheel (including slot machines, from which 90 percent of all revenue at tribal and nontribal casinos is derived). But IGRA also limited Indian sovereignty, as it opened the way for states to have a role to play in Indian country. Under the Supreme Court's ruling in *Cabazon,* states had no legal means of restricting Indian gaming within their borders. IGRA changed that.[17]

IGRA divided Indian gaming into three categories and prescribed different levels of regulation for each category. Class I gaming consisted of "social games solely for prizes of minimal value or traditional forms of Indian gaming," and its regulation was left solely in the hands of the tribes. Class II included bingo and several similar games, as well as un-banked[18] games such as poker. Class II games can be offered if the state permits anyone in the state to offer them; although the Indian tribes must comply with general state law in regards to hours of operation and pot-size limitations, the states have no formal role in the regulation of Class II games. Such games are regulated by the tribes in connection with the National Indian Gaming Commission. The regulation of Class III gaming is the part of IGRA that caused consternation among the Indian tribes. Class III gaming is any gaming that is not included in Classes I or II, including banked card games, casino games, slot machines, and pari-mutuel wagering.[19] The regulation of such gaming was subject to the same requirements as those games in Class II, but with one significant addition: in order to engage in Class III gaming, federally recognized tribes had to negotiate a compact with the state, subject to approval by the secretary of the interior. Suddenly, tribes that wished to establish self-reliance by offering gaming were put at the mercy of the states, from whom they had previously been independent, and who were often unsympathetic to the plight of the tribes.

Defenders of IGRA responded by noting that Congress did not leave the tribes vulnerable to state dictation, because it imposed on states a duty to negotiate in good faith with a tribe toward the formation of a compact and authorized the tribes to sue a state in federal court in order to compel performance of that duty. The United States Supreme Court, however, removed this protection in *Seminole Tribe of Florida v. Florida* (1996). When the Seminole Tribe sued the State of Florida for its refusal to enter into good-faith negotiations, Florida moved to dismiss the complaint on the ground that congressional authorization of the suit violated its sovereign immunity from suit in federal courts. In *Seminole Tribe of Florida v. Florida,* a five-member majority of the Supreme Court agreed, holding that Congress lacked power under the Commerce Clause to abrogate state sovereign immunity. This signaled to Native American tribes that they had to become actively involved in politics at both the federal and the state levels—through lobbying, through campaign contributions, through the backing of candidates, and through political organization—if they were to secure compacts providing for the kind and level of Indian gaming necessary to achieve self-reliance and economic self-sufficiency.

As a result of *Cabazon* and IGRA (and despite the negative consequences of *Seminole Tribe of Florida v. Florida*), tribal gaming has flourished; in 2014, $28.46 billion were wagered in 459 tribal casinos operated by 244 tribes in twenty-eight states from Connecticut to California. Tribal gaming has become Indian country's most effective economic-development tool, and the slot machine has become for many gaming tribes their "new buffalo"—a single source capable of fulfilling all of their needs, including jobs, schools, social services, and infrastructure. Federally recognized tribes with established reservations

have sought to enter into compacts with state governments to provide badly needed revenues for their tribal governments and members. The lure of casino revenues has also motivated tribes that lost or never had federal recognition, and tribes that lost most or all of
their lands to the Dawes Act and its successors, to reacquire federal recognition and reestablish their lands. The current Supreme Court has not been sympathetic to these efforts,
as *Carcieri v. Salazar* (2009), *Match-E-Be-Nash-She-Wish Band of Pottawatomi Indians v.
Patchack* (2012), and *Michigan v. Bay Mills Indian Community* (2014) show.

Carcieri involved the interpretation of the Indian Reorganization Act of 1934 (IRA),
which authorizes the secretary of the interior to acquire land and hold it in trust "for the
purpose of providing land for Indians." The IRA defines *Indian* to "include all persons of
Indian descent who are members of any recognized tribe now under Federal jurisdiction."
The Narragansett Tribe in Rhode Island, which lost federal recognition in 1880 but re-
gained it in 1983, asked the secretary of the interior to accept land into federal trust to
reestablish its reservation, and the secretary complied. The tribe asserted that it would use
the land to build apartments, but the State of Rhode Island worried that the Narragansett
might also use it to build a casino and that it would lose real estate taxes if the land were
placed in trust. So Rhode Island sued, arguing that the secretary lacked the authority to
acquire the land in question because the phrase *now under Federal jurisdiction* meant under
jurisdiction in 1934 when the act was passed. The lower federal courts concluded that the
meaning of *now* was ambiguous and that under the canons of construction customarily
applied under federal Indian law, the IRA was to be liberally construed in favor of the Indians, with all ambiguities resolved in their favor, and with tribal property rights and sovereignty preserved unless Congress's intent to the contrary was clear and unambiguous.
The Supreme Court, however, reversed. Justice Thomas declined to apply the canons and
held that "the phrase 'now under Federal jurisdiction' refers to a tribe that was under federal jurisdiction at the time of the statute's enactment."

In *Match-E-Be-Nash-She-Wish Band of Pottawatomi Indians v. Patchack,* the Court continued to complicate efforts by tribes to bring land into federal trust for gaming purposes.
The Band, an Indian tribe federally recognized in 1999, requested that the secretary take
into trust on its behalf a tract of land in Wayland Township, Michigan, which it intended
to use "for gaming purposes." The secretary took title to the property in 2009, one month
before the *Carcieri* decision. David Patchak, who lived nearby, filed suit in federal district
court asserting that the IRA did not authorize the secretary to acquire the property because
the band was not a federally recognized tribe when the IRA was enacted. Alleging a variety
of economic, environmental, and aesthetic harms as a result of the band's proposed use of
the property to operate a casino, he requested injunctive and declaratory relief reversing
the secretary's decision to take title to the land. Without reaching the merits, the district
court dismissed his suit, ruling that he lacked standing to sue, only to be reversed by the
Court of Appeals for the District of Columbia Circuit. In an 8–1 vote, the Supreme Court
affirmed the appellate court and held that Patchak had standing to challenge the secretary's
acquisition of the land. Speaking for the Court, Justice Kagan argued that the IRA requires
the secretary to acquire land with its eventual use in mind, after assessing the potential
conflicts that use might create. And, she continued, because the IRA encompasses the
land's use, neighbors to that use (like Patchak) are reasonable challengers of the secretary's
decisions, and their interests, whether economic, environmental, or aesthetic, come within
the IRA's regulatory ambit.

Finally, in *Michigan v. Bay Mills Indian Community*, Justice Kagan held for a five-member majority that tribal sovereignty prevented Michigan from suing the tribe in question
for operating a casino located outside of Indian country because Congress in IGRA had
not delegated the states that power. That would seem like a victory for the tribes, and a
reemergence of a more sympathetic Court, but the tribe's victory was pyrrhic, for Justice

Kagan made clear that Michigan could "resort to other mechanisms, including legal actions against the responsible [tribal] individuals" who were operating the casino.

THE CONTINUED VIABILITY OF THE CANONS OF CONSTRUCTION OF FEDERAL INDIAN LAW?

Perhaps because of the financial success of the gaming tribes and their aggressive use of casino profits to influence the political process, the Supreme Court over the course of the past decade has become decidedly less inclined to employ the canons of construction of federal Indian law to the tribes' advantage. As a result of its rulings in *Plains Commerce Bank, Carcieri,* and *Bay Mills,* tribal leaders now seek to keep cases from reaching the Supreme Court, believing that it is better to accept adverse decisions by lower courts, where the impact is limited, than risk having those adverse decisions affirmed by the Supreme Court and applied nationally. The 2013 Supreme Court decision in *Adoptive Couple v. Baby Girl* dramatically illustrates why. Justice Alito for a five-member majority refused to construe liberally the Indian Child Welfare Act of 1978, enacted to help preserve the cultural identity and heritage of Indian tribes, and thereby prevent a non-Indian family from adopting an Indian child.

NOTES

1. In discussing Native Americans, this chapter uses *tribes* and *nations* synonymously. For the reader who wants a comprehensive, definitive, and objective introduction into the subject of this chapter, there is no better source than the 1,622-page *Cohen's Handbook of Federal Indian Law* (Newark, NJ: LexisNexis, 2012).

2. This phrase is taken from Chief Justice John Marshall's famous opinion in *Cherokee Nation v. Georgia* (1831). For a perceptive analysis, see Jill Norgren, *The Cherokee Cases: The Confrontation of Law and Politics* (New York: McGraw-Hill, 1996).

3. Vine Deloria Jr. and Clifford Lytle, *The Nations Within: The Past and Future of American Indian Sovereignty* (New York: Pantheon Books, 1984), 2.

4. See David E. Wilkins, "Tribal-State Affairs: American States as 'Disclaiming' Sovereigns," *Publius: The Journal of Federalism* 28 (Fall 1998): 55–81.

5. Charles F. Wilkinson, *American Indians, Time, and the Law* (New Haven, CT: Yale University Press, 1987), 112.

6. See Henry E. Fritz, *The Movement for Indian Assimilation, 1860–1890* (Philadelphia: University of Pennsylvania Press, 1963); Francis P. Prucha, *American Indian Policy in Crisis: Christian Reformers and the Indian, 1865–1900* (Norman: University of Oklahoma Press, 1976); and Frederick E. Hoxie, *A Final Promise: The Campaign to Assimilate the Indians, 1880–1920* (New York: Cambridge University Press, 1984).

7. On the Indian Reorganization Act and its effects, see Graham D. Taylor, *The New Deal and American Indian Tribalism: The Administration of the Indian Reorganization Act, 1934–45* (Lincoln: University of Nebraska Press, 1980); on termination policy, see Larry W. Burt, *Tribalism in Crisis: Federal Indian Policy, 1953–1961* (Albuquerque: University of New Mexico Press, 1982); and on the transformation of Indian policy during the Nixon administration, see George Pierre Castile, *To Show Heart: Native American Self-Determination and Federal Indian Policy, 1960–1975* (Tucson: University of Arizona Press, 1998). Useful overviews include Russell L. Barsh and James Youngblood Henderson, *The Road: Indian Tribes and Political Liberty* (Berkeley: University of California Press, 1980); Stephen Cornell, *The Return of the Native: American Indian Political Resurgence* (New York: Oxford University Press, 1988); and Emma R. Gross, *Contemporary Federal Policy Toward American Indians* (Westport, CT: Greenwood Press, 1989).

8. Justice William Johnson offered considerably more support for tribal rights in his concurring opinion: "The uniform practice of acknowledging [the tribes'] right to soil, by purchasing from them, and restraining all persons from encroaching upon their territory, makes it unnecessary to insist upon their right to soil."

9. Quoted in Wilkinson, *American Indians, Time, and the Law,* 19.

10. Ibid., 21. For more general analyses of the General Allotment Act and its consequences, see Delos S. Otis, *The Dawes Act and the Allotment of Indian Lands* (Norman: University of Oklahoma Press, 1973); Loring B. Priest, *Uncle Sam's Stepchildren: The Reformation of United States Indian Policy, 1865–1887* (New Brunswick, NJ: Rutgers University Press, 1942); and Ronald L. Trosper, "Mind Sets and Economic Development on Indian Reservations," in *What Can Tribes Do?* edited by Stephen Cornell and Joseph P. Kalt (Los Angeles: University of California Indian Studies Center, 1992). Not every scholar has viewed the transfer of ownership from tribes to individuals as a negative development; see, for example, Terry L. Anderson, *Sovereign Nations or Reservations? An Economic History of American Indians* (San Francisco: Pacific Research Institute for Public Policy, 1995).

11. Wilkinson, *American Indians, Time, and the Law,* 8.

12. This ruling has been subjected to scathing critique. See, for example, David E. Wilkins, "The U.S. Supreme Court's Explication of 'Federal Plenary Power': An Analysis of Case Law Affecting Tribal Sovereignty, 1886–1914," in *Native American Sovereignty,* edited by John R. Wunder (New York: Garland, 1996).

13. Robert B. Porter, "Strengthening Tribal Sovereignty Through Peacemaking: How the Anglo-American Legal Tradition Destroys Indigenous Societies," *Columbia Human Rights Law Review* 28 (1997): 238.

14. 18 U.S.C. sec. 1162. For discussion of the threat to tribal autonomy posed by Public Law 280, see Carole Goldberg-Ambrose, *Planting Tail Feathers: Tribal Survival and Public Law 280* (Los Angeles: American Indian Studies Center, 1998).

15. 25 U.S.C. sec. 1326. Since adoption of this legislation, no Indian nation has consented to state assumption of jurisdiction. See Carole Goldberg, "Public Law 280 and the Problem of 'Lawlessness' in California Indian Country," in *Contemporary Native American Political Issues,* edited by Troy Johnson (Walnut Creek, CA: Alta Mira Press, 1999), 198.

16. 25 U.S.C. sec. 1301 et seq. For an attempt to unravel the intricacies of the criminal jurisdiction of tribal courts, see Robert N. Clinton, "Criminal Jurisdiction over Indian Lands: A Journey Through a Jurisdictional Maze," *Arizona Law Review* 18 (1976): 503–583.

17. See Ralph A. Rossum, *The Supreme Court and Tribal Gaming:* California v. Cabazon Band of Mission Indians (Lawrence: University Press of Kansas, 2011), 149–162.

18. A "banked" card game is one in which the house has an interest in the outcome of the game. In other words, the house will ensure available funds to pay all winners of a game, even if the aggregate of all losses in the game—losers' wagers in the game—is less than it takes to pay all winners.

19. "Pari-mutuel wagering" is a betting pool in which those who bet on competitors finishing in the first three places share the total amount bet, minus a percentage for the management.

SELECTED READINGS

The Federalist, Nos. 3, 42.

Ablavsky, Gregory. "Beyond the Indian Commerce Clause," *Yale Law Journal* 124 (2015): 1012–1090.

Anaya, S. James. *Indigenous Peoples in International Law.* New York: Oxford University Press, 2004.

Coffey, Wallace, and Rebecca Tsosie. "Rethinking the Tribal Sovereignty Doctrine: Cultural Sovereignty and the Collective Future of Indian Nations." *Stanford Law and Policy Review* 12 (2001): 191–210.

Cohen's Handbook of Federal Indian Law. 2012 ed. Newark, NJ: LexisNexis, 2012.

Deloria, Vine, Jr., and Clifford Lytle. *The Nations Within: The Past and Future of American Indian Sovereignty.* New York: Pantheon Books, 1984.

___, and David E. Wilkins. *Tribes, Treaties, and Constitutional Tribulations.* Austin: University of Texas Press, 1999.

Goldberg, Carole E., Kevin K. Washburn, and Philip P. Frickey, eds. *Indian Law Stories.* New York: Foundation Press, 2011.

Goldberg-Ambrose, Carole. *Planting Tail Feathers: Tribal Survival and Public Law 280.* Los Angeles: American Indian Studies Center, 1998.

Hoxie, Frederick E. *A Final Promise: The Campaign to Assimilate the Indians, 1880–1920.* New York: Cambridge University Press, 1984.

Kappler, Charles J. *Indian Affairs: Law and Treaties.* 7 vols. Washington, DC: Government Printing Office, 1904.

Light, Steven Andrew, and Kathryn R. L. Rand. *Indian Gaming and Tribal Sovereignty: The Casino Compromise.* Lawrence: University Press of Kansas, 2005.

Norgren, Jill. *The Cherokee Cases: The Confrontation of Law and Politics.* New York: McGraw-Hill, 1996.

Rossum, Ralph A. *The Supreme Court and Tribal Gaming:* California v. Cabazon Band of Mission Indians. Lawrence: University Press of Kansas, 2011.

Taylor, Graham D. *The New Deal and American Indian Tribalism: The Administration of the Indian Reorganization Act, 1934–45*. Lincoln: University of Nebraska Press, 1980.

Wildenthal, Bryan H. "Federal Labor Law, Indian Sovereignty, and the Canons of Construction." *Oregon Law Review* 86 (2007): 413–531.

Wilkins, David E. *American Indian Sovereignty and the U.S. Supreme Court: The Masking of Justice*. Austin: University of Texas Press, 1997.

___, and K. Tsianina Lomawaima. *Uneven Ground: American Indian Sovereignty and Federal Law*. Norman: University of Oklahoma Press, 2001.

Wilkinson, Charles F. *Indian Tribes as Sovereign Governments: A Sourcebook on Federal-Tribal History, Law, and Policy*. 2nd ed. Oakland, CA: American Indian Resources Institute, 2004.

Johnson v. McIntosh
21 U.S. (8 Wheat.) 543 (1823)

As a result of a July 5, 1773, land sale from the Illinois Indians and an October 18, 1775, land sale from the Piankeshaw Indians, Thomas Johnson acquired title to land in what would later become the state of Illinois. Upon his death in 1819, the property, of which he had never taken physical possession, was inherited by his son and grandson. In 1776, the Colony of Virginia, which under the terms of its royal charter of 1609 was given dominion over the lands in question by King James I, declared its independence from Great Britain. In 1783, the State of Virginia transferred ownership of these lands to the United States, and in 1818, the United States sold these lands to William McIntosh, who took possession of them. Upon inheriting these lands, Johnson's heirs also sought to take possession of them, only to find them occupied by McIntosh, whereupon the Johnson heirs brought an action of ejectment (i.e., an action for the recovery of the possession of land) in the district court for Illinois. The district court ruled for McIntosh, based on his purchase of the land from the United States. The case reached the US Supreme Court on a writ of error. Opinion of the Court: <u>Marshall</u>, Washington, Johnson, Livingston, Todd, Duval, Story.

THE CHIEF JUSTICE delivered the opinion of the Court.

The plaintiffs in this cause claim the land, in their declaration mentioned, under two grants, purporting to be made, the first in 1773, and the last in 1775, by the chiefs of certain Indian tribes, constituting the Illinois and the Piankeshaw Nations; and the question is, whether this title can be recognized in the Courts of the United States.

The facts, as stated in the case agreed, show the authority of the chiefs who executed this conveyance, so far as it could be given by their own people; and likewise show, that the particular tribes for whom these chiefs acted were in rightful possession of the land they sold. The inquiry, therefore, is, in a great measure, confined to the power of Indians to give, and of private individuals to receive, a title which can be sustained in the Courts of this country.

On the discovery of this immense continent, the great nations of Europe were eager to appropriate to themselves so much of it as they could respectively acquire. Its vast extent offered an ample field to the ambition and enterprise of all; and the character and religion of its inhabitants afforded an apology for considering them as a people over whom the superior genius of Europe might claim an ascendancy. The potentates of the old world found no difficulty in convincing themselves that they made ample compensation to the inhabitants of the new, by bestowing on them civilization and Christianity, in exchange for unlimited independence. But, as they were all in pursuit of nearly the same object, it was necessary, in order to avoid conflicting settlements, and consequent war with each other, to establish a principle, which all should acknowledge as the law by which the right of acquisition, which they all asserted, should be regulated as between themselves. This principle was, that discovery gave title to the government by whose subjects, or by whose authority, it was made, against all other European governments, which title might be consummated by possession.

The exclusion of all other Europeans, necessarily gave to the nation making the discovery the sole right of acquiring the soil from the natives, and establishing settlements upon it. It was a right with which no Europeans could interfere. It was a right which all asserted for themselves, and to the assertion of which, by others, all assented. Those relations which were to exist between the discoverer and the natives, were to be regulated by themselves. The rights thus acquired being exclusive, no other power could interpose between them.

In the establishment of these relations, the rights of the original inhabitants were, in no instance, entirely disregarded; but were necessarily, to a considerable extent, impaired. They were admitted to be the rightful occupants of the soil, with a legal as well as just claim to retain possession of it, and to use it according to their own discretion; but their rights to complete sovereignty, as independent nations, were necessarily diminished, and their power to dispose of the soil at their own will, to whomsoever they pleased, was denied by the original fundamental principle, that discovery gave exclusive title to those who made it.

While the different nations of Europe respected the right of the natives, as occupants, they asserted the ultimate dominion to be in themselves; and claimed and exercised, as a consequence of this ultimate dominion, a power to grant the soil, while yet in possession of the natives. These grants have been understood by all, to convey a title to the grantees, subject only to the Indian right of occupancy.

The history of America, from its discovery to the present day, proves, we think, the universal recognition of these principles. . . .

The United States . . . have unequivocally acceded to that great and broad rule by which its civilized inhabitants now hold this country. They hold, and assert in themselves, the title by which it was acquired. They maintain, as all others have maintained, that discovery gave an exclusive right to extinguish the Indian title of occupancy, either by purchase or by conquest; and gave also a right to such a degree of sovereignty, as the circumstances of the people would allow them to exercise.

The power now possessed by the government of the United States to grant lands, resided, while we were colonies, in the crown, or its grantees. The validity of the titles given by either has never been questioned in our Courts. It has been exercised uniformly over territory in possession of the Indians. The existence of this power must negative the existence of any right which may conflict with, and control it. An absolute title to lands cannot exist, at the same time, in different persons, or in different governments. An absolute, must be an exclusive title, or at least a title which excludes all others not compatible with it. All our institutions recognize the absolute title of the crown, subject only to the Indian right of occupancy, and recognize the absolute title of the crown to extinguish that right. This is incompatible with an absolute and complete title in the Indians.

We will not enter into the controversy, whether agriculturists, merchants, and manufacturers, have a right, on abstract principles, to expel hunters from the territory they possess, or to contract their limits. Conquest gives a title which the Courts of the conqueror cannot deny, whatever the private and speculative opinions of individuals may be, respecting the original justice of the claim which has been successfully asserted. The British government, which was then our government, and whose rights have passed to the United States, asserted a title to all the lands occupied by Indians, within the chartered limits of the British colonies. It asserted also a limited sovereignty over them, and the exclusive right of extinguishing the title which occupancy gave to them. These claims have been maintained and established as far west as the river Mississippi, by the sword. The title to a vast portion of the lands we now hold, originates in them. It is not for the Courts of this country to question the validity of this title, or to sustain one which is incompatible with it. . . .

However extravagant the pretension of converting the discovery of an inhabited country into conquest may appear; if the principle has been asserted in the first instance, and afterwards sustained; if a country has been acquired and held under it; if the property of the great mass of the community originates in it, it becomes the law of the land, and cannot be questioned. So, too, with respect to the concomitant principle, that the Indian inhabitants are to be considered merely as occupants, to be protected, indeed, while in peace, in the possession of their lands, but to be deemed incapable of transferring the absolute title to others. However this restriction may be opposed to natural right, and to the usages of civilized nations, yet, if it be indispensable to that system under which the country has been settled, and be adapted to the actual condition of the two people, it may, perhaps, be supported by reason, and certainly cannot be rejected by Courts of justice. . . .

After bestowing on this subject a degree of attention which was more required by the magnitude of the interest in litigation, and the able and elaborate arguments of the bar, than by its intrinsic difficulty, the Court is decidedly of opinion, that the plaintiffs do not exhibit a title which can be sustained in the Courts of the United States; and that there is no error in the judgment which was rendered against them in the District Court of Illinois.

Judgment affirmed, with costs.

Cherokee Nation v. Georgia
30 U.S. (5 Pet.) 1 (1831)

Claiming status as a foreign state, the Cherokee Nation of Indians brought suit in the United States Supreme Court, under the Court's original jurisdiction, against the State of Georgia. It did so under those provisions of Article III, Section 2, of the Constitution giving the Court jurisdiction in controversies in which a state of the United States or the citizens thereof and a foreign state, citizens, or subjects thereof are parties and original jurisdiction in all cases in which a state shall be a party. The Cherokee Nation sought an injunction to prevent the execution of various Georgia laws that sought to assert control over Cherokee lands within the state that were protected by treaty. The issue for the Court was whether the Cherokee Nation was a foreign state in the sense in which that term was used in the Constitution and, therefore, whether the Court had jurisdiction to hear the case. Opinion of the Court: <u>Marshall</u>, Johnson, Duval, McLean, Baldwin. Concurring opinions: <u>Johnson</u>; <u>Baldwin</u>. Dissenting opinion: <u>Thompson</u>, Story.

THE CHIEF JUSTICE delivered the opinion of the Court.

This bill is brought by the Cherokee nation, praying an injunction to restrain the state of Georgia from the execution of certain laws of that state, which, as is alleged, go directly to annihilate the Cherokees as a political society, and to seize, for the use of Georgia, the lands of the nation which have been assured to them by the United States in solemn treaties repeatedly made and still in force.

If courts were permitted to indulge their sympathies, a case better calculated to excite them can scarcely be imagined. A people once numerous, powerful, and truly independent, found by our ancestors in the quiet and uncontrolled possession of an ample domain, gradually sinking beneath our superior policy, our arts and our arms, have yielded their lands by successive treaties, each of which contains a solemn guarantee of the residue, until they retain no more of their formerly extensive territory than is deemed necessary to their comfortable subsistence. To preserve this remnant, the present application is made.

Before we can look into the merits of the case, a preliminary inquiry presents itself. Has this court jurisdiction of the cause? . . . Do the Cherokees constitute a foreign state in the sense of the constitution?

. . . The condition of the Indians in relation to the United States is perhaps unlike that of any other two people in existence. In the general, nations not owing a common allegiance are foreign to each other. The term foreign nation is, with strict propriety, applicable by either to the other. But the relation of the Indians to the United States is marked by peculiar and cardinal distinctions which exist no where else.

The Indian territory is admitted to compose a part of the United States. In all our maps, geographical treatises, histories, and laws, it is so considered. In all our intercourse with foreign nations, in our commercial regulations, in any attempt at intercourse between Indians and foreign nations, they are considered as within the jurisdictional limits of the United States, subject to many of those restraints which are imposed upon our own citizens. They acknowledge themselves in their treaties to be under the protection of the United States; they admit that the United States shall have the sole and exclusive right of regulating the trade with them, and managing all their affairs as they think proper. . . .

Though the Indians are acknowledged to have an unquestionable, and, heretofore, unquestioned right to the lands they occupy, until that right shall be extinguished by a voluntary cession to our government; yet it may well be doubted whether those tribes which reside within the acknowledged boundaries of the United States can, with strict accuracy, be denominated foreign nations. They may, more correctly, perhaps, be denominated domestic dependent nations. They occupy a territory to which we assert a title independent of their will, which must take effect in point of possession when their right of possession ceases. Meanwhile they are in a state of pupilage. Their relation to the United States resembles that of a ward to his guardian.

They look to our government for protection; rely upon its kindness and its power; appeal to it for relief to their wants; and address the president as their great father. They and their country are considered by foreign nations, as well as by ourselves, as being so completely under the sovereignty and dominion of the United States, that any attempt to acquire their lands, or to form a political connexion with them, would be considered by all as an invasion of our territory, and an act of hostility.

These considerations go far to support the opinion, that the framers of our constitution had not the Indian tribes in view, when they opened the courts of the union to controversies between a state or the citizens thereof, and foreign states.

. . . Be this as it may, the peculiar relations between the United States and the Indians occupying our territory are such brought by the Cherokee nation, praying an injunction to restrain the state of Georgia from the execution of certain laws of that state, which, as is alleged, go directly to annihilate the Cherokees as a political society, and to seize, for the use of Georgia, the lands of the nation which have been assured to them by the United States in solemn treaties repeatedly made and still in force.

If courts were permitted to indulge their sympathies, a case better calculated to excite them can scarcely be imagined. A people once numerous, powerful, and truly independent, found by our ancestors in the quiet and uncontrolled possession of an ample domain, gradually sinking beneath our superior policy, our arts and our arms, have yielded their lands by successive treaties, each of which contains a solemn guarantee of the residue, until they retain no more of their formerly extensive territory than is deemed necessary to their comfortable subsistence. To preserve this remnant, the present application is made.

Before we can look into the merits of the case, a preliminary inquiry presents itself. Has this court jurisdiction of the cause? . . . Do the Cherokees constitute a foreign state in the sense of the constitution?

. . . The condition of the Indians in relation to the United States is perhaps unlike that of any other two people in existence. In the general, nations not owing a common allegiance are foreign to each other. The term foreign nation is, with strict propriety, applicable by either to the other. But the relation of the Indians to the United States is marked by peculiar and cardinal distinctions which exist no where else.

The Indian territory is admitted to compose a part of the United States. In all our maps, geographical treatises, histories, and laws, it is so considered. In all our intercourse with foreign nations, in our commercial regulations, in any attempt at intercourse between Indians and foreign nations, they are considered as within the jurisdictional limits of the United States, subject to many of those restraints which are imposed upon our own citizens. They acknowledge themselves in their treaties to be under the protection of the United States; they admit that the United States shall have the sole and exclusive right of regulating the trade with them, and managing all their affairs as they think proper. . . .

Though the Indians are acknowledged to have an unquestionable, and, heretofore, unquestioned right to the lands they occupy, until that right shall be extinguished by a voluntary cession to our government; yet it may well be doubted whether those tribes which reside within the acknowledged boundaries of the United States can, with strict accuracy, be denominated foreign nations. They may, more correctly, perhaps, be denominated domestic dependent nations. They occupy a territory to which we assert a title independent of their will, which must take effect in point of possession when their right of possession ceases. Meanwhile they are in a state of pupilage. Their relation to the United States resembles that of a ward to his guardian.

They look to our government for protection; rely upon its kindness and its power; appeal to it for relief to their wants; and address the president as their great father. They and their country are considered by foreign nations, as well as by ourselves, as being so completely under the sovereignty and dominion of the United States, that any attempt to acquire their lands, or to form a political connexion with them, would be considered by all as an invasion of our territory, and an act of hostility.

These considerations go far to support the opinion, that the framers of our constitution had not the Indian tribes in, that we should feel much difficulty in considering them as designated by the term foreign state, were there no other part of the constitution which might shed light on the meaning of these words. But we think that in construing them, considerable aid is furnished by that clause in the eighth section of the third article; which empowers congress to "regulate commerce with foreign nations, and among the several states, and with the Indian tribes."

In this clause they are as clearly contradistinguished by a name appropriate to themselves, from foreign nations, as from the several states composing the union. They are designated by a distinct appellation; and as this appellation can be applied to neither of the others, neither can the appellation distinguishing either of the others be in fair construction applied to them. The objects, to which the power of regulating commerce might be directed, are divided into three distinct classes—foreign nations, the several states, and Indian tribes. When forming this article, the convention considered them as entirely distinct. . . .

The court has bestowed its best attention on this question, and, after mature deliberation, the majority is of opinion that an Indian tribe or nation within the United States is not a foreign state in the sense of the constitution, and cannot maintain an action in the courts of the United States.

A serious additional objection exists to the jurisdiction of the court. Is the matter of the bill the proper subject for judicial inquiry and decision? It seeks to restrain a state from the forcible exercise of legislative power over a neighbouring people, asserting their independence; their right to which the state denies. On several of the matters alleged in the bill, for example on the laws making it criminal to exercise the usual powers of self government in their own country by the Cherokee nation, this court cannot interpose; at least in the form in which those matters are presented.

That part of the bill which respects the land occupied by the Indians, and prays the aid of the court to protect their possession, may be more doubtful. The mere question of right

might perhaps be decided by this court in a proper case with proper parties. But the court is asked to do more than decide on the title. The bill requires us to control the legislature of Georgia, and to restrain the exertion of its physical force. The propriety of such an interposition by the court may be well questioned. It savours too much of the exercise of political power to be within the proper province of the judicial department. But the opinion on the point respecting parties makes it unnecessary to decide this question.

If it be true that the Cherokee nation have rights, this is not the tribunal in which those rights are to be asserted. If it be true that wrongs have been inflicted, and that still greater are to be apprehended, this is not the tribunal which can redress the past or prevent the future.

The motion for an injunction is denied.

JUSTICE THOMPSON, dissenting.

That a state of this union may be sued by a foreign state, when a proper case exists and is presented, is too plainly and expressly declared in the constitution to admit of doubt; and the first inquiry is, whether the Cherokee nation is a foreign state within the sense and meaning of the constitution.

The terms state and nation are used in the law of nations, as well as in common parlance, as importing the same thing; and imply a body of men, united together, to procure their mutual safety and advantage by means of their union. Such a society has its affairs and interests to manage; it deliberates, and takes resolutions in common, and thus becomes a moral person, having an understanding and a will peculiar to itself, and is susceptible of obligations and laws. Vattel, 1. Nations being composed of men naturally free and independent, and who, before the establishment of civil societies, live together in the state of nature, nations or sovereign states; are to be considered as so many free persons, living together in a state of nature. Vattel 2, §4. Every nation that governs itself, under what form soever, without any dependence on a foreign power, is a sovereign state. Its rights are naturally the same as those of any other state. Such are moral persons who live together in a natural society, under the law of nations. It is sufficient if it be really sovereign and independent: that is, it must govern itself by its own authority and laws. We ought, therefore, to reckon in the number of sovereigns those states that have bound themselves to another more powerful, although by an unequal alliance. The conditions of these unequal alliances may be infinitely varied; but whatever they are, provided the inferior ally reserves to itself the sovereignty or the right to govern its own body, it ought to be considered an independent state. Consequently, a weak state, that, in order to provide for its safety, places itself under the protection of a more powerful one, without stripping itself of the right of government and sovereignty, does not cease on this account to be placed among the sovereigns who acknowledge no other power. Tributary and feudatory states do not thereby cease to be sovereign and independent states, so long as self government, and sovereign and independent authority is left in the administration of the state. Vattel, c. 1, pp. 16, 17.

Testing the character and condition of the Cherokee Indians by these rules, it is not perceived how it is possible to escape the conclusion, that they form a sovereign state. They have always been dealt with as such by the government of the United States; both before and since the adoption of the present constitution. They have been admitted and treated as a people governed solely and exclusively by their own laws, usages, and customs within their own territory, claiming and exercising exclusive dominion over the same; yielding up by treaty, from time to time, portions of their land, but still claiming absolute sovereignty and self government over what remained unsold. And this has been the light in which they have, until recently, been considered from the earliest settlement of the country by the white people. . . .

The phraseology of the clause in the constitution, giving to congress the power to regulate commerce, is supposed to afford an argument against considering the Cherokees a foreign nation. The clause reads thus, "to regulate commerce with foreign nations, and among the several states, and with the Indian tribes." Constitution, Art. 1, §8. The argument is, that if the Indian tribes are foreign nations, they would have been included without being specially named, and being so named imports something different from the previous term "foreign nations."

This appears to me to partake too much of a mere verbal criticism, to draw after it the important conclusion that Indian tribes are not foreign nations. But the clause affords, irresistibly, the conclusion, that the Indian tribes are not there understood as included within the description, of the "several states;" or there could have been no fitness in immediately thereafter particularizing "the Indian tribes."

It is generally understood that every separate body of Indians is divided into bands or tribes, and forms a little community within the nation to which it belongs; and as the nation has some particular symbol by which it is distinguished from others, so each tribe has a badge from which it is denominated, and each tribe may have rights applicable to itself.

Cases may arise where the trade with a particular tribe may require to be regulated, and which might not have been embraced under the general description of the term nation, or it might at least have left the case somewhat doubtful; as the clause was intended to vest in congress the power to regulate all commercial intercourse, this phraseology was probably adopted to meet all possible cases; and the provision would have been imperfect, if the term Indian tribes had been omitted. . . .

And I am authorized by my brother Story to say, that he concurs with me in this opinion.

Worcester v. Georgia
31 U.S. (6 Pet.) 515 (1832)

Samuel A. Worcester, a citizen of Vermont and a Congregationalist missionary to the Cherokee Nation, was convicted in Gwinnett County

(Georgia) Superior Court and sentenced to four years of hard labor for violating an 1830 Georgia statute entitled "An Act to Prevent the Exercise of

Assumed and Arbitrary Power, by All Persons, Under Pretext of Authority from the Cherokee Indians, and Their Laws, and to Prevent White Persons from Residing Within That Part of the Chartered Limits of Georgia Occupied by the Cherokee Indians. . . ." The act prohibited "white persons" from "residing within the limits of the Cherokee nation without a license" and "without having taken the oath to support and defend the constitution and laws of the state of Georgia." The court rejected Worcester's argument that the Georgia statute was unconstitutional and void because the Constitution gave the power to establish and regulate trade and intercourse with the Indian tribes exclusively to the government of the United States and because this power had been exercised by treaties and by acts of Congress that were directly applicable to the Cherokees. His case was then brought before the US Supreme Court on a writ of error.* Opinion of the Court: <u>Marshall</u>, Johnson, Duval, Story, Thompson, McLean. Concurring opinion: <u>McLean</u>. Dissenting opinion: <u>Baldwin</u>.

THE CHIEF JUSTICE delivered the opinion of the Court.

This cause, in every point of view in which it can be placed, is of the deepest interest.

The defendant is a state, a member of the union, which has exercised the powers of government over a people who deny its jurisdiction, and are under the protection of the United States.

The plaintiff is a citizen of the state of Vermont, condemned to hard labor for four years in the penitentiary of Georgia; under color of an act which he alleges to be repugnant to the constitution, laws, and treaties of the United States.

The legislative power of a state, the controlling power of the constitution and laws of the United States, the rights, if they have any, the political existence of a once numerous and powerful people, the personal liberty of a citizen, are all involved in the subject now to be considered.

The defendant . . . avers, that the residence, charged in the indictment, was under the authority of the president of the United States, and with the permission and approval of the Cherokee nation. That the treaties, subsisting between the United States and the Cherokees, acknowledge their right as a sovereign nation to govern themselves and all persons who have settled within their territory, free from any right of legislative interference by the several states composing the United States of America. That the act under which the prosecution was instituted is repugnant to the said treaties, and is, therefore, unconstitutional and void. That the said act is, also, unconstitutional; because it interferes with, and attempts to regulate and control, the intercourse with the Cherokee nation, which belongs, exclusively, to congress; and, because, also, it is repugnant to the statute of the United States, entitled "an act to regulate trade and intercourse with the Indian tribes, and to preserve peace on the frontiers."

It has been said at the bar, that the acts of the legislature of Georgia seize on the whole Cherokee country, parcel it out among the neighbouring counties of the state, extend her code over the whole country, abolish its institutions and its laws, and annihilate its political existence.

From the commencement of our government, congress has passed acts to regulate trade and intercourse with the Indians; which treat them as nations, respect their rights, and manifest a firm purpose to afford that protection which treaties stipulate. All these acts . . . manifestly consider the several Indian nations as distinct political communities, having territorial boundaries, within which their authority is exclusive, and having a right to all the lands within those boundaries, which is not only acknowledged, but guaranteed by the United States.

In 1819, Congress passed an act for promoting those humane designs of civilizing the neighboring Indians, which had long been cherished by the executive. . . . This act avowedly contemplates the preservation of the Indian nations as an object sought by the United States, and proposes to effect this object by civilizing and converting them from hunters into agriculturists. Though the Cherokees had already made considerable progress in this improvement, it cannot be doubted that the general words of the act comprehend them. Their advance in the "habits and arts of civilization," rather encouraged perseverance in the laudable exertions still farther to meliorate their condition. This act furnishes strong additional evidence of a settled purpose to fix the Indians in their country by giving them security at home.

The treaties and laws of the United States contemplate the Indian territory as completely separated from that of the states; and provide that all intercourse with them shall be carried on exclusively by the government of the union.

. . . The settled doctrine of the law of nations is, that a weaker power does not surrender its independence—its right to self government, by associating with a stronger, and taking its protection. A weak state, in order to provide for its safety, may place itself under the protection of one more powerful, without stripping itself of the right of government, and ceasing to be a state. Examples of this kind are not wanting in Europe. "Tributary and feudatory states," says Vattel, "do not thereby cease to be sovereign and independent states, so long as self government and sovereign and independent authority are left in the administration of the state." At the present day, more than one state may be considered as holding its right of self government under the guarantee and protection of one or more allies.

The Cherokee nation, then, is a distinct community occupying its own territory, with boundaries accurately described, in which the laws of Georgia can have no force, and which the citizens of Georgia have no right to enter, but with the assent of the Cherokees themselves, or in conformity with treaties, and with the acts of congress. The whole intercourse between the United States and this nation, is, by our constitution and laws, vested in the government of the United States. . . .

It is the opinion of this court that the judgment of the superior court for the county of Gwinnett, in the state of Georgia, condemning Samuel A. Worcester to hard labor, in the penitentiary of the state of Georgia, for four years, was pronounced by that court under color of a law which is void, as being repugnant to the constitution, treaties, and laws of the United States, and ought, therefore, to be reversed and annulled.

United States v. Kagama
118 U.S. 375 (1886)

In Ex parte Crow Dog (1883), *the US Supreme Court overturned the conviction in federal court of an Indian who had murdered another Indian in Indian country. The Court reasoned that since Congress had not enacted specific legislation to grant jurisdiction to federal courts over this crime, jurisdiction was retained exclusively by tribal authorities. Congress responded with Section 9 of the Indian Appropriations Act of 1885—otherwise known as the Major Crimes Act of 1885. Among its various provisions, it gave jurisdiction to the courts of the United States for the crimes of murder, manslaughter, rape, assault with intent to kill, arson, burglary, and larceny committed on an Indian reservation within a state of the Union. In particular, it provided that all "Indians committing any of the above crimes against the person or property of another Indian or other person, within the boundaries of any State of the United States, and within the limits of any Indian reservation, shall be subject to the same laws, tried in the same courts and in the same manner, and subject to the same penalties, as are all other persons committing any of the above crimes within the exclusive jurisdiction of the United States." When Kagama of the Hoopa Indian Tribe was indicted for murder, a division of opinion between the judges on the Circuit Court for the District of California as to whether the Major Crimes Act was valid sent the case to the United States Supreme Court.* Opinion of the Court: Miller, Waite, Field, Bradley, Harlan, Woods, Matthews, Gray, Blatchford.

JUSTICE MILLER delivered the opinion of the Court.

The questions certified arise on a demurrer to an indictment against two Indians for murder committed on the Indian reservation of Hoopa Valley, in the State of California, the person murdered being also an Indian of said reservation.

[The] questions . . . are as follows: "Whether the provisions of said section 9, (of the act of Congress of March 3, 1885,) making it a crime for one Indian to commit murder upon another Indian, upon an Indian reservation situated wholly within the limits of a State of the Union, and making such Indian so committing the crime of murder within and upon such Indian reservation 'subject to the same laws' and subject to be 'tried in the same courts, and in the same manner, and subject to the same penalties as are all other persons' committing the crime of murder 'within the exclusive jurisdiction of the United States,' is a constitutional and valid law of the United States?" and "Whether the courts of the United States have jurisdiction or authority to try and punish an Indian belonging to an Indian tribe for committing the crime of murder upon another Indian belonging to the same Indian tribe, both sustaining the usual tribal relations, said crime having been committed upon an Indian reservation made and set apart for the use of the Indian tribe to which said Indians both belong?"

The indictment sets out in two counts that Kagama, alias Pactah Billy, an Indian, murdered Iyouse, alias Ike, another Indian, at Humboldt County, in the State of California, within the limits of the Hoopa Valley Reservation, and it charges Mahawaha, alias Ben, also an Indian, with aiding and abetting in the murder. . . .

The Constitution of the United States is almost silent in regard to the relations of the government which was established by it to the numerous tribes of Indians within its borders.

In declaring the basis on which representation in the lower branch of the Congress and direct taxation should be apportioned, it was fixed that it should be according to numbers, excluding Indians not taxed, which, of course, excluded nearly all of that race, but which meant that if there were such within a State as were taxed to support the government, they should be counted for representation, and in the computation for direct taxes levied by the United States. This expression, excluding Indians not taxed, is found in the Fourteenth Amendment, where it deals with the same subject under the new conditions produced by the emancipation of the slaves. Neither of these shed much light on the power of Congress over the Indians in their existence as tribes, distinct from the ordinary citizens of a State or Territory.

The mention of Indians in the Constitution which has received most attention is that found in the clause which gives Congress "power to regulate commerce with foreign nations and among the several States, and with the Indian tribes."

This clause is relied on in the argument in the present case, the proposition being that the statute under consideration is a regulation of commerce with the Indian tribes. But we think it would be a very strained construction of this clause, that a system of criminal laws for Indians living peaceably in their reservations, which left out the entire code of trade and intercourse laws justly enacted under that provision, and established punishments for the common-law crimes of murder, manslaughter, arson, burglary, larceny, and the like, without any reference to their relation to any kind of commerce, was authorized by the grant of power to regulate commerce with the Indian tribes. . . .

. . . [T]hese Indians are within the geographical limits of the United States. The soil and the people within these limits are under the political control of the Government of the United States, or of the States of the Union. There exist within the broad domain of sovereignty but these two. There may be cities, counties, and other organized bodies with limited legislative functions, but they are all derived from or exist in, subordination to one or the other of these. The territorial governments owe all their powers to the statutes of the United States conferring on them the powers which they exercise, and which are liable to be withdrawn, modified, or repealed at any time by Congress. What authority the State governments may have to enact criminal laws for the Indians will be presently considered. But this power of Congress to organize territorial governments, and make laws for their inhabitants, arises not so much from the clause in the Constitution in regard to disposing of and making rules and regulations concerning the Territory and other property of the United States, as from the ownership of the country in which the Territories are, and the right of exclusive sovereignty which must exist in the National Government, and can be found nowhere else. . . .

The Indian reservation in the case before us is land bought by the United States from Mexico by the Treaty of Guadaloupe Hidalgo, and the whole of California, with the allegiance of its inhabitants, many of whom were Indians, was transferred by that treaty to the United States.

The relation of the Indian tribes living within the borders of the United States, both before and since the Revolution, to the people of the United States has always been an anomalous one and of a complex character.

Following the policy of the European governments in the discovery of America towards the Indians who were found here, the colonies before the Revolution and the States and the United States since, have recognized in the Indians a possessory right to the soil over which they roamed and hunted and established occasional villages. But they asserted an ultimate title in the land itself, by which the Indian tribes were forbidden to sell or transfer it to other nations or peoples without the consent of this paramount authority. When a tribe wished to dispose of its land, or any part of it, or the State or the United States wished to purchase it, a treaty with the tribe was the only mode in which this could be done. The United States recognized no right in private persons, or in other nations, to make such a purchase by treaty or otherwise. With the Indians themselves these relations are equally difficult to define. They were, and always have been, regarded as having a semi-independent position when they preserved their tribal relations; not as States, not as nations, not as possessed of the full attributes of sovereignty, but as a separate people, with the power of regulating their internal and social relations, and thus far not brought under the laws of the Union or of the State within whose limits they resided.

Perhaps the best statement of their position is found in the two opinions of this court by Chief Justice Marshall in the case of the *Cherokee Nation v. Georgia* and in the case of *Worcester v. State of Georgia*. . . . [T]hey are spoken of as "wards of the nation," "pupils," as local dependent communities. In this spirit the United States has conducted its relations to them from its organization to this time. But, after an experience of a hundred years of the treaty-making system of government, Congress has determined upon a new departure—to govern them by acts of Congress. This is seen in the act of March 3, 1871, embodied in §2079 of the Revised Statutes: "No Indian nation or tribe, within the territory of the United States shall be acknowledged or recognized as an independent nation, tribe, or power, with whom the United States may contract by treaty; but no obligation of any treaty lawfully made and ratified with any such Indian nation or tribe prior to March third, eighteen hundred and seventy one, shall be hereby invalidated or impaired."

The case of *Crow Dog*, in which an agreement with the Sioux Indians, ratified by an act of Congress, was supposed to extend over them the laws of the United States and the jurisdiction of its courts, covering murder and other grave crimes, shows the purpose of Congress in this new departure. The decision in that case admits that if the intention of Congress had been to punish, by the United States courts, the murder of one Indian by another, the law would have been valid. But the court could not see, in the agreement with the Indians sanctioned by Congress, a purpose to repeal §2146 of the Revised Statutes, which expressly excludes from that jurisdiction the case of a crime committed by one Indian against another in the Indian country. The passage of the act now under consideration was designed to remove that objection, and to go further by including such crimes on reservations lying within a State.

Is this latter fact a fatal objection to the law? The statute itself contains no express limitation upon the powers of a State or the jurisdiction of its courts. If there be any limitation in either of these, it grows out of the implication arising from the fact that Congress has defined a crime committed within the State, and made it punishable in the courts of the United States. But Congress has done this, and can do it, with regard to all offences relating to matters to which the Federal authority extends. Does that authority extend to this case?

It will be seen at once that the nature of the offence (murder) is one which in almost all cases of its commission is punishable by the laws of the States, and within the jurisdiction of their courts. The distinction is claimed to be that the offence under the statute is committed by an Indian, that it is committed on a reservation set apart within the State for residence of the tribe of Indians by the United States, and the fair inference is that the offending Indian shall belong to that or some other tribe. It does not interfere with the process of the State courts within the reservation, nor with the operation of State laws upon white people found there. Its effect is confined to the acts of an Indian of some tribe, of a criminal character, committed within the limits of the reservation.

It seems to us that this is within the competency of Congress. These Indian tribes are the wards of the nation. They are communities dependent on the United States. Dependent largely for their daily food. Dependent for their political rights. They owe no allegiance to the States, and receive from them no protection. Because of the local ill feeling, the people of the States where they are found are often their deadliest enemies. From their very weakness and helplessness, so largely due to the course of dealing of the Federal Government with them and the treaties in which it has been promised, there arises the duty of protection, and with it the power. This has always been recognized by the Executive and by Congress, and by this court, whenever the question has arisen. . . .

The power of the General Government over these remnants of a race once powerful, now weak and diminished in numbers, is necessary to their protection, as well as to the safety of those among whom they dwell. It must exist in that government, because it never has existed anywhere else, because the theatre of its exercise is within the geographical limits of the United States, because it has never been denied, and because it alone can enforce its laws on all the tribes.

We answer the questions propounded to us, that the 9th section of the act of March, 1885, is a valid law in both its branches, and that the Circuit Court of the United States for the District of California has jurisdiction of the offence charged in the indictment in this case.

Lone Wolf v. Hitchcock
187 U.S. 553 (1903)

By an act of June 6, 1900, Congress abrogated various treaty agreements with the confederated tribes of the Kiowa, Comanche, and Apache Indians that provided that heads of families could select tracts of land within the reservation, not exceeding 320 acres, that would thereafter cease to be held by the tribes in common. Instead, they would be for the exclusive possession of the person making the selection, so long as he or his family continued to cultivate the land. Lone Wolf, on behalf of himself as well as all other members of the confederated tribes residing in the Territory of Oklahoma, brought suit in federal court against the secretary of the interior; he challenged the constitutionality of the act, asserting that by altering the allotment of certain lands to the Indians and by ceding to the United States 2 million acres of these lands, which would then be open to settlement by white men, the act violated the property rights of individual Indians who had acquired land under the language of the treaties. *If it were carried into effect, it would deprive them of their lands without due process of law. When the Court of Appeals for the District of Columbia ruled for the respondent, Lone Wolf appealed to the US Supreme Court.* Opinion of the Court: <u>White</u>, Fuller, Brewer, Brown, Shiras, Peckham, McKenna, Holmes. Concurring in the judgment: <u>Harlan</u>.

JUSTICE WHITE delivered the opinion of the Court.

The appellants base their right to relief on the proposition that . . . the confederated tribes of Kiowas, Comanches and Apaches were vested with an interest in the lands held in common within the reservation, which interest could not be divested by Congress in any other mode than that specified in the [treaty itself] and that as a result of the said stipulation the interest of the Indians in the common lands fell within the protection of the [Due Process Clause of the] Fifth Amendment to the Constitution of the United States, and such interest—indirectly at least—came under the control of the judicial branch of the government. We are unable to yield our assent to this view.

The contention in effect ignores the status of the contracting Indians and the relation of dependency they bore and continue to bear towards the government of the United States. To uphold the claim would be to adjudge that the indirect operation of the treaty was to materially limit and qualify the controlling authority of Congress in respect to the care and protection of the Indians, and to deprive Congress, in a possible emergency, when the necessity might be urgent for a partition and disposal of the tribal lands, of the power to act, if the assent of the Indians could not be obtained.

Now, it is true that in decisions of this court, the Indian right of occupancy of tribal lands, whether declared in a treaty or otherwise created, has been stated to be sacred, or as sometimes expressed, as sacred as the fee of the United States in the same lands. But in none of these cases was there involved a controversy between Indians and the government respecting the power of Congress to administer the property of the Indians. The questions . . . [rather] concerned the character and extent of such rights as respected States or individuals. . . .

Plenary authority over the tribal relations of the Indians has been exercised by Congress from the beginning, and the power has always been deemed a political one, not subject to be controlled by the judicial department of the government. Until the year 1871 the policy was pursued of dealing with the Indian tribes by means of treaties, and, of course, a moral obligation rested upon Congress to act in good faith in performing the stipulations entered into on its behalf. But, as with treaties made with foreign nations, the legislative power might pass laws in conflict with treaties made with the Indians.

The power exists to abrogate the provisions of an Indian treaty, though presumably such power will be exercised only when circumstances arise which will not only justify the government in disregarding the stipulations of the treaty, but may demand, in the interest of the country and the Indians themselves, that it should do so. When, therefore, treaties were entered into between the United States and a tribe of Indians it was never doubted that the *power* to abrogate existed in Congress, and that in a contingency such power might be availed of from considerations of governmental policy, particularly if consistent with perfect good faith towards the Indians. . . .

In view of the legislative power possessed by Congress over treaties with the Indians and Indian tribal property, we may not specially consider the contentions pressed upon our notice that . . . the treaty as signed had been amended by Congress without submitting such amendments to the action of the Indians, since all these matters, in any event, were solely within the domain of the legislative authority and its action is conclusive upon the courts.

. . . Indeed, the controversy which this case presents is concluded by the decision in *Cherokee Nation v. Hitchcock* (1902), decided at this term, where it was held that full administrative power was possessed by Congress over Indian tribal property. In effect, the action of Congress now complained of was but an exercise of such power, a mere change in the form of investment of Indian tribal property, the property of those who, as we have held, were in substantial effect the wards of the government. We must presume that Congress acted in perfect good faith in the dealings with the Indians of which complaint is made, and that the legislative branch of the government exercised its best judgment in the premises. In any event, as Congress possessed full power in the matter, the judiciary cannot question or inquire into the motives which prompted the enactment of this legislation. If injury was occasioned, which we do not wish to be understood as implying, by the use made by Congress of its power, relief must be sought by an appeal to that body for redress and not to the courts. The legislation in question was constitutional, and the demurrer to the bill was therefore rightly sustained.

Public Law 280
67 Stat. 588 (1953)

Before the enactment of Public Law 280 in 1953, the federal government and tribal courts shared exclusive jurisdiction over almost all criminal and civil matters involving Indians on the reservations. With its enactment, six "mandatory" states received jurisdiction over reservation Indians in all criminal matters and in civil causes of action. In 1968 Congress amended Public Law 280 to allow states, if they so choose, to retrocede to the federal government any or all of the jurisdiction they had acquired (25 U.S.C. §1323); it also required of all future "nonmandatory" states seeking to assume criminal or civil jurisdiction over reservation Indians that they obtain the consent of the tribes involved (25 U.S.C. §1326).

18 U.S.C. §1162. STATE JURISDICTION OVER OFFENSES COMMITTED BY OR AGAINST INDIANS IN THE INDIAN COUNTRY

(a) Each of the States or Territories listed in the following table shall have jurisdiction over offenses committed by or against Indians in the areas of Indian country listed opposite the name of the State or Territory to the same extent that such State or Territory has jurisdiction over offenses committed elsewhere within the State or Territory, and the criminal laws of such State or Territory shall have the same force and effect within such Indian country as they have elsewhere within the State or Territory:

State or Territory of Indian country affected

Alaska   All Indian country within the State, except that on Annette Islands, the Metlakatla Indian community may exercise jurisdiction over offenses committed by Indians in the same manner in which such jurisdiction may be exercised by Indian tribes in Indian country over which State jurisdiction has not been extended.

California   All Indian country within the State.

Minnesota   All Indian country within the State, except the Red Lake Reservation.

Nebraska   All Indian country within the State.

Oregon   All Indian country within the State, except the Warm Springs Reservation.

Wisconsin   All Indian country within the State.

(b) Nothing in this section shall authorize the alienation, encumbrance, or taxation of any real or personal property, including water rights, belonging to any Indian or any Indian tribe, band, or community that is held in trust by the United States or is subject to a restriction against alienation imposed by the United States; or shall authorize regulation of the use of such property in a manner inconsistent with any Federal treaty, agreement, or statute or with any regulation made pursuant thereto; or shall deprive any Indian or any Indian tribe, band, or community of any right, privilege, or immunity afforded under Federal treaty, agreement, or statute with respect to hunting, trapping, or fishing or the control, licensing, or regulation thereof.

28 U.S.C. §1360. STATE CIVIL JURISDICTION IN ACTIONS TO WHICH INDIANS ARE PARTIES

(a) Each of the States listed in the following table shall have jurisdiction over civil causes of action between Indians or to which Indians are parties which arise in the areas of Indian country listed opposite the name of the State to the same extent that such State has jurisdiction over other civil causes of action, and those civil laws of such State that are of general application to private persons or private property shall have the same force and effect within such Indian country as they have elsewhere within the State:

State or Territory of Indian country affected

Alaska   All Indian country within the State, except that on Annette Islands, the Metlakatla Indian community may exercise jurisdiction over offenses committed by Indians in the same manner in which such jurisdiction may be exercised by Indian tribes in Indian country over which State jurisdiction has not been extended.

California   All Indian country within the State.

Minnesota   All Indian country within the State, except the Red Lake Reservation.

Nebraska   All Indian country within the State.

Oregon   All Indian country within the State, except the Warm Springs Reservation.

Wisconsin   All Indian country within the State.

(b) Nothing in this section shall authorize the alienation, encumbrance, or taxation of any real or personal property, including water rights, belonging to any Indian or any Indian tribe, band, or community that is held in trust by the United States or is subject to a restriction against alienation imposed by the United States; or shall authorize regulation of the use of such property in a manner inconsistent with any Federal treaty, agreement, or statute or with any regulation made pursuant thereto; or shall confer jurisdiction upon the State to adjudicate, in probate proceedings or otherwise, the ownership or right to possession of such property or any interest therein.

(c) Any tribal ordinance or custom heretofore or hereafter adopted by an Indian tribe, band, or community in the exercise of any authority which it may possess shall, if not inconsistent with any applicable civil law of the State, be given full force and effect in the determination of civil causes of action pursuant to this section.

25 U.S.C. §1321. ASSUMPTION BY STATE OF CRIMINAL JURISDICTION

(a) Consent of United States; force and effect of criminal laws

The consent of the United States is hereby given to any State not having jurisdiction over criminal offenses committed by or against Indians in the areas of Indian country situated within such State to assume, with the consent of the Indian tribe occupying the particular Indian country or part thereof which could be affected by such assumption, such measure of jurisdiction over any or all of such offenses committed within such Indian country or any part thereof as may be deter-

mined by such State to the same extent that such State has jurisdiction over any such offense committed elsewhere within the State, and the criminal laws of such State shall have the same force and effect within such Indian country or part thereof as they have elsewhere within that State.

(b) Alienation, encumbrance, taxation, and use of property; hunting, trapping, or fishing

Nothing in this section shall authorize the alienation, encumbrance, or taxation of any real or personal property, including water rights, belonging to any Indian or any Indian tribe, band, or community that is held in trust by the United States or is subject to a restriction against alienation imposed by the United States; or shall authorize regulation of the use of such property in a manner inconsistent with any Federal treaty, agreement, or statute or with any regulation made pursuant thereto; or shall deprive any Indian or any Indian tribe, band, or community of any right, privilege, or immunity afforded under Federal treaty, agreement, or statute with respect to hunting, trapping, or fishing or the control, licensing, or regulation thereof.

25 U.S.C. §1322. ASSUMPTION BY STATE OF CIVIL JURISDICTION

(a) Consent of United States; force and effect of civil laws

The consent of the United States is hereby given to any State not having jurisdiction over civil causes of action between Indians or to which Indians are parties which arise in the areas of Indian country situated within such State to assume, with the consent of the tribe occupying the particular Indian country or part thereof which would be affected by such assumption, such measure of jurisdiction over any or all such civil causes of action arising within such Indian country or any part thereof as may be determined by such State to the same extent that such State has jurisdiction over other civil causes of action, and those civil laws of such State that are of general application to private persons or private property shall have the same force and effect within such Indian country or part thereof as they have elsewhere within that State.

(b) Alienation, encumbrance, taxation, use, and probate of property

Nothing in this section shall authorize the alienation, encumbrance, or taxation of any real or personal property, including water rights, belonging to any Indian or any Indian tribe, band, or community that is held in trust by the United States or is subject to a restriction against alienation imposed by the United States; or shall authorize regulation of the use of such property in a manner inconsistent with any Federal treaty, agreement, or statute, or with any regulation made pursuant thereto; or shall confer jurisdiction upon the State to adjudicate, in probate proceedings or otherwise, the ownership or right to possession of such property or any interest therein.

(c) Force and effect of tribal ordinances or customs

Any tribal ordinance or custom heretofore or hereafter adopted by an Indian tribe, band, or community in the exercise of any authority which it may possess shall, if not inconsistent with any applicable civil law of the State, be given full force and effect in the determination of civil causes of action pursuant to this section.

25 U.S.C. §1323. RETROCESSION OF JURISDICTION BY STATE

(a) Acceptance by United States.

The United States is authorized to accept a retrocession by any State of all or any measure of the criminal or civil jurisdiction, or both, acquired by such State pursuant to the provisions of section 1162 of title 18, section 1360 of title 28. . . .

25 U.S.C. §1324. AMENDMENT OF STATE CONSTITUTIONS OR STATUTES TO REMOVE LEGAL IMPEDIMENT; EFFECTIVE DATE

Notwithstanding the provisions of any enabling Act for the admission of a State, the consent of the United States is hereby given to the people of any State to amend, where necessary, their State constitution or existing statutes, as the case may be, to remove any legal impediment to the assumption of civil or criminal jurisdiction in accordance with the provisions of this subchapter. The provisions of this subchapter shall not become effective with respect to such assumption of jurisdiction by any such State until the people thereof have appropriately amended their State constitution or statutes, as the case may be.

25 U.S.C. §1325. ABATEMENT OF ACTIONS

(a) Pending actions or proceedings; effect of cession

No action or proceeding pending before any court or agency of the United States immediately prior to any cession of jurisdiction by the United States pursuant to this subchapter shall abate by reason of that cession. For the purposes of any such action or proceeding, such cession shall take effect on the day following the date of final determination of such action or proceeding.

(b) Criminal actions; effect of cession

No cession made by the United States under this subchapter shall deprive any court of the United States of jurisdiction to hear, determine, render judgment, or impose sentence in any criminal action instituted against any person for any offense committed before the effective date of such cession, if the offense charged in such action was cognizable under any law of the United States at the time of the commission of such offense. For the purposes of any such criminal action, such cession shall take effect on the day following the date of final determination of such action.

25 U.S.C. §1326. SPECIAL ELECTION

State jurisdiction acquired pursuant to this subchapter with respect to criminal offenses or civil causes of action, or with respect to both, shall be applicable in Indian country only where the enrolled Indians within the affected area of such Indian country accept such jurisdiction by a majority vote of the adult Indians voting at a special election held for that purpose. The Secretary of the Interior shall call such special election under such rules and regulations as he may prescribe, when requested to do so by the tribal council or other governing body, or by 20 per centum of such enrolled adults.

United States v. Lara
541 U.S. 193 (2004)

In Duro v. Reina, 495 U.S. 676 (1990), the United States Supreme Court held that an Indian tribe lacked sovereign authority to prosecute Indians who were not members of that tribe. In response, Congress in 1991 amended the Indian Civil Rights Act of 1968 to recognize the "inherent power" of Indian tribes to exercise criminal jurisdiction over "all Indians." Billy Jo Lara, a member of the Turtle Mountain Band of Chippewa Indians, was married to a member of the Spirit Lake Sioux Tribe and lived on the Spirit Lake Reservation in North Dakota. When federal police officers came to the reservation to arrest him for alleged public intoxication, he struck one of the officers. He pleaded guilty in the Spirit Lake Tribal Court to a charge of "violence to a policeman" (a violation of the Spirit Lake tribal code) and served ninety days in jail for that crime. He was subsequently charged in the United States District Court for the District of North Dakota by the federal government with the crime of assaulting a federal officer. Lara moved to dismiss the indictment as assertedly violative of the Double Jeopardy Clause of the federal Constitution's Fifth Amendment, but the district court denied the motion. A panel of the United States Court of Appeals for the Eighth Circuit initially affirmed; however, on rehearing en banc, the court of appeals reversed and ordered a remand, on the grounds that the tribal court, in prosecuting Lara, had exercised a federal prosecutorial power rather than the tribal court's own inherent tribal authority, that the "dual sovereignty" doctrine (holding that the Double Jeopardy Clause does not bar successive prosecutions brought by separate sovereigns) did not apply to the case at hand, and that the second prosecution therefore violated the Double Jeopardy Clause. Because of a disagreement among the circuits (the Ninth Circuit had reached the opposite conclusion), the Supreme Court granted certiorari. Opinion of the Court: Breyer, Rehnquist, Stevens, O'Connor, Ginsburg. Concurring opinion: Stevens. Concurring in the judgment: Kennedy; Thomas. Dissenting opinion: Souter, Scalia.

JUSTICE BREYER delivered the opinion of the Court.

This case concerns a congressional statute "recogniz[ing] and affirm[ing]" the "inherent" authority of a tribe to bring a criminal misdemeanor prosecution against an Indian who is not a member of that tribe—authority that this Court previously held a tribe did not possess. [See *Duro v. Reina* (1990).] We must decide whether Congress has the constitutional power to relax restrictions that the political branches have, over time, placed on the exercise of a tribe's inherent legal authority. We conclude that Congress does possess this power. . . .

We assume, as do the parties, that Lara's double jeopardy claim turns on the answer to the "dual sovereignty" question. What is "the source of [the] power to punish" nonmember Indian offenders, "inherent *tribal* sovereignty" or delegated *federal* authority?

We also believe that Congress intended the former answer. The statute says that it "recogniz[es] and affirm[s]" in each tribe the *"inherent"* tribal power (not delegated federal power) to prosecute nonmember Indians for misdemeanors. . . . [T]he statute seeks to adjust the tribes' status. It relaxes the restrictions, recognized in *Duro*, that the political branches had imposed on the tribes' exercise of inherent prosecutorial power. The question before us is whether the Constitution authorizes Congress to do so. Several considerations lead us to the conclusion that Congress does possess the constitutional power to lift the restrictions on the tribes' criminal jurisdiction over nonmember Indians as the statute seeks to do.

First, the Constitution grants Congress broad general powers to legislate in respect to Indian tribes, powers that we have consistently described as "plenary and exclusive." . . . This Court has traditionally identified the Indian Commerce Clause, U.S. Const., Art. I, §8, cl. 3, and the Treaty Clause, Art. II, §2, cl. 2, as sources of that power. . . .

The treaty power does not literally authorize Congress to act legislatively, for it is an Article II power authorizing the President, not Congress, "to make Treaties." But, as Justice Holmes pointed out, treaties made pursuant to that power can authorize Congress to deal with "matters" with which otherwise "Congress could not deal." And for much of the Nation's history, treaties, and legislation made pursuant to those treaties, governed relations between the Federal Government and the Indian tribes.

We recognize that in 1871 Congress ended the practice of entering into treaties with the Indian tribes. But the statute saved existing treaties from being "invalidated or impaired," and this Court has explicitly stated that the statute "in no way affected Congress' plenary powers to legislate on problems of Indians."

Second, Congress, with this Court's approval, has interpreted the Constitution's "plenary" grants of power as authorizing it to enact legislation that both restricts and, in turn, relaxes those restrictions on tribal sovereign authority. From the Nation's beginning Congress' need for such legislative power would have seemed obvious. After all, the Government's Indian policies, applicable to numerous tribes with diverse cultures, affecting billions of acres of land, of necessity would fluctuate dramatically as the needs of the Nation and those of the tribes changed over time. Congressional policy, for example, initially favored "Indian removal," then "assimilation" and the break-up of tribal lands, then protection of the tribal land base (interrupted by a movement toward greater state involvement and "termination" of recognized tribes); and it now seeks greater tribal autonomy within the framework of a "government-to-government relationship" with federal agencies. Such major policy changes inevitably involve major changes in the metes and bounds of tribal sovereignty.

Third, Congress' statutory goal—to modify the degree of autonomy enjoyed by a dependent sovereign that is not a State—is not an unusual legislative objective. The political branches, drawing upon analogous constitutional authority, have made adjustments to the autonomous status of other such dependent entities—sometimes making far more radical adjustments than those at issue here.

Fourth, *Lara* points to no explicit language in the Constitution suggesting a limitation on Congress' institutional authority to relax restrictions on tribal sovereignty previously imposed by the political branches.

Fifth, the change at issue here is a limited one. It concerns a power similar in some respects to the power to prosecute a tribe's own members—a power that this Court has called "inherent." In large part it concerns a tribe's authority to control events that occur upon the tribe's own land. And the tribes' possession of this additional criminal jurisdiction is consistent with our traditional understanding of the tribes' status as "domestic dependent nations." See *Cherokee Nation v. Georgia* (1831). Consequently, we are not now faced with a question dealing with potential constitutional limits on congressional efforts to legislate far more radical changes in tribal status. In particular, this case involves no interference with the power or authority of any State. Nor do we now consider the question whether the Constitution's Due Process or Equal Protection Clauses prohibit tribes from prosecuting a nonmember citizen of the United States.

Sixth, our conclusion that Congress has the power to relax the restrictions imposed by the political branches on the tribes' inherent prosecutorial authority is consistent with our earlier cases. True, the Court held in those cases that the power to prosecute nonmembers was an aspect of the tribes' external relations and hence part of the tribal sovereignty that was divested by treaties and by Congress. But these holdings reflect the Court's view of the tribes' retained sovereign status *as of the time* the Court made them. They did not set forth constitutional limits that prohibit Congress from changing the relevant legal circumstances, *i.e.*, from taking actions that modify or adjust the tribes' status.

. . . For these reasons, we hold . . . that the Constitution authorizes Congress to permit tribes, as an exercise of their inherent tribal authority, to prosecute nonmember Indians. We hold that Congress exercised that authority in writing this statute. That being so, the Spirit Lake Tribe's prosecution of Lara did not amount to an exercise of federal power, and the Tribe acted in its capacity of a separate sovereign. Consequently, the Double Jeopardy Clause does not prohibit the Federal Government from proceeding with the present prosecution for a discrete *federal* offense.

The contrary judgment of the Eighth Circuit is reversed.

JUSTICE KENNEDY, concurring in the judgment.

. . . The Court's analysis goes beyond this narrower rationale and culminates in a surprising holding: "For these reasons, we hold . . . that the Constitution authorizes Congress to permit tribes, as an exercise of their inherent tribal authority, to prosecute nonmember Indians." The Court's holding is on a point of major significance to our understanding and interpretation of the Constitution; and, in my respectful view, it is most doubtful. . . .

Lara . . . is a citizen of the United States. To hold that Congress can subject him, within our domestic borders, to a sovereignty outside the basic structure of the Constitution is a serious step. The Constitution is based on a theory of original, and continuing, consent of the governed. Their consent depends on the understanding that the Constitution has established the federal structure, which grants the citizen the protection of two governments, the Nation and the State. Each sovereign must respect the proper sphere of the other, for the citizen has rights and duties as to both. Here, contrary to this design, the National Government seeks to subject a citizen to the criminal jurisdiction of a third entity to be tried for conduct occurring wholly within the territorial borders of the Nation and one of the States. This is unprecedented. There is a historical exception for Indian tribes, but only to the limited extent that a member of a tribe consents to be subjected to the jurisdiction of his own tribe. The majority today reaches beyond that limited exception. . . .

The present case, however, does not require us to address these difficult questions of constitutional dimension. Congress made it clear that its intent was to recognize and affirm tribal authority to try Indian nonmembers as inherent in tribal status. The proper occasion to test the legitimacy of the tribe's authority, that is, whether Congress had the power to do what it sought to do, was in the first, tribal proceeding. There, however, Lara made no objection to the tribe's authority to try him. In the second, federal proceeding, because the express ratio- nale for the tribe's authority to try Lara— whether legitimate or not—was inherent sovereignty, not delegated federal power, there can be no double jeopardy violation. For that reason, I concur in the judgment.

JUSTICE THOMAS, concurring in the judgment.

As this case should make clear, the time has come to reexamine the premises and logic of our tribal sovereignty cases. . . . I write separately principally because [of] the Court's inadequate constitutional analysis. . . . In my view, the tribes either are or are not separate sovereigns, and our federal Indian law cases untenably hold both positions simultaneously. . . .

[T]his case raises important constitutional questions that the Court does not begin to answer. The Court utterly fails to find any provision of the Constitution that gives Congress enumerated power to alter tribal sovereignty. The Court cites the Indian Commerce Clause and the treaty power. I cannot agree that the Indian Commerce Clause "provide[s] Congress with plenary power to legislate in the field of Indian affairs." At one time, the implausibility of this assertion at least troubled the Court, see, *e.g., United States v. Kagama* (1886), and I would be willing to revisit the question.

Next, the Court acknowledges that "[t]he treaty power does not literally authorize Congress to act legislatively, for it is an Article II power authorizing the President, not Congress, "to make Treaties." This, of course, suffices to show that it provides *no* power to *Congress*, at least in the absence of a specific treaty. The treaty power does not, as the Court seems to believe, provide Congress with free-floating power to legislate as it sees fit on topics that could potentially implicate some unspecified treaty. Such an assertion is especially ironic in light of Congress' enacted prohibition on Indian treaties.

. . . The Federal Government cannot simultaneously claim power to regulate virtually every aspect of the tribes through ordinary domestic legislation and also maintain that the tribes possess anything resembling "sovereignty." In short, the history points in both directions.

The Court should admit that it has failed in its quest to find a source of congressional power to adjust tribal sovereignty. Such an acknowledgement might allow the Court to ask the logically antecedent question *whether* Congress (as opposed to the President) has this power. A cogent answer would serve as the foundation for the analysis of the sovereignty issues posed by this case. We might find that the Federal Government cannot regulate the tribes through ordinary domestic legislation and simultaneously maintain that the tribes are sovereigns in any meaningful sense. But until we begin to analyze these questions honestly and rigorously, the confusion that I have identified will continue to haunt our cases.

JUSTICE SOUTER, with whom JUSTICE SCALIA joins, dissenting.

. . . [W]e held in *Duro* that because tribes have lost their inherent criminal jurisdiction over nonmember Indians, any subsequent exercise of such jurisdiction "could only have come to the Tribe" (if at all) "by delegation from Congress." Three years later, in *South Dakota v. Bourland* (1993), we reiterated this understanding that any such "delegation" would not be a restoration of prior inherent sovereignty; we specifically explained that "tribal sovereignty over nonmembers cannot survive without express congressional delegation, and is therefore *not* inherent." Our precedent, then, is that any tribal exercise of criminal jurisdiction over nonmembers necessarily rests on a "delegation" of federal power and is not akin to a State's congressionally permitted exercise of some authority that would otherwise be barred by the dormant Commerce Clause. It is more like the delegation of lawmaking power to an administrative agency, whose jurisdiction would not even exist absent congressional authorization.

It is of no moment that we have given ostensibly alternating explanations for this conclusion. We have sometimes indicated that the tribes' lack of inherent criminal jurisdiction over nonmembers is a necessary legal consequence of the basic fact that the tribes are dependent on the Federal Government. At other times, our language has suggested that the jurisdictional limit stems from congressional and treaty limitations on tribal powers. What has never been explicitly stated, but should

come as no surprise, is that these two accounts are not inconsistent. Treaties and statutes delineating the tribal-federal relationship are properly viewed as an independent elaboration by the political branches of the fine details of the tribes' dependent position, which strips the tribes of any power to exercise criminal jurisdiction over those outside their own memberships. . . .

[T]here are only two ways that a tribe's inherent sovereignty could be restored so as to alter application of the dual sovereignty rule: either Congress could grant the same independence to the tribes that it did to the Philippines, or this Court could repudiate its existing doctrine of dependent sovereignty. The first alternative has obviously not been attempted, and I see no reason for us to venture down a path toward the second. To begin with, the theory we followed before today has the virtue of fitting the facts: no one could possibly deny that the tribes are subordinate to the National Government. Furthermore, while this is not the place to reexamine the concept of dual sovereignty itself, there is certainly no reason to adopt a canon of broad construction calling for maximum application of the doctrine. Finally, and perhaps most importantly, principles of *stare decisis* are particularly compelling in the law of tribal jurisdiction, an area peculiarly susceptible to confusion. And confusion, I fear, will be the legacy of today's decision, for our failure to stand by what we have previously said reveals that our conceptualizations of sovereignty and dependent sovereignty are largely rhetorical. . . .

I would therefore stand by our explanations in . . . *Duro* and hold that Congress cannot reinvest tribal courts with inherent criminal jurisdiction over nonmember Indians. It is not that I fail to appreciate Congress's express wish that the jurisdiction conveyed by statute be treated as inherent, but Congress cannot control the interpretation of the statute in a way that is at odds with the constitutional consequences of the tribes' continuing dependent status. What may be given controlling effect, however, is the principal object of the 1990 amendments to the Indian Civil Rights Act of 1968, which was to close "the jurisdictional void" created by *Duro* by recognizing (and empowering) the tribal court as "the best forum to handle misdemeanor cases over non-member Indians," I would therefore honor the drafters' substantive intent by reading the Act as a delegation of federal prosecutorial power that eliminates the jurisdictional gap. Finally, I would hold that a tribe's exercise of this delegated power bars subsequent federal prosecution for the same offense. I respectfully dissent.

California v. Cabazon Band of Mission Indians
480 U.S. 202 (1987)

The Cabazon and Morongo Bands of Mission Indians conducted bingo games on their reservations in Riverside County, California. The Cabazon Band also operated a card club for playing draw poker and other card games. These games were open to the public and were played predominantly by non-Indians coming onto the reservations. When the State of California and Riverside County sought to apply their gambling laws to the operation of these games, the tribes instituted an action for declaratory relief in federal district court, which entered summary judgment for the tribes. It held that neither the state nor the county had any authority to enforce its gambling laws on reservation lands. The Ninth Circuit Court of Appeals affirmed, and the state and county appealed. Opinion of the Court: <u>White</u>, Brennan, Marshall, Blackmun, Powell, Rehnquist. Dissenting opinion: <u>Stevens</u>, O'Connor, Scalia.

JUSTICE WHITE delivered the opinion of the Court.

The Cabazon and Morongo Bands of Mission Indians, federally recognized Indian Tribes, occupy reservations in Riverside County, California. Each Band, pursuant to ordinances approved by the Secretary of the Interior, conducts bingo games on its reservation. The Cabazon Band has also opened a card club at which draw poker and other card games are played. The games are open to the public and are played predominantly by non-Indians coming onto the reservations. The games are a major source of employment for tribal members, and the profits are the Tribes' sole source of income. The State of California seeks to apply to the two Tribes Cal. Penal Code Ann. §326.5. That statute does not entirely prohibit the playing of bingo but permits it when the games are operated and staffed by members of designated charitable organizations who may not be paid for their services. Profits must be kept in special accounts and used only for charitable purposes; prizes may not exceed $250 per game. Asserting that the bingo games on the two reservations violated each of these restrictions, California insisted that the Tribes comply with state law. Riverside County also sought to apply its local Ordinance No. 558, regulating bingo, as well as its Ordinance No. 331, prohibiting the playing of draw poker and the other card games. The Tribes sued the county in Federal District Court seeking a declaratory judgment that the county had no authority to apply its ordinances inside the reservations and an injunction against their enforcement. . . .

The Court has consistently recognized that Indian tribes retain "attributes of sovereignty over both their members and their territory," *United States v. Mazurie* (1975), and that "tribal sovereignty is dependent on, and subordinate to, only the Federal Government, not the States." It is clear, however, that state laws may be applied to tribal Indians on their reservations if Congress has expressly so provided. Here, the State insists that Congress has twice given its express consent: first in Public Law 280 in 1953 and second in the Organized Crime Control Act in 1970. We disagree in both respects.

In Public Law 280, Congress expressly granted six States, including California, jurisdiction over specified areas of Indian country within the States and provided for the assumption of jurisdiction by other States. In §2, California was granted broad criminal jurisdiction over offenses committed by or against Indians within all Indian country within the State. Section 4's grant of civil jurisdiction was more limited. In *Bryan v. Itasca County* (1976), we interpreted §4 to grant States jurisdiction over private civil litigation involving reservation Indians in state court, but not to grant general civil regulatory authority. We held, therefore, that Minnesota could not apply its personal property tax within the reservation. Congress' primary concern in enacting Public Law 280 was combating lawlessness on reservations. The Act plainly was not intended to effect total assimilation of Indian tribes into mainstream American society. We recognized that a grant to States of general civil regulatory power over Indian reservations would result in the destruction of tribal institutions and values. Accordingly, when a State seeks to enforce a law within an Indian reservation under the authority of Public Law 280, it must be determined whether the law is criminal in nature, and thus fully applicable to the reservation under §2, or civil in nature, and applicable only as it may be relevant to private civil litigation in state court.

The Minnesota personal property tax at issue in *Bryan* was unquestionably civil in nature. The California bingo statute is not so easily categorized. California law permits bingo games to be conducted only by charitable and other specified organizations, and then only by their members who may not receive any wage or profit for doing so; prizes are limited and receipts are to be segregated and used only for charitable purposes. Violation of any of these provisions is a misdemeanor. California insists that these are criminal laws which Public Law 280 permits it to enforce on the reservations.

Following its earlier decision in *Barona Group of Capitan Grande Band of Mission Indians, San Diego County, Cal. v. Duffy* (1982), which also involved the applicability of §326.5 of the California Penal Code to Indian reservations, the Court of Appeals rejected this submission. In *Barona,* applying what it thought to be the civil/criminal dichotomy drawn in *Bryan v. Itasca County,* the Court of Appeals drew a distinction between state "criminal/prohibitory" laws and state "civil/regulatory" laws: if the intent of a state law is generally to prohibit certain conduct, it falls within Public Law 280's grant of criminal jurisdiction, but if the state law generally permits the conduct at issue, subject to regulation, it must be classified as civil/ regulatory and Public Law 280 does not authorize its enforcement on an Indian

reservation. The shorthand test is whether the conduct at issue violates the State's public policy. Inquiring into the nature of §326.5, the Court of Appeals held that it was regulatory rather than prohibitory. This was the analysis employed, with similar results, by the Court of Appeals for the Fifth Circuit in *Seminole Tribe of Florida v. Butterworth* (1981), which the Ninth Circuit found persuasive.

We are persuaded that the prohibitory/regulatory distinction is consistent with *Bryan's* construction of Public Law 280. It is not a bright-line rule, however; and as the Ninth Circuit itself observed, an argument of some weight may be made that the bingo statute is prohibitory rather than regulatory. But in the present case, the court reexamined the state law and reaffirmed its holding in *Barona,* and we are reluctant to disagree with that court's view of the nature and intent of the state law at issue here.

There is surely a fair basis for its conclusion. California does not prohibit all forms of gambling. California itself operates a state lottery and daily encourages its citizens to participate in this state-run gambling. California also permits parimutuel horserace betting. Although certain enumerated gambling games are prohibited under Cal. Penal Code Ann. §330, games not enumerated, including the card games played in the Cabazon card club, are permissible. The Tribes assert that more than 400 card rooms similar to the Cabazon card club flourish in California, and the State does not dispute this fact. Also, as the Court of Appeals noted, bingo is legally sponsored by many different organizations and is widely played in California. There is no effort to forbid the playing of bingo by any member of the public over the age of 18. Indeed, the permitted bingo games *must* be open to the general public. Nor is there any limit on the number of games which eligible organizations may operate, the receipts which they may obtain from the games, the number of games which a participant may play, or the amount of money which a participant may spend, either per game or in total. In light of the fact that California permits a substantial amount of gambling activity, including bingo, and actually promotes gambling through its state lottery, we must conclude that California regulates rather than prohibits gambling in general and bingo in particular.

California and Riverside County also argue that the Organized Crime Control Act (OCCA) authorizes the application of their gambling laws to the tribal bingo enterprises. The OCCA makes certain violations of state and local gambling laws violations of federal law. . . . There is nothing in OCCA indicating that the States are to have any part in enforcing federal criminal laws or are authorized to make arrests on Indian reservations that in the absence of OCCA they could not effect. We are not informed of any federal efforts to employ OCCA to prosecute the playing of bingo on Indian reservations, although there are more than 100 such enterprises currently in operation, many of which have been in existence for several years, for the most part with the encouragement of the Federal Government. . . . [T]here is no warrant for California to make arrests on reservations and thus, through OCCA, enforce its gambling laws against Indian tribes.

Because the state and county laws at issue here are imposed directly on the Tribes that operate the games, and are not expressly permitted by Congress, the Tribes argue that the judgment below should be affirmed without more. They rely on the statement in *McClanahan v. Arizona State Tax Commission* (1973) that "[state] laws generally are not applicable to tribal Indians on an Indian reservation except where Congress has expressly provided that State laws shall apply." Our cases, however, have not established an inflexible *per se* rule precluding state jurisdiction over tribes and tribal members in the absence of express congressional consent. "[Under] certain circumstances a State may validly assert authority over the activities of nonmembers on a reservation, and . . . in exceptional circumstances a State may assert jurisdiction over the on-reservation activities of tribal members." [W]e [have, for example,] held that, in the absence of express congressional permission, a State could require tribal smokeshops on Indian reservations to collect state sales tax from their non-Indian customers. [The] . . . cases [in which we have done so] involved nonmembers entering and purchasing tobacco products on the reservations involved. The State's interest in assuring the collection of sales taxes from non-Indians enjoying the off-reservation services of the State was sufficient to warrant the minimal burden imposed on the tribal smokeshop operators.

This case also involves a state burden on tribal Indians in the context of their dealings with non-Indians since the question is whether the State may prevent the Tribes from making available high stakes bingo games to non-Indians coming from outside the reservations. Decision in this case turns on whether state authority is pre-empted by the operation of federal law; and "[state] jurisdiction is pre-empted . . . if it interferes or is incompatible with federal and tribal interests reflected in federal law, unless the state interests at stake are sufficient to justify the assertion of state authority." The inquiry is to proceed in light of traditional notions of Indian sovereignty and the congressional goal of Indian self-government, including its "overriding goal" of encouraging tribal self-sufficiency and economic development.

These are important federal interests. They were reaffirmed by the President's 1983 Statement on Indian Policy. More specifically, the Department of the Interior, which has the primary responsibility for carrying out the Federal Government's trust obligations to Indian tribes, has sought to implement these policies by promoting tribal bingo enterprises. . . . The Department of Housing and Urban Development and the Department of Health and Human Services have also provided financial assistance to develop tribal gaming enterprises. Here, the Secretary of the Interior has approved tribal ordinances establishing and regulating the gaming activities involved. The Secretary has also exercised his authority to review tribal bingo management contracts and has issued detailed guidelines governing that review.

These policies and actions, which demonstrate the Government's approval and active promotion of tribal bingo enterprises, are of particular relevance in this case. The Cabazon and Morongo Reservations contain no natural resources which can be exploited. The tribal games at present provide the sole source of revenues for the operation of the tribal governments and the provision of tribal services. They are also the major sources of employment on the reservations. Self-determination and economic development are not within reach if the Tribes cannot raise revenues and provide employment for their members. The Tribes' interests obviously parallel the federal interests.

California seeks to diminish the weight of these seemingly important tribal interests by asserting that the Tribes are merely marketing an exemption from state gambling laws. In *Washington v. Confederated Tribes of Colville Indian Reservation* (1980), we held that the State could tax cigarettes sold by tribal smokeshops to non-Indians, even though it would eliminate their competitive advantage and substantially reduce revenues used to provide tribal services, because the Tribes had no right "to market an exemption from state taxation to persons who would normally do their business elsewhere." . . . Here, however, the Tribes are not merely importing a product onto the reservations for immediate resale to non-Indians. They have built modern facilities which provide recreational opportunities and ancillary services to their patrons, who do not simply drive onto the reservations, make purchases and depart, but spend extended periods of time there enjoying the services the Tribes provide. The Tribes have a strong incentive to provide comfortable, clean, and attractive facilities and well-run games in order to increase attendance at the games. . . .

The State also relies on *Rice v. Rehner* (1983), in which we held that California could require a tribal member and a federally licensed Indian trader operating a general store on a reservation to obtain a state license in order to sell liquor for off-premises consumption. But our decision there rested on the grounds that Congress had never recognized any sovereign tribal interest in regulating liquor traffic and that Congress, historically, had plainly anticipated that the States would exercise concurrent authority to regulate the use and distribution of liquor on Indian reservations. There is no such traditional federal

view governing the outcome of this case, since, as we have explained, the current federal policy is to promote precisely what California seeks to prevent.

The sole interest asserted by the State to justify the imposition of its bingo laws on the Tribes is in preventing the infiltration of the tribal games by organized crime. To the extent that the State seeks to prevent any and all bingo games from being played on tribal lands while permitting regulated, off-reservation games, this asserted interest is irrelevant and the state and county laws are pre-empted. Even to the extent that the State and county seek to regulate short of prohibition, the laws are pre-empted. The State insists that the high stakes offered at tribal games are attractive to organized crime, whereas the controlled games authorized under California law are not. This is surely a legitimate concern, but we are unconvinced that it is sufficient to escape the pre-emptive force of federal and tribal interests apparent in this case.

We conclude that the State's interest in preventing the infiltration of the tribal bingo enterprises by organized crime does not justify state regulation of the tribal bingo enterprises in light of the compelling federal and tribal interests supporting them. State regulation would impermissibly infringe on tribal government, and this conclusion applies equally to the county's attempted regulation of the Cabazon card club. We therefore affirm the judgment of the Court of Appeals and remand the case for further proceedings consistent with this opinion.

JUSTICE STEVENS, with whom JUSTICE O'CONNOR and JUSTICE SCALIA join, dissenting.

Unless and until Congress exempts Indian-managed gambling from state law and subjects it to federal supervision, I believe that a State may enforce its laws prohibiting high-stakes gambling on Indian reservations within its borders. Congress has not pre-empted California's prohibition against high-stakes bingo games and the Secretary of the Interior plainly has no authority to do so. While gambling provides needed employment and income for Indian tribes, these benefits do not, in my opinion, justify tribal operation of currently unlawful commercial activities. Accepting the majority's reasoning would require exemptions for cockfighting, tattoo parlors, nude dancing, houses of prostitution, and other illegal but profitable enterprises. As the law now stands, I believe tribal entrepreneurs, like others who might derive profits from catering to non-Indian customers, must obey applicable state laws.

In my opinion the plain language of Public Law 280 authorizes California to enforce its prohibition against commercial gambling on Indian reservations.

Today the Court seems prepared to acknowledge that an Indian tribe's commercial transactions with non-Indians may violate "the State's public policy." The Court reasons, however, that the operation of high-stakes bingo games does not run afoul of California's public policy because the State permits some forms of gambling and, specifically, some forms of bingo. I find this approach to "public policy" curious, to say the least. The State's policy concerning gambling is to authorize certain specific gambling activities that comply with carefully defined regulation and that provide revenues either for the State itself or for certain charitable purposes, and to prohibit all unregulated commercial lotteries that are operated for private profit. To argue that the tribal bingo games comply with the public policy of California because the State permits some other gambling is tantamount to arguing that driving over 60 miles an hour is consistent with public policy because the State allows driving at speeds of up to 55 miles an hour.

In my view, Congress has permitted the State to apply its prohibitions against commercial gambling to Indian tribes. Even if Congress had not done so, however, the State has the authority to assert jurisdiction over appellees' gambling activities. We recognized this authority in *Washington v. Confederated Tribes;* the Court's attempt to distinguish the reasoning of our decision in that case is unpersuasive. In *Washington v. Confederated Tribes* (1980), the Tribes contended that the State had no power to tax on-reservation sales of cigarettes to non-Indians. The argument that we rejected there has a familiar ring:

The Tribes contend that their involvement in the operation and taxation of cigarette marketing on the reservation ousts the State from any power to exact its sales and cigarette taxes from nonmembers purchasing cigarettes at tribal smokeshops. The primary argument is economic. It is asserted that smokeshop cigarette sales generate substantial revenues for the Tribes which they expend for essential governmental services, including programs to combat severe poverty and underdevelopment at the reservations. Most cigarette purchasers are outsiders attracted onto the reservations by the bargain prices the smokeshops charge by virtue of their claimed exemption from state taxation. If the State is permitted to impose its taxes, the Tribes will no longer enjoy any competitive advantage vis-a-vis businesses in surrounding areas.

. . . Similarly, it is painfully obvious that the value of the Tribe's asserted exemption from California's gambling laws is the primary attraction to customers who would normally do their gambling elsewhere. The Cabazon Band of Mission Indians has no tradition or special expertise in the operation of large bingo parlors. Indeed, the entire membership of the Cabazon Tribe—it has only 25 enrolled members—is barely adequate to operate a bingo game that is patronized by hundreds of non-Indians nightly. How this small and formerly impoverished Band of Indians could have attracted the investment capital for its enterprise without benefit of the claimed exemption is certainly a mystery to me.

Appellants and the Secretary of the Interior may well be correct, in the abstract, that gambling facilities are a sensible way to generate revenues that are badly needed by reservation Indians. But the decision to adopt, to reject, or to define the precise contours of such a course of action, and thereby to set aside the substantial public policy concerns of a sovereign State, should be made by the Congress of the United States. It should not be made by this Court, by the temporary occupant of the Office of the Secretary of the Interior, or by non-Indian entrepreneurs who are experts in gambling management but not necessarily dedicated to serving the future well-being of Indian tribes.

I respectfully dissent.

Adoptive Couple v. Baby Girl
570 U.S. ___ (2013)

The Indian Child Welfare Act of 1978 (ICWA), establishes federal standards for state-court child custody proceedings involving Indian children. It was, as the Supreme Court described it in Mississippi Band of Choctaw Indians v. Holyfield *(1989), "the product of rising concern in the mid-1970's over the consequences to Indian children, Indian families, and Indian tribes of abusive child welfare practices that resulted in the separation of large numbers of Indian children from their families and tribes through adoption or foster care placement, usually in non-Indian homes." Congress found that "an alarmingly high percentage of Indian families [were being] broken up by the removal, often unwarranted, of their children from them by nontribal public and private agencies." This "wholesale removal of Indian children from their homes" prompted Congress to bar involuntary termination of a parent's rights in the absence of a heightened showing that serious harm to the Indian child is likely to result from the parent's "continued custody" of the child, 25 U. S. C. §1912(f); condition involuntary termination of parental rights with respect to an Indian child on a showing that remedial efforts have been made to prevent the "breakup of the Indian family," §1912(d); and provide placement preferences for the adoption of Indian children to members of the child's extended family, other members of the Indian child's tribe, and other Indian families, §1915(a).*

While Birth Mother was pregnant with Biological Father's child, their relationship ended and Biological Father (a member of the Cherokee Nation), agreed, in a text message, to relinquish his parental rights. Birth Mother put Baby Girl up for adoption through a private adoption agency and selected Adoptive Couple, non-Indians living in South Carolina. For the duration of the pregnancy and the first four months after Baby Girl's birth, Biological Father provided no financial assistance to Birth Mother or Baby Girl. Four months after Baby Girl's birth, Adoptive Couple served Biological Father with notice of the pending adoption. In the adoption proceedings, however, Biological Father sought custody and stated that he did not consent to the adoption. Following a trial, which took place when Baby Girl was two

years old, the South Carolina Family Court denied Adoptive Couple's adoption petition and awarded custody to Biological Father. At the age of twenty-seven months, Baby Girl was handed over to Biological Father, whom she had never met. The State Supreme Court affirmed, concluding that the ICWA applied because the child custody proceeding related to an Indian child; that Biological Father was a "parent" under the ICWA; that §§1912(d) and (f) barred the termination of his parental rights; and that had his rights been terminated, §1915(a)'s adoption placement preferences would have applied. The Supreme Court granted certiorari. Opinion of the Court: <u>Alito</u>, Roberts, Kennedy, Thomas, Breyer. Concurring opinions: <u>Thomas</u>, Breyer. Dissenting opinions: <u>Scalia</u>; <u>Sotomayor</u>, Scalia (in part), Ginsburg.

JUSTICE ALITO delivered the opinion of the Court.

This case is about a little girl (Baby Girl) who is classified as an Indian because she is 1.2% (3/256) Cherokee. Because Baby Girl is classified in this way, the South Carolina Supreme Court held that certain provisions of the federal Indian Child Welfare Act of 1978 required her to be taken, at the age of 27 months, from the only parents she had ever known and handed over to her biological father, who had attempted to relinquish his parental rights and who had no prior contact with the child. The provisions of the federal statute at issue here do not demand this result.

Contrary to the State Supreme Court's ruling, we hold that 25 U. S. C. §1912(f)—which bars involuntary termination of a parent's rights in the absence of a heightened showing that serious harm to the Indian child is likely to result from the parent's "continued custody" of the child—does not apply when, as here, the relevant parent never had custody of the child. We further hold that §1912(d)—which conditions involuntary termination of parental rights with respect to an Indian child on a showing that remedial efforts have been made to prevent the "breakup of the Indian family"—is inapplicable when, as here, the parent abandoned the Indian child before birth and never had custody of the child. Finally, we clarify that §1915(a), which provides placement preferences for the adoption of Indian children, does not bar a non-Indian family like Adoptive Couple from adopting an Indian child when no other eligible candidates have sought to adopt the child. We accordingly reverse the South Carolina Supreme Court's judgment and remand for further proceedings.

* * *

The Indian Child Welfare Act was enacted to help preserve the cultural identity and heritage of Indian tribes, but under the State Supreme Court's reading, the Act would put certain vulnerable children at a great disadvantage solely because an ancestor—even a remote one—was an Indian. As the State Supreme Court read §§1912(d) and (f), a biological Indian father could abandon his child in utero and refuse any support for the birth mother—perhaps contributing to the mother's decision to put the child up for adoption—and then could play his ICWA trump card at the eleventh hour to override the mother's decision and the child's best interests. If this were possible, many prospective adoptive parents would surely pause before adopting any child who might possibly qualify as an Indian under the ICWA. Such an interpretation would raise equal protection concerns, but the plain text of §§1912(f) and (d) makes clear that neither provision applies in the present context. Nor do §1915(a)'s rebuttable adoption preferences apply when no alternative party has formally sought to adopt the child. We therefore reverse the judgment of the South Carolina Supreme Court and remand the case for further proceedings not inconsistent with this opinion.

JUSTICE THOMAS, concurring.

I join the Court's opinion in full but write separately to explain why constitutional avoidance compels this outcome. Each party in this case has put forward a plausible interpretation of the relevant sections of the Indian Child Welfare Act (ICWA). However, the interpretations offered by respondent Birth Father and

the United States raise significant constitutional problems as applied to this case. Because the Court's decision avoids those problems, I concur in its interpretation. . . .

II

The ICWA asserts that the Indian Commerce Clause, Art. I, §8, cl. 3, and "other constitutional authority" provides Congress with "plenary power over Indian affairs." §1901(1). The reference to "other constitutional authority" is not illuminating, and I am aware of no other enumerated power that could even arguably support Congress' intrusion into this area of traditional state authority. The assertion of plenary authority must, therefore, stand or fall on Congress' power under the Indian Commerce Clause. Although this Court has said that the "central function of the Indian Commerce Clause is to provide Congress with plenary power to legislate in the field of Indian affairs," *Cotton Petroleum Corp. v. New Mexico* (1989), neither the text nor the original understanding of the Clause supports Congress' claim to such "plenary" power.

A

The Indian Commerce Clause gives Congress authority "[t]o regulate Commerce . . . with the Indian tribes." Art. I, §8, cl. 3. "At the time the original Constitution was ratified, 'commerce' consisted of selling, buying, and bartering, as well as transporting for these purposes." *United States v. Lopez* (1995) (Thomas, J., concurring). The term "commerce" did not include economic activity such as "manufacturing and agriculture," let alone noneconomic activity such as adoption of children.

Furthermore, the term "commerce with Indian tribes" was invariably used during the time of the founding to mean "'trade with Indians.'" And regulation of Indian commerce generally referred to legal structures governing "the conduct of the merchants engaged in the Indian trade, the nature of the goods they sold, the prices charged, and similar matters."

The Indian Commerce Clause contains an additional textual limitation relevant to this case: Congress is given the power to regulate Commerce "with the Indian tribes." The Clause does not give Congress the power to regulate commerce with all Indian persons any more than the Foreign Commerce Clause gives Congress the power to regulate commerce with all foreign nationals traveling within the United States. A straightforward reading of the text, thus, confirms that Congress may only regulate commercial interactions—"commerce"—taking place with established Indian communities—"tribes." That power is far from "plenary."

B

Congress' assertion of "plenary power" over Indian affairs is also inconsistent with the history of the Indian Commerce Clause. At the time of the founding, the Clause was understood to reserve to the States general police powers with respect to Indians who were citizens of the several States. The Clause instead conferred on Congress the much narrower power to regulate trade with Indian tribes—that is, Indians who had not been incorporated into the body-politic of any State . . .

III

In light of the original understanding of the Indian Commerce Clause, the constitutional problems that would be created by application of the ICWA here are evident. First, the statute deals with "child custody proceedings," not "commerce." It was enacted in response to concerns that "an alarmingly high percentage of Indian families [were] broken up by the removal, often unwarranted, of their children from them by nontribal public and private agencies." The perceived problem was that many Indian children were "placed in non-Indian foster and adoptive homes and institutions." This problem, however, had nothing to do with commerce.

Second, the portions of the ICWA at issue here do not regulate Indian tribes as tribes. Sections 1912(d) and (f), and §1915(a) apply to all child custody proceedings involving an Indian child, regardless of whether an Indian tribe is involved. This case thus does not directly implicate Congress' power to "legislate in respect to Indian tribes." *United States v. Lara* (2004). Baby Girl was never domiciled on an Indian Reservation, and the Cherokee Nation had no jurisdiction over her. Although

Birth Father is a registered member of The Cherokee Nation, he did not live on a reservation either. He was, thus, subject to the laws of the State in which he resided (Oklahoma) and of the State where his daughter resided during the custody proceedings (South Carolina). Nothing in the Indian Commerce Clause permits Congress to enact special laws applicable to Birth Father merely because of his status as an Indian.

Because adoption proceedings like this one involve neither "commerce" nor "Indian tribes," there is simply no constitutional basis for Congress' assertion of authority over such proceedings. Also, the notion that Congress can direct state courts to apply different rules of evidence and procedure merely because a person of Indian descent is involved raises absurd possibilities. Such plenary power would allow Congress to dictate specific rules of criminal procedure for state-court prosecutions against Indian defendants. Likewise, it would allow Congress to substitute federal law for state law when contract disputes involve Indians. But the Constitution does not grant Congress power to override state law whenever that law happens to be applied to Indians. Accordingly, application of the ICWA to these child custody proceedings would be unconstitutional.

* * *

Because the Court's plausible interpretation of the relevant sections of the ICWA avoids these constitutional problems, I concur.

JUSTICE SCALIA, dissenting.

. . . The Court's opinion, it seems to me, needlessly demeans the rights of parenthood. It has been the constant practice of the common law to respect the entitlement of those who bring a child into the world to raise that child. We do not inquire whether leaving a child with his parents is "in the best interest of the child." It sometimes is not; he would be better off raised by someone else. But parents have their rights, no less than children do. This father wants to raise his daughter, and the statute amply protects his right to do so. There is no reason in law or policy to dilute that protection.

JUSTICE SOTOMAYOR, with whom Justice Ginsburg and Justice Kagan join, and with whom Justice Scalia joins in part, dissenting.

A casual reader of the Court's opinion could be forgiven for thinking this an easy case, one in which the text of the applicable statute clearly points the way to the only sensible result. In truth, however, the path from the text of the Indian Child Welfare Act of 1978 (ICWA) to the result the Court reaches is anything but clear, and its result anything but right.

The reader's first clue that the majority's supposedly straightforward reasoning is flawed is that not all Members who adopt its interpretation believe it is compelled by the text of the statute; nor are they all willing to accept the consequences it will necessarily have beyond the specific factual scenario confronted here. The second clue is that the majority begins its analysis by plucking out of context a single phrase from the last clause of the last subsection of the relevant provision, and then builds its entire argument upon it. That is not how we ordinarily read statutes. The third clue is that the majority openly professes its aversion to Congress' explicitly stated purpose in enacting the statute. The majority ex-presses concern that reading the Act to mean what it says will make it more difficult to place Indian children in adoptive homes, but the Congress that enacted the statute announced its intent to stop "an alarmingly high percentage of Indian families [from being] broken up" by, among other things, a trend of "plac[ing] [Indian children] in non-Indian . . . adoptive homes." 25 U. S. C. §1901(4). Policy disagreement with Congress' judgment is not a valid reason for this Court to distort the provisions of the Act. Unlike the majority, I cannot adopt a reading of ICWA that is contrary to both its text and its stated purpose. I respectfully dissent.

I

Beginning its reading with the last clause of §1912(f), the majority concludes that a single phrase appearing there—"continued custody"—means that the entirety of the subsection is inapplicable to any parent, however committed, who has not previously had physical or legal custody of his child. Working back to front, the majority then concludes that §1912(d), tainted by its association with §1912(f), is also inapplicable; in the majority's view, a family bond that does not take custodial form is not a family bond worth preserving from "breakup." Because there are apparently no limits on the contaminating power of this single phrase, the majority does not stop there. Under its reading, §1903(9), which makes biological fathers "parent[s]" under this federal statute (and where, again, the phrase "continued custody" does not appear), has substantive force only when a birth father has physical or state-recognized legal custody of his daughter.

When it excludes noncustodial biological fathers from the Act's substantive protections, this textually backward reading misapprehends ICWA's structure and scope. Moreover, notwithstanding the majority's focus on the perceived parental shortcomings of Birth Father, its reasoning necessarily extends to all Indian parents who have never had custody of their children, no matter how fully those parents have embraced the financial and emotional responsibilities of parenting. The majority thereby transforms a statute that was intended to provide uniform federal standards for child custody proceedings involving Indian children and their biological parents into an illogical piecemeal scheme.

A

. . . The majority . . . asserts baldly that "when an Indian parent abandons an Indian child prior to birth and that child has never been in the Indian parent's legal or physical custody, there is no 'relationship' that would be 'discontinu[ed]' . . . by the termination of the Indian parent's rights." Says who? Certainly not the statute. Section 1903 recognizes Birth Father as Baby Girl's "parent," and, in conjunction with ICWA's other provisions, it further establishes that their "parent-child relationship" is protected under federal law. In the face of these broad definitions, the majority has no warrant to substitute its own policy views for Congress' by saying that "no 'relationship'" exists between Birth Father and Baby Girl simply because, based on the hotly contested facts of this case, it views their family bond as insufficiently substantial to deserve protection. . . .

II

C

The majority also protests that a contrary result to the one it reaches would interfere with the adoption of Indian children. This claim is the most perplexing of all. A central purpose of ICWA is to "promote the stability and security of Indian . . . families," 25 U. S. C. §1902, in part by countering the trend of placing "an alarmingly high percentage of [Indian] children . . . in non-Indian foster and adoptive homes and institutions." §1901(4). The Act accomplishes this goal by, first, protecting the familial bonds of Indian parents and children and, second, establishing placement preferences should an adoption take place, see §1915(a). ICWA does not interfere with the adoption of Indian children except to the extent that it attempts to avert the necessity of adoptive placement and makes adoptions of Indian children by non-Indian families less likely.

The majority may consider this scheme unwise. But no principle of construction licenses a court to interpret a statute with a view to averting the very consequences Congress expressly stated it was trying to bring about. Instead, it is the "judicial duty to give faithful meaning to the language Congress adopted in the light of the evident legislative purpose in enacting the law in question." *Graham County Soil and Water Conservation Dist. v. United States ex rel. Wilson* (2010) . . .

* * *

The majority opinion turns §1912 upside down, reading it from bottom to top in order to reach a conclusion that is manifestly contrary to Congress' express purpose in enacting ICWA: preserving the familial bonds between Indian parents and their children and, more broadly, Indian tribes' relationships with the future citizens who are "vital to [their] continued existence and integrity." §1901(3).

The majority casts Birth Father as responsible for the painful circumstances in this case, suggesting that he intervened "at the eleventh hour to override the mother's decision and the child's best interests." I have no wish to minimize the trauma of removing a 27-month-old child from her adoptive family. It bears remembering, however, that Birth Father took action to assert his parental rights when Baby Girl was four months old, as soon as he learned of the impending adoption. As the South Carolina Supreme Court recognized, "[h]ad the mandate of . . . ICWA been followed [in 2010], . . . much potential anguish might have been avoided[;] and in any case the law cannot be applied so as automatically to reward those who obtain custody, whether lawfully or otherwise, and maintain it during any ensuing (and protracted) litigation."

The majority's hollow literalism distorts the statute and ignores Congress' purpose in order to rectify a perceived wrong that, while heartbreaking at the time, was a correct application of federal law and that in any case cannot be undone. Baby Girl has now resided with her father for 18 months. However difficult it must have been for her to leave Adoptive Couple's home when she was just over 2 years old, it will be equally devastating now if, at the age of 3½, she is again removed from her home and sent to live halfway across the country. Such a fate is not foreordained, of course. But it can be said with certainty that the anguish this case has caused will only be compounded by today's decision.

I believe that the South Carolina Supreme Court's judgment was correct, and I would affirm it. I respectfully dissent.

———————

11

The Contract Clause

CHAPTER OUTLINE

Chapters 3 through 10 of this volume have examined various aspects of how governmental power is divided by the US Constitution. Chapters 3 through 6 examined the division of power within the federal government among the legislative, executive, and judicial branches (separation of powers). Chapters 7 through 9 examined the division of power between the federal government and the states (federalism). Chapter 10 examined the division of power between the federal government and Native American tribal governments. The remainder of this volume explores something different: property rights and how the Constitution and Court have protected them. This chapter focuses on a provision in the original Constitution—the Contract Clause of Article I, Section 10; Chapter 12 focuses on the Privileges or Immunities and Due Process Clauses of the Fourteenth Amendment and the Takings Clause of the Fifth Amendment.

Article I, Section 10, of the Constitution declares that no state shall pass any "Law impairing the Obligations of Contracts." This language was included in order to protect "vested rights"—those so fundamental to an individual that they must remain beyond governmental control.[1] Among the most important of these rights is the individual's right to security in the acquisition and possession of private property. The doctrine of vested rights thus precludes not only expropriation of an individual's property but also damaging interferences with future property interests, such as obligations embodied in contractual arrangements.[2]

James Madison's *Essay on Property*, first published in 1792 in the *National Gazette*, shows just how important property rights were for the Framers. He wrote:

> [Property] in its particular application means "that dominion which one man claims and exercises over the external things of the world, in exclusion of every other individual." In its larger and juster meaning, it embraces everything to which a man may attach a value and have a right; and which leaves to every one else the like advantage. In the former sense, a man's land, or merchandize, or money is called his property. In the latter sense, a man has property in his opinions and the free communication of them. He has a property of peculiar value in his religious opinions, and in the profession and practice dictated by them. He has property very dear to him in the safety and liberty of his person. He has an equal property in the free use of his faculties and free choice of the objects on which to employ them. In a word, as a man is said to have a right to property, he may be said to have a property in his rights.[3]

As noted in Chapter 1, a principal aim of the Constitution was to secure private rights (and especially property rights) from the danger of an overbearing majority and at the same time to preserve the spirit and form of popular government. This goal was underscored in an exchange between Roger Sherman and James Madison early in the Constitutional Convention. Sherman suggested that the objectives of the Union include no more than defense against foreign danger and internal disputes and the establishment of a central authority to make treaties with foreign nations and to regulate foreign commerce. In rejoinder, Madison argued that another such objective should be more effective provision "for the security of private rights, and the steady dispensation of justice." Interferences with these rights by state legislatures, Madison insisted, had been a principal force behind the calling of the convention.[4] And interferences there were. In Rhode Island, contemptuously referred to by many at the time as Rogues' Island, the legislature had passed a bill that allowed for the payment of debts with a worthless paper currency and made it a criminal offense, punishable by death by hanging without benefit of clergy, for a creditor to refuse to accept such payment.[5] Such acts of oppression by the majority were not confined to the smaller states: in Massachusetts, impoverished backcountry farmers led by Daniel

Shays had taken up arms against the government, demanding cheap paper money and a suspension of mortgage foreclosures.

The Framers adopted two principal defenses against the violation of property rights. At the national level, they relied upon the multiplicity of interests present in the extended republic they were creating. At the state level, where territorial and population restrictions precluded formation of a multiplicity of interests, the Framers trusted in the language of Article I, Section 10, whose prohibition of state laws that impair obligations of contracts helped to create a "constitutional bulwark in favor of personal security and private rights."

MARSHALL'S EXPANSION OF THE CONTRACT CLAUSE

In the hands of Chief Justice John Marshall, the Contract Clause became a powerful instrument for the protection of private property. The Marshall Court not only resisted any state encroachments on private contracts (i.e., contracts between individuals), but also expanded the scope of the term *contract* to include public contracts such as public grants and corporate charters.

Marshall's opinion for the Court in *Sturges v. Crowninshield* (1819) and his dissent in *Ogden v. Saunders* (1827) indicate how he sought to preserve private contractual relations against state interference. In *Sturges,* the Court invalidated a New York bankruptcy act because it applied to a debt incurred before the law was passed. Although the Constitution had given Congress the power to establish uniform nationwide bankruptcy laws, Marshall recognized that until Congress exercised its power in such a way as to exclude state legislation on the subject, the states were free to regulate "such cases as the laws of the Union may not reach." But, he continued, New York's law violated the Contract Clause by relieving debtors of preexisting financial obligations. Marshall went even further in *Ogden,* insisting that the Contract Clause prevented legislative impairments not only of contracts already in force but also of contracts entered into after the passage of the legislation in question. A bankruptcy law already in force before a contract was made, he declared, should be unconstitutional. In this case, however, Marshall was unable to persuade a majority of the Court to accept his point of view, and for the only time in his thirty-four years as chief justice, he was forced to dissent on a constitutional issue.[6] The general position taken by the Court majority was that a statute in effect at the time a contract is formed is "the law of the contract" and "a part of the contract," and therefore cannot be held to impair its obligation. In the words of Justice William Johnson, the Contract Clause is "a general provision against arbitrary and tyrannical legislation over existing rights, whether personal or property." Bankruptcy legislation, accordingly, is no more constitutionally infirm than laws regulating usurious contracts or the collection of gaming debts. Since *Ogden,* this view of insolvency laws has been maintained consistently by the Court.

Of even greater importance for the protection of the vested rights of private property was Marshall's expansion of the constitutional definition of a contract. In *Fletcher v. Peck* (1810), he extended the purview of the Contract Clause to public as well as private contracts, thereby making it applicable to transactions to which the state itself was a party. *Fletcher,* the first case in which a state statute was held void under the United States Constitution, originated in an action of the Georgia legislature, which in 1795 was induced by bribery to grant public lands, comprising much of what is now the states of Alabama and Mississippi, to four groups of purchasers known collectively as the Yazoo Land Companies.[7] Popular indignation forced the legislature in 1796 to rescind the grant on the ground that it had been secured by fraud. By that time, however, some of the land had been purchased by innocent third parties in New England and other parts of the country. These buyers contested the validity of the rescinding act, contending that the original grant could not be repealed without violating the Contract Clause. Marshall, speaking for a unanimous Court, agreed: "Is a clause to be considered as inhibiting the State from impairing the obligation of contracts between two individuals, but as excluding from that inhibition contracts made with itself? The words themselves contain no such distinction. They are general, and are applicable to contracts of every description." Declaring that a public grant qualified as a contractual obligation and could not be abrogated without fair compensation, he therefore held that the rescinding act was an unconstitutional impairment of the obligations of contract.

Marshall further broadened the Contract Clause's coverage of public contracts in *Dartmouth College v. Woodward* (1819), in which a corporate charter was held to be a contract protected from infringement by state legislatures. Although this case concerned a college, it fostered the economic development of the nation by assuring business corporations that they would be protected from political interference. As Marshall's biographer Albert J. Beveridge has noted, *Dartmouth College* was announced at the very time that corporations were coming into their own, "springing up in response to the necessity for larger and more constant business units and because of the convenience and profit of such organizations. Marshall's opinion was a tremendous stimulant to this natural economic tendency. It reassured investors in corporate securities and gave confidence and steadiness to the business world."[8]

THE DECLINE OF THE CONTRACT CLAUSE

Marshall's efforts to transform the Contract Clause into a powerful guarantor of vested property rights profoundly affected constitutional law for the remainder of the nineteenth century. In a definitive study of the Contract Clause, Benjamin F. Wright noted that, until 1889, it figured in about 40 percent of all Supreme Court cases involving the validity of state legislation. During that time, moreover, it provided the constitutional justification for seventy-five invalidations of state legislation on constitutional grounds—on almost half of all cases in which such legislation was held invalid by the Court.[9]

Over time, however, the Contract Clause has come to lose much of the potency that Marshall gave it. One of the principal reasons for the decline in the importance of the Contract Clause was the increased use of reservation clauses. As Justice Joseph Story pointed out in his *Dartmouth College* concurrence, states could insert, as a condition in a corporate charter, the power to "amend, alter, and repeal" the charter. Because such a reservation would be a part of the charter, legislative interference would not constitute an impairment of obligations of contract. Several states, taking Story's argument one step further, passed general legislation incorporating the reservation in all subsequently granted charters. Reservation clauses soon became quite common, and by 1865 fourteen states had written general reservation clauses into their constitutions.[10]

The Contract Clause's ability to protect vested rights was also diminished by the Court's strict construction of public contracts or grants after Chief Justice Roger Taney's famous opinion in *Charles River Bridge Company v. Warren Bridge Company* (1837). Taney insisted that any ambiguity in the terms of a grant "must operate against the adventurers [i.e., grantees] and in favor of the public," and that the grantees can claim only what is clearly given to them. Nothing could pass to the grantees by implication. "While the rights of private property are sacredly guarded," Taney observed, "we must not forget that the community also have rights, and that the happiness and well-being of every citizen depends on their faithful preservation."[11]

Yet a third contributor to the weakening of the Contract Clause was the rise of the doctrine of inalienable police power. Beginning with *Fertilizing Company v. Hyde Park* (1878), the Court has held that the states cannot contract away certain police powers. At issue in *Fertilizing Company* was a municipal ordinance—prohibiting the transportation of offal through the streets and forbidding the operation of such a factory within a certain distance of the town limits—that rendered valueless a franchise to operate a fertilizer factory. In upholding the ordinance, Justice Noah Swayne emphasized the principle that all grants are to be construed in favor of the state and argued that because the franchise grant contained no expressed exemption from the power to abate a nuisance, it had been made subject to the police power of the state. Two years later, in *Stone v. Mississippi,* the Court held that the grant of a twenty-five-year charter to operate a lottery was subject to later application of the police power and did not bar a subsequent statute prohibiting lotteries. The statute in question had been passed to implement a recently ratified provision of Mississippi's new constitution. Insisting that the power of governing is a trust committed by the people to the government, no part of which can be granted away, the Court found in the charter an implied agreement that the privilege granted by the state was subject to the exercise of police power: "Anyone who accepts a lottery charter does so with the implied understanding that the people may resume it at any time when the public good shall require. . . . He has in legal effect nothing more than a license to enjoy the privilege on the terms named for the specified time, unless it be sooner abrogated by the sovereign power of the State."[12] Since these two cases were decided, the Court has consistently upheld the supremacy of the state's police power against claims deriving from previously existing business franchises and public grants.

The doctrine of inalienable police power, like strict construction of public contracts and the use of reservation clauses, was aimed at ensuring that governments would retain the ability to govern. In reaction, those business interests that had traditionally relied on the Contract Clause for protection turned increasingly to the Due Process Clause of the Fourteenth Amendment, which in time became an even more important vehicle for the protection of vested property rights. This trend confirmed the decline of the once-potent Contract Clause. According to Professor Wright, "The displacement of the contract clause by due process of law is but an incident in the continuous development of an idea. The former clause had become too circumscribed by judicially created or permitted limitations, and its place was gradually taken by another clause where the absence of restrictive precedent allowed freer play to judicial discretion."[13]

The demise of the Contract Clause is perhaps nowhere more apparent than in *Home Building and Loan Association v. Blaisdell* (1934). At issue was a Depression era–inspired Minnesota act providing for a moratorium on mortgage payments. As law professor Lino A. Graglia has written, this debtor-relief measure was "precisely the sort that the Contract Clause was meant to preclude. The clause would have deprived the people of Minnesota of the power to deal with a crisis in the depths of the Great Depression by limiting farm foreclosures, even though impoverished farmers about to be rendered homeless by foreclosure were threatening violence against sheriffs and judges."[14] In fact, the Court upheld the measure by a 5–4 vote, declaring that states have a reserved power to protect the interests of their citizens in times of emergency. Writing for the majority, Chief Justice Charles Evans Hughes argued that "state power exists to give temporary relief from the enforcement of contracts in the presence of disasters due to physical causes such as fire, flood, or earthquake," and that the same power must exist "when the urgent public need demanding such relief is produced by other and economic causes." In the end, Hughes declared, "The question is no longer merely that of one party to a contract as against another, but of the use of reasonable means to safeguard the economic structure upon which the good of all depends. . . . The principle of this development is . . . that the reservation of the reasonable exercise of the protective power of the State is read into all contracts."[15]

As Graglia has noted, "By upholding the result of the political process in Minnesota, the decision served the cause of democracy, though not of constitutionalism."[16] The majority opinion in *Blaisdell* seems directly to contradict the principle embodied in the Contract Clause. And, as Graglia has argued elsewhere, it "required the Court to explicitly divorce constitutional law from the intent of the Framers and, therefore, from the Constitution, leaving it simply a vehicle for enactment of the policy views of the Justices."[17] In a lengthy dissent, Justice George Sutherland severely criticized the majority opinion on exactly these grounds. After describing the economic conditions that prevailed when the Constitution was adopted, Sutherland pointed out that the Contract Clause was specifically intended to prevent the states from mitigating the effects of financial emergency. He charged that in asserting that the Depression legitimated remedial actions by the state, the *Blaisdell* majority violated the intentions of those who wrote the Constitution. "With due regard for the processes of logical thinking," he wrote, "it legitimately cannot be urged that conditions which produced the rule may now be invoked to destroy it."

Many defenders of *Blaisdell* accept Justice Sutherland's analysis of the intent of the Framers but contend that the Court must adapt the Constitution "to the various crises of human affairs."[18] Not every defender of *Blaisdell* accepts Sutherland's analysis, however. Professor Gary Jacobsohn, for example, argues that Chief Justice Hughes's majority opinion reveals a deeper and more profound appreciation for the Framers' enterprise than does Sutherland's dissent. Admitting that Sutherland was correct in asserting that the Contract Clause was intended to protect creditors from their debtors (even in times of emergencies), Jacobsohn insists that "beyond this, there was a deeper intent, which was to promote the conditions of economic stability."[19] The emergency conditions created by the Depression threatened the stability necessary for sound financial arrangements in a commercial economy. "An appropriate response to this problem required a recognition of the radical changes that had occurred in the nation's economy since the time of the founding fathers. Its new complexity, a consequence of modern industrialization, commerce, and technology, meant that the interests of the society were intimately intertwined with the interests of the parties joined in a private contract."[20] According to Jacobsohn, Hughes, unlike Sutherland, recognized that in some circumstances, a temporary restraint of enforcement might be "consistent with the spirit and purpose of the constitutional provision and thus be found to be within the range of the reserved power of the State to protect the vital interests of the community." Hughes thus permitted the impairment of the obligations of a specific contract in order to preserve the principle embodied in the Contract Clause itself.

Although instructive, Jacobsohn's analysis of the "deeper intent" of the Framers raises a troubling question for defenders of *Blaisdell*: if the economic stability of the nation required the passage of a mortgage moratorium law, would it not have been more appropriate and in keeping with the Constitution's text for this law to have been passed by Congress rather than by a particular state legislature? Had Congress been persuaded that the economic stability of the nation required a mortgage moratorium law, it could have passed a law virtually identical to the Minnesota act, declaring therein that its provisions would go into effect in any state in which the mortgage foreclosure rate exceeded a predetermined level. A national problem, then, would have had a national solution, and no controversy would have arisen over the meaning of the Contract Clause, whose provisions are limited solely to the states.

Professor Wright has pointed out that Minnesota's mortgage moratorium law was a carefully drafted statute that attempted to protect the interests of the creditor and debtor alike.[21] Nonetheless, it could not possibly protect the interests of society as a whole as fully as could a national moratorium act. Only the multiplicity of interests present at the national level is sufficient to contribute to the protection of "the public good and private rights." Specifically, not every creditor affected by Minnesota's law resided in that state; many were spread across the country and had no effective voice in the Minnesota Legislature. To the extent that their interests were to be protected, they had to be protected at the national level. This point of view is in keeping with one of the principal means by which the ends of the Constitution are to be secured.

A CONTINUED RELEVANCE?

Many scholars of the Court believe that *Blaisdell* effectively ended the relevance of the Contract Clause. For them, the clause has become "a tail to the due process kite . . . , a fifth wheel to the Constitutional Law coach."[22] Decisions at the state and federal levels lend credence to this point of view.[23] The remarks by Judge Howard Baer of the New York Supreme Court for New York County in *Flushing National Bank v. Municipal Assistance Corporation* (1977) are illustrative. When the Emergency Moratorium Act of 1975, passed by the New York State Legislature to help New York City avoid bankruptcy, was challenged in his court for violating the Contract Clause (because it imposed a three-year moratorium on the repayment of $4.7 billion in outstanding short-term city debt), Judge Baer rejected this challenge, noting that both state and federal courts "have given priority to the public interest over strict compliance with the contract clause." He continued: "Numerous decisions . . . long ago repudiated the notion which plaintiff here espouses that the contract clause presents a rigid bar to the protection of vital public interests, recognizing instead the power, and indeed, the duty of states to prevent the literal enforcement of contractual terms in order to protect the health, safety, or welfare of their citizens."

United States Trust Company v. New Jersey (1977) indicated, however, that the Contract Clause has not become a dead letter—at least not in cases involving unilateral legislative impairment of government contracts. In *United States Trust,* the states were warned that they could not impair their obligations under contracts with private individuals in which the states receive direct, bargained-for benefits and are subject, in turn, to financial obligations that benefit the private parties to the contract. The reason is clear enough: in such instances, the states cannot be trusted to behave as referees, impartially acting in the best interests of the public. As Justice Harry Blackmun noted for the Court majority in *United States Trust,* "Complete deference to a legislative assessment of reasonableness and necessity is not appropriate because the State's self interest is at stake. A governmental entity can always find a use for extra money, especially when taxes do not have to be raised."[24]

Although *United States Trust* reflects that the Contract Clause remains a defense against self-interested governments that attempt to impair their financial obligations,[25] it would be a mistake to read too much into the case and conclude that it represents the beginning of the clause's revitalization.[26] As Douglas W. Kmiec has observed, the Contract Clause is "routinely subordinated to the modern Court's substantial deference to state legislative judgment in matters of economics."[27] Justice John Stevens's words in *Keystone Bituminous Coal Association v. DeBenedictis* (1987) capture well the current desuetude into which it has fallen: "Unlike other provisions in [Article I, Section 10], it is well settled that the prohibition against impairing the obligation of contracts is not to be read literally."[28]

Stevens's assessment should be especially troubling to members of the highly unionized public sector whose pensions, often much more generous than those received by taxpayers in the private sector, are increasingly acknowledged by parties across the political spectrum to be unsustainable. Does the Contract Clause remain as a viable constitutional limitation on state or local governments' ability to enact pension-reform laws—increasing the rates at which their employees must contribute to their pension funds, reducing or eliminating cost-of-living adjustments, increasing the retirement age, or even converting from defined-benefit to defined-contribution plans?

The Supreme Court has yet to directly address these issues, but two recent lower federal court opinions are suggestive of how it will approach them when the appropriate case presents itself. Both relied especially on two Supreme Court precedents, *Energy Reserves Group v. Kansas Power & Light Company* (1983) and *General Motors Corp. v. Romein* (1992) and employed a three-prong test to determine whether a law trenches impermissibly on the contractual rights of public employees. The first prong asks whether there is, in fact, a valid contract that has been substantially impaired; if so, the second prong asks whether the law serves a legitimate public purpose such as remedying a general social or economic problem and if such purpose is demonstrated; the third prong then inquires whether the means chosen to accomplish this purpose are reasonable and necessary.

The first lower federal court opinion was the unanimous opinion by Judge Richard J. Cardamore of the US Court of Appeals for the Second Circuit in *Buffalo Teachers Federation v. Tobe* (2006), a case that dealt with the issue of a wage freeze but by implication could perhaps cover the modification of pension programs as well. The three-judge appellate panel addressed a wage freeze prohibiting members of the plaintiff unions from receiving a 2 percent wage increase that the unions had negotiated as part of their labor contracts. The wage freeze was imposed by the Buffalo Fiscal Authority, created by the New York legislature to deal with Buffalo's chronic fiscal difficulties, after the tax increases and hiring freezes it had imposed were insufficient to close the Buffalo school district's budget gap. The panel agreed that the action substantially impaired the union members' contracts. Nonetheless, it upheld the wage freeze, noting that "courts have often held that the legislative interest in addressing a fiscal emergency is a legitimate public interest. We find no reason to reach a [contrary] conclusion. . . ." The wage freeze cleared the hurdle of the third prong as well, because "the temporary and prospective nature of the wage freeze" underscored its reasonableness. "The impairment here does not affect past salary due for labor already rendered or money invested. It only suspends temporarily the two percent increase in salary for services *to be* rendered."

The second lower federal court opinion was delivered by US District Court Judge Virginia Emerson Hopkins in *Taylor v. City of Gadsden* (2013). Judge Hopkins employed the same three-prong test and concluded on that basis that Gadsden, Alabama, did not violate the Contract Clause when it increased the required pension contributions of firefighter employees from 6 percent to 8.25 percent. She focused in particular on the first prong and concluded that "the plaintiffs actually had no contract with the city guaranteeing that they would never be required to pay more than 6 percent of their pay" toward their pensions, and, even if they did, that increasing their contribution from 6 percent to 8.25 percent did not substantially impair it.

Municipalities are increasingly filing for bankruptcy to void collective bargaining agreements, and, short of that drastic measure, they are also increasingly seeking unilaterally to abrogate agreements with public employee unions concerning salary and benefits, working conditions, and pensions. The *Buffalo Teachers Federation* and *City of Gadsden* decisions suggest that states and their political subdivisions may have the upper hand, the Contract Clause to the contrary, notwithstanding.

NOTES

1. See Gordon S. Wood, "The Origins of Vested Rights in the Early Republic," *Virginia Law Review* 85 (October 1999): 1421.

2. See Edward S. Corwin, "The Basic Doctrine of American Constitutional Law," *Michigan Law Review* 12 (February 1914): 255.

3. James Madison, "Essay on Property," in *The Writings of James Madison*, edited by Gaillard Hunt, 9 vols. (New York: G. P. Putnam's Sons, 1906), 6:101. For a contemporary reaffirmation of this view, see Justice Potter Stewart's opinion for the Court in *Lynch v. Household Finance Corporation* (1972).

4. Max Farrand, ed., *The Records of the Federal Convention of 1787*, 4 vols. (New Haven, CT: Yale University Press, 1937), 1:133–134.

5. See Andrew C. McLaughlin, *The Confederation and the Constitution, 1787–1789* (New York: Collier, 1962), 107–109.

6. Benjamin F. Wright, *The Contract Clause of the Constitution* (Cambridge, MA: Harvard University Press, 1938), 50.

7. For the details of this episode, see C. Peter Magrath, *Yazoo: Land and Politics in the New Republic; The Case of* Fletcher v. Peck (Providence, RI: Brown University Press, 1966).

8. Albert J. Beveridge, *The Life of John Marshall*, 4 vols. (Boston: Houghton Mifflin, 1919), 4:276. But see also Michael J. Klarman, "How Great Were the 'Great' Marshall Court Decisions?" *Virginia Law Review* 87 (October 2001). He challenges the widespread assumption that *Dartmouth College* and Marshall's other Contract Clause decisions were instrumental to American economic development during the first half of the nineteenth century: "As to the Contract Clause decisions more generally, their importance depends on two countervailing assumptions: (1) that in the absence of a constitutional mandate, states would renege on their promises; and (2) that in the presence of a constitutional mandate, states effectively were constrained from reneging on their promises. Yet, neither of these assumptions holds up under scrutiny" (1147).

9. Wright, *Contract Clause*, 95. Curiously, under the Taney Court, the Contract Clause also became a limitation on "judicial impairments" and not simply on "legislative enactments," as its language suggests (the clause, after all, refers to the "pass[ing]" of "Laws"). See Barton H. Thompson Jr., "The History of the Judicial Impairment 'Doctrine' and Its Lessons for the Contract Clause," *Stanford Law Review* 44 (July 1992): 1388–1418.

10. See Wright, *Contract Clause*, 84.

11. It must be emphasized that Taney's opinion in *Charles River Bridge Company* did not break with the Marshall tradition. Taney shared Marshall's view that "the rights of private property are sacredly guarded" and accepted without question Marshall's application of the Contract Clause to public as well as private contracts. See ibid., 62–63, 245–246.

12. 101 U.S. at 821. The police power prevails over private contracts with even greater force than over public contracts. As the Court observed in *Manigault v. Springs* (1905), "Parties by entering into contracts may not stop the legislature from enacting laws intended for the public good."

13. Wright, *Contract Clause*, 258.

14. Lino A. Graglia, "Constitutional Law: A Ruse for Government by an Intellectual Elite," *Georgia State University Law Review* 14 (July 1998): 772.

15. See Hadley Arkes, "On the Novelties of an Old Constitution: Settled Principles and Unsettling Surprises," *American Journal of Jurisprudence* 44 (1999): 15–42.

16. Graglia, "Constitutional Law," 772. Graglia continues: "In doing so, the Court missed its best, if not its only, chance to hold unconstitutional a law that really was."

17. Lino A. Graglia, "The Burger Court and Economic Rights," *Tulsa Law Journal* 33 (Fall 1997): 48.

18. See Chapter 1 and its discussion of the adaptive approach to constitutional interpretation. See also Samuel R. Olken, "Charles Evans Hughes and the *Blaisdell* Decision: A Historical Study of Contract Clause Jurisprudence," *Oregon Law Review* 72 (Fall 1993). Olken argues that Chief Justice Hughes "inherently perceived the Minnesota mortgage moratorium as presenting the Court with a classic problem in federalism over the limitations of state government" and therefore "crafted an opinion imbued with progressive notions of governmental authority and constitutional interpretation that essentially balanced the interests of individuals with the paramount objectives of the state in maintaining its economic structure" (603).

19. Gary J. Jacobsohn, *Pragmatism, Statesmanship, and the Supreme Court* (Ithaca, NY: Cornell University Press, 1977), 188.

20. Ibid., 192.

21. Wright, *Contract Clause*, 110.

22. Edward S. Corwin, *The Constitution of the United States of America: Analysis and Interpretation* (Washington, DC: Government Printing Office, 1953), 362.

23. At the federal level, see *Faitoute Iron & Steel Company v. City of Asbury Park* (1942), *East New York Savings Bank v. Hahn* (1945), and *El Paso v. Simmons* (1965).

24. Henry N. Butler and Larry E. Ribstein advance another possible use of the Contract Clause: to challenge the constitutionality of state statutes that regulate corporate takeovers. Operating from the premises of the "modern contractual theory of the corporation," they understand the "corporation as a set of contracts among shareholders, managers, creditors, and others" rather than "as a concession or franchise granted by the state" and therefore contend that the Contract Clause restrains the ability of states to alter the corporate contract. Butler and Ribstein, "Regulating Corporate Takeovers: State Anti-Takeovers Statutes and the Contract Clause," *University of Cincinnati Law Review* 57 (1988): 612.

25. See *Energy Reserves Group, Inc. v. Kansas Power & Light Co.* (1983), in which the Supreme Court held that a Kansas statute regulating the price of natural gas did not impair the energy company's contracts with a public utility in violation of the Contract Clause. Justice Blackmun held for the Court that the state statute did not violate Article I, Section 10, of the US Constitution, because "although the language of the Contract Clause is facially absolute, its prohibition must be accommodated to the inherent police power of the State 'to safeguard the vital interests of its people,'" which the state legitimately exercised when it protected "consumers from the escalation of natural gas prices caused by deregulation. The State reasonably could find that higher gas prices have caused and will cause hardship among those who use gas heat but must exist on limited fixed incomes." 459 U.S. at 417. Stanley H. Friedelbaum has summarized *Energy Reserves Group* as follows: "When the state has not sought to modify its own contractual obligations, . . . deferential principles generally apply, premised on standards of review traditionally linked to economic and social regulatory schemes." Friedelbaum, "Judicial Federalism: Current Trends and Long-Term Prospects," *Florida State University Law Review* 19 (Spring 1992): 1080.

26. "The limited significance of this partial revival of the Clause is indicated by the fact that no claim based upon it has prevailed in the nearly two decades since." Graglia, "Burger Court and Economic Rights," 66.

27. Douglas W. Kmiec, "Contracts Clause," in *The Oxford Companion to the Supreme Court of the United States,* edited by Kermit L. Hall (New York: Oxford University Press, 1992), 196.

28. 480 U.S. 470, 502 (1987).

SELECTED READINGS

The Federalist, No. 44.

Anderson, Michelle Wilde. "The New Minimal Cities," *Yale Law Journal* 123 (2014): 1118–1223.

Anenson, T. Leigh, Alex Slabaugh, and Karen Eilers Lahey. "Reforming Public Pensions," *Yale Law and Policy Review* 33 (2014): 1–74.

Befort, Stephen F. "Unilateral Alteration of Public Sector Collective Bargaining Agreements and the Contract Clause." *Buffalo Law Review* 59 (January 2011): 1–55.

Boyd, Steven R. "The Contract Clause and the Evolution of American Federalism, 1789–1815." *William and Mary Quarterly* 44 (1987): 537–541.

Buck, Stuart. "The Legal Ramifications of Public Pension Reform," *Texas Review of Law and Politics* 17 (2012): 25–96.

Burnham, William C. "Public Pension Reform and the Contract Clause," *Roger Williams University Law Review* 20 (2015): 523–584.

Ely, James W., Jr. *The Contract Clause in American History.* New York: Garland, 1997.

———. "The Protection of Contractual Rights: A Tale of Two Constitutional Provisions." *New York University Journal of Law & Liberty* 1 (2005): 370–403.

Epstein, Richard A. "Toward a Revitalization of the Contract Clause." *University of Chicago Law Review* 51 (Summer 1984): 703–751.

Fliter, John A., and Derek S. Hoff. *Fighting Foreclosure: The* Blaisdell *Case, the Contract Clause, and the Great Depression.* Lawrence: University Press of Kansas. 2012.

Kmiec, Douglas W., and John O. McGinnis. "The Contract Clause: A Return to the Original Understanding." *Hastings Constitutional Law Quarterly* (1987): 525–544.

Magrath, C. Peter. *Yazoo: Law and Politics in the New Republic; The Case of* Fletcher v. Peck. Providence, RI: Brown University Press, 1966.

Nedelsky, Jennifer. *Private Property and the Limits of American Constitutionalism: The Madisonian Framework and Its Legacy.* Chicago: University of Chicago Press, 1990.

Olken, Samuel R. "Charles Evans Hughes and the *Blaisdell* Decision: A Historical Study of Contract Clause Jurisprudence." *Oregon Law Review* 72 (Fall 1993): 513–602.

O'Neill, Johnathan. "Property Rights and the American Founding: An Overview," *Journal of Supreme Court History* 38 (2013): 109–129.

Story, Joseph. *Commentaries on the Constitution of the United States*. Vol. 3. Boston: Hilliard, Gray, 1833.

Thompson, Barton H., Jr. "The History of the Judicial Impairment 'Doctrine' and Its Lessons for the Contract Clause." *Stanford Law Review* 44 (July 1992): 1373–1466.

Woolhandler, Ann. "Public Rights, Private Rights, and Statutory Retroactivity." *Georgetown Law Journal* 94 (April 2006): 1015–1063.

Wright, Benjamin F. *The Contract Clause of the Constitution*. Cambridge, MA: Harvard University Press, 1938.

Fletcher v. Peck
10 U.S. (6 Cranch) 87 (1810)

In 1795, the Georgia Legislature was bribed into authorizing the sale of more than 35 million acres of land in what was known as the Yazoo tracts (located in the present states of Alabama and Mississippi) to four land companies for $500,000, or about 1.5 cents an acre, in return for a share of lands amounting to approximately $1,000 per legislator. An outraged Georgia electorate voted the bribed legislators out at the next election, and in 1796 the new legislature repealed the year-old land grant and voided all property rights created by it. It declared that because the 1795 law "was made without constitutional authority, and fraudulently obtained, it is hereby declared of no binding force or effect on this state, or the people thereof." Between the 1795 and 1796 acts, however, the four land companies sold off many parcels of the Yazoo tracts to purchasers who were unaware of the fraud behind the original land grants.

Among the purchasers were John Peck and Robert Fletcher, who were shareholders in a New England land company. To test the validity of their land titles, Peck, a Massachusetts resident, sold 15,000 acres of his Yazoo land to Fletcher, a citizen of New Hampshire, for $3,000. Fletcher then sued Peck in federal court for breach of contract, claiming that Peck could not convey clear title of the land to him. The Circuit Court for the District of Massachusetts found the 1795 act valid and the rescinding act of 1796 invalid and held that Peck had acquired clear title, which he conveyed to Fletcher. Fletcher appealed to the United States Supreme Court. Opinion of the Court: <u>Marshall</u>, Washington, Johnson, Livingston, Todd. Concurring opinion: <u>Johnson</u>. Not participating: Cushing, Chase.

THE CHIEF JUSTICE delivered the opinion of the Court.

The lands in controversy vested absolutely in the original grantees by the conveyance of the governor, made in pursuance of an act of assembly to which the legislature was fully competent. Being thus in full possession of the legal estate, they, for a valuable consideration, conveyed portions of the land to those who were willing to purchase. If the original transaction was infected with fraud, these purchasers did not participate in it, and had no notice of it. They were innocent. Yet the legislature of Georgia has involved them in the fate of the first parties to the transaction, and, if the act be valid, has annihilated their rights also.

The legislature of Georgia was a party to this transaction; and for a party to pronounce its own deed invalid, whatever cause may be assigned for its invalidity, must be considered as a mere act of power which must find its vindication in a train of reasoning not often heard in courts of justice. . . .

If a suit be brought to set aside a conveyance obtained by fraud, and the fraud be clearly proved, the conveyance will be set aside, as between the parties; but the parties of third persons, who are purchasers without notice, for a valuable consideration, cannot be disregarded. Titles which, according to every legal test, are perfect, are acquired with that confidence which is inspired by the opinion that the purchaser is safe. If there be any concealed defect, arising from the conduct of those who had held the property long before he acquired it, of which he had no notice, that concealed defect cannot be set up against him. He has paid his money for a title good at law, he is innocent, whatever may be the guilt of others, and equity will not subject him to the penalties attached to that guilt. All titles would be insecure, and the intercourse between man and man would be very seriously obstructed, if this principle be overturned. . . .

In this case the legislature may have had ample proof that the original grant was obtained by practices which can never be too much reprobated, and which would have justified its abrogation so far as respected those to whom crime was imputable. But the grant, when issued, conveyed an estate in fee-simple to the grantee, clothed with all the solemnities which law can bestow. This estate was transferable; and those who purchased parts of it were not stained by that guilt which infected the original transaction. Their case is not distinguishable from the ordinary case of purchasers of a legal estate without knowledge of any secret fraud which might have led to the emanation of the original grant. According to the well known course of equity, their rights could not be affected by such fraud. Their situation was the same, their title was the same, with that of every other member of the community who holds land by regular conveyances from the original patentee.

Is the power of the legislature competent to the annihilation of such title, and to a resumption of the property thus held? The principle asserted is, that one legislature is competent to repeal any act which a former legislature was competent to pass; and that one legislature cannot abridge the powers of a succeeding legislature.

The correctness of this principle, so far as respects general legislation, can never be controverted. But, if an act be done under a law, a succeeding legislature cannot undo it. The past cannot be recalled by the most absolute power. Conveyances have been made; those conveyances have vested legal estates, and, if those estates may be seized by the sovereign authority, still, that they originally vested is a fact, and cannot cease to be a fact.

When, then, a law is in its nature a contract, when absolute rights have vested under that contract; a repeal of the law cannot devest those rights; and the act of annulling them, if legitimate, is rendered so by a power applicable to the case of every individual in the community. . . .

The constitution of the United States declares that no state shall pass any bill of attainder, *ex post facto* law or law impairing the obligation of contracts.

Does the case now under consideration come within this prohibitory section of the constitution?

In considering this very interesting question, we immediately ask ourselves what is a contract? Is a grant a contract?

A contract is a compact between two or more parties, and is either executory or executed. An executory contract is one in which a party binds himself to do, or not to do, a particular thing; such was the law under which the conveyance was made by the [Georgia] governor. A contract executed is one in which the object of contract is performed; and this,

says Blackstone, differs in nothing from a grant. The contract between Georgia and the purchasers was executed by the grant. A contract executed, as well as one which is executory, contains obligations binding on the parties. A grant, in its own nature, amounts to an extinguishment of the right of the grantor, and implies a contract not to re-assert that right. A party is, therefore, always estopped by his own grant.

Since, then, in fact, a grant is a contract executed, the obligation of which still continues, and since the constitution uses the general term *contract*, without distinguishing between those which are executory and those which are executed, it must be construed to comprehend the latter as well as the former. A law annulling conveyances between individuals, and declaring that the grantors should stand seised of their former estates, notwithstanding those grants, would be as repugnant to the constitution as a law discharging the vendors of property from the obligation of executing their contracts by conveyances. It would be strange if a contract to convey was secured by the constitution, while an absolute conveyance remained unprotected.

If, under a fair construction of the constitution, grants are comprehended under the term *contracts,* is a grant from the state excluded from the operation of the provision? Is the clause to be considered as inhibiting the state from impairing the obligation of contracts between two individuals, but as excluding from that inhibition contracts made with itself?

The words themselves contain no such distinction. They are general, and are applicable to contracts of every description. If contracts made with the state are to be exempted from their operation, the exception must arise from the character of the contracting party, not from the words which are employed.

Whatever respect might have been felt for the state sovereignties, it is not to be disguised that the framers of the constitution viewed, with some apprehension, the violent acts which might grow out of the feelings of the moment; and that the people of the United States, in adopting that instrument, have manifested a determination to shield themselves and their property from the effects of those sudden and strong passions to which men are exposed. The restrictions on the legislative power of the states are obviously founded in this sentiment; and the constitution of the United States contains what may be deemed a bill of rights for the people of each state. . . .

It is, then, the unanimous opinion of the court, that, in this case, the estate having passed into the hands of a purchaser for a valuable consideration, without notice, the state of Georgia was restrained, either by general principles which are common to our free institutions, or by the particular provisions of the constitution of the United States, from passing a law whereby the estate of the plaintiff in the premises so purchased could be constitutionally and legally impaired and rendered null and void. . . .

Judgment affirmed with costs.

Dartmouth College v. Woodward
17 U.S. (4 Wheaton) 518 (1819)

In 1769, the British Crown granted a corporate charter to the trustees of Dartmouth College, conveying to them "forever" the right to govern the institution and to appoint their own successors. After remaining unchallenged through the Revolutionary era, the charter was dramatically altered in 1816. The Republican governor and legislature of New Hampshire, having concluded that the old charter was based on principles more congenial to monarchy than to free government, sought to bring the college under public control by enacting three laws that took control of the college from the hands of the Federalist-dominated trustees and placed it under a board of overseers appointed by the governor. The trustees turned for relief to the state's judiciary. Contending that the 1816 laws impaired the obligation of contract contained in the original charter of 1769, they brought an action against William Woodward, the secretary and treasurer of the college, to recover the college's records, corporate seal, and other corporate property temporarily entrusted to him by one of the 1816 acts. The New Hampshire Supreme Court upheld the legislature's acts, chiefly on the grounds that the college was essentially a public corporation whose powers were exercised for public purposes and that it was therefore subject to public control. The trustees of the college then appealed the case upon a writ of error to the United States Supreme Court. Opinion of the Court: <u>Marshall</u>, Washington, Johnson, Livingston, Story. Concurring opinions: <u>Washington</u>, Livingston; <u>Story</u>, Livingston. Dissent: <u>Duvall</u>.

THE CHIEF JUSTICE delivered the opinion of the Court.

It can require no argument to prove, that the circumstances of this case constitute a contract. An application is made to the crown for a charter to incorporate a religious and literary institution. In the application, it is stated, that large contributions have been made for the object, which will be conferred on the corporation, as soon as it shall be created. The charter is granted, and on its faith the property is conveyed. Surely, in this transaction every ingredient of a complete and legitimate contract is to be found. The points for consideration are, 1. Is this contract protected by the constitution of the United States? 2. Is it impaired by the acts under which the defendant holds?

1. On the first point, it has been argued, that the word *"contract,"* in its broadest sense, would comprehend the political relations between the government and its citizens, would extend to offices held within a state, for state purposes, and to many of those laws concerning civil institutions, which must change with circumstances, and be modified by ordinary legislation; which deeply concern the public, and which, to preserve good government, the public judgment must control. That even marriage is a contract, and its obligations are affected by the laws respecting divorces. That the clause in the constitution, if construed in its greatest latitude, would prohibit these laws. Taken in its broad, unlimited sense, the clause would be an unprofitable and vexatious interference with the internal concerns of a state, would unnecessarily and unwisely embarrass its legislation, and render immutable those civil institutions, which are established for purposes of internal

government, and which, to subserve those purposes, ought to vary with varying circumstances. That as the framers of the constitution could never have intended to insert in that instrument, a provision so unnecessary, so mischievous, and so repugnant to its general spirit, the term *"contract"* must be understood in a more limited sense. That it must be understood as intended to guard against a power, of at least doubtful utility, the abuse of which had been extensively felt; and to restrain the legislature in future from violating the right to property. That, anterior to the formation of the constitution, a course of legislation had prevailed in many, if not in all, of the states, which weakened the confidence of man in man, and embarrassed all transactions between individuals, by dispensing with a faithful performance of engagements. To correct this mischief, by restraining the power which produced it, the state legislatures were forbidden "to pass any law impairing the obligation of contracts," that is, of contracts respecting property, under which some individual could claim a right to something beneficial to himself; and that, since the clause in the constitution must in construction receive some limitation, it may be confined, and ought to be confined, to cases of this description; to cases within the mischief it was intended to remedy. . . .

The parties in this case differ less on general principles, less on the true construction of the constitution in the abstract, than on the application of those principles to this case, and on the true construction of the charter of 1769. This is the point on which the cause essentially depends. If the act of incorporation be a grant of political power, if it create a civil institution, to be employed in the administration of the government, or if the funds of the college be public property, or if the state of New Hampshire, as a government, be alone interested in its transactions, the subject is one in which the legislature of the state may act according to its own judgment, unrestrained by any limitation of its power imposed by the constitution of the United States.

But if this be a private eleemosynary institution, endowed with a capacity to take property, for objects unconnected with government, whose funds are bestowed by individuals, on the faith of the charter; if the donors have stipulated for the future disposition and management of those funds, in the manner prescribed by themselves; there may be more difficulty in the case. . . . It becomes then the duty of the court, most seriously to examine this charter, and to ascertain its true character. . . .

A corporation is an artificial being, invisible, intangible, and existing only in contemplation of law. Being the mere creature of law, it possesses only those properties which the charter of its creation confers upon it, either expressly, or as incidental to its very existence. These are such as are supposed best calculated to effect the object for which it was created. Among the most important are immortality, and, if the expression may be allowed, individuality; properties, by which a perpetual succession of many persons are considered as the same, and may act as a single individual. They enable a corporation to manage its own affairs, and to hold property, without the perplexing intricacies, the hazardous and endless necessity, of perpetual conveyances for the purpose of transmitting it from hand to hand. It is chiefly for the purpose of clothing bodies of men, in succession, with these qualities and capacities, that corporations were invented, and are in use. By these means, a perpetual succession of individuals are capable of acting for the promotion of the particular object, like one immortal being. But this being does not share in the civil government of the country, unless that be the purpose for which it was created. . . .

From the fact, then, that a charter of incorporation has been granted, nothing can be inferred, which changes the character of the institution, or transfers to the government any new power over it. The character of civil institutions does not grow out of their incorporation, but out of the manner in which they are formed, and the objects for which they are created. The right to change them is not founded on their being incorporated, but on their being the instruments of government, created for its purposes. The same institutions, created for the same objects, though not incorporated, would be public institutions, and, of course, be controllable by the legislature. The incorporating act neither gives nor prevents this control. Neither, in reason, can the incorporating act change the character of a private eleemosynary institution. . . .

. . . It appears, that Dartmouth College is an eleemosynary institution, incorporated for the purpose of perpetuating the application of the bounty of the donors, to the specified objects of that bounty; that its trustees or governors were originally named by the founder, and invested with the power of perpetuating themselves; that they are not public officers, nor is it a civil institution, participating in the administration of government; but a charity-school, or a seminary of education, incorporated for the preservation of its property, and the perpetual application of that property to the objects of its creation. . . .

This is plainly a contract to which the donors, the trustees and the crown (to whose rights and obligations New Hampshire succeeds) were the original parties. It is a contract made on a valuable consideration. It is a contract for the security and disposition of property. It is a contract, on the faith of which, real and personal estate has been conveyed to the corporation. It is, then, a contract within the letter of the constitution, and within its spirit also, unless the fact, that the property is invested by the donors in trustees, for the promotion of religion and education, for the benefit of persons who are perpetually changing, though the objects remain the same, shall create a particular exception, taking this case out of the prohibition created in the constitution.

It is more than possible, that the preservation of rights of this description was not particularly in the view of the framers of the constitution, when the clause under consideration was introduced into that instrument. It is probable, that interferences of more frequent occurrence, to which the temptation was stronger, and of which the mischief was more extensive, constituted the great motive for imposing this restriction on the state legislatures. But although a particular and a rare case may not, in itself, be of sufficient magnitude to induce a rule, yet it must be governed by the rule, when established, unless some plain and strong reason for excluding it can be given. It is not enough to say, that this particular case was not in the mind of the conven-

tion, when the article was framed, nor of the American people, when it was adopted. It is necessary to go further, and to say that, had this particular case been suggested, the language would have been so varied, as to exclude it, or it would have been made a special exception. The case being within the words of the rule, must be within its operation likewise, unless there be something in the literal construction, so obviously absurd or mischievous, or repugnant to the general spirit of the instrument, as to justify those who expound the constitution in making it an exception.

On what safe and intelligible ground, can this exception stand? There is no expression in the constitution, no sentiment delivered by its contemporaneous expounders, which would justify us in making it.

The opinion of the court, after mature deliberation, is, that this is a contract, the obligation of which cannot be impaired, without violating the constitution of the United States.

2. We next proceed to the inquiry, whether its obligation has been impaired by those acts of the legislature of New Hampshire, to which the special verdict refers?

From the review of this charter, which has been taken, it appears that the whole power of governing the college, of appointing and removing tutors, of fixing their salaries, of directing the course of study to be pursued by the students, and of filling up vacancies created in their own body, was vested in the trustees. On the part of the crown, it was expressly stipulated, that this corporation, thus constituted, should continue for ever. . . . By this contract, the crown was bound, and could have made no violent alteration in its essential terms, without impairing its obligation.

By the revolution, the duties, as well as the powers, of government devolved on the people of New Hampshire. It is admitted, that among the latter was comprehended the transcendent power of parliament, as well as that of the executive department. It is too clear, to require the support of argument, that all contracts and rights respecting property, remained unchanged by the revolution. The obligations, then, which were created by the charter to Dartmouth College, were the same in the new, that they had been in the old government. The power of the government was also the same. A repeal of this charter, at any time prior to the adoption of the present constitution of the United States, would have been an extraordinary and unprecedented act of power, but one which could have been contested only by the restrictions upon the legislature, to be found in the constitution of the state. But the constitution of the United States has imposed this additional limitation, that the legislature of a state shall pass no act "impairing the obligation of contracts." . . .

On the effect of this law . . . the whole power of governing the college is transferred from trustees, appointed according to the will of the founder, expressed in the charter, to the executive of New Hampshire. The management and application of the funds of this eleemosynary institution, which are placed by the donors in the hands of trustees named in the charter, and empowered to perpetuate themselves, are placed by this act under the control of the government of the state. The will of the state is substituted for the will of the donors, in every essential operation of the college. This may be for the advantage of this college in particular, and may be for the advantage of literature in general; but it is not according to the will of the donors, and is subversive of that contract, on the faith of which their property was given. . . .

It results from this opinion, that the acts of the legislature of New Hampshire, which are stated in the special verdict found in this cause, are repugnant to the constitution of the United States; and that the judgment on this special verdict ought to have been for the plaintiffs. The judgment of the state court must, therefore, be reversed.

Charles River Bridge Company v. Warren Bridge Company
36 U.S. (11 Peters) 420 (1837)

In 1785, the Massachusetts Legislature granted a charter to the Charles River Bridge Company, authorizing it to construct a bridge between Charlestown and Boston and to collect tolls for forty years. (In 1792, the charter was extended to seventy years.) This franchise replaced an exclusive ferry right granted to Harvard College in 1650, and provision was made for compensating Harvard for the impairment of its ferry franchise.

In 1828, however, the legislature incorporated the Warren Bridge Company and authorized it to construct another bridge, only 264 feet away from the Charles River Bridge on the Charlestown side and 825 feet away on the Boston side. No tolls were to be charged on the Warren Bridge after its construction costs were recovered or after a maximum period of six years. The Charles River Bridge Company entered state court and sought an injunction to prevent the erection of the Warren Bridge; then, after the bridge was constructed, they sought general relief, contending that the legislature, in authorizing the new bridge, had violated the Contract Clause. The Massachusetts Supreme Judicial Court dismissed the complaint, and the case went to the US Supreme Court on a writ of error. Opinion of the Court: Taney, Baldwin, Wayne, McLean, Barbour. Concurring opinion: McLean. Dissenting opinions: Story; Thompson.

THE CHIEF JUSTICE delivered the opinion of the Court.

The plaintiffs in error insist that the acts of the legislature of Massachusetts of 1785, and 1792, by their true construction, necessarily implied that the legislature would not authorize another bridge, and especially a free one, by the side of this, and placed in the same line of travel, whereby the franchise granted to the "proprietors of the Charles River Bridge" should be rendered of no value; and the plaintiffs in error contend, that the grant of the charter to the proprietors of the bridge is a contract on the part of the state; and that the law authorizing the erection of the Warren Bridge in 1828, impairs the obligation of this contract. . . .

This brings us to the act of the legislature of Massachusetts, of 1785, by which the plaintiffs were incorporated by the name of "The Proprietors of the Charles River Bridge;" and it is here, and in the law of 1792, prolonging their charter, that we must look for the extent and nature of the franchise conferred upon the plaintiffs.

Much has been said in the argument of the principles of construction by which this law is to be expounded, and what undertakings, on the part of the state, may be implied. The Court thinks there can be no serious difficulty on that head. It is the grant of certain franchises by the public to a private corporation, and in a matter where the public interest is concerned. The rule of construction in such cases is well settled, both in England, and by the decisions of our own tribunals. . . . "The rule of construction in all such cases, is now fully established to be this; that any ambiguity in the terms of the contract, must operate against the adventurers, and in favour of the public, and the plaintiffs can claim nothing that is not clearly given them by the act." . . .

. . . The object and end of all government is to promote the happiness and prosperity of the community by which it is established; and it can never be assumed, that the government intended to diminish its power of accomplishing the end for which it was created. And in a country like ours, free, active, and enterprising, continually advancing in numbers and wealth; new channels of communication are daily found necessary, both for travel and trade; and are essential to the comfort, convenience, and prosperity of the people. A state ought never to be presumed to surrender this power, because, like the taxing power, the whole community have an interest in preserving it undiminished. And when a corporation alleges, that a state has surrendered for seventy years, its power of improvement and public accommodation, in a great and important line of travel, along which a vast number of its citizens must daily pass; the community have a right to insist . . . "that its abandonment ought not be presumed, in a case, in which the deliberate purpose of the state to abandon it does not appear." The continued existence of a government would be of no great value, if by implications and presumptions, it was disarmed of the powers necessary to accomplish the ends of its creation; and the functions it was designed to perform, transferred to the hands of privileged corporations. . . . No one will question that the interests of the great body of the people of the state, would, in this instance, be affected by the surrender of this great line of travel to a single corporation, with the right to exact toll, and exclude competition for seventy years. While the rights of private property are sacredly guarded, we must not forget that the community also have rights, and that the happiness and well being of every citizen depends on their faithful preservation.

Adopting the rule of construction above stated as the settled one, we proceed to apply it to the charter of 1785, to the proprietors of the Charles River Bridge. This act of incorporation is in the usual form, and the privileges such as are commonly given to corporations of that kind. It confers on them the ordinary faculties of a corporation, for the purpose of building the bridge; and establishes certain rates of toll, which the company are authorized to take. This is the whole grant. There is no exclusive privilege given to them over the waters of Charles river, above or below their bridge. No right to erect another bridge themselves, nor to prevent other persons from erecting one. No engagement from the state, that another shall not be erected; and no undertaking not to sanction competition, nor to make improvements that may diminish the amount of its income. Upon all these subjects the charter is silent; and nothing is said in it about a line of travel, so much insisted on in the argument, in which they are to have exclusive privileges. No words are used, from which an intention to grant any of these rights can be inferred. If the plaintiff is entitled to them, it must be implied, simply, from the nature of the grant; and cannot be inferred from the words by which the grant is made.

The relative position of the Warren Bridge has already been described. It does not interrupt the passage over the Charles River Bridge, nor make the way to it or from it less convenient. None of the faculties or franchises granted to that corporation, have been revoked by the legislature; and its right to take the tolls granted by the charter remains unaltered. In short, all the franchises and rights of property enumerated in the charter, and there mentioned to have been granted to it, remain unimpaired. But its income is destroyed by the Warren Bridge; which, being free, draws off the passengers and property which would have gone over it, and renders their franchise of no value. This is the gist of the complaint. For it is not pretended, that the erection of the Warren Bridge would have done them any injury, or in any degree affected their right of property; if it had not diminished the amount of their tolls. In order then to entitle themselves to relief, it is necessary to show, that the legislature contracted not to do the act of which they complain; and that they impaired, or in other words, violated the contract by the erection of the Warren Bridge.

The inquiry then is, does the charter contain such a contract on the part of the state? Is there any such stipulation to be found in that instrument? It must be admitted on all hands, that there is none—no words that even relate to another bridge, or to the diminution of their tolls, or to the line of travel. If a contract on that subject can be gathered from the charter, it must be by implication; and cannot be found in the words used. Can such an agreement be implied? The rule of construction before stated is an answer to the question. In charters of this description, no rights are taken from the public, or given to the corporation, beyond those which the words of the charter, by their natural and proper construction, purport to convey. There are no words which import such a contract as the plaintiffs in error contend for, and none can be implied. . . .

Indeed, the practice and usage of almost every state in the Union, old enough to have commenced the work of internal improvement, is opposed to the doctrine contended for on the part of the plaintiffs in error. Turnpike roads have been made in succession, on the same line of travel; the later ones interfering materially with the profits of the first. These corporations have, in some instances, been utterly ruined by the introduction of newer and better modes of transportation, and travelling. In some cases, rail roads have rendered the turnpike roads on the same line of travel so entirely useless, that the franchise of the turnpike corporation is not worth preserving. Yet in none of these cases have the corporations supposed that their privileges were invaded, or any contract violated on the part of the state. The absence of any such controversy, when there

must have been so many occasions to give rise to it, proves that neither states, nor individuals, nor corporations, ever imagined that such a contract could be implied from such characters. It shows that the men who voted these laws, never imagined that they were forming such a contract; and if we maintain that they have made it, we must create it by a legal fiction, in opposition to the truth of the fact, and the obvious intention of the party. We cannot deal thus with the rights reserved to the states; and by legal intendments and mere technical reasoning, take away from them any portion of that power over their own internal police and improvement, which is so necessary to their well being and prosperity. . . .

The judgment of the supreme judicial court of the commonwealth of Massachusetts, dismissing the plaintiffs' bill, must, therefore, be affirmed, with costs.

JUSTICE STORY, dissenting.

I maintain that upon the principle of common reason and legal interpretation, the present grant carries with it a necessary implication that the legislature shall do no act to destroy or essentially to impair the franchise; that (as one of the learned judges of the state court expressed it), there is an implied agreement of the state to grant the undisturbed use of the bridge and its tolls, so far as respects any acts of its own, or of any persons acting under its authority. In other words, the state, impliedly, contracts not to resume its grants, or to do any act to the prejudice or destruction of its grant. I maintain, that there is no authority or principle established in relation to the construction of crown grants, or legislative grants; which does not concede and justify this doctrine. Where the thing is given, the incidents, without which it cannot be enjoyed, are also given. . . . I maintain that a different doctrine is utterly repugnant to all the principles of the common law, applicable to all franchises of a like nature; and that we must overturn some of the best securities of the rights of property, before it can be established. . . . I maintain, that under the principles of the common law, there exists no more right in the legislature of Massachusetts, to erect the Warren bridge, to the ruin of the franchise of the Charles River bridge, than exists to transfer the latter to the former, or authorize the former to demolish the latter. If the legislature does not mean in its grant to give any exclusive rights, let it say so, expressly; directly; and in terms admitting of no misconstruction. . . .

My judgment is formed upon the terms of the grant, its nature and objects, its design and duties; and, in its interpretation, I seek for no new principles, but I apply such as are as old as the very rudiments of the common law. . . .

Upon the whole, my judgment is, that the act of the legislature of Massachusetts granting the charter of Warren bridge, is an act impairing the obligation of the prior contract and grant to the proprietors of Charles River bridge; and, by the constitution of the United States, it is therefore utterly void.

I am for reversing the decree of the state court (dismissing the bill); and for remanding the cause to the state court for further proceedings, as to law and justice shall appertain.

Home Building and Loan Association v. Blaisdell
290 U.S. 398 (1934)

In 1933, at the depth of the Depression, Minnesota passed a mortgage moratorium act designed to prevent the loss of mortgaged property by individuals temporarily unable to meet their financial obligations. The act authorized the state courts, upon application of the mortgagor, to extend the period of redemption from foreclosure sales for such a period as the courts might deem equitable, but not beyond May 1, 1935. The act was to remain in effect "only during the continuance of the emergency and in no event beyond May 1, 1935." During the emergency period, the mortgagor was required to apply the income or reasonable rental value, as fixed by the courts, to the payment of taxes, interest, insurance, and the mortgage indebtedness. It was a carefully drafted statute that attempted to protect the interest of the creditor as well as that of the debtor. Despite the care that went into its drafting, the moratorium act did alter the arrangement of existing contracts and thus raised a question of whether the act was an unconstitutional impairment of the obligations of contract. This question was ultimately brought before the Supreme Court when John Blaisdell and his wife, owners of a lot that was mortgaged to the Home Building and Loan Association, applied to the District Court of Hennepin County for an extension of time so that they could retain ownership of their home. The district court extended the redemption period, and the Supreme Court of Minnesota affirmed the judgment. The loan company appealed. Opinion of the Court: Hughes, *Brandeis, Stone, Roberts, Cardozo. Dissenting opinion:* Sutherland, *Van Devanter, McReynolds, Butler.*

THE CHIEF JUSTICE delivered the opinion of the Court.

The state court upheld the statute as an emergency measure. Although conceding that the obligations of the mortgage contract were impaired, the court decided that what it thus described as an impairment was, notwithstanding the contract clause of the Federal Constitution, within the police power of the State as that power was called into exercise by the public economic emergency which the legislature had found to exist. Attention is thus directed to the preamble and the first section of the statute, which described the existing emergency in terms that were deemed to justify the temporary relief which the statute affords. . . .

In determining whether the provision for this temporary and conditional relief exceeds the power of the State by reason of the clause in the Federal Constitution prohibiting impairment of the obligations of contracts, we must consider the relation of emergency to constitutional power, the historical setting of the contract clause, the development of the jurisprudence of this Court in the construction of that clause, and the principles of construction which we may consider to be established.

Emergency does not create power. Emergency does not increase granted power or remove or diminish the restrictions imposed upon power granted or reserved. The Constitution was adopted in a period of grave emergency. Its grants of power to the Federal Government and its limitations of the power of the States were determined in the light of emergency and they are not altered by emergency. What power was thus granted and what limitations were thus imposed are questions which have always been, and always will be, the subject of close examination under our constitutional system.

While emergency does not create power, emergency may furnish the occasion for the exercise of power. . . . The constitutional question presented in the light of an emergency is whether the power possessed embraces the particular exercise of it in response to particular conditions. Thus, the war power of the Federal Government is not created by the emergency of war, but it is a power given to meet that emergency. It is a power to wage war successfully, and thus it permits the harnessing of the entire energies of the people in a supreme cooperative effort to preserve the nation. But even the war power does not remove constitutional limitations safeguarding essential liberties. When the provisions of the Constitution, in grant or restriction are specific, so particularized as not to admit of construction, no question is presented. Thus, emergency would not permit a State to have more than two Senators in the Congress, or permit the election of President by a general popular vote without regard to the number of electors to which the States are respectively entitled, or permit the States to "coin money" or to "make anything but gold and silver coin a tender in payment of debts." But where constitutional grants and limitations of power are set forth in general clauses, which afford a broad outline, the process of construction is essential to fill in the details. That is true of the contract clause. . . .

In the construction of the contract clause, the debates in the Constitutional Convention are of little aid. But the reasons which led to the adoption of that clause, and of the other prohibitions of Section 10 of Article I, are not left in doubt and have frequently been described with eloquent emphasis. The widespread distress following the revolutionary period, and the plight of debtors, had called forth in the States an ignoble array of legislative schemes for the defeat of creditors and the invasion of contractual obligations. Legislative interferences had been so numerous and extreme that the confidence essential to prosperous trade had been undermined and the utter destruction of credit was threatened. . . .

But full recognition of the occasion and general purpose of the clause does not suffice to fix its precise scope. Nor does an examination of the details of prior legislation in the States yield criteria which can be considered controlling. To ascertain the scope of the constitutional prohibition we examine the course of judicial decisions in its application. These put it beyond question that the prohibition is not an absolute one and is not to be read with literal exactness like a mathematical formula. . . .

Not only is the constitutional provision qualified by the measure of control which the State retains over remedial processes, but the State also continues to possess authority to safeguard the vital interests of its people. It does not matter that legislation appropriate to that end "has the result of modifying or abrogating contracts already in effect." . . . Not only are existing laws read into contracts in order to fix obligations as between the parties, but the reservation of essential attributes of sovereign power is also read into contracts as a postulate of the legal order. The policy of protecting contracts against impairment presupposes the maintenance of a government by virtue of which contractual relations are worth while,—a government which retains adequate authority to secure the peace and good order of society. This principle of harmonizing the constitutional prohibition with the necessary residuum of state power has had progressive recognition in the decisions of this Court. . . .

The legislature cannot "bargain away the public health or public morals." Thus, the constitutional provision against the impairment of contracts was held not to be violated by an amendment of the state constitution which put an end to a lottery theretofore authorized by the legislature. *Stone v. Mississippi* (1880). . . . The lottery was a valid enterprise when established under express state authority, but the legislature in the public interest could put a stop to it. A similar rule has been applied to the control by the State of the sale of intoxicating liquors. . . . The States retain adequate power to protect the public health against the maintenance of nuisances despite insistence upon existing contracts. . . . Legislation to protect the public safety comes within the same category of reserved power. . . . This principle has had recent and noteworthy application to the regulation of the use of public highways by common carriers and "contract carriers," where the assertion of interference with existing contract rights has been without avail. . . .

The argument is pressed that in the cases we have cited the obligation of contracts was affected only incidentally. This argument proceeds upon a misconception. The question is not whether the legislative action affects contracts incidentally, or directly or indirectly, but whether the legislation is addressed to a legitimate end and the measures taken are reasonable and appropriate to that end. Another argument, which comes more closely to the point, is that the state power may be addressed directly to the prevention of the enforcement of contracts only when these are of a sort which the legislature in its discretion may denounce as being in themselves hostile to public morals, or public health, safety, or welfare, or where the prohibition is merely of injurious practices; that interference with the enforcement of other and valid contracts according to appropriate legal procedure, although the interference is temporary and for a public purpose, is not permissible. This is but to contend that in the latter case the end is not legitimate in the view that it cannot be reconciled with a fair interpretation of the constitutional provision.

Undoubtedly, whatever is reserved of state power must be consistent with the fair intent of the constitutional limitation of that power. The reserved power cannot be construed so as to destroy the limitation, nor is the limitation to be construed to destroy the reserved power in its essential aspects. They must be construed in harmony with each other. This principle precludes a construction which would permit the State to adopt as its policy the repudiation of debts or the destruction of contracts or the denial of means to enforce them. But it does not follow that conditions may not arise in which a temporary restraint of enforcement may be consistent with the spirit and purpose of the constitutional provision and thus be found to be within the range of the reserved power of the State to protect the vital interests

of the community. It cannot be maintained that the constitutional prohibition should be so construed as to prevent limited and temporary interpositions with respect to the enforcement of contracts if made necessary by a great public calamity such as fire, flood, or earthquake. . . . The reservation of state power appropriate to such extraordinary conditions may be deemed to be as much a part of all contracts, as is the reservation of state power to protect the public interest in the other situations to which we have referred. And if state power exists to give temporary relief from the enforcement of contracts in the presence of disasters due to physical causes such as fire, flood or earthquake, that power cannot be said to be nonexistent when the urgent public need demanding such relief is produced by other and economic causes. . . .

It is manifest from this review of our decisions that there has been a growing appreciation of public needs and of the necessity of finding ground for a rational compromise between individual rights and public welfare. The settlement and consequent contraction of the public domain, the pressure of a constantly increasing density of population, the interrelation of the activities of our people and the complexity of our economic interests, have inevitably led to an increased use of the organization of society in order to protect the very bases of individual opportunity. Where, in earlier days, it was thought that only the concerns of individuals or of classes were involved, and that those of the State itself were touched only remotely, it has later been found that the fundamental interests of the State are directly affected; and that the question is no longer merely that of one party to a contract as against another, but of the use of reasonable means to safeguard the economic structure upon which the good of all depends. . . .

Applying the criteria established by our decisions we conclude:

1. An emergency existed in Minnesota which furnished a proper occasion for the exercise of the reserved power of the State to protect the vital interests of the community. The declarations of the existence of this emergency by the legislature and by the Supreme

Court of Minnesota cannot be regarded as a subterfuge or as lacking in adequate basis. . . . The finding of the legislature and state court has support in the facts of which we take judicial notice. . . .

2. The legislation was addressed to a legitimate end, that is, the legislation was not for the mere advantage of particular individuals but for the protection of a basic interest of society.

3. In view of the nature of the contracts in question—mortgages of unquestionable validity—the relief afforded and justified by the emergency, in order not to contravene the constitutional provision, could only be of a character appropriate to that emergency and could be granted only upon reasonable conditions.

4. The conditions upon which the period of redemption is extended do not appear to be unreasonable. . . . [T]he integrity of the mortgage indebtedness is not impaired; interest continues to run; the validity of the sale and the right of a mortgagee-purchaser to title or to obtain a deficiency judgment, if the mortgagor fails to redeem within the extended period, are maintained; and the conditions of redemption, if redemption there be, stand as they were under the prior law. . . . Also important is the fact that mortgagees, as is shown by official reports of which we may take notice, are predominantly corporations, such as insurance companies, banks, and investment and mortgage companies. These, and such individual mortgagees as are small investors, are not seeking homes or the opportunity to engage in farming. Their chief concern is the reasonable protection of their investment security. It does not matter that there are, or may be, individual cases of another aspect. The Legislature was entitled to deal with the general or typical situation. The relief afforded by the statute has regard to the interest of mortgagees as well as to the interest of mortgagors. The legislation seeks to prevent the impending ruin of both by a considerate measure of relief. . . .

5. The legislation is temporary in operation. It is limited to the exigency which called it forth. . . .

We are of the opinion that the Minnesota statute as here applied does not violate the contract clause of the Federal Constitution. Whether the legislation is wise or unwise as a matter of policy is a question with which we are not concerned. . . .

The judgment of the Supreme Court of Minnesota is affirmed.

JUSTICE SUTHERLAND, dissenting.

Few questions of greater moment than that just decided have been submitted for judicial inquiry during this generation. He simply closes his eyes to the necessary implications of the decision who fails to see in it the potentiality of future gradual but ever-advancing encroachments upon the sanctity of private and public contracts. The effect of the Minnesota legislation, though serious enough in itself, is of trivial significance compared with the far more serious and dangerous inroads upon the limitations of the Constitution which are almost certain to ensue as a consequence naturally following any step beyond the boundaries fixed by that instrument. And those of us who are thus apprehensive of the effect of this decision would, in a matter so important, be neglectful of our duty should we fail to spread upon the permanent records of the court the reasons which move us to the opposite view.

A provision of the Constitution, it is hardly necessary to say, does not admit of two distinctly opposite interpretations. It does not mean one thing at one time and an entirely different thing at another time. If the contract impairment clause, when framed and adopted, meant that the terms of a contract for the payment of money could not be altered *in invitum* by a state statute enacted for the relief of hardly pressed debtors to the end and with the effect of postponing payment or enforcement during and because of an economic or financial emergency, it is but to state the obvious to say that it means the same now. This view, at once so rational in its application to the written word, and so necessary to the stability of constitutional principles, though from time to time challenged, has never, unless recently, been put within the realm of doubt by the decisions of this court. . . .

The whole aim of construction, as applied to a provision of the Constitution, is to discover the meaning, to ascertain and give effect to the intent, of its framers and the people who adopted it. . . . The necessities which gave rise to the provision, the controversies which preceded, as well as the conflicts of opinion which were settled by its adoption, are matters to be considered to enable us to arrive at a correct result. . . . The history of the times, the state of things existing when the provision was framed and adopted, should be looked to in order to ascertain the mischief and the remedy. . . . As nearly as possible we should place ourselves in the condition of those who framed and adopted it. . . . And if the meaning be at all doubtful, the doubt should be resolved, wherever reasonably possible to do so, in a way to forward the evident purpose with which the provision was adopted. . . .

An application of these principles to the question under review removes any doubt, if otherwise there would be any, that the contract impairment clause denies to the several states the power to mitigate hard consequences resulting to debtors from financial or economic exigencies by an impairment of the obligation of contracts of indebtedness. . . .

The lower court, and counsel for the appellees in their argument here, frankly admitted that the statute does constitute a material impairment of the contract, but contended that such legislation is brought within the state power by the present emergency. If I understand the opinion just delivered, this court is not wholly in accord with that view. The opinion concedes that emergency does not create power, or increase granted power, or remove or diminish restrictions upon power granted or reserved. It then proceeds to say, however, that while emergency does not create power, it may furnish the occasion for the exercise of power. I can only interpret what is said on that subject as meaning that while an emergency does not diminish a restriction upon power it furnishes an occasion for diminishing it; and this, as it seems to me, is merely to say the same thing by the use of another set of words, with the effect of affirming that which has just been denied.

It is quite true that an emergency may supply the occasion for the exercise of power, depending upon the nature of the power and the intent of the Constitution with respect thereto. But we are here dealing not with a power granted by the Federal Constitution, but with the state police power, which exists in its own right. Hence the question is not whether an emergency furnishes the occasion for the exercise of that state power, but whether an emergency furnishes an occasion for the relaxation of the restrictions upon the power imposed by the contract impairment clause; and the difficulty is that the contract impairment clause forbids state action under any circumstances, if it have the effect of impairing the obligation of contracts. That clause restricts every state power in the particular specified, no matter what may be the occasion. It does not contemplate that an emergency shall furnish an occasion for softening the restriction or making it any the less a restriction upon state action in that contingency than it is under strictly normal conditions.

The Minnesota statute either impairs the obligation of contracts or it does not. If it does not, the occasion to which it relates becomes immaterial, since then the passage of the statute is the exercise of a normal, unrestricted, state power and requires no special occasion to render it effective. If it does, the emergency no more furnishes a proper occasion for its exercise than if the emergency were nonexistent. And so, while, in form, the suggested distinction seems to put us forward in a straight line, in reality it simply carries us back in a circle, like bewildered travelers lost in a wood, to the point where we parted company with the view of the state court. . . .

. . . The phrase, "obligation of a contract," in the constitutional sense imports a legal duty to perform the specified obligation of *that* contract, not to substitute and perform, against the will of one of the parties, a different, albeit equally valuable, obligation. And a state, under the contract impairment clause, has no more power to accomplish such a substitution than has one of the parties to the contract against the will of the other. It cannot do so either by acting directly upon the contract, or by bringing about the result under the guise of a statute in form acting only upon the remedy. If it could, the efficacy of the constitutional restriction would, in large measure, be made to disappear. . . .

I quite agree with the opinion of the court that whether the legislation under review is wise or unwise is a matter with which we have nothing to do. Whether it is likely to work well or work ill presents a question entirely irrelevant to the issue. The only legitimate inquiry we can make is whether it is constitutional. If it is not, its virtues, if it have any, cannot save it; if it is, its faults cannot be invoked to accomplish its destruction. If the provisions of the Constitution be not upheld when they pinch as well as when they comfort, they may as well be abandoned.

Being unable to reach any other conclusion than that the Minnesota statute infringes the constitutional restriction under review, I have no choice but to say so.

United States Trust Company v. New Jersey
431 U.S. 1 (1977)

A 1962 interstate compact between New York and New Jersey limited the ability of the Port Authority of New York and New Jersey to subsidize mass transit from revenues and reserves pledged as security for consolidated bonds issued by the authority. In 1974, in the face of an emerging national energy crisis, the New Jersey and New York Legislatures, acting concurrently, retroactively repealed the 1962 covenant. The United States Trust Company, a trustee and bondholder of the Port Authority, brought suit in a New Jersey superior court, attacking New Jersey's statutory repeal as a violation of the Contract Clause and seeking declaratory relief. The trial court dismissed the complaint on the grounds that the statute repealing the covenant was a reasonable exercise of New Jersey's police power. The New Jersey Supreme Court affirmed the decision, and the case was appealed to the Supreme Court. Opinion of the Court: Blackmun, Burger, Stevens, Rehnquist. Concurring opinion: Burger. Dissenting opinion: Brennan, White, Marshall. Not participating: Stewart, Powell.

JUSTICE BLACKMUN delivered the opinion of the Court.

. . . Whether or not the protection of contract rights comports with current views of wise public policy, the Contract Clause remains a part of our written Constitution. We therefore must attempt to apply that constitutional provision to the instant case with due respect for its purpose and the prior decisions of this Court. . . .

Although the Contract Clause appears literally to proscribe "any" impairment, this Court observed in *Blaisdell* that "the prohibition is not an absolute one and is not to be read with literal exactness like a mathematical formula." . . . Thus, a finding that there has been a technical impairment is merely a preliminary step in resolving the more difficult question whether that impairment is permitted under the Constitution. In the instant case, as in *Blaisdell*, we must attempt to reconcile the strictures of the Contract Clause with the "essential attributes of sovereign power" . . . necessarily reserved by the States to safeguard the welfare of their citizens. . . .

The States must possess broad power to adopt general regulatory measures without being concerned that private contracts will be impaired, or even destroyed, as a result. Otherwise, one would be able to obtain immunity from state regulation by making private contractual arrangements. . . .

Yet private contracts are not subject to unlimited modification under the police power. . . . Legislation adjusting the rights and responsibilities of contracting parties must be upon reasonable conditions and of a character appropriate to the public purpose justifying its adoption. . . . As is customary in reviewing economic and social regulation, however, courts properly defer to legislative judgment as to the necessity and reasonableness of a particular measure. . . .

When a State impairs the obligation of its own contract, . . . complete deference to a legislative assessment of reasonableness and necessity is not appropriate because the State's self-interest is at stake. A governmental entity can always find a use for extra money, especially when taxes do not have to be raised. If a State could reduce its financial obligations whenever it wanted to spend the money for what it regarded as an important public purpose, the Contract Clause would provide no protection at all.

Mass transportation, energy conservation, and environmental protection are goals that are important and of legitimate public concern. Appellees contend that these goals are so important that any harm to bondholders from repeal of the 1962 covenant is greatly outweighed by the public benefit. We do not accept this invitation to engage in a utilitarian comparison of public benefit and private loss. . . . The Court has not "balanced away" the limitation on state action imposed by the Contract Clause. Thus a State cannot refuse to meet its legitimate financial obligations simply because it would prefer to spend the money to promote the public good rather than the private welfare of its creditors. We can only sustain the repeal of the 1962 covenant if that impairment was both reasonable and necessary to serve the admittedly important purposes claimed by the State.

The more specific justification offered for the repeal of the 1962 covenant was the States' plan for encouraging users of private automobiles to shift to public transportation. The States intended to discourage private automobile use by raising bridge and tunnel tolls and to use the extra revenue from those tolls to subsidize improved commuter railroad service. Appellees contend that repeal of the 1962 covenant was necessary to implement this plan because the new mass transit facilities could not possibly be self-supporting and the covenant's "permitted deficits" level had already been exceeded. We reject this justification because the repeal was neither necessary to achievement of the plan nor reasonable in light of the circumstances.

The determination of necessity can be considered on two levels. First, it cannot be said that total repeal of the covenant was essential; a less drastic modification would have permitted the contemplated plan without entirely removing the covenant's limitations on the use of Port Authority revenues and reserves to sub-sidize commuter railroads. Second, without modifying the covenant at all, the States could have adopted alternative means of achieving their twin goals of discouraging automobile use and improving mass transit. Appellees contend, however, that choosing among these alternatives is a matter for legislative discretion. But a State is not completely free to consider impairing the obligations of its own contracts on a par with other policy alternatives. Similarly, a State is not free to impose a drastic impairment when an evident and more moderate course would serve its purposes equally well. . . .

We also cannot conclude that repeal of the covenant was reasonable in light of the surrounding circumstances. . . .

. . . In the instant case the need for mass transportation in the New York metropolitan area was not a new development, and the likelihood that publicly owned commuter railroads would produce substantial deficits was well known. As early as 1922, over a half century ago, there were pressures to involve the Port Authority in mass transit. It was with full knowledge of these concerns that the 1962 covenant was adopted. Indeed, the covenant was specifically intended to protect the pledged revenues and reserves against the possibility that such concerns would lead the Port Authority into greater involvement in deficit mass transit. . . .

. . . We cannot conclude that the repeal was reasonable in the light of changed circumstances.

We therefore hold that the Contract Clause of the United States Constitution prohibits the retroactive repeal of the 1962 covenant. The judgment of the Supreme Court of New Jersey is reversed.

JUSTICE BRENNAN, with whom JUSTICE WHITE and JUSTICE MARSHALL join, dissenting.

Decisions of this Court for at least a century have construed the Contract Clause largely to be powerless in binding a State to contracts limiting the authority of successor legislatures to enact laws in furtherance of the health, safety, and similar collective interests of the polity. In short, those decisions established the principle that lawful exercises of a State's police powers stand paramount to private rights held under contract. Today's decision, in invalidating the New Jersey Legislature's 1974 repeal of its predecessor's 1962 covenant, rejects this previous understanding and remolds the Contract Clause into a potent instrument for overseeing important policy determinations of the state legislature. At the same time, by creating a constitutional safe haven for property rights embodied in a contract, the decision substantially distorts modern constitutional jurisprudence governing regulation of private economic interests. I might understand, though I could not accept, this revival of the Contract Clause were it in accordance with some coherent and constructive view of public policy. But elevation of the Clause to the status of regulator of the municipal bond market at the heavy price of frustration of sound legislative policy-making is as demonstrably unwise as it is unnecessary. The justification for today's decision, therefore, remains a mystery to me, and I respectfully dissent. . . .

One of the fundamental premises of our popular democracy is that each generation of representatives can and will remain responsive to the needs and desires of those whom they represent. Crucial to this end is the assurance that new legislators will not automatically be bound by the policies and undertakings of earlier days. In accordance with this philosophy, the Framers of our Constitution conceived of the Contract Clause primarily as protection for economic transactions entered into by purely private parties, rather than obligations involving the State itself. . . . The Framers fully recognized that nothing would so jeopardize the legitimacy of a system of government that relies upon the ebbs and flows of politics to "clean out the rascals" than the possibility that those same rascals might perpetuate their policies simply by locking them into binding contracts.

I would not want to be read as suggesting that the States should blithely proceed down the path of repudiating their obligations, financial or otherwise. Their credibility in the credit market obviously is highly dependent on exercising their vast lawmaking powers with self-restraint and discipline, and I, for one, have little doubt that few, if any, jurisdictions would choose to use their authority "so foolishly as to kill a goose that lays golden eggs for them" . . . But in the final analysis, there is no reason to doubt that appellant's financial welfare is being adequately policed by the political processes and the bond marketplace itself. The role to be played by the Constitution is at most a limited one. . . . For this Court should have learned long ago that the Constitution—be it through the Contract or Due Process Clause—can actively intrude into such economic and policy matters only if my Brethren are prepared to bear enormous institutional and social costs. Because I consider the potential dangers of such judicial interference to be intolerable, I dissent.

Taylor, et al. v. City of Gadsden
958 F. Supp.2d 1287 (2013)

Joe Taylor and other firefighters employed by the City of Gadsden, Alabama, filed a putative class action lawsuit in US District Court for the Northern District of Alabama against the City of Gadsden and its mayor, Sherman Guyton, in his official capacity. Their complaint alleged that mandatory increases to their required pension contributions, imposed by a 2011 act of the Alabama Legislature, and subsequent resolutions of the City based on that act, violated the Contract Clause of Article I, Section 10 of the US Constitution. Opinion of the Court: US District Court Judge Virginia Emerson Hopkins.

JUDGE HOPKINS delivered the following Memorandum Opinion and Order of the Court:

. . . In this case, the plaintiffs contend that "the recent action of the City of Gadsden to increase the required pension contributions of firefighter employees from 6% to 8.25% of earnable compensation, as authorized by a recent act [Act 676] of the Alabama Legislature, constitutes an unlawful impairment of contractual obligations violative of Article I, Section 10 of the Constitution of the United States. . . ."

CONTRACT CLAUSE LAW

The Contract Clause of the United States Constitution provides: "No State shall . . . pass any . . . Law impairing the Obligation of Contracts." Judicial analysis of a Contract Clause claim has developed over time into several steps. In *General Motors Corp. v. Romein* (1992), the Supreme Court unanimously outlined the following framework for the initial evaluation of a claim brought under the Contract Clause:

Generally, we first ask whether the change in state law has "operated as a substantial impairment of a contractual relationship." This inquiry has three components: whether there is a contractual relationship, whether a change in law impairs that contractual relationship, and whether the impairment is substantial. . . .

The inquiry does not end when the court finds a contractual relationship and a change in law that substantially impairs that contractual relationship. To survive Contract Clause review, a legislative enactment that constitutes a substantial impairment of a contractual relationship must have a "significant and legitimate public purpose." The significant and legitimate public purpose may include "the remedying of a broad and general social or economic problem." However, "the public purpose need not be addressed to an emergency or temporary situation."

. . . In sum, therefore, a law or regulation that substantially impairs a contractual relationship does not violate the Contract Clause so long as it serves a significant and legitimate public purpose, is based on reasonable conditions, and is appropriate to the public purpose justifying its enactment. . . .

The defendants first argue that neither the Alabama legislature nor the City of Gadsden created a contractual relationship with the plaintiffs. They then argue that, if either did create such a relationship, requiring the plaintiffs to increase their contributions did not substantially impair the contractual relationship. Finally, the defendants argue that even if a substantial impairment of a contractual relationship exists, the acts of the legislature and the City are justified as reasonable and necessary to serve an important public purpose.

DO THE PLAINTIFFS HAVE A CONTRACT WITH THE CITY OF GADSDEN?

The plaintiffs seem at times to argue that *both* the State, through its enactments, *and* the City of Gadsden entered into a contract with them. Importantly, the State of Alabama is not a defendant in this case. Still, the complaint could be fairly read to say that the City created contractual rights in the plaintiffs when it adopted a pension program created by the State. . . .

ACTIONS BY THE LEGISLATURE

The plaintiffs do not set out one specific act of the legislature which they contend establishes contractual rights. Instead, they refer to numerous statutes and the RSA [Retirement System of Alabama] handbook.

Since they allege that Act 676, which increases the plaintiffs' contributions to the retirement plan, unconstitutionally interferes with their contract rights, the logical place to begin the analysis as to whether a contract was created is the statute which established the contribution rates in the first place. That statute states: "Effective January 1, 2001, and each pay period thereafter, each active employee who is a firefighter, law enforcement officer, or correctional officer, as defined in subsection (a), shall contribute to the Teachers' or Employees' Retirement System of Alabama *six percent* of his or her earnable compensation." . . .

DO THE ERS [EMPLOYEES' RETIREMENT SYSTEM] PROVISIONS CREATE, IN FAVOR OF THE PLAINTIFFS, A CONTRACTUAL RIGHT TO NEVER BE REQUIRED TO PAY MORE THAN 6% OF THEIR PAY TOWARDS THE SYSTEM?

A statutory enactment is generally presumed not to create "contractual or vested rights but merely declares a policy to be pursued until the legislature shall ordain otherwise." "[A]bsent some clear indication that the legislature intends to bind itself contractually, the presumption is that 'a law is not intended to create private contractual or vested rights.'"

Where a public contract allegedly arises out of statutory language, the hurdle under the first component of the first part of the test–proving that a contractual relationship exists—is necessarily higher, since "normally state statutory enactments do not of their own force create a contract with those whom the statute benefits."

This threshold requirement for the recognition of public contracts has been referred to as the "unmistakability doctrine." In *United States v. Winstar* (1996), the Supreme Court traced the history of the unmistakability doctrine from Justice Marshall's opinion in *Fletcher v. Peck* (1810), and explained its purpose. Because legislatures should not bind future legislatures from employing their sovereign powers in the absence of the clearest of intent to create vested rights protected under the Contract Clause, courts developed canons of construction disfavoring implied governmental contractual obligations. Thus, "'neither the right of taxation, nor any other power of sovereignty, will be held . . . to have been surrendered, unless such surrender has been expressed in terms too plain to be mistaken.'" The requirement that "the government's obligation unmistakably appear thus served the dual purposes of limiting contractual incursions on a State's sovereign powers and of avoiding difficult constitutional questions about the extent of State authority to limit the subsequent exercise of legislative power."

. . . Here, the court has no trouble finding no contractual rights were created. The plaintiffs have cited no statutory language, handbook provisions, or other materials which reflect "a clear intent by the legislature to create contractual rights." In other words, there is no indication that the legislature, and therefore the City, unmistakably has bound itself to *never* changing the contribution rate. . . . There is no evidence of any writing whereby the City of Gadsden agreed to never increase the percentage paid by firefighters. Even if the plaintiffs had contended, which they do not, that the ordinances of the City Council memorialize the contract, none of those ordinances state

that the amount of the contribution will *never* be increased.

IF THERE WAS A CONTRACT, AND THE CHANGE IN THE LAW IMPAIRS THAT CONTRACTUAL RELATIONSHIP, WAS THE IMPAIRMENT SUBSTANTIAL?

The defendants next argue that, if a contract exists, any impairment that the rights created in that contract was not substantial. In their response brief, the plaintiffs write: "First, defendants say nothing to support the notion that a 40% increase in the employees' contribution to their pension is not substantial. . . . The facts of that process are fully documented in the depositions of the employee negotiators, former Mayor Means and the other City officials involved. Nobody that testified suggested the amount of the increase was insubstantial." . . . The plaintiffs write, without citation to authority, "[b]y raising the contribution rates of employees who already hold vested pension rights with more than ten years of service, Gadsden substantially altered enforceable contractual interests. Those employees now have to pay 8.5% of their salary to maintain their already vested pension rights, rather than 6%."

The court does not agree. A "substantial impairment" can be the "total destruction of a contract." *Home Building & Loan Ass'n v. Blaisdell* (1934). However, the Supreme Court has recognized that "the actual line between permissible and impermissible impairments could well be drawn more narrowly." *U.S. Trust Co. of New York v. New Jersey* (1977). The extent of the impairment is only one "relevant factor in determining its reasonableness." "[T]he Supreme Court [also] looks at whether the impaired term was central to the contract, whether settled expectations have been disrupted, and whether the impaired right was reasonably relied on."

The plaintiffs have not shown or argued that keeping the employee compensation rate at 6% for firefighters *forever* was a central part of . . . their agreement to enter into the ERS. . . . Further, the RSA Handbook in existence in 2002, which the plaintiffs cite as forming part of the contract, states that "[t]he member's contribution rate is determined by statute and *subject to change by the Alabama legislature.*" (Emphasis added). "Under these circumstances, an employee's reasonable expectation from the Plan contract cannot include a guarantee that an employee contribution would never be required."

WERE THE LEGISLATURE AND THE CITY OF GADSDEN JUSTIFIED IN ENACTING THE CHANGES?

As shown above, a law or regulation that substantially impairs a contractual relationship does not violate the Contract Clause so long as it serves a significant and legitimate public purpose, is based on reasonable conditions, and is appropriate to the public purpose justifying its enactment. However, the court does not need to reach this issue, as it has already found no contract, and, even if there were a contract, the court has found that the plaintiffs' rights in the contract were not substantially impaired.

SUMMARY JUDGMENT FOR THE DEFENDANTS

Based on the foregoing, the defendants' motion for summary judgment will be GRANTED, [and] . . . it is hereby ORDERED, ADJUDGED, and DECREED that this case is DISMISSED, with prejudice, costs taxed as paid.

12

Economic Due Process and the Takings Clause

CHAPTER OUTLINE

Before the Civil War, the only constitutional restrictions on the power of the states to regulate economic activity were those found in Article I, Section 10, which prohibits the states from emitting bills of credit, making anything but gold or silver a tender in payment of debts, and passing *ex post facto* laws or laws impairing obligations of contracts. With the adoption of the Fourteenth Amendment in 1868, this situation changed. As briefly pointed out in Chapter 11 of Volume I, this amendment, especially through its Due Process Clause, supplied the Supreme Court with a potent weapon for invalidating state efforts at economic regulation and for protecting vested property rights. In the early part of the twentieth century, the Court wielded the Due Process Clause to strike down state laws that, in its estimation, arbitrarily, unreasonably, and capriciously interfered with the rights of life, liberty, and property.[1] During this period, various justices used the clause to justify substantive reviews of governmental actions, scrutinizing not only how, procedurally, the government acted, but also what, substantively, the government did.

As with the Contract Clause before it, substantive due process in the economic realm gradually lost its potency, and by the late 1930s it no longer represented a major obstacle to economic regulation by the states. Such obstacles as remain are now found in the limitations on punitive-damages awards established by the Court in *BMW v. Gore* (1996), the Takings Clause of the Fifth Amendment as incorporated to apply to the states, the Court's expanding interpretations of congressional power to regulate commerce among the several states, and the state constitutions themselves. Today, it is almost wholly within the realm of civil liberties that substantive due process retains its potency and continues to serve as a constitutional limitation not only on legislative and executive procedure, but also on legislative and executive power to act at all. This chapter traces the rise and decline of substantive due process in the economic realm, as well as its subsequent revival as a strong check on the substance of legislation infringing upon civil liberties. The chapter also explores the remaining significance of the Takings Clause as a check on state regulation of property rights.

THE FOURTEENTH AMENDMENT

The Fourteenth Amendment commands that "no state shall make or enforce any law which shall abridge the privileges or immunities of citizens of the United States; nor shall any State deprive any person of life, liberty, or property, without due process of law; nor deny to any person within its jurisdiction the equal protection of the laws." Out of an acrimonious debate over the specific intentions of the members of the Thirty-Ninth Congress who framed this amendment[2] has emerged general agreement as to what overall ends the amendment was intended to advance and as to how its three major provisions were to advance these ends. As a group, the Privileges or Immunities, Due Process, and Equal Protection Clauses were intended to place economic and civil liberties on the safe and secure foundation of federal protection, as follows:

- The Privileges or Immunities Clause was to protect substantive rights (e.g., freedom of speech, religious freedom, the right to engage in lawful occupations, freedom from improper police violence).
- The Due Process and Equal Protection Clauses were to protect procedural rights, with the former guaranteeing procedural safeguards and judicial regularity in the enforcement of those rights and the latter barring legislative and executive discrimination with respect to those substantive rights.

The Fourteenth Amendment can be visualized as a platform erected above the surface of state action for the protection of economic and civil liberties. In this metaphor, the

Privileges or Immunities, Due Process, and Equal Protection Clauses represent the platform's three legs: each performs different functions, yet collectively they render the platform stable and secure. The amendment's framers believed that all three legs were essential but that the Privileges or Immunities Clause would be the most important of the three, because it was designed to be the major load-bearing leg. This design is reflected clearly in Section 5 of the amendment, which provides that "Congress shall have power to enforce, by appropriate legislation, the provisions of this article." Looking at these provisions from the point of view of Congress, the Privileges or Immunities Clause provides the simplest framework for such enforcement legislation. Under that clause, Congress can set out, through a single act or a series of acts, a comprehensive list of the vast number of substantive rights that flow from US citizenship and make it unlawful for any state, or its agents, to abridge such substantive rights.[3] In contrast, the Due Process and Equal Protection Clauses, with their procedural emphases, represent far more elusive reference points for enforcement legislation, because of the formidable technical difficulties one faces to avoid unconstitutional vagueness and still frame statutes that protect persons from state deprivation of their lives, liberty, or property "without due process of law" or that guarantee "equal protection of the laws" without interference with essential classificatory schemes.

Just five years after the Fourteenth Amendment was ratified, however, the Supreme Court in *The Slaughter-House Cases* (1873) effectively kicked out the critical privileges-or-immunities leg and left the protective platform precariously supported by its two spindly procedural legs—due process and equal protection. To keep the platform of protections from collapsing altogether, subsequent Courts have found it imperative to increase substantially the size and strength of these procedural legs. Through judicial interpretation, the justices have added layer upon layer of meaning and coverage to these legs, in an effort to render secure those substantive economic and civil rights that were originally to have been protected by the Privileges or Immunities Clause.

THE EVISCERATION (AND POSSIBLE RECENT RESTORATION?) OF THE PRIVILEGES OR IMMUNITIES CLAUSE

In *Butcher's Benevolent Association v. Crescent City Live-Stock Landing and Slaughter-House Company*, more commonly known as *The Slaughter-House Cases* (1873), the Court upheld an act of the Louisiana Legislature that had conferred upon one firm what was in effect a monopoly of the slaughterhouse business in New Orleans. The plaintiffs had asserted, among other things, that the law in question was in violation of the Fourteenth Amendment. In a 5–4 decision, the Court rejected this claim, principally as a result of its especially narrow construction of the Privileges or Immunities Clause. Speaking for the majority, Justice Samuel F. Miller drew a distinction between state citizenship and national citizenship and, hence, between those privileges or immunities that accrued to an individual by virtue of state citizenship and those that stemmed from national citizenship. Only the latter, he insisted, were protected by the Fourteenth Amendment.

In distinguishing the privileges or immunities of state citizenship from those of national citizenship, Justice Miller quoted earlier decisions in an effort to demonstrate that the whole body of commonly accepted civil and economic rights—including the right to pursue lawful employment in a lawful manner, which lay at the heart of *The Slaughter-House Cases*—fell within the privileges or immunities of state citizenship. Such rights included "protection by the government, with the right to acquire and possess property of every kind, and to pursue and obtain happiness and safety, subject, nevertheless, to such restraints as the [state] government may prescribe for the general good of the whole." Miller contended that the framers of the Fourteenth Amendment had not intended to transfer this whole body of rights to the protection of the federal government. To interpret the amendment otherwise, he argued, would be to accept consequences "so serious, so far-reaching and pervading" that they would alter radically "the whole theory of the relations of the state and Federal governments to each other." This the Court refused to do, "in the absence of language which expresses such a purpose too clearly to admit of doubt."

Miller and the majority did not argue that national citizenship conferred no privileges or immunities. Although declining to define them precisely, they did suggest that such privileges or immunities included the right of a citizen "to come to the seat of the government to assert any claim he may have upon that government," the "right of free access to its seaports," and the right "to demand the care and protection of the Federal government over his life, liberty, and property when on the high seas, or within the jurisdiction of a foreign government." This list, however, left the whole body of traditional economic and civil rights solely under the protection of the states. As far as the federal Constitution was concerned, therefore, the privileges or immunities of the citizens of the separate states remained exactly as they had been before the Fourteenth Amendment was adopted. Justice Miller's argument prompted a frustrated Justice Stephen B. Field to complain in his dissent that if that was all the Privileges or Immunities Clause meant, "it was a vain and idle enactment, which accomplished nothing, and most unnecessarily excited Congress and the people on its passage." For Justice Field, the clause was intended to have a "profound significance and consequence." He argued that what the Privileges and Immunities Clause of Article IV, Section 2, "did for the protection of the citizens of one State against hostile and discriminating legislation of other States, the Fourteenth Amendment does for the protection of every citizen of the United States against hostile and discriminating legislation against him in favor of others, whether they reside in the same or in different states."

The *Slaughter-House* decision knocked out the only substantive (and, therefore, the most important) leg supporting the platform of economic and civil liberties erected by the Fourteenth Amendment. It was, in the words of Michael Kent Curtis, "one of the signal disasters of American judicial history."[4] In 1935, the Court made an initial effort to prop up this substantive leg and to restore the Privileges or Immunities Clause, holding in *Colgate v. Harvey* that the right of a US citizen to do business and place a loan in a state other than that in which he resided was a privilege of national citizenship. Just five years later in *Madden v. Kentucky* (1940), however, it expressly overturned that decision and returned to the old interpretation that "the right to carry out an incident of a trade, business, or calling such as the deposit of money in banks is not a privilege of national citizenship." And four years later in *Snowden v. Hughes* (1944), it again reaffirmed its narrow *Slaughter-House* interpretation when it held that the right to become a candidate for and be elected to a state office was an attribute of state citizenship, not a privilege of national citizenship. Those who had been denied this right, the Court declared, must look to their own state constitutions and laws for redress.[5]

Until 1999 it was altogether accurate to say that, with respect to the Privileges or Immunities Clause, the Court's decision in *The Slaughter-House Cases* remained good law. However, that year in *Saenz v. Roe,* the Court once again launched a campaign to restore the Privileges or Immunities Clause, invoking its language to strike down a durational residency requirement in California's welfare statute as an impermissible infringement on the right to travel and holding further that congressional approval of such a requirement did not resuscitate its constitutionality. Justice John Stevens held for a seven-member majority that a privilege and immunity of national citizenship is the right of travelers who elect to become permanent residents of a state "to be treated like other citizens of that State." Thomas dissented, arguing that Stevens attributed a meaning to the clause that was unintended when the Fourteenth Amendment was ratified. He faulted Stevens for failing to address the clause's "historical underpinnings." Yet, he declared, "because I believe that the demise of the Privileges and Immunities Clause has contributed in no small part to the current disarray of our Fourteenth Amendment jurisprudence, I would be open to reevaluating its meaning in an appropriate case." But, he continued, "before invoking the Clause, we should endeavor to understand what the framers of the Fourteenth Amendment thought it meant." And he went further: "We should also consider whether the Clause should displace, rather than augment, portions of our equal protection and substantive due process jurisprudence." He concluded by expressing his worry about the Court's sudden invocation of the Privileges or Immunities Clause: because Stevens used it to protect a right not expressly mentioned in the Constitution, will it become "yet another convenient tool for inventing new rights, limited solely by the 'predilections of those who happen at the time to be Members of this Court'"?

Interestingly, Thomas's dissent in *Saenz* gave great encouragement to Alan Gura, the brash young attorney who successfully argued in *District of Columbia v. Heller* that the Second Amendment secures to individuals the personal right to possess a firearm unconnected with service in a militia and to use that weapon for purposes of self-defense. Gura was retained to represent Otis McDonald, the petitioner in *McDonald v. Chicago,* where the question was whether the Second Amendment was incorporated by the Fourteenth Amendment to apply to the states. Gura gambled and devoted fifty-six of his sixty-three pages of argument in his initial brief to the Privileges or Immunities Clause argument. He so alarmed the National Rifle Association (NRA) that it filed a brief making selective incorporation under the Due Process Clause much more forcefully and at much greater length than did Gura's brief, asked for (and was granted) some of Gura's time during oral argument, and hired former solicitor general Paul Clement (who argued the government's case in *Heller*) to participate in the oral argument. The NRA's action proved to be wise, as Gura's efforts to rely on the Privileges or Immunities Clause were immediately challenged during oral argument; Chief Justice Roberts quickly questioned his reliance on the clause, noting that *The Slaughter-House Cases* had been good law for 140 years and adding that "it's a heavy burden for you to carry to suggest that we ought to overrule that decision." And, soon thereafter, Scalia challenged his argument in the following colloquy:

JUSTICE SCALIA: Mr. Gura, do you think it is at all easier to bring the Second Amendment under the Privileges and Immunities Clause than it is to bring it under our established law of substantive due?

MR. GURA: It's—

JUSTICE SCALIA: Is it easier to do it under privileges and immunities than it is under substantive due process?

MR. GURA: It is easier in terms, perhaps, of the text and history of the original public understanding of—

JUSTICE SCALIA: No, no. I'm not talking about whether—whether the *Slaughter-House Cases* were right or wrong. I'm saying, assuming we give, you know, the Privileges and Immunities Clause your definition, does that make it any easier to get the Second Amendment adopted with respect to the States?

MR. GURA: Justice Scalia, I suppose the answer to that would be no, because—

JUSTICE SCALIA: Then if the answer is no, why are you asking us to overrule 150, 140 years of prior law, when you can reach your result under substantive due [process]—I mean, you know, unless you are bucking for a—a place on some law school faculty—

(Laughter.)

MR. GURA: No. No. I have left law school some time ago and this is not an attempt to return.

> **JUSTICE SCALIA:** What you argue is the darling of the professoriate, for sure, but it's also contrary to 140 years of our jurisprudence. Why do you want to undertake that burden instead of just arguing substantive due process, which as much as I think it's wrong, . . . even I have acquiesced in it?
>
> (Laughter.)

Despite Roberts's and Scalia's questions, and the laughter they elicited, Thomas was unfazed. In a twenty-thousand-word solo opinion, he insisted that the right to keep and bear arms was an "inalienable right that pre-existed the Constitution's adoption" and a privilege and immunity that could be enforced against the states under the Fourteenth Amendment.

ECONOMIC REGULATION AND THE RISE
OF SUBSTANTIVE DUE PROCESS

The emasculation of the Privileges or Immunities Clause left the substantive economic and civil liberties guaranteed by that clause wholly dependent for support upon the Due Process and Equal Protection Clauses. The *Slaughter-House* majority, however, also construed these clauses narrowly.[6] In response to the plaintiffs' assertion that the Louisiana statute in question deprived them of their property without due process of law, the Court observed that "under no construction of that provision that we have ever seen, or that we deem admissible, can the restraint imposed by the State of Louisiana . . . be held to be a deprivation of property within the meaning of that provision."[7] And to a plea that the act deprived the plaintiffs of equal protection of the laws, the Court responded that the Equal Protection Clause had been aimed only at laws in the states "where the newly emancipated negroes resided, which discriminated with gross injustice and hardship against them as a class."

Over time, the Court has expanded and enlarged these narrow interpretations—these spindly legs—until today the Due Process and Equal Protection Clauses solidly support the protection of a vast array of substantive rights. (This chapter and Chapters 5 through 7 of Volume II explore the Court's expansion of the Due Process Clause, first in order to protect economic rights and subsequently in order to protect civil liberties. Chapters 8 through 10 in Volume II then explore the Court's somewhat later expansion of the Equal Protection Clause and how it has enlarged this procedural leg as well into a means of protecting substantive civil liberties. Finally, Chapter 11 of Volume II explores how the Court has employed these two clauses together to create and expand a generalized right to privacy, personal autonomy, and human dignity.)

The narrow procedural interpretation given the Due Process Clause in *The Slaughter-House Cases* gave way only gradually to a broader, more substantive understanding. In the significant case of *Munn v. Illinois* (1877), the Court reaffirmed the restrictive *Slaughter-House* interpretation and refused to hold that an Illinois statute that set maximum rates for grain elevators denied the elevator operators use of their property without due process of law. Chief Justice Morrison Waite argued that, since the days of the common law, grain elevators and warehouses had been recognized as businesses "clothed with a public interest" and as such were subject to public regulation by the legislature. Although he conceded that this regulatory power might be abused, the chief justice insisted that abuse "is no argument against the [law's] existence. For protection against abuses by legislatures the people must resort to the polls, not to the courts." In dissent, Justice Field argued that there was nothing in the character of the grain-elevator business that justified state regulation, and hence Illinois's legislation was "nothing less than a bold assertion of absolute power by the State to control at its discretion the property and business of the citizen, and fix the compensation he shall receive." To Field, this "unrestrained license" to regulate was incompatible with due process of law.

Field's broader conception of due process was articulated further by Justice Joseph Bradley in his concurring opinion in *Davidson v. New Orleans* (1878). Justice Miller, writing for the majority in *Davidson,* rejected a New Orleans landowner's claim that he had been deprived of his property without due process of law by being forced to pay a special assessment whose purpose (the draining of swamplands) allegedly would not benefit him. After confessing that "the Constitutional meaning or value of the phrase 'due process of law' remains today without that satisfactory precision of definition which judicial decisions have given to nearly all the other guarantees of personal rights found in the constitutions of the several States and of the United States," Justice Miller went on to declare that the phrase's meaning, however unclear, must be understood in a procedural sense only:

> It is not possible to hold that a party has, without due process of law, been deprived of his property, when, as regards the issues affecting it, he has, by the laws of the State, a fair trial in a court of justice, according to the modes of proceedings applicable to such a case. . . . This proposition covers the present case. Before the assessment could be collected, or become effective, the statute required that the tableau of assessments should be filed in the proper District Court of the State; that personal service of notice, with reasonable time to object, should be served on all owners who were known and within reach of process, and due advertisement made as to those who were unknown, or could not be found. This was complied with; and the party complaining here appeared, and had a full and fair hearing in the court of first instance, and afterwards in the Supreme Court. If this be not due process of law, then the words can have no definite meaning as used in the Constitution.

Justice Bradley, although agreeing with the decision, insisted that the Due Process Clause had a substantive dimension as well. Making explicit what was implicit in Justice Field's dissent in *Munn,* he argued,

> I think . . . we are entitled under the fourteenth amendment, not only to see that there is some process of law, but "due process of law," provided by the State law when a citizen is deprived of his property; and that, in judging what is "due process of law," respect must be had to the cause and object of the taking, whether under the taxing power, the power of eminent domain, or the power of assessment for local improvements, or none of these: and if found to be suitable or admissible in the special case, it will be adjudged to be "due process of law;" but if found to be arbitrary, oppressive, and unjust, it may be declared to be not "due process of law."

According to this view, the Due Process Clause requires courts to review not only how, procedurally, the government acts (procedural due process), but also what, substantively, the government does (substantive due process). If the Court discerns that a law is unreasonable—that is, "arbitrary, oppressive, and unjust"—then it is justified in declaring the law to be a denial of due process and, hence, constitutionally infirm.

These substantive due-process arguments did not originate with Justices Field and Bradley. As far back as 1856, in *Wynehamer v. New York,* the New York Court of Appeals (the state's highest court) had invalidated a Prohibition law on the grounds that such an exercise of the police power infringed on the economic liberty of tavern proprietors to practice their livelihood and therefore denied them due process of law.[8] Justices Field and Bradley, however, were the first to give expression to these sentiments at the level of the United

States Supreme Court, and the arguments they introduced in *Munn* and *Davidson* gained ascendancy in *Mugler v. Kansas* (1887) and *Allgeyer v. Louisiana* (1897) and received their clearest constitutional expression in *Lochner v. New York* (1905).

In *Mugler*, the Court upheld Kansas's Prohibition law but warned that it would begin examining the reasonableness of legislation. Justice John Marshall Harlan stressed that if "a statute purporting to have been enacted to protect the public health, the public morals, or the public safety has no real or substantial relation to those objects, or is a palpable invasion of rights secured by the fundamental law, it is the duty of the Courts to so adjudge." Then, in *Allgeyer*, the Court for the first time relied on substantive due process to invalidate state legislation. Louisiana had enacted legislation designed to regulate out-of-state insurance companies doing business in the state. Justice Rufus Peckham, writing for the majority, argued that the statute in question "is not due process of law, because it prohibits an act which under the federal constitution the defendant has a right to perform." The state's legitimate exercise of its police power, he contended, did not extend to "prohibiting a citizen from making contracts of the nature involved in this case outside of the limits of the jurisdiction of the state, and which are also to be performed outside of such jurisdiction." In the course of his opinion, Justice Peckham forthrightly announced the principle that the right to make contracts was a part of the liberty guaranteed by the Due Process Clause:

> The liberty mentioned in the [Fourteenth] Amendment means not only the right of the citizen to be free from the mere physical restraint of his person, as by incarceration, but the term is deemed to embrace the right of the citizen to be free in the enjoyment of all his faculties; to be free to use them in all lawful ways; to live and work where he will; to earn his livelihood by any lawful calling; to pursue any livelihood or avocation, and for that purpose to enter into all contracts which may be proper, necessary and essential to his carrying out to a successful conclusion the purposes above mentioned.

These substantive due-process arguments received their clearest expression in *Lochner v. New York,* in which the same Justice Peckham, the most libertarian member of the Court, was assigned the writing of the majority opinion and declared that New York had unreasonably and arbitrarily interfered with the "freedom of master and employee to contract with each other in relation to their employment" by passing a law limiting the number of hours a baker could work in a bakery.[9] Finding no valid health or safety reasons that could justify such a law, Peckham ruled that it amounted to an unreasonable deprivation of liberty (i.e., the liberty to contract) and violated the Due Process Clause. Justices John Marshall Harlan and Oliver Wendell Holmes each wrote separate dissents. Justice Harlan agreed with Peckham that there is "a liberty to contract which cannot be violated even under the sanction of direct legislative enactment," but charged the majority with "enlarging the scope of the Amendment far beyond its original purpose" and with "bringing under the supervision of this court matters which have been supposed to belong exclusively to the legislative departments of the several States." Justice Holmes penned one of his most memorable passages: "The Fourteenth Amendment does not enact Mr. Spencer's *Social Statics.* [In this work, Spencer presented an account of the development of human freedom and a defense of individual liberties based on the principles of social Darwinism.] . . . A constitution . . . is made for people of fundamentally differing views."

By embracing the notion of substantive due process, Justice Peckham assumed for the Court the very role that Justice Miller had warned against in *The Slaughter-House Cases:* it made the Court a "perpetual censor," reviewing the reasonableness of state efforts at economic regulation. It continued to play this role at least through *Adkins v. Children's Hospital* (1923), when it branded the District of Columbia's minimum-wage law for women and children "the product of a naked arbitrary exercise of power" and thus a violation of the Fifth Amendment's Due Process Clause. Prior to *Adkins,* the Court rarely played this role to strike down state laws; as Charles Warren made clear in two famous at the time but now largely forgotten articles in the *Columbia Law Review,* the Court had during this entire period upheld more than 90 percent of all due-process challenges to economic legislation by the states.[10] Thus, for example, in *Muller v. Oregon* (1908) and *Bunting v. Oregon* (1917), the justices upheld the constitutionality of state legislation that, respectively, limited the workday for women to ten hours and extended the same maximum-hours limitation to all mill and factory workers. Of decisive importance in both of these decisions, however, was the Court's belief that the regulations in question were a reasonable exercise of the state's police powers—not its post-*Adkins* conviction that any judicial inquiry into the substance or reasonableness of economic legislation was inappropriate.

THE DEMISE OF SUBSTANTIVE DUE PROCESS IN THE ECONOMIC REALM

As the Court's subsequent decision in *Adkins* makes apparent, *Muller* and *Bunting* did not represent a repudiation of substantive due process—in these cases, the Court merely judged that the economic regulations in question were reasonable; it did not conclude that it was inappropriate for the Court to make such judgments in the first place. The disavowal of substantive due process began somewhat later in *Nebbia v. New York* (1934), in which the Court, by a 5–4 vote, upheld the validity of a Depression-era law regulating the price of milk. The New York legislature had sought to prevent ruinous price cutting by establishing a milk control board with power to fix minimum and maximum retail prices, and the appellant claimed that enforcement of the milk price regulations denied him due process of law by preventing him from selling his product at whatever price he desired. In rejecting this claim, Justice Owen Roberts, speaking for the majority, declared, "So far as the requirement of due process is concerned, and in the absence of other constitutional restrictions, a state is free to adopt whatever economic policy may reasonably be deemed to promote public welfare, and to enforce that policy by legislation adapted to its purpose. The courts are without authority either to declare such policy, or, when it is declared by the legislature, to override it."

What was begun in *Nebbia* was completed in *West Coast Hotel Company v. Parrish* (1937). This case arose under a Washington State minimum-wage law that had been passed in 1913 and enforced continuously thereafter, quite irrespective of *Adkins.* In the midst of the intense political controversy generated by President Franklin Roosevelt's Court-packing plan, the Court upheld the law. Chief Justice Charles Evans Hughes insisted that the state legislature had the right to use its minimum-wage requirements to help implement its policy of protecting women from exploitative employers. He noted that "the adoption of similar requirements by many States evidences a deepseated conviction both as to the presence of the evil and as to the means adopted to check it. Legislative response to that conviction cannot be regarded as arbitrary or capricious, and that is all we have to decide." The chief justice then went even further: "Even if the wisdom of the policy is regarded as debatable and its effects uncertain, still the legislature is entitled to its judgment."

The Court's refusal in *Parrish* to contradict the judgment of the legislature on economic matters and its outright repudiation of substantive due process in the economic realm through its explicit overruling of *Adkins* remain controlling precedents. Subsequent decisions, in fact, suggest a reluctance to subject economic legislation to any constitutional test at all.[11] *Day-Brite Lighting v. Missouri* (1952) provides a clear example of this trend. In reviewing a state law that provided that employees could absent themselves from their jobs for four hours on election days and forbade employers from deducting wages for their absence, the Court admitted that the social policy embodied in the law was debatable but pointed out that "our recent decisions make plain that we do not sit as a superlegislature to weigh the wisdom of legislation nor to decide whether the policy it expresses offends the public welfare." This argument was repeated in *Williamson v. Lee Optical Company* (1955), which involved a statute that forbade any person but an ophthalmologist or an optometrist from fitting lenses to the face or duplicating or replacing lenses into frames, except on the prescription of an ophthalmologist or optometrist. After acknowledging that the law was "a needless, wasteful requirement in many cases," the Court went on to insist that "the day is gone" when it would strike down "state laws regulatory of business and industrial conditions, because they may be unwise, improvident, or out of harmony with a particular school of thought." Eight years later, in *Ferguson v. Skrupa* (1963), the Court applied the same reasoning in upholding a Kansas statute prohibiting anyone except lawyers from engaging in the business of debt adjustment, with Justice Hugo Black noting in his majority opinion that "it is up to legislatures, not courts, to decide on the wisdom and utility of legislation." The *Ferguson* opinion elicited some judicial protests, however. Despite his abiding commitment to judicial self-restraint, Justice John Harlan felt compelled to protest against what he perceived to be judicial abdication. In his concurrence, he insisted that even economic legislation must bear "a rational relation to a constitutionally permissible objective"—a relationship that he found to exist in the instant case.

PUNITIVE DAMAGES: AN EXCEPTION TO THE DEMISE OF SUBSTANTIVE DUE PROCESS IN THE ECONOMIC REALM?

Justice Black's words in *Ferguson,* echoing as they do Chief Justice Waite's opinion in *Munn v. Illinois,* highlight the full circle traveled by the Court in its consideration of the Due Process Clause and economic rights. The spindly due-process leg in *Munn,* which by *Lochner* had grown enormously in size and strength, had lost its muscularity by *Parrish* and atrophied to the spindly leg it once again became by *Williamson.* So it remained, at least until *BMW v. Gore* (1996), which raises the interesting question of whether the Court is not once again embracing substantive due process—if not to limit what legislatures can do, then at least to limit the size of punitive-damages awards that civil juries can impose.

In this case, the plaintiff brought suit in an Alabama court for $500,000 in compensatory and punitive damages against the American distributor of BMWs. He alleged that the failure to disclose that the top, hood, trunk, and quarter panels of the car he had purchased had been repainted at the automobile manufacturer's US vehicle preparation center—the result of damage caused by exposure to acid rain during transit between Germany and United States—constituted fraud under Alabama law. At trial, BMW acknowledged that it followed a nationwide policy of not advising its dealers, and hence its customers, of pre-delivery damage to new cars when the cost of repair did not exceed 3 percent of the car's suggested retail price. The cost of repainting the plaintiff's vehicle was $601.37 (or about 1.5 percent of its $40,750.88 suggested retail price) and therefore fell into that category. The jury returned a verdict finding BMW liable for compensatory damages of $4,000 (its judgment of how much less the plaintiff's car was worth because it had been repainted) and assessing $4 million in punitive damages (its judgment of the appropriate punishment for BMW for selling approximately one thousand repainted cars nationally for approximately $4,000 more than each was worth). The trial judge denied BMW's post-trial motion to set aside the punitive-damages award, holding, among other things, that the award did not violate the Due Process Clause of the Fourteenth Amendment as interpreted in two earlier damages cases: *Pacific Mutual Insurance Co. v. Haslip* (1991) and *TXO Production Corp. v.*

Alliance Resources Corp. (1993). The Alabama Supreme Court agreed, but it reduced the award to $2 million on the grounds that, in computing the amount, the jury had improperly multiplied Dr. Gore's compensatory damages by the number of similar sales in all states.

The Supreme Court, however, reversed the Alabama Supreme Court and held that the Due Process Clause of the Fourteenth Amendment prohibits a state from imposing punitive-damages awards that are "grossly excessive"—in this instance, a punitive-damages award that was five hundred times compensatory damages. Justice Stevens for a five-member majority identified three "guideposts" that led the Court to the conclusion that the Alabama courts had entered "the zone of arbitrariness" and deprived the defendant of "elementary notions of fairness": the degree of reprehensibility of the defendant's conduct, the ratio between the punitive award and the plaintiff's actual harm, and the difference between the courts' sanction and legislative sanctions authorized for comparable misconduct. In his dissent, Justice Antonin Scalia complained that these guideposts "mark a road to nowhere; they provide no real guidance at all." He observed that "the elevation of 'fairness' in punishment to a principle of 'substantive due process' means that every punitive award unreasonably imposed is unconstitutional; such an award is by definition excessive, since it attaches a penalty to conduct undeserving of punishment." He drew out the consequences: "If the Court is correct, it must be that every claim that a state jury's award of compensatory damages is 'unreasonable' (because not supported by the evidence) amounts to an assertion of constitutional injury. . . . By today's logic, every dispute as to evidentiary sufficiency in a state civil suit poses a question of constitutional moment, subject to review in this Court. That is a stupefying proposition." Justice Ruth Bader Ginsburg was in fundamental agreement; in her dissent, she likewise objected to the way in which the majority "leads us into territory traditionally within the States' domain" with "only a vague concept of substantive due process, a 'raised eyebrow' test, as its ultimate guide."

Several years passed before *BMW v. Gore* figured prominently in a subsequent Supreme Court opinion, allowing for speculation to develop over whether it was the beginning of a renewed judicial infatuation with substantive due process in the economic realm or whether it was merely an isolated, if provocative, exception. However, with its decision in *State Farm Mutual Automobile Insurance Company v. Campbell* (2003), the Court made it clear that *Gore* was no exception. In *Campbell,* the Court applied the three "guideposts" from *Gore* and held that an award of $145 million in punitive damages, where full compensatory damages were $1 million, was excessive and violated due process. Justice Kennedy for the six-member majority went so far as to argue that "few awards exceeding a single-digit ratio between punitive and compensatory damages . . . will satisfy due process." Justice Ginsburg in her dissent accused him of acting like a legislator rather than a judge when he suggested that if "compensatory damages are substantial, then a lesser ratio, perhaps only equal to compensatory damages, can reach the outermost limit of the due process guarantee."

Punitive-damages cases typically raise substantive due-process questions, but *Caperton v. Massey Coal Company* (2009) raised a procedural due-process question. A West Virginia jury returned a verdict that found the Massey Coal Company fraudulently liable in a coal contract dispute and awarded Caperton $50 million in compensatory and punitive damages. After the verdict but before the appeal, West Virginia held its 2004 judicial elections, in which Don Blankenship (Massey's chairman, chief executive officer, and president) supported Brent Benjamin, who successfully challenged Justice Warren McGraw, a member of the West Virginia Supreme Court, who was running for reelection. In addition to contributing the $1,000 statutory maximum to Benjamin's campaign committee, Blankenship donated almost $2.5 million to an independent political organization that opposed McGraw and supported Benjamin and spent more than $500,000 on independent expenditures—for direct mailings and letters soliciting donations as well as television and newspaper advertisements—in support of Benjamin's candidacy. When Massey's appeal was heard by the West Virginia Supreme Court, Justice Brent Benjamin refused to recuse himself—when challenged, he insisted that there was no "objective evidence" of bias on his part but merely a "subjective belief"—and joined the Court majority in a 3–2 decision overturning the jury's verdict and award. In a 5–4 decision, the US Supreme Court held in an opinion by Justice Kennedy that in this "extraordinary" case, the Due Process Clause required recusal whether or not actual bias existed or could be proved. Chief Justice Roberts wrote a spirited dissent, raising forty unanswered questions that Kennedy's opinion "quickly [brought] to mind. Judges and litigants will surely encounter others when they are forced to apply the majority's decision in different circumstances. Today's opinion requires state and federal judges simultaneously to act as political scientists (why did candidate X win the election?), economists (was the financial support disproportionate?), and psychologists (is there likely to be a debt of gratitude?)."

THE EMERGENCE OF SUBSTANTIVE DUE PROCESS IN THE CIVIL LIBERTIES REALM

With the possible exception of the Court's punitive-damages jurisprudence, what can be said with certainty is that the Court, for whatever reason, has not embraced substantive due process simultaneously in both the economic and the civil liberties realms. When substantive due process was at its height in the economic realm in the early part of the twentieth century, it was nonexistent in the realm of civil liberties, as *Buck v. Bell* (1927) makes abundantly clear.

In *Buck* the Court denied a substantive due-process objection to a 1924 Virginia statute that, on the grounds of the "health of the patient and the welfare of society," provided for the sexual sterilization of inmates of institutions supported by the state who were found to be afflicted with hereditary forms of insanity or imbecility. The preamble of the Virginia statute declared that the commonwealth was supporting in various institutions many "defective persons" who, if discharged, would become a menace, but who, if rendered incapable of procreating, might be discharged with safety and become self-supporting, with benefits both to themselves and to society; it also declared that experience had shown that "heredity plays an important part in the transmission of insanity, imbecility, etc." Justice Holmes upheld the sterilization of Carrie Buck, whom he described as a "feeble minded white woman," "the daughter of a feeble minded mother," and herself "the mother of an illegitimate feeble minded child." He argued first that the statute met all the requirements of procedural due process: "There can be no doubt that, so far as procedure is concerned, the rights of the patient are most carefully considered, and, as every step in this case was taken in scrupulous compliance with the statute and after months of observation, there is no doubt that, in that respect, the plaintiff in error has had due process of law." But, he noted, Carrie Buck also objected on substantive due-process grounds: "The attack is [also] upon the substantive law. It seems to be contended that in no circumstances could such an order be justified." The Court, however, was unpersuaded, and so, just four years after it had found in *Adkins* that a minimum-wage law for women and children was "the product of a naked arbitrary exercise of power," it held that Virginia's eugenics-inspired statute passed constitutional muster. Justice Holmes wrote for an eight-member majority (Justice Butler dissented but did not write an opinion) when he declared:

> We have seen more than once that the public welfare may call upon the best citizens for their lives. It would be strange if it could not call upon those who already

sap the strength of the State for these lesser sacrifices, often not felt to be such by those concerned, in order to prevent our being swamped with incompetence. It is better for all the world if, instead of waiting to execute degenerate offspring for crime or to let them starve for their imbecility, society can prevent those who are manifestly unfit from continuing their kind. The principle that sustains compulsory vaccination is broad enough to cover cutting the Fallopian tubes. Three generations of imbeciles are enough.[12]

At about the time that the Court was abandoning the protection of economic rights by substantive due process, it was beginning to embrace the concept to protect civil rights. The contemptuous disregard for the civil rights of Carrie Buck was soon replaced by a particular judicial solicitude for the rights of "discrete and insular minorities." In footnote 4 of the Court's opinion in *United States v. Carolene Products Company* (1938), decided just one year after its repudiation of substantive due process in the economic realm in *West Coast Hotel v. Parrish,* Justice Harlan Fiske Stone outlined a justification for "more exacting judicial scrutiny" where infringements of civil liberties were involved. The Court's subsequent embrace of substantive due process in the realm of civil liberties is a major theme in Volume II.

THE TAKINGS CLAUSE

Just as the Due Process Clause supplanted the Contract Clause as a means of protecting property rights, so, too, the Takings Clause of the Fifth Amendment as made applicable to the states by the Fourteenth Amendment appears to have supplanted due process. It states that private property shall not "be taken for public use, without just compensation." This language tacitly recognizes the inherent power of eminent domain of the federal and state governments; as the Court said in *Boom Co. v. Patterson* (1879), this power "appertains to every independent government. It requires no constitutional recognition; it is an attribute of sovereignty."

Prior to the adoption of the Fourteenth Amendment, the power of eminent domain of state governments was unrestrained by any federal authority. In *Barron v. Baltimore* (1833), the Court held that the just compensation provision of the Fifth Amendment did not apply to the states. In *Chicago, Burlington & Quincy Railroad Co. v. Chicago* (1897), however, the Court embraced the argument that the Due Process Clause of the Fourteenth Amendment afforded property owners the same measure of protection against the states as the Fifth Amendment did against the federal government. It ruled that, although a state "legislature may prescribe a form of procedure to be observed in the taking of private property for public use, . . . it is not due process of law if provision be not made for compensation. . . . The mere form of the proceeding instituted against the owner . . . cannot convert the process used into due process of law, if the necessary result be to deprive him of his property without compensation." Although the federal and state guarantees of just compensation flow from different sources, the standards used by the Court in dealing with the issues appear to be identical, whether they arise in federal or state cases.

The decision to condemn or expropriate private property for public use upon just compensation of the owner is a legislative one, and, over time, the Court has become increasingly reluctant to question whether the confiscated property has been taken for a "public use." Initially, the courts considered the term *public use* to be synonymous with *use by the public,* and they held the exercise of the power of eminent domain to be invalid if the property taken was conveyed to private individuals instead of being used, for example, for the construction of roads, schools, or parks. Beginning with *Clark v. Nash* (1905), however, the Supreme Court began to equate public use with any use conducive of the public interest or public welfare. The result has been that the public-use limitation on governments' power of eminent domain no longer limits the uses for which governments can take private property.

In *Clark* the Supreme Court held that Utah could authorize by statute an individual to condemn a right-of-way across his neighbor's land for the enlargement of an irrigation ditch, thereby enabling him to obtain water from a stream to irrigate his land, which otherwise would remain absolutely valueless. The Court held that "the validity of such statutes may sometimes depend upon many different facts, the existence of which would make a public use, even by an individual, where, in the absence of such facts, the use would clearly be private." The facts present in this case that convinced the Court that Utah's condemnation statute served the public interest—and therefore a public use—were the "climate and soil" of the "arid and mountainous States of the West" and the recognition by these states that "the cultivation of an otherwise valueless soil, by means of irrigation," was "absolutely necessary" for their "growth and prosperity."

Applying its equation of public use with the exercise of the police power in furtherance of the public interest, the Court has approved the widespread use of the power of eminent domain by federal and state governments in conjunction with private companies to facilitate urban renewal, destruction of slums, erection of low-cost housing in place of deteriorated housing, and the promotion of aesthetic values as well as economic ones. The leading modern case in this field is *Berman v. Parker* (1954). In it, the Court sustained a federal statute for the District of Columbia granting its redevelopment agency the power to acquire privately owned land in blighted areas by the use of eminent domain to eliminate slum and substandard housing conditions and to resell that land to other private individuals subject to conditions designed to accomplish these purposes. A unanimous Court held that the judiciary's role in determining whether eminent domain is being used for a public purpose "is an extremely narrow one." Courts must defer to the legislature on questions of eminent domain no less than on all other exercises of the police power: "When the legislature has spoken, the public interest has been declared in terms well-nigh conclusive. In such cases, the legislature, not the judiciary, is the main guardian of the public needs to be served by social legislation."

Against the argument that the taking of an individual's property merely to develop a better-balanced, more attractive community was not a proper public use, Justice William O. Douglas in *Berman v. Parker* declared that the values that governments can pursue in their exercise of eminent domain "are spiritual as well as physical, aesthetic as well as monetary. It is within the power of the legislature to determine that the community should be beautiful as well as healthy, spacious as well as clean, well-balanced as well as carefully patrolled. . . . If those who govern the District of Columbia decide that the Nation's Capital should be beautiful as well as sanitary, there is nothing in the Fifth Amendment that stands in the way." And against the argument that there is no public use involved when government takes the private property of one individual only to sell it in turn to another, the Court again showed its deference to the legislative branches: not only is the power of eminent domain "merely the means to the end," "but the means of executing the project are for Congress and Congress alone to determine, once the public purpose has been established."

Under the extraordinarily deferential standard laid down in *Berman v. Parker,* eminent domain can be exercised to achieve anything that is otherwise within the power of the legislature. *Hawaii Housing Authority v. Midkiff* (1984) and *Kelo v. City of New London* (2005) are the most important recent examples. In *Midkiff,* the Supreme Court unanimously upheld Hawaii's use of its power of eminent domain to acquire property from large landowners and transfer it to lessees living on single-family residential lots on the land. The purpose of this land-condemnation scheme was to reduce the concentration of landownership, and Justice O'Connor declared for a unanimous Court that "our cases make clear that empirical debates over the wisdom of takings—no less than debates over the wisdom of other kinds of socioeconomic legislation—are not to be carried out in the federal courts." And in *Kelo,* a sharply divided Court upheld the use of eminent domain for economic-development purposes in language so sweeping that Justice O'Connor, this time in dissent, declared that it had "effectively delete[d] the words 'for public use' from the Takings Clause."

The Takings Clause requires not only a "public use" for the property that is taken but also "just compensation" to the owner. *Just compensation* was defined by the Court in *Monongahela Navigation Co. v. United States* (1893) as "a full and perfect equivalent for the property taken." This has come to mean the market value of the property—that is, what a willing buyer would pay a willing seller. Because property is ordinarily taken under a condemnation suit upon the payment of the money award by the condemner, no interest accrues. However, if the property is taken in fact before payment is made, the courts have held that just compensation requires the payment of interest.

At its simplest, just compensation requires that, if real property is condemned, the market value of that property must be paid to the owner. Things, however, are seldom that simple: the many kinds of property and many uses of property cause problems in computing just compensation. For example, if only a portion of a tract of land is taken, the owner's compensation is to include any element of value arising out of the relation of the part taken to the entire tract, unless the taking has in fact benefited the owner, in which case the benefit may be subtracted from the value of the land condemned (even then, however, any benefit that the owner receives in common with everyone else from the public use to which the property is appropriated may not be subtracted). Moreover, the Court held in *Horne v. Department of Agriculture* (2015) that the Takings Clause and its requirement that the government pay just compensation "when it 'physically takes possession of an interest in property'" applies equally to both real property and personal property. As Chief Justice Roberts pithily explained it: "The Government has a categorical duty to pay just compensation when it takes your car, just as when it takes your home." At issue in *Horne* was the US Department of Agriculture's California Raisin Marketing Order, which required raisin growers to give a percentage of their crop to the government, free of charge (in 2002–2003, it ordered raisin growers to turn over 47 percent of their crop) to help maintain a stable raisin market. An eight-member majority held that the Takings Clause barred the government from imposing such a demand on growers without just compensation.

The courts have long held that legislatures are free to decide on the nature and character of the tribunals that determine compensation; as a consequence, they may be regular courts, special legislative courts, commissions, or administrative bodies. Proceedings to condemn land for the benefit of the United States are brought in the federal district court for the district in which the land is located.

When a government itself initiates a condemnation proceeding against someone's property, the question of whether that property has been "taken," with the consequent requirement of just compensation, does not arise. However, questions of whether there has been a taking do arise when physical damage results to property because of government action or when regulatory action limits activity on the property or otherwise deprives it of value.

In *Pumpelly v. Green Bay Co.* (1872), the Court determined that land can be "taken" in the constitutional sense by physical invasion or occupation by the government, as occurs when government floods land. More recently, it held in *Griggs v. Allegheny County* (1962) that operators of airports are required to compensate the owners of adjacent land when the noise, glare, and fear of injury occasioned by the low-altitude overflights during takeoffs and landings made the land unfit for the use to which the owners had applied it. Cases such as these, where the government has not instituted formal condemnation proceedings but instead property owners have sued for just compensation claiming that governmental action or regulation has "taken" their property, are described as "inverse condemnation."

Regulation may also deprive owners of most or all beneficial use of their property or may destroy the value of the property for the purposes to which it is suited. Does such regulation also constitute a taking? Initially, the Court flatly denied the possibility of compensation for this diminution of property values; however, in *Pennsylvania Coal Co. v. Mahon* (1922), it established as a general principle that "if regulation goes too far it will be recognized as a taking." But how far is "too far"?

Although the Court confessed in *Penn Central Transportation Co. v. City of New York* (1978) that it had failed to develop a "set formula to determine where regulation ends and taking begins," it has responded to increasing governmental regulation of property over the years—in terms of zoning and land-use controls, environmental regulations, and so on—by formulating general principles for determining whether a regulatory taking has occurred. One guideline had already been announced in *Armstrong v. United States* (1960): the regulation cannot force "some people alone to bear public burdens which, in all fairness and justice, should be borne by the public as a whole." Applying that guideline in *Nollan v. California Coastal Commission* (1987), Justice Scalia declared that, even if the California Coastal Commission was right in its belief that the public interest would be served by a continuous strip of publicly accessible beach along the coast, "that does not establish that the Nollans alone can be compelled to contribute to its realization" by requiring them to provide a public-access easement across their property as a condition for obtaining a building permit. The commission was free to serve this public interest, if it wished, "by using its power of eminent domain for this 'public purpose,'" but, Scalia insisted, if it wanted "an easement across the Nollans' property, it must pay for it."

Among the members of the Rehnquist Court, Justice Scalia was the most willing to enforce this guideline. Thus, in *Pennell v. City of San Jose* (1988), a case involving a rent-control ordinance that allowed administrative reductions on rent in case of "tenant hardship," Justice Scalia dissented from Chief Justice Rehnquist's majority decision that the case was not ripe for judicial resolution, reached the merits on the hardship provision, and expanded on the themes he had advanced in *Nollan*. He denied the landlords were the cause of the problem at which the hardship provision was aimed. Rather, he insisted that the provision was drafted "to meet a quite different social problem: the existence of some renters who are too poor to afford even reasonably priced housing. But that problem is no more caused or exploited by landlords than it is by the grocers who sell needy renters their food, or the department stores that sell them their clothes, or the employers who pay them their wages, or the citizens of San Jose holding the higher-paying jobs from which they are excluded." Moreover, Scalia continued, "Even if the neediness of renters could be regarded as a problem distinctively attributable to landlords in general, it is not remotely attributable to the particular landlords that the ordinance singles out—namely, those who happen to have a 'hardship' tenant at the present time, or who may happen to rent to a 'hardship' tenant in the future, or whose current or future affluent tenants may happen to decline into the 'hardship' category." He then delivered his primary point: "The fact that government acts through the landlord-tenant relationship does not magically transform general public welfare, which must be supported by all the public, into mere 'economic regulation,' which can disproportionately burden particular individuals."

Other guidelines have followed in the wake of *Thompson*. A second was spelled out in *Penn Central* itself: courts must consider the "economic impact of the regulation on the claimant and, particularly, the extent to which the regulation has interfered with reasonable investment-backed expectations."

A third guideline, announced in *Loretto v. Teleprompter Manhattan CATV Corp.* (1982), addresses physical invasions: when government permanently occupies or authorizes someone else to occupy property, the action constitutes a taking, and compensation must be paid regardless of the public interests served by the occupation or the extent of damage to the parcel as a whole. In that case, the Supreme Court held that a New York statute requiring landlords to allow television cable companies to install cable facilities in their apartment buildings constituted a taking, even though the facilities occupied no more than one and a half cubic feet of the landlords' property.

A fourth guideline was spelled out by the Court in *Agins v. City of Tiburon* (1980): a land-use regulation must "substantially advance legitimate governmental interests." Also applying that guideline in *Nollan*, Justice Scalia held for a five-member majority that the California Coastal Commission's extraction from the Nollans of a public-access easement across a strip of their beachfront property as a condition for obtaining a permit to enlarge their beachfront home did not "substantially advance" the state's legitimate interest in preserving the public's view of the beach from the street in front of the lot.

A fifth guideline was also announced in *Agins*: the regulation cannot deny a property owner "economically viable use of his land." The Court elaborated on this guideline in *Lucas v. South Carolina Coastal Council* (1992), a case in which a landowner was deprived of all "economically viable use" of his $1 million property when the state passed a coastal zone act, designed to prevent beach erosion, that prevented him from building a beachfront home on his property: "When the owner of real property has been called upon to sacrifice all economically beneficial uses in the name of the common good, that is, to leave his property economically idle, he has suffered a taking."

A sixth guideline was provided by the Court in *Tahoe-Sierra Preservation Council v. Tahoe Regional Planning Agency* (2002). In it, the Court held that no compensation is due to property owners who are temporarily deprived of all economically viable use of their land through, as in this case, the imposition of moratoriums on development imposed by governmental agencies during the process of drafting a comprehensive land-use plan.

And, a seventh guideline was articulated in *Dolan v. City of Tigard* (1994): local governmental agencies may not condition the approval of land-use permits on owners' relinquishment of a portion of their property unless there is a "nexus" and "rough proportionality" between the government's demand and the effects of the proposed land use. In *Dolan*, Chief Justice Rehnquist declared that "we see no reason why the Takings Clause of the Fifth Amendment, as much a part of the Bill of Rights as the First Amendment or Fourth Amendment, should be relegated to the status of a poor relation" and, upon applying this guideline, concluded that the City of Tigard, Oregon, violated the constitutional rights of Florence Dolan when it held that it would approve her application to expand her plumbing and electric supply store only if she dedicated 10 percent of her land to the city. In *Koontz v. St. John River Water Management District* (2013), the Court held that the government's demand for property from a land-use permit applicant must satisfy this guideline even when the government denies the permit and even when its demand is for money.

NOTES

1. For an especially useful essay on this matter, see Edward S. Corwin, "The Supreme Court and the Fourteenth Amendment," *Michigan Law Review* 7 (June 1909): 643.

2. See Raoul Berger, *Government by Judiciary: The Transformation of the Fourteenth Amendment* (Cambridge, MA: Harvard University Press, 1977); Jacobus Tenbroek, *Equal Under Law* (New York:

Macmillan, 1965); Alexander M. Bickel, "The Original Understanding and the Segregation Decision," *Harvard Law Review* 69, no. 1 (1955); Charles Fairman, "Does the Fourteenth Amendment Incorporate the Bill of Rights?" *Stanford Law Review* 2, no. 1 (1949); William W. Van Alstyne, "The Fourteenth Amendment, the 'Right to Vote,' and the Understanding of the Thirty-Ninth

Congress," in *1966 Supreme Court Review,* edited by Philip Kurland (Chicago: University of Chicago Press, 1966); and Alford H. Kelly, "Clio and the Court: An Illicit Love Affair," in *1965 Supreme Court Review,* edited by Philip Kurland (Chicago: University of Chicago Press, 1965).

3. See Corwin, "Supreme Court and the Fourteenth Amendment"; Tenbroek, *Equal Under Law,* 236–238; M. Glenn Abernathy, *Civil Liberties Under the Constitution,* 3rd ed. (New York: Harper and Row, 1977), 32–33; and Berger, *Government by Judiciary,* 18–19.

4. Michael Kent Curtis, "Resurrecting the Privileges and Immunities Clause and Revising the *Slaughter-House Cases* Without Exhuming *Lochner*: Individual Rights and the Fourteenth Amendment," *Boston College Law Review* 38 (December 1966): 105.

5. Unsuccessful attempts to broaden the scope of privileges and immunities include *Hague v. Committee for Industrial Organization* (1939), *Edwards v. California* (1941), and *Oyama v. California* (1948).

6. It could be said that, with respect to the Due Process and Equal Protection Clauses, the Court correctly identified the intentions of the Thirty-Ninth Congress in drafting these clauses and acted accordingly. Given its concurrent construction of the Privileges or Immunities Clause, however, the Court's fidelity to the intentions of the Thirty-Ninth Congress simply served to exacerbate matters and led directly to the development of substantive due process (discussed later). For an excellent treatment of the development of substantive due process, see Eugene W. Hickok and Gary L. McDowell, *Law vs. Justice: Courts and Politics in American Society* (New York: Free Press, 1993), 80–121.

7. The Court accepted without debate the procedural interpretation of due process. For differing views of what due process could have meant, however, see *Dred Scott v. Sandford* (1857), *Hepburn v. Griswold* (1870), and Edward S. Corwin, "Due Process of Law Before the Civil War," pts. 1 and 2, *Harvard Law Review* 24 (March 1911): 366ff.; (April 1911): 460ff.

8. As Justice Comstock put the question: "Do the prohibitions and penalties of the act for the prevention of intemperance, pauperism, and crime pass the utmost boundaries of mere regulation and police, and by their own force, assuming them to be valid and faithfully obeyed and executed, work the essential loss or destruction of the property at which they are aimed? . . . In my judgment, they do plainly work this result."

9. See David E. Bernstein's important recent revisionist book on *Lochner*: *Rehabilitating* Lochner: *Defending Individual Rights Against Progressive Reform* (Chicago: University of Chicago Press, 2011).

10. Charles Warren, "The Progressiveness of the United States Supreme Court," *Columbia Law Review* 13 (April 1913): 294–313, and "A Bulwark to the State Police Power: The United States Supreme Court," *Columbia Law Review* 13 (December 1913): 667–695.

11. Guy Miller Struve, "The Less-Restrictive-Alternative Principle and Economic Due Process," *Harvard Law Review* 80 (1967): 1463–1488.

12. Carrie Buck also objected on equal-protection grounds. Justice Holmes was equally unpersuaded here:

"But, it is said . . . this reasoning . . . fails when it is confined to the small number who are in the institutions named and is not applied to the multitudes outside. It is the usual last resort of constitutional arguments to point out shortcomings of this sort. But the answer is that the law does all that is needed when it does all that it can, indicates a policy, applies it to all within the lines, and seeks to bring within the lines all similarly situated so far and so fast as its means allow. Of course, so far as the operations enable those who otherwise must be kept confined to be returned to the world, and thus open the asylum to others, the equality aimed at will be more nearly reached."

SELECTED READINGS

Baude, William. "Rethinking the Federal Eminent Domain Power," *Yale Law Journal* 122 (2013): 1738–1825.

Berger, Raoul. *Government by Judiciary: The Transformation of the Fourteenth Amendment.* 2nd ed. Indianapolis: Liberty Fund, 1997.

Burnett, Guy F. *The Safeguard of Liberty and Property: The Supreme Court, Kelo v. New London, and the Takings Clause.* Lanham, MD: Lexington Books, 2014.

Chapman, Nathan S. and Michael W. McConnell, "Due Process as Separation of Powers," *Yale Law Journal* 121 (2012): 1672–1807.

Curtis, Michael Kent. "Resurrecting the Privileges and Immunities Clause and Revising the *Slaughter-House Cases* Without Exhuming *Lochner*: Individual Rights and the Fourteenth Amendment." *Boston College Law Review* 38 (December 1996): 1–106.

Eagle, Steven J. "Property Tests, Due Process Tests, and Regulatory Takings Jurisprudence." *Brigham Young University Law Review* (2007): 899–958.

Easterbrook, Frank H. "Substance and Due Process." In *1982 Supreme Court Review,* edited by Philip B. Kurland, Gerhard Casper, and Dennis Hutchinson. Chicago: University of Chicago Press, 1983.

Epstein, Richard A. *Takings: Property and the Power of Eminent Domain.* Cambridge, MA: Harvard University Press, 1985.

Kitch, Edmund W., and Clara Ann Bowler. "The Facts of *Munn v. Illinois.*" In *1978 Supreme Court Review,* edited by Philip B. Kurland and Gerhard Casper. Chicago: University of Chicago Press, 1979.

Krauss, Michael J. "Punitive Damages and the Supreme Court: A Tragedy in Five Acts." In *2006–2007 Supreme Court Economic Review.* Washington, DC: Cato Institute, 2007.

Labbe, Ronald M. and Jonathan Lurie, The Slaughterhouse Cases: *Regulation, Reconstruction, and the Fourteenth Amendment.* Lawrence: University Press of Kansas, 2005

McCloskey, Robert. "Economic Due Process and the Supreme Court: An Exhumation and Reburial." In *1962 Supreme Court Review,* edited by Philip B. Kurland. Chicago: University of Chicago Press, 1962.

Nelson, William E. *The Fourteenth Amendment: From Political Principle to Judicial Doctrine.* Cambridge, MA: Harvard University Press, 1988.

Porter, Mary Cornelia. "That Commerce Shall Be Free: A New Look at the Old Laissez-Faire Court." In *1976 Supreme Court Review,* edited by Philip B. Kurland. Chicago: University of Chicago Press, 1977.

Siegan, Bernard H. *Economic Liberties and the Constitution.* Chicago: University of Chicago Press, 1981.

Smith, Douglas G. "The Privileges and Immunities Clause of Article IV, Section 2: Precursor of Section 1 of the Fourteenth Amendment." *San Diego Law Review* 34 (May–June 1997): 809–857.

Somin, Ilya. *The Grasping Hand:* Kelo v. City of New London *and the Limits of Eminent Domain.* Chicago: University of Chicago Press, 2015.

Zuckert, Michael P. "Congressional Power Under the Fourteenth Amendment: The Original Understanding of Section Five." *Constitutional Commentary* 3 (1986): 123–147.

The Slaughter-House Cases
83 U.S. (16 Wallace) 36 (1873)

In 1869, the Louisiana Legislature passed an act designed to "protect the health of the City of New Orleans" by granting to the Crescent City Live-Stock Landing and Slaughter-House Company a twenty-five-year monopoly on the sheltering and slaughtering of animals in the city and surrounding parishes. The law required that all other butchers in the New Orleans area come to that company and pay for the use of its abattoir. Although the law was in response to a cholera epidemic and represented an attempt to end contamination of the city's water supply caused by the dumping of refuse into the Mississippi River by small independent slaughterhouses, the state legislature at the time was dominated by carpetbagger elements, and charges of corruption were rampant. The Butchers' Benevolent Association, a group of small, independent slaughterers who had been deprived of their livelihood by the legislation, challenged the act on the grounds that it violated the Thirteenth Amendment and the Privileges or Immunities, Due Process, and Equal Protection Clauses of the Fourteenth Amendment. A state district court and the Louisiana Supreme Court upheld the legislation, at which point this case, along with two others involving the same controversy, was brought to the United States Supreme Court on a writ of error. These three cases have come to be known simply as The Slaughter-House Cases. Opinion of the Court: <u>Miller</u>, Clifford, Davis, Strong, Hunt. Dissenting opinions: <u>Field</u>, Chase, Swayne, Bradley; <u>Bradley</u>; Swayne.

JUSTICE MILLER delivered the opinion of the Court.

The plaintiffs in error . . . allege that the statute is a violation of the Constitution of the United States in these several particulars:

That it creates an involuntary servitude forbidden by the thirteenth article of amendment;

That it abridges the privileges and immunities of citizens of the United States;

That it denies to the plaintiffs the equal protection of the laws; and,

That it deprives them of their property without due process of law; contrary to the provisions of the first section of the fourteenth article of amendment. This court is thus called upon for the first time to give construction to these articles.

. . . In the light of . . . recent . . . history, . . . and on the most casual examination of the language of these amendments, no one can fail to be impressed with the one pervading purpose found in them all, lying at the foundation of each, and without which none of them would have been even suggested; we mean the freedom of the slave race, the security and firm establishment of that freedom, and the protection of the newly made freeman and citizen from the oppressions of those who had formerly exercised unlimited dominion over him. . . .

We do not say that no one else but the negro can share in this protection. . . . But what we do say, and what we wish to be understood is, that in any fair and just construction of any section or phrase of these amendments, it is necessary to look to the purpose which we have said was the pervading spirit of them all, the evil which they were designed to remedy, and the process of continued addition to the Constitution, until that purpose was supposed to be accomplished, as far as constitutional law can accomplish it.

The first section of the fourteenth article, to which our attention is more specially invited, opens with a definition of citizenship—not only citizenship of the United States, but citizenship of the States. . . . "All persons born or naturalized in the United States, and subject to the jurisdiction thereof, are citizens of the United States and of the State wherein they reside." . . .

It declares that persons may be citizens of the United States without regard to their citizenship of a particular State, and it overturns the *Dred Scott* decision by making all persons born within the United States and subject to its jurisdiction citizens of the United States. . . . Not only may a man be a citizen of the United States without being a citizen of a State, but an important element is necessary to convert the former into the latter. He must reside within the State to make him a citizen of it, but it is only necessary that he should be born or naturalized in the United States to be a citizen of the Union.

It is quite clear, then, that there is a citizenship of the United States, and a citizenship of a State, which are distinct from each other, and which depend upon different characteristics or circumstances in the individual.

We think this distinction and its explicit recognition in this amendment of great weight in this argument, because the next paragraph of this same section, which is the one mainly relied on by the plaintiffs in error, speaks only of privileges and immunities of citizens of the United States, and does not speak of those of citizens of the several States. The argument, however, in favor of the plaintiffs rests wholly on the assumption that the citizenship is the same, and the privileges and immunities guaranteed by the Clause are the same.

The language is, "No State shall make or enforce any law which shall abridge the privileges or immunities of citizens of the United States." It is a little remarkable, if this clause was intended as a protection to the citizen of a State against the legislative power of his own State, that the word citizen of the State should be left out when it is so carefully used, and used in contradistinction to citizens of the United States, in the very sentence which precedes it. It is too clear for argument that the change in phraseology was adopted understandingly and with a purpose.

Of the privileges and immunities of the citizen of the United States, and of the privileges and immunities of the citizen of the State, and what they respectively are, we will presently consider; but we wish to state here that it is only the former which are placed by this clause under the protection of the Federal Constitution, and that the latter, whatever they may be, are not intended to have any additional protection by this paragraph of the amendment.

If, then, there is a difference between the privileges and immunities belonging to a citizen of the United States as such, and those belonging to the citizen of the State as such, the latter must rest for their security and protection where they have heretofore rested; for they are not embraced by this paragraph of the amendment.

The first occurrence of the words "privileges and immunities" in our constitutional history, is to be found in the fourth of the articles of the old Confederation. It declares "that . . . the free inhabitants of each of these States . . . shall be entitled to all the privileges and immunities of free citizens in the several States." . . .

In the Constitution of the United States, which superseded the Articles of Confederation, the corresponding provision is found in section two of the fourth article, in the following words: "The citizens of each State shall be entitled to all the privileges and immunities of citizens of the several States." . . .

That constitutional provision . . . did not create those rights, which it called privileges and immunities of citizens of the States. It threw around them in that clause no security for the citizen of the State in which they were claimed or exercised. Nor did it profess to control the power of the State governments over the rights of its own citizens.

Its sole purpose was to declare to the several States, that whatever those rights, as you grant or establish them to your own citizens, or as you limit or qualify, or impose restrictions on their exercise, the same, neither more nor less, shall be the measure of the rights of citizens of other States within your jurisdiction.

It would be the vainest show of learning to attempt to prove by citations of authority, that up to the adoption of the recent amendments, no claim or pretence was set up that those rights depended on the Federal government for their existence or protection, beyond the very few express limitations which the Federal Constitution imposed upon the States—such, for instance, as the prohibition against *ex post facto* laws, bills of attainder, and laws impairing the obligation of contracts. But with the exception of these and a few other restrictions, the entire domain of the privileges and immunities of citizens of the States, as above defined, lay within the constitutional and legislative power of the States, and without that of the Federal government. Was it the purpose of the fourteenth amendment, by the simple declaration that no State should make or enforce any law which shall abridge the privileges and immunities of citizens of the United States, to transfer the security and protection of all the civil rights which we have mentioned, from the States to the Federal government? And where it is declared that Congress shall have the power to enforce that article, was it intended to bring within the power of Congress the entire domain of civil rights heretofore belonging exclusively to the States?

All this and more must follow, if the proposition of the plaintiffs in error be sound. For not only are these rights subject to the control of Congress whenever in its discretion, any of them are supposed to be abridged by State legislation, but that body may also pass laws in advance, limiting and restricting the exercise of legislative power by the States, in their most ordinary and usual functions, as in its judgment it may think proper on all such subjects. And still further, such a construction followed by the reversal of the judgments of the Supreme Court of Louisiana in these cases, would constitute this court a perpetual censor upon all legislation of the States, on the civil rights of their own citizens, with authority to nullify such as it did not approve as consistent with those rights, as they existed at the time of the adoption of this amendment. The argument we admit is not always the most conclusive which is drawn from the consequences urged against the adoption of a particular construction of an instrument. But when, as in the case before us, these consequences are so serious, so far-reaching and pervading, so great a departure from the structure and spirit of our institutions; when the effect is to fetter and degrade the State governments by subjecting them to the control of Congress, in the exercise of powers heretofore universally conceded to them of the most ordinary and fundamental character; when in fact it radically changes the whole theory of the relations of the State and Federal governments to each other and of both these governments to the people; the argument has a force that is irresistible, in the absence of language which expresses such a purpose too clearly to admit of doubt.

We are convinced that no such results were intended by the Congress which proposed these amendments, nor by the legislatures of the States which ratified them.

Having shown that the privileges and immunities relied on in the argument are those which belong to citizens of the States as such, and that they are left to the State governments for security and protection, and not by this article placed under the special care of the Federal government, we may hold ourselves excused from defining the privileges and immunities of citizens of the United States which no State can abridge, until some case involving those privileges may make it necessary to do so.

But lest it should be said that no such privileges and immunities are to be found if those we have been considering are excluded, we venture to suggest some which owe their existence to the Federal government, its National character, its Constitution, or its laws. One of these is well described in the case of *Crandall v. Nevada*. It is said to be the right of the citizen of this great country, protected by implied guarantees of its Constitution, "to come to the seat of government to assert any claim he may have upon that government, to transact any business he may have with it, to seek its protection, to share its offices, to engage in administering its functions. He has the right of free access to its seaports, through which all operations of foreign commerce are conducted, to the subtreasuries, land offices, and courts of justice in the several States." . . .

Another privilege of a citizen of the United States is to demand the care and protection of the Federal government over his life, liberty, and property when on the high seas or within the jurisdiction of a foreign government. Of this there can be no doubt, nor that the right depends upon his character as a citizen of the United States. The right to peaceably assemble and petition for redress of grievances, the privilege of the writ of *habeas corpus*, are rights of the citizen guaranteed by the Federal Constitution. The right to use the navigable waters of the United States, however they may penetrate the territory of the several States, all rights secured to our citizens by treaties with foreign nations, are dependent upon citizenship of the United States, and not citizenship of a State. One of these privileges is conferred by the very article under consideration. It is that a citizen of the United States can, of his own volition, become a citizen of any State of the Union by a *bona-fide* residence therein, with the same rights as other citizens of that State. To these may be added the rights secured by the thirteenth and fifteenth articles of amendment, and by the other clause of the fourteenth, next to be considered.

But it is useless to pursue this branch of the inquiry, since we are of opinion that the rights claimed by these plaintiffs in error, if they have any existence, are not privileges and immunities of citizens of the United States within the meaning of the clause of the fourteenth amendment under consideration. . . .

The argument has not been much pressed in these cases that the defendant's charter deprives the plaintiffs of their property without due process of law. . . . We are not without judicial interpretation, . . . both State and National, of the meaning of this clause. And it is sufficient to say that under no construction of that provision that we have ever seen, or any that we deem admissible, can the restraint imposed by the State of Louisiana upon the exercise of their trade by the butchers of New Orleans be held to be a deprivation of property within the meaning of that provision.

"Nor shall any State deny to any person within its jurisdiction the equal protection of the laws." In the light of the history of these amendments, and the pervading purpose of them, which we have already discussed, it is not difficult to give a meaning to this clause. The existence of laws in the States where the newly emancipated negroes resided, which discriminated with gross injustice and hardship against them as a class, was the evil to be remedied by this clause, and by it such laws are forbidden. . . .

The judgments of the Supreme Court of Louisiana in these cases are

Affirmed.

JUSTICE FIELD, dissenting. . . .

The question presented is . . . one of the gravest importance, not merely to the parties here, but to the whole country. It is nothing less than the question whether the recent amendments to the Federal Constitution protect the citizens of the United States against the deprivation of their common rights by State legislation. In my judgment the fourteenth amendment does afford such protection, and was so intended by the Congress which framed and the States which adopted it.

The counsel for the plaintiffs in error have contended, with great force, that the act in question is also inhibited by the thirteenth amendment. . . .

. . . I have been so accustomed to regard it as intended to meet that form of slavery which had previously prevailed in this country, and to which the recent civil war owed its existence, that I was not prepared, nor am I yet, to give to it the extent and force ascribed by counsel. Still it is evident that the language of the amendment is not used in a restrictive sense. It is not confined to African slavery alone. It is general and universal in its application. . . .

It is not necessary, however, . . . to rest my objections to the act in question upon the terms and meaning of the thirteenth amendment. The provisions of the fourteenth amendment, which is properly a supplement to the thirteenth, cover, in my judgment, the case before us, and inhibit any legislation which confers special and exclusive privileges like these under consideration. . . . It first declares that "all persons born or naturalized in the United States, and subject to the jurisdiction thereof, are citizens of the United States and of the State wherein they reside." . . .

. . . It recognizes in express terms, if it does not create, citizens of the United States, and it makes their citizenship dependent upon the place of their birth, or the fact of their adoption, and not upon the constitution or laws of any State or the condition of their ancestry. A citizen of a State is now only a citizen of the United States residing in that State. The fundamental rights, privileges, and immunities which belong to him as a free man and a free citizen, now belong to him as a citizen of the United States, and are not dependent upon his citizenship of any State. . . .

The amendment does not attempt to confer any new privileges or immunities upon citizens, or to enumerate or define those already existing. It assumes that there are such privileges and immunities which belong of right to citizens as such, and ordains that they shall not be abridged by State legislation. If this inhibition has no reference to privileges and immunities of this character, but only refers, as held by the majority of the court in their opinion, to such privileges and immunities as were before its adoption specially designated in the Constitution or necessarily implied as belonging to citizens of the United States, it was a vain and idle enactment, which accomplished nothing, and most unnecessarily excited Congress and the people on its passage. With privileges and immunities thus designated or implied no State could ever have interfered by its laws, and no new constitutional provision was required to inhibit such interference. The supremacy of the Constitution and the laws of the United States always controlled any State legislation of that character. But if the amendment refers to the natural and inalienable rights which belong to all citizens, the inhibition has a profound significance and consequence.

What, then, are the privileges and immunities which are secured against abridgment by State legislation? . . . The terms, privileges and immunities, are not new in the amendment; they were in the Constitution before the amendment was adopted. They are found in the second section of the fourth article, which declares that "the citizens of each State shall be entitled to all privileges and immunities of citizens in the several States," and they have been the subject of frequent consideration in judicial decisions. In *Corfield v. Coryell* (1825), Mr. Justice Washington said he had "no hesitation in confining these expressions to those privileges and immunities which were, in their nature, fundamental; which belong of right to citizens of all free governments, and which have at all times been enjoyed by the citizens of the several States which compose the Union, from the time of their becoming free, independent, and sovereign;" and, in considering what those fundamental privileges were, he said that perhaps it would be more tedious than difficult to enumerate them, but that they might be "all comprehended under the following general heads: protection by the government; the enjoyment of life and liberty, with the right to acquire and possess property of every kind, and to pursue and obtain happiness and safety, subject, nevertheless, to such restraints as the government may justly prescribe for the general good of the whole." This appears to me to be a sound construction of the clause in question. The privileges and immunities designated are those *which of right belong to the citizens of all free governments.* Clearly among these must be placed the right to pursue a lawful employment in a lawful manner, without other restraint than such as equally affects all persons. . . .

What the clause in question did for the protection of the citizens of one State against hostile and discriminating legislation of other States, the fourteenth amendment does for the protection of every citizen of the United States against hostile and discriminating legislation against him in favor of others, whether they reside in the same or in different States. If under the fourth article of the Constitution equality of privileges and immunities is secured between citizens of different States, under the fourteenth amendment the same equality is secured between citizens of the United States. . . .

This equality of right, with exemption from all disparaging and partial enactments, in the lawful pursuits of life, throughout the whole country, is the distinguishing privilege of citizens of the United States. To them, everywhere, all pursuits, all professions, all avocations are open without other restrictions than such as are imposed equally upon all others of the same age, sex, and condition. The State may prescribe such regulations for every pursuit and calling of life as will promote the public health, secure the good order and advance the general prosperity of society, but when once prescribed, the pursuit or calling must be free to be followed by every citizen who is within the conditions designated, and will conform to the regulations. This is the fundamental idea upon which our institutions rest, and unless adhered to in the legislation of the country our government will be a republic only in name. The fourteenth amendment, in my judgment, makes it essential to the validity of the legislation of every State that this equality of right should be respected. . . .

JUSTICE BRADLEY, dissenting. . . .

In my view, a law which prohibits a large class of citizens from adopting a lawful employment, or from following a lawful employment previously adopted, does deprive them of liberty as well as property, without due process of law. Their right of choice is a portion of their liberty; their occupation is their property. Such a law also deprives those citizens of the equal protection of the laws, contrary to the last clause of the section.

It is futile to argue that none but persons of the African race are intended to be benefited by this amendment. They may have been the primary cause of the amendment, but its language is general, embracing all citizens, and I think it was purposely so expressed.

Munn v. Illinois
94 U.S. 113 (1877)

Pursuant to Article XIII of the Illinois Constitution of 1870, which empowered the state legislature to regulate the storage of grain, the Illinois General Assembly enacted a statute in 1871 that required grain warehouses and elevators to obtain operating licenses and established the maximum rates they could charge for the handling and storage of grain. Ira Y. Munn was convicted in county court of operating a grain warehouse without a license and of charging higher rates than those allowed by the law, and he was fined $100. The Illinois Supreme Court affirmed his conviction, and Munn brought the case to the US Supreme Court on a writ of error. Opinion of the Court: <u>Waite</u>, Clifford, Swayne, Miller, Davis, Bradley, Hunt. Dissenting opinions: <u>Field</u>; Strong.

THE CHIEF JUSTICE delivered the opinion of the Court.

The question to be determined in this case is whether the general assembly of Illinois can, under the limitations upon the legislative power of the States imposed by the Constitution of the United States, fix by law the maximum of charges for the storage of grain in warehouses at Chicago and other places in the State. . . .

It is claimed that such a law is repugnant— To that part of Amendment 14 which ordains that no State shall "deprive any person of life, liberty, or property, without due process of law." . . .

The Constitution contains no definition of the word "deprive," as used in the Fourteenth Amendment. To determine its signification, therefore, it is necessary to ascertain the effect which usage has given it, when employed in the same or a like connection.

While this provision of the amendment is new in the Constitution of the United States,

as a limitation upon the powers of the States, it is old as a principle of civilized government. It is found in Magna Charta, and, in substance if not in form, in nearly or quite all the constitutions that have been from time to time adopted by the several States of the Union. By the Fifth Amendment, it was introduced into the Constitution of the United States as a limitation upon the powers of the national government, and by the Fourteenth, as a guaranty against any encroachment upon an acknowledged right of citizenship by the legislatures of the States. . . .

When one becomes a member of society, he necessarily parts with some rights or privileges which, as an individual not affected by his relations to others, he might retain. . . . This does not confer power upon the whole people to control rights which are purely and exclusively private, . . . but it does authorize the establishment of laws requiring each citizen to so conduct himself, and so use his own property, as not unnecessarily to injure another. . . . From this source come the police powers. . . . Under these powers the government regulates the conduct of its citizens one towards another, and the manner in which each shall use his own property, when such regulation becomes necessary for the public good. In their exercise it has been customary in England from time immemorial, and in this country from its first colonization, to regulate ferries, common carriers, hackmen, bakers, millers, wharfingers, innkeepers, &c., and in so doing to fix a maximum of charge to be made for services rendered, accommodations furnished, and articles sold. To this day, statutes are to be found in many of the States upon some or all these subjects; and we think it has never yet been successfully contended that such legislation came within any of the constitutional prohibitions against interference with private property. . . .

This brings us to inquire as to the principles upon which this power of regulation rests, in order that we may determine what is within and what without its operative effect. Looking, then, to the common law, from whence came the right which the Constitution protects, we find that when private property is "affected with a public interest, it ceases to be *juris privati* only." This was said by Lord Chief Justice Hale more than two hundred years ago, in his treatise *De Portibus Maris,* . . . and has been accepted without objection as an essential element in the law of property ever since. Property does become clothed with a public interest when used in a manner to make it of public consequence, and affect the community at large. When, therefore, one devotes his property to a use in which the public has an interest, he, in effect, grants to the public an interest in that use, and must submit to be controlled by the public for the common good, to the extent of the interest he has thus created. He may withdraw his grant by discontinuing the use; but, so long as he maintains the use, he must submit to the control. . . .

. . . When private property is devoted to a public use, it is subject to public regulation. It remains only to ascertain whether the warehouses of these plaintiffs in error, and the business which is carried on there, come within the operation of this principle.

. . . It is difficult to see why, if the common carrier, or the miller, or the ferryman, or the innkeeper, or the wharfinger, or the baker, or the cartman, or the hackney-coachman, pursues a public employment and exercises "a sort of public office," these plaintiffs in error do not. They stand . . . in the very "gateway of commerce," and take toll from all who pass. Their business most certainly "tends to a common charge, and is become a thing of public interest and use." Every bushel of grain for its passage "pays a toll, which is a common charge," and, therefore, according to Lord Hale, every such warehouseman "ought to be under public regulation, viz., that he . . . take but reasonable toll." Certainly, if any business can be clothed "with a public interest, and cease to be *juris private* only," this has been. . . .

. . . For our purposes we must assume that, if a state of facts could exist that would justify such legislation, it actually did exist when the statute now under consideration was passed. For us the question is one of power, not of expediency. If no state of circumstances could exist to justify such a statute, then we may declare this one void, because in excess of the legislative power of the State. But if it could, we must presume it did. Of the propriety of legislative interference within the scope of legislative power, the legislature is the exclusive judge. . . .

We know that this is a power which may be abused; but that is no argument against its existence. For protection against abuses by legislatures the people must resort to the polls, not to the courts. . . .

We conclude, therefore, that the statute in question is not repugnant to the Constitution of the United States, and that there is no error in the judgment. . . .

Judgment affirmed.

JUSTICE FIELD, dissenting.

. . . I am compelled to dissent from the decision of the court in this case, and from the reasons upon which that decision is founded. The principle upon which the opinion of the majority proceeds is, in my judgment, subversive of the rights of private property, heretofore believed to be protected by constitutional guaranties against legislative interference. . . .

The question presented . . . is one of the greatest importance,—whether it is within the competency of a State to fix the compensation which an individual may receive for the use of his own property in his private business, and for his services in connection with it. . . .

. . . The court holds that property loses something of its private character when employed in such a way as to be generally useful. The doctrine declared is that property "becomes clothed with a public interest when used in a manner to make it of public consequence, and affect the community at large;" and from such clothing the right of the legislature is deduced to control the use of the property, and to determine the compensation which the owner may receive for it. When Sir Matthew Hale, and the sages of the law in his day, spoke of property as affected by a public interest, and ceasing from that cause to be *juris privati* solely, that is, ceasing to be held merely in private right, they referred to property dedicated by the owner to public uses, or to property the use of which was granted by the government, or in connection with which special privileges were conferred. Unless the property was thus dedicated, or some right bestowed by the government was held with the property, either by specific grant or by prescription of so long a time as to imply a grant originally, the property was not affected by any public interest so as to be taken out of the category of property held in private right. But it is not in any such sense that the terms "clothing property with a public interest" are used in this case. From the nature of the business under consideration—the storage of grain—which, in any sense in which the words can be used, is a private business, in which the public are interested only as they are interested in the storage of other products of the soil, or in articles of manufacture, it is clear that the court intended to declare that, whenever one devotes his property to a business which is useful to the public,—"affects the community at large,"—the legislature can regulate the compensation which the owner may receive for its use, and for his own services in connection with it.

If this be sound law, if there be no protection, either in the principles upon which our republican government is founded, or in the prohibitions of the Constitution against such invasion of private rights, all property and all business in the State are held at the mercy of a majority of its legislature. . . .

. . . It is only where some right or privilege is conferred by the government or municipality upon the owner, which he can use in connection with his property, or by means of which the use of his property is rendered more valuable to him, or he thereby enjoys an advantage over others, that the compensation to be received by him becomes a legitimate matter of regulation. Submission to the regulation of compensation in such cases is an implied condition of the grant, and the State, in exercising its power of prescribing the compensation, only determines the conditions upon which its concession shall be enjoyed. When the privilege ends, the power of regulation ceases.

There is nothing in the character of the business of the defendants as warehousemen which called for the interference complained of in this case. Their buildings are not nuisances; their occupation of receiving and storing grain infringes upon no rights of others, disturbs no neighborhood, infects not the air, and in no respect prevents others from using and enjoying their property as to them may seem best. The legislation in question is nothing less than a bold assertion of absolute power by the State to control at its discretion the property and business of the citizen, and fix the compensation he shall receive. The will of the legislature is made the condition upon which the owner shall receive the fruits of his property and the just reward of his labor, industry, and enterprise. . . . The decision of the court in this case gives unrestrained license to legislative will. . . . I am of opinion that the judgment of the Supreme Court of Illinois should be reversed.

Lochner v. New York
198 U.S. 45 (1905)

Joseph Lochner, a Utica, New York, bakery proprietor, was found guilty and fined $50 for violating an 1897 New York law that limited the hours of employment in bakeries and confectionery establishments to ten hours a day and sixty hours a week. When his conviction was sustained by the New York appellate courts, Lochner brought the case to the Supreme Court on a writ of error. Opinion of the Court: Peckham,

Fuller, Brewer, Brown, McKenna. Dissenting opinions: Harlan, Day, White; Holmes.

JUSTICE PECKHAM delivered the opinion of the Court.

The statute necessarily interferes with the right of contract between the employer and employees, concerning the number of hours in which the latter may labor in the bakery of the employer. The general right to make a contract in relation to his business is part of the liberty of the individual protected by the Fourteenth Amendment of the Federal Constitution. . . . Under that provision no State can deprive any person of life, liberty or property without due process of law. The right to purchase or to sell labor is part of the liberty protected by this amendment, unless there are circumstances which exclude the right. There are, however, certain powers, existing in the sovereignty of each State in the Union, somewhat vaguely termed police powers, the exact description and limitation of which have not been attempted by the courts. Those powers, broadly stated, . . . relate to the safety, health, morals and general welfare of the public. Both property and liberty are held on such reasonable conditions as may be imposed by the governing power of the State in the exercise of those powers, and with such conditions the Fourteenth Amendment was not designed to interfere. . . .

It must, of course, be conceded that there is a limit to the valid exercise of the police power by the State. There is no dispute concerning this general proposition. Otherwise the Fourteenth Amendment would have no efficacy and the legislatures of the States would have unbounded power, and it would be enough to say that any piece of legislation was enacted to conserve the morals, the health or the safety of the people; such legislation would be valid, no matter how absolutely without foundation the claim might be. The claim of the police power would be a mere pretext—become another and delusive name for the supreme sovereignty of the State to be exercised free from constitutional restraint. This is not contended for. In every case that comes before this court, therefore, where legislation of this character is concerned and where the protection of the Federal Constitution is sought, the question necessarily arises: Is this a fair, reasonable and appropriate exercise of the police power of the State, or is it an unreasonable, unnecessary and arbitrary interference with the right of the individual to his personal liberty or to enter into those contracts in relation to labor which may seem to him appropriate or necessary for the support of himself and his family? Of course the liberty of

contract relating to labor includes both parties to it. The one has as much right to purchase as the other to sell labor.

This is not a question of substituting the judgment of the court for that of the legislature. If the act be within the power of the State it is valid, although the judgment of the court might be totally opposed to the enactment of such a law. But the question would still remain: Is it within the police power of the State? and that question must be answered by the court.

The question whether this act is valid as a labor law, pure and simple, may be dismissed in a few words. There is no reasonable ground for interfering with the liberty of person or the right of free contract, by determining the hours of labor, in the occupation of a baker. There is no contention that bakers as a class are not equal in intelligence and capacity to men in other trades or manual occupations, or that they are not able to assert their rights and care for themselves without the protecting arm of the State, interfering with their independence of judgment and of action. They are in no sense wards of the State. Viewed in the light of a purely labor law, with no reference whatever to the question of health, we think that a law like the one before us involves neither the safety, the morals nor the welfare of the public, and that the interest of the public is not in the slightest degree affected by such an act. The law must be upheld, if at all, as a law pertaining to the health of the individual engaged in the occupation of a baker. It does not affect any other portion of the public than those who are engaged in that occupation. Clean and wholesome bread does not depend upon whether the baker works but ten hours per day or only sixty hours a week. . . .

We think the limit of the police power has been reached and passed in this case. There is, in our judgment, no reasonable foundation for holding this to be necessary or appropriate as a health law to safeguard the public health or the health of the individuals who are following the trade of a baker. . . .

We think that there can be no fair doubt that the trade of a baker, in and of itself, is not an unhealthy one to that degree which would authorize the legislature to interfere with the right to labor, and with the right of free contract on the part of the individual, either as employer or employee. In looking through statistics regarding all trades and occupations, it may be true that the trade of a baker does not appear to be as healthy as some other trades, and is also vastly more healthy than still others. . . .

. . . The act is not, within any fair meaning of the term, a health law, but is an illegal interference with the rights of individuals, both employers and employees, to make contracts regarding labor upon such terms as they may think best, or which they may agree upon with the other parties to such contracts. Statutes of the nature of that under review, limiting the hours in which grown and intelligent men may labor to earn their living, are mere meddlesome interferences with the rights of the individual, and they are not saved from condemnation by the claim that they are passed in the exercise of the police power and upon the subject of the health of the individual whose rights are interfered with, unless there be some fair ground, reasonable in and of itself, to say that there is material danger to the public health or to the health of the employees, if the hours of labor are not curtailed. . . .

It was further urged on the argument that restricting the hours of labor in the case of bakers was valid because it tended to cleanliness on the part of the workers, as a man was more apt to be cleanly when not overworked, and if cleanly then his "output" was also more likely to be so. . . . The connection, if any exists, is too shadowy and thin to build any argument for the interference of the legislature. If the man works ten hours a day it is all right, but if ten and a half or eleven his health is in danger and his bread may be unhealthful, and, therefore, he shall not be permitted to do it. This, we think, is unreasonable and entirely arbitrary. . . .

It is manifest to us that the limitation of the hours of labor as provided for in this section of the statute . . . has no such direct relation to and no such substantial effect upon the health of the employee, as to justify us in regarding the section as really a health law. It seems to us that the real object and purpose were simply to regulate the hours of labor between the master and his employees . . . in a private business, not dangerous in any degree to morals or in any

real and substantial degree, to the health of the employees. Under such circumstances the freedom of master and employee to contract with each other in relation to their employment, and in defining the same, cannot be prohibited or interfered with, without violating the Federal Constitution. . . .

Reversed.

JUSTICE HARLAN, with whom JUSTICE WHITE and JUSTICE DAY concur, dissenting.

I take it to be firmly established that what is called the liberty of contract may, within certain limits, be subjected to regulations designed and calculated to promote the general welfare or to guard the public health, the public morals or the public safety. . . .

Granting . . . that there is a liberty of contract which cannot be violated even under the sanction of direct legislative enactment, but assuming, as according to settled law we may assume, that such liberty of contract is subject to such regulations as the State may reasonably prescribe for the common good and the well-being of society, what are the conditions under which the judiciary may declare such regulations to be in excess of legislative authority and void? Upon this point there is no room for dispute; for, the rule is universal that a legislative enactment, Federal or state, is never to be disregarded or held invalid unless it be, beyond question, plainly and palpably in excess of legislative power. . . . If there be doubt as to the validity of the statute, that doubt must therefore be resolved in favor of its validity, and the courts must keep their hands off, leaving the legislature to meet the responsibility for unwise legislation. If the end which the legislature seeks to accomplish be one to which its power extends, and if the means employed to that end, although not the wisest or best, are yet not plainly and palpably unauthorized by law, then the court cannot interfere. In other words, when the validity of a statute is questioned, the burden of proof, so to speak, is upon those who assert it to be unconstitutional. . . . Let these principles be applied to the present case. . . .

It is plain that this statute was enacted in order to protect the physical well-being of those who work in bakery and confectionery establishments. . . . I find it impossible, in view of common experience, to say that there is here no real or substantial relation between the means employed by the State and the end sought to be accomplished by its legislation. . . . Nor can I say that the statute has no appropriate or direct connection with that protection to health which each State owes to her citizens, . . . or that it is not promotive of the health of the employees in question, . . . or that the regulation prescribed by the State is utterly unreasonable and extravagant or wholly arbitrary. . . . Still less can I say that the statute is, beyond question, a plain, palpable invasion of rights secured by the fundamental law. . . . Therefore I submit that this court will transcend its functions if it assumes to annul the statute of New York. It must be remembered that this statute does not apply to all kinds of business. It applies only to work in bakery and confectionery establishments, in which, as all know, the air constantly breathed by workmen is not as pure and healthful as that to be found in some other establishments or out of doors. . . .

. . . There are many reasons of a weighty, substantial character, based upon the experience of mankind, in support of the theory that, all things considered, more than ten hours' steady work each day, from week to week, in a bakery or confectionery establishment, may endanger the health, and shorten the lives of the workmen, thereby diminishing their physical and mental capacity to serve the State, and to provide for those dependent upon them.

If such reasons exist that ought to be the end of this case, for the State is not amenable to the judiciary, in respect of its legislative enactments, unless such enactments are plainly, palpably, beyond all question, inconsistent with the Constitution of the United States. We are not to presume that the state of New York has acted in bad faith. Nor can we assume that its legislature acted without due deliberation, or that it did not determine this question upon the fullest attainable information, and for the common good. We cannot say that the State has acted without reason nor ought we to proceed upon the theory that its action is a mere sham. Our duty, I submit, is to sustain the statute as not being in conflict with the Federal Constitution, for the reason—and such is an all-sufficient reason—it is not shown to be plainly and palpably inconsistent with that instrument. . . .

I take leave to say that the New York statute, in the particulars here involved, cannot be held to be in conflict with the Fourteenth Amendment, without enlarging the scope of the Amendment far beyond its original purpose and without bringing under the supervision of this court matters which have been supposed to belong exclusively to the legislative departments of the several States when exerting their conceded power to guard the health and safety of their citizens by such regulations as they in their wisdom deem best. . . .

JUSTICE HOLMES, dissenting. . . .

This case is decided upon an economic theory which a large part of the country does not entertain. If it were a question whether I agreed with that theory, I should desire to study it further and long before making up my mind. But I do not conceive that to be my duty, because I strongly believe that my agreement or disagreement has nothing to do with the right of a majority to embody their opinions in law. It is settled by various decisions of this court that state constitutions and state laws may regulate life in many ways which we as legislators might think as injudicious or if you like as tyrannical as this, and which equally with this interfere with the liberty to contract. Sunday laws and usury laws are ancient examples. A more modern one is the prohibition of lotteries. . . . The Fourteenth Amendment does not enact Mr. Herbert Spencer's *Social Statics*. . . . A constitution is not intended to embody a particular economic theory, whether of paternalism and the organic relation of the citizen to the State or of *laissez faire*. It is made for people of fundamentally differing views, and the accident of our finding certain opinions natural and familiar or novel and even shocking ought not to conclude our judgment upon the question whether statutes embodying them conflict with the Constitution of the United States.

. . . I think that the word liberty in the Fourteenth Amendment is perverted when it is held to prevent the natural outcome of a dominant opinion, unless it can be said that a rational and fair man necessarily would admit that the statute proposed would infringe fundamental principles as they have been understood by the traditions of our people and our law. It does not need research to show that no such sweeping condemnation can be passed upon the statute before us. A reasonable man might think it a proper measure on the score of health. Men whom I certainly could not pronounce unreasonable would uphold it as a first installment of a general regulation of the hours of work. . . .

West Coast Hotel Company v. Parrish
300 U.S. 379 (1937)

In 1913, the state legislature of Washington enacted a minimum-wage law covering women and minors. The law provided for the establishment of an Individual Welfare Commission, which was authorized "to establish such standards of wages and conditions of labor for women and minors employed within the State of Washington as shall be held hereunder to be reasonable and not detrimental to health and morals, and which shall be sufficient for the decent maintenance of women." Elsie Parrish, employed as a chambermaid by the West Coast Hotel Company, together with her husband brought suit to recover the difference between the wages paid her and the minimum wage fixed pursuant to the state law. The minimum wage for her job was $14.50 for a forty-eight-hour week. The trial court decided against Parrish and declared the law to be repugnant to the Due Process Clause of the Fourteenth Amendment. The Washington Supreme Court reversed the trial court and sustained the statute. The hotel company brought the case to the US Supreme Court on appeal. Opinion of the Court: <u>Hughes</u>, Brandeis, Stone, Roberts, Cardozo. Dissenting opinion: <u>Sutherland</u>, Van Devanter, McReynolds, Butler.

THE CHIEF JUSTICE delivered the opinion of the Court.

This case presents the question of the constitutional validity of the minimum wage law of the State of Washington. . . .

The appellant relies upon the decision of this Court in *Adkins v. Children's Hospital* (1923), which held invalid the District of Columbia Minimum Wage Act, which was attacked under the due process clause of the Fifth Amendment. . . . The state court has refused to regard the decision in the *Adkins* case as determinative and has pointed to our decisions both before and since that case as justifying its position. We are of the opinion that this ruling of the state court demands on our part a reexamination of the *Adkins* case. The importance of the question, in which many States having similar laws are concerned, the close division by which the decision in the *Adkins* case was reached, and the economic conditions which have supervened, and in the light of which the reasonableness of the exercise of the protective power of the State must be considered, make it not only appropriate, but we think imperative, that in deciding the present case the subject should receive fresh consideration. . . .

. . . The violation alleged by those attacking minimum wage regulation for women is deprivation of freedom of contract. What is this freedom? The Constitution does not speak of freedom of contract. It speaks of liberty and prohibits the deprivation of liberty without due process of law. In prohibiting that deprivation the Constitution does not recognize an absolute and uncontrollable liberty. Liberty in each of its phases has its history and connotation. But the liberty safeguarded is liberty in a social organization which requires the protection of law against the evils which menace the health, safety, morals and welfare of the people. Liberty under the Constitution is thus necessarily subject to the restraints of due process, and regulation which is reasonable in relation to its subject and is adopted in the interests of the community is due process.

. . . What can be closer to the public interest than the health of women and their protection from unscrupulous and overreaching employers? And if the protection of women is a legitimate end of the exercise of state power, how can it be said that the requirement of the payment of a minimum wage fairly fixed in order to meet the very necessities of existence is not an admissible means to that end? The legislature of the State was clearly entitled to consider the situation of women in employment, the fact that they are in the class receiving the least pay, that their bargaining power is relatively weak, and that they are the ready victims of those who would take advantage of their necessitous circumstances. The legislature was entitled to adopt measures to reduce the evils of the "sweating system," the exploiting of workers at wages so low as to be insufficient to meet the bare cost of living, thus making their very helplessness the occasion of a most injurious competition. The legislature had the right to consider that its minimum wage requirements would be an important aid in carrying out its policy of protection. The adoption of similar requirements by many States evidences a deepseated conviction both as to the presence of the evil and as to the means adapted to check it. Legislative response to that conviction cannot be regarded as arbitrary or capricious, and that is all we have to decide. Even if the wisdom of the policy be regarded as debatable and its effects uncertain, still the legislature is entitled to its judgment.

There is an additional and compelling consideration which recent economic experience has brought into a strong light. The exploitation of a class of workers who are in an unequal position with respect to bargaining power and are thus relatively defenceless against the denial of a living wage is not only detrimental to their health and well being but casts a direct burden for their support upon the community. What these workers lose in wages the taxpayers are called upon to pay. The bare cost of living must be met. . . . The community is not bound to provide what is in effect a subsidy for unconscionable employers. The community may direct its law-making power to correct the abuse which springs from their selfish disregard of the public interest. . . .

Our conclusion is that the case of *Adkins v. Children's Hospital* . . . should be, and it is, overruled. The judgment of the Supreme Court of the State of Washington is

Affirmed.

JUSTICE SUTHERLAND, dissenting.

It is urged that the question involved should now receive fresh consideration, among other reasons, because of "the economic conditions which have supervened"; but the meaning of the Constitution does not change with the ebb and flow of economic events. We frequently are told in more general words that the Constitution must be construed in the light of the present. If by that it is meant that the Constitution is made up of living words that apply to every new condition which they include, the statement is quite true. But to say, if that be intended, that the words of the Constitution mean today what they did not mean when written—that is, that they do not apply to a situation now to which they would have applied then—is to rob that instrument of the essential element which continues it in force as the people have made it until they, and not their official agents, have made it otherwise. . . .

The judicial function is that of interpretation; it does not include the power of amendment under the guise of interpretation. To miss the point of difference between the two is to miss all that the phrase "supreme law of the land" stands for and to convert what was intended as inescapable and enduring mandates into mere moral reflections. . . .

Coming, then, to a consideration of the Washington statute, it first is to be observed that it is in every substantial respect identical with the statute involved in the *Adkins* case. Such vices as existed in the latter are present in the former. And if the *Adkins* case was properly decided, as we who join in this opinion think it was, it necessarily follows that the Washington statute is invalid. . . .

Neither the statute involved in the *Adkins* case nor the Washington statute, so far as it is involved here, has the slightest relation to the capacity or earning power of the employee, to the number of hours which constitute the day's work, the character of the place where the work is to be done, or the circumstances or surroundings of the employment. The sole basis upon which the question of validity rests is the assumption that the employee is entitled to receive a sum of money sufficient to provide a living for her, keep her in health and preserve her morals. . . .

What we said further, in that case . . . is equally applicable here . . . : "A statute which prescribes payment without regard to any of these things and solely with relation to circumstances apart from the contract of employment, the business affected by it and the work done under it, is so clearly the product of a naked, arbitrary exercise of power that it cannot be allowed to stand under the Constitution of the United States." . . .

Williamson v. Lee Optical Company
348 U.S. 483 (1955)

In 1953, the Oklahoma Legislature passed a law that made it unlawful for any person other than a licensed ophthalmologist or optometrist to fit lenses to the face or to duplicate or replace lenses, except upon written prescriptive authority of a licensed ophthalmologist or optometrist. Lee Optical challenged the constitutionality of this law before a federal district court of three judges, alleging in part that it violated the Due Process Clause of the Fourteenth Amendment. The district court agreed, holding portions of the act unconstitutional, and the State of Oklahoma appealed to the Supreme Court. Opinion of the Court: <u>Douglas</u>, Warren, Black, Reed, Burton, Clark, Frankfurter, Minton. Not participating: Harlan.

JUSTICE DOUGLAS delivered the opinion of the Court.

An ophthalmologist is a duly licensed physician who specializes in the care of the eyes. An optometrist examines eyes for refractive error, recognizes (but does not treat) diseases of the eye, and fills prescriptions for eyeglasses. The optician is an artisan qualified to grind lenses, fill prescriptions, and fit frames.

The effect of §2 is to forbid the optician from fitting or duplicating lenses without a prescription from an ophthalmologist or optometrist. In practical effect, it means that no optician can fit old glasses into new frames or supply a lens, whether it be a new lens or one to duplicate a lost or broken lens, without a prescription. The District Court . . . rebelled at the notion that a State could require a prescription from an optometrist or ophthalmologist "to take old lenses and place them in new frames and then fit the completed spectacles to the *face* of the eyeglass wearer." . . . It held that such a requirement was not "reasonably and rationally related to the health and welfare of the people." . . . It was, accordingly, the opinion of the court that this provision of the law violated the Due Process Clause by arbitrarily interfering with the optician's right to do business.

The Oklahoma law may exact a needless, wasteful requirement in many cases. But it is for the legislature, not the courts, to balance the advantages and disadvantages of the new requirement. It appears that in many cases the optician can easily supply the new frames or new lenses without reference to the old written prescription. It also appears that many written prescriptions contain no directive data in regard to fitting spectacles to the face. But in some cases the directions contained in the prescription are essential, if the glasses are to be fitted so as to correct the particular defects of vision or alleviate the eye condition. The legislature might have concluded that the frequency of occasions when a prescription is necessary was sufficient to justify this regulation of the fitting of eyeglasses. Likewise, when it is necessary to duplicate a lens, a written prescription may or may not be necessary. But the legislature might have concluded that one was needed often enough to require one in every case. Or the legislature may have concluded that eye examinations were so critical, not only for correction of vision but also for detection of latent ailments or diseases, that every change in frames and every duplication of a lens should be accompanied by a prescription from a medical expert. To be sure, the present law does not require a new examination of the eyes every time the frames are changed or the lenses duplicated. For if the old prescription is on file with the optician, he can go ahead and make the new fitting or duplicate the lenses. But the law need not be in every respect logically consistent with its aims to be constitutional. It is enough that there is an evil at hand for correction, and that it might be thought that the particular legislative measure was a rational way to correct it.

The day is gone when this Court uses the Due Process Clause of the Fourteenth Amendment to strike down state laws, regulatory of business and industrial conditions, because they may be unwise, improvident, or out of harmony with a particular school of thought. . . . We emphasize again what Chief Justice Waite said in *Munn v. Illinois*, . . . "For protection against abuses by legislatures the people must resort to the polls, not to the courts." . . .

State Farm Mutual Automobile Insurance Company v. Campbell
538 U.S. 408 (2003)

In 1981, Curtis Campbell attempted to pass six vans traveling ahead of him on a two-lane Utah highway. To avoid a head-on collision with Campbell, a driver of a small car approaching from the opposite direction swerved onto the shoulder, lost control of his automobile, and collided with another vehicle, killing him and permanently disabling the driver of the vehicle into which he crashed. Campbell escaped without damage to his automobile or injury to himself. Although investigators and witnesses concluded that Campbell caused the accident, Campbell's insurer, State Farm Mutual Automobile Insurance Company, contested liability, declined to settle the ensuing claims for the $50,000 policy limit ($25,000 per claimant), ignored its own investigators' advice, and took the case to trial, assuring Campbell and his wife that they had no liability for the accident, that State Farm would represent their interests, and that they did not need separate counsel. In the ensuing wrongful-death and tort action, a Utah jury returned a judgment for $185,849—more than three times the policy limit—and State Farm refused to appeal. When the Utah Supreme Court denied Campbell's own appeal, State Farm agreed to pay the entire judgment; however, Campbell sued State Farm for bad faith, fraud, and intentional infliction of emotional distress. The trial court's initial ruling granting State Farm summary judgment was reversed on appeal. On remand, the court denied State Farm's motion to exclude evidence of similar out-of-state conduct, whereupon the jury found State Farm's decision not to settle to be unreasonable and awarded Campbell's estate (he had subsequently died) $2.6 million in compensatory damages and $145 million in punitive damages, which the trial court reduced to $1 million and $25 million, respectively. When the Utah Supreme Court reinstated the $145 million punitive-damages award, the Supreme Court granted certiorari. *Opinion of the Court:* Kennedy, Rehnquist, Stevens, O'Connor, Souter, Breyer. *Dissenting opinions:* Scalia; Thomas; Ginsburg.

JUSTICE KENNEDY delivered the opinion of the Court.

We address once again the measure of punishment, by means of punitive damages, a State may impose upon a defendant in a civil case. The question is whether . . . an award of $145 million in punitive damages, where full compensatory damages are $1 million, is excessive and in violation of the Due Process Clause of the Fourteenth Amendment to the Constitution of the United States. . . .

[I]n our judicial system compensatory and punitive damages, although usually awarded at the same time by the same decisionmaker, serve different purposes. Compensatory damages "are intended to redress the concrete loss that the plaintiff has suffered by reason of the defendant's wrongful conduct." By contrast, punitive damages serve a broader function; they are aimed at deterrence and retribution.

While States possess discretion over the imposition of punitive damages, it is well established that there are procedural and substantive constitutional limitations on these awards. The Due Process Clause of the Fourteenth Amendment prohibits the imposition of grossly excessive or arbitrary punishments on a tortfeasor. The reason is that "elementary notions of fairness enshrined in our constitutional jurisprudence dictate that a person receive fair notice not only of the conduct that will subject him to punishment, but also of the severity of the penalty that a State may impose." To the extent an award is grossly excessive, it furthers no legitimate purpose and constitutes an arbitrary deprivation of property.

Although these awards serve the same purposes as criminal penalties, defendants subjected to punitive damages in civil cases have not been accorded the protections applicable in a criminal proceeding. This increases our concerns over the imprecise manner in which punitive damages systems are administered. . . . Our concerns are heightened when the decisionmaker is presented . . . with evidence that has little bearing as to the amount of punitive damages that should be awarded. Vague instructions, or those that merely inform the jury to avoid "passion or prejudice," do little to aid the decisionmaker in its task of assigning appropriate weight to evidence that is relevant and evidence that is tangential or only inflammatory.

In light of these concerns, in [*BMW v.*] *Gore* [(1996)], we instructed courts reviewing punitive damages to consider three guideposts: (1) the degree of reprehensibility of the defendant's misconduct; (2) the disparity between the actual or potential harm suffered by the plaintiff and the punitive damages award; and (3) the difference between the punitive damages awarded by the jury and the civil penalties authorized or imposed in comparable cases. . . .

Under the principles outlined in *BMW v. Gore,* this case is neither close nor difficult. It was error to reinstate the jury's $145 million punitive damages award. We address each guidepost of *Gore* in some detail.

"The most important indicium of the reasonableness of a punitive damages award is the degree of reprehensibility of the defendant's conduct." We have instructed courts to determine the reprehensibility of a defendant by considering whether: the harm caused was physical as opposed to economic; the tortious conduct evinced an indifference to or a reckless disregard of the health or safety of others; the target of the conduct had financial vulnerability; the conduct involved repeated actions or was an isolated incident; and the harm was the result of intentional malice, trickery, or deceit, or mere accident. The existence of any one of these factors weighing in favor of a plaintiff may not be sufficient to sustain a punitive damages award; and the absence of all of them renders any award suspect. It should be presumed a plaintiff has been made whole for his injuries by compensatory damages, so punitive damages should only

be awarded if the defendant's culpability, after having paid compensatory damages, is so reprehensible as to warrant the imposition of further sanctions to achieve punishment or deterrence.

Applying these factors in the instant case, we must acknowledge that State Farm's handling of the claims against the Campbells merits no praise. The trial court found that State Farm's employees altered the company's records to make Campbell appear less culpable. State Farm disregarded the overwhelming likelihood of liability and the near-certain probability that, by taking the case to trial, a judgment in excess of the policy limits would be awarded. . . . While we do not suggest there was error in awarding punitive damages based upon State Farm's conduct toward the Campbells, a more modest punishment for this reprehensible conduct could have satisfied the State's legitimate objectives, and the Utah courts should have gone no further.

This case, instead, was used as a platform to expose, and punish, the perceived deficiencies of State Farm's operations throughout the country. The Utah Supreme Court's opinion makes explicit that State Farm was being condemned for its nationwide policies rather than for the conduct direct toward the Campbells. . . .

A State cannot punish a defendant for conduct that may have been lawful where it occurred. . . . A basic principle of federalism is that each State may make its own reasoned judgment about what conduct is permitted or proscribed within its borders, and each State alone can determine what measure of punishment, if any, to impose on a defendant who acts within its jurisdiction.

For a more fundamental reason, however, the Utah courts erred in relying upon this and other evidence: The courts awarded punitive damages to punish and deter conduct that bore no relation to the Campbells' harm. A defendant's dissimilar acts, independent from the acts upon which liability was premised, may not serve as the basis for punitive damages. A defendant should be punished for the conduct that harmed the plaintiff, not for being an unsavory individual or business. Due process does not permit courts, in the calculation of punitive damages, to adjudicate the merits of other parties' hypothetical claims against a defendant under the guise of the reprehensibility analysis, but we have no doubt the Utah Supreme Court did that here. . . .

Turning to the second *Gore* guidepost, we have been reluctant to identify concrete constitutional limits on the ratio between harm, or potential harm, to the plaintiff and the punitive damages award. We decline again to impose a bright-line ratio which a punitive damages award cannot exceed. Our jurisprudence and the principles it has now established demonstrate, however, that, in practice, few awards exceeding a single-digit ratio between punitive and compensatory damages, to a significant degree, will satisfy due process. In [*Pacific Mutual Life Insurance Co. v.*] *Haslip* [(1991)], in upholding a punitive damages award, we concluded that an award of more than four times the amount of compensatory damages might be close to the line of constitutional impropriety. We cited that 4-to-1 ratio again in *Gore*. The Court further referenced a long legislative history, dating back over 700 years and going forward to today, providing for sanctions of double, treble, or quadruple damages to deter and punish. While these ratios are not binding, they are instructive. They demonstrate what should be obvious: Single-digit multipliers are more likely to comport with due process, while still achieving the State's goals of deterrence and retribution, than awards with ratios in range of 500 to 1, or, in this case, of 145 to 1.

Nonetheless, because there are no rigid benchmarks that a punitive damages award may not surpass, ratios greater than those we have previously upheld may comport with due process where "a particularly egregious act has resulted in only a small amount of economic damages." The converse is also true, however. When compensatory damages are substantial, then a lesser ratio, perhaps only equal to compensatory damages, can reach the outermost limit of the due process guarantee. The precise award in any case, of course, must be based upon the facts and circumstances of the defendant's conduct and the harm to the plaintiff.

In sum, courts must ensure that the measure of punishment is both reasonable and proportionate to the amount of harm to the plaintiff

and to the general damages recovered. In the context of this case, we have no doubt that there is a presumption against an award that has a 145-to-1 ratio. The compensatory award in this case was substantial; the Campbells were awarded $1 million for a year and a half of emotional distress. This was complete compensation. The harm arose from a transaction in the economic realm, not from some physical assault or trauma; there were no physical injuries; and State Farm paid the excess verdict before the complaint was filed, so the Campbells suffered only minor economic injuries for the 18-month period in which State Farm refused to resolve the claim against them. The compensatory damages for the injury suffered here, moreover, likely were based on a component which was duplicated in the punitive award. Much of the distress was caused by the outrage and humiliation the Campbells suffered at the actions of their insurer; and it is a major role of punitive damages to condemn such conduct. Compensatory damages, however, already contain this punitive element. . . .

The third guidepost in *Gore* is the disparity between the punitive damages award and the "civil penalties authorized or imposed in comparable cases." . . . Here, we need not dwell long on this guidepost. The most relevant civil sanction under Utah state law for the wrong done to the Campbells appears to be a $10,000 fine for an act of fraud, an amount dwarfed by the $145 million punitive damages award. . . .

An application of the *Gore* guideposts to the facts of this case, especially in light of the substantial compensatory damages awarded (a portion of which contained a punitive element), likely would justify a punitive damages award at or near the amount of compensatory damages. The punitive award of $145 million, therefore, was neither reasonable nor proportionate to the wrong committed, and it was an irrational and arbitrary deprivation of the property of the defendant. The proper calculation of punitive damages under the principles we have discussed should be resolved, in the first instance, by the Utah courts.

The judgment of the Utah Supreme Court is reversed, and the case is remanded for proceedings not inconsistent with this opinion.

JUSTICE SCALIA, dissenting.

I adhere to the view expressed in my dissenting opinion in *BMW of North America, Inc. v. Gore* that the Due Process Clause provides no substantive protections against "excessive" or "'unreasonable'" awards of punitive damages. I am also of the view that the punitive damages jurisprudence which has sprung forth from *BMW v. Gore* is insusceptible of principled application; accordingly, I do not feel justified in giving the case *stare decisis* effect. I would affirm the judgment of the Utah Supreme Court.

JUSTICE GINSBURG, dissenting.

. . . In *Gore,* I stated why I resisted the Court's foray into punitive damages "territory traditionally within the States' domain." I adhere to those views. . . .

The large size of the award upheld by the Utah Supreme Court in this case indicates why damage-capping legislation may be altogether fitting and proper. Neither the amount of the award nor the trial record, however, justifies this Court's substitution of its judgment for that of Utah's competent decisionmakers. In this regard, I count it significant that, on the key criterion "reprehensibility," there is a good deal more to the story than the Court's abbreviated account tells. . . .

When the Court first ventured to override state-court punitive damages awards, it did so moderately. The Court recalled that "in our federal system, States necessarily have considerable flexibility in determining the level of punitive damages that they will allow in different classes of cases and in any particular case." Today's decision exhibits no such respect and restraint. No longer content to accord state-court judgments "a strong presumption of validity," the Court announces that "few awards exceeding a single-digit ratio between punitive and compensatory damages, to a significant degree, will satisfy due process." Moreover, the Court adds, when compensatory damages are substantial, doubling those damages "can reach the outermost limit of the due process guarantee." In a legislative scheme or a state high court's design to cap punitive damages, the handiwork in setting single-digit and 1-to-1 benchmarks could hardly be questioned; in a judicial decree imposed on the States by this Court under the banner of substantive due process, the numerical controls today's decision installs seem to me boldly out of order. . . .

United States v. Carolene Products Company
304 U.S. 144 (1938)

In what has become a famous footnote in an otherwise unimportant case, Justice Stone developed the justification for "more exacting judicial scrutiny" where infringements of civil liberties (as opposed to economic rights) are involved. Opinion of the Court: <u>Stone</u>, Hughes, Brandeis, Roberts. Concurring opinions: <u>Butler</u>; <u>Black</u>. Dissenting opinion: <u>McReynolds</u>. Not participating: Cardozo and Reed.

JUSTICE STONE delivered the opinion of the Court.

Regulatory legislation affecting ordinary commercial transactions is not to be pronounced unconstitutional unless in the light of the facts made known or generally assumed it is of such a character as to preclude the assumption that it rests upon some rational basis within the knowledge and experience of the legislators.[4]

---

[4]There may be narrower scope for operation of the presumption of constitutionality when legislation appears on its face to be within a specific prohibition of the Constitution, such as those of the first ten Amendments, which are deemed equally specific when held to be embraced within the Fourteenth. It is unnecessary to consider now whether legislation which restricts those political processes which can ordinarily be expected to bring about repeal of undesirable legislation, is to be subjected to more exacting judicial scrutiny under the general prohibitions of the Fourteenth Amendment than are most other types of legislation. Nor need we enquire whether similar considerations enter into the review of statutes directed at particular religious, or national, or racial minorities; whether prejudice against discrete and insular minorities may be a special condition, which tends seriously to curtail the operation of those political processes ordinarily to be relied upon to protect minorities, and which may call for a correspondingly more searching judicial inquiry.

Kelo v. City of New London
545 U.S. 469 (2005)

In 2000, New London, Connecticut, approved an integrated economic development plan designed to revitalize its Fort Trumbull area. The pharmaceutical company Pfizer, Inc., had announced that it would build a $300 million global research facility on a site immediately adjacent to Fort Trumbull, and the city, expecting the Pfizer facility to be a catalyst to the area's rejuvenation, included in its development plan the acquisition of land for new businesses that it hoped would be drawn to the area. With the plan approved, New London, through its development agent, purchased most of the property earmarked for the project from willing sellers and initiated condemnation proceedings against the owners of the rest of the property who refused to sell. Susette Kelo and eight other petitioners brought suit in New London Superior Court claiming that the taking of their properties violated the "public use" restriction in the Fifth Amendment's Takings Clause. The trial court granted a permanent restraining order prohibiting the taking of some of the properties. When the Connecticut Supreme Court, relying on Hawaii Housing Authority v. Midkiff *(1984) and* Berman v. Parker *(1954), reversed and upheld all of the proposed takings, the US Supreme Court granted certiorari.* Opinion of the Court: <u>Stevens</u>, Kennedy, Souter, Ginsburg, Breyer. Concurring opinion: <u>Kennedy</u>. Dissenting opinions: <u>O'Connor</u>, Rehnquist, Scalia, Thomas; <u>Thomas</u>.

JUSTICE STEVENS delivered the opinion of the Court.

In 2000, the city of New London approved a development plan that, in the words of the Supreme Court of Connecticut, was "projected to create in excess of 1,000 jobs, to increase tax and other revenues, and to revitalize an economically distressed city, including its downtown and waterfront areas." In assembling the land needed for this project, the city's development agent has purchased property from willing sellers and proposes to use the power of eminent domain to acquire the remainder of the property from unwilling owners in exchange for just compensation. The question presented is whether the city's proposed disposition of this property qualifies as a "public use" within the meaning of the Takings Clause of the Fifth Amendment to the Constitution. . . .

Petitioner Susette Kelo has lived in the Fort Trumbull area since 1997. She has made extensive improvements to her house, which she prizes for its water view. Petitioner Wilhelmina Dery was born in her Fort Trumbull house in 1918 and has lived there her entire life. Her husband Charles (also a petitioner) has lived in the house since they married some 60 years ago. In all, the nine petitioners own 15 properties in Fort Trumbull. Ten of the parcels are occupied by the owner or a family member; the other five are held as investment properties. There is no allegation that any of these properties is blighted or otherwise in poor condition; rather, they were condemned only because they happen to be located in the development area.

. . . Two polar propositions are perfectly clear. On the one hand, it has long been accepted that the sovereign may not take the property of *A* for the sole purpose of transferring it to another private party *B*, even though *A* is paid just compensation. On the other hand, it is equally clear that a State may transfer property from one private party to another if future "use by the public" is the purpose of the taking; the condemnation of land for a railroad with common-carrier duties is a familiar example. Neither of these propositions, however, determines the disposition of this case.

As for the first proposition, the City would no doubt be forbidden from taking petitioners' land for the purpose of conferring a private benefit on a particular private party. . . . On the other hand, this is not a case in which the City is planning to open the condemned land—at least not in its entirety—to use by the general public. Nor will the private lessees of the land in any sense be required to operate like common carriers, making their services available to all comers. But although such a projected use would be sufficient to satisfy the public use requirement, this "Court long ago rejected any literal requirement that condemned property be put into use for the general public." . . . The disposition of this case therefore turns on the question whether the City's development plan serves a "public purpose." Without exception, our cases have defined that concept broadly, reflecting our longstanding policy of deference to legislative judgments in this field.

In *Berman v. Parker* (1954), this Court upheld a redevelopment plan targeting a blighted area of Washington, D. C., in which most of the housing for the area's 5,000 inhabitants was beyond repair. Under the plan, the area would be condemned and part of it utilized for the construction of streets, schools, and other public facilities. The remainder of the land would be leased or sold to private parties for the purpose of redevelopment, including the construction of low-cost housing.

The owner of a department store located in the area challenged the condemnation, pointing out that his store was not itself blighted and arguing that the creation of a "better balanced, more attractive community" was not a valid public use. Writing for a unanimous Court, Justice Douglas refused to evaluate this claim in isolation, deferring instead to the legislative and agency judgment that the area "must be planned as a whole" for the plan to be successful. The Court explained that "community redevelopment programs need not, by force of the Constitution, be on a piecemeal basis—lot by lot, building by building."

In *Hawaii Housing Authority v. Midkiff* (1984), the Court considered a Hawaii statute whereby fee title was taken from lessors and transferred to lessees (for just compensation) in order to reduce the concentration of land ownership. We unanimously upheld the statute and rejected the Ninth Circuit's view that it was "a naked attempt on the part of the state of Hawaii to take the property of A and transfer it to B solely for B's private use and benefit." Reaffirming *Berman*'s deferential approach to legislative judgments in this field, we concluded that the State's purpose of eliminating the "social and economic evils of a land oligopoly" qualified as a valid public use. Our opinion also rejected the contention that the mere fact that the State immediately transferred the properties to private individuals upon condemnation somehow diminished the public character of the taking. "It is only the taking's purpose, and not its mechanics," we explained, that matters in determining public use. . . .

Those who govern the City were not confronted with the need to remove blight in the Fort Trumbull area, but their determination that the area was sufficiently distressed to justify a program of economic rejuvenation is entitled to our deference. The City has carefully formulated an economic development plan that it believes will provide appreciable benefits to the community, including—but by no means limited to—new jobs and increased tax revenue. As with other exercises in urban planning and development, the City is endeavoring to coordinate a variety of commercial, residential, and recreational uses of land, with the hope that they will form a whole greater than the sum of its parts. To effectuate this plan, the City has invoked a state statute that specifically authorizes the use of eminent domain to promote economic development. Given the comprehensive character of the plan, the thorough deliberation that preceded its adoption, and the limited scope of our review, it is appropriate for us, as it was in *Berman,* to resolve the challenges of the individual owners, not on a piecemeal basis, but rather in light of the entire plan. Because that plan unquestionably serves a public purpose, the takings challenged here satisfy the public use requirement of the Fifth Amendment.

To avoid this result, petitioners urge us to adopt a new bright-line rule that economic development does not qualify as a public use. Putting aside the unpersuasive suggestion that the City's plan will provide only purely economic benefits, neither precedent nor logic supports petitioners' proposal. Promoting economic development is a traditional and long accepted function of government. There is, moreover, no principled way of distinguishing economic development from the other public purposes that we have recognized. In our cases upholding takings that facilitated agriculture and mining, for example, we emphasized the importance of those industries to the welfare of the States in question; in *Berman,* we endorsed the purpose of transforming a blighted area into a "well-balanced" community through redevelopment; [and] in *Midkiff,* we upheld the interest in breaking up a land oligopoly that "created artificial deterrents to the normal functioning of the State's residential land market." . . . It would be incongruous to hold that the City's interest in the economic benefits to be derived from the development of the Fort Trumbull area has less of a public character than any of those other interests. Clearly, there is no basis for exempting economic development from our traditionally broad understanding of public purpose.

Petitioners contend that using eminent domain for economic development impermissibly blurs the boundary between public and private takings. Again, our cases foreclose this objection. Quite simply, the government's pursuit of a public purpose will often benefit individual private parties. For example, in *Midkiff*, the forced transfer of property conferred a direct and significant benefit on those lessees who were previously unable to purchase their homes. . . .

It is further argued that without a bright-line rule nothing would stop a city from transferring citizen *A*'s property to citizen *B* for the sole reason that citizen *B* will put the property to a more productive use and thus pay more taxes. Such a one-to-one transfer of property, executed outside the confines of an integrated development plan, is not presented in this case. While such an unusual exercise of government power would certainly raise a suspicion that a private purpose was afoot, the hypothetical cases posited by petitioners can be confronted if and when they arise. They do not warrant the crafting of an artificial restriction on the concept of public use.

Alternatively, petitioners maintain that for takings of this kind we should require a "reasonable certainty" that the expected public benefits will actually accrue. Such a rule, however, would represent an even greater departure from our precedents. "When the legislature's purpose is legitimate and its means are not irrational, our cases make clear that empirical debates over the wisdom of takings—no less than debates over the wisdom of other kinds of socioeconomic legislation—are not to be carried out in the federal courts." The disadvantages of a heightened form of review are especially pronounced in this type of case. Orderly implementation of a comprehensive redevelopment plan obviously requires that the legal rights of all interested parties be established before new construction can be commenced. A constitutional rule that required postponement of the judicial approval of every condemnation until the likelihood of success of the plan had been assured would unquestionably impose a significant impediment to the successful consummation of many such plans.

Just as we decline to second-guess the City's considered judgments about the efficacy of its development plan, we also decline to second-guess the City's determinations as to what lands it needs to acquire in order to effectuate the project. "It is not for the courts to oversee the choice of the boundary line nor to sit in review on the size of a particular project area. Once the question of the public purpose has been decided, the amount and character of land to be taken for the project and the need for a particular tract to complete the integrated plan rests in the discretion of the legislative branch."

In affirming the City's authority to take petitioners' properties, we do not minimize the hardship that condemnations may entail, notwithstanding the payment of just compensation. We emphasize that nothing in our opinion precludes any State from placing further restrictions on its exercise of the takings power. Indeed, many States already impose "public use" requirements that are stricter than the federal baseline. . . .

The judgment of the Supreme Court of Connecticut is affirmed.

JUSTICE O'CONNOR, with whom THE CHIEF JUSTICE, JUSTICE SCALIA, and JUSTICE THOMAS join, dissenting.

Over two centuries ago, just after the Bill of Rights was ratified, Justice Chase wrote:

An ACT of the Legislature (for I cannot call it a law) contrary to the great first principles of the social compact, cannot be considered a rightful exercise of legislative authority. . . . A few instances will suffice to explain what I mean. . . . [A] law that takes property from A. and gives it to B: It is against all reason and justice, for a people to entrust a Legislature with SUCH powers; and, therefore, it cannot be presumed that they have done it. *Calder v. Bull* (1798).

Today the Court abandons this long-held, basic limitation on government power. Under the banner of economic development, all private property is now vulnerable to being taken and transferred to another private owner, so long as it might be upgraded—*i.e.,* given to an owner who will use it in a way that the legislature deems more beneficial to the public—in the process. To reason, as the Court does, that the incidental public benefits resulting from the subsequent ordinary use of private property render economic development takings "for public use" is to wash out any distinction between private and public use of property—and thereby effectively to delete the words "for public use" from the Takings Clause of the Fifth Amendment. Accordingly I respectfully dissent.

. . . The Fifth Amendment to the Constitution, made applicable to the States by the Fourteenth Amendment, provides that "private property [shall not] be taken for public use, without just compensation." When interpreting the Constitution, we begin with the unremarkable presumption that every word in the document has independent meaning, "that no word was unnecessarily used, or needlessly added." In keeping with that presumption, we have read the Fifth Amendment's language to impose two distinct conditions on the exercise of eminent domain: "the taking must be for a 'public use' and 'just compensation' must be paid to the owner."

These two limitations serve to protect "the security of Property," which Alexander Hamilton described to the Philadelphia Convention as one of the "great objects of Government." Together they ensure stable property ownership by providing safeguards against excessive, unpredictable, or unfair use of the government's eminent domain power—particularly against those owners who, for whatever reasons, may be unable to protect themselves in the political process against the majority's will.

While the Takings Clause presupposes that government can take private property without the owner's consent, the just compensation requirement spreads the cost of condemnations and thus "prevents the public from loading upon one individual more than his just share of the burdens of government." The public use requirement, in turn, imposes a more basic limitation, circumscribing the very scope of the eminent domain power: Government may compel an individual to forfeit her property for the *public's* use, but not for the benefit of another private person. . . .

Where is the line between "public" and "private" property use? We give considerable deference to legislatures' determinations about what governmental activities will advantage the public. But were the political branches the sole arbiters of the public-private distinction, the Public Use Clause would amount to little more than hortatory fluff. An external, judicial check on how the public use requirement is interpreted, however limited, is necessary if this constraint on government power is to retain any meaning.

Our cases have generally identified three categories of takings that comply with the public use requirement, though it is in the nature of things that the boundaries between these categories are not always firm. Two are relatively straightforward and uncontroversial. First, the sovereign may transfer private property to public ownership—such as for a road, a hospital, or a military base. Second, the sovereign may transfer private property to private parties, often common carriers, who make the property available for the public's use—such as with a railroad, a public utility, or a stadium. But "public ownership" and "use-by-the-public" are sometimes too constricting and impractical ways to define the scope of the Public Use Clause. Thus we have allowed that, in certain circumstances and to meet certain exigencies, takings that serve a public purpose also satisfy the Constitution even if the property is destined for subsequent private use.

This case . . . presents an issue of first impression: Are economic development takings constitutional? I would hold that they are not. We are guided by two precedents about the taking of real property by eminent domain. In *Berman,* we upheld takings within a blighted neighborhood of Washington, D.C. The neighborhood had so deteriorated that, for example, 64.3% of its dwellings were beyond repair. It had become burdened with "over-crowding of dwellings," "lack of adequate streets and alleys," and "lack of light and air." Congress had determined that the neighbor-hood had become "injurious to the public health, safety, morals, and welfare" and that it was necessary to "eliminate all such injurious conditions by employing all means necessary and appropriate for the purpose," including eminent domain. Mr. Berman's department store was not itself blighted. Having approved of Congress' decision to eliminate the harm to the public emanating from the blighted neigh-borhood, however, we did not second-guess its decision to treat the neighborhood as a whole rather than lot-by-lot.

In *Midkiff*, we upheld a land condemnation scheme in Hawaii whereby title in real prop-erty was taken from lessors and transferred to lessees. At that time, the State and Federal Governments owned nearly 49% of the State's land, and another 47% was in the hands of only 72 private landowners. Concentration of land ownership was so dramatic that on the State's most urbanized island, Oahu, 22 land-owners owned 72.5% of the fee simple titles. The Hawaii Legislature had concluded that the oligopoly in land ownership was "skewing the State's residential fee simple market, inflating land prices, and injuring the public tranquility and welfare," and therefore enacted a condem-nation scheme for redistributing title.

In those decisions, we emphasized the im-portance of deferring to legislative judgments about public purpose. . . . Yet for all the em-phasis on deference, *Berman* and *Midkiff* hewed to a bedrock principle without which our public use jurisprudence would collapse: "A purely private taking could not withstand the scrutiny of the public use requirement; it would serve no legitimate purpose of govern-ment and would thus be void."

The Court's holdings in *Berman* and *Midkiff* were true to the principle underlying the Public Use Clause. In both those cases, the extraordi-nary, precondemnation use of the targeted property inflicted affirmative harm on soci-ety—in *Berman* through blight resulting from extreme poverty and in *Midkiff* through oligop-oly resulting from extreme wealth. And in both cases, the relevant legislative body had found that eliminating the existing property use was necessary to remedy the harm. Thus a public purpose was realized when the harmful use was eliminated. Because each taking *directly* achieved a public benefit, it did not matter that the property was turned over to private use. Here, in contrast, New London does not claim that Susette Kelo's and Wilhelmina Dery's well-maintained homes are the source of any social harm. Indeed, it could not so claim with-out adopting the absurd argument that any sin-gle-family home that might be razed to make way for an apartment building, or any church that might be replaced with a retail store, or any small business that might be more lucrative if it were instead part of a national franchise, is in-herently harmful to society and thus within the government's power to condemn.

In moving away from our decisions sanc-tioning the condemnation of harmful property use, the Court today significantly expands the meaning of public use. It holds that the sover-eign may take private property currently put to ordinary private use, and give it over for new, ordinary private use, so long as the new use is predicted to generate some secondary benefit for the public—such as increased tax revenue, more jobs, maybe even aesthetic pleasure. But nearly any lawful use of real private property can be said to generate some incidental benefit to the public. Thus, if predicted (or even guar-anteed) positive side-effects are enough to ren-der transfer from one private party to another constitutional, then the words "for public use" do not realistically exclude *any* takings, and thus do not exert any constraint on the emi-nent domain power. . . .

Finally, in a coda, the Court suggests that property owners should turn to the States, who may or may not choose to impose appropriate limits on economic development takings. This is an abdication of our responsibility. States play many important functions in our system of dual sovereignty, but compensating for our refusal to enforce properly the Federal Consti-tution (and a provision meant to curtail state action, no less) is not among them.

JUSTICE THOMAS, dissenting.

. . . I do not believe that this Court can eliminate liberties expressly enumerated in the

Constitution and therefore join [Justice O'Connor's] dissenting opinion. Regrettably, however, the Court's error runs deeper than this. Today's decision is simply the latest in a string of our cases construing the Public Use Clause to be a virtual nullity, without the slightest nod to its original meaning. In my view, the Public Use Clause, originally understood, is a meaningful limit on the government's eminent domain power. Our cases have strayed from the Clause's original meaning, and I would reconsider them. . . .

The most natural reading of the Clause is that it allows the government to take property only if the government owns, or the public has a legal right to use, the property, as opposed to taking it for any public purpose or necessity whatsoever. At the time of the founding, dictionaries primarily defined the noun "use" as "the act of employing any thing to any purpose." The term "use," moreover, "is from the Latin *utor,* which means 'to use, make use of, avail one's self of, employ, apply, enjoy, etc.'" When the government takes property and gives it to a private individual, and the public has no right to use the property, it strains language to say that the public is "employing" the property, regardless of the incidental benefits that might accrue to the public from the private use. The term "public use," then, means that either the government or its citizens as a whole must actually "employ" the taken property.

Granted, another sense of the word "use" was broader in meaning, extending to "convenience" or "help," or "qualities that make a thing proper for any purpose." Nevertheless, read in context, the term "public use" possesses the narrower meaning. Elsewhere, the Constitution twice employs the word "use," both times in its narrower sense. Article 1, §10 provides that "the net Produce of all Duties and Imposts, laid by any State on Imports or Exports, shall be for the Use of the Treasury of the United States," meaning the Treasury itself will control the taxes, not use it to any beneficial end. And Article I, §8 grants Congress power "to raise and support Armies, but no Appropriation of Money to that Use shall be for a longer Term than two Years." Here again, "use" means "employed to raise and support Armies," not anything directed to achieving any military end. The same word in the Public Use Clause should be interpreted to have the same meaning.

Tellingly, the phrase "public use" contrasts with the very different phrase "general Welfare" used elsewhere in the Constitution. See Article I, §8 ("Congress shall have Power To . . . provide for the common Defence and general Welfare of the United States"); preamble (Constitution established "to promote the general Welfare"). The Framers would have used some such broader term if they had meant the Public Use Clause to have a similarly sweeping scope. . . . The Constitution's text, in short, suggests that the Takings Clause authorizes the taking of property only if the public has a right to employ it, not if the public realizes any conceivable benefit from the taking.

The Constitution's common-law background reinforces this understanding. The common law provided an express method of eliminating uses of land that adversely impacted the public welfare: nuisance law. Blackstone and Kent, for instance, both carefully distinguished the law of nuisance from the power of eminent domain. Blackstone rejected the idea that private property could be taken solely for purposes of any public benefit. "So great . . . is the regard of the law for private property," he explained, "that it will not authorize the least violation of it; no, not even for the general good of the whole community." . . . When the public took property, in other words, it took it as an individual buying property from another typically would: for one's own use. The Public Use Clause, in short, embodied the Framers' understanding that property is a natural, fundamental right, prohibiting the government from "taking *property* from A. and giving it to B."

. . . There is no justification . . . for affording almost insurmountable deference to legislative conclusions that a use serves a "public use." To begin with, a court owes no deference to a legislature's judgment concerning the quintessentially legal question of whether the government owns, or the public has a legal right to use, the taken property. Even under the "public purpose" interpretation, moreover, it is most implausible that the Framers intended to defer to legislatures as to what satisfies the Public Use Clause, uniquely among all the express provisions of the Bill of Rights. We would not defer to a legislature's determination of the various circumstances that establish, for example, when a search of a home would be reasonable. . . . The Court has elsewhere recognized "the overriding respect for the sanctity of the home that has been embedded in our traditions since the origins of the Republic" when the issue is only whether the government may search a home. Yet today the Court tells us that we are not to "second-guess the City's considered judgments" when the issue is, instead, whether the government may take the infinitely more intrusive step of tearing down petitioners' homes. Something has gone seriously awry with this Court's interpretation of the Constitution. Though citizens are safe from the government in their homes, the homes themselves are not. Once one accepts, as the Court at least nominally does, that the Public Use Clause is a limit on the eminent domain power of the Federal Government and the States, there is no justification for the almost complete deference it grants to legislatures as to what satisfies it.

. . . *Berman* and *Midkiff* erred by equating the eminent domain power with the police power of States. Traditional uses of that regulatory power, such as the power to abate a nuisance, required no compensation whatsoever, in sharp contrast to the takings power, which has always required compensation. The question whether the State can take property using the power of eminent domain is therefore distinct from the question whether it can regulate property pursuant to the police power. In *Berman,* for example, if the slums at issue were truly "blighted," then state nuisance law, not the power of eminent domain, would provide the appropriate remedy. To construe the Public Use Clause to overlap with the States' police power conflates these two categories.

The "public purpose" test applied by *Berman* and *Midkiff* also cannot be applied in principled manner. "When we depart from the natural import of the term 'public use,' and substitute for the simple idea of a public possession and occupation, that of public utility, public interest, common benefit, general advantage or convenience . . . we are afloat without any certain principle to guide us." Once one permits takings for public purposes in

addition to public uses, no coherent principle limits what could constitute a valid public use. . . . I share the Court's skepticism about a public use standard that requires courts to second-guess the policy wisdom of public works projects. The "public purpose" standard this Court has adopted, however, demands the use of such judgment, for the Court concedes that the Public Use Clause would forbid a purely private taking. It is difficult to imagine how a court could find that a taking was purely private except by determining that the taking did not, in fact, rationally advance the public interest. The Court is therefore wrong to criticize the "actual use" test as "difficult to administer." It is far easier to analyze whether the government owns or the public has a legal right to use the taken property than to ask whether the taking has a "purely private purpose"—unless the Court means to eliminate public use scrutiny of takings entirely. Obliterating a provision of the Constitution, of course, guarantees that it will not be misapplied.

For all these reasons, I would revisit our Public Use Clause cases and consider returning to the original meaning of the Public Use Clause: that the government may take property only if it actually uses or gives the public a legal right to use the property.

The consequences of today's decision are not difficult to predict, and promise to be harmful. So-called "urban renewal" programs provide some compensation for the properties they take, but no compensation is possible for the subjective value of these lands to the individuals displaced and the indignity inflicted by uprooting them from their homes. Allowing the government to take property solely for public purposes is bad enough, but extending the concept of public purpose to encompass any economically beneficial goal guarantees that these losses will fall disproportionately on poor communities. Those communities are not only systematically less likely to put their lands to the highest and best social use, but are also the least politically powerful. If ever there were justification for intrusive judicial review of constitutional provisions that protect "discrete and insular minorities," *United States v. Carolene Products Co.* (1938), surely that principle would apply with great force to the powerless groups and individuals the Public Use Clause protects. The deferential standard this Court has adopted for the Public Use Clause is therefore deeply perverse. It encourages "those citizens with disproportionate influence and power in the political process, including large corporations and development firms" to victimize the weak.

Those incentives have made the legacy of this Court's "public purpose" test an unhappy one. In the 1950s, no doubt emboldened in part by the expansive understanding of "public use" this Court adopted in *Berman,* cities "rushed to draw plans" for downtown development. "Of all the families displaced by urban renewal from 1949 through 1963, 63 percent of those whose race was known were nonwhite, and of these families, 56 percent of nonwhites and 38 percent of whites had incomes low enough to qualify for public housing, which, however, was seldom available to them." Public works projects in the 1950s and 1960s destroyed predominantly minority communities in St. Paul, Minnesota, and Baltimore, Maryland. In 1981, urban planners in Detroit, Michigan, uprooted the largely "lower-income and elderly" Pole-

town neighborhood for the benefit of the General Motors Corporation. Urban renewal projects have long been associated with the displacement of blacks; "in cities across the country, urban renewal came to be known as 'Negro removal.'" Over 97 percent of the individuals forcibly removed from their homes by the "slum-clearance" project upheld by this Court in *Berman* were black. Regrettably, the predictable consequence of the Court's decision will be to exacerbate these effects.

The Court relies almost exclusively on this Court's prior cases to derive today's far-reaching, and dangerous, result. When faced with a clash of constitutional principle and a line of unreasoned cases wholly divorced from the text, history, and structure of our founding document, we should not hesitate to resolve the tension in favor of the Constitution's original meaning. For the reasons I have given, and for the reasons given in Justice O'Connor's dissent, the conflict of principle raised by this boundless use of the eminent domain power should be resolved in petitioners' favor. I would reverse the judgment of the Connecticut Supreme Court.

Horne v. Department of Agriculture
576 U.S. ___ (2015)

The Agricultural Marketing Agreement Act of 1937 authorizes the Secretary of Agriculture to promulgate "marketing orders" to help maintain stable markets for particular agricultural products. The marketing order for raisins established a Raisin Administrative Committee that imposes a reserve requirement—a requirement that growers set aside a certain percentage of their crop for the Government, free of charge. The Government then sells those raisins in noncompetitive markets, donates them, or otherwise disposes of them in a manner consistent with the purposes of the program. If any profits remain after subtracting the Government's expenses from administering the program, the net proceeds are distributed back to the raisin growers. In 2002–2003, raisin growers were required to set aside 47 percent of their raisin crop under the reserve requirement. In 2003–2004, 30 percent. The Horne family, raisin growers in California, refused to set aside any

raisins for the Government on the ground that the reserve requirement was an unconstitutional taking of their property for public use without just compensation. The Government fined the Hornes the fair market value of the raisins as well as additional civil penalties for their failure to obey the raisin marketing order.

The Hornes sought relief in federal court, arguing that the reserve requirement was an unconstitutional taking of their property under the Fifth Amendment. The Ninth Circuit rejected their argument that the reserve requirement was a Fifth Amendment taking; it determined that the requirement was not a per se taking because personal property is afforded less protection under the Takings Clause than real property and because the Hornes, who retained an interest in any net proceeds, were not completely divested of their property. The Ninth Circuit held that, as in cases allowing the government to set conditions on land use and development, the Government imposed a condition (the reserve requirement) in exchange for a Government benefit (an orderly raisin market). It also held that the Hornes could avoid relinquishing large percentages of their crop by "planting different crops." The Supreme Court granted certiorari. Opinion of the Court: <u>Roberts</u>, Scalia, Kennedy, Thomas, Ginsburg (as to Parts I and II), Breyer (as to Parts I and II), Alito, Kagan (as to Parts I and II). Concurring opinion: <u>Thomas.</u> Concurring in part and dissenting in part: <u>Breyer</u>, Ginsburg, Kagan. Dissenting opinion: <u>Sotomayor</u>.

CHIEF JUSTICE ROBERTS delivered the opinion of the Court.

Under the United States Department of Agriculture's California Raisin Marketing Order, a percentage of a grower's crop must be physically set aside in certain years for the account of the Government, free of charge. The Government then sells, allocates, or otherwise disposes of the raisins in ways it determines are best suited to maintaining an orderly market. The question is whether the Takings Clause of the Fifth Amendment bars the Government from imposing such a demand on the growers without just compensation.

I

The Agricultural Marketing Agreement Act of 1937 authorizes the Secretary of Agriculture to promulgate "marketing orders" to help maintain stable markets for particular agricultural products. The marketing order for raisins requires growers in certain years to give a percentage of their crop to the Government, free of charge. The required allocation is determined by the Raisin Administrative Committee, a Government entity composed largely of growers and others in the raisin business appointed by the Secretary of Agriculture. In 2002–2003, this Committee ordered raisin growers to turn over 47 percent of their crop. In 2003–2004, 30 percent.

Growers generally ship their raisins to a raisin "handler," who physically separates the raisins due the Government (called "reserve raisins"), pays the growers only for the remainder ("free-tonnage raisins"), and packs and sells the free-tonnage raisins. The Raisin Committee acquires title to the reserve raisins that have been set aside, and decides how to dispose of them in its discretion. It sells them in noncompetitive markets, for example to exporters, federal agencies, or foreign governments; donates them to charitable causes; releases them to growers who agree to reduce their raisin production; or disposes of them by "any other means" consistent with the purposes of the raisin program. Proceeds from Committee sales are principally used to subsidize handlers who sell raisins for export (not including the Hornes, who are not raisin exporters). Raisin growers retain an interest in any net proceeds from sales the Raisin Committee makes, after deductions for the export subsidies and the Committee's administrative expenses. In the years at issue in this case, those proceeds were less than the cost of producing the crop one year, and nothing at all the next.

. . . In 2002, the Hornes refused to set aside any raisins for the Government, believing they were not legally bound to do so. The Government sent trucks to the Hornes' facility at eight o'clock one morning to pick up the raisins, but the Hornes refused entry. The Government then assessed against the Hornes a fine equal to the market value of the missing raisins—some $480,000—as well as an additional civil penalty of just over $200,000 for disobeying the order to turn them over.

When the Government sought to collect the fine, the Hornes turned to the courts, arguing that the reserve requirement was an unconstitutional taking of their property under the Fifth Amendment. Their case eventually made it to this Court when . . . the Ninth Circuit . . . rejected the Hornes' argument that the reserve requirement was a per se taking, reasoning that "the Takings Clause affords less protection to personal than to real property," and concluding that the Hornes "are not completely divested of their property rights," because growers retain an interest in the proceeds from any sale of reserve raisins by the Raisin Committee. [It] . . . instead viewed the reserve requirement as a use restriction, similar to a government condition on the grant of a land use permit. See *Dolan v. City of Tigard*, (1994); *Nollan v. California*

Coastal Commission (1987). As in such permit cases, the Court of Appeals explained, the Government here imposed a condition (the reserve requirement) in exchange for a Government benefit (an orderly raisin market). And just as a landowner was free to avoid the government condition by forgoing a permit, so too the Hornes could avoid the reserve requirement by "planting different crops." Under that analysis, the court found that the reserve requirement was a proportional response to the Government's interest in ensuring an orderly raisin market, and not a taking under the Fifth Amendment. We granted certiorari.

II

The petition for certiorari poses three questions, which we answer in turn.

A

The first question presented asks "Whether the government's 'categorical duty' under the Fifth Amendment to pay just compensation when it 'physically takes possession of an interest in property' applies only to real property and not to personal property." The answer is no.

1

There is no dispute that the "classic taking [is one] in which the government directly appropriates private property for its own use." Nor is there any dispute that, in the case of real property, such an appropriation is a per se taking that requires just compensation. Nothing in the text or history of the Takings Clause, or our precedents, suggests that the rule is any different when it comes to appropriation of personal property. The Government has a categorical duty to pay just compensation when it takes your car, just as when it takes your home.

The Takings Clause . . . protects "private property" without any distinction between different types. The principle reflected in the Clause goes back at least 800 years to Magna Carta, which specifically protected agricultural crops from uncompensated takings. Clause 28 of that charter forbade any "constable or other bailiff" from taking "corn or other provisions from any one without immediately tendering

money therefor, unless he can have postponement thereof by permission of the seller."

The colonists brought the principles of Magna Carta with them to the New World, including that charter's protection against uncompensated takings of personal property. In 1641, for example, Massachusetts adopted its Body of Liberties, prohibiting "mans Cattel or goods of what kinde soever" from being "pressed or taken for any publique use or service, unless it be by warrant grounded upon some act of the generall Court, nor without such reasonable prices and hire as the ordinarie rates of the Countrie do afford." Virginia allowed the seizure of surplus "live stock, or beef, pork, or bacon" for the military, but only upon "paying or tendering to the owner the price so estimated by the appraisers." And South Carolina authorized the seizure of "necessaries" for public use, but provided that "said articles so seized shall be paid for agreeable to the prices such and the like articles sold for on the ninth day of October last."

. . . Nothing in this history suggests that personal property was any less protected against physical appropriation than real property. . . .

2

The reserve requirement imposed by the Raisin Committee is a clear physical taking. Actual raisins are transferred from the growers to the Government. . . . The Committee disposes of what become its raisins as it wishes, to promote the purposes of the raisin marketing order.

Raisin growers subject to the reserve requirement thus lose the entire "bundle" of property rights in the appropriated raisins . . . with the exception of the speculative hope that some residual proceeds may be left when the Government is done with the raisins and has deducted the expenses of implementing all aspects of the marketing order. The Government's "actual taking of possession and control" of the reserve raisins gives rise to a taking as clearly "as if the Government held full title and ownership," as it essentially does. . . .

B

The second question presented asks "Whether the government may avoid the categorical duty to pay just compensation for a physical taking of property by reserving to the property owner a contingent interest in a portion of the value of the property, set at the government's discretion." The answer is no.

The Government and dissent argue that raisins are fungible goods whose only value is in the revenue from their sale. According to the Government, the raisin marketing order leaves that interest with the raisin growers: After selling reserve raisins and deducting expenses and subsidies for exporters, the Raisin Committee returns any net proceeds to the growers. The Government contends that because growers are entitled to these net proceeds, they retain the most important property interest in the reserve raisins, so there is no taking in the first place. The dissent agrees, arguing that this possible future revenue means there has been no taking . . . That is not an issue here: The Hornes did not receive any net proceeds from Raisin Committee sales for the years at issue, because they had not set aside any reserve raisins in those years (and, in any event, there were no net proceeds in one of them).

C

The third question presented asks "Whether a governmental mandate to relinquish specific, identifiable property as a 'condition' on permission to engage in commerce effects a per se taking." The answer, at least in this case, is yes.

The Government contends that the reserve requirement is not a taking because raisin growers voluntarily choose to participate in the raisin market. According to the Government, if raisin growers don't like it, they can "plant different crops," or "sell their raisin-variety grapes as table grapes or for use in juice or wine."

"Let them sell wine" is probably not much more comforting to the raisin growers than similar retorts have been to others throughout history. . . . [P]roperty rights "cannot be so easily manipulated." . . . The Government and dissent rely heavily on *Ruckelshaus v. Monsanto Co.* (1984). There we held that the Environmental Protection Agency could require companies manufacturing pesticides, fungicides, and rodenticides to disclose health, safety, and environmental information about their products as a condition to receiving a permit to sell those products. While such information included trade secrets in which pesticide manufacturers had a property interest, those manufacturers were not subjected to a taking because they received a "valuable Government benefit" in exchange—a license to sell dangerous chemicals.

The taking here cannot reasonably be characterized as part of a similar voluntary exchange. In one of the years at issue here, the Government insisted that the Hornes turn over 47 percent of their raisin crop, in exchange for the "benefit" of being allowed to sell the remaining 53 percent. The next year, the toll was 30 percent. We have already rejected the idea that *Monsanto* may be extended by regarding basic and familiar uses of property as a "Government benefit" on the same order as a permit to sell hazardous chemicals. Selling produce in interstate commerce, although certainly subject to reasonable government regulation, is similarly not a special governmental benefit that the Government may hold hostage, to be ransomed by the waiver of constitutional protection. Raisins are not dangerous pesticides; they are a healthy snack. A case about conditioning the sale of hazardous substances on disclosure of health, safety, and environmental information related to those hazards is hardly on point.

III

[T]he Government briefly argues that if we conclude that the reserve requirement effects a taking, we should remand for the Court of Appeals to calculate "what compensation would have been due if petitioners had complied with the reserve requirement." The Government contends that the calculation must consider what the value of the reserve raisins would have been without the price support program, as well as "other benefits . . . from the regulatory program, such as higher consumer demand for raisins spurred by enforcement of quality standards and promotional activities." Indeed, according to the Government, the Hornes would "likely" have a net gain under this theory.

The best defense may be a good offense, but the Government cites no support for its hypothetical-based approach, or its notion that general regulatory activity such as enforcement of quality standards can constitute just compensation for a specific physical taking. Instead, our cases have set forth a clear and administrable rule for just compensation: "The Court has repeatedly held that just compensation normally is to be measured by 'the market value of the property at the time of the taking.'" The Government has already calculated the amount of just compensation in this case, when it fined the Hornes the fair market value of the raisins: $483,843.53. The Government cannot now disavow that valuation and does not suggest that the marketing order affords the Hornes compensation in that amount. There is accordingly no need for a remand; the Hornes should simply be relieved of the obligation to pay the fine and associated civil penalty they were assessed when they resisted the Government's effort to take their raisins. This case, in litigation for more than a decade, has gone on long enough.

The judgment of the United States Court of Appeals for the Ninth Circuit is reversed.

It is so ordered.

JUSTICE BREYER, with whom JUSTICE GINSBURG and JUSTICE KAGAN join, concurring in part and dissenting in part.

I agree with Parts I and II of the Court's opinion. However, I cannot agree with the Court's rejection, in Part III, of the Government's final argument. The Government contends that we should remand the case for a determination of whether any compensation would have been due if the Hornes had complied with the California Raisin Marketing Order's reserve requirement. In my view, a remand for such a determination is necessary.

The question of just compensation was not presented in the Hornes' petition for certiorari. It was barely touched on in the briefs. And the courts below did not decide it. . . . In my view, . . . the Takings Clause requires compensation in an amount equal to the value of the reserve raisins adjusted to account for the benefits received. And the Government does, indeed, suggest that the marketing order affords just compensation. Further, the Hornes have not demonstrated the contrary. Before granting judgment in favor of the Hornes, a court

should address the issue in light of all of the relevant facts and law.

* * *

Given the precedents, the parties should provide full briefing on this question. I would remand the case, permitting the lower courts to consider argument on the question of just compensation.

JUSTICE SOTOMAYOR, dissenting.

. . . Because the Order does not deprive the Hornes of all of their property rights, it does not effect a per se taking. I respectfully dissent from the Court's contrary holding.

. . . In my view, [w]here some property right is retained by the owner, no per se taking . . . has occurred. . . .

The Hornes . . . retain at least one meaningful property interest in the reserve raisins: the right to receive some money for their disposition. The Order explicitly provides that raisin producers retain the right to "[t]he net proceeds from the disposition of reserve tonnage raisins" and ensures that reserve raisins will be sold "at prices and in a manner intended to maxim[ize] producer returns," According to the Government, of the 49 crop years for which a reserve pool was operative, producers received equitable distributions of net proceeds from the disposition of reserve raisins in 42.

Granted, this equitable distribution may represent less income than what some or all of the reserve raisins could fetch if sold in an unregulated market. In some years, it may even turn out (and has turned out) to represent no net income. But whether and when that occurs turns on market forces for which the Government cannot be blamed and to which all commodities—indeed, all property—are subject. In any event, we have emphasized that "a reduction in the value of property is not necessarily equated with a taking," that even "a significant restriction . . . imposed on one means of disposing" of property is not necessarily a taking, and that not every "'injury to property by governmental action'" amounts to a taking. . . . I take us at our word: [An] action can[not] be called a per se taking . . . if there remains a property interest that is at most merely damaged. That is the case here; accordingly, no per se taking has occurred.

Nollan v. California Coastal Commission
483 U.S. 825 (1987)

The California Coastal Commission granted a permit to James and Marilyn Nollan to replace a small bungalow on their beachfront lot with a larger house upon the condition that they allow the public an easement to pass across their beach, which was located between two public beaches. The Nollans filed a petition for writ of administrative mandamus, asking the Ventura County Superior Court to invalidate the access condition. They argued that the condition could not be imposed absent evidence that their proposed development would have a direct adverse impact on public access to the beach. The court agreed and remanded the case to the commission for a full evidentiary hearing on that issue. On remand, the commission held a public hearing and made further factual findings; it reaffirmed its imposition of the condition, finding that the new house would increase blockage of the view of the ocean, thus contributing to the development of "a 'wall' of residential structures" that would prevent the public "psychologically . . . from realizing a stretch of coastline exists nearby that they have every right to visit." The Nollans filed a supplemental petition for a writ of administrative mandamus with the California Superior Court, arguing that imposition of the access condition violated the Takings Clause of the Fifth Amendment, as incorporated against the states by the Fourteenth Amendment. The superior court avoided the constitutional question but ruled in their favor on statutory grounds. In its view, the administrative record did not provide an adequate factual basis for concluding that replacement of the bungalow with the house would create a direct or cumulative burden on public access to the ocean. The commission appealed to the California Court of Appeals, which reversed, holding that the access condition violated neither California statutes nor the Takings Clause of the US Constitution. The Nollans appealed to the US Supreme Court. Opinion of the Court: <u>Scalia</u>, Rehnquist, White, Powell, O'Connor. Dissenting opinions: <u>Brennan</u>, Marshall; <u>Blackmun</u>; <u>Stevens</u>, Blackmun.*

JUSTICE SCALIA delivered the opinion of the Court.

Had California simply required the Nollans to make an easement across their beachfront available to the public on a permanent basis in order to increase public access to the beach, rather than conditioning their permit to rebuild their house on their agreeing to do so, we have no doubt there would have been a taking. To say that the appropriation of a public easement across a landowner's premises does not constitute the taking of a property interest but rather (as Justice Brennan contends) "a mere restriction on its use," is to use words in a manner that deprives them of all their ordinary meaning. Indeed, one of the principal uses of the eminent domain power is to assure that the government be able to require conveyance of just such interests, so long as it pays for them. . . . Perhaps because the point is so obvious, we have never been confronted with a controversy that required us to rule upon it, but our cases' analysis of the effect of other governmental action leads to the same conclusion. We have repeatedly held that, as to property reserved by its owner for private use, "the right to exclude [others is] 'one of the most essential sticks in the bundle of rights that are commonly characterized as property.'" . . .

Given, then, that requiring uncompensated conveyance of the easement outright would violate the Fourteenth Amendment, the question becomes whether requiring it to be conveyed as a condition for issuing a land-use permit alters the outcome. We have long recognized that land-use regulation does not effect a taking if it "substantially advance[s] legitimate state interests" and does not "den[y] an owner economically viable use of his land," *Agins v. Tiburon* (1980). Our cases have not elaborated on the standards for determining what constitutes a "legitimate state interest" or what type of connection between the regulation and the state interest satisfies the requirement that the former "substantially advance" the latter. They have made clear, however, that a broad range of governmental purposes and regulations satisfies these requirements. . . . The Commission argues that among these permissible purposes are protecting the public's ability to see the beach, assisting the public in overcoming the "psychological barrier" to using the beach created by a developed shorefront, and preventing congestion on the public beaches. We assume, without deciding, that this is so—in which case the Commission unquestionably would be able to deny the Nollans their permit outright if their new house (alone, or by reason of the cumulative impact produced in conjunction with other construction) would substantially impede these purposes, unless the denial would interfere so drastically with the Nollans' use of their property as to constitute a taking. . . .

The Commission argues that a permit condition that serves the same legitimate police power purpose as a refusal to issue the permit should not be found to be a taking if the refusal to issue the permit would not constitute a taking. We agree. Thus, if the Commission attached to the permit some condition that would have protected the public's ability to see the beach notwithstanding construction of the new house—for example, a height limitation, a width restriction, or a ban on fences—so long as the Commission could have exercised its police power (as we have assumed it could) to forbid construction of the house altogether, imposition of the condition would also be constitutional. Moreover (and here we come closer to the facts of the present case), the condition would be constitutional even if it consisted of the requirement that the Nollans provide a viewing spot on their property for passersby with whose sighting of the ocean their new house would interfere. Although such a requirement, constituting a permanent grant of continuous access to the property, would have to be considered a taking if it were not attached to a development permit, the Commission's assumed power to forbid construction of the house in order to protect the public's view of the beach must surely include the power to condition construction upon some concession by the owner, even a concession of property rights, that serves the same end. If a prohibition designed to accomplish that purpose would be a legitimate exercise of the police power rather than a taking, it would be strange to conclude that providing the owner an alternative to that prohibition which accomplishes the same purpose is not.

The evident constitutional propriety disappears, however, if the condition substituted for the prohibition utterly fails to further the end advanced as the justification for the prohibition. When that essential nexus is eliminated, the situation becomes the same as if California law forbade shouting fire in a crowded theater, but granted dispensations to those willing to contribute $100 to the state treasury. While a ban on shouting fire can be a core exercise of the State's police power to protect the public safety, and can thus meet even our stringent standards for regulation of speech, adding the unrelated condition alters the purpose to one which, while it may be legitimate, is inadequate to sustain the ban. Therefore, even though, in a sense, requiring a $100 tax contribution in order to shout fire is a lesser restriction on speech than an outright ban, it would not pass constitutional muster. Similarly here, the lack of nexus between the condition and the original purpose of the building restriction converts that purpose to something other than what it was. The purpose then becomes, quite simply, the obtaining of an easement to serve some valid governmental purpose, but without payment of compensation. Whatever may be the outer limits of "legitimate state interests" in the takings and land-use context, this is not one of them. In short, unless the permit condition serves the same governmental purpose as the development ban, the building restriction is not a valid regulation of land use but "an out-and-out plan of extortion." . . .

The Commission claims that it concedes as much, and that we may sustain the condition at issue here by finding that it is reasonably related to the public need or burden that the Nollans' new house creates or to which it contributes. We can accept, for purposes of discussion, the Commission's proposed test as to how close a "fit" between the condition and the burden is required, because we find that this case does not meet even the most untailored standards. The Commission's principal contention to the contrary essentially turns on a play on the word "access." The Nollans' new house, the Commission found, will interfere with "visual access" to the beach. That in turn (along with other shorefront development) will interfere with the desire of people who drive past the Nollans' house to use the beach, thus creating a "psychological barrier" to "access." The Nollans' new house will also, by a process not altogether clear from the Commission's opinion but presumably potent enough to more than offset the effects of the psychological barrier, increase the use of the public beaches, thus creating the need for more "access." These burdens on "access" would be alleviated by a requirement that the Nollans provide "lateral access" to the beach.

Rewriting the argument to eliminate the play on words makes clear that there is nothing to it. It is quite impossible to understand how a requirement that people already on the public beaches be able to walk across the Nollans' property reduces any obstacles to viewing the beach created by the new house. It is also impossible to understand how it lowers any "psychological barrier" to using the public beaches, or how it helps to remedy any additional congestion on them caused by construction of the Nollans' new house. We therefore find that the Commission's imposition of the permit condition cannot be treated as an exercise of its land-use power for any of these purposes. Our conclusion on this point is consistent with the approach taken by every other court that has considered the question, with the exception of the California state courts.

Justice Brennan argues that imposition of the access requirement is not irrational. In his version of the Commission's argument, the reason for the requirement is that in its absence, a person looking toward the beach from the road will see a street of residential structures including the Nollans' new home and conclude that there is no public beach nearby. If, however, that person sees people passing and repassing along the dry sand behind the Nollans' home, he will realize that there is a public beach somewhere in the vicinity. . . . The Commission's action, however, was based on the opposite factual finding that the wall of houses completely blocked the view of the beach and that a person looking from the road would not be able to see it at all.

Even if the Commission had made the finding that Justice Brennan proposes, however, it is not certain that it would suffice. We do not share Justice Brennan's confidence that the Commission "should have little difficulty in the future in utilizing its expertise to demonstrate a specific connection between provisions for access and burdens on access," . . . that will avoid the effect of today's decision. We view the Fifth Amendment's Property Clause to be more than a pleading requirement, and compliance with it to be more than an exercise in cleverness and imagination. As indicated earlier, our cases describe the condition for abridgment of property rights through the police power as a "*substantial* advanc[ing]" of a legitimate state interest. We are inclined to be particularly careful about the adjective where the actual conveyance of property is made a condition to the lifting of a land-use restriction, since in that context there is heightened risk that the purpose is avoidance of the compensation requirement, rather than the stated police power objective.

We are left, then, with the Commission's justification for the access requirement unrelated to land-use regulation: The Commission notes that there are several existing provisions of pass and repass lateral access benefits already given by past Faria Beach Tract applicants as a result of prior coastal permit decisions. The access required as a condition of this permit is part of a comprehensive program to provide continuous public access along Faria Beach as the lots undergo development or redevelopment. . . .

That is simply an expression of the Commission's belief that the public interest will be served by a continuous strip of publicly accessible beach along the coast. The Commission may well be right that it is a good idea, but that does not establish that the Nollans (and other coastal residents) alone can be compelled to contribute to its realization. Rather, California is free to advance its "comprehensive program," if it wishes, by using its power of eminent domain for this "public purpose," but if it wants an easement across the Nollans' property, it must pay for it.

Reversed.

JUSTICE BRENNAN, with whom JUSTICE MARSHALL joins, dissenting.

Appellants in this case sought to construct a new dwelling on their beach lot that would both diminish visual access to the beach and move private development closer to the public tidelands.

The Commission reasonably concluded that such "buildout," both individually and cumulatively, threatens public access to the shore. It sought to offset this encroachment by obtaining assurance that the public may walk along the shoreline in order to gain access to the ocean. The Court finds this an illegitimate exercise of the police power, because it maintains that there is no reasonable relationship between the effect of the development and the condition imposed.

The first problem with this conclusion is that the Court imposes a standard of precision for the exercise of a State's police power that has been discredited for the better part of this century. Furthermore, even under the Court's cramped standard, the permit condition imposed in this case directly responds to the specific type of burden on access created by appellants' development. Finally, a review of those factors deemed most significant in takings analysis makes clear that the Commission's action implicates none of the concerns underlying the Takings Clause.

Even if we accept the Court's unusual demand for a precise match between the condition imposed and the specific type of burden on access created by the appellants, the State's action easily satisfies this requirement. First, the lateral access condition serves to dissipate the impression that the beach that lies behind the wall of homes along the shore is for private use only. It requires no exceptional imaginative powers to find plausible the Commission's point that the average person passing along the road in front of a phalanx of imposing permanent residences, including the appellants' new home, is likely to conclude that this particular portion of the shore is not open to the public. If, however, that person can see that numerous people are passing and repassing along the dry sand, this conveys the message that the beach is in fact open for use by the public. Furthermore, those persons who go down to the public beach a quarter-mile away will be able to look down the coastline and see that persons have continuous access to the tidelands, and will observe signs that proclaim the public's

right of access over the dry sand. The burden produced by the diminution in visual access— the impression that the beach is not open to the public—is thus directly alleviated by the provision for public access over the dry sand. The Court therefore has an unrealistically limited conception of what measures could reasonably be chosen to mitigate the burden produced by a diminution of visual access. . . .

The fact that the Commission's action is a legitimate exercise of the police power does not, of course, insulate it from a takings challenge, for when "regulation goes too far it will be recognized as a taking." Conventional takings analysis underscores the implausibility of the Court's holding, for it demonstrates that this exercise of California's police power implicates none of the concerns that underlie our takings jurisprudence. . . .

. . . The character of the regulation in this case is not unilateral government action, but a condition on approval of a development request submitted by appellants. The state has not sought to interfere with any pre-existing property interest, but has responded to appellants' proposal to intensify development on the coast. Appellants themselves chose to submit a new development application, and could claim no property interest in its approval. They were aware that approval of such development would be conditioned on preservation of adequate public access to the ocean. The State has initiated no action against appellants' property; had the Nollans' not proposed more intensive development in the coastal zone, they would never have been subject to the provision that they challenge.

Examination of the economic impact of the Commission's action reinforces the conclusion that no taking has occurred. Allowing appellants to intensify development along the coast in exchange for ensuring public access to the ocean is a classic instance of government action that produces a "reciprocity of advantage." . . . Appellants have been allowed to replace a one-story 521-square-foot beach home with a two-story 1,674-square-foot residence and an attached two-car garage, resulting in development covering 2,464 square feet of the lot. Such development obviously significantly increases the value of appellants' property;

appellants make no contention that this increase is offset by any diminution in value resulting from the deed restriction, much less that the restriction made the property less valuable than it would have been without the new construction. Furthermore, appellants gain an additional benefit from the Commission's permit condition program. They are able to walk along the beach beyond the confines of their own property only because the Commission has required deed restrictions as a condition of approving other new beach developments. Thus appellants benefit both as private landowners and as members of the public from the fact that new development permit requests are conditioned on preservation of public access. . . .

. . . State agencies therefore require considerable flexibility in responding to private desires for development in a way that guarantees the preservation of public access to the coast. They should be encouraged to regulate development in the context of the overall balance of competing uses of the shoreline. The Court today does precisely the opposite, overruling an eminently reasonable exercise of an expert state agency's judgment, substituting its own narrow view of how this balance should be struck. Its reasoning is hardly suited to the complex reality of natural resource protection in the 20th century. I can only hope that today's decision is an aberration, and that a broader vision ultimately prevails. I dissent.

Lucas v. South Carolina Coastal Council
505 U.S. 1003 (1992)

In 1986, David Lucas paid $975,000 for two residential lots on the Isle of Palms, a barrier island situated to the east of Charleston, South Carolina. He intended to build single-family houses on them, such as were found on the immediately adjacent lots. At the time, Lucas's lots were not subject to South Carolina's coastal-zone building-permit requirements. In 1988, however, the South Carolina Legislature enacted the Beachfront Management Act, which had the direct effect of prohibiting Lucas from erecting any permanent habitable structures on his land. He filed suit against the newly created Coastal Council in the South Carolina Court of Common Pleas, contending that the Beachfront Management Act's ban on construction effected a taking of his property under the Fifth and Fourteenth Amendments and therefore required the payment of just compensation. He did not deny the validity of the act as a lawful exercise of South Carolina's police power; he simply contended that the act deprived him of all "economically viable use" of his property and that he was entitled to compensation, regardless of whether the legislature had acted in furtherance of a legitimate police-power objective. The state trial court agreed, finding that the ban had rendered Lucas's parcels "valueless," and ordered the Coastal Council to pay Lucas "just compensation" in the amount of $1,232,387.50. The Supreme Court

of South Carolina reversed. Because Lucas had not attacked the validity of the statute as such, it found itself bound to accept the uncontested findings of the South Carolina Legislature that new construction in the coastal zone of the sort that Lucas intended threatened South Carolina's beaches. It concluded, on the basis of Mugler v. Kansas *(1887) and a long line of cases that followed it, that when regulation is necessary to prevent "harmful or noxious uses" of property akin to public nuisances, no compensation is owed under the Takings Clause, regardless of the regulation's effect on the property's value. The US Supreme Court granted certiorari.* Opinion of the Court: Scalia, Rehnquist, White, O'Connor, Thomas. Concurring in the judgment: Kennedy. Dissenting opinions: Blackmun; Stevens. Separate statement voting to dismiss the writ of certiorari: Souter.

JUSTICE SCALIA delivered the opinion of the Court.

. . . Prior to Justice Holmes' exposition in *Pennsylvania Coal Co. v. Mahon* (1922), it was generally thought that the Takings Clause reached only a "direct appropriation" of property, *Legal Tender Cases* (1871), or the functional equivalent of a "practical ouster of [the owner's] possession." *Transportation Co. v. Chicago* (1879). Justice Holmes recognized in

Mahon, however, that if the protection against physical appropriations of private property was to be meaningfully enforced, the government's power to redefine the range of interests included in the ownership of property was necessarily constrained by constitutional limits. If, instead, the uses of private property were subject to unbridled, uncompensated qualification under the police power, "the natural tendency of human nature [would be] to extend the qualification more and more until at last private property disappear[ed]." These considerations gave birth in that case to the oft-cited maxim that, "while property may be regulated to a certain extent, if regulation goes too far it will be recognized as a taking." Nevertheless, our decision in *Mahon* offered little insight into when, and under what circumstances, a given regulation would be seen as going "too far" for purposes of the Fifth Amendment. In 70-odd years of succeeding "regulatory takings" jurisprudence, we have generally eschewed any "set formula" for determining how far is too far, preferring to "engag[e] in . . . essentially *ad hoc,* factual inquiries," *Penn Central Transportation Co. v. New York City* (1978). We have, however, described at least two discrete categories of regulatory action as compensable without case-specific inquiry into the public interest advanced in support of the restraint. The first encompasses regulations that compel the property owner to suffer a physical "invasion" of his property. In general (at least with regard to permanent invasions), no matter how minute the intrusion, and no matter how weighty the public purpose behind it, we have required compensation. For example, in *Loretto v. Teleprompter Manhattan CATV Corp.* (1982), we determined that New York's law requiring landlords to allow television cable companies to emplace cable facilities in their apartment buildings constituted a taking, even though the facilities occupied at most only 1 1/2 cubic feet of the landlords' property.

The second situation in which we have found categorical treatment appropriate is where regulation denies all economically beneficial or productive use of land. As we have said on numerous occasions, the Fifth Amendment is violated when land-use regulation "does not substantially advance legitimate state interests or denies an owner economically viable use of his land." We have never set forth the justification for this rule. Perhaps it is simply, as Justice Brennan suggested, that total deprivation of beneficial use is, from the landowner's point of view, the equivalent of a physical appropriation.

. . . On the other side of the balance, affirmatively supporting a compensation requirement, is the fact that regulations that leave the owner of land without economically beneficial or productive options for its use—typically, as here, by requiring land to be left substantially in its natural state—carry with them a heightened risk that private property is being pressed into some form of public service under the guise of mitigating serious public harm. We think, in short, that there are good reasons for our frequently expressed belief that when the owner of real property has been called upon to sacrifice all economically beneficial uses in the name of the common good, that is, to leave his property economically idle, he has suffered a taking.

The trial court found Lucas's two beachfront lots to have been rendered valueless by respondent's enforcement of the coastal-zone construction ban. Under Lucas's theory of the case, which rested upon our "no economically viable use" statements, that finding entitled him to compensation. Lucas believed it unnecessary to take issue with either the purposes behind the Beachfront Management Act, or the means chosen by the South Carolina Legislature to effectuate those purposes. The South Carolina Supreme Court, however, thought otherwise. In its view, the Beachfront Management Act was no ordinary enactment, but involved an exercise of South Carolina's "police powers" to mitigate the harm to the public interest that petitioner's use of his land might occasion. By neglecting to dispute the findings enumerated in the Act or otherwise to challenge the legislature's purposes, petitioner "concede[d] that the beach/dune area of South Carolina's shores is an extremely valuable public resource; that the erection of new construction, *inter alia,* contributes to the erosion and destruction of this public resource; and that discouraging new construction in close proximity to the beach/dune area is necessary to prevent a great public harm." In the court's view, these concessions brought petitioner's challenge within a long line of this Court's cases sustaining against Due Process and Takings Clause challenges the State's use of its "police powers" to enjoin a property owner from activities akin to public nuisances. . . .

It is correct that many of our prior opinions have suggested that "harmful or noxious uses" of property may be proscribed by government regulation without the requirement of compensation. However, we think the South Carolina Supreme Court was too quick to conclude that that principle decides the present case. . . .

A fortiori the legislature's recitation of a noxious-use justification cannot be the basis for departing from our categorical rule that total regulatory takings must be compensated. If it were, departure would virtually always be allowed. The South Carolina Supreme Court's approach would essentially nullify *Mahon's* affirmation of limits to the noncompensable exercise of the police power. . . .

Where the State seeks to sustain regulation that deprives land of all economically beneficial use, we think it may resist compensation only if the logically antecedent inquiry into the nature of the owner's estate shows that the proscribed use interests were not part of his title to begin with. This accords, we think, with our "takings" jurisprudence, which has traditionally been guided by the understandings of our citizens regarding the content of, and the State's power over, the "bundle of rights" that they acquire when they obtain title to property. Confiscatory regulations, i.e., regulations that prohibit all economically beneficial use of land, cannot be newly legislated or decreed (without compensation), but must inhere in the title itself, in the restrictions that background principles of the State's law of property and nuisance already place upon land ownership. . . .

On this analysis, the owner of a lake bed, for example, would not be entitled to compensation when he is denied the requisite permit to engage in a landfilling operation that would have the effect of flooding others' land. Nor the corporate owner of a nuclear generating plant, when it is directed to remove all improvements from its land upon discovery that the plant sits astride an earthquake fault. Such regulatory action may well have the effect of eliminating the land's only economically productive use, but it does not proscribe a productive use that was previously permissible under relevant property and nuisance principles. The use of these properties for what are now expressly prohibited purposes was always unlawful, and (subject to other constitutional limitations) it was open to the State at any point to make the implication of those background principles of nuisance and property law explicit. When, however, a regulation that declares "off-limits" all economically productive or beneficial uses of land goes beyond what the relevant background principles would dictate, compensation must be paid to sustain it. The "total taking" inquiry we require today will ordinarily entail (as the application of state nuisance law ordinarily entails) analysis of, among other things, the degree of harm to public lands and resources, or adjacent private property, posed by the claimant's proposed activities, the social value of the claimant's activities and their suitability to the locality in question, and the relative ease with which the alleged harm can be avoided through measures taken by the claimant and the government (or adjacent private landowners) alike. The fact that a particular use has long been engaged in by similarly situated owners ordinarily imports a lack of any common-law prohibition. So also does the fact that other landowners, similarly situated, are permitted to continue the use denied to the claimant.

We emphasize that to win its case South Carolina must do more than proffer the legislature's declaration that the uses Lucas desires are inconsistent with the public interest. As we have said, a "State, by *ipse dixit,* may not transform private property into public property without compensation. . . ." Instead, as it would be required to do if it sought to restrain Lucas in a common-law action for public nuisance, South Carolina must identify background principles of nuisance and property law that prohibit the uses he now intends in the circumstances in which the property is presently found. Only on this showing can the State fairly claim that, in proscribing all such beneficial uses, the Beachfront Management Act is taking nothing. . . .

The judgment is reversed and the cause remanded for proceedings not inconsistent with this opinion.

JUSTICE BLACKMUN, dissenting.

. . . This Court repeatedly has recognized the ability of government, in certain circumstances, to regulate property without compensation no matter how adverse the financial effect on the owner may be. More than a century ago, the Court explicitly upheld the right of States to prohibit uses of property injurious to public health, safety, or welfare without paying compensation: "A prohibition simply upon the use of property for purposes that are declared, by valid legislation, to be injurious to the health, morals, or safety of the community, cannot, in any just sense, be deemed a taking or an appropriation of property." *Mugler v. Kansas* (1887). On this basis, the Court upheld an ordinance effectively prohibiting operation of a previously lawful brewery, although the "establishments will become of no value as property."

Mugler was only the beginning in a long line of cases. In none of the cases did the Court suggest that the right of a State to prohibit certain activities without paying compensation turned on the availability of some residual valuable use. Instead, the cases depended on whether the government interest was sufficient to prohibit the activity, given the significant private cost.

Koontz v. St. Johns River Water Management District
570 U.S. ___ (2013)

The estate of Coy Koontz, Sr. sought permits to develop a section of his property from the St. Johns River Water Management District, which, under Florida law, requires permit applicants wishing to build on wetlands to offset the resulting environmental damage. Koontz offered to mitigate the environmental effects of his development proposal by deeding to the District a conservation easement on nearly three-quarters of his property. The District rejected Koontz's proposal and informed him that it would approve construction only if he (1) reduced the size of his development and deeded to the District a conservation easement on the resulting larger remainder of his property or (2) hired contractors to make improvements to District-owned wetlands several miles away. Believing the District's demands to be excessive in light of the environmental effects his proposal would have caused, Koontz filed suit under a state law that provides money damages for agency action that is an "unreasonable exercise of the state's police power constituting a taking without just compensation." The trial court found the District's actions unlawful because they failed the requirements of Nollan v. California Coastal Commission *(1987) and* Dolan v. City of Tigard *(1994). Those cases held that the government may not condition the approval of a land-use permit on the owner's relinquishment of a portion of his property unless there is a nexus and rough propor-* *tionality between the government's demand and the effects of the proposed land use. The District Court of Appeal affirmed, but the State Supreme Court reversed on two grounds. First, it held that petitioner's claim failed because, unlike in* Nollan *or* Dolan, *the District denied the application; and second, it held that a demand for money cannot give rise to a claim under* Nollan *and* Dolan. *Koontz petitioned the Supreme Court, which granted certiorari.* Opinion of the Court: Alito, Roberts, Scalia, Kennedy, Thomas. Dissenting opinion: Kagan, Ginsburg, Breyer, Sotomayor.

JUSTICE ALITO delivered the opinion of the Court.

Our decisions in *Nollan v. California Coastal Commission* (1987) and *Dolan v. City of Tigard* (1994) provide important protection against the misuse of the power of land-use regulation. In those cases, we held that a unit of government may not condition the approval of a land-use permit on the owner's relinquishment of a portion of his property unless there is a "nexus" and "rough proportionality" between the government's demand and the effects of the proposed land use. In this case, the St. Johns River Water Management District (District) believes that it circumvented *Nollan* and *Dolan* because of the way in which it structured its handling of a permit application submitted by Coy Koontz, Sr., whose estate is represented in this Court by Coy Koontz, Jr. The District did not approve his application on the condition that he surrender an interest in his land. Instead, the District, after suggesting that he could obtain approval by signing over such an interest, denied his application because he refused to yield. The Florida Supreme Court blessed this maneuver and thus effectively interred those important decisions. Because we conclude that *Nollan* and *Dolan* cannot be evaded in this way, the Florida Supreme Court's decision must be reversed.

I

A

In 1972, petitioner purchased an undeveloped 14.9-acre tract of land on the south side of Florida State Road 50, a divided four-lane highway east of Orlando. The property is located less than 1,000 feet from that road's intersection with Florida State Road 408, a tolled expressway that is one of Orlando's major thoroughfares. . . . Although largely classified as wetlands by the State, the northern section drains well. . . .

In 1984, in an effort to protect the State's rapidly diminishing wetlands, the Florida Legislature passed the Warren S. Henderson Wetlands Protection Act, which made it illegal for anyone to "dredge or fill in, on, or over surface waters" without a Wetlands Resource Management (WRM) permit. Under the Henderson Act, permit applicants are required to provide "reasonable assurance" that proposed construction on wetlands is "not contrary to the public interest," as defined by an enumerated list of criteria. Consistent with the Henderson Act, the St. Johns River Water Management District, the district with jurisdiction over petitioner's land, requires that permit applicants wishing to build on wetlands offset the resulting environmental damage by creating, enhancing, or preserving wetlands elsewhere.

Petitioner decided to develop the 3.7-acre northern section of his property, and in 1994 he applied to the District for MSSW and WRM permits. Under his proposal, petitioner would have raised the elevation of the north-

ernmost section of his land to make it suitable for a building, graded the land from the southern edge of the building site . . . , and installed a dry-bed pond for retaining and gradually releasing stormwater runoff from the building and its parking lot. To mitigate the environmental effects of his proposal, petitioner offered to foreclose any possible future development of the approximately 11-acre southern section of his land by deeding to the District a conservation easement on that portion of his property.

The District considered the 11-acre conservation easement to be inadequate, and it informed petitioner that it would approve construction only if he agreed to one of two concessions. First, the District proposed that petitioner reduce the size of his development to 1 acre and deed to the District a conservation easement on the remaining 13.9 acres. To reduce the development area, the District suggested that petitioner could eliminate the dry-bed pond from his proposal and instead install a more costly subsurface stormwater management system beneath the building site. The District also suggested that petitioner install retaining walls rather than gradually sloping the land from the building site down to the elevation of the rest of his property to the south.

In the alternative, the District told petitioner that he could proceed with the development as proposed, building on 3.7 acres and deeding a conservation easement to the government on the remainder of the property, if he also agreed to hire contractors to make improvements to District-owned land several miles away. Specifically, petitioner could pay to replace culverts on one parcel or fill in ditches on another. Either of those projects would have enhanced approximately 50 acres of District-owned wetlands. When the District asks permit applicants to fund offsite mitigation work, its policy is never to require any particular offsite project, and it did not do so here. Instead, the District said that it "would also favorably consider" alternatives to its suggested offsite mitigation projects if petitioner proposed something "equivalent."

Believing the District's demands for mitigation to be excessive in light of the environmental effects that his building proposal would have caused, petitioner filed suit in state court. Among other claims, he argued that he was entitled to relief under Fla. Stat. §373.617(2), which allows owners to recover "monetary damages" if a state agency's action is "an unreasonable exercise of the state's police power constituting a taking without just compensation."

II

A

We have said in a variety of contexts that "the government may not deny a benefit to a person because he exercises a constitutional right." *Regan v. Taxation With Representation of Washington* (1983). . . . *Nollan* and *Dolan* "involve a special application" of this doctrine that protects the Fifth Amendment right to just compensation for property the government takes when owners apply for land-use permits. Our decisions in those cases reflect two realities of the permitting process. The first is that land-use permit applicants are especially vulnerable to the type of coercion that the unconstitutional conditions doctrine prohibits because the government often has broad discretion to deny a permit that is worth far more than property it would like to take. By conditioning a building permit on the owner's deeding over a public right-of-way, for example, the government can pressure an owner into voluntarily giving up property for which the Fifth Amendment would otherwise require just compensation. So long as the building permit is more valuable than any just compensation the owner could hope to receive for the right-of-way, the owner is likely to accede to the government's demand, no matter how unreasonable. Extortionate demands of this sort frustrate the Fifth Amendment right to just compensation, and the unconstitutional conditions doctrine prohibits them.

A second reality of the permitting process is that many proposed land uses threaten to impose costs on the public that dedications of property can offset. Where a building proposal would substantially increase traffic congestion, for example, officials might condition permit approval on the owner's agreement to deed over the land needed to widen a public road. Respondent argues that a similar rationale justifies the exaction at issue here: petitioner's proposed construction project, it submits, would destroy wetlands on his property, and in order to compensate for this loss, respondent demands that he enhance wetlands elsewhere. Insisting that landowners internalize the negative externalities of their conduct is a hallmark of responsible land-use policy, and we have long sustained such regulations against constitutional attack.

Nollan and *Dolan* accommodate both realities by allowing the government to condition approval of a permit on the dedication of property to the public so long as there is a "nexus" and "rough proportionality" between the property that the government demands and the social costs of the applicant's proposal. Our precedents thus enable permitting authorities to insist that applicants bear the full costs of their proposals while still forbidding the government from engaging in "out-and-out . . . extortion" that would thwart the Fifth Amendment right to just compensation. Under *Nollan* and *Dolan* the government may choose whether and how a permit applicant is required to mitigate the impacts of a proposed development, but it may not leverage its legitimate interest in mitigation to pursue governmental ends that lack an essential nexus and rough proportionality to those impacts.

B

The principles that undergird our decisions in *Nollan* and *Dolan* do not change depending on whether the government approves a permit on the condition that the applicant turn over property or denies a permit because the applicant refuses to do so. We have often concluded that denials of governmental benefits were impermissible under the unconstitutional conditions doctrine. In so holding, we have recognized that regardless of whether the government ultimately succeeds in pressuring someone into forfeiting a constitutional right, the unconstitutional conditions doctrine forbids burdening the Constitution's enumerated rights by coercively withholding benefits from those who exercise them.

A contrary rule would be especially untenable in this case because it would enable the government to evade the limitations of *Nollan* and

Dolan simply by phrasing its demands for property as conditions precedent to permit approval. Under the Florida Supreme Court's approach, a government order stating that a permit is "approved if" the owner turns over property would be subject to *Nollan* and *Dolan*, but an identical order that uses the words "denied until" would not. Our unconstitutional conditions cases have long refused to attach significance to the distinction between conditions precedent and conditions subsequent. To do so here would effectively render *Nollan* and *Dolan* a dead letter.

The Florida Supreme Court puzzled over how the government's demand for property can violate the Takings Clause even though "no property of any kind was ever taken," but the unconstitutional conditions doctrine provides a ready answer. Extortionate demands for property in the land-use permitting context run afoul of the Takings Clause not because they take property but because they impermissibly burden the right not to have property taken without just compensation. As in other unconstitutional conditions cases in which someone refuses to cede a constitutional right in the face of coercive pressure, the impermissible denial of a governmental benefit is a constitutionally cognizable injury.

Nor does it make a difference, as respondent suggests, that the government might have been able to deny petitioner's application outright without giving him the option of securing a permit by agreeing to spend money to improve public lands. Virtually all of our unconstitutional conditions cases involve a gratuitous governmental benefit of some kind. Yet we have repeatedly rejected the argument that if the government need not confer a benefit at all, it can withhold the benefit because someone refuses to give up constitutional rights. Even if respondent would have been entirely within its rights in denying the permit for some other reason, that greater authority does not imply a lesser power to condition permit approval on petitioner's forfeiture of his constitutional rights. . . .

III

We turn to the Florida Supreme Court's alternative holding that petitioner's claim fails because respondent asked him to spend money

rather than give up an easement on his land. A predicate for any unconstitutional conditions claim is that the government could not have constitutionally ordered the person asserting the claim to do what it attempted to pressure that person into doing. For that reason, we began our analysis in both *Nollan* and *Dolan* by observing that if the government had directly seized the easements it sought to obtain through the permitting process, it would have committed a per se taking. The Florida Supreme Court held that petitioner's claim fails at this first step because the subject of the exaction at issue here was money rather than a more tangible interest in real property. Respondent and the dissent take the same position. . . .

. . . [I]f we accepted this argument it would be very easy for land-use permitting officials to evade the limitations of *Nollan* and *Dolan*. Because the government need only provide a permit applicant with one alternative that satisfies the nexus and rough proportionality standards, a permitting authority wishing to exact an easement could simply give the owner a choice of either surrendering an easement or making a payment equal to the easement's value. Such so-called "in lieu of" fees are utterly commonplace, and they are functionally equivalent to other types of land use exactions. For that reason . . . , we reject respondent's argument and hold that so-called "monetary exactions" must satisfy the nexus and rough proportionality requirements of *Nollan* and *Dolan*.

* * *

We hold that the government's demand for property from a land-use permit applicant must satisfy the requirements of *Nollan* and *Dolan* even when the government denies the permit and even when its demand is for money. The Court expresses no view on the merits of petitioner's claim that respondent's actions here failed to comply with the principles set forth in this opinion and those two cases. The Florida Supreme Court's judgment is reversed, and this case is remanded for further proceedings not inconsistent with this opinion.

JUSTICE KAGAN, with whom JUSTICE GINSBURG, JUSTICE BREYER, and JUSTICE SOTOMAYOR join, dissenting.

In the paradigmatic case triggering review under *Nollan* and *Dolan*, the government approves a building permit on the condition that the landowner relinquish an interest in real property, like an easement. The significant legal questions that the Court resolves today are whether *Nollan* and *Dolan* also apply when that case is varied in two ways. First, what if the government does not approve the permit, but instead demands that the condition be fulfilled before it will do so? Second, what if the condition entails not transferring real property, but simply paying money? . . .

I think the Court gets the first question it addresses right. The *Nollan-Dolan* standard applies not only when the government approves a development permit conditioned on the owner's conveyance of a property interest (i.e., imposes a condition subsequent), but also when the government denies a permit until the owner meets the condition (i.e., imposes a condition precedent). That means an owner may challenge the denial of a permit on the ground that the government's condition lacks the "nexus" and "rough proportionality" to the development's social costs that *Nollan* and *Dolan* require. Still, the condition-subsequent and condition-precedent situations differ in an important way. When the government grants a permit subject to the relinquishment of real property, and that condition does not satisfy *Nollan* and *Dolan*, then the government has taken the property and must pay just compensation under the Fifth Amendment. But when the government denies a permit because an owner has refused to accede to that same demand, nothing has actually been taken. The owner is entitled to have the improper condition removed; and he may be entitled to a monetary remedy created by state law for imposing such a condition; but he cannot be entitled to constitutional compensation for a taking of property. So far, we all agree.

Our core disagreement concerns the second question the Court addresses. The majority extends *Nollan* and *Dolan* to cases in which the government conditions a permit not on the transfer of real property, but instead on the payment or expenditure of money. . . . The boundaries of the majority's new rule are uncertain. But it threatens to subject a vast array of land-use regulations, applied daily in States and localities throughout the country, to heightened constitutional scrutiny. I would not embark on so unwise an adventure, and would affirm the Florida Supreme Court's decision.

I also would affirm for two independent reasons establishing that Koontz cannot get the money damages he seeks. First, respondent St. Johns River Water Management District (District) never demanded anything (including money) in exchange for a permit; the *Nollan-Dolan* standard therefore does not come into play (even assuming that test applies to demands for money). Second, no taking occurred in this case because Koontz never acceded to a demand (even had there been one), and so no property changed hands; as just noted, Koontz therefore cannot claim just compensation under the Fifth Amendment. The majority does not take issue with my first conclusion, and affirmatively agrees with my second. But the majority thinks Koontz might still be entitled to money damages, and remands to the Florida Supreme Court on that question. I do not see how, and expect that court will so rule.

I

. . . Koontz claims that the District demanded that he spend money to improve public wetlands, not that he hand over a real property interest. I assume for now that the District made that demand (although I think it did not). The key question then is: Independent of the permitting process, does requiring a person to pay money to the government, or spend money on its behalf, constitute a taking requiring just compensation? Only if the answer is yes does the *Nollan-Dolan* test apply. . . . [But] a requirement that a person pay money to repair public wetlands is not a taking. Such an order does not affect a "specific and identified propert[y] or property right"; it simply "imposes an obligation to perform an act" (the improvement of wetlands) that costs money. To be sure, when a person spends money on the government's behalf, or pays money directly to the government, it "will reduce [his] net worth"—but that "can be said of any law which has an adverse economic effect" on someone. Because the government is merely imposing a "general liability" to pay money—and therefore is "indifferent as to how the regulated entity elects to comply or the property it uses to do so"—the order to repair wetlands, viewed independent of the permitting process, does not constitute a taking. And that means the order does not trigger the *Nollan-Dolan* test, because it does not force Koontz to relinquish a constitutional right. . . .

The majority's approach . . . threatens significant practical harm. By applying *Nollan* and *Dolan* to permit conditions requiring monetary payments—with no express limitation except as to taxes—the majority extends the Takings Clause, with its notoriously "difficult" and "perplexing" standards, into the very heart of local land-use regulation and service delivery. Cities and towns across the nation impose many kinds of permitting fees every day. Some enable a government to mitigate a new development's impact on the community, like increased traffic or pollution—or destruction of wetlands. Others cover the direct costs of providing services like sewage or water to the development. Still others are meant to limit the number of landowners who engage in a certain activity, as fees for liquor licenses do. All now must meet *Nollan* and *Dolan*'s nexus and proportionality tests. The Federal Constitution thus will decide whether one town is overcharging for sewage, or another is setting the price to sell liquor too high. And the flexibility of state and local governments to take the most routine actions to enhance their communities will diminish accordingly. That problem becomes still worse because the majority's distinction between monetary "exactions" and taxes is so hard to apply. The majority acknowledges, as it must, that taxes are not takings. But once the majority decides that a simple demand to pay money—the sort of thing often viewed as a tax—can count as an impermissible "exaction," how is anyone to tell the two apart? . . .

At bottom, the majority's analysis seems to grow out of a yen for a prophylactic rule: Unless *Nollan* and *Dolan* apply to monetary demands, the majority worries, "land-use permitting officials" could easily "evade the limitations" on exaction of real property interests that those decisions impose. But that is a prophylaxis in search of a problem. No one has presented evidence that in the many States declining to apply heightened scrutiny to permitting fees, local officials routinely short-circuit *Nollan* and *Dolan* to extort the surrender of real property interests having no relation to a development's costs. And if officials were to impose a fee as a contrivance to take an easement (or other real property right), then a court could indeed apply *Nollan* and *Dolan*. That situation does not call for a rule extending, as the majority's does, to all monetary exactions. Finally, a court can use the *Penn Central* framework, the Due Process Clause, and (in many places) state law to protect against monetary demands, whether or not imposed to evade *Nollan* and *Dolan*, that simply "go too far."

In sum, *Nollan* and *Dolan* restrain governments from using the permitting process to do what the Takings Clause would otherwise prevent—i.e., take a specific property interest without just compensation. Those cases have no application when governments impose a general financial obligation as part of the permitting process. . . . By extending *Nollan* and *Dolan*'s heightened scrutiny to a simple payment demand, the majority threatens the heartland of local land-use regulation and service delivery, at a bare minimum depriving state and local governments of "necessary predictability." That decision is unwarranted—and deeply unwise. I would keep *Nollan* and *Dolan* in their intended sphere and affirm the Florida Supreme Court. . . .

III

Nollan and *Dolan* are important decisions, designed to curb governments from using their power over land-use permitting to extract for free what the Takings Clause would otherwise require them to pay for. But for no fewer than three independent reasons, this case does not present that problem. First and foremost, the government commits a taking only when it appropriates a specific property interest, not when it requires a person to pay or spend money. Here, the District never took or threatened such an interest; it tried to extract from Koontz solely a commitment to spend money to repair public wetlands. Second, *Nollan* and *Dolan* can operate only when the government makes a demand of the permit applicant; the decisions' prerequisite, in other words, is a condition. Here, the District never made such a demand: It informed Koontz that his applications did not meet legal requirements; it offered suggestions for bringing those applications into compliance; and it solicited further proposals from Koontz to achieve the same end. That is not the stuff of which an unconstitutional condition is made. And third, the Florida statute at issue here does not, in any event, offer a damages remedy for imposing such a condition. It provides relief only for a consummated taking, which did not occur here. The majority's errors here are consequential. The majority turns a broad array of local land-use regulations into federal constitutional questions. It deprives state and local governments of the flexibility they need to enhance their communities—to ensure environmentally sound and economically productive development. It places courts smack in the middle of the most everyday local government activity. As those consequences play out across the country, I believe the Court will rue today's decision. I respectfully dissent.

The Constitution of the United States of America

We the People of the United States, in Order to form a more perfect Union, establish Justice, insure domestic Tranquility, provide for the common defence, promote the general Welfare, and secure the Blessings of Liberty to ourselves and our Posterity, do ordain and establish this CONSTITUTION for the United States of America.

ARTICLE I

SECTION 1. All legislative Powers herein granted shall be vested in a Congress of the United States, which shall consist of a Senate and House of Representatives.

SECTION 2. [1] The House of Representatives shall be composed of Members chosen every second Year by the People of the several States, and the Electors in each State shall have the Qualifications requisite for Electors of the most numerous Branch of the State Legislature.

[2] No person shall be a Representative who shall not have attained to the Age of twenty five Years, and been seven Years a Citizen of the United States, and who shall not, when elected, be an Inhabitant of that State in which he shall be chosen.

[3] Representatives and direct Taxes shall be apportioned among the several States which may be included within this Union, according to their respective Numbers, which shall be determined by adding to the whole Number of free Persons, including those bound to Service for a Term of Years, and excluding Indians not taxed, three fifths of all other Persons. The actual Enumeration shall be made within three Years after the first Meeting of the Congress of the United States, and within every subsequent Term of ten Years, in such Manner as they shall by Law direct. The Number of Representatives shall not exceed one for every thirty Thousand, but each State shall have at Least one Representative; and until such enumeration shall be made, the State of New Hampshire shall be entitled to chuse three, Massachusetts eight, Rhode-Island and Providence Plantations one, Connecticut five, New-York six, New Jersey four, Pennsylvania eight, Delaware one, Maryland six, Virginia ten, North Carolina five, South Carolina five, and Georgia three.

[4] When vacancies happen in the Representation from any State, the Executive

Authority thereof shall issue Writs of Election to fill such Vacancies.

[5] The House of Representatives shall chuse their Speaker and other Officers; and shall have the sole Power of Impeachment.

SECTION 3. [1] The Senate of the United States shall be composed of two Senators from each State, chosen by the Legislature thereof, for six Years; and each Senator shall have one Vote.

[2] Immediately after they shall be assembled in Consequence of the first Election, they shall be divided as equally as may be into three Classes. The Seats of the Senators of the first Class shall be vacated at the Expiration of the Second Year, of the second Class at the Expiration of the fourth Year, and of the third Class at the Expiration of the sixth Year, so that one third may be chosen every second Year; and if Vacancies happen by Resignation, or otherwise, during the Recess of the Legislature of any State, the Executive thereof may make temporary Appointments until the next Meeting of the Legislature, which shall then fill such Vacancies.

[3] No person shall be a Senator who shall not have attained to the Age of thirty Years, and been nine Years a Citizen of the United States, and who shall not, when elected, be an Inhabitant of that State for which he shall be chosen.

[4] The Vice President of the United States shall be President of the Senate, but shall have no Vote, unless they be equally divided.

[5] The Senate shall chuse their other Officers, and also a President pro tempore, in the absence of the Vice President, or when he shall exercise the Office of the President of the United States.

[6] The Senate shall have the sole Power to try all Impeachments. When sitting for that Purpose, they shall be on Oath or Affirmation. When the President of the United States is tried, the Chief Justice shall preside: And no Person shall be convicted without the Concurrence of two thirds of the Members present.

[7] Judgment in Cases of Impeachment shall not extend further than to removal from Office, and disqualification to hold and enjoy any Office of honor, Trust or Profit under the United States: but the Party convicted shall nevertheless be liable and subject to Indictment, Trial, Judgment and Punishment, according to Law.

SECTION 4. [1] The Times, Places and Manner of holding Elections for Senators and Representatives, shall be prescribed in each State by the Legislature thereof; but the Congress may at any time by Law make or alter such Regulations, except as to the Places of chusing Senators.

[2] The Congress shall assemble at least once in every Year, and such Meeting shall be on the first Monday in December, unless they shall by Law appoint a different Day.

SECTION 5. [1] Each House shall be the Judge of the Elections, Returns and Qualifications of its own Members, and a Majority of each shall constitute a Quorum to do Business, but a smaller Number may adjourn from day to day, and may be authorized to compel the Attendance of absent Members, in such Manner, and under such Penalties as each House may provide.

[2] Each House may determine the Rules of its Proceedings, punish its Members for disorderly Behavior, and, with the Concurrence of two thirds, expel a Member.

[3] Each House shall keep a Journal of its Proceedings, and from time to time publish the same, excepting such Parts as may in their Judgment require Secrecy; and the Yeas and Nays of the Members of either House on any question shall, at the Desire of one fifth of those Present, be entered on the Journal.

[4] Neither House, during the Session of Congress, shall, without the Consent of the other, adjourn for more than three days, nor to any other Place than that in which the two Houses shall be sitting.

SECTION 6. [1] The Senators and Representatives shall receive a Compensation for their Services, to be ascertained by Law, and paid out of the Treasury of the United States. They shall in all Cases, except Treason, Felony and Breach of the Peace, be privileged from Arrest during their Attendance at the Session of their respective Houses, and in going to and returning from the same; and for any Speech or Debate in either House, they shall not be questioned in any other Place.

[2] No Senator or Representative shall, during the Time for which he was elected, be appointed to any civil Office under the Authority of the United States, which shall have been created, or the Emoluments whereof shall have been encreased during such time; and no Person holding any Office under the United States, shall be a Member of either House during his Continuance in Office.

SECTION 7. [1] All Bills for raising Revenue shall originate in the House of Representatives; but the Senate may propose or concur with Amendments as on other Bills.

[2] Every Bill which shall have passed the House of Representatives and the Senate, shall, before it become a Law, be presented to the President of the United States: If he approve he shall sign it, but if not he shall return it, with his Objections to that House in which it shall have originated, who shall enter the Objections at large on their Journal, and proceed to reconsider it. If after such Reconsideration two thirds of that House shall agree to pass the Bill, it shall be sent, together with the Objections, to the other House, by which it shall likewise be reconsidered, and if approved by two thirds of that House, it shall become a Law. But in all such Cases the Votes of both Houses shall be determined by Yeas and Nays, and the Names of the Persons voting for and against the Bill shall be entered on the Journal of each House respectively. If any Bill shall not be returned by the President within ten Days (Sundays excepted) after it shall have been presented to him, the Same shall be a Law, in like Manner as if he had signed it, unless the Congress by their Adjournment prevent its Return, in which Case it shall not be a Law.

[3] Every Order, Resolution, or Vote to which the Concurrence of the Senate and House of Representatives may be necessary (except on a question of Adjournment) shall be presented to the President of the United States;

and before the Same shall take Effect, shall be approved by him, or being disapproved by him, shall be repassed by two thirds of the Senate and House of Representatives, according to the Rules and Limitations prescribed in the Case of a Bill.

SECTION 8. The Congress shall have Power

[1] To lay and collect Taxes, Duties, Imposts and Excises, to pay the Debts and provide for the common Defence and general Welfare of the United States, but all Duties, Imposts and Excises shall be uniform throughout the United States;

[2] To borrow Money on the credit of the United States;

[3] To regulate Commerce with foreign Nations, and among the several States, and with the Indian Tribes;

[4] To establish an uniform Rule of Naturalization, and uniform Laws on the subject of Bankruptcies throughout the United States;

[5] To coin Money, regulate the Value thereof, and of foreign Coin, and fix the Standard of Weights and Measures;

[6] To provide for the Punishment of counterfeiting the Securities and current Coin of the United States;

[7] To Establish Post Offices and post Roads;

[8] To promote the Progress of Science and useful Arts, by securing for limited Times to Authors and Inventors the exclusive Right to their respective Writings and Discoveries;

[9] To constitute Tribunals inferior to the supreme Court;

[10] To define and punish Piracies and Felonies committed on the high Seas, and Offenses against the Law of Nations;

[11] To declare War, grant Letters of Marque and Reprisal, and make Rules concerning Captures on Land and Water;

[12] To raise and support Armies, but no Appropriation of Money to that Use shall be for a longer Term than two Years;

[13] To provide and maintain a Navy;

[14] To make Rules for the Government and Regulation of the land and naval Forces;

[15] To provide for calling forth the Militia to execute the Laws of the Union, suppress Insurrections and repel Invasions;

[16] To provide for organizing, arming, and disciplining, the Militia, and for Governing such Part of them as may be employed in the Service of the United States, reserving to the States respectively, the Appointment of the Officers, and the Authority of training the Militia according to the discipline prescribed by Congress;

[17] To exercise exclusive Legislation in all Cases whatsoever, over such District (not exceeding ten Miles square) as may, by Cession of particular States, and the Acceptance of Congress, become the Seat of the Government of the United States, and to exercise like Authority over all Places purchased by the Consent of the Legislature of the State in which the Same shall be, for the Erection of Forts, Magazines, Arsenals, dock-Yards, and other needful Buildings;—And

[18] To make all Laws which shall be necessary and proper for carrying into Execution the foregoing Powers, and all other Powers vested by this Constitution in the Government of the United States, or in any Department or Officer thereof.

SECTION 9. [1] The Migration or Importation of Such Persons as any of the States now existing shall think proper to admit, shall not be prohibited by the Congress prior to the Year one thousand eight hundred and eight, but a Tax or duty may be imposed on such Importation, not exceeding ten dollars for each Person.

[2] The Privilege of the Writ of *Habeas Corpus* shall not be suspended, unless when in Cases of Rebellion or Invasion the public Safety may require it.

[3] No Bill of Attainder or *ex post facto* Law shall be passed.

[4] No Capitation, or other direct, Tax shall be laid, unless in Proportion to the Census or enumeration herein before directed to be taken.

[5] No Tax or Duty shall be laid on Articles exported from any State.

[6] No preference shall be given by any Regulation of Commerce or Revenue to the Ports of one State over those of another; nor shall Vessels bound to, or from, one State be obliged to enter, clear, or pay Duties in another.

[7] No money shall be drawn from the Treasury, but in Consequence of Appropriations made by Law; and a regular Statement and Account of the Receipts and Expenditures of all public Money shall be published from time to time.

[8] No Title of Nobility shall be granted by the United States: And no Person holding any Office of Profit or Trust under them, shall, without the Consent of the Congress, accept of any present, Emolument, Office, or Title, of any kind whatever, from any King, Prince, or foreign State.

SECTION 10. [1] No State shall enter into any Treaty, Alliance, or Confederation; grant Letters of Marque and Reprisal; coin Money; emit Bills of Credit; make any Thing but gold and silver Coin a Tender in Payment of Debts; pass any Bill of Attainder, *ex post facto* Law, or Law impairing the Obligation of Contracts, or grant any Title of Nobility.

[2] No State shall, without the Consent of the Congress, lay any Imposts or Duties on Imports or Exports, except what may be absolutely necessary for executing its inspection Laws: and the net Produce of all Duties and Imposts, laid by any State on Imports or Exports, shall be for the Use of the Treasury of the United States; and all such Laws shall be subject to the Revision and Control of the Congress.

[3] No State shall, without the Consent of Congress, lay any Duty of Tonnage, keep Troops, or Ships of War in time of Peace, enter into any Agreement or Compact with another State, or with a foreign Power, or engage in War, unless actually invaded, or in such imminent Danger as will not admit of delay.

ARTICLE II

SECTION 1. [1] The executive Power shall be vested in a President of the United States of America. He shall hold his Office during the Term of four Years, and together with the Vice President, chosen for the same Term, be elected, as follows:

[2] Each State shall appoint, in such Manner as the Legislature thereof may direct, a Number of Electors, equal to the whole Number of Senators and Representatives to which the

State may be entitled in the Congress: but no Senator or Representative, or Person holding an Office of Trust or Profit under the United States, shall be appointed an Elector.

[3] The Electors shall meet in their respective States, and vote by Ballot for two Persons, of whom one at least shall not be an Inhabitant of the same State with themselves. And they shall make a List of all the Persons voted for, and of the Number of Votes for each; which List they shall sign and certify, and transmit sealed to the Seat of the Government of the United States, directed to the President of the Senate. The President of the Senate shall, in the Presence of the Senate and House of Representatives, open all the Certificates, and the Votes shall then be counted. The Person having the greatest Number of Votes shall be the President, if such Number be a Majority of the whole Number of Electors appointed; and if there be more than one who have such Majority, and have an equal Number of Votes, then the House of Representatives shall immediately chuse by Ballot one of them for President; and if no Person have a Majority, then from the five highest on the List the said House shall in like Manner chuse the President. But in chusing the President, the Votes shall be taken by States, the Representation from each State having one Vote; A quorum for this purpose shall consist of a Member or Members from two thirds of the States, and a Majority of all the States shall be necessary to a Choice. In every Case, after the Choice of the President, the Person having the greatest Number of Votes of the Electors shall be the Vice President. But if there should remain two or more who have equal Votes, the Senate shall chuse from them by Ballot the Vice President.

[4] The Congress may determine the Time of chusing the Electors, and the Day on which they shall give their Votes; which Day shall be the same throughout the United States.

[5] No person except a natural born Citizen, or a Citizen of the United States, at the time of the Adoption of this Constitution, shall be eligible to the Office of President; neither shall any Person be eligible to that Office who shall not have attained to the Age of thirty five Years, and been fourteen Years a Resident within the United States.

[6] In Case of the Removal of the President from Office, or of his Death, Resignation, or Inability to discharge the Powers and Duties of the said Office, the Same shall devolve on the Vice President, and the Congress may by Law provide for the Case of Removal, Death, Resignation or Inability, both of the President and Vice President, declaring what Officer shall then act as President, and such Officer shall act accordingly, until the Disability be removed, or a President shall be elected.

[7] The President shall, at stated Times, receive for his Services, a Compensation, which shall neither be increased nor diminished during the Period for which he shall have been elected, and he shall not receive within that Period any other Emolument from the United States, or any of them.

[8] Before he enter on the Execution of his Office, he shall take the following Oath or Affirmation:—"I do solemnly swear (or affirm) that I will faithfully execute the Office of President of the United States, and will to the best of my Ability, preserve, protect and defend the Constitution of the United States."

SECTION 2. [1] The President shall be Commander in Chief of the Army and Navy of the United States, and of the Militia of the several States, when called into the actual Service of the United States; he may require the Opinion, in writing, of the Principal Officer in each of the executive Departments, upon any Subject relating to the Duties of their respective Offices, and he shall have Power to grant Reprieves and Pardons for Offenses against the United States, except in Cases of Impeachment.

[2] He shall have Power, by and with the Advice and Consent of the Senate, to make Treaties, provided two thirds of the Senators present concur; and he shall nominate, and by and with the Advice and Consent of the Senate, shall appoint Ambassadors, other public Ministers and Consuls, Judges of the supreme Court, and all other Officers of the United States, whose Appointments are not herein

otherwise provided for, and which shall be established by Law, but the Congress may by Law vest the Appointment of such inferior Officers, as they think proper, in the President alone, in the Courts of Law, or in the Heads of Departments.

[3] The President shall have Power to fill up all Vacancies that may happen during the Recess of the Senate, by granting Commissions which shall expire at the End of their next Session.

SECTION 3. He shall from time to time give to the Congress Information of the State of the Union, and recommend to their Consideration such Measures as he shall judge necessary and expedient; he may, on extraordinary Occasions, convene both Houses, or either of them, and in Case of Disagreement between them, with Respect to the Time of Adjournment, he may adjourn them to such Time as he shall think proper; he shall receive Ambassadors and other public Ministers; he shall take Care that the Laws be faithfully executed, and shall Commission all the Officers of the United States.

SECTION 4. The President, Vice President and all civil Officers of the United States, shall be removed from Office on Impeachment for, and Conviction of, Treason, Bribery, or other high Crimes and Misdemeanors.

ARTICLE III

SECTION 1. The judicial Power of the United States, shall be vested in one supreme Court, and in such inferior Courts as the Congress may from time to time ordain and establish. The Judges, both of the supreme and inferior Courts, shall hold their Offices during good Behaviour, and shall, at stated Times, receive for their Services a Compensation which shall not be diminished during their Continuance in Office.

SECTION 2. [1] The judicial Power shall extend to all Cases, in Law and Equity, arising under this Constitution, the Laws of the United States, and Treaties made, or which shall be made, under their Authority;—to all Cases affecting Ambassadors, other public Ministers and Consuls;—to all Cases of admiralty and maritime Jurisdiction;—to Controversies to which the United States shall be a Party;—to Controversies between two or more States;—between a State and Citizens of another State;—between Citizens of different States;—between Citizens of the same State claiming Lands under Grants of different States, and between a State, or the Citizens thereof, and foreign States, Citizens or Subjects.

[2] In all Cases affecting Ambassadors, other public Ministers and Consuls, and those in which a State shall be Party, the supreme Court shall have original Jurisdiction. In all the other Cases before mentioned, the supreme Court shall have appellate Jurisdiction, both as to Law and Fact, with such Exceptions, and under such Regulations as the Congress shall make.

[3] The Trial of all Crimes, except in Cases of Impeachment, shall be by Jury; and such Trial shall be held in the State where the said Crimes shall have been committed, but when not committed within any State, the Trial shall be at such Place or Places as the Congress may by Law have directed.

SECTION 3. [1] Treason against the United States, shall consist only in levying War against them, or in adhering to their Enemies, giving them Aid and Comfort. No Person shall be convicted of Treason unless on the Testimony of two Witnesses to the same overt Act, or on Confession in open Court.

[2] The Congress shall have power to declare the Punishment of Treason, but no Attainder of Treason shall work Corruption of Blood, or Forfeiture except during the Life of the Person attained.

ARTICLE IV

SECTION 1. Full Faith and Credit shall be given in each State to the public Acts, Records, and judicial Proceedings of every other State. And the Congress may by general Laws prescribe the Manner in which such Acts, Records and Proceedings shall be proved, and the Effect thereof.

SECTION 2. [1] The Citizens of each State shall be entitled to all Privileges and Immunities of Citizens in the several States.

[2] A Person charged in any State with Treason, Felony, or other Crime, who shall flee from Justice, and be found in another State, shall on Demand of the executive Authority of the State from which he fled, be delivered up, to be removed to the State having Jurisdiction of the Crime.

[3] No Person held to Service or Labour in one State, under the Laws thereof, escaping into another, shall, in Consequence of any Law or Regulation therein, be discharged from such Service or Labour, but shall be delivered up on Claim of the Party to whom such Service or Labour may be due.

SECTION 3. [1] New States may be admitted by the Congress into this Union; but no new State shall be formed or erected within the Jurisdiction of any other State; nor any State be formed by the Junction of two or more States, or parts of States, without the Consent of the Legislature of the States concerned as well as of the Congress.

[2] The Congress shall have Power to dispose of and make all needful Rules and Regulations respecting the Territory or other Property belonging to the United States; and nothing in this Constitution shall be so construed as to Prejudice any Claims of the United States, or of any particular State.

SECTION 4. The United States shall guarantee to every State in this Union a Republican Form of Government, and shall protect each of them against Invasion; and on Application of the Legislature, or of the Executive (when the Legislature cannot be convened), against domestic Violence.

ARTICLE V

The Congress, whenever two thirds of both Houses shall deem it necessary, shall propose Amendments to this Constitution, or, on the Application of the Legislatures of two thirds of the several States, shall call a Convention for proposing Amendments, which, in either Case, shall be valid to all Intents and Purposes, as part of this Constitution, when ratified by the Legislatures of three fourths of the several States, or by Conventions in three fourths thereof, as the one or the other Mode of Ratification may be proposed by the Congress; Provided that no Amendment which may be made prior to the Year One thousand eight hundred and eight shall in any Manner affect the first and fourth Clauses in the Ninth Section of the first Article; and that no State, without its Consent, shall be deprived of its equal Suffrage in the Senate.

ARTICLE VI

[1] All Debts contracted and Engagements entered into, before the Adoption of this Constitution, shall be as valid against the United States under this Constitution, as under the Confederation.

[2] This Constitution, and the Laws of the United States which shall be made in Pursuance thereof; and all Treaties made, or which shall be made, under the Authority of the United States, shall be the supreme Law of the Land; and the Judges in every State shall be bound thereby, any Thing in the Constitution or Laws of any State to the Contrary notwithstanding.

[3] The Senators and Representatives before mentioned, and the Members of the several State Legislatures, and all executive and judicial Officers, both of the United States and of the several States, shall be bound by Oath or Affirmation, to support this Constitution; but no religious Test shall ever be required as a Qualification to any Office or public Trust under the United States.

ARTICLE VII

The Ratification of the Conventions of nine States shall be sufficient for the Establishment of this Constitution between the States so ratifying the Same.

Done in Convention by the Unanimous Consent of the States present the Seventeenth Day of September in the Year of our Lord one thousand seven hundred and Eighty seven and of the Independence of the United States of America the Twelfth In witness whereof We have hereunto subscribed our Names,

G° WASHINGTON—
Presdt and deputy from
Virginia

Delaware	Geo: Reed
	Gunning Bedford jun
	John Dickson
	Jaco: Broom
	James McHenry
Maryland	Dan of St Thos. Jenifer
	Danl. Carroll
Virginia	John Blair
	James Madison Jr.
	Wm. Blount
North Carolina	Richd. Dobbs Spaight
	Hu Williamson
	J. Rutledge
South Carolina	Charles Cotesworth
	Pinckney
	Charles Pinckney
	Pierce Butler
Georgia	Willian Few
	Abr Baldwin
New Hampshire	John Langdon
	Nicholas Gilman
Massachusetts	Nathaniel Gorham
	Rufus King
Connecticut	Wm. Saml. Johnson
	Roger Sherman
New York	Alexander Hamilton
	Wil: Livingston
New Jersey	David Brearley
	Wm. Paterson
	Jona: Dayton
Pennsylvania	B Franklin
	Thomas Mifflin
	Robt. Morris
	Geo. Clymer
	Thos. FitzSimons
	Jared Ingersoll
	James Wilson
	Gouv Morris

ARTICLES IN ADDITION TO, AND AMENDMENT OF, THE CONSTITUTION OF THE UNITED STATES OF AMERICA, PROPOSED BY CONGRESS, AND RATIFIED BY THE LEGISLATURES OF THE SEVERAL STATES, PURSUANT TO THE FIFTH ARTICLE OF THE ORIGINAL CONSTITUTION

AMENDMENT I [1791]

Congress shall make no law respecting an establishment of religion, or prohibiting the free exercise thereof; or abridging the freedom of speech, or of the press; or the right of the people peaceably to assemble, and to petition the Government for a redress of grievances.

AMENDMENT II [1791]

A well regulated Militia, being necessary to the security of a free State, the right of the people to keep and bear Arms, shall not be infringed.

AMENDMENT III [1791]

No Soldier shall, in time of peace be quartered in any house, without the consent of the Owner, nor in time of war, but in a manner to be prescribed by Law.

AMENDMENT IV [1791]

The right of the people to be secure in their persons, houses, papers, and effects, against unreasonable searches and seizures, shall not be violated, and no Warrants shall issue, but upon probable cause, supported by Oath or affirmation, and particularly describing the place to be searched, and the persons or things to be seized.

AMENDMENT V [1791]

No person shall be held to answer for a capital, or otherwise infamous crime, unless on a presentment or indictment of a Grand Jury, except in cases arising in the land or naval forces, or in the Militia, when in actual service in time of War or public danger; nor shall any person be subject for the same offence to be twice put in jeopardy of life or limb; nor shall be compelled in any criminal case to be a witness against himself, nor be deprived of life, liberty, or property, without due process of law; nor shall private property be taken for public use, without just compensation.

AMENDMENT VI [1791]

In all criminal prosecutions, the accused shall enjoy the right to a speedy and public trial, by an impartial jury of the State and district wherein the crime shall have been committed, which district shall have been previously ascertained by law, and to be informed of the nature and cause of the accusation; to be confronted with the witnesses against him; to have compulsory process for obtaining witnesses in his favor, and to have the Assistance of Counsel for his defense.

AMENDMENT VII [1791]

In suits at common law, where the value in controversy shall exceed twenty dollars, the right of trial by jury shall be preserved, and no fact tried by jury, shall be otherwise reexamined in any Court of the United States, than according to the rules of the common law.

AMENDMENT VIII [1791]

Excessive bail shall not be required, nor excessive fines imposed, nor cruel and unusual punishments inflicted.

AMENDMENT IX [1791]

The enumeration in the Constitution, of certain rights, shall not be construed to deny or disparage others retained by the people.

AMENDMENT X [1791]

The powers not delegated to the United States by the Constitution, nor prohibited by it to the States, are reserved to the States respectively, or to the people.

AMENDMENT XI [1798]

The Judicial power of the United States shall not be construed to extend to any suit in law or equity, commenced or prosecuted against one of the United States by Citizens of another State, or by Citizens or Subjects of any Foreign State.

AMENDMENT XII [1804]

The electors shall meet in their respective states and vote by ballot for President and Vice-President, one of whom, at least, shall not be an inhabitant of the same state with themselves; they shall name in their ballots the person voted for as President, and in distinct ballots the person voted for as Vice-President, and they shall make distinct lists of all persons voted for as President, and of all persons voted for as Vice-President, and of the number of votes for each, which lists they shall sign and certify, and transmit sealed to the seat of the government of the United States, directed to the President of the Senate;—The President of the Senate shall, in presence of the Senate and House of Representatives, open all the certificates and the votes shall then be counted;—The person having the greatest number of votes for President, shall be the President, if such number be a majority of the whole number of Electors appointed; and if no person have such majority, then from the persons having the highest numbers not exceeding three on the list of those voted for as President, the House of Representatives shall choose immediately, by ballot, the President. But in choosing the President, the votes shall be taken by states, the representation from each state having one vote; a quorum for this purpose shall consist of a member or members from two-thirds of the states, and a majority of all the states shall be necessary to a choice. And if the House of Representatives shall not choose a President whenever the right of choice shall devolve upon them, before the fourth day of March next following, then the Vice-President shall act as President, as in case of the death or other constitutional disability of the President.—The person having the greatest number of votes as Vice-President, shall be the Vice-President, if such number be a majority of the whole number of Electors appointed, and if no person have a majority, then from the two highest numbers on the list, the Senate shall choose the Vice-President; a quorum for the purpose shall consist of two-thirds of the whole number of Senators, and a majority of the whole number shall be necessary to a choice. But no person constitutionally ineligible to the office of President shall be eligible to that of Vice-President of the United States.

AMENDMENT XIII [1865]

SECTION 1. Neither slavery nor involuntary servitude, except as a punishment for crime whereof the party shall have been duly convicted, shall exist within the United States, or any place subject to their jurisdiction.

SECTION 2. Congress shall have power to enforce this article by appropriate legislation.

AMENDMENT XIV [1868]

SECTION 1. All persons born or naturalized in the United States, and subject to the jurisdiction thereof, are citizens of the United States and of the State wherein they reside. No State shall make or enforce any law which shall abridge the privileges or immunities of citizens of the United States; nor shall any State deprive any person of life, liberty, or property, without due process of law; nor deny to any person within its jurisdiction the equal protection of the laws.

SECTION 2. Representatives shall be apportioned among the several States according to their respective numbers, counting the whole number of persons in each State, excluding Indians not taxed. But when the right to vote at any election for the choice of electors for President and Vice-President of the United States, Representatives in Congress, the Executive and Judicial officers of a State, or the members of the Legislature thereof, is denied to any of the male inhabitants of such State, being twenty-one years of age, and citizens of the United States, or in any way abridged, except for participation in rebellion, or other crime, the basis of representation therein shall be reduced in the proportion which the number of such male citizens shall bear to the whole number of male citizens twenty-one years of age in such State.

SECTION 3. No person shall be a Senator or Representative in Congress, or elector of President and Vice-President, or hold any office, civil or military, under the United States, or under any State, who, having previously taken an oath, as a member of Congress, or as an officer of the United States, or as a member of any State legislature, or as an executive or judicial officer of any State, to support the Constitution of the United States, shall have engaged in insurrection or rebellion against the same, or given aid or comfort to the enemies thereof.

But Congress may by a vote of two-thirds of each House, remove such disability.

SECTION 4. The validity of the public debt of the United States, authorized by law, including debts incurred for payment of pensions and bounties for services in suppressing insurrection or rebellion, shall not be questioned. But neither the United States nor any State shall assume or pay any debt or obligation incurred in aid of insurrection or rebellion against the United States, or any claim for the loss or emancipation of any slave; but all such debts, obligations and claims shall be held illegal and void.

SECTION 5. The Congress shall have power to enforce, by appropriate legislation, the provisions of this article.

AMENDMENT XV [1870]

SECTION 1. The right of citizens of the United States to vote shall not be denied or abridged by the United States or by any State on account of race, color, or previous condition of servitude.

SECTION 2. The Congress shall have power to enforce this article by appropriate legislation.

AMENDMENT XVI [1913]

The Congress shall have power to lay and collect taxes on incomes, from whatever source derived, without apportionment among the several States, and without regard to any census or enumeration.

AMENDMENT XVII [1913]

The Senate of the United States shall be composed of two Senators from each State, elected by the people thereof, for six years, and each Senator shall have one vote. The electors in each State shall have the qualifications requisite for electors of the most numerous branch of the State legislatures.

When vacancies happen in the representation of any State in the Senate, the executive authority of such State shall issue writs of election to fill such vacancies: *Provided,* That the legislature of any State may empower the executive thereof to make temporary appointments until the people fill the vacancies by election as the legislature may direct.

This amendment shall not be so construed as to affect the election or term of any Senator chosen before it becomes valid as part of the Constitution.

AMENDMENT XVIII [1919]

SECTION 1. After one year from the ratification of this article the manufacture, sale, or transportation of intoxicating liquors within, the importation thereof into, or the exportation thereof from the United States and all territory subject to the jurisdiction thereof for beverage purposes is hereby prohibited.

SECTION 2. The Congress and the several States shall have concurrent power to enforce this article by appropriate legislation.

SECTION 3. This article shall be inoperative unless it shall have been ratified as an amendment to the Constitution by the legislatures of the several States, as provided in the Constitution, within seven years from the date of the submission hereof to the States by the Congress.

AMENDMENT XIX [1920]

The right of citizens of the United States to vote shall not be denied or abridged by the United States or by any State on account of sex.

Congress shall have the power to enforce this article by appropriate legislation.

AMENDMENT XX [1933]

SECTION 1. The terms of the President and Vice President shall end at noon on the 20th day of January, and the terms of Senators and Representatives at noon on the 3rd day of January, of the years in which such terms would have ended if this article had not been ratified; and the terms of their successors shall then begin.

SECTION 2. The Congress shall assemble at least once in every year, and such meeting shall begin at noon on the 3d day of January, unless they shall by law appoint a different day.

SECTION 3. If, at the time fixed for the beginning of the term of the President, the President elect shall have died, the Vice President elect shall become President. If a President shall not have been chosen before the time fixed for the beginning of his term, or if the President elect shall have failed to qualify, then the Vice President elect shall act as President until a President shall have qualified; and the Congress may by law provide for the case wherein neither a President elect nor a Vice President elect shall have qualified, declaring who shall then act as President, or the manner in which one who is to act shall be selected, and such person shall act accordingly until a President or Vice President shall have qualified.

SECTION 4. The Congress may by law provide for the case of the death of any of the persons from whom the House of Representatives may choose a President whenever the right of choice shall have devolved upon them, and for the case of the death of any of the persons from whom the Senate may choose a Vice President whenever the right of choice shall have devolved upon them.

SECTION 5. Sections 1 and 2 shall take effect on the 15th day of October following the ratification of this article.

SECTION 6. This article shall be inoperative unless it shall have been ratified as an amendment to the Constitution by the legislatures of three-fourths of the several States within seven years from the date of its submission.

AMENDMENT XXI [1933]

SECTION 1. The eighteenth article of amendment to the Constitution of the United States is hereby repealed.

SECTION 2. The transportation or importation into any State, Territory, or possession of the United States for delivery of use therein of intoxicating liquors, in violation of the laws thereof, is hereby prohibited.

SECTION 3. This article shall be inoperative unless it shall have been ratified as an amendment to the Constitution by conventions in the several States, as provided in the Constitution, within seven years from the date of the submission hereof to the States by the Congress.

AMENDMENT XXII [1951]

SECTION 1. No person shall be elected to the office of the President more than twice, and no person who has held the office of President, or acted as President, for more than two years of a term to which some other person was elected President shall be elected to the office of President more than once. But this Article shall not apply to any person holding the office of President when this Article was proposed by the Congress, and shall not prevent any person who may be holding the office of President, or acting as President, during the term within which this Article becomes operative from holding the office of President or acting as President during the remainder of such term.

SECTION 2. This article shall be inoperative unless it shall have been ratified as an amendment to the Constitution by the legislatures of three-fourths of the several States within seven years from the date of its submission to the States by the Congress.

AMENDMENT XXIII [1961]

SECTION 1. The District constituting the seat of Government of the United States shall appoint in such manner as Congress may direct: A number of electors of President and Vice President equal to the whole number of Senators and Representatives in Congress to which the District would be entitled if it were a State, but in no event more than the least populous State; they shall be in addition to those appointed by the States, but they shall be considered, for the purposes of the election of President and Vice President, to be electors appointed by a State; and they shall meet in the District and perform such duties as provided by the twelfth article of amendment.

SECTION 2. The Congress shall have power to enforce this article by appropriate legislation.

AMENDMENT XXIV [1964]

SECTION 1. The right of citizens of the United States to vote in any primary or other election for President or Vice President, for electors for President or Vice President, or for Senator or Representative in Congress, shall not be denied or abridged by the United States or any State by reason of failure to pay any poll tax or other tax.

SECTION 2. The Congress shall have power to enforce this article by appropriate legislation.

AMENDMENT XXV [1967]

SECTION 1. In case of the removal of the President from office or his death or resignation, the Vice President shall become President.

SECTION 2. Whenever there is a vacancy in the office of the Vice President, the President shall nominate a Vice President who shall take office upon confirmation by a majority vote of both Houses of Congress.

SECTION 3. Whenever the President transmits to the President pro tempore of the Senate and the Speaker of the House of Representatives his written declaration that he is unable to discharge the powers and duties of his office, and until he transmits to them a written declaration to the contrary, such powers and duties shall be discharged by the Vice President as Acting President.

SECTION 4. Whenever the Vice President and a majority of either the principal officers of the executive departments or of such other body as Congress may by law provide, transmit to the President pro tempore of the Senate and the Speaker of the House of Representatives their written declaration that the President is unable to discharge the powers and duties of his office, the Vice President shall immediately assume the powers and duties of the office as Acting President.

Thereafter, when the President transmits to the President pro tempore of the Senate and the Speaker of the House of Representatives his written declaration that no inability exists, he shall resume the powers and the duties of his office unless the Vice President and a majority of either the principal officers of the executive department or of such other body as Congress may by law provide, transmit within four days to the President pro tempore of the Senate and the Speaker of the House of Representatives their written declaration that the President is unable to discharge the powers and duties of his office. Thereupon Congress shall decide the issue, assembling within forty-eight hours for that purpose if not in session. If the Congress, within twenty-one days after receipt of the latter written declaration, or, if Congress is not in session, within twenty-one days after Congress is required to assemble, determines by two-thirds vote of both Houses that the President is unable to discharge the powers and duties of his office, the Vice President shall continue to discharge the same as Acting President; otherwise, the President shall resume the powers and duties of his office.

AMENDMENT XXVI [1971]

SECTION 1. The right of citizens of the United States, who are eighteen years of age or older, to vote shall not be denied or abridged by the United States or by any State on account of age.

SECTION 2. The Congress shall have power to enforce this article by appropriate legislation.

AMENDMENT XXVII [1992]

No law, varying the compensation for the services of the Senators and Representatives, shall take effect, until an election of representatives shall have intervened.*

---

*Adopted in 1992, 203 years after it was first proposed by James Madison and approved by the First Congress. Six states ratified the amendment in 1792, a seventh in 1873, an eighth in 1978, and thirty-two more recently, with Illinois becoming the thirty-eighth state to ratify it on May 12, 1992.

Justices of the Supreme Court

	Term	Appointed by	Replaced
*John Jay**	1789–1795	Washington	
John Rutledge	1789–1791	Washington	
William Cushing	1789–1810	Washington	
James Wilson	1789–1798	Washington	
John Blair	1789–1796	Washington	
James Iredell	1790–1799	Washington	
Thomas Johnson	1791–1793	Washington	Rutledge
William Paterson	1793–1806	Washington	Johnson
John Rutledge	1795	Washington	Jay
Samuel Chase	1796–1811	Washington	Blair
Oliver Ellsworth	1796–1800	Washington	Rutledge
Bushrod Washington	1798–1829	J. Adams	Wilson
Alfred Moore	1799–1804	J. Adams	Iredell
John Marshall	1801–1835	J. Adams	Ellsworth
William Johnson	1804–1834	Jefferson	Moore

*The names of the chief justices are italicized.

	Term	Appointed by	Replaced
Brockholst Livingston	1806–1823	Jefferson	Paterson
Thomas Todd	1807–1826	Jefferson	(new seat)
Gabriel Duval	1811–1835	Madison	Chase
Joseph Story	1811–1845	Madison	Cushing
Smith Thompson	1823–1843	Monroe	Livingston
Robert Trimble	1826–1828	J. Q. Adams	Todd
John McLean	1829–1861	Jackson	Trimble
Henry Baldwin	1830–1844	Jackson	Washington
James Wayne	1835–1867	Jackson	Johnson
Roger Taney	1836–1864	Jackson	Marshall
Philip Barbour	1836–1841	Jackson	Duval
John Catron	1837–1865	Van Buren	(new seat)
John McKinley	1837–1852	Van Buren	(new seat)
Peter Daniel	1841–1860	Van Buren	Barbour
Samuel Nelson	1845–1872	Tyler	Thompson
Levi Woodbury	1845–1851	Polk	Story
Robert Grier	1846–1870	Polk	Baldwin
Benjamin Curtis	1851–1857	Fillmore	Woodbury
John Campbell	1853–1861	Pierce	McKinley
Nathan Clifford	1858–1881	Buchanan	Curtis
Noah Swayne	1862–1881	Lincoln	McLean
Samuel Miller	1862–1890	Lincoln	Daniel
David Davis	1862–1877	Lincoln	Campbell
Stephen Field	1863–1897	Lincoln	(new seat)

	Term	Appointed by	Replaced
Salmon Chase	1864–1873	Lincoln	Taney
William Strong	1870–1880	Grant	Grier
Joseph Bradley	1870–1892	Grant	Wayne
Ward Hunt	1872–1882	Grant	Nelson
Morrison Waite	1874–1888	Grant	Chase
John Marshall Harlan	1877–1911	Hayes	Davis
William Woods	1880–1887	Hayes	Strong
Stanley Matthews	1881–1889	Garfield	Swayne
Horace Gray	1881–1902	Arthur	Clifford
Samuel Blatchford	1882–1893	Arthur	Hunt
Lucius Lamar	1888–1893	Cleveland	Woods
Melville Fuller	1888–1910	Cleveland	Waite
David Brewer	1889–1910	Harrison	Matthews
Henry Brown	1890–1906	Harrison	Miller
George Shiras	1892–1903	Harrison	Bradley
Howell Jackson	1893–1895	Harrison	Lamar
Edward White	1894–1910	Cleveland	Blatchford
Rufus Peckham	1895–1909	Cleveland	Jackson
Joseph McKenna	1898–1925	McKinley	Field
Oliver Wendell Holmes	1902–1932	T. Roosevelt	Gray
William Day	1903–1922	T. Roosevelt	Shiras
William Moody	1906–1910	T. Roosevelt	Brown
Horace Lurton	1909–1914	Taft	Peckham
Charles Evans Hughes	1910–1916	Taft	Brewer

	Term	Appointed by	Replaced
Edward White	1910–1921	Taft	Fuller
Willis Van Devanter	1910–1937	Taft	White
Joseph Lamar	1910–1916	Taft	Moody
Mahlon Pitney	1912–1922	Taft	Harlan
James McReynolds	1914–1941	Wilson	Lurton
Louis Brandeis	1916–1939	Wilson	Lamar
John Clarke	1916–1922	Wilson	Hughes
William Howard Taft	1921–1930	Harding	White
George Sutherland	1922–1938	Harding	Clarke
Pierce Butler	1922–1939	Harding	Day
Edward Sanford	1923–1930	Harding	Pitney
Harlan Stone	1925–1941	Coolidge	McKenna
Charles Evans Hughes	1930–1941	Hoover	Taft
Owen Roberts	1932–1945	Hoover	Sanford
Benjamin Cardozo	1932–1938	Hoover	Holmes
Hugo Black	1937–1971	F. Roosevelt	Van Devanter
Stanley Reed	1938–1957	F. Roosevelt	Sutherland
Felix Frankfurter	1939–1962	F. Roosevelt	Cardozo
William Douglas	1939–1975	F. Roosevelt	Brandeis
Frank Murphy	1940–1949	F. Roosevelt	Butler
James Byrnes	1941–1942	F. Roosevelt	McReynolds
Harlan Stone	1941–1946	F. Roosevelt	Hughes
Robert Jackson	1941–1954	F. Roosevelt	Stone
Wiley Rutledge	1943–1949	F. Roosevelt	Byrnes

	Term	Appointed by	Replaced
Harold Burton	1945–1958	Truman	Roberts
Fred Vinson	1946–1953	Truman	Stone
Tom Clark	1949–1967	Truman	Murphy
Sherman Minton	1949–1956	Truman	Rutledge
Earl Warren	1953–1969	Eisenhower	Vinson
John Harlan	1955–1971	Eisenhower	Jackson
William Brennan	1956–1990	Eisenhower	Minton
Charles Whittaker	1957–1962	Eisenhower	Reed
Potter Stewart	1958–1981	Eisenhower	Burton
Arthur Goldberg	1962–1965	Kennedy	Frankfurter
Byron White	1962–1993	Kennedy	Whittaker
Abe Fortas	1965–1969	Johnson	Goldberg
Thurgood Marshall	1967–1991	Johnson	Clark
Warren Burger	1969–1986	Nixon	Warren
Harry Blackmun	1970–1994	Nixon	Fortas
Lewis Powell	1972–1987	Nixon	Black
William Rehnquist	1972–1986	Nixon	Harlan
John Paul Stevens	1975–2010	Ford	Douglas
Sandra Day O'Connor	1981–2005	Reagan	Stewart
William Rehnquist	1986–2005	Reagan	Burger
Antonin Scalia	1986–2016	Reagan	Rehnquist
Anthony Kennedy	1988–	Reagan	Powell
David Souter	1990–2009	G. H. W. Bush	Brennan
Clarence Thomas	1991–	G. H. W. Bush	Marshall

	Term	Appointed by	Replaced
Ruth Bader Ginsburg	1993–	Clinton	White
Stephen Breyer	1994–	Clinton	Blackmun
John Roberts	2005–	G. W. Bush	Rehnquist
Samuel Alito	2006–	G. W. Bush	O'Connor
Sonia Sotomayor	2009–	Obama	Souter
Elena Kagan	2010–	Obama	Stevens

Glossary of Common Legal Terms

Abstention The doctrine under which the US Supreme Court and other federal courts choose not to rule on state cases, even when empowered to do so, so as to allow the issue to be decided on the basis of state law.

Advisory Opinion A legal opinion rendered at the request of the government or another party indicating how the court would rule if the issue arose in an adversary context.

Amicus Curiae "Friend of the court." A person or group not directly involved in a particular case that volunteers or is requested by the court to supply its views on the case (usually through the submission of a brief).

Appeal The procedure whereby a case is brought from an inferior to a superior court. In the Supreme Court, certain cases are designated as appeals under federal law and must be heard formally by the Court.

Appellant The party who appeals a decision from a lower to a higher court.

Appellate Jurisdiction The authority of a court to hear, determine, and render judgment in an action on appeal from an inferior court.

Appellee The party against whom an appeal to a superior court is taken and who has an interest in upholding the lower court's decision.

Arraignment The formal process of charging a person with a crime, reading the charge, and asking for and entering the plea.

Bail The security (cash or a bail bond) given as a guarantee that a released prisoner will appear at trial.

Bill of Attainder A legislative act declaring a person guilty of a crime and passing sentence without benefit of trial.

Brief A document prepared by counsel as the basis for an argument in court. It sets forth the facts of the case and the legal arguments in support of the party's position.

Case Law The law as defined by previously decided cases.

Certification A method of appeal whereby a lower court requests a higher court to rule on certain legal questions so that the lower court can make the correct decision in light of the answer given.

Certiorari, Writ of An order from a superior court to an inferior court to forward the entire record of a case to the superior court for review. The US Supreme Court can issue such writs at its discretion.

Civil Action A lawsuit, usually brought by a private party, seeking redress for a noncriminal act (e.g., a suit in negligence, contract, or defamation).

Class Action A lawsuit brought by one person or by a group on behalf of all persons similarly situated.

Comity Courtesy and respect. In the legal sense, the respect federal courts give to the decisions of state courts.

Common Law Principles and rules of action, particularly from unwritten English law, whose authority stems from long-standing usage and custom or from judicial recognition and enforcement of those customs.

Concurrent Powers Powers that can be exercised by both the national government and state governments.

Concurring Opinion An opinion submitted by a member of a court who agrees with the result by the court in a case but either disagrees with the court's reasons for the decision or wishes to address matters not touched on in the opinion of the court.

Declaratory Judgment A judicial pronouncement declaring the legal rights of the parties involved in an actual case or controversy but not ordering a specific action.

De Facto "In fact." The existence of something in fact or reality, as opposed to de jure (by right).

Defendant The person against whom a civil or criminal charge is brought.

De Jure "By right." Lawful, rightful, legitimate; as a result of official action, as opposed to de facto (in fact).

Dissenting Opinion An opinion submitted by a member of a court who disagrees with the result reached by the court.

Distinguish To point out why a previous decision is not applicable.

Diversity Jurisdiction The authority of federal courts to hear cases involving citizens of different states.

Dual Federalism The view that national powers should be interpreted so as not to invade traditional spheres of state activity.

Equity The administration of justice based upon principles of fairness rather than upon strictly applied rules found in the law.

Error, Writ of A writ issued by a superior court directing a lower court to send to the superior court the record of a case in which the lower court has entered a final judgment, for the purpose of reviewing alleged errors made by the lower court.

Exclusionary Rule The rule that evidence obtained by illegal means, such as unreasonable searches and seizures, cannot be introduced by the prosecution in a criminal trial.

Ex parte "From (or on) one side." A hearing in the presence of only one of the parties to a case, such as a hearing to review a petition for a writ of habeas corpus.

Ex Post Facto "After the fact." A law that makes an action a crime after it has already been committed.

Ex Rel. "By (or on) the information of." The designation of suit instituted by a state but at the instigation of a private individual interested in the matter.

Federal Question A case that contains a major issue involving the US Constitution, or US laws or treaties. (The jurisdiction of the federal courts is limited to federal questions and diversity suits.)

Habeas Corpus "You have the body." A writ inquiring of an official who has custody of a person whether that person is imprisoned or detained lawfully.

In Camera "In chambers." The hearing of a case or part of a case in private (without spectators).

Incorporation The process by which provisions of the Bill of Rights were applied as limitations on state governments through the Due Process Clause of the Fourteenth Amendment.

In Forma Pauperis "In the manner of a pauper." Permission for indigents to bring legal action without payment of the required fees.

Injunction A writ prohibiting the person to whom it is directed from performing some specified act.

In re "In the matter of; concerning." The designation of judicial proceedings in which there are no adversaries.

Judgment of the Court The ruling of the court (independent of the reasons for the court's ruling).

Judicial Review The power of a court to review legislation or other governmental action in order to determine its validity with respect to the US Constitution or state constitutions.

Juris Belli "Under the law of war." That part of the law of nations that defines the rights of belligerent and neutral nations during wartime.

Jurisdiction The authority of a court to hear, determine, and render final judgment in an action, and to enforce its judgments by legal process.

Justiciability The question of whether a matter is appropriate for judicial decision. A justiciable issue is one that appropriately can be decided by a court.

Litigant An active participant in a lawsuit.

Mandamus, Writ of "We command." A court order directing an individual or organization to perform a particular act.

Moot Unsettled, undecided. A moot question is one in which either the result sought by the lawsuit has occurred or the conditions have so changed as to render it impossible for the court to grant the relief sought.

Obiter Dicta (also called dictum or dicta) That part of the reasoning in a judicial opinion that is not necessary to resolve the case. Dicta are not necessarily binding in future cases.

Opinion of the Court The opinion that announces the court's decision and is adhered to by a majority of the participating judges.

Original Jurisdiction The authority of a court to hear, determine, and render judgment in an action as a trial court.

Per Curiam "By the court." An unsigned opinion by the court, or a collectively authored opinion.

Petitioner The party who files a petition with a court seeking action.

Plaintiff The party who brings a civil action or sues to obtain a remedy for an injury to his or her rights.

Plea Bargain Negotiations between the prosecution and defense aimed at exchanging a plea of guilty for concessions by the prosecution.

Police Power The power of the states to protect the health, safety, welfare, and morals of their citizens.

Political Question An issue that the court believes should be decided by a nonjudicial unit of government.

Precedent A prior case relied upon in deciding a present dispute.

Preemption The doctrine under which issues previously subject to state control are brought, through congressional action, within the primary or exclusive jurisdiction of the national government.

Prima Facie "At first sight." Evidence that, unless contradicted, is sufficient to establish a claim without investigation or evaluation.

Pro Bono "For the good." Legal services rendered without charge.

Ratio Decidendi "Reason for the decision." The principle of the case.

Remand To send back. In remanding a decision, a higher court sends it, for further action, back to the court from which it came.

Respondent The party against whom a legal action is taken.

Special Master A person designated by a court to hear evidence and submit findings and recommendations based on that evidence. The Supreme Court typically uses special masters in original jurisdiction cases.

Standing The qualifications needed to bring or participate in a case. To have standing to sue, plaintiffs must demonstrate the existence of a controversy in which they personally have suffered or are about to suffer an injury or infringement of a legally protected right.

Stare Decisis "Let the decision stand." The doctrine that a point settled in a previous case is a precedent that should be followed in subsequent cases with similar facts.

State Action Action by the state or by a private entity closely associated with it ("under color of state law"). The basis for redress under the Due Process and Equal Protection Clauses of the Fourteenth Amendments.

Stay To halt or suspend further judicial proceedings.

Subpoena An order to present oneself and to testify before a court, grand jury, or legislative hearing.

Subpoena Duces Tecum An order by a court or other authorized body that specified documents or papers be produced.

Tort Willful or negligent injury to the person, property, or reputation of another.

Ultra Vires "Beyond power." An action beyond the legal authority of the person or body performing it.

Vacate To make void, annul, or rescind.

Venue The jurisdiction in which a case is to be heard.

Vested Rights Long-established rights that government should recognize and protect and that a person cannot be deprived of without injustice.

Writ A written court order commanding the recipient to perform or refrain from performing acts specified in the order.

Table of Cases

Case titles in capital letters indicate cases that are reprinted in this volume. **Bold italic** page numbers indicate where the case is reprinted in this volume.